The New Arthurian Encyclopedia

EDITED BY

Norris J. Lacy

Associate Editors

Geoffrey Ashe, Sandra Ness Ihle,
Marianne E. Kalinke & Raymond H. Thompson

Garland Publishing, Inc.
New York & London 1996

Library of Congress Cataloging-in-Publication Data

The new Arthurian encyclopedia ; edited by Norris J. Lacy ; associate editors, Geoffrey Ashe . . . [et al.]. — Updated pbk. ed.
p. cm. — (Garland reference library of the humanities ; vol. 931)
Includes bibliographical references (p.) and index.
ISBN 0-8153-2303-4 (pbk. : alk. paper)
1. Arthur, King—Encyclopedias. 2. Great Britain—Antiquities, Celtic—Encyclopedias. 3. Great Britain—History—To 1066—Encyclopedias. 4. Britons—Kings and rulers—Encyclopedias. 5. Arthurian romances—Encyclopedias. I. Lacy, Norris J. II. Ashe, Geoffrey. III. Series.
DA152.5.A7N48 1996
809'.93351—dc20 95-36107
CIP

This volume is a completely revised and expanded edition of *The Arthurian Encyclopedia*, first published by Garland in 1986.

Paperback cover design by Lawrence Wolfson Design, New York
Paperback cover illustration: Cloisters Tapestry; Arthur as one of the Nine Worthies. Reprinted by permission of The Metropolitan Museum of Art, The Cloisters Collection, Munsey Fund, 1932, and Gift of John D. Rockefeller, Jr., 1947.

Printed on acid-free, 250-year-life paper

Manufactured in the United States of America

Contents

Preface

Until the publication of *The Arthurian Encyclopedia* in 1986, we had not had a reference work that offered, in encyclopedic form, a comprehensive and critical treatment of Arthurian subjects, artists, and works, both medieval and modern, in all languages. The gratifying success of that volume demonstrated both that a need existed for such a reference volume and that our work, to a considerable extent, filled that need. But it goes without saying that that volume was neither complete nor flawless, for what Dr. Johnson wrote of dictionaries in 1784 might be said as well of encyclopedias: "Dictionaries are like watches, the worst is better than none, and the best cannot be expected to go quite true."

We hope that this enlarged and revised edition, *The New Arthurian Encyclopedia*, will at least go almost "true." Like its predecessor, it deals with Arthuriana of all periods, from the earliest legends and texts to the present. Similarly, alongside literature, we have included history and chronicle, archaeology, art, film, and other media. The primary advantages of this volume over its predecessor lie in our having added a great deal of material, revised and expanded much more, updated the whole to 1990, and provided an index and a chronology of Arthurian events and works.

The original edition was incomplete mostly by design, though occasionally by oversight instead. In our revision, we have expanded the *Encyclopedia* from 700 entries to more than 1,200, with contributions from some 130 scholars rather than 94. Moreover, well over 100 of the original entries have been significantly expanded, substantially revised, or replaced, while a great many more have received minor revision or updating, particularly in regard to the accompanying bibliographical references.

In addition to the large number of brief and informative entries devoted to particular subjects, this volume, like its predecessor, includes a number of extended essays of two sorts. The first are those that treat major texts or authors (e.g., Malory, Tennyson, Chrétien de Troyes); these not only give the necessary information about their subjects but also provide analyses and critical evaluations. Second, we offer a number of surveys and essays on broader subjects. To those included in the original *Encyclopedia* (Arthur in the visual arts, manuscripts, Arthurian scholarship, surveys of English, French, German, Hispanic, Italian, Scandinavian, Celtic, and Middle Dutch literature), we have added treatments of such topics as Arthurian music, ballets, modern Dutch literature, Arthurian literature in the Czech lands, Arthurian chastity tests, Scandinavian Tristan material, the troubadours' use of Arthurian matter, Arthurian women, and Arthur in popular culture.

In the original volume, there were two areas in which we were rigorously selective: modern Arthurian literature, especially in English, and literary characters. Given the extraordinary proliferation of Arthurian texts, especially during the twentieth century, we considered it unnecessary to discuss a good many minor and marginal compositions. We have now expanded considerably in this area, and in fact a great many of the new entries in this edition treat modern texts, mostly in English but with additions also in French, German, Dutch, and other languages. Because some texts can no longer be located, and because others were still judged to be too marginal for inclusion, some gaps remain; we trust, however, that they are few and minor, and when we were in doubt we were generally inclined toward inclusiveness.

The first edition included discussion of some thirty major characters (Arthur, Merlin, Lancelot, Perceval, Tristan and Isolde, and the like); the new edition nearly triples that number. Even so, most minor characters are mentioned only in passing, usually in entries devoted to works in which they appear. Given the extent of the early legend and the degree to which writers have elaborated it ever since, a full glossary of characters would undeniably prove useful, but it would also be in itself a major undertaking that is beyond the scope and intent of this volume.

* * *

With a single but crucial exception, the organization of this edition is identical to that of the original. In the first edition, which was without an index, we listed most titles in alphabetical order and used cross-references to direct readers to the corresponding author entries. In this edition, we have eliminated those references but have provided instead a general index of authors, artists, titles, places, and subjects. The index offers an important advantage, beyond the gathering of references in a single section: it permits us to refer not only to the primary treatment of a topic but also to discussions found in other entries. Thus, for example, the reader who looks for "Malory" will be directed both to a major essay and to a number of entries concerning reworkings of his texts and his influence on other authors or artists. The index is extensive but not complete, and major figures, such as Arthur and Merlin, are of necessity indexed selectively.

The arrangement of material is intended to be simple and logical. Entries are alphabetized under their most obvious or distinctive element; for example, the essay on Arthur in the Visual Arts can be found under "V," not "A": VISUAL ARTS. Individual works are listed by author or artist rather than title, but the index cites titles and refers the reader to the correct entry. Entries on deceased authors include birth and death dates, where available. The few exceptions to our practice of devoting entries to authors rather than works concern texts of disputed or tentative authorship, those attributed to a translator rather than to an author or adapter, and anonymous works; in those cases, we list the entry under the title. Welsh titles are listed by English forms (since those are the forms most easily recognized by English readers); the original title follows. Other non-English titles are given in the original and accompanied by a translation.

Names of characters naturally varied a good deal from language to language and even within the literature of a single country. We have tried to list them under the most familiar form or, where that is in doubt, the form most prevalent in English. In practice, the spelling under which we list names will not often cause difficulties, and cross-references are rarely necessary. Within individual entries, we have kept names (e.g., Perceval or Parsifal, Guinevere or Guenevere) as they occur in the author or work in question.

In most cases, names of medieval authors who identify themselves by their places of origin are alphabetized under their first names; thus, Chrétien de Troyes is found under the letter "C." Custom has dictated a different system for a few names, however, and Jacob van Maerlant is under "M," rather than "J." When a name is not initially found, the alternative should be obvious. For medieval works like the *Roman d'Auberon*, which might be alphabetized under "R" or "A," we have generally taken the "Roman de" as an identification of genre, rather than as part of the title; that work will thus be listed as *AUBERON, ROMAN D'*. To facilitate attempts to locate material, we include a list of entries grouped by subject and by language.

Most entries are followed by bibliographical references that list editions and (where appropriate) translations and suggest material for further reading; those listings have been expanded and updated to reflect currents of Arthurian scholarship since the original *Encyclopedia*. In addition, we have similarly updated and enlarged the general bibliography that heads the volume. That bibliography nevertheless remains selective, both because we intend it as a general guide to the subject and because, to minimize duplication, we list few references to the major authors and subjects that receive a separate entry within the text.

Our contributors include a number of scholars whose assistance went well beyond what we could have asked of them, and we are pleased to express our gratitude to them. Debra Mancoff, of Beloit College, provided invaluable advice in preparing the list of entries and plates for Arthurian art, a complex area that, except for the Loomises' 1938 book, has been largely neglected until recently. Similarly, Christopher Kleinhenz, of the University of Wisconsin, Madison, offered substantial assistance in regard to Italian Arthuriana. We also owe a debt of gratitude to Leslie Alcock for his expert advice concerning Arthurian archaeology.

To those debts, acknowledged in the original encyclopedia, we have added others. Not least, we are grateful to our reviewers and to colleagues and readers who not only praised our work but brought deficiencies and omissions to our attention. In addition, we take pleasure in expressing our gratitude to Ruth Hamilton and the staff of the Newberry Library, for providing generous advice as well as illustrations, and to Alison Stones and, once again, Debra Mancoff, for their continuing assistance in that same area.

Finally, we are most grateful to Gary Kuris, of Garland Publishing, for the assistance and informed advice he offered at every turn. He is no less our collaborator than our editor.

N.J.L.
January 1991

The Contributors

NJL Norris J. Lacy, *Editor*
Washington University in St. Louis

GA Geoffrey Ashe, *Associate Editor*
Glastonbury, Somerset, England

SNI Sandra Ness Ihle, *Associate Editor*
University of Wisconsin

MEK Marianne E. Kalinke, *Associate Editor*
University of Illinois

RHT Raymond H. Thompson, *Associate Editor*
Acadia University

MA Muriel Aercke
University of Wisconsin

LA Lilian Armstrong
Wellesley College

CLB Cynthia L. Barnett
Springfield, Illinois

MSB M.S. Batts
University of British Columbia

RB Robert Baudry
Université Nationale,
Lubumbashi, Zaire

BBens Bernard Benstock
University of Miami

BB Bart Besamusca
University of Utrecht

FWB †Foster W. Blaisdell
Indiana University

PCB Phillip C. Boardman
University of Nevada, Reno

FB Fanni Bogdanow
University of Manchester

NB-C Nancy Bradley-Cromey
Sweet Briar College

EB Elisabeth Brewer
Emmanuel College, Cambridge

EJB E. Jane Burns
University of North Carolina

KB Keith Busby
University of Oklahoma

JPC James P. Carley
York University
North York, Ontario

MDC Mark Cumming
Memorial University of Newfoundland

RGD R.G. Dahms
University of New Brunswick

JRD Janine R. Dakyns
University of East Anglia

MLD Mildred Leake Day
Quondam et Futurus

PD Patrick Deane
University of Western Ontario

TJD Thurston J. Dox
Hartwick College

PJCF Peter J.C. Field
University College of North Wales, Bangor

PKF Patrick K. Ford
University of California, Los Angeles

MF Maureen Fries
Fredonia State University College

AEG †Aubrey E. Galyon
Iowa State University

LRG L.R. Galyon
Iowa State University

FGG Francis G. Gentry
University of Wisconsin

KHG K.H. Göller
Universität Regensburg

EGF Elke Görling-Fallenstein
Universität Salzburg

PHG Peter H. Goodrich
Northern Michigan University

MAG Alice Grellner
Rhode Island College

JLG †John L. Grigsby
Washington University

KRG Karin R. Gürttler
University of Montreal

CBH Constance B. Hieatt
University of Western Ontario

DLH Donald L. Hoffman
Northeastern Illinois University

LH Linda Hughes
Washburn University

MCH Margaret C. Hunt
Purdue University

REH Ruth E. Hamilton
Newberry Library

KH Kevin J. Harty
La Salle University

CSJ C. Stephen Jaeger
University of Washington

JDJ J.D. Janssens
Universitaire Faculteiten Sint-Aloysius, Brussels

SMJ Sidney M. Johnson
Indiana University

DK Douglas Kelly
University of Wisconsin

BK Beverly Kennedy
Marianopolis College

EDK Edward Donald Kennedy
University of North Carolina

WWK William W. Kibler
University of Texas

RWK Richard W. Kimpel
University of Western Ontario

ZK Zora Kipel
New York Public Library

CK Christopher Kleinhenz
University of Wisconsin

NK Naomi Kline
Plymouth State College

ESK Erik S. Kooper
University of Utrecht

RK Roberta Krueger
Hamilton College

JK Julia Kurtz
Lake Forest College

VML Valerie M. Lagorio
University of Iowa

LL Lauriat Lane, Jr.
University of New Brunswick

JML Joanne M. Lukitsh
Rice University

ACL Alan Lupack
Rossell Hope Robbins Library, University of Rochester

BTL Barbara Tepa Lupack
Empire State College, State University of New York

WCM William C. McDonald
University of Virginia

JPM J. Paul McRoberts
Pennsylvania State University

KGM Kenneth G. Madison
Iowa State University

DBM Dhira B. Mahoney
Arizona State University

DNM Debra N. Mancoff
Beloit College

PM Peter Meister
University of Virginia

UM Ulrich Müller
Universität Salzburg

LAM Louis A. Murillo
University of California, Berkeley

DN Daniel Nastali
Kansas City, Missouri

HN Helmut Nickel
Metropolitan Museum of Art

SJN Susan J. Noakes
University of Minnesota

JN James Noble
University of Western Ontario

JFO'G James F. O'Gorman
Wellesley College

RO'G Richard O'Gorman
University of Iowa

JPal Joseph Palermo
Virginia Polytechnic Institute and State University

MJP Marylyn J. Parins
University of Arkansas, Little Rock

LBP Linda B. Parshall
Portland State University

JP Jocelyn Price
University of Liverpool

VCR Virginia C. Raguin
College of the Holy Cross

SRR Stephen R. Reimer
University of Alberta

JR Jeff Rider
Wesleyan University

IJR Isidro J. Rivera
Wittenberg University

BFR Brynley F. Roberts
University College of Wales, Swansea

RJR Robert J. Rodini
University of Wisconsin

HRR Hans R. Runte
Dalhousie University

AAR Amelia Rutledge
George Mason University

VJS Vincent J. Scattergood
University of Dublin

PS Paul Schach
University of Nebraska

RCS Roger C. Schlobin
Purdue University (North Central)

SSch Siegrid Schmidt
Universität Salzburg

JAS James A. Schultz
University of Illinois, Chicago

DS-N Dayle Seidenspinner-Núñez
University of California, Irvine

HLS Harvey L. Sharrer
University of California, Santa Barbara

MSh Michael Sherberg
Washington University

TLS Thomas L. Sloan
Northeastern Illinois University

JLS Janet L. Smarr
University of Illinois

CNS Christopher Smith
University of East Anglia

NS Nathaniel Smith
Franklin & Marshall College

JWS James W. Spisak
Washington, D.C.

DS David Staines
University of Ottawa

HAS H. Alan Stewart
Memphis-Shelby County Public Library

WS Wayne Stith
University of Virginia

MS Marilyn Stokstad
University of Kansas

MAS M. Alison Stones
University of Pittsburgh

TT Toshiyuki Takamiya
Keio University

PWT Petrus W. Tax
University of North Carolina

BT Beverly Taylor
University of North Carolina

JHMT Jane H.M. Taylor
Oxford University

AT Alfred Thomas
Rutgers University, Newark

HT Hilary Thompson
Acadia University

FLT Frederick L. Toner
Texas Christian University

LT Laurel Tryforos
Roosevelt University

VU Veerle Uyttersprot
Universitaire Faculteiten Sint-Aloysius, Brussels

CVC Colette-Anne Van Coolput
Vlaamse Economische Hogeschool, Brussels

SLW Stephen L. Wailes
Indiana University

MWW Martin W. Walsh
University of Michigan

BJW Barry J. Ward
West Virginia University

PAW Patricia A. Ward
Wheaton College

RGW Robert G. Warnock
Brown University

JW Jean Watson
Southwestern College

MAW Muriel A. Whitaker
University of Alberta

JKW John Keith Wikeley
University of Alberta

CCW Charity Cannon Willard
Ladycliff College

HBW H. Bernard Willson
University of Leicester

SW Suzanne Wilson
Marquette University

JHW John H. Winant
Alexandria, Virginia

LDW Lenora D. Wolfgang
Lehigh University

JW-M Joanna Woods-Marsden
University of California, Los Angeles

LJW Leslie J. Workman
Studies in Medievalism

WW Werner Wunderlich
University of St. Gall

List of Entries Arranged by Category

The following list contains all the entries of the Encyclopedia, *arranged by category. Works by a known author are discussed in the author's entry. In general, chronicles are listed with* HISTORY, LEGEND, ARCHAEOLOGY, *rather than with the literature of the language in which they were written. In some cases, where those chronicles offer a clear literary, as well as historical, interest, they are also included under the appropriate literary category. A number of other duplications occur, the most common ones being the listing of place-names under* HISTORY *and* PLACES. *Owing to the large number of entries on literature in English, they have been divided into Early and Modern (although that division is general and not determined by a specific date).*

ARTS

CHARACTERS

HISTORY, LEGEND, ARCHAEOLOGY

LITERATURE

General

Celtic

"Dialogue of Arthur and Gwenhwyfar"
Dream of Rhonabwy
Gaelic Ballads
Geraint and Enid
Gododdin
Hélias, Pierre-Jakez
Irish Arthurian Literature
Langlais, Xavier de
Lorgaireacht an tSoidhigh Naomhtha
Mabinogi
Myrddin Poems
Owain
Peredur
Spoils of Annwfn
Taliesin
Triads
Welsh Arthurian Literature

Dutch

Dutch Arthurian Literature (Medieval)
Dutch Arthurian Literature (Modern)
Ferguut
Haar, Jaap ter
Historie van Merlijn
Lampo, Hubert
Lanceloet en het hert met de witte voet
Lancelot, Roman van
Lancelot-Compilatie
Lantsloot vander Haghedochte
Maerlant, Jacob van
Moriaen
Penninc and Pieter Vostaert
Perchevael
Riddere metter mouwen
Tristan
Velthem, Lodewijk van
Walewein ende Keye
Wrake van Ragisel

English, Early

Alliterative *Morte Arthure*
Anglo-Saxon Chronicle
Arthour and Merlin
Arthur
Arthur of Little Britain
Avowing of King Arthur, Sir Gawain, Sir Kay, and Baldwin of Britain
Awntyrs off Arthure at the Terne Wathelyn
"Boy and the Mantle"
Carle off Carlile
Caxton, William
Chaucer, Geoffrey
Chestre, Thomas
English Arthurian Literature (Medieval)
Foukes le Fitzwarin
Golagros and Gawane
Grene Knight
Here Begynneth the Lyfe of Joseph of Armathia with a Praysing to Joseph
Jeaste of Syr Gawayne
Joseph of Arimathie
"King Arthur and King Cornwall"
"King Arthur's Death"
Lancelot of the Laik
Layamon
"Legend of King Arthur"
Lovelich, Henry
Lydgate, John
Lyfe of Joseph of Armathy
Malory, Sir Thomas
"Marriage of Sir Gawain"
Parlement of the Thre Ages
Prose *Merlin* (2)
Short Metrical Chronicle
Sir Cleges
Sir Corneus, Romance of
Sir Degrevant
Sir Gawain and the Green Knight
Sir Gawan and Sir Galeron of Galloway
Sir Lambewell
Sir Lamwell
"Sir Lancelot du Lake"
Sir Landeval
Sir Perceval of Galles
Sir Tristrem
Stanzaic *Le Morte Arthur*
Syre Gawene and the Carle of Carlyle
Trevisa, John
Turke and Gowin
Wedding of Sir Gawain and Dame Ragnell
Ywain and Gawain

English, Modern Literature in

Adams, Oscar Fay
Aiken, Joan
Anderson, Poul
Anspacher, Louis K.
Arden, John, and Margaretta D'Arcy
Arnold, Matthew
Ashe, Geoffrey
Atterton, Julian
Atwood, Margaret
Austin, Martha Waddell
Babcock, William H.
Baden-Powell, Lord Robert
Badger, John D'Arcy
Bailey, Charles W.

Fawcett, Brian
Fawcett, Edgar
Fergusson, Adam
Field, Eugene
Field, Michael
Fielding, Henry
Finkel, George
Fisher, Robert
Ford, John M.
Forrest, Thorpe
Fortune, Dion
Frankland, Edward
French, Allen
Frere, John H.
Fry, Christopher
Fullarton, R. Macleod
Fuller, John G.
Furst, Clyde B.
Galloway, Christian F.J.
Gareth, David
Garner, Alan
Gash, Jonathan
Gemmell, David
Geoffrey Junior
Gibson, Wilfrid Wilson
Glasscock, Frederick Thomas
Glennie, John Stuart Stuart
Gloag, John
Glyn, Elinor
Godwin, Parke
Gray, Phoebe
Green, Robert Montraville
Gross, Joel
Guiterman, Arthur
Gunn, Thom
Gurr, David
Hagedorn, Hermann
Haldeman, Linda
Hamilton, Lord Ernest
Hanratty, Peter
Hardy, Thomas
Hare, Amory
Hawke, Simon
Hawker, Robert Stephen
Hayes, James Juvenal
Heard, John, Jr.
Hearne, Isabel
Heath-Stubbs, John
Heber, Reginald
Herbert, Kathleen
Hervey, Eleanora Louisa Montagu
Heywood, Thomas
Hildebrandt, Rita and Tim
Hill, Aaron
Hill, Graham
Hilton, William
Holdstock, Robert
Hole, Richard
Hollins, Dorothea
Horne, Richard Henry
Housman, Clemence
Hovey, Richard
Huemer, Richard
Hughes, Thomas
Hume, Cyril
Humphries, Rolfe
Hunter, Evan
Hunter, Jim
Hylton, John Dunbar
Ireland, William Henry
Jackson, Stephen
Jacobs, Maria
Jeter, K.W.
Jewett, Eleanore Myers
Johnson, Barbara Ferry
Johnson, Richard
Jones, David
Jones, Frank
Jones, Kathy, and Leona Aroha
Jones, Thomas Samuel, Jr.
Joyce, James
Juvenile Fiction in English
Kane, Gil, and John Jakes
Karr, Phyllis Ann
Katz, Welwyn Wilton
Kay, Guy Gavriel
Keith, Chester
Kendon, Frank
Kennealy, Patricia
King, Baragwanath
Kinross, Martha
Lange, M.R.
Lanier, Sterling E.
Laubenthal, Sanders Anne
Lawhead, Stephen R.
Lawrence, C.E.
Leader, Mary
Le Cain, Errol
Lee, Thomas Herbert
Levey, Sivori
Lewis, Charlton Miner
Lewis, C.S.
Leyden, John
Lindsay, Philip
Linwood, Mary
Lively, Penelope
Llewelyn, Morgan
Lodge, David
Lovell, Gerald
Lowe, Samuel E.

French

Artus de la Petite Bretagne
Atre périlleux
Auberon, Roman d'
Barjavel, René
Bataille de Loquifer
Bâtard de Bouillon
Bédier, Joseph
Benoit, Pierre
Béroul
Biket, Robert
Bliocadran Prologue
Briant, Théophile
Brun de la Montagne
Butor, Bauduin
Caradoc, Livre de
Carados
Châteaubriant, Alphonse de
Chevalier à l'épée
Chevalier du papegau
Chrétien de Troyes
Chrétien de Troyes, Burgundian Adaptations of
Claris et Laris
Cocteau, Jean
Continuations of *Perceval*
Cy nous dit
Delay, Florence
Didot-*Perceval*
Durmart le Gallois
Elucidation
Enfances Gauvain
Entrée d'Espagne
Escholier, Raymond, and Maurice Gardelle
Floriant et Florete
Folie Lancelot
Folie Tristan de Berne
Folie Tristan d'Oxford
Forme des tournoys au temps du roy Uterpendragon et du roy Artus
Foukes le Fitzwarin
French Arthurian Literature (Medieval)
French Arthurian Literature (Modern)
French Chivalric Romances, Eighteenth and Nineteenth Centuries
French Epic, Nineteenth Century
French Symbolism
Froissart, Jehan
Gaimar, Geffrei
Gargantuan Chronicles
Girart d'Amiens
Gliglois
Gogulor
Gonnot, Michot
Gracq, Julien
Graelent
Guénon, René
Guillaume le Clerc
Heldris de Cornualle
Hélias, Pierre-Jakez
Hunbaut
Huon de Bordeaux
Ilas et Solvas
Jean d'Outremeuse
Laforgue, Jules
Lancelot do Lac
Langlais, Xavier de
Livre d'Artus
Mantel mautaillié (*Lai du cort mantel*)
Marie de France
Maugin, Jean
Mélion
Mériadeuc (*Chevalier aux deux épées*)
Merveilles de Rigomer
Ogier le Danois, Roman d'
Ostroga, Yvonne
Paien de Maisières
Palamedes
Péladan, Joséphin
Perceforest
Perlesvaus
Pinget, Robert
Platin, Claude
Post-Vulgate Cycle
Prophécies de Merlin
Prose *Erec*
Prose *Merlin* (1)
Prose *Tristan*
Prose *Yvain*
Quinet, Edgar
Raoul de Houdenc
Renaut de Beaujeu
Robert de Blois
Robert de Boron
Roubaud, Jacques
Rusticiano da Pisa
Sala, Pierre
Samivel
Second Empire
Sept Sages de Rome
Sone de Nausay
Suite du Merlin
Thomas d'Angleterre
Tournier, Michel
Troubadours
Tyolet
Vaillant de Poitiers, Jean
Vallet à la cote mal tailliée
Vengeance Raguidel
Vian, Boris
Vilain qui devint riche et puis pauvre
Vulgate Cycle

German, Literature in

Wieland, Christoph Martin
Wigamur
Wigoleis vom Rade
Wippersberg, W. J. M.
Wirnt von Grafenberg
Wolf-Feuer, Käthe
Wolfram von Eschenbach
Workshop Moosach

Greek

Presbys Hippotes

Hebrew

Melekh Artus

Hispanic (Spanish, Portuguese, Provençal, Catalan)

Baladro del Sabio Merlín
Blandín de Cornualla
Broadsides (Spanish)
Carta enviada por Hiseo la Brunda a Tristán; Respuesta de Tristán
Cervantes Saavedra, Miguel de
Demanda do Santo Graal
Estoria de Merlín
Estoria del noble Vaspasiano
Ferreira de Vasconcelos, Jorge
Fructo de los tiempos
Gras, Mossèn
Jaufré
Josep Abaramatia, Livro de
Josep Abarimatia, Libro de
Lais de Bretanha
Lançarote de Lago
Martorell, Joanot, and Martí Joan de Galba
Montalvo, Garcí Rodríguez de
Persefores, Historia del noble rey
Salazar, Lope García de
Silva, António da, Mestre de Gramática
Spanish and Portuguese Arthurian Literature
Storia del Sant Grasal
Sumario de historia de los reyes de Bretaña
Tablante de Ricamonte
Torroella, Guillem de
Tristan in Spain and Portugal
Troubadours
Vives, Brother Juan
Zifar, Libro del Caballero

Italian

Alamanni, Luigi
Ariosto, Ludovico
Bel Gherardino
Berchet, Giovanni
Boccaccio, Giovanni
Boiardo, Matteo Maria
Boncompagno da Signa
Calvino, Italo
Cantare dei Cantari
Cantari
Cantari de Carduino
Cantari di Tristano
Chantari di Lancelotto
Conti dei Antichi Cavalieri
"Damigella di Scalot"
Dante Alighieri
Donna del Vergiù
Due Tristani
Entrée d'Espagne
Fatti de Spagna
Fazio degli Uberti
Febusso e Breusso
Fiorio e Biancifiore
Fossa, Matteo
Gatto Lupesco
Giovanni del Virgilio
Girone il Cortese
Gran Re Meliadus
Henricus of Settimello
Intelligenza
Italian Arthurian Literature
Lancelotto del Lago
Leopardi, Giacomo
Liombruno
Mare Amoroso
Moschino, Ettore
Nicolò degli Agostini
Novellino
Parsaforesto
Pieri, Paolino
Pucci, Antonio
Pulzella Gaia
Quando Tristano e Lancielotto combattettero al petrone di Merlino
Rusticiano da Pisa
Sette savi di Roma
Spagna
Tavola ritonda
Tristano Panciaticchiano
Tristano Riccardiano
Tristano Veneto
Tumiati, Domenico
Ultime imprese e morte di Tristano
Vendetta che fe Messer Lanzelloto de la morte di Miser Tristano
Vita di Merlino con le sue profetie

Japanese

Sōseki, Natsume

Latin

Andreas Capellanus
Arthur and Gorlagon
De Coniuge non Ducenda
De Ortu Waluuanii nepotis Arturi
Étienne de Rouen
Historia Meriadoci regis Cambrie
Liber de Compositione Castri Ambaziae
Map, Walter
Vera Historia de Morte Arthuri

Scandinavian

Breta sǫgur
Brother Robert
Erex saga
Eufemia
Gabons saga ok Vigoles
Gunnlaugr Leifsson
Hákon Hákonarson
Her Viegoleis med Guld Hiulet
Ivan Lejonriddaren
"Iven Erningsson"
Ívens saga
Ívint Herintsson
"Kvikkjesprakk"
Möttuls saga
Níels Jónsson
Old Swedish Legendary
Parcevals saga
Saga af Tristram ok Ísodd
Samsons saga fagra
Scandinavian Arthurian Literature
Sigurður Breiðfjörð
Skikkju rímur
Strengleikar
"Tistram og Isold"
"Tistram og Jomfru Isolt"
"Tístrams táttur"
Tistrans saga ok Indiönu
Tragoedisk Historie om den ædle og tappre Tistrand
Tristan in Scandinavia
"Tristram og Ísól bjarta"
"Tristrams kvæði"
Tristrams saga ok Ísöndar
Valvens þáttr

Slavic

Czech Arthurian Literature
Kuncewiczowa, Maria
Marek, Jiři
Povest' o Tryshchane
Švarc, Evgenij L.
Tomaszewski, Henryk

Tagalog

Tablante de Ricamonte sampo nang magasauang si Jofre at ni Bruniesen

Yiddish

Widwilt

PLACES

Albion
Avalon
Badon
Brittany
Brocéliande
Cadbury-Camelot
Caerleon
Camelot
Camlann
Castle Dore
Castle of Maidens
Corbenic
Dinas Emrys
Glastonbury
Gorre
Joyous Gard
Kelliwic
Logres
Lyonesse
Perilous Chapel
Sarras
Stonehenge
Tintagel
Val sans Retour
Winchester

THEMES, MOTIFS, OBJECTS

Bleeding Lance
Cave Legend
Chastity Tests
Dolorous Stroke
Excalibur
Grail
Nine Worthies
Perilous Seat
Questing Beast
Round Table

Sword in the Stone
Sword of the Strange Hangings
Tryst Beneath the Tree
Wasteland

MISCELLANEOUS

Arms and Armor
Ballets
Baltic Region, Arthurian Clubs in
Chivalry
Comics
Courtly Love
Experimental Theater
Films
Folklore
Frappier, Jean
Games
Henning, Doug
Heraldry
Holmes, Urban Tigner, Jr.
International Arthurian Society
Jung, Emma
Loomis, Roger Sherman
Manuscripts, Illuminated
Map, Walter
Marvels and the Marvelous
Masques
Matière de Bretagne
Medievalism
Merlin and the Prophetic Tradition
Nine Worthies
Philately
Popular Culture
Round Tables
Scholarship, Modern Arthurian
Tarot, Merlin
Television Series
Tournaments
Vinaver, Eugène
Weston, Jessie
Women, Arthurian

List of Illustrations

Selected Bibliography

The following bibliography is selective and comparatively brief; it is intended to offer suggestions for further reading. For additional information, the reader may consult the bibliographical information appended to most entries.

Several periodicals or series are devoted entirely to Arthurian subjects. The oldest of these is the Bibliographical Bulletin of the International Arthurian Society, *an annual that lists all the preceding year's publications on medieval Arthurian literature; it also includes several articles, a list of members of the Society, and Arthurian news.* Arthurian Interpretations *offers studies of Arthuriana, both medieval and modern.* Quondam et Futurus *is a newsletter that provides information on conferences, publications, and other matters and includes some articles and reviews.* Tristania *publishes articles on all aspects of the Tristan legend. Garland's* Arthurian Yearbook *publishes new studies and reprints important articles that are no longer easily available in their original form. Finally,* Arthurian Literature *offers extended studies, editions, and translations of Arthurian literature.*

I. BIBLIOGRAPHIES

Bibliographical Bulletin of the International Arthurian Society, 1 (1945)–41 (1989).

Last, Rex, ed. *The Arthurian Bibliography, 3*. Cambridge: Brewer, 1985.

———, ed. *The Arthurian Bibliography, III: Supplement 1979–1983*. Cambridge: Brewer, 1987.

Pickford, Cedric E., and Rex Last, eds. *The Arthurian Bibliography, I: Author Listing*. Cambridge: Brewer, 1981.

———, ———, and C.R. Barker, eds. *The Arthurian Bibliography, II: Subject Index*. Cambridge: Brewer, 1983.

Reiss, Edmund, Louise Horner Reiss, and Beverly Taylor. *Arthurian Legend and Literature: An Annotated Bibliography. I: The Middle Ages*. New York: Garland, 1984.

II. ANTHOLOGIES

Barber, Richard. *The Arthurian Legends: An Illustrated Anthology*. Woodbridge, Suffolk: Boydell, 1979.

Brengle, Richard L. *Arthur, King of Britain*. New York: Appleton-Century-Crofts, 1964.

Goodrich, Peter, ed. *The Romance of Merlin: An Anthology*. New York: Garland, 1991.

Hill, Joyce, ed. *The Tristan Legend: Texts from Northern and Eastern Europe in Modern English Translation*. Leeds: University of Leeds, Graduate Centre for Medieval Studies, 1977.

Lupack, Alan, ed. *"Arthur, the Greatest King": An Anthology of Modern Arthurian Poetry*. New York: Garland, 1988.

———, ed. *Arthurian Drama: An Anthology*. New York: Garland, 1991.

Matthews, John, ed. *An Arthurian Reader*. Wellingborough: Aquarian, 1988.

Wilhelm, James J., ed. *The Romance of Arthur II*. New York: Garland, 1986.

———, ed. *The Romance of Arthur III*. New York: Garland, 1988.

———, and Laila Zamuelis Gross, eds. *The Romance of Arthur*. New York: Garland, 1984.

III. GENERAL

Ashe, Geoffrey. *The Landscape of King Arthur*. Photographs by Simon McBride. Exeter: Webb and Bower, 1987.

Baswell, Christopher, and William Sharpe, eds. *The Passing of Arthur: New Essays in Arthurian Tradition*. New York: Garland, 1988.

Braswell, Mary Flowers, and John Bugge, eds. *The Arthurian Tradition: Essays in Convergence*. Tuscaloosa: University of Alabama Press, 1988.

Dean, Christopher. *Arthur of England: English Attitudes to King Arthur and the Knights of the Round Table in the Middle Ages and the Renaissance*. Toronto: University of Toronto Press, 1987.

Lacy, Norris J., and Geoffrey Ashe. *The Arthurian Handbook*. New York: Garland, 1988.

Lagorio, Valerie M., and Mildred Leake Day, eds. *King Arthur Through the Ages*. 2 vols. New York: Garland, 1990.

Moorman, Charles, and Ruth Moorman. *An Arthurian Dictionary*. N.p.: University Press of Mississippi, 1978.

Pors, Mette, ed. *The Vitality of the Arthurian Legend: A Symposium*. Odense: Odense University Press, 1988.

IV. HISTORY AND LEGEND

Alcock, Leslie. *Arthur's Britain: History and Archaeology A.D. 367–634*. London: Penguin, 1971.

———. *"By South Cadbury is That Camelot . . .": Excavations at Cadbury Castle 1966–70*. London: Thames and Hudson, 1972.

———. "Cadbury-Camelot: A Fifteen-Year Perspective." *Proceedings of the British Academy*, 68 (1982), 355–88.

Ashe, Geoffrey. "A Certain Very Ancient Book': Traces of an Arthurian Source in Geoffrey of Monmouth's *History*." *Speculum*, 56 (1981), 301–23.

———. *A Guidebook to Arthurian Britain*. Wellingborough: Aquarian, 1983.

———. *Avalonian Quest*. London: Methuen, 1982.

———, ed. *The Quest for Arthur's Britain*. London and New York: Praeger, 1968.

Barber, R.W. *Arthur of Albion*. London: Barrie and Rockliff, 1961.

———. *King Arthur: Hero and Legend*. New York: St. Martin, 1986.

Bromwich, Rachel. "Scotland and the Earliest Arthurian Tradition." *Bibliographical Bulletin of the International Arthurian Society*, 15 (1963), 85–95.

Carley, James P. *Glastonbury Abbey*. Woodbridge, Suffolk: Boydell and Brewer, 1988.

Chambers, E.K. *Arthur of Britain*. London: Sidgwick and Jackson, 1927.

Darrah, John. *The Real Camelot: Paganism and the Arthurian Romances*. London: Thames and Hudson, 1981.

Dumville, David. "Sub-Roman Britain: History and Legend." *History*, 62 (1977), 173–92.

Dunning, R.W. *Arthur: The King in the West*. New York: St. Martin, 1988.

Fletcher, Robert Huntington. *The Arthurian Material in the Chronicles, Especially Those of Great Britain and France*. Boston: Ginn, 1906; 2nd ed. Roger Sherman Loomis. New York: Franklin, 1966.

Jenkins, Elizabeth. *The Mystery of King Arthur*. New York: Coward, McCann and Geoghegan, 1975.

Jones, W. Lewis. *King Arthur in History and Legend*. Cambridge: Cambridge University Press, 1911.

Lindsay, Jack. *Arthur and His Times*. London: Muller, 1958.

Loomis, Roger Sherman. *Celtic Myth and Arthurian Romance*. New York: Columbia University Press, 1927.

———. *Wales and the Arthurian Legend*. Cardiff: University of Wales Press, 1956.

Morris, John. *The Age of Arthur*. New York: Scribner, 1973.

Newstead, Helaine. *Bran the Blessed in Arthurian Romance*. New York: Columbia University Press, 1939.

Paton, Lucy Allen. *Studies in the Fairy Mythology of Arthurian Romance*. Boston: Ginn, 1903; 2nd ed. Roger Sherman Loomis. New York: Franklin, 1960.

Radford, C.A. Ralegh, and Michael J. Swanton. *Arthurian Sites in the West*. Exeter: University of Exeter, 1975.

Schirmer, W.F. *Die frühen Darstellungen des Arthurstoffes*. Cologne: Opladen, 1958.

Treharne, R.F. *The Glastonbury Legends*. London: Cresset, 1967.

Westwood, Jennifer. *Albion: A Guide to Legendary Britain*. London: Granada, 1985.

Williams, Mary. "King Arthur in History and Legend." *Folklore*, 73 (1962), 73–88.

V. ARTHUR AND ARTHURIAN CHARACTERS

App, August J. *Lancelot in English Literature: His Role and Character*. Washington, D.C.: Catholic University of America Press, 1929.

Baker, Imogene. *The King's Household in the Arthurian Court from Geoffrey of Monmouth to Malory*. Washington, D.C.: Catholic University of America Press, 1937.

Busby, Keith. *Gauvain in Old French Literature*. Amsterdam: Rodopi, 1980.

Eisner, Sigmund. *The Tristan Legend: A Study in Sources*. Evanston, Ill.: Northwestern University Press, 1969.

Fox, Marjorie. "Merlin in the Arthurian Prose Cycle." *Arthuriana*, 2 (1929–30), 20–29.

Gollnick, James, ed. *Comparative Studies in Merlin from the Vedas to C.G. Jung*. Lewiston, N.Y.: Mellen, 1990.

Harding, Carol. *Merlin and Legendary Romance*. New York: Garland, 1988.

Haupt, Jürgen. *Der Truchsess Keie im Artusroman*. Berlin: Schmidt, 1971.

Jarman, A.O.H. *The Legend of Merlin*. Cardiff: University of Wales Press, 1960.

Kennedy, Elspeth. "King Arthur in the First Part of the *Prose Lancelot*." *Medieval Miscellany Presented to Eugène Vinaver*. Manchester: Manchester University Press, 1965, pp. 186–95.

Morris, Rosemary. *The Character of King Arthur in Medieval Literature*. Cambridge: Brewer, 1982.

Nitze, William A. "The Character of Gauvain in the Romances of Chrétien de Troyes." *Modern Philology*, 50 (1952–53), 219–25.

Noble, Peter. "The Character of Guinevere in the Arthurian Romances of Chrétien de Troyes." *Modern Language Review*, 67 (1972), 524–35.

Owen, D.D.R. "The Development of the Perceval Story." *Romania*, 80 (1959), 473–92.

Schoepperle, Gertrude. *Tristan and Isolt: A Study of the Sources of the Romance*. 2 vols. Frankfurt, 1913; 2nd ed. New York: Franklin, 1959.

Soudek, Ernst. *Studies in the Lancelot Legend*. Houston: Rice University Press, 1972.

Tolstoy, Nikolai. *The Quest for Merlin*. London: Hamish Hamilton, 1985.

Tyson, Diana B. "King Arthur as a Literary Device in French Vernacular History Writing of the Fourteenth Century." *Bibliographical Bulletin of the International Arthurian Society*, 33 (1981), 237–57.

Weston, Jessie L. *The Legend of Sir Gawain: Studies upon Its Original Scope and Significance*. London: Nutt, 1897.

———. *The Legend of Sir Lancelot du Lac*. London: Nutt, 1901.

———. *The Legend of Sir Perceval: Studies upon Its Origin, Development and Position in the Arthurian Cycle.* 2 vols. London: Nutt, 1906, 1909.

Zumthor, Paul. *Merlin le prophète: un thème de la littérature polémique de l'historiographie et des romans.* Lausanne: Payot, 1943.

VI. LITERATURE

Adams, Alison, Armel H. Diverres, Karen Stern, and Kenneth Varty, eds. *The Changing Face of Arthurian Romance: Essays on Arthurian Prose Romances in Memory of Cedric E. Pickford.* Cambridge: Brewer, 1986.

Barron, W.R.J. *English Medieval Romance.* London and New York: Longman, 1987.

Benson, Larry D. *Art and Tradition in Sir Gawain and the Green Knight.* New Brunswick, N.J.: Rutgers University Press, 1965.

———. *Malory's "Morte Darthur."* Cambridge: Harvard University Press, 1976.

Blakeslee, Merritt R. *Love's Masks: Identity, Intertextuality and Meaning in the Old French Tristan Poems.* Cambridge: Brewer, 1989.

Brinkley, Roberta F. *Arthurian Legend in the Seventeenth Century.* Baltimore: Johns Hopkins Press, 1932.

Bruce, James Douglas. *The Evolution of Arthurian Romance from the Beginnings Down to the Year 1300*, 2nd ed. 2 vols. Baltimore: Johns Hopkins Press, 1928.

Draak, Maartje. *Arthur en zijn Tafelronde.* The Hague, 1951.

Entwistle, W.J. *Arthurian Legend in the Literatures of the Spanish Peninsula.* London: Dent, 1925.

Faral, Edmond. *La Légende arthurienne: études et documents.* 3 vols. Paris, 1929.

Frappier, Jean. *Amour courtois et Table Ronde.* Geneva: Droz, 1973.

———. *Chrétien de Troyes.* Paris: Hatier, 1957.

Gardner, Edmund G. *The Arthurian Legend in Italian Literature.* London: Dent, 1930.

Goodman, Jennifer R. *The Legend of Arthur in British and American Literature.* Boston: Twayne, 1987.

Jackson, W.T.H. *The Anatomy of Love: The Tristan of Gottfried von Strassburg.* New York: Columbia University Press, 1971.

Kalinke, Marianne E. *King Arthur, North-by-Northwest: The "matière de Bretagne" in Old Norse-Icelandic Romances.* Copenhagen: Reitzel, 1981.

Köhler, Erich. *Ideal und Wirklichkeit in der höfischen Epik.* Tübingen: Niemeyer, 1956; 2nd ed., 1970.

Lacy, Norris J., Douglas Kelly, and Keith Busby, eds. *The Legacy of Chrétien de Troyes.* 2 vols. Amsterdam: Rodopi, 1987–88.

Lazar, Moshé. *Amour courtois et fin'amors dans la littérature du XIIe siècle.* Paris: Klincksieck, 1964.

Loomis, Roger Sherman, ed. *Arthurian Literature in the Middle Ages: A Collaborative History.* Oxford: Clarendon, 1959.

———. *The Development of Arthurian Romance.* New York: Harper and Row, 1963.

Loth, Joseph. *Contributions à l'étude des romans de la Table Ronde.* Paris, 1912.

Lumiansky, R.M., ed. *Malory's Originality.* Baltimore: Johns Hopkins University Press, 1964.

Marx, Jean. *Nouvelles Recherches sur la littérature arthurienne.* Paris: Klincksieck, 1965.

Merriman, James Douglas. *The Flower of Kings: A Study of the Arthurian Legend in England Between 1485 and 1835.* Lawrence: University Press of Kansas, 1973.

Owen, D.D.R., ed. *Arthurian Romance: Seven Essays.* New York: Barnes and Noble, 1971.

Poag, James F. *Wolfram von Eschenbach.* New York: Twayne, 1972.

Rosenberg, John D. *The Fall of Camelot: A Study of Tennyson's Idylls of the King.* Cambridge: Belknap, 1973.

Schmolke-Hasselmann, Beate. *Der arthurische Versroman von Chrestien bis Froissart.* Tübingen: Niemeyer, 1980.

Schultz, James A. *The Shape of the Round Table: Structures of Middle High German Arthurian Romance.* Toronto: University of Toronto Press, 1983.

Sharrer, Harvey L. *A Critical Bibliography of Hispanic Arthurian Material.* London: Grant and Cutler, 1977, Vol. 1: *Texts: The Prose Romance Cycles.*

Staines, David. *Tennyson's Camelot: The Idylls of the King and Its Medieval Sources.* Waterloo, Ont.: Wilfrid Laurier University Press, 1983.

Starr, Nathan Comfort. *King Arthur Today: The Arthurian Legend in English and American Literature, 1901–1953.* Gainesville: University of Florida Press, 1954.

Stevens, John. *Medieval Romance: Themes and Approaches.* London: Hutchinson, 1973.

Taylor, Beverly, and Elisabeth Brewer. *The Return of King Arthur: British and American Literature Since 1800.* Woodbridge, Suffolk: Boydell and Brewer; Totowa, N.J.: Barnes and Noble, 1983.

Thompson, Raymond H. *The Return from Avalon: A Study of the Arthurian Legend in Modern Fiction.* Westport, Conn.: Greenwood, 1985.

Varty, Kenneth, ed. *An Arthurian Tapestry: Essays in Memory of Lewis Thorpe.* Glasgow: French Department of the University, 1981.

Verbeke, W., J. Janssens, and M. Smeyers, eds. *Arturus Rex, 1: Catalogus.* Leuven: Leuven University Press, 1987.

Vinaver, Eugène. *Form and Meaning in Medieval Romance.* Leeds: Maney, 1966.

———. *The Rise of Romance.* Oxford: Clarendon, 1971.

Wapnewski, Peter. *Hartmann von Aue*, 3rd ed. Stuttgart: Metzler, 1967.

Wilson, Anne. *The Magical Quest: The Use of Magic in Arthurian Romance.* Manchester: Manchester University Press, 1988.

Wolfzettel, Friedrich, ed. *Artusroman und Intertextualität.* Giessen: Schmitz, 1990.

VII. ARTS

Gerould, G.H. "Arthurian Romance and the Date of the Relief at Modena." *Speculum*, 10 (1935), 355–76.

Harty, Kevin. "Cinema Arthuriana: Translations of the Arthurian Legend to the Screen." *Arthurian Interpretations*, 2 (1987), 95–113.

Haug, Walter. *Das Mosaik von Otranto: Darstellung, Deutung, und Bilddokumentation*. Wiesbaden: Reichert, 1977.

Loomis, Roger Sherman, and Laura Hibbard Loomis. *Arthurian Legends in Medieval Art*. London: Oxford University Press, 1938.

Mancoff, Debra N. *The Arthurian Revival in Victorian Art*. New York: Garland, 1990.

Newman, Ernest. *The Wagner Operas*. New York: Knopf, 1949.

Olschki, Leonardo. "La cattedrale di Modena e il suo rilievo arturiano." *Archivum Romanicum*, 19 (1935), 145–82.

Scherer, Margaret R. *About the Round Table*. New York: Metropolitan Museum of Art, 1945.

Whitaker, Muriel. *The Legends of King Arthur in Art*. Cambridge: Brewer, 1990.

VIII. THEMES, SYMBOLS, MOTIFS

Adolf, Helen. *Visio Pacis. Holy City and Grail: An Attempt at an Inner History of the Grail Legend*. State College: Pennsylvania State University Press, 1960.

Brown, Arthur C.L. "The Bleeding Lance." *PMLA*, 25 (1910), 1–59.

———. *The Origin of the Grail Legend*. Cambridge: Harvard University Press, 1943.

Bruce, James Douglas. "The Development of the Mort Arthur Theme in Mediaeval Romance." *Romanic Review* 4 (1913), 403–71.

Cosman, Madeleine Pelner. *The Education of the Hero in Arthurian Romance*. Chapel Hill: University of North Carolina Press, 1966.

Frappier, Jean. "Le Graal et la chevalerie." *Romania*, 75 (1954), 165–210.

Harward, Vernon J., Jr. *The Dwarfs of Arthurian Romance and Celtic Tradition*. Leiden: Brill, 1958.

Holmes, Urban Tigner, Jr., and M. Amelia Klenke. *Chrétien, Troyes, and the Grail*. Chapel Hill: University of North Carolina Press, 1959.

Jonin, Pierre. *Les Personnages féminins dans les romans français de Tristan au XII siècle: étude des influences contemporaines*. Aix: Ophrys, 1958.

Kahn Blumstein, Andrée. *Misogyny and Idealization in the Courtly Romance*. Bonn: Bouvier Verlag Herbert Grundmann, 1977.

Kennedy, Angus. "The Hermit's Role in French Arthurian Romance (c. 1170–1530)." *Romania*, 95 (1974), 54–83.

Lewis, Gertrud Jaron. *Das Tier und seine dichterische Funktion in Erec, Iwein, Parzival und Tristan*. Bern and Frankfurt: Herbert Lang, 1974.

Loomis, Laura Hibbard. "Arthur's Round Table." *PMLA*, 41 (1926), 771–84.

Loomis, Roger Sherman. "Arthurian Tradition and Folklore." *Folklore*, 69 (1958), 1–25.

———. "The Legend of Arthur's Survival." In *Arthurian Literature in the Middle Ages: A Collaborative History*. Oxford: Clarendon, 1959.

———. "The Visit to the Perilous Castle: A Study of the Arthurian Modifications of an Irish Theme." *PMLA*, 48 (1933), 1000–35.

———. *The Grail, From Celtic Myth to Christian Symbol*. Cardiff: University of Wales Press, 1963.

Marx, Jean. *La Légende arthurienne et le Graal*. Paris: Presses Universitaires, 1952.

Mott, Lewis F. "The Round Table." *PMLA*, 20 (1905), 231–64.

Muir, Lynette R. "The Questing Beast: Its Origin and Development." *Orpheus*, 4 (1957), 24–32.

Nelli, René, ed. *Lumière du Graal: études et textes*. Paris: Cahiers du Sud, 1951.

Newstead, Helaine. "The Besieged Lady in Arthurian Romance." *PMLA*, 63 (1948), 803–30.

Nitze, William A. "The Fisher King in the Grail Romances." *PMLA*, 24 (1909), 365–418.

———. "The Wasteland: A Celtic Arthurian Theme." *Modern Philology*, 43 (1945–46), 58–62.

Owen, D.D.R. *The Evolution of the Grail Legend*. Edinburgh and London: Oliver and Boyd, 1968.

Pickford, Cedric E. "Camelot." In *Mélanges de langue et de littérature médiévales offerts à Pierre Le Gentil*. Paris: SEDES, 1973.

Vinaver, Eugène. "King Arthur's Sword, or the Making of a Medieval Romance." *Bulletin of the John Rylands Library*, 40 (1957–58), 513–26.

Weston, Jessie. *From Ritual to Romance*. Cambridge: Cambridge University Press, 1920.

Chronology

The following chronology is both highly selective and, in some cases, approximate. It is selective for the obvious reason: a far longer listing, which would quickly get out of hand, would not necessarily be more useful. Consequently, we have included only a small number of the available titles and events, and for the twentieth century that percentage is by necessity minuscule. In addition to listing only a few names, we have in most cases included only a single title, or two at most, by authors and artists who have treated Arthurian themes repeatedly.

While a few dates in the Post-Roman period and the later Middle Ages are firmly established either within texts themselves or by scholarly assent, others remain vague. Very often, scholars are able to date texts only within a quarter- or even half-century, and Welsh compositions with far less precision than that. For example, scholars will often identify a Welsh work as being "probably from the thirteenth century," and in those instances (such as the "Three Welsh Romances") the date 1250 has been chosen arbitrarily. We are similarly arbitrary when there is an accepted range of dates (1136–38 for Geoffrey of Monmouth, 1200–15 for *Perlesvaus*). Thus, for the medieval period, the reader should consider the following dates to be a general guide. Our purpose is simply to provide a useful and accessible listing of events, literary texts, and artistic creations related to the Arthurian legends; the entries devoted to specific items will generally clarify problems of dating texts.

5th–6th CENTURIES

As Rome withdraws its forces from Britain, native Celtic, Christian leaders struggle against inroads of Saxon invaders. Sometime in this period, a British leader wins a victory against the Saxons, temporarily halting their advance. Though Arthur is mentioned in no contemporary documents that survive, his legend has its roots in this period.

410	Britain separates from Empire
425–50	Vortigern rules
450	Colonization of Brittany by British refugees from Saxon invasion
455–75	Arthur reigning in this period, according to Geoffrey of Monmouth
460	Ambrosius Aurelianus attacks Saxon enclaves
460–500	Cadbury refortified; Tintagel an important center
468	"King of Britons" crosses into Gaul
500	Siege of Mount Badon
540	Gildas, *De Excidio Britanniae*: reference to battle of Mount Badon
550	The name "Artorius" undergoes a revival of popularity, as witnessed in contemporary documents
575	Legendary activities of Myrddin (or Lailoken)

7th–11th CENTURIES

The stories about Arthur and Merlin enter oral tradition, especially in the "Celtic fringe" (Wales, Cornwall, Brittany). The tales are circulated to the Continent, perhaps by Breton storytellers.

600	*Gododdin*: may be first mention of Arthur by name
800	Nennius, *Historia Brittonum*: first mention of Arthur as *dux bellorum*; reference to supernatural gifts of Ambrosius Aurelianus, later to be known as Merlin
950	*Spoils of Annwfn*
	Annales Cambriae: reference to battle of Camlann, in which Arthur and Medraut fell
1019	*Legenda Sancti Goeznovii*: first "historical" mention of Arthur

1050 *Mabinogi*

Culhwch and Olwen

Welsh saints' lives

12th CENTURY

Arthur is mentioned in chronicles and saints' lives. The fictional biography by Geoffrey of Monmouth stimulates intense interest in the legends, which are cast as verse romances, beginning with Chrétien de Troyes in France. The legends have reached at least as far as Italy and Germany. In England, Arthur's "grave" is discovered.

1110 Perros Relief: first Arthurian sculpture

1125 William of Malmesbury, *Gesta Regum Anglorum*

1129 Henry of Huntingdon, *Historia Anglorum*

1130 Caradoc, *Vita Gildae*: first linking of Arthur and Glastonbury

1135 Modena Archivolt

1136–38 Geoffrey of Monmouth, *Historia Regum Britanniae*: first full "biography" of Arthur, first mention of Merlin by that name

1155 Wace, *Roman de Brut*: first mention of Round Table

1165 Otranto Mosaic

1160–90 Chrétien de Troyes: first romances focusing on Arthur's knights; first mention of Fisher King, Grail, Bleeding Lance, Camelot, Lancelot

1170 Marie de France, *Lanval* and *Chevrefueil*

1175 Thomas d'Angleterre, *Tristan*

1180 Eilhart von Oberge, *Tristrant*

1185 Andreas Capellanus, *De Amore*

Renaut de Beaujeu, *Le Bel Inconnu*

1190 Layamon, *Brut*: first Arthurian work in English

1191 Discovery of "Arthur's Grave," Glastonbury

Béroul, *Tristran*

1193 Giraldus Cambrensis, *De Principis Instructione*: records discovery of Arthur's body at Glastonbury

13th CENTURY

The period of the great prose cycles. The tales of Arthur and his knights are expanded to include the history of the Grail and Joseph of Arimathea. Arthurian works are composed in languages from Old Norse to Spanish.

1200 Robert de Boron: first cycle of Grail romances and first mention of Sword in the Stone, in *Merlin*

Gunnlaugr Leifsson, *Merlínusspá*

De Ortu Waluuanii

Perlesvaus: perhaps earliest prose Arthurian romance

Hartmann von Aue, *Erec* and *Iwein*

1210 Wolfram von Eschenbach, *Parzival*

Gottfried von Strassburg, *Tristan*

Wirnt von Grafenberg, *Wigalois*

1215–35 Vulgate Cycle: huge prose version of the Arthurian story, from the early Grail history to the death of Arthur; first mention of Galahad by name

1220 *Jaufré*

First illuminated Arthurian manuscript (Rennes 225)

1225 Der Stricker, *Daniel von dem blühenden Tal*

1226 Brother Robert, *Tristrams saga ok Ísöndar*: commissioned by Hákon IV of Norway

1230 Heinrich von dem Türlin, *Diu Crône*

1230–40 Post-Vulgate Cycle

1250 *Historia Meriodoci*

Three Welsh Romances

Wigamur

Prose *Tristan*: fully integrates Tristan story with Arthurian cycle

1260 Der Pleier, *Garel von dem blühenden Tal*

1261 Jacob van Maerlant, *Boec van Merline*

1270 Chertsey Abbey Tiles

Albrecht, *Der jüngere Titurel*

1275 Rusticiano da Pisa, *Compilation*: first Arthurian romance composed by an Italian

1279 *Melekh Artus*

1280 Penninc and Pieter Vostaert, *Roman van Walewein*

Tristano Riccardiano

1300 *Blandín de Cornualla*

Libro del Caballero Zifar

Sir Tristrem

Il Novellino

14th-15th CENTURIES

Arthurian compilations and lengthy prose romances. Flowering and eventual decline of Arthurian manuscript illustration. Medieval tradition culminates in Malory.

1303 *Herr Ivan Lejonriddaren*

1310 Jacques de Longuyon, *Les Voeux du paon*: first list of Nine Worthies (Arthur is first Christian worthy)

1313 Brother Juan Vives, Spanish translation of French Post-Vulgate

1320 *Arthur and Gorlagon*

Wienhausen Embroideries

1330 Winchester Round Table

Perceforest

1340 *Amadís*, original version

Tavola Ritonda

1380 Jehan Froissart, *Meliador*: last French Arthurian verse romance

Antonio Pucci, *Gismirante*

Thomas Chestre, *Libeaus Desconus*

Tandariáš a Floribella

1385 Cloisters Tapestry

1390 Alliterative *Morte Arthure*

1400 Stanzaic *Le Morte Arthur*

Runkelstein Murals

Saga af Tristan ok Ísodd

El Cuento de Tristán de Leonís

Sir Gawain and the Green Knight

1420 La Manta Murals

Louvre Tray

Anton Sorg, *Tristan*: first printed Arthurian book illustrated with woodcuts

1425 *The Avowing of King Arthur*

1450 Pisanello's murals at Mantua

Henry Lovelich, *History of the Holy Grail*

1460 Joanot Martorell and Martí Joan de Galba, *Tirant le Blanc*

1467 Ulrich Fuetrer, *Prosaroman von Lanzelot*

1470 Sir Thomas Malory, *Le Morte Darthur* (completed); last great Arthurian work of Middle Ages; influenced most future Arthurian texts in English

1485 William Caxton's printing of Malory

1490 Matteo Maria Boiardo, *Orlando Innamorato*

1498 Wynkyn de Worde: prints first illustrated Malory

16th-18th CENTURIES

Waning of interest in Arthur; descent into satire with Cervantes. Period of ballads, chapbooks, broadsides. Beginnings of modern Arthurian scholarship.

1508 Garci Rodríguez de Montalvo, *Amadís de Gaula*

1512-13 Polydore Vergil, *Anglica Historia*

1516 Ludovico Ariosto, *Orlando Furioso*

1525 Pierre Sala, *Tristan*

1527 Burghley Nef

1542 John Leland identifies Cadbury Castle as Camelot

1543-53 Hans Sachs, "Die Ehbrecherbruck," *Tragedia*

1554 Jean Maugin, *Nouveau Tristan*

1555 *I due Tristani*

1587 Thomas Hughes, *The Misfortunes of Arthur*

1590-96 Edmund Spenser, *The Faerie Queene*

1605 Miguel de Cervantes, *Don Quixote*

1610 Ben Jonson, *The Speeches at Prince Henry's Barriers*

1612 Michael Drayton, *Poly-Olbion*

1691 Henry Purcell and John Dryden, *King Arthur, or The British Worthy*

1695 Richard Blackmore, *Prince Arthur*

1730–31 Henry Fielding, *Tom Thumb*

1733 Thomas Arne, *The Opera of Operas*

1735 "Merlin's Cave" built at Richmond

1760 Aaron Hill, *Merlin in Love*

1767 John Mortimer, *Discovery of Prince Arthur's Tomb*

1789 Richard Hole, *Arthur: or, The Northern Enchantment*

19th CENTURY

Arthurian Revival. New editions of Malory and other works. Dyce and Tennyson give major impetus to Arthurian art; the Pre-Raphaelites and other artists cultivate Arthurian themes. Late in the century, Wagner's operas inspire artists and writers, especially in France and Germany.

1801 John Thelwall, *The Fairy of the Lake*

1810 Christoph Wieland, *Merlins weissagende Stimme*

1817–18 John Hookham Frere, *The Monks and the Giants*

1829 Thomas Love Peacock, *The Misfortunes of Elphin*

1832 Karl Immermann, *Merlin, eine mythe*

1834 Thomas S. Cooke, *King Arthur and the Knights of the Round Table*

1834–85 Alfred Lord Tennyson, *Idylls of the King*

1848 Founding of Pre-Raphaelite Brotherhood

1848–64 William Dyce, murals in the Queen's Robing Room

1850 William Holman Hunt, *The Lady of Shalott*

1854 Dante Gabriel Rossetti, *King Arthur's Tomb*: Rossetti's first Arthurian painting

1852 Matthew Arnold, *Tristram and Iseult*

1857 Oxford Union Murals

Moxon Tennyson

1858 William Morris, *The Defence of Guenevere*

1859 Gustave Doré, illustrations for *Idylls of the King*

1860 Edgar Quinet, *Merlin l'enchanteur*

1861 Henry Peach Robinson, *Lady of Shalott* (first Arthurian photograph)

1862 Dunlop Windows

1865 Richard Wagner, *Tristan und Isolde*

1875 Julia M. Cameron, photographs (first publication)

1875–77 Edward Burne-Jones, *The Beguiling of Merlin*

1880 Sidney Lanier, *A Boy's King Arthur*: most influential children's version of legends

1880–98 Edward Burne-Jones, *Arthur in Avalon*

1882 Algernon Swinburne, *Tristram of Lyonesse*

Richard Wagner, *Parsifal*

1885 Founding of *La Revue Wagnerienne*

1886 Karl Goldmark, *Merlin*

Jules Laforgue, *Lohengrin, fils de Parsifal*

1888 William Waterhouse, *The Lady of Shalott*

1889 Mark Twain, *A Connecticut Yankee in King Arthur's Court*

1890 Founding of Kelmscott Press

1890–1901 Edwin Austin Abbey, Boston Public Library murals

1891–98 Richard Hovey, *Launcelot and Guenevere*

1893–94 Aubrey Beardsley's illustrations for Dent *Morte D'Arthur*

1895 J. Comyns Carr, *King Arthur*

Ernest Chausson, *Le Roi Arthus* (performed 1903)

1897 James Archer, *La Mort d'Arthur*

George Frederick Watts, *Sir Galahad*

1897–1900 Karl Vollmöller, *Parcival*

1898 Wilhelm Hertz, *Die Sage von Parzival und dem Gral*

20th CENTURY

Arthurian literature flourishes, especially in English-speaking countries. Interest in Arthur leads to important advances in scholarship (including archaeology) and to the reentry of Arthurian themes into

popular culture (films, games, comics, and commercial enterprises). Explosion of novels after T.H. White.

1900 Joseph Bédier, *Tristan et Iseut*: most popular modern retelling of Tristan legend

Isaac Albéniz, *Merlin*

1902–24 Eduard Stucken, Grail Cycle

1903 Guillaume Apollinaire, *L'Enchanteur pourrissant*

Henry Hadley, *Merlin and Vivian* (published 1970)

Thomas Mann, *Tristan*

1903–10 Howard Pyle, illustrated retellings for children

1904 Edwin Porter, *Parsifal*: first Arthurian film (silent)

1905 Clemence Housman, *Sir Aglovale*

Ernest Rhys, *Lays of the Round Table*

Natsume Sōseki, *Kairo-kō*: A Dirge

1909 Emil Ludwig, *Tristan und Isolde*

1911 Walter Crane, illustrations for *King Arthur's Knights*

1911–45 Rutland Boughton, choral cycle

1912 Richard von Kralik, *Der heilige Gral*

1917 Arnold Bax, *Tintagel: A Symphonic Poem*

Edwin Arlington Robinson, *Merlin*

Gerhart Hauptmann, *Merlins Geburt*

1919 James Branch Cabell, *Jurgen*

1921 Edna St. Vincent Millay, "Elaine"

1922 Jacques Boulenger, *Les Romans de la Table Ronde*

T. S. Eliot, *The Waste Land*

Charles Connick, Princeton University Chapel Windows

Arthur Machen, *The Secret Glory*

1923 Thomas Hardy, *The Queen of Cornwall*

1925 René Guénon, *Le Roi du monde*

1926 John Erskine, *Galahad*

1927 E.A. Robinson, *Tristan*

Rodgers and Hart, *A Connecticut Yankee* (musical)

1928 John Masefield, *Midsummer Night*

1929 Joseph Bédier and Louis Artus, *Tristan et Iseut*

1930 G.K. Chesterton, "The Grave of Arthur"

1931 Frederick Ashton, *The Lady of Shalott*

1932 John Cowper Powys, *A Glastonbury Romance*

1930s Ralegh Radford, excavations at Tintagel

1934 Frank Kendon, *Tristram*

1936 Robert Gibbings, illustrations for Golden Cockerel Malory

1937 Jean Cocteau, *Les Chevaliers de la Table Ronde*

David Jones, *In Parenthesis*

1938 T.H. White, *The Sword in the Stone*

Charles Williams, *Taliessin Through Logres*

1939 Julien Gracq, *Au Château d'Argol*

James Joyce, *Finnegans Wake*

1940 Warwick Deeping, *The Man Who Went Back*

1943 Jean Cocteau, *L'Éternel Retour*

1944 Charles Williams, *The Region of the Summer Stars*

1945 C.S. Lewis, *That Hideous Strength*

1949 Tay Garnett, *A Connecticut Yankee in King Arthur's Court* (film)

International Arthurian Society founded

Julien Gracq, *Le Roi Pêcheur*

1952 David Jones, *The Anathemata*

Bernard Malamud, *The Natural*

1953 Boris Vian, *Le Chevalier de Neige*

1955 Naomi Mitchison, *To the Chapel Perilous*

Robert Pinget, *Graal Flibuste*

1956 E.M.R. Ditmas, *Gareth of Orkney*

1958 Xavier de Langlais, *Tristan hag Izold*

T.H. White, *The Once and Future King*: most popular modern treatment of Arthurian story

1958–59 John Steinbeck, *The Acts of King Arthur* (published 1976)

Italo Calvino, *Il cavaliere inesistente*

1960 Lerner and Loewe, *Camelot* (musical)

1961 Arthur Quiller-Couch and Daphne du Maurier, *Castle Dor*

1963 Margaret Atwood, *Avalon Revisited*

	The Sword in the Stone (film)
	Rosemary Sutcliff, *Sword at Sunset*
1966–70	Leslie Alcock, excavations at South Cadbury
1967	Maria Kuncewiczowa, *Tristan 1946*
	Joshua Logan, *Camelot* (film)
1969	Ruth Schirmer, *Tristan*
1970	Mary Stewart, *The Crystal Cave*
	Robert Newman, *Merlin's Mistake*
1971	Rosemary Sutcliff, *Tristan and Iseult*
1972	John Arden and Margaretta d'Arcy, *The Island of the Mighty*
	Sanders Anne Laubenthal, *Excalibur*
1973	Susan Cooper, *The Dark Is Rising*
	John Heath-Stubbs, *Artorius*
1974	Robert Bresson, *Lancelot du Lac* (film)
1975	Terry Gilliam and Terry Jones, *Monty Python and the Holy Grail* (film)
	Andre Norton, *Merlin's Mirror*
	Rick Wakeman, *The Myths and Legends of King Arthur and the Knights of the Round Table*
1976	Victor Canning, *The Crimson Chalice*
1976–79	Natalie Harder, *Recht mitten durch*
1977	Richard Monaco, *Parsival*
1977–	Jacques Roubaud and Florence Delay, *Graal-Théâtre*
1978	Thomas Berger, *Arthur Rex*
	Jim Hunter, *Perceval and the Presence of God*
	Walker Percy, *Lancelot*
	Eric Rohmer, *Perceval le Gallois* (film)
	Peter Vansittart, *Lancelot: A Novel*
1979	Jonathan Gash, *The Grail Tree*
1980	Roger Zelazny, "The Last Defender of Camelot"
	Richard Blank, *Parzival*
	Gillian Bradshaw, *Hawk of May*
	Parke Godwin, *Firelord*
1981	John Boorman, *Excalibur* (film)
	Tankred Dorst, *Merlin oder das wüste Land*
	Sharan Newman, *Guinevere*
1982	Marion Zimmer Bradley, *The Mists of Avalon*
	C.J. Cherryh, *Port Eternity*
	Phyllis Ann Karr, *Idylls of the Queen*
	Hans Jürgen Syberberg, *Parsifal* (film)
	Jane Yolen, *Merlin's Booke*
1983	Joy Chant, *The High Kings*
	Jacques Roubaud, *Le Roi Arthur au temps des chevaliers et des enchanteurs*
	Romain Weingarten, *Le Roman de la Table Ronde*
1984	René Barjavel, *L'Enchanteur*
	David Lodge, *Small World*
	Mary Stewart, *The Wicked Day*
1985	Richard Monaco, *Broken Stone*
1986	Anthony Powell, *The Fisher King*
1987	Persia Woolley, *Child of the Northern Spring*
1988	Peter Dickinson, *Merlin Dreams*
	Robertson Davies, *The Lyre of Orpheus*
1989	Michael Swanwick, "The Dragon Line"
1990	Donald Barthelme, *The King*
	Gene Wolfe, *Castleview*

THE NEW ARTHURIAN ENCYCLOPEDIA

Arthurian Britain

ACCOLON OF GAUL, in Malory (Book IV, Chapters 6–12), Morgan's lover. They conspire to kill Arthur, but in battle Accolon recognizes the King only after receiving a mortal blow from him. Accolon asks and receives forgiveness, but after his death his body is sent to Morgan. [NJL]

ADAMS, OSCAR FAY (1855–1919), American editor and author of *Post-Laureate Idyls and Other Poems* (1886). Combining Malory's *Morte Darthur* and familiar nursery rhymes, Adams parodies Tennyson's blank verse while satirizing chivalric romance. In "The Rape of the Tarts" ("The Queen of Hearts"), Iseult bakes tarts to console herself for Tristram's absence. Gawain, caught stealing the tarts, shares the tasty morsels with the Queen until warned of Mark's imminent return. Other burlesques are "At the Palace of King Lot" ("Sing a Song of Sixpence"), "The Return from the Grail Quest" ("Hark, hark, the dogs do bark"), and "The Maid's Alarm" ("Little Miss Muffet" and Tennyson's "Guenevere"). [MAW]

Adams, Oscar Fay. *Post-Laureate Idyls and Other Poems*. Boston: Lothrop, 1886.

AGRAVAIN, brother of Gawain, son of Lot and Morgause (or Anna), nicknamed *aux dures mains* ("of the hard hands"). He plays a prominent role in the Old French Prose *Lancelot* and *Mort Artu*, and subsequently in the various romances derived and adapted from these, including the Prose *Tristan* and Malory's *Morte Darthur*. His most significant deed is probably the public exposure of the affair of Lancelot and Guenevere, in which he is aided and abetted by Arthur's son, Mordred, and which is one of the catalysts in the downfall of the Round Table. His name in Old French already has overtones of "aggravation." [KB]

AIKEN, JOAN (DELANO), author of the children's book *The Stolen Lake* (1981). She tells how a girl called Dido Twite and a party from a nineteenth-century British man-of-war travel up country to Hy Brasil to visit the ancient, sinister Queen Ginevra. After the battle of Dyrham in 577, Ginevra had brought Lake Arianod, conveniently frozen into ice-blocks, with her to South America so that Arthur might return. The book offers a heady mixing of Arthurian and Inca material; among the lively characters is a sea captain's steward who is revealed as the once and future king. [CNS]

Aiken, Joan. *The Stolen Lake*. London: Jonathan Cape, 1981.

ALAIN (Alain le Gros), Perceval's father in the Didot-*Perceval* and *Perlesvaus*. Robert de Boron's *Joseph* identifies him as the son of Bron (as does the Didot-*Perceval*) but does not name his own son, noting only that the son is destined to be a keeper of the Grail. According to Robert, Alain and Bron, along with Petrus, are chosen to make their way to the west to await the Grail-keeper in Avalon. The Vulgate Cycle identifies Alain as the first Fisher King. (*See also* BRON.) [NJL]

ALAMANNI, LUIGI (1495–1556), poet, friend of Machiavelli, and exile from Florence. His *Avarchide* linked the Matter of Troy with the Matter of Britain. With the *Iliad* as his model, Alamanni has Arthur and Lancelot battle the usurper Claudius; the figure of Arthur is derived from Agamemnon, Lancelot from Achilles, Galehaut from Patroclus, and so on. Less ingenious but more traditionally Arthurian, Alamanni's *ottava rima* translation of the French prose text of *Gyron le Courtois*, was composed at the request of Francis I. This last major Arthurian text in Italian returns to the source of the Italian tradition by recounting the story of Giron derived from the *Compilation* of Rusticiano. [DLH]

Alamanni, Luigi. *Gyrone il Cortese di Luigi Alamanni, al Christianissimo et invittissimo Re Arrigo secondo*. Paris, 1548; Venice, 1549; Bergamo, 1757.

———. *La Avarchide del S. Luigi Alamanni, alla Sereniss. Madam Margherita di Francia, Duchessa di Savoia e di Berri*. Florence, 1570; Bergamo, 1761.

Gardner, Edmund G. *The Arthurian Legend in Italian Literature*. London: Dent, 1930, pp. 308–09, 329.

ALBION, in Geoffrey of Monmouth, an early name for Britain. Geoffrey explains that, colonized by a group of Trojans, Albion was then renamed Britain in honor of their leader Brutus, great-grandson of Aeneas. [NJL]

ALBRECHT, author of *Der jüngere Titurel*. For some time, scholars believed this thirteenth-century author identical with Albrecht von Scharfenberg. The relationship remains unsubstantiated, however, and recent scholarship treats Albrecht as a separate poet whose only known works are *Der jüngere Titurel* and a fragmentary dedication poem, the so-called *Verfasserfragment*.

Virtually all we know of Albrecht must be gleaned from the text of *Der jüngere Titurel*, which has been dated to ca. 1270. During most of this lengthy tale, the author/narrator adopts the fictive persona of Wolfram von Eschenbach. Speaking as "Wolfram," author of *Parzival*, *Willehalm*, and *Titurel*, he explains his intention to clarify the obscurities in *Parzival*, asserting that public demand has brought him to this undertaking (stanzas 86–87). Only near the end of the work, in stanza 5,883, does he claim authorship as "Albreht," without reference to his earlier misrepresentation.

It is generally accepted that Albrecht came from the southern part of German-speaking Europe, and that he began his work under the patronage of three unnamed princes (likely Markgraf Heinrich der Erlauchte von Meissen and his two sons, Albrecht and Dietrich). Apparently, Albrecht lost their support at a late stage in his composition of the story and was then forced to seek another donor. A desperate need for support is assumed to be the reason for Albrecht declaring his own identity so late in the poem, an argument supported by the *Verfasserfragment*, extant in just one copy and dated to 1272–73, in which Albrecht identifies himself as the author of the entire text of *Der jüngere Titurel* and dedicates his work to Ludwig II of Bavaria, appealing—in vain, as it turned out—for his sponsorship.

It is possible that Albrecht intended at least the sophisticated members of his audience to see through his Wolfram imitation, in fact to recognize his invention as a kind of culmination of Wolfram's work. Yet Albrecht did not make this easy. For not only does he pose as Wolfram, adopting his name, subject matter, vocabulary, and style, he also mimics many of his mannerisms as a narrator. Furthermore, *Der jüngere Titurel* sets out to "complete" the love story of Tschinotulander and Sigune, a tale first told in Wolfram's *Parzival* and *Titurel*. This central plot is framed by the history of the Grail, with Titurel's youth and the founding of Munt Salvasch serving as a preface and an abbreviated version of Parzival's adventures as a conclusion. Yet for all the echoes of Wolfram, Albrecht's work stands apart in its scale, moralizing piety, verbosity, and *geblümte Rede* (ornate style).

Der jüngere Titurel is a poetic achievement of daunting proportions. It is a formally and linguistically complex work of vast, almost encyclopedic learning, consisting of over 6,000 stanzas. The plot embraces more than a millennium of human history and follows its heroes through adventures on two continents and in the mythical Grail realm. We witness the founding of the Grail kinship by Titurel and later the building of the temple. (Albrecht's elaborate description of this architectural fantasy, stanzas 329–439, has been the subject of considerable debate. It has been claimed to embody architectural principles of both the late Romanesque and the high Gothic. It has been interpreted as the representation of a mystical experience of space and as the literary model for actual medieval buildings.) The central plot traces the search for an elusive object, not the Grail as in *Parzival*, but a bejeweled hound's leash. Here, the precious stones spell out a narrative, as in *Titurel*, but they also relate an allegorized lesson in virtue. A huge cast of characters is involved as well, including nearly all the names appearing in Wolfram's *Parzival* and many from *Willehalm*, and the story is enriched by religious and natural scientific lore drawn from a host of sources, most not yet identified. The tale is laced with a didactic commentary.

Der jüngere Titurel was well received by its early public, who accepted it as a work by Wolfram. During the first two centuries after its composition, it was lauded and repeatedly imitated. The sheer number of extant manuscripts attests its early popularity. From a total of eleven complete manuscripts and forty-six fragments, two are from the late thirteenth century, twelve from ca. 1300, thirty-two from the fourteenth century, and nine from the fifteenth. An incunabulum edition was printed at Strasbourg in 1477. Rediscovered in the Romantic era, *Der jüngere Titurel* was again treasured as Wolfram's masterpiece, falling from grace only in 1829, when Karl Lachmann scorned its literary qualities and disparaged the idea that Wolfram could have written such a "boring, dead, and affected" work. Lachmann's authority was enough to squelch scholarly enthusiasm for and interest in *Der jüngere Titurel* for some time. It has slowly regained its reputation, however, and the many studies devoted to it in the last two decades attest its continued significance within the history of late-medieval German literature. A complete critical edition is soon to be completed. [LBP]

Albrecht. *Albrecht von Scharfenberg: Der jüngere Titurel*, ed. K.A. Hahn. Quedlinburg and Leipzig: Basse, 1842.

———. *Albrechts von Scharfenberg Jüngerer Titurel*, ed. Werner Wolf (Vols. 1 and 2) and Kurt Nyholm (Vol. 3). Berlin: Akademie, 1955, 1968, and 1985 (last fascicle in progress).

Huschenbett, Dietrich. *Albrechts* Jüngerer Titurel. Munich: Fink, 1979.

Parshall, Linda B. *The Art of Narration in Wolfram's* Parzival *and Albrecht's* Jüngerer Titurel. Cambridge: Cambridge University Press, 1981.

Ragotzky, Hedda. *Studien zur Wolfram-Rezeption*. Stuttgart and Berlin: Kohlhammer, 1971.

Röll, Walter. *Studien zu Text und Überlieferung des sogennanten* Jüngeren Titurel. Heidelberg: Winter, 1964.

Schröder, Werner, ed. *Wolfram-Studien. VIII*. Berlin: Schmidt, 1984. (Papers from a 1982 colloquium devoted to Albrecht; includes bibliography.)

ALBRECHT VON SCHARFENBERG, a German poet of the thirteenth century, praised above Gottfried von Strassburg and Wolfram von Eschenbach in Ulrich Fuetrer's *Buch der Abenteuer* as a "giant" in the art of *geblümte Rede* (ornate style). Although for a time considered to be identical with Albrecht, author of *Der jüngere Titurel*, Albrecht von Scharfenberg is now held to be a separate poet. Fuetrer refers to three of his works, none of which survives: *Merlin*, *Seifrid de Ardemont*, and *Fraw Eren hof*. [LBP]

Nyholm, Kurt. *Albrechts von Scharfenberg* Merlin. Abo: Akademie, 1967.

Maak, Hans-Georg. "Zu Füetrers 'Fraw Eren hof' und der Frage nach dem Verfasser des *Jüngeren Titurel*. *Zeitschrift für deutsche Philologie*, 87 (1968), 42–46.

ALIXANDRE L'ORPHELIN, a prose narrative that relates Alixandre's duty and desire for vengeance on Marc of Cornwall. Marc treacherously slew his own brother, Alixandre's father. There is no definitive version of the story, which survives in adaptations in late manuscripts of the *Prophécies de Merlin*, the Prose *Tristan*, some late compilations, and, Englished, in Malory's *Morte Darthur*. It is therefore not a romance as such but rather an episode interpolated into various cycles, much like the Prose *Erec*. It could not have been written before the second half of the thirteenth century. [DK]

Pickford, Cedric E., ed. *Alixandre l'Orphelin*. Manchester: Manchester University Press, 1951.

ALLITERATIVE *MORTE ARTHURE*, a long narrative poem in Middle English (4,346 lines), composed near the end of the fourteenth century, possibly 1400–02. It survives in a unique manuscript, Lincoln Cathedral Library 91, an anthology compiled ca. 1440 by the Yorkshire scribe Robert Thornton. The poet is unknown, and the dialect of the original text not easily identifiable. Though originally considered West Midlands, it is most probably Northeast Midlands, passing through at least two stages of transcription, the text copied by Thornton being from a southwestern Lincolnshire exemplar, itself copied in eastern Lincolnshire.

Like other examples of the Alliterative Revival of the fourteenth century in England, the *Morte Arthure* uses the unrhymed alliterative long line, strongly resembling that of Old English poetry. The line falls regularly into two halflines, the A-verse and the B-verse, linked by the alliteration of stressed syllables. There are usually two (sometimes three) stressed syllables in the A-verse and one (sometimes two) in the B-verse, while the fourth stressed syllable remains unalliterated. The number of unstressed syllables varies. Thus, the most common alliterative pattern in the poem is aa/ax, but the poet manipulates the conventions with freedom and artistry, achieving a wide range of variations from the norm for different effects. Sometimes, he creates blocks of sound by running the same initial alliteration through several successive lines.

The poet also uses a highly specialized vocabulary, archaic terms associated with battle subjects, and technical terms describing armor, costume, cuisine, and so on. He employs frequent alliterative collocations (associational word clusters bound by ties of alliteration), drawing from a stock common to alliterative poets of the period. Though not itself composed orally, the poem may have been influenced by the techniques of oral-formulaic composition. Yet, despite the conventional features, the poet achieves great variation in his descriptions, being as adept at static pictures of idyllic landscapes as at scenes of violent action on the battlefield or at sea. His battle descriptions are both stylized and particularized, with vivid, concrete details, accurate references to contemporary fashion in armor or costume, and graphic portrayals of the brutality of war.

The structure of the poem is clear and well balanced, the narrative falling into four parts. Arthur, holding court at Carlisle, receives a demand from the emperor Lucius that he pay homage as a vassal of Rome. After his own vassals have pledged their support and made their battle vows, Arthur defies Lucius, and both sides prepare for war. Leaving Mordrede, his sister's son, as regent of England, Arthur embarks for France, dreaming a prophetic dream in which a dragon defeats a bear. Arriving in Brittany, he singlehandedly kills the giant of St. Michael's Mount, who has abducted and raped the Duchess of Brittany.

After two separate engagements with the emperor's forces and pagan allies, in which Gawayn and Cador each distinguishes himself against heavy odds, Arthur's forces meet the emperor's in a decisive battle. Lucius is killed and the vows made in council at Carlisle fulfilled, though Kayous, Bedwere, and many other British knights are lost. Instead of tribute, Arthur sends to Rome the coffins of his enemies.

Arthur then besieges a disloyal vassal, the Duke of Lorraine, at Metz. During the siege, Gawayn slips away from a foraging party and meets in single combat Priamus, a Greek knight fighting for Lorraine, who then brings his men over to the Arthurian side in the ensuing battle. After the surrender of Metz, Arthur continues southward into Italy, conquering Italian towns, until the Romans offer him the imperial crown.

At his peak of success, Arthur dreams that Fortune is turning him on her wheel and dashing him down. Next morning, he hears that Mordrede has usurped both his crown and his queen. Returning immediately to England, Arthur defeats Mordrede's pagan allies in a great sea battle, but in the ensuing land battle Gawayn's forces are outnumbered and he is killed. Arthur bitterly laments the death of his sister's son and vows vengeance on Mordrede. In the final battle in Cornwall, Arthur kills Mordrede but is himself fatally wounded. He is buried at Glastonbury, having appointed Cador's son Constantyne as his successor.

The poem clearly belongs to the Arthurian chronicle tradition, deriving ultimately from Geoffrey of Monmouth's *Historia Regum Britanniae*, transmitted through the *Bruts* of Wace and Layamon. The poet may have used as his sources all three chronicles, as well as that by Robert Mannyng of Brunne. The Charlemagne romance of *Sir Fierabras* (or the Middle English redaction *Sir Ferumbras*) may have suggested the Gawayn-Priamus episode, and the Alexandrian romance *Li Fuerres de Gadre* the foraging expedition. The motifs of the Nine Worthies and the avowing patterns may derive from the Alexandrian *Voeux du Paon*, or the Middle English *Parlement of the Thre Ages*. It has also been argued that the poet is alluding to contemporary history, especially the military campaigns of Edward III.

The genre of the *Morte Arthure* is difficult to define. It has been called a romance, an epic, a *chanson de geste*, a medieval tragedy of Fortune, and a "mirror" for kings. The difficulty of classifying the poem is related to the difficulty of interpreting its theme. It has been argued that Arthur's fall is the result not only of Fortune's capriciousness but also of his own moral degeneration from a champion of Christendom to an ambitious aggressor pursuing unjust wars. At what point Arthur's wars become unjust, however, is a matter of disagreement. The poem clearly celebrates the heroic virtues of courage against odds, of the fulfillment of battle-vows, of loyalty to leader and fellows, of the desire for fame; yet the poet seems ambivalent about the glories of war—even, it has been argued, condemnatory. Nevertheless, recent criticism has begun to challenge the view that the poet's treatment of heroic action is ironic and has sought to rehabilitate Arthur as an epic hero. Perhaps, the answer is that the poet is displaying the medieval ability to hold conflicting viewpoints in tension without their invalidating each other.

The *Morte Arthure* has influenced other works, such as the *Awntyrs off Arthure* and most notably Malory's *Morte Darthur*. Malory's "Noble Tale of King Arthur and the Emperor Lucius" (Caxton's Book V) is a free prose rendering, much condensed, of the first two-thirds of the poem, ending with Arthur's triumphal coronation in Rome. [DBM]

Hamel, Mary, ed. *Morte Arthure: A Critical Edition*. New York: Garland, 1984.

The Thornton Manuscript (Lincoln Cathedral MS. 91). Introduction by D.S. Brewer and A.E. Owen. London: Scolar, 1975; rev. 1977.

Stone, Brian, trans. *King Arthur's Death*. Harmondsworth: Penguin, 1988.

Benson, Larry D. "The Alliterative *Morte Arthure* and Medieval Tragedy." *Tennessee Studies in Literature*, 11 (1966), 75–88.

Göller, Karl Heinz, ed. *The Alliterative Morte Arthure: A Reassessment of the Poem*. Cambridge: Brewer, 1981.

Matthews, William. *The Tragedy of Arthur: A Study of the Alliterative "Morte Arthure."* Berkeley: University of California Press, 1960.

Obst, Wolfgang. "The Gawain-Priamus Episode in the Alliterative *Morte Arthure*." *Studia Neophilologica*, 57 (1985), 9–18.

AMBROSIUS AURELIANUS, a fifth-century British leader. He is the historical prototype of one of Geoffrey of Monmouth's kings, Aurelius Ambrosius, who checks the Saxon invasion unleashed by the policies of the previous king, Vortigern. In Welsh, the name *Ambrosius* becomes *Emrys*, and many Welshmen are still so called.

Ambrosius Aurelianus is the only fifth-century Briton actually named in the *De Excidio* of Gildas, written during the 530s or thereabouts. Gildas tells of Saxon mercenaries settling in Britain under the aegis of a *superbus tyrannus*, or "preeminent ruler," with whom Vortigern is usually identified. The Saxons revolted, raiding and ravaging everywhere. Their onslaught caused a migration of Britons overseas (the reference here is to the move to Armorica in northwest Gaul, which began the conversion of part of it into the Lesser Britain, or Brittany). Finally, the marauders withdrew to their settlements in the east of the island. Then, says Gildas, the surviving Britons recovered and launched a counter-offensive. Ambrosius enters his narrative as the war-leader who organizes it.

Gildas presents him as a "Roman," the son of parents who had "worn purple" and died in the Saxon devastation.

"Wearing purple" suggests an emperor but could mean merely that his father was of senatorial rank, like many imperial citizens of all nationalities. Gildas puts his counterattack after the British emigration, which can be roughly dated to the late 450s, so that the counterattack itself doubtless began in the 460s. The allusion to Ambrosius as a Roman has no ethnic content and probably points to a political leaning. Across the Channel in northern Gaul, a general named Aegidius had been attempting (with no help from the hapless emperors) to uphold the imperial system against barbarian pressures. His son Syagrius carried on his work, ruling from Soissons and at some point adopting the remarkable title "king of the Romans." Though Britain was now outside the empire, there are indications that the Britons who made new homes in Armorica may have done so through some agreement with these authorities; and the proimperial campaign of the king called Riothamus a few years after shows that the dominant Britons of the 460s had Roman rather than barbarian sympathies.

According to Gildas, Ambrosius's action against the Saxon settlements led to a period of doubtful warfare, culminating in a British success at the siege of Mount Badon somewhere about the year 500. Nothing shows when he ceased to be active personally. It has been thought that he was still in command at Badon, but Gildas does not name the commander on that occasion, and the only individual who is ever connected with it—admittedly, not till centuries afterward—is Arthur. In general, the rally that Ambrosius launched is associated with Arthur, too. Early materials shed no real light on the relation between them but hardly support the theory that they are the same person under different names.

Nennius mentions Ambrosius in the *Historia Brittonum*. Confusingly, he ignores him as a leader of anti-Saxon resistance, allotting that role first to Vortimer and later to Arthur. Ambrosius is spoken of as a rival whom Vortigern feared and then, after Vortigern's death, as a king holding paramountcy over lesser rulers. The only episode dealing with him at length is legendary—a story that introduces him in his youth as having prophetic gifts, displayed before Vortigern. At the end of it, he is made to say that his father was a Roman consul: perhaps an echo of Gildas, though it conflicts with the rest of the tale, which depends on his father being unknown.

In the same passage, Nennius calls him *Emrys gwledig* and says that Vortigern, awed by his prophecies, gave him the overlordship of western Britain—thus (it would seem) starting him on the career that made him formidable. Here, Nennius may at least be recording his true status, rather than when he calls him a paramount king. *Emrys gwledig* is the way Ambrosius is styled in Welsh tradition generally. The word *gwledig* comes to mean simply "prince," but its basic sense is "landholder"; and in its application to fifth-century figures it reflects a political reality of the time. Parts of Britain were governed by army commanders vested with regional powers. Ambrosius appears to have been one of them. Nennius is probably wrong to locate him in the west, which would mean essentially Wales. In some notes at the end of Nennius's main text, Ambrosius is stated to have fought Vitalinus (otherwise unknown) at Wallop in Hampshire, twelve years "from the reign of Vortigern"—a phrase taken to mean from the reign's beginning, which the same notes assign to 425. This suggests that he was asserting authority over the south or some part of it in 437. If so, he was already middle-aged at the time of his generalship against the Saxons, and he can scarcely have been the Britons' leader at Badon.

As to his position in the anti-Saxon campaign, Alcock plausibly pictures him as appointed to supreme command in the service of a high king, one of two or three who apparently reigned in Britain during the fifth century. He may be commemorated by a few place-names, such as Amesbury in Wiltshire, originally *Ambres-byrig*. In the Late Roman period, military forces were occasionally called after their leaders or nominal leaders. Ambrosius's men might have been the Ambrosiani; their chief's name could have been given to bases they used.

A Welsh Triad of uncertain provenance calls Ambrosius a fleet-owner. Conjecturally, he assembled shipping for the movement of Britons to Armorica, which developed from a flight of refugees into a more considered colonization, though not yet on a large scale. Some kind of British fleet existed in 468, when the army of the "king of the Britons" called Riothamus crossed to the Continent. Fleuriot has argued that this king actually was Ambrosius Aurelianus, "Riothamus" being a title. He draws attention to Breton place-names with *Aurilian* in them, and to traces of a tradition locating Ambrosius temporarily in Brittany. But there is no real evidence for Ambrosius's having held the sort of kingship implied, and a supervisory role in the overseas settlement would be enough to account for the facts. [GA]

Gildas. *De Excidio Britanniae*, Chapter 25.

Nennius, *Historia Brittonum*, Chapters 31, 40–42, 48, 66.

Alcock, Leslie. *Arthur's Britain*. London: Penguin, 1971, pp. 26–29, 105, 110, 358–59.

Bromwich, Rachel. *Trioedd Ynys Prydein*. Cardiff: University of Wales Press, 1961; 2nd ed. 1978, pp. 345–46.

Fleuriot, Léon. *Les Origines de la Bretagne*. Paris: Payot, 1980, pp. 170–76.

Morris, John. *The Age of Arthur*. New York: Scribner, 1973, pp. 48, 71, 95–97.

Wood, Ian. "The Fall of the Western Empire and the End of Roman Britain." *Britannia*, 18 (1987), 251–62.

ANDERSON, POUL, American science-fiction and fantasy writer, has two novels involving Arthurian characters. In *Three Hearts and Three Lions* (1961), Holger Carlsen, a Danish-American, is wounded in battle; he awakes in a world of romance as Ogier the Dane. Morgan le Fay figures prominently in the story, and Avalon is spoken of repeatedly; Charlemagne and Arthur are mentioned. *A Midsummer Tempest* (1974) posits a world in which everything that Shakespeare wrote was literal history. Oberon, Puck, and Ariel battle the Puritans—who threaten the existence of Faerie—in the English Civil War. King Arthur and the Knights of Avalon appear among the Royalist forces to turn King Charles's last stand, on Glastonbury Tor at Midsummer, into Cromwell's utter defeat. [SRR]

Anderson, Poul. *Three Hearts and Three Lions*. Garden City, N.Y.: Doubleday, 1961. (Originally serialized in 1953.)

———. *A Midsummer Tempest*. Garden City, N.Y.: Doubleday, 1974.

ANDREAS CAPELLANUS, author of *De Amore* (ca. 1185). This important, if not entirely serious, Latin prose treatise on courtly love includes a brief story about a young knight who must win the prize hawk from Arthur's court for his lady—but first he must slay two knights in double combat, obtain the hawk's gauntlet, and finally prove his lady's greater beauty in jousts at Arthur's court. When the knight finally achieves the hawk, he finds a parchment tied to it on which are written the rules of love. (*See also* COURTLY LOVE.) [MLD]

Andreas Capellanus. *De Amore*, ed. E. Trojel. Copenhagen, 1892; 2nd ed. Munich: Eidos, 1964.

ANDREW OF WYNTOUN, author of the *Original Chronicle of Scotland* (ca. 1420), a Scottish vernacular chronicle in verse, begins with the Creation, emphasizes general world history in Books I–V, and focuses on Scottish and British history in Books VI–IX. The account of Arthur is a brief summary of the war against Lucius (Book V, Chapter 13). Unlike some Scottish chroniclers, Andrew speaks favorably of Arthur, who was slain by "Mordred the traitor." He says that his source for the Arthurian story was the "Gestis Historiall" of "Huchone of the Auld Ryall." [EDK]

Andrew of Wyntoun. *The Original Chronicle of Andrew of Wyntoun*, ed. F.J. Amours. 6 vols. Edinburgh: Blackwood, 1903–14.

Kennedy, Edward Donald. "Chronicles and Other Historical Writing." In *A Manual of the Writings in Middle English*, ed. A.E. Hartung. New Haven: Connecticut Academy of Arts and Sciences, 1981–89, Vol. 8, pp. 2686–90, 2905–13.

ANFORTAS (Amfortas), in Wolfram von Eschenbach's *Parzival*, Parzival's maternal uncle and Grail King until succeeded by Parzival. Like the Fisher King in Chrétien de Troyes's *Perceval*, Anfortas is wounded and can be healed only if the correct question is asked. However, the question is not "Whom does the Grail serve?" but rather "Sire, what troubles you?"

In Wagner's *Parsifal*, Amfortas is wounded not in the genital area but in the side, and by the same spear that wounded Christ. He is eventually healed when Parsifal returns the Holy Spear to the Grail Brotherhood. [SW]

ANGLO-SAXON CHRONICLE, possibly dating from the ninth century, contains no specifically Arthurian material but offers indirect support to statements in Gildas and Nennius that Saxon advances were halted early in the sixth century. There is no mention of Saxon progress for a long time beginning with 527, a date too late to square exactly with Gildas and Nennius. [AEG]

Plummer, C., ed. *Anglo-Saxon Chronicle*. London, 1899.

ANNA, in Geoffrey of Monmouth's *Historia Regum Britanniae* and Wace's *Roman de Brut*, Arthur's sister and Uther and Ygerna's second child. Geoffrey says that Anna is the wife of King Lot of Lodonesia, but he also says that the wife of King Lot and the mother of Gawain and Mordred is the sister of Aurelius Ambrosius. To confuse the matter further, Geoffrey contends that the sister of Arthur is the wife of King Budicius of Brittany and the mother of Hoel. Whereas it is possible that Geoffrey had in mind two sisters for Arthur, several inconsistencies, particularly the ages of Gawain and Hoel, make this problematic. [SW]

ANNALES CAMBRIAE ("Annals of Wales"). This Latin chronicle records the battles of Badon and Camlann. It is attached to Nennius's *Historia Brittonum* in the Harley manuscript, and its date probably lies within the range 960–80. The text, however, is a composite formed by transcription of items from older chronicles. Several early entries are from Irish sources. The first that concern Britain are the ones mentioning Arthur. There are other copies with additional matter but nothing Arthurian.

The framework is a table of 533 years, against some of which events are noted. The years are numbered from a Year 1 best taken as A.D. 447. On that basis, the Arthurian entries come in 518 and 539. The first is: "The battle of Badon, in which Arthur carried the cross of Our Lord Jesus Christ on his shoulders for three days and three nights and the Britons were victors." The second is: "The strife of Camlann, in which Arthur and Medraut fell. And there was plague in Britain and in Ireland."

Odd as the Badon entry looks, it can be rationalized. "Shoulders" may mistranslate a Welsh word meaning "shield," so that the cross could be an emblem. Nevertheless, the "three days and nights" have a legendary air, and the date seems incompatible with the testimony of Gildas, who wrote when the battle was within living memory.

The second entry is the earliest known reference to Camlann and to Medraut, otherwise Mordred. Unlike other Welsh matter introducing Arthur, it looks like a plain statement, free from legend, and it has sometimes therefore been singled out as the only trustworthy evidence for him. But the late date, 539, casts serious doubt on it, and it hangs in a void unrelated to history. A claim that it proves Arthur's reality because it must have been posted from a contemporary record is no longer pressed. However, since (so far as is known) everyone named in the dozens of non-Arthurian entries did exist, there is a presumption that a real Arthur underlies these questionable phrases. Some of the entries are misdated or influenced by legend, but they never mention definitely fictitious persons. [GA]

Annales Cambriae, in Nennius, ed. and trans. John Morris under the title *British History and the Welsh Annals*. In *History from the Sources*. Chichester: Phillimore, 1980, Vol. 8.

Alcock, Leslie. *Arthur's Britain*. London: Penguin, 1971, pp. 45–55.

ANSPACHER, LOUIS K. (1878–1947), American author of *Tristan and Isolde* (1904), a verse tragedy in which Tristan and Isolde fall in love but remain chaste until they drink the love potion. Stabbed by a jealous Cornish lord, Tristan perishes, and Isolde dies by his side. King Mark says that he would have given up Isolde had he known all. [AEG]

Anspacher, Louis K. *Tristan and Isolde*. New York: Brentano, 1904.

ANTELAN, also known as *König Anteloy* ("King Anteloy"), an anonymous German narrative of thirty-three four-line stanzas, presumably composed at the end of the thirteenth or the beginning of the fourteenth century. The tale relates that Antelan, a dwarf king from Scotland (who also appears in a twelfth-century work belonging to the Alexander cycle, *Alexander und Anteloye*), is sent by three duchesses to King Arthur's court to seek adventure. Antelan confronts Parzival, Gawan, and Galleman in combat and easily defeats them. He refuses Parzival's invitation to stay at Arthur's court and returns home to report his adventure to the three duchesses. [MEK]

Scherer, W., ed. "Antelan." *Zeitschrift für deutsches Alterthum*, 3 (1872), 140–49.

Ertzdorff, Xenja von. "Linhart Scheubels Heldenbuch." In *Festschrift für Siegfried Gutenbrunner*, ed. Oskar Bandle, Heinz Klingenberg, and Friedrich Maurer. Heidelberg: Winter, 1972, pp. 33–46.

APOLLINAIRE, GUILLAUME (1880–1918), published *L'Enchanteur pourrissant* ("The Rotting Magician") in 1904; a new version appeared in 1909 with woodcuts by Derain. It is a fascinating but confused work, owing no doubt to the fact that it was one of the twenty-four-year-old author's earliest prose compositions.

The enchanter of the title is Merlin, whose fate, according to the author, was to be imprisoned by the spells he had imprudently revealed to Viviane, or Éviène, the Lady of the Lake. Apollinaire was inspired by the *Premier volume de Lancelot nouvellement imprimé à Paris suivi du second et du tiers volume*, edited in 1533 by Philippe Le Noir. In Apollinaire's story, we find an elaborate procession of characters and representatives of multiple mythologies (oriental, Greek, Hebraic, Scandinavian, Christian, Celtic) and a fantastic bestiary—all parading before the sepulcher of the immortal necromancer. Gauvain, for example, passes by, still linked to his solar mythology. All come in vain, however, since the charms transmitted by Merlin are by their nature invincible. We remain aware that their quest is condemned to failure from the start. The tedious impression is that of a surging mass, a kaleidoscope of conflicting mythologies. For Apollinaire offers us a curious mixture: erudition, a perceptive sense of diverse myths, and a propensity to treat them as an intellectual game, thereby precluding the expected effect of wonder and the supernatural.

In Merlin, Apollinaire may have wanted to represent his own fate as a "fatherless child"; in Viviane, the perfidy of woman toward the "Mal-Aimé." The author also suggests a number of his other personal obsessions (e.g., concerning menstrual blood) in the work. He doubtless wanted to recount an "inverted " quest: a pilgrimage of the "Magi" not to the cradle of a son of God but to the tomb of a son of the Devil. Attached to the work are some other fragments: e.g., the "Onirocritique" ("The Interpretation of Dreams"), in which we recognize Orqueneseles, the city that Gauvain sees and of which Guiromélans declares himself master, at the end of Chrétien's *Perceval*.

A story by Apollinaire, "Arthur, roi présent, roi futur" ("Arthur, Present and Future King"), included in *Le Poète assassiné* ("The Assassinated Poet") in 1914, recounts the legendary return of Arthur as king of Great Britain in the year 2105. His poem "Merlin et la vieille femme" ("Merlin and the Old Woman") evokes Merlin's eternal sleep and his love for Viviane. [RB]

Apollinaire, Guillaume. *L'Enchanteur pourrissant*, ed. Jean Burgos. Paris: Minard, 1972.

Baudry, Robert. "La Tradition du merveilleux et l'Enchanteur pourrissant." *Essays in French Literature*, 17 (1980). 36–49.

Forsyth, Louise Barton. "Apollinaire's Use of Arthurian Legend." *Esprit Créateur*, 12 (1972), 26–36.

ARCHER, JAMES (1823–1904), was characteristic of painters of the Arthurian Revival in that his interpretation was synthetic, drawing subjects from Tennyson and Malory. His extensive involvement with the Arthurian narrative is known through the lists of the Royal Scottish Academy and the Royal Academy of Arts in London, for many of his paintings are at present unlocated.

His earliest Arthurian painting was *La Mort D'Arthur* (1861, Manchester City Galleries), a theme he was to return to with subtle variations. His other works suggest that he sought to paint a full narrative of the legend; they include *King Arthur Obtains the Mystic Sword Excalibur* (1862, known through engraving), *Sir Lancelot Looks on Queen Guinevere* (1863, Private Collection), *The Parting of Arthur and Guinevere* (1865, known through oil study, Private Collection), *How Sir Lancelot and His Eight Fellows of the Round Table Carried Queen Guinevere from Almesbury to Glastonbury* (1869, unlocated), *The Death of Arthur* (1872, Private Collection), *The Dying King Arthur on the Island of Avalon Has a Vision of the San Grail* (1880, unlocated), *King Arthur in the Quest of His Mystic Sword Excalibur* (1880, unlocated), and *La Mort D'Arthur* (1897, unlocated). Archer's style was typical of the mid-Arthurian Revival, drawing upon both the Robing Room frescoes and the work of the Pre-Raphaelites as prototypes. [DNM]

Mancoff, Debra N. *The Arthurian Revival in Victorian Art*. New York: Garland, 1990, pp. 199–203.

1. James Archer, *Morte d'Arthur* (1897). (By permission of The Fine Art Society.)

ARDEN, JOHN, and MARGARETTA D'ARCY, authors (English and Irish, respectively) of *The Island of the Mighty* (1972), an epic three-part drama interweaving themes from Malory and the earliest Welsh poetry in the context of what has been called "The New Matter of Britain," that is, Arthur imagined in his original sixth-century milieu.

A political play in the manner of Brecht, *The Island of the Mighty* focuses not on the tragic fall of Arthur but on the contradictions within the sociopolitical situation as a whole, the "hero" merely exemplifying these to a marked degree. The trilogy dramatizes first a generation gap and then an ever-widening gap between political and artistic/philosophical realms. Part I, "Two Wild Young Noblemen: Concerning Balin and Balan and How Ignorant They Were," depicts the failure of Arthur's Romano-British military machine to stem an Angle invasion and, more importantly, to channel the desperate energies of British youth set adrift by the upheaval. Malory's pair of brothers die on each other's swords among the marginalized Picts, in a pagan succession ritual lifted directly from the pages of Frazer's *The Golden Bough*. Part II, "Oh the Cruel Winter: Concerning Arthur—How He Refused to See That the Power of His Army Was Finished," portrays the final collapse of Arthur's Roman "order" due to entanglements with opportunistic northern princes, Strathclyde and Gododdin, and the final ironic backlash of his brutal manipulation of native cults and beliefs. This section turns upon the pre-Lancelot triangle of Arthur, Gwenhwyvar, and Medraut, with the lady gradually coming to realize herself as an avatar of the goddess Branwen. A violent and abortive "Celtic Revival" ensues that precipitates the battle of Camlann. Part III, "A Handful of Watercress: Concerning Merlin—How He Needed to Be Alone and Then How He Needed Not to Be Alone," shows the descent into madness of the counselor/bard who had conspicuously betrayed his calling through the downward spiral of Parts I and II but who slowly recovers the sources of his vision as the Island painfully accommodates itself to the new era. The authors here graft the Irish saga of Mad Sweeney onto the Arthurian material, taking their hint from the similar madness of the early Welsh bard Myrddin.

The Island of the Mighty was originally conceived in the spirit of Indian folk drama, where epic subjects are realized in large units of playing time and fluid, stylized action punctuated by sung narrative. The play as produced by the Royal Shakespeare Company, however, was severely truncated in favor of the Arthur section, which provoked a "union action" on the part of the playwrights. They picketed their own premiere, claiming that their work had been grossly misinterpreted owing to the extensive cuts. The production proved a disaster, and the reviews, though mixed, were predominantly negative. The piece has not been professionally revived since, but an uncut production that met with the authors' approval was performed by students of King Alfred's College, under the direction of R. J. Ingram, during February 16–20, 1982. The playscript as a whole, however, has had its defenders, and there is a growing body of critical support for the Ardens' bold if overambitious theatrical conception. The play's subsequent influence upon the British stage is hard to gauge, but it no doubt helped point the way for such recent, radical experiments in historical drama as Howard Brenton's *The Romans in Britain* (1980), with its curious Arthurian epilogue. [MWW]

Arden, John, and Margaretta D'Arcy. *The Island of the Mighty: A Play on a Traditional British Theme in Three Parts*. London: Eyre Methuen, 1974.

———. "Playwrights on Picket." In *To Present the Pretense: Essays on the Theatre and Its Public*. London: Eyre Methuen, 1977, pp. 159–72.

Gray, Frances. *John Arden*. New York: Grove, 1982, pp. 129–45.

Hunt, Albert. *Arden: A Study of His Plays*. London: Eyre Methuen, 1974, pp. 157–64.

Malick, Javed. "The Polarized Universe of 'The Island of the Mighty': The Dramaturgy of Arden and D'Arcy," *New Theatre Quarterly*, 5 (1986), 38–53.

ARIOSTO, LUDOVICO (1474–1533), a member of the Este court in Ferrara and a major figure in the evolution of vernacular theater in modern Europe.

Ariosto completed the first edition of *Orlando Furioso* early in the sixteenth century (published in 1516) and revised it for a second edition published in 1522; major emendations and additions were incorporated into the final edition of 1532. A continuation of Matteo Maria Boiardo's *Orlando Innamorato*, the *Orlando Furioso* is recognized as the masterpiece of Italian chivalric romance, a blend of medieval Carolingian epic, *matière de Bretagne*, and the popular narrative traditions (*cantari*) of the Italian late Middle Ages. Structured upon three basic narrative lines—the war between Christian and pagan forces; the pursuit of the elusive Angelica by the love-crazed protagonist, Orlando; and the encomiastic celebration of the Este line in the marriage of Ruggiero and Bradamante—the forty-six-canto poem in octaves (*ottave*) is richly imbued with the structural and thematic elements of Arthurian romance.

Borrowing from Italian versions of Arthurian literature, in particular the *Vita di Merlino*, *Palamedes*, *Tristan*, the *Tavola Ritonda*, and the Prose *Lancelot*, the poem centers on the vagaries and vicissitudes of numerous victims of love, using the motif to underscore the multifaceted nature of human emotions and as a metaphor for the dichotomy between the ideals of chivalric tradition and the realities of a politically unstable Italy in the early decades of the sixteenth century. The titular hero, driven mad by a frustrated love and modeled after, among others, the lover of Iseult in the Prose *Tristan*, embarks upon a series of quests that, like those of his comrades Rinaldo and Ruggiero, reflect a personal voyage toward understanding, maturation, and, in his particular case, disillusionment. Ariosto borrows structural techniques from Arthurian tradition, especially interlace and a complex system of thematic cross-referencing. Of particular significance is the Arthurian tradition of enchantment and magic, which in Ariosto underscores the relativity and variable nature of the world. Numerous episodes derive directly from Arthurian sources in late-medieval *cantari*, including Rinaldo's adventures in the Caledonian Wood (Canto IV), based on Tristan's sojourn in the Forest of Danantes; names, such as that of the heroine Ginevra, whose story in Canto IV also contains numerous Arthurian elements; and figures with magical powers, such as the Arthurian sage Merlin. [RJR]

Ariosto, Ludovico. *Orlando Furioso*, ed. Giuseppe Campari and Angelo Ottolini, Milan: Hoepli, 1926.

———. *The Frenzy of Orlando: A Romantic Epic*, trans. Barbara Reynolds. 2 vols. Harmondsworth: Penguin, 1975–77.

Fatini, Giuseppe. *Bibliografia della critica ariostea, 1510-1956*. Florence: Le Monnier, 1958.

Gardner, Edmund G. *The Arthurian Legend in Italian Literature*. London: Dent, 1930.

Rajna, Pio. *Le Fonti dell' "Orlando Furioso."* Florence: Sansoni, 1876, 1900.

Rodini, Robert J., and Salvatore Di Maria. *Ludovico Ariosto: An Annotated Bibliography of Criticism, 1956–1980*. Columbia: University of Missouri Press, 1984.

ARMS AND ARMOR. Though Arthurian stories abound with battles and tournaments, factual descriptions of the arms and armor used are relatively rare. To a knightly audience, these would be thoroughly familiar and not need to be explained, except under special circumstances, such as to emphasize the richness of a champion's armament.

Three such descriptions of the arming of a knight are of special interest: first, the arming of King Arthur at the eve of the battle of Badon, in Geoffrey of Monmouth's *Historia Regum Britanniae* (ca. 1136); second, the arming of Erec in borrowed armor before the Joust of the Sparrowhawk, in Chrétien de Troyes's *Erec et Enide* (ca. 1170); finally, the arming of Sir Gawain in *Sir Gawain and the Green Knight* (ca. 1400).

The armings of Erec and Gawain give accurate accounts of the armor used during the twelfth and fourteenth centuries; they also demonstrate the proper way a knight should be armed, namely from his feet upward, in order to avoid unnecessary tiring and top-heaviness. Erec's armor consists of mail leggings (*chausses*) reinforced by separately buckled-on knee cops (*genouillières*) of solid plate, a mailshirt (*hauberk*), a helmet, and a shield. The term *hauberk* (from German *Halsberge* 'neck cover'), and the detail that Enide fastens Erec's *aventail* for him, indicate that this mailshirt had a hood (*coif*) with a face-covering flap, the *aventail*, and also mail mittens in one piece with its long sleeves, which made it impossible for Erec to tie the laces of the *aventail* himself. The helmet would have been a conical steel cap with a simple noseguard; the shield would be of the almond-shaped "Norman" type, with rounded top and drawn-out lower point covering the knight's entire left side from eye to knee.

Gawain, on the other hand, is being armed in the much more complicated armor of mail (*paunce*, related to German *Panzer*) and plates developed in the second half of the fourteenth century: articulated iron shoes (*sabatouns*), shin defenses (*greaves*), knee cops (*poleyns*), and thigh defenses (*cuishes*). After these, he dons mailshirt (*byrnie*); emblazoned surcoat (*cote-armure*); and arm defenses of *vambraces* for the forearms, *cowters* for the elbows, *rerebraces* for the upper arms, and *pauldrons* for the shoulders. The last items to be put on are the sword belt; the helmet, which now has an attached mail cape (*camail* and/or *aventail*) to replace the older *coif*; and finally the armored gloves (*gauntlets*). It was understood that proper arming of a knight could be done only with the help of a squire (or an obliging damsel, as in Erec's case). When the knight was in the saddle, his shield and lance would be handed to him by his squire (French *écuyer* 'shield bearer,' from *écu* 'shield'; German *Schildknappe* 'shield boy').

In striking contrast to these two descriptions, the arming of King Arthur in Geoffrey's *Historia* is not done in contemporary arms but with "a leather jerkin [*lorica*] worthy of so great a king. On his head . . . a golden helmet with a crest carved in the shape of a dragon; and across his shoulders a circular shield called Pridwen, on which was painted the likeness of the Blessed Mary, Mother of God." These elements—leather *lorica*, dragon-crested helmet, circular shield—correspond to actual weapons found in the seventh-century ship burial of Sutton Hoo, now in the British Museum. The faithful preservation of these details over a period of at least 500 years is another clue that Geoffrey had access to some earlier source, quite possibly "a very ancient book in the British language." High-ranking officers in the Late Roman army bore portraits of their emperors on their shields, as represented on the consular diptych of the commander-in-chief Stilicho (killed in 408); the icon of the Virgin Mary on Arthur's shield was a logical alternative for a Christian commander without an emperor above him.

Geoffrey also states that, when the Romans withdrew from Britain (assumed date 410), they left behind samples of their armor and weapons as models for the Britons to copy for their self-defense (Book VI, Chapter 3). After almost four centuries of Roman occupation, the tribal military traditions of Britain had dwindled away. Former Roman magistrates became local chieftains, or even kings, and

2-7. Arthurian Arms and Armor (drawings by Helmut Nickel).

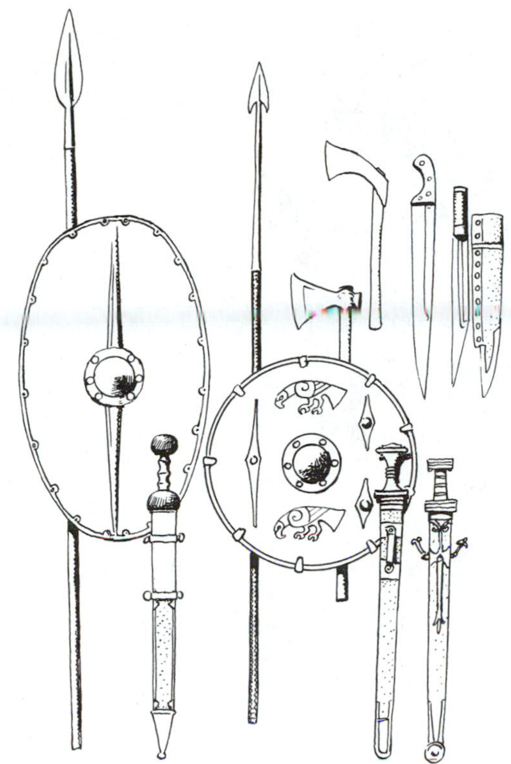

2. British and Germanic weapons.

4. Sarmatian cataphractarius with dragon standard.

3. Saxon and British warriors.

5. "Barbarian" armor in Late Roman Style (Sutton Hoo).

organized their followers as best they could. The wealthier among them would have helmets (*cassis* or *galea*), and short-sleeved mailshirts (*lorica hamata*), but the shield (Latin *scutum*; Welsh *ysquit*) would have been the main defense for practically every fighting man, with the possible exception of archers, who needed both hands to draw their bows. Shields were made of half-inch-thick wooden boards, covered with glued-on leather against splitting under a heavy blow and reinforced around the rim with bronze or iron mountings. Circular or oval in shape, they had a central

6. Erec and Enide (ca. 1170).

7. Gawain arming (ca. 1370).

handgrip. To accommodate the holding hand, a hole was cut into the shield board, covered by the iron shield boss (*umbo*).

Spears, bows and arrows, and swords—the latter mostly longer (ca. three feet) versions of the Roman *gladius*—were the weapons of offense.

The King Arthur of legend is the leader of the knights of the Round Table; the "historical Arthur" is generally thought to have been a Romanized British war-leader, who revived half-forgotten Roman cavalry tactics in order to repel the hit-and-run raids of sea-borne Saxon pirates.

The latest surviving muster roll of the Roman army, the *Notitia Dignitatum*, of ca. 425, shows that two-thirds of the forces stationed in Britain were cavalry, including the only two active regiments of heavy-armored cavalry, *cataphractarii*, in the west, and a unit of Sarmatian veteran troopers. *Cataphractarii* wore scale armor and helmets of eastern type, styled after the tribal armor of the Sarmatians, horse nomads from the Pannonian (Hungarian) steppes. Even their horses were armored with chanfrons of bronze-studded leather, and scale armor of bronze or horn for neck, breast, and crupper. Weapons were a long lance (*kontus*) and long cavalry swords. Their battle standard was a windsock-like *draco* on a pole. For parade purposes, highly decorative bronze helmets with lifelike modeled face masks were worn. Helmets, scale armor, and chanfrons have been found at Newstead (*Trimontium*). Two grave stelae of cataphractarii, one carrying a dragon banner, are in the Grosvenor Museum, Chester (*Urbs legionis*). (*See* CALVARY, ARTHURIAN.)

Archaeological evidence for Romano-British arms is scarce. The Britons were Christians, who did not believe in warlike gravegoods as did the Saxons. The latter were pagans who could look forward to a warrior's afterlife in Valhalla till Ragnarök. The main defense of a Saxon thegn was a round shield, of basically the same construction as the British type, though Saxon shields could have an extra carrying sling for the forearm; they also could have sharply pointed bosses to be used as effective weapons in counterattack. Body armor consisted of mailshirts, produced in the formerly Roman industrial centers of the Rhinelands, and *spangenhelms*, the "barbarian" helmet type, introduced into central Europe by eastern nomads, such as Sarmatians, Alani, and Huns. A particularly splendid type of *spangenhelm* seems to have been made at the court workshop of the Ostrogothic kings of Italy, at Ravenna, and distributed all over continental Europe, probably as diplomatic presents. Anglo-Saxon *spangenhelms* were distinguished by having crests, either dragon (Sutton Hoo helmet) or boar figurines (Benty Grange helmet); visor masks (*grim*) either covered the entire face or were frames around eyes and nose. However, not a single Germanic (or Viking) helmet with horns or wings has been found so far, though there are pre-Roman British and Gaulish horned helmets. The name of the Saxons is derived from *seax*, a machete-like long-knife, both tool and weapon; its sword-length version was the *scramasax* ("wound-knife"). The name of the Angles is probably related to *ango*, a barbed throwing spear or harpoon. A much-favored weapon that also was a handy tool on shipboard was the battle-axe, which also gave name to a tribe of the continental Saxons, the Longobards ("Long-axes"). The Franks were feared for their short-handled throwing axes, the *francisca*. The most treasured of weapons of a Germanic warrior was the sword (*spatha*); beautifully pattern-welded blades, whose surface markings evoked comparisons with dragon skin or twisting snakes, were produced in the Rhinelands, where mythical smiths, such as Wayland or Regin, to whom Siegfried once was apprenticed, were located, and where the cutlery center of Solingen still flourishes. Famous swords were given personal names; *Balmung* (Siegfried's sword), *Mimung* and *Nagelring* (products of Wayland), *Durendal* (Roland's sword), and of course Arthur's *Excalibur/Caliburnus*. (The intricate cross-cultural relations of the Migration Period and the so-called Dark Ages are shown in these sword names: *Balmung* is probably related to *Avalon*, where Geoffrey has Arthur's *Caliburnus* forged, whose name is derived from Latin *chalybs* 'steel,' which in turn comes from the *Kalybes*, a Sarmatian tribe of smiths in the Caucasus.) To enhance the value of a cherished sword, the maker richly mounted its hilt and scabbard in silver and gold. Ritual deposits of swords in sacred lakes are known from the province Angeln, the homeland of the Angles, at the Danish-German border. The motif of the Sword in the Lake might have its historical background in remembered occasions, when a priestess in charge of such a sacred lake would have retrieved a sword for a champion, to be returned after the hero's death. (*See also* HERALDRY; ROUND TABLES; SARMATIAN CONNECTION; TOURNAMENTS.) [HN]

Gamber, Ortwin. "Some Notes on the Sutton Hoo Military Equipment." *Journal of the Arms and Armour Society*, 10 (December 1982). 208–16.

Nickel, Helmut. "About Arms and Armor in the Age of Arthur." *Avalon to Camelot*, 1 (Fall 1983), 19–21.

Norman, A.V.B., and Don Pottinger, *Warrior to Soldier: English Weapons and Warfare, 449–1660*. London: Weidenfeld and Nicolson, 1966.

Robinson, H. Russell, and Ronald Embleton. *What the Soldiers Wore on Hadrian's Wall*. Newcastle-upon-Tyne: Graham, 1976.

Simkins, Michael, and Ronald Embleton. *The Roman Army from Hadrian to Constantine*. London: Osprey, 1979.

Wise, Terence. *Saxon, Viking and Norman*. London: Osprey, 1979.

ARNOLD, MATTHEW (1822–1888), wrote the first English modernization of the Tristan story, *Tristram and Iseult* (1852). His chief source was Dunlop's *History of Prose Fiction* (1814), which recounted Tristan's birth, voyage to Ireland disguised as a harper, wooing of Iseult for Mark, drinking of the love potion, secret meetings, marriage to Iseult of Brittany (Iseult of the White Hands), and deathbed reunion with Queen Iseult. From Southey's Malory, Arnold took the form of the hero's name, the Roman Wars episode (in which Malory's Tristram did not participate), and the phrase "passing weary" to describe Vivian's attitude to Merlin. The story of Merlin and Vivian came from Villemarqué's "Visite au Tombeau de Merlin" (*Revue de Paris*, 1837). Arnold's theme is the destructive power of love. He also seeks to evoke the ethos of Celtic poetry as defined in *On the Study of Celtic Literature* (1867): "the magical charm of nature" and the passionate melancholy of the characters' "adverse destiny."

In Part I, "Tristram" (373 lines of predominantly trochaic tetrameter), the hero in a delirious dream recalls his life with Iseult of Ireland, while his wife, "the sweetest Christian soul alive," watches by his bed. Part II, "Iseult of Ireland" (193 lines), consists of a rhapsodic duet in quatrains as the lovers are reunited. The exchange is soon terminated by their deaths. Part III, "Iseult of Brittany" (224 lines of heroic couplets), takes place a year later, after the lovers have been buried at Tintagel. The widowed Iseult tells her children (Arnold's addition) "an old world Breton history," the story of Merlin's beguilement. For the sexually frustrated heroine, Vivian's ability to enslave Merlin may be a wish-fulfilling dream of female power. Her patient suffering, loneliness, and social isolation represent a characteristic Arnoldian mode. [MAW]

Arnold, Matthew, *The Poetical Works of Matthew Arnold*, ed. C.B. Tinker and H.F. Lowry. London: Oxford University Press, 1960.

Buckler, William E. *On the Poetry of Matthew Arnold: Essays in Critical Reconstruction*. New York: New York University Press, 1982.

ART: *see* DECORATIVE ARTS (MEDIEVAL); VISUAL ARTS.

ARTHOUR AND MERLIN, the earliest English verse romance about Merlin. It emphasizes his role as Arthur's mage, with only fleeting references to his connection with the Holy Grail. Drawn from a chronicle of Arthur's career and the French Vulgate Cycle, and written as early as the middle or third quarter of the thirteenth century, the poem (ca. 9,900 lines) concerns the miraculous birth of Merlin, his aid to Uther Pendragon, the founding of the Round Table, and his great service to the young King Arthur.

A later rendition of this romance, the so-called "jüngere version" (ca. 2,000 lines) contained in four varying fifteenth-century manuscripts, recounts the history only up until the death of Pendragon, Uther's brother, so that it concentrates on Merlin, the mage, and his pre-Arthurian activities. There is also an interesting colophon giving Glastonbury as the burial site for Pendragon, whereas in the earlier version both Pendragon and Uther are buried at Stonehenge. The poem offers an interesting contrast with the two later English translations of the Merlin saga, Lovelich's *Merlin* and the Prose *Merlin*, both of which concern Merlin's role as the prophet of the Holy Grail. An English chapbook version, *A Lytel Treatyse of þe Byrth and Prophecye of Marlyn*, appeared in 1510. [VML]

Kölbing, Eugen, ed. *Arthour and Merlin.* Heilbronn: Henniger, 1890.

Ackerman, Robert W. "The English Rimed and Prose Romances." In *Arthurian Literature in the Middle Ages*, ed. Roger Sherman Loomis. Oxford: Clarendon, 1959, pp. 485–86.

ARTHUR, an early fifteenth-century English verse chronicle (642 lines), is an interpolation in a Latin chronicle of the kings of Britain found in Longleat MS 55. Based upon some version of Wace's *Brut*, it tells of Arthur's war against the Romans. Details not in known versions of Wace include Arthur's burial at Glastonbury and the inscription on Arthur's tomb ("Hic jacet Arthurus, rex quondam rexque futurus"), which are also found in the Thornton Manuscript of the Alliterative *Morte Arthure* and in Malory's *Morte Darthur*. [EDK]

Furnivall, Frederick J., ed. *Arthur.* London: Oxford University Press, 1864.

Finlayson, J. "The Source of 'Arthur,' an Early Fifteenth-Century Verse Chronicle." *Notes and Queries*, n.s., 7 (1960), 46–47.

Göller, Karl Heinz. *König Arthur in der englishchen Literatur des späten Mittelalters.* Göttingen: Vandenhoeck and Ruprecht, 1963, pp. 57–66.

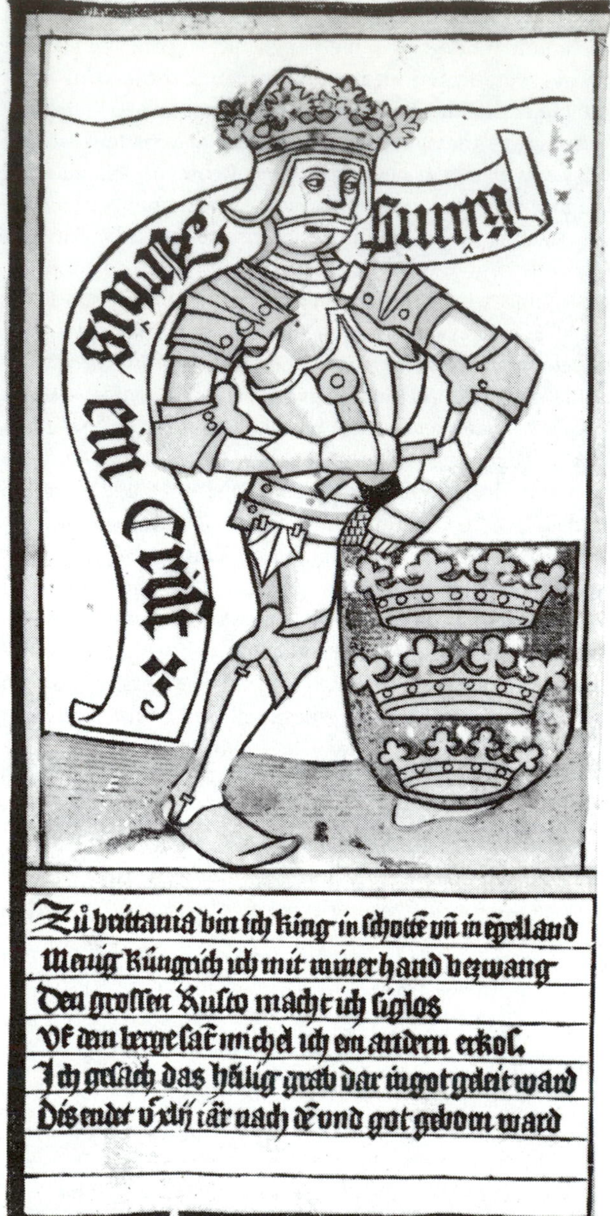

8. Woodcut, "King Artus," for a Nine Worthies series (ca. 1475), Bern, Burgerbibliothek, Cod. A45, p. 309. (Courtesy Bern Burgerbibliothek.)

ARTHUR, CHARACTER OF. Although attempts to identify the historical Arthur continue, the King is largely a creation of romance, and it is hardly surprising that his character changes and grows and that he presents occasional inconsistent traits from text to text. In pseudo-chronicles (e.g., Wace), the depiction is understandably that of a military leader, since the legend of Arthur was just being forged and developed and since his prestige would henceforth be based in large part on his having subjugated much of the world and imposed himself as its leader. Even in such texts, however, Arthur's concern for peace and justice balances his warlike traits; it is in Wace that, having brought an extended period of peace to the world, he establishes the Round Table to promote equality and harmony.

Much of Arthurian literature is only marginally, if at all, about Arthur. In the course of the Middle Ages, emphasis shifts quickly to Lancelot and Guenevere, to Perceval, Galahad, or Gawain, to Tristan and Isolde. However, in Celtic material more than in French or other romances, Arthur does often play the central and dominant role, undertaking wars, hunts, and quests, succeeding thereby in gaining both glory and territory for himself. At the same time, in works like *Culhwch and Olwen*, Arthur, although a glorious and famous king, is closely associated with magic and the supernatural: the Welsh Arthur, not surprisingly, participates extensively in the Celtic mythological tradition.

Beyond the chronicles, the Celtic material, and certain other texts (e.g., the Middle English works), the emphasis on Arthur as warrior and conqueror is reduced. Romance authors generally abandon interest in large-scale wars in favor of more localized battles, tourneys, and (especially) the presentation of Arthur as sovereign and patriarch rather than warrior. He is most consistently presented as wise, generous, and magnanimous. He is kind and forgiving, trustworthy and loyal. On the other hand, he is sometimes seen as indecisive or, conversely, petulant and stubborn, even when his own interests or those of the court may be compromised. For example, in Chrétien de Troyes's *Erec et Enide* Arthur insists on conducting the hunt for the white stag, even though he is told—and does not appear to doubt—that the hunt will inevitably lead to dissension and trouble at court.

Arthur may act hastily, but he rarely reacts in anger, other than righteous indignation. An exception is offered by the Alliterative *Morte*, but most often he is presented as even-tempered to the point of blandness. In the *Mort Artu*, we may be startled by an absence of outrage when Arthur is told of Lancelot's sin with Guenevere: he becomes pale, comments that all this is *merveilles*, and lapses into silence. Of course, his passivity may be less a function of his traditional character than of the *Mort Artu* poet's individual presentation—the King will react with near indifference even to the Queen's death—but in most texts he is shown to be even-tempered, even-handed, and calm.

The King appears on occasion to be a somewhat feeble patriarch. In Chrétien's *Yvain*, for example, Arthur is unable to stay awake after a feast; he retires to the Queen's chamber for a nap, causing puzzlement and grumbling on the part of his knights. The essential fact here and in other texts, however, is that his prestige is never—or almost never—compromised by his personal weaknesses. Whether he is nodding off at awkward moments, suffering fools (like Kay) a bit too gladly, or risking the harmony of the court by commanding everyone to play his white-stag game, his authority and glory remain intact. Indeed, they remain intact even when the ethic and efficacy of the Arthurian court itself are questioned. (It should be noted that occasional works, such as Robert Biket's *Lai du cor* and other settings of chastity tests, often indulge in humor at Arthur's expense; this is, however, a minority view of the King.)

As Rosemary Morris notes, Arthur was an ideal Christian hero, and in various texts, such as *Culhwch and Olwen*, he is presented as God's elect. In some works that recount the withdrawal of the Sword in the Stone, it is by that phenomenon that God chooses Arthur as king. Yet, as early as Chrétien, authors begin to hint that the court and its kind of chivalry are ineffective or flawed ideals. Once the Grail quest becomes a preoccupation of Chrétien and his successors, the writers imply—and sometimes indicate explicitly—that the quest can be accomplished only by a renunciation of Arthurian chivalry and adherence to a higher code.

Nevertheless, it is only by implication (however clear) that Arthur is himself diminished, and within the context of his court and world he remains respected and revered. It appears that there are in a sense two Arthurs: one of them is a human being, illustrious, wise, but quite human nonetheless; the other is an image, identified with the ideals of Camelot and the Round Table. The natural, if rare, frailties of the human king seldom compromise the image, even when the distinction between the two widens progressively, and the most fascinating settings of the Arthurian legend are often those that show Arthur as human and imperfect.

If later authors have not often made fundamental changes in the character of Arthur, they have in a number of cases concentrated more heavily on one side of that character than on the other. Some accounts have deified him and thereby robbed him of most of his humanity, but other writers have successfully resisted that temptation, presenting Arthur as subject to doubts, fears, and jealousies. Among many notable treatments of the monarch, we might conclude with two. Thomas Berger comically traces Arthur's development from a naive youth (and a pompous one, who reacts to the news that he will be king by immediately adopting the royal "we") to a great ruler who nonetheless retains his human traits; and T.H. White shows us, far better than most writers, an Arthur who is at the end an old man, feeble and exhausted, sad and near despair, an old man sustained—but barely—by hope. [NJL]

Morris, Rosemary. *The Character of King Arthur in Medieval Literature*. Cambridge: Brewer, 1982.

Thompson, Raymond H. *The Return from Avalon: A Study of the Arthurian Legend in Modern Fiction*. Westport, Conn.: Greenwood, 1985.

ARTHUR, ORIGINS OF LEGEND. Though the legend of Arthur is a phenomenon of history, taking shape over a roughly known period, historical research alone fails to establish how it began. With (for example) Alexander and Charlemagne, who likewise inspired medieval romance, history gives a simple answer: the hero was a real person, with a documented career. The question "Was Arthur a real person?" cannot be answered in the same direct manner. His reality is not proved, or for that matter disproved, by the strictly historical evidence. Barring some new discovery, the only way to arrive at even a cautious conclusion is to appraise this in conjunction with data of other types.

A manifest obstacle is that the medieval authors who developed the Matter of Britain had little interest in authenticity. They were not writing historical fiction in the modern sense. Like all medieval storytelling based on ancient material, Arthurian romance updated it, portraying kingship, warfare, costume, and much else in contemporary terms, however idealized and fantasized, and giving pride of place to themes of contemporary interest, such as chivalry and courtly love. There is no direct route from the romances back to any underlying reality. Geoffrey of Monmouth, who prepared the ground by creating Arthur's official biography, is an author of a different kind: he undoubtedly *uses* history and is somewhat closer to whatever facts there may be. But he, too, updates, as in his description of Arthur's court at Caerleon, and where he can be checked, as in his version of the preceding Roman period, his fictionalization is so palpable as to deprive him of any credit as a historian. Nothing he says can be trusted by itself as a statement of fact.

Most investigators who have sought a "historical Arthur" by historical methods have dismissed Geoffrey and the romancers from any consideration at all. That exclusion has led in practice to another. It is assumed that there can be no evidence directly concerning Arthur outside Britain, because his activities overseas, however important and circumstantial Geoffrey and some romancers make them, are part of the literary fantasy. (The possibility of Breton information, handed down from emigrant Britons in Arthur's time, has generally been ignored.) Within the tacitly agreed limits, the evidence is twofold. First, there is a miscellany of data, almost entirely of Welsh provenance, showing the nature of the tradition before Geoffrey. Second, there is another body of data, augmented by archaeology, from which a vague picture can be formed of the course of events in Britain during the fifth and sixth centuries, when Arthur supposedly lived. Historians have tried to evaluate the former and bring it into relation with the latter.

An early Welsh allusion occurs in the *Gododdin* series of poems, composed toward 600 and ascribed to the northern bard Aneirin. The poems commemorate the fallen in a battle against the Angles at *Catraeth*, probably Catterick in Yorkshire. Arthur is mentioned in passing as proverbial for martial prowess. It is not implied that he was one of the northern warriors himself, or contemporary with them. The line may be an interpolation, but no cogent reason exists for thinking so, and even if it is it must still be quite early. Other poems, in the so-called Book of Taliesin and the Black Book of Carmarthen, also name Arthur as a famous warrior and refer to a band of followers. The "Stanzas of the Graves" say his grave is a mystery, and in this connection a Cornish anecdote told by Hermann of Tournai attests a folk-belief in his immortality. The cryptic Welsh verses entitled *The Spoils of Annwfn* involve him and his followers in an otherworld quest, a possible Celtic antecedent of the quest of the Grail.

Such bardic and folkloric items, though not numerous in the early centuries, demonstrate a rooted tradition that the Welsh developed from older materials—perhaps from heroic lays current among their forebears, the Celtic inhabitants of Britain before the Saxon ascendancy. Arthur's appearances in several fabulous "Lives" of Welsh saints also make him a military figure, with troops at his command and sometimes a royal title, if a rather uncertain one. The Triads, and the *Mabinogion* tale *Culhwch and Olwen*, show that by the late eleventh century a Welsh Arthurian saga had grown up portraying him as a formidable warrior-prince with a large entourage comprising historical, quasi-historical, and purely fantastic characters.

While these poems and stories may be thought to give a cumulative impression of a real original, a great man remembered and glorified, the factual element in them must be scanty. But Wales supplies two Latin texts giving what looks like substantiation. These are the ninth-century *Historia Brittonum*, ascribed to Nennius, and the tenth-century *Annales Cambriae*. The former speaks of Arthur as *dux bellorum*, the war-leader of the kings of the Britons, and lists twelve battles that he won against the Saxons and probably their Pictish allies. The twelfth battle is Badon, a major victory attested by Gildas much earlier, though Gildas does not name the Britons' commander. The *Annales* also refer to Badon and add the "strife of Camlann" in which Arthur fell, together with Medraut (Mordred).

Some historians have accepted Nennius and the *Annales* as more or less reliable here. The chief justification for doing so is plausibility. The other body of data, on the post-Roman situation in general, suggests that an Arthur who led antibarbarian resistance can at least be credibly fitted in. Britain was separated from the empire in 410 and passed into a long phase of transition and trouble. Though the wilder jeremiads of Gildas can be discounted, there is no good reason to doubt that Saxon auxiliaries stationed in Britain did revolt toward the middle of the fifth century; that a period of widespread raiding, which involved Picts as well, was followed by a respite and partial British recovery; that, while subsequent Saxon land-taking progressed without conflict in many places, a fluctuating warfare continued for years in others; and that in the first half of the sixth century, after the British success at Badon, all major Saxon encroachment ceased for a time. Alone among Rome's provincials, the Britons became self-governing before the barbarians moved in, fought back when they did, and more than once appeared to have halted their advance. This pattern of rescue-from-disaster would accord with Arthur's career in Nennius. As British war-leader, he could have been, at some crucial stage, the principal rescuer. For this reason, the Britons' resurgence has been described as the "Arthurian Fact," meaning the fact of history that he came to symbolize, whether he existed or not.

Scholars favoring the view that he did exist, on the basis of the Welsh matter, made various suggestions during the 1930s and decades ensuing. R.G. Collingwood envisaged Arthur as holding the Late Roman military office of *Comes Britanniarum*, Count of the Britains, and employing cavalry to defeat the pedestrian Saxons. The cavalry theory has outlived Collingwood's presentation of it. Much of its original force depended on the assumption that all the battles in Nennius's list were genuine, the inference being that, as they are apparently widely scattered, Arthur must have been mobile and ubiquitous. Kenneth Jackson, while rejecting most of Collingwood's thesis, found likely locations for some of the battles, which confirmed that Arthur's activities were believed to have ranged far and wide. Jackson regarded him as probably though not certainly real; if real, he was a "supreme British commander of genius" active principally in southern Britain. Leslie Alcock, having shown that Cadbury Castle (allegedly Camelot) was reoccupied and refortified in about the right period, interpreted Arthur much as Jackson did and proposed Cadbury as a base from which he operated. During this phase of scholarship, his royal status was usually regarded as a product of legend, but in 1973 John Morris presented him as a sort of emperor.

Four years later, the use of the Welsh matter as historical evidence was crushingly criticized by David Dumville, and the pursuit of Arthur along this line came to a virtual halt. Alcock retired into agnosticism. The documents, it must be acknowledged, are inadequate. They may contain factual material, but they are insufficient for proof or even convincing reconstruction. They supply no reference to Arthur that comes anywhere near to being contemporary, except perhaps the *Gododdin* line, and that is uncertain and uninformative. They offer or imply hopelessly inconsistent dates for him, spreading him out, as an active campaigner, over a stretch of eighty or ninety years. They never give a chronological fix: that is, they never synchronize him with known history outside Britain. Moreover, not a single Welsh text makes a plain historical statement about him, acceptable as free from legend. Even Nennius's fairly sober account is called in question by the assertion that Arthur singlehandedly slew 960 enemies at Badon, a feat that shows him to be already legendary.

One or two historians have picked out the Camlann entry in the *Annales* as a solitary scrap of firm evidence. But it was written in the tenth century; it cannot be related to known history; and the late date that it gives, 539, can hardly be reconciled with the rest of Arthur's quasi-historical record. The only logical way to handle it would be to drop the rest altogether and postulate an Arthur doing nothing of note at all but perish at Camlann fighting another Briton. That step has occasionally been taken. But it seems a *reductio ad absurdum*, implying that the whole Arthurian legend grew round a petty chief—one among dozens—with no victories to his credit, no role in the struggle against the Saxons, and an inglorious exit. To confine Arthur to Camlann merely replaces one mystery with another.

The failure of the purely historical approach is proved in the end by the contradictions among those who have attempted it. Some have made Arthur a local leader, some a national one. Some have put him in the fifth century, some around the beginning of the sixth, some, by a radical reinterpretation, toward the end of it. N.K. Chadwick even hazarded the notion, if noncommitally, that the only original Arthur was a Scottish prince in Argyll, who was probably born ca. 570. Fully as daunting are the disagreements over Arthur's home territory. An influential school of thought has favored the north, mainly on the ground that the oldest poetic allusions to him are northern. But there need not be more in this than the fact that the first memorable poets in Welsh happened to be northerners. Opponents have retorted that Arthur is far more believable as a leader in the south, where Saxons were numerous and aggressive, and have pointed out that, while stories of him occur widely, the only ones identifying a birthplace, a headquarters, or a grave all belong to Cornwall and Somerset. Archaeology indeed has shown that all three places (Tintagel, Cadbury, Glastonbury) were important at roughly the time the stories indicate. This triple result implies some knowledge of the period on the storytellers' part, but it does not prove the presence of any specific individual.

In the midst of these perplexities, one fact does emerge, the significance of Arthur's name. It is the Welsh form of the Roman name Artorius, and clearly suggests a real person born in the fifth century, when the custom of giving children Roman names still flourished among the Britons. Furthermore, a revival of this particular name late in the sixth century, when the custom in general was almost defunct, strongly hints that, somewhat earlier, an Arthur had flourished who had become a national hero.

The name tells against the conjecture, which the character of the Welsh matter has sometimes encouraged, that Arthur is not a man but a myth: perhaps a Celtic god, euhemerized. Plainly, such a figure is not likely to have borne a Roman name, and a human one at that. Advocates of the myth theory have failed to find a god called Artorius or to give "Arthur" a viable alternative etymology. Arthur's saga certainly involved touches of what may be described as mythification—he may, for instance, owe something to Bran—but the notion of him as wholly mythical or divine has proved unsustainable. Would-be reconstructions by Raglan, Darrah, and others are more completely incompatible than their historical counterparts. No one who definitely denies Arthur has succeeded in accounting for the facts without him. Most followers of the long debate have been inclined, after all, to conclude that there is a real person lurking somewhere. Despite the difficulties, it is easier on balance to believe that he did exist than that he did not.

Given such an outcome—only barely positive and in the eyes of skeptics not even that—an issue that arises is whether the starting point might be reached by some other path. If so, the figure of Arthur might come into better focus, and the ostensibly historical data might be better assessed. The question "Was he a real person?" leads to no certain answer, but the question "How did his legend originate, what facts is it rooted in?" can broaden the scope of the inquiry by taking the literary process into account, with the hope of attaining fresh historical insight by way of it. In particular, this question brings Geoffrey of Monmouth back into the discussion. Rightly ruled out as a historian or a direct source for history, he can return as an imaginative writer who uses it. The nature of the history that he uses is a proper subject to explore.

It might be supposed that this exploration can shed no further light, because, when Geoffrey wrote of Arthur, he merely adopted him from the Welsh and inflated the Welsh material already reviewed. That is one frequent assumption; another is that his notorious claim to have drawn on an additional work, an "ancient book in the British language," is bogus. Yet, whether or not he had an ancient book, the assumption about his sources is questionable. The Arthur story contrasts eloquently with other parts of the text. His narrative of the villain Vortigern is indeed purely Welsh, an expansion of Nennius. But his narrative of the hero Arthur is a great deal more. Welsh quasi-historical matter underlies only about one-fifth of it. The rest is quite different in substance and atmosphere, and different also from the Welsh Arthur saga, which he hardly seems to know. The anti-Saxon campaign, which for Nennius is the whole point, is not central but introductory. Promoting Arthur to a kingship without parallel, Geoffrey devotes half the story of his reign to embroilments with the empire and warfare in Gaul, of which the Welsh give no hint.

Also, Geoffrey transforms the denouement. When he first foreshadows Arthur's career, in the *Prophetiae Merlini*, he seems to picture it as ending in Gaul. When he comes to compose the actual narrative, he does bring in the Welsh tradition, returning Arthur to Britain to fall at Camlann. But, in defiance of the Welsh, he makes Mordred a traitorous deputy ruler who intrigues with barbarians. The disaster is still intertwined with the Gallic warfare, and Arthur's final destination is *Insula Avallonis*, which does not precisely Latinize the Welsh *Avallach* but does echo the name of a real place in Burgundy—Avallon.

As remarked, since Arthur's activities overseas have normally been dismissed as invention, it has been taken for granted that no relevant historical sources exist outside Britain. But Geoffrey's account of the Gallic warfare suggests that this is another assumption that may fairly be challenged. In view of the climactic importance he gives it, and the lack of any Welsh prototype, it is reasonable to wonder whether he found materials for it in continental records.

To reject such an inquiry on the ground that he simply made it all up is to imply that he is doing something here that he never does anywhere else, from Julius Caesar on, that is, fabricate a long, major piece of narrative out of absolutely nothing. Even his wildly fictitious account of Arthur's court has its antecedent in the Welsh tale *Culhwch and Olwen*. His normal method of composition does call for a background search.

Vital here are his indications of date. Curiously, he supplies what the Welsh matter never does, a chronological fix. Arthur's Gallic campaigning occurs, as he says three times, in the reign of Leo, clearly the eastern emperor Leo I, who reigned from 457 to 474. Similar if less certain clues narrow the range to 468–74 and may even reduce it to 469–70. This agrees with the observation of Sharon Turner, as long ago as 1799, that Geoffrey's Arthur is based, here at least, on the "king of the Britons" called Riothamus who led a British army through Gaul at exactly that time, playing a part in the last agonies of the western empire. The sources here are contemporary or early, so that one manifest difficulty raised by the Welsh matter—its remoteness in time from the events—does not arise.

Features of his career, pieced together from Jordanes, Sidonius, and Gregory of Tours, confirm Geoffrey's use of it and the likelihood of a lost historical source (even an "ancient book") assembling the scattered details. Riothamus advanced to the neighborhood of Burgundy. He was betrayed by a deputy ruler who treated with barbarian enemies. He is last located in Gaul among the Burgundians. He disappears after a fatal battle with no recorded death. The line of his retreat shows him moving in the direction of the actual Avallon. All these themes are introduced in Geoffrey's account of Arthur, and so, if garbled, are several contemporary names besides Leo's. While the politics of the war are different, its modification for the King's greater glory is in keeping with Geoffrey's literary conduct in other places, and its true character is still vestigially visible.

Riothamus means "supreme king" or "supremely royal" and was probably a title or honorific applied to a British high king, so that the personal name of the man thus styled is unknown. There are signs that, in fictionalizing him under the name of Arthur and implying his identity with the war-leader of the Welsh, Geoffrey was not indulging in fancy without precedent. The author of the Breton *Legend of St. Goeznovius* apparently refers to the same king and calls him Arthur, and at least six chroniclers give dates and particulars for Arthur, not derived from Geoffrey, that point the same way. Credibly, "Arthur" (Artorius) was Riothamus's name or at any rate was supposed to have been his name long before Geoffrey, who used a source, probably Breton, affirming the identity. One possibility is that the name is a sobriquet inspired by an earlier Artorius, the imperial commander Lucius Artorius Castus, who led an expedition from Britain to Gaul to suppress a rebellion. A second commander leading an expedition from Britain to Gaul might have been hailed in panegyric, or commemorated in poetry, as a "second Artorius."

Riothamus existed, and therefore supplies a point of origin for at least part of Arthur's pseudo-biography, the Gallic part. The further question is whether the Welsh tradition requires a separate Arthur-figure, real or fictitious, or whether, as Geoffrey and others would imply, Riothamus-called-Arthur could account for this, too. Any answer must be speculative, since nothing is known of his activities in Britain before he shipped his army to Gaul. However, in the situation of the 450s and 460s he could have fought the

Britons' enemies at all the more-or-less identified places on Nennius's list. The most relevant archaeological site is Cadbury–Camelot, and on the basis of Alcock's revised assessment (1983) Riothamus is the only documented person who qualifies as its royal refortifier.

As Arthur-Riothamus (to coin a term), hypothetically high king in succession to Vortigern, he is an arguable original for the insular legend as well as the continental. The other military leader, Ambrosius, might have been a general in his service while he reigned in Britain and regent during his absence abroad. More important to the case than guesswork like this is the question whether a fifth-century high king could have been transformed by bards and storytellers into the Arthur of the Welsh, who is less clearly royal and, though undatable, is sometimes associated with persons belonging to the sixth century. The parallel here might be the treatment by German minstrels of Theodoric, the great Gothic king of Italy, who in the *Nibelungenlied* is reduced to the warlike noble Dietrich of Bern and made anachronistically a companion of Attila. On this showing, Geoffrey reunited a figure who had been split up, though the result was a literary creation, not a reinstatement of historical truth.

If the question "Was Arthur a real person?" is pressed, a defensible answer would be: "The Arthur of Geoffrey and the romancers is a legend, but he has a real original, the British high king who went to Gaul." The feasibility of regarding this man as the *only* original must remain an open question. King Arthur may be a composite like Merlin. Certainly, Riothamus, who fades from the scene ca. 470, cannot explain the association of Arthur with Badon and Camlann. He can explain another seeming anomaly, the date 542, which Geoffrey gives for Arthur's passing, because recognized processes of error could have derived it from 470. But Badon and Camlann might be thought to demand a second Arthur-figure. This, however, is far from definite. To judge from a Welsh poem about a battle at *Llongborth* (Portchester?), a military body called Arthur's Men existed, or was believed to have existed, independently of his presence and perhaps after his departure. Poetic allusions to Arthur's Men at Badon, Camlann, and indeed other battles might have been misconstrued as implying that Arthur was there in person: a misconstruction that is demonstrably possible, because it has been laid on the Llongborth poem itself. Obviously, this is only one of many problems remaining unsolved. (*See also* CHRONICLES, ARTHUR IN; *GOEZNOVII, LEGENDA SANCTI*; LEO I; LUCIUS; RIOTHAMUS; SARMATIAN CONNECTION; SCHOLARSHIP, MODERN ARTHURIAN; SULPICIUS.)

[GA]

Alcock, Leslie. *Arthur's Britain.* London: Penguin, 1971, pp. 1-141, 351–64.

Ashe, Geoffrey. "A Certain Very Ancient Book." *Speculum*, 56 (April 1981), 301–23.

———. *The Discovery of King Arthur.* New York: Doubleday, 1985, Part II.

———. "The Historical Origins of the Arthurian Legend." In *The Vitality of the Arthurian Legend: A Symposium*, ed. Mette Pors. Odense: Odense University Press, 1988, pp. 25–43.

Chambers, E.K. *Arthur of Britain.* London: Sidgwick and Jackson, 1927, pp. 1–99, 168–232.

Collingwood, R.G., and J.N.L. Myres. *Roman Britain and the English Settlements.* London and New York: Oxford University Press, 1937, pp. 321–26.

Dumville, David. "Sub-Roman Britain: History and Legend." *History*, 62 (1977), 173–91.

Dunning, R.W. *Arthur: The King in the West.* New York: St. Martin, 1988, pp. 23-32, 111–42.

Jackson, Kenneth Hurlstone. "The Arthur of History" and "Arthur in Early Welsh Verse." In *Arthurian Literature in the Middle Ages*, ed. Roger Sherman Loomis. Oxford: Clarendon, 1959, pp. 1–19.

Morris, John. *The Age of Arthur.* New York: Scribner, 1973, pp. 87–141.

ARTHUR AND KALETVWLCH (ARTHUR A KALETVWLCH), a short Welsh prose narrative, dating perhaps from the fourteenth century, that offers an account of Arthur from his conception and birth to his coronation. Included is the story of Arthur's drawing the sword (here named Kaletvwlch) from the stone. [NJL]

Davies, J.H. "A Welsh Version of the Birth of Arthur." *Y Cymmrodor*, 24 (1913), 247–64. (Edition.)

ARTHUR AND GORLAGON, Latin prose, whose extant text dates from the early fourteenth century. Arthur's queen tells him that he does not know the heart, nature, or ways of women. Challenged by her, Arthur goes on a quest for the answer, an answer that Gorlagon gives him by telling the story of a king (Gorlagon himself) who is turned into a werewolf by his lecherous, traitorous wife. Analogues for the story of the werewolf exist in Celtic and in oriental folktales. [MLD]

Kittredge, George L., ed. "Arthur and Gorlagon." *Harvard Studies and Notes in Philology and Literature,* 8 (1903), 149–275.

ARTHUR OF LITTLE BRITAIN. The hero of this sixteenth-century prose translation by Sir John Bourchier, Lord Berners, of the French romance *Artus de la Petite Bretagne* is the son of the Duke of Brittany. The best knight in the world, Arthur demonstrates his prowess in feats of arms and encounters with marvelous creatures. He ends the enchantments of the Port Noire and wins the hand of the fair Florence, daughter of King Emendus. [JN]

Utterson, E.V., ed. *The History of the Valiant King Arthur of Little Britain*. London: White, Cochrane, 1814.

ARTHURIAN REVIVAL. The renewed interest in Arthurian literature in the early nineteenth century did not significantly affect the visual arts until the reign of Queen Victoria. The Arthurian Revival in the arts was in fact a Victorian phenomenon, built upon the ideas and sensibilities of the Gothic Revival but endowed with the high moral values and modernized chivalric ideals of the subsequent era. The course of the Arthurian Revival followed Victorian history, flowering shortly after the coronation, developing through the reign, and waning at the end of the epoch. In this way, the Arthurian Revival reflected the rise and decline of the idealism of the Victorian era.

After centuries of neglect, the Arthurian legend was introduced into the repertoire of the British painter as a patriotic allegory. In 1848, the government, upon the suggestion of Prince Albert, requested that William Dyce design and execute a program of frescoes based on the Arthurian legend in the Queen's Robing Room in the new palace at Westminster. Using Malory as his text, Dyce personified the ideal qualities of British manhood in the heroes of the legend, and his moral stance foreshadowed Tennyson's interpretation in the *Idylls of the King*. The frescoes provided the absent prototype, both in heroic form and didactic interpretation, that endured through the course of the Revival.

The Robing Room frescoes stimulated wide interest in Arthurian iconography in the 1850s. The Pre-Raphaelites, already drawn to the poetry of Tennyson, addressed the new subject with energy and ingenuity. Tennyson's influence was in ascendance, and the Moxon Tennyson disseminated Arthurian interest. The first publication of the *Idylls*, in 1859, placed him on an equal footing with Malory as a literary source for the arts.

Arthurian interest came to fruition in the 1860s and 1870s; every sector of the Victorian art world embraced the expanding iconography. Academic artists, including James Archer, Joseph Noël Paton, and Thomas Woolner, followed the example set by Dyce, depicting monumental figures engaged in noble action, while the Pre-Raphaelites, notably Edward Burne-Jones, Dante Gabriel Rossetti, and Arthur Hughes, preferred poignant vignettes of love. Overall, the favored subjects included Sir Galahad, Elaine of Astolat, the adventures of Sir Lancelot, and the death of Arthur. Narrative interpretation supplanted allegorical personification, but Dyce's moral didacticism and physical types were maintained. Sources from Tennyson and Malory were freely mixed, and new subjects were invented, such as Arthurian landscape, depicting archaeological sites, and portraits of legendary *femmes fatales*, inspired by the work of Dante Gabriel Rossetti. Book illustration enjoyed enormous popularity, especially editions of Tennyson's poetry, illustrated by Gustave Doré and Julia Margaret Cameron. During these decades, the visual arts caught up with the literary tradition and enjoyed a parallel course of equal strength and invention.

During the last decades of the century, Arthurian art betrayed the decline of Victorian aspiration. Subjects implying the failure of the vision, particularly the Lady of Shalott and the death of Arthur, drew unprecedented attention, especially in the circle of Academic artists, such as John Lyston Byam Shaw, Frank Dicksee, and John William Waterhouse. The heroic figure type was replaced with an attenuated, even androgynous, form, seen in the work of Burne-Jones and especially Aubrey Beardsley. By the turn of the century, Arthurian interest was vestigial, as seen in late Pre-Raphaelite imitators like Sidney Meteyard and in decadent aesthetes like Frank Cadogan Cowper. The tragedy of World War I dealt the death blow to the last shreds of Victorian idealism and likewise to the Arthurian Revival.

The Arthurian Revival shared only the basic subject matter with the medieval development in the arts. In origin, in form, and in meaning, it was distinct. Brought into being as inspirational allegory, it maintained a moral implication and a monarchical association to the end of its course. The aesthetic was medieval only in superficial details of costume and setting; it reflected instead current taste. Visual conventions allowed the viewer to read the narrative, and a specific iconography was codified. Ultimately, even the subject matter was contemporary, incorporating new writings and revised interpretations of traditional materials. These differences distinguish the Arthurian Revival as a revival in the fullest sense, not simply imitating the past but revitalizing the tradition itself. (*See also* MEDIEVALISM.) [DNM]

Fredeman, William E. "Dozing in Avalon." In *The Passing of Arthur: New Essays in Arthurian Tradition*, ed. Christopher Baswell and William Sharpe. New York: Garland, 1988.

Mancoff, Debra N. *The Arthurian Revival in Victorian Art*. New York: Garland, 1990.

Simpson, Roger. *Camelot Regained: The Arthurian Revival and Tennyson, 1800–1849*. Woodbridge, Suffolk: Boydell and Brewer, 1989.

ARTMANN, HANS CARL, contemporary Viennese poet who is one of the most versatile and adventuresome

Austrian authors. He repeatedly employs characters and storylines from Arthurian literature in his poems, such as a brief cycle written in 1953–54. The poem found at the center of this cycle, "ginevra verrät sich im schlaf und der könig antwortet ihr mit einem gedicht" ("Guenevere reveals herself while asleep, and the king responds with a poem"), shows Artmann's playful mastery of language, being composed in a form of pseudo-Cymric. [UM/WCM]

Donnenberg, Josef, ed. *Pose, Possen and Poesie: Zum Werke Hans Carl Artmanns*. Stuttgart: Akademischer Heinz, 1981.

ARTUS DE LA PETITE BRETAGNE, a fourteenth-century French prose romance, concerning the quest undertaken by Artus (who is not Arthur but is named after him) to liberate an enchanted castle and to win love. It was translated into English in the sixteenth century, as *Arthur of Little Britain*, by John Bourchier, Lord Berners. [NJL]

Le Livre du vaillant et preux chevalier Artus, fils du duc de Bretagne. Lyon: Jean de la Fontaine, 1493.

ASHE, GEOFFREY, turns from Arthurian history to fiction and philosophy in his novel *The Finger and the Moon*. Investigating Allhallows, a school of magic near Glastonbury, freelance writer "Geoffrey" learns that myths like the Arthurian legend captivate because they represent our collective memory of a "proto-realm" where the separation of science and religion, of the rational self and the eternal, now subconscious, "proto-self," had not yet developed. [RWK]

Ashe, Geoffrey. *The Finger and the Moon*. London: Heinemann, 1973.

ATRE PÉRILLEUX, L' ("The Perilous Cemetery"), an anonymous French verse romance of 6,676 lines dating from about the middle of the thirteenth century. The hero is Gauvain, who sets out in search of Arthur's abducted cupbearer after Keu has unsuccessfully made the attempt. Three maidens tell Gauvain (incognito) that they are lamenting his own death at the hands of three wicked knights. Gauvain does not reveal his identity but promises to "avenge" the victim, eventually forcing one of the killers to bring him back to life. He beheads a devil who has imprisoned a damsel in a tomb in the Perilous Cemetery and then kills the knight, Escanor, who had abducted the cupbearer. Gauvain is incognito for most of the romance and is known as *cil sans nom* ("he without a name").

The author of *L'Atre périlleux* seems to have drawn on *La Vengeance Raguidel* and *Meraugis de Portlesguez*, as well as Chrétien's *Yvain* and *Lancelot*. Many of the motifs and incidents are familiar from other romances: Gauvain's false death, his incognito, his being loved for his reputation alone, his succeeding where Keu fails. The intertextual links between Chrétien and the "epigonal romances," of which *L'Atre périlleux* is one, and among the epigonal romances themselves, are complex and deserve closer examination. Scholars nowadays generally regard the relations among particular romances in intertextual and reception-oriented terms rather than as mere sources and influences. In this respect, *L'Atre périlleux* occupies a position of some interest in the evolution of Arthurian verse romance.

L'Atre périlleux is a successful romance remarkable for being one of the few poems (along with the *Mériadeuc*) of which Gauvain is actually the hero rather than an important adjunct figure. The restoration of Gauvain to the position of hero can be seen as one of the varied responses to his general decline in status in the first quarter of the thirteenth century. [KB]

Woledge, Brian, ed. *L'Atre périlleux*. Paris: Champion, 1936.
Busby, Keith. "Diverging Traditions of Gauvain in Some of the Later Old French Verse Romances." In *The Legacy of Chrétien de Troyes*, ed. Norris J. Lacy, Douglas Kelly, and Keith Busby. 2 vols. Amsterdam: Rodopi, 1988, Vol. 2, pp. 93–109.
Woledge, Brian. *L'Atre périlleux: études sur les manuscrits, la langue, et l'importance littéraire du poème, avec un spécimen du texte*. Paris: Champion, 1930.

ATTERTON, JULIAN, English author of the novel *The Last Harper* (1983), which tells the story of the boy Gwion, who, after his village is destroyed by Germanic raiders, flees to the court of Urien of Rheged. When Myrddin, who has begun to train Gwion, is fatally wounded, he gives the boy his harp and a new name, Taliesin. Taliesin then becomes harper to Owain, whose father, Urien, has also been killed. [ACL]

Atterton, Julian. *The Last Harper*. London: MacRae, 1983.

ATWOOD, MARGARET (ELEANOR), contemporary Canadian poet, fiction writer, and literary critic, employed the Arthurian myth in "Avalon Revisited" (1963), an early sequence of seven short poems: "The Kings," "Recollections of Vivien," "The Betrayal of Arthur," "Elaine in Arcadia," "The Rider," "The Apotheosis of Guinevere," and "The King." Reflecting a young poet's exploration of the possibilities of recreating myth, the seven impressionistic reworkings are less interesting for their vague Arthurian origin than for the theme of loneliness and isolation so prevalent in Atwood's later work. Atwood's postgraduate studies in English at Harvard University centered on Victorian literature, and the Victorian poets, especially Tennyson, stand behind these brief forays into Arthurian legend. [DS]

Atwood, Margaret Eleanor. "Avalon Revisited." *The Fiddlehead*, 55 (1963), 10-13.

AUBERON, ROMAN D', a French composition, dating from the second half of the thirteenth century, that serves as a prologue to the *chanson de geste* entitled *Huon de Bordeaux*. The text relates a number of experiences of Auberon and his parents (Morgan la Fay and Julius Caesar), including his own appearance in Arthur's court. (*See also* HUON DE BORDEAUX.) [NJL]

Subrenat, Jean, ed. *Le Roman d'Auberon, prologue de Huon de Bordeaux*. Geneva: Droz, 1973.

AURELIUS AMBROSIUS, Arthur's uncle in Geoffrey of Monmouth. He is based on the historical figure Ambrosius Aurelianus. In Geoffrey's narrative, Aurelius and his brother Uther are sons of King Constantine. As children, they live after Constantine's death at the Breton court, where their guardians have taken them to keep them safe from the usurper Vortigern. Growing up, Aurelius becomes renowned for his generosity, truthfulness, and skill with weapons. He returns to Britain with Uther, and the Britons acknowledge him as their rightful sovereign.

Aurelius besieges Vortigern in a fort; it catches fire and Vortigern perishes. Next, he defeats the Saxons whom the usurper allowed to settle in Britain, captures their leader Hengist, and executes him for his many atrocities. He restores the churches destroyed in the Saxon ravaging. Wishing to set up a monument for 460 nobles whom Hengist massacred, he sends Uther to Ireland with Merlin to bring back a megalithic circle called the Giants' Ring. Merlin dismantles it by his arts, the stones are shipped to Britain, and he reassembles them on Salisbury Plain—the origin of Stonehenge. Aurelius does not live much longer. When he is ill, a vengeful son of Vortigern hires a Saxon to pose as a doctor and give him poison. He is buried at Stonehenge and Uther succeeds him.

The connection with the actual Ambrosius Aurelianus—or with the little that is known of him—is tenuous. Gildas, the sole early authority, speaks of him as a war-leader only. Nennius, however, calls him a king in passing, doubtless a sufficient hint. Geoffrey seems to put the whole reign in the 430s, whereas Gildas implies that Ambrosius was alive much later. Even if Geoffrey was aware of the discrepancy, it was forced on him by the invented family relationships, within an original scheme in which Arthur was a contemporary of the emperor Leo I. [GA]

Geoffrey of Monmouth. *Historia Regum Britanniae*, Book VI, Chapters 5 and 8; Book VIII, Chapters 1-16.

"AUSGLEICHUNG, DIE" ("The Adjustment"). Clemens Brentano's and Achim von Arnim's famous collection of folksongs *Des Knaben Wunderhorn* (1806-08) contains one Arthurian ballad, "Die Ausgleichung." The ballad is an adaptation and conflation of matter first attested in Robert Biket's *Lai du cor* and in *Le Mantel mautaillié*. In the ballad, King Arthur obtains a magic mantle from a fay for the express purpose of testing Guenevere. The Queen, in turn, obtains from a dwarf a magic drinking horn to prove her husband. When King and Queen are disgraced by horn and mantle, the royal couple demand that those present also be tested. The only faithful pair are an old knight and his young wife. They turn out to be a fay and a dwarf, presumably the very ones who had provided the mantle and the drinking horn in the first place. The dwarf and fay return the mantle and horn to Arthur and Guenevere—but only after having emptied the horn and spilled a drop of the wine on the mantle. Now King and Queen and all present can make use of the objects without embarrassment: the horn does not spill and the mantle fits. The ballad ends, however, on a sour note: in the course of the years, the stain on the mantle widens and the horn rings ever more hollow. [MEK]

Von Arnim, Ludwig Achim, and Clemens Brentano, eds. "Die Ausgleichung." In *Des Knaben Wunderhorn: Alte deutsche Lieder*. Berlin: Rütten and Loening, 1966, Vol. 1, pp. 333-35.

AUSTIN, MARTHA WADDELL, author of *Tristram and Isoult* (1905). Austin's dramatic poem exonerates the lovers because of their innate nobility, contrasted with Mark's treachery. The poem's Arthur, perceived as coldly upright, resembles Tennyson's, and Guinevere is depicted as envious of the two lovers. Austin works out these contrasts in rather mannered verse, and her final scene has overtones of Wagner's music drama. [AAR]

Austin, Martha W. *Tristram and Isoult*. Boston: Poet Lore, 1905.

AVALON. Geoffrey of Monmouth gives the name *Avalon* to an otherworldly island of Celtic mythology. In his Latin, it is *Insula Avallonis*. He mentions the place twice in the *Historia Regum Britanniae*, saying that Arthur's sword was forged there and that he was carried there after his last battle so that his wounds might be attended to. The meaning Geoffrey attaches to the name emerges in his poetic *Vita Merlini*, where he introduces the island as the *Insula Pomorum*, or "isle of apples," which, he adds, is called Fortunate. It lies vaguely over western waters and is the home of Morgan—i.e., Morgan le Fay—here depicted as a kindly enchantress heading a sisterhood of nine. In Geoffrey's poem, the bard Taliesin tells how Arthur was taken there after Camlann in a boat piloted by Barinthus, an authority on seafaring who also figures in the Irish tale of *St. Brendan's Voyage*. Morgan placed Arthur on a bed made of gold, examined his major wound, and undertook to heal him if he would stay in Avalon for a long time under her care.

This account is related to much older beliefs, and even realities. Geoffrey pictures Avalon as one of the Fortunate Isles of classical myth. He speaks of self-sown grain, vines that flourish without tending, and inhabitants who live for a century or more. But he combines all this with genuine Celtic motifs. The nine sisters are like the nine maidens who have custody of the magic cauldron in *The Spoils of Annwfn*. Moreover, the first-century geographer Pomponius Mela refers to a group of nine virgin priestesses actually living on the Ile de Sein off the coast of Brittany. Reputedly, they could cure the sick, foretell the future, control the weather, and assume animal disguises. Their talents resemble Morgan's as Geoffrey describes them. She herself, in her origins, is a Celtic goddess.

9. MS Paris, Bibliothèque Nationale, f.fr. 120, fol. 590v: Battle between Lancelot and Gauvain. (Paris, Bibliothèque Nationale.)

In Welsh, Geoffrey's island is *Ynys Avallach*. His "apple" etymology is probably right, the apples being paradisal or magical fruit like those of the Hesperides, or of Celtic otherworld regions portrayed elsewhere. However, a king called Avallach (variously spelled) occurs in Welsh genealogical and legendary matter and is supposed to rule over the island and to be Morgan's father. There may be nothing more here than coincidence followed by confusion. Another curious point is that Geoffrey's spelling of the name, whether or not he invented it, would scarcely be a true Latin equivalent for the Welsh. His *Insula Avallonis* is influenced, perhaps through Breton channels, by the name of a real place in Burgundy, Avallon. This is of Gaulish derivation and certainly does have the "apple" meaning. Geoffrey's use of it, coupled with hints in his *Prophetiae Merlini* and elsewhere, may indicate a different version of Arthur's passing.

Apart from what Geoffrey transmits himself, little is known of the way the island was regarded before him. The Irish sea-god Manannan ruled over an elysian otherworld isle to which the epithet *ablach* was given, meaning "rich in apple-trees." There is obviously some connection, but the Irish parallel remains unenlightening. Some have thought that Avalon was an abode of departed spirits. Evidence is lacking, and indeed, as the story of Arthur's sojourn develops, the whole point is that he is not a departed spirit; he is still alive through enchantment and will continue in Avalon till the day comes for his return. Wace and Layamon note this as a Breton belief, and several authors follow inventively in the same path.

Their Avalon tends to drift into other climes, and Morgan goes with it. Étienne de Rouen in *Draco Normannicus* (ca. 1169) takes Arthur to the Antipodes, though his intention may be satirical. Others do not venture so far. The author of *Floriant et Florete* (ca. 1250) seems to identify Avalon with Sicily, an opinion that passes from romance into folklore. The resulting Sicilian presence of Morgan is the reason for the term *Fata Morgana* applied to a mirage phenomenon in the Straits of Messina. A fourteenth-century poem about the hero Ogier places Avalon in the east near the Earthly Paradise, and a Danish redaction of it points to India. But the chronicler Jean des Preis, or d'Outremeuse, toward 1400, tells of Ogier's meeting with Arthur in a Mediterranean Avalon, where Morgan houses them in a palace surrounded by pools and fruit-trees, and both enjoy immortality and perpetual youth. The Majorcan poet Guillem Torroella, in *La Faula* (1360–70), describes a voyage on a whale's back to an island that is likewise in the Mediterranean and is clearly meant to be Avalon. The narrator enters Morgan's palace, and she shows him paintings of Arthurian characters. A young man in her company turns out to be Arthur. He has healed his wounds by bathing in the water of the River Tigris, which flows from the Earthly Paradise, and his youth is annually restored by visits of the Holy Grail.

Back in England, a different story was told at Glastonbury. The monks of its abbey claimed that Glastonbury itself was Avalon, in a comparatively mundane sense, as Arthur's last earthly destination, where he died and was buried. It is not known whether they said this before 1191, when they announced that they had exhumed him, together with a cross bearing the island's name in the form *Avalonia*. At all events, the equation was widely publicized after that and accepted by Giraldus Cambrensis, Robert de Boron, and the anonymous author of *Perlesvaus*. It was probably helped by a lingering sense of "otherness" at Glastonbury, rooted in its strange topography and non-Christian associations.

Malory is unclear about Arthur's end. The King is carried off in a barge by a company of ladies including Morgan, apparently Avalon-bound, but Malory allows that he *may* have been buried at Glastonbury and that the ladies *may* simply have brought his body there, in which case the Avalon = Glastonbury equation holds. Tennyson rules it out. Arthur goes away over the water to a sort of paradise:

> . . . the island-valley of Avilion
> Where falls not hail, or rain, or any snow,
> Nor ever wind blows loudly; but it lies
> Deep-meadow'd, happy, fair with orchard-lawns
> And bowery hollows crown'd with summer sea.

This is to come full circle, more or less, to Geoffrey's Fortunate Isle. [GA]

Geoffrey of Monmouth. *Historia Regum Britanniae*, Book IX, Chapter 4; Book XI, Chapter 2.

———. *Vita Merlini*, 11. 908–40.

Ashe, Geoffrey. *Avalonian Quest*. London: Methuen, 1982; rev. ed. Fontana, 1984, pp. 51, 70–73, 246–47.

Bromwich, Rachel. *Trioedd Ynys Prydein*. Cardiff: University of Wales Press, 1961; 2nd ed. 1978, pp. 266–68.

Cavendish, Richard. *King Arthur and the Grail*. London: Weidenfeld and Nicolson, 1978, pp. 35, 118–21.

Loomis, Roger Sherman, ed. *Arthurian Literature in the Middle Ages*. Oxford: Clarendon, 1959, pp. 65–68, 92–93.

AVOWING OF KING ARTHUR, SIR GAWAIN, SIR KAY, AND BALDWIN OF BRITAIN, THE,

AVOWING OF KING ARTHUR, SIR GAWAIN, SIR KAY, AND BALDWIN OF BRITAIN, THE, a tail-rhyme romance of 1,148 lines in sixteen-line stanzas, extant only in the Liverpool Ireland Manuscript of post-1450, though written somewhat earlier and farther south in the West Midlands.

Arthur, accompanied by three knights, hunts a ferocious boar in Inglewood Forest. In the tradition of the *gab* or boast, he vows to slay and cut the boar up, Gawain and Kay vow vigil and errantry overnight, and Baldwin vows never to be jealous of any woman, nor fear death, nor deny hospitality. Arthur accomplishes his vow, and, in keeping with their traditional characterization, Kay fails in combat with Sir Menealf over a captured maiden and Gawain succeeds, avenging Kay and winning the damsel.

Arthur sends a roadside ambush and a minstrel-spy to test Baldwin and then visits him himself. Baldwin fulfills all his vows, even though the King sets up an elaborately misleading situation in his wife's chamber. "Explaining" his triple vow, Baldwin tells Arthur three stories of his campaign experiences in a Spanish castle. All the stories have analogues in European or classical literature and are not specifically Arthurian.

A fearless, genial hunter and host, Baldwin is reminiscent of the Green Knight in *Sir Gawain and the Green Knight*, with which this romance also shares a predilection for triadic arrangements, fitt divisions, a difficult boar hunt, and a preoccupation with the meaning and application of chivalric institutions. The vows move from response to a specific adventure to chivalry's characteristic construction of relations (where the maiden can become an object of pledge for the knights, like the boar with which she is carried to court), to Baldwin's larger perspective. His vows are conditions of life, not specific acts. His awareness of female competition for survival contrasts with Arthur's naiveté, but his exemplary stories give no guarantees or explanations, showing only that chivalric codes may as well be adhered to as not, since defining the appropriate moment to fear death, be jealous, or withhold food is not obvious or easy in the light of experience. [JP]

Dahood, Roger, ed. *The Avowing of King Arthur*. New York: Garland, 1984.

French, W.H., and C.B. Hale, eds. *Middle English Metrical Romances*. New York: Russell and Russell, 1930 (but see also R. Dahood, "Dubious Readings in the French and Hale Text of *The Avowing of King Arthur*." *Notes and Queries*, n.s., September 1971, 323–26).

AWNTYRS OFF ARTHURE AT THE TERNE WATHELYN, THE, an unusual English Arthurian poem of the late fourteenth century (the four manuscripts, however, all date from the fifteenth century). The poem consists of fifty-five stanzas of thirteen lines each (715 lines in all) and has a highly intricate structure. The rhyme scheme is ababababcdddc; the first nine lines are four-beat and the final four (the "wheel") are two-beat alliterating lines. The stanzas are linked by the repetition of a word or phrase from the last line of one stanza in the first line of the next (stanza linking or iteration). A similar phenomenon occurs between the two parts of a stanza, though less regularly.

The poem itself consists of two parts, not very convincingly linked. In the first half, the ghost of Guinevere's mother, emerging from Tarn Wadling, appears to Guinevere and Gawain. She warns them that the sumptuousness of the court will lead to damnation. Gawain anxiously inquires what will happen to those who have taken other kings' lands without any right. The spirit then prophesies that Arthur's covetousness, and Fortune's Wheel, will cause his fall. The second part seems to provide an exemplum that justifies the ghost's accusations. Galeron, a Scottish knight whose lands had been won by Arthur (through deceit, he says), fights with Gawain, to whom they had been given. Arthur stops the combat when Gawain is about to win; Galeron resigns his claim, is made a knight of the Round Table, and is restored to his lands.

The source for the second part is unknown, but the first part goes back to the *Trentals of St. Gregory* (also known in a Middle English version). The topographical names relate the story to the north (Cumberland). Its author was influenced by *Sir Gawain and the Green Knight*, which he may be "citing" when he says that Galeron wounded Gawain, dressed in green, on his neck with a sword. Remarkable is the social criticism implied by Gawain's question to the spirit and her reply. [ESK]

Gates, Robert J., ed. *The Awntyrs off Arthure at the Terne Wathelyne*. Philadelphia: University of Pennsylvania Press, 1969.

Hanna, Ralph, III, ed. *The Awntyrs off Arthure at the Terne Wathelyn*. Manchester: Manchester University Press, 1974.

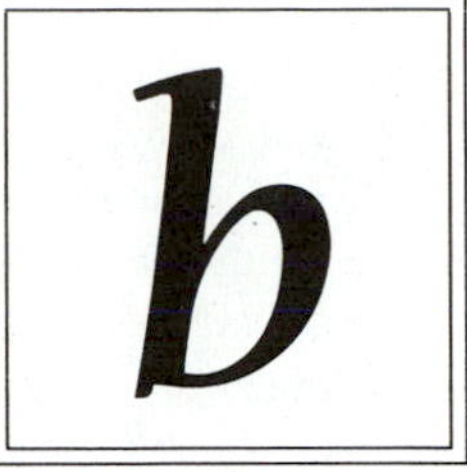

BABCOCK, WILLIAM H(ENRY) (1849–1922), wrote *The Two Lost Centuries of Britain* (1890), a historical account of the fifth and sixth centuries, and followed it with *Cian of the Chariots* (1898), a rambling and sentimental historical romance that warns against religious intolerance in an untraditional account of Arthur's struggle against the Saxons. [RHT]

Babcock, William H. *The Two Lost Centuries of Britain*. Philadelphia: Lippincott, 1890.

———. *Cian of the Chariots: A Romance of the Days of Arthur Emperor of Britain and His Knights of the Round Table, How They Delivered London and Overthrew the Saxons After the Downfall of Roman Britain*. Boston: Lothrop, 1898.

BADEN-POWELL, LORD ROBERT (1857–1941), founder of the Boy Scouts and the Girl Guides. When he established Scouting, Baden-Powell explicitly linked the movement with the fellowship of Arthur and the Knights of the Round Table. In *Yarns for Boy Scouts Told Round the Camp Fire*, Baden-Powell retold the story of the Round Table, claiming that Arthur was the real founder of British Scouts and that the Scouts were modern-day knights seeking the Holy Grail. [KJH]

Baden-Powell, Robert. *Yarns for Boy Scouts Told Round the Camp Fire*. London: Pearson, 1909.

Rosenthal, Michael. *The Character Factory: Baden-Powell and the Origin of the Boy Scout Movement*. New York: Pantheon, 1986.

BADGER, JOHN D'ARCY, Canadian publisher, brought out in 1972 a sequence of fifty-six irregular sonnets, *The Arthuriad*. Each of the sonnets is accompanied by a lengthy free-verse commentary; more polemical than poetic, they offer a reinterpretation of the Arthurian and Christian myths in an argument for the universal adoption of a "radical-centrist" political humanism. [SRR]

Badger, John D'Arcy. *The Arthuriad*. Toronto: Pendragon House, 1972.

BADON. According to Gildas, the Britons won a decisive victory over the Saxon invaders at the "siege of Mount Badon" (*obsessio Badonici montis*). This was the climax of a struggle with varying fortunes, beginning from the counterattack against the Saxon settlements launched by Ambrosius Aurelianus. Badon brought a spell of relative peace and order. In his own time, Gildas laments, the Britons have lost respect for their fathers' achievement and are fighting among themselves; but he has no doubt about the achievement. He does not name any British commander at the battle. Later, the commander is said to have been Arthur.

Badon presents three main problems: its date, its location, and Arthur's connection with it.

Gildas makes a puzzling statement about the date. It is usually understood as follows: "The year of Badon . . . was the year of my birth; as I know, one month of the forty-fourth year since then has already passed." His probable date of composition suggests that Badon was fought in the late 490s or early 500s. This is certainly the likeliest meaning. But Bede seems to have read Gildas in another text, now lost, because he takes the "forty-fourth year" quite differently and reckons the period from the Saxons' first settlement in Britain, with Badon coming at the end of it. As he dates the settlement around the middle of the fifth century, the result turns out to be quite similar. Gildas's involved Latin has even been construed in a third sense, as saying the battle took place in the forty-fourth year from the British counterstroke that began the war, a reading that might shift it definitely from the last decade of the fifth century into the first decade of the sixth. On any showing, however, it belongs about the year 500. Gildas wrote when it was still within living memory, and he is unlikely to be far wrong whatever his meaning actually is. The irreconcilability of the date given for Badon in the *Annales Cambriae*, 518, is therefore a reason for treating that chronicle's Arthurian entries with reserve.

Gildas's British victory ca. 500, followed by a long lull, accords fairly well with archaeological and historical data.

Generally speaking, there were no more Saxon encroachments for several decades, and some evidence for a reverse migration back to the Continent suggests that in Britain the advance was halted. There are even arguable traces of local withdrawals. The only question arises from entries in the *Anglo-Saxon Chronicle* claiming continued progress by the West Saxons in Hampshire and victories won by them, in contrast with Gildas's assertion of a respite. Archaeology, however, shows that these Saxons were few and their progress was meager, while their battles in the *Chronicle* are skirmishes only, or fictitious. Gildas may have regarded them as not worth mentioning. He may not even have heard of them.

As to Badon's whereabouts, it was in the south of Britain. The settlements of northern Angles were still unorganized and in most areas sparse. A defeat in that quarter would not have deterred the Saxon kings established in Kent and elsewhere. The word *mons* 'mountain' or 'hill' has often been supposed to refer to a hill fort. Several placenames with the element *Bad-* in them do denote hill forts or locations close by. There has been speculation about a folk-hero or demigod called Badda, who was associated with hill forts and might have given his name to several. Against the year 667, the *Annales Cambriae* note a "second battle of Badon," which is unlikely to have been in the same place as the first.

Given the hill-fort assumption, historians have tried to pick out a particular one as Gildas's. Some have favored Badbury Rings in Dorset, though it is hard to see how enough Saxons could have been there early enough. Liddington Castle in Wiltshire has a village of Badbury near its foot, and excavation has shown that its earthwork defenses were refurbished at about the right time. Geoffrey of Monmouth locates the battle at Bath, where the baths, in one of the manuscripts of Nennius, are called *balnea Badonis*. One or two modern authors have agreed, pointing, for instance, to the hill fort of Solsbury just outside the town. There are other candidates.

Almost everything that is said about Badon rests on probabilities only. It need not have been a hill fort at all. Very likely it was, but nothing shows who was besieging whom, or which group or groups of Saxons took part. The proved British reoccupation of hill forts suggests that the Britons were the besieged, in which case the victory may have come through a sortie or a relief operation. Its impact would have been moral rather than material. No battle conceivable at that time could have inflicted such losses as to deprive the Saxons of the manpower and resources for further war. Badon would have been decisive as an unnerving catastrophe far from their home bases, perhaps involving the death of a king and consequent loss of leadership.

Lastly, there is the problem of Arthur's role. He is first presented as the victor by Nennius in the ninth century and next by the *Annales* in the tenth. Both references are dubious not only because of the long interval but because of apparently legendary touches that call them in question. The early Welsh have little to say about this battle—it is not in the Triads, for instance—and it seems to have carried no great weight in the making of Arthur as they imagined him. On the other hand, there is no alternative candidate as the British commander. Ambrosius would almost certainly have been too old, and probably dead. The commander would surely have been a man of some note, remembered afterward for the victory, and it may be doubted whether a *totally* unconnected Arthur could have supplanted him in tradition and effaced his name. (*See also* ARTHUR, ORIGINS OF LEGEND.) [GA]

Gildas. *De Excidio Britanniae*, ed. and trans. Michael Winterbottom under the title *The Ruin of Britain*, and Nennius, *Historia Brittonum*, ed. and trans. John Morris under the title *British History and the Welsh Annals*. In *History from the Sources*. Chichester: Phillimore, 1978, 1980, Vols. 7 and 8.

Alcock, Leslie. *Arthur's Britain*. London: Penguin, 1971, pp. 26–27, 45–55, 67–71.

Chambers, E.K. *Arthur of Britain*. London: Sidgwick and Jackson, 1927, pp. 197–201.

Morris, John. *The Age of Arthur*. New York: Scribner, 1973, pp. 112–15.

BAILEY, CHARLES W., N.S. MILLICAN, and G.R. HAMMOND, collaborated on *The Quest of the Golden Fleece and Other Plays from Epic Poetry* (1929). This contains four plays for use in schools, of which "King Arthur and the Knights of the Round Table" is one. The Coming of Arthur is told in a Prologue, and the sequence of scenes ends with a tableau of the Passing of Arthur. The text is freely adapted from Tennyson and is illustrated with photographs and diagrams. [EB]

Bailey, C.W., N.S. Millican, and G.R. Hammond. "King Arthur and the Knights of the Round Table." In *The Quest of the Golden Fleece and Other Plays from Epic Poetry*. London: Nelson, 1929.

BAIRD, EDWARD, wrote "They Went South by Severn" (1944) as "A Fragment of the Arthurian Saga." It appears with three tales and a number of poems in *Brighid and the Dun Cow*, and tells how a boat brings Myrddhin and a knightly stranger to Glastonbury. The latter is Arthur, who declares his identity to great public acclamation. [EB]

Baird, Edward. *Brighid and the Dun Cow*. Dudley, Birmingham: Herald, 1946.

BAKER, SIR RICHARD (1568–1645), author of *A Chronicle of the Kings of England*, a history of grand dimensions that dealt with the kings of Britain and England from Roman times until, in the third edition, the reign of Charles I. As to Geoffrey of Monmouth, Baker is ambivalent yet goes on to give a version of Arthur's life that closely follows Geoffrey. In a somewhat defensive summation, Baker concludes that there were enough truly wonderful actual deeds to ascribe to Arthur that his life cannot be looked upon as a fable. [JHW]

Baker, Sir Richard. *A Chronicle of the Kings of England*, 3rd ed. London, 1660.

BALADRO DEL SABIO MERLÍN, EL ("The Shriek of Merlin the Sage"), a Spanish romance based upon an earlier Hispanic translation of the *Merlin* branch of the Post-Vulgate *Roman du Graal*. It survives in two versions: a 1498 incunabulum and a 1535 imprint. Although there is strong evidence pointing to the original translation of the *Roman du Graal* as a single work—sections of the three branches are preserved together in a late fifteenth-century copy of a translation attributed to one Joannes Bivas in 1313 and in Lope García de Salazar's history of England within his *Libro de las bienandanzas e fortunas*, compiled between 1461 and 1467—at some point the *Baladro* was separated from the first branch. In the 1535 imprint, however, the adapter considered the *Baladro* to form the first part of the *Demanda del Sancto Grial*, the third branch of the Spanish adaptation of the *Roman du Graal*. The recent discovery of two early fourteenth-century fragments of a Galician-Portuguese translation of the Post-Vulgate *Merlin* makes it clear that the *Baladro* reflects a tendency by later adapters of Arthurian romance to modify the original with material from other sources. In this case, the author or editor of the *Baladro* incunabulum made use of two fifteenth-century Spanish sentimental romances—the *Siervo libre de amor*, by Juan Rodríguez del Padrón, and *Grimalte y Gradissa*, by Juan de Flores—and prophecies derived ultimately from Geoffrey of Monmouth's *Historia Regum Britanniae*, as well as adding preliminary and concluding remarks of his own apparent creation. Some critics also believe that a series of *Baladro* adventures involving Baudemagus, adventures ascribed to a mysterious *Conte del Brait*, were the invention of the Spanish author, but the question remains unresolved. The adapter of the 1535 imprint also made a change, appending a series of cryptic prophecies attributed to Merlin concerning Spanish history, material taken from an earlier text of prophecies surviving in Castilian and Catalan manuscript copies. [HLS]

Bohigas Balaguer, Pedro, ed. *El Baladro del Sabio Merlín según el texto de la edición de Burgos de 1498*. 3 vols. Barcelona, 1957–62.

Bonilla y San Martín, Adolfo, ed. *El Baladro del Sabio Merlín, primera parte de la Demanda del Sancto Grial*. In *Libros de caballerías, primera parte: Ciclo artúrico-Ciclo carolingio*. Madrid: Bailly-Baillière, 1907, pp. 3–162.

BALIN and BALAN, two brothers who fought for Arthur in his war against King Lot (see Malory's Book II). Balin (also called Balin le Sauvage and The Knight with Two Swords) killed Garlon, and when King Pellam tried to avenge this death Balin inflicted the Dolorous Stroke on him. Eventually, the two brothers kill each other in battle (without recognizing each other) and are buried in the same tomb. Merlin sets Balin's sword in the stone, from which Galahad will eventually draw it. (*See also* DOLOROUS STROKE.) [NJL]

BALLETS have been inspired by the Arthurian legend during the twentieth century. The earliest was Frederick Ashton's *The Lady of Shalott* (London, 1931), to music by Sibelius, but more interest has been shown in the Tristan story, which was reworked for ballet several times using Wagner's music: by Léonide Massine (*Mad Tristan*, New York, 1944; libretto and scenery by Salvador Dali), by Herbert Ross (New York, 1958), and by Maurice Béjart (*Les Vainqueurs*, "The Conquerors," Brussels, 1969). Ashton used the music of Englishman Arnold Bax for *Picnic in Tintagel* (New York, 1952), and in Berlin in 1965 Tatjana Gsovsky based her Tristan ballet on a new composition by Boris Blacher. The unexpected death of John Cranko in 1973 prevented the realization of his plan to produce a Tristan ballet to music by Hans Werner Henze, spread out over three evenings, at the Stuttgart State Opera. Henze's composition *Tristan* (1973) was, however, used as ballet music by Glen Tetley (Paris, 1976).

More recently, the career of King Arthur inspired the pantomime drama of Henryk Tomaszewski (1981) as well as the *Artus-Sage* by John Neumeier, performed for the first time at the Hamburg State Opera in 1982 and then revised in 1986. Both dance versions relate the entire history of Arthur, from the winning of the sword to his death, including the search for the Grail; Neumeier based his version chiefly on music from the Middle Ages as well as on that of Sibelius, as Ashton had done in 1931. [UM/WLS]

Seipt, Angelus. "Artus-Sage und Tanz." In *Artus-sage*. Hamburg: State Opera Program Guide, 1986.

BALTIC REGION, ARTHURIAN CLUBS IN. For several centuries, during the later Middle Ages and beyond, an

Arthurian cult flourished in a number of Baltic towns, including Danzig, Riga, Culm, and Elbing. The documents that remain from the period are not literary texts but rather charters and lists of rules for the societies (known by a variety of names, such as Artushof or Societas Arturi), which were a combination of a social or fraternal organization with a merchants' exchange. Among the activities of the clubs were annual festivities, in presumed imitation of Arthur's court, during which members dressed in chivalric costumes and held tournaments. (*See also* ROUND TABLES.) [NJL]

Schlauch, Margaret. "King Arthur in the Baltic Towns." *Bibliographical Bulletin of the International Arthurian Society*, 11 (1959), 75–80.

BAN DE BENOIC (Ban of Benwick), a French king, brother of Bors and father of Hector de Maris and of Lancelot. The Vulgate Cycle recounts his early alliance with Arthur and also his eventual death at the hand of Claudas. As a result of that death, the Lady of the Lake was able to take the young Lancelot away with her. [NJL]

BARBOUR, JOHN (ca. 1316–1396), archdeacon of Aberdeen, wrote the *Bruce*, the great epic-chronicle of medieval Scotland. Although Barbour appealed to the patriotism of the Scots, unlike some later Scottish writers he admires Arthur and refers to him as a valorous king who was slain treacherously by Mordred, his sister's son; the Arthurian story, like those of Troy, Alexander, and Julius Caesar, is for Barbour an exemplum about treason. [EDK]

Barbour, John. *Barbour's Bruce*, ed. M.P. McDiarmid and J.A.C. Stevenson. 2 vols. Edinburgh: Blackwood, 1980, 1981.

Kennedy, Edward Donald. "Chronicles and Other Historical Writing." In *A Manual of the Writings in Middle English*, ed. A.E. Hartung. New Haven: Connecticut Academy of Arts and Sciences, 1981–89, Vol. 8, pp. 2681–86, 2891–904.

BARING, MAURICE (1874–1945), English writer, responds seriously to his subject in his sonnet "Tristram and Iseult," dated 1903, and in his blank-verse drama of the same name. The lovers figure too in the sestet of the sonnet "Le Prince Errant." The tone changes to good-humored banter in "From the Diary of Iseult of Brittany" in *Lost Diaries* (1913) and the more successful "Camelot Jousts." The latter, first appearing in the London *Morning Post* and later published with similar pieces in 1910 in *Dead Letters*, takes the form of an exchange of correspondence between Arthur and Guinevere. Arrangements for a tourney at Camelot are discussed as if it were an Edwardian weekend party, and the Queen is catty about Mark and Iseult. "In Memoriam A.H.," first printed in the *New Statesman* on April 7, 1917, reverts to a more solemn manner; Baring finds comfort in the thought that his friend Auberon Herbert, Captain Lord Lucas of the Royal Flying Corps, who fell in action on November 3, 1916, will have found welcome among the Knights of the Round Table in the City of the Grail. [CNS]

Baring, Maurice. *Dead Letters*. London: Constable, 1910.

———. *Lost Diaries*. London: Constable, 1913.

———. *Collected Poems*. London: Heinemann, 1925.

BARJAVEL, RENÉ, French author of *L'Enchanteur* ("The Magician," 1984), one of the most successful modern French treatments of Arthurian material. The novel centers on Merlin's relationship with Viviane and on the Grail quest. According to Barjavel, Merlin had already established the Round Table and sent knights off to seek the Grail before Arthur was crowned. Moreover, the magician (rather than the Gornemant of traditional accounts) served as Perceval's tutor, preparing him for the quest. *L'Enchanteur* offers a prehistory involving the Grail: originally a cup fashioned by Eve in order to receive the blood flowing from Adam's side, it was broken by an angel after the Fall and eventually repaired prior to the Last Supper and the events involving Joseph of Arimathea.

Barjavel effectively balances the high seriousness of the Grail quest with playfulness and humor and presents a Merlin whose devotion to that quest coexists uneasily with personal, erotic interests and sexual frustration. [NJL]

Barjavel, René. *L'Enchanteur*. Paris: Denoël, 1984.

BARTHELME, DONALD (1931–1989), American author of *The King* (1990), a novel in which Arthur is king during World War II. The world of chivalry is set against the modern world, especially when Arthur refuses to allow the construction of an atomic bomb because "it's not the way *we* wage war." Though there is a great battle between Arthur's forces and Mordred's, Arthur survives, as does Mordred, who becomes a Nazi. The book does not have the tragic end that Guinevere says legend requires. Instead, it concludes with Lancelot lying under an apple-tree dreaming of Guinevere. His recurring romantic dream is a diversion from the recurring brutality of war. Barthelme's story suggests that the one is as much an enduring part of human existence as the other. [ACL]

Barthelme, Donald. *The King*. New York: Harper and Row, 1990.

BATAILLE DE LOQUIFER, LA ("The Battle with Loquifer"), a French verse composition, dating from ca. 1230 and extant in two versions, as well as a prosification; it has been attributed to Graindor de Brie. The main action, recounting Renouart's battle with the giant Loquifer, is non-Arthurian, but one of the versions has Renouart transported by Morgan la Fay to Avalon, where he encounters Arthur and other knights of his court. [NJL]

Barnett, Monica, ed. *La Bataille Loquifer*. Oxford: Blackwell, 1975.

BÂTARD DE BOUILLON, LE ("The Bastard of Bouillon"), an anonymous fourteenth-century northern French *chanson de geste* that narrates the hard-fought arrival and settlement of the first Crusaders in Jerusalem. The *chanson* is interrupted in the middle (ll. 3,291–743) by a fairytale-like intermission that contains Arthurian material. In this brief but intense section, the auditor/reader is introduced to King Artus and his sister Morgue. Their kingdom, located near the Red Sea, is surrounded by a huge cloud. The poet includes such standard Arthurian fare as the motif of the identification of the most valiant knight by means of the ivory olifant (horn). Another conventional test to discover the flower of Christian knighthood is set in Artus's magic garden: the candidates have to pluck a rose over which two heavily armed robots keep a close watch. At the conclusion of the intermission, Artus presents his visitors with a white horse, to be reserved for the future use of the "Bâtard" himself, who is only a child at the moment of these events.

Le Bâtard de Bouillon is allied thematically to the Arthurian material, using the prominent topos of "bastardry linked with evil." In the *chanson*, this fateful combination will cause the Crusaders' visions of the Holy Land to collapse. [MA]

Cook, Robert F., ed. *Le Bâtard de Bouillon*. Geneva: Droz, 1972.
———, and Larry S. Crist, eds. *Le Deuxième Cycle de la Croisade: deux études sur son développement*. Geneva: Droz, 1972.

BÄUMER, GERTRUD (1873–1954), was active in the German women's movement (1904–33) and in the Reichstag. In 1927, she began to write about history and sociocultural politics. In *Die drei Göttlichen Komödien des Abendlandes* ("The Three Divine Comedies of the West"), she retells the Parzival story, linking it to Goethe's *Faust* and Dante's *Divine Comedy*. Rhymed passages presented as manuscript citations are intended to suggest fidelity to the original. [SSch/PM]

Bäumer, Gertrud. *Die drei Göttlichen Komödien des Abendlandes: Wolframs Parsifal, Dantes Divina Comedie, Goethes Faust*. Münster and Regensburg: Regensburger Verlagsbuchhandlung, 1949.

BEARD, DAN(IEL CARTER) (1850–1941), American author and illustrator instrumental in organizing the Boy Scouts in the United States. Beard illustrated the first edition of Mark Twain's *A Connecticut Yankee in King Arthur's Court*. His illustrations are sometimes faithful to the text but often have their basis only in the satiric spirit of the book. Many of them offer social commentary. For example, Merlin, Twain's villain, is depicted as Tennyson and The Slavedriver as robber baron Jay Gould. Beard commonly uses allegorical drawings: some suggest the superiority of the American ideal of advancement through ability over the British system of inherited privileges, but others suggest the similarities between British society, in which superiority is based on titles, and American society, which allows for superiority based on wealth. Twain was delighted with Beard's work: "There are a hundred artists who could have illustrated any other of my books, but only one who could illustrate this one. It was a lucky day I went netting for lightning bugs and caught a meteor." [ACL]

Beard, Dan. *Hardly a Man Is Now Alive: The Autobiography of Dan Beard*. New York: Doubleday, Doran, 1939.
Twain, Mark. *A Connecticut Yankee in King Arthur's Court*, illus. Dan Beard. New York: Webster, 1889.

BECKER, KONRAD, Austrian artist, wrote and directed *Parzival* in 1984 in Vienna, describing the play as a "Rituelle Oper nach Wolfram von Eschenbach" ("A Ritualistic Opera After Wolfram von Eschenbach"). As is often the case in German literature, particularly that of recent times, Wolfram's hero is interpreted in terms of initiation and self-discovery. Mythical and alchemical motifs unite in a multimedia production with word, music, scenery, and slides. Although the play has enjoyed little acclaim, it is typical of a certain contemporary trend in the interpretation of Arthurian tales. [UM/PWM]

BEDE, in the *Historia Ecclesiastica Gentis Anglorum* (A.D. 731), gives an account of the Germanic invasion of Britain, taken mostly from Gildas. He refers to the battle of Badon but does not mention Arthur. He writes that the leaders of the Saxons were two brothers named Hengist and Horsa and gives genealogies of Saxon kings. Bede's work was used by later writers, such as Geoffrey of Monmouth and Layamon. [AEG]

Bede. *Opera Historica*, ed. C. Plummer. London, 1896.

BÉDIER, (CHARLES MARIE) JOSEPH (1864–1938), in 1903 succeeded Gaston Paris in the Chair of French Medieval Language and Literature at the Collège de France; in 1921 he was elected to the Académie Française. In addition to seminal work on the origins of French epic poetry and the first major study of the fabliaux, Bédier edited and translated the *Roman de Tristan par Thomas* (2 vols., 1902–05). He is best known to Arthurians for his graceful reconstitution of the legend of *Tristan et Iseut*, which has been frequently reprinted since its first appearance in 1900. In collaboration with Louis Artus, Bédier used his *Tristan* as the basis for a stage play; the drama, with incidental music by Paul Ladmirault, was produced in 1929. [WWK]

Bédier, Joseph. *Le Roman de Tristan et Iseut*. Paris: Piazza, 1900.

BEDIVERE. The career of Bedivere, or Bedwyr as he is called in Welsh, has undergone five distinct developments. In early Welsh tradition, he is renowned for his valor and for his close friendship with Arthur and Kay. *Culhwch and Olwen* comments upon his skill with a spear, despite his having but one hand, and notes that he never shrank from an enterprise on which Kay was bound. Geoffrey of Monmouth preserves these two features in his portrayal of Bedivere, and he is followed by later chroniclers. Bedivere acts as Arthur's cupbearer and is later created Duke of Normandy. He and Kay accompany the King when he kills the Giant of Mont St.-Michel. He is then slain in the battle against the Romans.

Despite this early prominence, Bedivere is virtually ignored in the romances. He acts as Arthur's constable rather than butler, and like both the King and Kay he usually remains at court while newer heroes ride forth to win renown.

This neglect is reversed in the English Stanzaic *Le Morte Arthur*, which introduces the third development in Bedivere's career. Here, Bedivere, rather than Girflet as in the Vulgate *Mort Artu*, is the surviving companion who casts Arthur's sword Excalibur into the mere after the battle of Camlann. He spends his remaining years praying by the King's tomb in the hermitage at Glastonbury. His role in the story of Arthur's death is preserved by Malory and most later authors.

Tennyson introduces the fourth development when he has Bedivere narrate "The Coming of Arthur." Other authors who use Bedivere as narrator include George Finkel, Catherine Christian, and Roy Turner.

In modern Arthurian fiction, Bedivere has regained his early prominence, and he has even started to replace Lancelot as Guenevere's lover. Concerned to create a credible picture of the Dark Ages, yet wishing to preserve the tragic motif of the trusted friend who betrays his king, Rosemary Sutcliff makes Bedivere the Queen's lover in *Sword at Sunset*. Her lead has been followed by Gillian Bradshaw, Mary Stewart, and John M. Ford. [RHT]

Thompson, Raymond H. "'The Old Order Changeth . . .': Bedivere in Arthurian Literature." In *Moderne Arthusrezeption*, ed. Kurt Gamerschlag. Wissenschaftliche Buchgesellschafft, forthcoming.

BEK, THOMAS, OF CASTELFORD, a Yorkshireman to whom a verse chronicle of British, Scottish, and English history, written ca. 1327, has traditionally been attributed; 39,674 lines survive in a single manuscript, Göttingen University Library Codex MS Hist. 740. Although the later part does not follow any known source closely, the account of Arthur follows Geoffrey of Monmouth, with some details taken from Wace, Robert of Gloucester, Pierre de Langtoft, and others. Only the part of the chronicle covering the coronation of Arthur through the death of Cadwallader (ll. 19,715–27,466) has been edited, but Perrin gives a detailed account of the contents of the manuscript. [EDK]

Castelford, Thomas. *Thomas Castelford's Chronicle*, ed. in part by Frank Behre. Göteborg: Elanders, 1940.

Kennedy, Edward Donald. "Chronicles and Other Historical Writing." In *A Manual of the Writings in Middle English*, ed. A.E. Hartung. New Haven: Connecticut Academy of Arts and Sciences, 1981–89, Vol. 8, pp. 2624–25, 2809–11.

Perrin, M.L. *Über Thomas Castelfords Chronik von England*. Boston: Ginn, 1890.

BEL GHERARDINO, an Italian *cantare* thought to have been composed in the mid-fourteenth century, tells the story of the love of the knight Gherardino for the White Fairy. Some episodes may be based on Marie de France's *Lanval*. Cited by Boccaccio in the *Corbaccio*, it is considered one of the best *cantari* from an aesthetic viewpoint. Other possible influences include the anonymous *Graelent* and, especially, the French *Parthenopeus de Blois*. [SJN]

Balduino, A., ed. *Cantari del Trecento*. Milan: Marzorati, 1970.
Levi, Ezio, ed. *Fiore di leggende: cantari antichi*. Bari: Laterza, 1914.

BENOIT, PIERRE (1886–1962), published *Montsalvat* in 1957; in this novel he transposed the Grail quest to the France of 1944. A history professor and a student embark on the quest, which takes them to Montsalvy, to Montségur, to the monastery of Montserrat (where they recognize the enchanted setting of the *Parsifal*). The Grail, which in this novel has evil powers, causes the death of two German officers who are seeking it and leads also to the loss of the professor's daughter, wife, and companion. After suffering from a fever, the professor finds the Grail at Montsalvy and transports it to the Holy Land. This work, replete with Wagnerian and Catharist influences, succeeds better than most such efforts in providing a modern setting for the quest while remaining faithful to the spirit of its medieval predecessors. [RB]

Benoit, Pierre. *Montsalvat*. Paris: Michel, 1957.
Baudry, Robert. "Le *Montsalvat* de Pierre Benoit: une quête occitane et catalane du Graal." In *Actes du Colloque International sur le Merveilleux*. Narbonne: Cahiers du CERMEIL, 1985, Vol. 2, no. 5, pp. 14–22.
———. "Echos arthuriens dans les romans de Pierre Benoit." In *Actes du XIII Congrès International Arthurien*. Leuven, 1990.

BERCHET, GIOVANNI (1783–1851), a leading figure of the Italian Romantic movement and an active fighter in the struggle to liberate Italy from Austria, composed (in 1835) ballads of "Tristano e Isotta" and "Lancilotto e Ginevra" translated from the 1555 edition of the Spanish *Cancionero de romances*. [DLH]

Berchet, Giovanni. *Opere*, ed. Egidio Ballorini. Bari: Laterza, 1911, Vol. 1, pp. 285–87.

BERGER, THOMAS, author of *Arthur Rex* (1978), the finest ironic fantasy on the Arthurian legend written in the twentieth century. The story is loosely based upon Malory's version, supplemented by material from romances like *Sir Gawain and the Green Knight*. Berger has a keen eye for the ridiculousness inherent in romance conventions, which he parodies in such observations as: "Knights did perish only in battles and ladies from love." He also delights in ironic reversal for comic purposes: when Morgan la Fey discovers that her evil schemes are invariably frustrated, she reforms, convinced that "corruption were sooner brought amongst mankind by the forces of virtue."

Human imperfection does finally doom Arthur's idealistic dream of a nobler world. However, the heroic struggle of Arthur and his knights to achieve that dream, though it leads them from one comic misadventure to the next, wins our admiration. Since they do not fear to behave generously, even when it makes them ridiculous, they succeed beyond all expectations in an impossible task. This reversal of expectations, whereby apparently naive and foolish behavior turns out to be the noblest wisdom, creates not only one of the most appreciative responses to Arthurian legend but also a profound controlling vision in the novel. [RHT]

Berger, Thomas. *Arthur Rex: A Legendary Novel*. New York: Delacorte, 1978.
Thompson, Raymond H. "Humor and Irony in Modern Arthurian Fantasy: Thomas Berger's *Arthur Rex*." *Kansas Quarterly*, 16 (Summer 1984), 45–49.

BERNAL, A.W., reverses the premise of Mark Twain's *A Connecticut Yankee in King Arthur's Court* when he uses a time machine to bring Galahad forward in time for a brief visit to the 1940 World's Fair at New York in his humorous science-fiction story "King Arthur's Knight in a Yankee Court" (1941). [RHT]

Bernal, A.W. "King Arthur's Knight in a Yankee Court." *Amazing Stories*, April 1941, 43–69.

BĒROUL is the author of a late twelfth-century Tristan romance written in Anglo-Norman French and preserved as a single long fragment (of almost 4,500 lines of octosyllabic verse) in manuscript Paris, B.N. f. fr. 2171, a defective and carelessly executed codex dating from the second half of the thirteenth century. Of Béroul himself nothing is known; he names himself twice in the text but is not mentioned elsewhere. Some scholars, citing textual evidence in the form of internal contradictions and stylistic inconsistencies, have concluded that Béroul was more than one person, but thus far theories of multiple authorship have not gained general acceptance. His *Tristran* has been dated as early as the 1160s and 70s and as late as the last decade of the twelfth

u temps que
se peu hercu
les et theseus
regnerent en
grece. Et es
toit iuge du peuple disrael
ung homme Jair qui fut
le iii. apres Josue alors fut
regnant en Sirie ung tres
puissant roy nomme Diodicias
qui tenoit soubz lui et sa
seigneurie la plus part de
perse de mede et mezopota
me et ny avoit pour lors
par les parties orientalles
dont il ne fust cremu et re
doubte plus que nul autre
Et tant que par sa force et
par sa grant chevalerie q
estoit en lui il avoit conquis

century; the latter view is supported by line 3,849, which refers to *le mal dagres*, an apparent reference to an illness suffered by crusaders at Acre in the winter of 1190–91.

Béroul's *Tristran* is clearly related to the German *Tristrant* of Eilhart von Oberge. Both belong to what is generally called the primitive or common version of the Tristan legend. That is, scholars presume that this text remains relatively faithful to a hypothetical archetype and thus descends from a more primitive, noncourtly stage of the legend, whereas the so-called courtly version, an example of which is the *Tristan* by Béroul's contemporary Thomas d'Angleterre, integrates the work thoroughly into the current of courtly love.

The fragment begins with the encounter of Tristran and Iseut under the tree in which her husband Mark is hiding. The lovers, realizing that they are being spied upon, emphatically proclaim their innocence and their fidelity to Mark, thereby allaying his suspicions. The text continues with the episode in which the dwarf spreads flour on Iseut's floor in order to detect Tristran's footprints in the event he visits her at night; the scene in which Tristran, having been taken prisoner, asks permission to enter a chapel and pray, whereupon he leaps to freedom from a window; Mark's delivering Iseut to a colony of lepers, for their pleasure and her punishment; and the lovers' life of hardship in the forest, during which Mark once discovers them sleeping with a bare sword between them and erroneously concludes that they are guiltless.

The potion that has bound them together in love was concocted to last only three years (whereas it had been of limitless effect in the "courtly" version of the legend); when it wanes, the lovers regret their lives of sin; Iseut returns to court, but Tristran's enemies persuade Mark to exile him. There follows the long episode in which Iseut, tested in the presence of Arthur and his knights, succeeds in exonerating herself by swearing an equivocal oath to the effect that the only two men who have ever been between her thighs are her husband and the leper (in fact, Tristran in disguise) who carried her across a ford the day before. At the end of the fragment, Tristran ambushes and kills one of the lovers' enemies and brings his hair to show Iseut; when he arrives, they discover another of their enemies spying on them, Tristran immediately kills him, and the text breaks off in mid-sentence.

The *Tristran* is but marginally Arthurian, reflecting the independent origin of the Tristan legend and the comparatively recent merger of the two legends. King Arthur is mentioned several times, and Iseut makes it clear that his prestige was firmly established at the time by insisting that he be present to give credence to her oath of innocence and to protect her should any other accusations be leveled against her.

As with most Tristan and Isolde romances, Béroul's text presents a cyclical form. Despite their (occasional) best intentions, the young lovers repeatedly fall back into their sinful ways; Mark becomes suspicious, initially refuses to believe he is being betrayed (by both of them: Iseut is his wife, while Tristran is both his vassal and his nephew), and is finally convinced; the lovers resolve to reform; after a period of abstinence on their part, the cycle repeats itself. This is a highly ironic and ambiguous text. Appearances are always deceiving. When the lovers appear most innocent, they are consistently the most guilty. When Mark thinks them innocent, he is being tricked, or else he is misinterpreting the evidence. Even the lovers' desire to reform is motivated by less than noble impulses: they have no particular desire to live a life of Christian purity and virtue, but they are willing to make the effort if that will return them to a life of luxury, comfort, and wealth at the court.

Despite the potential tragedy of the lovers' passion, Béroul's poem is characterized by humor and, in many passages, by a tone far closer to that of the fabliaux than to the courtly romance. His style is lively and engaging, bearing many of the marks (such as frequent addresses to *Seigneurs*, "lords") of both public presentation and authorial personality. Although usually good-natured, his wit sometimes has a decidedly sharp edge, but throughout the work authorial sympathies, and consequently those of Béroul's readers, remain consistently with the lovers. [NJL]

Béroul. *The Romance of Tristran*, ed. and trans. Norris J. Lacy. New York: Garland, 1989.

Barteau, Françoise. *Les Romans de Tristan et Iseut: introduction à une lecture plurielle*. Paris: Larousse, 1972.

Blakeslee, Merritt R. *Love's Masks: Identity, Intertextuality and Meaning in the Old French Tristan Poems*. Cambridge: Brewer, 1989.

Noble, Peter. *Beroul's "Tristan" and the "Folie of Berne."* London: Grant and Cutler, 1982.

Reid, T.B.W. *The "Tristan" of Béroul: A Textual Commentary*. Oxford: Blackwell, 1972.

Varvaro, Alberto. *Il "Roman de Tristan" de Béroul*. Turin: Bottega d'Erasmo, 1963. (Published in Great Britain as *Beroul's "Romance of Tristan,"* trans. John C. Barnes. Manchester: Manchester University Press, 1972.)

BERRY, CHARLES WALTER, wrote *The Round Table—Arthur* (1930) and *Arthurian Reverie* (1939). The former offers a so-called Socratic dialogue about the Arthurian legend, with some passages in verse, ending with special reference to the Grail legend and its association with Glastonbury. The latter purports to be an "instructive Vade Mecum to Arthurian legend" under various headings. [EB]

10. MS Oxford, Bodleian, Douce 383, fol. 1, illustration from *Guiron le Courtois*: the court of King Diodecias of Syria; the King enthroned; in the bottom border, the arms of Engelbert of Nassau. (Bodleian Library, Oxford.)

Berry, Charles Walter. *The Round Table—Arthur: A Conversation Between Two Knights of the Round Table Club.* London: Methuen, 1930.

———. *Arthurian Reverie.* London: Buckley, 1939.

BERTILAK (BERCILAK, BERNLAK) **DE HAUTDESERT,** Gawain's generous host in *Sir Gawain and the Green Knight.* The two men agree to an exchange of winnings, and for three days Bertilak goes out hunting while his wife tries to seduce Gawain. The host gives the game he has killed to Gawain, and the latter gives him the kisses he has received from the woman, withholding only a green sash she gave him to protect him from harm. The hero leaves to complete a beheading contest with the Green Knight, who thereafter reveals that he and Bertilak are one and that the entire intrigue was arranged by Morgan. [SW]

BIDDER, GEORGE, British author of *Merlin's Youth* (1899), a narrative poem in three parts, written in six-line stanzas (abbacc) with interspersed lyrics of various types including ballad form. Set in Dark Age Britain, this original poem depicts Merlin's love for Yberha, a supernatural woman who is leader of a wolf pack. Given the choice of marrying her as a powerless maid or waiting until he has learned her magic, Merlin chooses the latter. He completes the additional task of driving the enemy from the land, only to be rejected because he succeeded through magic rather than prowess. Embittered, Merlin withdraws to a cave, whence he rules the world through his spells. [MAW]

Bidder, George. *Merlin's Youth.* Westminster: Constable, 1899.

BIKET, ROBERT, author of the 580-line *Lai du cor* ("The Lai of the Horn"), composed during the second half of the twelfth century. The lai is an early setting of the Arthurian chastity test, involving a drinking horn, made by a fay, which will spill its contents on cuckolds. Arthur tries to drink from it and is thoroughly soaked, after which Guenevere explains that she is guilty of having once given a ring to a young man. Arthur forgives her, especially when the horn also empties its contents on all the other men at court except Caradoc.

The *Lai du cor* is notable for its unusual (and archaic) six-syllable line and for Robert's humorous irreverence toward Arthur. Variants of the test are found in "The Boy and the Mantle," *Caradoc, Ain Hupsches Vasnachtspill von Künig Artus, Dis Ist Frauw Tristerat Horn von Saphoien,* and *The Romance of Sir Corneus.* [NJL]

Biket, Robert, *The Anglo-Norman Text of Le Lai du Cor,* ed. C.T. Erickson. Oxford: Blackwell, 1973.

BINYON, LAURENCE (1869–1943), English poet, art historian, orientalist, and Keeper of Prints and Drawings at the British Museum, is now best known for the Remembrance Day favorite "For the Fallen." He also wrote *Tristram's End* (1913), an ode; *Arthur, A Tragedy* (1923); and the unfinished *Madness of Merlin* (1947), which he described as "dialogue arranged as story rather than drama." *Tristram's End* is divided into three parts, the first and third in iambic lines of varying length and irregular rhyme, the second in eight-line stanzas that represent the alternating voices of the lovers as they recall the past. Binyon utilizes the Thomas-Gottfried tradition of the black and white sails, the lying wife, and the lovers' deathbed reunion in Brittany. The second Isoud takes the bodies to Cornwall, where Mark recognizes that they have been not traitors but victims.

Arthur, A Tragedy illustrates Binyon's ambition to restore blank-verse drama to the modern stage. It was produced at London's Old Vic Theatre in 1923, with incidental music by Edward Elgar. The plot, derived from Malory, presents the final events of Arthur's reign: the tournament at Astolat and Elaine's fatal love, the Mordred–Agravain entrapment of Lancelot and Guenevere, the siege of the Joyous Gard, Guenevere's return to Arthur at the pope's command, and her withdrawal to a nunnery. In a departure from the *Morte Darthur,* Arthur and Guenevere meet and are reconciled before Arthur proceeds to the last battle and Avalon.

In *The Madness of Merlin,* Binyon wanted to treat the sage independently of the Arthur story. He turned to Celtic traditions of prophetic madmen (Myrddin and Lailoken) who withdrew to the forests of the Scottish Lowlands after defeat in battle. Geoffrey of Monmouth's *Vita Merlini* (ca. 1150) was the chief source. In addition to Merlin (a Welsh prince), the characters include his wife, Gwendolen; his sister, Gwyndyth, married to King Redderech ("an example of excessive idealism"); St. Kentigern, the bard Taliesin, and the minstrel Peredur; and a peasant, Himlian, who bears Merlin's son. Though Merlin is twice rescued from the wilderness, he refuses to be saved, thus illustrating, in Binyon's words, "the way things always turn out differently from what one expects." The mystical poetry is considerably better than average. [MAW]

Binyon, Laurence. *Arthur, A Tragedy.* London: Heinemann, 1923.

———. *The Madness of Merlin.* London: Macmillan, 1947.

BIRTH OF MERLIN, THE, OR THE CHILDE HATH FOUND HIS FATHER, a 1662 play originally attributed to William Rowley and William Shakespeare. Dealing with the Saxon invasion of Britain and promoting as thesis the superiority of Christian over pagan, the play depicts the gradual development of a complex Merlin who, at the end, prophetically announces the coming of Arthur. *The Birth of Merlin* has only rarely been performed. The play was translated into German by Ludwig Tieck (*Die Geburt des Merlin*, 1829). (*See also* SHAKESPEARE, WILLIAM.) [NJL]

Rowley, William, and William Shakespeare (attributed). *The Birth of Merlin*. London: Tho. Johnson and H. Marsh, 1662.

Shakespeare, William, and William Rowley (attributed), with additional chapters by R.J. Stewart, Denise Coffey, and Roy Hudd. *The Birth of Merlin, or the Childe Hath Found His Father*. Shaftesbury: Element, 1989. (See review by S. Schoenbaum, *Times Literary Supplement*, February 2–8, 1990.)

BISCHOFF, DAVID, author of *Star Spring*, a science-fiction novel with a convoluted plot, part of which involves a search for the Grail in a computer-generated fantasy world. Ultimately, this Grail is less than holy, representing the reintegration of the divided personality of an alien villain. Before the questers learn of these darker implications, they are assisted by Galahad and Merlin. [ACL]

Bischoff, David. *Star Spring: A Space Operetta*. New York: Berkley, 1982.

BISHOP, FARNHAM, and ARTHUR GILCHRIST BRODEUR set their highly idealized and sentimental historical romance *The Altar of the Legion* (1926) in sinking Lyonesse shortly after Arthur's death. King Owain ap Urien and the black-cloaked Irish cavalry known as his "ravens" (figures developed from *The Dream of Rhonabwy*) help in the heroic resistance against the Saxons. [RHT]

Bishop, Farnham, and Arthur Gilchrist Brodeur. *The Altar of the Legion*. Boston: Little, Brown, 1926.

BLACKMORE, SIR RICHARD (1654–1729), composed two English verse epics based on Arthurian themes: *Prince Arthur: An Heroick Poem: In Ten Books* (1695) and *King Arthur: An Heroick Poem: In Twelve Books* (1697). As early as Michael Drayton, English writers had suggested that Arthur should be the subject of an English national epic closely modeled on classical forms, and Blackmore set out to realize this aim. In the preface to *Prince Arthur*, his first published work, Blackmore outlined the criteria of the epic form according to the categories of Le Bossu: "a feign'd or devis'd Story of an *Illustrious Action*, related in Verse, in an *Allegorical, Probable, Delightful* and *Admirable* manner, to cultivate the Mind with Instruction of Virtue." He was concerned in particular with the moral aspect of literature (he especially deplored the abuses of the Restoration stage) and wished, moreover, to show how Christian theology could be incorporated into the epic. *Prince Arthur* opens with Arthur's return to Britain to reclaim the crown after the Saxon overthrow of Uter's kingdom. The poem includes accounts of Lucifer's attempts to thwart Arthur's purpose, an analysis of the development of Christianity, a catalogue of the kings of Britain (leading up to the reign of William and Mary), and various battles. It culminates in a final single combat between Tollo and Arthur for the hand of Ethelina and the control of the kingdom. The chief historical authority for the poem is Geoffrey of Monmouth's *Historia Regum Britanniae*, which has been recast stylistically with Vergil as a model—the poem opens, for example, with a clear echo of the *Aeneid*: "I sing the *Briton* and his Righteous Arms." There are also borrowings from both Spenser and Milton. Much of the interest, however, lies in the allegorical adaptations of the source material. There are many obvious identifications of contemporaries: Arthur is an immediately recognizable portrayal of King William, Octa is James II, Ethelina is Queen Mary, the wise Pascentius is Thomas Osborne, Earl of Danby, and so forth.

Prince Arthur was highly popular, especially with King William, who—after Mary's death and a Jacobite attempt to reclaim the throne—wished to see his cause presented in the most favorable light. It is therefore not surprising that Blackmore's knighthood and the publication of *King Arthur* occurred in the same year. This second Arthuriad opens with the Gallic lords (the Huguenots) imploring Arthur to intervene against the outrages of King Clotar (Louis XIV). Although Arthur is tempted by Lucifer, and his troops become temporarily dispirited, he finally returns and decapitates Clotar, and we see the beginning of an age of peace. Apart from the political allegory, Blackmore includes in this poem discussions of many contemporary themes, such as Lockean psychology and the Newtonian cosmology. He is especially aware of Milton as a model, and although *King Arthur* was less popular than *Prince Arthur* had been Blackmore probably helped to advance Milton's reputation during the early eighteenth century.

Blackmore had strong supporters for his poetry, but he was also attacked by many of the great writers of his day, Defoe, Swift, and Pope, for example. In particular, through Pope's *Peri Bathous* the name Blackmore is often unjustly viewed by historians of literature as almost synonymous with poetaster. [JPC]

Blackmore, Richard. *Prince Arthur: An Heroick Poem in Ten Books.* 3rd ed. corrected. London: Printed for Awnsham and John Churchil at the Black Swan in Pater-Noster Row, 1696.

———. *King Arthur: An Heroick Poem in Twelve Books.* London: Printed for Awnsham and John Churchil at the Black Swan in Pater-Noster Row, and Jacob Tonson at the Judges Head near the Inner-Temple-gate in Fleet-street, 1697.

Brinkley, Roberta F. *Arthurian Legend in the Seventeenth Century.* Baltimore: Johns Hopkins Press, 1932.

Solomon, Harry M. *Sir Richard Blackmore.* Boston: Twayne, 1980.

BLAISE (Blayse, Bleise), in Robert de Boron's *Joseph* and *Merlin* and the Didot-*Perceval*, Merlin's companion, who records the story of Joseph of Arimathea and the Grail as it is dictated to him by Merlin. In Malory's *Morte Darthur*, Blaise is Merlin's tutor from birth. In Tennyson's *Idylls of the King* ("The Coming of Arthur"), Blaise tells Bellicent, Queen of Orkney, that the infant Arthur was mysteriously washed ashore at Tintagel. The name appears to be a variant of "Bleheris," the name of a twelfth-century Welsh storyteller mentioned by Giraldus Cambrensis, Thomas d'Angleterre, and others. [SW]

BLAKE, WILLIAM (1757–1827), incorporates Arthurian figures and patterns into the powerful mythic narrative of his epic poem *Jersualem, the Emanation of the Giant Albion*, composed during the first two decades of the nineteenth century. Blake's complex treatment of his Arthurian materials derives from the enigmatic view, expressed in his *Descriptive Catalogue* of 1809, that the "stories of Arthur are the acts of Albion, applied to a Prince of the fifth century, who conquered Europe, and held the Empire of the world in the dark age, which the Romans never again recovered." On the one hand, Arthur is for Blake only a particular British "Prince of the fifth century," a limited representation of the larger and more important Albion, the gigantic figure of Britain whose progress he traces in *Jerusalem*. Thus, Arthur appears at the beginning of the poem's third chapter as the "hard cold constrictive Spectre" of Albion, which is his circumscribed and (in isolation) dangerous faculty of Reason; in Blake's personal mythology, Arthur becomes Albion's antagonist, a Druid, an empirical philosopher in the tradition of Bacon, Newton, and Locke, and a Satanic enemy and tempter of Christ. On the other hand, the undying tale of Arthur's "death, or sleep, and promise to return again" (as Blake describes it in the *Descriptive Catalogue*) provides Blake with a potent analogue for the death and resurrection of Albion, which constitute the central action of his poem. Though Blake does not attempt a British epic deriving exclusively or even primarily from the matter of Arthur, he does combine Arthurian materials with biblical and personal myths in a major prophetic work of far-reaching political significance for modern Britain. [MDC]

Blake, William. *The Poetry and Prose of William Blake*, ed. David V. Erdman. Garden City, N.Y.: Doubleday, 1965.

Ashe, Geoffrey. *Camelot and the Vision of Albion.* London: Heinemann, 1971.

Damon, S. Foster. *A Blake Dictionary.* London: Thames and Hudson, 1973.

BLANDÍN DE CORNUALLA, an anonymous Provençal verse romance (2,394 lines) of apparent Catalan authorship dating from the late thirteenth century or first half of the fourteenth. Inspired ostensibly by Arthurian romance, the author narrates in linear fashion, with some humor and irony, the adventures of two friends from Cornwall, the knights Blandín de Cornualla and Guiot Ardit de Miramar, ending the tale with their respective marriages to the sisters Brianda and Irlanda, whose names may betray his familiarity with the Tristan story. The romance emphasizes chivalric ideals and includes troubadour themes and imagery as well as stock romance characters and situations. [HLS]

Pacheco, Arseni, ed. *Blandín de Cornualla i altres narracions en vers dels segles XIV i XV.* Barcelona: Edicions 62, 1983.

BLANK, RICHARD, German film director who made a television movie (of approximately ninety minutes' duration) of Wolfram's *Parzival* in 1980. Using the translation by Wolfgang Mohr (1977), Blank presents the story in an anti-illusionistic manner, with references to the modern world. Blank's film thus differs both from popular fantasy movies (for example, *Excalibur* and Veith von Fürstenberg's Tristan story of 1981, *Feuer und Schwert*) and from the highly stylized Arthurian films of Robert Bresson and Eric Rohmer. [UM/WCM]

Müller, Ulrich. "Parzival 1980—auf der Bühne im Fernsehen und im Film." In *Mittelalter-Rezeption II*, ed. Jürgen Kühnel, Hans-Dieter Mück, Ursula Müller, and Ulrich Müller. Göppingen: Kümmerle, 1982.

BLEEDING LANCE, a lance or spear that first appeared in Chrétien de Troyes's *Perceval*, where it was associated with the Grail in the ceremony in the Fisher King's castle. It was carried by a youth, and from its tip came a drop of blood. Here and in subsequent romances, it remained in direct relationship with the ritual of the Grail. This lance soon came into association with the apocryphal legend of Longinus, the blind Roman soldier whose spear pierced the side of Christ while he hung on the cross (see, e.g., the Continuations of Chrétien's *Perceval*, the Didot-*Perceval, Durmart le Gallois*). The romances also claim for the Lance the power of healing (e.g., *Estoire, Queste*) as well as the role of avenger (e.g., *Estoire, Merlin* Continuation), which led J.D. Bruce to ascribe to it in the Vulgate Cycle the twofold attributes of God: wrath and mercy. Originally, this was not the same weapon as that which wounded the Fisher King, but it became so identified in Wolfram's *Parzival*, in the various romances of the Vulgate Cycle, and in Malory. Though in Chrétien the blood issuing from the spear tip does not seem to flow into the Grail, as a result of Robert de Boron's equating of the Grail with the cup of the Last Supper the blood became the Blood of Christ, emblem of the Real Presence (e.g., *Perlesvaus, Queste*). Upon the death of Galaad in the *Queste* (Perceval in the Manessier Continuation), the Lance and the Grail were removed by a hand from heaven, never to reappear. [RO'G]

West, G.D. *An Index of Proper Names in French Arthurian Prose Romances*. Toronto: University of Toronto Press, 1978. pp. 186–87.

BLIND HARRY wrote the *Wallace* (ca. 1476–78), the Scottish verse epic-chronicle in twelve books inspired by Barbour's *Bruce*, as a thinly veiled attack on the pro-English policies of James III. Harry, once thought to have been an uneducated blind minstrel, was apparently a literate writer who drew upon written sources. Although the work is biased against the English, Harry admired the "gud king Arthour," compares his hero, Wallace, to him, and, in a passage echoing Barbour's Arthurian allusion, says that Arthur, like Ector, Alexander, and Julius Caesar, was destroyed through cowardice. (*See also* CHRONICLES, SCOTTISH.) [EDK]

Blind Harry. *Harry's Wallace*, ed. M.P. McDiarmid. 2 vols. Edinburgh: Blackwood, 1968–69.

Kennedy, Edward Donald. "Chronicles and Other Historical Writing." In *A Manual of the Writings in Middle English*, ed. A.E. Hartung. New Haven: Connecticut Academy of Arts and Sciences, 1981–89, Vol. 8, pp. 2692–99, 2915–24.

BLIOCADRAN PROLOGUE, an 800-line prologue to the *Conte del Graal* of Chrétien de Troyes, appearing in two of its fifteen manuscripts and in the Prose *Perceval* of 1530. Date and authorship are unknown, but it was probably composed in the early thirteenth century, somewhat after the work of Robert de Boron but before the *Perlesvaus*. The poem, in seven episodes, tells the story of Perceval's father, named Bliocadran, who dies in a tournament when Perceval is born. His widow flees the court to preserve her son from knowledge of arms and chivalry.

Bliocadran is the sole survivor of twelve brothers. His wife and people beg him not to go to tournaments, since all his brothers have died in them. Yet, when Bliocadran's first child is about to be born, a messenger arrives with news of a tournament announced by the King of Wales, and Bliocadran insists on going. He is mortally wounded in the tournament and lingers two days.

Bliocadran's son had been born three days after he left for the tournament. When the child is seven months old, his mother decides to flee to the waste forest to keep her son from ever hearing about chivalry. She pretends to be going on a pilgrimage to St. Brendan of Scotland. The lady, her attendants, and all her belongings are assembled at Calfle on the coast of Wales. After reaching the waste forest, they search fifteen days for a proper site. Fourteen years pass, and Bliocadran's people have given the lady and her son up for lost. The mother has told her son that, when hunting in the forest, if he should see men "dressed as though they were covered with iron" (l. 757), they would be devils; he is to retreat, cross himself, and say his Credo. The next day, when he returns from hunting, his mother asks him what he found. "Diversion and pleasure" is his answer. The mother does not inquire further, and the young man says no more.

The *Bliocadran Prologue* is an eludication of the material contained in lines 407–88 (Roach edition) of Chrétien de Troyes's *Conte del Graal*, where Perceval's mother reveals to him that his father had been a renowned knight who had been wounded, impoverished, and exiled in the waste forest under unspecified circumstances after the death of Utherpendragon. Although the *Prologue* changes some of the narrative details (there are eleven brothers in the *Prologue* who die in combat instead of two brothers, and the father dies in a tournament instead of grieving fatally over the deaths of his two older sons), it nevertheless dramatizes Chrétien's narrative theme: the fear of the havoc wrought by chivalric pursuits that caused Perceval's mother to protect her son by raising him in ignorance of the existence of chivalry.

Because the *Prologue* is an elaboration of unexplained material in Chrétien's *Perceval*, it can be considered another Perceval "continuation" or Perceval romance (Romance of Perceval's Father). (*See also* CONTINUATIONS.) [LDW]

Wolfgang, Lenora D., ed. *Bliocadran: A Prologue to the Perceval of Chrétien de Troyes*. Tübingen: Niemeyer, 1976.

Brugger, Ernst. "Bliocadran, the Father of Perceval." In *Medieval Studies in Memory of Gertrude Schoepperle Loomis*, ed. Roger Sherman Loomis. Paris: Champion, 1927, pp. 147–74.

Newstead, Helaine. "Perceval's Father and Welsh Tradition." *Romanic Review*, 36 (1945), 3–31.

Thompson, Albert Wilder. "The Text of the *Bliocadran*." *Romance Philology*, 9 (1955–56), 205–09.

BLUNT, WILFRID SCAWEN (1840–1922), British poet and adventurer, who selected "The Wisdom of Merlin" (1914) as the epilogue for his collected verse, claiming that it "gives an old man's view . . . of the philosophy of living." Consisting of over 100 triplet stanzas—mostly platitudes on the necessity of passionate love—the poem is only of slight Arthurian interest. Two sonnets, "The Morte D'Arthur" and "Le Roi Est Morte. Vive Le Roi!," more directly celebrate the enduring vitality of Arthurian story. [DN]

Blunt, Wilfrid Scawen. *The Poetical Works*. London: Macmillan, 1914.

BOCCACCIO, GIOVANNI (1313–1375). Although Boccaccio certainly had French romances available to him during his youth at the Angevin court of Naples, his use of Arthurian materials began only after his return to Florence, continuing then to the end of his life. The *Amorosa Visione* (1342) lists many Arthurian knights and ladies in its triumph of Fame (Canto 11), while Lancelot and Tristan reappear in the triumph of Love (Canto 29). Both categories are subsequently overturned in the triumph of Fortune, and the narrator is urged by his guide to turn from these worldly matters to the pursuit of salvation. In the *Elegia di Madonna Fiammetta* (1343–44), the heroine compares her love tragedy to Isolt's (Chapter 8) and that of other tragic heroines in order to claim pridefully that her own misery is greater than all others'. Like Dante's Francesca, Fiammetta is an example of the destructive powers of obsessive passion, who, although still alive at the end of her tale, has clearly descended into a state of damnation and despair. The lusty widow of the *Corbaccio* (1355) is satirically characterized as reading Arthurian love stories instead of prayer books, and as becoming sexually aroused by these readings. The book is a misogynistic tirade intended to cure a hapless lover of his erroneous love.

More complex is the use of Arthurian materials in the *Decameron* (1349–51). The book's subtitle, "Prencipe Galeotto" (Prince Galehaut), has been variously interpreted as a defense of the work's erotic contents (Boccaccio is a go-between, a friend to lovers) or as a reference to *Inferno*, Canto 5, and thereby a warning about the reader's moral responsibility for the way one reads and acts. The latter interpretation seems reinforced by Tale 10.6, in which a king falls in love with two sisters named Ginevra and Isotta (Guenevere and Isolde) but then vanquishes his own lust and has them honorably married. He thus avoids Francesca's sinful imitation of the Arthurian lovers' example and becomes explicitly a positive example of behavior to be imitated. Hollander has pointed out that Boccaccio in his preface begs his women readers not to let the plague description frighten them from reading on ("di più avanti leggere")—thus negatively evoking the last line of Francesca's speech in hell: "that day we read no farther" ("quel giorno più non vi leggemmo avante"). The use of the Lancelot story as pornography by the bawdy widow of the *Corbaccio* further supports the connection between allusions to this tale and the problem, already recognized by Dante, of authors' versus readers' responsibility for the influence of literature on behavior. It has even been suggested that "Galeotto" unmasks the dangerous seductions of fiction itself, and that the *Decameron* narrators therefore distance themselves from the historical world to emphasize the distinction between reality and fiction. There is some disagreement as to the relevance of Dante's *Inferno*, Canto 5, to Boccaccio's subtitle; but Boccaccio's continual imitation of Dante's writing makes such an allusion probable. Thus, Dante would be a formative influence on Boccaccio's own views of the Lancelot legend, making moral questions paramount. The *Amorosa Visione* seems to reinforce this concern with moral interpretation. For the *Elegia*, too, it is important that the famous Arthurian love stories are tragedies. The *Decameron* narrator claims to be finally freed from the miseries of excessive love and, alluding to Ovid's *Remedia Amores*, offers to help distract ladies from such melancholy passion. He is thus scarcely a go-between to their loves.

Besides the "Galeotto" subtitle, the *Decameron* contains very little Arthurian reference; but a few tales bear perhaps some resemblance to Arthurian materials. An indirect connection has been suggested between the story of Alatiel (2.7) and strands of a complex romance within the Old French Prose *Tristan* of the previous century. The theme of the eaten heart, occurring in a tale (4.9) derived from the Provençal *vida* of Guillem de Cabestaing, can also be found in the "Lai Guiron" sung by Ysolt in the marriage segment (Sneyd fragment, ll. 781–90) of Thomas's *Tristan*. In any case, even though the *Novellino*, an earlier collection of Italian *novelle* known to Boccaccio, had drawn directly from Arthurian legends for a number of tales, Arthurian stories were not a major or direct source for the *Decameron*.

De Casibus Virorum Illustrium (1355–62) recounts the history of King Arthur, drawn mainly from Geoffrey of Monmouth, but adds to it the twelve rules of the Round Table. Boccaccio's chapter was cited in turn by Lydgate. Boccaccio avoids any reference to fabulous adventures and prefaces the narrative by commenting that Arthur's fame makes his inclusion in this book of histories seem necessary despite serious doubts about the historical truth of the matter. Emphasizing Arthur's military career, he suggests that Arthur's pride in conquests abroad led to his destruction at home. His final moral is that only humble things endure.

In all, Boccaccio's treatment of Arthurian materials seems remarkably negative. The famous King and his loving knights offer moral examples of what to avoid, not what to imitate. Dante may well have been a powerful influence on this attitude. [JLS]

Bruce, J. Douglas. "A Boccaccio Analogue in the Old French Prose Tristan." *Romanic Review*, 1 (1910), 384–94.

Gardner, Edmund G. *The Arthurian Legend in Italian Literature*. London: Dent, 1930, pp. 228–38.

Mazzotta, Giuseppe. "The *Decameron*: The Marginality of Literature." *University of Toronto Quarterly*, 42 (Fall 1972), 68–69.

Padoan, Giorgio. "Mondo Aristocratico e Mondo Communale nell'Ideologia e nell'Arte de Giovanni Boccaccio." *Studi sul Boccaccio*, 2 (1964), 124–25.

Viscardi, Antonio. "Arthurian Influences on Italian Literature from 1200 to 1500." In *Arthurian Literature in the Middle Ages*, ed. Roger Sherman Loomis. Oxford: Clarendon, 1959, pp. 419–29.

BODMER, JOHANN JACOB (1698–1783), a Swiss-German professor of history, is known primarily for his contributions to the literary theory of his time, which resulted in the liberation of German literature from the artificial constraints of French classical models, and for his collection of medieval German manuscripts, which was a major factor in the revival of interest in medieval German literature. Ironically, his own lack of talent as a creative writer is revealed in his abridged translations of parts of Wolfram's *Parzival* (*Der Parcival*, 1753, and *Gamuret*, 1755), both based on a 1477 printing of a composite of two manuscripts and both written in inappropriate, stiff hexameters. A later ballad, "Jestute" (1781), relating the Jeschute-Orilus episode from *Parzival*, was also of little literary significance. [RWK]

Bender, Wolfgang. *J.J. Bodmer und J.J. Breitinger*. Stuttgart: Metzler, 1973.

BOECE, HECTOR, first principal of the University of Aberdeen, wrote the influential Latin chronicle *Scotorum Historiae* (1527). Boece's story of Arthur diverges markedly from earlier accounts and carries to an extreme the sentiments against Arthur that were implicit in John of Fordun's chronicle. From Fordun's account, it incorporate's Arthur's illegitimacy and weak claim to the throne but adds several new elements: Arthur's conquests are limited to Britain; Arthur recognizes Mordred as his successor but is persuaded to break the treaty, thus causing hostilities to be renewed; Guenevere is taken prisoner and held by the Picts for the rest of her life.

J.B. Black describes the chronicle as a "wild welter that recalls the grotesque pages of Geoffrey of Monmouth." John Bellenden, at the request of James V of Scotland, translated Boece's *Scotorum Historiae* into Middle Scots prose in 1531. He shortened the Arthurian section somewhat but maintained Boece's bias against Arthur. He noted that Gawain fought on Arthur's side "against his native people." Also at the request of James V, William Stewart translated Boece's history into 61,000 lines of Scottish verse in 1535. He adds considerably to Boece's Arthurian account, calling Arthur the most unfortunate of all British kings, one punished by God for being "faithless and untrue" to King Mordred. (*See also* JOHN OF FORDUN.) [EDK]

Boece, Hector. *Scotorum Historiae*. Paris: Ascensius, 1527.

Bellenden, John, trans. *The Chronicle of Scotland Compiled by Hector Boece*, ed. R.W. Chambers, E.C. Batho, and H.W. Husbands. 2 vols. Edinburgh: Blackwood, 1938, 1941.

Black, J.B. "Boece's *Scotorum Historiae*." In *University of Aberdeen: Quatercentenary of the Death of Hector Boece*. Aberdeen: University of Aberdeen Press, 1937, pp. 30–53.

Brie, Friedrich. *Die nationale Literatur Schottlands*. Halle: Niemeyer, 1937, pp. 317–53.

Fletcher, Robert Huntington. *The Arthurian Material in the Chronicles, Especially Those of Great Britain and France*. Boston: Ginn, 1906; 2nd ed. Roger Sherman Loomis. New York: Franklin, 1966, pp. 245–48.

Göller, K.H. "König Arthur in den schottischen Chroniken." *Anglia*, 80 (1962), 390–404.

BOIARDO, MATTEO MARIA (1441–1494), was associated at various periods of his life with the Este court at Ferrara, serving from 1480 to 1482 as Ercole d'Este's representative in the city of Modena and from 1487 until his death as governor of Reggio. His literary fame rests on an influential collection of love poems, the *Amorum libri tres* or *Canzoniere*, which are noteworthy examples of Petrarchan lyrics of courtly elegance, and on the most significant chivalric romance of the fifteenth century, the *Orlando Innamorato*, which, left unfinished at the poet's death, served as the starting point for the composition of Ariosto's *Orlando Furioso*, completed early in the following century. Traditionally, Boiardo has been credited with having realized in his lengthy poem (three books totaling sixty-nine cantos) a fusion of Carolingian epic tradition and the *matière de Bretagne*, creating thereby a unique Italian genre. Though in truth such a fusion occurs in works predating the *Orlando*

Innamorato, Boiardo's poem, in its reflection of the culture and ideals of Italian Renaissance court life during the golden age of Este patronage, is the first masterpiece of the Italian romance genre and the earliest to manifest a sophisticated use of such narrative techniques as interlace. It is well known that Ferrara and similar northern Italian courts were fascinated by medieval epic traditions and that the Este library contained numerous Arthurian romances familiar to Boiardo and other courtiers. Boiardo's work continued and developed the fourteenth- and fifteenth-century *cantari* tradition and also served the literary and aesthetic tastes of a court audience. The framework of the poem is essentially Carolingian, recounting the struggle of the Christian forces of Charlemagne with those of the pagan Agramante. However, the focus of the romance is on the Arthurian elements, including the innumerable fantastic adventures of knights-errant, magic fountains and enchanted forests, and particularly love, which has frequently been seen as the motive force behind a highly energized series of complex episodes, commencing with that of the hero-protagonist, Orlando. A transformation of the French Roland, Orlando becomes a victim of the ineluctable forces of love, represented by Angelica, the daughter of the King of Cathay, sent to undermine the valor of the Christian armies. Boiardo borrows episodes, locales, and characters from Arthurian tradition, transforming them into a tapestry of courtly elegance and sensibility with a markedly international Gothic flavor. [RJR]

Boiardo, Matteo Maria. *Orlando Innamorato di Matteo Maria Boiardo rifatto da Francesco Berni*. Florence: Sansoni, 1971.

———. *Orlando Innamorato*, trans. Charles Stanley Ross. Berkeley: University of California Press, 1989.

Franceschetti, Antonio. "*L'Orlando Innamorato* e gli ideali cavallereschi nella Ferrara del Quattrocento." In *Atti del R. Istituto Veneto di Scienze, Lettere ed Arti*. Venice: Classe di scienze morali e lettere, 1971–72, pp. 315–33.

Gardner, Edmund G. *The Arthurian Legend in Italian Literature*. London: Dent, 1930.

Molinaro, Julius A. *Matteo Maria Boiardo: A Bibliography of Works and Criticism from 1487–1980*. Ontario: Canadian Federation for the Humanities, 1987.

Rajna, Pio. *Le Fonti dell' "Orlando Furioso."* Florence: Sansoni, 1876, 1900.

BONCOMPAGNO DA SIGNA refers in his *Cedrus* (1194–1203) to companies of young men in many parts of Italy, some of which have taken the name of the "fellowship of the Round Table" (*de tabula rotonda societas*). In *De Amicitia* (ca. 1205), he provides the first reference in Italy to Iseult. In a rhetorical handbook, he provides a sample letter in which a teacher informs a lazy student that he is not likely to graduate before Arthur returns to Britain. [DLH]

Boncompagno da Signa. *Cedrus*. In *Briefsteller und Formelbucher des elften bis vierzehnten Jahrhunderts*, ed. Ludwig Ritter von Rockinger. Munich, 1863.

———. *Amicitia de maestro Boncompagno da Signa*, ed. S. Nathan. Rome, 1909.

Gardner, Edmund G. *The Arthurian Legend in Italian Literature*. London: Dent, 1930, pp. 9–10.

BOND, FREDERICK BLIGH (1864–1945), English archaeologist and psychic. After having been forced to abandon his excavations at Glastonbury Abbey, he produced a series of nine "Glastonbury Scripts," purporting to be communications from the spirits of the Brothers of the twelfth-century "Company of Avallon" (whom Bond also called "The Watchers") regarding the antiquities of Glastonbury. One of these scripts, partly produced by automatic writing, is a metrical account of the "true" story of "King Arthur and the Quest of the Holy Grail" (1925). [SRR]

Bond, Frederick Bligh. *The Story of King Arthur and How He Saw the Sangreal: of His Institution of the Quest of the Holy Grail: and of the Promise of the Fulfillment of That Quest in the Latter Days*. Glastonbury: Privately printed, 1925; repr. in *The Glastonbury Scripts, Nos. I to IX*. Glastonbury: Hartes, 1934.

BOND, NANCY, author of a fantasy for juveniles, *A String in the Harp* (1976). In this first novel, a young boy, Peter, is drawn back from the twentieth century to sixth-century Wales after discovering the tuning fork for Taliesin's harp. Though the novel focuses on his adventures in time and his struggle to return the key to Taliesin's grave and keep it from an ambitious and evil museum curator, the actual heart of the book is the boy's difficulty in coping with the death of his mother and his estrangement from his sisters and his grieving and withdrawn father. [RCS]

Bond, Nancy. *A String in the Harp*. New York: Atheneum, 1976.

BOOK ILLUSTRATION (AMERICAN). Arthurian illustration in the United States is represented chiefly by juvenile books. Americans shared the Victorian conviction that Malory's *Morte Darthur* (in abridged forms) provided models of gentlemanly behavior. The most significant promoter of "the high nobility of spirit that moved these excellent men" was "the father of American illustration,"

11. Howard Pyle, illustration for Tennyson's *The Lady of Shalott* (New York: Dodd, Mead, 1881). (Courtesy of The Newberry Library, Chicago.)

Howard Pyle (1853–1911), whose personal identification with a romantic past was expressed in *The Story of King Arthur and His Knights* (1903), *The Story of the Champions of the Round Table* (1905), *The Story of Sir Launcelot and His Companions* (1907), and *The Story of the Grail and the Passing of Arthur* (1910). The books are lavishly decorated with Beardsleyesque headpieces, tailpieces, and full-page pen-and-ink drawings featuring enigmatic ladies, neo-Gothic furnishings, and complexly patterned dress and armor.

American editions of popular British juveniles commonly featured American artists. In 1917, Pyle's most famous pupil, N.C. Wyeth (1882–1945), provided nine watercolors for Sidney Lanier's *The Boy's King Arthur* (1880), combining brilliantly costumed medieval characters with the landscapes and muscular farm horses of the Brandywine Valley. Louis Rhead (1857–1926), introducing a 1923 reprint of Knowles's *King Arthur and His Knights* (1862), deplored the artists' failure to research sixth-century social history and revealed that his own stylistic sources were the Book of Kells and Abbey's Grail decorations for the Boston Public Library. The result is medieval pastiche with Pre-Raphaelite leanings.

In the last thirty years, a conscious imitation of medieval manuscripts has characterized much illustration. Gustaf Tenggren's muscular heroes in golden armor occupy a primitive Nordic world to complement Sterne and Lindsay's *King Arthur and the Knights of the Round Table* (1962). For Keith Baines's *Sir Thomas Malory's Le Morte d'Arthur* (1963), Enrico Arno's black-and-white line drawings imitate Gothic manuscripts. Ruth Robbins's *Taliesin and King Arthur* (1970), with its two-dimensional figures, frontal positioning, and marginalia, suggests Anglo-Saxon sources. Herschel Levit in Mary MacLeod's *King Arthur* (1963) combines Romanesque forms with turquoise and crushed-strawberry colors. Virgil Burnett's sophisticated full-page drawings for Silverstein's *Sir Gawain and the Green Knight: A Comedy for Christmas* (1974), with their contorted, bare-branched trees, snakey-haired lady, and symbolic candles and toads, recall Beardsley and Rackham. In general, American artists have been less successful than the British in developing original visualizations of Arthurian romance. [MAW]

Mahoney, Bertha E., L.P. Latimer, and Beulah Folmsbee. *Illustrators of Children's Books*. Boston: Horn Book, 1947– (with supplements).

Pitz, Henry C. *Howard Pyle: Writer, Illustrator, and Founder of the Brandywine School*. New York: Potter, 1975.

BOOK ILLUSTRATION (BRITISH). An important aspect of Victorian medievalism was the revived interest in the Arthurian legends, particularly as found in Malory's *Morte Darthur* and Tennyson's *Idylls of the King*. Tennyson's works invited illustration. Woodcut designs by Dante Gabriel Rossetti, Holman Hunt, and Daniel Maclise accompanied the Arthurian compositions in Moxon's 1857 edition of *Poems*, and in 1866–67 the folio editions of four idylls, "Elaine," "Vivien," "Guinevere," and "Enid," contained thirty-six steel-engravings designed by the eminent Alsatian artist Gustave Doré. Although he fails to encapsulate the poet's moral concerns, Doré evocatively portrays a romantic wilderness of misty lakes, dense forests, pounding seas, and castle-topped crags.

From 1870 to 1940, the predominant influence on Arthurian illustration was Pre-Raphaelitism. Landscapes recreated with some botanical accuracy, neo-Gothic furnishings, bright colors, complexity of pattern and symbol, and senuously beautiful women were the illustrator's stock in trade. The most extensive pictorial cycle in this tradition was the series of forty-eight watercolors provided by W. Russell Flint for the Medici Society's deluxe *Morte* (1910–11). What seems to determine Flint's choice of subjects is the opportunity to present ladies in various degrees of nakedness. Though he clearly found the Grail quest uncongenial, his secular scenes, with their tapestries, carved pillars, rose gardens, and swan-decorated lakes, opulently convey the ambience of courtly society.

William Morris's view of a book as a unified work of art with all the visual elements in harmony—type, illustration, border, page layout, paper, binding—resulted in the production of several profusely decorated Malorys, generally in limited editions. An immediate response to the Kelmscott

12. Arthur Rackham, illustration for the Medici Society's *Le Morte Darthur* (London, 1920). (Courtesy of The Newberry Library, Chicago.)

books was J.M. Dent's *Morte D'Arthur* (1893–94), which contained twenty-one full-page illustrations and 585 headings, borders, initials, and ornaments by the then-unknown Aubrey Beardsley. Though a Burne-Jones influence was evident in the early chapters, Beardsley soon developed the Art Nouveau style characterized by whiplash line, abstract floral motifs, and starkly contrasted black-and-white forms. Even more original was his treatment of content, for his knights, lethargic and spiritless, are completely dominated by their mistresses and the fays. Far from glorifying chivalric romance, Beardsley satirized it, shocking Victorian sensibilities with his effeminate heroes, androgynous nudes, lecherous satyrs, and sensual angels.

While the Beardsley drawings were economically reproduced by a new photomechanical process, Charles Gere and Robert Gibbings returned to the art of wood-engraving. In the twenty-seven cuts that Gere supplied in 1913 for the Ashendene Press Malory, the Burne-Jones Kelmscott style is applied to such conventional subjects as Arthur's wedding feast, Tristram and Isolde's shipboard drink, and Arthur's departure for Avalon. The Golden Cockerel *Morte* (1936) shows that Robert Gibbings was more decorator than illustrator, for he seldom illustrates specific incidents. Such botanical forms as spearlike grass and stylized trees provide a continuum for human figures energetically engaged in the rituals of knight-errantry.

Because the Victorians saw Malory's knights as exemplars of gentlemanly behavior, abridged editions for juveniles became the most popular form of presentation. The audience justified the use of illustrations that would convey not only the sense of a historical past (occurring anywhere between the sixth and sixteenth centuries), but also an aura of magic and mystery. The most popular abridgments, like Sir James Knowles's *King Arthur and His Knights* (1862), Sidney Lanier's *The Boy's King Arthur* (1880), and Alfred W. Pollard's *The Romance of King Arthur and His Knights of the Round Table* (1917), were illustrated by various artists, including Walter Crane, Arthur Rackham, A.G. Walker, Innes Fripp, H.J. Ford, Lancelot Speed, and Walter Hodges.

Recently, a diversification of texts has extended the range of pictorial subjects. Errol Le Cain's picture book *King Arthur's Sword* (1968) uses collage and unrealistic color to present a comic fantasyland for the amusement of young readers. The eccentricities of T.H. White's *The Book of Merlyn* (1977) are enhanced by Trevor Stubley's clever black-and-white drawings of anthropomorphic animals and a dunce-capped Merlin. Translations and adaptations of medieval metrical romances have provided opportunities for mingling realism and fantasy, as in Dorothy Braby's color engravings for Gwyn Jones's *Sir Gawain and the Green Knight* (1952), where elegance of costume and sinuosity of line are enhanced by the subtle use of pink, olive, and aquamarine. The well of Arthurian inspiration shows no signs of going dry. [MAW]

Bland, David. *A History of Book Illustration*. London: Faber and Faber, 1969.

Crane, Walter. *Of the Decorative Illustration of Books Old and New*. London: Bell, 1972 (1896).

Mancoff, Debra N. *The Arthurian Revival in Victorian Art*. New York: Garland, 1990, pp. 250–74.

Muir, Percy. *Victorian Illustrated Books*. London: Batsford, n.d.

Whalley, Joyce Irene, and Tessa Rose Chester. *A History of Children's Book Illustrations*. London: John Murray; Victoria and Albert Museum, 1988.

Whitaker, Muriel. "Illustrating Caxton's Malory." In *Studies in Malory*, ed. James W. Spisak. Kalamazoo, Mich.: Medieval Institute Publications, 1985, pp. 279–319 and illustrations.

———. *The Legends of King Arthur in Art*. Cambridge: Brewer, 1990.

BOORMAN, JOHN, British filmmaker whose *Excalibur*, released in 1981, has enjoyed a sharply divided critical reception. Boorman himself indicated that he was determined "to tell the whole story of the *Morte Darthur*," whose author, Thomas Malory, Boorman saw as the "first hack writer." Boorman's determination notwithstanding, *Excalibur* is not a cinematic translation of Malory.

13. Uther with Excalibur, from John Boorman's *Excalibur* (1981).

Boorman has instead been free with his sources, conflating materials, as is directorial practice, to suit his needs. Here, Arthur is the Grail King, but the Grail is stripped of any Christian associations. In a film where the king and the land are one, the Grail is the central symbol of a not always clearly defined pagan fertility ritual. The vision of the Grail offered by the film's screenplay (jointly authored by Boorman and Rospo Pallenberg) owes as much to that of Jessie Weston as it does to that of Malory.

The central and only fully developed character in

Excalibur is Merlin, played by Nicol Williamson, who links the past and the future. Events in the film revolve around a trinity of women, Igrayne, Guinevere, and Morgana (the film's conflation of the traditionally separate characters of Morgawse, Nimue, and Morgan le Fay), and their complex relations with Arthur, Lancelot, and Merlin.

The film does succeed in effectively blending fantasy and magic with realistic portrayals of martial violence. Filmed on several Irish locations with admirable cinematography by Alex Thompson, *Excalibur* is often sumptuous and spectacular to see—and to hear. The soundtrack includes selections from Carl Orff's *Carmina Burana*. [KJH]

Anonymous. "Dossier: *Excalibur*." *Positif*, 247 (October 1981), 29–43.

Kennedy, Harlan. "The World of King Arthur According to John Boorman." *American Film*, 6 (March 1981), 30–37.

Shichtman, Martin B. "Hollywood's New Weston: The Grail Myth in Francis Ford Coppola's *Apocalypse Now* and John Boorman's *Excalibur*." *Postscript*, 4 (Fall 1984), 35–48.

BOROWSKY, MARVIN, portrays Arthur in *The Queen's Knight* (1955) as an illiterate oaf who, though brought to the throne by Mordred and Merlin as a straw-king, rallies the realm with peasant good sense. Lancelot is all that Arthur is not—a doughty warrior, a proud nobleman, and a great lover. Guinevere cannot resist him, though she comes to respect her husband. The kingdom falls because Arthur, who tries his utmost, cannot unite all that is best in it. Borowsky's novel is insightful, if somewhat clumsy in technique. [CNS]

Borowsky, Marvin. *The Queen's Knight*. New York: Random House, 1955.

BORS (Bohort), in the Vulgate Cycle and Malory's *Morte Darthur*, Lancelot's cousin. With Perceval and Galahad, Bors goes to Sarras, achieves the quest of the Grail, and is the only one to return to Arthur's court. Afterward, he is a go-between for Lancelot and Guenevere, is made king of Claudas's lands, fights Mordred with Arthur, becomes a hermit, and eventually dies in the Crusade to Jerusalem. [SW]

BOSS, ELEANOR, tells the story of the Grail in *In Quest of the Grail* (1930). The book, probably intended for young readers, consists of quotations from Tennyson's "The Holy Grail" interspersed with connecting passages of exposition and commentary in prose. [EB]

Boss, Eleanor. *In Quest of the Grail*. London and Edinburgh: Marshall, Morgan and Scott, [1930].

BOSTON PUBLIC LIBRARY MURALS. The second-floor Delivery Room of the Boston Public Library (McKim, Mead and White, architects, 1887–95) contains a frieze depicting The Quest of the Holy Grail, by Edwin Austin Abbey (1852–1911), executed in two stages between 1890 and 1901. There are fifteen scenes of varying width based upon a great many literary sources, from Robert de Boron to Tennyson, and arranged to "suit the exigencies of pictorial treatment," with the scarlet figure of Galahad as "the brilliant recurring note" (Abbey). The narrative begins with The Vision (or Infancy of Galahad) and continues through his Vigil, The Siege Perilous, The Departure or Benediction, The Castle of the Grail and the Failure, The Loathly Damsel, The Conquest of the Seven Deadly Sins, The Key to the Castle, Delivering the Captive Virtues, Leaving Blanchefleur, Amfortas Released, Galahad Departs, The Voyage to Sarras, Sarras, and The Golden Tree and Achievement of the Grail. [JFO'G]

Baxter, Sylvester. *The Legend of the Holy Grail*. Boston: Curtis and Cameron, 1904.

BOTTOMLEY, GORDON (1874–1948), published in 1929 a collection of short dramas intended to demonstrate the continuing vitality of spoken verse in the theater. In *Merlin's Grave*, a one-act play, a young woman is revealed to be the Lady of the Lake returned to renew Merlin's confinement. [DN]

Bottomley, Gordon. *Scenes and Plays*. New York: Macmillan, 1929.

BOUGHTON, RUTLAND (1878–1960), British composer, devoted much of his last forty years to a grandiose cycle of Arthurian operas. Only the earlier parts were ever produced, and they were far less successful than *The Immortal Hour*, a setting of Fiona Macleod's Celtic drama, or *The Queen of Cornwall*, based on Thomas Hardy's mummers' play. The music for the operas remains unpublished. Turning first to the theme when collaborating with the poet Reginald Buckley, who wrote the libretto for the first two parts, Boughton developed it as the expression of his conviction that Christianity was declining and would be sup-

14. Edwin Austin Abbey, "The Tree of Life." (Courtesy of the Trustees of the Boston Public Library.)

planted by socialism. The five parts of the cycle are *The Birth of Arthur, The Round Table* (culminating in Arthur's proclamation of the quest of the Grail), *The Lily Maid* (about Elaine's love for Lancelot), *Galahad* (which contains Boughton's ideas about the function of the arts), and *Avalon* (with Arthur's death).

Among the composer's other Arthurian works are the choral pieces *Chapel in Lyonesse* (1905) and *King Arthur Had Three Sons*. Boughton was also instrumental in founding the Glastonbury Festival, with support from George Bernard Shaw, Thomas Hardy, and other eminent figures. (*See also* MUSIC.) [CNS]

Buckley, Reginald, and Rutland Boughton. *The Music Drama of the Future*. London: Reeves, 1911.

Hurd, Michael. *Immortal Hour: The Life and Period of Rutland Boughton*. London: Routledge and Kegan Paul, 1962.

BOWER, WALTER, abbot of Inchcolm, wrote between 1440 and 1447 a continuation of John of Fordun's *Chronica Gentis Scotorum*, which survives in two versions, the first known as the *Scotichronicon*, the second as the *Book of Cupar*. In revising Fordun's account of Arthur's reign, Bower stressed Arthur's illegitimacy and emphasized that the Scot Mordred should have been king. [EDK]

Bower, Walter. *Scotichronicon*, ed. and trans. D.E.R. Watt. Aberdeen: Aberdeen University Press, 1987, Vol. 8.

Johannis de Fordun. *Chronica Gentis Scotorum*, ed. W.F. Skene. Edinburgh: Edmonston and Douglas, 1871.

———. *John of Fordun's Chronicle of the Scottish Nation*. trans. F.J.H. Skene, ed W.F. Skene. Edinburgh: Edmonston and Douglas, 1872.

Kelly, Susan. "The Arthurian Material in the *Scotichronicon* of Walter Bower." *Anglia*, 97 (1979), 431–38.

Kennedy, Edward Donald. "Chronicles and Other Historical Writing." In *A Manual of the Writings in Middle English*, ed. A.E. Hartung. New Haven: Connecticut Academy of Arts and Sciences, 1981–89, Vol. 8, pp. 2679–80, 2891.

Withrington, John. "The Arthurian Epitaph in Malory's *Morte Darthur*." *Arthurian Literature*, 7 (1987), 103–44.

BOWERS, GWENDOLYN, in two historical romances for juveniles, deals with an adolescent's maturation and rise to knighthood. In *Brother to Galahad* (1963), Hugh of Alleyn acts as Galahad's squire on the Grail quest, subsequently witnesses King Arthur's defeat, and finally comprehends that his quest involves the cultivation of his own Welsh heritage. In *The Lost Dragon of Wessex* (1957), an orphan, Wulf, discovers his descendance from Arthur's bard, Taliessin, whose family was entrusted with the safekeeping of Arthur's insignia of power, a dragon-shaped armring. According to Merlin, its reappearance 350 years later would signal the succession of an even greater king. Wulf's presentation of the armring to King Alfred fulfills the prophecy. [RHT/RWK]

Bowers, Gwendolyn. *The Lost Dragon of Wessex*. New York: Walck, 1957.

———. *Brother to Galahad*. New York: Walck, 1963.

"BOY AND THE MANTLE, THE." The hero of this sixteenth-century English ballad preserved in the Percy Folio is Craddocke, a figure familiar to readers of the French romances as Caradoc Briebras. Craddocke's success derives from the fact that his wife, alone among the women assembled at Carlisle, has remained faithful to her husband. Only she is able to pass the test of the magic mantle. Similarly, Craddocke is the only male in Arthur's court who is able to meet the cuckold's challenge of carving the boar's head and of drinking from a magical horn. This ballad bears comparison with a number of other Arthurian works, most notably with the *Cort Mantel* and Robert Biket's *Lai du cor*. [JN]

Child, Francis James, ed. *The English and Scottish Popular Ballads*. Boston: Houghton-Mifflin, 1884, pp. 1–14; repr. New York: Dover, 1965. Vol. 1, pp. 257–74.

BRADLEY, MARION ZIMMER, American author of *The Mists of Avalon* (1982). Set in Romano-Celtic Britain of the late fifth century, this fantasy relates the Arthurian legend from the viewpoint of the women in the saga: Igraine, wife of Gorlois; their daughter, Morgaine; Igraine's younger sister, Morgause, later Lot's queen; Igraine's half-sister Viviane, Lady of the Lake, priestess of the Mother Goddess on the Holy Isle of Avalon, and mother of Lancelot; her descendants Niniane and Nimue; and Gwenhwyfar, Arthur's queen. Morgaine is the focal character. The central struggle in the book is between the older religions (Druids, early Christians, and worshipers of the Mother Goddess) and a narrow-minded Christianity, with both beliefs headquartered on the Holy Isle of Avalon (Glastonbury). This continuing conflict provides the background for the rise and fall of Arthur, who, fusing the royal bloods of both pagan and Christian groups, is destined to effect peace in Britain. Bradley follows the Arthurian legend faithfully, incorporating the conception of Arthur by Uther and Igraine; the conception of Mordred (known as Gwydion) by Arthur and his half-sister (though here Morgaine, rather than Morgause); Arthur's crowning, marriage to Gwenhwyfar, and establishing of the Companions of the Round Table; the love affair between Gwenhwyfar and Lancelot; Galahad's conception by Lancelot and Elaine; the love affair between Morgaine, married to Uriens, and Accolon; the Grail quest; Galahad's achievement of the Grail and holy death; Arthur's and Mordred's killing of each other; Lancelot's death at Glastonbury. The major departures from the legend are the close familial ties among all of the women, except the Christian Gwenhwyfar, thereby creating a pagan sorority; the pagan Grail hallows, which included Excalibur, all euhemerized into the Christian Holy Grail and Sacred Spear; and Arthur's appointing first Galahad, then Mordred as his heir. Bradley's concern with the pagan Arthurian women necessarily lessens her emphasis on the history of Arthur and depicts Christianity as a repressive, interloping religion. Yet the novel ends on a note of reconciliation of Arthurian past and present, paganism and Christianity. Given its feminist thrust, it represents an original and at times engrossing account of the Arthurian legend. [VML]

Bradley, Marion Zimmer. *The Mists of Avalon*. New York: Knopf, 1982.

Day, Mildred Leake, Review of *The Mists of Avalon*. *Avalon to Camelot*, 1 (1983), 27.

BRADLEY, WILL, author of a romantic fantasy, *Launcelot and the Ladies* (1927), in which the protagonist relives scenes from the love triangle formed by Launcelot, Guenevere, and Elaine (a fusion of the two Elaines). Given a comparable choice in his own life, he marries the younger, unattached woman. [RHT]

Bradley, Will. *Launcelot and the Ladies*. New York and London: Harper, 1927.

BRADSHAW, GILLIAN, author of an Arthurian trilogy. The series begins with *Hawk of May* (1980), narrated by Gwalchmai (Hawk of May, Gawain's name in Welsh). At fourteen, about to be initiated by his mother, Morgawse, into "Darkness," the boy recoils in horror, escapes, and spends three years in the Isles of the Blessed. He returns to seek service with a reluctant Arthur, from whom he learns the dark secret of Medraut's incestuous origin. In *Kingdom of Summer* (1981), which begins nine years later, Rhys ap Sion, Gwalchmai's servant, tells the story of his master's ill-fated love affair with Elidan. The central action of the story is the struggle between Morgawse, the Queen of Darkness, and Gwalchmai, the Champion of Light. In the end, Morgawse is beheaded by Agravain, and Gwalchmai finds Elidan, but he receives no forgiveness and leaves her without learning that Gwynn, a Percival-like character, is his son. *In Winter's Shadow* (1982) shifts the focus to Gwynhwyfar, whose first-person narrative of her passion for Bedwyr, her love for Arthur, her fear and hatred of Medraut, and her guilt and shame for her part in the breakup of the Family, written years later in a convent where she is abbess, is a gripping and convincing account from the Queen's perspective. Medraut, whom she had tried to poison, exposes the lovers. Bedwyr, in trying to rescue her, accidentally kills Gwynn. This inspires in Gwalchmai a passion for revenge that leaves the empire vulnerable to Medraut's usurpation and the ensuing tragedy. Bradshaw borrows material from a variety of traditional sources, and she integrates it with skill to produce a convincing, if increasingly somber, vision of the Arthurian legend. [MAG]

Bradshaw, Gillian. *Hawk of May*. New York: Simon and Schuster, 1980.

———. *Kingdom of Summer*. New York: Simon and Schuster, 1981.

———. *In Winter's Shadow*. New York: Simon and Schuster, 1982.

BRAN (Bran the Blessed), a Celtic sea-deity, or the son of one, reputed to have performed marvelous exploits. He appears (as Bendigeidfran, "Bran the Blessed") in the second branch of the *Mabinogi* and is mentioned in the Triad of Three Fortunate Concealments, where his severed head—a powerful talisman—was buried to protect Britain from invasion, and in that of Three Unfortunate Disclosures, in which Arthur dug it up.

Bran is considered by some to be the inspiration for, or the prototype of, Bron the Fisher King. The association with the latter is strengthened by Bran's death from a wound made by a poisoned spear (the Fisher King having suffered from a poisoned wound through the thigh or genitals). Bran also possessed a magic horn—a horn of plenty that produced food and drink whenever they were desired—and some advocates of the Celtic theories relate that horn to the Grail, which, in Chrétien de Troyes's *Perceval*, contains a single Mass wafer capable of sustaining life indefinitely. There is a possibility that other characters, in particular Perceval's father, may also be descended from Bran; indeed, the mystery surrounding the name and identity of Bran makes him a versatile figure, and a character of the same name has even turned up (in Susan Cooper's series The Dark Is Rising, from the 1960s and 70s) as the son of Arthur and Guinevere. [NJL]

Newstead, Helaine. *Bran the Blessed in Arthurian Romance*. New York: Columbia University Press, 1939.

BRANDSTETTER, ALOIS, professor of medieval literature at the University of Klagenfurt, is one of the leading short-story writers in contemporary Austrian literature. *Die Burg* ("The Castle," 1986) belongs to the genre of academic novels: the narrator, a teaching assistant in medieval literature whose name is Arthur, tells of his unsuccessful quest for an academic career. A great number of Arthurian motifs and themes appear. The union of Arthurian and academic worlds notwithstanding, few similarities obtain between Brandstetter's novel and David Lodge's *Small World* (1984). [UM/PWM]

Brandstetter, Alois. *Die Burg*. Salzburg and Vienna: Residenz, 1986.

BRANGAENE (Brangwain, Brangien, Bringvain), Isolde's handmaid, who accompanies her on the fateful voyage to Britain, where Isolde is to marry King Mark of Cornwall. Brangaene brings a love potion, which is intended for Isolde and Mark, but Isolde and her escort, Tristan, mistakenly drink it during the voyage and become lovers. Isolde persuades Brangaene to take her place on her wedding night, so that Mark will believe the woman he has married is a virgin. Her name may derive from the Welsh "Branwen," a figure in the second branch of the *Mabinogi*, but as Brangien she appears first in French texts of the late twelfth century. [SW]

BRENTON, HOWARD, provoked controversy through violent language and action and by a merciless indictment of militaristic colonialism when *The Romans in Britain* was produced at London's National Theatre in 1980. Act I depicts Julius Caesar's invasion of Britain; Act II juxtaposes Britain in 515 and modern Ireland. At the end of the play, Arthur's name is mentioned to evoke a lost golden age. [CNS]

Brenton, Howard. *The Romans in Britain*. London: Eyre Methuen, 1980.

BRESSON, ROBERT, French director, whose controversial 1974 film *Lancelot du Lac* recounts the aftermath of the unsuccessful quest for the Grail and of Lancelot's failure to keep his promise to God not to continue his affair with Guenevere. Critical reaction to the film varied widely. Bresson's supporters termed it admirable, tender, and passionate, a cinematic poem that stands as one of his most beautiful masterpieces. Detractors saw it as arid, sterile, and pretentious. Despite such severe criticism, the film won the 1974 International Critics' Prize, which was, however, refused.

For the general outlines of its plot, the film owes much to the thirteenth-century *Mort Artu*. Bresson's interests, however, include more than simply charting the demise of Arthur's court. Originally entitled *The Grail*, the film is an apocalyptic meditation on the downfall of the Middle Ages because of the era's loss of a sense of the spiritual, which the Grail (intentionally absent from the film) symbolizes.

The film opens with Lancelot's unsuccessful return from the quest for the Grail. His failure to learn from the quest the value of the spiritual over the secular sets into motion a pattern of events that detail in gory bleakness the downfall of Camelot. But thanks to Bresson's use of anachronisms, the film is at times strikingly modern in its concerns. No one, the film seems to say, finds salvation, not Arthur, not his court—and especially not Lancelot, who dies in battle staring heavenward and murmuring Guenevere's name. [KJH]

Hanlon, Lindley. *Fragments: Robert Bresson's Film Style.* Rutherford, N.J.: Fairleigh Dickinson University Press, 1986.

Sloan, Jane. *Robert Bresson: A Guide to References and Resources.* Boston: G.K. Hall, 1983.

Williams, Alan. "On the Absence of the Grail." *Movietone News*, 47 (January 1976), 10–13.

BRETA SQGUR ("Sagas, or Stories, of the Britons"), the Old Norse version of Geoffrey of Monmouth's *Historia Regum Britanniae*. They are a free translation, with many additions and substitutions. Contractions and omissions, however, are much more common, particularly in the second half of the work. There are two redactions, and in each the *Breta sǫgur* follow *Trójumanna saga* (the Old Norse version of the Fall of Troy), and this probably accounts for one significant difference from Geoffrey. Geoffrey's dedication and his description of Britain are replaced by five chapters on the adventures of Aeneas. Chapter 6 then picks up Geoffrey's account of Brutus. The main narrative of the *Breta sǫgur* continues to follow that of Geoffrey's *Historia*, though within individual episodes the order of events is often varied. The Old Norse translator was more interested than Geoffrey in Christianity and, for example, substitutes the standard hagiographic story of St. Ursula for Geoffrey's secular version. He also takes particular interest in English ecclesiastical history. Other changes reflect the *Breta sǫgur*'s northern orientation. For example, Hengist and Horsa are accompanied by the hero Þiðrikr, and the list of Scandinavian countries occupied by Arthur is expanded. Geoffrey's *Prophetiae Merlini* appear in their proper place in a verse translation known as *Merlínusspá*, made by the Icelandic monk Gunnlaugr Leifsson. The *Breta sǫgur* conclude with an account of the West Saxon kings, which is not drawn from Geoffrey. Many minor variations and omissions may derive from the Latin exemplar, and others are almost certainly misreadings of the Latin. The *Breta sǫgur* were probably written early in the thirteenth century, although a slightly later date is also possible. Although both manuscripts in which the *Breta sǫgur* are preserved are Icelandic, it is uncertain whether the work was composed in Iceland or in Norway. The author of the *Breta sǫgur* is unknown, but the whole may be the work of Gunnlaugr Leifsson or one of his contemporaries.

[CLB]

Finnur Jónsson, ed. *Hauksbók, udgiven efter de Arnamagnæanske Håndskrifter No. 371, 544 og 675, 4° samt forskellige Papirhåndskrifter.* Copenhagen: Det kongelige nordiske Oldskrift-Selskab, 1892–96, pp. 231–301.

BREWER, GEORGE M., first presented *The Holy Grail* (1933), "A Whitsuntide Mystery of the Quest of the Soul," in the Church of the Messiah in Montreal. Written in blank verse and prose, the play moves from Christ's tomb in Jerusalem to Avalon, where Joseph of Arimathea and his brother Brons (Bran), the Fisher King, are commanded by the Archangel Gabriel to bear the Holy Grail and Spear of Longinus. There the Grail is identified with Keridwen's Cauldron of Plenty, while the Spear is used by Salome to wound Brons in a jealous rage. Five hundred years later, Percivale heals Brons and saves the repentant Salome (Kundrie), when he elevates the Grail while the Grail theme from Wagner's *Lohengrin* is played on the organ. [HT]

Brewer, George M. *The Holy Grail: A Whitsuntide Mystery of the Quest of the Soul.* Montreal: Printed for the author at The Herald Press, 1933.

BRIANT, THÉOPHILE, French author of the 1975 novel *Le Testament de Merlin*. Briant, who uses the Arthurian story as a framework for the presentation of philosophical views, depicts the magician as the founder of chivalry and tells us that it was Merlin, and not Arthur, who killed Mordred on Salisbury Plain. Merlin's power also prevented Arthur's death and permitted his departure for Avalon, after which the magician retired to Brocéliande to live with Viviane and to offer revelations of esoteric truths to his young friend Adragante. [NJL]

Briant, Théophile. *Le Testament de Merlin.* Nantes: Ballanger, 1975.

BRICKDALE, ELEANOR FORTISCUE (1872–1945), English illustrator best known for her interpretations of British literature in watercolor. Brickdale represents the third generation of the Pre-Raphaelite Arthurian vision. The exhibition of *Lancelot du Lake* in 1896 marked her debut in the Royal Academy as an artist in black-and-white, but wide recognition came in the first decades of the twentieth century with one-woman thematic shows in small London galleries. Many of these collections were subsequently published. In 1911, thirty-seven works, most drawn from Tennyson, were presented at the Leicester Gallery, resulting in two illustrated volumes of *Idylls of the King* (London: Hodder and Stoughton, 1910–12), the first a deluxe edition with twenty-one plates and the second a smaller and less expensive collection of twelve plates based on the first four *Idylls*, "Enid," "Vivien," "Elaine," and "Guinevere." Although heralded in the press as a "Pre-Raphaelite Revivalist" (*Truth*, June 20, 1901), Brickdale demonstrated little of the ethereality or decorative interest of Edward Burne-Jones or Dante Gabriel Rossetti; her style was instead distinguished by a strong narrative conception, reminiscent of Ford Madox Brown, and a solidity of figure and density of composition influenced by Walter Crane. After World War I, she abandoned Arthurian imagery, turning her attention to the design of war memorials and stained glass. The productivity of her last years was inhibited by failing health and incipient blindness. [DNM]

Taylor, G.L. *Centenary Exhibition of Works by Eleanor Fortiscue Brickdale 1872–1945.* Oxford: Ashmolean Museum, 1972.

BRIDIE, JAMES (pseudonym of Osborne Mavor; 1888–1951). Bridie contrasts civilization with natural life in the primitive utopia of Ultima Thule in *Holy Island* (1942). Though Margause, queen of Orkney, is Arthur's sister, little else is Arthurian in the play. *Lancelot* (written 1939, produced 1945) chronicles traditional events in modern language to show the knight's fall from grace when Merlin tricks him into sleeping with Elaine. A stage direction characterizes Arthur as an "etherealised Blimp." [CNS]

Bridie, James. *Lancelot* and *Holy Island.* In *Plays for Plain People.* London: Constable, 1944.

Bannister, Winifred. *James Bridie and His Theatre.* London: Rockliff, 1955.

BRITTANY, "Lesser" Britain as distinct from "Great" Britain: the northwest peninsula of France, inhabited by the Bretons, people of British descent whose ancestors played a major role in Arthurian legend-making. Under the Roman Empire, it was part of the somewhat larger territory of Armorican Gaul. Colonization from Britain began during the last phase of the empire in the West.

Welsh tradition associates the settlement with the emperor Maximus, who was proclaimed in Britain in 383 and captured Rome in 388 but was overthrown soon after. His army included numerous Britons, and according to the Welsh he allotted them lands on the Continent. Nennius (early ninth century) says: "He gave them many districts from the lake on top of Mount Jove to the city called Quentovic, as far as the Western Mass, that is the Western Ridge. They are the Armorican British, and they never came back, even to the present day." Nennius's statement spreads them out widely; by implication, it was the settlement in what is now Brittany that survived.

The story is enlarged on in the *Mabinogion* tale *The Dream of Macsen Wledig.* Here, Macsen—Maximus himself—marries the British princess Elen, and, when her brother Cynan brings a British army to Rome to aid him, he rewards Cynan's warriors for the consequent victory with a free hand in Armorica. They kill the men and marry the women, cutting out their tongues to prevent them from corrupting the British language with speech of their own. This is an onomastic legend. *Llydaw*, the Welsh name for Brittany, is made out to have been derived from *lled* 'half' and *taw* 'silent,' because only the male half of the population could speak.

Cynan or (in Breton) Conan, surnamed Meriadoc, is also depicted as the founder in the *Legend of St. Goeznovius.* Its author knows the tongue story but seems not to know the reason for it, so the point is lost. This Breton version says nothing of Maximus and treats Conan's colonization as a purely British enterprise.

There is some evidence for a British presence in Armorica at least as early as these accounts imply. But the first serious colonization took place in the late 450s, being marked historically by a reference to a "bishop of the Britons," Mansuetus, as attending a council at Tours in 461. Gildas describes the overseas movement as a flight of refugees from the Saxon ravagings, and so at first it presumably was. Yet the bulk of the emigration seems to have come from southwestern Britain, a long way from the Saxon enclaves. It is likely that some Britons went over in a more deliberate way by arrangement with Aegidius, the Roman ruler of northern Gaul, and cooperated during the next decade or so in coastal defense and other measures of control. The migrant leaders included people of wealth and education (Gildas says they took many books with them), and they apparently helped in the repulse and containment of Saxon marauders occupying the lower Loire valley. However, nothing suggests a cohesive mass settlement, transforming the character of the region, as early as this. The supposed case for it depends wholly on the assumption that a large British force that operated in Gaul ca. 468–70 was recruited in Armorica, implying a large British population already there. But the little that is recorded about this army indicates that most if not all of it came directly from Britain, and with the army eliminated as evidence not much remains.

The next step, in the later fifth century, was the beginning of an influx of "saints"—ecclesiastics, most of them Welsh, who crossed over from Britain and were active in organizing Breton communities. In the first half of the sixth century, a fresh wave of general emigration, on a larger scale, finally converted most of Armorica into "Brittany"; the names "Brittany" and "Armorica" became interchangeable. The country was nominally subject to the kings of the Franks but kept a decided character of its own. The earlier Armorican people were absorbed. Breton developed as a language in its own right, evolved from the Celtic British speech of the imperial era, like Welsh and Cornish. Brittany had local dynasties and retained economic and cultural ties with Cornwall. Several regional rulers may have held some kind of authority on both sides of the Channel.

Brittany's traditions of Arthur were strong, but mainly oral, so that their nature is a matter of inference rather than knowledge. To judge from the *Legend of St. Goeznovius*, they were built on a genuine historical foundation. But motifs of a poetic and fanciful sort may have originated here, too. Notable is the idea of Arthur's immortality and destined return, which is often mentioned as a Breton belief by a series of authors beginning with Henry of Huntingdon (*see* Return, Legends of Arthur's). Geoffrey of Monmouth shows a pro-Breton bias, pointing to his use of materials from that quarter, perhaps brought to England by Bretons returning to their ancestral island with the Norman conquerors, as many did. If the "ancient book in the British language" that he claims as his source had any reality, it is more likely to have come from Brittany than from Wales.

Breton stories, spread abroad by minstrels through France and beyond, probably underlie much Arthurian romance on the Continent. Arthur holds court in Brittany in Chrétien's *Cligés* and explicitly at Nantes in Wolfram's *Parzival*. Brittany figures in the Tristan legend and may have supplied some of its elements. Wace, who first mentions the Round Table, claims to have heard of it from the Bretons. He also mentions the enchanted forest of Brocéliande, in the heart of their country. He was disappointed with it himself, but it reappears in romance, and its remnants harbor Arthurian folklore to this day—as do other Breton locations. [GA]

Cavendish, Richard. *King Arthur and the Grail*. London: Weidenfeld and Nicolson, 1978, pp. 7, 23–26.

Chadwick, N.K. "The Colonisation of Brittany from Celtic Britain." *Proceedings of the British Academy*, 51 (1966).

———. *Early Brittany*. Cardiff: University of Wales Press, 1969.

Fleuriot, Léon. *Les Origines de la Bretagne*. Paris: Payot, 1980.

Hoepffner, Ernest. "The Breton Lais." In *Arthurian Literature in the Middle Ages*, ed. Roger Sherman Loomis. Oxford: Clarendon, 1959, pp. 112–21.

BROADSIDES were single sheets of paper that contained printing on only the front, or *recto*, side; the size of the sheet fluctuated between folio and sixteenmo. If the printing extended onto the reverse side as well, the page was called a "broadsheet"; when these sheets were folded together once, twice, or more times, they formed a small pamphlet termed a "chapbook" or "cheapbook," a forerunner of the modern paperback. Although the subject matter and style of these sheets were quite heterogeneous, ranging from verse to prose, from religious tract to bawdy tale, from bucolic poem to popular song, the broadside was particularly associated with the transmittal of a specific genre of popular literature, the ballad.

The practice of printing ballads on broadsides, first documented during the latter half of the fifteenth century, can be traced to the confluence of several causes: the decline of the professional minstrel, the invention of movable type (increasing literacy among the populace), and an insatiable demand for inexpensive reading material. Indeed, the broadside ballad may be seen as one of the first forms of popular literature produced on a mass scale. It was simple to print, it was within the reach of even the poorest as it sold for only pennies, and it could be hawked anywhere. The broadside ballad attained maximum popularity during the sixteenth and seventeenth centuries; thereafter, although it lingered on until the late nineteenth century, it was supplanted in large measure by the production of chapbooks. From the sixteenth through the eighteenth centuries, a Gothic typeface called "Black-Letter" was used; from the eighteenth century onward, the Black-Letter type was replaced with a Roman type called "White-Letter." The text was printed in four columns, and then the page was divided in half, each leaf being sold separately. Frequently, a decorative woodcut illustration preceded the text.

The broadside was an ephemeral form of literature; as

such, it was destined for momentary consumption: to be read, reread, and then discarded. Consequently, the broadsides that have survived until the modern era represent only a small fraction of the thousands printed during the Renaissance and Baroque.

The history of the broadside ballad has been intertwined from the first with that of the Arthurian tradition. The earliest broadsides in England, dating from the last two decades of the fifteenth century, were the work of the presses of William Caxton, the first editor of Thomas Malory's *Le Morte Darthur*. Other famous collectors of broadside ballads, such as Sir Walter Scott and Alfred Lord Tennyson, participated in the later Arthurian Revival. Two of the earliest broadsides, from ca. 1508, treat Arthurian themes: one is a version of *Sir Eglamour*, and the other is a metrical romance of *Golagros and Gawane*. Other examples of Arthurian ballads that circulated on broadsides include "Sir Lionel," "The Boy and the Mantle," "King Arthur and King Cornwall," and "The Marriage of Sir Gawain."

Broadsides are of invaluable worth to scholars, as they attest to the ceaseless fluctuations wrought by word-of-mouth dissemination: the addition or deletion of characters, the rearrangement of existing scenes, and the insertion of new material. From the broadside, scholars can more accurately trace the evolution of cycles like the Arthurian, for these texts, reflecting the oral tradition, help to bridge the gap between the different manifestations of the material in manuscript form. [JK]

Child, Francis James, ed. *The English and Scottish Popular Ballads*. Boston: Houghton-Mifflin, 1884.

Shepherd, Leslie. *The Broadside Ballad: A Study in Origins and Meaning*. Wakefield, West Yorkshire: E.P., 1978.

BROADSIDES (SPANISH), or *pliegos sueltos* ("loose sheets") as they are termed in Spanish, derive their name from the format in which they were sold. Analogous to their English counterparts, they consisted of a page folded in half lengthwise, each half being sold separately. Printers of broadsides in Spain also made use of a Gothic type (*letra gótica*), placed woodcut illustrations above the text, and frequently indicated the melody to which the ballad was to be sung. The practice in Spain of printing ballads on broadsides follows the same chronology as the rest of Europe, with the sixteenth and seventeenth centuries being the period of greatest production.

Broadsides play a pivotal role in the history of Spanish literature, for they are a direct link with the late Middle Ages. If it were not for the printers and collectors who became interested in the oral-traditional literature circulating around them and who rescued such literature from oblivion by preserving it on broadsides, an entire literary epoch would have been lost. Even more significantly, broadsides were the raw material from which the compilers of the sixteenth- and seventeenth-century songbooks drew their versions of ballads and other songs. Such is the case with the only three ballads of Arthurian material that have survived on the Iberian peninsula: one deals with Tristan and Isolde ("Herido está don Tristán") and the other two with Lancelot ("Nunca fuera caballero" and "Tres hijuelos había el rey"). Precious relics of a much larger ballad cycle, these three poems hint at what must have been a flourishing Arthurian tradition on the Iberian peninsula. [JK]

Rodríguez-Moñino, Antonio, ed. *Diccionario de pliegos sueltos poéticos (siglo XVI)*. Madrid: Castalia, 1970.

BROCÉLIANDE. The forest of Brocéliande, identified with the forest of Paimpont about midway between Dinan and Rennes in modern-day Brittany, was famous throughout the Middle Ages for its enchantments, in particular its storm-making spring, known sometimes as the fountain of Barenton. The spring is central to Chrétien de Troyes's *Yvain* and is mentioned by Giraldus Cambrensis. Wace in a famous passage of his *Roman de Rou* recounts how he traveled to Brocéliande to seek the marvels about which the Bretons spoke but was unable to find any: "I saw the forest and I saw the land; I looked for marvels, but I did not find them" (*Roman de Rou*, ed. Holden, ll. 6,393–95). In the sequels to the Old French prose romances devoted to Merlin, Brocéliande is the site of the enchanted prison in which Niniane holds Merlin captive. The forest is also mentioned in the Old French *Tournoiement Anticrist*, by Huon de Méry, in *Claris et Laris*, and in *Brun de la Montagne*, as well as in the German romance of *Garel von dem blühenden Tal*, by Der Pleier. [WWK]

BRON (Hebron), Joseph of Arimathea's brother-in-law and Alain's father; were it possible to trace him back far enough, he might well be related to Bran the Blessed. In Robert de Boron's romance *Joseph*, he catches a fish, which he places on the Grail table, and is thereafter known as the Rich Fisher. One seat at the table is reserved for Bron's son or grandson—Robert contradicts himself here—and we learn that Alain himself will have a son who is to be a keeper of the Grail. Eventually, Alain and then a certain Petrus depart for the west, to the "vales of Avaron" or Avalon; later, Bron follows them, taking with him the Grail, which he has received from Joseph.

In the Didot-*Perceval*, Perceval is the son of Alain and thus the grandson of Bron, the Fisher King. At the end of the romance, Perceval heals Bron's wounds by asking the Grail question. The old king instructs Perceval about the Grail and then dies, to be replaced by the young man. [NJL]

Newstead, Helaine. *Bran the Blessed in Arthurian Romance*. New York: Columbia University Press, 1939.

BROOKE, MAXEY, author of a number of stories, including an Arthurian mystery, "Morte d'Alain: An Unrecorded Idyll of the King" (1969). Merlin's apprentice recounts how his master solved a mystery surrounding the murder of one of Arthur's knights. [SRR]

Brooke, Maxey. "Morte d'Alain: An Unrecorded Idyll of the King." In *Rogues' Gallery: A Variety of Mystery Stories*, ed. Walter Gibson. Garden City, N.Y.: Doubleday, 1969, pp. 265–73.

BROOKS, BENJAMIN GILBERT, British poet, provides a surreal vision of the end of Arthur's reign in "Camelot" (1919). Guenivere is a Middle Eastern queen, Gawaine her executioner, and Modred slays Arthur in the midst of decadent splendor as Camelot falls in some 200 lines of extravagant imagery. [DN]

Brooks, Benjamin. *Camelot*. Oxford: Blackwell, 1919.

BROTHER ROBERT, active during the first half of the thirteenth century, produced in 1226 a Norwegian translation of Thomas d'Angleterre's *Tristan* entitled *Tristrams saga ok Ísöndar*. This translation, the only complete version of the Thomas branch of the legend, influenced the dissemination of Tristan material in Scandinavia and exerted influence especially in Iceland, where a ballad, "Tristrams kvæði," and a prose adaptation, *Saga af Tristram ok Ísodd*, were produced. Robert's name also appears in *Elis saga* (a translation of *Elie de St. Gille*, a *chanson de geste*), but with the title "Abbot." Scholars have associated Robert with the Norwegian translations of several Arthurian works made during King Hákon's reign (1217–63): *Ívens saga* and *Parcevals saga* (based on Chrétien de Troyes's *Yvain* and *Perceval*), *Möttuls saga* (a version of the fabliau *Le Mantel mautaillié*), and *Strengleikar* (a collection of twenty-one lais). His nationality is unknown, but his name suggests Anglo-Norman origins. Given the ties with England during Hákon's reign, Brother Robert may have been a cleric associated with Norwegian monasteries, at Lyse or Hovedøya, which maintained close ties with England. Although Robert's name is linked with certainty only to two translations, they were both commissioned by King Hákon and thus attest the Norwegian king's interest in French fiction and his role in the transmission of Arthurian material in Scandinavia. (*See also* TRISTAN IN SCANDINAVIA; *TRISTRAMS SAGA OK ÍSÖNDAR*.) [IJR]

Leach, Henry G. *Angevin Britain and Scandinavia*. Cambridge: Harvard University Press, 1921.

Schach, Paul. "Some Observations on the Translations of Brother Robert." In *Les Relations littéraires franco-scandinaves au Moyen Âge: Actes du Colloque de Liège*. Paris: Société d'Édition "Les Belles Lettres," 1975, pp. 117–35.

BROUGH, WILLIAM (1826–1870), British journalist and dramatist. His *King Arthur, or the Days and Knights of the Round Table* is a "Christmas Extravaganza" that relies heavily on puns, horseplay, and parody. It was first performed at the Theatre Royal, Haymarket, December 26, 1863, with Ellen Terry as Tristram. According to Brough, it is "founded on the various legends of 'the Blameless King' including Tennyson's fanciful 'Idylls' and the author's own idyl fancies." Lavish costumes, scenery, machinery, and music make it a multimedia production, as the actors cavort through the Saxon kidnaping of Guenevere, the enchantments of Arthur and Merlin, and Morgan's nefarious schemes. All are reunited at the Christmas feast. [MAW]

Brough, William. *King Arthur, or the Days and Knights of the Round Table*. In *Lacy's Acting Edition of Plays, Dramas, Farces, Extravaganzas*. London: Thomas Hailes Lacy, n.d., Vol. 61.

BROWNJOHN, ALAN CHARLES, uses catchy West Indian rhythms for his sardonic "Calypso for Sir Bedivere." The traditional tale of the knight hesitating about casting the sword into the lake is transformed, as the worldly-wise Bedivere discovers it is impossible to deceive the wise old king who had been outsmarting everybody since Excalibur came into his possession. [CNS]

Brownjohn, Alan. "Calypso for Sir Bedivere." In *Warrior's Career*. London: Macmillan, 1972; and in *Collected Poems, 1952–83*. London: Secker and Warburg, 1983.

BRUCE, SIR CHARLES (1836–1920), was a British colonial governor whose *The Story of Queen Guenevere and Sir Lancelot of the Lake* (1865) was adapted from a work by Wilhelm Hertz. Written in octosyllabic couplets, it follows Malory's *Morte Darthur* from the lovers' entrapment to their deaths. Departures from this source include Arthur's depiction as "a weary old man" with a young wife; the reconciliation of Arthur and Guenevere in Lancelot's castle, where the Queen nurses her wounded husband; Gawain's suicide in preference to reconciliation; Mordred's jealous passion for the Queen; and Lancelot's supervision of Arthur's burial. The mad Mordred, having fatally stabbed Guenevere, confesses the crime to the priest, Lancelot. In the ensuing fight, Mordred dies and Lancelot is fatally wounded. He succumbs at Guenevere's deathbed, and, like Tristan and Isolde, they are buried together. [MAW]

Bruce, Sir Charles. *The Story of Queen Guenevere and Sir Lancelot of the Lake*. London: Longman, Green, 1865.

BRUMM, CHARLES, World War I poet who describes his *In Quest of the Holy Grail* (1921) as "withered leaves from my war diary." Taking his inspiration from medieval knights who symbolize "man's pursuit of the highest and holiest," Brumm calls for a brotherhood to make war on the idea of war so that the Holy Grail may be achieved. Though not strictly Arthurian, the poems utilize chivalric imagery. [MAW]

Brumm, Charles. *In Quest of the Holy Grail: A Hermit's War Lyrics*, rev. ed. London: Daniel, 1921.

BRUN DE LA MONTAGNE, a late fourteenth-century French adventure romance in monorhyme couplets. It survives, incomplete, in a single manuscript (Paris, B.N. fr. 2170). The broad outline of the plot, however, is evident from the three predictions made by fays at his birth. Brun's father, Butor, has his son left overnight in the forest of "Bersillant," where the three fays' predictions are overheard. The first two predict that he will be of exceptional beauty and courtesy and that he will be a champion in war and tournament. But the third fay announces that he will be unfortunate in love, so much so that he will see his beloved prefer a hunchbacked dwarf whom she will marry before his very eyes. One of the first two fays secretly places a golden ring on his finger. For the rest of his life, he will be under her protection. Later she announces his fate but comforts him with the promise that after ten years he will find a new, happier love. Most of the remainder of the plot is taken up with combat. It breaks off just as he declares his love and is spurned.

Arthurian elements punctuate the slow-moving plot. The forest where Brun's adventures occur has obvious affinities with Brocéliande. Brun himself is nicknamed Tristan because of his unhappiness in love. Arthur is in the background as lord of the forest and the fairies. The castle where Brun meets his cruel love belongs to Morgain la Fee. [DK]

Meyer, Paul, ed. *Brun de la Montagne*. Paris: Firmin Didot, 1875.

BRUNDAGE, BURR C., American poet who wrote *The King Who Cast No Shadow* (1986), a volume in free verse, which presents Arthur against a background of conflict between the Roman and the Celtic influences in Britain. The title refers to the fact that the Arthur of legend is just a name and so casts no shadow, even though a real man who "left a shadow" lies behind the legend. [ACL]

Brundage, Burr C. *The King Who Cast No Shadow*. Lanham, Md.: University Press of America, 1986.

BRUNNER, JOHN, British writer of science fiction, wrote a novel using Arthurian motifs, *Father of Lies* (1968). Under the influence of Tennyson's Arthurian tales, a young boy in Victorian England, with a fantastic power of mental projection, turns his father's baronial estate into Logres, an Arthurian kingdom with himself as absolute ruler. There are dragons and ogres, his people speak Old English, and radios and cars will not work within his sphere of influence. In the mid-twentieth century, a group of university students, investigating inconsistencies in the Ordnance Survey map, stumble into this realm, release the boy's father (trapped inside an oak-tree from which he would speak oracularly when invoked), and help to destroy the child-tyrant and bring his people into the modern era. [SRR]

Brunner, John. *Father of Lies*. New York: Belmont, 1968. (Bound together with *Mirror Image*, by Bruce Duncan.)

BRUTUS, legendary founder of Britain, according to Geoffrey of Monmouth, who explains that Brutus was the great-grandson of Aeneas. Arriving in Albion, Brutus established himself as king and renamed the island after himself (a spurious but not atypical example of medieval etymologizing). He established his capital at a new city called New Troy, later to become London. His name provided the title for Wace's *Roman de Brut*, Layamon's *Brut*, and other chronicles. [NJL]

BRYHER (pseudonym of Annie Winifred Ellerman; 1894–1983), English editor and author of the historical novel *Ruan* (1960), which is set in sixth-century Britain. Inspired by a harper's tale of Gawain setting forth on a voyage to Avalon, a young Cornish boy rejects a secure life ashore for that of a sailor and eventually himself embarks on a voyage to search for a mysterious western island. The author's fascination with Avalon is seen again in *Visa for Avalon* (1965), a novel in a contemporary setting with a number of Arthurian allusions. [RHT]

Bryher. *Ruan*. New York: Pantheon, 1960.

———. *Visa for Avalon*. New York: Harcourt, Brace, World, 1965.

BUCHANAN, GEORGE. Although considered a Scottish humanist, Buchanan followed Hector Boece fairly closely in the account of Arthur that he presented in his *Rerum Scoticarum Historia* (1582); changes from the source tend to make Arthur's character worse than it is in Boece. He also finds the account of Arthur's conception a fiction invented by Merlin and Uther to lessen Igerne's shame, and he has Guenevere help Mordred plan Arthur's downfall. (*See also* BOECE, HECTOR.) [EDK]

Buchanan, George. *Rerum Scoticarum Historia*. Edinburgh: Arbuthnet, 1582.

———. *The History of Scotland*, trans. John Watkins. London: Fisher, Jackson, 1827.

Göller, K.H. "König Arthur in den schottischen Chroniken." *Anglia*, 80 (1962), 390–404.

BULLA, CLYDE ROBERT, promotes truthfulness, persistence, and loyalty in his children's story *The Sword in the Tree* (1956). Deprived of his home by a devious uncle, eleven-year-old Shan journeys to King Arthur's court, where, despite Sir Kay's intimidation, he convinces Arthur to send Sir Gareth to help rescue his father and his castle. [RWK]

Bulla, Clyde Robert. *The Sword in the Tree*. New York: Crowell, 1956.

BULWER-LYTTON, EDWARD GEORGE (1803–1873), wrote two Arthurian poems, "The Fairy Bride" (1853), a brief tale of a young knight's unhappy encounter with an unearthly lover, and *King Arthur* (1848), a twelve-book epic recounting the triumph of Arthur and his Britons over a Saxon invasion. In *King Arthur*, Bulwer-Lytton creates his own narrative, rather than reshape traditional Arthurian materials, and fashions his own personal allegory of Arthur's career as the genesis of British political freedom. He recasts Guenevere as two separate persons (Arthur's bride, Genevieve, and Lancelot's bride, Genevra), thereby eliminating the issue of Lancelot's and Guenevere's adultery, which is central to the Arthurian poems of his contemporaries Tennyson and Morris.

Bulwer-Lytton's son, Edward Robert Bulwer Lytton, himself wrote three Arthurian poems. [MDC]

Lytton, Edward George Earle Lytton Bulwer-. *King Arthur*. London: Colburn, 1848.

Bulwer-Lytton, Victor Alexander. *The Life of Edward Bulwer, First Lord Lytton*. 2 vols. London: Macmillan, 1913.

BURGESS, ANTHONY, British author, examined aspects of Welsh and Israeli nationalism while following the fortunes of two interrelated families through the first half of this century in his novel *Any Old Iron* (1989). Excalibur, the "iron" of the title, figures in the story as the sword of Attila and Arthur. Preserved for centuries by the Benedictines, it is captured by the Russians in World War II and then stolen back to Britain by one of the novel's major characters. There, it becomes a symbol for the Sons of Arthur, a Welsh nationalist group. [DN]

Burgess, Anthony. *Any Old Iron*. London: Hutchinson, 1989.

BURGHLEY NEF. Ship models made of precious materials were often used as incense boats, reliquaries, and votive offerings in the late Middle Ages. Secular pieces, known as nefs, may originally have been made as drinking vessels; they were related only in the most general form to these ecclesiastical pieces. The Burghley Nef (Victoria and Albert Museum, London) has a nautilus shell for its hull, and the poop and fo'c'sle are formed of ornamental open battlements. Fully rigged, swarming with sailors, and armed with so many guns that one cannon seems to be aimed at the main mast, this fantastic creation glides over a silver sea on the back of a silver mermaid. The nef also has cast-silver passengers, a young couple seated in front of the main mast who seem to have been playing chess but now clasp hands and gaze fondly at each other. The figures depicted can only be Tristan and Isolde on the voyage to Cornwall. Although the salt is a Renaissance piece, in date and in some ways in style, bearing the Paris hallmarks for 1527–28, its type is of

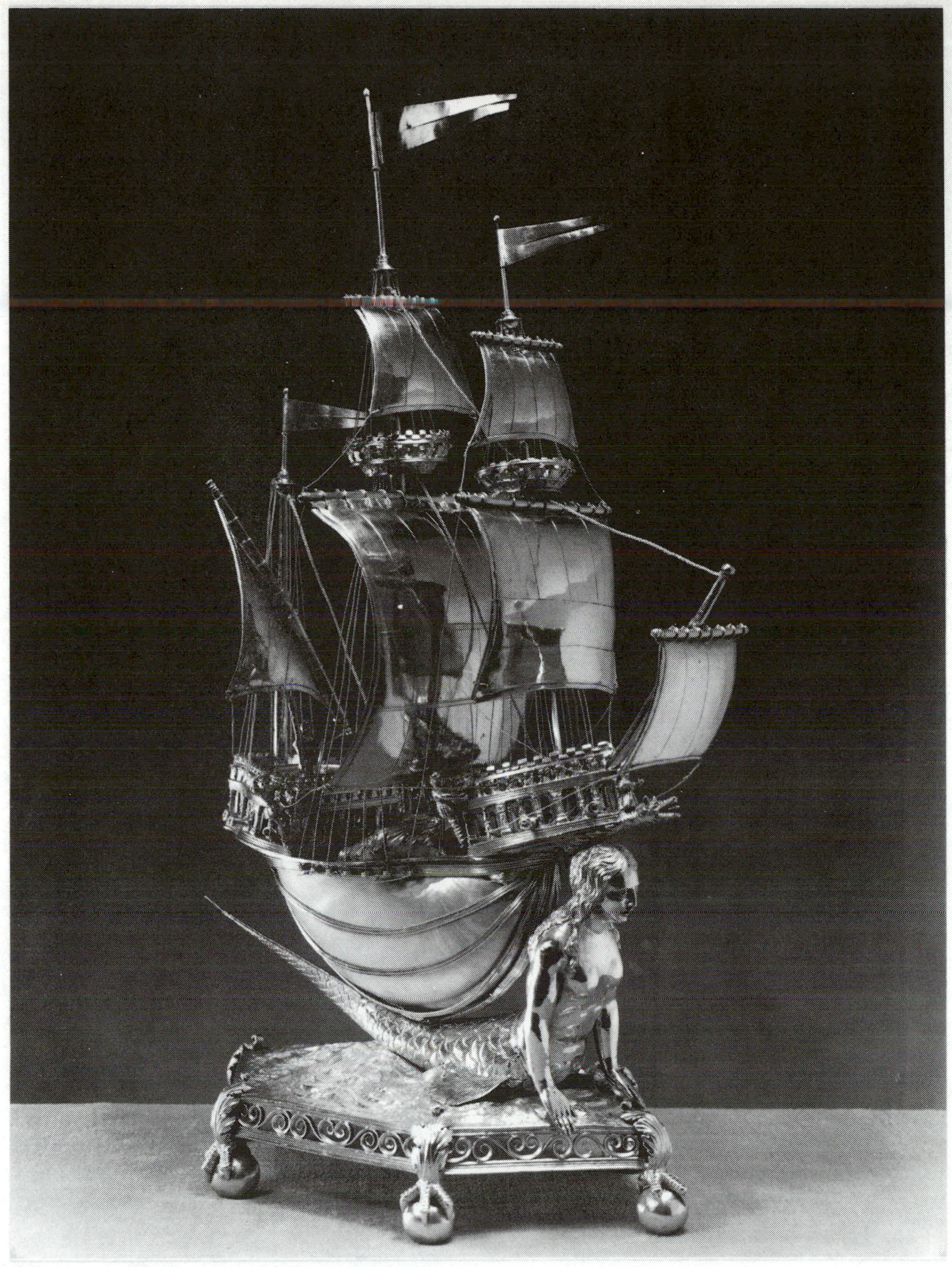

15. Burghley Nef. (Victoria and Albert Museum, London.)

16. Edward Burne-Jones, *Arthur at Avalon*. (Courtesy Museo de Arte de Ponce, Puerto Rico.)

medieval origin, such as described and illustrated in French and English sources from at least the fourteenth century. [MS]

Oman, Charles. *Medieval Silver Nefs*. London: Victoria and Albert Museum, 1963.

BURNE-JONES, EDWARD (1833–1898), a painter who featured Arthurian subjects throughout his oeuvre. It is his visual interpretation that is associated with the mid- to late Arthurian Revival. His attenuated figures, floating in a dreamlike setting, were influential; his style provided the prototype for the later Victorian painters, such as Edwin Austen Abbey and John William Waterhouse, and even more extensively for book illustrators, especially Aubrey Beardsley, Walter Crane, and Arthur Rackham.

Burne-Jones became acquainted with Arthurian subjects at Exeter College, Oxford, in 1853, when he was introduced to the poetry of Tennyson by his friend William Morris. In 1855, Morris gave him the Southey edition of *Le Morte Darthur*, a volume he had coveted but could not afford. Their mutual enthusiasm for Malory influenced Pre-Raphaelite painter Dante Gabriel Rossetti, as seen in the Oxford Union Murals project (1857), in which Burne-Jones painted *The Death of Merlin*. His interest in Tennyson revived in 1858, when he met the poet and was inspired to draw many Arthurian subjects, including *Sir Galahad* (Fogg Art Museum, Cambridge).

In the next two decades, his elongated figure style and evocative Arthurian vision gained maturity. The former

17. Edward Burne-Jones, *The Beguiling of Merlin*. (Lady Lever Art Gallery, Port Sunlight.)

is seen in the Dunlop Windows project (1862), while the latter emerged in such non-Arthurian but chivalric works as *The Merciful Knight* (1863, Birmingham City Art Gallery) and *Le Chant d'Amour* (1865, Museum of Fine Arts, Boston). The innocent dream world took on erotic connotations in *The Beguiling of Merlin* (1875–77, Lady Lever Art Gallery, Port Sunlight), in which he blended ideas from Tennyson and French romance.

In the last decades of his life, his Arthurian interest increased. A sketchbook of 1885 (British Museum, London) contains extensive notes on Arthurian heraldry, foreshadowing the decorative-arts designs of the subsequent years, including the Rottingden Windows (1886, Victoria and Albert Museum, London) and the Stanmore Hall Tapestries (1891–94, Collection, Duke of Westminster), both illustrating the quest for the Holy Grail. In 1895, he designed scenery and costumes for J. Comyns Carr's drama *King Arthur* (lost, known through sketchbooks). He was to have illustrated a luxury edition of *Le Morte Darthur* for Morris's Kelmscott Press; the project was abandoned, but he did design a frontispiece and title page for each of the two volumes of Sebastian Evans's *The High History of the Holy Graal* (London: Dent, 1898). His culminating work was *Arthur in Avalon* (1880–98, Museum of Art, Ponce, Puerto Rico), an enormous project, unfinished at his death. The artist felt it to be the summation of all his ideals in art. He defined his Arthurian vision in writing to Thomas Rooke, who was on holiday in Avallon, Burgundy, in 1886: "But how is it that you are at Avalon, where I have striven to be with all my might." [DNM]

Arts Council of Great Britain. *The Paintings, Graphic and Decorative Work of Sir Edward Burne-Jones*. Great Britain: The Arts Council of Great Britain, 1975.

Burne-Jones, Georgiana. *Memorials of Edward Burne-Jones*. 2 vols. London: Macmillan, 1906.

Harrison, Martin, and Bill Waters. *Burne-Jones*. New York: Putnam, 1973.

Poulson, Christine. "Costume Designs by Burne-Jones for Irving's Production of *King Arthur*." *Burlington Magazine*, 128 (January 1986), 324–28.

BURNHAM, JEREMY, and TREVOR RAY, authors of *Raven* (1977), a fantasy for adolescents based upon their own screenplay for a British television series of the same name. A rebellious youth emerges as reluctant leader of a conservationist movement to save an ancient network of caves linked with Arthur's cave legend. There are suggestions that the hero is Arthur reborn and that his mentor is Merlin. [RHT]

Burnham, Jeremy, and Trevor Ray. *Raven*. London: Corgi, 1977.

BUTOR, BAUDUIN. Author of four drafts of the beginning of a thirteenth-century Arthurian prose romance in French. Following a prologue, the narrator recounts King Constant de Logre's death, which leaves three young sons at the mercy of Vertigier, who is seeking to usurp the throne. This narrative draws on material already presented in Geoffrey of Monmouth's *Historia Regum Britanniae* and Wace's *Roman de Brut* and elaborated in Robert de Boron's *Merlin*. One of the drafts presents, in addition, the loves of Pandragus, one of Constant's sons, and Libanor.

The text was written on the blank leaves and in the margins of manuscript Paris, B.N. fr. 1446 (probably an autograph manuscript). The author names as his patrons the Count of Flanders Guy de Dampierre and his son-in-law Hughes de Châtillon; the first two drafts also name Jean II d'Avesnes, who was Count of Hainaut under the name of Jean I and nephew and rival of the Count of Flanders.

Since Guy de Dampierre was consistently presented both as Count of Flanders and Marquis of Namur, the four texts must have been composed while Guy had both titles, that is, between 1263 and 1297. Moreover, since Butor identifies Hughes de Châtillon as the Count of Blois, the composition must postdate 1292, when Hugh received that title. The third prologue is dated 1295.

Bauduin Butor describes his work as a *contes desrimez* (a prosified or "de-rhymed" tale); whether it is the prosification of a verse text or an original composition in prose is uncertain. The same expression is found in the *Cassidorus*, a sequel to the *Sept Sages de Rome*, also written for Guy de Dampierre. As a result, Lewis Thorpe suggested that Butor may also have been the author of *Cassidorus*. The hypothesis was originally accepted but later rejected by Joseph Palermo, the editor of the *Cassidorus*. [C-AVC]

Flutre, L.F. "Le Roman de *Pandragus et Libanor* par Baudouin Butor: texte inédit de la fin du XIIIe siècle." *Romania*, 94 (1973), 57–90.

Thorpe, Lewis. "Les 'contes desrimez' et les premiers romans en prose." In *Mélanges de langue et de littérature du Moyen Age et de la Renaissance offerts à Jean Frappier*. Paris: Droz, 1970, Vol. 2, pp. 1031–41.

———. "The Four Rough Drafts of Bauduins Butors." *Nottingham Medieval Studies*, 12 (1968), 3–20; 13 (1969), 49–64; 14 (1970), 41–63.

BUTTS, W. MARLIN, wrote *The Youth of King Arthur* (1935), a short play for young people "originally produced at Camp Camelot, Foxboro, Mass." Using archaic diction, it depicts Arthur's success in withdrawing the sword from the stone, as told in Malory. [RHT]

Butts, W. Marlin. *The Youth of King Arthur: A Legendary Play in Five Scenes*. East Boston: Published by the author, 1935.

C

CABELL, JAMES BRANCH (1879–1958), American novelist whose most famous work was *Jurgen: A Comedy of Justice* (1919). This picaresque romance recounts the adventures of Jurgen, a thirteenth-century pawnbroker in the mythical realm of Poictesme, married to a shrewish wife, Dame Lisa. Like Faust, he magically regains his youth and embarks on an amatory odyssey through time, his conquests including a pliant Guenevere, the Lady of the Lake, and Helen of Troy.

Although the Arthurian characters are peripheral, *Jurgen* follows the pattern of many twentieth-century American works on Arthur, in that it satirizes the excesses of Arthur's chivalric world, such as nonpareil yet adulterous ladies, jousting at the drop of a lance, and overly idealistic tenets for establishing a social order in a Christian world. Cabell ironically mocks the restrictive sexual and religious mores of his own time; the book was banned and of course became a bestseller. *Jurgen*, however, is a witty, erudite comedy, if not of justice then of human nobility battling with and being undercut by human frailty. It is in every way the best work in Cabell's eighteen-volume Biography of the Life of Manuel, and represents an original adaptation of Arthurian material.

Among the many restless figures searching for their heart's desire in *Something About Eve* (1927), another volume in the Manuel series, is Merlin. His confinement in an enchanted tower in the company of a loving Nimuë was voluntary, he confides, but he eventually tired of domestic bliss, in contrast to the protagonist, Gerald, who chooses to abandon his heroic quest for the comforts of domesticity.

In "The Eighth Letter: To Sir Galahad of the Siege Perilous" (1934), the author criticizes the "supernal holiness" that destroyed the "genial and broad-minded spirit of compromise" necessary for the survival of Arthur's kingdom.
[VML/RHT]

Cabell, James Branch. *Jurgen: A Comedy of Justice*. New York: McBride, 1919.

———. *Something About Eve: A Comedy of Fig-Leaves*. New York: McBride, 1927.

———. "The Eighth Letter: To Sir Galahad of the Siege Perilous." In *Ladies and Gentlemen: A Parcel of Reconsiderations*. New York: McBride, 1934, pp. 109–21.

———. *The Letters of James Branch Cabell*, ed. Edward Wagenknecht. Norman: University of Oklahoma Press, 1975.

Cover, James P. *Notes on Jurgen*. New York: McBride, 1928.

CADBURY-CAMELOT. Cadbury Castle, an Iron Age hill fort beside the village of South Cadbury in Somerset, has three features of Arthurian interest: first, its longstanding designation by the name *Camelot*; second, a miscellany of local folklore related to this; and third, its proved reoccupation and refortification during the period within which Arthur supposedly lived.

There was never a castle here in the medieval sense. The hill itself is the castle, being made so by its huge system of earthwork ramparts, now largely overgrown with woods but still exposed in places. The topmost bank of the fout encircles an eighteen-acre enclosure, rising to a summit plateau 500 feet above sea level. John Leland, in his *Itinerary* (1542), wrote: "At the very south end of the church of South-Cadbyri standeth Camallate, sometime a famous town or castle. . . . The people can tell nothing there but that they have heard say Arthur much resorted to Camalat."

Leland uses the name as if it were an accepted one. Arguably, he is merely speculating, prompted by the place-name *Camel* that occurs in the neighborhood. By itself, this hardly seems a sufficient explanation, and folklore may also have played a part. A version of the Arthurian cave legend probably already existed here. In its modern form, it asserts that a pair of gates concealed in the hillside swing open once a year, revealing the sleeping king. There is sixteenth-century evidence for the highest part of the hill being known as Arthur's Palace. Further legends, recorded in more recent times, may or may not be old. On Midsummer Eve or Midsummer Night or Christmas Eve (it is doubtful which, and it may be only every seven years), the ghosts of Arthur and his knights ride across the hilltop and out through the ancient gateway in the fortifications. Below, a track running toward Glastonbury is Arthur's Hunting Causeway, and on winter nights, it is said, spectral riders and horses can be heard on it. The nearby River Cam is eligible as Camlann, the scene of the battle in which Arthur fell.

After Leland, other antiquaries, such as Stukeley, take up the "Camelot" theme, and the name appears on maps, justifying its use to distinguish this Cadbury from others. Any deeper significance must depend on definitions. The Camelot of the romancers who created it is a medieval dream-city that it would be futile to seek anywhere. It has, however, the special attribute of being peculiarly King Arthur's capital; no other monarch reigns there; and Cadbury

18. Cadbury Castle, aerial view. (Photograph courtesy of Simon McBride.)

could be claimed as "the real Camelot" so far as anything ever was, if it were connected in some way with the original Arthur, having (for example) been refurbished as his personal citadel. It would be the far-off reality behind the Camelot of the romancers. This is a possibility that the archaeology of the site may be held to raise.

The principal excavation was carried out during 1966-70 under the direction of Leslie Alcock. It confirmed an Iron Age settlement on the plateau, with which the defenses were associated. This survived undisturbed for some time after the Roman conquest of southern Britain. Then the hill was stormed and captured. The inference is that Cadbury was a center of resistance in some unrecorded British revolt, possibly an offshoot of Boudicca's in A.D. 60-61. The Roman period was followed by a complete gap, after which the dating evidence of imported pottery attests reoccupation.

This phase of the site—Cadbury 11, in Alcock's terminology—may have begun ca. 460 or at any time over the next few decades, but not much after 500. Buildings belonging to it include a timber hall on the plateau, in the "Arthur's Palace" area, and a gatehouse reminiscent of Roman auxiliary forts. However, the most striking feature is embedded in the topmost bank: a drystone wall about sixteen feet thick running around the entire perimeter, a distance of nearly three-quarters of a mile. This massive enhancement of the rampart incorporated pieces of Roman masonry and was bound together by a framework of wooden beams. Celtic, not Roman, in style, it was a fairly sophisticated structure embodying an impressive amount of labor.

At the time of its discovery, Cadbury 11 was interpreted as an army base. Since the scale and elaborateness of the refortification were archaeologically unmatched in that period, the results permitted a connection with Arthur conceived as the war-leader of Welsh tradition. Over the next few years, it was widely assumed that Cadbury's apparent uniqueness was accidental, and the excavation of other hill forts would refute it. This did not happen. Reoccupation during the same period was proved in various places, but the stone-and-timber defensive work remained without a contemporary parallel in the archaeology of England and Wales. Comparable structures were found in Scotland but were markedly smaller and had no gatehouses. In a 1982 reassessment, Alcock suggested that Cadbury was a political center rather than a military one, the seat of a king with resources of wealth and manpower unequaled, on the existing evidence, in the Britain of his time.

Considered historically, such a view raises the issue of the British high kingship that appears to have existed at least in name during much of the fifth century. It is interesting that Vortigern, a holder of this office, is portrayed by Nennius as trying to build himself a personal fortress on a hill in Wales. Moreover, he uses "timber and stones," as at Cadbury. Though the story may be fictitious, it hints that "timber and stones" were regarded as the proper materials for a high king's citadel. A project like the one ascribed to Vortigern might have been actually undertaken at Cadbury by a successor.

Whether this successor can be meaningfully equated with Arthur is a question outside the scope of archaeology. (*See* ARTHUR, ORIGINS OF LEGEND.) But the nature of Cadbury 11 makes it less likely that Leland's Camelot identification was a pure guess. Somehow, he hit on what is easily the most appropriate site throughout Britain. Even a modern archaeologist could not have picked it out on a visual appraisal alone, without excavation. As perhaps at Castle Dore and Tintagel, some kind of tradition is probable. The actual romantic name need not have been part of it, since by the sixteenth century "Camelot" was familiar as the name of Arthur's home, and Leland could simply have applied it to a place where he understood that home to have been.

A literary by-product of the work at Cadbury was the choice of this location for Camelot by novelists, such as Marion Zimmer Bradley, Catherine Christian, and Mary Stewart. [GA]

Alcock, Leslie. *"By South Cadbury Is That Camelot . . .": Excavations at Cadbury Castle 1966–70*. London: Thames and Hudson, 1972, Chapters 1–4, 8.

———. "Cadbury-Camelot: A Fifteen-Year Perspective." *Proceedings of the British Academy*, 68 (1983).

CAEN CAPITAL, a capital in the church of St.-Pierre, Caen, illustrating two scenes from Arthurian romances—Lancelot crossing the Sword Bridge and Gawain on the Perilous Bed—together with non-Arthurian material (the Capture of the Unicorn, Aristotle Ridden by Phyllis, Samson and the Lion, and the Pelican in Her Piety). In the context of these well-known symbols of Christian sacrifice (the pelican, the unicorn), strength and protection (Samson), and the power of Women (Phyllis, the Virgin), the adventures of Arthur's knights, who fight temptations and evil powers in the service of their ladies, take on moral implications that make them acceptable for inclusion as church decoration. The selection and depiction of the Arthurian scenes seem to have been inspired by early fourteenth-century Parisian ivory caskets, thus the capital can be dated at mid-fourteenth century. [MS]

Loomis, Roger Sherman, and Laura Hibbard Loomis. *Arthurian Legends in Medieval Art*. London: Oxford University Press, 1938, pp. 71–72; figs. 138–39.

CAERLEON, a small town by the River Usk in Gwent, at the southeast corner of Wales. Its name means "City" (originally "Fort") "of the Legion." As the Roman *Isca Silurum*, it combined a military establishment with a center of civilian population. It has been proposed as the "City of the Legion" that is the scene of Arthur's ninth battle in Nennius. In this context, however, Caerleon is a less probable candidate than Chester, the Roman base near the northern end of the Welsh borderlands.

Caerleon's chief importance in Arthurian literature is as the place where Geoffrey of Monmouth has Arthur hold a plenary court, after organizing the conquests made in his first Gallic campaign. Geoffrey may have chosen it simply because it was near his native Monmouth and he had seen the ruins, which in the twelfth century were still conspicuous. In fact, he mentions them (Book IV, Chapter 19). His lavish description of the court prepares the way for the romancers' concept of Camelot as a special Arthurian capital. Here also, he locates the convent to which Guenevere retires.

Today, thanks to excavation and preservation, a large part of the complex of Roman buildings has survived. The amphitheater is the finest specimen in Britain. Before it was restored to daylight, it was covered by an accumulation of earth that concealed the structure but kept the shape, a hollow oval. The resulting mound was claimed locally as the true Round Table, the idea being that the knights sat facing inward as the original spectators did.

Caerleon has a version of the cave legend. A mysterious stranger in a three-cornered hat guided a farmer to a cave where a thousand of Arthur's soldiers lay asleep, waiting till they should be needed. One detail, that their heads were resting on guns, suggests that this tale is hardly one of the earliest forms of the legend. [GA]

Geoffrey of Monmouth. *Historia Regum Britanniae*, Book IX, Chapters 12–15; Book XI, Chapter 1.

Ashe, Geoffrey. *A Guidebook to Arthurian Britain*. Wellingborough: Aquarian, 1983, pp. 57–60.

CALDECOTT, MOYRA, South African-born British writer. A specialist in novels set in the Bronze Age and in reworkings of Celtic myth, Caldecott has written two short novels touching on Arthurian materials. *The King of Shadows* (1981) is based mainly on the story of the rivalry between Gwynn ap Nudd, the Lord of Annwn, and Gwythyr ap Greidyawl for the love of Creiddylad, as is found in *Culhwch and Olwen*. *Taliesin and Avagddu* (1983) retells the story of the birth of Taliesin and his support of his ugly brother Avagddu in the winning of a beautiful young girl. The story is closely based on the Welsh poems attributed to the bard Taliesin and set in the time of Arthur. [PCB]

Caldecott, Moyra. *The King of Shadows: A Glastonbury Story*. Frome, Somerset: Privately printed at The Hunting Raven Press, 1981.

———. *Taliesin and Avagddu*. Frome, Somerset: Bran's Head, 1983.

CALVINO, ITALO (1923–1985), Italian author of the 1959 novel *Il cavaliere inesistente* ("The Nonexistent Knight"), set in the time of Charlemagne and including the Knights of the Holy Grail ("i Cavalieri del San Gral"). These knights function like automata, according to the impulses communicated to them by the Grail. They are therefore half-somnambulistic, half-robot in their actions and ceremonies. Human concerns do not sway them, only the impulse—even when violent—of the Grail, which is never seen or described physically. They are eventually overcome by peasants, who drive them away when the Knights refuse to relinquish their demands for food even when the peasants cannot provide enough for themselves. One character, Torrismondo, is said to be the son of the Knights of the Grail, born after they robbed his mother, Sofronia, of her virginity. [DK]

Calvino, Italo. *Il cavaliere inesistente*. Turin: Einaudi, 1959.

CAMDEN, WILLIAM (1551–1623), an antiquarian of primary importance, is best known for his *Britannia*, a comprehensive and monumental work, one of the first great systemized surveys of Britain in its entirety. Published in Latin in 1586, it was edited, revised, and expanded by the author in 1587, 1590, 1594, 1600, and 1607. The first edition in the English language appeared in 1610.

Camden rejects Geoffrey of Monmouth's assertion that Brutus was founder of the British race. Instead, he suggests that the Gauls, more closely linked than the Trojans in proximity, language, and customs, were more likely candidates. This opinion reflects the gradual erosion of Tudor interest in the Trojan lines in favor of links with France or even the Saxons. Camden accepts Arthur's historicity, and the *Britannia* is full of references to him. He identifies Tintagel and Camelford, both in Cornwall, with Arthur's birth and death. The Somerset chapter links Cadbury Castle with Nennius's list of Arthurian victories. Camden connects Badon Hill with Bath, citing Gildas. Of great importance is his publication of a drawing of the famed lead cross believed to have been found during the disinterment of what were reputedly Arthur's, and perhaps Guenevere's, remains at Glastonbury. [JHW]

19. William Camden, leaden cross from "Arthur's Grave" at Glastonbury. (Courtesy of the Kenneth Spencer Research Library, University of Kansas.)

Camden, William. *Camden's Britannia, Newly Translated into English: With Large Additions and Improvements*, published by Edmund Gibson. London: F. Collins, 1695.

Kendrick, T.D. *British Antiquity*. London: Methuen, 1950.

Piggott, Stuart. *William Camden and the Britannia*. London, 1951, Vol. 37, pp. 199–217.

CAMELOT, Arthur's principal residence and preferred castle. Although later descriptions of the castle appear to owe a good deal to Geoffrey of Monmouth's depiction of Caerleon, Camelot is not mentioned prior to Chrétien de Troyes in the late twelfth century, in whose work it occurs but once (at the beginning of *Lancelot*—and even there it is not present in all manuscripts). It was during the thirteenth century that Camelot became prominent, especially in the Vulgate Cycle of romances. From that time on, it served as the point of departure for the Grail questers, and in the *Mort Artu* Gawain expressed his desire to be buried at Camelot, which had obviously become by that time the ideological, as well as geographical, center of the Arthurian world. The ultimate ruin of Camelot, according to *Palamedes* and the Spanish *Demanda del Sancto Grial*, was the work of the aged Mark, who, hearing that Lancelot was dead, invaded Logres, destroying Joyous Gard, Lancelot's tomb, Camelot, and the Round Table.

During the thirteenth century, various writers described Camelot in considerable physical detail. The castle was surrounded by plains, with a forest and a river nearby. There was at least one church, and there was, naturally enough, a town or city around or near the castle.

There is nothing surprising about Camelot, at least in terms of its physical presentation: it is a beautiful city and an extraordinary castle, but it could not have been significantly different from many another city or castle. Only two facts set it apart from others: first, it eventually takes on religious as well as ideological overtones (certain knights even being baptized there); second, it is not clear where it is. Malory identifies Camelot with Winchester, but other writers are far less specific. In certain texts, it appears to be located in southern England, but few works will permit us to be any more precise than that.

Scholars continue to look for Camelot, and some believe they have found it (or its prototype) at Cadbury-Camelot. But while a good deal of energy has been expended on the search for the "actual" Camelot, it is clear that Camelot's geographical imprecision, whether conscious or not, is a stroke of genius on the part of romance authors: for Camelot, located nowhere in particular, can be anywhere. In the world of Arthurian romance, it is less a specific place than a state of mind, a source of inspiration, an idea.

Modern versions of the legend have generally maintained this lack of precision. Camelot, in effect, is the center of the Arthurian universe, and no more geographical detail is needed. On the other hand, authors almost universally update the castle itself, transforming it into a typical if unusually opulent castle of the High Middle Ages, complete with drawbridges, portcullises, and crenelated towers. Such a transformation is carried very nearly to its logical conclusion in the film version of *Camelot*, which uses the Castle of Coca (Segovia) as Camelot. [NJL]

Pickford, Cedric E. "Camelot." In *Mélanges de langue et de littérature médiévales offerts à Pierre Le Gentil*. Paris: SEDES, 1973.

CAMERON, JULIA MARGARET (1815–1879). In the fall of 1874, Alfred Tennyson asked his close friend Julia Margaret Cameron to provide photographic illustrations of subjects from his *Idylls of the King* and other poems. These photographs, which used family members, friends, and sometimes strangers as models, were produced for reproduction as wood-engraved frontispieces to a cabinet edition of Tennyson's *Works* (London: Henry S. King and Company, 1874–76, 10 vols.; Cameron photographs used in Volumes 6, 7, and 9). Cameron, disappointed at the meager wood-engravings and confident that she could capitalize upon the contemporary popularity of the *Idylls*, published her photographs with Tennyson's encouragement in two volumes of gift books, *Illustrations to Tennyson's "Idylls of the King" and Other Poems* (London: Henry S. King and Company, 1875). The first volume, apparently released in time for Christmas sales, consists of subjects from the *Idylls of the King*, and the second volume, published in May 1875, features three photographs from the *Idylls* and nine from other Tennyson poems. The two volumes are otherwise identical in title and format: a frontispiece photographic portrait of Tennyson by Cameron; a sonnet in honor of Cameron by Charles Turner; twelve photographs, each preceded by a page with an excerpt, reproduced in a facsimile of Cameron's handwriting, from the Tennyson text illustrated in the photograph.

The *Idylls* chapters illustrated in the first volume are "Gareth and Lynette," "Geraint and Enid," "Merlin and Vivien," "Lancelot and Elaine," "The Holy Grail," "Guinevere," and "The Passing of Arthur," and in the second volume "Lancelot and Elaine" and "The Passing of Arthur." Cameron sequenced the *Idylls* subjects in both volumes to follow the course of Camelot; her choice of incident emphasized the experiences of the women characters, who are represented as active, exerting power over passive and reactive male characters. The heroic figure of King Arthur concludes the sequence of *Idylls* photographs in both volumes, but visual parallels between the photographs of King Arthur and Elaine elevate her fantasy of love into one of the major events of Cameron's representation of the *Idylls*.

The two volumes of the *Illustrations* were Cameron's first and only publication of her photographs in book form, but individual subjects were sold separately. Cameron aspired to the commercial success Gustave Doré enjoyed for his *Idylls* engravings; the print run of the *Illustrations* is not known, but variations in production details suggest a limited number. The London *Times* reviewed the first volume of the *Illustrations* on February 1, 1875, and the photograph of "The Parting of Lancelot and Guinevere" was reproduced on the cover of *Harper's Weekly* on September 1, 1877. Cameron's account of the project is given in a series of letters (now in the collection of the Gilman Paper Company, New York City), partially reprinted by Gernsheim. [JL]

Gernsheim, Helmut. *Julia Margaret Cameron: Her Life and Photographic Work*, 2nd ed. Millerton, N.Y.: Aperture, 1975.

20. Julia Margaret Cameron, "So Like a Shattered Column Lay the King." (Gernsheim Collection, Harry Ransom Humanities Research Center, The University of Texas at Austin.)

CAMLANN (Camlan), in Welsh literature the scene of Arthur's last battle, in which he clashed fatally with Mordred, and most of the combatants perished on both sides. Neither Gildas nor Nennius mentions such a battle. It appears first in the tenth-century *Annales Cambriae* as "the strife of Camlann, in which Arthur and Medraut fell." The date is given as Year 93 of the chronicle, probably 539.

Nothing is said here to make Mordred a villain, or

even to show that he and Arthur were opposed. Early bardic allusions are favorable to him. In the Triads, however, the enmity and tragedy are clearly emerging. Camlann is one of the three "futile battles," in which Arthur not only fought Mordred but through some unexplained lapse of judgment allowed many of his troops to join his opponent. A strong and sad tradition makes the battle a massacre with so few survivors that they are individually named. The Welsh have much more to say about Camlann than about Badon.

The name corresponds to the British *Camboglanna* 'crooked bank' (i.e., of a river), or less probably *Cambolanda* 'crooked enclosure.' There is a place called Camlan today, a valley in Merioneth with a small river flowing down it, but several rivers have the "crooked" element in their names. Geoffrey of Monmouth chooses the Camel in Cornwall. Another candidate is the Somerset Cam, which is near Cadbury-Camelot. A multiple burial is said once to have come to light in the fields below the hill. The original British form *Camboglanna* is actually found as the name of a Roman fort on Hadrian's Wall, allegedly though questionably Birdoswald, high above the River Irthing, which runs through a valley and is suitably crooked. Naturally, this fort has been favored as the site.

Wherever the battle was, it may be accepted as historical. The question is whether the involvement of Arthur is also historical. On the face of it, this is a different case from that of Badon, because bards would have wished to connect him with a victory but not with a dismal inter-British quarrel. Perhaps, then, the facts were too clear to set aside. Yet an Arthurian battle in 539 (no other source offers any alternative) seems very late; it is suspect because the same chronicle almost certainly errs about Badon; and it is further suspect in view of evidence from the Welsh saints' lives that legend did come to involve Arthur in activities extending far into the sixth century, activities that were certainly fictitious.

Nevertheless, some scholars have picked out the Camlann entry in the *Annales* as the one reliable Arthurian statement, partly because it is free from manifest legend, partly on the ground that, although it occurs in a tenth-century text, it was copied (or may plausibly be supposed to have been copied) from a contemporary record. But the form of the name tells against this argument. If it started as *Camboglanna*, it would have become *Camlann* in Welsh, but it would have passed through an intermediate form *Camglann* and taken a long time doing so. Hence, the *Annales* entry mentioning "Camlann" is not contemporary or anything like it. A copyist might have modernized the older spelling, but it cannot be proved that the older spelling was there for him to modernize.

While Arthur's involvement with Camlann could be authentic, it could also be one of many cases of his association over the centuries with battlefields and other sites up and down Britain. Geoffrey's Camel location may itself be due to this process. There was indeed a battle beside the Camel, and local legend grew to be highly circumstantial about it, indicating a field near Slaughter Bridge a mile above Camelford. The battle, however, was probably one between the Cornish and the West Saxons, fought in 823. Camlann's identification with the Birdoswald fort raises a special difficulty, because the triadic version of Arthur's quarrel with Mordred places this in Cornwall, with Arthur living at Kelliwic. Furthermore, the *Mordred/Modred* form of the name, which replaces the Welsh *Medraut* or *Medrawd*, is Cornish and implies a Cornish tradition. Geoffrey is at least looking in a plausible direction. But Birdoswald is a long way from Cornwall.

The problem is not made simpler by traces of another account of Arthur's end. In the *Prophetiae Merlini*, which Geoffrey inserts in his *Historia Regum Britanniae*, he makes the prophet foretell Arthur's career and predict a mysterious passing that seems to be in Gaul. When he came to write the actual story, Geoffrey introduced Camlann, but the denouement is still interwoven with events overseas, wholly foreign to the Welsh version, as is Geoffrey's portrayal of Mordred as Arthur's traitorous deputy. In the Vulgate Cycle and Malory, while Mordred's villainy is retained, Camlann as such disappears again. The final and fatal battle is fought near Salisbury.

Camlann probably happened; Arthur's name was connected with it by the tenth century; and, if it was discreditable, there may have been a reason for that connection that was more compelling than pure fancy. On the other hand, all would-be reconstructions of a real Camlann with a real Arthur in it fall short of conviction. Also, there are grave obstacles to the belief that he was active so late. This difficulty might be overcome by the hypothesis of a minor Arthur, who perished in the battle and was absorbed into a saga originating from an earlier leader. Another possibility is suggested by a Welsh poem about a battle fought by the West Country ruler Geraint. Though this mentions Arthur, it does not say that he was present in person, but an ambiguity in the wording has led to its being construed as saying that he was. An early bardic lament over Camlann might have introduced his name in the same way, with the same result. (*See also* ARTHUR, ORIGINS OF LEGEND.) [GA]

Alcock, Leslie. *Arthur's Britain*. London: Penguin, 1971, pp. 45–55, 67.

Ashe, Geoffrey. *A Guidebook to Arthurian Britain*. Wellingborough: Aquarian, 1983, pp. 61, 65–66.

Bromwich, Rachel. *Trioedd Ynys Prydein*. Cardiff: University of Wales Press, 1961; 2nd ed. 1978, pp. 160–62.

CAMPBELL, (WILLIAM) WILFRED (1858?–1918), Canadian rector, civil servant, and author, tells the story of Lancelot, ending with his guilt-haunted death in the

Last Battle, in "Sir Lancelot" (1892), a poem in blank verse with Tennysonian echoes. His play *Mordred*, written in July and August of 1893 but never staged, is a melodramatic account of how a hunchbacked Mordred avenges the scorn and rejection that his disfigurement prompts at court. Ill-fated love and a misguided concern with appearance are the central themes. [EB/RHT]

Campbell, Wilfred. "Sir Lancelot." In *The Dread Voyage: Poems*. Toronto: Briggs, 1893, pp. 39–51.

———. *Mordred: A Tragedy in Five Acts, Founded on the Arthurian Legend of Sir Thomas Malory*. In *Mordred and Hildebrand: A Book of Tragedies*. Ottawa: Durie, 1895, pp. 1-106.

CANNING, VICTOR, British author of three Arthurian novels, published separately as *The Crimson Chalice* (1976), *The Circle of the Gods* (1977), and *The Immortal Wound* (1978); these were later issued together as *The Crimson Chalice* (1978). The setting of the stories is Late Roman Britain in transition from the fragmented society of Roman magistrates and Celtic tribes to the unified realm of Arturo, here depicted as the son of Baradoc, a Celtic chieftain, and Gratia, a British Roman. Their story and that of Arturo's early efforts toward defeating the Saxons are given in greater detail in the first book than much of the traditional Arthurian material in the subsequent works.

Canning's Arthur-figure, Arturo, is a picaresque visionary. Outlawed by Prince Geraint, the Celtic leader, and by the ambitious Ambrosius, he proceeds to steal cavalry mounts and to recruit men bored by standard military routine, in order to form an attack force against the Saxons and force an awareness of his strength upon the established leaders. Arturo views himself as a man inspired by the gods—this justification is offered throughout the novel for any act on his part.

Canning gives Arturo two wives. The first, Daria, a love-match, is murdered at Ambrosius's behest. The second, Gwennifer, corresponds to the Guenevere of legend; childless, she engages in love affairs, but this does not lead to conflict and friction, since Arturo is, here as always, treated as somehow above the obstacles and potential tragedies of the story. The Arturo of the latter portions of the novel is bland when compared with the rebellious child and young soldier. The major exceptions to this approach are the loss of Daria, which is deeply felt, and the inevitable compromise between vision and reality. The action reaches its climax in the battle of Mount Badon. By contrast, the closing pages of the story, when the aging Arthur, forewarned by a detailed dream, goes to the final encounter with Mordreth, are perfunctory.

Canning retains the general outlines of the Arthurian story, even to a kind of Grail, a silver chalice that functions more as a talisman for Arturo than as the object of a spiritual quest for his knights. On the whole, however, Canning's imaginative recreations and Arturo's faith in the "immortal wound," the cyclical existence of the chosen hero, tend to overshadow or even diminish the power of the tale. [AAR]

Canning, Victor. *The Crimson Chalice*. New York: Morrow, 1978.

CANTARE DEI CANTARI, a kind of omnibus *cantare* in fifty-nine stanzas; it includes many ancient stories as well as material from the Roland and Arthurian cycles. The Arthurian material (stanzas 39–47) contrasts the Old and New Tables, and the poet refers to Arthur, Lancelot and Guenevere, Tristan and Isolde, the Grail quest, and other Arthurian characters and themes. Composed in Italy about 1380, it was assigned its suggestive title by its nineteenth-century editor. [SJN]

Rajna, Pio, ed. "Il Cantare dei Cantari e il Sirventese del Maestro di tutte le arti." *Zeitschrift für romanische Philologie*, 2 (1878), 220-54, 419-37.

Gardner, Edmund G. *The Arthurian Legend in Italian Literature*. London: Dent, 1930, pp. 270-72.

CANTARI, popular narrative poems taking their generic name from a substantivization of the Italian verb *cantare* 'to sing.' They were sung in the piazzas by performer-poets called *canterini*, *cantastorie*, or *cantambanchi* (from *cantari in banca*, singers on the platform designated for such entertainments). *Cantari* were usually composed in *ottava rima* and often divided into *giornate* (a section suitable for performance in one day, or *giorno*) of about fifty octaves. These works are difficult to date, individually or as a genre, since the manuscripts or early printed books that transmit them to us are necessarily later transcriptions of poems possibly transmitted orally for generations. Most scholars believe, however, that performances of *cantari* were frequent in Italy from the second half of the thirteenth century until the end of the fifteenth, first in such Tuscan centers as Florence (where the *canterini* had a *banco* in the piazza of S. Martino al Vescovo), Siena, Lucca, and Pisa, and later farther north at Bologna, Venice, and especially Verona. In the fifteenth century, *cantari* became popular entertainments in the south as well, particularly at Naples. *Canterini* strove to keep the audience's attention by combining in rapid succession accounts of astonishing deeds, evocations of mysterious atmosphere, and descriptions of luxurious costume and decor. To the same end, they often in a single *cantare* sang about some characters whose celebrated names could attract an audience and about others, less well known or entirely new, whose stories could be elaborated without the constraints imposed by traditional plots. In this way, *canterini* made use of many stock figures from ancient myth and history, from the tales of Roland, and from Arthurian literature but often mentioned such figures only in passing. One of the few *cantari* by an author whose name is known to us, Antonio Pucci's mid-fourteenth-century *Gismirante*, is typical in this regard: the protagonist's dying father recommends, as the *cantare* opens, that he travel to Arthur's court and make himself known to Tristan and Lancelot, whose names are not mentioned again—though Arthur is alluded to several more times, as feeling affection for Gismirante, conducting a court with special customs, granting Gismirante's wish for knighthood, bidding him farewell, and serving as the endpoint of a journey Gismirante hopes (unsuccessfully) to make with his chosen lady. In the second *cantare* of *Gismirante*, Arthur and his circle are absent entirely, no doubt because they have served their purpose for Pucci, in attracting an audience. Because such heterogeneity of source and plot was typical of the genre, it is impossible to discriminate definitively a body of *cantari* that can be labeled "Arthurian": such a well-known figure as Lancelot, for example, is likely to be introduced in many *cantari* that nonetheless do not give him a continuing or important role, just as a "guest star" might appear in one episode of a television series in need of higher ratings. Among the *cantari* most frequently studied today, however, several are notable for their Arthurian content: *Bel Gherardino, Cantare dei cantari, I Cantari di Carduino, I Cantari di Tristano, Li Chantari di Lancellotto, La Donna del Vergiù, Febusso e Breusso, Fiorio e Biancifiore, Liombruno, La Pulzella Gaia,* and *Quando Tristano e Lancielotto combattettero al petrone di Merlino.* [SJN]

Balduino, A. *Cantari del Trecento*. Milan: Marzorati, 1970.

Gardner, Edmund G. *The Arthurian Legend in Italian Literature*. London: Dent, 1930, pp. 239–72.

Picone, M., and M. Bendinelli Predelli, eds. *I Cantari: Struttura e tradizione*. Florence: Olschki, 1984.

CANTARI DI CARDUINO, I, have been dubiously attributed to Antonio Pucci (1318–1388), bell-ringer and town crier of the commune of Florence, and date to the 1370s. The *primo cantare*, reminiscent of the *enfances* of Perceval, tells of the murder of Arthur's favorite knight, Dondinello, by jealous barons and the flight of his widow and infant son into the forest, where the child is raised in the fear of God and ignorance of knights and knighthood. At the age of twelve, he discovers knights hunting in the forest, and, although they pursue him as a wild man, he determines to serve their leader, Arthur. At court, Carduino impresses the knights with his rusticity and his appetite. A damsel accompanied by a dwarf interrupts the feast with a request that Arthur provide her with a champion who will liberate her city and her sister from the enchantments of an evil sorcerer. The *secondo cantare*, reminiscent of tales featuring Gawain's son or brother, recounts the adventures of Carduino and the enchanted city. On his way to the city, he is assaulted by giants and lusty ladies in a series of castles, and he encounters and kills Calvano's brother, Aguerisse, thus unwittingly avenging his father's murder. When he arrives at the enchanted city, he sees a rocky wasteland infested with dragons and other beasts. Challenged by a strange knight, Carduino defeats him in combat, finds his ring, and, breaking it, releases the city from enchantment. When he kisses the chained serpent, she is transformed into the angelically beautiful Beatrice. The quest is completed, the expected marriage is celebrated, a glorious progeny is prophesied, and all ends happily. The *Carduino* is a masterpiece of popular Italian literature. It is of great importance to literary history because it represents a variant, and possibly more authentic, version of the *enfances* of Perceval than that found in Chrétien and because it represents an important branch of the Fair Unknown/*fier baiser* story type. It is of particular importance to students of English literature because of its resemblance to the verse romances *Sir Perceval of Galles* and *Libeaus Desconus* and to Malory's "Tale of Sir Gareth." [DLH]

Rajna, Pio, ed. *Cantari di Carduino giuntovi quello di Tristano e Lancillotto quando combattettero al petrone di Merlino*. Bologna: Romagnoli, 1873.

CANTARI DI TRISTANO, I, dating from the second half of the fourteenth century, are a group of six *ottava rima* narratives of episodes from the life of Tristan. The *Bataglia* recounts the combat of Tristano and Lancilotto at Merlin's stone, or *peron*, when Tristano had expected to meet and fight, for the honor of the queen, his rival Palamides. It is not until Tristano utters the name "Isotta" that Lancilotto and Tristano realize that they are fighting for the honor of different queens. The *Cantare di Lasancis* tells of the return to Camelot after the combat at the *peron* and Tristano's discovery that Marco has imprisoned Isotta. As he leaves for Cornwall, Lasancis arrives demanding to avenge his brother, who was killed by Lancilotto; the fragment ends before the combat begins. In *I Cantari del "Falso Scudo"* ("The False Shield"), Tristano appears in only the first *cantare*, where he is listed as one of those defeated by the Knight with the Enchanted Shield. He does not appear in the second *cantare*, which deals briefly with Galasso (Galahad) and his defeat of the Knight with the Enchanted Shield. In *Le ultime imprese di Tristano* ("The Last Deeds of

Tristan"), Tristano embarks on the quest of the Grail but abandons the pursuit to defend the chastity of a damsel pursued by the infamous Knight Without Pity. *La morte di Tristano* and *La vendetta di Lancilotto* are the best known of the *cantari*. The first tells how Marco kills Tristano with the lance of Morgan le Fay and how Isotta, overcome by the force of Tristano's last embrace, dies with him. The *Vendetta* recounts the Arthurian campaign led by Lancilotto to avenge the death of Tristano. The *cantari* as a group are important evidence of the extent of Tristano's popularity in Italy, but the narratives, although competent, are derivative and the verse is undistinguished. [DLH]

Bertoni, Giulio, ed. *Cantari di Tristano*. Modena: Società Tipografica Modenese, 1937.

Rajna, Pio, ed. *I Cantari di Carduino guintovi quello di Tristano e Lancielotto quando combattettero al petrone di Merlino*. Bologna: Romagnoli, 1873.

Wilhelm, James J., trans. "Cantare on the Death of Tristan." In *The Romance of Arthur III*. New York: Garland, 1988.

CAPGRAVE, JOHN (1393–1464), Augustinian friar from Norfolk whose works include saints' lives, biblical commentaries, theological treatises, the *Nova Legenda Angliae* (*see* DE SANTO JOSEPH AB ARIMATHIA), and the *De Illustribus Henricis*. He is the author of the English *Abbreuiacion of Cronicles* (1462–63), a chronicle of the "most famous thingis" that have happened in the world drawn primarily from the *Chronicon Pontificum et Imperatorum* of Martinus Polonus and the St. Albans chronicles of Thomas Walsingham. Capgrave gives a brief account of Arthur's conquests and of his being wounded and taken to Avalon, and he also tells of the twelfth-century discovery of Arthur's body at Glastonbury and of Edward III's interest in the Round Table. [EDK]

Capgrave, John. *The Chronicle of England (from the Creation to 1417)*, ed. F.C. Hingeston. London: Longman, 1848.

———. *John Capgrave's Abbreuiacion of Cronicles*, ed. Peter J. Lucas. London: Oxford University Press, 1983.

Kennedy, Edward Donald. "Chronicles and Other Historical Writing." In *A Manual of the Writings in Middle English*, ed. A.E. Hartung. New Haven: Connecticut Academy of Arts and Sciences, 1981–89, Vol. 8, pp. 2668–70, 2882–86.

CARADOC, LIVRE* (or *ROMAN*) *DE, a romance embedded in the First Continuation of Chrétien de Troyes's *Perceval* (*see* CONTINUATIONS). Though it has no independent manuscript existence, it could be excerpted without damage to the narrative of either the Continuation or itself. The *Livre* appears in all three redactions of the Continuation and varies in length from some 3,300 to 5,800 lines. The biography of Caradoc consists of three parts: 1) He is born to Ysave, Arthur's niece, and to her adulterous lover, Eliavrés, a sorcerer. Despite his bastard birth, Caradoc remains the legitimate heir of his father, King Caradoc of Nantes. As a newly dubbed knight in King Arthur's court, Caradoc alone accepts the challenge of the Beheading Game, a motif made famous in English literature by *Sir Gawain and the Green Knight*. Caradoc escapes unscathed because the challenger, who turns out to be his legitimate father, relents. 2) Caradoc imprisons his mother in a tower in Nantes; he rescues a maiden, Guigner, on his way back to join Arthur; he establishes his reputation as the best knight of the court. He learns that Eliavrés has visited his mother, goes back to Nantes, and humiliates the sorcerer. The wicked couple take revenge on the hero by attaching to his arm a deadly serpent, which will slowly sap his life away in two years' time. But he is saved by Guigner and her brother. She immerses herself in a vat of milk while Caradoc sits in a tub of vinegar. As the viper leaps to the sweeter host, the brother slashes off its head, but not without cutting off the maiden's nipple, which is later restored in gold by a magic shield. 3) Caradoc passes the supreme test of the drinking horn. Only he can drink its enchanted wine without spilling a drop, because he alone in the court possesses a truly faithful lover, Guigner. A variant of the latter episode may be found in Robert Biket's *Lai du cor*. The *Livre de Caradoc* has been rarely studied and obviously merits further scholarly attention. [JLG]

Roach, William, ed. *The Continuations of the Old French "Perceval" of Chrétien de Troyes: The First Continuation*. 3 vols. (Vol. 2 with Robert H. Ivy, Jr.) Philadelphia: American Philosophical Society, 1949–52.

CARADOC OF LLANCARFAN, author of the *Vita Gildae* ("Life of St. Gildas"), a work (ca. 1130) drawing on romance literature and hagiography. This is the first known text to associate King Arthur with Glastonbury. According to the *Vita*, King Melwas of the Summer Region carried off Guenevere, and Arthur, "the tyrant," brought all the forces of Devon and Cornwall to Glastonbury to retrieve her; the abbot of Glastonbury, however, accompanied by Gildas, obtained her release. In this episode, Caradoc explains that the origin of the name "Glastonbury" is from "Isle of Glass" (and by implication that "Somerset" derives from "Summer Region"). The etymologies both carry otherworldly implications, which paved the way for the later association of Glastonbury with Avalon. [JPC]

Mommsen, Theodorus, ed. *Vita Gildae Auctore Caradoco Lancarbanensi*. In *Monumenta Germaniae Historica, Auctores Antiquissimori 13. Chronica Minora 3*. Berlin: Weidmann, 1898, pp. 107–10.

CARADOS, a late fourteenth-century French abridgment of the *Livre de Caradoc* (from the First Continuation). The *Carados*, which retains the story of the chastity test but substitutes a cup for the horn, is embedded in the *Renart le Contrefait*. [NJL]

Raynaud, Gaston, and Henri Lemaître, eds. *Le Roman de Renart le Contrefait*. Paris: Champion, 1914, Vol. 1, pp. 46–47.

CARLE OFF CARLILE, THE, an early sixteenth-century balladlike poem (500 lines), preserved in the Percy Folio, is a later version of *Syre Gawene and the Carle of Carlyle*. The two texts are incomplete but complement each other; both derive from the same tail-rhyme romance, whose metrical pattern is still visible in *The Carle* in the regular occurrence of three-stress instead of four-stress lines. The beheading that disenchants the Carl it shares with *The Turke and Gowin*. [ESK]

Madden, Frederic, ed. *Syre Gawayne*. London: Bannatyne Club, 1839.

Kurvinen, Auvo, ed. *Sir Gawain and the Carl of Carlisle in Two Versions*. Helsinki, 1951.

CARMICHAEL, DOUGLAS, author of the novel *Pendragon* (1977), a recreation of the twelve battles that Arthur fought to consolidate his kingdom. The book incorporates both early lore and later legends into an account that eschews magic in favor of rational explanations, provides psychological motivation for familiar incidents, and makes action-packed battle scenes come alive. [MAG]

Carmichael, Douglas. *Pendragon*. Hicksville, N.Y.: Blackwater, 1977.

CARPENTER, RHYS (1889–1980), American scholar and archaeologist, composed a dramatic poem, *The Tragedy of Etarre* (1912), based upon the story, from the fourth book of Caxton's Malory, of Pelleas's unrequited love for Etarre and of Gawain's treacherous intervention. Although written as dialogue, in blank verse, and divided into acts and scenes (with some stage directions), it is nevertheless a dramatic poem rather than a play. [SRR]

Carpenter, Rhys. *The Tragedy of Etarre: A Poem*. New York: Sturgis and Walton, 1912.

CARR, J. COMYNS (1849–1916), was a reviver of Arthurian drama. His *King Arthur* was produced at London's Lyceum in January 1895, with Henry Irving as King Arthur, Forbes Robertson as Launcelot, and Ellen Terry as Guenevere. Incidental music was by Sir Arthur Sullivan (who conducted the first-night performance), and Edward Burne-Jones designed the scenery, costumes, and armor. The Prologue presents Arthur's acquisition of Excalibur at the Magic Mere while a Chorus of Lake Spirits comments prophetically. The four acts—"The Holy Grail," "The Queen's Maying," "The Black Barge," "The Passing of Arthur"—compress Malory's time scheme. Conflict is provided by Morgan and her son, Mordred. Launcelot wrestles with the demands of Elaine (whose love predates Guenevere's), Arthur, the Queen, and God. *Tristram and Iseult* (1906), a somewhat Wagnerian version, covers events enacted in Cornwall and Ireland but departs from tradition by casting Andret as Tristram's murderer. (*See also* Music.) [MAW]

Carr, J. Comyns. *King Arthur: A Drama in a Prologue and Four Acts*. London: Macmillan, 1895.

———. *Tristram and Iseult: A Drama in Four Acts*. London: Duckworth, 1906.

Goodman, Jennifer R. "The Last of Avalon: Henry Irving's *King Arthur* of 1895," *Harvard Library Bulletin*, 32 (1984), 239–55.

CARTA ENVIADA POR HISEO LA BRUNDA A TRISTÁN; RESPUESTA DE TRISTÁN ("Isolde's Letter to Tristan; Tristan's Reply"), a highly rhetorical epistolary exchange in Spanish between Isolde of Cornwall and Tristan, the former complaining of Tristan's marriage to Isolde of the White Hands and Tristan defending his actions. The work is contained in an early sixteenth-century manuscript copy (Madrid, Biblioteca Nacional 22021). The Isolde letter is adapted from a similar but shorter and less rhetorical letter found in most redactions of the Prose *Tristan*, but Tristan's reply would seem to be the creation of the Spanish author. The letters demonstrate a tendency in late-medieval Spain to fuse Arthurian and sentimental material, with the rhetoric of the letters betraying that of the sentimental romance, a genre that began to develop in Spain in the fifteenth century and that made extensive use of letters. The Isolde letter in fact incorporates actual lines from one such romance, *Grimalte y Gradissa*, by Juan de Flores. While the letters may have been extracted from a remodeled Spanish Prose *Tristan*—curiously, *Grimalte y Gradissa* material is also found in a 1501 printing of the Spanish Prose *Tristan*—they may have been simply a rhetorical exericse. [HLS]

Sharrer, Harvey L. "Letters in the Hispanic Prose Tristan Texts: Iseut's Complaint and Tristan's Reply." *Tristania*, 7 (1981–82), 3–20.

CASE, CLARENCE MARSH (1874–1946), wrote *The Banner of the White Horse* (1918), a story of the Anglo-Saxon conquest for younger readers, in which the hero is "a shadowy forerunner of the shadowy King Arthur." The author claims to have purposely softened the harshness of the times and relieved the darkness of paganism. [EB]

Case, Clarence Marsh. *The Banner of the White Horse: A Tale of the Saxon Conquest*. London: Harrap, 1918.

CASTLE DORE, an earthwork fort near Fowey in Cornwall, involved in the Cornish localization of the Tristan story. Inhabited during the last three centuries B.C., it was vacant during the Roman era, but excavation has shown that from the fifth century A.D. onward the enclosure contained sizable timber buildings. These suggest a princely or royal household. The place's closeness to the old trackway across Cornwall may have given it a continuing importance, as perhaps happened also with Castle Killibury, the likeliest candidate for Kelliwic.

Several Tristan localities are to be found in this neighborhood, such as Lantyan (Béroul's *Lancien*) and the parish of St. Sampson, with its church at Golant. Just outside Fowey is the Tristan Stone, a transplanted monument that formerly stood much nearer to Castle Dore. Its inscription shows that it once marked the grave of "Drustanus, son of Cunomorus." The first name is a form of "Tristan." The second Latinizes *Kynvawr*, the name of a king who reigned in Cornwall during the first half of the sixth century. Castle Dore was doubtless a residence of his.

A ninth-century Life of St. Paul Aurelian identifies Cunomorus with Mark. This identification played a part in localizing the Tristan tale hereabouts. The claim that the localization is history rather than fancy, and that the man commemorated by the inscription is *the* Tristan, depends on the Mark = Cunomorus equation being correct. It is not widely accepted, but it has its supporters. If, as the inscription states, Tristan was the king's son and not his nephew, Iseult (whether as a real person or as a creature of imagination) would have had to be a young stepmother. Poets might have altered the relationship to make the situation more acceptable. [GA]

Ashe, Geoffrey. *A Guidebook to Arthurian Britain*. Wellingborough: Aquarian, 1983, pp. 76–78.

Bromwich, Rachel. *Trioedd Ynys Prydein*. Cardiff: University of Wales Press, 1961; 2nd ed. 1978, pp. 444–46.

Ditmas, E.M.R. *Tristan and Iseult in Cornwall*. Gloucester: Roberts, 1969, pp. 72–73.

Radford, C.A. Ralegh. "Castle Dore." In *The Quest for Arthur's Britain*, ed. Geoffrey Ashe. London: Pall Mall, 1968, pp. 94–100.

CASTLE OF MAIDENS, in Geoffrey of Monmouth's *Historia Regum Britanniae*, a castle founded by King Ebraucus, who is a contemporary of the biblical King David, and located on Mount Agned or Mont Dolerous ("Sad Mountain"). In the Second Continuation, a maiden explains to Perceval that the Castle of Maidens was built by four maidens and appears deserted to wandering knights. She explains further that, if a knight strikes the table in the castle, food will mysteriously appear. With this explanation, Perceval falls asleep. When he awakens the next day, the castle has vanished. In other texts, such as the Prose *Tristan*, the Castle of Maidens is a meeting place for Arthur's court, or, as in the Third Continuation and the Vulgate Cycle, is inhabited by women who for one reason or another need to be rescued. [SW]

CAVALRY, ARTHURIAN. Opinions about the use of cavalry by the "historical Arthur" range from R.G. Collingwood's blunt "King Arthur's knights are myths" (*Antiquity*, 3 [1929], 292) to Robert Graves's vision of "mounted commandos" led by "a heroic British cavalry general named Arturius" (Introduction, *Le Morte d'Arthur*, ed. Keith Baines, New York, 1962). As usual, the truth seems to be somewhere in the middle.

Though the adventures of King Arthur's knights of the Round Table are admittedly largely fiction, the earliest historians mention Arthur as a "warlord," *dux bellorum*, and fighting against the invading Saxons, at the turn of the sixth century (Nennius; *Annales Cambriae*). Gildas reports that after the withdrawal of the Roman army the Britons were advised to see to their own defense; this was done using Roman equipment as models. The muster roll of the Late Roman army, *Notitia Dignitatum* (ca. 425), shows that two-thirds of the Roman forces in Britain were cavalry, under the command of the *Dux Britanniarum* and the Count (*Comes*) of the Saxon Shore. Among these cavalry units were the only two regiments of *cataphractarii* in western Europe, as well as two regiments of *stablesiani*, one of *scutarii*, two of Taifali, and one *cuneus* (troop) of Sarmatian veterans. *Cataphractarii* were the heaviest type of cavalry, wearing cuirasses of leather with bronze scales, segmented helmets, and leg defenses; their horses were armored with scale bardings and chanfrons of bronze-studded leather with strainer-like eyeguards. Weapons were ten-foot-long lances (*contus*) and long cavalry swords, worn on a shoulder baldric. *Stablesiani* and *scutarii* were medium-heavy cavalry with scale armor, but on unarmored horses. Taifali were eastern European horse nomads like the Sarmatians, with an ancient heavy-cavalry tradition. The armament of the *cataphractarii* was in fact modeled on that of the Sarmatians; presumably the Taifali were similarly equipped.

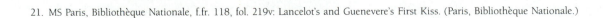

21. MS Paris, Bibliothèque Nationale, f.fr. 118, fol. 219v: Lancelot's and Guenevere's First Kiss. (Paris, Bibliothèque Nationale.)

The Sarmatians, according to Herodotus, were the offspring of adventurous Scythian youths and Amazons, and became the first heavy-armored cavalry known in the West, when the emperor Marcus Aurelius recruited 8,000 of them as auxiliaries for the Roman army, in A.D. 175. The bulk of them, 5,500 in all, were sent to northern Britain to fight the Picts. After their term of service (twenty-five years) had expired, they were not returned to their homeland, Pannonia (Hungary), as was standard procedure, but were settled in Lancashire at *Bremetannacum* (Ribchester). The fact that 250 years later, in the *Notitia Dignitatum*, they were still listed as Sarmatian veterans suggests that they had preserved their tribal identity fairly well. Besides their scale armor for men and horses, other tribal features were a battle standard in shape of a windsock-like dragon on a pole, and the worship of their god of war as a naked sword planted upright in the ground or a platform. When the Sarmatian auxiliaries arrived in Britain, they were attached to the Sixth Legion; that legion's *praefectus* was a certain Lucius Artorius Castus, who had served in Pannonia earlier in his career. It is possible that his name became a title, the way Caesar's name did, with the Sarmatian troopers. When the regular army withdrew from Britain in the early fifth century, the military settlement of the Sarmatian veterans at *Bremetennacum*, guarding the Lancashire coast against Irish pirates, seems to have stayed on. They might have become the cavalry of the "Historical Arthur," when worse danger threatened from the Saxons. In any case, the place-names in Nennius's list of twelve battles won by Arthur against the Saxons—Castell Guinnion/*Vinonia* (Binchester); Mons Agned/*Trimontium* (Newstead); Bregomion/*Bremetennacum* (Ribchester); *Urbs legionis* (Chester)—are all, if their interpretation is right, garrisons of Late Roman cavalry.

In Geoffrey of Monmouth's *Historia*, the tide of battle is turned repeatedly by the prowess of Armorican cavalry; Armorica (Brittany) was an area with an unusually high concentration of Alanic settlers. The Alans, another eastern tribe of horse nomads, kept their heavy-cavalry equipment and tactics up to the Norman invasion of England in 1066 (the left wing of Duke William's cavalry was commanded by Alan the Red, Duke of Brittany). (*See also* SARMATIAN CONNECTION.) [HN]

Bachrach, Bernard. "The Origin of Armorican Chivalry." *Technology and Culture*, 10 (1969), 166–71.

Eadie, N.W. "The Development of Roman Mailed Cavalry," *Journal of Roman Studies*, 57 (1967), 161–73.

Gamber, Ortwin. "Kataphrakten, Clibanarier, Normannenreiter." *Jahrbuch der kunsthistorischen Sammlungen*, 64 (1968), 7ff.

Nickel, Helmut. "Wer waren König Artus' Ritter?," *Waffen- und Kostümkunde*, 1 (1975), 1–28.

Nicolle, David. *Arthur and the Anglo-Saxon Wars*. London: Osprey, 1984.

Seeck, Otto, ed. *Notitia Dignitatum*. Berlin, 1876.

CAVE LEGEND. According to the Welsh "Stanzas of the Graves," in the Black Book of Carmarthen, Arthur's grave is a mystery. William of Malmesbury confirms this in his *Gesta Regum Anglorum* (ca. 1125): "The grave of Arthur is nowhere beheld." Therefore, William adds, "ancient songs" prophesy his reappearance. The idea that his grave could not be found because he had none, being immortal, seems to have originated in Brittany and spread to Cornwall, and thence to Wales. Its more literary form, deriving from the Bretons, was that he was in the enchanted isle of Avalon. But a folk-belief of another kind took hold among the Welsh and in parts of England and Scotland: that he was asleep in a cave until his messianic return. Both the principal versions of his survival, the island story and the cave story, may have their ancestry in the Celtic myth reported by Plutarch (in two dialogues, *Concerning the Face That Appears in the Orb of the Moon* and *The Obsolescence of Oracles*), about a banished god sleeping in a cave in a western island.

There are two real caves bearing Arthur's name, in Anglesey and Herefordshire. But the typical form of the legend makes his cave an elusive place that can be found only on rare occasions. Usually, it houses more than the King—a company of slumbering knights, or a royal treasure, or both. Sometimes, indeed, Arthur himself is absent, presumably in another cave. One location, which is probably of very long standing, is Cadbury Castle in Somerset: Cadbury-Camelot. Others are Craig-y-Ddinas in Glamorgan, Alderley Edge in Cheshire, Richmond Castle in Yorkshire, Sewingshields in Northumberland, and the Eildon Hills near Melrose in Scotland. At least nine more have been recorded besides these.

The legend varies from place to place, but it commonly includes an account of someone entering the cave with unhappy results. At Craig-y-Ddinas, a Welshman is said to have been guided into it by an English wizard. He saw the King and his knights asleep in a circle, their heads pointing outward. They wore armor, and weapons lay beside them. Within the circle were a heap of gold and a heap of silver. The magician told the Welshman that Arthur was sleeping till the time when he should wake and restore justice and peace throughout Britain. Meanwhile, it was permissible for the visitor to carry off some of the treasure, but he must not disturb the knights. If one of them woke, he would ask if it was day, and then the only way to escape unscathed was to reply, "No, sleep on." Also, the treasure must on no account be squandered. The Welshman succeeded in getting out with some gold, but he did squander it and came back alone for more. The second time, he had forgotten the formula; several of the knights woke up, gave him a beating, and ejected him from the cave. For the rest of his days, he was infirm from the beating and very poor, and he could never find the entrance again.

In English and Scottish versions, the intruder is tested in other ways and fails through panic or confusion.

He may be confronted with magical objects, such as a sword and a horn, which he uses wrongly. At Sewingshields, Arthur actually does wake, but the victim fails to complete the ritual and he goes back to sleep. The Melrose story is told by Walter Scott. Canonbie Dick, a horse-dealer, was riding home one night with a pair of horses that he had been unable to sell. A stranger in antique clothing offered to buy them, paying with obsolete gold coins. The same thing happened several times. Dick became curious about the stranger's dwelling. The stranger—who was in fact the mysterious poet Thomas the Rhymer—warned him that he must not show fear and led him through a doorway into a vast torchlit chamber under the Eildon Hills, full of sleeping knights and horses. On a table lay a sword and a horn. Thomas told Dick that he must choose whether to draw the sword or blow the horn. Dick blew the horn and learned too late that this was wrong: it was the act of a man summoning help and therefore showed fear. With a noise like thunder, the knights began to stir, and Dick's fear became genuine enough. A violent wind swept him out of the cave, and the door closed behind him. He told his tale to some shepherds and fell dead. Naturally, no one else ever found the entrance. It is said to have been in an odd-looking rocky hillock called the Lucken Hare, where witches used to hold meetings.

Though this folklore-Arthur lay hidden from the world, he could emerge in phantasmal form and join the legendary Wild Hunt, careering among the clouds with other heroes, and occasionally descending to earth. At Cadbury, he had both a cave and a "hunting causeway." Accompanied by his knights, he became a spectral huntsman in France as well as Britain. About 1211, Gervase of Tilbury mentions this belief (attested also by Gatto Lupesco), together with another giving him a permanent place of concealment in Mount Etna. Doubtless, this was an importation into Sicily by Normans or by Bretons in Norman service. The Sicilian Arthur is awake at least some of the time and talks to people from outside. But the notion of an undying king or hero asleep underground spread widely through medieval Europe, attaching itself to other characters. Whether all the variants were derived from Arthur by way of his vogue in romance it is impossible to tell, because in most cases written records fail to show when or how the beliefs arose. The most famous was almost certainly imitative. This was the German legend of Emperor Frederick II slumbering inside the Kyffhäuser mountain. After a couple of centuries, the sleeper's identity changed, and he became Frederick I, Barbarossa, as he is still.

There is a similar ambiguity at several of the Welsh locations. The person in the cave is normally supposed to be Arthur, but according to some he is Owen Lawgoch, a medieval Welsh patriot. Loomis indicates that versions of the legend were still quite widely accepted during the nineteenth century, and in fact it has survived into the twentieth. While the remote origins of this motif may lie in Celtic myth, the folklorist Jennifer Westwood has pointed out that it has always or nearly always attached itself to historical persons, not fairy-tale characters. Its association with Arthur is therefore an argument for his historicity in some sense. (*See also* FOLKLORE; RETURN, LEGENDS OF ARTHUR'S; TOPOGRAPHY AND LOCAL LEGENDS.) [GA]

Ashe, Geoffrey, *A Guidebook to Arthurian Britain.* Wellingborough: Aquarian, 1983, pp. 83–84.

Chambers, E.K. *Arthur of Britain.* London: Sidgwick and Jackson, 1927, pp. 221–30.

Loomis, Roger Sherman, ed. *Arthurian Literature in the Middle Ages.* Oxford: Clarendon, 1959, pp. 68–71.

Rhys, John, *Celtic Folklore.* 2 vols. Oxford: Clarendon, 1901, Vol. 2, pp. 457–61.

Westwood, Jennifer. *Albion: A Guide to Legendary Britain.* London: Granada, 1985.

CAWEIN, MADISON J. (1865–1914), author of a pioneer American adaptation of Malory material, *Accolon of Gaul* (1889), based on *Morte Darthur*, Book IV, Chapters 6–15. Written in heroic couplets with Keatsian ornamentation and Tennysonian characters (including Vivian and Dagonet), the poem depicts a young Accolon whose vow of chastity is negated by Morgane's amorous aggressiveness, as his vow of chivalric loyalty is negated by her devious plots against Arthur and Urience. [MAW]

Cawein, Madison J. *Accolon of Gaul with Other Poems.* Louisville, Ky.: Morton, 1889.

CAXTON, WILLIAM (ca. 1422–1491). Though the thirty years Caxton spent as a mercer are often eclipsed by his introduction of printing to England, the diplomacy and business sense he gained during this period are at least partially responsible for the success of his middle-age venture. After serving as Governor of the English Nation at Bruges for nine years, Caxton began a translation of the *Recuyell of the Histories of Troy*, demand for which caused him to take up printing. Having learned the trade under Johan Veldener, he opened a shop in Bruges, where he printed five other books besides the *Recuyell.* Two years later, he introduced printing to England, choosing Chaucer's *Canterbury Tales* as his first title in folio, and opened a shop at Westminster, from which he issued over 100 (extant) titles.

For a pioneer printer, Caxton had a remarkable range of tastes—or certainly a clear sense of the tastes of his readership. He published the works of the great writers of antiquity in translation (including Ovid, Vergil, and Cicero), prose romances (*Blanchard and Eglantyne, The Four Sons of Aymon*), mythical stories (*The History of Jason*), beast fables (*Reynard the Fox*, Aesop's *Fables*), religious and philosophical works (*The Curial*, Boethius's *Consolation, The Moral Proverbs* of Christine de Pizan), historical works (Trevisa's translation of Higden's *Polychronicon*, a *Description of Britain*), chivalric romances (*Paris and Vienne*), and also grammar books, vocabularies, statutes of the realm, indulgences, and other miscellaneous pieces. Most of all, he published the best literature England had to offer at the time, including the *Canterbury Tales, Troilus and Criseyde, Confessio Amantis, Le Morte Darthur*, and many of the minor works of Chaucer and Lydgate.

Universal as Caxton's tastes were, he showed a marked preference for chivalric literature, an interest that dates at least as far back as his association with the Duchess of Burgundy (ca. 1470) and probably farther. Before publishing *Le Morte Darthur* in 1485, he translated and printed *Godfrey of Bouillon* and *The Ordre of Chyualry* (in whose prologue and epilogue, respectively, he mentioned the stories of Arthur), and afterward *Charles the Grete, Paris and Vienne*, and *The Fayttes of Armes and Chyualry*. The works on Godfrey, Charlemagne, and Arthur were apparently planned as a series designed to honor the three Christian Worthies. It should not be surprising that the work honoring the English Worthy, Sir Thomas Malory's *Morte Darthur*, is the one for which Caxton is most remembered.

Caxton finished printing *Le Morte Darthur* on July 31, 1485; the book most likely took about ten months to print. Only one typeface was used, type 4*, probably because there are no running heads or titles. Five-line woodcut initials are used at the beginning of each of the twenty-one books, and a similar three-line series is used for chapter beginnings. Otherwise, the folio is not decorated: there are no illustrations or borders, which suggests that there was no decoration in the manuscript Caxton printed from. This book survives in two extant copies: the only complete one is housed in the Pierpont Morgan Library in New York; the other, which lacks eleven of the original leaves, is in the John Rylands University Library in Manchester. Aside from two sheets that were completely reset, there are few variant readings between the two copies.

Caxton divided Malory's text into twenty-one books and 506 chapters and added a table of rubrics, a prologue, and a colophon. The table and prologue were printed after the rest of the text was set, as the signatures indicate; this may account for the discrepancies between the table and the text itself. The basis for Caxton's layout cannot be fully determined, since his exemplar is no longer extant, but it is worth noting that nineteen of the twenty book divisions have some counterpart in the only manuscript version of Malory's work, which was in his office while the *Morte* was being printed.

Caxton's role as editor of *Le Morte Darthur* is unclear. His English is a more "standard" dialect than that of the manuscript, and his version is generally regarded as the more readable; but without his copy text we cannot ascertain how much of the version can be assigned to Caxton. The section in which the two versions differ most is that of Arthur's War with Lucius, Caxton's Book V, which is twice as long in the manuscript as it is in the printed text. Scholarly debate on this issue has produced two conflicting arguments. Some, after comparing his text with the manuscript, have charged Caxton with revising the Roman War episode and by extension the entire work. Others, citing Caxton's statement in his prologue and his editorial habits with other texts, believe that he did in fact print "according to his copy," and that someone else—perhaps Malory himself—revised the text he printed. Even if we follow Caxton's critics, the revision attributed to him is not an unreasonable exercise of editorial duty.

Caxton's prologue to *Le Morte Darthur* is unlike his others, notably in what he leaves out. He fails to identify a patron, though Anthony Wydville is surely the "certain gentleman" he mentions. This may be because Richard III, who had ordered Wydville's execution two years earlier, still had the crown when the *Morte* was published. He also fails to dedicate the work, perhaps because the most likely recipient of such praise would have been Edward IV. And he gives us very little information about the author, though Malory's own political connections may have prevented this. Such political risks, along with other hesitations expressed in his prologue, make us wonder that Caxton decided to publish *Le Morte Darthur* at all. Had he not, Arthurian literature from the sixteenth century to the present might well have been deprived of its major English source.

[JWS]

Spisak, James W. *Caxton's Malory: A New Edition of Sir Thomas Malory's Le Morte Darthur Based on the Pierpont Morgan Copy of William Caxton's Edition of 1485*. 2 vols. Berkeley: University of California Press, 1983.

Blake, N.F. *William Caxton: A Bibliographical Guide*. New York: Garland, 1985.

Hellinga, Lotte. *Caxton in Focus*. London: British Library, 1982.

Painter, George D. *William Caxton: A Quincentennial Biography of England's First Printer*. London: Chatto and Windus, 1976.

Rutter, Russell. "William Caxton and Literary Patronage." *Studies in Philology*, 84 (1987), 440–70.

CELIDON (Celyddon, Cat Coit Celidon), in Nennius's *Historia Brittonum*, the location of Arthur's seventh battle, where Arthur fought the Picts and Angles. However, because Bede's *Historia Ecclesiastica* mentions an alliance that was reached between the Picts and Angles in the middle of the fifth century, the date of Arthur's battle at Celidon conflicts with the dates of Arthur's battles at Badon and at Camlann, which, according to Gildas's *De Excidio Britanniae* and the *Annales Cambriae*, are fifty years later. The forest of Celidon includes Dumfries and Selkirkshire and extends to the upper Clyde and Tweed. Celidon is said to have been frequented by Lailoken, the "Wild Man of the Woods" who supposedly instigated an inter-British battle at Arfderydd (Arthuret) in the late sixth century and later went insane. In addition, Myrddin, who later appears as Merlin in Geoffrey of Monmouth, is thought to have lived in the forest of Celidon. The Welsh *Hoianau* states that he wandered in the woods for fifty years, hiding with a pig in an invisible apple-tree. [SW]

CELTIC ARTHURIAN LITERATURE: *see* GAELIC BALLADS; IRISH ARTHURIAN LITERATURE; WELSH ARTHURIAN LITERATURE.

CELTIC INFLUENCES ON ARTHURIAN LEGEND: *see* SCHOLARSHIP, MODERN ARTHURIAN.

CERDIC, reputed founder of the West Saxon dynasty and a figure in Arthurian speculation. According to the *Anglo-Saxon Chronicle*, he landed on the shore of Southampton Water in 495. He and his son and followers gradually established control over other Saxon groups on the Hampshire coast. Despite alleged successes against the local Britons, it is nowhere stated that Cerdic penetrated far inland. Under his successors, however, his little realm grew into the kingdom of Wessex. One of its kings was Alfred the Great, from whom a line of descent can be traced to modern royalty.

Archaeology confirms an early Saxon presence in the area indicated, but on a small scale. Gildas's testimony seems to imply that he has not heard of this inroad, or thinks it negligible, and Nennius's *Historia Brittonum* says nothing of Cerdic or his people, though it gives pedigrees for the Kentish, East Anglian, Mercian, and Northumbrian dynasties. Nevertheless, Cerdic has been proposed as an opponent of Arthur and even as the Saxon commander at the battle of Badon. The notion may have been inspired by Henry of Huntingdon, whose Arthur paragraph is inserted, rather vaguely, at a point where it can be construed as making the two contemporary. Versions of their inferred conflict occur in Higden and John of Glastonbury. Gibbon adopts it, and so do Alfred Duggan in his novel *Conscience of the King* (1951) and John Heath-Stubbs in his poem *Artorius* (1973).

Obscure as Cerdic is, his reality is probable because of his name, which no Wessex court-genealogist would have invented. It is not Anglo-Saxon but British, appearing early in Welsh and Latin forms. Nennius mentions "Ceretic" as Vortigern's interpreter in his dealings with Hengist; St. Patrick addresses a letter to the officers of the northern chief "Coroticus"; Geoffrey of Monmouth has a post-Arthurian British king called "Kareticus." There are other relevant instances.

It has been conjectured that Cerdic was the son of a British noble and a Saxon wife. He may have migrated to Armorica, where settlers of both ethnic stocks were more or less coexisting. Here, aided perhaps by his parentage, he could have recruited a mixed following, returning with this to assert some territorial claim, in defiance of the neighboring British authorities. The British element in his small domain would soon have been swamped by incoming Saxons. [GA]

Campbell, James, ed. *The Anglo-Saxons*. Ithaca, N.Y.: Cornell University Press, 1982, p. 37.

Morris, John. *The Age of Arthur*. New York: Scribner, 1973, pp. 103–04, 323–25.

CERVANTES SAAVEDRA, MIGUEL DE (1547–1616), Spanish author of *Don Quixote* (1605, 1615). This, the first modern novel, is also the final and comical turn to the insanity of Arthurian heroes, such as Yvain, Lancelot, and Amadís. Adventures in Part I parody the Arthurian quest of gratuitous adventure, and in Part II the hoax-enchantment of Dulcinea recreates the abduction-rescue pattern of Chrétien de Troyes's Lancelot-Guenevere story, though there is no direct influence. Cervantes's hero, who aspires to surpass the Knights of the Round Table, styles himself as knight in imitation of Amadís de Gaula and Lanzarote (Lancelot) of Castilian ballads; Sancho recalls the figure of Arthurian dwarfs. Arthurian influence is most evident in the episode of the penitent knight (Part I, Chapter 25), the enchantments in the cave and the hoax enchanter Merlin (Part II, Chapters 23 and 35), and in the themes of "dueñas y doncellas" ("dames et damoiseles") and of Arthur's return in the form of a raven (Part I, Chapter 13). [LAM]

Entwistle, William J. *The Arthurian Legend in the Literatures of the Spanish Peninsula*. London: Dent, 1925.

Murillo, L.A. *The Golden Dial*. Oxford: Dolphin, 1975.

Williamson, Edwin. *The Halfway House of Fiction:* Don Quixote *and Arthurian Romance*. Oxford: Clarendon, 1984.

CHAMBERLAIN, HOUSTON STEWART (1855–1927), son-in-law of Richard Wagner and literary, musical, and cultural historian. Chamberlain provides Wagner's *Parsifal* with psychological motivation and coherence through three fairy tales—*Weihnachtsmärchen*, *Ostermärchen*, and *Pfingstmärchen* (Christmas, Easter, and Pentecost Tales). The first two bridge Acts II and III of Wagner's cryptic opera, while the third rounds off Wagner's work by depicting Parsifal's death and the succession of his son, Lohengrin, as Grail King. [RWK]

Chamberlain, Houston Stewart. *Parsifal-märchen*. Munich: Bruckmann, 1900.

Golther, Wolfgang. *Parzival und der Gral in der Dichtung des Mittelalters und der Neuzeit*. Stuttgart: Metzler, 1925, pp. 336–38.

CHANT, JOY (pseudonym of Eileen Joyce Rutter), English librarian and author of *The High Kings* (1983). She focuses on significant episodes in Arthur's career to create a dramatic narrative frame for a book that is beautifully illustrated by George Sharp. Within this frame, bards recite traditional stories of past rulers and of Arthur himself, drawn from Geoffrey of Monmouth and Welsh tradition. Each episode and its accompanying story are preceded by a short explanation of some aspect of Celtic life relevant to the stories. The 1987 paperback edition, which lacks illustrations, restores cuts made in the text of the first edition. [RHT]

Chant, Joy. *The High Kings*, illus. George Sharp. New York: Bantam, 1983.

———. *The High Kings*, rev. ed. London: Unwin, 1987.

CHANTARI DI LANCELOTTO, LI, or *La struzione della Tavola Ritonda* ("The Destruction of the Round Table"), are seven *ottava rima* narratives of late fourteenth-century Italy that recount the fall of Camelot in a manner similar to that of the English Stanzaic *Morte Arthur*, which is also derived from the Vulgate *Mort Artu*. The seven sections into which the narrative is divided seem to reflect the duration of performances by the *cantastorie*, who were accustomed to perform on Sundays and feast days from noon to three and then, after an interval, until Vespers. The *cantari* narrate the destruction of the Round Table as follows: 1) Mordarette warns Artù that he is being dishonored by his wife and Lancelotto; Artù plans a tournament at Winchester (Vincestri) to see if Lancelotto will accompany the court or remain with the Queen. Lancelotto arrives in disguise; the Fair Maid of Astolat (Sgaleotto) falls in love with him and dies of despair. 2) A ship carries her body to Camelot, where it is discovered by Chalvano (Gawain). Ginevra (Guenevere) plans a dinner party, at which a knight is poisoned and Ginevra held responsible. Lancelotto rescues her from harm, but when he visits her later in her chambers he is ambushed by Chalvano and his brothers. Although Lancelotto escapes, the Queen is taken into custody. 3) Lancelotto rescues Ginevra as she is about to be burned at the stake, but accidentally murders Chalvano's brother, Ghueriesse (Gareth), in the attempt. 4) Artù and his troops besiege Joyous Gard until, through the intervention of the pope, it is agreed that the Queen will be returned to her husband. 5) Chalvano demands vengeance for the death of his brother and is mortally wounded in the subsequent assault on Lancelotto's French domain. 6) Mordarette rebels, and the Round Table is shattered in the course of the climactic battle on Salisbury Plain. Gilfrette (rather than the traditional Lucan) is given the task of returning Excalibur to the waves. When he finally succeeds, Artù is taken onto the mysterious ship and Camelot is burned and pillaged. 7) Following the death of Lionello, Lancelotto becomes a hermit, and, dying in holiness, is buried between his friend Galeotto (Galehaut) and his son, Galahad (Galeotto).

In addition to their merit as an effective popular narrative of the fall of Camelot, the *Chantari di Lancelotto* provide the only evidence that the French Vulgate tradition of the Arthurian legend was known in Italy. [DLH]

Griffiths, E.T., ed. *Li Chantari di Lancelotto*. Oxford: Clarendon, 1924.

Gardner, Edmund G. *The Arthurian Legend in Italian Literature*. London: Dent, 1930, pp. 265–67.

CHAPMAN, VERA, in her Three Damosels (or Arthurian) trilogy—*The Green Knight* (1975), *The King's Damosel* (1976), and *King Arthur's Daughter* (1976)—pioneered the female narration in modern Arthurian fiction. These fantasies are indebted to Malory and *Sir Gawain and the Green Knight*, but they demonstrate considerable originality. The borrowed and created narrators provide a refreshing vision of the twelfth century. Of particular note is Chapman's creation of Arthur's daughter, Ursulet ("the small bear," Princess/Queen of all England), and her slavery in *King Arthur's Daughter*; her amplification of the raped and unhappily married Lynett of Lyonesse in *The King's Damosel*; and the fell motivation for the Beheading Game in *The Green Knight*.

The tales are set generations apart, but they are unified by characters who age and reappear and by the brooding, ever-present specter of Arthur's archenemy, Morgan le Fay. The series focuses on the more magical events of the Arthurian legend (e.g., Bertilak's shape-shifting beneath Morgan's wand, Ursulet's achieving of the Holy Grail). However, the series' major accomplishment is its portrayal of strong women maturing in a chaotic, complex, and sorcerous time. [RCS]

Chapman, Vera. *The Green Knight.* London: Collings, 1975.
———. *The King's Damosel.* London: Collings, 1976.
———. *King Arthur's Daughter.* London: Collings, 1976.

CHASE, MARY ELLEN (1887–1973), American educator and author of two works that contain Arthurian allusions. In *Dawn in Lyonesse* (1938), the narrator's reading of the story of Tristan and Isolde gives her insight into a comparable bond between her husband and friend, while in "A Candle at Night" (1942) it leads her to forgive her friend for falling in love with her fiancé. [RHT]

Chase, Mary Ellen. *Dawn in Lyonesse.* New York: Macmillan, 1938.
———. "A Candle at Night." *Collier's*, May 9, 1942, 17, 74–77.

CHASTITY TESTS are a favorite motif in Arthurian literature. Chastity-testing devices, chiefly magic drinking horns and mantles (H 411.4 and H 411.7, respectively, in the Stith Thompson *Motif Index*) appear either as the central motif generating the plot, as in some lays and ballads, or as the focus of a major episode in a longer narrative. Most Arthurian chastity-testing tales derive from two twelfth-century French lays, Robert Biket's *Lai du cor* and the anonymous *Lai du cort mantel* (also known as *Le Mantel mautaillié*). In the former, the inability of a knight to drink from a magic horn without spilling its contents signals not his own infidelity but rather that of his beloved, and in the latter the infidelity of women is revealed by an ill-fitting magic mantle. Common to the two lays as well as the many narratives inspired by them is the public nature of the test: the infidelity of women is always exposed at a social gathering.

In both the *Lai du cor* and the *Lai du cort mantel*, the one flawless woman is the beloved of Caradoc (in Welsh, Caradawc Vreichvras), namely, Tegau Eurvron, who according to the Welsh "Triads of the Island of Britain" has in her possession a mantle, a goblet, and a knife. These presumably are the chastity-testing devices appearing throughout Arthurian literature. Of the three objects, the knife was literarily the least productive, but it does appear in conjunction with the horn and the mantle in the ballad "The Boy and the Mantle."

The drinking-horn test from the *Lai du cor* inspired similar tests in French, German, and English literature. It occurs in the *Livre de Caradoc*, embedded in the First Continuation (ca. 1200), which was subsequently included in abridged form (the *Carados*) in the fourteenth-century *Roman de Renart le Contrefait* (here, the vessel is a cup). The magic horn was introduced into the Tristan matter in the thirteenth-century Prose *Tristan*, and in the fifteenth century it entered both English and German literature in the *Romance of Sir Corneus* and the *Meisterlied* "Dis ist Frauw Tristerat Horn von Savoien," respectively.

In German literature, an additional chastity-testing device was depicted, a bridge that does not carry the unfaithful or otherwise imperfect lover (Thompson, H 411.8). The magic bridge appears in the thirteenth-century *Jüngerer Titurel* and in the presumably derivative sixteenth century *Meisterlied* "Die Ehbrecherbruck." When unfaithful lovers attempt to cross the bridge, they fall off. Whereas chastity tests are generally aimed at women, the author of the fifteenth-century German Shrovetide play *Vasnachtspil mit der Kron* features a crown that, when tried on by men, produces horns on the head of all but the faithful lover.

The magic mantle is the most usual chastity-testing device. Mantle tales are found in medieval as well as modern Arthurian literature, taking such forms as lay, ballad, novel, and even opera libretto. Common to the mantle-test compositions is the following plot: at Whitsun a messenger arrives at King Arthur's court and asks for a boon. Without knowing the nature of the request, the King agrees to grant it, only to learn that all the ladies, including Guenevere, are to try on a precious mantle fashioned by a fay. The woman whom the garment fits will receive it. The peculiar virtue of the mantle is its ability to expose unfaithful wives or lovers. One beautiful woman after another tries on the mantle, without, however, being aware of its special character, and is led in disgrace to her seat, while Kay, the steward, takes it upon himself to interpret the mantle's ill fit and reveal the nature of the sexual transgression. After presumably all the women at Arthur's court have miserably failed the test, the messenger fears he will have to depart without having found a faithful woman. But a final search is made of the premises, and a maiden is found, who had absented herself from the feasting because she was indisposed. Over the objections of her beloved, Caradoc, who fears the worst, she tries on the mantle, and it fits her. The couple then depart, taking the mantle with them.

The earliest literary attestation of the mantle-test tale is the *Lai du cort mantel*. Roger Sherman Loomis considered the mantle test to be of Welsh origin, since the Welsh Triads mention that Tegau Gold-breast, the wife of Caradawc Vreichvras, possessed the chastity-testing mantle. Even though there seemed to be widespread knowledge of the mantle of Tegau Gold-breast in Wales, there is no evidence that the Welsh tradition antedates the French lay. Furthermore, the Byzantinist Renée Kahane has noted that a variant of the chastity-testing mantle was already known to Byzantine folklore. A collection of historical and topological memorabilia, the *Pátria Kōnstantinoupóleōs* ("The Antiquities of Constantinople"), a work dating ca. 1000, mentions a chastity test in connection with the Xenón of Theophilus (829–42), a hostelry for the needy. In the days of Emperor Constantine the Great (r. 306–37), a statue of Aphrodite situated next to a brothel was used to test the chastity of women. When those who were unchaste walked past the statue, their outer garments were raised—in one redaction by a supernatural force, in another, by the women themselves—so as to uncover their private parts. It is possible that the author of the *Lai du cort mantel* not only was acquainted with Robert Biket's *Lai du cor* but also knew of the Byzantine tradition, under the influence of which he transformed Biket's horn into a magic mantle. Regardless of the origin of the motif, however, all the literary magic-mantle tales derive ultimately from the *Lai du cort mantel*.

The *Lai du cort mantel* is the source of the thirteenth-century German *Der Mantel* and the Old Norse *Möttuls saga*, which was translated during the reign of King Hákon Hákonarson, who ruled Norway from 1217 to 1263. Both the German and the Old Norse versions are characterized by a lengthy encomium of King Arthur, which is not found in the French lay. *Der Mantel* and *Möttuls saga* in turn are the source of subsequent mantle tales and episodes. From the fifteenth century, two German mantle-test compositions are extant, the *Meisterlied* "Lanethen Mantel" and a *Fastnachtspiel* entitled *Der Luneten Mantel*. Despite the titles, the two compositions are quite dissimilar, in part because the Shrovetide play extends the chastity test beyond Arthur's court to include the wives of mighty kings and emperors. *Möttuls saga*, a prose narrative, inspired the composition of the *Skikkju rímur* ("Mantle Rhymes"), a fourteenth-century Old Icelandic metrical version. The *rímur* modify and expand the mantle story by incorporating the wedding guests from *Erex saga*, the Old Norse-Icelandic version of Chrétien de Troyes's *Erec et Enide*. As in the German Shrovetide play, the *rímur* extend the mantle test to guests at King Arthur's court.

An English ballad from the sixteenth century, "The Boy and the Mantle," not only transmits the mantle test from the *Lai du cort mantel* but also incorporates two additional chastity tests. While the ladies submit to the trial by mantle, the knights undergo two tests: they must carve a wild boar's head and drink out of a magic horn without spilling its contents. Failure to succeed in the tasks indicates not their own lack of fidelity, however, but rather that of their ladies. The carving and drinking tests thus may be interpreted as a validation of the mantle test. Whereas the origin of the carving test is obscure (one should note, however, that the Welsh Triads mention a knife in addition to the horn and mantle), the trial by drinking horn presumably derives from the *Lai du cor*. "The Boy and the Mantle" provided the inspiration for Stephen Jackson's 1903 novel *The Magic Mantle*.

Except for its lack of an Arthurian setting, the ballad known as "The Magic Cloak," which belongs to the Gaelic Fionn Cycle and dates from the early fifteenth century, transmits a version of the Arthurian mantle tale. The ballad relates how six wives boast at a drinking party that nowhere on earth can there be found women as chaste as they. Their bragging is prelude to the appearance of a maiden wearing a seamless white robe that shields only the spotless wife. Conan's wife tries on the mantle, but it leaves her breast exposed. The chieftain becomes so enraged that he kills her; but the other women live to tell the tale. The ballad concludes with a curse on the bearer of the mantle. Although scholars are not agreed about the ballad's relationship to the existing Arthurian tales, recent scholarship favors the thesis that the Irish mantle story is more likely to derive from the Arthurian versions than vice versa.

Several mantle episodes and references are embedded in longer works, both Arthurian and non-Arthurian. The most extensive occurs in Ulrich von Zatzikhoven's *Lanzelet* (ll. 5,679–6,157), dated to the very end of the twelfth century. The episode is nearly half the length of the *Lai du cort mantel*. Here, the mantle test does not reveal a woman's failure to be faithful to her knight but rather woman's—as well as man's—failure to adhere to the conventions of the courtly game of love. Two additional Lancelot-romances, the one French, the other Dutch, incorporate the mantle story. In the *Vengeance Raguidel*, dated to the early thirteenth century and written by a certain Raoul, possibly Raoul de Houdenc, a page informs Gawain that a mantle test had taken place at Arthur's court during his absence and summarizes the events (ll. 3,928–61). In the first quarter of the fourteenth century, this romance was incorporated in abridged form in the Dutch *Lancelot*, where the page's account of the mantle test occurs in ll. 12,504–27. In Heinrich von dem Türlin's monumental romance *Diu Crône*, women's fidelity is tested not only by means of the magic mantle but also by means of a cup and glove. In Iceland, the non-Arthurian *Samsons saga fagra* contains a mantle test and also relates how the mantle came to be woven. The saga enlarges on the power of the magic mantle: in addition to testing feminine faithfulness, it can be used to identify thieves.

Two dialogues contain references to the mantle. Johannes von Tepl's *Ackermann aus Böhmen* ("Plowman from Bohemia"), a dialogue between Death and a plowman dated between 1401 and 1405, mentions the gift of a mantle, which the plowman's wife was able to take untorn and untainted to her grave. The puzzling reference is clarified in the slightly later but related *Tkadleček* (1409), a Czech dialogue between a weaver, whose beloved has been unfaithful to him, and Misfortune. In *Tkadleček*, Honor is said to possess a mantle that fits only women who do not waver in their honor, a garment presumably inspired by the Arthurian chastity-test mantle.

Literary sources relate that the chastity-testing mantle had become something of a relic in the Middle Ages. Sir Thomas Gray (d. 1369?) tells us in his *Scalacronica* that the mantle could still be seen in his own day in Glastonbury, whereas Raimon de Perillos, who left an account of a trip he took from Avignon to Dublin at the end of the fourteenth century, informs us that the mantle could be viewed in Dover, together with Gawain's skull. A century later, Caxton confirms in the preface to his edition of *Le Morte Darthur* (1485) that "Cradocks mantel" may be seen in the castle of Dover.

The mantle tale was revived in modern times in Germany. In 1778, Johann Gottfried Herder published his German translation of "The Boy and the Mantle," and Clemens Brentano and Achim von Arnim included in their famous collection of folksongs *Des Knaben Wunderhorn* ("A Boy's Magic Horn," 1806–08) the ballad "Die Ausgleichung" ("The Adjustment"). The ballad relates that King Arthur and Queen Guenevere obtained from a dwarf a magic mantle and a magic horn, respectively, to test each other. Additional members of Arthur's court are tested, and only a very old knight and his very young wife turn out to be faithful to each other.

Of greater significance than the two ballads is Benedikte Naubert's novel *Der kurze Mantel* ("The Short Mantle"), which was published in a collection of four volumes (1789–93) entitled *Neue Volksmährchen der Deutschen* ("New Folktales of the Germans") and which subsequently inspired the composition of an opera libretto and a *Singspiel*. Naubert, who knew both the English ballad and a sixteenth-century French prose redaction, *Le Manteau mal taillié*, combined the mantle, drinking-horn, and boar-carving tests with material from the German folktale about Frau Holle, a good fay who punishes lazy and impertinent women but rewards those who are diligent and industrious. In effect, *Der kurze Mantel* is a piece of negative criticism of the Arthurian world, which is depicted as controlled by lascivious women. The mantle test vindicates the one pure woman at Arthur's court, who had been banished as the result of Guenevere's false accusations.

Naubert's novel inspired Friedrich August Clemens Werthes to publish in 1800 *Das Pfauenfest* ("The Feast of Peacocks"), which was set to music by Johann Rudolf Zumsteeg, concertmaster to the court of Duke Frederick I. The *Singspiel* was premiered at the Hoftheater in Stuttgart on February 24, 1801, and was well received. A version derivative of both the *Singspiel* and Naubert's novel appeared under the title "Lenora" in Johann Peter Lyser's collection of tales entitled *Abendländische Tausend und eine Nacht* ("Occidental Thousand and One Nights"), published in 1838. Unlike Werthes's musical version of the mantle tale, an opera libretto in three acts entitled *Der Zaubermantel* ("The Magic Mantle"), by Karl Franz van der Velde, although published in 1816–17, was never set to music. [MEK]

Child, Francis James, ed. *The English and Scottish Popular Ballads*. Boston and New York: Houghton-Mifflin, 1884; New York: Folklore Press, 1956, Vol. 1, pp. 257–71.

Kalinke, Marianne E., ed. *Mǫttuls saga: With an Edition of* Le Lai du cort mantel *by Philip E. Bennett*. Copenhagen: Reitzel, 1987, esp. pp. xiii–xxxiii.

Thompson, Stith. *Motif Index of Folk-Literature*, 2nd ed. 6 vols. Bloomington: Indiana University Press, 1955.

CHÂTEAUBRIANT, ALPHONSE DE (1877–1951), French author of *La Réponse du Seigneur* ("The Lord's Response"), a 1933 novel that explicitly acknowledges its Grail quest theme. A student seeking adventures in Brittany follows a path through the forest and comes upon a manor with open doors (cf. *Perceval*). He enters and finds a company assembled for a funeral ceremony (cf. the Gauvain Continuation). An old man in pain, a sort of Maimed King, takes the youth to be the long-awaited hero, his spiritual heir. In a scene reminiscent of Chrétien de Troyes's *Lancelot* and of Sigune from Wolfram's *Titurel*, a dwarf leading them from a cemetery informs the young man that the latter is the only hero "capable of transforming everything evil into good." During the evening, the master initiates him into the legend of the Grail, an ineffable object manifested as a butterfly, lace, a flower. Contemplation of it permits an apotheosis by which earthly chivalry is made celestial. Upon his departure, the youth is given this marvelous talisman; he returns to the world but then retires to a monastery (cf. *La Queste del Saint Graal* and the Third Continuation).

It is notable that, though a germanophile, Châteaubriant was nonetheless the first French writer of the period to turn for inspiration to French versions of the Grail story rather than to Wagner. [RB]

Châteaubriant, Alphonse de. *La Réponse du Seigneur*. Paris: Grasset, 1933.

CHAUCER, GEOFFREY (1340?–1400), names Arthurian figures and uses some Arthurian narrative motifs in the *Canterbury Tales*. In *The Squire's Tale*, the youthful squire tells a chivalric romance of suitably amorous aspiration. Gawain and Lancelot are cited as exemplars of courtesy and courtly behavior but seen as remote and long-gone (ll. 95–97, 287). Like *Sir Thopas*, with its mention of "Sir Lybeux" (l. 900) and "Sire Percyvall" (l. 916, and see *Sir Percyval of Galles*), these later Arthurian allusions are oblique and wry in comparison with those of the Chaucerian *Roman de la Rose* translation (ll. 1,199, 2,209).

The Wife of Bath's Tale offers a short (408 lines) but complex reworking of the Loathly Lady theme. Unlike his counterparts in ballad and Middle English romance (*The*

Wedding of Sir Gawain and Dame Ragnell, "The Marriage of Sir Gawain"), the protagonist is not Gawain but an unnamed Arthurian knight. Having raped a maiden, he is granted his life by the Queen if he can say what it is that all women desire. Tutored by an old hag, the knight gives the correct answer to the assembled ladies of the court but is appalled when, as her promised reward, the hag claims him in marriage. On their wedding night, she answers his objections to her low birth, poverty, and age with a sermon principally on the theme that "he is gentil that dooth gentil dedis" (l. 1,170) and offers him the choice of having her ugly and faithful, or fair and sought-after. Resigning the choice to her, the knight effectively gives her the sovereignty women desire; she promises him permanent fairness and constancy.

Other Middle English Arthurian narratives (notably *Sir Gawain and the Green Knight*) use the delayed articulation of female roles to revise the ethical categories of chivalric protagonists. Here, the knight's initial act of rape provokes reconsideration of personal identity and its consequent rights and obligations in the more general terms of marriage rather than chivalry. Chaucer juxtaposes folkloric, patristic, and courtly elements in a complex redirection of romance, affecting nonchivalric identities. The Loathly Lady's entirely inner-directed account of what constitutes a person challenges the knight's sense of how far birth, possessions, and appearance make identity, but she nonetheless acknowledges his creaturely need in her permanent fairness. The tale's Arthurian setting functions to place this realistic and accommodating application of the ideology of *gentilesse* as possible nowhere but in Faery, where mutual rights, obligations, and identities can be renegotiated. Often seen as wish-fulfillment for its teller, the tale is less a romance illustrating an individual psyche, than an exemplum to provoke reevaluation of the ideologies of personal and social identity in us all. [JP]

Chaucer, Geoffrey, *The Riverside Chaucer*, ed. Larry D. Benson. Boston: Houghton Mifflin, 1987.

———. *The Wife of Bath's Prologue and Tale*, ed. J. Winny. Cambridge: Cambridge University Press, 1965.

Carruthers, M. "The Wife of Bath and the Painting of Lions." *PMLA*, 94 (1979), 209–22.

Patterson, Lee. "For the Wyves of Bathe: Feminine Rhetoric in the *Roman de la Rose* and the *Canterbury Tales*." *Speculum*, 58 (1983), 656–95.

Silverstein, T. "The Wife of Bath and the Rhetoric of Enchantment." *Modern Philology*, 58 (1961), 153–73.

CHAUSSON, ERNEST (1855–1899), French composer, devoted much energy in his final years to *Le Roi Arthus* (Opus 23), an opera for which he wrote, following Wagner's example, both the libretto and the music. It was first performed in Brussels four years after his death. The theme is Lancelot's passion for Guenevere. Their love is betrayed by the self-seeking Mordred. After agonies of remorse, Guenevere strangles herself and Lancelot is slain in battle, but Arthus, magnanimous and idealistic, achieves immortality as he is borne away across the sea. Chausson responds creatively to Wagner's influence without losing individuality, and in its lyricism and respect for the rhythms of French speech the opera looks forward to *Pelléas et Mélisande*. Chausson also composed the symphonic poem *Viviane* (1882). [CNS]

Barricelli, J.-P., and Leo Weinstein, *Ernest Chausson*. Norman: Oklahoma University Press, 1955.

Hunt, Tony. "Ernest Chausson's 'Le Roi Arthus.'" *Arthurian Literature*, 4 (1985), 127–54.

CHERRYH, C.J. (pseudonym of Carolyn Janice Cherry). In her thoughtful science-fiction novel *Port Eternity* (1982), a spacecraft is marooned in another dimension where its human occupants are threatened by aliens. The crew are "made people"—cloned from special genetic combinations, then conditioned to order for human owners. Influenced by Tennyson's *Idylls of the King*, their owner had modeled them on Arthurian characters: Lancelot, Mordred, Vivien, Gawain, Percival, Lynette, and Elaine of Astolat. Their attempts to cope with the external threat on the one hand, and the internal pressure to act out their traditional roles on the other, provide penetrating insight into the problems created for us all by our conditioned attitudes. [RHT]

Cherryh, C.J. *Port Eternity*. New York: DAW, 1982.

Thompson, Raymond H. *The Return from Avalon: A Study of the Arthurian Legend in Modern Fiction*. Westport, Conn.: Greenwood, 1985.

CHERTSEY ABBEY TILES, surviving fragments of a thirteenth-century pavement, illustrate the Anglo-Norman version of the romance of *Tristan* by Thomas d'Angleterre. The abbey, ten miles from Windsor, enjoyed royal patronage under the Plantagenets, and W.R. Lethaby has suggested that the tiles were made in 1270 for a "King's Chapel" funded by Henry III. Among the identified subjects are thirty-five scenes from *Tristan*, three of Richard Coeur de Lion, and a number of hunts and combats.

The tiles, an inch thick and nine and a half inches in diameter, were made of dark red clay stamped with a design, and the resulting impression was filled with white

22. Chertsey Abbey Tile: Tristan Harping. (The Trustees of the British Museum.)

clay. Each composition was in a rondel, encircled by an inscription and enframed in a foliate patterned square. Other pavements of this type have been identified, including that of the Abbey of Halesowen near Birmingham, where some of the Chertsey Abbey tile molds were reused, but the Chertsey program appears to have been the most magnificent.

In the nineteenth century, Manwaring Shurlock, a retired physician, recognized the source of the tiles as *Tristan* and published his findings in *Tiles from Chertsey Abbey* (London, 1885). The surviving narrative concentrates on Tristan's youth: his boyhood adventures, his arrival at the court of Cornwall, and his combat with Marhaus. By coincidence, or by censorious design, only three tiles depict the scenes after Tristan and Isolde drink the potion. The tiles are presently scattered; the largest collection is in the British Museum in London, with other examples in the Victoria and Albert Museum, London, and the Survey Archaeological Society Museum at Guilford. [DNM]

Lethaby, W.R. "The Romance Tiles of Chertsey Abbey." *Walpole Society Annual*, 2 (1912–13), 69–80.

Loomis, Roger Sherman. *Illustrations of Medieval Romance on Tiles of Chertsey Abbey*. Urbana: University of Illinois Press, 1916.

CHESTER, NORLEY (pseudonym of Emily Underdown), adapted the Grail legends for children in *Knights of the Grail. Lohengrin: Galahad* (1907). Galahad, "the youngest and bravest knight," is presented as a model: "for the pure of heart all things are possible and those who would wear the victor's crown must seek it with no thought of self." Lancelot's role as the knight who fails through sensuality and pride is transferred to Perceval. [MAW]

Chester, Norley. *Knights of the Grail. Lohengrin: Galahad*. London, Edinburgh, Dublin, and New York: Nelson, 1907.

CHESTERTON, FRANCES ALICE (1875–1938), the wife of G.K. Chesterton, composed "Sir Cleges" (1924), a didactic play for children based on the medieval version. After giving all his goods to the poor, the impoverished Cleges finds ripe cherries on a tree at Christmas, a gift of Virgin Mary. He presents them to Arthur, who rewards him by restoring his land. [RHT]

Chesterton, Frances Alice. "Sir Cleges (Christmas Play of the Arthurian Legend)." In *Three Plays for Children*. London and New York: French, 1924.

CHESTERTON, G(ILBERT) K(EITH) (1874–1936), in his eighteen-line poem "The Myth of Arthur" launches a characteristically vigorous and witty onslaught on dry-as-dust scholarship that would banish poetry from life by its over-cautious approach to such figures as Arthur. "The Grave of Arthur," published in 1930 with attractive illustrations by Celia Fiennes, is an incantatory poem in twelve four-line stanzas on the theme "dead is the King who shall not die." [CNS]

Chesterton, G.K. "The Myth of Arthur." In *Collected Poems*. London: Parker, 1927, p. 58.

———. *The Grave of Arthur*. London: Faber and Faber, 1930.

CHESTRE, THOMAS, generally thought to be the author of *Libeaus Desconus* and *Sir Launfal*. *Libeaus Desconus* is a late fourteenth-century stanzaic tail-rhyme version of the Fair Unknown story. The English version includes more motifs than Renaut de Beaujeu's *Le Bel Inconnu*, and Chestre probably used several variant versions of Fair Unknown romances. Though not always highly regarded by modern critics, Chestre's text survives in one seventeenth- and five fifteenth-century manuscripts.

Lybeaus is announced by the narrator to be Gawain's son, Gyngalyn, but he himself remains ignorant of his identity in a solitary rural upbringing, in which his mother calls him Bewfiz. He is named Lybeaus Desconus by King Arthur when he requests knighthood and the next Arthurian adventure. Initially scorned by this adventure's maiden and dwarf messengers, Lybeaus nonetheless successfully undertakes an escalating series of prowess-testing encounters en route to rescuing the Lady of Synadoun from imprisonment. He defeats Sir William Salebraunche, William's three brothers, and two giants, sending them vanquished to Arthur's court. His messenger-damsel fails to win a beauty contest, but he defeats the winning lady's knight in combat and sends Arthur the prize gerfalcon. He also fights to retain the hound of Sir Otes de Lyle the huntsman, thus indicating competence for another chivalric pursuit.

Lybeaus further experiences the interrelations of knightly prowess and love in a long *recreantise* from his quest with the Ile d'Or sorceress Dame Amoure. Rebuked by his messenger-damsel, Lybeaus re-proves himself, in a long joust with the steward of Synadoun, as being worthy of hospitality, worthy of the quest, and worthy of being Gawain's kin. He then tackles the two clerks oppressing the Lady of Synadoun; after earthquakes, other deceptive appearances, and difficult combats, he prevails and with his kiss frees the Lady of Synadoun from existence as a lamia. The romance concludes with their bridal feast and Arthurian rejoicing. [JP]

Sir Launfal is a fourteenth-century lay of 1,044 lines that survives in a single manuscript (London, B.L. Cotton Caligula A II). It is the work of a minstrel who identifies himself at the conclusion of the piece as Thomas Chestre. Though his primary source was an English couplet version of *Sir Landeval*, Chestre recounts his lay in the stanzaic form characteristic of the English tail-rhyme romances—i.e., in twelve-line stanzas rhyming aabccbddbeeb, aabaabccbddb, or aabaabccbccb.

From *Sir Landeval*, Chestre derived the rudiments of his narrative of the magnanimous young Sir Launfal, who leaves Arthur's court in disgrace, takes a fairy mistress during his absence from Carlisle, loses his mistress as a consequence of boasting about her to Guinevere, and is ultimately reunited with his lover and vindicated by her of the false charges leveled against him by the Queen. As all students of the poem have recognized, Chestre's indebtedness to *Sir Landeval* is marked: the later poet omits few of the details found in his original and in some passages takes over whole lines and fragments of lines from his primary source. Indeed, the verbal similarities between Chestre's poem and *Sir Landeval* are such that it would appear that Chestre was working with a version of *Sir Landeval* very similar to that which survives in Oxford, Bodl. MS Rawlinson C 86.

To the version of the Launfal story preserved in *Sir Landeval*, however, Chestre added a good deal of material borrowed from other sources. From the anonymous lay of *Graelent*, for example, Chestre derived the motif of Guinevere's animosity toward Launfal, most of the incidents that take place at the mayor's dwelling during Launfal's exile from Arthur's court, and the account of the disappearance of Gyfre after Launfal's fateful encounter with the amoral Guinevere. According to Roger Sherman Loomis, the tournament and Sir Valentine episodes in *Sir Launfal* are also borrowed, in this case from a source or sources no longer extant. In short, the only parts of the poem believed to be of Chestre's own invention are the episodes concerning Launfal's relations with Sir Hugh and Sir John and with his former servant, the mayor.

Interestingly, it is not Chestre's lack of originality but his lack of refinement that has most frequently occasioned comment by critics of *Sir Launfal*. With only a few exceptions, students of the poem have charged that the work is unsophisticated and that, given the behavior of its principal characters, its moral tone is dubious at best. Although there is an element of validity in these charges, particularly when *Sir Launfal* is compared with extant romances intended for an aristocratic audience, we ought always to bear in mind that this lay was almost certainly composed for and recited to a popular audience acquainted only through fiction with the principles of chivalric action and decorum. [JN]

Chestre, Thomas. *Lybeaus Desconus*, ed. Maldwyn Mills. London: Oxford University Press, 1969.

———. *Sir Launfal*, ed. A.J. Bliss. London and Edinburgh: Nelson, 1960.

CHETWIN, GRACE, English-born teacher and novelist. In *Out of the Dark World* (1985), a novel for younger readers, Meg lives on Long Island, New York, but her heritage is Welsh. With her gift of second sight and an ability to travel through dreams and time, and with the assistance of Rhiannon/Morgan le Fay, she rescues a cousin who has been confined in a computer in a future time. [HT]

Chetwin, Grace. *Out of the Dark World*. New York: Lothrop, Lee and Shepard, 1985.

CHEVALIER À L'ÉPÉE, LE ("The Knight of the Sword"), a brief (1,206-line) French Gauvain romance composed at the time of, or shortly after, Chrétien de Troyes. The work may be by the same author (who signs himself Paien de Maisières) who wrote *La Mule sans frein*. The author plays amusingly on Gauvain's traditional lack of constancy by contrasting him in this work to others far more fickle than he. [NJL]

Johnson, R.C., and D.D.R. Owen, eds. *Two Old French Gauvain Romances*. New York: Barnes and Noble, 1973.

CHEVALIER DU PAPEGAU, LE ("The Knight of the Parrot"), an independent French prose romance from the late fourteenth or early fifteenth century, preserved in a single manuscript (Paris, B.N. f. fr. 2154). In the story, the newly crowned Arthur sets out to liberate a lady from her oppressor. The short narrative is so action-filled that it defies summary, but it is characterized by a strong use of supernatural elements, such as the Fish-Knight and the parrot that gives its name to the romance. This latter is kept in a splendid golden cage and carried on horseback; it sings songs to Arthur and advises him on his course of action.

The title of *Le Chevalier du papegau* probably plays on that of Chrétien de Troyes's *Le Chevalier au lion* (*Yvain*), but the symbolic and narrative function of the parrot is much reduced when compared with that of the lion in Chrétien's romance. As is the case with many later Arthurian romances, the *Papegau* has to be seen as a response to earlier tradition, knowledge of which is assumed by the author on the part of the audience. The generally comic tone of the work suggests not so much a degeneration of the romance form as a blurring of the generic parameters between romance, *nouvelle*, and fabliau. [KB]

Heuckenkamp, Ferdinand, ed. *Le Chevalier du Papegau*. Halle: Niemeyer, 1896.

Vesce, Thomas E., trans. *The Knight of the Parrot* (*Le Chevalier du papegau*). New York: Garland, 1986.

Taylor, Jane H.M. "The Fourteenth Century: Context, Text, and Intertext." In *The Legacy of Chrétien de Troyes*, ed. Norris J. Lacy, Douglas Kelly, and Keith Busby. 2 vols. Amsterdam: Rodopi, 1987, Vol. 1, pp. 267–332.

CHIVALRY. It is impossible to define chivalry adequately in a few paragraphs, because the term denoted differing states and obligations, depending on whether we are dealing with the early or the late Middle Ages, with political and social reality or literary inspiration, with secular or religious contexts, and so on. We can, however, make some generalizations. In its origins, "chivalry" refers to a purely military status (the very word *chevalier* in French suggests a mounted soldier). Yet it quickly developed into far more than that. It was generally an indication of social standing, and in its literary expression it could develop into an elaborate code, inextricably linked up in complex ways with courtly love.

The *Ordene de chevalerie*, an early thirteenth-century French treatise on the theory of knighthood, enumerates the knight's duties: to love God and be willing to spill his blood for Him; to possess justice and loyalty, protecting the poor and the weak; to remain clean in flesh and pure in spirit, avoiding in particular the sin of lechery; and, remembering that death is before us all, to strive for candor and flee from pride. In a more practical piece of advice, the knight is told not to witness false judgment or treason, never to deny his protection to a lady or maiden, to be abstemious, and to attend Mass daily.

Other treatises, as well as descriptions of the practice of chivalry, emphasize that honor, prowess, and loyalty are the knight's cardinal virtues; important corollaries include generosity, compassion and pity, courtesy, courage, and religious zeal. Although chivalry was an ideal—indeed, an ideal that may have been only infrequently attained, and perhaps never in actual warfare—it abounded in practical axioms, including the prohibition against a healthy and armed knight attacking another who is unarmed, injured, or afoot. Indeed, if a knight unhorsed his opponent, he was required, in principle, either to allow the other to remount or to dismount and continue the battle on foot. Similarly, a knight was expected to accord rest or respite to one who requested it, treat a defeated opponent with honor, and in general follow the dictates of "fair play."

Following Painter, it is customary to divide the subject of chivalry into three categories: Feudal Chivalry, Religious Chivalry, and Courtly Love. Feudal chivalry, largely summarized above, is the service of one's feudal lord or king; in exchange for protection and a fief, the knight owed fealty to the lord, and the crucial qualities in his service were prowess (courage, strength, and skill in the use of weapons) and loyalty. Religious chivalry, according to which we are all God's vassals, added to these virtues piety, temperance, and chastity (and, of course, adherence to the tenets and causes of the church and, secondarily, to the demands of the prince). Courtly love wedded the adoration of the lady to the chivalric ethic, holding love to be an ennobling, even perfecting, force. Adoration, fidelity, and the acquisition of certain social graces assumed an importance approaching—in some cases, surpassing—that of military skills and devotion to political or religious causes.

Accordingly, medieval literature, Arthurian or other, could emphasize the knight's obligation to God, to the king and the social order, or to a lady; alternatively, writers could attempt a synthesis of two or all of these obligations. Such a synthesis was not always comfortable or effective. In earlier French romances, such as those by Chrétien de Troyes, the knight often fails to understand that chivalry and love are, or can be, compatible. Thus, Chrétien's heroes may err by neglecting chivalry (Erec) or by neglecting the lady for the pleasures of knighthood (Yvain). In Chrétien's *Lancelot*, however, the service of the lady is clearly paramount, and it is that service that gives meaning to the chivalric vocation. In later works, such as the French Vulgate Cycle, the quest for the Grail assumes priority, as a higher conception of chivalry supplants both courtly love and the political/social functions of knighthood. Malory often sees the demands of chivalry as incompatible with those of love: the successful Grail quester must keep himself pure, whereas the earlier French poets sometimes interpreted "purity" in a relative way. For Galahad, amorous satisfaction would interfere with his higher calling.

Whatever the particular conception of chivalry, certain virtues remained constant. Constancy itself, the single-minded devotion to a goal, was the ideal. The knight was sworn to uphold the good and overturn evil, and he was obligated to protect the poor, the weak, the downtrodden, such as widows, maidens, and orphans. Generosity, as Chrétien reminds us, is the queen of virtues, for knights as for others. This ideal entailed various practices, from offering hospitality to bestowing gifts to freeing captives on their word. Conversely, the knight must himself be honest and trustworthy, keeping his word and his promises.

Moreover, a knight's reputation was carefully cultivated and prized, since it was considered an accurate indication of his character; but in building and nurturing that reputation, he often sought adventure for its own sake, savoring the pleasure of successful martial, or amatory, encounters. While such events—or at least the martial ones—might usefully hone the knight's skills, a number of texts, most notably Chrétien's *Perceval*, offered examples of knights who sought adventure solely for the purpose of acquiring glory, without understanding that only unswerving service to an ideal or to a person could give meaning and value to chivalry.

Not surprisingly, there grew up around general chivalric precepts a code of social conduct that could become very complex and that could, and sometimes did, become little more than meaningless ritual. It was normally assumed that a knight should possess the social graces and abilities expected of the nobility (the low-born being generally excluded from chivalric ranks), and certain knights, such as Gawain, took obvious pleasure in demonstrating their mastery of manners, conversational skills, and techniques of seduction. Discretion and restraint were considered virtues, but these too could go awry. Chrétien's Perceval is advised, for example, not to talk excessively, and he mistakes such trivial rules for the more important precepts of chivalry. The possibility of such error, of cultivating ritual instead of performing useful service, was exploited by a number of authors, who used Gawain or other knights as examples of chivalry gone wrong.

Since the king was considered to be God's vassal (as his knights were his), Arthur was, not unexpectedly, the most honorable and virtuous of men. This conception of the King appears not to have been compromised even when writers of romance presented him as largely passive or ineffectual. In Chrétien, for example, Arthur's military power and his own prowess often appear to have been neutralized, so that he is unable to respond forcefully to a stranger's threats at court (in *Lancelot*) or prevent the theft of a valued gold cup (in *Perceval*). Yet the opening lines of *Yvain* praise Arthur's exemplary valor, which teaches others to be brave and courteous. He is noted for having never failed to keep his word, and he is consistently presented as the repository of the highest chivalric virtues, from generosity to courtesy to honesty. (*See also* COURTLY LOVE.) [NJL]

Broughton, Bradford B. *Dictionary of Medieval Knighthood and Chivalry*. 2 vols. Westport, Conn.: Greenwood, 1986–88.

Busby, Keith, ed. *Raoul de Houdenc: "Le Roman des eles"; The Anonymous "Ordene de Chevalerie."* Amsterdam: Benjamins, 1983.

Gies, Frances. *The Knight in History*. New York: Harper and Row, 1984.

Keen, Maurice. *Chivalry*. New Haven: Yale University Press, 1984.

Painter, Sidney. *French Chivalry*. Baltimore: Johns Hopkins University Press, 1940.

CHRÉTIEN DE TROYES, the greatest French writer of medieval romance. Some would consider him the inventor of the genre, although that would do a serious injustice to the authors of the romances of antiquity, composed around, and shortly after, the middle of the twelfth century. In any event, Chrétien was without a doubt instrumental both in the elaboration of the Arthurian legend and in the establishment of the ideal form for the diffusion of that legend.

We know virtually nothing of Chrétien's life, although some information can be drawn from his own references to his work. For example, in the prologue to *Cligés* he tells us that he had translated or adapted several Ovidian works (entitled in his text *Les Commandemanz d'Ovide, L'Art d'amors*, and *Le Mors de l'espaule*) and that he had composed a work about Isolde and King Mark; none of these works is extant. He also lists another Ovidian adaptation, the metamorphosis (or *muance*) "de la hupe et de l'aronde et del rossignol"; this text, from Ovid's Philomela story, does exist in a version that may be his. In addition, we have from Chrétien two brief lyric poems and the five Arthurian romances for which he is known today. A romance entitled *Guillaume d'Angleterre* (a pseudo-hagiographic narrative) bears the name "Crestiiens," and scholars disagree about the identification of this author with Chrétien de Troyes. His romances are written in octosyllabic couplets, the standard narrative form of the period.

Presumably, Chrétien was from Troyes or, at least, had spent a good part of his active life there; both his name and certain dialectal features of his language support this contention. We do not know when he was born. There is considerable difference of opinion concerning the dates of his romances. Some scholars (e.g., Luttrell) conclude that Chrétien's primary literary activity took place in the 1180s, while others suggest that he composed his romances some time between the late 1150s—in the *Chevalier de la charrete*, he refers to Marie de Champagne as *ma dame de Chanpaigne*, indicating that her marriage to Henry the Liberal, which took place as early as 1159, predated the composition of this work—and ca. 1190. His final romance, *Le Conte del Graal*, was dedicated to Philip of Flanders, who died in 1191.

Chrétien's first Arthurian romance was *Erec et Enide*, followed by *Cligés*, *Le Chevalier de la charrete* ("The Knight of the Cart," also known as *Lancelot*), *Le Chevalier au lion* ("The Knight with the Lion," or *Yvain*), and *Le Conte del Graal* ("The Story of the Grail," or *Perceval*). Two manuscripts (Paris, B.N. f. fr. 794 and 1450) preserve all five of the romances; approximately thirty others contain one or more of them.

Certain common threads run through Chrétien's romances, despite differences of tone, subject matter, and artistic maturity. The most obvious of these threads is the Arthurian setting and the author's literary exploration of the notion of Arthurian chivalry. Arthur and his court remain at the center of the society examined by Chrétien, but Arthur himself is never the center of a romance (indeed, in *Yvain* he becomes something of a doddering, ineffective old man, although his authority is never questioned and the respect he receives diminishes only slightly). Chrétien's emphasis is instead on the trials, errors, and ultimate triumphs of his hero, on the hero's love interests, and on the relationship, often uncomfortable until perfected through trials or pain, of that love with the social demands of chivalry. It is also possible to see the works as exploring the problem of the individual vs. the couple, the couple vs. society, or self-interest vs. the social utility of knighthood. Generalizing further, we can state that, while Chrétien's works may not include a genuine *Bildungsroman*, they do generally trace the development of characters from naiveté to sophistication and from ignorance to understanding. This is true to a significant degree even for the heroes who, like Yvain or Lancelot, are knights accomplished and respected—but nonetheless flawed—even when we first meet them.

Erec et Enide develops with clarity the potential conflicts between love and chivalry; the latter term is taken to include service to others, the quest for adventure, and concern for one's reputation. Once Erec wins his bride, he neglects his public duties, causing others to grumble. Enide herself laments the rumors about him and the responsibility she may bear for those rumors. Overhearing her expression of concern, and presumably doubting her love and devotion, he commands her—without explanation—to prepare to leave with him. There follows a period of wandering, hardship, and pain. Erec imposes silence on Enide, but she repeatedly disobeys him in order to warn him of approaching danger. Ironically, it is through disobedience, indicating concern for his welfare rather than for her own, that she proves her love for him.

The period of wandering in fact constitutes a test for both of them, providing proof of her love and of his chivalric (i.e., public, active) competence, of his ability to tend to his public duties while remaining the loving husband. Readers, not surprisingly, have frequently thought him to have an odd way of expressing his love: her husband requires Enide to go without sleep and indulge his apparently petulant actions. But neither the narrator nor Enide herself appears to entertain any doubts in this regard. In exploring ways to reconcile the lover's devotion with the knight's duty, Chrétien's first romance dramatizes a problem that will concern him repeatedly while at the same time offering the first of several solutions to that problem.

Chrétien's next romance, *Cligés*, resembles his first in a number of ways but also differs from it significantly. The primary difference is in the structure: Chrétien recounts the story of Alexandre (Cligés's father) before that of the hero himself. In so doing, Chrétien appears to be making systematic reference to the Tristan story, and some critics have contended in fact that he is composing an "anti-Tristan." Yet, despite this bipartite division, the poem's general complexion, both technical and ideological, identifies it as Chrétien's composition.

The similarity of this work to *Erec et Enide* resides in the dramatization of a "before/after" duality; here, however, the contrast is not between an earlier and a later stage of a single knight's development but between the levels of courtly sophistication of two consecutive generations. The first is Alexandre's, which is non- or "proto-courtly" (in Peter Haidu's term). The work is Chrétien's most rhetorical romance, with Alexandre, among others, indulging in extensive and self-conscious interior monologues on the subject of love and his beloved. In the course of his monologues, he grapples poorly with the subject, although his lack of subtlety in no way diminishes the intensity of his love. By contrast, Cligés proves himself a comfortable inhabitant of the courtly world, dealing easily and adroitly with the rhetoric and with the sensations of love.

The romance offers more specific reminiscences of the Tristan legend, in addition to a number of explicit references to it. Cligés loves Fénice, but she is married to his uncle Alis (Isolde had of course been the wife of Tristan's uncle). Fénice loves him, also, but she insists that she will not repeat the actions of Isolde, whose body was possessed by one man while her heart belonged to another. This dilemma provides the principal ethical problem of the second part of the romance, and Fénice does indeed find a solution.

That solution involves her taking a potion that causes her to appear to be dead. Once her "death" is established, she is free to live with Cligés—Fénice, the Phoenix, survives her death—and fully indulge her love for him. Clearly, the solution is equivocal and not entirely honorable. The lovers have in fact succeeded not in solving their problem but only in evading it. On the other hand, Fénice is apparently more interested in her reputation than in her ethics, and therein she has been successful: people cannot say, as they said of Isolde, that she divided her love between two men.

Le Chevalier de la charrete ("The Knight of the Cart"), or *Lancelot*, may well be Chrétien's best-known romance. It is known, first of all, for its dedication to Marie de Champagne and, second, for its depiction and apparent glorification of adulterous love. In a quest for Guenevere, who has been abducted from the court, Lancelot has the opportunity to find her more quickly if he accepts a ride in a cart reserved ordinarily for criminals. Mindful of his status and reputation, he hesitates briefly but then steps into the cart. When he eventually arrives in Guenevere's presence, she rejects him, and we learn that it is because of his reluctance to ride in the cart. Apparently, he has offended her by putting concern for his reputation before concern for her. The remainder of the romance is a series of trials undertaken to expiate his offense. Among his adventures, for example, is a tourney in which the Queen commands him to do "his worst," proving thereby that he is now willing to suffer for her sake the humiliation he had avoided before.

Near the end, Chrétien left off the writing of this romance, for reasons unknown to us, although the lack of evidence has not prevented some critics from speculating that he personally disapproved of the subject, imposed on him by his patroness. Godefroy de Leigny finished the romance according to a plan, he tells us, provided him by Chrétien.

There is some indication that Chrétien may have been composing *Lancelot* and *Yvain* (also known as *Le Chevalier au lion*) at the same time. Yet the two romances differ considerably. The *Lancelot* has a discursive, somewhat loose structure, whereas *Yvain* is highly composed and almost "classically" structured. Moreover, the adulterous relationship of the former is replaced by marital love in *Yvain*. The latter work is in fact closer, in inspiration and subject matter, to *Erec et Enide* than to *Lancelot*; indeed, it is from certain points of view the mirror image of *Erec et Enide*. On the other hand, all these works share, with Chrétien's other romances, a binary opposition between two stages of the hero's progress, a "before/after" opposition, with the dividing line being an offense or error committed by the hero.

Erec, as we have seen, neglects chivalry in favor of love: Yvain does the opposite. He wins Laudine's love, after killing her husband, but immediately after his marriage he yields to the persuasive powers of Gauvain, who has asked his friend to accompany him in his quest for adventure. Laudine reluctantly gives him leave for one year; he later loses her love when he fails to return within the time granted him. The remainder of the romance depicts Yvain's grief and madness and his subsequent attempts to expiate his offense. During his wandering, he is accompanied and aided by a lion whose life he had saved. The lion, thought by some to represent Christ or grace, more likely symbolizes Yvain's own perfected ideal of service and devotion. The adventures through which Yvain accomplishes his expiation are intricately interlaced with one another in a pattern that gives clear evidence, if evidence were needed, of Chrétien's attention not only to elaboration of theme but to structure and composition as well.

If, in terms of form and the effective elaborations of theme, *Yvain* is Chrétien's best romance, his final romance, *Perceval*, or *Le Conte del Graal*, has proved the most fascinating. Part of its fascination is doubtless due to the intriguing possibilities of its unfinished state—possibilities that were exploited in a number of Continuations and adaptations when Chrétien, whether because of death or for other reasons, left his romance without an ending. The character of Perceval himself has also appealed to audiences, as he develops from comical bumpkin to Grail knight. Yet the primary appeal of the work must be the Grail itself.

Although the word "grail" existed before Chrétien, it originally meant simply "dish"; it was Chrétien who first attached special significance to the word. (It must be pointed out in passing that it was not, in his work, the chalice of the Last Supper or the vessel in which Christ's blood was collected: those were innovations made by writers after Chrétien: *see* GRAIL; ROBERT DE BORON.) For him, it was a beautiful and mysterious vessel, whose function is initially unknown to Perceval. In fact, the very *mystery* of the Grail, rather than its specific use, is of prime importance in the work. And the Grail procession itself, in a mysterious disappearing castle, with a bleeding lance and a strange infirm host, provides a fascinating narrative core for this remarkable work.

It is entirely appropriate for the Grail to be a mystery to Perceval. Although endowed with exceptional physical gifts, he is seriously deficient in knowledge and insight. At the beginning of the work, he does not even know what knights and churches are. When he learns about knights, he immediately resolves to become one; typically, however, he confuses the possession of armor with the status of knighthood. In valuing the trappings of chivalry (equipment, reputation, and the thrill of combat) over its ethical and social concerns, he shares a failing with a number of Chrétien's other characters, from Gauvain to the early Lancelot; the distinction between Perceval and the others resides in his naiveté and in the consistent comedy of his actions.

When he decides not to inquire about the Grail procession, he is acting typically, since he had been told that a knight is careful not to talk excessively. His failure to ask that question is the critical turning point of the work, as he later learns that the question would have cured the Fisher King, the castle's inhabitant, and would have restored the fertility of his land. This error corresponds to the crisis that we have noted in Chrétien's other works, and it requires a similar expiation. In this case, however, the hero's errors are multiple, for in addition to failing to cure the Fisher King Perceval learns that his abrupt departure from home had caused the death of his own mother. Furthermore, he had along the way taken a lady, Blancheflor, as his love, and yet he repeatedly postpones his return to her, just as he had postponed the Grail question and his return to his mother.

Perceval's adventures are abruptly interrupted, and the author turns his attentions to Gauvain. Eventually, the latter's adventures are themselves interrupted by a brief (300-line) but crucial return to Perceval. In this episode, which takes place on Good Friday, Perceval speaks with a holy hermit, rediscovers God, and hears the explanation of the Grail castle and of his own past failings. This episode alone is responsible for imbuing the work with a largely religious meaning. Afterward, the focus returns to Gauvain, and we learn no more of Perceval in the remainder of this unfinished romance.

Gauvain undertakes an extraordinary series of mostly trivial and frequently comical adventures in a strange realm, where only once, in a castle inhabited by Arthur's mother, does he encounter characters and situations with which he is at ease. The odd interlace of sequences devoted separately to Perceval and to Gauvain, and the suddenness of Chrétien's shifts from one to the other, have led a good many critics to conclude that the story of Gauvain was intended to be a separate romance but that the vagaries of manuscript transmission had fused the two sequences into one. Specific structural and thematic correspondences between the two halves provide evidence, however, that they were intended to be part of the same romance, and the opportunity for further revision might have enabled Chrétien to provide a more graceful transition. Gauvain's adventures appear to be designed as a counterpoint to those of Perceval, providing an inverted reflection of earlier events: the early portions of the romance depict the contact of a naive Perceval with a worldly, courtly Arthurian realm; the Gauvain sections show the difficulties encountered by the quintessentially courtly knight in a decidedly uncourtly land.

Perceval may have been interrupted by Chrétien's death; in any case, the poet's career obviously ended at this point. However, during that career, Chrétien was largely responsible for perfecting a literary form that was to remain central to French literature from that time on. His mastery of narrative form and style, the subtlety of his psychological portraits, and the appeal of his themes established him as a consummate artist. Those who came after developed numerous varieties of romance, but they all owed a good deal to Chrétien de Troyes, and in many cases they express their debt to him directly, by praise and acknowledgment, or indirectly, by appropriating motifs or even textual matter. It is reasonable to conclude that they could not have accomplished what they did were it not for their illustrious precursor. [NJL]

Chrétien de Troyes. Les Romans de Chrétien de Troyes: *Erec et Enide*, *Le Chevalier de la charrete*, and *Le Chevalier au lion (Yvain)*, ed. Mario Roques (Paris, 1952, 1958, 1960); *Cligés*, ed. A. Micha (Paris, 1957); *Le Conte du Graal (Perceval)*, ed. Félix Lecoy (Paris, 1973).

———. *Erec et Enide*, ed. and trans. Carleton W. Carroll. New York: Garland, 1987.

———. *Lancelot, or The Knight of the Cart*, ed. and trans. William W. Kibler. New York: Garland, 1981.

———. *The Knight with the Lion, or Yvain*, ed. and trans. William W. Kibler. New York: Garland, 1985.

———. *Li Contes del Graal*, ed. Rupert T. Pickens, trans. William W. Kibler. New York: Garland, 1990.

Frappier, Jean. *Chrétien de Troyes*. Paris: Hatier, 1957. (English translation published as *Chrétien de Troyes: The Man and His Work*, trans. Raymond J. Cormier. Athens: Ohio University Press, 1982.)

Kelly, Douglas, ed. *The Romances of Chrétien de Troyes: A Symposium*. Lexington, Ky.: French Forum, 1985.

Lacy, Norris J. *The Craft of Chrétien de Troyes*. Leiden: Brill, 1980.

———, Douglas Kelly, and Keith Busby, eds. *The Legacy of Chrétien de Troyes*. 2 vols. Amsterdam: Rodopi, 1987–88.

Topsfield, L.T. *Chrétien de Troyes: A Study of the Arthurian Romances*. Cambridge: Cambridge University Press, 1981.

CHRÊTIEN DE TROYES, BURGUNDIAN ADAPTATIONS OF. Chrétien de Troyes at the court of Burgundy presents a curious problem because the prose versions of the only two of his works that were known there fail to mention his name. These are *Cligés* (Leipzig, Universitätsbibliothek 108) and *Erec et Enide* (Brussels, Bibl. Roy. 7235, and a partial text in Paris, B.N. f. fr. 363), both preserved in single, paper copies dating from the middle of the fifteenth century. Wendelin Foerster, who published both texts as appendices to his editions of the original poems, was of the opinion that the Leipzig and Brussels manuscripts were the work of the same scribe, although G. Doutrepont, in his discussion of the Burgundian *mises en prose*, considered the dialect of the two texts sufficiently different to indicate two scribes, and possibly two editors. Indeed, the techniques of the two prose versions differ, for the editor of *Erec et Enide* constantly abbreviates passages from the poem, including a number of descriptions of combats that would seemingly have been to the taste of a Burgundian audience. He sees Enide's trials as comparable to the patient Griselda's. The Prose *Cligés* has also been altered in a number of instances, sometimes abbreviated, but also with details frequently added, apparently to conform to tastes different from those of an earlier audience. In general, analyses of love and other such emotions are omitted, although a passage concerning the hero's encounter with a lovelorn maiden in a forest is introduced as motivation for his appreciating Fénice's sorrow at his absence and his decision to return to Greece from King Arthur's court. That there are no other known copies of either work, however, suggests that the prose versions did not meet with the

Duke of Burgundy's approval, nor that of other book collectors at his court.

There was, however, an independent version of the first part of *Erec et Enide* included in the compilation of Arthurian material centering on *Guiron le Courtois* prepared for one Burgundian bibliophile, Louis de Bruges, Lord of Gruthuyse (Paris, B.N. f. fr. 363), although here Erec appears merely as one of the knights who fight against the champion of the tournament at Val Brun, where he does not meet with success, although his life is spared through Enide's intervention. [CCW]

Chrétien de Troyes. *Sämtliche erhaltene Werke nach allen bekannten Handschriften*, ed. Wendelin Foerster. 4 vols. Halle: Niemeyer, Vol. 1 (*Cligés*), 1884; Vol. 3 (*Erec et Enide*), 1890.

Doutrepont, Georges. *Les Mises en prose des épopées et des romans chevaleresques du XIVe au XVIe siècle*. Brussels: Mémoires de l'Académie Royale de Belgique, Classe de Lettres, 1939, pp. 261–64.

Lathuillère, Roger. *Guiron le Courtois: étude de la tradition manuscrite et analyse critique*. Geneva: Droz, 1966.

CHRISTIAN, CATHERINE, wrote *The Sword and the Flame* (1978; published in the United States as *The Pendragon*, 1979), a historical novel set in a Romano-Celtic Britain more pagan than Christian. Narrated by Arthur's closest companion, Bedivere, the story encompasses Arthur's youth, Lancelot and Guenevere's adultery, the Grail quest, and Medraut's treachery. Though sometimes interesting for its treatment of tradition, the novel is too often an uninspired reworking of Malory. [VML]

Christian, Catherine. *The Sword and the Flame: Variations on a Theme of Sir Thomas Malory*. London: Macmillan, 1978. (Published in the U.S. as *The Pendragon*. New York: Knopf, 1979.)

CHRONICLE OF SCOTLAND IN A PART (THE SCOTTIS ORIGINALE), an anonymous short chronicle in Middle Scots (ca. 1460) that presents Arthur as a tyrant, a "huris sone" who was made king by the "devilry of Merlin," while the true heirs, Mordred and Gawain, were passed over because they were Scottish; therefore, Mordred, "in his rychtwyse querele," slew Arthur. It is an extreme development of the version of the Arthurian story presented by John of Fordun. (*See also* JOHN OF FORDUN.) [EDK]

Scott, W., D. Laing, and T. Thomson, eds. *The Chronicle of Scotland in a Part*. In *Bannatyne Miscellany*. Edinburgh: Bannatyne Club, 1855.

The Scottis Originale. In *The Asloan Manuscript*, ed. William A. Craigie. Edinburgh: Blackwood, 1923, pp. 185–96.

Alexander, Flora. "Late Medieval Scottish Attitudes to the Figure of King Arthur: A Reassessment." *Anglia*, 93 (1975), 17–34.

Kennedy, Edward Donald. "Chronicles and Other Historical Writing." In *A Manual of the Writings in Middle English*, ed. A.E. Hartung. New Haven: Connecticut Academy of Arts and Sciences, 1981–89, Vol. 8, pp. 2692, 2914–15.

CHRONICLES, ARTHUR IN. There is no mention of Arthur in the English traditions of the fifth and sixth centuries preserved in the *Anglo-Saxon Chronicle*. Its silence, however, implies nothing either way about his reality, because, while it names a few of the Britons' leaders (Vortigern, for instance), it omits those who inflicted reverses on the Saxons, such as Ambrosius. Hence, the presumably successful Arthur would have had no place in it. His first appearance in a chronicle is in the tenth-century *Annales Cambriae*, a Welsh document that associates him with the battles of Badon and Camlann, assigned to 518 and 539 or thereabout. The provenance of these entries is unknown, and the date given for Badon seems to clash with the earlier testimony of Gildas. The Camlann entry proves at least that there was a Welsh tradition of that battle before Geoffrey of Monmouth.

William of Malmesbury (*Gesta Regum Anglorum*, 1125) mentions Arthur as leading British resistance to the Saxons in association with Ambrosius. Henry of Huntingdon, in his *Historia Anglorum* (ca. 1129), draws mainly on Anglo-Saxon matter for this period but adds an account of Arthur in a vague retrospect of "those times" inserted between 527 and 530. It is based on Nennius's list of his battles. Henry calls him "the leader of the soldiers and kings of Britain."

Geoffrey's transformation of Arthur into a quasi-historical monarch, with a detailed and grandiose career, completely alters his status. Where medieval historiography touches on post-Roman Britain, Geoffrey's story is commonly accepted in substance. Two authors taking a skeptical or hostile view, Giraldus Cambrensis and William of Newburgh, are distinguished spokesmen for what long remains a minority opinion. Yet there is a recurrent awareness that the story presents difficulties, especially with dating. Chroniclers' use of it varies widely in fullness and credulity.

Welsh adapters and translators of Geoffrey, in the chronicles known as *Bruts*, follow him fairly closely. Among the works written in England, the most important are by Pierre de Langtoft, Robert Mannyng (Robert of Brunne or Bourn), and John Hardyng. In the hands of these authors and many others, Geoffrey's narrative is treated selectively, sometimes modified by the authors' own fancies and sometimes augmented with material from romance. In the end, the problems arising from more genuine history, which fails to confirm Geoffrey and often casts obvious suspicion on him, become too intractable. In Polydore Vergil (1534), a definite skepticism has set in. Raphael Holinshed (1577) can still make a serious attempt to harmonize Arthur with Anglo-Saxon and other evidence, but he drifts into speculations and contradictions that leave everything in confusion.

Scotland's chroniclers, such as John of Fordun (ca. 1385), also try to follow Geoffrey. With less of the critical spirit than their English counterparts, they are subversive instead through a difference of attitude. Repelled by Geoffrey's account of war waged by Arthur against the Scots, and by the Plantagenets' adoption of him as in effect a king of England, Scottish chroniclers tend to alter the values of the story and make him unsympathetic. The extreme of this process is represented by Hector Boece (1527), whose Arthur is the faithless and licentious ruler of a contemptible nation.

On the Continent, Arthur is overwhelmingly a king of romance, and interest in the historical aspect is slight. Some chroniclers mention him briefly, usually echoing Geoffrey, if with reservations. A few, such as Jean des Preis, or d'Outremeuse (late fourteenth century), exploit the romances to elaborate his career in ways of their own. There are traces, however, of a historical tradition that is independent of Geoffrey or nearly so. This places Arthur's *floruit* in and around the 460s and associates him with real persons—notably Aegidius, a Roman ruler of northern Gaul—of whom Geoffrey knows nothing.

A glimpse of it can perhaps be caught in a recension of a chronicle Geoffrey may have used himself, that of Sigebert of Gembloux, who died in 1112. Between 1138 and 1147, a writer known as the Monk of Ursicampum (Ourscamp) compiled an enlarged version of Sigebert's chronicle. He introduced matter from Geoffrey but with certain questions, raising the possibility that Arthur might be the same as the British king known as Riothamus, documented in Gaul ca. 468–70. A separate hint at this equation occurs in the *Chronicles of Anjou*, where, in a passage generally derived from Geoffrey, Arthur's betrayer becomes *Morvandus*. This suggests a conflation of "Mordred" and "Arvandus," the name of an imperial prefect who did betray Riothamus. Allusions to Arthur consistent with the equation, though not offering it in plain terms, appear in Albericus Trium Fontium (1227–51), the *Salzburg Annals* (thirteenth century), Martinus Polonus (ca. 1275), Jacques de Guise (late fourteenth century), and Philippe de Vigneulles (1525). With one or two minor corrections, genuinely required in the interests of accuracy, these could all be derived from a single source giving Arthur a sixteen-year reign running from about 454 to 470. The English chronicler John Capgrave concurs. Such a reign would allow him to be the immediate successor of Vortigern, as implied by the apparently independent account—also continental—in the *Legend of St. Goeznovius*. (*See also* Chronicles, Scottish; Chronicles in English.) [GA]

Ashe, Geoffrey. *The Discovery of King Arthur*. New York: Doubleday, 1985, pp. 106–11.

Chambers, E.K. *Arthur of Britain*. London: Sidgwick and Jackson, 1927, pp. 100–32.

Day, Mildred Leake. "Report from the International Arthurian Congress." *Quondam et Futures*, September 1987, 6–11.

Fletcher, Robert Huntington. *The Arthurian Material in the Chronicles, Especially Those of Great Britain and France*. Boston: Ginn, 1906; 2nd ed. Roger Sherman Loomis. New York: Franklin, 1966.

Fleuriot, Léon. *Les Origines de la Bretagne*. Paris: Payot, 1980, pp. 110, 227.

CHRONICLES, SCOTTISH. References to Arthur in Scottish Arthurian chronicles can be positive or negative; and it is easy to account for the chroniclers' reactions by considering both the ultimate source of their information, Geoffrey of Monmouth's *Historia Regum Britanniae*, and the feelings of Scottish nationalism that developed in the late Middle Ages and that found expression in the chronicles. In Geoffrey of Monmouth, the Picts and the Scots are Arthur's enemies; Arthur conquers Scotland; and Arthur's kingdom is eventually destroyed by the traitorous Scot Mordred. Yet Geoffrey's account is not completely biased against the Scots, for Arthur has in it some important Scottish allies: Loth of Lodonesia, Gawain, and King Auguselus.

As one might expect, when the Scots began to write their own chronicles, their reactions to this material were mixed, and by the late fifteenth and sixteenth centuries the use of it, by some chroniclers at least, was colored by feelings of nationalism and by their antagonism toward the English, who had accepted the British Arthurian history as a part of their own nation's past glory. Some, like Barbour, Andrew of Wyntoun, and Blind Harry, accept Arthur's reputation uncritically and refer to him with admiration as a great British king; their allusions to him, however, are brief, and they make little effort to tell much of the Arthurian story. Others accept the fact that Arthur was a great king, but they are also skeptical or critical. John Leslie, for example, in his brief account of Arthur, doubts the stories of Arthur's foreign conquests. John of Fordun and John Major give more detailed accounts than any of the above; and although they admire Arthur they point out that he was illegitimate and that the true heirs to the throne were Mordred and Gawain, who were passed over because they were too young. This view that Scots, not Arthur, should have ruled Britain, popularized by John of Fordun's fourteenth-century chronicle, became the basis for bitter attacks on Arthur in the fifteenth-century *Chronicle of Scotland in a Part* and in the sixteenth-century chronicles of Boece, Bellenden, Stewart, and Buchanan. (*See also* Andrew of Wyntoun; Barbour, John; Blind Harry; Boece, Hector; Bower, Walter; Buchanan, George;

CHRONICLE OF SCOTLAND IN A PART; JOHN OF FORDUN; LESLIE, JOHN; MAJOR, JOHN.) [EDK]

Alexander, Flora. "Late Medieval Scottish Attitudes to the Figure of King Arthur: A Reassessment." *Anglia*, 93 (1975), 17–34.

Brie, Friedrich. *Die nationale Literatur Schottlands*. Halle: Niemeyer, 1937, pp. 317–53.

Fletcher, Robert Huntington. *The Arthurian Material in the Chronicles, Especially Those of Great Britain and France*. Boston: Ginn, 1906; 2nd ed. Roger Sherman Loomis. New York: Franklin, 1966, pp. 245–48.

Göller, K.H. "König Arthur in den schottischen Chroniken." *Anglia*, 80 (1962), 390–404.

Kennedy, Edward Donald. "Chronicles and Other Historical Writing." In *A Manual of the Writings in Middle English*, ed. A.E. Hartung. New Haven: Connecticut Academy of Arts and Sciences, 1981–89, Vol. 8, pp. 2679–80, 2891.

CHRONICLES IN ENGLISH. The Middle English chroniclers who wrote about Arthur generally followed the story of the rise and fall of Arthur as it was presented in Geoffrey of Monmouth's *Historia Regum Britanniae*. Although most of the chroniclers knew some of the Arthurian romances and borrowed from them details and names of some characters, like Lancelot and Yvain, they generally did not make major changes in Geoffrey's account. They apparently distinguished between what they considered to be the basically true account in Geoffrey and the basically fictitious ones in romance. Although a few Latin chroniclers, like Ranulf Higden and William of Newburgh, had doubts about the truth of Geoffrey's *Historia*, they were in the minority. In fact, most of the English chroniclers, in contrast to Higden, William, and some of the Scottish chroniclers, were enthusiastic about Arthur and portrayed him not as the weak king of some of the French romances (Chrétien's *Chevalier de la charrete*, parts of the Vulgate Cycle) but as the heroic figure developed by Geoffrey. This may at first seem surprising, since Arthur was British and an enemy of the Saxons, the ancestors of the English. Admittedly, Layamon may have been more interested in drawing a parallel to the later Norman Conquest than in praising the British; but the attitude of most of the chroniclers seems to be similar to the attitude of Caxton, who in his preface to Malory's *Morte Darthur* (1485) explains that noble gentlemen told him that he should print the history of Arthur, the "noble king and conqueror," rather than that of any of the other Nine Worthies, since Arthur "was a man born within the realm, and [was] king and emperor of the same." Caxton, like most earlier English chroniclers, looked upon Arthur's reign as one of the great periods in the history of the land they now inhabited. Although by the sixteenth century there was considerable skepticism about the truth of the Arthurian story, a skepticism fostered particularly by the chronicle of the humanist historian Polydore Vergil, the Tudor monarchs' claim to have been descended from Arthur did much to keep the legend alive. (*See also* ARTHUR; BEK, THOMAS, OF CASTELFORD; CAPGRAVE, JOHN; CHRONICLES, ARTHUR IN; CHRONICLES, SCOTTISH; HARDYNG, JOHN; HIGDEN, RANULF; LAYAMON; MANNYNG, ROBERT, OF BRUNNE; PROSE *BRUT*; ROBERT OF GLOUCESTER; *SHORT METRICAL CHRONICLE*; TREVISA, JOHN.) [EDK]

Fletcher, Robert Huntington. *The Arthurian Material in the Chronicles, Especially Those of Great Britain and France*. Boston: Ginn, 1906; 2nd ed. Roger Sherman Loomis. New York: Franklin, 1966, pp. 193–98.

Göller, Karl Heinz. *König Arthur in der englischen Literatur des späten Mittelalters*. Göttingen: Vandenhoeck and Ruprecht, 1963, pp. 19–40, 57–66.

Gransden, Antonia. *Historical Writing in England, c. 550 to c. 1307*. London: Routledge and Kegan Paul, 1974.

———. *Historical Writing in England, c. 1307 to the Early Sixteenth Century*. Ithaca, N.Y.: Cornell University Press, 1982.

Kendrick, T.D. *British Antiquity*. London: Methuen 1950.

Kennedy, Edward Donald. "Chronicles and Other Historical Writing." In *The Manual of the Writings in Middle English*, ed. A.E. Hartung. New Haven: Connecticut Academy of Arts and Sciences, 1988, Vol. 8.

CHRONICON DE LANERCOST ("Lanercost Chronicle"), an anonymous chronicle in Latin prose, dating from the fourteenth century, that recounts a 1216 meeting between Arthur and the bishop of Winchester. The two dined together, and then, to ensure that others would believe the bishop's account, Arthur gave him the power to produce a butterfly at will simply by opening his fist. [NJL]

Stevenson, Joseph, ed. *Chronicon de Lanercost*. Edinburgh: Maitland Club, 1839.

CHRONICON MONTIS SANCTI MICHAELIS IN PERICULO MARIS ("Chronicle of St. Michael's Mount"), Breton in origin and perhaps predating Geoffrey of Monmouth's *Historia*, records in its initial entry that Arthur was king of Britain in 421. The *Chronicle* is part of the remains of the library of Mont St.-Michel and is preserved in manuscript Avranches 213. [MLD]

Migne, J.P., ed. *Chronicon Montis Sancti Michaelis in Periculo Maris*. In *Patrologia Latina*. Paris: Migne, 1855, Vol. 202, col. 1323.

CHURCHYARD, THOMAS (1520?–1604), a minor English poet, wrote *The Worthines of Wales* (1587), a largely topographical poem dedicated to Queen Elizabeth, who Churchyard says is descended from Arthur. Churchyard defends the historicity of Arthur against the attacks of writers like Polydore Vergil; argues that Caerleon, the site of Arthur's court, should be as famous as Troy and Athens; and inserts prose passages from Geoffrey of Monmouth into the poem to suggest that England owes no allegiance to "Romish practises." [ACL]

Churchyard, Thomas. *The Worthines of Wales*. London: G. Robinson, 1587; repr. New York: Franklin, 1967.

Millican, Charles Bowie. *Spenser and the Table Round: A Study in the Contemporaneous Background for Spenser's Use of the Arthurian Legend*. Cambridge: Harvard University Press, 1932.

CIARDI, JOHN (1916–1986), American poet who wrote "Launcelot in Hell" (1961), a monologue by a proud and boastful Launcelot that gives a deromanticized account of the final days of Arthur's realm. Launcelot tells how he loved Guinevere (whom he calls a "mare to be mounted," and whose conversion he despises), killed Arthur, and threw the King's sword into a swamp. He does not regret having caused a war for a queen originally "worth damnation" and says that he would have fought the King even without her because no one but Arthur dared to meet him in battle. [ACL]

Ciardi, John. "Launcelot in Hell." In *In the Stoneworks*. New Brunswick, N.J.: Rutgers University Press, 1961.

CLARE, HELEN, author of *Merlin's Magic* (1953). Merlin sends a group of modern children on a magical treasure hunt. They meet several Arthurian characters while learning that the true treasure is the human imagination. [RHT]

Clare, Helen. *Merlin's Magic*. London: Lane, 1953.

CLARIS ET LARIS, a two-part romance of over 30,000 lines that tells the story of two friends, Claris and Laris. Claris marries Lidoine after the death of her husband, the King of Gascony. Laris is carried off by a fay, Madoine, and eventually rescued by Claris. The second half of the poem concerns the affair of Laris with Marine, sister of Yvain, whose father, Urien, is besieged by King Tallas of Denmark, who in turn has designs on Marine. Claris and Laris, together with Gauvain and Yvain, vanquish Tallas, but Laris is taken prisoner. After a series of lengthy quests, Merlin helps Brandaliz find and liberate Laris.

The romance is well structured in the balance between the two parts, and the narrative seems to have been influenced by the *entrelacement* (structural interlace) of the prose romances. Begun in 1268, *Claris et Laris* is one of the last Old French verse romances, and the author draws on a wide variety of stock motifs and earlier works, such as the romances of Chrétien de Troyes, the Continuations of the *Perceval*, Wace's *Brut*, the Didot-*Perceval*, and the *Perlesvaus*. Particularly interesting is the way in which the author specifically alludes to some of these other works and incorporates them into his own composition. *Claris et Laris* is written in a lively manner and is imbued with a slightly subversive sense of humor.

Claris et Laris can be compared in length, tone, and structure with Girart d'Amiens's *Escanor* (with which it is roughly contemporary); both works have a tendency to accrete already existing material into a kind of *summa arthuriana* best seen perhaps in the later prose compilations (e.g., some redactions of the Prose *Tristan* or the work of Michot Gonnot). [KB]

Alton, Johann, ed. *Claris et Laris*. Tübingen: Bibliothek des literarischen Vereins in Stuttgart, 1884.

Kelly, Douglas. "'Tout li sens du monde' dans *Claris et Laris*." *Romance Philology*, 36 (1982–83), 406–17.

Klose, Martin. *Der Roman von Claris und Laris in seinen Beziehungen zur altfranzösischen Artusepik*. Halle: Niemeyer, 1916.

Schmolke-Hasselmann, Beate. *Der arthurische Versroman von Chrestien bis Froissart*. Tübingen: Niemeyer, 1980, pp. 166–69.

CLARKE, GRAHAM, British artist who wrote and illustrated *Balyn and Balan* (1970), an impressive hand-printed folio volume, in which twenty-three wood and lino illustrations depicting scenes from Balyn's adventures complement the text, a very brief and simple version of Malory's tale of Balyn (based on Roger Lancelyn Green's retelling). [ACL]

Clarke, Graham. *Balyn and Balan*. Boughton Monchelsea, Kent: Ebenezer, [1970].

CLAUDAS, in the *Perlesvaus*, the Vulgate Cycle, and Malory's *Morte Darthur*, King of Terre Deserte. Claudas is the enemy of Ban (Lancelot's father), Bors, and Arthur. When

Claudas fights Ban, the child Lancelot is taken away by the Lady of the Lake. In Malory, Claudas raises Bors's sons, Lionel and Bors the younger, who accidentally kill Claudas's son, Dorin. Claudas is eventually defeated by Ban, Bors, and Arthur. [SW]

CLIES, the German version of Chrétien de Troyes's *Cligés*, presumably composed ca. 1230, of which only fragments are extant today. According to Rudolf von Ems (ca. 1200–ca. 1252), both Konrad Fleck (ca. 1220) and Ulrich von Türheim (ca. 1230) composed a *Clies*; it is more likely that there existed only one version of the romance, and that Ulrich wrote the conclusion to a work left incomplete by Fleck. In a recently discovered fragment that contains text from the latter half of the romance, the author identifies himself as "Vlrich von Tureheim." The romance was well known in Germany; a number of medieval German writers refer to it, including Wolfram von Eschenbach. [MEK]

Bachmann, Albert. "Bruchstücke eines mhd. Cliges." *Zeitschrift für deutsches Alterthum*, 32 (1888), 123–28.

Vizkelety, András. "Neue Fragmente des mhd. Cligés-Epos aus Kalocsa (Ungarn)." *Zeitschrift für deutsche Philologie*, 88 (1969), 409–32.

CLIGÉS, in Chrétien de Troyes's second romance, *Cligés*, the chief character and nephew of Gawain. Cligés inherits the kingdom of Constantinople, but his uncle Alis usurps his throne. Cligés and Alis's wife, Fénice, fall in love and are united when Fénice escapes Alis by feigning death. The romance also survives in a later Burgundian adaptation, and in addition, the fragmentary German *Clies* is a reworking of Chrétien's text. [SW]

CLOSS, HANNAH (1905–1953?), English author of the historical novel *Tristan* (1940), which employs impressionistic and stream-of-consciousness techniques to relate the traditional love story of Tristan and Isolde. Events are often filtered through the mind of the hero, who is dreamer and poet as well as warrior. The images thus gain an imaginative intensity that vividly evokes the lovers' passions. [RHT]

Closs, Hannah. *Tristan*. London: Dakers, 1940.

COCTEAU, JEAN (1889–1963), French author of the three-act play *Les Chevaliers de la Table Ronde*, written in 1937. In the play, Ginifer, a servant of Merlin, assumes the identities of various characters (Gauvain, Galaad, Guenièvre) to confound Artus, the King, and his entourage. Although Merlin initially enjoys the favor of Artus, he is an evil character who uses his servant and his own powers to enchant (*intoxiquer*) the castle. Galaad breaks the spell, but the rebirth of the castle brings about pain and travail, including the death of the Queen and her lover. The play was first performed at the Théâtre de l'Œuvre on October 14, 1937.

Cocteau also used Arthurian material in his film *L'Éternel Retour* (1943; dir. Jean Delannoy). This screenplay transposes the Tristan legend into the twentieth century. The author retains the name Marc but transposes Tristan into Patrice and Iseut into Natalie (the final syllables of the new names echoing the first syllables of the originals). After rescuing Natalie from an oafish drunkard and bully named Morolt, Patrice persuades her to marry his aging uncle Marc, but the young people soon fall madly in love through the action of a potion. The "enemies" are the Frossins, the family of his deceased first wife, and particularly their dwarf son, Achille. Despite a number of innovations, Cocteau is quite faithful to the early versions of the legend in his transposition of several episodes, such as the white sail, here a scarf, announcing the return of his mistress.

In 1951, a radio adaptation of *L'Éternel Retour* was made by Georges Beaume, with music by Georges Auric. [NJL]

Cocteau, Jean. *Les Chevaliers de la Table Ronde*. In *Œuvres complètes de Jean Cocteau*. Geneva: Marguerat, 1948, Vol. 6.

23. From Jean Cocteau, *L'Éternel Retour* (1943). (Courtesy of The Newberry Library, Chicago.)

———. *Three Screenplays*, trans. Carol Martin-Sperry. New York: Grossman, 1972.

Savage, Edward B. *The Rose and the Vine*. Cairo: American University at Cairo Press, 1961, pp. 133–56.

COHEN, MATT, Canadian author of the story *Too Bad Galahad* (1972), which ironically reverses the hero's traditional role as perfect knight by presenting him as failed schoolmaster, would-be dragonslayer swallowed by dragon, inept lover, and quester unable to identify the Grail until he is about to die. Conflated time, word play, and antiromantic views of Malorian characters and events produce a wittily irreverent modernization. [MAW]

Cohen, Matt. *Too Bad Galahad*. Toronto: Coach House, 1972.

COLIN, PHILIPP, and CLAUS WISSE. Between 1331 and 1336, they translated and adapted two of the French continuators of Chrétien's *Perceval*, Wauchier de Denain and Manessier, into German. Helping them in the translation was a Strassburg Jew, Sampson Pine. The result of their efforts, *Der nüwe Parzefal* (36,426 lines), was inserted between Books 14 and 15 of Wolfram von Eschenbach's *Parzival*, which also was revised in many places and received an Alsatian dialect coloring.

Colin and Wisse were both from Strassburg goldsmith families that are attested in Strassburg documents from 1265 and 1148, respectively. In his epilogue, Colin reports that Lady Love and Lady Generosity have chosen his patron, Ulrich von Rappoltstein, to provide for the production of this work of literature. Ulrich, a member of the high nobility, was indeed touched by Lady Generosity and paid 200 pounds for the task.

The episodic nature of the *Nüwe Parzefal* is its most striking characteristic. It is a bourgeois work by bourgeois authors, and as a result the adventurous and the fantastic are given great play. Parzefal must cede equal time and space—indeed sometimes more—to Gawan, whose adventures are narrated in great detail. In this work, both Gawan and Parzefal achieve entry into the Grail castle, and on the third occasion Parzefal is offered the crown, which he refuses in order to ride out on more adventures. The original concept of the hero as found in Wolfram's work—that only the best knight, who has conquered his own deficiencies, is worthy of the Grail—is lost. Further, the inner integrity and value of the courtly-chivalric world, which is the key element in Wolfram's *Parzival*, disappears behind the bourgeois coating of the Colin-Wisse version. *Der nüwe Parzefal* is found in the Donaueschingen Hs. 97 (D) from the fourteenth century and is presumed to be the original. A copy, likewise from the fourteenth century, is found in the Bibliotheca Casanatensis in Rome (R). [FGG]

Schorbach, Karl, ed. *Parzifal, von Claus Wisse und Philipp Colin*. Strassburg: Trübner, 1888.

Wittmann-Klemm, Dorothee. *Studien zum "Rappoltsteiner Parzifal."* Göppingen: Kümmerle, 1977.

COLLINS, (EDWARD JAMES) MORTIMER (1827–1876), English mathematician, antiquary, poet, and novelist, whose *The Inn of Strange Meetings and Other Poems* (1871) contains Arthurian selections. For example, "Merlin," in ballad form, describes the seer's sleep in Brocéliande, which is seen as a blessed relief from "the fever of life." [MAW]

Collins, Mortimer. *The Inn of Strange Meetings and Other Poems*. London, Edinburgh, Dublin, and New York: Nelson, 1907.

COLUM, PADRAIC (1881–1972), Irish-American author of *The Boy Apprenticed to an Enchanter* (1920). Merlin helps the boy Eean defeat his master, an evil magician. Merlin is considered least among the three great enchanters of the world because he would rather love than be wise. However, since love and loyalty are important in this children's fantasy, Merlin does find happiness with Vivien, following her possessive incarceration of him and his subsequent promise of devotion. [HT]

Colum, Padraic. *The Boy Apprenticed to an Enchanter*. New York: Macmillan, 1920.

COMICS. The Arthurian legend in comics has generally served as source material for the creation of original adventure stories. The American newspaper comic strip *Prince Valiant* (1937–), the earliest major work on an Arthurian theme, is also the most famous. Writer-illustrator Harold R. (Hal) Foster (1892–1982), working in the tradition of Howard Pyle, created the young exiled prince of Thule, who first comes to Arthur's court as squire to Gawain and eventually becomes a knight of the Round Table. Val journeys to Africa and North America in the course of his adventures, as well as participating in more traditionally Arthurian episodes. An ongoing story chronicled in weekly installments for over fifty years (since 1980, by Cullen and John Cullen Murphy), *Prince Valiant* is generally acknowledged to be one of the high achievements in the comics medium. There have been adaptations of the strip published as novels and as a game (*see* GAMES), and a motion-picture version was released in 1953.

Foster's creation of Prince Valiant has been followed by the introduction, in comic books, of still more knights of the Round Table. These include the Shining Knight (*Adventure Comics*, 1941) and the Black Knight (1955), both of whom owe their empowerment to Merlin. Merlin also figures in the origins of several other comic-book heroes, such as the Demon (1972) and the patriotic superhero Captain Britain (1976). Other comic books have retold the original legends, adapted film or television versions, or have featured new adventures of traditional Arthurian characters.

Recent years have seen English-language comic books and their readership growing more sophisticated, with a correspondingly greater sophistication in the handling of Arthurian themes. *Camelot 3000* (1982–85), by Mike Barr and Brian Bolland, deals with the return of Arthur and his knights in the year 3000 to save Britain from the threat of an invasion from outer space. A more personal approach to the theme of Arthur's return is presented in Matt Wagner's *Mage* (1984), the story of a seemingly ordinary man who finds himself reluctantly involved in a struggle between magical forces of good and evil, and is eventually revealed as the reborn Arthur. [HAS]

Germany has seen its own series of Arthurian comic books. The team of Götz Altenburg, Gunther Herbst, Joachim Honnef, et al. has created thirty installments, aimed at adults, of *Sir Roland the Lionhearted*. The plots usually follow a basic pattern: monsters or villains threaten a country and its people; Roland is charged by Arthur (or, occasionally, fate) with liberating the land; after the hero or his allies have fallen into the enemy's hands, they manage to escape through force or trickery and to overwhelm their foes. The castle of Camelot is here located in the Odenwald. Other motifs are taken from various legend cycles. [SSch/PM]

Altenburg, Götz. *Ritter Roland: Der Kämpfer mit dem Löwenherz*. Bergisch-Gladbach: Bastei Verlag Gustav Lübbe, 1980–81.

Saba, Ann. "Harold R. Foster: Drawing upon History." *Comics Journal*, 102 (1985), 61–84.

Stewart, H. Alan. "King Arthur in the Comics." *Avalon to Camelot*, 2 (1986), 12–14.

CONDWIRAMURS, in Wolfram von Eschenbach's *Parzival*, Lohengrin's mother, Parzival's wife, King Tampenteire's daughter, Sigune's cousin, and Gurnemanz's niece. In the German tradition of Arthurian Grail stories, Blancheflor, Perceval's sweetheart and Gornemant's niece in Chrétien de Troyes, is replaced by Condwiramurs. [SW]

CONEY, MICHAEL GREATREX, Canadian author of *Fang, the Gnome* (1988) and its sequel *King of the Scepter'd Isle* (1989), a highly original science-fiction treatment of Arthurian legend. Avalona, the mother of Merlin and mentor of Nyneve, uses her special powers to alter the "happentracks," the many frames of existence created by the different choices that are possible to people. The chivalric legend of King Arthur is one of those happentracks, and it merges with those both of Nyneve and of the gentle gnomes, whose origins, as their adventurous leader Fang discovers, turn out to be extraterrestrial. Arthur and the gnomes discover the limits of individual freedom when they find themselves caught up in a destiny neither can escape, the former doomed to act out the stories that have been told about him, the latter conditioned by the genetic engineers who designed them, and both subject to the manipulations of the happentracks. [RHT]

Coney, Michael Greatrex. *Fang, the Gnome*. New York: New American Library, 1988.

———. *King of the Scepter'd Isle*. New York: New American Library, 1989.

CONSTANTINE (1), Arthur's grandfather in Geoffrey of Monmouth. A prince from the offshoot British kingdom in Armorica (given an unhistorically early foundation), he comes to Britain by invitation near the beginning of the fifth century, to organize defense against marauding barbarians. Completely successful, he is rewarded with the crown. He has three sons: Constans, who becomes a monk; Aurelius Ambrosius; and Uther, the future father of Arthur. After reigning over Britain for ten years, Constantine is assassinated by a Pict. The crafty Vortigern persuades Constans to leave his monastery and become king. Constans is a puppet in Vortigern's hands, and presently he, too, is assassinated. Suspicion falls on Vortigern. Constantine's other sons are still children, and their guardians take them to the Breton court for safety. Vortigern seizes the crown. When the princes are grown up, however, they return and depose him, so that the royal house continues, producing Arthur in the next generation.

Constantine is vaguely based on a soldier who in 407 was proclaimed emperor as Constantine III by the Roman army in Britain. He may have been British, and he did have a son Constans who was a monk and left his monastery. Taking most of the troops overseas, he achieved control of

Gaul and Spain. After various campaigns and dealings, he surrendered in 411 to a general of Honorius, the legitimate western emperor, but was murdered. Constans was already dead.

Constantine III's removal of troops from Britain was a prime cause of its severance from the empire, which occurred in 410. Left unprotected against the assaults of Saxons and other barbarians, the Britons turned against him. Honorius authorized them to arm in their own defense, with the result that they became self-governing. Geoffrey's independent fifth-century Britain is founded, to that extent at least, on historical fact. [GA]

Geoffrey of Monmouth. *Historia Regum Britanniae*, Book VI, Chapters 4–8.

CONSTANTINE (2), Arthur's successor. Geoffrey of Monmouth makes him a cousin, taking the name and a few particulars from Gildas, who denounces a king so called. Gildas's Constantine ruled only in Dumnonia, now known as the West Country. His conversion into a king of all Britain is incompatible with any historical possibility. [GA]

Geoffrey of Monmouth. *Historia Regum Britanniae*, Book XI, Chapters 2–4.

CONTI DEI ANTICHI CAVALIERI ("Tales of the Knights of Old," dating from the thirteenth century) devotes one of its twenty *novelle* to the story of the Castle Pleur and its horrifying custom, which requires Brunor, brought to the castle by a storm, to do battle with the lord and then to marry the widow when he is victorious. Their son Galehaut attempts to abolish such customs everywhere and eventually comes into conflict with Arthur. The conflict is resolved when Galehaut joins Tristan and Lancelot to follow Arthur. [DLH]

Papa, Pasquale, ed. "Conti di Antichi Cavalieri." *Giornale storico della letterature italiana*, 3 (1884), 192–217.

CONTINUATIONS OF *PERCEVAL*. About 1190, probably interrupted by death, Chrétien de Troyes abandoned his *Conte del Graal* (*Perceval*), which he had undertaken for Count Philip of Flanders. But even Chrétien's failure became a momentous literary event, for his unfinished *Perceval* engendered writing and debate that have endured to the present. The mystery of the Grail, the Bleeding Lance, and the respective roles of Perceval and Gauvain were heady matters in the early thirteenth century, a ripe opportunity for imitators who perhaps believed that they might participate in Chrétien's glory, like Godefroy de Leigny, who brought to a close the *Chevalier de la charrete*.

Chrétien's *Perceval* ends abruptly at line 9,234 (in the Hilka text). A first continuator picked up the story at this point and added 9,500 to 19,600 lines (depending on the various manuscript traditions) but came to no conclusion. A second continuator took over the plot where the first ended, lengthened it by some 13,000 lines, but still failed to complete the task. A third continuator, Manessier, added 10,000 lines more, with, finally, a conclusion. Gerbert de Montreuil compiled an enormous Fourth Continuation of some 17,000 lines, which survives in two manuscripts, where it is inserted between the Second and Third Continuations. Gerbert managed to compose an ending, but it has been lost in the manuscript tradition. In sum, the Continuations amount to an augmentation of more than 58,000 lines. One manuscript, Paris, B.N. f. fr. 12576, contains a "total" Perceval romance, including Chrétien's, which adds up to 63,550 octosyllabic lines.

The First Continuation was once attributed to Wauchier de Denain and even to Chrétien de Troyes. When it was shown that the author was unidentifiable, many scholars during the first half of the twentieth century persisted in naming him the Pseudo-Wauchier. Whoever he was, he probably composed his sequel ca. 1200, certainly no earlier than 1190. Until William Roach completed his multivolume edition, the manuscript tradition remained thoroughly confused. Now, thanks to his achievement, we can discern three redactions, a Short, a Mixed, and a Long. The Short, which is very likely the earliest, betrays the disadvantage of inadequate links to its predecessor, the *Perceval* of Chrétien. The Long Redaction, though probably later than the others, is tied closely to Chrétien, for most of the episodes left dangling by him are completed. In all redactions, Perceval is no longer the protagonist, and is in fact absent from the action except when he appears almost coincidentally in a tournament where another warrior, Caradoc, is declared the best knight. Gauvain has replaced Perceval to the extent that the First Continuation becomes, especially in the Short Redaction, almost an independent romance and is therefore often entitled the *Gauvain-Continuation*. The main events are 1) Gauvain's clash with Guiromelant, who is able nevertheless to marry Clarissant, Gauvain's sister, with King Arthur's help; 2) the siege of the castle of Brun de Branlant, during which Gauvain seduces the sister of Bran de Lis; 3) the adventures of Caradoc, an independent romance inserted with little transition, and sometimes called the *Livre* (or *Roman*) *de Caradoc*; 4) Arthur's attack on the Chastel Orguellos, which involves two duels by

Gauvain; 5) Gauvain's Grail visit, including a breathtaking episode wherein Gauvain ventures into a dark chapel near the sea at the end of a long bower of trees; 6) the misadventures of Gauvain's brother Guerrehet. Though the First Continuation lacks unity, its carefully wrought episodes can capture today's reader by their artistry of suspense.

The Second Continuation is often labeled the *Perceval-Continuation*, because in it Perceval returns to the forefront. Composed shortly after the First—i.e., ca. 1200—it appears to be signed by a Gauchier de Donaing (1. 31,421), who has been identified as the author of hagiographical works under the patronage of Philip of Flanders and his niece Johanna. The attribution was generally considered fraudulent until G. Vial set forth a convincing case in favor of Gauchier's authorship. The continuator lacks the spark of his predecessors; he fails to distinguish personalities among his characters and relies on repetitions and common motifs (empty castles, meals, ritual exchange of names) to lend unity to his story. He relates in a simple, straightforward manner Perceval's loss of the White Stag's head, his long quest to retrieve it, and finally his return to the Grail castle, where he meets only partial success. There, he attempts to piece together his broken sword, but a hairline fissure remains, symbolizing his failure to reach perfection. The author abandons his tale at this point.

Manessier's Continuation is normally numbered third because that is its place in most manuscripts. Probably ca. 1230, certainly no earlier than 1211 or later than 1244, he picks up the story with Perceval in the Grail castle and brings it to an end with the hero triumphantly crowned Grail King. Alongside Perceval's adventures come those of Sagremor and Gauvain. Perceval learns many answers at the very outset, so that much suspense is destroyed. Links to predecessors include a return to the chapel of the Black Hand, the repair by Triboet of the broken sword (as predicted in Chrétien's *Perceval*), Calogrenant's death, and echoes of the adventure of the Joie de la Cour (in Chrétien's *Erec et Enide*), but new characters and themes are introduced, notably the appearance of the Devil in several disguises. After the Fisher King's death, Perceval reigns for seven years in his place, then retires to the forest to finish his life as a hermit. The narrator surmises that the Grail, the Lance, and the silver plate must have accompanied him to heaven.

At about the same time as Manessier, Gerbert attached his Fourth Continuation to the end of the Second Continuation and imagined his own ending. Because of its survival in two manuscripts as an interpolation between the Second Continuation and Manessier, it appears to be third in the series, for the redactors concealed its conclusion. To avoid confusion, it is wise to refer to the third and fourth by their authors. Gerbert names himself five times in the first third of his poem and some scholars have identified him as Gerbert de Montreuil, the author of the *Roman de la violette*. His style is far sprightlier than the Second Continuation's rather tiresome language, and the tale holds many surprises, such as the sudden appearance of the Gate of Heaven, an invitation to bed by a maiden, an attack by two monstrous serpents, and above all a complete Tristan episode. Gerbert often relies on proverbs to prove a point. His final episode puts Perceval back in the Grail castle, where he manages to mend the broken sword perfectly. [JLG]

Roach, William, ed. *The Continuations of the Old French "Perceval" of Chrétien de Troyes*. 5 vols. Philadelphia: University of Pennsylvania Press/American Philosophical Society, 1949–83.

Gerbert de Montreuil. *La Continuation de Perceval*, ed. Mary Williams (Vols. 1 and 2) and Marguerite Oswald (Vol. 3). 3 vols. Paris: Champion, 1922, 1925, 1975.

Busby, Keith. *Gauvain in Old French Literature*. Amsterdam: Rodopi, 1980.

Corley, Corin F.V. *The Second Continuation of the Old French Perceval*. London: Modern Humanities Research Association, 1987.

Gallais, Pierre. *L'Imaginaire d'un romancier français de la fin du XIIe siècle: description raisonnée, comparée et commentée de la Continuation-Gauvain, première suite du Conte du Graal de Chrétien de Troyes*. 4 vols. Amsterdam: Rodopi, 1988–89.

Ivy, Robert H. *The Manuscript Relations of Manessier's Continuation of the Old French* Perceval. Philadelphia: University of Pennsylvania Press, 1951.

Vial, Guy. "L'Auteur de la deuxième continuation du *Conte du Graal*." *Travaux de linguistique et de littérature*, 16 (1978), 519–30.

CONVERSE, FLORENCE, American novelist and poet who published three Arthurian poems. "Tintagel" (1921) contrasts how much we know about Tintagel—how large it looms in the legends—with the limited vision of the Arthurian figures for whom Tintagel was important. In "Merlin Met Morgan-le-Fay" (1922), the young girl Morgan meets Merlin as he carries the baby Arthur down a country lane. She announces her plans to be schooled in sorcery and to plague her brother when he is king. "The Grail" (1897) urges us to see beyond the multitude of transient views and visions of the Grail, which are summarized, to the saving quest it represents, for Logres still lies waste. [PCB]

Converse, Florence. *Collected Poems*. New York: Dutton, 1937.

COONEY, ELLEN, American poet, author of *The Quest for the Holy Grail*, a sequence of poems using symbolism from the Tarot and from traditional Grail stories. Though the poems focus more on symbolism and imagery than narrative, they do combine to give a loose sense of a quest for and achievement of the Grail. [ACL]

Cooney, Ellen. *The Quest for the Holy Grail.* San Francisco: Duir, 1981.

COOPER, JEREMY, British author of *Ruth* (1986), a first novel that updates Tennyson's story of the Lady of Shalott. Secluded in a mock-Gothic priory near Glastonbury, the ailing heroine daydreams of the Holy Grail while she works on a painting, in the Pre-Raphaelite style, of Merlin, Lancelot, and Guinevere. Her attempt to escape this secure but unsatisfying retreat leads eventually to the harsh world of psychiatric wards and the sad victims they house. [RHT]

Cooper, Jeremy. *Ruth.* London: Hutchinson, 1986.

COOPER, SUSAN, British-American author best known for her Dark Is Rising series, which is composed of *Over Sea, Under Stone* (1965), *The Dark Is Rising* (1973), *Greenwitch* (1974), *The Grey King* (1975), and *Silver on the Tree* (1977).

In modern-day Britain, a changing group of young protagonists seek magical truths and personhood. Will Stanton serves as the series's focus, particularly in *The Dark Is Rising.* Here, he discovers that he is the lastborn of the "Old Ones," a line of immortal guardians with supernatural powers. They are opposed by a well-drawn and enigmatic evil force, known as the "Dark." The Dark is rising for a last assault upon humanity, and the books describe how talismans of power are collected to aid the forces of Light: the Drew children find the Grail; Will Stanton gathers the six signs of power; then, with the aid of a strange albino boy who turns out to be Bran (the Blessed), son of King Arthur and Queen Guenevere, he goes on to win the golden harp and crystal sword. The young people are aided by Merriman (Merlin), a senior member of the Old Ones; but since they are forced to rely largely upon their own resources, they grow rapidly in maturity and understanding. However, it is a Welsh shepherd in whom the personal goals of the series—the union of love, wisdom, and compassion—find their culmination.

The series introduces into a modern setting elements drawn from Celtic and Arthurian legends. Within this context, Will Stanton's world becomes a dual one in which the superficial and mundane are continually overlaid with true visions of a titanic and elemental psychomachia. Curiously for a juvenile series, Christianity is viewed as an inaccurate, if successful, mythos and an inadequate defense against the Dark.

Like many romances, Cooper's novels are short on characterization. But despite their reliance on existing mythology and archetypes, they represent a genuinely mythopoeic effort that deserves to be numbered among the most successful of twentieth-century juvenile fantasies. [RCS]

Cooper, Susan. *Over Sea, Under Stone.* London: Cape, 1965.
———. *The Dark Is Rising.* New York: Atheneum, 1973.
———. *Greenwitch.* New York: Atheneum, 1974.
———. *The Grey King.* New York: Atheneum, 1975.
———. *Silver on the Tree.* New York: Atheneum, 1977.

CORBENIC (Carbonek), in the Vulgate Cycle, the magical castle in which the Fisher King guards the Grail. In the *Queste del Saint Graal*, Galahad, Perceval, and Bors arrive at Corbenic, signaling the end of the castle's travails; it is there that Galahad succeeds in joining the pieces of the broken sword. In Malory's *Morte Darthur*, Bors and Lancelot visit Corbenic, not realizing its magical character and not seeing the Grail completely. "Corbenic" may derive from "cor benoit" ("blessed body"), a reference to the sacrificed body of Christ, which is manifested in the eucharistic sacrament and, according to some texts, appears in the Grail. [SW]

COURTLY LOVE, a term first used by Gaston Paris in an 1883 article. It may well be a misleading designation for the medieval phenomenon it is supposed to identify. A good many scholars criticize the term and propose that it be abandoned. That is unlikely to occur, owing to its familiarity and usefulness. It is often, and probably erroneously, used interchangeably with *fin'amors*, which is the proper term for a conception of love propounded by the Provençal troubadours. A question that has occupied a good many scholars is whether courtly love, in northern France especially, was a historical and cultural phenomenon or simply a literary convention. It certainly was the latter, at least, and it is in its literary manifestations that it bears on the Arthurian legend.

The danger in talking about courtly love is that one is tempted—and sometimes obliged—to deal with it as a monolithic and uniform system, a code that was firmly established and rarely questioned. Such a notion is entirely mistaken. The troubadours presented in general a system of illicit and passionate love, but though many saw love as more ennobling when not consummated, others insisted that one would have to be a fool to waste one's effort without hope of recompense. For some, that recompense could be a smile or a word; for others, it could be nothing less than sexual pleasure.

Imported into northern France, this system of love was further developed and was even codified, although perhaps not seriously. Two names prominent in that development are Andreas Capellanus and Chrétien de Troyes, contemporaries at the court of Marie de Champagne during the second half of the twelfth century. Andreas is the author of *De Amore*, a treatise that purports to record "courts of love" at the court. These "courts," in which a problem concerning love was proposed, discussed, and decided, are themselves the subject of much discussion. They may never have taken place, or, if they did, they may have been nothing more than literary or social exercises, a kind of cultivated parlor game. It may well be that Andreas, inspired by Ovid, intended his work as humor or parody, but that very fact would likely confirm the existence of courtly love, at least as a literary construct. Andreas even goes so far as to offer a list of the "rules of love," according to which love and marriage are incompatible; a true lover eats and sleeps very little, thinks only of his lady, and turns pale in her presence; one can love only one person (but can be loved by many); and so on.

The text that offers the best-known elaboration of the courtly love situation (and, incidentally, the one to which the term itself was first applied) is Chrétien de Troyes's *Lancelot*, or *Le Chevalier de la charrete*. In that romance, it is clear that the duty of the lover, as the lady's vassal, is to serve her faithfully, with no thought of his own welfare. Thus, Guenevere rejects him not because, in order to come to her, he rode in a cart reserved for criminals but because he hesitated momentarily before doing so; apparently, he was briefly reluctant to dishonor himself, and that concern is incompatible with a system in which all must be subordinated to the service of the lady. Later in the work, he must expiate his sin by humiliating himself repeatedly in a tourney.

As these examples suggest, there is an inherent contradiction between the demands of courtly love and those of chivalry, as the later is developed in practice. The knight's duty is to serve (society, the court and king, or individuals in need), but in so doing he gains a reputation for valor and courage, and it is generally important for him not to compromise that reputation. Love, however, imposes higher demands than those of chivalry, at least in *Lancelot*. In other works, the tensions between a knight's duty to his lady and his duty to himself and his chivalric calling are worked out in various ways; later, that tension will be replaced by a different one: between earthly chivalry and the higher calling of the Grail quest. Yet the ideals of courtly love (the lady on a pedestal, served unstintingly by a man who derives his joy from that service) will continue to influence literature throughout the Middle Ages and well beyond.

Jean Frappier proposed a concept of "Arthurian love," which he defined as *fin'amors* in a Breton context, or the synthesis of *fin'amors* and Celtic fairy lore. The result is an amorous enchantment, the reflection in literature of a traditional motif: the love of a fairy for a chosen mortal. Marie de France's *Lanval* develops that motif explicitly, while other works are implicitly and subtly influenced by its spirit and conventions. This Arthurian love is by no means contrary to the spirit of what we generally call "courtly love"; rather, it extends it and invests it with a particular tonality lacking in works not part of the *matière de Bretagne*. (*See also* CHIVALRY.)

[NJL]

Frappier, Jean. *Amour courtois et Table Ronde*. Geneva: Droz, 1973, pp. 43–56.

Lazar, Moshé. *Amour courtois et "fin'amors" dans la littérature du XIIe siècle*. Paris: Klincksieck, 1964.

Newman, F.X., ed. *The Meaning of Courtly Love*. Albany: State University of New York Press, 1968.

COUTTS, FRANCIS (FRANCIS BURDETT MONEY-COUTTS NEVILL, FIFTH BARON LATYMER; 1852–1923), who was influenced by Tennyson and also read Malory, repeatedly turned to Arthurian themes. "The Maid of Astolat, a Dirge," with its haunting refrain, is included in *Chords* (1877). The cheery lyric "Queen Guenevere's Maying" is found in *The Alhambra and Other Poems* (1888), along with "A Ballad of Cornwall," a sprightly retelling of an episode from the story of Sir Tristram and "la Beale Isoud." "Glastonbury" is nostalgically evoked in *Musa Verticordia* (1905), and *Egypt and Other Poems* (1912) contains "The Death Song of Guenevere," in which she laments her loss of Arthur's love, and "Ettard's Troth," a vigorous, laconic ballad relating Sir Gawain's betrayal of Sir Pelleas's trust. *The Romance of King Arthur* (1907), a revision and expansion of a trilogy of lyric dramas after Malory that had first appeared in 1897, comprises a prologue, *Uther Pendragon*, the poetic dramas *Merlin* and *Launcelot du Lake*, and the poem *The Death of Launcelot*. This is Coutts's major Arthurian work, but it is flawed by pseudo-antique diction. Coutts also wrote the libretto, after Malory, for Isaac Albéniz's opera *Merlin* (1902).

In his essay "King Arthur" in *Ventures in Thought* (1915), Coutts pays tribute to Tennyson's presentation of Arthur while arguing that his manner is too lyrical when epic or dramatic treatment is needed; he also discusses archaeological discoveries at South Cadbury and argues for a historical Arthur. In "Parsifal," he dismisses Wagner's opera as a travesty of the historical Perceval theme. [CNS]

Money-Coutts, F.B. *Chords*. Privately printed, 1877.

———. *The Alhambra and Other Poems*. London: Lane, 1888.

Coutts, Francis. *Musa Verticordia*. London: Lane, 1905.
———. *The Romance of King Arthur*. London: Lane, 1907.
———. *Egypt and Other Poems*. London: Lane, 1912.
———. "King Arthur" and "Parsifal." In *Ventures in Thought*. London: Lane, 1915.

COX, IRVING E., teacher and writer of science fiction, is the author of an Arthurian story, "Lancelot Returned" (1957). In Hollywood in the 1950s, Sir Lancelot comes to rescue a young girl from an "evil enchantress," her actress mother. The studio public-relations man, whom the mother calls in to help her daughter and in whose voice the story is told, is unable to save the girl from death but watches as her spirit rides off into a ghostly forest with Lancelot. [SRR]

Cox, Irving E. "Lancelot Returned." *Fantastic Universe*, 8 (October 1957), 58–68.

CRAIG, ALEC (ALEXANDER GEORGE CRAIG), socialist writer of tracts espousing freedom of expression and sexual reform. *The Voice of Merlin* (1946) is a book-length dramatic poem describing the life of Merlin and the reign of Arthur through a series of flashbacks narrated by the dying mage. Merlin is the manipulative power behind Arthur's throne, acting out first his own desire for power and then his lust for Nimue, who finally abandons him. In the crucial act of his tragedy, he substitutes himself for Uther in Igraine's bed. When Merlin tells the newly crowned Arthur that *he* is his father, Arthur reveals that his half-sister Margawse is his mistress. [PCB]

Craig, Alec. *The Voice of Merlin*. London: Fortune, 1946.

CRAM, RALPH ADAMS (1863–1942), American architect and author of *Excalibur: An Arthurian Drama*. In this play, completed in 1893 but not published until 1909 (and intended as the first part of a trilogy, which was never finished), Merlin sees himself as God's deputy on earth and Arthur as a tool for carrying out his grand design. The king's love for Guinevere causes him to defy Merlin and to lose Excalibur; but at the end of the play Merlin regains the sword, which symbolizes the right to rule, for Arthur. [ACL]

Cram, Ralph Adams. *Excalibur: An Arthurian Drama*. Boston: Richard G. Badger/The Gorham Press, 1909.

CRAMER, HEINZ TILDEN VON, German radio and film director who has written short stories, essays, science fiction, and opera libretti (for Hans Werner Henze among others). In his only Arthurian play, the radio drama *The Once and Future King* (Gemeinschaftsproduktion des Süddeutschen und Bayerischen Rundfunks, 1982), Cramer attempts to synthesize treatments of Arthurian material by T.H. White and Thomas Malory. In the first part ("Morning"), he shows Arthur's adolescent development. The sorcerer Merlin, who affords Arthur glimpses into the world from the perspective of animals, prods the future king into critical thought. In the second part ("Evening"), traveling singers advance the idea of the Round Table and its demise. The old king philosophizes at the same time on violence, power, and war. A story about a unicorn that is cruelly slain in a sincere attempt simply to capture it shows that through wrong execution even the will to do good can result in senseless destruction. [EGF/PM]

Cramer, Heinz Tilden von. *Einst und in alle Zukunft König: Ein Spiel vom Herrn Artus nach Terence Hanbury White and Sir Thomas Malory*. Unpublished manuscript (Archivexemplar Nr. 1943 und 1944), Süddeutscher Rundfunk Stuttgart, Hörspielredaktion.

CRANE, WALTER (1845–1915), English illustrator. By the 1870s, Walter Crane's reputation was established as an illustrator of inexpensive color-plate books for children. He had already shown an interest in medieval art and literature, and like his contemporary William Morris he later sought to reconcile his enthusiasm for the Middle Ages with his attraction to socialist ideals. Crane's most ambitious project of book illustration was for an edition of Spenser's *Faerie Queene*, issued in nineteen parts between 1894 and 1897 with black-and-white illustrations, a publishing venture comparable to the Dent *Morte D'arthur* with Aubrey Beardsley's illustrations in 1893–94. Crane's only specifically Arthurian illustrated works, *King Arthur's Knights* (1911) and *The Knights of the Round Table* (1915), selected stories retold for juveniles by Henry Gilbert, appeared at the end of his career, and belong to the pictorial style of a younger generation of illustrators who were using the new, commercially successful three-color printing process. These late works retain little of the distinctive quality of Crane's best illustrations. The names he gave to his two sons, Lionel and Lancelot, reflect Crane's long personal attraction to Arthurian legends. [TLS]

Massé, Gertrude. *Bibliography of First Editions of Books Illustrated by Walter Crane*. London: Chelsea, 1923.
Spencer, Isobel. *Walter Crane*. London: Studio Vista, 1975.

24. Walter Crane, "Sir Galahad Brought to King Arthur's Court." (Courtesy of the John M. Wing Foundation, The Newberry Library.)

CROSFIELD, TRUDA H., set her historical romance *A Love in Ancient Days* (1908) in a credibly portrayed Roman Britain. Arthur, as war-leader, remains in the background. Influenced by theosophy, the author saw herself as the reincarnation of her heroine. [EB]

Crosfield, Truda H. *A Love in Ancient Days*. London: Mathews, 1908.

CULHWCH AND OLWEN, an important Welsh Arthurian tale extant in two manuscripts: a complete copy in the Red Book of Hergest, ca. 1400, and an incomplete one in the White Book of Rhydderch, ca. 1325. On the evidence of the orthography and certain linguistic features of the text, it has been estimated that the tale took more or less its present shape sometime shortly before the eleventh century. It is therefore perhaps the earliest extant vernacular prose text from Wales.

The youth Culhwch has a curse placed upon him by his stepmother that he shall have no woman until he has Olwen, daughter of the giant Ysbaddaden. As a result of the curse, Culhwch is filled with love and longing for the maiden. On his father's advice, he makes for the court of Arthur, his cousin, to seek his help. Arthur sends seven of his men to accompany Culhwch on his quest, and in time they locate the maiden and enter into the presence of the giant. The giant imposes a series of seemingly impossible tasks that Culhwch must accomplish before he can wed the daughter. With the help of Arthur and his men, the tasks are indeed accomplished, the giant is killed, and Culhwch marries Olwen. Thus, the story is at one level a common type of folktale, the Giant's Daughter, embellished by a number of motifs well known to folklorists: the jealous stepmother, love for an unseen maiden, the oldest animals, the helper animals, the impossible tasks, and so on. But in its entirety the story is much more than this, and Culhwch and Olwen are insignificant characters in the tale, except insofar as they precipitate its major events. The bulk of the narrative is given over to two important catalogues and to adventures of Arthur and his men.

Before we leave Culhwch, however, it is worthwhile to look briefly at the Celtic traditions to which he belongs. Pigs were sacred animals to the Celts or at least occupied a special place in their mythological traditions. One of the nicknames of the Gaulish Mercury was *Moccus* 'boar,' and votive objects in the shape of a boar have been found at various sites sacred to the Celts. In early Irish and Welsh literature, swine play an important role, sometimes as objects of the hunt, sometimes as transformed humans of special destinies. Swineherds are shapeshifters and enjoy special status, mythologically speaking. In the Welsh Triads, we meet *Henwen* 'Ancient White (or Blessed),' a sow of mythic proportions, whose travels around Wales constitute a veritable Welsh cosmogony. In the present tale, the longest sustained adventure is Arthur's fight with Twrch Trwyth, a human king turned boar. All this has significance for the opening paragraph of the tale, which recounts Culhwch's birth. His mother went mad, we are told, and abandoned civilization. She gave birth to her son in an enclosure (*cul*) for pigs (*hwch*), whereupon she regained her senses; the boy was brought to the court by the swineherd. The Celtic evidence suggests strongly that in these briefly narrated events we have embedded the kernel of a myth about the birth of the swine-god; though the key elements in the myth were preserved, they were minimized and underplayed in favor of the Arthurian matter.

When Culhwch gets to Arthur's court, he is confronted by Glewlwyd Gafaelfawr, Arthur's porter, whom we encounter in a dialogue poem in the thirteenth-century Black Book of Carmarthen. After being admitted, Culhwch comes before Arthur, identifying himself and proclaiming his relationship. Arthur welcomes him and grants him any request he may wish to make. Naturally, Culhwch requests that Arthur get Olwen for him, and he ensures his request by invoking it in the name of Arthur's entire (presumably) retinue of warriors and courtly attendants. Over 200 names are recited by Culhwch, and the list goes on for nearly six pages, in one translation. Readers do well to pay close attention to the list, for it contains references to a wealth of tradition that has not otherwise survived. A handful of names belong to characters drawn directly from early Irish saga. Some are frivolous inventions of the author/redactor: the three maidservants Drwg, Gwaeth, and Gwaethaf Oll ("Bad, Worse, and Worst of All"), or Naw son of Seithfed ("Nine son of Seventh"), and others were probably invented for purely euphonious reasons. But the core represents names of characters that surely were traditional: among them a prodigious runner, a remarkable seer, and characters that are renowned for their leaping, eating, and hearing. Some in the list are bare names; others are characterized by an epithet or even a sentence or two that suggests a much fuller underlying tradition. For example, "Teithi Hen son of Gwynnan, whose kingdom was overrun by the sea; he barely escaped and came to Arthur. From the time he came there, his knife had this peculiarity: no haft would ever remain on it. Because of that he became sick and enfeebled while he was alive, and then he died of it."

The other catalogue in *Culhwch and Olwen* is the list of some forty tasks imposed upon Culhwch by Ysbaddaden as conditions of his betrothal to Olwen. This catalogue is a more reasoned one than the list of the members of Arthur's court. The first half comprises tasks relating to the material preparations for the wedding feast and the ritual shaving of Ysbaddaden himself; the second half of the list pertains to the hunting of Twrch Trwyth, between whose ears lie the razor, comb, and shears necessary for shaving the giant. In this catalogue, we again find tantalizing references to lost branches of the tradition. There is no direct connection between the list of tasks and the rest of the story, however, for fewer than half of them are ever accomplished, and those that are are done without regard for the order in which they were imposed.

The picture of Arthur and his court portrayed in *Culhwch and Olwen* is an intriguing one. Glewlwyd Gafaelfawr identifies himself at the beginning as Arthur's porter on New Year's Day and names four assistants who discharge that office for the rest of the year. None is permitted to enter Arthur's hall unless he is the son of a true king or a craftsman. The hall is well stocked with foods and wines drunk from solid gold horns, and visitors and wayfarers receive the same fare in adjacent lodgings. Arthur is called the chief of the nobles of Britain, and his fame has spread far and wide. His porter declares or implies that he has been with Arthur in Scandinavia, Europe, India, Corsica, Greece, and in several mythical kingdoms, too. He declares further that two-thirds of his own and of Arthur's life are past. Arthur's chief lieutenant is Cei (Kay), and Bedwyr (Bedivere) appears to be second only to Cei. True to his behavior in a good many other medieval romances. Arthur does not set out on the quest himself but delegates seven of his best men, led by Cei and Bedwyr, to help Culhwch.

After the tasks have been enumerated and imposed upon Culhwch, the men return to Arthur's court, having already accomplished the last-named task. Arthur asks which of the tasks should be attempted first (ignoring the fact that one has been accomplished already), and at this point he joins the action. From here on, Arthur plays the dominant role in the story. He rescues the divine Mabon son of Modron from his watery prison, successfully hunts a wolf-bitch and her two whelps in his ship Prydwen (after he has surrounded them, God restores to them their former human shape), and makes peace between Gwyn son of Nudd, the king of the Welsh otherworld, and his immortal enemy. Following that, he attacks Ireland, overcomes its army, and carries off a special cauldron full of Irish treasures. Next, he takes up the hunting of Twrch Trwyth, the longest episode in the tale. He pursues him from Ireland to Wales, from Wales to Brittany, and thence to Cornwall. After much fierce fighting and heavy casualties on both sides, the razor and shears are snatched from Twrch Trwyth in the mouth of the Severn, and in Cornwall Arthur's men succeed in snatching the comb. Thereupon, Twrch Trwyth charges into the sea and is not heard from again. Arthur goes off to Celliwig in Cornwall to bathe and rest. In one last adventure, Arthur encounters the "pitch-black witch from the Valley of Grief in Hell's back country" and overcomes her, cutting her in half with his knife.

It can be seen clearly that, while Arthur is portrayed as a great king whose reputation is far-flung, his activities are far from those of the feudal overlord of romance. Rather, he is like the hero in a wonder tale, aided by magic and accompanied by men with supernatural gifts, and his chief opponent has affinities with the divine animals of Celtic mythological tradition. Though the frame story of Culhwch's wooing of Olwen is important and generically grounded in Celtic narrative tradition, the tale is essentially Arthurian and contains a wealth of information about the native Welsh Arthur and his court. [PKF]

Evans, J. Gwenogvryn, ed. *The White Book Mabinogion*. Pwllheli, 1907.

Bromwich, Rachel, and D. Simon Evans, eds. *Culhwch ac Olwen*. Cardiff: University of Wales Press, 1988.

Ford, Patrick K., trans. *The Mabinogi and Other Medieval Welsh Tales*. Berkeley: University of California Press, 1977.

Loomis, Richard M., trans. "The Tale of Culhwch and Olwen." In *The Romance of Arthur*, ed. James J. Wilhelm and Laila Zamuelis Gross. New York: Garland, 1984, pp. 27–55.

Bromwich, Rachel. *Trioedd Ynys Prydein*. Cardiff: University of Wales Press, 1961; 2nd ed. 1978.

Edel, Doris. "The Catalogues in *Culhwch and Olwen* and Insular Celtic Learning." *Bulletin of the Board of Celtic Studies*, 30 (1983), 253–67.

Foster, Idris Llewelyn. "*Culhwch and Olwen* and *Rhonabwy's Dream*." In *Arthurian Literature in the Middle Ages*, ed.

Roger Sherman Loomis. Oxford: Clarendon, 1959, pp. 31–43.

Jarman, A.O.H., and Gwilym Rees Hughes. *A Guide to Welsh Literature I.* Swansea: Davies, 1976.

MacCana, Proinsias. *Celtic Mythology*. London: Hamlyn, 1970.

CUNDRY (Kundrie, Cundrie), in Wolfram von Eschenbach's *Parzival*, daughter of King Lot of Norway, sister of Gawain, niece of Arthur, and wife of Lischois Gwelljus, Duke of Gowerzin. Cundry is one of four queens and 400 maidens who live in the Schastel Marveile. She is not to be confused with Cundry La Surziere, the loathly damsel who reproaches Perceval for not having asked the appropriate question during his visit to the Grail castle.

In Wagner's *Parsifal*, Kundry is a complex character who despite her nobler instincts becomes an agent of evil when the magician Klingsor casts a spell on her. Her efforts to corrupt Parsifal by seduction fail; the hero's renunciation of sensual pleasures and his affirmation of pure love eventually establish him as the redeemer of the other characters. [SW]

CURRY, JANE (LOUISE), American artist and author of *The Sleepers* (1968), an exciting fantasy for younger readers, in which four children discover Arthur and his knights sleeping in an underground cavern in the Eildon Hills. With the help of Myrddin (Merlin), they foil a plot by Morgan le Fay and Medraut to destroy the Sleepers and capture the thirteen Treasures of Prydein (Britain). [RHT]

Curry, Jane. *The Sleepers.* New York: Harcourt, Brace and World, 1968.

CY (CI) NOUS DIT, an anonymous fourteenth-century French composition preserved in some twenty manuscripts, consists of nearly 800 exempla, fables, and other narratives, all of them beginning with the words "Cy nous dit que . . ." ("here we are told that . . .") and concluding with a statement of the moral significance of the tale. A reference to Tristan and Isolde's tryst beneath the tree in which Mark is hiding is followed by a moral concluding that we should keep ourselves free of evil, for the King watches us from above. The tryst is depicted in a miniature from a Chantilly manuscript of the *Cy nous dit.* [NJL]

Loomis, Roger Sherman, and Laura Hibbard Loomis. *Arthurian Legends in Medieval Art.* London: Oxford University Press, 1938, p. 28.

CZECH ARTHURIAN LITERATURE. Arthurian texts written in Czech date only from the middle to the end of the fourteenth century, but references to Arthurian matter in Bohemia go back a century earlier. The name of Arthur is first found in lyric verse composed by *Minnesinger* resident at the court of the Přemyslide kings in Prague. The knight Friedrich von Sonnenburg compared his patron, Přemysl Otakar II, to King Arthur and Alexander the Great. It was the role of the German poets to compare their masters to chivalric heroes in order to enhance their prestige and standing among the German princes in the empire. A further reference to Arthurian culture occurs in Book II of the *Chronicon Aulae Regiae*, by Peter of Zittau, where we find the first description of a joust in the Czech lands. Certain young noblemen approach their king, John of Luxemburg, with the request that he establish a Round Table to spread his fame and reputation abroad. Responding to this flattery, John duly invites German counts and princes to Prague, where he has built a wooden structure to house the festivities. But not a single guest arrives, prompting the author to reflect on the folly of such enterprises when they are inadequately publicized.

Courtly romance in Czech arose during the reign of John's son, Charles IV (r. 1347–78). Czech literature blossomed at this period, encompassing all the genres then current in the West—satire, fabliau, epic, romance, lyric, drama, and secular and theological prose. However, only two courtly romances with an Arthurian theme are extant: *Tandariáš a Floribella* and *Tristram a Izalda*.

Tandariáš is based on *Tandareis und Flordibel*, by the Austrian poet Der Pleier, working perhaps in Salzburg between 1240 and 1270. The Czech poem, written in octosyllabic verse with a standard trochaic meter, is preserved in three manuscripts, dated 1463, 1472, and 1483. Internal linguistic evidence (morphology and rhymes) suggests that the poem was composed ca. 1380. *Tandariáš* has traditionally been dismissed as inferior to its courtly German model, but it is in fact quite different in conception and realization from Der Pleier's poem. One-tenth the size of the source, it is more reminiscent of the popular English tail-romances of the period. The emphasis is placed on a dynamic plot, which is punctuated by lively realistic dialogue in order to make Der Pleier's amorphous tale of love, loss, and reconciliation more accessible to the Czech burgher audience. The story is basically the same, with the exception of three episodes absent from Der Pleier's work: the conquest of the dwarf oppressing the Christian queen and the subsequent scene with the dwarf at Artuš's (Arthur's) court; the conquest of the heathen oppressing the Queen of the Maidens; and the distribution of the rewards by Artuš.

Der Pleier depicts an idealized courtly world set a generation later than the events described in the classical romances of Hartmann von Aue and Wolfram von Eschenbach. Each character in the German romances is given a distinct pedigree. The anonymous Czech author, however,

25. MS Paris, Bibliothèque Nationale, f.fr. 343, fol. 3: Galahad at the Pentecost Feast (from *La Queste del Saint Graal*). (Paris, Bibliothèque Nationale.)

assumes that his audience is unfamiliar with the Arthurian stories, and introduces Arthur with a minstrel formula; "There was a king,/his name was Arthur" (l. 1). He concentrates on three main heroes, Tandariáš, Floribella, and Artuš; the minor characters remain nameless, with the exception of three lesser figures, Cayn, Gwan, and Gawin, necessary to link events in the story. There are 118 characters mentioned in Der Pleier, but only seven in the Czech version. By restricting the number of characters, the author simplifies the story for his audience, which was unaccustomed to the elaborate genealogy of Arthurian romance.

The Czech reworking is more realistic and down-to-earth than its German source. The characters, stripped of their aristocratic courtly demeanor, are reduced to the level of everyday humanity. The headstrong Floribella, unlike her German counterpart, does not indulge in long soliloquies addressed to *frauwe Amûr* but prefers action to contemplation. She tests the hero's devotion by getting up earlier every day to see if he is standing dutifully at her door. Similarly, Tandariáš is quite different from his prototype, Tanderois; he loses his courtly veneer and becomes a simple knight-errant. The author gives Tandariáš a mission to fight against the heathen and their oppression of the true Christian faith. The story is thus remodeled on exemplary lines as a tale of true love and fidelity triumphing over injustice and barbarism, consistent with the generally moralizing function of Czech literature in the Middle Ages. In addition to restructuring the story and adding certain episodes, the Czech author also includes certain realistic features of characterization that make the heroes seem more immediate and plausible than their somewhat two-dimensional German equivalents. Artuš bellows with anger when he hears of Tandariáš's exploits; Floribella cries out at the tournament when she espies her beloved in the lists and is rebuked by the Queen for her unseemly behavior. At one point, she is so distressed at her lover's absence that she suffers a nosebleed, an example of psychosomatic parallelism and a formula signaling distress, one that also occurs in the Middle English romance *Athelston*. Tandariáš behaves in a boisterous fashion incompatible with his courtly status; for example, he is so delighted to see Floribella at her window that he throws his companions over his shoulder like a farmboy.

Tristram a Izalda, dated to the end of the fourteenth century, is a conflation of three German sources: Eilhart's *Tristrant* (twelfth century), Gottfried von Strassburg's courtly version, and Heinrich von Freiberg's continuation of Gottfried's unfinished masterpiece. Its 9,000 verses make it the longest narrative poem in medieval Czech literature. The text, preserved in two manuscripts, the Strahov MS (A), dated 1449, and the Brno MS (B), dated 1483, is of particular importance because it offers a complete version of the Tristan story. Less well conceived and structured than *Tandariáš*, *Tristram* is yet a vigorous retelling of the story, shorn of the courtly ethos of the sources. Like *Tandariáš*, *Tristram* has been regarded as an uninspired translation of the German models; but it has little in common with the aristocratic world of Eilhart or Gottfried. Written with a burgher audience in mind, it evokes workaday attitudes accessible to the rising new middle classes. Instead of a noble conception of love, we find a universal treatment of love and fidelity not limited to a refined circle of *edele herzen* but available to all regardless of class and background. Tristram is neither a feudal warrior, a minstrel, nor a courtly lover but a simple knight or, in the scenes based on Heinrich, a comic figure akin to the *joculatores* tradition of the mystery plays.

Tristram is a hodgepodge of styles, from lyrical formulae interpolated at random to burlesque features reminiscent of the satires and fabliaux. It is interesting as an example of Czech medial-style realism, whereby the characters are made more vivid than in the sources through the use of exterior gesture and movement to signal an inner psychological state. In the scene set in the wilderness, where Tristram is credited with the invention of fishing, the Czech author adds certain lively touches to the characters' actions: for example, Izalda takes a pin from her veil and gives it to Tristram, who uses it to make a hook for a fishing rod (ll. 4,681–84). In the love-potion episode (based on Eilhart), Isalde's long monologues addressed to *frauwe Amûr* are omitted, as they deflect attention from the narrative; the Czech author prefers to explore the relationship between the characters through dialogue rather than the soliloquy favored by the courtly sources. Sometimes, the realism goes so far that the border between romance and fabliau becomes blurred. In the final scene, where the two Izaldas meet over Tristram's corpse, their confrontation in the Czech version is close to a fishwives' brawl. The first Izalda strikes her rival on the side with the comment, "You are like a wolf that steals sheep," an example of folk animal imagery typical of medieval Czech texts. On the linguistic level, *Tristram* contains a rich variety of proverbs, sayings, and idioms drawn from the everyday language, further evidence that the poem was not intended for a noble, but for a heterogeneous, audience. [AT]

Bamborschke, Ulrich, ed. *Das altčechische Tristan-Epos*. 2 vols. Wiesbaden: Harrassowitz, 1968, 1969.

———, ed. *Der altčechische Tandariuš*. Berlin, 1982.

Brušák, Karel. "Some Notes on *Tandariáš a Floribella*, a Czech 14th Century Chivalrous Romance." In *Gorski vijenac: A Garland of Essays Offered to Professor Elizabeth Mary Hill*, ed. Robert Auty et al. Cambridge: Modern Humanities Research Association, 1970, pp. 44–56.

Thomas, Alfred. "The Treatment of the Love Theme in the Old Czech Tristram." *Die Welt der Slaven*, 30 (1985), 260–68.

———. *The Czech Chivalric Romances Vévoda Arnošt and Lavryn in Their Literary Context*. Göppingen: Kümmerle, 1989.

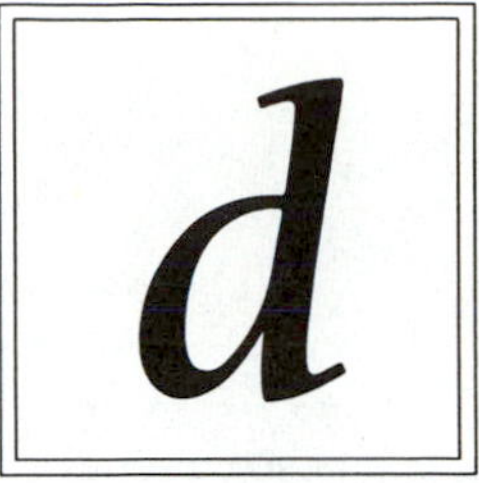

"DAMIGELLA DI SCALOT" ("Lady of Scalot"), Tale 82 of the *Novellino*, recounting the story of the lady of Scalot (Shalott), whose corpse arrives mysteriously at Camelot after she dies of love for Lancelot. The story offers early evidence of Italian interest in Arthurian texts (in this case, the French *Mort Artu*) and exemplifies the process by which romance episodes were adapted to the formal requirements of the brief Italian *novella*. (*See also* NOVELLINO, IL.) [MSh]

Segre, Cesare, ed. "Il *Novellino*." In *La prosa del Duecento*, ed. Cesare Segre and Mario Marti. Milan: Riccardo Ricciardi, 1959, pp. 793–881.

———. *Structures and Time: Narration, Poetry, Models*, trans. John Meddemmen. Chicago: University of Chicago Press, 1979, pp. 58–64.

DANE, CLEMENCE (pseudonym of Winifred Ashton; 1888–1965). Dane's *The Saviours* (1942) consists of seven poetic radio plays narrated by Merlin and structured around the figure of *Artus redivivus*, returning in Britain's hours of need as King Alfred, Robin Hood, Elizabeth and Essex, Lord Horatio Nelson, and the Unknown Warrior of World War I. The series ends with Arthur, recognized as the indomitable spirit of Britain, predicting his next return, which would coincide with the onset of World War II. [VML]

Dane, Clemence. *The Saviours*. London and Toronto: Heinemann, 1942.

DANTE ALIGHIERI (1265–1321) alluded to Arthurian romance no more than some half-dozen times, yet no student of medieval literature can fail to wonder about the relationship between the greatest body of medieval secular literature and the man who was arguably the greatest secular poet of the age. Dante is known for his insistence that morally and intellectually serious literature could be written in the vernacular and for his realization in the *Divine Comedy* of this notion, still controversial in the early fourteenth century. Did he see Arthurian literature as an illustrious example of what he wished vernacular literature to do, or instead as a dangerous countermodel?

An attempt to answer this perennial question must be based on a survey of Dante's allusions to Arthurian literature. Three are rather minor. In *Inferno*, Canto 5, l. 67, he pairs Tristan with Paris, to end the parade of those damned through love. He alludes to Mordred and names Arthur in a periphrasis (*Inferno*, Canto 32, ll. 61–62), affirming that two damned souls encountered deep in the infernal realm of treachery called "Caina" were even more worthy to be there than Mordred. In a different vein, in a lyric poem addressed to his "first friend," Guido Cavalcanti, Dante expresses the wish that the two of them, with their friend Lapo Gianni, might by enchantment be put together in a marvelous boat ("Guido, i' vorrei che tu e Lapo ed io/fossimo presi per incantamento/e messi in un vasel . . .") and that "il buono incantatore" would then send certain ladies to join in their fantastic journey; it is entirely possible that the setting Dante evokes is derived from Arthurian romance and that the "good enchanter" is Merlin.

More suggestive of Dante's view of the Arthurian corpus than these minor allusions are a key reference in the treatise on the vernacular known as the *Vulgari Eloquentia* and a cluster of allusions (in *Inferno*, *Paradiso*, and *Convivio*) to the Lancelot romance. Dante probably first grappled with the problem that his linguistic treatise tries to resolve under the influence of Brunetto Latini, the learned Florentine writer and public servant whom Dante (*Inferno*, Canto 15, ll. 82–85) mentions as having taught him much; for Brunetto, an exile in France from 1260 to about the time of Dante's birth (1265), wrote his famous encyclopedic work, the *Livre dou Tresor*, in French, affirming that language's superiority for didactic purposes to his native Tuscan. By implication, it might seem that Dante came to disagree with his "master," if the *Comedy*, in Italian, is taken to be didactic, even encyclopedic, in character—though his explicit disagreement with Brunetto in matters of language has to do not with Brunetto's championing of French but instead (*Vulgari Eloquentia*, Book 13) with his decision to write (probably another work, the didactic poem entitled *Il Tesoretto*) in a merely municipal, Florentine, dialect. In any case, Brunetto raised the question of the adequacy of the Romance vernaculars to specific literary genres, and Dante makes a preliminary attempt to answer it early in the *Vulgari*

Eloquentia, Book 9, Chapter 2), stating that Italian, Provençal, and French each might be legitimately seen as the best vernacular for different reasons: Italian because it is the closest to (Latin) grammar and therefore the most logical; Provençal because it was the language of the foremost love poets, the troubadours; and French because it dominates the field of vernacular prose, both didactic and narrative. It is in this context that Dante cites, together with instances of the *matière d'antiquité*, Arthurian romance ("Arturi regis ambages pulcerrimae"). This allusion (tangentially suggesting, not surprisingly, that Dante did not know the verse texts of the Arthurian cycle, including the work of Chrétien) indicates that Dante thought Arthurian prose literature a very important achievement indeed, establishing French as a major language by revealing, together with other prose works, a narrative capacity in the *langue d'oïl* comparable in quality to the rigorous grammaticality of the language of the Italian peninsula.

In this context, Dante's most famous allusion to Arthurian romance, in the Paolo and Francesca episode of *Inferno*, Canto 5, has puzzled many who have taken Dante, through the voice of Francesca, to be condemning the Lancelot romance and its author for an immorality that has led her to eternal damnation: "Galeotto fu il libro, e chi lo scrisse" ("A Galahaut was the book and the one who wrote it"). Dante, however, is here by no means condemning Arthurian literature but rather a pair of its readers: he puts Paolo and Francesca in hell, not the Lancelot author. The Paolo and Francesca episode is related to and illuminated by two other Dantesque allusions to the Lancelot cycle. In *Paradiso*, Canto 16, ll. 14–15, Dante compares Beatrice's laugh to the Lady of Malohaut's cough at the moment of Guenevere's "first mistake" ("primo fallo"); however this comparison is to be interpreted, it suggests Dante's awareness that characters within the story are alert to Guenevere's "mistake," implying that readers are not obliged to adopt the viewpoint of the sinning protagonists of the episode. More conclusive in this regard is Dante's allusion in his vernacular treatise on the nature of poetry, *Convivio*, Book IV, Chapter 28, Section 8, to Lancelot's end, as a monk repentant of the adultery that kept him from fulfilling his high mission. Dante makes clear that Paolo and Francesca miss the warning provided by the disastrous conclusion of Lancelot and Guenevere's relationship because they do not finish reading the book: "non vi leggemmo piu avanti" ("we read no further"). He is himself fully aware that the Lancelot author provided such a warning, and his reader must be, too, if Paolo and Francesca's situation is to succeed in teaching the reader anything important. Thus, the high judgment of Arthurian literature expressed in the *Vulgari Eloquentia* is not diminished in any way by the Paolo and Francesca episode. [SJN]

Dante Alighieri. *Opere*, ed. Michele Barbi et al. 2nd ed. Florence: Società Dantesca Italiana, 1960.

Delcorno, Daniela Branca. "Romanzi arturiani." In *Enciclopedia Dantesca*. Rome: Istituto della Enciclopedia Italiana, 1973, pp. 1028–30.

Noakes, Susan. "The Double Misreading of Paolo and Francesca." *Philological Quarterly*, 62 (1983), 221–39.

DAVEY, FRANK, Canadian poet, composed a series of free-verse lyrics, *The King of Swords* (1972), describing the end of a love affair in terms of the life and death of Arthur. The seamier side of the Arthurian myth is used as an illustration, both sexual and social, of modern times. [SRR]

Davey, Frank. *The King of Swords*. Vancouver: Talonbooks, 1972.

DAVID, PETER, author of *Knight Life* (1987), an amusing but slight novel depicting Arthur's return and his successful campaign, as Arthur Penn, to be elected mayor of New York. His supporters and enemies include incarnations of earlier Arthurian figures: an eight-year-old Merlin, Morgan, and characters with such names as Moe Dredd, Gwen DeVere, and Percy Vale. [NJL]

David, Peter. *Knight Life*. New York: Ace, 1987.

DAVIDSON, JOHN (1857–1909), Scottish poet and playwright. In his poem "The Last Ballad" (1899), Lancelot struggles against his consuming passion for Guinevere by performing valiant deeds and acts of penance. He even sinks into madness, from which he is healed by his son, Galahad, before he finally accepts its inevitability. "Lancelot" (1903), Davidson's play about the adultery between the lovers, was rejected by the London theaters and never performed. [RHT]

Davidson, John. "The Last Ballad." In *The Last Ballad and Other Poems*. London and New York: Lane, 1899, pp. 1–23.

DAVIES, ROBERTSON, Canadian novelist, playwright, and critic, has published two novels with Arthurian themes: *What's Bred in the Bone* (1985) and *The Lyre of Orpheus* (1988). In the former, Francis Cornish struggles to reconcile his romantic heritage, the legend of Arthur, with reality and his destiny as an artist. *The Lyre of Orpheus*, which takes place after Cornish's death, features a more explicitly Arthurian plot, as money from Francis's estate is used to complete and produce *Arthur of Britain, or The Magnanimous Cuckold*, an unfinished and apparently fictitious opera by E.T.A. Hoffmann. In the process, Arthur Cornish (Francis's nephew), his wife, Maria, and their best friend find themselves reenacting the Arthurian triangle. In both works, Davies argues the necessity of assuming a personal myth in order to flourish as an artist and human being—and the dangers of living the wrong one. They are part of a series about the life and influence of Francis Cornish, which began with *The Rebel Angels* (1981). [REH]

Davies, Robertson. *What's Bred in the Bone*. Toronto: Macmillan; New York: Viking Penguin, 1985.

———. *The Lyre of Orpheus*. Toronto: Macmillan; New York: Viking Penguin; Harmondsworth: Penguin, 1988.

DAVIS, GEORGENE, author of *The Round Table* (1930), a lyric poetic drama on Arthur, set in sixth-century Britain, concentrating on the intrigue among the Round Table company, especially Guinevere, Lancelot, and Gawain. The work proves once again how difficult it is, especially with plot alterations, to transform the Arthurian legend into drama, despite the author's explicit stage directions. [VML]

Davis, Georgene. *The Round Table: A History Drawn from Unreliable Sources*. Rutland, Vt.: Tory, 1930.

DAWSON, CONINGSBY (1883–1959), produced an Arthurian *Pilgrim's Progress* in the allegorically cumbersome novel *The Road to Avalon* (1911). The Christian protagonist of this quest to bring Arthur back from Avalon encounters personified vices and virtues, and he discovers in the end that he has become Arthur himself. [DN]

Dawson, Coningsby. *The Road to Avalon*. London: Hodder and Stoughton, 1911.

DE ANGELO, MICHAEL, author of *Cyr Myrddin* (1979), tells of Merlin's preparation for his role as Arthur's precursor in this *Bildungsroman*. The portrayal of the young Merlin—here a prince of the Pendragon family—as he learns life's hard lessons, is sufficiently appealing to offset the novel's contrived incidents and characterizations. [DN]

De Angelo, Michael. *Cyr Myrddin: The Coming of Age of Merlin*. Everett, Wash.: Gododdin, 1979.

DE BEVERLEY, THOMAS (pseudonym of George Newcomen), includes six Arthurian poems, almost all in blank verse, in *The Youth of Sir Arthour, The Quest of the Sangraele and Other Poems* (1925): "The Youth of Sir Arthour," "The Story of Nimue," "The Birth of Sir Galahad," "Sir Percival's Vision," "The Achievement of the Sangraele and the Death of Sir Galahad," and "Sir Uwain's Daughter." [EB]

De Beverley, Thomas. *The Youth of Sir Arthour, The Quest of the Sangraele and Other Poems*. London: Macdonald, 1925.

DE CUNIUGE NON DUCENDA ("Against Marriage"), a popular satire on marriage written in Latin verse in the mid-thirteenth century. Although the introduction to the recent edition by A.G. Rigg suggests that the protagonist is the Arthurian hero Gawain, the poem has no other connection to the body of Arthurian romance. The protagonists in the various manuscripts carry many names—Gawain, William, Gilbert, Walter, Golias, Michael, Colin, Calvin, Robert, Andrew, John—but Gawain and its variants are most common. The context is the misery of marriage for a hard-working man who must support a family—certainly not a situation that the chivalrous and royal Sir Gawain ever faced. The Gawain of the satire is apparently a namesake of the hero of romance, this in itself adding to the satire. [MLD]

Rigg, A.G., ed and trans. *Gawain on Marriage*. Toronto: Pontifical Institute of Mediaeval Studies, 1986.

DE ORTU WALUUANII NEPOTIS ARTURI ("On the Rise of Gawain, Arthur's Nephew"), a Latin prose romance about the birth, boyhood, and early adventures of Gawain. Gawain, illegitimate son of Arthur's sister Anna, is trained in arms by the emperor of Rome. Unaware of his name and royal blood, he is known only as "Knight of the Surcoat." His early adventures are undertaken as a Roman cavalry officer and include two major quests: first, single combat against a Persian champion to raise the siege of

Jerusalem; and second, military aid for Arthur of Britannia, menaced by raiders on his northern border. The first quest is interrupted by battles with pirates on land and at sea, pirates who even use the dreaded Greek Fire. The second quest is interrupted when Gawain, unwittingly, must confront both Arthur and Kay for passage of the last ford before he reaches Caerleon. Gawain is victorious, but Arthur, humiliated, refuses to allow Gawain to fight at his side against the raiders. Nevertheless, Gawain saves Arthur from defeat at the Castle of Maidens. Arthur rewards Gawain's brilliant victory by revealing to him his lineage and accepting him as nephew and knight. Although ascribed by John Bale to Robert of Torigni (Abbot of Mont St.-Michel, 1154–86), the work is variously dated from the last quarter of the twelfth century to the last quarter of the thirteenth. Another Arthurian romance in Latin, *Historia Meriadoci*, is considered to be by the same author. [MLD]

Day, Mildred Leake, ed. and trans. *The Rise of Gawain, Nephew of Arthur (De ortu Waluuanii nepotis Arturi)*. New York: Garland, 1984.

DE SANCTO JOSEPH AB ARIMATHIA, a prose work printed by Richard Pynson in 1516. It is an epitome of Joseph's life contained in Capgrave's *Nova Legenda Angliae* and John of Glastonbury's *Cronica*, stressing the Glastonbury account of Joseph's commission by St. Philip to evangelize Britain, his founding of the oratory of Our Lady at Glastonbury, and his subsequent holy life and burial at the abbey there. [VML]

Skeat, Walter W., ed. *Joseph of Arimathie*. London: Trübner, 1871, pp. 33–34.

DEAL, BABS H(ODGES), American writer, ingeniously transposes Arthurian legend to the setting of United States college football in *The Grail: A Novel* (1963). It is fascinating to identify traditional characters in new roles, as the Arthur-Guenevere-Lancelot triangle is reenacted by the coach, his wife, and his Louisiana French quarterback, though the final effect is to trivialize the legend. [RHT]

Deal, Babs H. *The Grail: A Novel*. New York: McKay, 1963.

DECORATIVE ARTS (MEDIEVAL). Arthurian themes are often found in the decorative arts of the Middle Ages. Among the most popular were stories of the great lovers, such as Tristan and Lancelot, or themes having religious overtones, such as the Grail legend. King Arthur was represented as one of the three Christian Worthies, or in the larger context of the Nine Worthies, seldom as presiding over the Round Table. And even in this relatively select group, certain subjects caught the imagination of artists and—we must suppose—of patrons as well: Sir Lancelot crossing the Sword Bridge, Sir Gawain on the Perilous Bed, Sir Yvain charging through the castle gate with his horse caught by the portcullis, Tristan and Isolde playing chess in a garden or on the voyage to Cornwall and spied on by King Mark. This "Tryst Beneath the Tree" was the single most popular Arthurian subject. From Germany to England, artists represented the jealous King Mark's deception in painting and embroidery, wood and ivory carving, metal- and enamelwork. The subject lent itself to representation in the visual arts because the complex narrative could be condensed into a single image, and the composition permitted considerable flexibility. Mark observed the lovers from the branches while the water below reflected his features. The symmetrical composition around the tree and fountain or pool, with paired figures left and right and paired faces above and below, could be adapted to the round, square, or quatrefoil frame (e.g., mirror-back or box), and when an irregular shape had to be covered (e.g., a misericord or comb) the foliage and water could spread out over the requisite surface. The story might be made explicit by the use of elegant banderoles, like comic-strip speech balloons, as it is on a boxwood comb from eastern France or Switzerland (Museum of Fine Arts, Boston).

Literary description of Arthurian subjects, although often exaggerated and fanciful, indicates the popularity and extraordinary richness of the decorative arts of the late Middle Ages. Inventories, surviving from the fourteenth and fifteenth centuries, confirm the existence of great treasures. Since objects were admired for their intrinsic value, as well as for their workmanship, they were traded, pawned, seized as booty, and used as exchange. Owners had little hesitation in melting down works of art for the precious metals they contained, and when new items were desired, old-fashioned pieces were sent to the goldsmith. Thus, of all the pieces listed in medieval inventories, only a handful have survived to the twentieth century. Fortunate indeed is the museum or the private collector who can boast of a gold cup, ivory box, or enameled knife having secular scenes. Church treasures were able to survive, either because of conservatism of taste or the sanctity surrounding the object, be it reliquary, cross, or candlestick. Decorative artworks made from humbler materials fared little better. Instead of being lost because of the value of their materials, they were discarded as worthless or destroyed accidentally. The wells and garbage pits of cities have contained treasure troves for the archaeologist and student of the decorative arts. Thus, tiles, woodwork, leather, ceramics, or ordinary textiles are as rare and precious as the more ostentatious products of the jeweler's skill.

The most glamorous of all objects in the decorative arts were the table fountains used to dispense wine, rose-water, or perfumes. One such fountain survives (Cleveland Museum of Art), and fragments of others may have been incorporated into other works. Descriptions do exist in literature and inventories; not surprisingly, the Tryst Beneath the Tree lent itself to adaptation as a fountain. The inventory made in 1353 of the belongings of John the Good of France describes a silver fountain with Tristan and Isolde beneath a vine (surely a misunderstanding of the tree). The base of a fourteenth-century French goblet (now in Milan) also represents the meeting. The most spectacular late-medieval table decoration, the Burghley Nef (Victoria and Albert Museum, London), shows the lovers as they played chess aboard the ship taking them to Cornwall. Other metalwork may not be as rich, but it does serve to remind us of the popular art of the time. Bronze pendants used for decoration and identification of horses and hounds might be gilt and enameled with figures from the romances. Tristan and Isolde represented as lovers holding the fatal goblet can be seen on a fourteenth-century Catalan pendant (Metropolitan Museum of Art, New York).

From the smallest to the largest scale, Arthurian stories appear. Walls might be painted with the romances, as evidenced by surviving murals and tapestries. Even the floors were enriched with ornamental tiles (e.g., Chertsey Abbey Tiles, British Museum). Personal possessions—ivory, bone, or boxwood boxes, combs, hair-parters, and mirror-cases—also treated the romances of Tristan, Lancelot, and Gawain. But the complete popularization of the Arthurian heroes as seen in the minor arts came in the new medium of printing. The makers of woodblocks for playing cards reduced the great King Arthur to a king in a deck of cards, and in a Provençal deck of the mid-fifteenth century the noble Lancelot, along with Ogier, Roland, and Valery, becomes one of the four knaves. (*See also* Burghley Nef; Chertsey Abbey Tiles; Embroidery (Medieval); Ivory; Louvre Tray; Misericords; Stained Glass; Tapestry.) [MS]

Hind, Arthur, *An Introduction to a History of Woodcut*. London: Constable, 1935.

Loomis, Roger Sherman, and Laura Hibbard Loomis. *Arthurian Legends in Medieval Art*. London: Oxford University Press, 1938.

Verdier, Philippe. *The International Style*. Catalogue, Walters Art Gallery, Baltimore, 1962.

Whitaker, Muriel. *The Legends of King Arthur in Art*. Cambridge: Brewer, 1990.

DEEPING, (GEORGE) WARWICK (1877–1950), English author of four sentimental historical romances with Arthurian connections. The borrowings are only general in *The Man on the White Horse* (1934) and *The Man Who Went Back* (1940). Even *Uther and Igraine* (1903) departs widely from tradition in its account of virtuous love between Arthur's parents.

Artorius himself appears to rally resistance against the Saxons in *The Sword and the Cross*, which was published posthumously in 1957. The central hero, however, is Gerontius, whose valor in battle contrasts sharply with his deference in love for the beautiful Igerna. [RHT]

Deeping, Warwick. *Uther and Igraine*. New York: Outlook, 1903.

———. *The Man on the White Horse*. London: Cassell; New York: Knopf, 1934.

———. *The Man Who Went Back*. London: Cassell, 1940.

———. *The Sword and the Cross*. London: Cassell, 1957.

DELAY, FLORENCE, and JACQUES ROUBAUD, French scholars and authors, have begun a series of ten stage plays about the Grail and King Arthur. The six that appeared in print prior to 1988 were written in musical, mostly unpunctuated prose. Bearing the overall title of *Graal Théâtre*, the project, described by the authors as *relativement mégalomane*, depicts the Grail and Arthurian cycle from Joseph of Arimathea to the death of Arthur. Sources include a large number of primarily French Grail and Arthurian works from Robert de Boron and Chrétien de Troyes to the later prose versions, as well as the *Mabinogi* and the much-read investigations of Jean Markale. The three plays about Merlin, Gawain and the Green Knight, and Lancelot—each lasting three hours—were performed with great success by the Marcel Maréchal Company in the Nouveau Théâtre National de Marseille in 1979. Though acclaimed, the project is at an apparent standstill. In ambition and achievement, it warrants comparison with Dorst's *Merlin* (1981). (*See also* Roubaud, Jacques.) [UM/PWM]

Delay, Florence, and Jacques Roubaud. *Graal Théâtre*. 2 vols. Paris: Gallimard, 1977, 1981.

Roubaud, Jacques. *Graal fiction*. Paris: Gallimard, 1978.

Hochberg, Brigitte. "Graal Théâtre." In *Mittelalter-Rezeption III*, ed. Jürgen Kühnel, Hans-Dieter Mück, Ursula Müller, and Ulrich Müller. Göppingen: Kümmerle, 1987.

Müller, Ulrich. "Parzival 1980—auf der Bühne, im Fernsehen und im Film." In *Mittelalter-Rezeption II*, ed. Jürgen Kühnel, Hans-Dieter Mück, Ursula Müller, and Ulrich Müller. Göppingen: Kümmerle, 1987.

DE LINT, CHARLES, Canadian author of the fantasy *Moonheart* (1984). In an old house in modern Toronto, an assorted group of people are caught up in a terrifying struggle between magic-wielders from the past, including the bard Taliesin, and discover how dangerous is the evil that lies within us all. [RHT]

De Lint, Charles. *Moonheart*. New York: Ace, 1984.

DELL, FLOYD (1887–1969), American author of *King Arthur's Socks* (1916). This one-act play set in Camelot, Maine, is Arthurian in name only. Gwen Robinson, wife of Professor Arthur Robinson, and Lance Jones, an artist, declare their love for each other. Gwen, unwilling to damage a comfortable marriage, darns Arthur's socks as Lance leaves to marry their friend Vivien. [AEG]

Dell, Floyd. *King Arthur's Socks and Other Village Plays*. New York: Knopf, 1922.

DEMANDA DO SANTO GRAAL, A ("The Quest of the Holy Grail"). The Portuguese *Demanda do Santo Graal* and the Spanish *Demanda del Sancto Grial* both derive from a common source: the last branch of the Post-Vulgate *Roman du Graal*, which was translated into a western Ibero-Romance language, probably Galician-Portuguese, either at the end of the thirteenth century or in the early fourteenth. At some point, the *Demanda* branch became a separate romance, surviving as such in a fifteenth-century Portuguese manuscript (Vienna, Nationalbibliothek 2594) and in two Castilian imprints (Toledo, 1515, and Seville, 1535). However, the title apparently came to signify the whole Arthurian story as told in the Post-Vulgate texts. The fifteenth-century copy of the Portuguese *Livro de Josep Abaramatia*, for example, refers to this text as the first part of the *Demanda do Santo Graal*, and the Castilian *Baladro del Sabio Merlín* of 1535 calls the *Baladro* the first part of the *Demanda*. The *Demandas* contain material presumed to have formed part of the now-lost sections of French Post-Vulgate text, including the epilogue of Mark's second invasion of Arthur's kingdom. The Portuguese version reflects more accurately than the Spanish the original language of the French and is frequently cited by critics for its qualities of style, and selections from it continue to be included in contemporary Portuguese school texts. [HLS]

Magne, Augusto, ed. *A Demanda do Santo Graal: Reprodução facsimilar e transcrição crítica do códice 2594 da Biblioteca Nacional de Viena*. 3 vols. Rio de Janeiro: Instituto Nacional do Livro, 1944.

Bonilla y San Martín, Adolfo, ed. *La demanda del Santo Grial*. In *Libros de caballerías, primera parte: Ciclo artúrico–Ciclo carolingio*. Madrid: Bailly-Baillière, 1907, pp. 163–338.

26. Aubrey Beardsley, "How Sir Bedivere Cast the Sword Excalibur into the Water," from the Dent *Morte D'Arthur*. (Courtesy of the Kenneth Spencer Research Library, University of Kansas.)

DENT *MORTE D'ARTHUR*, a two-volume edition, was published in installments in 1893 and 1894 by John M. Dent and illustrated by a hitherto unknown artist, Aubrey Beardsley (1872–1898). Intended to rival the luxury editions of the Kelmscott Press, it featured over 400 drawings in black-and-white, including full-page vignettes, chapter headings, and decorative borders. Varying stylistically, Beardsley's early drawings recall Burne-Jones, while the later contributions exhibit his mature aesthetic, reflecting the decadent spirit of the late Arthurian Revival and transforming the heroic characters into androgynous phantoms. [DNM]

Malory, Sir Thomas. *Morte D'arthur*, London: Dent, 1893–94.

———. *Dent Morte Darthur*, 2 vols. Woodbridge, Suffolk: Boydell and Brewer, 1985 (facsimile).

Mancoff, Debra N. *The Arthurian Revival in Victorian Art*. New York: Garland, 1990, pp. 243–45, 260–264.

Whitaker, Muriel. "'Flat Blasphemies'—Beardsley's Illustrations for Malory's *Morte Arthur*." *Mosaic*, 8 (1975), 67–75.

DIALOG ETRE ARZUR ROE D'AN BRETOUNET HA GUYNGLAFF, AN ("Dialogue Between Arthur and Guynglaff"), a Breton text, of which 247 lines survive, concerning Guynglaff, a sort of "wildman of the woods" who is also a prophet and magician and thus a Merlin figure. Guynglaff is questioned by Arthur about the events that will precede the end of the world. Following his answers, the text offers a sequence typical of the "Merlin's prophecies" type of story in which a prophet, fictionally located in the past, is able to foretell contemporary events; Guynglaff predicts invasions, wars, and various catastrophes that are to occur during the 1580s. As that date indicates, the extant version of the *Dialog* dates from the end of the sixteenth century or the early seventeenth; Dom Louis Lepelletier, in his eighteenth-century copy of the lost original, added the date 1619. It may well be, however, that the work is derived from a considerably older tradition, updated by the near-contemporary references. [NJL]

Largillière, René, ed. "Le Dialogue entre Arthur et Guinclaff." *Annales de Bretagne*, 38 (1929), 627–74.

Piriou, Jean-Pierre. "Un Texte en moyen-breton: *Le Dialogue entre Arthur, Roi des Bretons, et Guynglaff.*" In *Actes du 14e Congrès International Arthurien*. Rennes: Presses Universitaires de Rennes, 1985, Vol. 2, pp. 473–99.

"DIALOGUE OF ARTHUR AND GWENHWYFAR," a Welsh poem extant in two manuscripts, the older of which is dated to the sixteenth century. One version consists of twelve stanzas of three or four lines each, the other has ten stanzas of three lines each. The two versions are sufficiently dissimilar to show that they derive from different manuscript (or perhaps oral) sources. The argument of the poem is quite obscure, and one critic has suggested that there must have been accompanying prose passages to provide the setting for the verses. One thing does seem clear: the poem is not a dialogue between Arthur and Gwenhwyfar (Guenevere) but rather a dialogue involving Melwas and Gwenhwyfar, and perhaps Cei (Kay). Mary Williams argued that the dialogue was part of a mystery ritual in which Melwas was the one who sought to be initiated and Gwenhwyfar played the role of the goddess whose cult it was. Cei would be involved as the initiator or hierophant. Professor Jackson, on the other hand, insists that the poem can be understood only by reference to the abduction of Guenièvre by Meleagant in Chrétien's *Lancelot* and that it relates the appearance of Melwas (Meleagant) at Arthur's court, where he challenges Arthur to entrust the Queen to one of his knights as escort. The verse dialogue, then, would be between Melwas and Gwenhwyfar, speaking of Cei's qualifications, or maybe between Melwas and Cei himself. All three names occur in the dialogue, which is characterized by boasting, and the longer version appears to end in a fight between Cei and Melwas. [PKF]

Jackson, Kenneth Hurlstone. "Arthur in Early Welsh Verse." In *Arthurian Literature in the Middle Ages*, ed. Roger Sherman Loomis. Oxford: Clarendon, 1959, pp. 12–19.

Williams, Mary. "An Early Ritual Poem in Welsh." *Speculum*, 13 (1938), 38–51.

DICKINSON, PETER, British novelist, questions the values of both medieval and modern society in *The Weathermonger* (1968), a fantasy for younger readers. The book describes a Britain plunged back into medieval ways when a misguided chemist prematurely awakens Merlin. Young Geoffrey and his eleven-year-old sister race across England in a vintage Rolls Royce, pursued by irate lords and peasants, and persuade Merlin to resume his hibernation.

Merlin figures again in *Merlin Dreams* (1988), this time as a shaman who seeks escape from his powers in an enchanted sleep beneath a stone. He wakes occasionally, recalling from his earlier life some image that is then transformed in his dream from a historical setting to one of medieval romance. This becomes the frame for a series of perceptive and ironic tales that employ various Arthurian motifs. The book is beautifully illustrated by Alan Lee. [CBH/RHT]

Dickinson, Peter. *The Weathermonger*. London: Gollancz, 1968.

———. *Merlin Dreams*. London: Gollancz, 1988.

DIDOT-*PERCEVAL*. The title of this early (ca. 1220–30) French prose text has been established to avoid confusion with Chrétien de Troyes's romance, with the *Queste del Saint Graal*, or even with the *Perlesvaus*. The name comes from the former owner, Ambroise Firmin-Didot, whose manuscript was the basis of the first edition by Eugène Hucher in 1875. A second manuscript, however, in the Biblioteca Estense at Modena, offers a more coherent version of the tale. Both surviving redactions probably stem from a prose reworking of Robert de Boron's lost *Perceval*, which followed chronologically his two earlier "branches": *Joseph d'Arimathie* and *Merlin*. The manuscript tradition is so entangled that it has been difficult to separate the parts. The Didot-*Perceval* contains a final section dealing with Arthur's last days, a kind of *Mort Artu*, derived indirectly from Geoffrey of Monmouth's *Historia Regum Britanniae* but offering no serious deviations from Wace's adaptation. The author remains anonymous, though Loomis has suggested that Robert himself was responsible for the flaws in the surviving text. It has also been proposed that a clumsy continuator added the Perceval story without reliance on a *Perceval* by Robert (who may never have written one). The Didot-

Perceval clashes frequently with Robert's works, principally because of interpolations apparently based on Chrétien and the Second Continuation. The date of composition cannot be pinned down, but we can surmise that it occurred in the second or third decade of the thirteenth century, surely after the Second Continuation and before Manessier. It is, then, an early example of French prose, produced in the same epoch as Villehardouin's *Conqueste de Constantinople.*

The events are much compressed at the tale's beginning, so that the slow progression of Perceval's self-awareness is lacking. He is in this version the son of Alain le Gros, who sends him to Arthur's court. There, he sits in a forbidden seat at the Round Table, which causes darkness to cover the skies, a stone to split, and a voice to sound that rebukes Arthur for allowing the seat to be occupied against Merlin's warnings and announces the presence of the Grail, which a superior knight must seek in order to reestablish order and to rid Britain of enchantments. Thus begins the Grail quest by all the knights of the Round Table. Perceval vows never to remain two nights in one lodging until he has found the Grail. His adventures include a hunt for the White Stag, the loss of his lady's hound (both themes borrowed from the Second Continuation), a battle with the Knight of the Tomb, the perilous ford, the children in the tree, visits to his hermit uncle and the Fisher King (from Chrétien), encounters with Merlin, and finally his successful questions about the Grail, which restore health to the Fisher King, cause the sundered stone to be mended, reveal all secrets of the Grail, and win for him the privilege of remaining in the Fisher King's house. Thereafter, Arthur occupies center stage. He conquers France, campaigns against the Romans, and earns that crown also. He is betrayed and mortally wounded by Mordred, then taken away to Avalon. Merlin reports these events to Perceval and then disappears.

The bland characterization of Perceval makes him no different from any banal chivalric hero. The carefully studied naiveté that distinguishes him in Chrétien's story becomes a glaring self-confidence as he demands, almost childishly, to sit in the thirteenth chair at the Round Table. As soon as he abandons knighthood to act as guardian of the Grail, Gauvain replaces him at the pinnacle of chivalry. The atmosphere changes abruptly after Perceval's success at the Fisher King's house; it becomes less religious and more political. Arthur demonstrates his courtesy by remaining polite in the face of insults leveled against him by Roman ambassadors. He gains the allegiance of his barons by distributing among them the lands his army has conquered in France. He wins a moral triumph over those he vanquishes and in the end earns their respect by persuasion rather than force. Character study, however, interests the author much less than straightforward narration of events. [JLG]

Roach, William, ed. *The Didot-Perceval*. Philadelphia: University of Pennsylvania Press, 1941.

Pickens, Rupert T. "*Mais de çou ne parole pas Crestiens de Troies*: A Re-examination of the Didot-*Perceval*." *Romania*, 105 (1984), 492–510.

DILLON, ARTHUR, published his drama *King Arthur Pendragon* in 1906. It is based on Malory and on the poetic translations of the Arthurian legends by Sebastian Evans. Five acts of verse, in various meters and in stilted historical language, present a wide range of traditional material with some emphasis on the sense of decline and fall and conclude with the passing of Arthur. [CNS]

Dillon, Arthur. *King Arthur Pendragon*. London: Mathews, 1906.

DINADAN, Tristan's amiable and loyal companion. In the Prose *Tristan*, where he first appears, Dinadan comments upon the codes of chivalric behavior with amused skepticism, professing not to understand why knights endure hardship in order to win the favor of courtly ladies, when there are other women who can be charmed easily. In Malory's *Morte Darthur*, Dinadan composes a song that ridicules Mark of Cornwall, but he rarely expresses an opinion that is inconsistent with his good-natured humor. [SW]

DINAS EMRYS ("Ambrosius's Fort"), the Welsh name for a hill fort on the southern fringe of Snowdonia, in Nant Gwynant near Beddgelert. The Ambrosius in question is Ambrosius Aurelianus, known in Welsh as *Emrys gwledig* (*gwledig* 'prince' or 'landholder'). Nennius identifies him with a legendary boy-prophet who outfaced King Vortigern and his magicians—reputedly, here. Vortigern wanted to build a stronghold on top of the hill. When the building materials kept disappearing through subsidence, his magicians advised a human sacrifice. Yet the boy intended as the victim confounded them by revealing a subterranean pool and other strange things. He then gave his name as Ambrosius. Nennius adds *Emrys gwledig* to make it quite clear and says that Vortigern handed over the place to him. This is the original Welsh view of the lad's identity. Geoffrey of Monmouth, however, makes him out to have been the young Merlin, explaining away "Ambrosius" as an alternative name. A later legend follows Geoffrey, asserting that before Merlin left the neighborhood he hid a golden, treasure-filled cauldron, which will be found only by the person for whom it is intended.

Excavation of the hill fort has uncovered various

features within its earthworks. There was a Roman building, and nearby there actually was a pool. During the second half of the fifth century, a platform of ground above a swampy hollow was built on and occupied by a prosperous household, seemingly Christian. Presumably, at some unknown stage in legend-weaving, the chief occupant was said to have been Ambrosius. This localization of the name and story may have been due to a prior association with Vortigern, the other main character. A tradition recorded in the seventeenth century tells of a combat in the valley below between a giant and a warrior, Owein (Eugenius), who was a son of the Roman emperor Maximus. Since Vortigern supposedly married one of this emperor's daughters, Owein—who figures in a Triad—would have been his brother-in-law. It may be that a dynastic saga, only a fragment of it preserved by Nennius, was the reason for Vortigern himself being located here. [GA]

Geoffrey of Monmouth. *Historia Regum Britanniae*, Book VI, Chapters 17–19.

Nennius. *Historia Brittonum*, Chapters 40–42.

Alcock, Leslie. *Arthur's Britain*. London: Penguin, 1971, pp. 214–15.

Bromwich, Rachel. *Trioedd Ynys Prydein*. Cardiff: University of Wales Press, 1961; 2nd ed. 1978, p. 346.

Hawkes, Jacquetta. *A Guide to the Prehistoric and Roman Monuments in England and Wales*. London: Cardinal, 1973.

"DIS IST FRAUW TRISTERAT HORN VON SAPHOIEN" ("This Is Lady Tristerat of Savoy's Horn"), an anonymous fifteenth-century *Meisterlied* based on the tale first attested in Robert Biket's *Lai du cor*. A young lady bearing a magic drinking horn arrives at King Arthur's court one day. The horn has been sent by Lady Tristerat to test the fidelity of the ladies at Arthur's court. That man who is able to drink from the horn without spilling a drop has a faithful wife. First Arthur and then the kings of mighty lands attempt to empty the horn without mishap. Only the king of Spain succeeds, and his wife, the most beautiful woman present, turns out to be the only faithful lady. [MEK]

Bruns, Paul Jacob. "Zwei Erzählungen im Meistergesang." In *Beiträge zur kritischen Bearbeitung unbenutzter alter Handschriften, Drucke und Urkunden*. Braunschweig: Reichard, 1802–03, pp. 139–43.

DITMAS, E(DITH) M.R., British historian and folklorist, in *Gareth of Orkney* (1956) retells Malory's tale for juveniles. The addition of minor characters, social history, Welsh and Cornish geography, and the events of Gareth's year as kitchen-boy, along with the rationalization of the source's supernatural elements, produces a credible historical novel. Ditmas was also the author of a nonfiction work, *Tristan and Iseult in Cornwall* (1969). [MAW]

Ditmas, E.M.R. *Gareth of Orkney*. London: Faber and Faber, 1956.

———. *Tristan and Iseult in Cornwall*. Gloucester: Roberts, 1969.

DODERER, HEIMITO VON (1896–1966), born in Vienna and one of the most significant novelists of the twentieth century to write in the German language. Doderer believed that not content but form was essential for great prose and practiced this in his numerous short stories, novellas, and novels. In 1953, he published an Arthurian novella, *Das letzte Abenteuer* ("The Last Adventure"), which he had begun in 1917 and completed by 1936. The novella, characterized by Doderer in the autobiographical epilogue as "escapism" (p. 126), is a bridal-quest narrative in which the protagonist, Ruy de Fanez, accompanied by his young squire Gauvain (knighted in the course of the tale), sets out to woo the widowed duchess Lidoine of Montefal, who is also desired by a rival named Gamuret. The names Gauvain, Lidoine (from *Claris et Laris*), and Gamuret (from Wolfram von Eschenbach's *Parzival*) suggest the novella's proximity to Arthurian literature, as does the basic situation of the wooer who has to overcome a fierce dragon in order to win the desired bride. Nonetheless, Doderer turns Arthurian conventions around: the mature rivals for the hand of Lidoine (the hero is forty) decide after all that she is not worth their undertaking difficult adventures and agree to assume the role of wooers on behalf of the young knight Gauvain. The novella concludes with the hero's "last adventure," his death in battle. [MEK]

Doderer, Heimito von. *Das letzte Abenteuer: Erzählung*. Stuttgart: Reclam, 1953.

———. "The Last Adventure," trans. Vincent Kling. *Southern Humanities Review*, 22 (1988), 113–68.

Waidson, H.M. "Heimito von Doderer: *Das letzte Abenteuer*." *Books Abroad*, 42 (1968), 375–78.

DOLOROUS STROKE, in the *Suite du Merlin* and Malory, the blow dealt King Pellean (Pellam) by Balain; the blow reduces Logres to a wasteland. Thereafter, the maimed king remains ill for many years until cured by Galahad. [NJL]

DONNA DEL VERGIÙ, LA, an Italian *cantare* closely related to the French *Châtelaine de Vergi*. Composed ca. 1330, and containing Arthurian allusions, it is atypical of the *cantare* genre because of its tragic ending. [SJN]

Levi, Ezio, ed. *Fiore di leggende: cantari antichi*. Bari: Laterza, 1914.

DORÉ, GUSTAVE (1832–1883), French illustrator. Although he illustrated *Jaufry the Knight of the Fair Brunissende: A Tale of the Times of King Arthur* in 1856, Doré's most significant contribution to Arthurian art was his illustration of Tennyson's *Idylls of the King*. Already famous for his editions of Dante, the Bible, Cervantes, and others, Doré was commissioned by Moxon & Co., Tennyson's publisher, to provide thirty-six wash drawings for the immensely popular 1859 *Idylls*, nine for each of Tennyson's four poems: "Enid," "Vivien," "Elaine," and "Guinevere." His work was then copied by English steel-engravers rather than being carved into wood blocks, Doré's usual practice. The illustrated poems were issued separately in folio editions from 1867 to 1868, by Moxon in London and by Hachette in Paris (trans. Francisque Michel). In 1868, the separate editions were gathered into one volume, for which Doré added a frontispiece depicting Tennyson surrounded by his Arthurian characters, with some creatures of Doré's invention. The illustrations were popular, especially in England, and went through several editions.

Doré's illustrations for the *Idylls* have never been accorded the critical esteem reserved for those he prepared for *Don Quixote* or the *Divine Comedy*, partly for technical reasons. The English steel-engravers are thought to have distorted Doré's expression, and in any case Doré had less control over the engraving process than he did when working in France. The illustrations are also uneven in quality, and his depiction of women often weak; in "King Arthur Reading the Letter of Elaine," the dead Elaine is actually propped up in a sitting position, mouth and eyes open, looking more besotted than dead. Yet the best are equal to Doré's most famous work and create a magical, otherworldly realm of Arthurian legend that has helped fix the imagery of Tennyson's poetry, and Arthurian fantasy, in readers' minds from the 1860s onward.

Highly romantic, the engravings most typically depict dramatic moments of action or violence, or characters in quiet contemplation amid scenes of fantastic castles, crumbling ruins, or sublime landscapes. The best known of these include "Yniol Shows Prince Geraint His Ruined Castle" and "Edyrn, His Lady and Dwarf, Journey to Arthur's Court" from "Enid"; "The Knights' Progress" from "Vivien"; "King Arthur Discovering the Skeletons of the Brothers" and "The Body of Elaine on Its Way to King Arthur's Palace" from "Elaine"; and "The Joyous Sprites" from "Guinevere."

Opinion is divided on the degree of fidelity between poem and illustration. Doré could read Tennyson only in translation, and the December 21, 1867, *Athenaeum* complained that his work had "neither the scenery nor the sentiment of Mr. Tennyson" (p. 845). It is true that Doré sometimes ignored central passages to illustrate lines of subordinate interest in the poem. Yet such engravings as "The King's Farewell" from "Guinevere" follow closely the details of the text: like Tennyson, Doré gives us a prone Guinevere groveling at Arthur's feet. And if Tennyson's text was the starting point for many of Doré's own details, Doré's imagery may have influenced idylls issued after 1868. Responding to the description of a Camelot "strange, and rich, and dim" in "The Holy Grail" (published late in 1869), the December 14, 1869, *Daily Telegraph* observed that "this is by no means the only passage where the poet has drawn in his verse a scene that Doré alone could render, and Doré himself could hardly surpass with his audacious pencil. . . . Perhaps the poet has insensibly caught the air of his last and greatest illustrator; certainly there is a picturesque grandeur about some of the descriptions in this volume which finds no parallel in former works of Tennyson" (p. 5d). The reviewer's speculation about Doré's influence is impossible to verify but indicates how closely poem and illustration could be identified for nineteenth-century and later audiences.

Samuel F. Clapp argues that a defining trait of Doré is the fusion of highly realistic detail with the unreal and supernatural, a combination suited to Tennyson's poetic technique of minute natural and psychological description embedded in a matrix of otherworldly legend, plangent diction, and mellifluous blank verse. Offering an alternative world that is nonetheless highly realized, Doré's illustrations also share the aesthetic appeal of much fantasy art and literature of the nineteenth and twentieth centuries. [LH]

Clapp, Samuel F. "Voyage au pay des mythes." In *Gustave Doré: 1832–1883*. Strasbourg: Musée d'Art Moderne, 1983.

Mancoff, Debra N. *The Arthurian Revival in Victorian Art*. New York: Garland, 1990, pp. 157–60.

Richardson, Joanna. *Gustave Doré: A Biography*. Cassell: London, 1980.

Whitaker, Muriel. *The Legends of King Arthur in Art*. Cambridge: Brewer, 1990, pp. 223–25.

DORST, TANKRED, one of the best-known dramatists in modern-day Germany. Many critics regard his *Merlin oder das Wüste Land* ("Merlin or the Wasteland," 1981), written in collaboration with Ursula Ehler, as the first major dramatic work of the 1980s. The play has had several successful productions since its premiere in Düsseldorf in 1981. *Merlin*, possessing a multidimensional scope, depicts the

27. Gustave Doré, "Uther Finds the Crown," for Tennyson's *Idylls of the King* (1859). (Courtesy of the Kenneth Spencer Research Library, University of Kansas.)

complete story of Arthur and the Grail, from origins to decline and fall. Without abridgment, the play requires almost an entire day of staging, and fifty actors are necessary for the more than 100 scenes. Dorst's literary sources include Malory's *Morte Darthur*, T.H. White's *The Once and Future King*, the seventeenth-century play *The Birth of Merlin* (in the German rendering of Ludwig Tieck), Immermann's *Merlin*, and T.S. Eliot's *The Waste Land*. Dorst strives for a kind of universal world-theater, in the tradition of Goethe's *Faust* or a great "mystery play." His *Merlin* contains a baroque profusion of images and is unique in its blending of drama, epic storytelling, and song. It relates the story of Merlin, the son of the Devil, in a grotesque manner that relies on many anachronisms with contemporary relevance. In opposition to his father's schemes, Merlin seeks to engender a better, civilized world. The collapse of this civilization is depicted, however, and, in contrast to the English Arthurian tradition, no principle of hope informs the conclusion. The "elite utopia" of the Round Table that Merlin creates must perish because of human inadequacy, and the ending is a cosmic catastrophe that destroys the entire world. Critics observed that *Merlin* reflected the mood of Europe at the onset of the 1980s. Dorst's stage spectacular has found various reshapings and continuations in recent years. Arrangements of the songs and the performance in 1984 of the popular Austrian group Schmetterlinge ("Butterflies") metamorphosed *Merlin* into a kind of musical at the Wiener Volkstheater, a production widely seen over Austrian television. George Gruntz, the theatrical composer and jazz musician who had written the score for a 1983 staging of *Merlin* in Zurich, composed a jazz suite and a "Scenic Jazz Oratorio," *The Holy Grail of Jazz and Joy*, both inspired by Dorst's play. *The Holy Grail*, lasting seventy-five minutes, also reworks Tennyson and gives a strongly pacifist interpretation to the story of King Arthur. Its premiere in October 1985, at a festival for modern art in Styria, was held in a huge cave; Austrian television arranged for a broadcast.

In 1986, the Berlin experimental and avant-garde theater Zum Westlichen Stadthirschen staged a two-hour version of Dorst's extravaganza, *Artus Suchbild* ("Wanted: King Arthur"), with only five actors playing various roles. A great stir arose in 1987 over the production of *Parzival: Auf der anderen Seite des Sees* ("Parzival: On the Other Side of the Lake"), a collaboration of Tankred Dorst, Ursula Ehler, and Robert Wilson, the avant-garde Texas director. Performed at the Thalia Theater in Hamburg, this work, filled with mysterious images and nonverbal techniques, presents the Grail quest of Parzival, played by Christopher Knowles, as unsuccessful, symbolizing a failed attempt at socialization. Dorst has repeatedly attempted to shed new light on the Parzival figure of Wolfram von Eschenbach. His interpretations include a prose sketch, *Der nackte Mann* ("The Naked Man," 1986); a scenario for a TV movie, not yet made (soon to be published by Rüdiger Krohn); and a stage play, *Heinrich oder Die Schmerzen der Phantasie* ("Henry or the Agonies of Phantasy," first performed in 1985 in Düsseldorf), a variation on the Parzival theme. [UM/WGM]

Dorst, Tankred, with Ursula Ehler. *Merlin oder das Wüste Land*. Frankfurt: Suhrkamp, 1981.

Dorst, Tankred. *Der nackte Mann: Mit fartbigen Zeichnungen von Johannes Brützke*. Frankfurt: Insel, 1986.

Krohn, Rüdiger. "'Die Geschichte widerlegt die Utopie?': Zur Aktualität von Tankred Dorsts Bühnenspektakel 'Merlin oder Das Wüste Land.'" *Euphorion*, 78 (1984).

Müller, Ulrich. "Mittelalter-Musicals. Eine kommentierte Übersicht. Mit einem Anhang über mittelalterliche Themen in der U- und E-Musik 1977–1984." In *Forum: Materialien und Beiträge zur Mittelalter-Rezeption I*, ed. Rüdiger Krohn. Göppingen: Kümmerle, 1986.

DRAESEKE, FELIX AUGUST BERNHARD (1835–1913), one of the few German composers of nineteenth-century "medieval operas" (other than Richard Wagner) who is deserving of some note. His opera *Merlin* (1900–05), a free reworking of Immermann's play, was first performed posthumously in Gotha (1913). [UM/WCM]

Fischer, Jens Malte. "Singende Recken und blitzende Schwerter." In *Akten des DFG-Symposions zur Mittelalter-Rezeption*, ed. Peter Wapnewski. Stuttgart: Metzler, 1985.

Roeder, Erich. *Felix Draeseke: Der Lebens- und Leidensweg eines deutschen Musikers*. 2 vols. Dresden, 1932; Berlin, 1937.

DRAKE, DAVID (ALLEN), author of *The Dragon Lord* (1982), a sword-and-sorcery fantasy about an Irish warrior who serves Arthur against the Saxons. Arthur and his followers, who include Lancelot, Gawain, and Merlin, exhibit the pride and sadistic violence typical of figures in the genre. This Arthurian world forms the setting for Neil Randall's *Storm of Dust* (1987), a solo fantasy gamebook (*see* GAMES) with an introduction by Drake outlining the genesis of the novel. [RHT]

Drake, David. *The Dragon Lord*. New York: Doherty, 1982.

Randall, Neil. *Storm of Dust: A Crossroads Adventure in the World of David Drake's Dragon Lord*. New York: Doherty, 1987.

DRAYTON, MICHAEL (1563–1631), English author of *Poly-Olbion* (1612), a poem celebrating the topography of Britain, in which Arthurian material is related to geographical details associated with Arthur. Drayton's Arthur is chiefly the Arthur of Geoffrey of Monmouth, though he may have been influenced by Camden, Holinshed, and Malory. Drayton accepts the historicity of Arthur. [AEG]

Drayton, Michael. *Works*, ed. J. William Hebel. Oxford: Oxford University Press, 1933, Vol. 4.

DREAM OF RHONABWY, THE (BREUDWYT RHONABWY), a thirteenth-century (?) Welsh prose tale the single medieval copy of which is found in the fourteenth-century Red Book of Hergest. The story is given a precise setting in terms of geography and date. Iorwerth, an otherwise unattested brother of Madog ap Maredudd, prince of Powys (died 1159), became an outlaw. The prince mustered his warband to seek him throughout his land.

Rhonabwy and his companions on the quest were quartered in the house of one Heilyn Goch (the Red), apparently a historical figure, but its filthy condition and the flea-infested blankets they were given made sleep impossible. Rhonabwy retired and lay upon a yellow ox-skin, whereupon he was granted a vision of Arthurian Britain. The greater part of the tale relates this dream, which portrays the Arthurian age as one of gigantic heroes, with whom Rhonabwy's puny contemporaries are contrasted. Rhonabwy sees a succession of armies, swordbearers, servitors, and messengers, whose rich dress and equipment are colorfully described. Arthur and Owain play chess while a group of squires complain that Arthur's men are attacking Owain's ravens, followed by a second group protesting that the ravens are now killing Arthur's men, a battle that is ended when Arthur crushes the chessmen and Owain lowers his standard. Bards sing Arthur's praise in incomprehensible poetry, and his enemies ask for a fortnight's truce. The commotion of the armies arising to follow Arthur to Cornwall awakens Rhonabwy. The tale is a succession of narrative but colorful non sequiturs, and the illogical realism of a dream world with its convoluted standards of behavior is well presented. The tale is comedy of a high order and is intended to be satirical on more than one level. It explodes the myths of the heroic Arthurian age, as of bardic poetry, and derides the age of Madog ap Maredudd, but its narrative method seems to parody accepted conventions of interlace and digressive description. It is a consciously composed story: the scribe's colophon, noting that the tale was read, never recited, is explained by its status in the repertoire as a literary not a traditional tale, rather than by the explanation offered that the wealth of descriptive detail overtaxed the memories of storytellers. [BFR]

Richards, G.M., ed. *Breudwyt Rhonabwy*. Cardiff: University of Wales Press, 1948.

Jones, Gwyn, and Thomas Jones, trans. *The Mabinogion*, 2nd ed. London: Dent, 1974.

Jarman, A.O.H., and Gwilym Rees Hughes. *A Guide to Welsh Literature I*. Swansea: Davies, 1976.

DRYDEN, JOHN (1631–1700), English poet, whose *King Arthur, The British Worthy* (1691), a "Dramatik Opera," is little indebted to the Arthur of history or romance. The plot concerns King Arthur's battle with Oswald, the pagan leader of the Saxons, for the control of Great Britain. Both men are also contending for Emmeline, the beautiful and blind daughter of the Duke of Cornwall. Arthur emerges victorious from a complicated series of trials, influenced by Spenser and Tasso, which include adventures in an enchanted forest where Emmeline is held captive and Arthur's temptation by sirens. Arthur defeats Oswald in single combat and is united with Emmeline, whose sight Merlin has restored. The work was lavishly staged, with music by Henry Purcell. The piece, begun in 1684, was intended to be a political allegory flattering Charles II. William and Mary were on the throne when it was produced in 1691, and Dryden wrote that he was compelled to alter it greatly owing to the current political situation. [AEG]

Dryden, John. *The Dramatic Works*, ed. Montague Summers. London: Nonesuch, 1931–32, Vol. 6.

DUE TRISTANI, I ("The Two Tristans"), an Italian romance published in Venice in 1555. The first book is a translation or close adaptation of the Spanish *Don Tristán de Leonís*, except for a long interpolation in which Tristan and Isolde have two children, whom they name after themselves, and in which a sorceress falls in love with Tristan. This book offers the story of Tristan and Isolde's love, Mark's suspicions and periodic reconciliations with Tristan, and the lovers' death in each other's arms. Book 2 is the story of the younger Tristan and Isolde. The former is crowned King of Cornwall by Mark, who assumes that he is the son of Isolde of the White Hands, and is later knighted by Arthur and given his father's seat at the Round Table. Guenevere falls in love with him, but he evades her advances. The end of the work recounts a number of strange adventures and concludes with the marriage of Isolde to King Juan of Castile and that of Tristan to the Infanta Maria. [NJL]

L'Opere magnanime dei due Tristani, cavalieri della Tavola Ritonda. Venice: Tramezzino, 1555.

Gardner, Edmund G. *The Arthurian Legend in Italian Literature*. London: Dent, 1930, pp. 295–303.

DUGGAN, ALFRED LEO (1903–1964), author of historical novels both for adults and for young readers. His novel *Conscience of the King* (1951) is the picaresque autobiography of the part-Saxon Coroticus son of Eleutherius, who later assumes the name Cerdic Elesing. The elderly Cerdic recalls how he successfully manipulated and destroyed all who were obstacles to his total independence, except for Arthur at Mount Badon, his one "mistake." His constant self-justification is maintained in ironic tension with the novel's title. [AAR]

Duggan, Alfred Leo. *Conscience of the King*. New York: Coward-McCann, 1951.

DU MAURIER, GEORGE (1834–1896), parodied the enthusiasm for Arthurian subjects in a loose burlesque of "The Lady of Shalott": "A Legend of Camelot," published in five installments in *Punch* in March 1866. His verses mocked those of Tennyson and Morris, his flowing-tressed women and posturing men imitated those of William Holman Hunt and Dante Gabriel Rossetti, and his format satirized the Moxon Tennyson. [DNM]

Ormond, Leonée. "A Mid-Victorian Parody: George Du Maurier's 'A Legend of Camelot.'" *Apollo*, 85 (January 1967), 54–59.

DUNLOP WINDOWS. In 1862, Bradford merchant Walter Dunlop commissioned a set of thirteen stained-glass panels for the music room in his house at Harden Grange near Bingley, Yorkshire, from the newly founded design firm Morris, Marshall and Falkner. William Morris was given full artistic freedom for the commission. He chose the tragedy of Tristram as told by Malory as the subject, and he hired only Pre-Raphaelite artists: Ford Madox Brown, Edward Burne-Jones, Arthur Hughes, Valentine Prinsep, and Dante Gabriel Rossetti. The subjects were *The Birth of Tristram* (Hughes), *The Slaying of Sir Marhaus* (Rossetti), *Sir Tristram Demands La Belle Isounde* (Prinsep), *Sir Tristram Drinks the Love Potion with La Belle Isounde* (Rossetti), *The Madness of Sir Tristram* and *The Marriage of Sir Tristram to Isounde les Blanc Mains* (both Burne-Jones), *The Lovers at Camelot* (Morris), *Sir Tristram Slaine by King Mark* (Brown), *The Tomb of Tristram and Isounde* (Burne-Jones), and *King Arthur, Sir Lancelot, Queen Guenevere*, and *Isounde les Blanc Mains* (all Morris).

The windows were a unified program in clear composition and graceful, medievalized figure style. The narrative sequence was presented with outstanding clarity, each panel placed in order and linked to the next with an inscription. The Dunlop Windows, now in the City Art Gallery, Bradford, were the most successful of the Pre-Raphaelite ensembles. [DNM]

Sewter, A. Charles. *The Stained Glass of William Morris and His Circle*. 2 vols. New Haven: Yale University Press, 1974.

Wroot, Herbert E. "Pre-Raphaelite Windows at Bradford." *International Studio*, 63 (1917), 69–73.

DURMART LE GALLOIS, a French romance of nearly 16,000 lines, difficult to date precisely, but certainly of the thirteenth century, and in any case before 1244. After an affair with the wife of his father's seneschal, Durmart comes to his senses and attempts to win the love of the Queen of Ireland, whom he has never met but whose beauty he has heard of. He meets her without being aware of her identity, wins a sparrowhawk for her, and then sets out to find her, rescues Guenevere from an aggressor, and wins a tournament. He refuses to join the Round Table until he has found his love. Coming unawares to Ireland, he finds the queen besieged in Limerick by Nogant, who eventually flees (on a camel!) rather than face a combat with Durmart. The queen and Durmart are married. At the end of the romance, Durmart founds an abbey and visits Rome, which he frees from the pagans.

Like many romances of the period, *Durmart le Gallois* was written in the wake of the success of Chrétien de Troyes, and its nature is determined largely by the author's attempts to come to grips with the master's legacy. While it shows knowledge of other texts, it responds largely to the *oeuvre* of Chrétien, particularly *Erec et Enide*, *Cligés*, and *Yvain*. *Durmart* has recently been termed an "anti-*Erec*," in that it seems to provide an explanation (other than Chrétien's) of the crisis in Erec and Enide's marriage. The author of *Durmart* has his hero commit his error (loving the lowly seneschal's wife) at the beginning of the romance and devotes the rest of the poem to his expiation. It is suggested that whereas Erec creates problems for himself by marrying below his station (the daughter of a poor vavassor), Durmart, a close relative of King Arthur, avoids the same mistake by finally marrying the Queen of Ireland. Some epigones, such as Raoul de Houdenc, respond to Chrétien with burlesque or parody, but the author of *Durmart* adopts a more moralizing and religious tone, particularly visible in the events described at the end of the romance. *Durmart le Gallois* is another part of the legacy of Chrétien de Troyes. [KB]

Gildea, Joseph, ed. *Durmart le Gallois: roman arthurien du treizième siècle*. 2 vols. Villanova, Pa.: Villanova University Press, 1965–66.

Blumenfeld-Kosinski, Renate. "Arthurian Heroes and Convention: *Meraugis de Portlesguez* and *Durmart le Gallois*." In *The Legacy of Chrétien de Troyes*, ed. Norris J. Lacy, Douglas Kelly, and Keith Busby. 2 vols. Amsterdam: Rodopi, 1988, Vol. 2, pp. 79–92.

Schmolke-Hasselmann, Beate. *Der arthurische Versroman von Chrestien bis Froissart*. Tübingen: Niemeyer, 1980, pp. 139–48.

DUTCH ARTHURIAN LITERATURE (MEDIEVAL). Arthurian material must have been popular in the Netherlands very early. This is proved by Flemish proper names (e.g., Iwain and Walewainus) that appear in charters from the beginning of the twelfth century. Later on, it was not only in Flanders that Arthurian romances were in vogue. From manuscript transmissions beginning in the second half of the thirteenth century, it appears that Arthurian romances were also written, copied, recited, and read in Brabant, Limburg, and Holland.

The manuscript transmission of Middle Dutch Arthurian literature is a peculiar business. Four complete manuscripts have been transmitted, as well as fragments of eighteen codices. A remarkable fact is that two of those manuscripts contain nearly all of the Middle Dutch Arthurian romances. Manuscript The Hague, K.B. Hs. 129 A 10, known under the collective term *Lancelot-Compilatie*, contains no fewer than ten romances; and in the codex Burgersteinfurt, Fürst zu Bentheimsche Schlossbibliothek B 37, three romances have been preserved: the *Historie van den Grale*, the *Boec van Merline*, and the *Merlijn-Continuatie*.

Current scholarship regards few of these as faithful translations from the Old French. Of the oldest Old French verse romances, only Chrétien de Troyes's *Perceval* was transposed literally into Middle Dutch, as appears from the Liège *Perchevael* fragments, which date to the thirteenth century. In addition, the Vulgate *Lancelot-Queste-Mort* was translated twice. A faithful verse translation is preserved in the *Lancelot-Compilatie*, and the so-called Rotterdam fragments contain an extremely literal prose translation of the Prose *Lancelot*. The *Suite-Vulgate du Merlin*, too, was translated. In 1326, Lodewijk van Velthem completed his verse translations, the *Merlijn-Continuatie*.

A large number of Middle Dutch Arthurian romances are adaptations from the Old French. The oldest are adaptations of the *Vengeance Raguidel*, under the title *Wrake van Ragisel*, and of Thomas's *Tristan*, both in fragments dating from the thirteenth century. The *Fergus* was also adapted into Middle Dutch, probably in the second half of the thirteenth century. The text, under the title *Ferguut*, has been transmitted in a codex dated ca. 1350. The Old French Prose *Lancelot* was not only transmitted twice but also adapted once. This verse adaptation, *Lantsloot vander Haghedochte*, has been transmitted in fragmentary form. Some 6,000 lines are extant from a splendid manuscript that must have once contained over 100,000. Finally, mention should be made of the adaptations by Jacob van Maerlant, who ca. 1261 transposed prose versions of Robert de Boron's *Joseph d'Arimathie* and *Merlin* into Middle Dutch (*Historie van den Grale* and *Boec van Merline*).

One Arthurian romance occupies an exceptional position in regard to the question of whether the work is a translation or an adaptation. The *Torec*, attributed to Jacob van Maerlant, goes back to an Old French Arthurian romance (*Torrez chevalier au cercle d'or*), but the source has not survived.

Five romances do not seem to go back to an Old French source. Four of these have been preserved in the *Lancelot-Compilatie: Lanceloet en het hert met de witte voet*, *Moriaen*, *Van den Riddere metter mouwen*, and *Walewein ende Keye*. These were written mainly in the second part of the thirteenth century. From the same period dates one of the high points of Middle Dutch Arthurian romance: the *Roman van Walewein*, by Penninc, who did not manage to finish his work. Pieter Vostaert completed the romance, which comprises about 11,200 lines. The well-considered structure of the work is based on Aarne-Thompson Tale Type 550 (cf. Grimm's *Der goldene Vogel*).

In the *Lancelot-Compilatie*, versions of a number of Arthurian romances have been transmitted that occupy an exceptional position. These are adaptations of Middle Dutch Arthurian romances. Responsible for these versions is the compiler of the *Lancelot-Compilatie*, who inserted abbreviated versions of the *Perchevael*, the *Riddere metter mouwen*, and the *Wrake van Ragisel* in his composite codex. (Of the other romances found in the *Lancelot-Compilatie*, the *Moriaen* was inserted unchanged, *Lanceloet en het hert met de witte voet* was probably abbreviated, and of the *Torec* and *Walewein ende Keye* no fragments have survived.)

After the fourteenth century, the popularity of Arthurian romances appears to have waned. This may be deduced from the lack of manuscript transmissions after that date and the scant dispersion of the material in chapbooks. Only one chapbook, the *Historie van Merlijn* (ca. 1540), has been partly preserved. [BB]

Berteloot, A. "Artus in den Niederlanden: Ein Überblick." In *Studia Belgica: Aufsätze zur Literatur- und Kulturgeschichte Belgiens*, ed. Hans-Joachim Lope. Bern, 1980, pp. 17–28.

Besamusca, Bart. *Repertorium van de Middelnederlandse Arturepiek: Een beknopte beschrijving van de handschriftelijke en gedrukte overlevering*. Utrecht, 1985.

Gerritsen, W.P. "Artus IV. Mittelniederländische Literatur." In *Lexikon des Mittelalters*. Munich: Artemis, 1980. Vol. 1, cols. 1085–87.

Sparnaay, Hendricus. "The Dutch Romances." In *Arthurian Literature in the Middle Ages*, ed. Roger Sherman Loomis. Oxford: Clarendon, 1959, pp. 443–61.

Verbeke, W., J. Janssens, and M. Smeyers, eds. *Arturus Rex, 1: Catalogus*. Leuven: Leuven University Press, 1987.

DUTCH ARTHURIAN LITERATURE (MODERN). Arthur and related topics were known in the sixteenth-century Netherlands. In the treatise *Institutio Principis Christiani* (1516), Erasmus, the emperor Charles V's counselor, mentions Arthurian romances and calls them stupid, without any instructive value. The comment suggests that Arthurian literature must have been well known at Charles's court, but the romances circulating there were doubtless French.

After the Middle Ages, indigenous Dutch Arthurian literature appears to have gone into hibernation until the end of the eighteenth century. The Amsterdam scholar Balthazar Huydecoper (1695–1778) collected manuscripts and rare prints. In 1772, he published the *Rijmkroniek van Melis*

Stoke ("Rhymed Chronicle of Melis Stoke," 3 vols.), in which he quoted manuscripts he had acquired, among them the manuscripts of *Walewein* and *Ferguut*. The Enlightenment was concerned mainly with the historical and documentary value of ancient works, the literary value of which was believed to be negligible. Henric van Wijn was the first to offer a historical survey of the earliest literature in *Historische en letterkundige avondstonden* ("Historical and Literary Evening-Hours," 1800). In this book, Van Wijn announced the publication of *Ferguut*, but he never executed his plan. (The first to publish *Ferguut*, in 1838, was L.G. Visscher of Utrecht.) Van Wijn's judgment of Arthurian romances, typical of the eighteenth century, is negative. A similar view was expressed in B.H. Lulofs's *Handboek van den vroegsten bloei der Nederlandsche Letterkunde* ("Manual of the Earliest Flowering of Dutch Literature," 1845).

The beginning of serious interest in medieval literature and specifically in Arthurian literature starts with W.J.A. Jonckbloet, author of the first true literary histories, *Geschiedenis der Middelnederlandsche Dichtkunst* ("History of Middle Dutch Poetry," 3 vols., 1851–55) and *Geschiedenis der Nederlandsche Letterkunde* ("History of Dutch Literature," 2 vols., 1868–72; 4th printing, 6 vols., 1888–92). In 1846, he published the *Roman van Walewein* (the volume with commentary appeared in 1848) and the first part of his *Lancelot* (i.e., the Hague *Lancelot-Compilatie*); the second part appeared three years later. In 1880, J. van Vloten published the Grail-Merlin cycle with the misleading title *Jacob van Maerlants Merlijn, naar het eenig bekende Steinforter handschrift uitgegeven* ("Jacob van Maerlant's Merlin, Published from the Only Known Steinfort Manuscript").

Interest in the Middle Ages, however, was not restricted to scholarly editions of texts and other philological activities. Tennyson's Arthurian works did not go unnoticed in the Netherlands; the *Idylls* were translated into Dutch by Soera Rana (pseudonym of Isaac Esser; 1845–1920) as *Tennyson's Idyllen van den Koning* (Amsterdam, 1896). Louis Couperus (1863–1923) published a collection of poems in a similar style: *Williswinde* (1895). The verse novel *Walewein* (1890), by M.C.H. Betz, is one of the best examples of the neoromantic interest in Arthurian themes and gives clear evidence of Tennyson's influence.

At the turn of the century, and especially after the First World War, Arthurian material became very popular. In 1903, Marie Loke translated Joseph Bédier's Tristan reconstruction. Couperus published *Het zwevende schaakbord* ("The Floating Chessboard"), an ironic, melancholy continuation of the *Roman van Walewein*, first in installments in *De Haagsche Post* from October 1917 until June 1918 and then in a single volume in 1922. Arthur van Schendel (1874–1946) adapted Gottfried von Strassburg's Tristan story in *Tristan en Isolde* (1920). Marie Koenen (1879–1959) adapted the Perceval story in *Parcival* in 1920 and wrote *Bretonsche legenden* ("Breton Legends") in 1927. In 1921, P.C. Boutens (1870–1943) published *Liederen van Isoude* ("Songs of Isolde"). Stijns Streuvels (1871–1969) based his *Tristan en Isolde* (1924) on the German *Tristrant und Isalde* of 1484, and in 1941 J.W.F. Weremeus Buning summarized the story of the lovers in *De ware geschiedenis van Tristan en Isolde* ("The True Story of Tristan and Isolde").

In more recent literature, Arthurian themes have inspired mainly magic-realistic authors. Maria Jacques wrote a novel about love and death, *De visserkoning* ("The Fisher King," 1978), based on the Grail theme. The most important author inspired by the Grail is Hubert Lampo, whose novels include *De heks en de archeoloog* ("The Witch and the Archaeologist," 1967) and *Wijlen Sarah Silbermann* ("The Late Sarah Silbermann," 1980). He also treated the mysteries of Glastonbury in *Zeg maar Judith* ("Judith," 1983) and wrote the script of the documentary *In de voetsporen van Koning Arthur* ("In the Footsteps of King Arthur," 1981), as well as essays on Arthurian subjects.

Arthur appears frequently in Dutch juvenile literature, both translations and original works. Among noteworthy translations is that of Rosemary Sutcliff's Arthurian trilogy, rendered into Dutch as *Schild en kruis* ("The Light Beyond the Forest," 1981), *Zwaard en kroon* ("The Sword and the Circle," 1983), and *Afscheid van een koning* ("The Road to Camlann," 1984). Other authors whose Arthurian works have been translated into Dutch are G. Aick, Roger Lancelyn Green, Harold R. Foster and Max Trell, Howard Pyle, Selina Hastings, and Anthony Mockler.

King Arthur and the knights of the Round Table also appear in original Dutch works. D.L. Daalder published *De ridders van de tafelronde* ("Knights of the Round Table") in 1952, and H. de Bruijn's *Koning Arthur en zijn ridders* ("King Arthur and His Knights") appeared in 1953. In 1958, Leo Roelants published a collection of legends, including that of Lohengrin, in *Het heldenboek: Sagen en legenden* ("Book of Heroes: Sagas and Legends"). The protagonist of *Parzival*, by J. Bovée, is also featured in a 1959 play by A. de Nolf, *De Graal: Een spel van Parzival in 4 bedrijven* ("The Grail: A Parzival Play in Four Acts"). Leon Benedikt concentrated on Lancelot in the 1965 *Sir Lancelot*, an adaptation of English television scripts.

The best-known modern Dutch writer to deal with Arthurian themes is Jaap ter Haar, author of *De geschiedenis van Koning Arthur* ("The Story of King Arthur," 1962); in 1963 he retold the stories of Lohengrin, Tristan and Isolde, and others in *De grote sagen van de donkere Middeleeuwen* ("Great Legends of the Middle Ages"). In 1983, Frank Herzen combined cartoons with story in *Ridders van de tafelronde: naverteld uit oude bronnen voor jeugdige lezers* ("Knights of the Round Table: Retold from Ancient Sources for Young Readers") and in *Het zwaard van Brittannië* ("The Sword of Britannia," the sword being Excalibur). Together with Gerrit Stapel, he created two cartoon strips for the magazine *Taptoe* (Volume '80): *Lancelot* and *Gawain en de Groene Ridder* ("Gawain and the Green Knight"). [JDJ]

Aardse, Karel. "Couperus te Camelot." *Literatuur*, 1 (1984), 120-28.

———. "Viermaal Koning Arthur en zijn ridders." *Literatuur*, 3 (1986), 223-30. (On juvenile literature.)

Janssens, Jozef. "Het naleven van Koning Arthur." In *Arturus Rex, 1: Catalogus*, ed. W. Verbeke, J. Janssens, and M. Smeyers. Leuven: Leuven University Press, 1987, pp. 303-10.

DYCE, WILLIAM (1806-1864), British history painter and, owing to his frescoes in the new palace at Westminster, primary contributor to the Arthurian Revival in Victorian painting. The palace, begun in 1836, was extensively decorated in fresco painting. The Fine Arts Commission, comprising government officials and leaders of the art world, oversaw the vast undertaking, which was intended to depict the glories of British history and culture in an allegorical mode. Of all the rooms in the palace, the Queen's Robing Room, where the monarch prepared for her appearance in the House of Lords, was seen to have the greatest symbolic significance and therefore posed a special iconographical problem.

The solution was found when Dyce observed to the president of the Commission, Prince Albert, that Malory's *Morte Darthur* was a British equivalent of the German national epic the *Nibelungenlied* and that the Arthurian legend, neglected in the arts, would provide a suitable subject for the monarch's chamber in the new Palace at Westminster. Albert, who admired the allegorical interpretation of the *Nibelungenlied* in King Ludwig of Bavaria's Munich Residenz, communicated Dyce's suggestion to the Fine Arts Commission, the governing board responsible for the decoration of the Palace, and in 1848 Dyce was invited to design and execute a cycle of seven frescoes based on the Arthurian legend for the Queen's Robing Room.

Dyce approached the Commission as a history painter rather than a devotee of popular medievalism. Before formulating his interpretation, he read extensively in sources as diverse as Davies's *Mythology of the English Druids* (1809), Dunlop's *History of Fiction* (1814), and Herbert's *Britannia After the Romans* (1836). His major source was Malory's *Morte Darthur* in the Southey edition (1817). In accordance with the traditions of history painting, Dyce strove to express the noblest actions of his subjects in order to evoke empathy in his viewers. He resolved to "consider the companions of the Round Table as personifications of certain moral qualities which make up the ancient idea of Chivalric greatness." His first design, however, *Piety: The Knights of the Round Table Departing on the Quest for the Holy Grail* (1849; National Gallery of Scotland, Edinburgh) was rejected by the Commission. A higher moral tone, free from mystical associations, was demanded, and Dyce quickly learned to edit the legend. The completed frescoes show the King and his champions as exemplars of Victorian moral virtue. The subjects were *Religion: The Vision of Sir Galahad and His Company* (1851), *Generosity: King Arthur Unhorsed, Spared by Sir Lancelot* (1852), *Courtesy: Sir Tristram Harping to La Belle Isolde* (1852), *Mercy: Sir Gawaine Swearing to Be Merciful and Never Be Against Ladies* (1854), and *Hospitality: The Admission of Sir Tristram to the Fellowship of the Round Table*, which was near completion at the artist's death in 1864 and finished according to his design by C.W. Cope. The remaining designs, *Courage: The Combat Between King Arthur and the Five Northern Kings* and *Fidelity: Sir Lancelot Rescuing Queen Guenevere from King Meliaguance*, were abandoned, and drawings do not survive. The ensemble was completed in 1868 with the addition of eighteen bas-relief oak panels at the dado, depicting narrative scenes from Arthur's history and the quest for the Grail, carved by H.H. Armstead (1828-1875).

The frescoes in the Robing Room constitute the first and most significant monument of the Arthurian Revival. As the first Victorian artist to address Arthurian themes, Dyce set the prototype. He abjured archaeological specificity for a universalized setting in his compositions and rejected narrative illustration for allegorical personification. For style and figure type, Dyce turned to the works of the High Renaissance, most notably those of Raphael. His work was indebted to medieval examples only for subject matter and superficial details. The cycle was intended to be a discourse on chivalric virtue, exemplifying characteristics associated with the knights of the Round Table but preserved in the conduct of the modern British gentleman.

His massive, sculpturesque figures, based on those in German history painting, and simple yet theatrical settings became standard conventions. The physical identities he formulated—a broad-chested, bearded, middle-aged King; a heroic, dark Lancelot; a tawny-haired Gawaine; a long-haired, mustachioed, brunette Tristram; and a fair, athletic Galahad—endured until the end of the century. Above all, Dyce's moral interpretation, guided by the censorious scrutiny of the Prince and the Commission, gave Arthurian imagery a didactic iconology, and his expurgated Arthuriad foreshadowed the tone of Tennyson's *Idylls of the King*. [DNM]

Boase, T.S.R. "The Decoration of the New Palace at Westminster." *Journal of the Warburg and Cortauld Institutes*, 17 (1954), 319-58.

Mancoff, Debra N. "'An ancient idea of Chivalric greatness': The Arthurian Revival and Victorian History Painting." In *The Arthurian Tradition: Essays in Convergence*, ed. Mary Flowers Braswell and John Bugge. Tuscaloosa: University of Alabama Press, 1988, pp. 127-43.

———. *The Arthurian Revival in Victorian Art*. New York: Garland, 1990, pp. 93-97, 113-137.

Pointer, Marcia. *William Dyce (1806-1864): A Critical Biography*. Oxford: Clarendon Press, 1979.

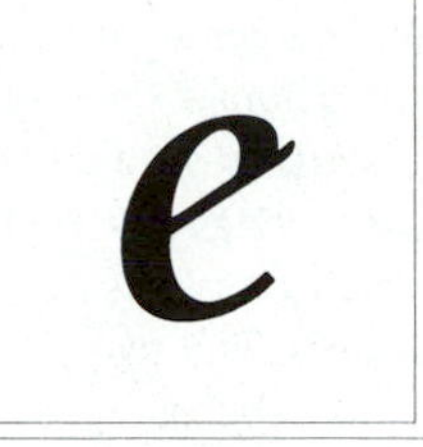

EAGER, EDWARD (McMAKEN) (1900–1964), introduces the Arthurian world in one fairly amusing episode ("What Happened to Katharine") of the children's book *Half Magic* (1954). Launcelot du Lac appears in fulfillment of four youngsters' daydreams; they save him from Morgan le Fay's machinations, and Katharine unhorses him in a joust. It all proves the power of the imagination of children brought up on *The Boy's King Arthur* and *A Connecticut Yankee in King Arthur's Court*. [CNS]

Eager, Edward. *Half Magic*. London: Macmillan, 1954.

ECTOR (Hector, Auctor, Antor), introduced in Malory's *Morte Darthur* as Kay's father and Arthur's foster-father. Ector is given Arthur by Merlin, who instructs him to entrust his own son Kay to a wetnurse. When Arthur successfully draws the sword from the stone, Ector reveals Arthur's identity. In most modern texts, Arthur knows all along that he is not Ector's true son and, until Ector discloses his true identity after he draws the sword from the stone, believes he is a bastard. [SW]

EDOLANZ, a German romance, presumably dating from the middle of the thirteenth century, of which only 380 verses are transmitted in two fragments. The extant text depicts Edolanz's rescue of Gawain and a queen by vanquishing the giant who had held them captive; his encounter with a dwarf who warns him against riding into a magic forest; his assistance to citizens of a town under siege; and his victory over a knight in a contest for a sparrowhawk that takes place at the court of King Arthur. As is the case in the fragment *Segremors*, the author of *Edolanz* employs rhyming couplets but indicates the conclusion of narrative segments with rhyming triplets. [MEK]

"Edolanz." In *Mittelhochdeutsche Übungsstücke*, ed. Heinrich Meyer-Benfey. Halle: Niemeyer, 1909, pp. 154–59.

Hoffmann von Fallersleben, Heinrich. "Gawain: Drei Bruchstücke." *Altdeutsche Blätter*, 2 (1840), 148–52.

Schönbach, Anton. "Neue Bruchstücke des Edolanz." *Zeitschrift für deutsches Alterthum*, 25 (1881), 271–87.

EILHART VON OBERGE. In line 9,446 of the Middle High German *Tristrant*, the author names himself as "von Hobergin her Eylhart." Despite scholarly efforts on the one hand to identify the author with a certain Eilhart attested in documents as hailing from Oberg near Braunschweig, and on the other hand to seek his home in the middle Rhine area, his identity and origins remain uncertain.

Scholars date the composition of *Tristrant* as early as 1170, but not later than 1190. The work is the oldest complete Tristan romance. Eilhart's *Tristrant* has in the past been considered an infelicitous translation of a French source, but contemporary scholarship (e.g., Buschinger) inclines to discern in the remarkable quadripartite structure of the romance the work of an adapter, rather than a translator, of a French original. Eilhart's French source, like Béroul's, was the so-called *Estoire*.

Eilhart's *Tristrant* deviates substantially from the classic and better-known tale of tragic love transmitted in Thomas's and Gottfried von Strassburg's fragmentary versions and in the thirteenth-century Norwegian translation of Thomas's *Tristan, Tristrams saga ok Ísöndar*. Because Mark wants Tristrant to inherit his throne, he really has no intention of getting married. When his courtiers continue to importune him regarding marriage, he hits upon what seems to be an impossible task. He has seen two swallows fight over a woman's beautiful hair and vows not to marry any woman but the one from whose head the hair has come. Tristrant is charged with the bridal quest. Since he does not realize that Isalde is the woman he seeks, he orders his helmsman to steer clear of Ireland, where he had earlier been healed of the poisoned wound that Morhold had inflicted on him. His plans to avoid Ireland, a country hostile to strangers, are thwarted, however, by a terrible storm that drives the ship onto Irish soil. When Tristrant is revived by Isalde after having slain the dragon, he recognizes in her the woman he is seeking.

The most significant discrepancy between Eilhart's version and the romance deriving from Thomas's *Tristan* pertains to the love potion. In Eilhart's work, the love philter is so powerful for a period of four years that the lovers cannot bear to be parted for even half a day. But after four years the effect of the potion begins to wane, and one day during their forest sojourn the lovers suddenly cannot bear the hardships of their existence any longer and take steps to escape. Tristrant returns Isalde to her husband after he has confessed his sin to a hermit. Although the lovers part of their own accord and Tristrant eventually marries a second Isalde, with whom he is said to be happy, they are still under the spell of a powerful albeit less effective outside force. Tristrant continues his secret assignations with Isalde. Their relationship is not without shadow. In one episode, Tristrant, disguised as a leper, seeks out Isalde. She fails to recognize him and scornfully sends him away. Tristrant reacts with bitterness, and the lovers are reconciled only when Tristrant learns that Isalde has been wearing a hairshirt that she will not remove until she has been reassured of his love once more.

A number of episodes in Eilhart's romance are tinged by an uncourtly or precourtly tone. When the lovers are discovered in *flagrante delicto* by King Mark, he orders Tristrant to be broken on the wheel but Isalde to be burned. Her sentence is modified, however, at the suggestion of a leprous duke, who proposes that she be handed over to him to be raped by every member of his leprous retinue.

Tristrant contains a fair share of humorous, even farcical, elements. As a member of King Arthur's hunting party, Tristrant is able to enjoy the hospitality of King Mark's court for one night. Nonetheless, Mark is quite suspicious. Since Mark and Isalde, as well as Arthur and his knights, sleep in communal quarters, Mark arranges to have the floor of the hall studded with sharp projecting blades. Not unexpectedly, Tristrant makes his way to Isalde's bed and is badly cut. To cover up for one of their own, Arthur's knights accept Kay's suggestion to stage a brawl, during which everyone is badly cut.

Some of the episodes in *Tristrant* have analogues in other fiction. During one of his journeys to visit Isalde, Tristrant gets involved in three contests in which he surpasses others: throwing the javelin, leaping over a ditch, and casting a stone. Although he is in disguise, his superiority in these sports identifies him. The episode is reminiscent of Gunther's and Siegfried's experiences in their quest for Brünhild. In another episode, Kehenis, the brother of Tristrant's wife, wishes to enjoy the sexual favors of Gymele, Isalde's handmaiden. Prompted by Isalde, Gymele places a magic pillow under his head, so that he quickly falls asleep. The incident is analogous to similar incidents in the so-called maidenking romances in Icelandic literature.

Tristrant adopts many disguises in order to be able to conduct his illicit relationship with Isalde. He appears as leper, as pilgrim, and as fool. In the last disguise, he manages to lead a double life at court: Mark's fool by day and Isalde's lover by night.

The ending of Eilhart's *Tristrant* diverges significantly from that in the versions deriving from Thomas's romance. When Tristrant and Isalde have died, Mark learns about the magic potion and deeply regrets his former actions. He has the lovers buried in one grave, on which he plants a rosebush (Isalde) and a grapevine (Tristrant). The two plants grow and intertwine in such a manner as to become inseparable. [MEK]

Eilhart von Oberge. *Tristrant: Édition diplomatique des manuscrits et traduction en français moderne avec introduction, notes et index*, ed. and trans. Danielle Buschinger. Göppingen: Kümmerle, 1976.

———. *Tristrant: Synoptischer Druck der ergänzten Fragmente mit der gesamten Parallelüberlieferung*, ed. Hadumod Bussmann. Tübingen: Niemeyer, 1969.

———. *Eilhart von Oberge's Tristrant*, trans. J.W. Thomas. Lincoln: University of Nebraska Press, 1978.

Buschinger, Danielle. "La Structure du *Tristrant* d'Eilhart von Oberg." *Études germaniques*, 27 (1972), 1–26.

Gottzmann, Carola L. *Artusdichtung*. Stuttgart: Metzler, 1989.

Lichtenstein, Franz, ed. *Eilhart von Oberge*. Strassburg: Trübner, 1877.

EISELEY, LOREN (1907–1977), American anthropologist, museum curator, essayist, and poet, who wrote three poems using Arthurian characters and themes. In "New Men, New Armor" (1973), the Green Knight, the Lord of the Spring, is seen to have the ultimate victory over Gawain and Arthur, who lie dead, never to awaken. To the same point, Arthur and his sleeping warriors under the hill are addressed by Merlin in "I, Merlin, Say It" (1973); Merlin urges an end of the dream of return, for death, the great leveler, brings all things to the same end. In "Druid Born" (1977), the scientist-scribe-narrator confronts a druid-born poet in a debate about the future. Arthur, Merlin, and Excalibur are taken as symbols of human aspiration and wisdom, but the debate ironically takes place beneath an oak that has no birds in it. [PCB]

Eiseley, Loren. *The Innocent Assassins*. New York: Scribner, 1973.

———. *Another Kind of Autumn*. New York: Scribner, 1977.

ELAINE OF ASTOLAT. Often identified simply as the *demoiselle d'Escalot* (e.g., in the Vulgate *Mort Artu*) or the Fair Maid of Astolat, she is the woman who falls in love with Lancelot and dies of grief when he does not reciprocate. A

28. Gustave Doré, "The Lady of Shalott," from Tennyson's *Idylls of the King* (1859). (Courtesy of the Kenneth Spencer Research Library, University of Kansas.)

barge eventually arrives at Camelot, bearing her body and a letter attributing her death to Lancelot's rejection of her. It is Malory who names her Elaine and gives her home as Astolat. Tennyson follows Malory in the *Idylls of the King*, referring to her as "the lily maid of Astolat," but he also adapts the name to create "The Lady of Shalott," who is required to view the world through a mirror and who dies when "she look'd down to Camelot." The character is doubled in Natsume Sōseki's *Kairo-kō: A Dirge*. The Japanese text, drawing heavily on Tennyson and presumably on Malory as well, has the Lady of Shalott die when she looks away from her mirror and directly at Lancelot; but we later meet Elaine of Astolat, whose story roughly parallels the traditional account of her love for Lancelot, her death as a result of unrequited love, and the boat bearing her body to court. [NJL]

ELAINE OF CORBENIC. Unnamed in most French texts, the mother of Galahad is called Elaine by Malory. As daughter of King Pelles, keeper of the Grail, she is descended from Joseph of Arimathea, but in order to join the holy line to that of Lancelot, she must first seduce the reluctant knight. Convinced through enchantment that she is Guenevere, Lancelot hastens to Elaine's bed, where he engenders not only the Grail Knight but also a mountain of trouble with the jealous Queen. Modern authors portray her as either naive (John Erskine, Marion Zimmer Bradley, Will Bradley) or sanctimonious (Naomi Mitchison, Parke Godwin). Godwin and Catherine Christian fuse her with Elaine of Astolat. [RHT]

ELGAR, SIR EDWARD (1857–1934), English composer who revealed his interest in chivalry in *The Black Knight*, with a text by H.W. Longfellow after Ludwig Uhland; in his selection of Keats's lines "When chivalry/Lifted up her lance on high" as the epigraph for his overture *Froissart*; and in his acknowledgment of Tintagel and Venice as the places of inspiration of his Second Symphony. Elgar came out of semiretirement to write incidental music for Laurence Binyon's *Arthur*, which was first performed in London's Old Vic Theatre in 1923. Using restricted resources—strings, flute (doubling piccolo), clarinet, two cornets, percussion, harp, and piano—Elgar composed evocative music to link the scenes of the tragedy. "Elaine Asleep" is elegiac, contrasting with the bustle of "The Banqueting Hall at Westminster"; "Arthur's Passage to Avalon," with its plaintive tolling bell, provides a fine conclusion. Elgar assigned no opus number to the score, which remained unpublished during his lifetime. The music survives, however, as an attractive orchestral suite. [CNS]

Elgar, Edward. *The Starlight Express Suite: King Arthur Suite*. (Recording.) Bournemouth Sinfonietta conducted by George Hurst. Chandos: CBT 1001.

Moore, J.N. *Edward Elgar: A Creative Life*. Oxford: Oxford University Press, 1984.

ELIOT, T(HOMAS) S(TEARNS) (1888–1965), ventured into the Arthurian world, specifically the Grail story, in *The Waste Land*, a poem in five parts, first published in the *Criterion* (October 1922) and one of the most important and influential poems of the twentieth century.

In "Notes on the Waste Land," Eliot writes: "Not only the title, but the plan and a good deal of the incidental symbolism of the poem were suggested by Miss Jessie L. Weston's book on the Grail legend: *From Ritual to Romance*." For Eliot, the center of the Grail story is the Wasteland and its sexually maimed Fisher King, whose healing leads to his kingdom's restoration. Using the city as an objective correlative of the modern human condition, Eliot interprets his environment as a wasteland, cut off from its traditions and spiritually and intellectually dead. The poem alludes to many of the figures and symbols from the Grail story. A figure on one of the Tarot cards, Eliot explains, "I associate, quite arbitrarily, with the Fisher King himself." He depicts an urban equivalent of Brons "fishing in the dull canal." Similarly, by means of his allusions and notes, he directs his readers to Paul Verlaine's *Parsifal* (recalling the washing of Parsifal's feet before he enters the Grail castle) and to Richard Wagner's *Tristan und Isolde* (recalling Tristan's death in Brittany as Isolde sails toward him). In the poem's final section, "What the Thunder Said," the Chapel Perilous, where the hero of medieval legend has to spend a night, is now "only the wind's home," another symbol of the dead world that is Eliot's universe in *The Waste Land*.

As Eliot's notes did not appear until the poem was printed as a book (December 1922), and as they seem to emphasize the Grail story more than the poem does, there has been disagreement as to the extent to which the notes, and so the Grail story itself, are a part of the poem. Eliot himself explained that "when it came to print *The Waste Land* as a little book . . . it was discovered that the poem was inconveniently short, so I set to work to expand the notes, in order to provide a few more pages of printed matter, with the result that they became the remarkable exposition of bogus scholarship that is still on view to-day. I have sometimes thought of getting rid of the notes, but now they can never be unstuck. They have had almost greater popularity than the poem itself. . . . It was just, no doubt, that I should pay tribute to the work of Miss Jessie Weston; but I regret having sent so many enquirers off on a wild goose chase after Tarot cards and the Holy Grail." [DS]

Eliot, T.S. *Poems: 1905–1925*. London: Faber and Gwyer, 1925, pp. 63–92.
———. *On Poetry and Poets*. London: Faber and Faber, 1957, pp. 109–10.

ELLIS, THOMAS (EVELYN) (1880–1922), Eighth Baron Howard de Walden, composed *Lanval* (1908), a drama in blank verse, and *The Cauldron of Annwn* (1922), a collection of three poetic dramas in rhyming verse based on the *Mabinogi* (*Children of Don; Dylan, Son of the Wave;* and *Bronwen*) and reminiscent of W.B. Yeats. Against a background of "drifting grey shadows," the ancient enmities of Celtic chieftains are tragically played out, but when the "wild deeds die away," "the islands fair/Stand mystic still." The three were set to music by Josef Charles Holbrooke (1887–1919). [EB]

Ellis, Thomas. *Lanval: A Drama in Four Acts*. London: Davy, 1908.
———. *The Cauldron of Annwn*. London: T. Werner Laurie (privately printed), 1922.

ELUCIDATION, THE, a thirteenth-century French prologue of 484 lines, found in one of the fifteen manuscripts of *Le Conte del Graal* of Chrétien de Troyes, in the Prose *Perceval* of 1530, and in the fourteenth-century *Der nüwe Parzefal* of Colin and Wisse.

The author says he is beginning the best of all stories, *Le Conte del Graal*, whose secret will not be revealed until the tale is told, according to the authority of "maistre Blihis." The poem will tell how Logres falls into decline and how the custom of the wells is lost when the maidens who served travelers from them are ravished and their golden cups stolen, first by King Amangon. As a result, the court of the Rich Fisher can never be found again. The knights of the Round Table set out to restore the wells and protect the maidens. They find maidens with armed knights in the forest. Gauvain conquers Blihos Bliheris, who goes back to Arthur's court and tells how the maidens are descendants of those ravished by Amangon, and they are forced to wander until the court of the Rich Fisher is found again. Percevaus and Gauvain find the court, and it is also found seven other times in seven "branches" (*souviestemens*) of the story. The land is revived, but evil folk set up the Castel Orguellous, which Arthur subdues after a siege of four years. The last eight lines of the *Elucidation* are lines 61–68 of the *Conte del Graal*, where Chrétien promises "rimoier le mellor conte . . . Qui soit contés en cort roial" ("to put into rhyme the best story ever told in a royal court," *Elucidation*, ll. 479, 481). [LDW]

Thompson, Albert Wilder, ed. *The Elucidation: A Prologue to the Conte del Graal*. New York: Institute of French Studies, 1931.
Hilka, Alfons, ed. *Der Percevalroman*. Halle: Niemeyer, 1932, pp. 417–29.
Bruce, James Douglas. *The Evolution of Arthurian Romance*, 2nd ed. 2 vols. Baltimore: Johns Hopkins Press, 1928, Vol. 2, pp. 85–89.

EMBROIDERY (MEDIEVAL). Descriptions of embroidered hangings and clothing attest to the widespread use of Arthurian material as inspiration for needlework; however, little of this secular embroidery has survived. Of the German medieval embroideries dating from the fourteenth century, six depict the story of Tristan, and others, the adventures of Gawain and Yvain. Among the finest depictions of the Tristan story are the so-called Wienhausen embroideries, worked by nuns in the Cistercian convent of Wienhausen in Hanover. The designers seem to have had access to a lost version of the *Tristan*, for they include details found in neither Eilhart von Oberge nor Gottfried von Strassburg.

Large linen panels (the largest, 12 feet 3 inches by 7 feet 8 inches) were embroidered in colored wool in horizontal bands. In the earliest of the three Wienhausen embroideries (ca. 1310), the story is told as a continuous narrative in three bands of pictures and text alternating with four rows of arcades enclosing heraldic shields. In the two later embroideries (dated ca. 1325 and ca. 1340), the scenes are divided only by text bands and foliage or architectural elements. Other Tristan embroideries are to be found in Luneburg (fragments of white linen embroidered in white, green, and yellow illustrating the bath, the tryst, and the ship), Erfurt (a linen tablecloth 14 by 3 feet, from the Benedictine convent at Wurzburg embroidered in red and blue, ca. 1370), the Victoria and Albert Museum, London (fragments of a larger piece stitched together, related to the Erfurt embroidery in style and technique), and Regensburg (a large, 9-by-4-foot linen panel worked in bright-colored wool and representing famous lovers including Tristan and Isolde's tryst by the tree). Other German embroidery designers represented the story of Gawain and the lady Orgeluse as told by Wolfram von Eschenbach (Brunswick Museum, from the Benedictine convent of Kreuzkloster, related to the Wienhausen embroideries, second quarter of the fourteenth century) and the adventures of Yvain, made ca. 1325 for the banker Johannes Malterer of Freiburg and his wife, Anna (Augustinermuseum, Freiburg in Breisgau). The Freiburg embroidery is a linen strip 16 feet by 26 inches worked in colored wool, with a border of roses enclosing a series of eleven spiked quatrefoils that frame scenes demonstrating the wiles of women. In the two Yvain scenes, the

29. Embroidery, German, fourteenth century, "Tristan and Isolde Beneath the Tree." (Courtesy of the Board of Trustees of the Victoria and Albert Museum.)

Knight of the Lion kills Ascalon and is presented to Laudine.

The Tristan story inspired Sicilian needleworkers to create pictorial linen quilts in which figures, setting, text, and decorative frames were worked in low relief by means of fine stitchery and cotton padding. Heraldic devices suggest that two quilts, one now in the Victoria and Albert Museum, London, and the other in the Bargello, Florence, were made for the wedding of Piero di Luigi Guicciardini and Laodamia Acciaiuoli in 1395. Depicted are scenes from Tristan's youth, his championship of King Mark and Cornwall against Ireland, and his victory over Amoroldu, the knight who treacherously wounded him. The fragment of a third quilt, the so-called Pianetti quilt, had Tristan and Isolde as a central medallion. The Italian quilts do not seem to depend on any single surviving manuscript for their iconography but rather combine incidents from the *Tavola Ritonda*, the *Cuento de Tristán de Leonís*, and the Stanzaic *Le Morte Arthur*, with additional details unique to the quilts. [MS]

Loomis, Roger Sherman, and Laura Hibbard Loomis. *Arthurian Legends in Medieval Art*. London: Oxford University Press, 1938, pp. 50–55, 67–68, 72–73, 78–79, figs. 76–86, 128, 143–44, 167 (German); pp. 63–65; figs. 117–19 (Italian).

Schuette, Marie. *Gestickte Bildteppiche und Decken des Mittelalters*. 2 vols. Leipzig, 1927, 1930.

EMERSON, RALPH WALDO (1803–1882), American essayist and poet whose interest in Arthurian legend is reflected in his journals, notebooks, and lectures. He uses Merlin to symbolize the figure of the ideal poet in five poems: "Politics," "The Harp," "Merlin I," "Merlin II," and "Merlin's Song" (1846–67). [RHT]

Emerson, Ralph Waldo. *The Complete Works of Ralph Waldo Emerson*, ed. Edward Waldo Emerson. Boston: Houghton-Mifflin, 1904, Vol. 9.

Taylor, Beverly, and Elisabeth Brewer. *The Return of King Arthur: British and American Arthurian Literature Since 1800*. Woodbridge, Suffolk: Boydell and Brewer, 1983.

ENFANCES GAUVAIN, LES ("The Youth of Gauvain"), two fragments (712 lines) of an early thirteenth-century French manuscript that tell of the birth and early life of Gauvain. According to the first fragment, Gauvain is the child of Arthur's sister, Morcades (Morgause), and her page, Lot. The child is entrusted to Gauvain le Brun, who gives it his own name and then sets it adrift on the sea in a cask. The second fragment tells how the child is rescued by a fisherman who learns of the circumstances of his birth and brings him to Rome, where he is educated and knighted by the pope. Similar events are related in Wace's *Brut*, the *Perlesvaus*, and the *De Ortu Waluuanii*. [KB]

Meyer, Paul. "Les Enfances Gauvain." *Romania*, 39 (1910), 1–32.

ENGAR, KEITH, wrote *Merlin's Tale of Arthur's Magic Sword* (1982), a play for children that recounts Arthur's birth and boyhood, culminating in his triumphant withdrawal of the sword from the stone. Merlin is central to the plot. Lot is ambitious and Morgan le Fay vengeful, but Kay's younger sister Marion uncovers their conspiracy. [HT]

Engar, Keith. *Merlin's Tale of Arthur's Magic Sword*. New Orleans: Anchorage, 1982.

ENGLISH ARTHURIAN LITERATURE (MEDIEVAL). The Arthurian legend enjoyed great popularity in England during the Middle Ages. The story of Arthur was celebrated in chronicle and romance throughout the twelfth to the sixteenth centuries, taking its impetus both from the belief that Arthur had been King of Britain and from a large influx of French Arthurian romances. Although the chronicle and romance traditions are distinct, English romancers, using primarily French sources, tended in many cases to imbue their stories with heroic, noncourtly elements from the chronicles, thus creating a peculiarly English type of Arthurian romance.

English romance emerged late, at a time when French romance bore only a faint resemblance to the model of Chrétien de Troyes. But the romance mode had already penetrated English literature through various forms: the chronicle, which reflected chivalric idealism; saints' lives, whose characters' had adventures similar to those of knights; and lyric, where courtly love was celebrated. Similarly, chivalric orders based on Arthur's Round Table and tournaments in imitation of romance indicated the degree to which the romance ideal had been assimilated by aristocratic society.

The Arthurian chronicle tradition, based on Geoffrey of Monmouth's *Historia Regum Britanniae*, for the most part presented the Arthurian story as true. The chronicles tended to stress the role of Arthur as a strong and powerful king, whereas the romances, based on the French, particularly Chrétien de Troyes, present him more often in a passive role, remaining at court while his knights go off in search of adventure. Except for the Scottish chronicles, which were generally critical of Arthur for national reasons, he was seen as an English warrior-hero, and it is that aspect of his career, rather than the courtly, that is recorded in chronicle accounts. The English Arthurian chroniclers include Robert of Gloucester, Thomas Bek of Castelford, Robert Mannyng of Brunne, John Trevisa, John Capgrave, and John Hardyng. The anonymous *Arthur*, the *Short Metrical Chronicle*, and the English Prose *Brut* also survive. These chronicles, mostly in verse, span the thirteenth through the fifteenth centuries.

Layamon's *Brut*, written in the late twelfth century, is one of the earliest stories of Arthur in English. Basing his work on Wace's *Roman de Brut*, a French adaptation of Geoffrey of Monmouth's *Historia*, Layamon removes many of the courtly features found in the French author, recalling Geoffrey's more military Arthurian world. He increases the Arthurian material to about a third of the work, while also imbuing it with Anglo-Saxon culture. Although it was another seventy-five years before true Arthurian romance began appearing in England, there were no doubt oral versions of French romances and Celtic stories available. When the romances were eventually written down, many of them took an attitude toward Arthurian romance rather more like that of Layamon than of their French originals.

The English Arthurian romances use a variety of verse forms as well as prose. Many of the shorter tail-rhyme romances are believed to have been composed for oral delivery, whereas others are clearly the products of clerkly authors. The alliterative poems, deriving from Old English metrics, are surely among these. Regardless of their origins, the English romances, with a few major exceptions, are less courtly and sophisticated, but simpler and shorter than their French predecessors. Emphasis remains on dramatic action and adventure rather than on love and psychological *finesse*; nonetheless, even in the most sophisticated romances, such as *Sir Gawain and the Green Knight* and Malory's *Morte Darthur*, these very "English" qualities contribute to the overall narrative effect.

Robert W. Ackerman has usefully divided the English Arthurian romances, except for Malory, into three categories: works whose main concern is with periods or episodes in King Arthur's life; romances taken from the French Vulgate *Estoire del Saint Graal* and *Merlin*, giving the early history of the Grail; and, the largest number, those romances about individual Arthurian knights.

The first English romance about Arthur's early life and battles, and, in fact, one of the earliest English Arthurian romances, is *Arthour and Merlin*. It includes an account of Merlin's part in Uther's succession to the crown and the birth and crowning of Arthur, followed by a version of Arthur's battles against the rebellious kings. It is believed to follow closely a lost variant version of the French Vulgate Cycle; it stresses campaigns and battles over love and courtesy. The fourteenth-century Alliterative *Morte Arthure*, an account of Arthur's life and death, follows primarily the chronicle tradition, leaving out any mention of the love between Lancelot and Guenevere, and stressing honor and battles over courtly courtesy. Its style is more epic than romance. Conversely, the Stanzaic *Le Morte Arthur*, approximately contemporary with the alliterative poem, is a condensation/adaptation of the French Vulgate *Mort Artu* and thus does include the love between Lancelot and Guenevere. The final battle leading to the end of Arthur's kingdom is therefore the result of complex romance plot elements derived from the French rather than of the simple usurpation of Arthur's throne by Mordred found in the alliterative poem. Although differing greatly, both of these romances offer effective literary portrayals of the Arthurian world. Malory later used both in his version.

The early sixteenth century produced the remaining works featuring Arthur himself as hero. Two versions of the same ballad are "The Legend of King Arthur" and "King Arthur's Death." A fragmentary ballad, "King Arthur and King Cornwall," features magical adventures, and magic is also important in John Bourchier, Lord Berners's *Arthur of Little Britain*, a sixteenth-century translation of the French romance *Artus de la Petite Bretagne*.

Although the actual quest for the Grail appears in Middle English only in Malory, there are some works dealing with the early history of the Grail and Joseph of Arimathea. The popularity of this part of the Arthurian story may be due to its connections with Glastonbury. The discovery of Arthur and Guenevere's grave by the monks at Glastonbury in 1191 could be used by the English kings to their glory. The example of Arthur's kingdom as model of chivalry and feudal devotion could serve to inspire greater loyalty in their own followers. The *Joseph of Arimathie* (ca. 1375) is an early alliterative poem based on the *Estoire del Saint Graal*. The most complete English account of Joseph of Arimathea and the Grail is to be found in Lovelich's *History of the Holy Grail* (ca. 1450), also an adaptation of the *Estoire*. Lovelich also produced a *Merlin* in verse, a translation of the French Vulgate *Merlin*. An anonymous Prose *Merlin* (ca 1450), another close translation of the French Vulgate, is more complete and brings the story up to the birth of Lancelot.

The majority of Middle English Arthurian romances relate the adventures of individual knights; most of them take Gawain as central figure. In England, Gawain seems to have been in fact more popular than Arthur himself. Other Arthurian knights are for the most part the subjects of only one or two works each. Gawain is already Arthur's nephew in Geoffrey of Monmouth's *Historia*, his character established as counselor and military leader. In the French tradition, however, Gawain's reputation is progressively undermined by his exploits as lover, comic foil, rash figure, and by his exposure in the prose romances as spiritually inadequate to achieve the quest for the Grail. In contrast, English romancers, except for Malory, hold to the notion of a noble, chivalric Gawain, partially perhaps to uphold the seriousness of his presentation in chronicles but also in deference to his successful completion of tests in folk tradition. The Gawain romances fall largely into three groups: those containing the themes of beheading, of testing, or of the Imperious Host; those in which the main subject is the performance of vows; and those using the Loathly Lady theme.

The beheading/testing/Imperious Host group comprises poems from the early fifteenth to the early sixteenth centuries. *Syre Gawene and the Carle of Carlyle* (ca. 1400) and the later balladlike version, *The Carle off Carlile* (ca. 1500), both contain the Imperious Host and beheading themes, and *The Turke and Gowin* (ca. 1500) contains both the testing and beheading plots. *The Grene Knight* (ca. 1500), a late condensation of *Sir Gawain and the Green Knight*, of course includes both the beheading and testing themes.

Among the Gawain poems concerning the performance of vows are two alliterative poems: *The Awntyrs off Arthure at the Terne Wathelyn* (after 1375) and the Scottish *Golagros and Gawane* (late fifteenth century). In spite of its title, *The Awntyrs* is generally considered a Gawain poem since he accepts the challenge to joust and is very much the hero of the work. *The Avowing of King Arthur, Sir Gawain, Sir Kay, and Baldwin of Britain* (ca. 1425), although including the performance of vows by all the knights named in the title, is also considered a Gawain poem because it shares characters and setting with *The Awntyrs off Arthure* and *The Wedding of Sir Gawain and Dame Ragnell*.

The Loathly Lady theme is represented in *The Wedding of Sir Gawain and Dame Ragnell* (ca. 1450), "The Marriage of Gawain" (a fifteenth-century ballad), and Chaucer's *Wife of Bath's Tale* (1392–94). Although the plots are quite similar, it is generally agreed that Chaucer's source is earlier than that for the other two works.

The Jeaste of Syr Gawayne, a romance of the fifteenth century, is unrelated to other Gawain poems in English. It is primarily a seduction story, based on two passages in the First Continuation of Chrétien's *Perceval*.

Although demonstrating varying degrees of narrative sophistication, none of these poems develops the strands of the Gawain stories in English as fully as *Sir Gawain and the Green Knight*. An alliterative poem written 1370–90, it is the earliest of the English Gawain poems; its author is believed to have been well educated and familiar with courtly life. The *Gawain*-poet combines the themes of beheading, temptation, and performance of vows in a poem distinguished by its tightly patterned structure and effective use of visual imagery. The poem, which is structurally complex and verbally controlled, presents a richly ambivalent view of romance adventure.

The remaining romances on individual knights are for the most part adaptations of the French. *Lancelot of the Laik*, the only Middle English romance, apart from Malory, in which Lancelot plays a dominant role, is a late fifteenth-century Scottish rehandling of the first portion of the French Prose *Lancelot*. A late fragmentary ballad, "Sir Lancelot du Lake," survives; it is probably based on Malory. *Ywain and Gawain*, a romance from the first half of the fourteenth century, is in fact about Ywain rather than Gawain; it is a close adaptation of Chrétien's *Yvain* (*Le Chevalier au lion*). The single poem on Perceval, the early fourteenth-century *Sir Perceval of Galles*, appears to be based on Chrétien's *Perceval* (*Le Conte del Graal*), although it omits the Grail theme. It also omits the Gawain episodes, and resembles less the French romance than a typical folktale of an innocent hero who overcomes all adversities. The late thirteenth-century poem *Sir Tristrem* is a condensed version of the French *Tristan* by Thomas d'Angleterre. It is, however, no longer a love story raising moral issues but an adventure story with a plot to appeal to a popular audience, preserving little of the original meaning. The fourteenth-century *Sir Cleges* is a folktale or secular saint's legend, rather than an adaptation of Chrétien de Troyes's *Cligés*, as its title might suggest.

The story of Sir Launfal, a form of the Fairy Mistress story, exists in four lays that ultimately derive from Marie de France's *Lai de Lanval*. The three shorter anonymous lays, *Sir Landeval*, *Sir Lambewell*, and *Sir Lamwell*, are believed to stem from a lost Middle English translation of Marie's lai, while the longer *Sir Launfal*, by Thomas Chestre, is a version of *Sir Landeval* augmented with other material. Thomas Chestre is also believed to be the author of the late fourteenth-century poem *Libeaus Desconus*, a story about Gawain's son, Gyngalyn, based on the Fair Unknown motif found in Renaut de Beaujeu's *Le Bel Inconnu*.

The chastity test found in some French romances is represented in Middle English Arthurian romance by *The Romance of Sir Corneus* (1450) and the later ballad "The Boy and the Mantle." In the test, a husband's ability to drink from a horn proves that he is not a cuckold. Traditionally, the testing takes place in either the court of Arthur or that of King Mark. Another early fifteenth-century romance of adventure, *Sir Degrevant*, is only marginally Arthurian; the hero is early identified as a knight of the Round Table, but there the relationship ends.

The most complete Middle English treatment of the Arthurian story is Sir Thomas Malory's fifteenth-century prose *Morte Darthur*. Using primarily French Arthurian prose romances (Vulgate, Post-Vulgate, Prose *Tristan*), Malory begins his story with Merlin's part in the begetting of Arthur and ends with the destruction of Arthur's kingdom; he includes Tristan material and the quest for the Grail, the only such account in Middle English. Besides his French sources, Malory also drew from the Alliterative *Morte Arthure* and the Stanzaic *Le Morte Arthur*, indicating some familiarity with English Arthurian romance. No mere translator, Malory consistently adapted his material to his own conception of the Arthurian story, pruning away what he felt did not belong. The result is an abbreviated, direct, immediate account of the Arthurian story that has remained popular for many centuries and that became the source for much later Arthurian literature. His version of the Arthurian world, fusing idealistic aspiration with human limitations, provides an inclusive, yet poignant and tragic narrative romance.

Whether tail-rhymed, alliterative, or written in prose, whether courtly or popular, English Arthurian works retain their own character in spite of many borrowings from other literatures, mainly French. The elaborate interlace of the French prose cycles never made its way into English romance, nor did the analysis of questions of love found in Chrétien. English romance relies instead on action, adventure, and direct speech to produce straightforward narrative about knightly conflicts and values. [SNI]

Barber, Richard W. *King Arthur, Hero and Legend*. Woodbridge, Suffolk: Boydell and Brewer, 1986.

Barron, W.R.J. *English Medieval Romance*. London and New York: Longman, 1987.

Dean, Christopher. *Arthur of England: English Attitudes to King Arthur and the Knights of the Round Table in the Middle Ages and the Renaissance*. Toronto: University of Toronto Press, 1987.

[Loomis], Laura A. Hibbard. *Medieval Romance in England*. New York: Oxford University Press, 1924.

Loomis, Roger Sherman, ed. *Arthurian Literature in the Middle Ages*. Oxford: Clarendon, 1959.

Mehl, Dieter. *The Middle English Romances of the Thirteenth and Fourteenth Centuries*. London: Routledge and Kegan Paul, 1969.

ENGLISH, ARTHURIAN LITERATURE IN (MODERN). 1) FICTION. The popularity of prose fiction about the Arthurian legend is a relatively recent phenomenon in English. Even in the Middle Ages, romances in prose were heavily outnumbered by those in verse, although they tried to make up in length what they lacked in numbers. This pattern persisted into the nineteenth century, but it has been dramatically reversed in the twentieth.

As the Middle Ages gave way to the Renaissance, literary tastes changed and Arthurian legend proved to be one of the casualties. For some time, medieval romances remained popular and even spawned imitations during the late sixteenth and early seventeenth centuries. Among them were a few episodic prose romances loosely associated with Arthurian legend. Best known are *Tom a Lincolne* (1599–1607), by Richard Johnson, and *History of Tom Thumb, the Little* (1621), a prose version of the popular ballad. Such works seek merely to take advantage of the dwindling popularity of Arthurian legend by using it as unimportant background to a series of independent adventures. Typically, they depart widely from tradition.

For the rest of the seventeenth and all of the eighteenth centuries, prose fiction shared the neglect into which Arthurian legend sank, and it was not until the Romantic movement led to a revival of interest in the Middle Ages that the situation improved. The publication of medieval Arthurian romances in the early nineteenth century, especially Malory's *Morte Darthur*, provided the impetus for new versions, but the century belonged to poetry as far as Arthurian legend was concerned, for novels were few and insignificant, with the exception of two ironic works: Thomas Love Peacock's *The Misfortunes of Elphin* (1829) and Mark Twain's *A Connecticut Yankee in King Arthur's Court* (1889). (*See* MEDIEVALISM.)

Poetry, along with drama, continued to dominate the early part of the twentieth century, but the number of novels grew steadily after the First World War, then markedly after the Second. This growth has been matched by a sharp decline in the number of plays and longer poems, so that, while short poems have remained popular, prose fiction is now the dominant literary form for dealing with the Arthurian legend. This fiction can be divided into five broad categories: retellings, realistic fiction, historical fiction, science fiction, and fantasy. They are distinguished by their attitude toward setting.

Retellings are either translations or modernizations of versions composed in the Middle Ages. Since most are aimed at younger readers, they tend to simplify their material to varying degrees and to remove elements that are deemed morally unsuitable (*see* JUVENILE FICTION). The setting of the sources is reproduced with little change. These stories, particularly when retold with skill by an author like Rosemary Sutcliff, serve to introduce Arthurian legend to a wide public.

Unlike fantasy, *realistic fiction* offers what is intended to be a rational explanation for the Arthurian element that it introduces into a contemporary setting. It is thus realistic in its treatment of this element, as opposed to others, like character and plot. Several novels are mystery thrillers that borrow items with Arthurian associations in constructing their plots. Thus, in Jonathan Gash's *The Grail Tree* (1979), the best of these, murder is committed to steal an ornate silver casket that holds a cup reputed to be the Grail. (*See* MYSTERY AND SUSPENSE FICTION.) More common are novels that transpose parts of the legend into a modern setting, although the borrowings may be made elaborately explicit in some cases or merely vaguely evoked in others. The love story of Tristan and Isolde has inspired *Castle Dor* (1961), by Sir Arthur Quiller-Couch and Daphne du Maurier. That of Lancelot and Guenevere has been ingeniously transposed to the settings of United States college football in Babs H. Deal's *The Grail: A Novel* (1963) and gothic romance in Nicole St. John's *Guinever's Gift* (1977). The Grail quest forms the basis of John Cowper Powys's mystical novel *A Glastonbury Romance* (1933) and of Walker Percy's penetrating exploration of appearance and reality in *Lancelot* (1978). David Gurr's *The Ring Master* (1987) and Robertson Davies's

The Lyre of Orpheus (1988) carry the process of transposition one step farther, for the lives of the central characters follow not just traditional Arthurian patterns but those found in the specific Arthurian operas that are performed in each novel.

Historical fiction, which is a much larger category, places events back in Arthur's day. This may be either during the Dark Ages (the years between the withdrawal of Roman protection at the beginning of the fifth century and the final tide of Anglo-Saxon conquest in the last half of the sixth) or else during the High Middle Ages pictured in the romances that were the literary sources for the modern versions.

Among the novels set in the Dark Ages, a few focus upon events before or after Arthur's career, like Adam Fergusson's political satire of postcolonial experience, *Roman Go Home* (1969), and Kathleen Herbert's *The Lady of the Fountain* (1982), which places the traditional tale in North Britain a generation after Arthur's death; or else upon the lives of figures who have only brief contact with him, like Cerdic, the protagonist of Alfred Duggan's *Conscience of the King* (1951). Those in which the Arthurian element plays an important role, however, range from the harshly realistic to the sentimentally romantic. Since the former type of novel presents the bleak reality of life in a cruel age, it is usually pessimistic in mood, as in the works of Edward Frankland, John Masefield, Henry Treece, and Peter Vansittart. Here, the vices of ambition, cruelty, and treachery so loudly castigated by Gildas overwhelm the impulses toward positive goals.

Much more common have been novels that emphasize the aspirations and achievements of Arthur in order to create a more optimistic mood. Though some of these are tiresomely sentimental, many offer involving stories and challenging insights: in *Porius* (1951) John Cowper Powys probes the psychological causes of the political divisions that ruined Britain; and the Arthurian novels of Victor Canning and Mary Stewart measure the role of destiny in the rise and fall of Arthur's realm.

The complex range of traditional material has created structural problems for all the historical novelists, and only Rosemary Sutcliff has met them successfully. Her novels *The Lantern Bearers* (1959) and *Sword at Sunset* (1963) introduce us to heroes who learn the important lesson of compassion: it can be exercised only at the cost of personal suffering, but to neglect it invites even greater loss.

Although the Dark Ages have been the usual setting for historical fiction about Arthur in recent years, the High Middle Ages proved more popular prior to the 1960s. Fiction in this setting can be divided into four groups: psychological novels, sentimental romances, juvenile adventure stories, and sentimental comedies. The psychological novels focus upon character development to account for the behavior of the knights and ladies of Arthur's court. Thus, John Erskine ironically scrutinizes the idealism of Palamede in *Tristan and Isolde: Restoring Palamede* (1932), Hannah Closs recreates the rapturous passion of the lovers in *Tristan* (1940), and Jim Hunter discovers the existential dilemma of the Grail quest in *Percival and the Presence of God* (1978).

30. Andrew Wyeth, "Merlin Advising Arthur." (Courtesy of The Newberry Library, Chicago.)

Like the medieval prose romances upon which they are modeled, the sentimental romances suffer from long and episodic plots, as well as tiresome sentimentality. At their best, as in Clemence Housman's *The Life of Sir Aglovale de Galis* (1905), they can offer penetrating insights into the gap between illusion and reality that destroyed the Round Table, but such moments seem hardly worth the tedium.

The juvenile fiction is intended to entertain and to offer both moral and historical instruction to young readers. Books like Eugenia Stone's *Page Boy for King Arthur* (1949) not only give a picture of life in a medieval castle but also warn against the perils of irresponsible conduct. They succeed only when they create a truly sympathetic hero, as E.M.R. Ditmas does in *Gareth of Orkney* (1956).

The high moral tone of many Arthurian works also provoked an ironic response. In the pages of popular magazines like *Saturday Evening Post*, stories by P.G. Wodehouse, Don Marquis, and T.G. Roberts poked amiable fun at the impractical behavior of Arthurian heroes in medieval romance.

Science fiction has rarely been used to treat the Arthurian legend. Andre Norton accounts for Merlin's powers as extraterrestrial technology in *Merlin's Mirror* (1975), and in her series The Keltiad (1984–) Patricia Kennealy creates a Celtic culture in a space-faring future. Apart from Mark Twain's *A Connecticut Yankee in King Arthur's Court*, however, which can just as easily be considered a fantasy, by far the finest Arthurian science-fiction novel is C.J. Cherryh's *Port Eternity* (1982), which makes skillful use of the legend to explore the problems caused by role-playing. Borrowings from Arthurian legend also occur in *science fantasy*, a hybrid form that combines elements from both science fiction and fantasy. The most intriguing are three recent novels, *The Last Knight of Albion: The Quest for Mordred* (1986) and *The Book of Mordred* (1988), by Peter Hanratty, and Michael Greatrex Coney's *Fang, the Gnome* (1988), all of which explore the conflict between reality and the world of idealized romance.

The largest category of Arthurian fiction, especially in recent years, is *fantasy*, which is distinguished from other literary genres in that the element of the marvelous is crucial. In low fantasy, no explanation is offered for nonrational phenomena, which thus tend to be mysterious and frightening. High fantasy creates a secondary world where nonrational events are accounted for by a supernatural power that is acceptable within that world.

A few low fantasies make use of Arthurian legend. The most common group are horror novels in a modern setting, like Fred Saberhagen's *Dominion* (1982), where Merlin and Nimue confront each other again, and Philip Michaels's *Grail* (1982), where the forces of good and evil battle for the sacred vessel. In addition, two fine juvenile novels deserve mention for the skill with which they use the supernatural as a means to develop character: William Mayne's *Earthfasts* (1966) borrows the cave legend attached to Arthur; in Nancy Bond's *A String in the Harp* (1976) the young hero finds Taliesin's harp-tuning key.

Apart from a couple of didactic fantasies, like John Cowper Powys's *Morwyn* (1937), the many Arthurian high fantasies can be readily divided into three main groups: mythopoeic, heroic, and ironic. In mythopoeic fantasy, the struggle between good and evil is waged directly between supernatural powers, and it usually takes place in a contemporary setting. Thus, Charles Williams relates a powerful story of spiritual conflict in a disbelieving world as competing parties search for the Holy Grail in *War in Heaven* (1930); and C.S. Lewis condemns the dehumanizing aspects of scientific progress in *That Hideous Strength* (1945).

The protagonists of these novels develop a deeper understanding of life, but only at the cost of personal loss and suffering. This pattern is adopted also in the best of the mythopoeic novels for younger readers, those by Alan Garner and Susan Cooper. The discovery of supernatural powers by the young protagonists must be paid for by a loss of innocence on the one hand and an increased burden of responsibility on the other. At the end of Garner's *The Moon of Gomrath* (1963), the hearts of both Susan and Colin are filled with yearning after they have seen and heard the Wild Hunt; and in Cooper's *The Dark Is Rising* (1973) Will Stanton's newly awakened powers as an Old One are put to a terrifying test. Where the protagonists do not discover latent supernatural powers of their own, their growth to maturity is a less intense experience, as can be seen in Andre Norton's *Steel Magic* (1965) and Jane Curry's *The Sleepers* (1968).

These fantasies introduce Arthurian legend into a modern setting through such devices as rediscovering the Grail; or wakening Merlin from the spell cast upon him by Nimue; or making Merlin, Arthur, and Morgan le Fay immortal, sometimes dwelling in Avalon, sometimes asleep in a cavern. Guy Gavriel Kay's Fionavar Tapestry series (1984–86) varies this pattern by moving its protagonists from the modern world to an alternative world where figures from Arthurian tradition are enlisted in the struggle against the forces of evil.

Robert Newman and Gillian Bradshaw, however, set their mythopoeic fantasies back in Arthur's day. Newman returns to the High Middle Ages in *The Testing of Tertius* (1973), and he proceeds to teach his young protagonists that they must conquer their own subconscious fears before they can assist Merlin and Arthur in the struggle against evil. Bradshaw returns to the Dark Ages in her Arthurian trilogy (1980–82). Gwalchmai (Gawain), in the service of "Light," helps Arthur lead the struggle against the forces of "Dark" served by Morgawse. At considerable cost, they win early successes, only to watch them fade at the end, undone by human weakness and folly. Gwalchmai bitterly discovers that "even the best intentions of those devoted to Light can create Darkness."

The largest group among the fantasies is the heroic, some of which are placed in a modern setting. Peter Dickinson's *The Weathermonger* (1968), Roger Zelazny's "The Last Defender of Camelot" (1980), and Simon Hawke's Wizard series (1987–) achieve this by reviving Merlin from his long sleep. The modern world is linked to the past by visions in Will Bradley's *Launcelot and the Ladies* (1927), by time travel in Meriol Trevor's *Merlin's Ring* (1957), and by magic "sendings" in Welwyn Wilton Katz's *The Third Magic* (1988).

Most of the heroic fantasies are set entirely in Arthur's day. Some, like H. Warner Munn's Arthurian novels, David Drake's *The Dragon Lord* (1982), and Keith Taylor's Bard series (1981–), belong to the category popularly known as sword and sorcery, and these introduce new and violent heroes into a particularly brutal Dark Age setting. Dee Morrison Meaney also makes use of the Dark Ages as the setting for his account of the love between Tristan and Iseult in *Iseult* (1985), but he paints a less savage picture, while in her Heirs to Byzantium trilogy (1987–88) Susan Schwartz explores the Dark Ages in a world with an alternative history.

Others set their stories in the High Middle Ages, notably Vera Chapman's trilogy of The Three Damosels (1975–76), Phyllis Ann Karr's *Idylls of the Queen* (1982), and Jane Yolen's *Merlin's Booke* (1986). Chapman offers a valuable female perspective on a predominantly masculine world, even if the situations often seem romantically contrived; Karr provides a sympathetic appraisal of some of the less attractive figures in Arthurian legend, as Kay painstakingly solves the mystery of who murdered Sir Patrise with a poisoned apple; Yolen's lyrical tales offer different perspectives on Merlin and the women with whom he was associated. Peter Dickinson's *Merlin Dreams* (1988) gets the best of both worlds by using a Dark Age frame for a series of tales set in the High Middle Ages. Ruth Collier Sharpe also places her gothic melodrama *Tristram of Lyonesse* (1949) in Arthur's day, but she creates a disconcertingly anachronistic setting that recalls the seventeenth century.

Four authors of heroic fantasy to date have covered the complete story of Arthur's rise and fall. The best-loved version is undoubtedly T.H. White's *The Once and Future King* (1958). Like Malory, whose *Morte Darthur* forms the basis of his series, White creates a true mood of tragedy because he imparts a keen sense that something precious has been lost. With Arthur, there fade the bright hopes of childhood for a better world. Parke Godwin, by contrast, strikes a more positive note in *Firelord* (1980). His Arthur is one of the most attractive portraits of the King in modern fiction, balancing idealism with humorous pragmatism, compassion with heroic self-sacrifice. The development of these qualities, moreover, provides a firm structure for the novel. The sequel, *Beloved Exile* (1984), continues in a more somber mood the story of Guenevere after Arthur's death. Marion Zimmer Bradley's *The Mists of Avalon* (1982) is one of those rare Arthurian novels told from the female point of view. Morgaine is the central figure in this account of the conflict waged between tolerance and intolerance, both at a political level, where it is fought between adherents of the older religions and those who practice a dogmatic Christianity, and at a personal level, where the characters must struggle to reconcile their own conflicting impulses. The failure to resolve this conflict dooms Arthur's kingdom. Sharan Newman's trilogy about Guinevere (1981–85) also focuses upon the role of a woman, in this case the Queen as she is caught in the social and political turmoil of Arthur's realm.

Godwin, Bradley, and Newman set their novels in the Dark Ages, but like White the authors of the ironic fantasies discovered a richer potential for humor in the world of romance set in the High Middle Ages. The earliest ironic fantasies reacted against the lofty moral tone of many Victorian treatments of Arthurian legend, most notably Tennyson's *Idylls of the King*. The most famous is Mark Twain's *A Connecticut Yankee in King Arthur's Court*, whose hero, Hank Morgan, journeys back in time to Arthur's day. Twain uses Hank to reveal the comedy inherent in the exaggerations of medieval romance and to criticize the ignorance and callousness of society. However, when Hank mercilessly turns the weapons created by his advanced technology against those who oppose his rule at the end of the novel, he makes it abundantly clear that the target of Twain's satire is as much society in his own day as in the Middle Ages. Indeed, the author treats Arthurian legend itself with an underlying affection that is evident in such episodes as that in which Arthur carries a child dying of smallpox down to its mother.

In Twain's work are found the three major elements of ironic fantasies about the Arthurian legend: satire of humanity's self-destructive impulses, comedy at the expense of our foolish pretensions, and a poignant affection for the aspirations of high romance. Least common is the satire, but it has gained rapidly in popularity since the publication of John Steinbeck's *The Acts of King Arthur* in 1976. Starting as a simplified retelling of Malory, this novel increasingly expands upon its source, developing notes of disillusionment not found there. The next year, 1977, saw the appearance of both *The Book of Merlyn*, T.H. White's bitter conclusion to *The Once and Future King*, and the first part of Richard Monaco's apocalyptic series on the Grail. They were followed in 1978 by Robert Nye's *Merlin*, where events are fittingly presided over by Satan.

More numerous have been the fantasies that combine comedy with warm affection for the legend. Several are written for younger readers, including Robert Newman's *Merlin's Mistake* (1971), which teaches its young protago-

31. Roy Morgan, lithograph for *Sir Gawain and the Green Knight* (London: Lion and Unicorn, 1956). (Courtesy of The Newberry Library, Chicago.)

nists not to take life at face value. Those for adults include James Branch Cabell's *Jurgen* (1919), John Myers Myers's *Silverlock* (1949), and Naomi Mitchison's *To the Chapel Perilous* (1955), all of which use figures from Arthurian legend to teach their protagonists some valuable, albeit unexpected, lessons about life.

More recently, Thomas Berger, in *Arthur Rex* (1978), has made delightful use of such ironic techniques as parody and ironic reversal to probe the comedy of Arthurian romance. As he lies dying, Arthur despairs over "the triumph of perfect evil over imperfect virtue, which is to say, of tragedy over comedy. For have I not been a buffoon?" He is comforted, however, by the ghost of Gawaine, who reminds him that they did at least live their lives "with a certain gallantry." It is this gallantry, this heroic struggle to create a better world, however impractical the task given humankind's flawed nature, that distinguishes the heroes of the ironic fantasies. In the final analysis, the authors prefer their noble folly to the destructive cynicism of the real world that destroys them.

In the hands of modern authors, Arthurian tradition continues to modify and grow, and while no new heroes have won general acceptance some old ones have gained fresh prominence, most notably Kay, Bedivere, Mordred, and Merlin. Women and children are also paid more attention, and they play a much more active role in events that shape Arthur's world than they did in the medieval romances. The range and popularity of prose fiction about the Arthurian legend have continued to widen throughout the twentieth century. Though no works of postmedieval fiction can stand comparison with the romances of Chrétien de Troyes or Malory, nonetheless some first-rate novels have been written, and they amply repay critical attention. These achievements offer convincing evidence of the vitality of the Arthurian legend in prose fiction.

2) DRAMA. Of all the literary forms in English, drama has proven the least successful for Arthurian legend. The few dramatists of note who have treated the legend have produced work that is inferior by their own standards, while minor authors, despite some promising performances, have never risen above their limitations.

Arthurian drama first appeared during the Renaissance, when the surge of patriotism in England during the reign of Elizabeth I excited great interest in the chronicle play. However, though the history of Britain recounted in the chronicles provided the source for such well-known plays as *Gorboduc* (1561), by Thomas Sackville and Thomas Norton, and Shakespeare's *King Lear* (1605–06) and *Cymbeline* (1609–10), the Arthurian episodes were largely ignored. The earliest Arthurian play, *The Misfortunes of Arthur*, by Thomas Hughes, was performed before Elizabeth I in 1588. Modeled upon Seneca's *Thyestes*, it covers the events following Arthur's return from the Continent to deal with Mordred's rebellion and Guenevora's adultery. Stress is placed on the importance of loyalty to the monarch if the horrors of civil war are to be avoided, a message that was of contemporary political concern.

Only three other Arthurian dramas have survived from this period. In Ben Jonson's *The Speeches at Prince Henry's Barriers* (1610), Arthur and Merlin are among the characters who praise the achievements of the more recent English rulers, most notably James I and his son, for whom the masque was performed. Thomas Middleton's *Hengist* (also known as *The Mayor of Queenborough*) and *The Birth of Merlin*, sometimes attributed to William Rowley, were published in 1661 and 1662, respectively, but were composed perhaps forty years earlier. Both offer melodramatic versions of the invasion of the Saxons and their wars against the Britons, and like many contemporary works they emphasize such elements as lust, treachery, and intrigue. The best parts of these undistinguished plays are their humorous subplots, which are coarse but vigorous.

As the Renaissance gave way to the Augustan Age, interest in the Arthurian legend declined. John Dryden's "Dramatik Opera" *King Arthur*, with music by Henry Purcell and a variety of striking stage effects, was a briefly popular success when it was produced in 1691. The plot, however, departs drastically from tradition in its sentimentalized account of the struggle between Arthur and Oswald, leader of the Saxons, for possession of both Britain and "Fair, Blind, Emmeline," daughter of the Duke of Cornwall. Henry Fielding's witty burlesque *The Tragedy of Tragedies; or The Life and Death of Tom Thumb the Great* (1730) won a more enduring popularity by parodying the very exaggerations of heroic tragedy that are so evident in Dryden's play. William Hilton's *Arthur, Monarch of the Britons, A Tragedy* (1759), on the other hand, returns to the chronicles for its account of Arthur's war against Mordred.

As the eighteenth century drew to a close and the Romantic movement began, conditions improved for a revival of interest in Arthurian legend. John Thelwall's closet drama *The Fairy of the Lake* (1801), however, looks back to Dryden's opera as the inspiration for its story, in which the Lady of the Lake assists Arthur and Guenevere against the wicked Rowenna. As the nineteenth century progressed, interest in Arthurian legend grew, but chiefly among the poets. Occasional plays, such as Reginald Heber's *Morte D'Arthur* (1841), were written and performed, but they were rarely printed and did not reach a wide audience.

The closing decades of the nineteenth century and opening decades of the twentieth witnessed an astonishing revival of Arthurian drama. First to achieve popular success was *King Arthur*, by J. Comyns Carr, produced at London's Lyceum Theatre in 1895, with Henry Irving in the title role and incidental music by Sir Arthur Sullivan. In the United States, Richard Hovey was engaged in an ambitious cycle of Arthurian plays, *Launcelot and Guenevere: A Poem in Dramas*, which appeared between 1891 and 1907. The peak years for Arthurian drama were the 1920s, which saw the appearance of Laurence Binyon's *Arthur, A Tragedy*, John Masefield's *Tristan and Isolt*, and Thomas Hardy's *The Famous Tragedy of the Queen of Cornwall*, all three of which are marked by firm structure and dramatic power. Despite some penetrating psychological insights, the predominant mood of Arthurian plays of this era is romantic and sentimental, and this is reflected by their interest in love and its tragic consequences. The affair between Lancelot and Guenevere attracted such dramatists as Henry Newbolt, Francis Coutts, Georgene Davis, Wilfred Campbell, and Ernest Rhys; the passion of Tristan and Isolde found sudden popularity during the opening years of the twentieth century in the hands of Michael Field, Martha Kinross, Arthur Symons, and others; and, though the story proved less popular than the former two, Merlin's fateful infatuation with Nimue/Vivien found favor with Ethel Mumford, as well as Binyon and Coutts. Even treatments of the Grail story by the likes of T. Hilhouse Taylor and George Brewer give untraditional importance to love, influenced by Wagner's opera *Parsifal*.

These playwrights look to medieval romance, or works based upon it, for their material. However, the plays written since the outbreak of the Second World War have signaled a concern for realism by turning back to history and chronicle. In *The Saviours* (1942), a series of radio plays by Clemence Dane that invokes the heroic spirit of resistance against desperate odds, both Merlin and Arthur play important roles; and Archibald Fleming MacLiesh's *The Destroyers* (1942) uses the story of Mordred's rebellion to condemn the destruction of war. Merlin appears again in *Thor, with Angels* (1948), Christopher Fry's play about the coming of Christianity among the Saxons, and Arthur rallies Romano-British resistance against the invaders in Robert Sherriff's *The Long Sunset* (1955). More recently, *The Island of the Mighty* (1973), by John Arden and Margaretta D'Arcy, has carried this realism still farther in order to present an antiromantic picture of Arthur and his followers.

Arthurian drama has thus passed through four distinct phases. The heroic and melodramatic mood of the sixteenth and seventeenth centuries led to parody in the eighteenth; the romantic and sentimental mood of the nineteenth and early twentieth centuries has in its turn yielded to the realism and antiromanticism of the past thirty years. It is too early to decide how long this present trend will continue, but the current popularity of fantasy suggests that a new direction may well await Arthurian legend. Indeed, the success of musicals like *Camelot* (1960), by Frederick Loewe and Alan Jay Lerner, and of films like John Boorman's *Excalibur* (1981) suggests that the time is ripe for a revival of a new heroic mood in the theater. Whether Arthurian legend will at last find worthy expression as drama nevertheless remains to be seen. (*See* EXPERIMENTAL THEATER.)

3) POETRY. As the Middle Ages waned, so did interest in the Arthurian legend. During the Renaissance, readers continued to enjoy medieval romances, but few authors chose them as the source for new work. Their attention had shifted from feudalism and romance to new political concerns and classical models. For a while, the Tudor attempt to reinforce their claim to the throne as descendants of Arthur stimulated interest in the chronicle account of his reign, and this was reinforced by patriotic sentiment during the reign of Elizabeth I. Yet this association with the monarchy worked against the legend when the Stuarts fell out of favor in the seventeenth century. Eighteenth-century rationalism and admiration of the classics condemned Arthur to obscurity, and it was not until the Romantic movement that conditions improved for an Arthurian revival. This culminated in the second half of the nineteenth century in the poetry of Tennyson, which firmly secured the legend's popularity, a popularity that has persisted to this day. Poetry remained the most important literary form for treatment of the Arthurian legend until the Second World War, when it yielded its preeminence to prose fiction.

Despite the popularity of medieval romances throughout most of the sixteenth century, it was not until the patriotic enthusiasm of the closing decades that a new work appeared. This was Edmund Spenser's *The Faerie Queene*, an impressive allegorical epic that was little more than half finished when the poet died in 1599. The ostensible hero is the youthful Prince Arthur, who represents the virtue of magnanimity, and he spends his time searching for Gloriana, the Faerie Queene. However, in order to develop his allegory Spenser divorces Arthur from tradition and pushes him into the background for most of the story.

A more traditional, albeit brief, account of Arthur's career, based upon the chronicles, figured in a handful of poems from the early years of the seventeenth century, Robert Chester's *Love's Martyr* (1601) traces Arthur's descent from Joseph of Arimathea. Thomas Heywood's *Troia Britanica* (1609) includes one short stanza on Arthur in its record of the kings of Britain. Arthur was added to the historical examples used to offer political lessons in the 1610 edition of *The Mirror for Magistrates*, although Vortigern and Uther were listed as early as 1578. In *Poly-Olbion* (1612), Michael Drayton gives Arthur considerable attention in his description of the legends associated with locations throughout Britain.

This largely antiquarian interest in Arthur was but a ripple in the ebbing tide. More typical of the seventeenth century was the response of John Milton, Ben Jonson, and John Dryden, all of whom abandoned plans to write an Arthurian epic in favor of other projects. Jonson and Dryden each composed a play in which Arthur appeared, but it was not until the end of the century that another Arthurian poem was published. This was Richard Blackmore's epic *Prince Arthur* (1695), and it proved so popular that two years later he published another, *King Arthur*. Since both are allegories of contemporary political events—Arthur is King William, his foes are James II and Louis XIV—they have lost most of their interest for modern readers.

The eighteenth century, with its devotion to reason, dismissed Arthurian romance with the scorn it felt for the "barb'rous" Middle Ages. A few minor poems about Merlin were written during the first half of the century, but it was not until the Romantic revival that the situation changed. At first, attention to Arthurian legend was confined to the publication of medieval romances by scholars and of poems by obscure talents like Thomas Warton (1777), Richard Hole (1789), and John Leyden (1803). When greater writers turned to the legend, however, the results proved disappointing. William Blake incorporates Arthurian elements into his prophetic epic poem *Jerusalem, the Emanation of the Giant Albion*, composed during the first two decades of the nineteenth century, but this can hardly be considered an Arthurian work. Walter Scott's *The Bridal of Triermain* (1813) is a slight piece, interesting primarily for its wry humor at the expense of Arthur and his court. William Wordsworth's "The Egyptian Maid" (1835) is an imaginative but sentimental allegory of the Grail legend. Two other poems from this period, John Hookham Frere's *The Monks and the Giants* (1817–18), which makes use of Arthur and his knights to poke fun at Italian chivalric romance, and Reginald Heber's *Morte D'Arthur* (1830), which deals with events surrounding Guenevere's marriage, are both incomplete. Though not without merit, neither is particularly successful.

A new generation of poets was now coming to the fore, and they were to raise Arthurian legend to its greatest heights since the Middle Ages. Preeminent among them was Alfred, Lord Tennyson, whose first Arthurian poem, "The Lady of Shalott," was published in 1832. Based upon an Italian version of the tale of Elaine of Astolat, the poem is impressive for its rich imagery and its treatment of the theme of illusion and reality. It reappeared in a revised version in 1842 as part of a collection that included three more Arthurian poems: "Sir Launcelot and Queen Guinevere," which celebrates the lovers' passion; "Sir Galahad," a vigorous monologue in praise of purity; and "Morte d'Arthur," in which the circumstances of Arthur's departure for Avalon after the battle of Camlann reflect the nineteenth-century anxiety over change. These poems aroused public interest in Arthurian legend and an anticipation that the great epic treatment it deserved would at last be written. This anticipation was not to be disappointed.

Tennyson's *Idylls of the King* appeared over a number of years. The first sign of what was to come was an 1857 trial edition of only six copies of two of the idylls, *Enid and Nimuë: or, The True and the False*. Nimuë's name was then changed to Vivien, and in 1859 the two poems were published, together with poems on Elaine and Guinevere, as *The True and the False: Four Idylls of the King*. In 1869, Tennyson expanded this initial framework when he published "The Coming of Arthur," "The Holy Grail," "Pelleas and Ettarre," and "The Passing of Arthur," the last of which is an expansion of the "Morte d'Arthur." "Gareth and Lynette" and "The Last Tournament" followed in 1872, and in 1873 "Enid" was divided into two separate idylls, "The Marriage of Geraint" and "Geraint and Enid." "Balin and Balan," composed 1872–74 but not published until 1885, completed the twelve idylls.

In covering the career of Arthur from birth to death, Tennyson develops him into a symbol of "ideal manhood closed in real man," as he explains in the epilogue, "To the Queen." The central conflict is "Sense at war with Soul," the glorious attempt to establish the ideal kingdom on earth that fails, finally, through human weakness. Although each idyll focuses upon a separate episode in the legend, they are all influenced by this controlling vision. Thus, Tennyson modifies the traditional order of the tales to emphasize the progression from early success to later failure: the triumphant war against the Romans is shifted to the beginning of Arthur's reign. The poet also modifies the traditional characters: Arthur is absolved of all blame and placed firmly at the center of the poem; by contrast, Lancelot is burdened with guilt and Tristram reduced to a scornful, world-weary cynic. The links between the tales are reinforced by the developing patterns of imagery and symbol. The significance of both the color white and the naked babe changes from innocence and hope at the beginning of the poem to cold and death at the end.

Tennyson's achievements greatly stimulated the revival of interest in Arthurian legend, which found expression in both art and literature. Much of the poetry produced is of inferior quality: the moments of genuine humor in Edward Bulwer-Lytton's *King Arthur* (1848) fail to redeem an overly ambitious and episodic narrative; despite its vigor, Robert Stephen Hawker's *Quest of the Sangraal* (1864) fades into mystical obscurity; George du Maurier's *A Legend of Camelot* (1866) is an amusing parody of absurdities in the poetry of both Tennyson and the Pre-Raphaelites, but it grows tedious once the novelty wears off; Thomas Westwood's *The Sword of Kingship* (1866), which describes Arthur's early years, and *The Quest of the Sancgreall* (1868)—like Ralph Fullarton's *Merlin* (1890), Madison Cawein's *Accolon of Gaul* (1889), and Ernest Rhys's "The Story of Balin and Balan: From the *Morte d'Arthur*" (1897)—are imitations of Tennyson, and they suffer by comparison.

The greater talents of Matthew Arnold, William Morris, and Algernon Swinburne yielded more impressive results. Arnold's *Tristram and Iseult* (1852), the first English modernization of the story, warns against the destructive power of love. At the same time, the poem stresses the value of the human imagination that finds expression in legend. True to his own dictum, Arnold ingeniously incorporates the tale of how Vivian enchants Merlin into his poem to give greater force to his twin themes. Morris wrote several Arthurian poems, the best-known of which is "The Defence of Guenevere" (1858). The Queen here offers a passionate, albeit self-incriminating, defense of her affair with Launcelot, in which may be seen a justification for following the creative impulse. Swinburne's *Tristram of Lyonnesse* (1882) recreates the lovers' intense passion, burning all the more fiercely because of the obstacles it encounters; his *The Tale of Balen* (1896) is a more conventional, if well-paced, reworking of Malory's version of the tragic tale.

Poetry on the Arthurian legend was not confined to long narrative verse. Tennyson's shorter poems inspired others to evoke a more lyrical mood, and the steady outpouring of this kind of writing has continued unabated in the twentieth century. Among the earliest to appear were three poems by Bulwer-Lytton's son, Edward Lytton, who wrote under the pseudonym of Owen Meredith. The best of these was "The Parting of Launcelot and Guenevere: A Fragment" (1855), which explores the tensions and quarrels between the lovers. These same tensions account for Lancelot's madness in John Davidson's "The Last Ballad" (1899) and Kaufmann Spiers's "The Madness of Lancelot" (1909).

A more popular motif was the passionate yearning of one lover for another, be it Lancelot for Guenevere in Swinburne's "Lancelot," an early poem that was not published until 1925, or Sinclair Lewis's "Launcelot" (1904), his first published poem; or both together in Morris's "King Arthur's Tomb" (1858), Stephen Phillips's "The Parting of Launcelot and Guinevere" (1907), and Edward Hunt's "The Parting of Lancelot and Guinevere" (1908). It is Elaine who longs for Lancelot in Edna St. Vincent Millay's "Elaine" (1921); Iseult for Tristan in "Joyeuse Garde," another early poem by Swinburne, and Sara Teasdale's "At Tintagil" (1926); and Tristan for Iseult in Lauriston Ward's "Tristan in Brittany" (1902), Frederic Manning's "Tristram" (1910), and Millay's "Tristan" (1954). This yearning is a central feature in poems that poignantly describe the deaths of Tristan (Laurence Binyon, 1901; James Ormerod, 1928; Sydney Smith, 1948) and Lancelot (Condé Benoist Pallen, 1902; Francis Coutts, 1907; Edgar Lee Masters, 1916). By contrast, John Ciardi's powerful poem "Launcelot in Hell" (1961) presents us with an unrepentant sinner who boasts with defiant scorn that he deliberately slew the cuckold monarch out of lust for Guenevere, "a mare to be mounted."

Merlin's fate also attracted attention. Its inevitability is revealed in Gordon Bottomley's dramatic poem "Merlin's Grave" (1929), when the wizard wakens from his enchanted sleep only to be beguiled again by an endlessly reborn Lady of the Lake. In M. Jourdain's "Merlin" (1910), his sleep is an escape from the ravages of time into a union with an undying Nature. In Thom Gunn's "Merlin in the Cave: He Speculates Without a Book" (1955), he is trapped in the contemplation of his own metaphysics rather than by any external power. Both Laurence Binyon's dramatic poem *The Madness of Merlin* (1947) and R.S. Thomas's "Taliesin 1952" return to earliest tradition for their account of Merlin driven mad by the sight of slaughter.

Gawain was the subject of a handful of poems, including three by Charlton Lewis (1916), Yvor Winters (1937), and David Schubert (1974), all inspired by the fourteenth-century English verse romance *Sir Gawain and the Green Knight*. His reputation for casual love affairs is criticized in two poems by Richard Hovey, "Launcelot and Gawaine" (1888) and "The Last Love of Gawaine" (1898). Rhys Carpenter is more sympathetic to him in his long dramatic work *The Tragedy of Etarre: A Poem* (1912), in which the inexperienced knight is seduced by the lady, as in French versions of the story. Gawain's susceptibility to unattached damsels is recalled in Jessie Weston's "Knights of King Arthur's Court" (1896), where he sings a song in praise of them all, in contrast to Tristan and Lancelot, who confine their devotion to their respective ladies, and to Perceval, who thinks only of the Grail quest.

The Grail quest proved a source of inspiration for others also. Alfred Graves's "The Coming of Sir Galahad and a Vision of the Grail" (1917) and the many poems collected in A.E. Waite's *The Book of the Holy Graal* (1921) glorify its mysticism; Vachel Lindsay uses it as a rallying cry against such contemporary problems as "trafficking in young girls" in "Galahad, Knight Who Perished" and drinking in "King Arthur's Men Have Come Again" (1923); and Grail imagery pervades the work of David Jones (1937–74).

The moralistic and sentimental mood of such pieces inevitably prompted humorous parodies. Both Oscar Adam's *Post Laureate Idylls* (1886), which includes poems like " The Rape of the Tarts," and Edward Hamley's "Sir Tray: An Arthurian Idyl" (1873), which relates the later life of the Lady of Shalott, satirize Tennyson's *Idylls*. Don Marquis pokes fun at the lovers in "Lancelot and Guinevere" and "Tristram and Isolt" (1922); Maggie Ross comments sardonically upon the hero's reputation both as a lover and as a warrior in "Gawain the Impossible" (1971); Eugene Field narrates how a smart trader, much like Mark Twain's Connecticut Yankee, swindles Arthur and his knights in "A Proper Trewe Idyll of Camelot" (1889).

For most, however, Arthurian legend has inspired a less critical admiration. This is particularly noticeable in the lyrical poems that use a place with legendary associations to prompt philosophical meditations. Tintagel leads Binyon (1894), Roden Noel (1902), Nancy Turner (1928), and L. Sprague de Camp (1967) to ponder the *ubi sunt* ("Where are they now?") theme. To Stanley James (1927), Avalon is the place "where the broken dreams are gone," while to Fred Cogswell (1966) its timeless beauty beckons us amidst this "Clock-heavy world." To Charles Dalmon, Camelot is an alluring dream (1929), though to Gustav Davidson (1922) and to Gail White (1972) it is a dream betrayed by the passion of Lancelot and Guenevere. G.K. Chesterton's "The Grave of Arthur" (1930) reflects upon the paradox of a king who may never have lived but whose legend will never die; amidst the peril of war, Francis Brett Young's "Hic Jacet Arthurus Rex Quondam Rexque Futurus . . ." (1944) celebrates his heroic defiance in the face of doom; Marian

Boyle's "Artorius Rex Invictus" (1987) summons him to return and restore a Golden Age.

Among the most interesting developments in modern Arthurian poetry has been the appearance of sequences of short poems. The earliest was Ernest Rhys's *Lays of the Round Table* (1905), a collection of romantic poems based upon incidents in Malory. The early emphasis upon the suffering that love brings prepares the reader for the Grail quest and the passing of Arthur in the second part of the collection. Coutts mixes drama and verse in *The Romance of King Arthur* (1907), which consists of two plays framed by two long poems: the first deals with Arthur's birth, the second with the deaths of Launcelot and Guenevere. John Masefield's *Midsummer Night and Other Tales in Verse* (1928) imaginatively embroiders traditional material in a series of poems that move from Arthur's begetting to the hope for his return.

These three were first published in Britain, but of the six sequences that have appeared more recently four were published in Canada, the remaining two in the United States. Margaret Atwood's "Avalon Revisited" (1963) is a series of short poems that focus upon the role of women. In the last, "The King," she concludes that Arthur is not in Avalon, despite all the tales, "Only those queens that were His three mortal wounds." Jack Spicer's *The Holy Grail* (1964) explores the response of the chief members of Arthur's court to the Grail. John D'Arcy Badger's sequence of fifty-six sonnets, *The Arthuriad* (1972), attacks the modern vices of cruelty, fanaticism, and selfishness and calls for a return to the values of moderation that Arthur stands for. Frank Davey's *The King of Swords* (1972) describes the end of a love affair in terms of the life and death of Arthur. Mickey Byrd invokes the Merlin legend in *Merlin and Vivien: A Texas Sonnet Sequence* (1977). Maria Jacobs captures the poignancy of loss felt not only by the separated lovers but also by Mark over their betrayal in her cycle of twenty poems, "Iseult, We Are Barren" (1987).

Despite the proliferation of short poems on the Arthurian legend, longer poems have continued to appear, and the compositions of T.S. Eliot, Edwin Arlington Robinson, and Charles Williams represent the greatest achievements in Arthurian literature during the first half of the twentieth century. Robinson's *Merlin* (1917), *Lancelot* (1920), and *Tristram* (1927), all set in the last days of Arthur's rule, are permeated by a sense of loss. Recognizing their own weakness and failure, the characters nonetheless attain a stoic fortitude with which to confront their doom. Eliot's *The Waste Land* (1922), one of the most important poems of the twentieth century, reveals the relevance of the Grail legend to modern experience. Charles Williams's unfinished Arthurian cycle, published in *Taliessin Through Logres* (1938) and *The Region of the Summer Stars* (1944), explores the mystical significance of the Grail story. The downfall of Arthur's kingdom results from spiritual failure: an egotistical self-love that breeds disorder.

The remaining poems have been less impressive. The favorite subject has been the love between Tristan and Isolde, retold by An Philibin (1924), Ernest Reynolds (1930), Frank Kendon (1934), Florence Pomeroy (1958), and George Saul (1969). Episodes from Malory form the basis of Rhys Carpenter's *The Tragedy of Etarre: A Poem* (1912), the three Arthurian poems of Sidney Wright (1926–30), Clyde Furst's *Merlin* (1930), and Robert Green's *The Round Table: An Arthurian Romance Epic* (1955). More innovative have been Martyn Skinner's *Merlin or the Return of Arthur* (1951) and *The Return of Arthur* (1955, 1959), and John Heath-Stubbs's *Artorius* (1973). Skinner brings back Arthur and Merlin to support freedom and religious faith against repression and barbarism in the year 2000; Heath-Stubbs uses the Arthurian story to comment upon contemporary life.

The many literary allusions and the wry humor of Heath-Stubbs's poem make it one of the most entertaining treatments of the legend in verse. However, the range of forms with which the poet experiments throughout the poem means that it has as much in common with the sequences of short poems as it does with longer narrative verse. The present trend in Arthurian poetry is clearly toward the former, and in the hands of skilled practitioners like Atwood and Heath-Stubbs these works give ample evidence that the poetic form remains vigorous, even though it has been overshadowed by prose fiction in recent years. [RHT]

Dean, Christopher. *Arthur of England: English Attitudes to King Arthur and the Knights of the Round Table in the Middle Ages and the Renaissance*. Toronto: University of Toronto Press, 1987.

Merriman, James Douglas. *The Flower of Kings: A Study of the Arthurian Legend in England Between 1485 and 1835*. Lawrence: University Press of Kansas, 1973.

Northup, Clark S., and John J. Parry. "The Arthurian Legends: Modern Retellings of the Old Stories." *Journal of English and Germanic Philology*, 43 (1944), 173–221.

Reid, Margaret J.C. *The Arthurian Legend: Comparison of Treatment in Modern and Mediaeval Literature*. Edinburgh and London: Oliver and Boyd, 1938.

Reimer, Stephen R. "The Arthurian Legends in Contemporary English Literature, 1945-1981." *Bulletin of Bibliography*, 38 (1981), 128-38, 149.

Staines, David. "King Arthur in Victorian Fiction." In *The Worlds of Victorian Fiction*, ed. Jerome H. Buckley. Cambridge: Harvard University Press, 1975, pp. 267–93.

Starr, Nathan Comfort. *King Arthur Today: The Arthurian Legend in English and American Literature, 1901–1953*. Gainesville: University of Florida Press, 1954.

Taylor, Beverly, and Elisabeth Brewer. *The Return of King Arthur: British and American Arthurian Literature Since 1800*. Woodbridge. Suffolk: Boydell and Brewer, 1983.

Thompson, Raymond H. "Arthurian Legend and Modern Fantasy." In *Survey of Modern Fantasy Literature*, ed. Frank N. Magill. Edgehill Cliffs, NJ.: Salem, 1983, Vol. 5, pp. 2299–315.

———. *The Return from Avalon: A Study of the Arthurian Legend in Modern Fiction*. Westport, Conn.: Greenwood, 1985.

ENID (Ēnide), Geraint's wife and Ynywl's daughter in the Welsh *Geraint* and Erec's wife in Chrétien de Troyes's *Erec et Enide*, Hartmann von Aue's *Erec*, Tennyson's *Idylls of the King*, and other works. Enid suffers greatly when her husband suspects that, for her, self-interest and public opinion outweigh her concern for him. [SW]

ENTRÉE D'ESPAGNE, L' ("The Entry into Spain"), an incomplete Franco-Italian romance epic dated ca. 1300–50, by an anonymous Paduan of considerable literary skill and erudition. The elaborate *unicum* manuscript probably circulated among the courts of Mantua, Ferrara, and the prehumanistic circles of Padua. Testimony to francophilism in both language and content, it forms a 15,805-line prelude to the Oxford *Chanson de Roland*, narrating events of the Spanish campaign including the battle for Pamplona, conquest of which takes place in the sequel, *Prise de Pampelune*. The poet was familiar with much extant epic and romance, as well as texts now lost; the brief Oxford allusions to Nobles are amplified to a major episode, in which the friction between Charles and Roland that is a major theme of the first 11,000 lines escalates to violent confrontation. Part 2, opening with a second prologue claiming greater originality of material, reveals the influence of Arthurian texts despite the Paduan's declaration that his "gloriose cançons" is unlike "les flabes d'Artu." The Roland who abandons the French campaign is depicted as a *chevalier errant* wandering aimlessly through trackless forests. A restorative fountain in the wilderness is the site of his *plantus*, in which Roland's lamentation over loss of chivalric status recalls the exiled Tristan. The author mentions Galahad, Meliadus, and others, and he evokes the Grail quest as a model of resolute activity. Roland's questlike voyage to the Orient, initially undertaken as a vindictive act after Charles had struck him with a mailed glove, develops into an educative experience for the hero. Denying even his name during the initial *aventures*, Roland wins back his identity as heroic and courtly knight via a series of trials. Having established himself as the finest knight serving the Persian Sultan, Roland is ready to return to Spain and carry on the fight for Pamplona. Immediately prior to his reunion with the French, he encounters the hermit Samson, an episode that suggests parallels between the two men in their quest for chivalric and spiritual perfection and recalls episodes from Grail texts. The Roland who rejoins Charles has a new sense of the Christian uses of knighthood transcending the *Entrée*'s earlier epic and secular romance models. [NB-C]

Thomas, Antoine, ed. *L'Entrée d'Espagne: chanson de geste franco-italienne, publiée d'après le manuscrit unique de Venise.* 2 vols. Paris: Champion, 1913.

EREC (Geraint), Enid's husband in the Welsh *Geraint*, Chrétien de Troyes's *Erec et Enide*, Hartmann von Aue's *Erec*, Alfred Tennyson's *Idylls of the King* ("The Marriage of Geraint" and "Geraint and Enid"), and other works. After their marriage, Erec forgets his knightly duties and Enid believes she is to blame. Her doubts are misinterpreted by her husband, who subjects her to many cruel adventures, in order to test her loyalty. Only in Hartmann von Aue's *Erec* does Enid merit Erec's harsh treatment. [SW]

EREX SAGA, an Old Icelandic prose adaptation of Chrétien de Troyes's *Erec et Enide*. There is no internal indication of time or circumstance of origin, as there is for *Ívens saga*, but it seems reasonable to assume that the original translation was connected with the court of the Norwegian king Hákon Hákonarson (r. 1217–63), responsible for the translation of *Tristrams saga, Ívens saga* (probably), and several other works of like provenance. The two primary manuscripts are Icelandic and from the seventeenth century; two small vellum fragments from ca. 1500 preserve only nine lines of text.

Erex, one of King Arthur's twelve champions, rides out unarmed one day to accompany the Queen. He is forced to suffer insults and a blow from a dwarf, the servant of an unknown knight. After obtaining his arms, Erex rides after the knight and defeats him in a joust. He thereby avenges the disgrace and coincidentally wins the hand of the fair Evida. Erex now devotes himself to his bride to such an extent that some accuse him of neglecting his knightly duties. When he hears of this, he sets out with Evida on a series of adventures to reestablish his reputation. In the course of this journey, Erex manages, among other things, to defeat eight robbers, fight an evil earl, and rescue knights and ladies from giants, a flying dragon, and a band of seven armed men. He concludes by defeating a single champion in a wondrous garden. Erex, fully rehabilitated, can now return to Arthur's court, where he is crowned king, since his father has died. Erex and Evida go to their kingdom, rule it well, and have two distinguished sons.

The saga thus reproduces much of the general outline of its French original, but it rearranges and condenses episodes, adds two new ones (the dragon and the seven armed men), and supplies a brief epilogue. There are changes in characterization, motivation, and the role of women. We have here a clear attempt at adaptation to an indigenous model, the sagas of the Icelanders. [FWB]

Blaisdell, Foster W., ed. *Erex saga Artuskappa*. Copenhagen: Munksgaard, 1965.

———, and Marianne E. Kalinke, trans. *Erex Saga and Ívens Saga*. Lincoln: University of Nebraska Press, 1977.

Barnes, Geraldine. "Arthurian Chivalry in Old Norse." *Arthurian Literature*, 7 (1987), 50–102.
Kalinke, Marianne E. *King Arthur, North-by-Northwest*. Copenhagen: Reitzel, 1981.

ERNST, PAUL (1866–1933), sets his *Jugendstil* comedy *Ritter Lanval* ("Knight Lanval," 1906) in the enchanted forest of Avalun, where the chastity test is a magic bridge that throws unfaithful lovers into the water, and where the true love between Sir Lanval and a water nymph triumphs over the disagreeable Arthur and Guenevere, who try Lanval for *lèse majesté* when he refuses to breach an amorous confidence. [RWK]

Ernst, Paul. *Ritter Lanval: Lustspiel in drei Aufzügen*. Leipzig: Insel, 1906.

ERSKINE, JOHN (1879–1951), American author of two Arthurian novels, both urbane, witty, and thoroughly modern in outlook. The first, *Galahad* (1926), is the story of Elaine, a level-headed, strong-willed girl determined to have a child by Lancelot, resourceful enough to succeed, and clever enough to bide her time until Lancelot acknowledges his son and takes him to court. There, Guinevere, who enjoys manipulating knights, turns Galahad into a priggish idealist who censures his parents when he discovers that they are not married, walks away from Guinevere when he learns that she and Lancelot are lovers, and goes off in search of the Grail. Lancelot, on his way to a tournament, meets the second Elaine and is unwittingly the cause of her death. Lancelot, later as a religious, ponders the ironies of his life. Erskine ignores the tragic and smiles gently but knowingly at the romantic aspects of the story.

In *Tristan and Isolde* (1932), he again explores what happens to an idealist who discovers the truth about the people he admires. In this case, it is Palamede, who journeys from the East to find the idealized people described by his Christian slave/tutor. What he finds in Cornwall is Isolde, for whom he cultivates a hopeless love; Brangain, whom he rescues and who loves him, but with a clear-eyed sense of herself as a real person; and a sadly disillusioning view of chivalric knighthood in the persons of Mark, Tristan, and Segurade. In the end, Palamede is baptized, wounds Tristan, brings Isolde to him, and leaves for the Holy Land, hotly pursued by Brangain in a denouement that reads like a comedy of errors.

Erskine returned briefly to the Arthurian legend in a series entitled "Seven Tales from King Arthur's Court." Published in *The American Weekly* (February 4–March 17, 1940), they retell, in contemporary idiom with occasional lively touches of irreverence, seven stories based loosely upon Malory. [MAG/RHT]

Erskine, John. *Galahad: Enough of His Life to Explain His Reputation*. New York: Grosset and Dunlap, 1926.
———. *Tristan and Isolde: Restoring Palamede*. Indianapolis: Bobbs-Merrill, 1932.

ESCHOLIER, RAYMOND (1882–?), **and MAURICE GARDELLE,** French authors who, in *Le Secret de Montségur* ("The Secret of Montségur," 1952), adopt the thesis of the Catharist Grail propounded by Otto Rahn in his *Kreuzzug gegen Gral* ("Grail Crusade," 1933). The pilgrim of this Grail quest is Richard Wagner himself, who in 1850 at Montségur encounters the last keepers of the secret of the Grail, the owner of a castle and her daughter. The daughter, watched over by the Spirit, eventually disappears mysteriously in a Pyrenees cave that contains the Catharist treasure, including the Grail.

Influenced by Rahn, this work also reflects persistent local legends according to which the Grail is still hidden in the caves of Montségur. In turn, this novel doubtless inspired Pierre Benoit's *Montsalvat* five years later. [RB]

Escholier, Raymond, and Maurice Gardelle. *Le Secret de Montségur*. Paris: La Colombe, 1952.

ESTORIA DE MERLĨN, LA, a fragmentary fourteenth-century Spanish translation of the French Post-Vulgate *Merlin*; it narrates the beginning portion of Merlin's life, from his birth to his dictation of Arthur's story to Blaise. [NJL]

Pietsch, Karl, ed. *Spanish Grail Fragments*. Chicago: University of Chicago Press, 1924, Vol. 1, pp. 57–81.

ESTORIA DEL NOBLE VASPASIANO, LA ("The History of the Noble Vespasian"), a late-medieval adaptation of a prosified version of the late twelfth- or early thirteenth-century French poem *La Venjance Nostre Seigneur* concerning the destruction of Jerusalem. Two Spanish incunabula (ca. 1491–94 and 1499), a Portuguese incunabulum (1496), and a seventeenth-century Spanish manuscript copy survive. Distinguishing these texts from extant French, Provençal, and Catalan versions of *La Venjance Nostre Seigneur* is Emperor Vespasian's allegorical vision—derived from Evalach's vision in the *Estoire del Saint Graal*, the first branch of the Vulgate Cycle—of a child entering a doorless room, a phenomenon that convinces Vespasian of the authenticity of Jesus Christ's Incarnation. An interpolated reference to Joseph of Arimathea's imprisonment would also seem to be taken from the *Estoire del Saint Graal*. [HLS]

Bonilla y San Martín, Adolfo, ed. *La destruición de Jerusalén*. In *Libros de caballerías, segunda parte*. Madrid: Bailly-Baillière, 1908, pp. 377–401.

Hook, David, and Penny Newman, eds. *Estoria do muy nobre Vespesiano Emperador de Roma (Lisbon, 1496)*. Exeter: University of Exeter, 1983.

ÉTIENNE DE ROUEN, author of *Draco Normannicus* ("The Norman Dragon"), a rhymed Latin chronicle completed ca. 1169. For 350 lines in the second book, Étienne tells about the exchange of letters between King Arthur and Henry II over the rights of sovereignty of Brittany. Arthur boasts of his battle with Lucius Hiberius and adds details not in Geoffrey of Monmouth. He has been healed by his sister Morgana, a nymph who has granted him earthly immortality in a kingdom in the southern hemisphere. Arthur retains his ultimate authority over Brittany but grants Henry feudal rights as his vassal. [MLD]

Étienne de Rouen. *Draco Normannicus*, ed. Richard Howlett. In *Chronicles of the Reigns of Stephen, Henry II, and Richard I*. London: Longman, Trübner, 1855, Vol. 2, pp. 589ff.

EUFEMIA (d. 1312), queen of Hákon Magnússon of Norway (r. 1299–1319), commissioned the translation into Swedish of three chivalric romances. These works, composed in 1303 on the occasion of the marriage of Eufemia's daughter Ingeborg to Duke Erik of Sweden, are known collectively as the *Eufemiavisor*. Included in the collection are *Flores och Blanzeflor* (a translation of the French *Floire et Blancheflor*), *Hertig Fredrik* (a tale whose original is not extant in French or Norwegian), and *Ivan Lejonriddaren* (a translation of Chrétien de Troyes's *Yvain*). Only the last translation belongs to the corpus of Arthurian literature. *Ivan Lejonriddaren* shares some affinities with *Ívens saga*, the Norwegian version of *Yvain* translated during the reign of Hákon Hákonarson (r. 1217–63), but scholars disagree concerning the source of the Swedish translation. The popularity of this work extended into Denmark, where it was in turn translated into Danish. Eufemia's contribution lies in the dissemination of Arthurian materials and in the exportation of Norwegian literary tastes into the rest of Scandinavia. [IJR]

Leach, Henry G. *Angevin Britain and Scandinavia*. Cambridge: Harvard University Press, 1921.

Ståhle, Carl Ivar. "Eufemiavisorna." In *Kulturhistorisk leksikon for nordisk middelalder fra vikingetid til reformationstid*. Copenhagen: Rosenkilde and Bagger, 1958–78, Vol. 4, cols. 55–57.

EVERNDEN, MARGERY, wrote a number of plays for children, including *King Arthur's Sword* (1959). The three acts, culminating in Arthur's triumphant withdrawal of the sword from the stone, reveal Arthur's kindness, Kay's pride, Merlin's scheming, and Guinivere's fascination with the boy who becomes King of England. [HT]

Evernden, Margery. *King Arthur's Sword*. Chicago: Coach House, 1959.

EWERS, HANNS HEINZ (1871–1943), German writer who, after flirting with National Socialism, fell out of Nazi favor in 1935. His play *Das Mädchen von Shalott* (1921) takes up the story of Guenevere's adultery with Lancelot, which causes the downfall of the Maiden of Shalott; Arthur closes his eyes to the affair. In a parallel story, Ewers recasts the plot in Vienna at the turn of the century. Here, the psychoanalyst Sigmund Freud, the painter Gustav Klimt, and the poet P. Altenberg uncover the background of a young girl who has committed suicide because of "someone who acted irresponsibly" (i.e., Lancelot). [EGF/PWM]

Ewers, Hanns Heinz. *Das Mädchen von Shalott und andere Dramen*. Munich: Georg Müller, 1921, pp. 1–78.

EXCALIBUR, Arthur's sword, called Caliburnus (Latin *chalybs* 'steel') by Geoffrey of Monmouth. Through much of the medieval French tradition—e.g., Chrétien's *Perceval* (l. 5,902) and the Prose *Lancelot*—the sword belonged at one time to Gawain, but in later works it is the exclusive property of the King. In certain texts, and in popular Arthurian lore, Excalibur is also the Sword in the Stone, but such an identification is incompatible with the tradition, found in such texts as Post-Vulgate Cycle and Malory, whereby the sword is given to Arthur, and finally taken from him, by a hand in the lake. Merlin, who brings Arthur to the Lady of the Lake to receive Excalibur, informs the King that the scabbard is worth far more than the sword itself, for the former will protect its bearer from injury. Despite this fact, it is the sword rather than its scabbard that has captured the imagination of later writers and readers.

In the Vulgate *Mort Artu*, Arthur orders Girflet to throw the sword into the enchanted lake in order that it not fall into corrupt hands. Twice Girflet disobeys, first exchanging Excalibur for his own sword, then hiding it while throwing the scabbard into the water. Twice rebuked by Arthur, he finally throws the sword into the lake, where a hand emerging from the water catches it, brandishes it, and then disappears. In Malory and in the English tradition in general, it is instead Bedivere who returns the sword to the lake, and in John Boorman's film *Excalibur*, it is Perceval who does so. (*See also* ARMS AND ARMOR.) [NJL]

EXPERIMENTAL THEATER. Not exclusively the province of major stages, Arthurian themes have also enjoyed hospitality in smaller, experimental theaters. In England, Timothy Porter and his Green Branch company of Bristol, and, since ca. 1970, the Foot's Barn tent theater, have consistently drawn on Arthurian subject matter, in most cases emphasizing Celtic elements. A successful marionette version of *Sir Gawain and the Green Knight* was produced in 1979 by the Movingstage Marionette Company of London. In Glastonbury, Ariadne Productions, a community-theater association, undertook *Passages About Gwenhwyfar*, by Kathy Jones and Leona Aroha, in 1989. The Tristan story is especially favored by such theatrical companies. Examples are the folk opera *Trystan and Essylt*, by Porter (1980); a Tristan play mounted by the Foot's Barn (1972); the *Ballade von Tristan und Isolde* (1980), by the Ensemble Parable of Prague, Czechoslovakia, which used striking, great wooden figures; "Sortilège" (1981), performed by the Théâtre Tel Quel of Lausanne, Switzerland; and "Tristan und Isolde" (1981), a production of the Austrian ensemble Theaterbrett Wien. These and similar performances are unfortunately poorly documented and only rarely published as texts. (*See also* BECKER, KONRAD; DORST, TANKRED; HARDER, NATHALIE; THEATER DER FIGUREN; WORKSHOP MOOSACH.) [UM/WCM]

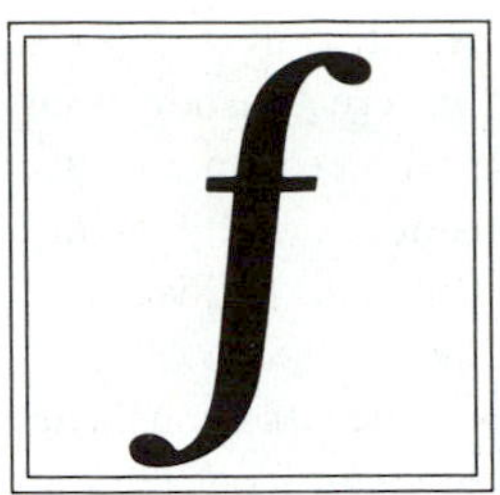

FAHRNER, RUDOLF, German professor whose specialty was the history of ideas. His play *Launcelot* (1971), based on Malory and written in a pseudo-medieval diction, depicts the Round Table, the jousts of its knights, their intrigues, and their influence on a hesitant King Arthur. The focus is on Launcelot and his love for Queen Guinevere. Launcelot weathers all hostilities and stays true to the Round Table, even after its downfall, when his love for Guinevere finds fulfillment through abstinence. [EGF/PM]

Fahrner, Rudolf. *Launcelot*. Munich: Als Manuscript gedruckt bei Georg Aglassinger (Offset), 1971.

FALSE GUENEVERE, in the Vulgate Cycle, the half-sister and double of Guenevere. Both girls were born on the same night, but the False Guenevere was born to the wife of their father's seneschal. Their father's enemies attempt to kidnap Guenevere on her wedding night and place the False Guenevere in her stead, but their plan is foiled. The False Guenevere later accuses her half-sister of not being the woman Arthur married, thereby temporarily tricking Arthur into believing he is her husband. However, when the False Guenevere becomes ill and confesses her deceit, Arthur returns to Guenevere. [SW]

FARADAY, W. BARNARD, author of *Pendragon* (1930), a rambling and sentimental historical romance about Arthur as *dux bellorum* in the struggle against the Saxons. The book is redeemed by some entertaining passages of verbal humor and by its portrayal of the keen-witted Gwendaello (Guenevere). [RHT]

Faraday, W. Barnard. *Pendragon*. London: Methuen, 1930.

FATTI DE SPAGNA, LI, a fourteenth-century Lombard narrative of fifty-six chapters, of which 1–38 are modeled on a lost version of the *Entrée d'Espagne*, 39–46 on a continuation of the *Entrée*, and 47–56 on the *Chanson de Roland*. Its principal innovation from romance is the motivation for Ganelon's betrayal in the irresistible love offered him by Braidamante, wife of King Marsile. Although not specifically an Arthurian text, the work uses numerous motifs characteristic of the Matter of Britain. (*See also* ENTRÉE D'ESPAGNE.) [NB-C]

Ruggieri, Ruggero M., ed. *Li Fatti de Spagna*. Modena: Società Editrice Modenese, 1951.

FAULKNER, NANCY (ANNE IRVIN), American author of *Sword of the Winds* (1957), a juvenile novel set in sixteenth-century Cornwall. The young hero discovers Arthur and his knights sleeping beneath Tintagel castle and becomes the agent through which Arthur's might is turned against the Spanish Armada. [DN]

Faulkner, Nancy. *Sword of the Winds*. Garden City, N.Y.: Doubleday, 1957.

FAULKNER, WILLIAM (1897–1962), American novelist. *Mayday* (1926), a story that Faulkner originally hand-lettered and illustrated himself, is the tale of Sir Galwyn of Arthgyl, a young knight in quest of the ideal woman he envisions. On his quest, which leads ultimately to disillusionment and death, Galwyn meets and kills Tristram, and he spends a brief time with Yseult, who, despite her beauty, cannot hold his interest very long. [ACL]

Faulkner, William. *Mayday*. Notre Dame, Ind.: University of Notre Dame Press, 1978.

FAWCETT, BRIAN, Canadian poet. His *Tristram's Book* (1981), a sequence of fifty-three blank-verse lyrics, uses the love story of Tristram and Iseult as a frame for exploring the growth and decline of a contemporary love affair. The poems were recorded as a radio performance for five voices and aired on CFRO-Vancouver Cooperative Radio on June 30, 1980. [RHT]

Fawcett, Brian. *Tristram's Book. Capilano Review*, 19 (1981).

FAWCETT, EDGAR (1847–1904), American author of *The New King Arthur: An Opera Without Music* (1885), an entertaining parody in the style of W.S. Gilbert that sets out to improve upon Tennyson's "creditable" treatment of Arthurian legend. [RHT]

Fawcett, Edgar. *The New King Arthur: An Opera Without Music*. New York and London: Funk and Wagnalls, 1885.

FAZIO DEGLI UBERTI (ca. 1301–1367), a Tuscan poet who makes several references to Arthurian material in *Il Dittamondo*. In this encyclopedic poem in *terza rima*, he narrates his journey through the known world under the guidance of Solinus, the famed classical geographer. During the visits to Brittany (Book IV, Chapter 22) and Great Britain (IV, 23–26), Fazio describes numerous sites by their association with Arthurian characters: for example, Tintagel is recalled as the place where the ivy plant united the tombs of Tristan and Isolde (IV, 22, ll. 100–09); London is the location of the tower that Guenevere defended against Mordred (IV, 23, ll. 52–53); Gaunes is alluded to as the scene of the death of Dorins, son of Claudas, the usurper king (IV, 22, ll. 91–92). Among the many other references are Camelot (laid to ruin by Mark; IV, 23, l. 58), the Castle of the Dolorous Gard (where Lancelot began his chivalric career; IV, 23, ll. 55–57), the castle of Penevric (in which Erec and Enide consoled themselves; IV, 23, ll. 61–62), and the valley where Tristan slew the giant Nabon (IV, 23, ll. 70–72). The wide variety of sources for these place-names and the legends associated with them—e.g., *Lancelot, Tristan, Mort Artu, Palamedes, Erec et Enide*—attests to the broad culture and synthesizing attitude of Fazio degli Uberti and suggests the extent of general penetration of Arthurian material into Italy by the middle of the fourteenth century. [CK]

Fazio degli Uberti. *Il Dittamondo e le rime*, ed. Giuseppe Corsi. 2 vols. Bari: Laterza, 1952.
Gardner, Edmund G. *The Arthurian Legend in Italian Literature*. London: Dent, 1930, pp. 222–28.

FEBUSSO È BREUSSO, an Italian *cantare* thought by Branca to be the oldest extant representative of this genre (ca. 1325–35). The work retells the cavern episode from *Palamedes*. Its narrator is an old man who recounts to the unpolished knight Breusso the famous deeds of the mighty Febusso. Each of the six *cantari* of which the work is composed comprises, on average, sixty octaves. This is somewhat longer than the portion of a *cantare* thought to have been performed in one day, which was about forty or fifty octaves. [SJN]

Branca, Vittore. *Il cantare trecentesco e il Boccaccio del Filostrato e del Teseida*. Florence: Sansoni, 1936.

FERGUSSON, ADAM, British politician and journalist, satirized contemporary postcolonial experience in *Roman Go Home* (1969). After Rome grants independence to Britain, the unscrupulous Vortigern seizes power by murdering his brother Constans, only to become a puppet of the Marxist Saxon mercenaries whom he hires to prop up his corrupt regime. [RHT]

Fergusson, Adam. *Roman Go Home*. London: Collins, 1969.

FERGUUT, a Middle Dutch verse adaptation of the Old French *Fergus* by Guillaume le Clerc. The adaptation, probably written in the second half of the thirteenth century, runs to 5,604 lines. Up to the moment when Ferguut sets out to look for his beloved (l. 2,202), the Middle Dutch poet follows his Old French model, after which he increasingly follows his own path. In doing this, he ignores the historical implications of the *Fergus*. The topography of the *Ferguut*, for instance, is almost completely arbitrary, in contrast with the French source. The text is extant in one manuscript, Leiden, University Library Ltk. 191, dating from ca. 1350. [BB]

Rombauts, E., Norbert de Paepe, and Max J.M. de Haan, eds. *Ferguut*. Culemborg: Tjeenk Willink, 1976.
Spahr, Blake L., "Ferguut, Fergus, and Chrétien de Troyes." In *Traditions and Transitions: Studies in Honor of Harold Jantz*, ed. L.E. Kurth et al. Munich: Delp, 1972, pp. 29–36.

FERREIRA DE VASCONCELOS, JORGE, author of the *Memorial das Proezas da Segunda Távola Redonda* ("Record of the Achievements of the Second Round Table"), a sixteenth-century Portuguese romance of chivalry. It continues the story of the Round Table beyond Arthur's death, giving Sagramor, one of Arthur's younger knights, heroic prominence. The creation of a second Round Table was an apparent pretext for the description in the romance of an actual tournament, held in 1552 at Xabregas, where Prince Dom João was armed as a knight, reflecting the desires of the Portuguese court for grandeur corresponding to that of medieval myth. The work was printed in Coimbra in 1567 but may have been composed shortly after the 1552 tournament. [HLS]

Ferreira de Vasconcelos, Jorge. *Memorial das Proezas da Segunda Tavola Redonda*. Coimbra: João de Barreyra, 1567; 2nd ed. Lisbon, 1867.

Moisés, Massaud. *A Novela de Cavalaria no Quinhentismo Português: O Memorial das Proezas da Segunda Tavola Redonda de Jorge Ferreira de Vasconcelos*. São Paulo: Universidade de São Paulo, 1957.

FIELD, EUGENE (1850–1895), American poet who wrote two poems on Arthurian themes. "The Vision of the Holy Grail," set in Pelles's court, contrasts earthly cheer with the joy of the Grail. In "A Proper Trewe Idyll of Camelot," when Arthur and the knights overdrink, a stranger from "ye West" leads off the ladies of Camelot to make a deal with the Chicago Board of Trade. Field also wrote "The Tragedie of Elaine," a humorous review of a play about Elaine of Astolat. [ACL]

Field, Eugene. "A Proper Trewe Idyll of Camelot." In *A Little Book of Western Verse*. New York: Scribner, 1890.

———. "The Tragedie of Elaine." In *The Clink of the Ice and Other Poems Worth Reading*. Chicago: Donohue, 1905.

———. "The Vision of the Holy Grail." In *John Smith, U.S.A.* Chicago: Donohue, 1905.

FIELD, MICHAEL, was the pseudonym of two English writers, Katharine H. Bradley (1846–1914) and Edith E. Cooper (1862–1913), whose interest in Tristan produced verse drama: "Tristan de Leonois" in *The Accuser* (1911) and *The Tragedy of Pardon* (1911). The latter's cast includes Mark, Tristan, Jovelin, his son Kahedin, the Bishop of Thames, Melot (a dwarf), Kurvenal, three Iseults, and Brangaena. The scenes range from Dublin, Tintagel, Caerleon, and the Cornish Forest to Parmenie and Arundel. Plot elements include the love elixir, the persecution of Brangaena, Iseult's trial by ordeal, the love grotto, the significant sail, the joint burial, and the Wagnerian *Liebestod* motif. [MAW]

Field, Michael. *The Tragedy of Pardon*. London: Sidgwick and Jackson, 1911.

———. "Tristan of Leonois." In *The Accuser*. London: Sidgwick and Jackson, 1911, pp. 77–149.

Sturge Moore, T., and D.C. Sturge Moore, eds. *Works and Days from the Journal of Michael Field*. London: John Murray, 1933.

FIELDING, HENRY (1707–1754), enjoyed success as a comic dramatist before turning to the novel. His *Tragedy of Tragedies; or The Life and Death of Tom Thumb the Great* appeared before the London public in a number of versions. *Tom Thumb; A Tragedy*, in two acts, was first performed as an afterpiece at the Little Theatre on April 24, 1730, and ran for forty nights. The text, with alterations, was published soon after, with a preface, prologue, and epilogue guying Colley Cibber's style. On November 30, 1730, a new act, not by Fielding but possibly by Thomas Cooke, was added; it was a malicious satire on the selection of Colley Cibber as Poet Laureate, in succession to Laurence Eusdon. The play appeared in definitive three-act form on March 24, 1731. *The Battle of the Poets* was omitted, but there was additional dramatic material and a new preface, ascribed to H. Scriblerius Secundus, and an apparatus of mock-critical notes by the same author, who is, of course, Fielding. In 1733, Eliza Haywood and William Hatchett fashioned an opera out of *Tom Thumb*, and Thomas Arne wrote the music. That year, the libretto was set again, by the Saxon composer Johann Friedrich Lampe, but the work was performed only once. In 1780, Kane O'Hara took elements from both the play and libretto for *Tom Thumb, A Burletta*, which was produced repeatedly throughout the nineteenth century.

Tom Thumb portrays the misfortunes of its diminutive hero. King Arthur wishes to reward his favorite's victories by bestowing the hand of his daughter Huncamunca, but jealous Queen Dollallolla and, in the later version, Glumdalca, Queen of the Giants, thwart the plan. A satire on pedantic criticism and heroic drama, *Tom Thumb* parodies such playwrights as Dryden, Lee, Otway, Young, Theobald, and Thomson. Fielding's verve ensures that his play still amuses after many of his butts have been almost forgotten. [CNS]

Fielding, Henry. *Tom Thumb*. In *Burlesque Plays of the Eighteenth Century*, ed. Simon Trussler. London: Oxford University Press, 1969.

———. *The Tragedy of Tragedies*. In *Eighteenth-Century Comedy*, ed. W.D. Taylor and Simon Trussler. London: Oxford University Press, 1969.

Dudden, F. Homes. *Henry Fielding: His Life, Works and Times*. 2 vols. Oxford: Clarendon, 1952.

FILMS. Arthurian film had its beginning in 1904 with an unsuccessful attempt to bring a version of *Parsifal* to the screen. Hoping to capitalize on the successful 1903 first New York production of Wagner's work, Edwin Porter, Thomas Edison's principal director, shot a film version of the opera consisting of eight scenes. The film features elaborate sets and some trick photography, but the acting is highly exaggerated to suggest that the actors are singing as they stand or move about the set. Edison himself hoped to synchronize phonographic recordings of the music from the opera with the film, but the technology for such a venture did not yet exist.

Inadequate technology marred two other early attempts to bring productions of opera to the screen. In 1912, Mario Caserini directed a second version of *Parsifal* that was much more detailed than Porter's film had been in its presentation of Wagner's opera; in 1921, Maurice Mariaud attempted a version of *Tristan et Yseut*. As outdoor setting for his film, Mariaud chose the cliffs of the Riviera as stand-ins for those of early Celtic Cornwall and Ireland.

In 1917, Edison's production company weighed in with a second Arthurian film, *Knights of the Square Table, or The Grail*. With a screenplay by James A. Wilder, then Commissioner of the Boy Scouts, the film reflects the link between Scouting and the Round Table established at the inception of the Scout Movement by Lord Robert Baden-Powell. *Knights* skillfully tells parallel stories of two groups of boys, one Scouts, the other ne'er-do-wells, whose leader's sole possession is a copy of Howard Pyle's *The Story of the Champions of the Round Table*, which he consults in an ill-considered attempt to set up his own fellowship of knights. The Scouts prove true knights, and in the closing frames of the film the Grail and Grail Knight appear to heal the leader of the ne'er-do-wells and to show him that the Scout way is the true way to knightly fellowship.

More successful were early films based on literary sources. In 1909, Vitagraph released *Lancelot and Elaine*, a free rendering of Tennyson's poem from *Idylls of the King*. The film is notable for camera shots inside a dark cave and closeups of the tournament in which Lancelot fights to win the Queen's favor.

In 1921, Fox released *A Connecticut Yankee at King Arthur's Court*, the first of several screen adaptations of Twain's novel. The screenplay misses no opportunity to add touches of contemporaneity to the film. The subtitles include references to the Volstead Act, Tin Lizzies, and the Battle of Argonne. The success of this silent version of Twain's novel doubtless contributed to Fox's decision to make a talking version, released in 1931 as *A Connecticut Yankee*. Will Rogers plays Twain's hero, while Myrna Loy and Maureen O'Sullivan appear as Morgan le Fay and Alisande. This film version proved such a commercial success that it was rereleased in 1936.

Paramount released a third film version of Twain's novel in 1949, *A Connecticut Yankee in King Arthur's Court*. Truer to the details of Twain's plot than either the 1921 or the 1931 screen versions, this film is in many ways the least successful. The production showcases the musical talents of Bing Crosby, who stars in the title role, but the directional method used throughout the film calls for the plot to advance not by dramatic interaction but rather by song mixed with silly dialogue. Twain's novel returned to the screen for a fourth time in 1979 in a Disney film released in the United States as *The Unidentified Flying Oddball* and in Great Britain as *The Spaceman and King Arthur*. In the film, a NASA malfunction sends astronaut Tom Trimble and a look-alike robot companion back to the sixth century at time-warp velocity. If not the most successful of film adaptations of Twain's novel, *Oddball* may nonetheless be the funniest.

In the 1940s, film versions of the legend of Arthur took a number of original turns. In 1942, comedy combined with the British war effort in Marcel Varnel's *King Arthur Was a Gentleman*, the story of Arthur King, a sad-sack British soldier, who imagines he finds Excalibur. When King is ordered to the front, he uses the sword to perform a series of heroic acts, only to have his faith in the talisman shattered when friends convince him that the sword is not Excalibur. Also reflecting conditions during the Second World War is *L'Éternel Retour*, Jean Delannoy's modernized version of the Tristan story from a screenplay by Jean Cocteau (1943), with a score by Georges Auric. Made during the Occupation, the film, for all its success in adapting the Tristan story, is at times less than subtle in its racism. Cocteau's screenplay adds to the Tristan story a sinister, if not pathological, family, the Frossins. The Frossin parents are dark and devious, and their son is a dwarf, while the blond hero and heroine are clearly portrayed as superior. In 1949, Hollywood weighed in with an Arthurian cliffhanger, Columbia's *Adventures of Sir Galahad*. True to its genre, this fifteen-part serial presents a convoluted plot heavily indebted to bits and pieces of the legend of Arthur.

The 1950s saw the industry's widespread use of CinemaScope in action and adventure films, and directors and producers readily turned to the legends of Arthur and his knights as sources. In 1953, MGM released *The Knights of the Round Table*, a film which, despite the studio's claims to fidelity to its source in Malory, presents a curious jumble of Arthuriana. In 1953, Twentieth Century-Fox followed with *Prince Valiant*, based on Hal Foster's long-running comic strip, and Warwick and Columbia released *The Black Knight*, whose contrived plot shows Mark of Cornwall in league with Saracens, who, when they are not attempting to overthrow Arthur, use Stonehenge for human sacrifice. The model for each of these films is the movie western, but here knights in armor doing battle take the place of cowboys giving chase. The range of possibilities that CinemaScope afforded directors to shoot spectacle rather than an interest in Arthuriana was the primary motivation behind the decisions to make these three films.

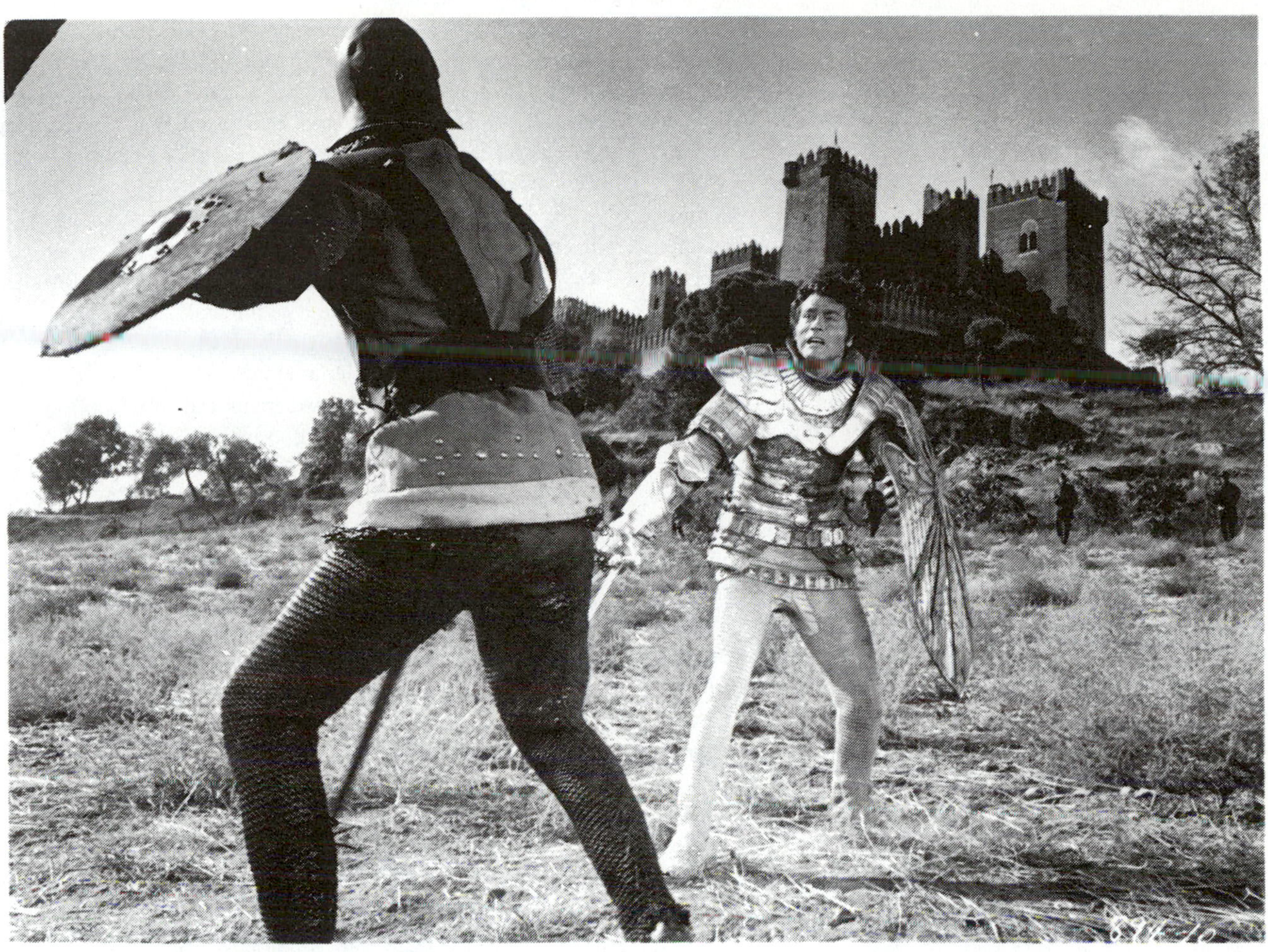

32. From the film *Camelot* (1967).

The first film to deal unhesitatingly with the adultery between Lancelot and Guinevere was *The Sword of Lancelot*, released in Great Britain as *Lancelot and Guinevere* (1963). Loosely based on Malory, the film too clearly favors the two lovers, who are much younger than Arthur. In *Siege of the Saxons*, also released in 1963, another much-too-old Arthur is murdered by a vassal, who is in turn defeated by Arthur's daughter, Katherine, and her Robin Hood–like champion.

In 1965, Disney released *The Sword in the Stone*, an animated version of the first book of T.H. White's tetralogy, *The Once and Future King*. Though an example of Disney animation at its best, *Sword* is less successful as an adaptation of White's novel. The movie introduces Mad Madame Mim as Merlin's nemesis and spends too much time on their silly battle of wits. More successful in adapting parts of White's novel was the 1967 film version of the Broadway play *Camelot*. Directed by Joshua Logan, the film focuses on the love between Lancelot and Guinevere and its tragic consequences, albeit on a one-dimensional level appropriate to a movie musical.

In the 1970s, no fewer than seven motion pictures about the legend of Arthur came to the screen. The French director Yvan Lagrange went to Iceland in 1972 to film *Tristan et Iseult*. The film adds nothing new to the legend of the doomed lovers, but it does focus the viewer's attention on the conflict between love and war, which the director sees at the heart of this oft-retold legend. In 1973, the British director Stephen Weeks attempted a low-budget version of *Sir Gawain and the Green Knight*. In both this film, *Gawain and the Green Knight*, and a big-budget remake, *The Sword of the Valiant*, released ten years later, Weeks proves himself a director incapable of dealing with the complexities of one of the masterpieces of medieval literature.

Much more successful—and some would argue one of the best examples of Arthurian film—is Robert Bresson's *Lancelot du Lac*, released in 1974 and indebted to the *Mort Artu* for the general outlines of its plot. Also successful, but in a totally different way, is the 1975 film *Monty Python and the Holy Grail*, featuring vintage Python slapstick and irreverence. What is being lampooned in the film is not, however, the legend of Arthur but rather earlier film treatments of that legend. *King Arthur, The Young Warlord*, also made in 1975, seems never to have been released commercially, although it does exist as a ninety-minute videotape.

Here, the young Arthur is pitted against Saxons, Picts, and Jutes in his attempt to save his own people and unite England.

Clearly the most authentically medieval example of Arthurian film is Eric Rohmer's *Perceval le Gallois* (1978), which carefully follows its source, Chrétien de Troyes's *Le Conte del Graal*, in retelling the story of Perceval. Rohmer, however, cuts Gawain's final adventures from Chrétien's unfinished text and substitutes in their place a version of the medieval passion play in which Perceval takes the central role in a true union with Christ. Considerably less interesting is the 1979 *Tristan and Isolt*, subsequently released on videotape under the title *Lovespell*, one of a series of movies Richard Burton, in the role of King Mark, made late in his career solely for financial reasons. The film has a score by the Irish group The Chieftains.

In 1980, Richard Blank directed a totally different version of the story of Perceval. In a ninety-minute film for German television, Blank interlaced the plot of Wolfram von Eschenbach's *Parzival* with references to the modern world. In 1981, a second German director, Veith von Fürstenberg, made his debut with a film of the Tristan story, *Feuer und Schwert—Die Legende von Tristan und Isolde*. To his medieval sources, themselves often a jumble of conflicting details, von Fürstenberg adds some personal touches: Isolde knowingly gives Tristan the potion and later bears him a child. Not successful commercially, the film does offer a visually poetic version of the legend that is its source.

More successful, and much more controversial, has been Hans-Jürgen Syberberg's film version of Wagner's *Parsifal* (1981–82), for some *the* opera movie of all time. Set in a labyrinth constructed out of the cracks and crevices in an oversized model of Wagner's death mask, Syberberg's film succeeds where earlier attempts to bring Wagner to the screen had failed. Also mixed in its critical reception has been *Excalibur* (1981), John Boorman's version of Malory's *Morte Darthur*. Boorman's vision of the Grail is stripped of any Christian associations. Here, the land and the King are one, in an ill-defined pagan fertility ritual. The legend of Arthur combines with the quest for the American dream in George A. Romero's *Knightriders*, a film released during the same week as *Excalibur*. Romero examines the values of Arthurian society as they are practiced by a group of motorcycle stunt-riders who travel, armor-clad, throughout west-

33. From Eric Rohmer's *Perceval le Gallois* (1978).

ern Pennsylvania from country fair to country fair in search of a simpler and better way of life.

Arthur the King, a movie made for CBS television in 1982 and aired in 1985, attempts to retell the story of Arthur through the eyes of an American tourist who falls into a hole in the ground at Stonehenge and lands in an icy cave housing Merlin and his lover, Niniana. There is little to suggest a clear line from the film back to any recognizably medieval source. More interesting, if not always successful, is a BBC2 "silent version" of Malory's work that aired in 1984 as *The Morte D'Arthur*. Part drama, part mime, the film stars the Royal Shakespeare Company's John Barton as the knight-prisoner Sir Thomas Malory, who narrates events from the last two books of the *Morte* as they are brought to life in a series of choreographed scenes. More detailed in its use of Malory is *The Legend of King Arthur*, a coproduction of the BBC, Time-Life Television, and the Australian Broadcasting Commission. The eight-part series of thirty-minute episodes was shown originally on BBC1 in 1979.

Indiana Jones and the Last Crusade (1989), the final film in Steven Spielberg's trilogy about the archaeologist-adventurer, casts Jones as a latter-day Grail knight. In one scene reminiscent of Romero's *Knightriders*, Jones, riding a motorcycle with sidecar, jousts with a German solder. *Crusade* also introduces the hero's father, Henry, a medievalist, who joins forces with his son to keep the Grail—here as in the medieval tradition possessive of healing powers—from falling into the hands of the Nazis.

Finally, two Scandinavian films have presented reworkings of the legend of Tristan and Isolde. *I skugga Hrafsina* ("In the Shadow of the Raven"), an Icelandic-Swedish production (1988) directed by Hrafn Gunnlaugsson, has a somewhat more tenuous connection to the Arthurian tradition. The main characters, Trausti (Tristan) and Isolde, are caught up in a feud, but the source of the feud is religious rivalry rather than a love triangle. In contrast, Danish director Jytte Rex's *Isolde* (1989) presents the contemporary complications of the legend's familiar triangle, here a young librarian, Isolde; her ex-husband, a crafty politician; and her new lover, a mercenary soldier. [AG/KJH]

Harty, Kevin J. "Cinema Arthuriana: A Bibliography of Selected Secondary Materials," *Arthurian Interpretations*, 3 (Spring 1989), 119–37.

———. "Cinema Arthuriana: Translations of the Arthurian Legend to the Screen." *Arthurian Interpretations*, 2 (Fall 1987), 95–113.

———. "Film Treatments of the Legend of King Arthur." In *King Arthur Through the Ages*, ed. Valerie M. Lagorio and Mildred Leake Day. New York: Garland, 1990, Vol. 1, pp. 278–90.

FINKEL, GEORGE, former British naval officer, wrote an Arthurian novel entitled *Twilight Province* (1967). In this demythologizing and highly militaristic account, Bedwyr records the struggle against the Saxons of a small Roman settlement in the north of Britain and the subsequent attempt to unite the Romans throughout the island under Artyr as *dux bellorum*. [SRR]

Finkel, George. *Twilight Province*. Sydney: Angus and Robertson, 1967. (Published in the U.S. as *Watch Fires to the North*. New York: Viking, 1968.)

FIORIO E BIANCIFIORE, an Italian *cantare* of the thirteenth or early fourteenth century, containing Arthurian allusions, thought to be the principal source of Boccaccio's *Filocolo*. It may be even older than *Febusso e Breusso*, in which case it would be the earliest extant *cantare*. It is closely related to the French non-Arthurian romance *Floire et Blancheflor*. [SJN]

Branca, Vittore. *Il cantare trecentesco e il Boccaccio del Filostrato e del Teseida*. Florence: Sansoni, 1936.

Reinhold, Joachim H. *Floire et Blancheflor: étude de littérature comparée*. Paris: Larose, 1906.

FISCHER, HANS WALDEMAR (1876–1945), German editor and writer. The epilogue to his *Tristan und Isolde* (1947) describes the author's debt to a variety of traditions, but especially to contemporary criticism. Attempting to relax the prejudices that shape our image of the Middle Ages, he explains why he has combined Tristan, Arthurian, and Grail material in his adaptation. The Tristan material nevertheless clearly dominates: Arthurian and Grail passages appear in only four of twenty-seven chapters. [SSch/PM]

Fischer, Hans Waldemar. *Tristan und Isolde: Der grosse Roman von Liebe und Tod*. Berlin: Deutsche Buchgemeinschaft, 1932.

FISHER, ROBERT, American comedy writer who is the author of an allegory for younger readers, *The Knight in the Rusty Armor* (1987). The knight, trapped in his armor of insecurity and false idealism, is sent on a quest by Merlin. He is reborn, freed from his armor, after traveling the path of truth and passing tests in the Castles of Silence, of Knowledge, and of Will and Daring. [HT]

Fisher, Robert. *The Knight in the Rusty Armor*. North Hollywood, Calif.: Melvin Powers/Wiltshire Book Company, 1987.

FISHER KING, the keeper of the Grail; sometimes called the Rich Fisher. Perhaps an avatar of Bran the Blessed, the Fisher King is the wounded occupant of the Grail castle in Chrétien de Troyes's *Perceval* and other works. He and his land could have been restored had Perceval asked about the Grail procession; Perceval's failure to do so necessitates the Grail quest. Eventually, Chrétien's hero learns that the Fisher King is his cousin (although in other texts he is Perceval's uncle or grandfather). Chrétien does not give him a name, but in Wolfram von Eschenbach he is called Anfortas.

In the work of Robert de Boron, the Fisher King is identified with Hebron or Bron, Joseph of Arimathea's brother-in-law, who catches the fish that is placed on the Grail table. The Didot-*Perceval* continues and concludes the story of the Fisher King, as the work's hero returns to the Grail castle, asks the Grail question, and cures the king. [NJL]

FLORIANT ET FLORETE, a French romance of 8,278 lines, probably written in the third quarter of the thirteenth century. Floriant is the posthumous son of a king of Sicily. He is abducted by Morgan le Fay, educated, and sent to Arthur's court, where he remains only briefly, having to return to Sicily to defend his mother, who is besieged by the wicked seneschal of the Emperor of Constantinople. During the battle, in which he is assisted by Arthur, Floriant falls in love with the emperor's daughter, Florete, whom he marries after defeating the seneschal. After accusations of inactivity, Floriant sets out, as *li Biaus Sauvages* ("the Fair Savage"), in the company of Florete, proves his prowess once more, and settles down in Palermo. A white stag one day leads him to Morgan's castle, where Florete is also taken. The conclusion of the romance is lacking.

The author uses the "lost childhood" motif found elsewhere (e.g., the Prose *Lancelot* and Ulrich von Zatzikhoven's *Lanzelet*) and the marriage-crisis-resolution structure found in Chrétien de Troyes's *Erec* and *Yvain*. *Floriant et Florete* is unusual in other respects, however: it prefaces the hero's central adventures with the story of his parents, of his birth, childhood, and early deeds (perhaps reflecting the shape of Chrétien's *Cligés* and the Tristan story); the central events take place in Sicily, not in Arthur's Britain; Gauvain is, exceptionally, said to be married. The romance was turned into prose in the fifteenth century. [KB]

Lévy, Claude M.L., ed. *Le Roman de Floriant et Florete ou le chevalier qui la nef maine*. Ottawa: Éditions de l'Université d'Ottawa, 1983.

Williams, Harry F., ed. *Floriant et Florete*. Ann Arbor: University of Michigan Press, 1947.

FOLIE LANCELOT, LA ("The Madness of Lancelot"), a French prose romance, dating from ca. 1230, that offers episodes concerning Lancelot's madness and the youthful adventures of Perceval and Galahad. The work is based on material from the Vulgate and from the Prose *Tristan*; it appears to provide narrative preparation for the *Mort Artu*. [NJL]

Bogdanow, Fanni, ed. *La Folie Lancelot: A Hitherto Unidentified Portion of the Suite du Merlin Contained in MSS. B.N. fr. 112 and 12559*. Tübingen: Niemeyer, 1965.

FOLIE TRISTAN DE BERNE, LA ("The Madness of Tristan"), some 574 lines that relate essentially the same material as the Oxford *Folie*. Tristan's allusions to his past adventures are less rigorously organized than in Oxford, the style is less polished, and the text is more closely related to Béroul's *Tristran* than to Thomas's. Composed in the late twelfth century and preserved in a single, rather defective, manuscript, Bern Library 354, the Berne *Folie* is in a northeastern dialect of Old French. [WWK]

Bédier, Joseph, ed. *Les Deux Poèmes de la Folie Tristan*. Paris: Didot, 1907.

Hoepffner, Ernest, ed. *La Folie Tristan de Berne*. Paris: Les Belles Lettres, 1934.

Payen, Jean-Charles, ed. and trans. *Tristan et Yseut*. Paris: Garnier, 1974.

FOLIE TRISTAN D'OXFORD, LA, a twelfth-century Old French poem of 998 lines that recounts how Tristan, banished from King Mark's court, disguises himself as a fool in order to see Queen Iseut. At court, he amuses Mark with his wit as he makes allusions to his past with Iseut. After Mark leaves for a hunt, Iseut remains skeptical until Tristan is warmly greeted by the dog Husdent. The work is found in a single manuscript in Oxford's Bodleian Library (Douce d 6) immediately after a truncated text of Thomas's *Tristan*, to which it is closely related. [WWK]

Bédier, Joseph, ed. *Les Deux Poèmes de la Folie Tristan*. Paris: Didot, 1907.

Hoepffner, Ernest, ed. *La Folie Tristan d'Oxford*. Paris: Les Belles Lettres, 1938.

Payen, Jean-Charles, ed. and trans. *Tristan et Yseut*. Paris: Garnier, 1974.

FOLKLORE. Despite the existence of the large number of carefully composed literary texts that take Arthur as their subject, his legend is inextricably bound up with the conventional materials of folklore. There have been attempts to establish a folk origin for Arthurian romances themselves, in the form of pagan rituals, the memory of which was preserved in oral tradition, expanded, and finally fixed in written form. Those attempts have not been wholly persuasive, and most scholars would hesitate to go so far. It is nonetheless clear that popular beliefs very early grew up around Arthur; moreover, the relation of folklore and literary tradition is certainly reciprocal: while folk-motifs were often recast in literary form, the dissemination and popularity of that literature clearly gave rise, in turn, to a great many of the popular beliefs about Arthur and Arthurian subjects. Such a view has had the support of a good number of scholars, including Roger Sherman Loomis, who concluded that, although some elements of Arthurian stories "survive in Celtic and other folktales collected within the last century, it would be a mistake to infer their origin in 'folklore' in the strict sense of that term." At the same time, certain of the beliefs commonly associated with Arthur also have folk attachments to other heroes as well: for example, the motif identified by Stith Thompson as "king asleep in a mountain" (D1960.2 in the Thompson *Motif-Index*; cf. A571) is attached to Arthur, Barbarossa, King Marko, Holger Danske, and others.

In any event, we need to make a distinction between "Arthurian lore" (such as the Sword in the Stone and Avalon) and folklore per se, which provides traditional material appropriated by many authors, including those of Arthurian romances. In the former category, by far the most common beliefs about Arthur concern the durable legends of his survival and return (Thompson A580: culture hero's expected return). A number of English, Welsh, Breton, and other stories have traditionally been told about the discovery of Arthur and his knights in various circumstances, such as sleeping in a cave or riding in a nocturnal hunt (Thompson E501, the "wild hunt"). Some versions that present them as sleeping insist that a call for help in their presence would immediately rouse the knights and bring them forth to battle the enemies of England. A fourteenth-century text, the *Lanercost Chronicle*, records the story of a bishop who met Arthur face to face; to ensure that the bishop would be believed when recounting the meeting, Arthur magically gave him the power to produce a butterfly whenever he opened his fist. Other accounts of the cave legend include such details as a shepherd's (or wanderer's) discovery of the knights sleeping beside a stack of gold and one of silver; he is invited to take what he wants from either pile, and Arthur stirs and asks if it is time for his return. In at least one instance, the tale is so specific as to provide a name for the intruder: Potter Thompson.

In contrast to the detail of such stories, other folk-beliefs are much more general associations, as witness the link, mentioned as early as Cervantes and attested in Cornwall and Somerset during the last century, between Arthur and birds, especially the raven and the chough or crow. The reason for the association is often not clear; attempts at explanation usually follow Don Quixote's notion that, not only has Arthur survived his apparent death to await the hour of his return, but he lives on specifically in the form of a raven. This belief has led at times to a popular proscription against killing ravens.

Folk-beliefs are also responsible for the expansion or modification of Arthur's lineage and personal associations. In 1865, Robert Hunt recorded several such beliefs; one traces the Argyle family back to Constantine, Arthur's grandfather. Of course, some attempts to link up families (e.g., the Plantagenets, Tudors, or Stuarts) with King Arthur have far less to do with folklore than with calculation and political motivation. Other associations, while scarcely more fanciful than many of the political claims, are the genuine product of popular belief; for example, Jack the Giant-Killer was sometimes identified as the tutor of Arthur's son, and Tom Thumb (or Thomas of the Thumb) as the King's favorite dwarf.

Arthurian names and themes are popularly associated with numerous places—more than 600, according to some estimates. Certain of these associations are supported by specific romance motifs, such as the identification of the Fountain of Barenton as the storm-producing spring in Chrétien de Troyes's *Yvain*, while others result simply from a popular tendency to attach Arthurian names (especially Arthur, Tristan, and Merlin) and motifs to mysterious or evocative locations. Arthurian connections abound in particular areas: for example, Arthur's habitation has been located in England, Wales, Ireland, Scotland, and Brittany. Brittany claims not only the magic fountain and Merlin's Stone beside it, but the location of Merlin's tomb (also in Brocéliande), his birthplace (the Île de Sein, although Carmarthen also claims it), the Val sans Retour (the Valley of No Return, where the enchantress Morgan imprisoned false lovers), and even a dolmen near Trébeurden that is sometimes taken as Arthur's gravestone. Breton folklore has, moreover, its variant of the story of Merlin entombed by Viviane, an island named Île Tristan on which Isolde and her lover supposedly spent portions of their exile, and several islands and towns popularly identified as Avalon. Local legend has it that Lancelot, Mark, and other characters are of Breton origin, and ruins have in some cases been identified as their castles, including Joyous Guard. Finally, the alignments of stones at Carnac are said to have been an invading army turned to stone; the feat is traditionally attributed to St. Cornély, but occasionally to Merlin.

At least three places outside Brittany also claim Merlin's grave (Drumelzier, Marlborough, and Bardsey), while other names of places or objects include Merlin's Tree, Merlin's Rock, Merlin's Cave, Merlin's Bridge, Tristan's

Cairn, Guinevere's Monument, Arthur's Seat, Arthur's Fountain, Arthur's Fold, Arthur's Bed, Arthur's Chair, Arthur's Table, Arthur's Bridge, Arthur's Stone, Arthur's Wood, Arthur's Yard, the King's Crag and the Queen's Crag, and a great many others. Most often, the name was obviously attached to the place long after the Arthurian period, a phenomenon that, again, reflects the popularity of Arthurian themes and their ability to stimulate as well as reflect folk-beliefs.

It is hardly surprising that Arthurian and other romances cast much folk material in literary form. They draw heavily on traditional motifs, many of which Loomis and others traced to sources in Celtic myth and folklore. For example, while legend offers numerous examples of stakes supporting severed human heads (Thompson H901.1; Q421.1), Loomis suggests that the Celtic world provides the only folk antecedent for the particular situation of Chrétien de Troyes's *Erec et Enide*, in which a final stake is specifically reserved for the hero's head.

Folk-motifs that Arthurian romances share with many other tales and texts include the storm-producing spring (Thompson D2143.1.1) and the Giant Herdsman from Chrétien de Troyes's *Yvain* (F531.6.17.5; G152), the Underwater Bridge from his *Lancelot* (F842.2.3.2), chastity tests (H400–455; see esp. H411.4, H411.7, H411.8), the beheading test from *Sir Gawain and the Green Knight* and other romances (M221), fairy mistresses, such as the one in Marie de France's *Lanval* (F302ff.), the question-test found in the Perceval stories (C651), and, perhaps, the cauldron of plenty, in the form of the Grail (D1472.1.19–33). (*See also* Cave Legend; Glastonbury; Grail; Joseph of Arimathea; Return, Legends of Arthur's; Topography and Local Legends; Welsh Arthurian Literature). [NJL]

Ashe, Geoffrey. *A Guidebook to Arthurian Britain*. Wellingborough: Aquarian, 1983.

Bett, Henry, and Eric Fraser. *English Legends*. London: Batsford, 1950.

Briggs, Katharine M. *A Dictionary of British Folk-Tales in the English Language*. 4 vols. London: Routledge and Kegan Paul, 1971.

Brown, A.L. "Camlann and the Death of Arthur." *Folklore*, 72 (1961), 612–21.

Darrah, John. *The Real Camelot: Paganism and the Arthurian Romances*. London: Thames and Hudson, 1981.

Hunt, Robert. *Popular Romances of the West of England; or, The Drolls, Traditions, and Superstitions of Old Cornwall*. London: Hotten, 1865.

Johnson, W. Branch. *Folktales of Brittany*. New York: Stokes, 1927.

Jones, Gwyn. *Welsh Legends and Folk-Tales*. London: Oxford University Press, 1955.

Loomis, Roger Sherman. "Arthurian Tradition and Folklore." *Folklore*, 69 (1958), 1–25.

Rhys, John. *Celtic Folklore*. 2 vols. Oxford: Clarendon, 1901.

Thompson, Stith. *Motif-Index of Folk-Literature*, 2nd ed. 6 vols. Bloomington: Indiana University Press, 1955.

FORD, JOHN M., American author of science fiction and fantasy, anachronistically envisions Arthur's court in an age of railways in his poem "Winter Solstice, Camelot Station" (1988). His award-winning fantasy *The Dragon Waiting* (1983) is set in a world with an alternative history that includes stories of King Arthur and a ritual drama known as "Arthur's Court." [RHT]

Ford, John M. *The Dragon Waiting: A Masque of History*. New York: Simon and Schuster, 1983.

———. "Winter Solstice, Camelot Station." In *Invitation to Camelot: An Arthurian Anthology of Short Stories*, ed. Parke Godwin. New York: Ace, 1988, pp. 243–50.

FORME DES TOURNOYS AU TEMPS DU ROY UTERPENDRAGON ET DU ROY ARTUS, LA ("The Form of Tournaments in the Time of King Utherpendragon and King Arthur"), a French prose composition dating from the later fifteenth century. The treatise describes Arthurian tournaments, gives a list of the oaths sworn by Arthurian knights, names some 150 knights of the Round Table, and explains their coats of arms. [NJL]

Blangy, Auguste, Comte de, ed. *La Forme des tournois au temps du Roy Uter et du Roy Artus, suivie de l'Armorial des Chevaliers de la Table Ronde*. Caen, 1897.

FORREST, THORPE, British author of *Builders of the Waste* (1899), a historical novel set in sixth-century Britain. Dutigirn, a Romanized Briton and a leader of the Angles, proposes to Brenda, the daughter of Aurelius, only to discover that she loves an Anglian prince, Aella. Their love is doomed because she is Christian and he pagan. There is little Arthurian content, though Urien of Reged, father of Owain, has received his kingdom from "the mysterious Arthur." [MAW]

Forrest, Thorpe. *Builders of the Waste*. London: Duckworth, 1899.

FORTUNE, DION (pseudonym of Violet Firth Evans; 1890–1946), through her leadership of an occult society and her book *Avalon of the Heart* (1934), helped popularize Glastonbury as a site of ancient spiritual importance in the 1920s and 1930s. She embodied her idiosyncratic psychological theories and religious mysticism in bizarre depictions of Morgan le Fay and Merlin in the fantasy novel *The Sea Priestess* (1938). A sequel with slighter Arthurian associations and even murkier plot, *Moon Magic*, was published posthumously in 1956. [DN]

Fortune, Dion. *Avalon of the Heart*. London: F. Muller, 1934; expanded as *Glastonbury: Avalon of the Heart*. Wellingborough: Aquarian, 1986.

———. *The Sea Priestess*. London: Published by the author, 1938; new ed. York Beach, Maine: Samuel Weiser, 1978.

———. *Moon Magic*. London: Aquarian, 1956: new ed. York Beach, Maine: Samuel Weiser, 1978.

FOSSA, MATTEO (d. 1516), of Cremona, composed the *Innamoramento di Galvano* ("Gawain's Falling in Love"), a revision of the tale of Gawain and the Pulzella Gaia, Morgan's daughter, who captivates Gawain and forbids him to reveal their love. The text is derived from the Italian tradition of the *cantare*. [DLH]

Gardner, Edmund G. *The Arthurian Legend in Italian Literature*. London: Dent, 1930, p. 308.

FOUKES LE FITZWARIN, an Anglo-Norman composition, probably written in Shropshire shortly after 1250. Devoted to the history of the medieval Fitzwarin family, and especially to Foukes III, the text becomes "Arthurian" by including the story of Arthur's squire Cahus, as it occurs in the *Perlesvaus*. Originally written in verse, the work is extant only in a fourteenth-century prose redaction; there is some evidence that a Middle English adaptation was made but subsequently lost. [NJL]

Hathaway, E.J., P.T. Ricketts, C.A. Robson, and A.D. Wilshire, eds. *Foukes le Fitz Waryn*. Oxford: Blackwell, 1975.

FOUQUÉ, FRIEDRICH BARON DE LA MOTTE (1777–1843), Prussian nobleman of Huguenot descent. First active as a military officer, he became one of the most successful authors of the German Romantic movement. Fouqué's reputation had waned sufficiently during his lifetime that he was, however, unable to find a publisher for his lengthy epic *Parcival* (1831–32). It is being prepared for publication from his literary remains by Frank Rainer Max and Ursula Rautenberg. *Parcival* is a tripartite, educational verse-novel in which a romantic revivification of the Middle Ages is professedly combined with an impressive enthusiasm for poetic experimentation. [UM/WCM]

Max, Frank Rainer, and Ursula Rautenberg. In *Mittelalter-Rezeption II: Gesammelte Vorträge des 2. Salzburger Symposions*, ed. Jürgen Kühnel, Hans-Dieter Mück, Ursula Müller, and Ulrich Müller, Göppingen: Kümmerle, 1982.

FRANKLAND, EDWARD (1884–1958), English author who developed his "Medraut and Gwenhwyvar," a short story about Arthur marching to fight the Saxons while his wife and nephew plot betrayal, into the historical novel *The Bear of Britain* (1944). Arthur is too honorable to seize absolute power after his victory at Badon, and his achievement is squandered through the selfish ambition of others. The somber vision is inspired by Gildas's diatribe against the greed, folly, treachery, and corruption of the British rulers. [RHT]

Frankland, Edward. *The Bear of Britain*. London: MacDonald, 1944.

———. "Medraut and Gwenhwyvar." In *England Growing*. London: MacDonald, 1944, pp. 15–21.

FRAPPIER, JEAN (1900–1974), professor at the University of Paris-Sorbonne (1948–69). Frappier demonstrated broad interests in the major genres of medieval literature and philology and an abiding concern with the Renaissance, but his primary legacy was the furtherance of Arthurian studies. The demand for his works on *La Mort le Roi Artu, Le Roman breton, Étude sur Yvain, Le Mythe du graal*, and *Chrétien de Troyes* required that all of these be reissued at least once. Frappier's books are an indispensable point of departure for scholarly investigations, since he excelled at compressing the discoveries and theories of his predecessors into clear perspectives. He distilled his own carefully balanced interpretations from reasoned foundations and skillful reading of the texts. On the question of origins of French Arthurian romance, he tended toward acceptance of Celtic sources but never denied the possibility of learned (ecclesiastic) or popular influences, or the role of individual creativity. A bibliography of his works to 1969 may be found in *Mélanges Frappier*, Vol. 1 (1970). [JLG]

Foulon, Charles. "Jean Frappier (1900–1974)." *Bibliographical Bulletin of the International Arthurian Society*, 27 (1979), 238–41.

Malkiel, Yakov. "Jean Frappier: Dedication and Necrology (1900–74)." *Romance Philology*, 30 (1976), 4–8.

FRENCH, ALLEN (1870–1946), American educator, historian, and author of a historical romance for juveniles, *Sir Marrok* (1902), in which a noble knight of Uther's court, who is transformed into a werewolf by an evil enchantress, nonetheless continues to protect his vassals. This didactic story extols the virtues of gratitude and fortitude in adversity, while it warns against being deceived by appearances. [RHT]

French, Allen. *Sir Marrok: A Tale of the Days of King Arthur.* New York: Century, 1902.

FRENCH ARTHURIAN LITERATURE (MEDIEVAL). If the modern Arthur is to a considerable extent the property of the English-speaking world, it is only slight exaggeration to suggest that, in his literary manifestations, he is the invention of the French Middle Ages. Arthur so captured the imagination of medieval French writers and audiences that he and his knights served as the primary source of inspiration for narrative poets during at least two centuries (the twelfth and thirteenth), and the popularity of Arthurian themes continued nearly unabated well into the sixteenth.

The history of Arthurian fiction in France begins in 1155, when Wace adapted Geoffrey of Monmouth's *Historia Regum Britanniae*. The resulting text, entitled *Roman de Brut*, stands between chronicle and romance, going well beyond Geoffrey's creation to offer imaginative accounts of conversations and emotions. Wace's most remarkable innovation was his introduction of the Round Table, Arthur's attempt to abolish precedence and preclude jealousies.

A few years after Wace wrote his *Brut*, France produced its greatest writer of Arthurian romance, Chrétien de Troyes. In the late twelfth century—though there is controversy about the precise dates—Chrétien wrote the five romances that largely set the shape and direction of Arthurian literature for some time to come. His works are *Erec et Enide*, *Cligés*, *Lancelot* or *Le Chevalier de la charrete* (which presented and apparently glorified the illicit love of Lancelot and Guenevere), *Yvain* or *Le Chevalier au lion*, and the unfinished *Perceval* or *Le Conte del Graal*, in which Chrétien introduces the Grail into world literature. In his treatment of Arthurian themes and of the King himself, Chrétien established several precedents that would be followed by most romancers. First, although the Arthurian court would remain the prestigious locus of much action, the romances centered not on Arthur but on other heroes. Second, Chrétien developed the "episodic romance," ignoring the chronicle form in order to present events occurring over a more limited period, often of months or a year or two. Finally, he presented Arthur himself as a patriarch, and sometimes a passive or ineffective figure, who nonetheless retains his authority. In the structure of his romances, Chrétien favored a procedure that emphasized the hero's initial failure and eventual progress by juxtaposing him with another character (usually Gauvain) or, in the case of *Cligés*, with a different generation.

During the last decade of the twelfth century or the first years of the thirteenth, Robert de Boron wrote *Le Roman du Graal* ("The Romance of the Grail"), known also as the *Joseph d'Arimathie*, in which he transformed the Grail from Chrétien's holy but mysterious object into a relic whose identity and religious significance are entirely clear: it is the vessel of the Last Supper, in which Joseph of Arimathea later collected Christ's blood after the Deposition.

Robert also composed a *Merlin* romance, and while only a fragment of it survives, it is known through two forms of a prose version: a part of the Vulgate Cycle and an introduction to the *Suite du Merlin*. We also have a prose Perceval romance, known as the Didot-*Perceval*, which may be the prosification of a lost work by Robert. Following the conclusion of the Grail quest, the Didot-*Perceval* turns abruptly to an account, similar to that given by Wace, of Arthur's conquests, his betrayal by Mordred, and his departure for Avalon. These sequences may themselves have been derived from a *Mort Artu* composition by Robert.

Both because Chrétien's *Perceval* was unfinished and because of the appeal of the Grail quest as a theme, the way was now clear for poets to compose sequels to his work, in order to bring that quest to a conclusion. Of course, the quest is in theory infinitely expandable, and the authors of the Continuations were nothing if not expansive. There were four Continuations, in verse, following alternately the adventures of Perceval and those of Chrétien's other hero, Gauvain. The first two date from ca. 1200; the first is a Gauvain-Continuation once attributed to "Wauchier de Denain," while the second, signed by "Gauchier de Donaing" develops Perceval's adventures. The third and fourth were composed ca. 1230, one by Manessier, the other by Gerbert de Montreuil. These two follow Perceval until he becomes Grail King. Taken together, the Continuations added nearly 60,000 lines to Grail literature.

The late twelfth and the thirteenth centuries produced a number of independent (i.e., noncyclic) romances, such as the *Perlesvaus*, an early (ca. 1200–10) example of prose composition, in which Gauvain, like Perceval, fails the Grail test and Perceval frees the Grail castle. But most notably, the thirteenth century produced the imposing Arthurian prose cycles, characterized by length and increasing complexity, with multiple quests and interlaced adventures. The great Vulgate Cycle of Arthurian romance, from the first half of the century, consists of five works: the *Estoire del Saint Graal* and *Merlin* (probably written after the other three, before which they stand in the sequence established within the cycle), the *Lancelot*, *La Queste del Saint Graal*, and *La Mort Artu*. The Vulgate develops further the Joseph of Arimathea connection, the love of Lancelot and Guenevere, the choice and progress of Galahad as perfect Grail knight, and the Arthurian apocalypse.

A prose composition known as the *Livre d'Artus* ("The Book of Arthur") coincides in the beginning with the Merlin portion of the Vulgate but soon diverges from it to recount a long series of Gauvain adventures.

The Vulgate was followed quickly by the Post-Vulgate, a cycle dating from 1230–40 and sometimes called the "Pseudo-Robert de Boron" cycle. The Post-Vulgate is not preserved intact, but it has been largely reconstructed, partially on the basis of extant translations in Spanish and Portuguese. The structure of the cycle corresponds generally to that of the Vulgate, with the addition of a continuation of the Vulgate *Merlin*, the *Suite du Merlin* or the Huth *Merlin*, and sequences taken from the Prose *Tristan* and with one major deletion: most of the *Lancelot*. The effect is a shift of emphasis from the story of Lancelot and Guenevere's adulterous love to the Grail story.

The traditions of thirteenth-century Arthurian texts, especially concerning Merlin and Lancelot, are exceedingly complex. For example, in addition to the Vulgate *Lancelot* and a section of it adapted for the Post-Vulgate, there is also a noncyclic prose *Lancelot* whose narrative development, unlike that of the Vulgate romance, gives no indication that it was intended to be followed by a *Queste* or a *Mort Artu*.

While Arthur and the Grail quest were being treated at length, another theme and set of characters were proving to have great popularity. The story of Tristan, Isolde, and Mark, while originally part of a different tradition, was soon attached, however loosely, to the Arthurian world. During the twelfth century, both Béroul and Thomas d'Angleterre composed Tristan romances, although both survive only in substantial fragments. The two texts apparently derive from different traditions. Thomas's work, which belongs to the so-called "courtly branch" of the legend, clearly shows courtly influences and emphasizes amorous rhetoric and the introspective analysis of emotion. Béroul's text, which the manuscript names *Tristran*, is a descendant of the "common" or "primitive" tradition, meaning only that it is thought to be more closely related to a hypothetical archetype; the characters are more tortured than ennobled by love, and Béroul's narration is direct, realistic (sometimes to the point of shock), and witty.

Since the Tristan story was by nature episodic, involving brief encounters, separations, reconciliations, and further separations, a number of writers offer us the account of a single episode or a restricted sequence of events. For example, Tristan may return to court in disguise to see Isolde (the two versions of *Folie Tristan*), assume the role of a minstrel (*Tristan Ménestrel*, inserted into the Fourth Continuation of *Perceval*), or imitate birdcalls to offer her a pretext for joining him outside (*Tristan Rossignol*). However, the best-known French Tristan text, after those of Béroul and Thomas, is *Chevrefueil*, Marie de France's lai that recounts a meeting of the lovers in the forest. Marie's only other Arthurian lai is *Lanval*, concerning a knight who rebuffs Guenevere's advances and then takes a fairy mistress.

In contrast to these brief texts, the lengthy thirteenth-century Prose *Tristan* links the lovers' story to those of Lancelot and Guenevere and to the Grail history. Here, Tristan is a friend of Lancelot and an active participant in the Grail quest, and the Prose *Tristan* completes the fusion of the Tristan story with those of Arthur, his knights, and the Grail.

Although the best-known romances from the twelfth and thirteenth centuries deal with the Grail quest, a number of writers chose instead to follow other paths, and one of the popular subjects was Gauvain. Throughout Chrétien's work, he had played a significant role, as a consummate knight but usually as a foil for the hero, and in *Perceval* he clearly has certain obvious defects, notably pride, impetuousness, and frivolity. Later poets seized on his flaws and composed a number of "non-Grail" romances, most of them relatively short, in which, without being an object of derision, Gauvain becomes either a comical figure or a means of charting the progressive decline of chivalry. In *Gliglois*, he loses the lady he loves to a squire who serves her more humbly and devotedly. *La Mule sans frein* ("The Mule Without a Bridle") comically transforms him into an uncharacteristically devoted knight but has him unstintingly pursue a largely pointless quest. His flaws and, in some cases, those of the Arthurian chivalric system are further explored in *Le Chevalier à l'épée* ("The Knight with the Sword"), *La Vengeance Raguidel* ("The Vengeance of Raguidel"), *Hunbaut*, *L'Atre périlleux* ("The Perilous Cemetery"), and Robert de Blois's *Beaudous*. On the other hand, the author of *Yder* departs from this tradition and presents a Gauvain who is unreservedly deserving of praise.

Gauvain has only a minor role in Renaut de Beaujeu's *Le Bel Inconnu* ("The Fair Unknown"), as his son Guinglain is its principal character. Guinglain, who appears also in the First Continuation, will reappear in the sixteenth century, in Claude Platin's *Giglan*.

The vogue of literary cycles that gave us the Vulgate and Post-Vulgate also produced *Les Sept Sages de Rome* ("The Seven Sages of Rome"), a series of prose romances dating from the thirteenth and fourteenth centuries. Though the original romances that constitute the cycle are non-Arthurian, they spawned several continuations that exploit themes from Arthurian romance or that, in the case of the *Roman de Laurin*, are explicitly Arthurian. Laurin is an emperor of Constantinople who travels to Arthur's court and undertakes adventures involving Arthur, Mordred, Gauvain, and other knights of the Round Table. Other continuations that, although not Arthurian, recast material such as the lion theme from Chrétien's *Yvain* or the cart scene from his *Charrete*, are the romances entitled *Cassidorus*, *Pelyarmenus*, *Helcanus*, and *Kanor*.

Chrétien's *Perceval*, with its sharp division into two distinct but related stories, appears to have begun something of a trend, and a number of romances and lais, from that time on, were thematically or structurally bipartite. The two parts of the work often present double quests, one of them usually conducted by Gauvain; examples are *Meraugis de Portlesguez*, *Le Chevalier as deus espees* ("The Knight with Two Swords"), and *Hunbaut*. Some romances, such as *Les Mervelles de Rigomer* ("The Marvels of Rigomer") and *Claris et Laris*, multiply the quests. Other works that present a bipartite structure include the lai *Tyolet*, which recounts Perceval's childhood and follows that with the story of Tyolet, who cuts off a stag's foot for a maiden. *Escanor*, late in the thirteenth century, devotes its first half to a love story involving Kay before turning to a sequence in which Gauvain is accused of murder.

By the end of the thirteenth century, romances were no longer being written in verse, although an exception is the fourteenth-century *Meliador*, by Jehan Froissart. Moreover, most romances of the late Middle Ages were increasingly lengthy and complex works that often extend the boundaries, temporal as well as geographical, of the Arthurian romance. *Perceforest*, consisting of a staggering 531 chapters, relates, for example, that Alexander the Great established the work's hero as British king and that the civilization founded by Perceforest is eventually destroyed by Caesar. In *Ysaïe le Triste*, on the other hand, Tristan's son inhabits a post-Arthurian world where the King's chivalric system is a decided anachronism.

Alongside those works, the late Middle Ages have left us vast compilations of Arthurian material, such as those by Jean Vaillant, Michot Gonnot, and Rusticiano da Pisa. The romance entitled *Palamedes* consisted of two large divisions, one devoted to Tristan's father, Méliadus, and the other to Guiron le Courtois. The two parts were sometimes separated and during the sixteenth century were published as distinct romances, each half titled after its primary character. Among other late-medieval Arthurian works should be noted the Burgundian prose adaptations of Chrétien de Troyes's poems, as well as a Prose *Erec* and a Prose *Yvain* inspired by Chrétien's characters but based only distantly, if at all, on his work.

The popularity of Arthurian themes during the Middle Ages and the tendency to deflect the focus of romances from Arthur onto other characters gave us, from relatively early until the close of the medieval period, a number of works that were only partly or incidentally Arthurian. Béroul's *Tristran*, as already noted, provides an illustration of this phenomenon, for it develops only one major episode that is explicitly Arthurian. Romances that are less than fully Arthurian also include *Claris et Laris*, where, in the second half of the narrative, the title characters are joined in their exploits by Gauvain and Yvain, with Merlin playing a significant role in the denouement. Whether we consider *Claris et Laris* to be a fundamentally non-Arthurian romance to which some Arthurian characters are added, or instead a text in which, as in many another romance, new characters are being brought into the Arthurian sphere, may depend simply on our point of view. Other examples are yet more problematical. Heldris de Cornualle's *Roman de Silence* (thirteenth century) is Arthurian in little more than Merlin's presence in the final episode, and the thirteenth-century *Sone de Nausay* (or *Nansay*) includes several episodes involving Grail material and reference to Joseph of Arimathea.

Finally, some romances offer no more than an incidental reference to Arthur's court. *Floris et Lyriopé*, by Robert de Blois, who also composed *Beaudous*, develops an intrigue that requires the hero Floris to leave his country for a year. He decides to spend the year at Arthur's court; yet the text merely records that fact, without focusing on the period or the court and without offering any details of his stay. In this extreme, but not unique, case, we are clearly dealing with a fundamentally non-Arthurian text, but the simple reference to the King, when any other king and court would have done as well, offers sure evidence of the pervasive vogue of the Matter of Britain during the Middle Ages. [NJL]

Frappier, Jean. *Amour courtois et Table Ronde*. Geneva: Droz, 1973.

———, and Reinhold R. Grimm, eds. *Le Roman jusqu'à la fin du XIIIe siècle*. Heidelberg: Winter, 1978.

Lacy, Norris J. "The Typology of Arthurian Romance." In *The Legacy of Chrétien de Troyes*, ed. Norris J. Lacy, Douglas Kelly, and Keith Busby. 2 vols. Amsterdam: Rodopi, 1987–88, Vol. 1, pp. 33–56.

Loomis, Roger Sherman, ed. *Arthurian Literature in the Middle Ages*. Oxford: Clarendon, 1959.

Pickford, Cedric E. "The Maturity of the Arthurian Prose Romances," *Bibliographical Bulletin of the International Arthurian Society*, 34 (1982), 197–206.

Schmolke-Hasselmann, Beate. *Der arthurische Versroman von Chrestien bis Froissart: Zur Geschichte einer Gattung*. Tübingen: Niemeyer, 1980.

FRENCH ARTHURIAN LITERATURE (MODERN). The sixteenth century continued both the medieval interest in Arthurian literature and the tendency toward compilations, translations, adaptations and modernizations, prosifications, and expansions of those stories. Examples are *Le Chevalier doré* (a condensation of *Perceforest*), the French prose *Amadis de Gaule* (translation by Nicolas de Herberay), a *Lancelot du Lac* printed in 1533, *L'Hystoire du Saint Graal* (1516), *Le Noble Chevalier Gauvain* (1540), and *Perceval le Gallois* (1530). The popularity of these works is indicated by the fact that several of them went through a large number of editions and reprintings: Frappier notes that the *Petit Artus de Bretagne* was printed fourteen times between 1493 and 1584, and other romances, such as the Prose *Lancelot*, *Meliadus*, and the *Prophécies de Merlin*, saw seven or eight reprintings during the sixteenth century.

Despite the tendency to expand earlier works, the

end of the Middle Ages and the sixteenth century did on occasion offer abridgments of long texts or cycles. For example, the fifteenth-century *Histoire du Sainct Graal abrégée* ("Abridged History of the Holy Grail") is an abbreviated version of the Vulgate Cycle; the sixteenth-century *Histoire de Lancelot du Lac* performs a similar abridgment of the three sections of the *Lancelot*.

A few sixteenth-century French writers composed new Arthurian works. Pierre Sala, author of a new redaction of *Yvain*, in the 1520s wrote a *Tristan* romance in which he combines some original material with themes taken from earlier texts, especially the thirteenth-century Prose *Tristan*. The Tristan story also provided the material for Jean Maugin, who updated the legend to appeal to "modern" tastes, in his *Nouveau Tristan* (1554).

Arthurian texts fascinated certain French Renaissance writers, among them Rabelais. (*See* GARGANTUAN CHRONICLES.) Even though Rabelais did not write an Arthurian romance, that influence is apparent in some of his techniques and also in his specific references to Giglan, Gauvain, the Grail, Gallehault, Lancelot, Merlin, Perceforest, and Artus de Bretaigne. Other writers from the Renaissance, though not composing Arthurian works, give us an indication of the esteem in which the Arthurian legend was held. Ronsard, in the preface to the *Franciade*, suggested that Lancelot, Tristan, Gauvain, and Artus should serve as subjects for France's national epics, and du Bellay, in his *Deffense et Illustration de la langue françoyse,* speaks of "ces beaux vieulx romans Françoys, comme un *Lancelot,* un *Tristan*, ou autres." Arthurian texts were considered to be important more as national history or linguistic material than as literary creations. Nonetheless, they were valued by a good many writers of the time.

But tastes were changing. Montaigne included *Lancelot du Lac* in a class he called *tel fatras de livres* ("a hodgepodge of books") good only for the amusement of children; he insisted that he did not know even their titles, much less the works themselves. Although interest in Arthur never disappeared entirely from France, it diminished radically toward the end of the sixteenth century, and from that time forward the attitude of the French toward Arthurian subjects may seem to border on indifference. Of course, interest waned in England as well during the seventeenth and eighteenth centuries, but far less than in France, and the nineteenth-century rediscovery of Arthurian themes in France was a minor phenomenon by contrast to the Arthurian Revival in England. Postmedieval French Arthurian renderings amount to a small percentage of those available in English. Reasons for such a difference in national appeal are not immediately apparent. It will not suffice to suggest that there were other heroes in competition with Arthur, for either they themselves have stirred French imaginations less than he or, as in the case of Napoleon, they have fascinated readers and writers of only a particular and often quite limited period.

A partial explanation is provided by the French Renaissance's rejection of virtually everything "medieval," a view shared by the Neoclassical (seventeenth-century) authors and theorists, who sought classical and sometimes biblical models for their creations. Arthur's fall from favor was all but inevitable in such a climate. It should be noted, however, that this rejection was only "official," and popular tastes often ignored official opinion. The very condition of Arthurian literature at that time doubtless contributed to that rejection. The tales had by then been reworked, expanded, fused, divided, and further expanded to such a point that many of them had lost a good deal of their coherence and vigor; they virtually self-destructed. Arthur's decline, if inevitable, might nevertheless have been retarded had not France lacked one important element: a writer with the vision and talent necessary to capture the spirit of the legend, fix its form, and present it in a way that could fire the imagination of future ages. France had indeed had such writers during the twelfth and thirteenth centuries, with Chrétien de Troyes and the authors of the Vulgate, but no one with comparable ability was writing Arthurian literature two centuries later. As Jean Frappier has noted, "It was our misfortune not to have had a Thomas Malory at the end of the Middle Ages." In the more recent past, he might also have noted the absence of a Tennyson.

Whatever the cause, the seventeenth century saw a clear diminution of interest in Arthuriana. Although the Bibliothèque bleue presented many medieval works to the public, that series neglected many Arthurian texts. On the other hand, Arthurian romances were championed by Jehan Chapelain in his *La Lecture des vieux Romans* ("The Reading of Ancient Romances") and by Marc Vulson, Sieur de la Colombière in *Le Vray Théâtre d'Honneur et de Chevalerie, ou le miroir héroïque de la noblesse* ("The True Theater of Honor and Chivalry, or the Heroic Mirror of Nobility," 1648). Dedicating the book to Mazarin and intending it as a manual of instruction for the young Louis XIV, Vulson gives lessons of nobility and chivalric procedure by recounting events of the Arthurian story, in which Arthur, Guenevere, Morgan, and a number of the knights of the Round Table are presented briefly.

The seventeenth century gave us a number of original Arthurian works that, as had often been the case during the Middle Ages, focused far more on other characters than on Arthur. Merlin, for example, became a popular figure in seventeenth-century French theater and ballet. The influence of Cervantes is apparent in such writings, some of which adopt or adapt his title. In 1640, Guérin de Bouscal entitled his play with ballet *Don Quichot de la Manche*, a work that contributed, as did most of these Merlin pieces, to the decline of the sorcerer's reputation. Mlle Béjart reworked Bouscal's text, and her *Don Quichot ou les Enchantements de Merlin* ("Don Quixote or the Enchantments of Merlin") was presented by Molière's troupe in 1660. The year 1671 saw the composition of Rosidor's *Les Amours de Merlin*, a comedy in one act, and the Comédie Française in 1687 presented

Merlin peintre ("Merlin the Painter"), which was probably written by Thuellerie. In 1690, Dancourt presented *Merlin déserteur*, whose author he may also be, and Jacques Siret (known as Raisin l'aîné) wrote *Merlin Gascon*. Dating also from the mid-seventeenth century (ca. 1643), but not so specifically dealing with Merlin, is *Le Libraire du Pont-Neuf ou les romans* ("The Pont-Neuf Bookseller, or The Romances"), a ballet featuring "les Chavaliers de la Table-Ronde."

The following century saw a number of popularizations of Arthurian legend, of generally unremarkable quality. The Marquis de Paulmy d'Argenson made serveral romances known through summaries he published in *Mélanges tirés d'une grande bibliothèque* ("A Miscellany from a Great Library"). La Curne de Sainte-Palaye (1697–1781) was among the more successful disseminators of the Arthurian material, insisting in a series of papers that it was a valuable source of historical information. Not unexpectedly, authors who prepared adaptations or original compositions generally altered the tone and themes of their predecessors to make them correspond to contemporary tastes. For example, Le Comte de la Vergue de Tressan, in *Extraits de romans de chevalerie* ("Excerpts of Romances of Chivalry"), transformed the story of Tristan and Isolde from a tale of passion and tragedy into simple pastoral. The Bibliothèque universelle des romans (1775–89), in which Tressan's work appeared, published versions of numerous medieval works, including some of Chrétien de Troyes's romances.

Some significant treatments of Arthurian subjects throughout the nineteenth century came from writers who now are little more than historical footnotes. For example, in 1812 the Baron Creuzé de Lesser presented a modern French verse rendering of *Les Chevaliers de la Table Ronde*, a little-known work that nonetheless holds considerable interest. M.F. Marchangy's lengthy prose composition *La Gaule poétique* (1813–17) attained great popularity during its day, though it largely neglects Arthur in favor of Charlemagne.

A number of far less obscure nineteenth-century authors were inspired by Arthur. Not surprisingly, the Symbolist poets and their precursors adopted Arthurian themes. Maeterlinck, Verlaine, Laforgue, and others dealt ostensibly with medieval, including Arthurian, materials, but in fact their immediate source of inspiration was less often medieval than modern—Tennyson or Wagner, for example. The lyric poets of the time drew heavily from Wagner, composing pseudo-Arthurian poems either inspired by the operas or written in praise of the composer and publishing them in such journals as *La Revue Wagnérienne* (founded 1885) and *Le Saint-Graal* (1892). Poets like Gabriel Mourey (1865–1943), Stuart Merrill (1863–1915), Edouard Dujardin (1861–1949), Jean Ajalbert (1863–1947), and Paul Verlaine (1844–1896) devoted texts to Parsifal, Lohengrin, and Tristan and Isolde, as well as to "Hommage à Wagner." In *Sagesse*, Verlaine, the best known of the group, had presented his own imprisonment in terms of Arthurian themes; he also composed a *Parsifal* sonnet now known primarily because T.S. Eliot included a line from it in *The Waste Land*: "Et, ô ces voix d'enfants chantant dans la coupole!" ("And ô those children's voices, singing in the dome!").

Joséphin Péladan (1859–1918), in *La Queste du Graal* (1892), collected lyrical excerpts from his novels and dedicated the volume to Wagner; he also included a section devoted to Parsifal in *Le Secret des troubadours* (1906) and used Arthurian material in an 1892 play entitled *Le Mystère du Graal* ("The Mystery of the Grail"). Other authors inspired by Wagnerian themes are Edouard Schuré (1841–1929), who composed a drama on *Merlin l'enchanteur*, and the Count Villiers de L'Isle-Adam (1838–1889), who included characters from *Parsifal* and a transposition of the *Liebestod* from *Tristan und Isolde* in his poetic drama *Axel*. Jules Laforgue (1860–1887) used his *Lohengrin, fils de Parsifal* ("Lohengrin, Son of Parsifal," 1886) as a vehicle to present a satirical view of love and marriage.

A good many French writers used the Arthurian legend for eccentric personal or political ends. A prominent

34. "The Death of Elaine," illustration for Victorin de Joncières's lyric drama *Lancelot* (Paris: Delay, 1900). (Courtesy of The Newberry Library, Chicago.)

example is Edgar Quinet (1803–1875), who in his 900-page epic *Merlin l'enchanteur* (1860) exploited Arthuriana to lament France's dispirited and decadent state and to provide a vehicle for his attacks on Louis-Napoleon. He took Merlin as a symbol of the French spirit and nation and also as an incarnation of Quinet himself, whose exile was reflected in that of the enchanter. Similarly, Victor de Laprade (1812–1883) used his *La Tour d'ivoire* ("The Ivory Tower," 1865) to provide an attack on the empire.

Throughout this period, as indeed since the sixteenth century, the interest in Arthurian literature in France was fostered as much by the popularizing efforts of scholars and editors as by the original work of poets, novelists, and dramatists. Hersart de La Villemarqué published *Les Romans de la Table Ronde et les contes des anciens Bretons* ("The Romances of the Round Table and the Tales of the Ancient Bretons," 1842) and *Myrdhinn ou l'enchanteur Merlin, son histoire, ses oeuvres, son influence* ("Myrdhinn or Merlin the Magician, His History, Works, and Influence," 1862), and from 1868 to 1877 Paulin Paris prepared five volumes of *Les Romans de la Table Ronde*, adapted into modern French. Although Paris's work influenced modern notions of the Middle Ages and its literature, it appears to have met with limited popular success.

The situation is radically different with Joseph Bédier. At the turn of the century, Bédier presented what has now established itself as the "standard" version of the Tristan story. *Le Roman de Tristan et Iseut* has gone through hundreds of editions and has been translated into a number of languages. Bédier's work has served in fact as one of the primary sources of inspiration for much of the French Arthurian literature of the twentieth century. His closest rival in that regard is Wagner, with Tennyson, the Pre-Raphaelites, and occasionally Malory also exercising significant literary influence.

Several other works, especially dramas, were based on the Tristan legend during the last years of the nineteenth century and the early part of the twentieth. Most are of little more than historical interest. Prior to Bédier's publication, Armand Silvestre's *Tristan de Léonis* was seen briefly at the Comédie-Française in 1897. *La Tragédie de Tristan et Iseult* of Stéphane-Georges de Bouhélier-Lepelletier, better known as Saint-Georges de Bouhélier (1876–1947), had a brief run in Paris in 1923. Six years later, a dramatic version of *Tristan et Iseut*, credited to Bédier himself and to Louis Artus, with music by Paul Ladmirault, received lavish critical praise. Gabriel Mourey, mentioned above, was inspired by Bédier's original *Tristan* to make detailed plans with Claude Debussy for a Tristan opera. Unfortunately, they never completed the work, and only a few measures remain of the music.

Although the appeal of Arthur for the twentieth century has been, as was suggested above, far weaker in France than in England or the United States, the legend has continued to attract a good deal of attention. *Les Romans de la Table Ronde* is the collective title given to two modernized adaptations of French Arthurian materials, by Jacques Boulenger (4 vols., 1922) and Pierre D'Espezel (4 vols., 1960). Xavier de Langlais (1906–1975) offered a retelling of the full Arthurian story in his five-volume *Le Roman du Roi Arthur* (completed in 1971), adapting Old French texts and adding material from Celtic, German, and other sources. In addition, there have been reconstructions and other semipopular renderings of Arthurian texts, especially of Tristan romances, as well as modern French translations of many medieval romances, including those of Chrétien de Troyes.

A certain number of major twentieth-century authors, most notably Guillaume Apollinaire (1880–1918) and Jean Cocteau (1889–1963), have been attracted to Arthurian themes but, instead of retelling or recreating them, have used them for their metaphorical value. For example, in *L'Enchanteur pourrissant* ("The Putrescent Magician," 1904) Apollinaire exploited the traditionally demonic aspects of Merlin, whom he presents as an antichrist. The work presents the declaimed sentiments of characters gathered around the decaying corpse of Merlin. Some critics have seen *L'Enchanteur pourrissant*, a kind of "antigospel" that parodies scripture, as a violent attack on Christianity itself.

Cocteau used Arthurian material successfully in drama and film. His play *Les Chevaliers de la Table Ronde* ("The Knights of the Round Table," 1937; original title *Blancharmure*, "Whitearmor") contrasts the "'intoxication" of Merlin's spells with Galahad's liberating efforts—or detoxification, since the work apparently offers a metaphor for Cocteau's own opium addiction. Cocteau's 1943 screenplay *L'Éternel Retour* ("The Eternal Return"), which was filmed by Jean Delannoy and featured music by Georges Auric, transposed the Tristan and Isolde legend into a modern setting.

The Grail story and quest attracted René Guénon (1886–1951), whose *Le Roi du monde* ("The King of the World," 1925) is a full "history" of the Grail, from its origin in the emerald that fell from Lucifer's forehead. Julien Gracq recast both the Parsifal legend, in *Au Château d'Argol* ("The Castle of Argol," 1949), and the story of Perceval and the Fisher King, in his 1949 drama *Le Roi Pêcheur* ("The Fisher King").

Lancelot was the subject of the ambitious and successful *Le Chevalier de neige* ("The Snow Knight"), by Boris Vian (1920–1959), whose source was Jacques Boulenger's modernization of the Vulgate Cycle. A drama of epic proportions, presented in 1953 and then made into a three-act opera in 1957, *Le Chevalier de neige* treats the story of Lancelot and Guenevere, from the knight's first arrival at court until the death of both of them and the departure of the wounded King Arthur for Avalon. Georges Delerue composed the music for the opera, as well as songs and dances for the play.

Although it is not at all unusual for writers to update the Arthurian legend, as Cocteau did in *L'Éternel Retour*, the most striking example of such translation may well be provided by Pierre Benoit (1886–1962), in his 1957 novel

Montsalvat, in which the Grail quest occurs in occupied France.

The later 1970s and the 1980s have seen a quickening of interest in Arthurian subjects. Théophile Briant, Romain Weingarten, and René Barjavel published novels taking Merlin as their central focus. Briant's 1975 *Le Testament de Merlin* ("Merlin's Testament") is an imaginative recreation of the Merlin story as preamble to the presentation of an esoteric philosophy. Weingarten's *Le Roman de la Table Ronde, ou le livre de Blaise* ("The Romance of the Round Table, or the Book of Blaise," 1983) uses a method of interlace reminiscent of medieval procedures to tell much of the Arthurian story. Barjavel's 1984 *L'Enchanteur* ("The Magician") is perhaps the best of the recent Arthurian novels, offering a deft mixture of tones, from the expression of lofty sentiments concerning the Grail quest to the eroticism, and frequent frustration, of Merlin's relationship with Viviane, and to a taste for linguistic playfulness and wit.

Jacques Roubaud returned Arthur to the center of attention in his 1983 *Le Roi Arthur au temps des chevaliers et des enchanteurs* ("King Arthur in the Time of Knights and Magicians"), in which he presents Arthur's forebears and the earlier parts of the King's own career. With Florence Delay, Roubaud is also the author of *Graal Théâtre*, a project begun in 1977 and expected to run to ten volumes.

In addition to specifically Arthurian texts, French writers have frequently produced works in which the Arthurian element is elusive or questionable. Often, there is little more than a name or series of images, or perhaps the conventions of a quest, to generate Arthurian resonances. For example, the title of André Gide's *Voyage d'Urien* ("The Voyage of Urien," 1892) has Arthurian connotations, Urien being traditionally the father of Yvain. However, Gide's work, while announcing a voyage, is instead an "anti-voyage," a fact indicated by the pun in the title: *Voyage d'Urien* or *Voyage du rien* ("Voyage of Nothing"). Although Gide gives Arthurian or pseudo-Arthurian names to some characters other than Urien—Morgain, Eric, Agloval—these characters do not necessarily have their usual Arthurian identities; beyond the names and vaguely developed conventions of a quest, the work is not really "Arthurian" at all.

Like Gide's title, that of Robert Pinget's 1955 novel *Graal Flibuste* (definitive edition 1966) implies an Arthurian connection, but apart from that title ("Grail" + "Piracy"), which is the name of the monarch of a bizarre wasteland, the novel offers only a strange parody of a quest, with no beginning, ending, or purpose. Moreover, no Grail is seen, much less achieved. The novel is an antiquest that is hardly more Arthurian than Gide's.

A final example is a story by Michel Tournier, whose Arthurian interests are undeniable, as witness his preface to Pierre Champion's modern French version of *Tristan et Iseut* (1979). Tournier's "Tristan Vox," a story included in *Coq de bruyère* (1978), is Arthurian only in that the main character, a radio announcer, takes the name Tristan only to begin receiving love letters from a woman who signs herself "Isolde." Although such compositions as those of Gide, Pinget, and Tournier are at best marginally Arthurian, they demonstrate clearly that the stories of Arthur, Tristan, and Merlin have consistently exerted an influence on French letters out of proportion to the simple number of texts that are included in the usual discussion of modern French Arthurian literature. (*See also* French Chivalric Romances, Eighteenth and Nineteenth Centuries; French Epic, Nineteenth Century; French Symbolism; Gargantuan Chronicles; Second Empire.) [NJL]

Barber, Richard. *King Arthur in Legend and History*. London: Sphere, 1973.

Brinkley, Roberta F. *Arthurian Legend in the Seventeenth Century*. Baltimore: Johns Hopkins Press, 1932.

Dakyns, Janine R. *The Middle Ages in French Literature, 1850–1900*. London: Oxford University Press, 1973.

Lacy, Norris J., and Geoffrey Ashe. *The Arthurian Handbook*. New York: Garland, 1988, pp. 153–62.

Pickford, Cedric E. "The Maturity of the Arthurian Prose Romances," *Bibliographical Bulletin of the International Arthurian Society*, 34 (1982), 197–206.

Reid, Margaret Jane. *The Arthurian Legend: Comparison of Treatment in Modern and Mediaeval Literature; A Study in the Literary Value of Myth and Legend*. Edinburgh: Oliver and Boyd, [1938].

FRENCH CHIVALRIC ROMANCES, EIGHTEENTH AND NINETEENTH CENTURIES, were primarily extracts and adaptations of the prose Vulgate Cycle of medieval Arthurian literature.

The eighteenth century was characterized by the stirrings of an interest in the Middle Ages, but attitudes toward the period were ambivalent. Voltaire saw chivalry as a "counterweight to the general savagery of the customs" of the Middle Ages (*Essai sur les moeurs*). Scholars and historiographers of the Enlightenment began to study medieval historical and literary texts as a means of understanding that culture. One of the most influential of these scholars was La Curne de Sainte-Palaye (1697–1781), a member and director of the Académie des Inscriptions, a center for historical and archaeological research. A student of Old French and Old Provençal, as well as a collector and collator of manuscripts, Sainte-Palaye in 1743 gave a paper before the Académie, "Mémoire concernant la lecture des anciens romans de chevalerie." He justified the utility of reading chivalric romances because they conveyed information concerning medieval history, genealogy, geography, feudal duties, and customs. This paper served as an introduction to five other papers between 1746 and 1753: "Mémoires sur l'ancienne chevalerie considérée comme un établissement politique et militaire," published first by the Académie and then separately in 1759, 1781, and 1826 (in an edition by Charles Nodier). This work was enormously influential in exciting interest in chivalry in western Europe. Voltaire's remark, cited above, reflects this interest. The "Mémoires" were translated into English in 1784 and into German from 1789 to 1791. If for Sainte-Palaye chivalry was a coherent system created by the early monarchy, the real importance of his work was its appeal to a changing sensibility in France and western Europe. Chivalry and chivalric romances were of interest, not for scholarly reasons first of all, but because the popular imagination was increasingly attracted to primitivism, the gothic, sentimentalism, and sensibility.

The appetite and habits of the general reading public reveal these new tastes. Such romances as the seventeenth-century *L'Astrée* and translations of Ariosto, Boiardo, and Tasso continued to be popular. Readers liked popular versions of late-medieval or pseudo-medieval romances, often connecting chivalry with gallantry. The manuscript source of a particular romance did not matter to the general public, although some old texts began to appear in print. Late-medieval Arthurian material, *Amadis of Gaul*, and adaptations of *chansons de geste* all constituted "romances."

Arthur himself never captured the hearts of the reading public in the way that Charlemagne did. Nevertheless, there was a considerable vogue in the later eighteenth and in the nineteenth centuries for extracts and adaptations of Arthurian material, primarily from the prose Vulgate Cycle; these emphasized the storyline in a simple style. Chapbooks, sold by *colporteurs* in the provinces, were available in the provinces in the Bibliothèque bleue series, which included *Artus de Bretagne*, *Lancelot du Lac*, and *La Reine Genièvre*. The wealthier subscribed to the Bibliothèque universelle des romans (1775–89), edited by the Marquis de Palmy and later by J.F. Bastide; the Comte de Tressan also served on the editorial committee. The library of Palmy included fourteenth- and fifteenth-century manuscripts and early books that were used for the extracts published in the Bibliothèque; Sainte-Palaye also furnished material from his library. Palmy published extracts of the *Lancelot du Lac*, *Histoire du Saint Gréal*, *Roman du Roi Artus*, *Roman de Merlin*, and *Perceval le Gallois*. From the library of Sainte-Palaye, the Bibliothèque published versions of the *romans* of Chrétien de Troyes, including the *Aventures du chevalier Eric et de la belle Enide*, *Chevalier au lion*, and *Chevalier à la charette*. The Comte de Tressan claimed that "all the old romances of the Round Table, drawn by the Bretons from the old and fabulous chronicles of Melkin and Tézelin, were written in Latin by Rusticien de Puise" and were translated during the reign of Philippe Auguste ("Discours Préliminaire sur les romans français").

The popularity of these versions of Arthurian romances, along with the Tristan and Amadis stories, continued in the nineteenth century, even after *colportage* was outlawed early in the Second Empire. The Nouvelle Bibliothèque bleue, edited by le Roux de Lincy, appeared in 1842, and the Bibliothèque bleue, edited by Delvau, reprinted thirty chapbooks in three volumes (1859–60); Delvau included the stories *Lancelot du Lac* and *La Reine Genièvre*.

Interest in Breton material was aroused when poetic and prose versions of folk material began to appear. La Villemarqué, for example, published his *Contes populaires des anciens Bretons, précédés d'un Essai sur l'origine des épopées chevaleresques de la Table Ronde* in 1842, and by 1860 a third, enlarged, edition had appeared with the title *Les Romans de la Table Ronde et les contes des anciens Bretons*.

Paulin Paris recognized this continuous popular interest in the Arthurian romance, but, representing the emergence of modern medieval scholarship, he wished to base his versions on medieval texts. His prose version of this material appeared in five volumes between 1868 and 1877 as *Les Romans de la Table Ronde mis en nouveau langage*. Paris claimed to be the only person of his time to have read all the romances "of the cycle of Arthur." His version begins with Merlin and Arthur and ends with the adventures of "Mordret." Paris gave precedence over the romances of Chrétien to the "primordial" Arthurian cycle, which he ordered as follows: *Joseph d'Arimathie et Merlin* (Robert de Boron); *Continuations du Merlin* (*Le Livre d'Artus, Gauvain, Perceval*); *Lancelot du Lac*; *La Mort d'Artus*; *Tristan*, *Le Saint-Graal, La Quête du Saint-Graal, les dernières parties du Lancelot* (Vulgate). Paris's version, while more satisfying than the popular versions that preceded it, still owes its essential narrative form to the Vulgate Cycle. [PAW]

Estève, Edmond. "Le Moyen Âge dans la littérature du XVIIIe siècle." *Revue de l'Université de Bruxelles*, 29 (1923–24), 353–82.

Gossman, Lionel. *Medievalism and the Ideologies of the Enlightenment: The World and Work of La Curne de Sainte-Palaye*. Baltimore: Johns Hopkins University Press, 1969.

FRENCH EPIC, NINETEENTH CENTURY.

Writers of the nineteenth century were driven by the desire to write epics, a carryover of the classical notion that the epic was the "highest" genre. If we enlarge the definition of the epic to include works in both prose and poetry of national or universal scope, a continuous epic tradition can be traced in nineteenth-century France. During the empire and Restoration, numerous epics on historical and heroic themes in the classical tradition were written, of which several concerned Charlemagne, such as d'Arlincourt's *Charlemagne ou la Caroléide* (1810) and Millevoye's *Charlemagne* (1812). Arthurian material received scant attention because of the political and national concerns of the period. An exception is Auguste François Creuzé de Lesser's poem of twenty cantos of decasyllables *Les Chevaliers de la Table Ronde* (1811), later called *La Table Ronde*. It was followed by *Amadis de Gaule* (1813) and *Roland* (1815). By 1839, *La Table Ronde* had appeared in its sixth edition, this time in a volume with the other two poems, *La Chevalerie, ou les histoires du moyen âge . . . Poèmes sur les trois grandes familles de la chevalerie romanesque*. Creuzé de Lesser described the chivalric stories as a "second mythology after that of the Greeks." Lancelot and Tristan are "the most brilliant heroes of the Round Table," while Guinevere and Yseult are "veritable Helens." In sythesizing the Arthurian material, Creuzé de Lesser claimed that the search for the Holy Grail was the unifying element of the poem. Actually, this epic and the two that followed it were a reproduction in verse form of the popular versions of chivalric romances sold to the public in chapbooks in the late eighteenth century. *La Table Ronde* begins with the history of Arthur and Merlin, follows the stories of Lancelot and Tristan, includes the story of Perceval and the Grail (the Fisher King is in Fingal's Cave!), and concludes with the death of Arthur and the disappearance of the Grail.

La Gaule poétique, by M.F. Marchangy (1813–17), was a series of prose narratives in eight volumes of the history of France as related to poetry, the arts, and "eloquence." Although not strictly an epic, *La Gaule poétique* deserves mention because of its great popularity. Marchangy gives much attention to Charlemagne but almost ignores Arthur. The section "On Chivalry" owes much to eighteenth-century sources, particularly La Curne de Sainte-Palaye. There, Marchangy mentions Arthur in connection with the heraldic arms of three knights of the Round Table: "Romance writers, in their fabulous stories, attribute the origin of this order to the King Arthur of Brittany who perhaps never existed."

In the so-called "humanitarian epics" that emerged from the new social and political consciousness of the century, the Arthurian legend figures in only one work, Edgar Quinet's *Merlin l'enchanteur* (1860), a prolix prose epic in twenty-four books. In the preface, Quinet claims that his subject is "the legend of the human soul up to death, and beyond death." Trying to reconcile all legends into a single one, Quinet chose the figure of Merlin, "the soul of French tradition." Quinet's narrative has nothing to do with the Arthurian literary tradition. His Merlin stands for the French spirit and for Quinet himself, who spent years in exile because of his opposition to the Second Empire of Louis-Napoleon. Contemporaries admired Quinet's book as a daring political allegory attacking Napoleon III. Merlin enchants Gaul, blesses the origins of the French nation (Arthur's chosen kingdom), and erects a Round Table of stone. He leaves the kingdom, performing exploits throughout Europe (which stand for the accomplishments of the French nation), only to return to find Arthur's kingdom in decline. Merlin then loses his power to enchant and withdraws into a kind of entombment representative of Quinet's own exile and the loss of French freedom. Eventually, the Satan of the poem is pardoned and Arthur and his kingdom are restored in spirit.

This nineteenth-century Arthurian epic material represents an obscure and curious footnote to the story of the role of Arthurian legend in French culture. (*See also* Second Empire.) [PAW]

Dakyns, Janine R. *The Middle Ages in French Literature, 1850–1900*. London: Oxford University Press, 1973.

Hunt, Herbert J. *The Epic in Nineteenth-Century France*. Oxford: Blackwell, 1941.

FRENCH SYMBOLISM. Symbolist poets of the 1880s and 1890s cultivated states of soul that they often chose to portray in a medieval guise. Their Middle Ages were nebulous and subjective in reaction against Parnassian precision and impersonality. Poems and plays were steeped in an atmosphere of immemorial time that can often loosely be called Arthurian: magic forests and towers, melancholy knights, palely loitering ladies, bedraggled banners, and defaced escutcheons. Their sources were scarcely ever directly medieval, though medieval studies had gathered momentum after the Franco-Prussian War, and from 1880 onward medieval literature was taught in secondary schools. The Symbolist Middle Ages derived from recent, and for the most part non-French, versions of the period. Tennyson, Poe, the Pre-Raphaelites, Wagner. Ludwig of Bavaria's Arthurian fantasies enthralled these poets, who preferred to see the past through the eyes of a modern mediator. Maurice Maeterlinck's Arthurian names were, he claimed, taken from Malory, but they were really adaptations or compounds of those in the *Idylls of the King*. An important precursor of the Symbolists was Paul Verlaine (1844–1896), who produced some fine poems, including the first two of the collection *Sagesse* (1881), in which medieval imagery is a vehicle for personal emotion. The moral climate in which the poet lived during his two years' imprisonment (1873–75) for wounding Rimbaud is translated into an Arthurian landscape that hauntingly dramatizes Verlaine's inner strife and remorse. His prison is transmuted into a magic castle in which he forges a new soul for himself. Tennyson's *Idylls* were an important source of inspiration for these poems. Another interesting work in which Arthurian material was used as a vehicle for complex modern sentiment is Jules Laforgue's *moralité légendaire* in prose, *Lohengrin, fils de Parsifal* (1886), a satire on contemporary love and marriage. Lohengrin arrives on his swan to rescue and marry Elsa, a disgraced Vestal Virgin. A burlesque honeymoon ensues, ending in Lohengrin's escape from the marriage bed when his pillow turns into the swan and carries him into outer space. There are undertones of astringent self-mockery in Verlaine's intense confessional seriousness; Laforgue fuses comic inventions with stinging irony; but most French poets around this time were thoroughgoing idealists rather than ironists, and for them Arthurian material was conducive to an atmosphere of soulful melancholy. It was fashionable to give literary magazines names like *Le Saint-Graal* (1892) and *Durendal* (1894). [JRD]

Verlaine, Paul. *Sagesse*, ed. V.P. Underwood. London: Zwemmer, 1944.

Bowden, M.M. *Tennyson in France*. Manchester: Manchester University Press, 1930.

Dakyns, Janine R. *The Middle Ages in French Literature, 1851–1900*. London: Oxford University Press, 1973.

Ramsey, Warren. *Jules Laforgue and the Ironic Inheritance*. New York: Oxford University Press, 1953.

FRERE, JOHN H. (1769–1846), English civil servant and author (writing under the pseudonym Whistlecraft) whose unfinished Arthurian burlesque in *ottava rima*, *The Monks and the Giants* (1817–18), was intended to "put a coat of varnish" on the story of King Arthur. Aside from Arthurian characters (a courteous Gawain, a restless and inventive Tristram, a Launcelot who is the best of British knights "except perhaps Lord Wellington in Spain") and traditional motifs (Christmas feast, loathly lady, distressed damsels), the material is largely original. In Cantos I and II, the knights' attack on the giants' stronghold succeeds not because of prowess but because the enemy has used stones from their protective wall to bombard the attackers. Cantos III and IV deal with an earlier event, the severance of good relations between the giants and the neighboring monks, "poor proficients in divinity," whose constant bell-ringing has "rous'd their irrational gigantic anger." Frere's object is to ridicule, by means of puns, slang, plebeian diction, pointless digression, and the citing of pseudo-authorities, the style of Italian chivalric romance. A second motive may be to criticize allegorically the British campaigns against Napoleon in Spain, events that had led to Frere's censure and removal from office. In writing *ottava rima* burlesque, Frere angled in the same waters as Byron; in Waller's words: "Byron caught the big fish, but Frere had shown him where to cast his line." [MAW]

Frere, John Hookham. *The Monks and the Giants*. London: Murray, 1821.

FROISSART, JEHAN (1337–after 1404), the greatest chronicler of the Hundred Years War, was also an important love poet and the author of the last French Arthurian verse romance, *Meliador*. Throughout his life, Froissart was in the service of various noble patrons. In 1361, he went to England in the entourage of Philippa of Hainaut, the queen of Edward III, and remained in her service until her death in 1369. During this period, he composed an early version of his *Meliador*, of which only fragments remain. Then, between 1383 and 1388, following the death of his patron Wenceslas of Brabant and wishing to restore an idealized chivalric "paradise lost," Froissart revised his romance, which, although incomplete at the end, nonetheless runs to 30,499 octosyllabic lines in manuscript Paris, B.N. f. fr. 12557, which preserves it for us.

The poem tells of a series of five tournaments arranged by Floree for the hand of her cousin Hermondine of Scotland. Knights come to England from all of western Europe to vie for Hermondine, but it is soon evident that she is destined for Meliador of Cornwall. Meliador's sister, Phenonee, is the second "prize" of the series of tournaments, and she is won by Agamanor of Normandy.

The poem is set in the early years of the kingdom of King Arthur, before the adventures of Gawain, Lancelot, Perceval, and Galahad. A direct link to Arthur's legend is afforded by the introduction of Agravain and Sagremore later in the romance, as well as by situating the final tournament at Camelot. The poem breaks off, however, before this tournament can be completed, but not before Agravain is able to woo and win Floree, the organizer of the tournaments.

Meliador is lengthy and repetitious but intricately interlaced and carefully organized. Like *Perceforest* from the same period, it presents new heroes and new adventures, and is not simply a reworking of previous romances. [WWK]

Froissart, Jean. *Meliador*, ed. A. Longnon. 3 vols. Paris: Firmin Didot, 1895–99.

Dembowski, Peter F. *Jean Froissart and His "Meliador": Context, Craft, and Sense*. Lexington, Ky.: French Forum, 1983.

FRUCTO DE LOS TIEMPOS ("Fruit of the Times"), a Spanish compilation of British history, including a summary of the Arthurian legend, was written in 1509 in behalf of Catherine of Aragon by her tutor, Rodrigo de Cuero. Bearing the full title *Historia de Inglaterra llamada Fructo de los tiempos* and followed by a *Relación de Ynglaterra, Gales, Escocia e Yrlando*, the work is a generally literal translation of the St. Albans Chronicle as first printed in 1497 by Wynkyn de Worde with the title *Cronycles of Englonde with the Fruyte of Tymes*, to which a *Descrypcyon of Englonde* was added in the 1502 printing, the latter corresponding to Cuero's appended *Relación*. Two manuscripts of the Spanish text survive: Real Biblioteca de El Escorial X.ii.20, an apparent autograph copy of which only the *Relación* section has been edited; and Salamanca, Biblioteca Universitaria 1850, the latter preserving a portion of the Arthurian story now missing in MS X.ii.20. [HLS]

Malfatti, C.V., ed. *The Descrypcyon of Englonde, An Addition to St. Albans Chronicle First Printed by Wynkyn de Worde, London 1502, Facsimile of British Museum G 5997; Transcription of the Abridged Spanish Translation Relacion de Ynglaterra, Gales, Escocia e Yrlanda por Rodrigo de Cuero, Londres 1509, Escorial MSS. X-II-20.* Barcelona: Sociedad Alianza de Artes Gráficas, 1973.

FRY, CHRISTOPHER, British verse-playwright, was the author of *Thor, with Angels*, prepared for performance in Canterbury Cathedral in 1948. Merlin is the seer who paid for his immortality with his soul. He foretells, and is part of, the reawakening Christian spirit in England under Ethelred. He hints at Joseph's coming to England with the Grail and mentions the miracle at Glastonbury. [HT]

Fry, Christopher. *Thor, with Angels*. London: Oxford University Press, 1949.

FUETRER, ULRICH, German painter and poet generally believed to have been born in the Bavarian town of Landshut in the early fifteenth century. This assumption is given credibility through Fuetrer's statement in his *Bayerische Chronik* that his father lost several thousand *guldin* during the Landshut rebellion of 1410. Fuetrer himself is first mentioned in Munich municipal receipts from 1453 in his capacity as a painter. From 1482 to 1496, he appears in the Munich municipal tax records as owning a house. It is assumed that he died before October 1496, since his wife, who was then listed as the house's owner, was put in the pillory and subsequently banished from Munich.

As a painter, Fuetrer was more a craftsman than an independent artist. In 1465, he painted the Andreaskapelle of the monastery in Tegernsee. From 1476 to 1478, he worked on the interior decoration of the old City Hall in Munich, and from 1486 to 1495 he was active at the court of Duke Albrecht IV. From this latter period, his decoration of Schloss Grünwald is particularly noteworthy. Fuetrer was a highly regarded member of his guild and held the honorary office of one of the "Four."

Both as a painter and as a writer, Fuetrer must be regarded more as a skilled and conscientious adapter and reviser than as an independent poet of genius. All of his works were composed in connection with the Wittelsbach court in Munich, and all are dedicated to Duke Albrecht IV. Fuetrer probably gained access to the court through the mediation of Jakob Püterich von Reichertshausen (d. 1469); there, he managed to cultivate a select circle of friends and patrons who provided him with solid support and aided him in gaining and maintaining the esteem of the ducal court. It is worthy of note that, although Fuetrer spent the last decade of his life at the court as an occasional painter (1486–95), he was more highly regarded for his poetic talents, in spite of the fact that he had completed most of his literary works before this time. His works include *Prosaroman von Lanzelot* ("Prosa-Lanzelot," ca. 1467), *Das Buch der Abenteuer I* (1473–78), *Die Bayerische Chronik* ("Bavarian Chronicle," 1478–81), *Das Buch der Abenteuer II* (finished before 1484), and *Der strophische Lanzelot* ("Stanzaic Lanzelot," begun before 1484 and finished in 1487).

Fuetrer's *Prosaroman von Lanzelot* is an abridgment of the *Prosa-Lancelot* text found in the *P* manuscript and the *k* fragment. Aside from a few minor interpolations, Fuetrer's work remains true to the original.

In the first book of *Das Buch der Abenteuer* ("The Book of Adventures") Fuetrer uses Albrecht's *Der jüngere Titurel* as the framework within which he recounts the tales of Wolfram von Eschenbach's *Parzival*, Heinrich von dem Türlin's *Crône*, and *Lohengrin* as one continuous story. In addition, he interpolates a Trojan War narrative and the history of Merlin as more or less independent episodes. In the second book (so named by Fuetrer) are seven independent tales without a definite framework: *Floreis und Wigoleis*, *Seifrid de Ardemont*, *Meleranz*, *Iban*, *Persibein*, *Poytislier*, and *Flordimar*.

All of the stories in both books are adaptations of older works, although for some of Fuetrer's narratives it is at present impossible to determine which older texts or poets served as models. Fuetrer ascribes two, *Merlin* and *Seifrid de Ardemont*, to Albrecht von Scharfenberg, whose *oeuvre*, however, has not been transmitted.

In spite of the fact that Fuetrer worked from models, his achievement should not be belittled. He was extraordinarily well-read and he succeeded in blending the various Arthurian and Grail works into a cohesive whole. As one critic has put it, it seems as if Fuetrer read all available texts and then made a "card-index" of the characters, motifs, and adventures, which he then rearranged into one continuous story. Since Fuetrer leaves out all digressive episodes that may have appeared in his sources but that would not further the flow of the narrative, it is almost impossible to determine with any certainty which text was used for any specific part of his own work. The *Buch der Abenteuer* contains 5,644 *Titurel* strophes of seven lines apiece. It is Fuetrer's most important achievement as a writer and offers insight into the reception of medieval literature during the late Middle Ages and early Renaissance.

In the *Strophische Lanzelot*, Fuetrer revises his original *Prosaroman von Lanzelot* in order to bring the Lanzelot tale into harmony with the events described in his *Buch der*

Abenteuer. Only a few of the 5,700 *Titurel* strophes have been published.

Fuetrer is one of the more fascinating personalities of the late-medieval and early humanistic period, and through his poetic efforts one gains an appreciation of the literary interest of the Wittelsbach court at the beginning of the "modern" era. The time was doubtless gone when an audience could identify with the exploits of the Arthurian heroes, when the listeners or readers might be able to recognize lessons in tales that would have application to their own lives. Nonetheless, the stories of the Arthurian knights exercised a definite attraction on the courtly audiences toward the end of the fifteenth century, and they viewed this literature as part of their cultural heritage and therefore worthy of preservation, even if in a form and style more commensurate with their own tastes and outlook. [FGG]

Fuetrer, Ulrich. *Poytislier aus dem Buch der Abenteuer von Ulrich Fuetrer*, ed. Friederike Weber. Tübingen: Niemeyer, 1960.

———. *Persibein: Aus dem Buch der Abenteuer*, ed. Renate Munz. Tübingen: Niemeyer, 1964.

———. *Wigoleis*, ed. Heribert A. Hilgers. Tübingen: Niemeyer, 1975.

———. *Lannzilet (Aus dem "Buch der Abenteuer") Str. 1–1122*, ed. Karl-Eckhard Lenk. Tübingen: Niemeyer, 1989.

Buschinger, Danielle, and Wolfgang Spiewok. "Ulrich Füetrer—ein Hofdichter?" *Jahrbuch der Oswald von Wolkenstein Gesellschaft*, 4 (1986–87), 95–102.

Gottzmann, Carola L. *Artusdichtung*. Stuttgart: Metzler, 1989.

Kern, Peter. "Ulrich Füetrers 'Flordimar': Bearbeitung eines Artusromans des 13. Jahrhunderts?" *Zeitschrift für deutsche Philologie*, 107 (1988), 410–31.

FULLARTON, R(ALPH) MACLEOD, in *Merlin: A Dramatic Poem* (1890), applies Tennysonian morality—Sense at War with Soul—to the Merlin-Vivien material. Merlin, an Arthurian knight, possesses a magical ring that puts to sleep "Whomso the wearer will/So long the wearer please." Vivien's acquisition of the ring gives her power to overcome her enemies, including Merlin, whom she marries. Surprisingly, Morgan is a beneficent character who uses her crucifix to waken the hero from the first magic sleep but fails to save him from the rocky death that Merlin accepts as God's will. [MAW]

Fullarton, R. Macleod. *Merlin: A Dramatic Poem*. Edinburgh and London: Blackwood, 1890.

FULLER, JOHN G(RANT), broadened the comedy and softened Twain's satire in his dramatic adaptation of *A Connecticut Yankee in King Arthur's Court* (1941). The Yankee is a young engineer, transported to Camelot by an electric shock, who chooses to reject modern life and to return to Arthur's world at the end of the play. [DN]

Fuller, John G. *A Connecticut Yankee in King Arthur's Court*. Boston: Baker, 1941.

FURST, CLYDE B. (1873–1931), American author of *Merlin*, a blank-verse poem in which Merlin is described as rising above the conflict between "the saint and fiend within his veins." He devotes his life to serving church and state and makes medicine, education, and art available to the people. [ACL]

Furst, Clyde B. *Merlin*. New York, 1930.

FUSELI, HENRY (1741–1825). Johann or Hans-Heinrich Füssli or Fuessli, known as Henry Fuseli after he moved to England, was born in Zurich. A member of the Royal Academy and famous for his illustrations for the works of Shakespeare and Milton, Fuseli also created paintings and drawings inspired by themes from Spenser's *The Faerie Queene*. Some of these Arthurian illustrations were engraved by P. Tomkins for Macklin's *Poet's Gallery* (e.g., *The Dream of Prince Arthur*, 1788). [MS]

g

GABONS SAGA OK VIGOLES, or *Saga af Viegoleis með Gullhiólit* ("Saga of Viegoleis with the Golden Wheel"), is the title given to two different Icelandic translations of the Danish chapbook *Her Viegoleis med Guld Hiulet*, which was first published in 1656. The Danish chapbook is in turn a translation of the fifteenth-century German prose redaction of Wirnt von Grafenberg's *Wigalois*. Shortly after the publication of the Danish chapbook in 1656, Magnús Jónsson í Vigur (b. 1637) translated the work into Icelandic, probably between the years 1656 and 1683. His translation is preserved in two late seventeenth-century manuscripts.

A different, anonymous, translation of the Danish chapbook is extant in only one eighteenth-century manuscript. Since the Danish chapbook was printed several times during the first half of the eighteenth century, the source of the second Icelandic translation was presumably one of the eighteenth-century editions. [MEK]

Nyerup, Rasmus. *Almindelig Morskabslæsning i Danmark og Norge igjiennem Aarhundreder*. Copenhagen: Seidelin, 1816, pp. 125–33.

Seelow, Hubert. *Die isländischen Übersetzungen der deutschen Volksbücher*. Reykjavik: Stofnun Árna Magnússonar, 1989.

GAELIC BALLADS. A limited but significant number of Gaelic ballads contain explicit references to Arthurian characters or provide substantial thematic correspondences to Arthurian romances. Although versions of some ballads have been recorded in modern oral tradition, the subject matter does not differ from that found in medieval Arthurian literature.

"Am Bròn Binn" ("The Sweet Sorrow"), found only in Scottish oral versions, recounts the tale of a beautiful girl seen in a dream and Sir Bhalbha's (or Fios-falaich's or the King of the Britains') quest to find her. John L. Campbell discovered contemporary examples in oral tradition in the Hebrides, and researchers from the School of Scottish Studies found others in Barra and on mainland Scotland. Most versions follow essentially the same storyline. A knight or king dreams of a beautiful woman and determines to find her. He follows his quest for seven weeks before he finds her imprisoned by a powerful *Fear Mór* ("great man"). Through a ruse and the seductive power of her music, she manages to lull the *Fear Mór* to sleep, whereupon she kills him and joins her questing knight. Critics have identified the tale as one of the Sir Gawain stories.

"Am Bròn Binn" underwent some changes during oral transmission, resulting in several versions that substantially alter the sensibility of the original. "Bàs Artuir" ("The Death of Arthur"), first recorded ca. 1775, transforms the story into the tale of an evil woman who lures the questing hero to his death. As the title indicates, Gawain of "Am Bròn Binn" has now become King Arthur, and the focus has shifted from the quest to the death by deceit of the hero. In later versions of "Bàs Artuir," an episode of the killing of a giant is integrated into the plot along with a bizarre love triangle. Gawain/Arthur, having killed the giant who has held the beautiful woman captive, is rejected as the woman leaps into the grave of her slain captor and immediately dies herself. We are left with the clear impression that her "rescue" was not at all to her liking.

"Laoidh an Bhruit" ("The Lay of the Mantle") is first recorded in the sixteenth-century Book of the Dean of Lismore (Scotland) and the early seventeenth-century Duanaire Finn (Ireland). It recounts how Fionn, his followers, their ladies, and a serving girl are boasting of their high morals when a girl appears wearing a wonderful mantle with special properties—it will cover only those who are completely faithful. The presence of this familiar chastity test, related to those in the *Mantel mautaillié*, the *Lai du cor*, and other French and Celtic texts, is considered by some scholars to be significant evidence concerning the Celtic origins of the Arthurian story.

Finally, among the Gaelic ballads of the Arthurian tradition is "Laoidh an Amadáin Mhóir" ("The Lay of the Great Fool"). Found in both published collections and oral circulation, in Scotland and Ireland, it recounts the test of the Great Fool upon his reaching adulthood. Its storyline is reminiscent of Fair Unknown romances and some elements of *Sir Gawain and the Green Knight*. The date of composition is not known, though some time in the late sixteenth or early seventeenth century seems most probable. [BJW]

Collinson, Francis. *The Traditional and National Music of Scotland*. London: Routledge and Kegan Paul, 1966.

Gillies, William. "Arthur in Gaelic Tradition." *Cambridge Medieval Celtic Studies*, 2 (Winter 1981), 47–72.

GAHERIS (Guirres, Generez, Gaheret, Guinrez), in the First Continuation of Chrétien's *Perceval*, Gawain's brother, who suffers an unexplained shameful incident and later avenges the knight Brangemuer, the son of a mortal and a fairy. In some romances, Gaheris and Gareth are the same character. Malory tells us that Gaheris is the son of Lot and Morgause and the brother of Gawain, and that he kills his mother when he finds her with Lamorak, Pellinore's son, because Pellinore had killed his father. Later, Gaheris, along with his brothers Gawain, Agravain, and Mordred, slays Lamorak. He meets his own death when Lancelot rescues Guenevere from the stake. The Vulgate Cycle portrays Gaheris as a good knight who never approved of his brother's plot to expose Guenevere and Lancelot's affair. T.H. White's *Once and Future King* further improves Gaheris's character, stating that Agravaine, not Gaheris, killed Morgause. [SW]

GAIMAR, GEFFREI, author of an Anglo-Norman adaptation, now lost, of Geoffrey of Monmouth's *Historia Regum Britanniae*. To his adaptation, done in the 1140s, he appended a history of England through the reign of William Rufus; the sequel refers to his version of the *Historia*, but the latter has been replaced in the manuscripts by that of Wace. [NJL]

GALAHAD (Galaad), the son of Lancelot and the perfect Grail knight. In the Vulgate Cycle, Lancelot, whose baptismal name was also Galahad, fathers the future hero while lying with Pelles's daughter but—under the influence of a potion—thinking her to be Guenevere. Galahad's story is told primarily in the *Queste del Saint Graal*, where, having been knighted, he arrives at Arthur's court, following predictions, signs, and marvelous events, and passes the tests of the Perilous Seat and the Sword in the Stone. He is thus recognized as the future hero of the Grail quest. Later, he will heal the wounded king and will die in ecstasy after seeing directly the mystery of the Grail.

Galahad was the preordained hero of the quest, and we are told that he remained virgin throughout his life, thereby compensating for his impure conception. His physical beauty and his prowess are as evident as his moral perfection. Although details vary from text to text, his character and his role remain constant; Malory, for example, retains the French account virtually unaltered. In both, and in later tradition, Galahad is "the culmination," as Jean Frappier noted, "of the effort to fuse chivalry with religion." [NJL]

Lot-Borodine, Myrrha. "Christ-Chevalier: Galaad." In *De l'amour profane à l'amour sacré: études de psychologie sentimentale au Moyen Âge*. Paris: Nizet, 1961.

GALEHAUT (Galahalt), in the Vulgate Cycle, the Prince of the Lointaines ("Faraway") Isles, of Surluse, and of the Scillies. Galehaut is one of Arthur's earliest foes; he invades Arthur's kingdom when Arthur refuses to yield to him. Galehaut is also Lancelot's friend and confidant, who arranges Lancelot's first clandestine meeting with Guenevere. In turn, Guenevere serves as a go-between for Galehaut and her friend and confidante, the Lady of Malehaut. Because of his friendship with Lancelot, Galehaut hides Lancelot and Guenevere in Surluse when the False Guenevere temporarily usurps Guenevere's matrimonial claim. Later, when he is seriously ill and hears false rumors about Lancelot's death, Galehaut becomes so weakened and dismayed that he dies. Lancelot buries his friend not only in his castle, Joyous Guard, but also in his personal tomb. In Dante's *Inferno*, Galehaut is portrayed as a go-between for Paolo and Francesca; Boccaccio's *Decameron* has as its subtitle "Prencipe Galeotto," which has been variously interpreted. [SW]

GALLOWAY, CHRISTIAN F.J., wrote *The Exploits of Lancelot* (1924), a humorous account in pseudo-medieval prose of Lancelot's encounters with various damsels. The medieval setting is updated to include such amenities as telephones at Camelot. [EB]

Galloway, Christian F.J. *The Exploits of Lancelot*. London: Stockwell, 1924.

GAMES. The growth of interest in fantasy fiction during the past three decades has given rise to the development of role-playing games, such as *Dungeons & Dragons*. Some of these incorporate into their character lists figures from legend, including the Arthurian. Arthur and his best-known knights are used as warriors at the highest levels of play, while Merlin and Morgan le Fay are prominent among the magic-users. Individual adventure modules used in such games may also employ an Arthurian setting; for example, "The Pillar of Clinschor" (1983), written by Shari and Sam Lewis, sends a group of adventurers with Merlin to seize a castle from Clinschor and Morgan le Fay.

35. MS Paris, Bibliothèque Nationale, f.fr. 342, fol. 186: Lancelot Rescues Guenevere. (Paris, Bibliothèque Nationale.)

While Arthurian tradition is but a small component of most role-playing games, which draw upon folklore and legend from many lands, it comprises the entire setting in *Knights of the Round Table* (1978), designed by Phil Edgren, *Hidden Kingdom* (1983), designed by Jon McClenahan and Stanley Dokupil, and *King Arthur Pendragon* (1985), designed by Greg Stafford. This last, which achieved the greatest success, encourages characters to develop not only combat skills but also chivalrous qualities, such as loyalty and courtesy, and abilities like dancing and hunting, through a range of experiences similar to those one might encounter in the pages of medieval romance. It is supported by a series of adventure and information books, including *The King Arthur Companion*, by Phyllis Ann Karr. Based primarily upon Malory, this offers copious notes upon characters and places.

Stafford also designed *Prince Valiant, the Storytelling Game* (1989), based upon the comic strip created by Hal Foster. This combines the setting of fifth-century Europe with elements drawn from medieval romance. Frames from the comic strip are used to illustrate the rules, which have been simplified to make the game more accessible, while continuing to encourage the development of chivalrous, as well as warlike, skills.

Role-playing games have spread from North America to other countries, including France, where *La Table Ronde* has been designed by Anne Vétillard and produced by Jeux Descartes as part of their series Premières Légendes. Its purpose is to involve players in adventures set in the world of Arthurian romance. The basic game includes a rule book and a guidebook with information on both Arthurian legend and medieval society. It is supported by two adventure modules.

Arthurian legend has also provided the inspiration for board games, both general, as in Parker Brothers' battle game *Camelot*, and specific, as in *Knights of Camelot* (1980), by Glenn and Kenneth Rahman; *King Arthur and the Knights of the Round Table* (1988), by Matthew Hill et al.; *King Arthur's Knights* (1978); and *Merlin* (1980). This last pair were also designed by Greg Stafford: the object of the former is to prove oneself worthy of membership in the Round Table through a series of encounters, adventures, and quests; the latter reenacts a magical duel between Merlin and Morgan le Fay, both aided by their respective assistants. To fit the rules of play, the Arthurian characters have been simplified, but, even so, most of these board games remain complex.

From fantasy role games have recently developed solo fantasy gamebooks, which are often illustrated. The reader chooses among several courses of action at vital stages of the adventure, then turns to the appropriate section to discover the consequences. Among those that borrow Arthurian elements are Ellen Kushner's *Knights of the Round Table* (1988), in which younger readers undertake a series of adventures based upon those of Sir Gareth to prove themselves worthy of becoming knights of the Round Table, and J.H. Brennan's *Grail Quest I: The Castle of Darkness* (1984), where Merlin sends the reader off to rescue Guenevere from an enchanted fortress, though the perils encountered are the monsters and traps typical of role games rather than Arthurian tradition. Brennan continues this "Arthurian" format in subsequent gamebooks in the Grail Quest series, which are subtitled *The Den of Dragons*, *The Gateway of Doom*, *Voyage of Terror*, *Kingdom of Horror*, *Realm of Chaos*, *Tomb of Nightmares*, and *Legion of the Dead*. In Neil Randall's *Storm of Dust* (1987), a gamebook based upon the sword-and-sorcery world created in David Drake's *Dragon Lord*, the reader encounters the specter of Uther Pendragon among the trials posed by a quest for the Grail. [RHT]

Particularly since 1978, computer gamers have embraced fantasy and science-fiction themes, and many of the games developed for home computers have borrowed from Arthurian legend. There are three types of computer games: graphic adventures, text-only adventures, and war-game simulations. Arthurian themes have appeared in all of these.

Great Britain led the way for Arthurian computer games. The text adventure *The Quest for the Holy*

Grail resembles the film *Monty Python and the Holy Grail* more than the *Morte Darthur*; but another text-only game, *Grail*, follows the legends more closely. Two popular graphic adventures, *Avalon* and *The Dragontorc of Avalon*, deal with Merlin during the reign of Vortigern; and British gamers can rescue Guinevere from danger in another text game, *Cavelon*.

Arthurian computer games began to appear in America in 1982, beginning with two graphic adventures for the Atari system: *King Arthur's Heir* (Epyx) and Douglas Crockford's *Galahad and the Holy Grail* (Atari Program Exchange). In the former, the player must prevent a nuclear holocaust predicted by Merlin; he or she will then be named heir to Camelot. The latter, also a graphic adventure, includes references to Monty Python, though Crockford also summarizes the Grail legend, includes a limited bibliography and filmography, and precedes game play with a speech by Sir Gawain taken from Keith Baines's rendering of the *Morte Darthur*.

The game *Excalibur* by Chris Crawford, Larry Summers, and Valerie Atkinson (Atari Program Exchange, 1983) is of the war-game variety. The player assumes the persona of Arthur and must rule all aspects of his kingdom. *Excalibur* includes a sixty-three-page book that retells the legend. The game's wealth of detail offers the most complete vicarious experience of all the Arthurian games.

Two other computer games are text adventures: *Brimstone*, by James Paul (Brøderbund, 1986), and *The Holy Grail* (Hayden Software, 1986). *Brimstone* is of the new "electronic novel" genre of text adventures: more attention is paid to literary description, documentation, and ease of interaction with the computer, including a larger vocabulary. The only true Arthurian element, however, is Gawain's final encounter with the Green Knight. A lengthy hardcover book sets the scene for game play; the game is compatible with Apple, Commodore, IBM, and Atari systems. *The Holy Grail*, which confines itself to the Grail quest, is no longer available.

The computer-game industry is volatile. Of the American games mentioned here, only *Brimstone* and *Galahad and the Holy Grail* are readily available; *Excalibur* has limited availability through its designers. The best source for the older games is through computer-user groups or advertisements in computer magazines. Arthurian themes, however, will no doubt continue to appear in computer games, providing young people contact with Malory and the Arthurian legends that they may not otherwise acquire. [LAT]

Brennan, J.H. *Grail Quest I: The Castle of Darkness*. London: Fontana/Armada, 1984.

Fawcett, Bill, ed. *Wizards*. Chicago: Mayfair Games, 1983.

Karr, Phyllis Ann. *The King Arthur Companion*. Albany, Calif.: Chaosium, 1983.

Randall, Neill. *Storm of Dust: A Crossroads Adventure in the World of David Drake's Dragon Lord*. New York: Doherty, 1987.

Stafford, Greg. *King Arthur Pendragon*. Albany, Calif.: Chaosium, 1985. (Game.)

———, with William Dunn, Lynn Willis, and Charlie Krank. *Prince Valiant, the Storytelling Game*. Albany, Calif.: Chaosium, 1989.

Vétillard, Anne. *La Table Ronde*. Paris: Jeux Descartes, n.d. (Game.)

GARETH (Gareth of Orkney), also known in Malory as Beaumains (because of his "large-handedness" or generosity). He and Gaheret are brothers in some texts, fused into a single character in others. Gareth is Gawain's favorite brother. Arriving at court (in Malory's Book VII), Beaumains is mocked by Kay but welcomed, and eventually knighted, by Lancelot. He falls in love with Lyones and suffers—because their love is thwarted by her sister—until Arthur gives him to her in marriage. In the Vulgate *Mort Artu* and in Malory, Gareth dies at the hand of Lancelot, who does not recognize him in the melee surrounding Guenevere's rescue by her lover. His death, which saddens Lancelot and angers Gawain, precipitates the final tragedy, or, as the *Mort Artu* calls it, the war that will have no end. It has been suggested that there may have been a French romance (now lost) concerning Beaumains; in any event, the striking resemblance of Malory's tale to the situation of *Fergus* and perhaps to that of Chrétien de Troyes's Laudine convinced Roger Sherman Loomis, in *Arthurian Tradition and Chrétien de Troyes*, that those various narrative sequences shared a common and doubtless oral origin. [NJL]

GARETH, DAVID, exposes the dangers of religious fanaticism inherent in the pursuit of the Grail in his short story "Sir Mador Seeks the Grail" (1987). The narrator is Lancelot. [RHT]

Gareth, David. "Sir Mador Seeks the Grail." *The Round Table*, 1987, 18–30.

GARGANTUAN CHRONICLES. During the early sixteenth century, a number of tales, first oral and then written, grew up in France about the mythical giant Gargantua, best known today as one of Rabelais's heroes. The works are designated collectively as Gargantuan Chronicles, and while they are without exception far less remarkable than Rabelais's work, they retain some interest both as possible inspirations for his books and for the Arthurian content of several of them. Worthy of particular note are the

1532 *Les Grandes et Inestimables Cronicques du grant et enorme geant Gargantua* ("The Great and Inestimable Chronicles of the Huge and Enormous Giant Gargantua," referred to by Rabelais in his Prologue to *Pantagruel*) and *Les Croniques admirables du puissant roy Gargantua* ("The Admirable Chronicles of the Powerful King Gargantua"), which probably dates from 1534. The latter text, published by one of its editors as *The Tale of Gargantua and King Arthur*, was at one time attributed to Rabelais himself but is generally accepted as the work of one François Girault, who left his name in an acrostic near the end of the text. His work served as the source for a translation (now lost) into Elizabethan English.

The two works, and certain other texts about Gargantua, tell much the same story, with variations in detail and length (the 1532 text presenting little more than an outline of the events developed in some detail in Girault's version). According to these texts, Merlin created Gargantua's parents, Grandgosier and Gallemelle, from whale bones and from Lancelot's blood and the clippings of Guenevere's fingernails. When Gargantua was still a youth, Merlin took him to England, where he joined the company of Arthur's knights. He served Arthur for 200 years, defeating giants and entire armies; eventually, he was taken away to a faerie otherworld by Melusine (or, in some versions of the story, by Morgain). Arthur remains for the most part a colorless figure, whose most obvious trait is incompetence. Merlin is a more prominent character, but he serves primarily as a catalyst for the action and as an intermediary between Arthur and Gargantua. The focus, as in Rabelais, remains on the fabulous and often comical exploits of Gargantua. A number of events in the stories occur as well in Rabelais's work, but the latter contented himself with referring frequently to Arthurian characters and motifs, without writing a genuinely Arthurian story. [NJL]

Françon, Marcel, ed. *Les Cronicques admirables du puissant roy Gargantua*. Rochecorbon: Gay, 1956.

Girault, François. *The Tale of Gargantua and King Arthur*, ed. Huntington Brown. Cambridge: Harvard University Press, 1932.

GARNER, ALAN, English writer best known in Arthurian circles for his Alderley books, *The Weirdstone of Brisingamen* (1960) and *The Moon of Gomrath* (1963). Garner does not name the king who sleeps with his warriors in a cavern, but the Alderley Edge legend upon which the story is based and other hints identify him as Arthur (*see* CAVE LEGEND). Two modern children discover the cave and learn of the critical role played by the magical Weirdstone in the stasis. Their struggle to help the immortal and grandfatherly (if powerful) wizard Cadellin to preserve it from the forces of evil, led by the Morrigan, causes a growth in maturity that brings loss as well as gain. Of particular note are Garner's vivid settings, drawn in large part from his native Alderley in Cheshire, and his powerful recreations of the forces unleashed by the "Old Magic," especially the Wild Hunt. Garner skillfully manages to balance the human and the supernatural in these books.

Though not specifically Arthurian, two other Garner fantasies of interest are the tragic *Elidor* (1965), which uses the Wasteland and Fisher King motifs, and *The Owl Service* (1967), which draws heavily upon the Welsh *Mabinogi*.

Garner returned to the Arthurian cave legend, in this case the version attached to Richmond in Yorkshire, for his libretto for *Potter Thompson*. With music composed by Gordon Crosse, this "music drama" was first produced by Michael Elliott and performed by the Finchley Children's Music Group in London on January 9, 1975. [RCS/RHT]

Garner, Alan. *The Weirdstone of Brisingamen: A Tale of Alderley*. London: Collins, 1960; rev. ed. London: Penguin, 1963.

———. *The Moon of Gomrath*. London: Collins, 1963.

———. *Potter Thompson: A Music Drama in One Act*. Music composed by Gordon Crosse. Oxford: Oxford University Press, 1985.

GASH, JONATHAN (pseudonym of John Grant), British mystery novelist, in whose *The Grail Tree* (1979) the rakish antique dealer and detective Lovejoy undertakes a search for the Holy Grail when its owner is murdered. Lovejoy learns that although the Grail is an ancient pewter cup preserved at Lindisfarne, its desirability was enhanced in the seventeenth century when it was encased in a silver and crystal tree to which great artisans subsequently added adornments. [DN]

Gash, Jonathan. *The Grail Tree*. London: Collins, and New York: Harper and Row, 1979.

GATTO LUPESCO, a late thirteenth-century writer, in his poem *Detto* presents himself as a minstrel who, during his wandering, encounters two English knights who have unsuccessfully sought Arthur at Mongibello. Although there are earlier references in Latin and French, this is the first Italian allusion to Arthur's association with Mount Etna (*see* CAVE LEGEND). [DLH]

De Bartholomeis, V. *Rime giullareschi e popolari d'Italia*. Bologna, 1926, p. 24.

Monaci, E. *Crestomazia italiana dei primi secoli*. Citta di Castello, 1912, p. 449.

Gardner, Edmund G. *The Arthurian Legend in Italian Literature*. London: Dent, 1930, pp. 14–15.

GAWAIN (Walwanus, Gauvain, Gawein, Gwalchmei, Walewein), son of King Lot of Lothian and Orkney and of Morgause (or Anna), Arthur's sister or half-sister. Gawain appears to have northern, possibly Scottish, origins, but it is impossible to trace him back to a historical model, however shadowy. Like Kay and Bedivere, Gawain may have early associations with Arthur in Celtic tradition, although the evidence in his case is less clear. The equivalence between Gawain and Gwalchmei appears first in the Welsh romances and translations of Geoffrey of Monmouth's *Historia Regum Britanniae*, but Gwalchmei does appear in *Culhwch ac Olwen* and in some Welsh Triads, where the influence of Geoffrey or Chrétien is unlikely. Another possible indication of a distant Celtic origin may be the phenomenon of his strength waxing and waning with the sun in some romances; this could suggest a relationship with a solar deity. An early mention of the Latin Walwanus, probably inspired by popular British insular tradition, is to be found in William of Malmesbury's *Gesta Regum Anglorum*, but the character first appears in a role of any importance in Geoffrey of Monmouth. However, occurrences of the name Walwanus (and variants) in charters suggest the popularity of stories about him in the eleventh century on the Continent.

In Geoffrey of Monmouth, Gawain is a valiant warrior who aids his lord and king in various campaigns. The uncle-nephew (sister's son) relationship is of particular importance in creating an intimate bond between the two that enables Gawain to function as counselor and putative heir to the throne. In Wace's adaptation of Geoffrey, Gawain has already assumed a courtly aspect and praises the virtues of love and chivalry rather than war. It is Chrétien de Troyes who first allots a major role to Gawain in his romances. Gawain functions as a friend of the hero and as a model whom young knights aspire to emulate. Often, the hero of the romance becomes involved in an undecided combat with Gawain, in Chrétien's later romances the implication being that the hero is the moral victor. Chrétien seems to take a more critical attitude toward Gawain and the way of life he represents as his career progresses, and particularly in *Lancelot* and *Perceval* he is unfavorably contrasted with the hero and made the butt of some burlesque humor. Chrétien seems particularly concerned with Gawain's blind adherence to custom and frivolous attachment to the opposite sex. Even though *Perceval* is unfinished, it seems clear that Gawain is bound to fail where Perceval will succeed.

Both the burlesque and more serious strains are taken up in later Old French romance, the burlesque aspect being prevalent in the post-Chrétien verse romances (e.g., *Le Chevalier à l'épée* and *La Vengeance Raguidel*) and the serious criticism coming to the fore in the Grail romances, especially in the Vulgate *Queste*, where Gawain is depicted as a hardened and unrepentant sinner. His narrative role in the Vulgate Cycle is particularly important, and most notably in the *Mort Artu*. Here, his actions can best be seen in his relationship to his four brothers, Agravain, Mordred, Gaheriés, and Guerrehés (the similarity between the names of the last two understandably caused confusion among scribes and adapters). He initially attempts to dissuade the malcontents Agravain and Mordred from revealing the affair between Lancelot and Guenevere, but when he learns that Lancelot has killed Gaheriés, Guerrehés, and Boort, during the rescue of Guenevere, his love for Lancelot turns to an implacable desire for vengeance, and he becomes one of the catalysts in the events that lead up to Arthur's death.

In the Prose *Tristan*, he is an out-and-out murderous villain, no respecter of persons or property. As of this point (ca. 1230), authors wishing to depict Gawain therefore had various choices open to them: they could portray him as a real hero, as a somewhat comic figure, or as a true villain. Later French literature shows him in all of these roles.

Outside France, all authors of Arthurian romances were familiar with the French tradition, and it is interesting to note that the portrayal of Gawain varies geographically. In Germany, he remains by and large the same figure as in France, although Wolfram von Eschenbach in his *Parzival* is less harsh on him than Chrétien in *Perceval*; he becomes the hero proper of a lengthy Grail romance, *Diu Crône*, by Heinrich von dem Türlin. Gawain seems to have enjoyed considerable popularity in the Low Countries, where a special form of the name, Walewein, developed very early; the portrayal of him in Middle Dutch literature (with the exception of some texts directly dependent on French models) is almost uniformly positive, and he is named *der avonturen vader* ("the father of adventures"). Why the portrayal of Gawain in some Germanic literatures should be so positive is difficult to say, but the case of Middle English is at least partly explicable. There is in Middle English a marked reluctance to take over any of the negative features of the French Gawain, and Middle English romance in many ways restores Gawain to a position of respect and dignity. The author of *Sir Gawain and the Green Knight*, for example, shows a Gawain who is almost but not quite perfect. Other texts, such as *Syre Gawene and the Carle of Carlyle*, portray an unimpeachably courteous and valiant knight, or at least one whose actions are not criticized. One possible explanation for this is that English authors and audiences regarded Gawain as a British hero and that it was considered unseemly to show such a figure in a poor light. A similar tendency is visible in the restoration in English literature of the French Arthur from a weak and indecisive monarch to a great warrior-king. Malory departs from this pattern of favorable treatment of Gawain in Middle English, however, when he follows his sources by presenting Arthur's nephew in an unflattering role. His lead was followed by Tennyson and most postmedieval writers, though some recent novels, by authors like Gillian Bradshaw, have shown him to better advantage once again.

Curiously, French literature, where Gawain occurs more often than anywhere else, rarely shows him in the role of a real hero, setting out on a quest he is destined to achieve, or falling properly in love. This occurs, however, in some of the transformations mentioned above, and it is this flexible, nonhero status in Old French literature (but with heroic potential) that rendered the figure of Gawain so serviceable. Authors could use Gawain as part of a design transformed to their own needs, where he might turn out to be a hero or an adjunct, courteous or not, and so on. But on the whole, despite lapses into frivolous love affairs, the figure of Gawain remains by and large admirable, with the exception of the Vulgate *Queste* and the Prose *Tristan*. A wicked Gawain of this kind is after all less useful to authors, for a debased and debauched knight makes neither a good foil for the hero of a romance nor a good hero himself. [KB]

Busby, Keith. *Gauvain in Old French Literature*. Amsterdam: Rodopi, 1980.

Whiting, B.J. "Gawain: His Reputation, His Courtesy, and His Appearance in Chaucer's *Squire's Tale*." *Medieval Studies*, 9 (1947), 189–234.

GEMMELL, DAVID, British writer of heroic fantasy fiction, tells the story of Uther Pendragon's youth in *Ghost King* (1988). Under the guidance of immortals who have been the gods and heroes of past cultures, and after a series of Tolkienesque adventures, Uther becomes High King of Britain. Arthurian elements are inventively incorporated into a gory and highly fantasized narrative. [DN]

Gemmell, David. *Ghost King*. London: Century Hutchinson, 1988.

GEOFFREY JUNIOR (pseudonym of William John Courthope; 1842–1917), author of *The Marvellous History of King Arthur in Avalon* (1904), a pseudo-chronicle in archaic diction. This account of Arthur and his knights, beguiled into forgetful pleasure in Avalon by Morgan le Fay, is a political allegory attacking abuse of the parliamentary system in Britain. [RHT]

[Courthope, William John]. *The Marvellous History of King Arthur in Avalon and the Lifting of Lyonnesse: A Chronicle of the Round Table Communicated by Geoffrey of Monmouth, Ed. with Introduction and Notes by Geoffrey Junior*. London: Murray, 1904.

GEOFFREY OF MONMOUTH, author of the *Historia Regum Britanniae* ("History of the Kings of Britain"), a twelfth-century Latin work first given this title—implied by the preface—in Jerome Commelin's 1587 edition. This is the work that made Arthur a quasi-historical monarch with an "official" biography. It is one of the most important books of the Middle Ages. Besides planting highly erroneous notions of British history, it supplied a basis and framework for Arthurian romance and exerted an influence extending through Spenser, Shakespeare, and many others. *The Faerie Queene* includes compressed verse paraphrases of large portions of it.

Presumably born at Monmouth in southeast Wales, Geoffrey may have been Welsh. However, he shows an interest in Brittany and a pro-Breton bias that suggest that his family came from across the Channel, as numerous Bretons did in the wake of the Norman Conquest. His father's name is said to have been Arthur. From 1129 to 1151, Geoffrey was a minor cleric and seemingly a teacher at Oxford, where schools already existed though the university did not. Charters relating to church properties reveal that he was acquainted with Walter, archdeacon of the diocese, whose name figures in his scanty account of his sources. After 1151, Geoffrey was in London and was consecrated bishop of the Welsh see of St. Asaph. This appointment tells in favor of his being of Breton stock, since under the Anglo-Norman monarchy Welshmen were not usually made bishops of Welsh sees. Owing to the turbulence of the country, it is unlikely that he ever took up residence. He died in 1154 or 1155.

His first published work was a series of *Prophetiae Merlini* ("Prophecies of Merlin"). He gave this to the world in the 1130s, while he was still busy with the *Historia*, and later incorporated it into the larger work, as supposedly uttered by Merlin. Hence, the *Historia* is now the context in which to find it. The germ of the *Prophetiae* is a Welsh tradition that Merlin (or rather Myrddin—the familiar form of the name is Geoffrey's) foretold the overthrow of the Saxons and the destruction of their usurped realm of England, in a Celtic resurgence. Most of the text, however, is Geoffrey's invention. Its oracular imagery refers to Arthur as "the Boar of Cornwall" and gives a few recognizable allusions to real events, but in the main it is hopelessly obscure except in its foreshadowing of a restored Celtic Britain. Nevertheless, there were medieval commentators who professed to expound these "Prophecies," which were still well enough known in the sixteenth century for Rabelais to gibe at them.

The *Historia Regum Britanniae* was completed ca. 1138. The best of the many copies is the Cambridge University Library MS 1706, though it needs supplementing from one or two others. There are slight indications that no extant copy reproduces the original and that the *Historia* as now known is a revision datable to the 1140s. An appreciably different "Variant Version" remains puzzling. Geoffrey seems to have attempted more than one dedication. He addresses himself to Robert, Earl of Gloucester, and also to Waleran, Count of Mellent.

His most obvious aim is to glorify the Britons of old, ancestors of the Welsh and Bretons. He bewails their disunion and degeneration, which led to the loss of most of their territory to the English; but through the prophetic Merlin he holds out hope to their descendants. A second obvious aim is to please the Normans, by whom the English have in turn been conquered. Geoffrey seeks to show not only that their island realm has an august pedigree but that their lands on the Continent once belonged to Britain, so that there are precedents for Norman claims on both sides of the Channel. Deeper issues may well be raised by the portrayals of Merlin and of Arthur himself, the inspired prophet and the messianic ruler. To these, a key should perhaps be sought in Judeo-Christian apocalyptic literature and a transfer of themes from the biblical Chosen People to the Britons—an idea for which Gildas supplied a hint.

After a conventionalized description of Britain, the *Historia* opens in the age of classical epic. Geoffrey recalls Vergil's account of Aeneas, who, after the fall of Troy, is said to have led a party of Trojans to Italy, these being the ancestors of the Romans. Vergil introduces Aeneas's son Ascanius, and Geoffrey makes out that Ascanius's grandson Brutus led a further migration. He freed several thousand Trojans from slavery in Greece and took them to the island of Albion, which was promptly renamed "Britain" after himself. Basically, this is a Welsh legend found in Nennius, but Geoffrey vastly expands it. Albion, he says, was uninhabited except for a few giants, mostly in Cornwall. The Trojan settlers—now "Britons"—eliminated the giants and created a kingdom, with a capital on the Thames called New Troy, subsequently London.

From Brutus, Geoffrey goes on to a long series of further kings. They include Leir, the original King Lear, with his three daughters. Most of the kings are imaginary, though in some cases Geoffrey has taken names from Welsh princely genealogies that actually apply to a much later period. Two of the most important of his kings are the brothers Belinus and Brennius. Belinus is a euphemerized Celtic god; Brennius is a Gallic king who sacked Rome in 390 B.C. and is here (slightly misspelled) converted into a Briton. Toward the time of the Roman conquest, Geoffrey begins to adopt characters from Welsh stories preserved in the *Mabinogion*.

With the advent of Julius Caesar, he is somewhat constrained by authentic history. Yet he avoids admitting that Britain was ever conquered by Rome. Oddly at first sight, this archpatriot never mentions the heroic leaders of anti-Roman resistance, Caratacus and Boudicca. The truth is that he does not need them, because he denies the conquest itself. By agreement with the emperors, Britain survives as a tributary state within the imperial system, and its kings continue under a Roman overlordship that is only intermittently felt. Geoffrey ingeniously portrays some of the emperors, Constantine the Great for instance, as Britons or demi-Britons or Britons-by-marriage, and simply includes them in his line of kings.

He makes much of the legendary origin of Brittany, reputedly settled by Britons as a result of the activities of the pretender Maximus. Brittany, in the narrative, quickly becomes a kingdom in its own right. Meanwhile, the insular Britons are overrun by Picts, Scots, and other barbarians, and after one rescue expedition the Romans abandon them to their fate. Through the diplomacy of the archbishop of London, a Breton prince, Constantine, comes over to organize the island's defense and is made king. He has three sons—Constans, Aurelius Ambrosius, and Uther, the last being the destined father of Arthur.

Constantine is assassinated, and the sinister Vortigern disposes of Constans also and takes over the sovereignty. The two younger princes find haven in Brittany. Vortigern invites the heathen Saxons, led by Hengist, to settle in Britain as auxiliary troops. The alliance is cemented by his marriage to Hengist's daughter. Hengist contrives a massacre of the British nobles at a conference, and the Saxons ravage the country. Vortigern, hated and rejected by most of his people, flees to Snowdonia and tries to build a fortress there. The foundations keep crumbling away. Vortigern's magicians tell him he must find a boy without a father, kill him, and sprinkle his blood upon the stones. Here, Geoffrey is following an older Welsh tale in Nennius, but the outcome is different. A lad is found whose mother conceived by an incubus, and he is brought to the building site. His name is Merlin: thus the enchanter makes his debut on the stage of major literature. He reveals what the magicians did not know, that the foundations collapse because they are over a pool. Moreover, the pool has two dragons in it, a red one and a white one. When brought out into the light of day, the dragons fight; they represent the Britons and Saxons. Merlin utters his prophecies, portending doom for Vortigern and warning him that the rightful princes Aurelius and Uther are on the point of returning to Britain.

He speaks truly. They overthrow and slay the usurper and curb the Saxons, though inconclusively. Aurelius's reign is short. Uther, called Pendragon, succeeds him and begets Arthur with the aid of Merlin's magic. Geoffrey's narrative now rises toward its climactic phase, a glorious rebirth after catastrophe. Arthur becomes king while still in his teens. He routs the Saxons, not quite expelling them from Britain but reducing them to subjection. His decisive victory is at Bath (Geoffrey's interpretation of Badon), where he wields a sword called Caliburn forged in the Isle of Avalon. Then he crushes the Picts and Scots in the north and, having "restored Britain to its earlier dignity," marries Guenevere. But the restoration is only a beginning. He invades and conquers Ireland and, as an afterthought, Iceland.

Arthur now reigns in peace and prosperity for twelve years. He creates an order of knighthood that accepts men of note from all nations. His fame spreads widely, and, aware of the awe that he inspires, he conceives the notion of conquering Europe. He starts with Norway and Denmark, and then invades Gaul, still tenuously held by the Roman Empire. Vanquishing its governor, Frollo, in single combat, he reorganizes the Roman territories under his own rule, employing his cupbearer, Bedivere, and his seneschal, Kay.

In a second spell of peace, Arthur holds court magnificently at the former Roman city of Caerleon-upon-Usk. Geoffrey's description of Arthurian Caerleon is the major literary step toward the Camelot of romance. An embassy arrives from the Roman ruler Lucius demanding tribute and the restitution of conquered lands. Lucius is here styled Procurator of the Republic, though later he is once or twice called an emperor. The ambiguity of his status hints at a hazy consciousness on Geoffrey's part of the nullity of the last western emperors. By contrast, Lucius's eastern colleague, Leo, is an "emperor" unequivocally.

Arthur rejects the Roman demands and takes an army over to Gaul, where he defeats Lucius and penetrates Burgundy, but before he can pursue his more grandiose visions he is recalled to Britain by a revolt. His treacherous nephew Mordred, left in charge as his deputy, has seized the crown and made a deal with the Saxons. Arthur crushes the rebellion beside the River Camel in Cornwall but is mortally wounded and "carried off to the Isle of Avalon for his wounds to be attended to." Thus, cryptically, his reign ends. Geoffrey leaves the door open for the folk-belief in the King's immortality, but he never affirms it. The rest of the *Historia* gives a distorted though not totally fanciful account of the Britons' eventual collapse and the Saxon triumph, closing the line of kings with Cadwallader in the seventh century. After him, the remaining Britons maintain their independence in Wales only and are called Welsh.

There is no doubt that Geoffrey is a writer of fiction and can never be relied on for facts. Yet there is equally no doubt that he makes use of older materials, both genuine history and preexisting legend. Besides Roman historians, he draws upon Gildas, Nennius, Bede, and probably the *Annales Cambriae*, as well as Welsh genealogical and hagiographic matter. But the main problem with his sources is a statement he makes in a dedicatory preface: that the *Historia* is translated from "a certain very ancient book written in the British language," which was given him by Archdeacon Walter. No trace of the book exists today, and Geoffrey's claim is quite inadmissible as it stands, if only because the *Historia* contains many things, such as a reference to Normans in Arthur's army, that could not have been in an "ancient" source. The claim is therefore usually dismissed as a pure fabrication, like similar claims by other medieval authors.

Geoffrey, however, is very positive about this book in the British language. Mentioning three contemporary historians, Caradoc of Llancarfan, William of Malmesbury, and Henry of Huntingdon, he advises them to leave the kings of the Britons alone, because he has the book and they do not. He alleges further that Walter brought it *ex Britannia*. In Geoffrey's time, "the British language" might mean either Welsh or Breton, which had a common ancestor in the Late British tongue of the fifth century and had not diverged very widely from each other. But *Britannia* suggests Brittany rather than Wales.

Geoffrey makes one specific assertion about the book's contents, that it gave him material on the downfall of Arthur. In his Arthur story, it is noteworthy that known Welsh sources cannot account for more than about one-fifth of the total and that Geoffrey presents an Arthur who is not really like the warrior-prince of the Welsh and has a downfall quite at variance with the Welsh tradition of Mordred, or "Medraut." In dealing with the recognized villain, Vortigern, he merely enlarges on what the Welsh have to say; in dealing with the hero, Arthur, he might be expected to do the same but instead does something significantly different. Half the story is taken up with the Gallic warfare. Judged purely by allocation of space, Geoffrey's Arthur is more a Gallic conqueror than anything else. The emphasis, and the denouement, have no real Welsh antecedents. A theory that Geoffrey makes Arthur campaign on the Continent in imitation of Maximus, or the Norman kings, may carry some weight but fails to take the full measure of the problem. Arguably, he did have a lost source, perhaps a Breton chronicle or narrative poem portraying Arthur in a role unknown to the Welsh. Such a text could not have been "ancient" in the sense of being as early as the fifth or sixth century, because Late British and its immediate derivatives were not written languages. But it might have been a Breton redaction of a truly ancient Latin original.

That possibility is linked with Geoffrey's chronological scheme. It cannot be made entirely coherent, but he arranges the family relationships, and other matters, so as to put most of Arthur's reign in the third quarter of the fifth century. Though he brings in some characters who are undoubtedly later, such anachronisms do not call the main structure in question. In particular, he says three times that Arthur's Gallic warfare occurred during the emperorship of Leo, evidently Leo I, who was eastern emperor from 457 to 474. For Arthur's passing, directly afterward, he gives the date 542, and this is so completely at odds with almost everything else that it is likely to have arisen from a mistake or corruption.

Now it has been shown that recognized processes of error could have derived 542 from 470, a date within Leo's reign, which precisely fits certain historical events that Geoffrey seems to have had in mind at this point. The error would imply a primary source using the chronology of Victorius of Aquitaine, counting the years from Christ's Passion. This was employed during the late fifth century but on the Continent was superseded by the *Anno Domini* method during the sixth. In other words, Geoffrey's dating of the Gallic warfare and Arthur's demise can be harmonized, and fixed within Leo's reign, on the hypothesis of source material that used Victorius's system and was therefore early. The Breton *Legend of St. Goeznovius*, and some chronicle references to Arthur, point to a similar tradition about his *floruit*. (*See* ARTHUR, ORIGINS OF LEGEND; CHRONICLES, ARTHUR IN; *GOEZNOVII, LEGENDA SANCTI*; RIOTHAMUS.)

Geoffrey's third work was the *Vita Merlini* ("Life of Merlin"), a long poem in hexameters (ca. 1150). When he wrote the *Historia*, he had picked up the name of the northern bard Myrddin and applied it, modified and Latinized, to the young prophet who confounded Vortigern's magicians. He then learned more about this bard, including the fact that he lived much later. According to the Welsh, Myrddin was driven out of his mind at a battle in Cumbria in 575 and roamed through the northern forests uttering prophetic ravings. In his poem, Geoffrey uses the story after his own fashion, with a certain fudging of dates. The poem introduces another bard, Taliesin, who is made to say that after Arthur's last battle he accompanied the wounded King to the paradisal "island of apples," Avalon. Here, the enchantress Morgen reigned as chief of nine sisters, and she undertook to heal Arthur's wounds if he remained on the island. Morgen, who in romance becomes the sinister Morgan le Fay, is here entirely benign. There is still no commitment as to her royal patient's eventual fate.

To revert to the *Historia*: though Geoffrey established the "official" account of Arthur, together with some of the characters and motifs, his work was by no means the only creative force behind Arthurian romance. But the romances largely presupposed it and acquired conviction and verisimilitude by fitting more or less into the purportedly factual frame that it provided. Wace, in his French verse adaptation, entitled the *Roman de Brut* after Brutus, refers to Arthurian tales already current and explains that these adventures took place during the long peace following the King's first cycle of warfare. Besides Wace's version, there are several Welsh chronicles based on Geoffrey and also known by Brutus's name. The Welsh *Bruts* are more strictly quasihistorical and less relevant to romance. (*See also* PROSE *BRUT*.) [GA]

Geoffrey of Monmouth. *The Historia Regum Britanniae of Geoffrey of Monmouth*, ed. Neil Wright. Cambridge: Brewer, 1985.

———. *The History of the Kings of Britain*, trans. Lewis Thorpe. London: Penguin, 1966.

———. *Vita Merlini*, ed. and trans. John Jay Parry. Urbana: University of Illinois Press, 1925.

Ashe, Geoffrey. "A Certain Very Ancient Book." *Speculum*, 56 (1981), 301–23.

Chambers, E.K. *Arthur of Britain*. London: Sidgwick and Jackson, 1927, pp. 20–99.

Crick, Julia. *Summary Catalogue of the Manuscripts of the "Historia Regum Britanniae" of Geoffrey of Monmouth*. Cambridge: Brewer, 1989.

Hoffman, Donald J. "The Third British Empire." *Interpretations*, 15 (1984), 1–10.

Kendrick, T.D. *British Antiquity*. London: Methuen, 1950.

Parry, John Jay, and Robert A. Caldwell. "Geoffrey of Monmouth." In *Arthurian Literature in the Middle Ages*, ed. Roger Sherman Loomis. Oxford: Clarendon, 1959, pp. 72–93.

Piggott, Stuart. "The Sources of Geoffrey of Monmouth." *Antiquity*, 15 (1941).

Tatlock, J.S.P. *The Legendary History of Britain*. Berkeley: University of California Press, 1950.

GERAINT AND ENID, probably written in the thirteenth century, one of the "three Welsh romances." (*Owain* and *Peredur* are the others.) *Geraint* is the closest of the three to the corresponding romance by Chrétien de Troyes, in this case *Erec et Enide*, though the hero's name is that of a late sixth- or early seventh-century king of Dumnonia (southwest Britain), rather than the Breton hero referred to in French. Geraint, one of Arthur's knights, wins Enid's hand after successfully competing for the prize of a sparrowhawk in a tournament. After their marriage, the couple are recalled to Geraint's patrimony because of the feebleness of his father the king, but the young husband neglects his duties as ruler and knight because of his overriding affection for his wife. One morning, she inadvertently reveals the courtiers' criticism of their prince to Geraint, who mistakenly, and inexplicably, takes her words to mean that she is unfaithful to him. He orders her roughly to ride out with him, but through a series of trials she eventually convinces him of her constancy and care for him. On the return journey to their court, Geraint in a final adventure overcomes the knight of the hedge of mist and destroys its enchantment. Though the first part of the story is clearly set in southwest Wales, and Geraint's country is realistically placed in the southwest peninsula, the rest of the romance has no geographical location, and Geraint's later adventures with his wife are poorly motivated. The first part is a taut, well-constructed narrative, the second more rambling. Stylistically, the narrative shows many of the rhetorical devices of Middle Welsh storytelling and pays such an attention to legal details and traditional nomenclature that, whatever its immediate origins may be, Chrétien's romance or its source, the story has been successfully put into a Welsh mold. [BFR]

Jones, Gwyn, and Thomas Jones, trans. *The Mabinogion*, 2nd ed. London: Dent, 1974.

Jarman, A.O.H., and Gwilym Rees Hughes. *A Guide to Welsh Literature I*. Swansea: Davies, 1976.

GERMAN ARTHURIAN LITERATURE (MEDIEVAL). Arthurian legends began to be adapted in Germany in the last decades of the twelfth century. We can only guess how transmission took place. We have reason to believe that influential princely patrons became acquainted with Old French Arthurian poems through their relationship with courts in France or during the Crusades. They themselves procured the manuscripts and had them adapted or translated into German. A well-known example is the landgrave Hermann of Thuringia, who provided the original versions for Herbort's *Lied von Troje* and Wolfram von Eschenbach's *Willehalm*. In only one case are we told how the original of an Arthurian story came to Germany, to be transposed there into a Middle High German verse romance. At the end of his *Lanzelet*, Ulrich von Zatzikhoven mentions a French book written by an Anglo-Norman. It had belonged to Hugo de Morville, one of the hostages given in 1194 to the German emperor Henry VI by King Richard the Lionhearted.

We must assume that Old French Arthurian poems were also transmitted orally, as testified by Wirnt von Grafenberg in his *Wigalois*, where he affirms that a page had told him the story. Very often, however, the indications of sources in German Arthurian romances are fictitious. This is the case with the authorities cited by Heinrich von dem Türlin and by Der Pleier; and the philological controversy over Wolfram's Provençal "Kyot," whom he quotes as an authority for the final parts of his *Parzival*, is still not settled. In addition to the literary sources that constitute the major part of the Arthurian tradition in Germany, we must take into account a nonliterary stream of Arthurian narrative that had preserved a precourtly image of King Arthur, transmitted, presumably, by Breton minstrels, who traveled widely throughout Europe.

The classical German Arthurian romance follows Chrétien de Troyes closely with regard to content, substance, and structure; the Arthurian epics of the thirteenth and fourteenth centuries develop more and more into an amalgamation of all kinds of European narrative traditions. The sources used are not limited to the Old French Arthurian romances, lais, and fabliaux but also integrate elements of the antique and Byzantine romance, French and German heroic epic, fairy tales, and legends of every provenance, including historical and pseudo-historical documents. At an early stage, legends had been absorbed in French as well as in German romance, such as the Arthurian and the Tristan legends (especially by Eilhart von Oberge and Heinrich von dem Türlin, but not Gottfried von Strassburg) and the Knight of the Swan legend (Wolfram). In tracing the evolution of German Arthurian romance, we must give special consideration to the interdependence, filiations, and continuations of these works.

The variety of literary and nonliterary sources also accounts for the varying concepts of King Arthur's role and function in German Arthurian literature. Although certain fundamental characteristics remain relatively constant, the concept of King Arthur and his court undergoes considerable modification and stands for different models of social values and ethics.

The two founders of courtly Arthurian romance in Germany are Hartmann von Aue and Wolfram von Eschenbach. The first German Arthurian romance is Hartmann's *Erec*, probably composed ca. 1180 or later, followed by *Iwein* about twenty years afterward. Both are adaptations of Chrétien's verse romances. *Iwein* closely follows Chrétien, but the adaptation of *Erec* contains a number of significant modifications that have led to the speculation that Hartmann also used a source close to the *Mabinogi* tale *Geraint and Enid* or to the Old Icelandic *Erex saga*. There are, however, no cogent reasons to doubt that Hartmann translated Chrétien's *Erec* in substance if not always in wording. The same applies to Wolfram's *Parzival* (1200–10).

The third classical author, Gottfried von Strassburg, created in his *Tristan* a romance that was to have a profound effect on the development of the Tristan-matter in Germany but that stands outside the pale of Arthurian literature in respect to characters, structure, and motivation. Unlike Hartmann and Wolfram, Gottfried did not affect the development of Arthurian romance in Germany.

Although Hartmann's *Erec* and *Iwein* retain the general pattern and sequence of adventures of their French models, a distinct shift of focus is noticeable, with the aspect of service and reward being reinforced. Hartmann's romances reflect the self-perception and self-assertion of the *ministeriales*, or lower gentry, and their striving for social recognition and integration into the hereditary nobility on the basis of the services they rendered. Thus, Hartmann relegates Erec's royal attributes to the background and stresses his dependence on King Arthur—the relationship between the Arthurian knight and the sovereign being founded on the mutual respect for the moral and social values of service and merit—and accentuates Enite's state of poverty: she, like Erec, has to undergo a series of tests in order to earn her new royal status. Hartmann clearly distinguishes between the two courses of adventures that Erec must undergo, assigning a higher degree of social consciousness and maturity to the second course, with its culmination in the *Joie de la curt* episode and the liberation of the eighty widows (not found in Chrétien's *Erec*), an act of social commitment. The religious and eschatological interpretations of this episode, based on Erec's *saelden wec* ("path to salvation"), should not blind us to the fact that its motivations are rooted in a sociopolitical reality, one that is distinct from that of French vassalage as exemplified in Chrétien's *Erec*.

Hartmann's *Iwein* shows a critical distancing. Not only is the court occasionally called into question as the paradigm of morality and courtly joy, and of the protective and integrating forces of the Arthurian world, but the very concept of the chivalric adventure also becomes ambivalent. Iwein's assault on Askalon, for example, is qualified as an act of brutality, resulting in his usurpation of his adversary's possessions. Adventure, the *raison d'être* of knightly existence, turns into an end in itself. Iwein's fault consists not only in his violation of Laudine's order, the missing of the deadline, but in his failure to perform his duties and responsibilities as the coregent and protector of Laudine's estate. Hartmann therefore emphasizes the second course of adventures, all of which are achieved in the true spirit of chivalric action, that is, the succoring of people in distress. In spite of the ironic overtones, especially apparent in *Iwein*, Hartmann's Arthurian romances present a princely *speculum virtutum* ("mirror of virtues") aimed at the realization of moral, social, and political aspirations in harmony with the divine order. Hartmann set the standard for the evolution of Arthurian romance in Germany; he was widely imitated, especially in regard to his skill with language and versification.

If Hartmann was an adapter of Chrétien, Wolfram, despite his debt to the French poet, must be considered a recreator and innovator. He probably used two different versions of Chrétien's unfinished *Perceval* in the course of his redaction and perhaps knew the so-called *Bliocadran Prologue* as well as parts of the First Continuation. His *Parzival* brings the quest of the Grail to a conclusive end, and the scope of this voluminous work of some 25,000 verses—of which eighty-four manuscripts and fragments are extant—is widened and deepened to embrace the vital questions of the medieval world. It is amazing to what extent Wolfram succeeds in amalgamating the enormous amount of material derived from heterogeneous literary and nonliterary sources into a coherent whole.

Among the striking differences from Chrétien's *Perceval*—the concept of the Grail and the Grail society; the addition of the two initial Gahmuret books, which, together with the Feirefiz episode of the final books, constitute the frame of the Parzival-Gawan strands of the narrative—one aspect deserves particular consideration: the historicization of the story. Whereas Chrétien's *Perceval* unfolds in a fairy-tale world undefined in time and space, Wolfram places his *Parzival* in a geographical, historical, and social context that, although fictitious, allows for references to the great issues of medieval society. This historicization is seen in the Gahmuret books and their undogmatic view of heathendom; in Trevrizent and the community of the Grail, reflecting the lay movements of religious reformation and the orders of knighthood; in Wolfram's theological speculations on guilt and redemption, reflecting the controversy from Augustine to the mystics and lay reformers; in his concern with names and family relationships, in accord with the importance of noble descent in medieval society. Arthur's kingdom is one among many, with cleavages between allies and enemies, and is set in a realistic framework of kindred relations, with their inherent conflicts, which reflect the situation of medieval society in Germany. The Grail kingdom, however, represents Wolfram's vision of a new human order guided by spiritual forces. The Grail itself becomes the cosmic symbol of the third eschatological realm of humankind when the reunification of Orient and Occident is achieved by Feirefiz's and Parzival's offspring, the legendary Priest-King John, and Loherangrin, the Knight of the Swan (Loherangrin had already in the twelfth century been connected with the House of Godefroy de Bouillon, the first Christian king of Jerusalem).

Wolfram's *Parzival* attained long-lasting success throughout the Middle Ages and eventually eclipsed the romances of his predecessor Hartmann. Wirnt von Grafenberg began his *Wigalois* in Hartmann's manner but, under the impact of the first books of *Parzival*, turned to imitate Wolfram. For centuries, Albrecht's *Jüngerer Titurel*, whose main source is the *Parzival*, was attributed to Wolfram's authorship. In the fourteenth century, Claus Wisse and Philipp Colin readapted the *Parzival* and expanded it to some 37,000 lines with the translation of the French Continuations of Chrétien's *Conte del Graal*. In the fifteenth century, Ulrich Fuetrer included the story of Parzival in his *Buch der Abenteuer*.

Wolfram's two *Titurel* fragments, composed in a strophic form close to the *Nibelungenlied* and the *Kudrun*, focus on the infant love of Schionatulander and Sigune, whose tragic end is related in *Parzival*, and on the allegory of courtly virtues inscribed on the precious leash of Gardevias, the hunting dog. Though not in any direct relation to the Arthurian subject matter, this episode gave rise to the voluminous expansion of the Schionatulander and Sigune story in Albrecht's *Jüngerer Titurel* and to the enthusiastic reception it met in the late Middle Ages.

Beside the courtly Arthurian epic modeled on Chrétien evolved the so-called romance of entertainment. The earliest German representatives of this genre are Ulrich von Zatzikhoven's *Lanzelet* (1194–1205) and Wirnt von Grafenberg's *Wigalois* (1210–15). *Lanzelet* represents the "primitive" type of Arthurian romance, in which the integration of an archaic narrative substratum, mostly Celtic in origin, and chivalric courtly ethics is intended but not attained. Precourtly influences surface in the episodes of Ginover's abduction and liberation by Arthur and his knights, which go back to an earlier Celtic version of the abduction story. Ulrich did not know Chrétien's *Chevalier de la charrete* and the doctrine of courtly love it exhibits (the adulterous relation between Lancelot and Guenevere and the total submission of the lover to his mistress's demands, defying all rules of feudal allegiance and loyalty), nor was he familiar with the structural and ideological model of classical Arthurian romance. Lanzelet's adventures are only loosely connected to each other and are not governed by the principle of higher perfectibility. Nonetheless, *Lanzelet* introduced a number of common features of Arthurian lore, especially those related to the Lancelot tradition, such as the hero's infancy and upbringing by a fairy on an island of blissfulness, his unknown identity, the realm of the dead and its demonic guardians (the Valerin episode), and the tests of virtue and chastity, which enjoyed a great popularity among the lesser writers of Arthurian romance.

Wirnt von Grafenberg, a Franconian probably in the service of the counts of Andechs, composed his verse romance *Wigalois* while in the entourage of Otto I, Duke of Meran, after a French source transmitted orally (as he claims in lines 11,686 ff.). The work reveals striking similarities to Renaut de Beaujeu's French romance *Le Bel Inconnu* and the late prose romance *Le Chevalier du papegau*. The *Wigalois* must have been widely read and appreciated, as attested by thirteen manuscripts and twenty-three fragments, references and borrowings by later authors, adaptations in verse and prose, and translations into Danish, Icelandic, and even Yiddish. Episodes from the romance were represented in the frescoes (ca. 1400) of Runkelstein castle near Bolzano. Wirnt's *Wigalois*, like the *Lanzelet*, contains narrative material that can be traced back to Celtic myth and legend: Gawein's abduction into a fabulous land; Wigalois's childhood there and his unrevealed identity; Roaz's netherworld realm, identified here with the Christian concept of the fiendish and heathenish powers; and landscape inhabited by dragons, monsters, and ghosts. The romance, however, is characterized by confidence in divine guidance and in Christian faith and piety, which overcome all evil. Crusader influences can also be traced, as well as those of the Revelation of John. Scholarship has noted the resemblance to the contemporary situation, particularly apparent in the lion episode.

King Arthur's court serves only as the traditional setting for the initial adventure of the hero, a mere literary relic with little relevance to the action. Wirnt's ideal of the sovereign is not represented by Arthur, nor are his moral values embodied in the courtly and chivalric Arthurian world, but in a Christian kingship grounded in medieval moral theology, whose ideal representative is Wigalois. A number of components contribute to the dissociation from the traditional structure of courtly Arthurian romance. First, the relationship between father (Gawein) and son (Wigalois) is emphasized much more than the relationship between the hero and Arthur. Second, Wigalois makes his appearance at Arthur's court already as the accomplished, perfect hero, thus eliminating one of the most important structural elements of Arthurian romance—the protagonist's striving for chivalric and moral stature in order to gain the recognition and honors of Arthurian society. Wigalois's liberation of Korentin is undertaken in the name of the Arthurian court, but in the course of events the connections with the court are disrupted. Wigalois's greatest deed of chivalry does not culminate in the recognition of Arthur's circle. The prevalent Christian import of the Korentin adventure, and the religious tendency of the work as a whole, did not fit into an Arthurian world in its established literary typology.

Heinrich von dem Türlin's *Diu Crône* ("The Crown," ca. 1230) is an extraordinary compilation of motifs and episodes derived from almost every known Arthurian and Grail romance, from Old French lais and fabliaux, and from fairy tales and legends. This most voluminous Arthurian verse romance (30,041 lines) apart from the *Jüngerer Titurel* is like a gigantic sponge, absorbing all sorts of fabulous

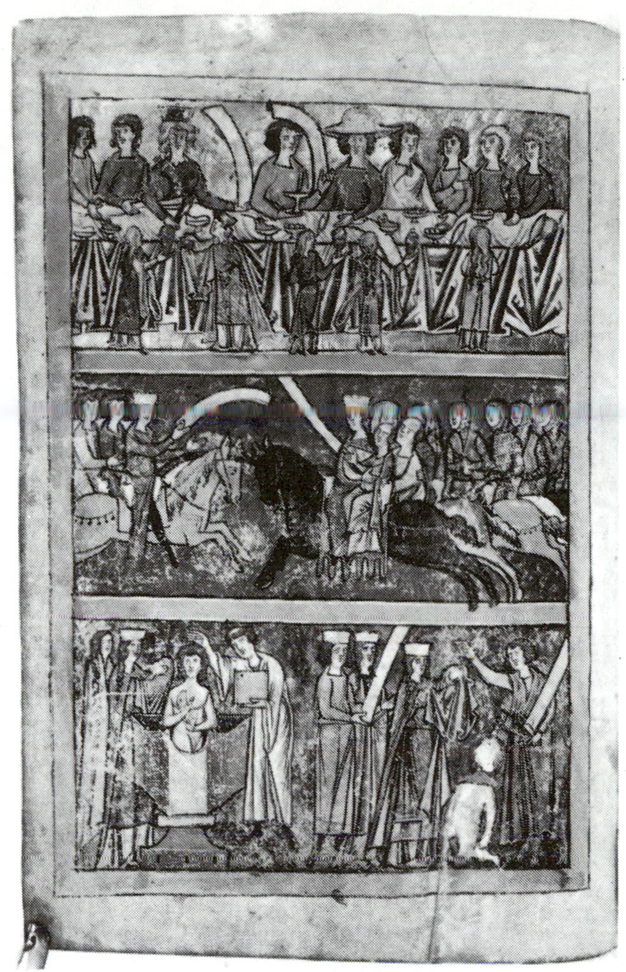

36. MS Munich, Bayerische Staatsbibliothek, cgm 19, fol. 50v: Grail Feast from *Parzival*; Parzival and Condwiramur; Baptism of Feirefiz. (Courtesy Bayer, Staatsbibliothek, Munich.)

material. In the tradition of a *vita*, the romance starts with Arthur's birth and childhood but soon breaks off for lack of subject matter (Heinrich did not know Geoffrey's *Historia* or Wace's *Brut*). This portrait of an ideal Arthur, illustrating a young king favored by fortune, gives place in the Gazosein episode to a representation of King Arthur like that encountered in popular epics and jocular poetry. It was Heinrich's intent to make his King Arthur the ideal sovereign, embodying the ideal of courtly, chivalric, and princely life. The earlier approach, though, is treated conventionally, leading to a loss of substance of courtly and ethical values. These values no longer stand for the individual efforts and aspirations toward a higher state of accomplishment; courtly existence, as represented by Heinrich, is deprived of all vitality. The second approach falls to the level of rustic and grotesque comedy. The incompatibility of these two devices—of royal and courtly representation on the one hand and of the knight-errant on the other—turns the romance of King Arthur into the romance of Gawein. Nevertheless, a remarkable change in the perception of Arthur's kingship can be observed: Heinrich's attempt to reactivate the role of the King is probably a reflection of the new ideal of the *rex et miles*, which led to kingship taking on knightly forms of life.

The same tendency is recognizable in Der Stricker's *Daniel von dem blühenden Tal* ("Daniel of the Blossoming Valley," 1220–30) but is realized in a quite different manner. It is the non-Arthurian elements that stamp this romance with its special characteristics and account for its exceptional position among German Arthurian epics. These elements have their origin in the heroic epic and explain the hybridity of *Daniel*'s substance and form. To mention just a few: courtly love, the moving force of courtly Arthurian romance, is of no importance at all. Furthermore, the lengthy descriptions of single and mass combats, shaped by the model of the *Song of Roland*, in which Arthur takes the field as commander-in-chief and dreaded, awe-inspiring fighter, are contrary to the classical Arthurian romance. This reversion to the precourtly ideal of kingship demonstrates Der Stricker's rejection of the narrative and symbolic structure of the Arthurian world in its traditional form. Instead of the traditional courtly values, we find political cleverness and energy; instead of moral exemplariness, pragmatism. Even if the quest for adventure and the individual chivalric actions of the protagonist are maintained, they are dominated by the idea of common welfare and social ethics, at the base of which are unconditional feudal faith and allegiance. The reevocation of these ideals, though not absent in classical Arthurian romance, exalts the precourtly ideal of vassalage seen in the heroic epic. In King Arthur, Der Stricker portrays another Charlemagne.

Der Pleier, a widely read man from the vicinity of Schärding on Inn, Austria, who perhaps belonged to the lower nobility, is the author of three Arthurian verse romances written between 1260 and 1280. These works tend to reestablish the ideal values of the past and set them against the decay and corruption of the poet's own times. For a long time considered a minor epigone who exploited his predecessors to the verge of plagiarism, Der Pleier and his contribution to the renewal of Arthurian literary tradition have been reevaluated by recent scholarship. Although he mostly borrows his material from Hartmann, Wolfram, Ulrich, Wirnt, Gottfried, Albrecht, and precourtly German epic, he is a talented and imaginative narrator, who combines the conventional elements of Arthurian lore into well-constructed plots of his own. His *Garel von dem blühenden Tal*, as the title indicates, is an anti-*Daniel*, or corrective model in the tradition of classical Arthurian romance, in keeping with Der Stricker's general plan. The work must have met with the approval of his public: the Runkelstein muralist included scenes from it in his exhibition of Arthurian chivalry. The romance *Meleranz* combines elements derived from *Seifrid de Ardemont*, a mermaid fairy tale that goes back to the French lai *Graelent*, and such traditional Arthurian motifs as the liberation of prisoners and noble ladies pressed by unwelcome suitors, combats against a tyrannical lord, villains living on robbery and exploitation, and a heathen king, but all are placed in a more realistic setting. *Tandareis und Flordibel* amalgamates episodes from various sources—*Erec*, *Iwein*, *Parzival*, *Wigalois*, *Lanzelet*, *Willehalm*, *Lanval*, and *Graelent*—the action being set in motion by the well-known motif of the grant of a boon. The French book that Der Pleier pretends to have translated into German (ll. 4,066ff. and 18,304ff.) is invented. The poet's concern is the preservation and transmission of courtly values, and his Arthurian romances are to be understood as guides to chivalric rules of behavior, as exemplified by Arthur and his circle.

Konrad von Stoffeln's *Gauriel von Muntabel* (late thirteenth century) likewise amalgamates fairy-tale and Arthurian components into a new plot, here the combination of the motif of the offended fay, as in *Lanval* and *Graelent*, with the journey to the otherworld, as in *Désiré*, set into an Arthurian framework. Although Konrad maintains the narrative scheme of Arthurian romance (as seen, above all, in Hartmann), the underlying principle is not enhancement to attain a higher status but simply cumulation and seriality. Nonetheless, Konrad shows a manifest interest in heraldry; he himself may have belonged to the Hohenstoffeln family of the Hegau in southwestern Germany.

Wigamur, written ca. 1250 or later by an unknown author probably from eastern Swabia, treats Arthurian matter on the level of jocular poetry. Marked by comic and burlesque elements, the fable is constructed on such common features as the abduction of the infant hero by a supernatural creature, his unknown identity, his association with an animal (here the eagle—though the association has no function in the tale), the legal contest between two damsels, the combat against a heathen king, and the revelation of the protagonist's noble descent. Arthurian knighthood is taken up with jousting and tilting, and the pleasures of the table are extensively described. The original significance of the Round Table has been lost. King Arthur, no longer the immobile center around which others move, appears as the leader of his knights on the scene of action. The Arthurian episodes have no distinguishing quality, nor do they have a symbolic meaning.

Albrecht's *Jüngerer Titurel* (ca. 1270) marks both the culmination and the point of disintegration of German Arthurian verse romance. Little is known about the author; he calls himself only by his Christian name at the end of the book. He often has been identified with Albrecht von Scharfenberg, whom Ulrich Fuetrer mentions in his *Buch der Abenteuer* and to whom he attributes two romances, *Seifrid de Ardemont* and *Merlin*. Albrecht was long considered merely the continuator of Wolfram. He certainly did adapt and integrate his main source, the *Parzival* and the *Titurel* fragments, exploiting the most incidental motifs and episodes and reassembling them to form new narrative complexes. These concentrate on the history of the Grail and the Grail family: the erection of the marvelous Grail temple by Titurel, the love of Tschionatulander and Sigune and the story of the hunting dog's leash, Gahmuret's and Tschionatulander's exploits in the East, Parzival's quest for the Grail, and the removal of the Grail to India, the fabulous realm of the Priest-King John.

The moving force behind Albrecht's work is its eschatological vision; his concern is religious and moral instruction. Whereas in the Arthurian romances of Heinrich von dem Türlin and of Der Pleier the Arthurian world occupies a central position, deriving its justification from the supremacy of courtly and chivalric existence, in the *Jüngerer Titurel* this supremacy is given to the transcendental order of eternal life, the sole guiding principle of existence. Albrecht introduces historical dimensions, such as his fixation of Arthur's reign to the sixth century; his references to Troy, Alexander, Rome, Charlemagne, and other Christian kings and martyrs; his allusion to the conflict between Hohenstaufen and Guelph; his genealogy of the Grail Kings. Albrecht's concept of history is eschatological and typological rather than chronological; events and personalities, whether real or fictitious, are seen not in their temporality but in their relation to the eternal. Albrecht writes the history of the Grail through analogy to the Scriptures. In the *Jüngerer Titurel*, chivalric action, guaranteeing peace and order, proves ineffectual. The most valorous and noble representatives of chivalry perish; combat and belligerency take on a worldwide dimension, reflecting a permanent human condition. King Arthur excels on the battlefield, but his victories do not restore peace. The Round Table breaks up, and Arthur's attempts to reconcile the antagonistic forces bear no fruit. In the final sequences of the romance, Arthur and his court completely disappear; Arthur himself is last mentioned as a founder of monasteries. The order of the future is projected into the theocratic realm of Prester John, who personifies the two great forces of the medieval world, kingship and priesthood. But this realm, the prefiguration of Paradise, lies in the Orient, not in the Occident.

Der jüngere Titurel was widely read (fifty-seven manuscripts survive) and appreciated. Jakob Püterich von Reichertshausen calls it the "haubt ob teutschen buochen" ("greatest of German books") in his *Ehrenbrief* (1462), and Count Gerhard von Sayn recommends it in his last will to his sons as the mirror of courtly virtues (1491). Ulrich Fuetrer uses it as the frame to his *Buch der Abenteuer*.

The attraction of Arthurian lore for the thirteenth-century Middle High German epic is also shown by a number of fragments related more or less directly to Arthurian tradition. *Der Mantel*, an adaptation of the French *Le Mantel mautaillié*, is ascribed to Heinrich von dem Türlin, but his authorship has recently been called into question; *Segremors* (three fragments of 433 lines) relates the adventures and friendship of this lesser-known knight of the Round Table with Gawein; *Edolanz* (380 lines) is similar to *Segremors*; *Manuel und Amande* (272 lines) presents the usual adventures and alludes to the legend of Arthur's death and expected return.

Simultaneously with the metrical versions of Arthurian romance, Germany produced a prose version of the French Vulgate *Lancelot*, the earliest fragments of which have been dated to the thirteenth century; the only complete manuscript (Heidelberg) belongs to the fifteenth. Linguistically, the Munich fragment and the Würzburg-Berlin manuscript show Low German (Ripuaric) characteristics, which has led to the assumption that the *Lancelot* may have been transmitted through Flanders and the Netherlands. The three parts of the German *Prosa-Lancelot* (ca. 1250) deal with Lancelot, the Grail quest and Galahad, and the death of King Arthur. The German redactor was a gifted translator, as well as an innovator, there being no German prose style tradition of its own.

Efforts to revive the literary convention of Arthurian lore were undertaken in the late Middle Ages. In the fourteenth century, two Strassburg goldsmiths, Philipp Colin and Claus Wisse, with the help of Sampson Pine, translated the Continuations of Chrétien's *Perceval* and inserted them between Books 14 and 15 of Wolfram's rearranged *Parzival*, unaware of the underlying concept and leading ideas of the Middle High German original. The *Nüwe Parzefal*, an enormous rhymed compilation executed between 1331 and 1336 for Count Ulrich von Rappoltstein, is of poor quality. Adventures are interchangeable and monotonous, the mystery of the Grail is no longer comprehended, and the idea of Arthurian chivalry is reduced to the knight-errant's feats of arms. Colin and Wisse were occasional writers and versemongers of bourgeois extraction with no higher poetic aspirations. Their primary interest was remuneration, and in this respect their patron's literary tastes and interests are more revealing than the redactors'.

In the fifteenth century, Ulrich Fuetrer produced the *Prosaroman von Lanzelot* (ca. 1467), an adaptation of the German *Prosa-Lancelot*; *Das Buch der Abenteuer* (ca. 41,500 lines in *Titurel* stanzas, published in two parts between 1473 and 1483); *Der strophische Lanzelot* (ca. 39,000 lines, also in *Titurel* stanzas, completed by 1487); and *Die Bayerische Chronik* (1478–81). All his literary works are dedicated to or composed on behalf of Duke Albrecht IV of Bavaria. The duke's interest in medieval chivalry and courtly ethics was due not only to the literary revival of traditional Arthurian romance but also to the fact that the models of the past manifestly served his purpose of princely and courtly self-representation and idealization. *Das Buch der Abenteuer* begins with an introductory book of the history of the Grail and the Grail Kings, followed by that of the Round Table. The main parts contain adaptations of the history of the Trojan War (Konrad von Würzburg), *Merlin*, *Parzival*, *Diu Crône*, *Lohengrin*, *Floreis und Wigoleis*, *Seifrid de Ardemont*, *Meleranz*, *Iban*, *Persibein*, *Poytislier*, *Flordimar*, and *Lancelot*. Ulrich, a talented writer and a great admirer of Wolfram, belonged to the literary circle of Jakob Püterich von Reichertshausen, which was close to the Wittelsbach court.

Das Buch der Abenteuer marks the end of almost four centuries of Arthurian reception and innovation in Germany. The sixteenth century is the epilogue to a great tradition of courtly romance, with the appearance of bourgeois genres and the invention of the printed book. Hans Sachs, the Nuremburg shoemaker and poet, uses Arthurian topics and episodes in his facetiae, histories, and *Meistersang* (e.g., "Die Ehbrecherbruck," 1545). Abridged versions in prose made their appearance in the second half of the fifteenth century, such as Wirnt von Grafenberg's *Wigalois* (1472), reprinted several times, and along with the so-called *Volksbücher* (*Lanzelot*, *Oliver und Artus*, *Tristan*, and others), in vogue during the sixteenth century, they satisfied a large public's fancy for popular and fantastic adventure stories, but the idea of Arthurian kingship and knighthood had waned. [KRG]

Bindschedler, Maria. "Die Dichtung um König Artus und seine Ritter." *Deutsche Vierteljahresschrift für Literaturwissenschaft und Geistesgeschichte*, 31 (1957), 84–100.

Brogsitter, Karl Otto. *Artusepik*. Stuttgart: Metzler, 1965; 2nd ed. 1971.

Emmel, Hildegard. *Formprobleme des Artusromans und der Graldichtung: Die Bedeutung des Artuskreises für das Gefüge des Romans im 12. und 13. Jahrhundert in Frankreich, Deutschland und den Niederlanden*. Bern: Francke, 1951.

Gottzmann, Carola L. *Artusdichtung*. Stuttgart: Metzler, 1989.

Gürttler, Karin R. *"Künec Artûs der guote": Das Artusbild der höfischen Epik des 12. und 13. Jahrhunderts*. Bonn: Bouvier Verlag Herbert Grundmann, 1976.

Schultz, James A. *The Shape of the Round Table: Structures of Middle High German Arthurian Romance*. Toronto: University of Toronto Press, 1983.

GERMAN ARTHURIAN LITERATURE (MODERN). 1) INTRODUCTION. The appearance of Arthurian themes in postmedieval German literature must be seen as an offshoot of a more general revival of interest in German medieval culture, beginning in the mid-eighteenth century. The medieval tradition had little appeal for the German writers of the seventeenth and early eighteenth centuries. They were more concerned with providing German literature with a poetics that would elevate it to the level of the French Classicists, whom they viewed as their literary and theoretical models. This century-and-a-half hiatus was broken by the influence of the theories of the Swiss-German professor Johann Jacob Bodmer. Reacting against the artificiality of the French Classicists, he attempted to understand the internal process of poetic creation itself, which he studied in the literature of various cultures, including medieval Germany. Despite the importance of Bodmer's more general literary theories, however, his poetic translations of medieval works lacked literary quality and were perhaps too premature to have an impact.

It was the German Romantic movement at the turn of the nineteenth century that was responsible for the tremendous revival of medieval culture as a source for creative literature. Faced with religious and political fragmentation and the threat of Napoleonic occupation, many German Romantics developed an idealistic interest in the Catholicism and perceived political unity of the medieval period. This interest in their own past, coupled with a concern for poetic spontaneity, led them to research, collect, and imitate the sagas, fairy tales, and folksongs of the past and to write numerous works set in the Middle Ages. In fact, the Romantics can be seen as providing the impetus for the great wave of historical fiction and drama that swept Germany in the nineteenth century.

Yet, although Romantics, such as the famous Schlegel brothers, expressed great interest in Arthurian literature, they produced little of it. Understandably, German writers would be more likely to exploit their own mythical, historical, and literary past, especially their "national epic," the *Nibelungenlied*, rather than the Matter of Britain. Though there was an almost unbroken stream of adaptations of the *Nibelungen* material from 1803 on, adaptation of Arthurian materials in the Romantic Age was at best sporadic and not very original. Here, and among the Preromantics, it was generally limited to poetic allusions to Merlin the prophet, often independent of specific Arthurian associations, or else consisted of translations of French versions of Arthurian stories, the prime source being Count Tressan's Bibliothèque universelle des romans (1775–89), or else attempted to translate or rework parts of Wolfram von Eschenbach's *Parzival* or Gottfried von Strassburg's *Tristan*.

With few exceptions, German Arthurian literature of the nineteenth and twentieth centuries was based on Wolfram and Gottfried. Production of postmedieval German Arthuriana could thus not expand until critical editions of Wolfram's and Gottfried's works, by such editors and translators as Eberhard von Groote (*Tristan*, 1821), Friedrich von der Hagen (*Tristan*, 1823), Karl Lachmann (*Parzival*, 1833), San Marte (*Parzival*, 1836), Karl Simrock (*Parzival* and *Titurel*, 1842), and Hermann Kurz (*Tristan*, 1844), made this material accessible to a wider public as a potential source for creative writers. Christoph Heinrich Myller's earlier publication of Bodmer's medieval *Parzival* and *Tristan* manuscripts (1784–85) had little impact because they lacked the critical apparatus that would have made these difficult works understandable. This was not as true of the *Nibelungenlied*, the style and language of which were much more straightforward.

In quantitative terms, the greatest interest in Arthurian literature (again limited primarily to the Tristan and Parzival material) occurred in the late nineteenth and early twentieth centuries. This can be traced directly to two factors: first, the success of Richard Wagner's operas *Tristan und Isolde* (1859), *Parsifal* (1877–82), and, to a lesser extent, *Lohengrin* (1847), all of them depending heavily on translations of Wolfram and Gottfried; second, the Neoromantic development in German literature at the turn of the twentieth century, which shared with the Romantic movement of the preceding century a degree of nationalism, nostalgic idealism, and religious fervor. This development, or literary echoes of it, extended into the 1920s.

The political and social atmosphere of the National Socialist era did not favor the production of Arthurian literature, which was never extensive under the best of circumstances, and the literature of the postwar years exhibits a concern for more pressing contemporary issues. From the 1970s on, however, interest in German medieval history and literature is revealed by an increased publication of new editions and translations of medieval works; critical writings on them; literary, film, and stage adaptations; and even novels about the lives of Wolfram and Gottfried. This renewed interest reflects the desire of each of the two modern German states, particularly the German Democratic Republic, to establish its own cultural identity with a continuous tradition.

The general receptivity of the Federal Republic of Germany to English and American literature, television programming, films, and technology as well as an international interest in fantasy literature of all kinds has also had a significant effect on the reception of Arthurian themes into German literature. The multivolume Arthurian novels of T.H. White, Rosemary Sutcliff, Mary Stewart, Susan Cooper, Gillian Bradshaw, Sharan Newman, and Richard Monaco have all appeared in German in recent years, and the 1983 translation of Marion Zimmer Bradley's *The Mists of Avalon* was on the German bestseller list for sixty-five weeks. English and American cartoons, video games, and films based on Arthurian literature or rich in Arthurian motifs are finding their way to the German public as well. Although the films by Richard Blank (*Parzival*, 1980, based on Wolfram), Klaus Lindemann (*Tristans Klage* ["Tristan's Lament"], produced for television in 1976, broadcast in 1979), Veith von Fürstenberg (*Feuer und Schwert* ["Fire and Sword"], 1981–82, based on Gottfried), and Hans-Jürgen Syberberg (*Parsifal*, 1982, based on Wagner) are still embedded in the somewhat narrow German Arthurian tradition, American films consistently command about fifty percent of the West German film market. The exponential increase in the exposure of the German public to English and American developments in Arthuriana is impressive. It is too early, however, to assess or predict the full impact of this phenomenon.

2) FICTION. Except for Johann Jacob Bodmer's verse-renderings of parts of Wolfram's *Parzival*; the epic *Tristan* fragments by Schlegel, Rückert, and Immermann; and the mixture of verse and prose narrative in the translations by Felix von Hofstaeter (1741–1814) of Ulrich von Zatzikhoven's *Lanzelet* and of Ulrich Fuetrer's *Lanzelet*, *Froner Gral*, and *Theurer Merlin*, all found in his *Altdeutsche Gedichte aus den Zeiten der Tafelrunde* ("Old German Poems from the Times of the Round Table," 1811), the occurrence of German Arthuriana in narrative form is relatively infrequent before the appearance of Wagner's *Parsifal*, and it largely relies upon contemporary foreign versions of medieval material.

In 1804, Friedrich Schlegel published a *Geschichte des Zauberers Merlin* ("Story of Merlin the Magician"), a translation by Schlegel's future wife, Dorothea, of the medieval French *Roman de Merlin*. Schlegel criticized his fellow Romantics for resorting to the newer, often abridged, versions of such medieval materials in Tressan's Bibliothèque universelle des romans, which served as a source for Christoph Martin Wieland's blank-verse narrative *Geron der Adelige* ("The Noble Geron," 1777), and probably also for his brief prose summary of Merlin's life, *Merlin der Zauberer* ("Merlin the Magician," 1777), In the verse narrative *Die Päpstin Johanna* ("Pope Johanna," 1813, prose version published posthumously, 1848), by the Romantic poet and novelist Achim von Arnim (1781–1831), Merlin is alluded to because of the symbolism of his birth from the union of a demon and a fairy (or demon and human). He thus embodies the conflict between good and evil with which Johanna is faced when the Devil uses deception to achieve her election as pope. Ludwig Tieck's tale of the *Leben und Thaten des kleinen Thomas, genannt Däumchen* ("Life and Times of Little Tom Thumb," 1811, in his collection *Phantasus*), with Tom's birth prophesied by the magician Merlin, sets a combination of the English and German versions of the fairy tale against an Arthurian background. Another magician, Klinschor, owner of the Castle of Wonders in the Gawain adventure in Wolfram's *Parzival*, is reduced to the figure of a mentor-poet in the legend of the *Minnesinger* competition at the Wartburg, adapted by Friedrich von Hardenberg (known as Novalis, 1772–1801) for his idealistic Romantic novel fragment *Heinrich von Ofterdingen* (1802). Despite their interest in Arthurian literature, the German Romantics preferred historical or quasi-historical characters and settings for their own works. Though the subjects of Benedikte Naubert's writings were typically Romantic in this sense, her depiction of the Arthurian Middle Ages as immoral and ephemeral was not.

The German interest in Arthuriana during the later nineteenth and early twentieth centuries shifted its focus to the medieval literary tradition of Wolfram's *Parzival* and Gottfried's *Tristan*, with Neoromantic developments stimulated especially by Wagner's *Parsifal* and *Tristan und Isolde*. However, whereas the Parzival material is dealt with in prose and poetry as well as dramatic works, the Tristan story occurs almost exclusively in dramatic adaptations.

The Merlin material, although still adapted occasionally, appeared more often in drama than fiction. The narrative *Merlins Wanderungen* ("Merlin's Travels," 1887), by Rudolf von Gottschall (1823–1909), takes up the conflict of values that Merlin represents as a result of his combined demonic-human origin. Lienhard's novella *Merlin der Königsbarde* ("Merlin, Bard of the King," 1900), which is typical of the Neoromantic idealism of his other works, makes Merlin a folk-hero. Paul Heyse (1830–1914) uses the title *Merlin* as a metaphor for the modern Merlin-Niniane love relationship, which his novel (1892) depicts. In Gerhart Hauptmann's mystical novel fragment *Der neue Christophorus* ("The New St. Christopher"), the first chapter of which was published in 1932 as *Merlins Geburt* ("Merlin's Birth"), a boy born of a demon and an earth spirit serves a religious apprenticeship under Father Christophorus, who perceives in him the new savior of humankind.

Metaphorical titles were also used to evoke associations with the Grail in novels with an otherwise non-Arthurian modern setting. This is the case with *Die Abendburg* ("The Evening Castle," 1909), by Bruno Wille (1860-1928), and *Montsalvasch* (1912), by Erwin Guido Kolbenheyer (1878-1962). In other novels by Kolbenheyer, particularly *Amor Dei* (1908) and *Meister Johannes Pausewang* (1910), it is clear that the author has again been influenced by the Grail motifs of quest and idealism, which is also the case with the novel *Wiltfeber, der ewige Deutsche* ("Wiltfeber, the Wandering German," 1912), by Hermann Burte (1879-1960). In the 1908 novel *Zwölf aus der Steiermark* ("Twelve from Styria"), by Rudolph Hans Bartsch (1873-1952), the medieval parallel is all too obvious and borders on the ridiculous when twelve idealistic poets band together to form a vegetarian order. On the other hand, the title of the historical novel *Parzival* (1878), by Albert Emil Brachvogel (1824-1878), is misleading, since the work deals with the decline of the Knights Templar around 1300, with only occasional mention of the Grail theme.

A number of mediocre works produced in the Neoromantic enthusiasm of the turn of the century can be grouped together as more or less free adaptations of Wolfram's *Parzival*, with some Wagnerian influence: *Parzival* (an edition for the German household with pictures and facsimiles, 1888), by Emil Engelmann (1837-1900); *Parzival, ein Abenteuerroman* ("Parzival, An Adventure Novel," 1911), by Will Vesper (1882-1962); *Der Liebesgral* ("The Love Grail," 1913), a free rendering of only the Schionatulander and Gahmuret stories in novel form by Georg Terramare (1889-1948); *Lohengrin* (1913) and *Parsival* (1914), both longer prose narratives by Gerhart Hauptmann; and *Flamme über die Welt: Die Sagen Parzival, Tristan, Merlin* ("Flame over the World: The Parzival, Tristan, and Merlin Legends," 1926), one of a trilogy of shorter narrative volumes on historical, mythological, and literary figures by Siegfried von der Trenck (1882-1951). The best of these reworkings of Wolfram's text are the 1898 version *Die Sage von Parzival und dem Gral* ("The Legend of Parzival and the Grail"), by Wilhelm Hertz (1835-1902), and *Parzival der Gralsucher* ("Parzival, Seeker of the Grail," 1922), by Hans von Wolzogen (1855-1934). Finally, the three fairy tales (1892-94) of Houston Stewart Chamberlain (1855-1927), *Weihnachtsmärchen, Ostermärchen*, and *Pfingstmärchen* (Christmas, Easter, and Pentecost Tales), derive directly from Wagner's *Parsifal*. The first two present the insights gained by Parsifal during periods of introspection on Christmas Eve and the eve preceding the Good Friday on which he regains the Grail, i.e., between Acts II and III of Wagner's opera. The third tale depicts Parsifal's death and is meant to span the gap between Wagner's *Parsifal* and *Lohengrin*.

The German interest in Arthuriana was curtailed during the National Socialist era and the period of social disruption immediately following World War II. Only Thomas Mann's novel *Der Erwählte* ("The Holy Sinner," 1951), based on the medieval Gregorius legend of Hartmann von Aue and written during Mann's self-imposed exile in America, is rich in Arthurian allusions.

Emphasis on the German cultural heritage by both the East and West German states since the 1970s has led to an increase in editions, translations, and adaptations of German medieval Arthurian works. Although it is difficult to draw the line between free translation or adaptation and creative writing, adapters of medieval romances in the German Democratic Republic were often accused of making ideological changes to render their versions more "socialistically" relevant. Günter de Bruyn's *Tristan und Isolde* (1975) and Werner Heiduczek's *Seltsame Abenteuer des Parzival* ("Unusual Adventures of Parzival," 1974) are examples of two such East German prose works. Lily Hohenstein's *Die Nächte in St. Wendelin: Der Lebensroman Wolframs von Eschenbach* ("Nights in St. Wendelin: The Life of Wolfram von Eschenbach," 1969) and Bruno Gloger's *Dieterich: Vermutungen um Gottfried von Strassburg* ("Dieterich: Assumptions About Gottfried von Strassburg," 1976), are biographical novels and, in a sense, literary-historical fiction.

In the Federal Republic of Germany, there was a similar awakening of interest in the rewriting of medieval German epics, for example, Ruth Schirmer's *Tristan* (1969). However, the importance of English and American cultural and literary phenomena added a dimension lacking in the modern Arthurian fiction of the German Democratic Republic. Successful German translations of popular Arthurian adaptations by a whole spectrum of English and American writers, from Mark Twain to Marion Zimmer Bradley, appeared in the 1970s and 1980s. This has led to an increased familiarity with a broader Arthurian tradition among the German readership. The appearance of works centered on Arthur and Merlin, such as Maria Christiane Benning's *Merlin der Zauberer und König Artus* ("Merlin the Magician and King Arthur," 1958, reissued in 1980), Ulla Leippe's *Artussagen neu erzählt* ("The Legends of Arthur Retold," 1978—one of a series of children's books), Walter Schneider's television script *König Arthur* (1974), and Kurt Vethake's *König Arthur* (1975), a radio play for children, all indicate a broadening of the German Arthurian horizon.

3) DRAMA. The dramatization of Arthurian material in German literature was the domain of late nineteenth- and early twentieth-century writers, primarily under the influence of Richard Wagner's operas; earlier writers preferred to adapt the material to epic or poetic forms. The Postromantic, or *Biedermeier*, author August von Platen (1796-1835)

37. MS Munich, Bayerische Staatsbibliothek, cgm 51, fol. 90r: *Tristan*: Tristan and Isolde Go into Exile; Mark Arrives at Cave; Tristan and Isolde Return to Court. (Courtesy Bayer, Staatsbibliothek, Munich.)

planned to dramatize the Merlin and Tristan materials (1827–28) but did not proceed beyond sketches. Friedrich de la Motte Fouqué's *Parcival* remained unpublished, and *Die Geburt des Merlin oder Das Kind hat seinen Vater gefunden* (1829), by the Romantic Ludwig Tieck, is merely an excellent translation of the Elizabethan drama *The Birth of Merlin, or The Child Hath Found His Father* (1662). Two obscure late Romantic *Tristan* tragedies (1854 and 1858) by Friedrich Roeber (1819–1901) and Joseph Weilen (1828–1889) are of minimal significance.

Only one Arthurian drama stood out as an exception to this reluctance to dramatize, Immermann's *Merlin: Eine Mythe* (1832), a philosophical Postromantic work that was meant to be read and that has in fact never been successfully performed. Merlin, the son of Satan and intended Antichrist, rebels against his father and presumptuously tries to save humankind by making Arthur rather than Titurel the King of the Grail. Merlin, however, seduced and robbed of his powers by Niniane, fails Arthur in his search for the Grail. Arthur and his knights perish, and Merlin dies dedicating himself to God rather than submitting to Satan. This pessimistic blend of romanticism and rationalism, which combines multiple Merlin traditions from a variety of sources, including Schlegel's translation of the Merlin story and Tieck's translation of *The Birth of Merlin*, deals basically with the inevitable incompatibility of the divine and worldly, or demonic, sides of human nature.

The Neoromanticism at the turn of the twentieth century, accompanied by the interest in medieval German Arthurian works generated by Wagner's operas, led to a surge of literary production based primarily on Gottfried's *Tristan* and Wolfram's *Parzival*, and on Wagner's adaptations of them. Almost all of the Tristan adaptations were in dramatic form, not only because of the strong influence of Wagner but also because writers saw in the inevitable tragic outcome of the Tristan and Isolde love affair a potential for adaptation as tragic drama. Whether this perception was incorrect or the literary ability to realize it too limited, these *Tristan* dramas were never successful.

The Parzival material was adapted to all genres, not least among them drama. A number of Grail plays were little more than dramatic trivializations: August Reissmann's *Das Gralspiel: Parsifal der reine Tor oder die Ritter von Salvator* ("The Grail Play: Parsifal the Ultimate Fool or The Knights of Salvator," 1833), a parody of Wagner; Wilhelm Henzen's *Parsival, ein Mysterium* ("Parzival, A Mystery Play," 1889); Paul Matzdorfs *Parsival, ein Jugendlichenspiel* ("Parsival, A Play for Young People," 1915); Emmanuel von Bodman's *Der Gral* (written 1915, published 1925); Friedrich Johann Pesendorfer's *Rosmunda, die Gralskönigin, eucharistisches Schauspiel für die Mädchenbühne* ("Rosmunda, the Grail Queen, Eucharistic Stage Play for Girls," 1916); Hans Rhyn's *Parzival und Kondwiramur* (1924); Gustav Renner's *Merlin* (1912). This last play, despite its title, explores the problems of striving and guilt normally associated with Parzival.

Wagner's impact is underscored both by the appearance of new Arthurian operas (for example, Goldmark's *Merlin*, 1886, with considerable contributions from Immermann's earlier play, and Felix Draeseke's *Merlin*, 1913) and also by the addition of musical elements to Parzival dramas in an attempt to enhance their effect. *Titurel* (1891), by Karl Schäfer (1849–1915), fluctuates between opera and drama and offers a depiction of the Sigune-Schionatulander love story as a prelude to the Grail legend. *Der heilige Gral* ("The Holy Grail," 1912), by Richard von Kralik, is a prelude to the story as adapted by Wagner and deals with Amfortas's loss of the Holy Lance. A choir of angels imitates Wagner's chorus. Although Kralik also wrote a *Merlin* drama (1913) emphasizing the Niniane (Viviane) episode, it was his attraction to the religious-mystical idealism of the Grail quest that most typified his Neoromantic work. The idealism of Friedrich Lienhard was more heroic than mystical; it is reflected in his numerous medieval themes, including his drama *König Arthur* (1900). This depicts the tragedy of Arthur, who tolerates Guinevere's adultery with Lancelot in order to preserve the integrity of his ideal of the Round Table.

By far the most prolific author of Arthurian literature at this time was Eduard Stucken, whose Grail cycle, or dramatic epos as it has been called, consists of eight plays: *Gawan* (1901), *Lanval* (1903), *Lanzelot* (1909), *Merlins Geburt* ("Merlin's Birth," 1912), *Tristram und Ysolt* (1916), *Das verlorene Ich* ("The Lost Self," 1922), *Vortigern* (1924), *Zauberer Merlin* ("Merlin the Magician," 1924). In this protracted frenzy of Neoromantic *Jugendstil* creativity, Stucken juggled plots and characters in order to transform the Grail quest into the central thread connecting Arthurian themes based on the most diverse sources, including Immermann's *Merlin: Eine Mythe*. Finally, two additional dramas were connected only indirectly to the Arthurian tradition. Rudolf König's *Der Gral, eine Dichtertragödie aus dem deutschen Mittelalter* ("The Grail, A German Medieval Tragedy of Poets," 1914) deals with the genesis of the medieval Claus Wisse-Philipp Colin *Der nüwe Parzefal*, which extends Wolfram's work by 37,000 lines. Gerhart Hauptmann's drama fragment *Galahad* (1908–14) used the title metaphorically to evoke the play's theme, the struggle of youthful innocence against temptation.

Interest in German Arthurian literature faded with the decline of Neoromanticism. National Socialist idealism was not oriented toward Arthuriana, and literature of the immediate postwar years reflected disillusionment rather than idealism. Arthurian interest did not revive until the 1970s, when each of the two German states emphasized the German cultural heritage as the basis for its new individual national identity. Although a revival of German medieval literature has led to new versions of the Parzival and Tristan materials, these have not generally been in dramatic form. Two West German adaptations of Wolfram's *Parzival* are Nathalie Harder's puppet play (1976–79) and a play by the experimental Munich theatrical company Workshop Moosach called *Flechtungen: Der Fall Partzifall* ("Weavings: The Partzifall Case," 1978), which interweaves incidents in the lives of two types of social outcast, an institutionalized psychiatric patient and the Parzival character of Wolfram's work.

Tankred Dorst made a more important contribution to modern German Arthuriana in his monumental drama *Merlin oder das Wüste Land* ("Merlin or the Wasteland," 1981). Written in colloquial German with generous amounts of irony, humor, and absurdity, which do much to demythologize even the most mythological parts of the tradition, the play is a pessimistic allegory presenting the whole rise and decline of King Arthur and his knights, and Merlin with them. Conceived for an international theater festival in Hamburg, Dorst's *Merlin* is particularly significant as an indication of the recent developments in German Arthurian adaptation. It reflects not only a readiness on the part of German writers to incorporate modern English and American Arthurian motifs and allusions but also the growing spirit of internationalism in German literature and culture in general.

4) POETRY. Verse epics or narratives, such as Bodmer's *Der Parcival* (1753) and *Gamuret* (1755), Wieland's *Geron der Adelige* (1777), the *Lanzelot und Ginevra* (1860) of Wilhelm Hertz (1835–1902), and the *Tristan* fragments by Schlegel, Rückert, and Immermann, are ambitious undertakings of varying success. It is sometimes difficult to distinguish creative poetry from translation in verse. The same can be said of Hofstaeter's *Altdeutsche Gedichte aus den Zeiten der Tafelrunde* (see above), which contains translations of Zatzikhoven's *Lanzelet* and Fuetrer's *Lanzelet, Froner Gral*, and *Theurer Merlin*. Lyric poetry, on the other hand, tends to draw on individual incidents and characters to create a mood. The character Merlin is the first to predominate in postmedieval German lyric poetry, with Parzival becoming more prevalent beginning with the post-Wagnerian Neoromanticism at the turn of the twentieth century. The principal exceptions to this generalization are Bodmer's poetically poor ballad "Jestute" (1781), and two poems in *Das Knaben Wunderhorn: Alte deutsche Lieder* ("The Youth's Magic Horn: Old German Songs," 1806–08), an extensive collection of German lyric folk-poetry by Achim von Arnim (1781–1831) and Clemens Brentano (1778–1842). The title poem of this collection, "Das Wunderhorn," is a variation on the chastity-horn theme from the medieval French *Lai du cor*, by Robert Biket. A second Arthurian poem, "Die Ausgleichung" ("The Adjustment"), combines this theme with an adaptation of the related *Mantel mautaillié*.

In poems based on the Merlin material, further Arthurian associations are either lacking or minor. For his second "Kophtisches Lied" ("Coptic Song," 1787), the great Classicist Goethe borrowed the role of the oracular Merlin, prophesying from his grave, from Ariosto's *Orlando Furioso*. Goethe may also have had the old magician Merlin in mind when writing his ballad "Der Zauberlehrling" ("The Sorcerer's Apprentice," 1797). Merlin's grotto-grave in the forest of Brocéliande figures again in Wieland's long elegiac poem *Merlins weissagende Stimme aus seiner Gruft* ("Merlin's Prophetic Voice from His Grave," 1810), in which the prophet bemoans the loss of the golden age of Arthurian chivalry and, by implication, the passing of the German Classical Age of Weimar.

The theme of Merlin's forest entombment or confinement by Niniane (or Viviane), or his voluntary isolation in nature, provided a convenient formula for the Romantic poets. In Immermann's philosophical poem "Merlins Grab" ("Merlin's Grave," 1818), Merlin represents the spirit of nature as a source of enlightenment and consolation for those who are openminded enough to accept his advice. In his later poem "Merlin im tiefen Grabe" ("Merlin in the Deep Grave," 1833), written as a second epilogue to his 1832 drama *Merlin: Eine Mythe*, an older and disillusioned Immermann laments the human inability to escape the confinement within modern society and so to benefit from the rejuvenating force of nature. Nikolaus Lenau, on the other hand, depicts only the positive aspect of Merlin's association with nature in the course of his description of Merlin reveling in the physical and spiritual enjoyment of a tempest in the fifth of his *Waldlieder* ("Forest Songs," 1843).

The Swabian Romantic Ludwig Uhland offers a poetic rendition of the basically non-Arthurian story of "Merlin der Wilde" ("Merlin the Wild Man," 1829), taken from a summary of Geoffrey's *Vita Merlini*. Merlin, depressed at the death of his three brothers, prefers to contemplate the mysteries of nature, from which he derives strength and prophetic insight, rather than remain at the court of his brother-in-law, King Roderick. The poem is dedicated to Uhland's friend and fellow poet Karl Mayer (1786–1870), whom he praises as a "modern Merlin." In a poem sent to Uhland out of gratitude for this compliment, Mayer humbly rejects the comparison and applies it to Uhland instead. Wolfgang Müller von Königswinter (1816–1873) uses the same basic story in his *Merlin der Zauberer* ("Merlin the Magician," 1857), but in this version it is not Merlin as the man of nature who is emphasized. Here he is Niniane's lover, and he uses his wisdom to resolve the conflict that arises from his revelation of the love affair of Guinevere, the king's daughter.

The poetic depiction of the Merlin-Niniane relationship is, however, not usually this positive. In the third of his *Katharina* poems (1835), Heinrich Heine compares the lover to Merlin, the suitor entranced by his mistress. The lover's mistress, however, may be interpreted as anything from political freedom to abstract beauty or nature. "In der Winternacht" ("In the Winter Night," 1840–50), by Gottfried Kinkel (1815–1882), presents this same stereotype, but here lacking any deeper significance. Finally, two poems by the later Romantic Alexander Kaufmann (1817–1893), "Unter den Reben" ("Among the Grapevines," 1852) and "Merlin und Niniane" (1852), present love, embodied in Niniane, and thought, embodied in Merlin, as two sides of the human spirit that are not compatible when pursued without compromise.

Except for Bodmer's ballad "Jestute," mentioned previously, and Goethe's uncompleted poetic narrative *Die Geheimnisse* ("The Secrets," 1784), in which the depiction of an isolated brotherhood of priests offers striking parallels to the Grail community of the Parzival story, without any direct reference to it, the Parzival material is largely neglected in German poetry until the end of the nineteenth century, when its potential for mystical interpretation is drawn on by writers of various antinaturalist movements, but primarily those of Neoromanticism.

"Neoromanticism" is often used loosely to encompass several related trends, such as mysticism, impressionism, and *Jugendstil*, among others, not all of which necessarily occur in the works of all Neoromantic poets and not all of which are characteristics only of Neoromanticism. In Karl Vollmöller's cycle of poems *Parcival* (1897–1900), the coherence of the Parzival story and its relationship to medieval sources are lost in an aestheticism of bombastic metaphor and *Jugendstil* nature descriptions. This is also true, but to a considerably lesser extent, of Albrecht Schaeffer's verse novel *Parzival* (1922), which omits most of the Arthur and Gawain material, and confuses the roles of other characters, but does include Merlin as a secondary figure. *Das Nordlicht* ("The Northern Light," 1910), a lyric poem of epic dimensions (some 30,000 lines) by Theodor Däubler (1876–1934), lies somewhere between Neoromanticism and Expressionism and also suffers from an overabundance of cryptic imagery. The persona of this poem is transformed into various historical and mythological figures (including Parzival), whose striving represents humanity's upward struggle toward a mystical union with the light of salvation.

The Neoromantic prose, drama, and poetry of Friedrich Lienhard are more straightforward and give expression to an idealism tinged with chauvinism. His poem "Parsifal und der Büsser" ("Parsifal and the Penitent"), contained in his collection of poetry *Lichtland* ("Land of Light," 1912), shows two equally valid paths to salvation, the penitent's self-denial and Parzival's knightly battle in his search for the Grail castle. A similar idealism is expressed in *Der Stern des Bundes* ("The Star of the Order," 1914), a cycle of 100 untitled poems by Stefan George (1868–1933). George, although generally considered a Neoclassicist, was nevertheless influenced by the Grail literature at the turn of the century. He uses the term *templeis*, Wolfram's designation for a Knight of the Grail, to refer to members of an elite group that must be established in order to achieve the spiritual rebirth of humanity. A religious-philosophical movement among Catholic writers in Vienna is reflected in the works of Richard von Kralik, whose poetic chronicle *Die Gralsage* ("The Legend of the Grail," 1907) overambitiously attempts to compress almost all German medieval Grail and Round Table traditions, with additions from some French sources, into one connected verse epic.

A break with Neoromanticism can be seen in the works of Ernst Stadler (1883–1914), an early Expressionist whose poems in *Der Aufbruch* ("The Start," or, in a political sense, "The Awakening," 1914) express the importance of action and challenge. This volume contains "Parzival vor der Gralsburg" ("Parzival Before the Grail Castle"), in which a voice from the castle admonishes Parzival to turn back and convert his quest for the Grail into productive activity for humankind and to earn his reward through suffering for this cause.

As already mentioned, Arthurian literature ceased to be of importance in the years before, during, and immediately after World War II, when writers focused on issues of more pressing relevance. With the revival of interest in medieval literature beginning in the 1970s, and with the German readiness to accept English and American cultural trends, it is possible that such references may expand to include more than the limited Arthurian tradition of earlier German literature. The poetry of H.C. Artmann, an avid fan of all Arthuriana as early as the 1950s, may represent a step in this direction. However, modern poetry like that of Artmann, with its departure from traditional forms, is often based on free association of words, ideas, and symbols, and it relies on the reader's familiarity with the elements that make up these associations. The poems of Artmann that draw on a wide spectrum of Arthurian references, for example, are unlikely to be appreciated by readers who are unfamiliar with the allusions. It is as yet uncertain to what extent a broader conception of the Arthurian tradition will develop among German poets and whether Artmann's predilection for Arthurian allusion in poetry is an anomaly or the reflection of things to come.

5) CHILDREN'S LITERATURE. The adaptation of Arthurian legend for children's literature in Germany is a relatively recent phenomenon. In the late nineteenth and early twentieth centuries, interest in Arthuriana was rekindled by the Neoromantic movement and the success of Richard Wagner's operas. However, it focused upon the specifically German tradition represented by Gottfried von Strassburg's *Tristan* and Wolfram von Eschenbach's *Parzival*. Moreover, since stories of illicit love were considered inappropriate reading for young people, *Tristan* was generally not adapted for children, while the few adaptations of *Parzival* for this group omitted most of the Gawain sections. The results, by authors like Richard Weitbrecht (*Deutsches Heldenbuch*, 1887), Emil Engelmann (*Parzival*, with pictures, 1888), and Gustav Bornhak (*Parzival*, 1910), were unmemorable.

After World War II, interest in Arthurian legend took a somewhat different turn in each of the two modern German states, both of which looked to their past as part of an attempt to reestablish a sense of cultural continuity and integrity. In the German Democratic Republic, modern Arthuriana continued to follow the more limited German tradition and was not a common source for children's literature. Werner Heiduczek's *Seltsame Abenteuer des Parzival* ("Curious Adventures of Parzival," 1974) seems at first glance to be an adaptation for children, with large print, colorful illustrations, and simplification of plot. The ironic tone, however, bordering on cynicism, is inconsistent with this outward format, which must then be interpreted as part of the author's ironic intent.

Although the Federal Republic shared the concern for German tradition, as can be seen in Nathalie Harder's puppet play *Parzival* (1976–79), it was also receptive to English and American cultural influences. These influences resulted in translations not only from medieval non-German Arthurian tradition, in anthologies like *Die Ritter der Tafelrunde* ("The Knights of the Round Table," 1957) and Ulla Leippe's *Artussagen neu erzählt* ("Arthurian Legends Newly Told," 1978) and in radio plays like Kurt Vethake's *König Arthur* (1975), but also from modern fiction. Almost half of the three dozen or so Arthurian works translated from English since 1970 are for a juvenile readership. They include translations of T.H. White's *The Once and Future King* as *Der König auf Camelot* (1976; 7th ed. 1984), Susan Cooper's five-volume The Dark Is Rising series as *Wintersonnenwende* (1977–85), and Rosemary Sutcliff's *The Lantern Bearers* as *Drachenschiffe drohen am Horizont* (1962; 5th ed. 1983), as well as her imaginative modernizations of earlier material.

Although the list of Arthurian works is short compared with the total amount of children's literature that has been translated, it has been growing rapidly in terms of both new translations and repeat editions. It reflects German receptivity toward a more international Arthurian tradition and toward English and American literature in general. [RWK]

Frenzel, Elisabeth. *Stoffe der Weltliteratur: Ein Lexikon dichtungsgeschichtlicher Längsschnitte*, 6th ed. Stuttgart: Kröner, 1983.

Golther, Wolfgang. *Parzival und der Gral in der Dichtung des Mittelalters und der Neuzeit*. Stuttgart: Metzler, 1925.

Hermand, Jost. "Gralsmotive um die Jahrhundertwende." *Deutsche Vierteljahresschrift*, 36 (1962), 521–43.

Müller, Ulrich. "Das Nachleben der mittelalterlichen Stoffe." In *Epische Stoffe des Mittelalters*, ed. V. Mertens and Ulrich Müller. Stuttgart: Kröner, 1984, pp. 435–59.

———. "Parzival 1980—auf der Bühne, im Fernsehen und im Film." In *Mittelalter-Rezeption II*, ed. Jürgen Kühnel, Hans-Dieter Mück, Ursula Müller, and Ulrich Müller, Göppingen: Kümmerle, 1982.

———. "Das Suchen nach dem gestrigen Tag: ARTus und ARTmann oder die Okulation des Mittelalters durch H.C. Artmann." In *Pose, Possen und Poesie: Zum Werke Hans Carl Artmanns*, ed. Josef Donnenberg. Stuttgart: Akademischer Verlag, 1981, pp. 19–34.

Weiss, Adelaide Marie. *Merlin in German Literature*. Washington, D.C.: Catholic University of America Press, 1933.

GESTA REGUM BRITANNIAE ("Deeds of the Kings of Britain"), a mid-thirteenth-century chronicle, perhaps by William of Rennes, that is a Latin hexameter adaptation of Geoffrey of Monmouth's *Historia*, perhaps influenced by later accounts. Arthur is the greatest of all heroes for the author, who mentions the belief that he is not dead. Merlin uses magic songs to accomplish his wonders, such as changing the shape of Uther, who had to stay three nights with Igraine to beget Arthur. [AEG]

Michel, Francisque, ed. *Gesta Regum Britanniae*. Bordeaux: Gonnouilhow, 1862.

GIBSON, WILFRID WILSON (1878–1962), one of England's Georgian poets, drew on the lives of country folk for his poetic dialogues. In "The Queen's Crags" (1912), a young Northumberland farmhand reveals to an older companion the encounters he has had with Queen Guinevere on past Midsummer Eves. [DN]

Gibson, Wilfrid Wilson. *Poems*. New York: Macmillan, 1929.

GILDAS, author of *De Excidio Britanniae* ("On the Ruin of Britain"), the only early work covering the phase of British history to which Arthur is commonly assigned. A statement in the text seems to place Gildas's birth somewhere about the year 500. Reputedly, he was the son of a chief in the Clyde area. Like several other Britons of future fame, he attended the school in Wales founded by St. Illtud. His style shows that either he studied elsewhere in addition, or the curriculum was broader and more Roman than might be expected. Certainly a cleric of some sort, he is generally supposed to have been a monk and, according to William of Malmesbury, he spent some time in the Glastonbury community; a passage in *De Excidio* may at least suggest an acquaintance with it. He is said to have gone to Brittany and founded the monastery at Rhuys. The *Annales Cambriae* put his death in or about 572.

He probably wrote *De Excidio* in the 540s—certainly not much before or after. It is a long diatribe in convoluted but far from contemptible Latin, addressed to British princes and clerics and especially to five regional kings whom he denounces individually. "Ruin" in the title refers to the disruption and destruction caused by the Saxon occupation of parts of Britain that began in the fifth century. Hence, the title is sometimes given in a longer form, with the word "conquest," *De Excidio et Conquestu Britanniae*. Gildas's theme is that the Britons brought the disaster on themselves by their sins, and national repentance is overdue. This message helped to inspire a large-scale monastic movement. It is chiefly because of his influence that Gildas has the title of saint, despite his uncharitable outlook.

Known as "the Wise" (meaning "learned"), he is a source of history but not primarily a historian. His retrospect of Roman and post-Roman Britain simply supplies him with topics for moralizing. Much of the history is grossly distorted. Though he speaks of Latin as "our language," and of Britons as "citizens," he has almost lost sight of Britain's Romanization under the empire and regards most of its people as merely conquered and more or less contemptible. When he reaches the fifth century, he is still blundering badly, but while his post-Roman story indicates a sequence and chronology of events that cannot be wholly accepted, it is right as to the general trend and probably somewhat nearer truth than falsehood.

He says that a British governing council, together with a *superbus tyrannus* or "preeminent ruler" (in this context, the conventional translation "proud tyrant" is misleading), invited Saxons from across the North Sea to settle in Britain as auxiliary troops. The *superbus tyrannus* is usually taken to be the man elsewhere called Vortigern; their identity is assumed by Bede, whose account of this period is largely a shorter paraphrase of *De Excidio*. Gildas explains that the Saxons were hired to fight the "peoples of the north," meaning principally the Picts. The arrangement crumbled when many more arrived and growing demands for supplies could not be met. The Saxons revolted and ravaged Britain, raiding across to the western sea. One effect was a British emigration (identifiable as a move to Armorica in northwest Gaul, which launched Brittany). At last, the Saxons retired within their authorized settlements. Then came a British recovery, both military and moral. Its organizer was Ambrosius Aurelianus, one of the few persons of whom Gildas approves. Decades of fluctuating warfare came to a victorious climax at the siege of Mount Badon, which Gildas seems to date to the year of his own birth, ca. 500. It brought a spell of comparative peace and order. But he laments that in his own time the Britons are backsliding and fighting among themselves, and the outlook is ominous.

Gildas's allusion to Badon is a well-known crux. Welsh tradition ascribes this triumph to Arthur and to no one else. But Gildas does not name the commander or refer plainly to Arthur at all. A reader might infer that there was no such person, or that he was a minor chief later exaggerated by legend. Either conclusion could be right, but the substance and style of *De Excidio* make both unsafe. Gildas records only historical facts as material for his sermon. If he did not think Arthur relevant to it, he would have seen no cause to mention him. He is oddly reluctant to name names in general, before his own contemporaries. Throughout the fifth century, Ambrosius is the only Briton he does name. If an explanation for his Arthurian silence is needed, it could lie in clerical rancor, since Arthur may have been "bad" by his standards; or Arthur may have flourished after his time, or substantially before it, beyond living memory. There are too many unknowns. The only safe statement is that Gildas is evidence for the war-effort with which Arthur is associated, but not for Arthur personally.

A medieval theory, sometimes echoed by modern scholarship, distinguished two Gildases—the author and the saint. Hagiography, however, treats them as the same person, and that assumption may be allowed to stand. A Breton "Life" composed in the ninth century has nothing of Arthurian interest, but another by a Welshman, Caradoc of Llancarfan, is important. He wrote it ca. 1130. He says Gildas had a brother, Hueil, a brigand and rebel but a popular hero, whom Arthur put to death. Gildas, grief-stricken, became Arthur's enemy, but eventually they were reconciled. Later, Melwas, King of Somerset, abducted Arthur's wife, "Guennuvar," and kept her at Glastonbury when Gildas was there. Arthur came to rescue her with troops from Devon and Cornwall, but the watery terrain hampered his movements. Gildas and the abbot mediated, the kings made peace, and the lady was restored.

Caradoc's two Arthur episodes are akin to those in other saints' lives. They present him unsympathetically as a foil for the saint, who forgives and helps him. However, this "Life" has several points of interest for the formation of legend. First, because of it, Gildas's omission of Arthur from *De Excidio* paradoxically became part of the story: Gildas, according to Giraldus Cambrensis, did write about him, but destroyed what he had written because of the killing of Hueil. Second, the Queen's abduction reappears in romance, with Melwas becoming Meleagant, and Lancelot. replacing her husband as rescuer. Third, this is the earliest proved connection of Arthur with Glastonbury. Finally, Welsh storytellers embroider the Hueil episode, one result being that the stone on which Arthur beheaded him can still be seen in the marketplace at Ruthin.

Excavated remains of buildings on Glastonbury Tor are datable to roughly this period, and have been held to give credibility to Melwas—perhaps, if they are remains of a stronghold, but their interpretation is doubtful. [GA]

Gildas. *De Excidio Britanniae*, ed. and trans. Michael Winterbottom under the title *The Ruin of Britain*. In *History from the Sources*. Chichester: Phillimore, 1978, Vol. 7.

Alcock, Leslie. *Arthur's Britain*. London: Penguin, 1971, pp. 21–29, 121–22.

Jackson, Kenneth Hurlstone. "The Arthur of History." In *Arthurian Literature in the Middle Ages*, ed. Roger Sherman Loomis. Oxford: Clarendon, 1959, pp. 1–11.

Lapidge, Michael, and David Dumville, eds. *Gildas: New Approaches*. Woodbridge, Suffolk: Boydell and Brewer, 1984.

GILES, REV. J.A. (1808–1881). A Fellow of Christ Church College, Oxford, during the mid-nineteenth century, Giles's major claim was that he walked in the literary footsteps of Aaron Thompson, the first translator into the English language of Geoffrey of Monmouth's history of British kings. Giles updated Thompson's English version and examined Thompson's principal Latin source. In 1842, Giles produced his edition of Thompson's 1718 translation, adding little to the text but bringing much of the language up to date. The 1842 book was followed in 1848 by *Six Old English Chronicles*, which contained not only the Thompson update but English translations of Gildas, Nennius, and Saxon chroniclers as well. In 1844, he published a Latin version of Geoffrey, the first to be printed in England. He must be given credit for keeping the Matter of Britain alive, both in vernacular and scholarly terms, by editing the first English reprint of Geoffrey's history in more than 125 years and the first Latin version in more than 250 years. [JHW]

Geoffrey of Monmouth. *The British History of Geoffrey of Monmouth, in twelve books, translated from the Latin by A. Thompson, Esq., a new edition, revised and corrected by J.A. Giles LL.D.* London: Bohn, 1842.

Giles, J.A., ed. *Galfridi Monumentensis Historia Britonum*. In *Scriptores Monasticio*. London: Nutt, 1844.

———. ed. *Six Old English Chronicles*. London, 1848; repr. London: Bell and Daldy, [1870?].

GIOVANNI DEL VIRGILIO. In a 1325 pastoral poem addressed to Albertino Mussato of Padua, Giovanni del Virgilio praises a certain Lycidas as the poet who had celebrated the love of Iseult; a fourteenth-century scholiast (tentatively identified as Boccaccio) identifies this Lycidas as Lavato de' Lovati (d. 1309), a Paduan poet, six lines of whose Latin poem on Iseult have been preserved in Mediceo Laurenziana, plut. xxxiii, cod. 31. [DLH]

Gardner, Edmund G. *The Arthurian Legend in Italian Literature*. London: Dent, 1930, pp. 217–18.

GIRALDUS CAMBRENSIS (ca. 1146–1222/3). In nine, or about half, of his numerous works, Gerald of Wales made passing references to either Arthur or his contemporary, Merlin Ambrosius. Concerning Arthur, Gerald says little, only noting that according to British traditions Irish kings paid tribute to Arthur and that Roman ambassadors came to his court at Caerleon, where also Dubricius, archbishop of Caerleon, ceded the metropolitan see to the King's uncle, St. David, bishop of Menevia, subsequently known as St. David's. In addition, in *De Principis Instructione* (ca. 1193) and *Speculum Ecclesiae* (ca. 1215), Gerald recorded the 1191 discovery of the bodies of Arthur and Guenevere at Glastonbury and their reburial in the abbey there.

When treating British—that is, Welsh—traditions, Gerald appears to be of two minds. He believed in prophecies and included several by Merlin Ambrosius as well as many others from Celtic sources. But Gerald did not trust Geoffrey of Monmouth and twice revealed reservations concerning Geoffrey's version of history. [KGM]

Gerald of Wales. *Giraldi Cambrensis Opera*, ed. J.S. Brewer et al. 8 vols. London: Longman, 1861–91.

Bartlett, Robert. *Gerald of Wales, 1146–1223*. Oxford: Clarendon, 1982.

Gransden, Antonia. *Historical Writing in England, c. 550 to c. 1307*. London: Routledge and Kegan Paul, 1974.

Richter, Michael. *Giraldus Cambrensis: The Growth of the Welsh Nation*. Aberystwyth: National Library of Wales, 1976.

GIRART D'AMIENS, who also wrote *Méliacin*, is the author of *Escanor*, a romance of nearly 26,000 lines dated to ca. 1280. It may have been presented in 1279 to Eleanor of Castile, since the prologue and epilogue contain dedications to Eleanor, her husband, Edward I of England, and their children. Edward is known to have been an Arthurian enthusiast, and like other English royalty used the Arthurian story for political purposes, in particular to strengthen claims to territories in northern England and Scotland.

One of the two main plots concerns Kay, who falls in love during a tournament with Andrivete, daughter of Canor of Northumberland. Kay, however, returns to court without confessing his love, and Andrivete narrowly escapes being married for political motives by her uncle to someone of inferior social status. In the other plot, Gauvain is accused by Escanor le Beau of the murder of a cousin. Gauvain hesitates to defend himself against the accusation, and Gifflet's brother Galantivet defeats the accuser. In the meantime, Escanor le Grand, uncle of Escanor le Beau, captures Gifflet when he is unable to take Gauvain. Gauvain finally defeats Escanor le Beau and the two are reconciled.

Although much of the narrative is formed by stock motifs, the author does depart from convention in his portrayal of Kay as a timid lover and Gauvain as somewhat of a coward. An aura of religiosity pervades the end of the romance. Much of the plot hinges on necromancy and the supernatural, and the influence of the prose romances, especially the Prose *Tristan*, is particularly strong. Composed during the same period, *Escanor* has much in common in terms of narrative structure and treatment of subject matter with the romance of *Claris et Laris*. [KB]

Girart d'Amiens. *Escanor*, ed. Heinrich Michelant. Tübingen: Bibliothek des Literarischen Vereins in Stuttgart, 1886.

Schmolke-Hasselmann, Beate. *Der arthurische Versroman von Chrestien bis Froissart*. Tübingen: Niemeyer, 1980, pp. 222–28.

Schulze-Busacker, Elisabeth. "'Gauvain li malparlier': le rôle de Gauvain dans le roman d'*Escanor*." In *Lancelot, Yvain, Gauvain (Colloque arthurien belge de Wégimont)*. Paris: Nizet, 1984, pp. 113–23.

GIRFLET (Giflet), a minor knight of the Round Table, who appears in many texts, including Chrétien de Troyes's *Erec et Enide* and *Perceval*, the First Continuation, Gerbert de Montreuil's Continuation, Béroul's *Tristran*, the Prose *Tristan*, *Hunbaut*, *La Vengeance Raguidel*, and the Vulgate Cycle. In the Vulgate, Girflet fights with Arthur against Mordred and, when Arthur is mortally wounded, is instructed to throw Excalibur into a nearby lake. When Girflet finally obeys Arthur's command, a hand emerges from the water, seizes Excalibur, and vanishes. In subsequent texts, Girflet is killed when Lancelot rescues Guenevere from the stake, and it is Bedivere who casts Excalibur into the water. [SW]

GIRONE IL CORTESE, an Italian translation of the 150l(?) French edition of *Gyron le Courtois*, a portion of the *Compilation* of Rusticiano da Pisa (Rusticien de Pise). In its focus on Girone, the Italian text has all but detached its hero from the traditional cycles of Arthur and Tristan to present an extended account of a nearly independent knight-errant. While there are lengthy digressions from the central storyline, the heart of the narrative is the chivalric friendship between Girone and Danain, and the strain placed on that friendship when Danain, leaving to pursue his vendetta against the Brothers of the Savage Land, leaves his wife, the Lady of Malehaut (Maloanco), in the custody of his friend, Girone, who promptly falls in love with her. The narrative includes a history of Girone's family, the House of Bruni, beginning with the dramatic entrance of the last knight of the Tavola Vecchia, the 120-year-old Branor Bruni, into Arthur's court, where he overcomes Tristan, Lancelot, and Arthur himself. The romance then concentrates on the adventures of Girone and Danain. In the longest sequence of interpolated adventures, Breunis Senza Pietà is tricked by a lady he loves and is trapped in a cave where he discovers richly appointed chambers, the effigies of a knight and a lady, and an ancient knight. This knight turns out to be Girone's grandfather, and he relates the adventures of the House of Bruni to Breunis, who mends his ways after hearing of these marvels of chivalry. The narrative returns to Girone, whose adventures at the Perilous Pass reunite him with Danain and the Good Knight Without Fear, who goes on to endure a series of adventures in the Vale of Servitude that do not conclude until the *Meliadus*, the second volume of the *Compilation*. After an encounter with Hellin the Red, the vile scion of an incestuous union, Girone and Danain part at a crossroad, Danain taking the path to the Tower of False Pleasure and Girone the path to the Tower of Wrath, in which he and his wife are both imprisoned. Girone's wife gives birth to a son, Galinans, who is fostered in evil ways by the lord of the Tower, and the last chapter of the *Girone* abandons the titular hero to tell of the death of his wicked son at the hands of Palamides. Despite its peculiarly unsatisfactory ending, the result of its position as merely a portion of the *Compilation*, *Girone il Cortese* is a reasonably lively romance, more coherent than its source and possessing a quality that raises it above the level of mere translation. It is also, of course, a belated translation into his native language of the earliest Arthurian romance composed by an Italian. [DLH]

Tassi, Francesco, ed. *Girone il Cortese; romanzo cavalleresco di Rustico o Rusticiano da Pisa*. Florence: Società Tipografica, 1855.

Gardner, Edmund G. *The Arthurian Legend in Italian Literature*. London: Dent, 1930, pp. 47–59.

GLASSCOCK, FREDERICK THOMAS (1871–1934), English founder of a fellowship based on King

Arthur's Round Table and author of *King Arthur . . . and the Twofold Quest*, a play recounting events of the Arthurian legends, in which each scene is assigned a symbolic value. Glasscock developed his sometimes idiosyncratic reading of the legends in *The Symbolic Meaning of the Story of King Arthur* (1929). *The Book of the Order of the Fellowship of the Knights of the Round Table of King Arthur* (1929) outlines the procedures for becoming a member of and advancing in the fellowship that Glasscock established at King Arthur's Hall, Tintagel, and whose members wished to "keep the principles of King Arthur before them as a standard for their everyday life." [ACL]

[Glasscock, Frederick]. *The Book of the Order of the Fellowship of the Knights of the Round Table of King Arthur*. King Arthur's Hall, Tintagel: n.p., [1929].

———. *The Symbolic Meaning of the Story of King Arthur*. King Arthur's Hall, Tintagel: n.p., [1929].

———. *King Arthur: The Symbolic Story of King Arthur and the Knights of the Round Table and the Twofold Quest*. King Arthur's Hall, Tintagel, 1931.

GLASTONBURY, a small town in Somerset with a ruined abbey; Glastonbury has an immensely long history and is the focus of much legend and speculation. It has several Arthurian connections: as the scene of the first known version of the abduction of Guenevere; as the site of Arthur's reputed grave; as a place associated in some way with the Grail; and as the retreat to which Lancelot and others retire as hermits.

Glastonbury lies in and around a cluster of hills, of which the highest is the Tor, a curious whaleback formation visible a long way off. The country round about, as far as the Bristol Channel, is low and level. In the last centuries B.C. and the early Christian era, much of it was swampy and much was under water. From most angles, the hill-cluster would then have had the appearance of an island, though it was not completely so. In the neighborhood, till about the period of the Roman conquest, two Celtic lake-villages stood on ground artificially built up above the water-line. These were centers of the La Tène culture. Artifacts testify to developed crafts and wide-ranging trade. The land was

38. Glastonbury Abbey, general view of ruins. (Courtesy the Bettmann Archive/ BBC Hulton.)

eventually drained and the sea excluded, but the image of the hill-cluster's insularity persisted and was the reason for two controversial names applied to it: *Ynys-witrin*—i.e., the Isle of Glass—and *Avalon*.

Some etymologists believe that the oldest name was *Glastonia*, derived from a Celtic word meaning "blue-green," or more specifically "woad," the plant from which blue-green dye was made: this was a place where woad grew. *Glastonbury* is the Anglo-Saxon *Glaestingabyrig*, supposedly the result of the Saxons' coining the word *Glaestingas* for the dwellers in Glastonia and then adding *byrig*, meaning a town or inhabited spot. By a further complication, *Glast* or *Glasteing* is sometimes given as a personal name, that of the founder of the settlement.

Ynys-witrin, the Glass Island, is a Celtic form, quoted in early records as predating the Saxon occupation of this area in the seventh century. Its claim to priority has been disputed, on the ground of its being due to a misapprehension that the syllable *Glas* was literally "glass": an error implying the English language, in however early a shape, and therefore subsequent to the Saxons' advent. This is by no means certain. Amid so much confusion, the sole certainty is that the etymological roots lie deep.

As for *Avalon*, it became attached to Glastonbury because of Arthur. The place was asserted to have been his last earthly destination after his fatal wounding, the true Avalon. This claim cannot be documented before the announcement of the discovery of his grave in 1191. But the magical name seems to have owed its acceptability here to a far older otherworldly aura, which was a legacy of pre-Christian beliefs and practices.

In the Celtic scheme of things, Glastonbury's hill-on-island topography was intensely numinous. Moreover, the Tor is encircled by a system of paths or terraces, heavily weathered but still traceable over long distances. They may in part be strip lynchets, created by medieval agriculture, but a case exists for the view that the system is basically a kind of labyrinth, a great ritual work assignable to the same era as other ritual works, such as Stonehenge and Silbury. Also, there are recurrent, perhaps related, allusions to a folk-belief that the Tor is hollow, a point of entry to the underworld or otherworld that figures in the Welsh poem *The Spoils of Annwfn*. Collen, a wandering Welsh saint, is said to have actually entered the hill and tried to exorcize the underworld king Gwyn-ap-Nudd. A tower that now surmounts the hill is all that remains of a church dedicated to St. Michael, built in the fourteenth century to replace a previous church that collapsed in an earthquake. The dedication to the angelic conqueror of infernal powers may hint at a belief that these powers were present and active—an excusable suspicion after the earthquake, since in Britain the destruction of buildings from that cause is practically unknown.

Whatever its pagan past, Glastonbury was arguably the home of the first British Christian community, the first at any rate that held together and survived. It undoubtedly has a continuity without parallel in England. A Celtic-type settlement of British monks was already in being when the Saxons arrived, in a year chronicled as 658. By then, the conquerors were Christians themselves, and the community continued without a break, under the lavish patronage of the kings of Wessex. Saxon and Irish monks presently joined it. Under St. Dunstan in the tenth century, Glastonbury became a major Benedictine abbey, and during the Middle Ages it was the greatest in England, or an equal-first with Westminster. But as to how the original community had come to be there, neither documentation nor archaeology can provide a firm answer, and imagination has flourished freely.

William of Malmesbury, writing ca. 1130, gives a transcript from an alleged charter dated 601 in which a king made the monastery a grant of land. Opinions are divided as to its authenticity. An apparent allusion by Gildas, if accepted, would push back the monastery's existence sixty years farther, and it is likely that there were hermits earlier than that. A small community may have taken shape on and around the Tor before the monastic settlement of the abbey site. Excavations in 1964–66 uncovered foundations of buildings on the summit that were not later than the sixth century and could have belonged to the fifth, though their nature and use remain uncertain. A spring below the Tor, now called Chalice Well and possibly sacred before Christianity, would have given a reliable water supply.

However, the fact at the center of all the early tradition is that within the abbey precinct, on the spot now occupied by the Lady Chapel, a church once stood that was so ancient that there was no trustworthy record of its foundation. William of Malmesbury gives a long account of it. A wattle building with reinforcements of timber and lead, it was known simply as the *vetusta ecclesia*, or Old Church. The dedication was to the Virgin Mary, from which it would appear that the original builders were under devotional influences hard to parallel so early in Britain. It was around the immensely venerated Old Church that the Christian legends of Glastonbury grew. William notes a current belief that it was built in the first century by disciples of Christ himself. He speaks cautiously and names no names. But by a process of interpolation in William's book, and the concoction of spurious charters, the abbey improved its early history and eventually put a name to the disciples' leader: Joseph of Arimathea.

Other legend-making had already made a deep mark in William's time, thanks probably to Irishmen who had formerly conducted the monastic school. St. Patrick, for instance, was said to have come to Glastonbury and even to have been buried there. Gildas was also claimed as a resident, perhaps more credibly, and it is in Caradoc's "Life" of him that Arthur makes an early appearance. Writing, like William, ca. 1130, Caradoc tells how King Melwas of the Summer Land (Somerset) carried off Guenevere and kept her in a stronghold at Glastonbury. Arthur came to rescue

SITE OF KING ARTHUR'S TOMB.
IN THE YEAR 1191 THE BODIES OF
KING ARTHUR AND HIS QUEEN WERE
SAID TO HAVE BEEN FOUND ON THE
SOUTH SIDE OF THE LADY CHAPEL.
ON 19TH APRIL 1278 THEIR REMAINS WERE
REMOVED IN THE PRESENCE OF
KING EDWARD I AND QUEEN ELEANOR
TO A BLACK MARBLE TOMB ON THIS SITE.
THIS TOMB SURVIVED UNTIL THE
DISSOLUTION OF THE ABBEY IN 1539

39. Glastonbury Abbey, site of "Arthur's Tomb." (Courtesy of Britain on View Photographic Library, BTA/ETB.)

her with troops from Devon and Cornwall, but the watery terrain hindered his army's movements. Gildas and the abbot mediated, the kings made peace in the "temple of holy Mary"—that is, the Old Church—and the lady was restored. Traces of this tale can be picked out in Chrétien de Troyes's *Lancelot*.

A linkage of Glastonbury with Arthur was established, therefore, before Geoffrey of Monmouth. Geoffrey himself ignored the place; his Isle of Avalon is not here, probably not anywhere. But in 1190–91, the monks gave the connection a more sensational form by exhuming Arthur's remains in their own cemetery and publicizing the find. Though accounts of this event vary somewhat, Giraldus Cambrensis reports it in careful detail soon afterward, and the main story is sufficiently clear.

The location of Arthur's grave had long been a mystery, here and elsewhere, as William of Malmesbury attests. But a Welsh or Breton bard divulged the secret to Henry II: Arthur was buried in Glastonbury Abbey's graveyard, between two "pyramids" or memorial pillars. Henry passed the news on. In 1190 or early 1191, the abbot ordered an excavation. Seven feet down, the diggers struck a stone slab and found underneath it a cross made of lead with the inscription Hic Iacet Sepultus Inclitus Rex Arturius in Insula Avalonia, "Here lies buried the renowned King Arthur in the Isle of Avalon." Nine feet farther down, they unearthed the coffin, a hollowed-out log. Inside were the bones of a tall man, who had apparently been killed by a blow on the head, because the skull was fractured. Some smaller bones, with a lock of hair that crumbled when touched, were interpreted as Guenevere's. The bones were deposited in two chests and transferred, in 1278, to a marble tomb before the high altar in the main abbey church. There they lay till the sixteenth-century rifling and vandalism that followed the dissolution of the monasteries.

Historians have often dismissed the grave as a fabrication and a publicity stunt. In 1184, most of the abbey, including the Old Church, had burned down. Money was needed for rebuilding, and, while Henry II had supplied it and encouraged others to do so, his successor, Richard I, did not. Besides the assumed usefulness of the grave for fund-raising, a political motive has also been discerned. Proof that Arthur was dead, and would never return as a Celtic champion, was calculated to weaken Welsh morale in resisting the English.

Both motives are credible, yet despite the confidence with which they are often affirmed, both are modern speculations devoid of documentary basis. No evidence exists that the monks did try to raise money by exploiting the grave or that it was ever employed as a weapon against the Welsh. In 1958, the archaeologist Ralegh Radford showed that the story had curious points of plausibility in the light of the graveyard's known history. Five years later, he completed an excavation south of the Lady Chapel proving that the monks had indeed dug where they said and had reached a layer of early burials.

The charge of complete falsehood being thus exploded, the question is not whether they found a grave but whose grave they found. This turns on the inscribed cross. It has disappeared, but William Camden gives a facsimile of one side of it in his *Britannia* (1607). If, as Giraldus claims, there was a mention of Guenevere, it was presumably on the other. The wording, particularly the epithet *inclitus*, might suggest that the inscription is based on Geoffrey and therefore a twelfth-century forgery. On the other hand, the style and irregularity of the lettering can be held to indicate an earlier date, conceivably much earlier. Furthermore, the standard twelfth-century Latinization of "Arthur" was not "Arturius," as on the cross, but "Arturus," as in Geoffrey. Up to 1191, "Arturius" can be paralleled only in Adamnan's seventh-century *Life of St. Columba*, where the person referred to is Prince Arthur of Argyll. In other words, it occurs only as a very early form.

To a certain extent, the hypothesis of a fraud is self-destructive. If Arthur's grave carried so much weight as to be worth elaborately faking, Welshmen or others might have been expected to challenge the claim and perhaps to ex-

40. Glastonbury Abbey, section of ruins. (Courtesy of Britain on View Photographic Library, BTA/ETB.)

hibit rival graves. This seems never to have happened. Folklore and fancy have offered several Camelots, several caves where Arthur lies sleeping, and so forth. For practical purposes, the King has only the one grave. Whether or not an original Arthur-figure actually *was* buried at Glastonbury (or reburied under unknown circumstances after interment elsewhere), a Welsh or Breton tradition may have said he was and become too firmly established to retract once it leaked out to Henry II. In that case, the grave with its identification, if fraudulent, could have been in the same class as some of the forged charters that Glastonbury was especially apt at producing. Such documents are not exactly fakes in the modern sense; they are attempts to give substance and color to beliefs that were held quite sincerely and sometimes even, in principle, correctly.

Glastonbury's known connection with the Christianized Grail begins soon after the exhumation. In Robert de Boron's *Joseph d'Arimathie*, the Grail has to be conveyed to the far west, to the Vales of Avaron. By "Avaron," Robert certainly intends "Avalon," and it is equally plain that his allusion is to the low-lying country of central Somerset; mythology or Geoffrey might have supplied an "Isle" of Avalon, but not "Vales." The author of *Perlesvaus* (early thirteenth century) professes to have adapted a Latin text at a religious house in the Isle of Avalon, where (he says) Arthur and Guenevere now lie. He, also, manifestly means Glastonbury. Neither of these romances shows whether the authors really had anything more in mind than some vague tale of Christians coming to the place in the apostolic era, the kind of tale that William of Malmesbury had already noted and been doubtful about. As for Joseph of Arimathea himself, though romance brings him to Britain, it never states explicitly that he came to Glastonbury, as monastic legend asserted.

That idea is first documented in an interpolated text of William, composed at the abbey toward the mid-thirteenth century. The writer of the relevant passage describes Joseph's arrival in A.D. 63, at the head of a party of twelve, and the building of the Old Church. His story is not a mere borrowing from Grail romance—indeed, it is incompatible with it—and the relation between Joseph's two roles, as Grail-bearer and as founder of Christian Glastonbury, is obscure. The fourteenth-century chronicler John of Glastonbury does slightly interweave them, and he also quotes a bizarre "prophecy" ascribed to a British bard called Melkin, which may preserve fragments of a separate legend. However, the precise statement that Joseph brought the Grail to Glastonbury does not seem to have been made, at least in any work of note, before Tennyson.

The *Perlesvaus* author's claim to have done research on the spot has been contested, because, it is urged, his description of Avalon's monastic site in the reign of Arthur does not fit the abbey. That is true, but it does fit the approach to Glastonbury Tor by way of an old road. The author knows the area, and is using a tradition of early Christian settlement on the higher ground. As observed, this may have a historical basis. A variant emerges at the end of Malory's work, where, after Arthur has gone, Lancelot and other survivors retire from the world to live as hermits in a retreat between two wooded hills "beside" Glastonbury. Malory's description would apply to the space between the Tor and Chalice Hill, which is adjacent to it.

Henry VIII dissolved the abbey in 1539, and the last abbot, Richard Whiting, was convicted on trumped-up charges and hanged on the Tor. Held briefly by the crown, the property passed into private hands. Over the next centuries, a series of owners used the buildings as a quarry for salable stone, till very little was left. The Church of England acquired the site in 1908, and the ruined remnants are carefully preserved.

Glastonbury has continued to show its capacity for myth-making and spell-weaving. The parent specimen of its famous Holy Thorn, a local tree that blossoms approximately at Christmas, is reputed to have sprung from Joseph of Arimathea's staff—but the miracle is first spoken of only as late as 1716. Glastonbury's real historic potency—as a religious center, as a fountainhead of Arthurian legend, and in political and cultural ways not considered here—has proved to be by no means a thing of the past. Besides a revival of pilgrimage, the modern town has witnessed a striking influx of mystics, theorists, and spiritual seekers. These have further enlarged its mythology. A notion about a visit by Christ himself (of unknown provenance, but hardly ancient) has won wide support. Chalice Well, the spring near the Tor's foot, is the holy place of a fellowship with beliefs of its own. A popular theory asserts that huge zodiacal figures are traced in the surrounding landscape and that their symbolism supplies keys to Arthurian stories, notably *Perlesvaus*. This idea, though quasi-archaeological, has not commended itself to archaeologists. [GA]

William of Malmesbury. *De Antiquitate Glastoniensis Ecclesiae*, in Scott, below.

Ashe, Geoffrey. *Avalonian Quest*. London: Methuen, 1982; rev. ed. Fontana, 1984.

Carley, James P. *Glastonbury Abbey*. Woodbridge, Suffolk: Boydell and Brewer, 1988.

Lagorio, Valerie M. "The Evolving Legend of St. Joseph of Glastonbury." *Speculum*, 46 (1971), 209–31.

Radford, C.A. Ralegh. "Glastonbury Abbey." In *The Quest for Arthur's Britain*, ed. Geoffrey Ashe. London: Pall Mall, 1968, pp. 119–38.

Rahtz, Philip. "Glastonbury Tor." In *The Quest for Arthur's Britain*, ed. Geoffrey Ashe. London: Pall Mall, 1968, pp. 139–53.

Robinson, Joseph Armitage. *Two Glastonbury Legends*. Cambridge: Cambridge University Press, 1926.

Scott, John. *The Early History of Glastonbury*. Cambridge: Brewer, 1981.

Treharne, R.F. *The Glastonbury Legends*. London: Cresset, 1967.

GLENNIE, JOHN STUART STUART (ca. 1840–after 1906), barrister, antiquarian, and widely traveled ethnologist, published in 1869 *Arthurian Localities*—an expanded version of his article "Arthurian Scotland" (*Macmillan's Magazine*, December 1867)—to expound the theory that Arthur was active in southern Scotland. *King Arthur or the Drama of the Revolution* (1867–70) was designed to show the development of humanity in the period since the French Revolution. Only two parts of the grandiose prose-poem were completed, the "Prologue" and "Overture" and "The Quest for Merlin." [CNS]

Glennie, John Stuart Stuart. *Arthurian Localities: Their Historical Origin, Chief Country and Fingalian Relations*. Edinburgh: Hertford, 1869.

———. *King Arthur: or the Drama of the Revolution*. 2 vols. London: Trübner, 1867–70.

GLIGLOIS, an anonymous French Gauvain romance composed in verse (ca. 3,000 lines) during the first half of the thirteenth century. The romance is available only in an edition prepared by Livingston from earlier notes, the unique manuscript of the work having been destroyed in the Turin fire of 1904. The hero, Gliglois, is contrasted with Gauvain. Both of them love the same woman, Beauté, but Gauvain does nothing to win her (apparently relying on his reputation and his traditional appeal to women), while his squire, Gliglois, serves her faithfully and patiently, thus gaining her love. The originality of this work lies in its removing fame and status as preconditions to success in love. The *Gliglois* was composed by an author of limited talent, but it is a competent romance, a straightforward, clear, and realistic narrative. [NJL]

Livingston, Charles H., ed. *Gliglois: A French Romance of the Thirteenth Century*. Cambridge: Harvard University Press, 1932.

GLOAG, JOHN (1896–1981), English author of *Artorius Rex* (1977), which concerns a Romano-Celtic Arthur of Britain, his wars, victories, loves, sorrows, triumphs, and tragedies, as written by one Caius Geladius (Sir Kay) at the request of the emperor Justinian. Artorius (Arthur) ends as an impotent king, deserted by a sluttish Gwinfreda (Guenevere), his aged companions, and Merlin. [VML]

Gloag, John. *Artorius Rex*. New York: St. Martin, 1977.

GLOGER, BRUNO, East German historian, wrote the novel *Dieterich: Vermutungen um Gottfried von Strassburg* ("Dieterich: Speculations About Gottfried von Strassburg") in 1976. Gloger adroitly places Gottfried's fragmentary version of *Tristan* in the frame of a fictional biography of the medieval poet. [UM/WCM]

Gloger, Bruno. *Dieterich: Vermutungen um Gottfried von Strassburg*. Berlin: Union, 1976.

Gernentz, Hans-Joachim. "Bruno Gloger: Vermutungen um Gottfried von Strassburg." In *Rezeption deutscher Dichtung des Mittelalters*. Greifswald: Ernst-Moritz-Arndt-Universität, 1982.

GLYN, ELINOR (1864–1943), American author of popular romances, loosely transposes the love triangle of Arthur-Guinevere-Lancelot into a contemporary upper-class English setting in her sentimental romance *Guinevere's Lover* (1913). A self-preoccupied Guinevere narrates the story. [RHT]

Glyn, Elinor. *Guinevere's Lover*. New York: Appleton, 1913. (Published in England as *The Sequence, 1905–1912*. London: Duckworth, 1913.)

GODFREY OF VITERBO, an ecclesiastic in the service of the emperor Frederick Barbarossa (r. 1152–90), retold Geoffrey of Monmouth's stories of Vortigern and the tower, the search for Merlin, and the conception of Arthur in his universal history *Pantheon* (1169–91). [DLH]

Godfrey of Viterbo. *Godefridi Viterbiensis Pantheon sive Universitatis libri qui Chronici appellantur XX*. Basle, 1559.

Gardner, Edmund G. *The Arthurian Legend in Italian Literature*. London: Dent, 1930, pp. 6–8.

GODODDIN, THE, a series of laments, ascribed to the northern bard Aneirin, for a company of British nobles who assembled in the kingdom of Manau Guotodin, around Edinburgh, and rode south to *Catraeth* (possibly Catterick in Yorkshire), where they fell into battle against the Angles. The date of this campaign is ca. 600, and the *Gododdin* poems, or those that are genuinely Aneirin's, belong to that time.

One stanza mentions a warrior named Gwawrddur as having "glutted the ravens" (that is, killed adversaries) "though he was not Arthur." The apparent sense is that he was a great fighter even though not equal to the greatest of all. Arthur is clearly proverbial for prowess in war. How much significance should be attached to the stanza is uncertain, since it may be an interpolation by a later poet, though there is no cogent reason for thinking so. [GA]

Jackson, Kenneth Hurlstone. *The Gododdin: The Oldest Scottish Poem*. Edinburgh: Edinburgh University Press, 1969.

GODWIN, PARKE, American author of the Arthurian novels *Firelord* (1980), *Beloved Exile* (1984), and *The Last Rainbow* (1985). *Firelord* is notable in that it presents the story of Arthur against the background of a complex society made up of the remnants of Roman culture in Britain, the various settled Celtic tribes, and the remaining survivors of the nomadic, Pictish tribes. Godwin's Arthur, though brought up by the Romano-Celtic family of Uther, is here depicted as part Pict. He is also a visionary—Merlin appears as an aspect of Arthur's own character, and Arthur's encounter with his Pictish side has the quality, at least in its beginning and ending, of a dreamlike otherworld experience.

Godwin's strengths lie not only in his effectively realized society but in the various characters of the novel, especially Guenevere. She is Arthur's equal in strength of character and in her classical training, and it is the clash of their strengths, combined with the frustrations of their love relationship, that leads to their tragic discord. In Guenevere more than in Arthur can be found the clearest evidence of the all-but-impossible struggle to forge unity from disparate elements of society.

Beloved Exile continues the story of Guenevere after Arthur's death at the hands of Modred, son of Arthur's Pictish wife, Morgana. Guenevere attempts to retain control of the fragmenting society that her husband had forged. She is forced to work with those of Arthur's allies whom her conflict with Arthur has alienated and, just as Arthur had to come to terms with his Pictish side by living for a time with Morgana and her family, Guenevere, in an extended period of Saxon captivity, comes to value the qualities of a culture greatly different from her own. Godwin's deliberately romantic departures from the conventions of the Arthurian legend are effective in that they permit the author to establish a parallel between Arthur and Guenevere—the "alien" experience that humanizes each. Both novels are characterized by a vigorous, humorously ironic narrative tone.

The Last Rainbow moves back in time to the life of St. Patrick before his mission to Ireland. Forced to live among Pictish nomads, the young missionary learns, through physical and spiritual suffering, to temper his ferocious Christian zeal. He later encounters Ambrosius Aurelianus, who has begun his struggle for British autonomy.

Godwin also includes Arthurian elements in three short stories. "The Lady of Finnigan's Hearth" (1977) combines lightheartedness and poignancy: after the ennui of afterlife in heaven, Isolde returns to earthly existence in modern America, where she encounters the jaded, drunken Marty Finnigan. Set in the High Middle Ages, "The Last Rainbow" (1978) offers an ironic warning against greed and ambition when a bishop demands treasure and the Grail from one of the Faerie. "Uallannach" (1988)—which means "love" in the language of the Prydn—returns to the realm of *Firelord* to describe again the fatal encounter between Arthur and Modred, this time from the latter's point of view. The story appears in an anthology of original Arthurian tales edited by Godwin.

Godwin's work is representative of the characteristic trends of Arthurian fiction in the 1970s and 1980s in its attempts to combine anthropological and archaeological fidelity with modern narrative techniques and concerns. [AAR/RHT]

Godwin, Parke. "Finnigan's Hearth." *Fantastic*, 26 (September 1977); repr. in *The Fire When It Comes*. Garden City, N.Y.: Doubleday, 1984, pp. 45–76.

———. "The Last Rainbow," *Fantastic*, 27 (June 1978); repr. in *The Fire When It Comes*. Garden City, N.Y.: Doubleday, 1984, pp. 112–45.

———. *Firelord*. Garden City, N.Y.: Doubleday, 1980.

———. *Beloved Exile*. New York: Bantam, 1984.

———. *The Last Rainbow*. New York: Bantam, 1985.

———. "Uallanach." In *Invitation to Camelot: An Arthurian Anthology of Short Stories*, ed. Parke Godwin. New York: Ace, 1988, pp. 83–107.

GOETHE, JOHANN WOLFGANG (1749–1832), a prolific writer in all genres, is known to world literature primarily as the greatest German Classicist and as the author of *Faust*. Like most Classicists, Goethe was not particularly interested in Arthurian literature, although he does express agreement with Friedrich Schlegel's positive evaluation of Wolfram's *Parzival*. In fact, the name "Merlin" is the only direct reference that Goethe makes to any Arthurian character in his own poetic works., In his second "Kophtisches Lied" ("Coptic Song," 1787), he employs the image of Merlin the prophet borrowed from Ariosto's *Orlando Furioso*. Goethe's oracular Merlin, lying in his grave, gives advice to wise men only, since it is futile to offer wisdom to fools. A less specific image of Merlin as the old magician may be reflected in his famous ballad "Der Zauberlehrling" ("The Sorcerer's Apprentice," 1797). In addition, in his poetic narrative fragment *Die Geheimnisse* ("The Secrets," 1784) it is difficult to ignore the parallel between Wolfram's Grail community and Goethe's depiction of a contemplative order of twelve knight-priests whose old leader Humanus (Titurel?) will be replaced by a younger wandering "templar" (Parzival?). [RWK]

Goethe, Johann Wolfgang. *Werke*, ed. Erich Trunz. Hamburg: Christian Wegner, 1948–60, Vols. 1 and 2.

Golther, Wolfgang. "Goethe's 'Geheimnisse.'" In *Parzival und der Gral*. Stuttgart: Metzler, 1925, pp. 286–88.

Weiss, Adelaide Marie. "Goethe." In *Merlin in German Literature*. Washington, D.C.: Catholic University of America Press, 1933, pp. 69–72.

GOEZNOVII, LEGENDA SANCTI ("Legend of St. Goeznovius"). "Goeznovius" is a late Latinization of *Goueznou*, the name of a saint of Brittany. Its Welsh equivalent is *Gwyddno*. Goueznou was born in Wales but was one of many ecclesiastics who helped to create a Lesser Britain in Armorican Gaul. Contradictory datings put him in the sixth or seventh century, the former being more likely. In any case, he has no personal connection with Arthur. The relevance of the *Legenda Sancti Goeznovii* lies in the prologue. This contains the only early historical narrative in which Arthur is mentioned plainly, with no obviously dubious or fantastic touches.

Undoubtedly written in Brittany, *Goeznovius* is one of several historical works cited in the fourteenth-century *Chronique de Saint Brieuc*. The substance of it survives in a fifteenth-century manuscript formerly at Nantes Cathedral. According to an introductory sentence, its author is a cleric named William and its date is 1019. Passages of narrative prose alternate with liturgical verse. The prologue takes up the first two prose sections, setting the stage for the saint's career. Referring to an "Ystoria Britanica," the author sketches the Britons' first colonization of Armorica. He puts it before the fifth century, like Nennius and Geoffrey of Monmouth. Part of what he says is legend, but he gives local information that carries some weight. The next prose section traces the fifth-century events leading to the migration of British saints overseas. This has rhetorical phrases but nothing manifestly fictitious.

It tells how Vortigern, as usurping ruler of Britain, brought into the country Saxon auxiliaries, who inflicted great suffering on the Britons. "Presently" (*postmodum*, suggesting sooner-rather-than-later), they were largely cleared from the island and reduced to subordination by "the great Arthur, king of the Britons." Arthur's victories extended to Gaul. Then, he was "summoned from human activity," a phrase that might refer to death or an uncertain end but need not endorse the folk-belief in his immortality. Thereafter, the way was open for the Saxons to go again into the island. Their renewed depredations went on "through the times of many kings, Saxons and Britons, striving back and forth." Numerous holy men were martyred; others migrated to Brittany.

This prologue was long neglected as an Arthurian source because of its dismissal by J.S.P. Tatlock, who claimed that its date, 1019, was spurious, that it was later than Geoffrey of Monmouth, and that it was simply a précis of his *Historia Regum Britanniae*. Eventually, Fleuriot reopened the question and defended 1019 as correct. However, *Goeznovius* cannot be derived from the *Historia* whatever its date. It tells a story different from Geoffrey's: glaringly different, in its account of the beginnings of Brittany; and just as surely, if not quite so glaringly, in its account of Arthur and his aftermath. It contains matter that occurs in other contexts but not in Geoffrey, proving the use of a prior tradition independent of him. More important, within its concise limits it gives a sounder summary of fifth-century British affairs than any other comparable document. Even if its author did read the *Historia*, he could not have distilled such an account from it without some other, more factual, source enabling him to select and emend.

While Arthur himself is the unknown factor, the credibility of the setting in which the text places him justifies attention to its Arthurian testimony. Here, he succeeds Vortigern directly, without Geoffrey's two intervening reigns. On this showing, his battles in Britain would belong to the anarchic period of the Saxon revolt. The Saxons' withdrawal into a limited area, probably ca. 460, is attested by Gildas. Arthur's incursion into Gaul can be reasonably related to British activities overseas, and to a campaign of Romans and Franks against the Saxons in the Loire valley, in which there is evidence for British participation. This happened toward the close of the 460s. Saxon landings in Britain at new points—"going again into the island"—are confirmed by the *Anglo-Saxon Chronicle*, which assigns them to the period from 477 on, consistently with Arthur's having left the scene by then, as *Goeznovius* indicates. The breakup of Britain into small warring kingdoms, and the beginning of the saints' migration, are also in accord with the apparent course of events in the late fifth century.

Goeznovius therefore tells a story that fits history quite well and is nowhere in outright conflict with known facts. It is of course too distant from the events to use directly as historical evidence, but its substantial rightness warrants respect for whatever tradition it embodies. The story makes Arthur prominent in the 460s, and perhaps a little before and after. This agrees with Geoffrey's single but repeated chronological fix for him, putting his Gallic warfare in the reign of the eastern emperor Leo I (457–74). It cannot be merely derived from that, because the date is indicated in a different way, by implication and circumstance without names. The concurrence is one of several facts suggesting that both Geoffrey and the *Goeznovius* author are thinking of the "king of the Britons" who is documented in Gaul ca. 468–70 as Riothamus and for some shared and older reason are calling him Arthur.

Goeznovius implies continental sources of information. The Breton monastery of Rhuys may have contributed. Gildas was its reputed founder; the community possessed copies of his work and may be supposed to have had historical interests. Early in the tenth century, the monks fled from the Norse to Berry in central France. Ebbon, the seigneur of Déols, took them under his protection till the danger was past and they could return. Déols was the scene of the final battle in Riothamus's continental campaign. A local legend or even record of that battle, and the events leading up to it, could have gone back to Brittany with the monks and helped to form the conception of Arthur. [GA]

Ashe, Geoffrey. "A Certain Very Ancient Book." *Speculum*, 56 (1981), 301–23.

Chambers, E.K. *Arthur of Britain*. London: Sidgwick and Jackson, 1927, pp. 92–94, 241–43.

Fleuriot, Léon. *Les Origines de la Bretagne*. Paris: Payot, 1980, p. 277.

Tatlock, J.S.P. "The Dates of the Arthurian Saints' Legends." *Speculum*, 14 (1939), 345–65.

GOGULOR, a thirteenth-century French verse fragment (136 lines) of a Fair Unknown romance. It concerns a young knight who does battle with a giant named Gogulor to prevent the latter from marrying a young woman against her will. The name of Gogulor also appears in Gerbert's Continuation of Chrétien de Troyes's *Perceval*. [NJL]

Livingston, Charles H. "Fragment d'un roman de chevalerie." *Romania*, 66 (1940–41), 85–93.

GOLAGROS AND GAWANE, a Middle Scots poem of 1,362 lines, written toward the end of the fifteenth century. No manuscript has been preserved; the poem's survival is due to the activities of the first Scottish printers, Walter Chepman and Androw Myllar, who printed it in 1508. Only one copy is now known to exist. The stanza structure is the same as that of *The Awntyrs off Arthure at the Terne Wathelyn*, except that it lacks the linking features.

The story is based on two originally unrelated episodes of the First Continuation of Chrétien de Troyes's *Perceval*. In the first part, Kay the "crabbit" is, as so often, made the foil of Gawain the "gracious." When Arthur and his knights at the end of a day come upon a beautiful city, Kay offers to go and buy victuals there. He soon returns with no more than a thrashing for his boorish behavior, so that Gawain has to put things right again. In the second and longer part, Arthur tries to defeat a knight, Golagros, who had up till then held his lands as an independent lord. At the suggestion of Sir Spynagros, who replaces the Brandelis of the French text, Arthur sends three envoys, but they return empty-handed, in spite of the sugar-coated courtesy of their request. After a siege and a series of combats, Golagros is brought to submission by Gawain, who once more proves his perfect knighthood by agreeing to go through a mock defeat to allow Golagros to save face. In the original, he had done so to preserve the life of Golagros's *amie*, and this change, and the tone of the dialogue between Gawain and Golagros, confirm that the poem's main concern is with knightly honor and prowess. In Golagros, these are rewarded when Arthur releases him from his allegiance. [ESK]

The Knightly Tale of Golagros and Gawane. Edinburgh: Chepman and Myllar, 1508.

Madden, Frederic, ed. *Syr Gawayne*. London: Bannatyne Club, 1839.

GOLDMARK, KARL (1830–1915), a Hungarian composer who had great success with the opera *Die Königin von Saba* (1875). His Arthurian opera *Merlin* (premiere in Vienna, 1886; revised version in Frankfurt, 1904) is based on Immermann's play of the same name. Jens Malte Fischer compared it favorably with other "medieval" operas, such as *Le Roi Arthus* (1903), by Ernest Chausson. [UM/WCM]

Fischer, Jens Malte. "Singende Recken und blitzende Schwerter." In *Akten des DFG-Symposions zur Mittelalter-Rezeption*, ed. Peter Wapnewski. Stuttgart: Metzler, 1985.

GONNOT, MICHOT, is known for having recopied and signed five manuscripts in the library of Jacques d'Armagnac, Duke of Nemours (Paris, B.N. fr. 93, 99, 112, 916; Bibliothèque de l'Arsenal 5121). The first volume completed, MS 99, bears the date 1463; the others were transcribed between that year and the arrest of the duke in spring 1476. Michot Gonnot describes himself as a priest living at Crozant (Creuse). In MS 112 occurs the name of Micheau Gantelet of Tournai, written over an erased portion of the manuscript. While Pickford did not dismiss the possibility that the copyist resided briefly in Tournai, the reference may instead be an attempt to conceal any link between this manuscript and Jacques d'Armagnac, after the latter's decapitation.

It is generally accepted that Michot Gonnot is also the compiler of MS 112, which claims to bring together, in a vast new synthesis, materials drawn for the most part from French prose Arthurian romances of the thirteenth century. The compilation includes reworkings of the Vulgate *Lancelot*, *Queste*, and *Mort Artu*, as well as an abridgment of the Prose *Tristan* and portions of other romances. Although incomplete—the first and fifth "books" are lost—this *summa* offers considerable interest as an indication of the reception and reinterpretation of the *matière de Bretagne* in the fifteenth century and as evidence of the continuing appeal of the Arthurian world at the close of the Middle Ages.

[C-AVC]

Pickford, Cedric E. "A Fifteenth-Century Copyist and His Patron." *Medieval Miscellany Presented to Eugène Vinaver*, ed. F. Whitehead, A.H. Diverres, and F.E. Sutcliffe. Manchester, 1965.

———. *L'Évolution du roman arthurien en prose vers la fin du moyen âge d'après le manuscrit 112 du fonds français de la Bibliothèque Nationale*. Paris: Nizet, 1960.

GORLOIS, Duke of Cornwall, husband of Ygerna, and generally the father of Morgause, Elaine, and Morgan. Because Uther Pendragon desires Ygerna, a battle ensues between Uther and her husband. Merlin transforms Uther into the likeness of Gorlois and, while Ygerna's husband is on the battlefield, Uther enters Gorlois's castle at Tintagel, in which Ygerna has been barricaded, and beds her, thereby begetting Arthur. Meanwhile, Gorlois is killed in battle. Gorlois first appears in Geoffrey of Monmouth's *Historia Regum Britanniae*. Malory's *Morte Darthur* begins with a detailed account of the circumstances surrounding Arthur's conception but never refers to Gorlois by name. Gorlois reappears in later texts, such as Alfred Tennyson's *Idylls of the King*.

[SW]

GORNEMANZ (Gornemant de Gohort), in Chrétien de Troyes's *Perceval*, Blancheflor's uncle and Perceval's tutor, who teaches Perceval the rudiments of chivalry and advises him to avoid excessive speech, which results in the young man's failure to ask the question about the Grail. In Gerbert de Montreuil's Continuation, Gornemant is confused with the Fisher King; he disappears from subsequent Old French texts. However, his character is strengthened in the German tradition. In Wolfram von Eschenbach's *Parzival*, Gurnemanz is Condwiramurs's uncle and Parzival's tutor, as well as Prince of Graharz and Schenteflur's father.

[SW]

GORRE (Gore), in Chrétien de Troyes's *Lancelot*, the Vulgate Cycle, and Malory's *Morte Darthur*, Baudemagus's kingdom, to which Meleagant takes Guenevere when he abducts her from Arthur's court. Gorre is surrounded by water and is accessible by two magical bridges, a sword and an underwater passageway. The Vulgate says that Gorre borders on Sugales and is adjacent to Logres. It also refers to the outskirts of Gorre, where Baudemagus's prisoners are kept, as Terre Foraine ("Foreign Land"). In Malory, Gorre belongs to Urien, king of Rheged, but is ruled by Baudemagus.

[SW]

GOTTFRIED VON STRASSBURG, author of the classical version of the romance of Tristan and Isolde. An unfinished poem of some 19,500 lines in Middle High German rhymed couplets, it is a complex and difficult work composed in the first decade of the thirteenth century. A drastically reduced synopsis follows.

Tristan is conceived on the deathbed of his father, Rivalin. His mother, who revives her dying lover by the fulfillment of their mutual desire, dies herself in giving birth to the child she had conceived. Tristan, so named because of the tragic circumstances of his birth, is kidnaped from his foster parents, becomes the favorite of King Mark of Cornwall, and eventually leads a wooing expedition to win Princess Isolde of Ireland as the bride of King Mark. But on the ship from Ireland to Cornwall, Tristan and Isolde by mistake drink the magic potion intended for Mark and Isolde, and it seals their eternal love. Their life consists of deflecting the attempts of Mark and his courtiers to expose the love affair. At one point, they are banished from the court by Mark and lead an idyllic life in a secret forest glade, living in a lovers' temple. But they return to court and eventually are discovered in bed together by Mark himself. Tristan must leave and begins a life of wandering and longing for his beloved. Gottfried's version breaks off when

Tristan is about to marry a woman named Isolde of the White Hands, but we learn from the preserved fragments of Gottfried's source, Thomas d'Angleterre, that the two marry, though the marriage remains unconsummated. Tristan eventually dies from a poisoned wound, and shortly before his death he sends for Isolde the Fair of Ireland, his true love. The ship sent for her is to hoist white sails if she is aboard, black if not. She comes to her dying lover with a cure, but the jealous Isolde of the White Hands lies to Tristan and tells him that the approaching ship has black sails. He dies of grief, and upon her arrival, the true Isolde clasps the body of her dead lover and breathes her last.

The story of Tristan and Isolde had an odd fate in the Middle Ages. It was well known and popular, but no complete version has survived, except for the Old Norse-Icelandic *Tristrams saga ok Ísöndar*, a Norwegian translation from 1226, and the Czech *Tristram a Izalda* (late fourteenth century). All other extant versions are fragments. There is an Old French *Tristran*, by the Norman-French poet Béroul, hard to date but probably from the last third of the twelfth century. The German poet Eilhart von Oberge composed a Tristan romance ca. 1170, bringing the story to a conclusion but omitting several episodes that—as they are present in Béroul—may go back to a lost original. These "precourtly" versions have in common a roughcut concept of love. The love potion and the fatal passion of the protagonists are seen as a regrettable tragic fate that breaks over the lovers against their will; the love potion wears off after four years. It was left to a certain Thomas d'Angleterre to reshape the conception of love into the sublime glorification of passion that we have in Gottfried's version. Thomas, an Anglo-Norman, wrote his poem for someone at the court of Henry II of England, probably ca. 1170, though the dating varies between 1155 and 1190. His patroness may have been none other than Eleanor of Aquitaine, wife of Henry and ardent devotee of courtly literature. Gottfried mentions Thomas as the true master of the tale. Thomas understood courtly ideals and courtly love much better than did Eilhart or Béroul, and he transformed the legend of Tristan and Isolde into the story of passion alienating individuals from society and raising them above it in their struggle to defend their relationship from detection. Gottfried adapted Thomas's version, and he turned the legend into the vehicle of a dark and tragic, lofty and transcendent view of love. But he did a great deal more with it.

Arthurian romance, set in the landscape of Celtic fairy tale and drawing on the half-legend, half-myth of an ancient King Arthur of the Britons, presents itself to the modern reader as a fusion of Celtic and English traditions. For some time, Arthurian scholarship was dominated by the quest for the sources and analogues of twelfth- and thirteenth-century romance in Celtic materials. This point of departure is understandable, though a firm textual basis for it never existed. It is the approach to the *body* of the Arthurian materials. But their heart and soul—sensibilities, ethical values, mores of the heroes and heroines—are to be sought not in prehistoric Britain but in the courts and cathedral schools of the twelfth century. The sublime dream vision of the Arthurian knight questing for love, adventure, and identity in fairy-tale forests was dreamed by worldly, humanistic clerics who sought to educate and entertain the lay nobles and court society with paragons of chivalric conduct. "Courtly" ideals and the figure of the courtly-chivalric knight are creations of this class of men. So was King Arthur, and so were the romances of his knights. Some of these authors, Chrétien de Troyes prominent among them, were influenced by the humanist thinking of the twelfth-century schools and were exposed to the fertile climate of ideas that arose in the so-called "renaissance of the twelfth century." There is a strong element of classical revival in the ethical ideals of Arthurian romance, and it is no coincidence that the earliest romances were medieval recastings of the epics of antiquity—the Trojan War and the wanderings of Aeneas, for example. These intellectual obligations are especially evident in Gottfried. He stands out clearly among his contemporaries as a man of learning, a virtuoso poet, and a connoisseur of court life. As a stylist, he is the most important master of the German language before Goethe. His view of humanity, his mastery of classical poetic forms, the amalgamation of these with Christian forms, and his depiction of the ideal courtier anticipate ideals and poetic practices of the Renaissance in the fifteenth and sixteenth centuries. It is apparent that he was educated in the humanist cathedral schools. He is a master of classical literature; his poem is replete with classical and mythological allusion. He inclines more to allegory than any contemporary vernacular poet, and particularly in his use of this technique we can see his obligations to twelfth-century humanism.

What we know of Gottfried von Strassburg, beyond his title *Meister* and his association with Strassburg, we glean from his work. We know nothing about his biography, but a great deal about his thinking, his tastes, his attitudes toward love, women, education, music, poetry, courts, and kings. A remarkable and important passage in his *Tristan* is the part that modern scholars call the "literary excursus." It interrupts and in a subtle way continues and comments on the ceremony of young Tristan's knighting. Faced with the task of describing the knightly splendor of the investiture, the preparation of the clothes for Tristan and the thirty pages knighted with him, he is reminded of the many poets who have gone before him and tailored, trimmed, and dyed the clothes of knighthood with their words. He praises Heinrich von Veldeke as the originator of courtly language in German, Hartmann von Aue for his clarity and transparence, a certain Blicker von Steinach for the soaring flight of his words and ideas (in an epic poem now lost). But an unnamed poet comes in for a drubbing. This "comrade of the hare" skips about on the "field of words" and lays claim to the laurel wreath, which Gottfried had set on the head of Hartmann. This poet writes in an obscure and uncourtly way, projecting the illusion of profundity in the way that carnival conjurers turn lead to gold and dust to pearls to dupe children. His target is undoubtedly Wolfram von Eschenbach. In this passage, Gottfried reveals himself as something of a literary critic, and his survey of poets might be called the earliest piece of literary criticism in the vernacular literature of the Middle Ages. He appears to set himself up as a judge of poetry and arbiter of taste, one of those who have the right to bestow the laurel wreath on their contemporaries. The ceremony of crowning poets with the laurel wreath originated in classical antiquity. It was not practiced in the Middle Ages prior to the fourteenth century, so far as is known, and Gottfried's use of it appears to be metaphorical. But even as a metaphor his bestowing of the laurel wreath on Hartmann shows us something important about Gottfried's self-awareness and about his perception of the contemporary literary scene. He sees his contemporaries as successors of the great poets of antiquity, and to underscore this indebtedness he ascribes to each of the poets he praises a classical or pagan source of inspiration: Veldeke has his wisdom from the well of Pegasus, from which all inspiration derives; Blicker's words and meanings are washed and dyed in the fountain of the fairies; Hartmann wears the laurel wreath, symbol of Apollo's favor. The same is true of the two lyric poets he names: Reinmar von Hagenau sings with the tongue of Orpheus, and the love songs of Walther von der Vogelweide are inspired by the goddess of love, Venus. Toward the end of the excursus, Gottfried places himself in the same line of descent in his invocation of the Muses and Apollo, the most artful and elaborate example of that form that any medieval poet produced, and that includes Alain of Lille and Dante. Having conjured up all his illustrious contemporaries, he finds himself speechless before the example of their eloquence, and he seeks the aid of the nine Muses sitting on their thrones on Mount Helicon and of their leader, Apollo. If they will send him a single drop of their abundant inspiration, it will restore his flagging powers and burnish his words like pure gold. But then he calls on certain beings "up there in their heavenly choirs" to grant him the inspiration of "True Helicon, the highest throne." This inspiration will render his words transparent like an exquisite jewel. It is an example of the double invocation, common in the traditions of Christian humanism: the inspiring spirits of pagan antiquity are to combine their powers with those of Christian tradition, here referred to in the classicizing epithet "True Helicon." It is a form that we encounter in Alain of Lille's *Anticlaudianus*, in Dante's *Divine Comedy*, in Petrarch's *Africa*, and in a great many works from the Renaissance of the fifteenth and sixteenth centuries. It implies a humanist poetic program synthesizing classical and Christian inspiration, though setting the former subordinate to the latter. Here, as in a number of other places, we see clearly Gottfried's obligations to the traditions of Christian humanism.

These are also evident in one of the most remarkable and original passages that Gottfried added to the tale received from Thomas d'Angleterre, the allegory of the cave of lovers. In Thomas, the lovers abandon the court of King Mark and spend a period of time living in isolation in a distant forest. It is an idyllic scene, which Thomas modeled on the forest idyll in the *Legend of St. Giles*. But Gottfried outbids his source. He takes over the concept of an idyllic life in the forest (in Béroul and Eilhart it was nasty and brutish), and adds the lovers' temple, ingeniously wrought in prehistoric times by giants who used it for their secret amorous rendezvous. This "cave of lovers," set in a beautiful landscape, is described in great detail. After some talk about the lovers' life there (they sing, read sad tales of tragic love, and nourish themselves by gazing into each others' eyes), he returns to the lovers' temple and begs the indulgence of his readers to hear the real significance of its architecture. He proceeds to explain the parts of the cave allegorically: the smoothness of the walls stands for love's simplicity, their height is aspiration, the green of the floor stands for constancy; the crystal bed represents the purity and transparency of love. The exegesis continues at length. Scholarly debate about the sources of the cave allegory has shown that Gottfried in part borrowed techniques of allegory at home in the Christian tradition of cathedral allegory and applied them to an adulterous love affair. The problematic nature of such a borrowing has not escaped readers, and it raises the important and difficult question of Gottfried's relation to Christianity. One reader has made of him a heretic, or sympathizer with heresy, who attempts by sacrilegious borrowings to reduce Christian forms of thought and expression to a shambles, using them to exalt a dubious love relationship. Another reader accepts this spiritualizing of love as thoroughly in harmony with Christian sensibilities. A third has denied that the cave allegory has any relation to the Christian tradition but is derivable from the epithalamial tradition of late antiquity and secular love allegories. Yet another denies this view and claims that the cave allegory is quite consistent with worldly, humanistic forms of Christian thought, in fact serves as a good example of the program mapped out in the invocation, the cooperation of the pagan and the Christian traditions. In any case, it is certain that Gottfried in his cave allegory and elsewhere in his work introduced to the romance a spiritualized conception of human passion, set parallel to religious devotion.

There are other passages that underscore Gottfried's problematic relationship to Christianity. In his prologue, he

41. MS Paris, Bibliothèque Nationale, f.fr. 755, fol. 115: Banquet at Tournament of Lonazep. (Paris, Bibliothèque Nationale.)

Yseut.
Rovart.
pal.
lanc. T.
Gah. dv. un

offers the story to the readers as "bread to the living"; through the story, the lovers "live on though they are dead." The eucharistic overtones are distinct, and they would seem to imply an analogy between the lovers and Christ, between the reading of their tale and the taking of the sacramental bread. Most puzzling and troublesome is an apparent attack on Christ's pliant nature that Gottfried added to the story after the famous scene of Isolde's ordeal by the hot iron. The queen is forced to prove her innocence before a court by carrying a glowing iron. When the day and place are set, Isolde arranges for Tristan to happen by disguised as a pilgrim. She asks that the "pilgrim" carry her from her ship to the place of the ordeal so that she will not be profaned before this numinous event by the touch of worldly men. The disguised Tristan carries her, but slips and tumbles to the ground, landing on top of her. She then proceeds to take the oath of innocence, swearing that no man has ever lain with her except her husband, and of course that pilgrim, whom all have just seen lying in her lap. She carries the iron and is not burned. Gottfried's comment: "Then and there it was made perfectly clear and manifest to all that Christ for all his virtue shifts like a sleeve in the wind. . . . He is at the service of all whether their affairs are upright or deceitful." It may be, as some readers have suggested, that Gottfried did not like ordeals, and his words suggest, "This is the kind of creature that men turn Christ into by foolish institutions like the ordeal." But since he earlier depicted the battle between Tristan and Morold uncritically as a trial by combat in which God renders judgment, this explanation is not compelling. However we read the passage, it is hard to escape the conclusion that it is based on some highly unmedieval suspension of the reverence appropriate to the name of Christ. This and other ambiguous uses of Christian symbolism and thought urge on us the conclusion that Gottfried's relationship to Christianity is troubled and unorthodox. Despite the efforts of modern scholars, it remains unexplained.

In origin, the tale of Tristan and Isolde is a love story. But it is worth noting that they do not fall in love until around Gottfried's line 12,000—that is, approximately halfway through the entire work (assuming that the finished work would have reached around 24,000 lines). Up to that point, the story is concerned with Tristan's parents (ca. 1,800 lines) and with Tristan's youth, education, entry into court, battles, intrigues, and courting of Isolde for King Mark (ca. 10,000 lines). The figure of the young Tristan is on center stage in the first and longest part of the romance, and this is understandable. Thomas and Gottfried created a hero who is quite untypical in Arthurian romance. He is highly educated, he makes his way by his wit, charm, beauty of appearance and manners, and talents in hunting, music, and foreign languages. The knight of Arthurian romance finds his destiny alone in the forest of adventure, facing adversaries natural and supernatural, whom he overcomes by his strength, knightly prowess, and constancy. By contrast, in *Tristan* intellectual and personal qualities are in the foreground. We wait long until Tristan fights on horseback, and in Gottfried's entire romance occurs not a single tourney, that most popular event of the typical Arthurian romance. Young Tristan is not first and foremost a knight, but rather a courtier and artist. He is kidnaped from his foster parents by Norwegian merchants, who admire his talents in chess and language, his bearing and presence, and imagine that they can turn a profit by selling this child prodigy. Released and washed up on the shore of Cornwall, he impresses the king's hunting party by a dazzling mastery of hunting customs and the French terms for them. At court, the king marvels at his abilities in music, which Tristan highlights by a calculated show of modesty, a well-known courtier's strategy of winning favor. After these and other shows of skill, he wins the love of King Mark (who, unknown to both, is his uncle), becomes his private minstrel and master huntsman, and stands at the pinnacle of favor. Tristan's early successes at court are the result not of chivalric prowess, the least important of his abilities, but rather of what Baldesar Castiglione would call *cortegiania* 'courtiership.' The Tristan romance in the version of Thomas-Gottfried introduced a new character into Arthurian romance: the courtier-knight. The court is the main theater of events; its intrigues account for a good part of the action; the mentality of the courtier accounts for the motivations of the characters. Also, the central event of the plot is one of the favorite motifs of court literature and court life: the clandestine love affair concealed through deception. The institution of the ruler's court has had an influence on western literature and art that is easy to underestimate. The courtly version of the Tristan romance is one good example of this influence, and it would not be inaccurate to call Gottfried's version a "courtier romance."

We have examined the literary-philosophical unity into which Gottfried transformed the tale he had received. But now we want to consider it from another angle: the rediscovery of its earliest form by reference to Celtic analogues. This approach is fraught with the danger of hypothesizing on thin evidence, a danger that did not prevent an earlier generation of scholars from attempting reconstructions as interesting as they are unverifiable. Apart from the risk of inaccuracy, another danger is the illusion created by this approach that the preserved versions of the romance are fragmented bits of a lost unity, not autonomous works of art arising out of a vital and genial attempt of a single poet to come to terms with his own world and time.

We can say with some certainty that the names of the main characters are traceable to Britain of the sixth or seventh century. In the Irish chronicles of the Picts, we find from the eighth century a *Talorcan filius Drostan* and a *Drest filius Talorcan*. *Drostan*, or *Drest*, appears to be a name common among Pictish chieftains, though it occurs also among the Celts of Britain. The name appears in Welsh Triads (which date in their written form from the thirteenth century or later but preserve earlier material) as *Drystan*, or *Trystan, son of Tallwch*. The same sources tell us that Drystan was the lover of Essylt, the wife of his uncle March. The Triads postdate the French and German romances and must be suspected of French influence, but the name *Tallwch* is not suspect. It is fully the equivalent in sound of the *Talorc* of the chronicles. Yet the love relationship between Drystan and Essylt, wife of King March, cannot be located in Celtic sources that predate the twelfth- and thirteenth-century romances, however strong the probability of a Celtic tradition may be.

Historians of Celtic literature tell us that the original core of the Tristan legend was a tradition that Drust rescued a princess from her fate as a tribute for a foreign oppressor; that she recognized her deliverer as he lay in a bath and thwarted the attempt of a false claimant to rob Drust of his due glory. This nucleus is preserved in the tenth-century version of the Irish saga *The Wooing of Emer*. We can gain some understanding of the genesis of the love story by reference to another Irish tale, the elopement of Diarmaid and Gráinne, believed to have existed as early as the ninth century. Gráinne, wife of the Irish chieftain Fionn, is taken with a passion for her husband's nephew, the hero Diarmaid. He rejects her, but she forces him by a magic spell to become her lover. They flee to the forest, are pursued by Fionn, and suffer hardship and deprivation in their flight.

The question whether the story of Tristan and Isolde is in its origins Celtic is perhaps superfluous. There are also Persian and Hellenistic elements in the versions from the twelfth and thirteenth centuries. But from the comparison with Celtic analogues we can learn a great deal about the transformation that the love motif experienced. Earlier versions seem to have depicted the Isolde figure as a witch who ruthlessly imposes her will on a reluctant lover. The love of the two is dangerous and demonic. In these early versions, the social order, the loyalty of hero to chieftain and of nephew to uncle, are unquestioned values. In the version of Eilhart, the love potion is still seen as a curse imposed on the hero and heroine by a catastrophic chance from which they are eventually released. This crude conception of love shows us by contrast the refinements of the Thomas-Gottfried version. Here, the love potion imposes a relationship on Tristan and Isolde for which their own psyches destined them. The love is affirmed even in its most negative aspects: the disruption of the social order, the betrayal of friendship and blood relationship. Gottfried has imbued an illicit love with a pathos, a sense of the elevation of the lovers through the destructive bond that unites them. How differently society and its highest representative, King Mark, are depicted in the romance: Mark is a weakling and a coarse, sensual, shortsighted man, who, as Gottfried states openly, gets what is coming to him. His court consists of cowards, villains, and low intriguers. The whole thrust of the romance and the lovers' efforts is to thwart society's attempts to expose the love relationship. It is cultivated as a high ideal, and even the tragedy is seen as elevating and exalting. In the courtly version of the Tristan romance, loyalty to king, uncle, and society is the questioned value, not the passion of "noble hearts." (*See also* Tristan in Modern German Versions.) [CSJ]

Gottfried von Strassburg. *Tristan*, ed. Reinhold Bechstein, re-ed. Peter Ganz. Wiesbaden: Brockhaus, 1978.

———. *Tristan . . . with the Surviving Fragments of the Tristan of Thomas*, trans. A.T. Hatto. Harmondsworth: Penguin, 1960.

Batts, Michael. *Gottfried von Strassburg*. New York: Twayne, 1971.

Jackson, W.T.H. *The Anatomy of Love: The Tristan of Gottfried von Strassburg*. New York: Columbia University Press, 1971.

Jaeger, C. Stephen. *Medieval Humanism in Gottfried von Strassburg's Tristan und Isolde*. Heidelberg: Winter, 1977.

Stevens, Adrian, and Roy Wisby, eds. *Gottfried von Strassburg and the Medieval Tristan Legend*. Cambridge: Brewer, 1990.

GOVERNAL (Kurneval, Gouvernail), Tristan's tutor and squire. Kurneval, in Eilhart von Oberge, accompanies Tristan on his journey to Ireland, to fetch Isolde for King Mark of Cornwall, and on the journey's fateful return, when Tristan and Isolde mistakenly drink the love potion intended for Mark and Isolde. In Béroul, Eilhart, and other texts belonging to the "primitive" version, he provides advice and material help in Tristan's resistance to Mark's persecutions. [SW]

GRACQ, JULIEN (pseudonym of Louis Poirier). French writer. From an early age, Gracq admired Wagnerian drama, and in 1939 his *Au Château d'Argol* offered a "demonic version" of *Parsifal*. The figure of the hero seems to pale before the theme of Amfortas's wound; for example, the blood from the wound flows into the Grail, profaning the myth by reversing the holy liquid from the direction it took in the First Continuation.

Gracq's four-act play *Le Roi Pêcheur* was presented in 1949. (A preface to the printed edition of 1945 recommends the adaptation of medieval myths.) As the title suggests, the playwright transfers emphasis from Perceval, who does not appear until the second act, to the Grail King. The young hero assumes a solar character, borrowed from Gauvain, and his silver armor contrasts with the black clothing of Amfortas. The work is inspired as much by Wolfram von Eschenbach as by Wagner. It reestablishes the duality of Gornemant and Trévrizent, whom Wagner confused. Amfortas remains the Fisher King, since his wound, the result of his seduction by Kundry, prevents his hunting. The Grail is by now all but forgotten, and its guardians are languishing. But Kundry, now converted, resists Clingsor's order once again to seduce the young hero, and she comes to his aid instead. Departing from Wagner's version, but following the tradition established by Chrétien de Troyes, Perceval does not ask about the Grail procession, and an exuberant vegetation—a rather surrealistic inversion of the "Wasteland"—progressively suffocates the glacial Manor, cursed by the Wound.

At a time when Anouilh, Sartre, Giraudoux, and Cocteau were grafting modern psychology onto Greek myths, Gracq was making a similar effort in regard to medieval myth, although his demystification and humanization of legendary characters, while accenting their realism, weakens the supernatural element.

The work is somewhat static, since the main characters, like Kundry and Perceval, evolve little or not at all, but the language, on the other hand, is magnificent. The critics were unjustly brutal toward the play, and it has only rarely been revived. [RB]

Gracq, Julien. *Au Château d'Argol*. Paris: Corti, 1939.

———. *Le Roi Pêcheur*. Paris: Corti, 1945; repr. in *Œuvres complètes*, ed. Bernhild Boie. Paris: Gallimard, 1989, pp. 325–96, 1239–71.

Baudry, Robert. "Julien Gracq et la légende du Graal." In *Actes du Colloque International sur Julien Gracq*. Angers: Presses de l'Université d'Angers, 1981.

Dandrea, Claude. "Le Roi Pêcheur et la légende du Graal." In *Actes du Colloque International sur Julien Gracq*. Angers: Presses de l'Université d'Angers, 1981.

Douchin-Shahin, Andrée. "La Survivance du mythe au vingtième siècle: 'Le Roi Pêcheur' de Julien Gracq." *Symposium*, 40 (Fall 1986), 173–208.

McLendon, Will L. "Thèmes wagnériens dans les romans de Julien Gracq." *French Review*, 41 (1968), 539–48.

GRAELENT, an anonymous Breton lai of 756 lines, from the early thirteenth century, not actually Arthurian, but notable for its utilization of basically the same story as Marie de France's *Lanval*. The existence of *Graelent* suggests that the Arthurian setting of *Lanval* is not original but a later accretion. [KB]

Tobin, Prudence Mary O'Hara, ed. *Les Lais anonymes des XIIe et XIIIe siècles: édition critique de quelques lais bretons*. Geneva: Droz, 1976.

Weingartner, Russell, ed. and trans. *Graelent and Guingamor: Two Breton Lays*. New York: Garland, 1984.

GRAIL (Graal). We must distinguish at the outset between the French word *graal* (which became *grail* in English) and the thing or things it came to designate in medieval literature.

The word itself is not shrouded in mystery. It is one of the numerous reflexes of medieval Latin *gradale*, a word that meant "by degree," "in stages," applied to a dish or platter that was brought to the table at various stages or servings during a meal. In the early thirteenth century, Helinand of Froidmont wrote: "Gradalis autem sive gradale gallice dicitur scutella lata et aliquantulum profunda in qua pretiosae dapes cum suo jure divitibus solent apponi gradatim, . . . et dicitur vulgari nomine *graalz*" (". . . a wide and somewhat deep dish in which costly meats with their broth are customarily placed for the rich, . . . and it is commonly called a 'grail'") (Migne, *Patrologia Latina*, Vol. 212, col. 814). As a common noun, it figures in inventories of precious plate as early as 1010 as *gradales duas de argento*, and *grassalete argentei* from an inventory dated 1294. Even in some early literary texts, the word is found with the simple meaning of dish or plate, without any of the overtones of sacredness or splendor it came to acquire: "Sire, dist il, Deus te gart de tot mal! Ersoir mangai o toi a ton gräal" ("Sir, said he, may God protect you from all harm! Yesterday evening, I ate with you from your grail"—*Roman d'Alexandre*). Although not perhaps in widespread use, the word *graal* was undeniably common enough in Old French and designated some sort of dish or serving vessel.

The prodigious fortune of the word was due directly to Chrétien de Troyes. In his *Perceval*, or *Le Conte del Graal*, the youth Perceval, seated on a couch next to the Fisher King, beholds a magnificent procession that, at each course of the repast, emerges from a chamber at one end of the hall, passes before the table, and disappears into another chamber. The first to appear is a young boy holding a bleeding lance; he is followed by two youths with candelabra. Finally,

Un graal entre ses deus mains
Une damoisele tenoit,
Qui avec les vallés venoit,
Bele et gente et bien acesmee. . . .
Li graaus, qui aloit devant,
De fin or esmeré estoit;
Presc̈ieuses pierres avoit
El graal de maintes manieres,
Des plus riches et des plus chieres
Qui en mer ne en terre soient;
Totes autres pierres passoient
Celes del graal sanz dotance.

("A beautiful and comely maiden who accompanied the youths held a grail in her hands. . . . The grail, borne ahead of the procession, was worked with fine gold, and there were in the grail many precious stones, the finest and most costly in the world; surely the stones in the grail surpassed all others.") That Chrétien designated the vessel *un graal* is proof that he regarded the word as a common noun, a platter or dish of costly workmanship. In a later passage, we learn that the *graal* does not contain a pike, a salmon, or a lamprey (suggesting a rather large serving platter not unlike that described by Helinand), rather

D'une sole oiste le sert on,
Que l'en en cel graal li porte;
Sa vie sostient et conforte,
Tant sainte chose est li graals.
Et il, qui est esperitax
Qu'a se vie plus ne covient
Fors l'oiste qui el graal vient.

("He [the old king] is provided with a single Mass wafer, which is brought to him in the grail; and it sustains his life, such a holy thing is the grail. And he is so spiritual that he needs nothing more than the wafer contained in the grail.") Noteworthy are the spiritual overtones absent in the first appearance of the *graal*. Here, the ancient king is sustained over the years by the single Mass wafer contained in the vessel.

But even though we know much about the *graal* at this stage, we remain in complete ignorance where Chrétien derived the elements of his mysterious procession, or for that matter why a grail was conceived as the centerpiece of this splendid ritual. In all likelihood, Chrétien drew on some ancient myth of food-producing vessels, perhaps but not necessarily of Celtic origin, of the type catalogued by Stith Thompson (D1472.1.19 to D1472.1.33), cauldrons of plenty, cornucopias, etc., and applied the name of an ornate platter to the vessel, thereby with one stroke providing the foundation for the myth of the Grail, or Holy Grail.

The story would have doubtless remained there, a mysterious procession with at its center a jewel-encrusted and luminous vessel that had the power to produce food, if it had not been for an author who wrote some ten or fifteen years after Chrétien left his *Perceval* unfinished. Robert de Boron recognized the possibilities of the *graal* as he read about it in Chrétien. Whereas the latter left the reader wondering what precisely the *graal* was and what function it had in the narrative, Robert was most specific. It was the vessel of the Last Supper used by Joseph of Arimathea to catch Christ's blood after the Deposition and was later placed at the center of an altarlike table where a sort of "service" was held. Finally, it was transported to Arthurian Britain by Joseph's family to become henceforth the Holy Grail (*Le Saint Graal*). Robert transformed Chrétien's enigmatic vessel, *un graal*, into *le Graal*, a type of Christian chalice and symbol of Christ's real presence. The transition from a vessel producing food for the body to the vessel of the Christian cult, the chalice, which produces nourishment for the soul, was an obvious one in an age imbued with Christian typology.

In the many works in which this precious vessel appears, the Grail or Holy Grail assumes many forms and functions, although in all cases it retains its basic power as a food-provider or is associated with food consumption at table. In Chrétien, it seems clearly a platter that sustains the old king in the second chamber. In Robert, it is a cup used at table that assumed later characteristics of the Mass chalice and whose service broke the famine. In Wolfram von Eschenbach's *Parzival*, it is a "thing" called a Grail, a stone or *lapsit exillis* that produces an abundance of the most savory foods. In the First Continuation of the *Perceval*, the Rich Grail, floating about the hall, provides food and drink to all in attendance. Manessier, in his Continuation, depicts the Grail carried by a maiden as in Chrétien. The Welsh *Peredur* presents the gruesome spectacle of a great salver carried by two maidens in which a man's head is found swimming in blood. In the *Perlesvaus*, the Grail is, as in Robert's poem, the vessel used by Joseph to collect the blood of Christ, but it causes rejuvenation and is carried in a ceremony before Gauvain, who perceives in it visions of a chalice, then the form of a child (signifying the real body of Christ), and finally the Crucifixion. In the Prose *Lancelot*, the Grail assumes the shape of a chalice. In the *Queste del Saint Graal*, as in Malory, it becomes synonymous with the beatific vision and is an object of a quest by Bors, Perceval, and the pure knight Galahad. When the quest is achieved, a hand descends from heaven and removes the Grail forever from its earthly, sinful abode. What is most astonishing is that, in the midst of this wealth of story and Christian legend, the official Church kept complete silence, never approving or condemning its many and shifting fictions.

The appeal of the Holy Grail is not limited to the Middle Ages. With the fascination for medieval literature and culture manifested in the nineteenth century, the Grail once again became associated with the arduous yearnings after mystical experience. Tennyson, Wagner, T.S. Eliot, T.H. White, and Charles Williams all wrote about the struggle between the forces of good and evil centering on the possession of the most sacred of vessels, the Holy Grail. (*See also* SCHOLARSHIP, MODERN ARTHURIAN.) [RO'G]

Loomis, Roger Sherman. *The Grail: From Celtic Myth to Christian Symbol*. Cardiff: University of Wales Press, 1963.

Marx, Jean. *Nouvelles Recherches sur la littérature arthurienne*. Paris: Klincksieck, 1965.

Nitze, William A., and Harry F. Williams. *Arthurian Names in the Perceval of Chrétien de Troyes*. Berkeley: University of California Press, 1955, pp. 275–78.

O'Gorman, Richard. "Ecclesiastical Tradition and the Holy Grail." *Australian Journal of French Studies*, 6 (1969), 3–8.

Owen, D.D.R. *The Evolution of the Grail Legend*. Edinburgh: Oliver and Boyd, 1968.

GRAN RE MELIADUS, IL ("The Great King Meliadus"), an Italian translation (1558–59) of the French *Meliadus de Leonnoys*. Set in the early years of Arthur's reign, it describes the love of Meliadus for the Queen of Scotland, recounts the former's exploits, and presents the illustrious youth of Tristan (who is three years old when the story opens). The events of this work are entwined with those of *Girone il Cortese*, as the French texts from which they derive had once been parts of the same work (*see* PALAMEDES). [NJL]

Gardner, Edmund G. *The Arthurian Legend in Italian Literature*. London: Dent, 1930, pp. 47–63.

GRAS, MOSSÈN, fifteenth-century author of the *Tragèdia de Lançalot*, a Catalan incunabulum version of the *Mort Artu*. From the nine surviving leaves, it is evident that Gras condensed the initial episodes of the *Mort Artu* and gave a sentimental treatment to the love triangle of Lancelot, Guenevere, and the Maid of Astalot, using rhetoric commonly found in Hispanic sentimental romances of the fifteenth century. [HLS]

Gras, Mossèn. *Tragèdia de Lançalot*, ed. Martín de Riquer. Barcelona: Quaderns Crema, 1984.

GRAY, PHOEBE, sets her sentimental novelette *Little Sir Galahad* (1915) in contemporary United States. Little Sir Galahad is a brave little cripple and member of the "Galahad Knights," a boys' club dedicated to performing good deeds and acts of chivalry. [EB]

Gray, Phoebe. *Little Sir Galahad*. London: Stanley Paul, 1915.

GREEN, ROBERT MONTRAVILLE, American physician whose fifty-year avocation as a student of Arthurian legend produced *The Round Table* (1955), a poetic retelling of the story from Vortigern and the boy Merlin to Arthur's coronation. Although composed in dated Tennysonian blank verse—some 18,000 lines in all—the narrative is well paced, and Malory's storyline is embellished with additions from Marie de France and other sources. [DN]

Green, Robert Montraville. *The Round Table: An Arthurian Romance Epic*. Boston: Eliot, 1955.

GRENE KNIGHT, THE, a late (ca. 1500) tail-rhyme version of that pearl of English Arthurian romances, *Sir Gawain and the Green Knight*. *The Grene Knight* is a perfect example of the disastrous effect that the combination of popular demand and lack of poetic skill and feeling could produce. In spite of its abbreviated form (516 lines), the poem shows no trace of the concentration of its famous ancestor, in which every detail matters; the poem spoils what tension is left by revealing everything beforehand, without, however, explaining anything. Thus, we are told who the Green Knight is (a Sir Bredbeddle), and why he travels to Arthur's court (to lure away Sir Gawain, who is loved by his wife), but not why he should be transformed into a *green* knight, especially as his arrival at court causes no consternation. Lack of competence at times has hilarious results, as when the Green Knight politely sets "his head vp on againe" before shaking hands in parting with the King. The rest of the story is in the same vein: Gawain is tempted only once by the Lady, but with three kisses, while the Green Knight is hunting hinds, boars, foxes, etc.; these winnings they share instead of exchanging them. The Lady gives Gawain a white "lace"; it duly saves his neck, and the next day the two knights return to Arthur's court together. The story explains, the poet says, why the Knights of the Bath wear a white "lace" until they have performed a deed of valor (which seems to agree with contemporary practice). Some peculiar details: Morgan is called Aggteb, the Green Knight lives at Castle Hutton in the West Country, and Arthur resides at Carlisle in the unidentified Castle of Flatting, in the Forest of Delamore (i.e., Delamere Forest, Cheshire). [ESK]

Madden, Frederic, ed. *Syr Gawayne*. London: Bannatyne Club, 1839.

GROOS, LUDWIG, begins his German "epic poem" *Parzival und sein Narr* ("Parzival and His Fool," 1949) with the hero telling his story to a fool. The fool takes Parzival to a hermit, who tells of his own search for the meaning of life and sends him on a search for the Grail, which will bring him truth and faith. The fool, whom Parzival recognizes as an aspect of himself, is allowed to accompany the hero on his search. [SSch/PWM]

Groos, Ludwig. *Parzival und sein Narr: Episches Gedicht*. Düsseldorf: Renaissance, 1949.

GROSS, JOEL, American author of *The Lives of Rachel* (1984), a historical romance about a series of Jewish women, each named Rachel. They live at different periods in history, but all are distinguished for their courage and self-sacrifice. One of them, a skilled metalworker, falls in love with Artorius, the British war-leader, and helps make the sword Excalibur with which he defeats the Saxons. [RHT]

Gross, Joel. *The Lives of Rachel*. New York: New American Library, 1984.

GUENEVERE (Guinevere, Guenièvre, Gwenhwyfar, Gaynour, Guenhumare, Ginevra), the wife of King Arthur and mistress of Lancelot du Lac.

Geoffrey of Monmouth's *Historia* (ca. 1136) identifies Guenevere as a noble Roman whom Arthur married for her surpassing beauty and whom his nephew Mordred also married after usurping his uncle's throne. Guenevere's guilt and fear of Arthur's wrath in both Wace's *Brut* (ca. 1155) and Layamon's *Brut* (ca. 1200) could indicate that she was a willing accomplice in Mordred's treachery, but Hardyng's *Chronicle* (ca. 1457) probably reflects the reality of any early-medieval queen caught in her circumstances when it says that she was forced to wed the traitor. The Alliterative *Morte Arthure* (ca. 1400) is unique in concluding that Guenevere is the mother of Mordred's two sons. All the English chronicles comment on the misfortune of her barrenness as Arthur's wife; however, Welsh tradition maintained that she bore him sons. The Welsh also preserved the tradition of her infidelity, blaming her to such an extent that in some parts of the country, as recently as the end of the last century, it was regarded as an insult to a girl's moral character to call her Guenevere.

Lanval, a late twelfth-century romance in which Marie de France characterizes Arthur's queen as a seductress, may reflect this Welsh tradition, since Ulrich von Zatzikhoven's *Lanzelet* (1195) does not corroborate Marie's judgment of the Queen's character. At the same time, even though it is allegedly based upon a French (*welschez*) book, the German romance exhibits no awareness of a liaison between Guenevere and Lancelot. This seems to have been the invention of another Marie, Countess of Champagne. Chrétien de Troyes claims to have received from her both the *matière* and the *sen* of his *Chevalier de la charrete* (ca. 1178). The title refers to Lancelot, who loves and serves his lady, the beautiful and haughty Queen, with a fervor akin to religious adoration and protests that he owes all his knightly worth to her love. Approximately fifty years later, the anonymous author(s) of the French prose romances of Arthur now known as the Vulgate Cycle decided to incorporate Chrétien's love story. They glorify the love affair in the early part of the *Lancelot*, where the Lady of the Lake assures the young Queen that she is not wrong to love the best knight in the world. Later, however, they condemn their love as the cause of Lancelot's failure in the *Queste del Saint Graal* and as one of the causes of the fall of the Round Table in the *Mort Artu*.

Sir Thomas Malory conflates the romance and chronicle traditions in his *Morte Darthur* (1469–70), with the result that his portrait of Guenevere is richer and more subtle than that of any of his sources. She is the epic Queen of history and chronicle, bounteous of her gifts to the knights of the Round Table, and she is also the tragic heroine of romance, deserving of our pity for having been given in marriage to a man she must respect but cannot love, and fated to love a man she cannot marry. Malory praises Guenevere as a "trew lover" and gives her an exceptionally "good ende" by suggesting that she and Lancelot are finally united in spirit after each has renounced the vanities of this world for the "perfeccion" of the religious life.

Modern English versions of Guenevere's life and love all derive ultimately from Malory and at the same time reflect the different values and intentions of their authors. Alfred, Lord Tennyson, portrays Guenevere in his *Idylls of the King* (1859) as a fallen woman who grovels on her knees before a Victorian husband godlike in forgiveness. T.H. White domesticates the love in his *Once and Future King* (1939–40), portraying Guenevere as just plain "Jenny" to her "Lance" and imagining that Arthur benevolently overlooks their affair until his kinsmen force him to take action. Thomas Berger suggests in *Arthur Rex* (1978) that Guenevere seduced Lancelot in order to prove her power and in so doing, perhaps inadvertently, calls attention to the real powerlessness of women, even of queens, in medieval society. A more sympathetic handling of this theme appears in Sharan Newman's *Guinevere* (1981), *The Chessboard Queen* (1983), and *Guenevere Evermore* (1985), a trilogy retelling Arthurian legend from Guenevere's point of view. By contrast, a few novels, like Parke Godwin's *Firelord* (1980) and *Beloved Exile* (1984), portray Guenevere as the inheritor of a matriarchal tradition and a powerful ruler in her own right. [BK]

DiPasquale, Pasquale, Jr. "Malory's Guinevere: Epic Queen, Romance Heroine and Tragic Mistress." *Bucknell Review*, 16 (1968), 86–102.

Weston, Jessie L. *The Legend of Sir Lancelot du Lac*. London: Nutt, 1901.

GUÉNON, RENÉ (1886–1951), in *Le Roi du Monde* (1925), an esoteric treatise on Arthurian history, interpreted the Grail legend in light of his belief in a Revelation prior to all religions and available to all humanity. According to Guénon, the angels shaped the Grail from an emerald that fell from the forehead of Lucifer at the time of his fall. The Grail was entrusted to Adam until he was dismissed from Eden; it was later recovered by Seth, the representative of order and stability. Between Seth and Christ, the Druids may have been the Grail guardians. The work goes on to make the Grail the cup of the Last Supper and to connect it with Joseph of Arimathea, with Nicodemus (who helped transport it to Britain), and with the establishment of the Round Table by Arthur and Merlin. Constructed by Arthur, according to Merlin's plans, the Table was to receive the Grail once it was achieved. The essential role of the knights of the Round Table seems to be the Grail quest; the Grail doubtless represents both the Book (*grad(u)ale*), i.e., tradition, and the Vase (*grasale*), the primordial state recovered by the one who achieves this supreme degree of knowledge. The Grail, the "Book of Life," is often associated with the Lance, the symbol of the "Axis of the World." The blood flowing from the Lance corresponds to the dew emanating from the "Tree of Life," the vital principle intimately related to blood. Montsalvat, the "Mont du Salut" that holds the Grail, represents the sacred isle, the polar mountain, the Land of Immortality (identical with the earthly paradise), in the "Center of the World." [RB]

Guénon, René. *Le Roi du Monde*. Paris: Gallimard, 1925.

———. "L'Ésotérisme du Graal." In *Lumières du Graal*. Paris: Cahiers du Sud, 1951, pp. 37–49.

Baudry, Robert. "De la Loire au Nil, ou l'itinéraire spirituel de René Guénon." In *Loire et Littérature*. Angers: Presses de l'Université d'Angers, 1989, pp. 327–48.

Le Nabour, Eric. "René Guénon, prophète des temps modernes." *Historia*, 479 (November 1986), 98–104.

GUILLAUME LE CLERC. Not to be confused with the author of the *Bestiaire*, this Guillaume wrote *Fergus*, a romance sometimes named *Fergus et Galienne*, written between 1200 and 1233, possibly at the request of Alan of Galloway to celebrate his marriage in 1209. Scotland is the setting, scholars believe, and a Scottish lord, a son-in-law of Henry I of England, may have been a historical model for the hero, at least in name. The action begins in a forest near Glasgow, but the plot is hardly more than a rearrangement of Chrétien de Troyes's *Perceval*, *Yvain*, and *Erec*, with echoes of his *Lancelot* and perhaps even *Cligés*. Fergus earns fame as the *Chevalier au bel escu* ("Knight of the Fair Shield"), a hint that the author may have also imitated Renaut de Beaujeu's *Bel Inconnu*. The romance was translated into Dutch in the fourteenth century. [JLG]

Guillaume le Clerc. *Ferguut*, ed. E. Rombauts, N. de Paepe, and M.J.M. de Haan. Culemborg: Tjeenk Willink, 1976.

———. *The Romance of Fergus*, ed. Wilson Frescoln. Philadelphia: Allen, 1983.

GUIOMAR, in the Vulgate Cycle, Guenevere's cousin and one of Morgan's first lovers. Morgan's affair with Guiomar results in a dispute between Morgan and Guenevere, which leads to Guiomar's exile and Morgan's interest in witchcraft. [SW]

GUIRON LE COURTOIS: *see PALAMEDES; RUSTICIANO DA PISA.*

GUITERMAN, ARTHUR (1871–1943), New York journalist and poet who wrote ballads, humorous verse, and opera librettos. A number of his ballads are on legendary themes, including seven using Arthurian materials (1921). "To Sir Thomas Mallory" addresses Malory as a fellow poet who has been silent for too long. In "King Arthur and the Half-Man," the giant Keudawd Pwyll is defeated by Arthur. Merlin weds a fairy named Trinali in "The Perfect Marriage." "Lancelot" repeats Sir Ector's lament at the death of Lancelot. "Legend" deals with the cave legend. When Tristram sends Yseult a fairy bell in "Queen Yseult's Bell," she throws it into the sea so as not to be happier than her beloved. "Gawaine's Choice," a version of a scene in Malory, shows Uwaine, Marhaus, and Gawaine choosing among three ladies who offer quests. [PCB]

Guiterman, Arthur. *A Ballad-Maker's Pack*. New York: Harper, 1921.

GUNN, THOM (THOMSON WILLIAM GUNN), British poet, in "Merlin in the Cave: he speculates without a book," uses twelve seven-line stanzas to present the existential worries—"This cave is empty, and is very cold"—of humankind grown old vainly seeking certainties, only to realize that life is a process in which one's nature is determined by choice and action. [CNS]

Gunn, Thom. "Merlin in the Cave: he speculates without a book." *Poetry*, 83 (June 1955), 131–34; repr. in *The Sense of Movement*. London: Faber and Faber, 1957.

GUNNLAUGR LEIFSSON (d. 1218 or 1219), an Icelandic monk of the Benedictine monastery of Þingeyrar and the author of several hagiographic works. He translated Geoffrey of Monmouth's *Prophetiae Merlini* into Icelandic verse as *Merlínusspá* and may have had a hand in *Breta sǫgur*, the Old Norse translation of Geoffrey's *Historia*.

Merlínusspá is preserved in only one of the Icelandic manuscripts of the *Breta sǫgur*, although the other surviving manuscript refers to it. *Merlínusspá* was translated ca. 1200, and both manuscripts give the author as Gunnlaugr Leifsson. Gunnlaugr turned Geoffrey's Latin prose into Old Norse poetry. His understanding of the tradition of vatic poetry that Geoffrey was imitating is clearly indicated by his choice of the Eddic verse form *fornyrðislag* ("old story meter"). *Fornyrðislag* is also the meter of the *Vǫluspá* ("Sibyl's Prophecy"), a Scandinavian prophetic poem composed probably no later than the tenth century. Gunnlaug's *Merlínusspá* in fact contains several specific verbal echoes of *Vǫluspá* and other Eddic poetry.

Merlínusspá is divided into two sections that appear to have been transposed in the manuscript. Part 1 has a few verses of introduction and then translates the middle of Geoffrey's *Prophetiae*. The last few verses of Part 1 are a drastic condensation of the end of the *Prophetiae*. Part 2 opens with an extended introduction about Vortigern, Merlin, and the two dragons. It then translates the *Prophetiae* up to the point at which Part 1 begins. With the exception of those passages that he eliminates, Gunnlaug's translation is close and careful. Many of his changes are minor, dictated by the poetic form in which he was working. Gunnlaug's more substantial changes seem intended to make the poem clearer. In particular, he expands passages and changes words to make explicit references to Arthur and to other events that occur later in Geoffrey's *Historia*. Such familiarity with the *Historia Regum Britanniae* as a whole makes it extremely unlikely that Gunnlaugr was working from a separate "Libellus Merlini." [CLB]

Finnur Jónsson, ed. *Hauksbók, udgiven efter de Arnamagnæanske Håndskrifter No. 371, 544 og 675, 4° samt forskellige Papirhåndskrifter*. Copenhagen: Det kongelige nordiske Oldskrift-Selskab, 1892–96, pp. 271–83.

GURR, DAVID, Canadian author of *The Ring Master* (1987), a subtle and ironic novel in which the rise and fall of Nazi Germany is played out as "a striking production" of Wagner's Ring Cycle. As a friend of Hitler, the naive narrator, Edwin Casson-Perceval, has a vital role in this real-life performance, for he is the incestuous lover of his sister, a famous Wagnerian opera soprano (Siegmund to her Sieglinde); but he also plays the role of his namesake, the Fool, in *Parsifal*, desperately excavating various sites in a misguided search for the Grail, until he finally recognizes that it is no other than his sister's (and perhaps his own) daughter. [RHT]

Gurr, David. *The Ring Master*. Toronto: McClelland and Stewart, 1987.

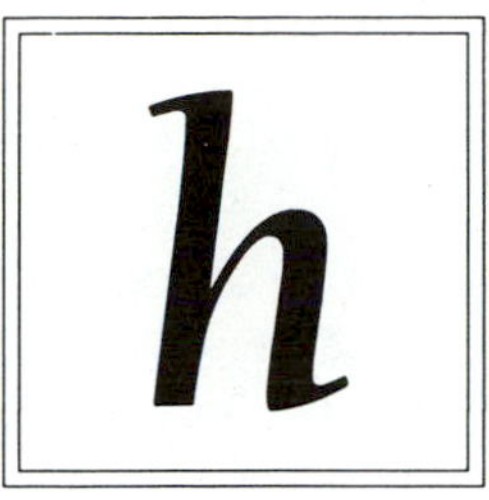

HAAR, JAAP TER, one of the most important modern Dutch adapters of Arthurian legends. He retold the stories of Tristan and Isolde and others in his 1963 *De grote sagen van de donkere Middeleeuwen* ("Great Legends of the Dark Ages"), published *Parcival* in 1967, and wrote the script of "In de voetsporen van Koning Arthur" ("In the Footsteps of King Arthur"), a 1981 documentary for Belgian Radio and Television. His most notable Arthurian publication, however, may be *Koning Arthur* ("King Arthur," 1967), a brief but interesting retelling whose usual classification as juvenile fiction does it something of an injustice.

Although Harr includes in his novel most of the familiar incidents of the Arthurian story, he casts some of them in a decidedly original form, often tracing events to human motives and efforts rather than to supernatural or other forces beyond the characters' control. For example, Merlin steals Kay's and Arthur's swords so that the latter will pull the sword from the stone, a feat he is able to accomplish only because the magician has revealed to him the secret mechanical device that holds the sword in place. Eventually, when Camelot begins to crumble, it does so not merely because of the love (here unconsummated) of Lancelot and Guinevere, nor does it result from the conflicts inherent in Arthur's system of justice and chivalry. Rather, Harr presents Modred as the mastermind of the entire cataclysm: it is he who sends a message asking Lancelot to come to Guinevere's chamber and then arranges for them to be discovered and for Lancelot's men to rescue him. Eventually, Guinevere is to undergo ordeal by fire (rather than be burned as legal punishment, as in most accounts), and it is Modred who has Lancelot informed, knowing that the latter will rescue the Queen and that, as a result, Arthur will go to war against him. The villain's plans work flawlessly until he incites Arthur's enmity by declaring himself king. Eventually, although Arthur has been called "once and future king," he and Modred kill each other, there being no mention of Avalon or Arthur's survival. [NJL]

Haar, Jaap ter. *Koning Arthur*. Bussum: Van Dishoeck, Van Holkema and Warendorf, 1967. (Published in the U.S. as *King Arthur*, trans. Marian Powell. New York: Crane Russak, 1973.)

———. *Parcival*. Bussum: Van Dishoeck, Van Holkema and Warendorf, 1967.

HAGEDORN, HERMANN (1882–1964), American educator, editor, and writer, in his one-act play *The Silver Blade* (1907) describes how Guinevere falls in love with Lancelot, who has come to escort her to her wedding with Arthur. Knowing that betrayal is inevitable, she contemplates suicide but chooses the path of least resistance. His short poem "The Song of the Grail Seekers" (1909) expresses the knights' "unquenchable yearning." [RHT]

Hagedorn, Hermann. *The Silver Blade*. Berlin: Ungar, 1907.

———. "Song of the Grail Seekers." In *A Troop of the Guard and Other Poems*. Boston: Houghton Mifflin, 1909, p. 67.

HÁKON HÁKONARSON, King of Norway (r. 1217–63), encouraged the translation of French literature of his time. Ultimately, his efforts established a body of translated works that was accessible not only in Norway but also in the rest of Scandinavia. The earliest work commissioned by Hákon is *Tristrams saga*, a translation of Thomas's *Tristan*. Written in 1226, this translation represents the only complete version of the Thomas-branch of the Tristan legend. According to its preface, *Tristrams saga* was translated by "Brother Robert." His name occurs in association with *Elis saga*, a translation of *Elie de St. Gille, a chanson de geste*, also made at Hákon's behest. The remaining translations that originated in Hákon's court are anonymous and include works that contain Arthurian material: *Ívens saga*, a version of Chrétien de Troyes's *Yvain; Möttuls saga*, a rendering of the fabliau *Le Mantel mautaillié*; and *Strengleikar*, a significant compilation of the lais of Marie de France. It is also possible that two additional translations of Arthurian material—*Parcevals Saga* and *Erex saga*, based on Chrétien's *Perceval* and *Erec et Enide*—were also translated during this period. The extant manuscripts of these two translations do not mention Hákon's patronage. The literary activity at Hákon's court was influenced by close ties to Angevin England, which provided King Hákon with model and material. The translations share a common style characterized by rhetorical embellishment, rhythmic prose, and artistic elaboration. Hákon's patronage occupies an important position in the spread of Arthurian literature in the North. Many of these translations reached Iceland, where they were recopied or, as in the case of *Tristrams saga*, adapted. A similar influence is present in Sweden, where *Ivan Lejonriddaren*, a translation of *Yvain*, was probably indebted to *Ívens saga*. These contributions position Hákon at the center of the international movement of Arthurian literature in Scandinavia. [IJR]

Leach, Henry G. *Angevin Britain and Scandinavia*. Cambridge: Harvard University Press, 1921.

HALDEMAN, LINDA, American writer, uses a long-lived Merlin's talents as an enchanter to provide the magic spell that will enable an exchange between a fairy and a human in *The Lastborn of Elvinwood* (1978), a fantasy in a contemporary setting. [RHT]

Haldeman, Linda. *The Lastborn of Elvinwood*. Garden City, N.Y.: Doubleday, 1978.

HALM, FRIEDRICH (pseudonym of Eligius Franz Joseph Reichsfreiherr von Münch-Bellinghausen; 1806–1871), wrote romantic plays and realistic novellas. In the dramatic poem *Griseldis* (premiered December 30, 1835), Halm transplants the Patient Griselda motif to Arthur's court. At Guinevere's instigation and with Arthur's approval, Griseldis must undergo tests of her loyalty and devotion (give away her son, leave the court in disgrace) for no apparent reason. The Queen is eventually humiliated by the simple maiden's endurance, and Lancelot, recognizing Guinevere's evil character, soberly rides back home to France. [EGF/PWM]

Halm, Friedrich. *Griseldis: Dramatisches Gedicht in fünf Aufzügen*. Vienna: Gerold, 1837; repr. Berlin, Leipzig, Vienna, and Stuttgart: Deutsches Verlagshaus Bong, n.d., pp. 57–126.

HAMILTON, LORD ERNEST (1858–1939), author of *Launcelot: A Romance of the Court of King Arthur* (1926), echoes Malory so assiduously as to give the effect of parody. In this version, Pelles is a converted Norseman, Launcelot is Elaine's husband, and Guenevere is a lecherous, deceitful liar who lures the hero to Vortigern's tower under false pretense, seduces him, and plans to murder Elaine. The complexities of the situation baffle the hero, but then, as the author tells us, "Sir Launcelot was a man of simple mind." [MAW]

Hamilton, Lord Ernest. *Launcelot: A Romance of the Court of King Arthur*. London: Methuen, 1926.

HANDKE, PETER, a leading Austrian author, makes surprising use of the Parzival figure in his dramatic text *Das Spiel vom Fragen oder Die Reise zum sonoren Land* ("The Play of the Query, or the Voyage to the Sonorous Land," 1989). Handke treats the themes of communication breakdown and the crisis of language. The protagonist, whose "action" resides in fragmented and disordered conversations, is called Parzival. Handke thus contributes to the German Parzival tradition, according to which this character, especially in Wolfram's *Parzival*, claims recognition as the prototypical seeker and questioner. The play premiered in Vienna on January 16, 1990. [UM/WCM]

Handke, Peter. *Das Spiel vom Fragen oder Die Reise zum sonoren Land*. Frankfurt: Suhrkamp, 1989.

HANRATTY, PETER, blends science fiction and fantasy in two novels that set Arthur's chivalric world in pre-Roman Britain. In *The Last Knight of Albion: The Quest for Mordred* (1986), Percevale, last survivor of the Round Table, seeks revenge against Mordred for using an atomic bomb, obtained from extraterrestrial aliens, at Camlann. Over the years, he loses most of his illusions about life, but when called upon to defend a town against a marauding army he rediscovers the importance of self-sacrifice, the quality that motivated the best among Arthur's followers.

The Book of Mordred (1988) follows the earlier career of Mordred, from his childhood in a forest haunted by fairies, through his education at Arthur's court and Glastonbury, where he reads Plato, to his successful quest for the Grail in the company of Lancelot and Galahad. Mordred emerges as an intelligent and idealistic young man whose efforts to help others are constantly frustrated by the ignorance and prejudice of those around him. [RHT]

Hanratty, Peter. *The Last Knight of Albion: The Quest for Mordred*. New York: Bluejay, 1986.
———. *The Book of Mordred*. Lake Geneva, Wisc.: New Infinities Productions, 1988.

HARDER, NATHALIE, contemporary German artist, adapted the *Parzival* of Wolfram von Eschenbach for the puppet theater (1976–79). Titled *Recht mitten durch: Eine Miniature aus dem Mittelalter nach Wolfram von Eschenbach—ein Traum aus dem Mittelalter*, the dreamlike piece is performed in two and a half hours with over fifty marionettes. Harder takes as interpretive models Eric Rohmer's film *Perceval le Gallois* (1978) and C.G. Jung's depth-psychology. The play has been performed successfully in Berlin and elsewhere. [UM/WCM]

HARDT, ERNST (1876–1946), whose five-act drama *Tantris der Narr* ("Tristram the Jester," 1909) won for its author a leading place among German dramatists and poets. The play recounts Iseult's lament after Tristram has been ordered from Mark's court and marries Iseult of Brittany, Mark's condemnation of her to a leper's life, her two rescues by a disguised Tristram, and finally Tristram's death. This is a dramatic and moving treatment of the legend. [VML]

Hardt, Ernst. *Tantris der Narr*. Leipzig: Insel, 1909.

———. *Tristram the Jester*, trans. John Heard, Jr. Boston: Badger, 1913; rev. ed. *Poet-Lore*, 43 (1936), 229–78, 289–327.

42. Thomas Hardy, Tintagel, from *The Queen of Cornwall*. (Courtesy of The Newberry Library, Chicago.)

HARDY, THOMAS (1840–1928), author of *Queen of Cornwall* (1923). In this "new version of an old story arranged as a play for mummers in one act," Tristram, deceived by the white-handed Iseult, appears disguised at Mark's court, where he is killed by Mark. Iseult of Ireland kills her husband and then jumps to her death from a cliff. [AEG]

Hardy, Thomas. *The Famous Tragedy of the Queen of Cornwall at Tintagel in Lyonnesse*. London and New York: Macmillan, 1923.

Clark, S.L., and J.N. Wasserman. *Thomas Hardy and the Tristan Legend*. Heidelberg: Winter, 1983.

HARDYNG, JOHN (1378–ca. 1465), wrote two versions of his verse chronicle of Britain and England that covers the period from the legendary settling of Britain to the mid-fifteenth century. The first version (ca. 19,000 lines), found in only one manuscript (Lansdowne 204) and so far unedited, was completed by 1457 for presentation to Henry VI. A second version (ca. 12,600 lines) was prepared for Richard, Duke of York (d. 1460), and this version was revised for Edward IV and was in its final form by 1464. This shorter version survives in twelve manuscripts and three fragments, and Richard Grafton printed two editions of it, along with his own prose continuation, in 1543.

Although Hardyng's political sympathies are Lancastrian in the first version and Yorkist in the second, an important political message in both versions was that England should conquer Scotland. Undoubtedly, much of his reason for writing the chronicle was to answer Scottish nationalist historians like John of Fordun who claimed that Scotland was historically independent of England. Hardyng's rhyme-royal stanzas are usually dismissed as doggerel, but his chronicle has been valued for some of the information it gives about events in fifteenth-century England. His use of the Arthurian legend is also of interest, for he draws upon material, such as the Joseph of Arimathea legend and Galahad's Grail quest, that other English chroniclers usually ignored. And few writers could speak more enthusiastically about the glories of Arthur's reign. The chronicle was a minor source for both Malory's *Morte Darthur* and Spenser's *Faerie Queene* and was one of the most frequently cited chronicles of the sixteenth and seventeenth centuries. Besides contributing to Spenser's knowledge of the legendary history of Britain and giving Malory a number of details, such as Arthur's coronation as Roman emperor at the end of Tale II, Hardyng, writing in the tradition of what Gransden calls chivalric historiography, could have influenced both Spenser and Malory's conceptions of Arthurian chivalry. (*See also* John of Fordun.) [EDK]

Hardyng, John. *The Chronicle of John Hardyng*, ed. Henry Ellis. London: Rivington, 1812.

Göller, Karl Heinz. *König Arthur in der englischen Literatur des späten Mittelalters*. Göttingen: Vandenhoeck and Ruprecht, 1963, pp. 34–38.

Gransden, Antonia. *Historical Writing in England. c. 1307 to the Early Sixteenth Century*. Ithaca, N.Y.: Cornell University Press, 1982, pp. 274–87.

Kennedy, Edward Donald. "Chronicles and Other Historical Writing." In *A Manual of the Writings in Middle English*, ed. A.E. Hartung. New Haven: Connecticut Academy of Arts and Sciences, 1981–89, Vol. 8, pp. 2644–47, 2836–45.

———. "John Hardyng and the Holy Grail." *Arthurian Literature*, 8 (1989), 185–206.

———. "Malory and His English Sources." In *Aspects of Malory*, ed. Toshiyuki Takamiya and Derek Brewer. Cambridge: Brewer, 1981, pp. 27–55.

Lagorio, Valerie M. "The Evolving Legend of St. Joseph of Glastonbury." *Speculum*, 46 (1971), 209–31.

Withrington, John. "The Arthurian Epitaph in Malory's *Morte Darthur*." *Arthurian Literature*, 7 (1987), 103–44.

HARE, AMORY (pseudonym of Amory Hare Hutchinson), author of *Tristram and Iseult: A Play* (1930). Hare's work is inspired by Bédier, although he is aware of the scholarly tradition and of poems by John Masefield and Edwin Arlington Robinson. The play focuses on the pine-tree and flour episodes and depicts the major characters to good effect in the setting of a Cornish court full of jealousy and unrest. [AAR]

Hare, Amory. *Tristram and Iseult: A Play*. Gaylordsville, Conn.: Slide Mountain, 1930.

HARLEY *BRUT*, a French verse translation, from the mid-twelfth century, of Geoffrey of Monmouth's *Historia*. Extant in five fragments (London, B.L. Harley 1605), it ends before Arthur's battle with Rome. [NJL]

Blakey, Brian. "The Harley *Brut*: An Early French Translation of Geoffrey of Monmouth's *Historia Regum Britanniae*." *Romania*, 82 (1961), 44–70.

HARTMANN VON AUE, one of the outstanding poets of the so-called "blossom-time" of Middle High German courtly literature. A younger contemporary, Gottfried von Strassburg, says of him in his *Tristan* that his stories are full of color and ornament and that the inner meaning and outer form are in complete harmony. This is no exaggeration. Hartmann's works testify to his considerable poetic skill and reveal him as a writer who used his gifts in the service of the courtly society in which he lived, as a firm upholder and energetic propagator of its ideals and values. He has a strong sense of courtliness and deep religious convictions.

Hartmann's main literary output consists of four narrative poems in rhymed couplets: two Arthurian romances, *Erec* and *Iwein*, whose sources were almost certainly Chrétien's *Erec et Enide* and *Yvain*; and two shorter, non-Arthurian poems, *Gregorius* and *Der arme Heinrich*. He also wrote a dialogue, or disputation, between the body and heart of a young man (himself) on the subject of love, the *Klage* ("complaint"), as well as fifteen love songs and three crusade songs. Although it is impossible to give precise dates for any of Hartmann's compositions, the sequence of his narrative poems, or "court epics," is thought to have been *Erec*, *Gregorius*, *Der arme Heinrich*, and *Iwein*. The *Klage* was perhaps his earliest work. He may have actually taken part in a Crusade, but even if he did, which is by no means universally accepted, we cannot decide whether it was in 1189/90 or in 1197. His love poetry cannot be dated either, such is the paucity of information available concerning Hartmann's personal life and affairs. He was almost certainly not born before 1150 and was still alive ca. 1210, though probably dead by 1220. His literary career may have begun ca. 1180, and *Iwein* is likely to have been completed by 1205. These rough estimates are based on what little we know of his relations with contemporary literary figures, such as Wolfram von Eschenbach and Gottfried von Strassburg.

In *Der arme Heinrich*, Hartmann refers to himself as *dienestman . . . ze Ouwe* ("vassal at Aue"), which implies that, like many classical Middle High German poets, he was a member of the unfree but up-and-coming knightly class of *ministeriales*. He wrote and probably also performed for courtly audiences; for his livelihood and for the needs of his profession—manuscripts of sources (particularly French); working materials, such as parchment; scribes; and time and leisure to write—he must have been dependent on a noble patron or patrons, but we do not know whom. But he may well have served some time at the court of the Dukes of Zähringen, who held extensive lands in southern Germany, Switzerland, and eastern France, since it is generally agreed that he hailed from the Upper Rhine region. There were probably other patrons too; even the Hohenstaufens may have employed him. Although he wrote in the standard Middle High German "poet's language," his dialect was almost certainly Swabian, which at that time was spoken in part of what is now northern Switzerland. The place- and/or family-name *Ouwe* ("land on water") cannot be pinpointed, since what would now be "Au" appears as the final syllable of many place-names. Eglisau near Schaffhausen and Reichenau (Lake Constance) have both been popular suggestions, though a more modern one is Au near Freiburg, where a ministerial family of the Zähringer is known to have lived.

In *Iwein* and *Der arme Heinrich*, Hartmann describes himself as a knight who had been taught to read what he found written in books. From this, and from his obvious ability to read the texts of his sources (both French and Latin, it would seem), it may be deduced that he attended a monastic or cathedral school, perhaps Reichenau. In *Gregorius*, he describes the education of the hero in such a school, and though we cannot be sure that this has any autobiographical relevance or not, it seems certain that, judging from his poetic achievements, Hartmann was well acquainted with the *Trivium* (Grammar, Rhetoric, and Dialectic). He is a complete master of contemporary poetic techniques, and his skillful use of parallelism, antithesis, and paradox suggests dialectical training. Furthermore, his firm grasp of fundamental medieval religious ideas, as revealed particularly in *Gregorius* and *Der arme Heinrich*, may well have been the result of some theological instruction, however rudimentary. He is clearly proud of his schooling, which, he says, enabled him to read "all sorts of books" and which was probably more comprehensive and thorough than that of most laymen of his time and class. His education, indeed, may well have been sponsored by a noble patron.

Hartmann's two Arthurian romances, like Chrétien's *Erec* and *Yvain*, are both essentially problem-tales. In *Erec*, a fairly free adaptation of Chrétien that runs to a little more than 10,000 lines, he shows how the newly wed hero neglects his courtly and chivalric duties because of overindulgence in sexual activity, and how he subsequently redeems himself through deeds of knightly prowess in the service of fellow human beings. In *Iwein*, just over 8,000 lines and much closer to Chrétien, the opposite is the case: the hero, also newly wed, leaves his wife, Laudine, after a week and becomes so immersed in the pursuit of knightly fame and glory that he fails to keep his promise to return to her by an agreed deadline of one year. This ethical problem, too, must be solved by the hero before he can be regarded as a perfect knight.

In both his Arthurian epics, Hartmann's main preoccupation is with courtly, chivalric, and Christian ethics, particularly with reference to the protagonists, the hero and his wife in *Erec* and Iwein and his wife's maidservant, Lunete, in the later poem. In the earlier work (of which the beginning, some 100 lines, is missing, and which has some further lacunae), the hero's lack of balance between sexual love and chivalry (*verligen*) causes him to lose the respect of his court, who blame his marriage to Enite for what has happened. Although Enite hears what people are saying about them, she doesn't complain to Erec because she is afraid of losing him. When he does find out, as a result of a mistake on Enite's part, he immediately rides out in search of adventure, taking Enite with him but making her ride some distance ahead and forbidding her to speak to him on pain of death. He treats her with the minimum of courtesy.

On several occasions during the ensuing adventures, Enite saves Erec's life at the risk of losing her own, but in doing so she has to break her promise not to speak to him. She thus shows a higher order of loyalty to and love for her husband (*triuwe*) than she would have done if she had kept her promise and not spoken to him, for he would then have been killed. But this is not how Erec sees it: for him, her disobedience is not *triuwe* but its very opposite. In his eyes, she has failed to show her loyalty to him as her husband, and so each time she disobeys him his anger increases, though he does not carry out his threat to kill her. But Enite remains staunchly loyal throughout, and the two are finally reconciled when the hero comes to realize his wife's true worth and seeks her forgiveness for mistreating her. According to the narrator, he felt he had to "test" her to be sure that she was a good wife, and she has indeed passed the test.

Erec's last, supreme adventure is the so-called "joi de la curt," in which he liberates the knight Mabonagrin and his wife from their self-imposed isolation from courtly society in a miraculous garden and so restores the "joy of the court," the loss of which was caused by their withdrawal. This situation is analogous to that of Erec and Enite themselves earlier, which was so damaging to their reputations. Now, having repaired that damage, the hero is able to free Mabonagrin and his wife from this comparable situation, which occurred because the wife, afraid of losing her husband to other women, made him promise to stay shut up with her in the garden until another knight came and defeated him, a promise that Mabonagrin wanted to break but would not. But if he had done so, he would have shown a higher order of *triuwe* than he actually showed to his wife by staying in the garden with her and so neglecting his social duties.

The problem confronting Erec and Enite after their *verligen* is how to "order" their love for each other, that is, how to reconcile it with their duties to themselves and to those members of courtly society who depend on them as their rulers. The inordinate, all-excluding sexual love of the protagonists leads to disaster, and to rehabilitate himself Erec knows that he must go out on adventure and prove himself as a knight. What is more, he feels that Enite, who was also implicated in the *verligen* and who has behaved so strangely that he has lost faith in her as a wife, should come with him. Both must make themselves acceptable again to their fellows and to God. Erec, though overreacting to what he sees as his wife's failure to give him full wifely support and loyalty and treating her far more harshly than she deserves, finally recovers his chivalric reputation as a result of his exploits, and in so doing he "orders" his love for Enite, acknowledging that through her incomparable display of loyalty and constancy to him on the adventures, when she unselfishly placed his safety above her own, she has proved herself to be a good wife. Both have redeemed themselves: their mutual love is integrated into the wider framework of their lives in and responsibilities to courtly society. Unlike their manifest "self-love" as newlyweds, their love now partakes, in keeping with the strong religious accent of the poem, of the nature of *caritas* itself, ordered love for God and one's neighbor.

The "ordering of love" is also central to the ethical development of the hero in *Iwein*. Like that of Erec to Enite, Iwein's marriage to Laudine also goes wrong, but for different reasons. It is a union hastily arranged by Lunete, who, after Iwein has killed Ascalon, Laudine's husband, in his successful attack on the magic fountain of Breziljan, persuades her mistress that his killer would be the best replacement as defender of the fountain, since in defeating him he has demonstrated his obvious knightly superiority. Iwein has no objections, having fallen in love with the beautiful and partly naked Laudine as he watched her lament the loss of Ascalon. His love for her is pure sexual passion, and hers for him, if it can be called love at all, is the direct result of her need to have a new defender of the fountain. That their marriage should collapse is hardly surprising. Almost immediately after their wedding, Gawein reminds the hero of what happened to Erec and persuades him to ask Laudine for leave of absence to go out on knightly adventure and so avoid *verligen*. This he obtains, but forgets to return after the agreed period of one year, thus breaking his solemn oath (*triuwe*) to his wife and committing the opposite offense to that of Erec. He shows inordinate love for knighthood.

Laudine's reaction to Iwein's *untriuwe* is harsh: she sends Lunete to Arthur's court to denounce him publicly, and in his shame and remorse the hero takes leave of his senses and wanders naked in the forest like an animal until he is cured by a magic salve, the application of which symbolizes his ethical rebirth. All his subsequent adventures, altruistic and compassionate in character, are concerned not so much with Iwein's self-glorification, but rather to show that his love is no longer exclusively for himself, but for his fellows. One of them, highly symbolic, tells how he comes upon a fight between a lion and a serpent, representing good and evil respectively, and intervenes on the side of the "nobler" animal, helping it to overcome its adversary. The lion, perhaps intended to recall the lion of Judah, shows its gratitude (*triuwe*) by becoming the hero's faithful companion and comrade-in-arms; Iwein then becomes known as the "knight with the lion." Eventually, he is received back into his wife's favor when he asks for her forgiveness for his *untriuwe* and she reciprocates by apologizing to him for having caused him so much sorrow and pain, by overreacting to his unintentional failure to keep his promise and inflicted such public humiliation on him.

The hero, it is clear, cannot return to his wife and regain her favor until he has accomplished his later adventures of compassion and charity. But once this has happened, he has proved that his love for her is ordered and their marriage can be repaired and reestablished on a basis of mutual *caritas*, or *triuwe*. In both his romances, in fact, Hartmann concentrates his ethical message in this virtue, which at its highest level is essentially love for God and one's neighbor. He makes it very clear that it is not a straightforward concept but takes many forms and exists at different levels and in different "orders." In his ethical approach, as has been frequently indicated, he is greatly influenced by the medieval Christian idea of *ordo*. Sexual love is not intrinsically bad, but because it is such a powerful emotion it can easily become "inordinate" and so must be integrated into the wider love of *caritas*, the highest order of *triuwe*.

It is universally accepted that *Iwein* is the most polished and sophisticated of all Hartmann's poems, and for this reason it is assumed to have been the last of his compositions, the culmination of his artistic career. With its wealth of parallelism, antithesis, and paradox, the poem shows unmistakable signs of Hartmann's training in rhetoric and dialectic. Nowhere is this sophistication more strikingly revealed than in his ironic and often humorous depiction of the goings-on at the court of King Arthur. Through irony, he draws scathing attention to the obvious flaws of the court and its conventional code of conduct and limited conception of knightly adventure, and shows in the career of his hero, an outstanding knight, how this is overcome and a new chivalric ideal established.

Hartmann's Arthurian romances owe much to Chrétien, who provides the basic story in both cases. Nevertheless, the German poet, one of the three "great masters" of the courtly epic (the other two are Wolfram von Eschenbach and Gottfried von Strassburg), is no mere imitator of a French model. His undoubted individuality, poetic imagination, and creativity are clearly visible if we compare his adaptations of the Erec and Iwein stories with Chrétien's originals. Hartmann brings to their full realization the latent ethical and religious potentialities of his French sources. [HBW]

Hartmann von Aue. *Erec*, ed. Albert Leitzmann; 6th ed. Christoph Cormeau and K. Gärtner. Tübingen: Niemeyer, 1985.

———. *Erec*, trans. Thomas L. Keller. New York: Garland, 1986.

———. *Iwein: Eine Erzählung*, ed. G.F. Benecke and Karl Lachmann; 7th ed. Ludwig Wolff. Berlin: De Gruyter, 1968.

———. *Iwein*, ed. and trans. Patrick M. McConeghy. New York: Garland, 1984.

Cormeau, Christoph, and Wilhelm Störmer. *Hartmann von Aue: Epoche—Werk—Wirkung*. Munich: Beck, 1985.

Gottzman, Carola L. *Artusdichtung*. Stuttgart: Metzler, 1989.

Neubuhr, Elfriede. *Bibliographie zu Hartmann von Aue*. Berlin: Schmidt, 1977, rev. 1987.

Wapnewski, Peter. *Hartmann von Aue*. Stuttgart: Metzler, 1962; 7th ed. 1979.

HAUPTMANN, GERHART (1862–1946), Nobel Prize-winner (1912) and one of the most important German poets and dramatists of the twentieth century, often used medieval subject matter. Written for his twelve-year-old son, Benvenuto, *Parsival* (1914) and *Lohengrin* (1913) freely adapt the stories of Wolfram von Eschenbach, Robert de Boron, and Richard Wagner. These prose narratives, which center on Parsival, the seeker after God, and the world of the Grail, are characterized by an adolescent sentimentality. From 1917 to 1944, Hauptmann worked on an unfinished novel, *Der neue Christophorus* (originally to be called *Merlin*). This fragment, heavy with myth and mysticism, concerns an "earthman," a new Merlin, conceived in death by an ancient "superman" and born in a coffin. He is to be initiated into the great esotericism of the German nationality and of humanity by Pater Christophorus. The work stands clearly in the German Merlin tradition as set down by Immermann. Hauptmann also left unfinished the drama *Galahad* (1908–14). [UM/WCM]

Hauptmann, Gerhart. *Lohengrin*. Berlin: Ullstein, 1913.

———. *Parsival*. Berlin: Ullstein, 1914.

HAWKE, SIMON (pseudonym of Nicholas Yermakov), American writer, sets his lively fantasy series in a future where magic has replaced fossil fuels as an energy source for technology. In *The Wizard of 4th Street* (1987), the Dark Ones try to escape their ancient imprisonment and regain power over humankind, but they find themselves opposed by an alliance formed by Morgan le Fay, her son Modred, two descendants of her sisters Elaine and Morgause, and Merlin, whose reawakening from his long enchantment had ushered in the new age of magic after the collapse of the age of technology. In *The Wizard of Whitechapel* (1988), the struggle takes on Gothic tones when one of the escaped Dark Ones sets werewolves and a murderer modeled on Jack the Ripper loose upon London in an effort to trap and destroy his opponents. In *The Wizard of Sunset Strip* (1989), the action shifts to Los Angeles, where the protagonists get involved in plans to make an Arthurian film and receive help against the Dark Ones from the spirit of Gorlois. [RHT]

Hawke, Simon. *The Wizard of 4th Street*. New York: Popular Library/Warner, 1987.

———. *The Wizard of Whitechapel*. New York: Popular Library/Warner, 1988.

———. *The Wizard of Sunset Strip*. New York: Popular Library/Warner, 1989.

HAWKER, ROBERT STEPHEN (1803–1875), published his mystical poem *The Quest of the Sangraal* in 1864. Though based upon Malory, it reduces the number of Grail questers to four: Lancelot, Tristram, Perceval, and Galahad. Three more parts were planned but never completed. When a revised version was published in *Cornish Ballads* (1869), it was accompanied by Arthurian poems that had previously appeared in magazines. "King Arthur's Waes-hael" (1861) is a Christmas carol; "Queen Guennivar's Round" (1864) is a song celebrating Cornwall's daughters as the nymphs of the tide at Dundagel; and "The Doom-Well of St. Madron" (1855) shows Mordred's lack of faithfulness exposed by a magic well. [RHT/PCB]

Hawker, Robert Stephen. *The Quest of the Sangraal: Chant the First*. Exeter: Published for the author, 1864.

———. *Cornish Ballads and Other Poems*. Oxford and London: Parker, 1869.

HAYES, JAMES JUVENAL, in his slight piece *Sir Kay: A Poem in the Old Style* (1923), recounts how Kay, while still a young and romantic knight, meets and falls in love with a faerie maiden. Unable to find her again, he becomes the bitter-tongued seneschal of romance tradition, seeking death in combat with stronger knights. [RHT]

Hayes, James Juvenal. *Sir Kay: A Poem in the Old Style*. [Sioux City, Iowa]: Dark Harp, [1923].

HEARD, JOHN, JR. (1889–?), not only translated Ernst Hardt's *Tantris der Narr* (1909) as *Tristram the Jester* (1913; rev. ed. 1936) but also composed the poem "The Marriage of Tristram" (1942). Resentful at his long banishment, Tristram marries Isolde of Brittany, but his love for Isolde of Ireland is rekindled on his wedding night when he learns of her death. Boarding the funeral vessel, he claims her as his "ever-lasting bride" and harps their wedding song as they sail into the west. [RHT]

Heard, John, Jr., trans. *Tristram the Jester: A Play in Five Acts from the German of Ernest Hardt*. Boston: Badger, 1913; rev. ed. *Poet-Lore*, 43 (1936), 229–78, 289–327.

———. "The Marriage of Tristram." *Poet-Lore*, 48 (1942), 72–83.

HEARNE, ISABEL, tells the "tale of a woman's heart" in *Queen Herzelied* (1911), a poetic play in three acts. This account of his mother's desire to prevent Parzival's departure concludes with her death as he sets out, clad in a fool's dress that she has made for him in a futile attempt to deter him from leaving. [EB]

Hearne, Isabel. *Queen Herzelied: An Episode in the Boyhood of the Hero, Parzival*. London: Nutt, 1911.

HEATH-STUBBS, JOHN, contemporary English poet, composed a version of the tales of Arthur, published in 1973 under the title *Artorius*. This retelling of the tales owes as much to classical Greek literature and to Northrop Frye's theory of literary genres as it does to Geoffrey of Monmouth or Malory. The twelve parts, each corresponding to a sign of the zodiac, are grouped into four sections corresponding to the seasons. Within each of these four sections, one part is in heroic verse (with heavy alliteration, reminiscent of Anglo-Saxon heroic poetry), the other two in various genres ranging from Aristophanic comedy to Pindaric ode or Sophoclean tragedy. The complete cycle recounts the life of Arthur from the spring of his victory on Mount Badon to the winter of his last battle and his passing to Avalon; it is offered, according to the opening Invocation (to Calliope and the other muses), as a paradigm of human life: ". . . his seasons' progress/From spring's heyday to high summer and harvest,/And lastly to the laggard lagoon of old age/ Where his son supplants him and the cycle returns."

Like Geoffrey of Monmouth, Heath-Stubbs invites comparisons between the Arthurian story and the *Aeneid* of Vergil. Like Aeneas, Arthur journeys to the underworld and is shown a vision of the future of Britain. Like the *Aeneid*, *Artorius* includes considerable discussion of the nature of leadership and of empire; though Arthur's capabilities in battle prove his worth, he long resists the urgings of his people to take the imperial crown, and he speaks at length about the nature of the *imperium*. Further, this theme is coupled to the themes of history and the telling of history, of the nature of antiquity and of story (and several of the "interludes" between books have to do with poets, critics, and historians, and their often ineffectual and sometimes ludicrous attempts to grapple with the past). *Artorius* is a rich blending of ancient literary traditions, using the story of Arthur as a vehicle for an exploration of the very nature of literary tradition. There is considerable learning and subtlety displayed here, and the poem rewards the careful and knowledgeable reader.

Two other poems by Heath-Stubbs have Arthurian connections. "The Triumph of the Muse," like *Artorius*, is concerned with the nature of poetic traditions; here, that concern is expressed through a satirical view of modern poetry. In a dream (retold in six cantos in *terza rima*), the poet is taken by the spirit of Sigmund Freud (in the process of expiating his sins) on a flight (with deliberate echoes of Chaucer's *The Hous of Fame* and Dickens's *A Christmas Carol*) to Helicon and the temple of the Muses. Here, he sees gathered the ancient poets of various times and countries, and the bulk of the poem is a catalogue of brief descriptions of these poets. Merlin and Taliesin are included among the poets of the ancient Celts. The Muse then appears and offers to grant lasting fame to any of the modern poets who can prove themselves worthy, and the poet sees a host (including some of his friends, he says) rush forward to offer their verses; several of these modern poets are described in somewhat disparaging terms. While owing much to Dante and Chaucer in terms of the "vision" and the meter, the style of the piece is very like the mock-heroic of Byron's *Don Juan*. "The Lament of Tristan" is a short lyric in two six-line stanzas. Tristan, late in life, laments that the month of May no longer brings to him the softness and sweetness of birds and flowers, but only rocks and ships and the cold sea. [SRR]

Heath-Stubbs, John. "The Lament of Tristan." In *Beauty and the Beast*. London: Routledge and Kegan Paul, 1943.

———. "The Triumph of the Muse." In *The Triumph of the Muse and Other Poems*. London: Oxford University Press, 1958.

———. *Artorius: A Heroic Poem in Four Books and Eight Episodes*. London: Enitharmon, 1973.

———. *Collected Poems, 1943–1987*. Manchester: Carcanet, 1987. (Reprints all three of the other works listed here.)

HEBER, REGINALD (1783–1826), bishop and hymnologist, wrote two Arthurian fragments. *Morte D'Arthur* (1812), an epic in Spenserians, presents a victorious Arthur married to Ganora (Guenevere), supposedly a villager, who longs for her forester-lover Cadual (Lancelot in disguise). Morgue and her son Mordred provide plot complications. *The Masque of Gwendolen* (1816) combines Merlin, Titania, and the Loathly Lady. Heber's moralistic treatment prefigures Tennyson. [MAW]

Merriman, John Douglas. *The Flower of Kings: A Study of the Arthurian Legend in England Between 1485 and 1835*. Lawrence: University Press of Kansas, 1973.

HECTOR (ECTOR) **DE MARIS** (des Mares), Lancelot's brother and King Ban's son in the French Vulgate Cycle and later texts. Although Hector goes on the quest for the Grail, he is denied admittance to the Grail castle because of his worldly ways. When Arthur and Lancelot are at cross-purposes, he sides with his brother and later helps him rescue Guenevere from the stake. After Lancelot dies, Hector joins Bors and the other knights in the Crusade to Jerusalem, where he meets his death. [SW]

HEIDUCZEK, WERNER, East German writer, based his 1974 novel *Die seltsamen Abenteuer des Parzival* ("The Curious Adventures of Parzival") on Wolfram's epic, but wanted to present the tale "in a way that seems believable." Through changes in emphasis and in actual content, as well as by his own use of language, Heiduczek depicts Parzival as a reason-dominated individual responsible for his own fate and unmasks the Arthurian court as a decadent aristocracy, in contrast to the Grail kingdom, which exhibits humanitarian principles. [SSch/PM]

Heiduczek, Werner. *Die seltsamen Abenteuer des Parzival: Nach Wolfram von Eschenbach neu erzählt*. Berlin: Neues Leben, 1974.

HEIN, CHRISTOPH, important East German fiction writer and playwright, employed medieval subject matter in a topical vein in his novella *Drachenblut* ("Dragonblood," 1982; earlier title: *Der fremde Freund*, "The Unknown Friend"). He is therefore in the mainstream of literary reception of the Middle Ages in the former German Democratic Republic. His play *Die Ritter der Tafelrunde* ("The Knights of the Round Table," 1989), concentrates on a few leading figures of the Arthurian legend: Arthur, Parzival, Lancelot, Orilus, Kay, Mordred, Guenevere, and Cunneware. Almost all of them have grown old; resigned, they live in the past, doubtful of the future. They are members of a society in transition. The play can be interpreted as criticism of a ruling stratum that no longer has faith in its own ideals.

The play, which for political reasons had only an unofficial opening night in Dresden in March 1989, is one of the most important literary texts reflecting the situation leading to the *Wende*, or upheaval, that was to rock East Germany in the autumn of 1989. [UM/WCM]

Hein, Christoph. *Die Ritter der Tafelrunde*. Frankfurt: Luchterhand Literaturverlag, 1989.

HEINE, HEINRICH (1797–1856), one of the great lyric poets of later German Romanticism and at the same time, through his irony and scathing satire, one of its strongest critics. In the third of his nine *Katharina* poems (1835), Heine alludes to the entrancement of the lover in the traditional Merlin-Niniane story. However, Heine's reference may be to an incapacitating fixation not only for a mistress but for any abstract ideal, such as beauty, nature, or political freedom. [RWK]

Heine, Heinrich. *Werke und Briefe*, ed. Hans Kaufmann. Berlin: Aufbau, 1962, Vol. l.

Spencer, Hanna. *Heinrich Heine*. Boston: Twayne, 1982.

Weiss, Adelaide Marie. "Heinrich Heine." In *Merlin in German Literature*. Washington, D.C.: Catholic University of America Press, 1933, pp. 126–28.

HEINRICH VON DEM TÜRLIN, German poet of the first half of the thirteenth century. Heinrich may have been a descendant of the distinguished family of freedmen recorded under the name of *von/vor/pey dem Turlin/Turleine* (*de Portula*) in the ducal town of St. Veit on Glan/Carinthia. He may also be identical with one Heinrich von dem Turlein, a witness recorded on a deed, dated 1229, of Count Albert I of Gorce and Tyrol. Heinrich names himself on four occasions in his *Diu Crône*, the first reference occurring in the acrostic ll. 182–216; and Rudolf von Ems praises him in his *Alexander* (ll. 3,219–28). There is no testimony as to where Heinrich lived and worked, although various conjectures have been advanced, such as the court of Duke Bernhard of Carinthia, or the court of Duke Frederic II in Vienna; neither is there evidence as to his social status (commoner or *ministerialis*) or occupation (chancery or military service). The only indication Heinrich himself provides in the *Crône* (ll. 2,973–82) leads to the assumption that his native country lay somewhere in the southeastern part of the Empire, which is corroborated by the Bavarian-Austrian linguistic characteristics of the poem. He must have received an excellent education; he read Latin and French and had an astounding knowledge of German and French literature.

Heinrich has been linked with the anonymous *Der Mantel*, a fragment of 994 lines, and he is the author of the voluminous Arthurian romance *Diu Crône* ("The Crown," 30,041 lines). The *Mantel* fragment, an adaptation of the Old French fabliau *Le Mantel mautaillié*, relates a chastity and fidelity test at Arthur's court. Variants of this motif occur twice in the *Crône*, with the goblet and glove tests. The fragment must have been composed before the *Crône*, as proven by Heinrich's self-quotation (*Crône*, ll. 23,502–05).

"Allr Âventiure Krône" is the title given by Rudolf von Ems (*Alexander*, l. 3,219) to Heinrich's Arthurian romance, supported by lines 29,916–21 and 29,966–90 in *Diu Crône*, where Heinrich compares his work to a crown adorned with precious stones.

The hero of the countless adventures, which are grouped into four sequences of different length and framed by five great feasts at Arthur's court, is Gawein, despite Heinrich's announced intention to write the story of King Arthur (ll. 164–74). The main episodes of the first part of the romance are Ginover's abduction by Gasozein, the proposed single combat between Arthur and Gasozein (which never takes place), and Ginover's liberation by Gawein. These episodes constitute the first sequence, interlaced by the Sgoidamur-Amurfina sequence of the magic bridle and Gawein's captivity at Amurfina's castle. The double wedding of the couples Gawein-Amurfina and Gasozein-Sgoidamur at Arthur's court in Karidol concludes the first part (ll. 13,860–934). The second part has two main sequences: the quest for the Grail, with Gawein's first visit to the Grail castle, and the Vrou Saelde (Lady Fortune) and Fimbeus-Giramphiel sequence, with the acquisition of Fimbeus's magic girdle, Gawein's visit at Ordohorht, the allegorical castle of Vrou Saelde, and the bestowal of the ring of fortune. The climax is reached with Gawein's successful Salie adventure (inspired by the Gawein books of the *Parzival*), his invitation to Arthur followed by another great feast at Arthur's court, and the delivery of the ring of fortune to Arthur (ll. 21,819–22,989). The anticlimax, initiated by the appearance of the knight on the ibex and by the glove test, leads to the loss of the magic stone of Fimbeus's girdle and the ring of fortune. Gawein, Keii, Lanzelet, and Calocreant then depart from Karidol and after another series of fabulous adventures recover the magic objects and restore them to Arthur. The Grail sequence finds its conclusion with the deliverance of the Grail company and its eternal rest in the realm of the dead. A feast of joy at Karidol celebrates the reunion of the four Arthurian knights (ll. 29,744–910).

It is impossible to enumerate all the adventures Gawein encounters as knight-errant. Many of them, traditionally assigned to other heroes of the Round Table, like Parzival, Iwein, and Lanzelet, are now attributed to Gawein to enhance his status and prestige as the outstanding representative and defender of the Arthurian world. They are occasionally interspersed with critical comments, for instance in the episode of the deliverance of the Grail castle, where Heinrich stresses the exemplariness of his protagonist compared with Parzival's failure. Thus, Gawein is the model of all chivalric virtues, the favorite of Lady Fortune, successful in all his endeavors like the hero of fairy tales who undergoes no evolution or crisis.

The mostly negative criticism that *Diu Crône* has received is not quite justified; recent studies have led to a reevaluation. Heinrich's merit resides in his inventiveness and his ability to combine a variety of subject matters and motifs of Arthurian and non-Arthurian provenance into a coherent plot, even if a great number of episodes are to be considered padding, introduced for their elements of fantasy rather than for their significance within the narrative structure of the romance.

Heinrich's sources range from Chrétien de Troyes's *Perceval* and *Lancelot*, Old French lais and fabliaux (such as *La Mule sans frein*, *Le Chevalier à l'épée*, the *Lai du cor*), and the Continuations of the *Perceval* to the German Arthurian romances of Ulrich von Zatzikhoven, Hartmann von Aue, and Wolfram von Eschenbach and to German heroic epics and other sources, not all of which have been traced. Heinrich's narrative technique varies from courtly stylization to realistic descriptions, including comic and burlesque elements. The most remarkable feature of the *Crône* is its tendency to desymbolize and demystify (particularly apparent in the Grail episodes) in favor of rationalization, realistic imagery, and allegorization. (*See also* MANTEL, DER.) [KRG]

Heinrich von dem Türlin. *Diu Crône*, ed. G.H.F. Scholl. Stuttgart, 1852.

———. *The Crown: A Tale of Sir Gawein and King Arthur's Court*, trans. J.W. Thomas. Lincoln: University of Nebraska Press, 1989.

Cormeau, Christoph. *"Wigalois" und "Diu Crône": Zwei Kapitel zur Gattungsgeschichte des nachklassischen Aventiureromans*. Munich: Artemis, 1977.

Heller, Edmund Kurt. "A Vindication of Heinrich von dem Türlin, Based on a Survey of His Sources." *Modern Language Quarterly*, 3 (1942), 67–82.

Kratz, Bernd. "Zur Kompositionstechnik Heinrichs von dem Türlin." *Amsterdamer Beiträge zur älteren Germanistik*, 5 (1973), 141–53.

Schultz, James A. *The Shape of the Round Table: Structures of Middle High German Arthurian Romance*. Toronto: University of Toronto Press, 1983.

HEINRICH VON FREIBERG, author of a continuation of Gottfried von Strassburg's incomplete *Tristan*. Composed at the behest of Reimund von Lichtenburg, Heinrich's *Tristan* is dated ca. 1285–90. Unlike Ulrich von Türheim, an earlier continuator, Heinrich von Freiberg masters the language of courtly romance and approximates the style of his revered master, Gottfried. The sources for Heinrich's continuation are Eilhart von Oberge's *Tristrant* and Ulrich von Türheim's *Tristan*. Heinrich's continuation opens with a prologue (84 lines) in which he contrasts Gottfried's artistic mastery with his own deficiency. The tale proper commences with Tristan's betrothal and marriage to Îsôt Blanschemanîs (Isolde of the White Hands). Tristan explains his failure to consummate the marriage as the result of an oath to the Virgin Mary to live chastely for one year. Heinrich draws on and incorporates Eilhart's hunting episode, in which Tristan and Arthur's knights are severely wounded by a trap that King Mark has set in his hall. Heinrich borrows Eilhart's motif of the intertwining rose and vine, but like Ulrich before him he reverses the plants: Mark plants the rose over Tristan's body and the vine over Îsôt's. [MEK]

Heinrich von Freiberg. *Tristan*, ed. Reinhold Bechstein. Leipzig: Brockhaus, 1877.

Buschinger, Danielle. "À propos du *Tristan* de Heinrich von Freiberg." *Études germaniques*, 33 (1978), 53–64.

HEISELER, HENRY VON (1875–1928), wrote mainly lyrical and dramatic works and translated Pushkin and the English Romantics. In his "wedding play" *Der junge Parzival*, he depicts the hero's arrival in Pelrapeire and his marriage to Condwiramur. Heiseler's *Tristan* remains in notebook form. The plot was to have begun with the magic potion. [SSch/PM]

Heiseler, Henry von. *Der junge Parzival: Ein Hochzeitsspiel*. In *Sämtliche Werke*. Heidelberg: Lambert Schneider, 1965, pp. 565–601.

———. *Tristan: Szenenentwurf*. In *Sämtliche Werke*. Heidelberg: Lambert Schneider, 1965, p. 602.

HELDRIS DE CORNUÄLLE, author of the *Roman de Silence* (6,706 lines), which dates probably to the second half of the thirteenth century. Heldris is otherwise unknown, and it is uncertain whether "Cornuälle" refers to Cornwall in England, Cornuaille in Brittany, or the hamlet of La Cornuaille (Maine-et-Loire). The French verse romance relates how a woman, Silence, brought up as a man, achieves success as a minstrel and then as a knight before marrying and settling into matrimony. Medieval mysogyny, which appears in several digressions critical of women, is curiously countered by the example of Silence herself and by the implied criticism of inheritance only through male offspring. It is in fact the King of England's arbitrary imposition of male-line inheritance that impels Silence's parents to hide her sex. There are also general tirades against the decline in morals in the author's times.

The Arthurian material is brought in principally in a final episode in which Merlin identifies Silence as a woman. The episode is an adaptation of the theme of Merlin's sardonic laughter in the Vulgate *Estoire de Merlin*; there are also elements that were perhaps influenced by Geoffrey of Monmouth's *Vita Merlini*, his *Historia Regum Britanniae*, and Wace. [DK]

Heldris de Cornuälle. *Le Roman de Silence*, ed. Lewis Thorpe. Cambridge: Heffer, 1972.

———. *Roman de Silence*, trans. Regina Psaki. New York: Garland, 1990.

HÊLIAS, PIERRE-JAKEZ, in his 1965 drama *An Isild A-Heul* or *Yseult seconde* ("Yseult the Second"), offers a new version of the romance of Tristan and Yseult, written in Breton and translated into French by the author himself. The play, in three acts and an epilogue, faithfully follows the legendary story of a Tristan divided between his fatal love for the first Yseult and his love for his wife, the second Yseult. However, the work transforms the traditional perspective by presenting the drama from the point of view of the second Yseult, usually neglected in treatments of the myth. The author attempts also to explore the psychology of the characters, especially of the second Yseult and Tristan, in some detail. The risk in such an endeavor is that it tends to reduce the legend into an ordinary conflict of a man torn between conjugal love and adulterous passion. [RB]

Hélias, Pierre-Jakez. *An Isild A-Heul*. Brest: Brud-Nevez, 1964. (Translated into French by the author as *Yseult seconde et le Jeu de Gradion*. Paris: Galilée, 1965.)

HENNING, DOUG, American magician, designed the "Magic Musical" *Merlin*, which opened on February 13, 1983, in the Mark Hellinger Theatre, New York, and played for almost a year. With light reference to Merlin, it concentrated on Henning's illusionistic arts. The other participating authors were Richard Levinson and William Link (book), Don Black (lyrics), Elmer Bernstein (music). [UM/WLS]

Müller, Ulrich. "Mittelalter-Musicals. Eine kommentierte übersicht. Mit einem Anhang Über mittelalterliche Themen in der U-und E-Musik 1977–1984." In *Forum: Materialien und Beiträge zur Mittelalter-Rezeption I*, ed. Rüdiger Krohn. Göppingen: Kümmerle, 1986.

HENRICUS OF SETTIMELLO provides Italy's first reference to Tristan in his *Elegia de diversitate fortunae et philosophiae consolatione* ("Elegy on the Diversity of Fortune and the Consolation of Philosophy," ca. 1193). In addition to suggesting that only Tristan has suffered more than he has, the author establishes Arthur as a model of excellence and twice refers to the promise of his return. [DLH]

Henricus of Settimello. *Henricii Septimellensis Elegia sive de Miseria*, ed. A. Marigo. Padua, 1926.

Gardner, Edmund G. *The Arthurian Legend in Italian Literature*. London: Dent, 1930, p. 8.

HENRY OF HUNTINGDON (d. ca. 1154) based the account of the Arthurian period in his *Historia Anglorum* (ca. 1129) primarily on Bede, the *Anglo-Saxon Chronicle*, and perhaps Nennius. He lists the twelve battles of Arthur, inserting the list between the *Chronicle* entries for 527 and 530. He suggests, moreover, that the sites are now unknown. Henry is also the author of the *Epistola ad Warinum* (ca. 1139), a letter in which he writes that Robert of Torigni, then in charge of the manuscript collection at Bec, has shown him a book by Geoffrey of Monmouth on the history of the kings of Britain. He summarizes the book, including some details about Arthur's final battle that are not in surviving texts of the *Historia Regum Britanniae* and adding that the Bretons deny Arthur's death and still await his return. Many of the later chroniclers, such as Robert of Torigni, supplemented Geoffrey of Monmouth's dry account of the last battle with details from Henry's more spirited version. [JPC]

Henry of Huntingdon. *Epistola ad Warinum*. In *Chronicles of the Reigns of Stephen, Henry II, and Richard I*, ed. Richard Howlett. London: Longman, Trübner, 1885.

———. *Henrici Archidiaconi Huntendunensis Historia Anglorum*, ed. Thomas Arnold. London: Longman, 1879.

HENZE, HANS WERNER, German composer of *Tristan, prelude für klavier, tonbänder und orchester* (1973). This orchestral work quotes medieval music (the *Lamento di Tristano*) and music by Brahms, Chopin, and Wagner (*Tristan und Isolde*, as well as the Wesendonk song "Im Treibhaus"). Further, it uses verses by Thomas d'Angleterre, translated into English, that describe Isolde's death. The piece depicts the "total misery of humanity," by use of strong expression and a montage technique. In 1980, the television director Karl Lindemann attempted to transpose the sound and the "plot" of the composition into a visual production for the First Program of German Television (ARD). In 1976, Henze's composition had been used in Paris by Glen Tetley for a Tristan ballet, but plans of choreographer John Cranko to produce together with Henze a ballet trilogy about the Tristan story remained unrealized at Cranko's death in 1973. [UM/WLS]

Henze, Hans Werner. *Musik und Politik: Schriften und Gespräche 1955–1975*. Munich: Deutscher Taschenbuch-Verlag, 1976.

Müller, Ulrich. "Mittelalterliche Dichtungen in der Musik des 20. Jahrhunderts III: Das Tristan-und-Isolde-Oratorium von Frank Martin (nach Joseph Bédier). Mit einem Ausblick auf die Tristan-Komposition von Hans Werner Henze." In *Tradition und Entwicklung: Festschrift Eugen Thurnher*, ed. Werne Bauer, Achim Masser, and Guntram A. Plangg. Innsbruck: Innsbruck University, 1982.

HER VIEGOLEIS MED GULD HIULET ("Sir Viegoleis with the Golden Wheel"), the title of the oldest extant edition of the Danish chapbook. It dates from the year 1656 and is a translation of an anonymous German prose redaction (dated 1472) of Wirnt von Grafenberg's *Wigalois*. The German chapbook exists in two branches, the younger of which is characterized by a rather modern language, and it is presumably this younger version that is the source of the Danish chapbook. The Danish translator had command of neither his own language nor of German. The Danish chapbook was translated into Icelandic, and this version is known as *Gabons saga ok Vigoles*. [MEK]

Jacobsen, J.P., Jørgen Olrik, and R. Paulli, eds. *En smuck lystig Historie/Om den berømmelige Ridder oc Heldt Her Vigoleis med Guld Hiulet*. In *Danske Folkebøger fra 16. og 17. Aarhundrede*. Copenhagen: Det danske Sprog-og Litteraturselskab, 1921, Vol. 4.

HERALDRY. Heraldry—the use of a shield device and a helmet crest to identify a knight in battle and tournament—was traditionally one of the distinctive features that set a knight apart from other members of medieval society. The custom originated in the twelfth century, when the newly introduced visored helmet made the face of its wearer unrecognizable. Though in classical antiquity and the Dark Ages individual warriors could be known by their personal shield emblems, true heraldry is different insofar as shield devices and helmet crests are hereditary within a family and carry legal status, on seals for instance, beyond mere marks of recognition. They were also displayed on banners, horse trappings, and the surcoats covering the knights' armor; from the latter use, it became customary to call them "coats-of-arms."

By the time the great Arthurian epics were composed, heraldry had become so firmly established as an integral part of knightly culture that neither the authors nor their audience could imagine the knights of the Round Table without proper heraldic bearings.

The "historical Arthur" lived in the preheraldic Dark Ages, and his famous dragon banner is definitely derived from the battle standard of Late Roman auxiliary cavalry. But his dragon helmet crest, which according to Geoffrey of Monmouth's *Historia* (ca. 1136) he had inherited from his father, Uther Pendragon, is an example of how true heraldry came into being.

King Arthur's shield device seems to have been first a cross and/or an icon of the Virgin Mary, as reported in the *Annales Cambriae* and in Nennius's *Historia Brittonum* (ca. 800). Though he is said to have carried these "on his shoulders," this might result from a confusion of Welsh *ysqwyt* "shield" and *ysqwyd* "shoulder" in the translation into Latin from a hypothetical Welsh source. From the fourteenth century on, however, the shield charges attributed to King Arthur are three crowns, probably meant to indicate his superiority over ordinary kings. In the fifteenth century, after the idea had taken hold that these three crowns stood for his three realms of North Wales, South Wales, and Logres, their number was increased up to thirteen, to represent all the kingdoms allegedly conquered by him. The color of Arthur's shield is usually red, though in French sources it is blue, corresponding to the French royal arms.

Some authors of Arthurian epics were experts in heraldry—Chrétien de Troyes seems to have been a herald himself, and Wolfram von Eschenbach and Hartmann von Aue were knights—and went to considerable lengths to describe their heroes' armorial bearings. There is occasional disagreement among competing authors and also with the illustrators of the manuscripts about the charges borne by their favorite heroes, in much the same way that the authors of the Grail romances disagree about the exact nature of the Grail, but these arms by themselves conform to the accepted rules of heraldry, though they might become marked as something out of the ordinary by frequent application of the unusual tinctures *vert* (green) and *purpure* (purple).

(It will be useful to define a few of the more common heraldic terms: *Or* [French] = "gold" or yellow; *Argent*

[French] = "silver" or white; *Gules* [Persian *gûl* 'a rose'] = red; *Azure* [Arabic *az'raq* 'sky'] = blue; *Sable* [the Siberian mink] = black; *Vert* [French] green; *Purpure* = purple.)

Shortly after the middle of the fifteenth century, a roll of arms, *Les Noms, Armes, et Blasons des Chevalliers et Compaignons de la Table Ronde*, was compiled as an appendix to the famous *Livre des tournoys*, by King René d'Anjou (ca. 1455), which gave detailed instructions how a tournament should be held "according to the rules set up at the time of King Uterpendragon and King Artus and his Knights of the Round Table." Of this Arthurian roll of arms, the three most important copies in the United States are in Cambridge (Harvard University Library, Holer 1), in New York City (Pierpont Morgan Library 16), and in Baltimore (Walters Art Gallery). Among these, the Harvard roll is the earliest, ca. 1470, but it lists the shields and names of only 150 knights, while the Morgan copy (ca. 1500), gives names and shields of 175 knights together with brief descriptions of their achievements and their appearances, such as the color of their eyes and hair; the Walters roll (ca. 1510) is the most comprehensive, adding the knights' crests, shield supporters, and "reasons" (mottoes). The author of this Arthurian roll of arms is thought to have been Jacques d'Armagnac, Duke of Nemours, who was married to a niece of King René. Interestingly enough, many of the arms of the lesser knights, which had to be filled in because they would not be recorded in the romances, were borrowed from a contemporary (ca. 1440) handbook of heraldry. *Le Traitié du Blazon d'Armes*, by Clément Prinsault, dedicated by its author to Jacques "filz de monseigneur le duc de Nemours."

Some of these arms are directly related to motifs in the tales, such as the arms of Yvain, "le Chevalier au Lion," who bears: *Azure, a lion, Or*, and those of Lancelot: *Argent, three bends gules*, referring to his having the strength of three ordinary men. Others are "canting arms," representing a wordplay on the knight's name, such as Tristram de Lyonesse's: *Vert, a lion Or*, Sir Brumor de la Fontaine's: *Quarterly Or and sable, a fountain argent over all*, or Sir Brandelis des Vaulxsur's: *Gules, three swords* (brands) *erect argent*. On occasion, a scribal error can change a charge, such as Sir Kay's: *Sable, a chief argent*, which he bears in the early French romance *Durmart le Gallois* (ca. 1240) to indicate his position as seneschal and "head" of Arthur's household, into *two keys argent*, in the armorial roll. This makes sense, too, but is the result of reading *clefs* 'keys' instead of *chef* 'chief.' Sometimes, an entirely new character is created by such a mistake. For instance, in the Arthurian roll is listed Bauiers le Forcenné, who owes his existence to a misunderstanding of the description of the banner (*baniers*) of Sagramours le Desrée in the Second Continuation of *Perceval*: "Aprés recoisi Sagremor/Qui baniers de noir et d'or/Portoit, ce sanbloit, gironees. . . ." Interestingly, it is the spurious Sir Bauiers who retains the arms gyronny, while Sagramours's shield is changed to: *Sable, two stars Or, on a canton argent a star sable*. In some cases, heraldry is used for comic relief. In Wolfram's *Parzival*, King Hardiess of Gaskon bears the forepart of a griffin in his shield, while his retainers bear the griffin's hindquarters!

Owing to the complexity of traditions in Arthurian epics, the arms even of champions of the first magnitude can differ fundamentally from author to author. For instance, Chrétien does not mention Gawain's arms at all, though he gives detailed descriptions of the blazons of a number of minor knights. Wolfram, who makes it a special point that for his *Parzival* he did not follow Chrétien, but a rival authority, "Kyot the Provençal," has Gawain wearing a surcoat with two *gampilûns* of sable in appliqué work. This is a variant of the single *gampilûn* borne by his cousin, Ilinot, Arthur's son. The *gampilûn* has escaped zoological classification so far; most likely, it is a Germanic phonetic rendering of the dragonlike heraldic *gamelyon*, whose name was later reassigned to the now more familiar chameleon!

In the thirteenth-century French romances *Durmart*, *Escanor*, and the Second Continuation of *Perceval*, Gawain's arms are: *Argent, a canton gules*, with related blazons for his brothers. These are probably "canting arms" in French, derived from the name of their father, King Loth of Orkney, because *lot* means "section," and a canton can be considered to be a section of a shield.

According to Geoffrey of Monmouth, Gawain was educated in Rome and was given his arms (not described) by Pope Sulpicius (alas, a pope unknown to all other historians); in the *Perlesvaus*, Gawain received from Pope Gregory the Great the shield of Judas Maccabeus; *Gules, an eagle Or*. In "official" fifteenth-century tradition, as represented by the roll of arms attributed to Jacques d'Armagnac, Gawain bears: *Purpure, a double-headed eagle Or*, a device derived from both the shield of Judas Maccabeus and the emblem of the Holy Roman Empire. Again, his brothers share the same arms with appropriate differences.

Gawain's most famous armorial bearings, however, are those assigned to him in *Sir Gawain and the Green Knight* (ca. 1365): *Gules, a pentangle Or*, the "Seal of Solomon, that the English call 'the endless knot.'" The *Gawain*-poet's elaborate explanation that this "devys" is a symbol of Gawain's being perfect in his five senses, in the dexterity of his five fingers, in his reverence of the five wounds of Christ, in his love for the Queen of Heaven and her five joys, and in his five virtues makes it clear that the pentangle is a strictly personal badge and not his inherited family coat-of-arms. When in the fourteenth century tournament armor developed away from battle armor, it became fashionable for knights to have garnitures of two shields, a "shield for War," of the traditional triangular shape bearing the family arms, and a "shield for Peace," a squarish targe with a cutout for couching the lance, displaying the personal badge for use in tournaments and other peaceful pursuits. Therefore, when Gawain went on his quest for the Green Chapel, he quite properly took along his "shield for Peace." The reason the *Gawain*-poet chose the pentangle as Gawain's "devys" might

43–46. Arthurian Heraldry. (Drawings by Helmut Nickel.)

43a. King Arthur's shield: standard version, early fifteenth century. Three golden crowns in either red (English) or blue (French tradition) field.

43b. King Arthur's full arms, late version French style: Azure, thirteen crowns Or; crest: a dragon Or issuant from a crown; mantlings: party azure and Or, lined ermine; supporters: two white greyhounds collared gules; motto: "Pendragon." The greyhounds are probably borrowed from the arms of the contemporary king of England, Henry VII.

43c. King Arthur's arms, late version English (Tudor) style: Quarterly, 1 and 4 Vert, a cross Argent, in the cantel the Virgin and Child Or, 2 and 3 Gules, three crowns in pale Or.

44a. Gawain's shield. Gules, a pentangle Or.

44b. The two versions of Sir Kay's arms: Sable, a chief Argent (left) and Azure, two keys Argent.

44c. The arms of Bauiers le Forcenné and of Sagramours le Desrée: Gyronny of sable and Or (originally Sagramours's) (left) and Sable, two stars Or, on a canton Argent a star sable.

have been that he saw a "canting" reference to Gawain's home country, Orkney in *Or-knit*, the golden knot.

Though the heraldry of the Arthurian roll of arms was accepted as authentic and perpetuated in handbooks of heraldry up to the nineteenth century, nothing of it—with exception of the shield of Sir Galahad—was incorporated into *Le Morte Darthur*. Surprisingly, Sir Thomas Malory's monumental work contains only a handful of heraldic descriptions. For this reason, modern retellers of the tale, such as Tennyson and T.H. White, and particularly illustrators like Howard Pyle, N.C. Wyeth, Robert Ball, and Hal Foster, have had to rely on their own imagination. It is heartening to see, though, that the designer of "King Arthur's Merry-go-round" in Disneyland *did* research the "authentic" shields of

(a)

(b)

(c)

(d)

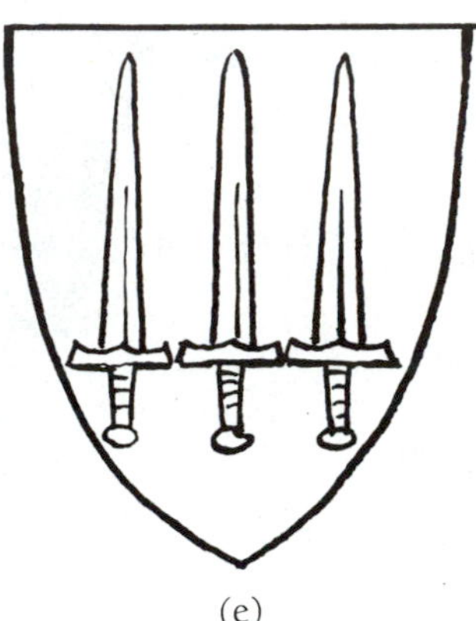

(e)

45. (a) Yvain "le Chevalier au Lion": Azure, a lion Or. (b) Lancelot du Lac: Argent, three bends Gules. (c)-(e) "Canting arms." (c) Tristram of Lyonesse: Vert, a lion Or. (d) Brumor de la Fontaine: Quarterly Or and Sable, a fountain Argent over all. (e) Brandelis de Vaulxsur: Gules, three swords (brands), erect argent, hilts Azure.

the knights of the Round Table from the roll of arms of Jacques d'Armagnac! (*See also* Arms and Armor; Round Tables; Tournaments.) [HN]

Brault, Gerard J. *Early Blazon: Heraldic Terminology in the Twelfth and Thirteenth Centuries with Special Reference to Arthurian Literature*. London: Oxford University Press, 1972.

Crompton, N.J.R. "Mediaeval Symbolic Heraldry." *The Coat of Arms*, 8 (October 1964), 166-68.

de Blangy, Alphonse. *La Forme des tournois au temps du roy Uter et du roy Artus, suivi de l'Armorial des chevaliers de la Table Ronde*. Caen, 1897.

Nickel, Helmut. "Arthurian Heraldry." *Avalon to Camelot*, 1 (1984), 11-12.

Pastoureau, Michel. *Armorial des chevaliers de la Table Ronde*. Paris: Léopard d'Or, 1983.

Sandoz, Edouard. "Tourneys in the Arthurian Tradition." *Speculum*, 19 (1944), 389-420.

Scott-Giles, C.W. "Some Arthurian Coats of Arms." *The Coat of Arms*, 8 (October 1965), 332-39, and 9 (January 1966), 30-35.

Timpson, George F. "Heraldry in Wolfram's Parzival." *The Coat of Arms*, 4 (July 1957), 278-81.

HERBERT, KATHLEEN, British author of two historical novels set in the Dark Ages. *The Lady of the Fountain* (1982) transposes the traditional story, found in the *Mabinogi* and Chrétien de Troyes's *Yvain*, to north Britain a generation after Arthur's death. Owain, son of King Urien of Cumbria, and Taniu, daughter of King Loth of Lothian (and half-sister of Gawain), eventually find happiness together, but the bitter suffering that they must first undergo is both a harsh learning experience and a reflection of the British kingdoms' struggle for survival against not only Anglian and Pictish invaders but, more deadly yet, each other's pride and treachery. *Queen of the Lightning* (1983) is also set in north Britain, but in the seventh century, when folk-memories of Urien and Owain are still potent among their descendants. [EB/RHT]

Herbert, Kathleen. *The Lady of the Fountain*. Frome, Somerset: Bran's Head, 1982.

———. *Queen of the Lightning*. London: Bodley Head, 1983.

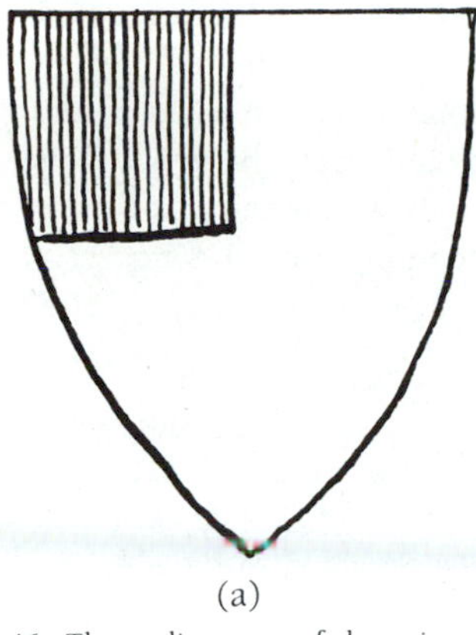
(a)

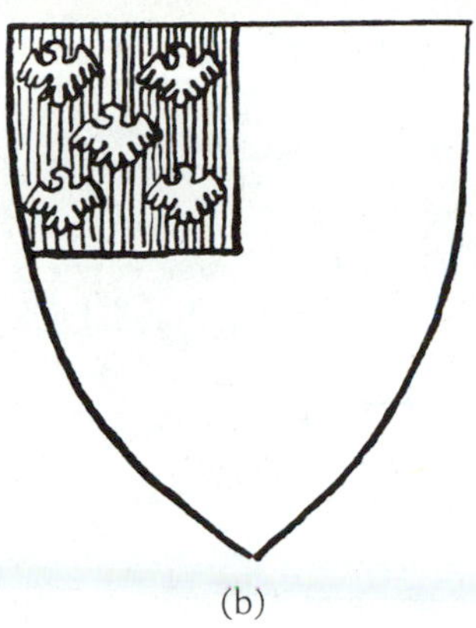
(b)

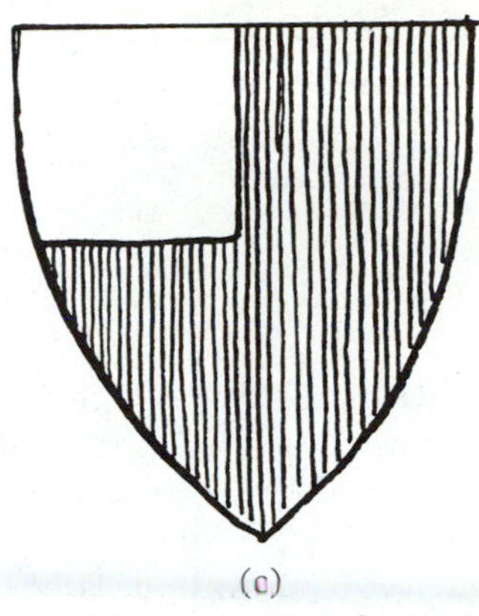
(c)

46. The earlier arms of the princes of Orkney: (a) Gawain: Argent, a canton Gules; (b) Gareth: Argent, a canton Gules, semé with eagles Or; (c) Mordred: Gules, a canton Argent.

(d)

(e)

(f)

The later arms of the princes of Orkney: (d) Gawain: Purpure, a double-headed eagle Or; (e) Gareth: Purpure, a double-headed eagle Or, over all a bendlet Gules; (f) Mordred: Purpure, a double-headed eagle Or, a chief Argent.

HERDER, JOHANN GOTTFRIED (1744–1803). In his *Volkslieder, Erster Theil*, published in Leipzig, 1778, Johann Gottfried Herder included "Der Knabe mit dem Mantel: Ein Rittermährchen." This is a German translation of the medieval English ballad "The Boy and the Mantle," which ultimately derives from *Le Mantel mautaillié* and the *Lai du cor*. It seems plausible that the modern German writers who adapted the mantle tale—Benedikte Naubert, F.A.C. Werthes, and Karl Franz van der Velde—were familiar with Herder's German translation. [MEK]

Herder, Johann Gottfried. "Der Knabe mit dem Mantel: Ein Rittermährchen." In *Herders Poetische Werke*, ed. Carl Redlich. Berlin: Weidmann, 1885, Vol. 1, pp. 244–50.

HERE BEGYNNETH THE LYFE OF JOSEPH OF ARMATHIA WITH A PRAYSING TO JOSEPH, printed by Richard Pynson in 1520, is a poetic tribute to Joseph, his apostolic missions in the Holy Land, the city of Sarras, France, and England, his founding of Glastonbury Abbey and burial there, and an extensive list of posthumous miracles. *A Praysing to Joseph* extols him as Glastonbury's great healer, obviously promoting the abbey's pilgrimage interests. [VML]

Skeat, Walter W., ed. *Joseph of Arimathie*. London: Trübner, 1871.

HERVEY, MRS. T.K. (ELEANORA LOUISA MONTAGU) (1811–1903), author of *The Feasts of Camelot* (1863), a collection of tales told by members of and visitors to Arthur's court at Camelot on the feasts of Whitsuntide and Christmas. The stories, many of which are original, show the influence of Chaucer and the Gothic novel. Even the traditional material is reshaped so as to remove much of the moral impropriety surrounding characters like Tristram and Morgan. [ACL]

Hervey, Mrs. T.K. *The Feasts of Camelot, with the Tales That Were Told There.* London: Bell and Daldy, 1863.

HERZELOYDE, in Wolfram von Eschenbach's *Parzival*, the wife of Gahmuret, the mother of Parzival, the granddaughter of Titurel, and the sister of Amfortas (the Grail King), Trevrizent, Schoysiane, and Repanse de Schoye (the Grail-bearer). Herzeloyde is the Queen of Wales, Anjou, and Norgales and was won by Gahmuret in a jousting tournament. The name does not occur prior to Wolfram. [SW]

HEYWOOD, THOMAS (1573–1641), author of a prose compilation, *The Life of Merlin* (1641), which initiated a vogue for attaching Merlin's name to political and other kinds of prophecies during the troubled last years of King Charles I's reign and the succeeding Commonwealth. The *Life of Merlin* is in many ways a piece of hack work in spite of Heywood's own credulity and genuine interest in prognostication. Heywood gives as his main authority for the truth of the predictions Alain of Lille's "explanation or Comment upon *Merlins* Prophesies, the original being extracted out of *Jeffrey* of *Monmouth*." For the historical aspect of his text he also relies heavily on Robert Fabyan's *New Chronicles of England and of France*. [JPC]

Heywood, Thomas. *The Life of Merlin, Surnamed Ambrosius; His Prophecies and Predictions Interpreted, and Their Truth Made Good by Our English Annals: Being a Chronographical History of All the Kings and Memorable Passages of This Kingdom, from Brute to the Reign of King Charles.* London: J. Okes, 1641; repr. Carmarthen: J. Evans, 1812.

Baines, Barbara J. *Thomas Heywood.* Boston: Twayne, 1984.

Brinkley, Roberta F. *Arthurian Legend in the Seventeenth Century.* Baltimore: Johns Hopkins Press, 1932.

Clark, Arthur Melville. *Thomas Heywood: Playwright and Miscellanist.* Oxford: Blackwell, 1931.

HIGDEN, RANULF (d. 1363/4), a Benedictine monk from Cheshire, wrote the *Polychronicon*, a Latin universal chronicle that was the most popular source of world history in England until the publication of Ralegh's *History of the World* in the seventeenth century. There are at least 118 manuscripts. It was translated into English by John Trevisa in 1387 and by an anonymous translator in the fifteenth century. Fragments of four other Middle English translations have also survived. Higden based his Arthurian section primarily upon Henry of Huntingdon and William of Malmesbury. Unlike many English chroniclers, he doubted the reliability of Geoffrey of Monmouth, wondering why none of the continental chroniclers mention Arthur's conquest of thirty kingdoms. (*See also* TREVISA, JOHN.) [EDK]

Higden, Ranulf. *Polychronicon Ranulphi Higden*, ed. C. Babington and J.R. Lumby. 9 vols. London: Longman, 1865–86, Vol. 5, pp. 328–38.

Kennedy, Edward Donald. "Chronicles and Other Historical Writing." In *A Manual of the Writings in Middle English*, ed. A.E. Hartung. New Haven: Connecticut Academy of Arts and Sciences, 1981–89, Vol. 8, pp. 2656–61, 2866–77.

Taylor, John. *English Historical Literature in the Fourteenth Century.* Oxford: Clarendon, 1987, pp. 96–103 and passim.

———. *The Universal Chronicle of Ranulf Higden.* Oxford: Clarendon, 1966.

HILDEBRANDT, RITA and TIM, American wife-and-husband team whose illustrated science-fiction novel, *Merlin and the Dragons of Atlantis* (1983), is set millennia in the past. Both the dragons and Merlin's skills are products of highly developed sciences in Atlantis and Lemuria, lost when they are engulfed. Tim, a well-known artist and illustrator of science fiction and fantasy, provides the illustrations for Rita's text. [RHT]

Hildebrandt, Rita and Tim. *Merlin and the Dragons of Atlantis.* Indianapolis and New York: Bobbs-Merrill, 1983.

HILL, AARON (1685–1750), author of the "pantomime opera" *Merlin in Love, or: Youth Against Magic*, printed in 1760 but perhaps composed as early as 1740. The work, which includes recitatives, dances, and airs, is the story of Merlin, "a conjurer, with his wand, long beard, and trailing robe," who uses magic to steal Columbine from her lover, Harlequin. In revenge, she takes Merlin's wand and transforms him into an ass and then sings, in the last of the twenty-five airs: "The wife may take warning, as well as they can,/Still thus, will it come to pass!/Let a *young* woman loose, at an *old* cunning man;/The conjurer proves but an ass." There is no evidence that *Merlin in Love* was ever performed. [NJL]

Hill, Aaron. *Merlin in Love, or: Youth Against Magic.* In *Dramatic Works.* London, 1760, Vol. 1.

HILL, GRAHAM, author of the play *Guinevere*. Performed at the Court Theatre in London on October 13, 1906, the play is a melodramatic account of the love between Launcelot and Guinevere and its tragic consequences. [RHT]

Hill, Graham. *Guinevere: A Tragedy in Three Acts*. London: Mathews, 1906.

HILTON, WILLIAM (fl. 1740), an obscure English poet whose *Poetical Works* (1775–76) included *Arthur, Monarch of the Britons, a Tragedy* (1759). The drama utilized the account of Arthur's downfall found in Geoffrey of Monmouth's *Historia*. Arthur's dying assertion, "Britons must be free," illustrates a patriotic intention appropriate to the conflicts of the Seven Years' War then being waged. [MAW]

Merriman, James Douglas. *The Flower of Kings: A Study of the Arthurian Legend in England Between 1485 and 1835*. Lawrence: University Press of Kansas, 1973.

HINZE, CHRIS, important Dutch composer and jazz musician. In collaboration with the lyricist James Batton, Hinze composed *Parzival*, a work almost two hours long, which premiered at the Holland Festival in 1976 (recording on Keytone, KYT 2-101, 1976, 2 LPs). Hinze himself describes *Parzival* as "programme music comprising the total music of our time, with particular emphasis on jazz." Hinze and Batton, to lend their material contemporary resonance, drew on various sources, but primarily the *Parzival* of Wolfram von Eschenbach. The monumental composition requires for performance a symphony orchestra, synthesizer, a big band, jazz ensemble, soloists, and a classical as well as a "soul" choir. [UM/WCM]

HISTORIA MERIADOCI REGIS CAMBRIE ("The Story of Meriadoc, King of Cambria"), a Latin prose romance about the prince of the kingdom of Cambria (pre-Saxon Wales), who, after surviving an attempted assassination by his uncle, fights as a young knight in the cause of royal justice. With Arthur's help, he brings his usurping uncle to trial for the murder of his father. As Arthur's champion in three judicial duels, he not only defeats the contending knights but acts to prevent Arthur from unjust acquisition of their lands. Then, laying aside his reign in Cambria in favor of his twin sister and her husband, King Urien, he takes the position of a mercenary in the service of the Emperor of the Alamanni in order to bring peace to the warring realms of Europe—for war is no more than a judicial duel between kings and, like the judicial duels fought in Arthur's court, not a system of justice but a contest of power. Meriadoc, however, is compromised by his position as a mercenary, and although he defeats the King of the Land from Which No One Returns and rescues the Emperor's only daughter, he falls victim to the Emperor's political necessity. In the end, he must act on his own in the cause of justice; and it is the Emperor's enemy, the King of Gaul, who finally grants Meriadoc his just reward.

The romance is dated variously from the last quarter of the twelfth century to the last quarter of the thirteenth. Although attributed by John Bale to Robert of Torigni, abbot of Mont St.-Michel from 1154 to 1186, the work is generally considered anonymous. The same author also wrote *De Ortu Waluuanii* ("The Rise of Gawain"). [MLD]

Day, Mildred Leake, ed. and trans. *The Story of Meriadoc, King of Cambria (Historia Meriadoci, Regis Cambrie)*. New York: Garland, 1988.

HISTORIE VAN MERLIJN. In 1926, Nijhoff discovered two quires in the Royal Library at Brussels, eight pages in all, of a Dutch chapbook, the *Historie van Merlijn* (now with the signature Oude Druk V.H. 27526 A). They were found wrongly bound in a copy of the *Cronijcke van Vlaenderen int corte van 621–1532*. This work was printed by Symon Cock at Antwerp in 1539. The *Historie van Merlijn* was also printed by Symon Cock between 1534 and 1544. The chapbook is an adaptation of an English one, *A Lytel Treatyse of þe Byrth and Prophecye of Marlyn*. This is a version of the Middle English *Arthour and Merlin* and was printed in London in 1510. [BB]

Kronenberg, M.E., ed. "Een onbekend volksboek van Merlijn (c. 1540)." *Tijdschrift voor Nederlandsche Taal- en Letterkunde*, 48 (1929), 18–34.

Pesch, Pierre N.G. "Het Nederlandse volksboek van *Merlijn*: bron, drukker en datering." In *Liber amicorum Leon Voet*, ed. F. de Nave. Antwerp, 1985, pp. 303–28.

HOËL, name of several kings or lords of Bretagne (most often clearly identified as continental Brittany) or of Breton cities, in a number of Arthurian texts: Geoffrey of Monmouth's *Historia Regum Britanniae*, Wace's *Roman de Brut*, various Arthurian chronicles, Renaut de Beaujeu's *Bel In-*

connu, the *Suite du Merlin*, Marie de France's lai *Guigemar*, various Tristan romances, and Malory.

Geoffrey, who first made Hoël a significant character, presented him as Arthur's ally and nephew: "Hoelus filius sororis Arturi ex Budicio, rege Armoricanorum Britonum, generatus" ("Hoël the son of Arthur's sister, his father being Budicius, King of the Armoricans"). Geoffrey's text is contradictory, because elsewhere he gives Arthur only one sister: she is Anna, wife of King Lot and mother of Gawain and Mordred; yet Hoël is never identified as Gawain's and Mordred's brother. This confusion continues in Wace's work. In certain Latin chronicles and in Malory, Hoël is Arthur's cousin.

The *Suite du Merlin* presents not only a Hoël who is Arthur's ally but also a character of the same name who is Duke of Tintagel and the first husband of Igerne, Arthur's mother. In the Tristan tradition, King Hoël of Brittany is the father of Iseut of the White Hands and of Kaherdin.

[C-AVC]

Blaess, Madeleine. "Arthur's Sisters." *Bibliographical Bulletin of the International Arthurian Society*, 8 (1956), 69–77.

Fletcher, Robert Huntington. *The Arthurian Material in the Chronicles, Especially Those of Great Britain and France*. Boston: Ginn, 1906; 2nd ed. Roger Sherman Loomis. New York: Franklin, 1966.

HOHENSTEIN, LILY (1896–1981), German writer, in her novel *Ich, Wolfram von Eschenbach* (1958), offers more than a purported autobiography of the author of the medieval German *Parzival*. She transposes this Arthurian romance to a historical medieval setting, portraying Wolfram as a secularized Parzival and *Parzival* as the romanticization of Wolfram's own life. Ironically, the reader must have an acquaintance with Wolfram's masterpiece in order to understand Hohenstein's fictional account. [RWK]

Hohenstein, Lily. *Ich, Wolfram von Eschenbach*. Vienna, Berlin, and Stuttgart: Neff, 1958. (Published in East Germany as *Die Nächte in St. Wendelin: Der Lebensroman Wolframs von Eschenbach*. Rudolstadt: Greifenverlag, 1969; 2nd ed. 1973.)

HOLDSTOCK, ROBERT, English writer who won the World Fantasy Award for *Mythago Wood* (1984), a novel that evolved from an earlier novella. He uses Jungian theories of archetypes and the collective unconscious to create a magical English forest where mythic figures, including Arthur, Peredur, and the huntress Guiwenneth (Guenevere?), come to life, and where the hero seeks Lavondyss (Avalon). The search is continued in *Lavondyss* (1988).

Under the pseudonym of Chris Carlsen, Holdstock wrote *Berserker: The Bull Chief* (1977). This sword-and-sorcery fantasy of more than usual violence is the second in a series about a warrior cursed to be endlessly reborn as a berserker, in this case in fifth-century Ireland. He helps Arthur in his war against the Saxons but is murdered for his pains. Guenevere is transformed into a savage Irish warrior queen named Grania. [RHT]

Carlsen, Chris. *Berserker: The Bull Chief*. London: Sphere, 1977.

Holdstock, Robert. *Mythago Wood*. New York: Arbor House, 1984.

———. *Lavondyss*. London: Gollancz, 1988.

HOLE, RICHARD (1746–1803), Anglican clergyman and archetypal Pre-Romantic, wrote *Arthur, or the Northern Enchantment in Seven Books* (1789). Conflict ensues between Arthur (aided by Merlin, the father of Arthur's beloved Inogen) and Hengist the Saxon (aided by the Fatal Sisters). Disguise, shape-shifting, monsters, and magic castles are romantic motifs, but the heroic couplets and epic conventions produce a classical effect. [MAW]

Hole, Richard. *Arthur, or the Northern Enchantment*. London: G.G.J. and J. Robinson, 1789.

Merriman, James Douglas. *The Flower of Kings: A Study of the Arthurian Legend in England Between 1485 and 1835*. Lawrence: University Press of Kansas, 1973.

HOLLINS, DOROTHEA, published *The Quest: A Drama of Deliverance* in 1910. She explores myth with the aid of poetry and music to express Christian theosophical idealism with affinities, as she remarks, to the thought of the German philosopher R.C. Eucken (1846–1926) and the South African-born writer Olive Schreiner (1853–1920). In Scene 1, Arthur desires Galahad to seek purity and wholeness of spirit, yet despite prayer and aspiration they have to leave the quest to others, such as Dante and Sir Philip Sidney. [CNS]

Hollins, Dorothea. *The Quest: A Drama of Deliverance*. London: Williams and Norgate, 1910.

HOLMES, URBAN TIGNER, JR. (1900–1972), for most of his career a professor of romance philology at the University of North Carolina at Chapel Hill. Holmes's most significant contribution to Arthurian studies was his controversial Judeo-Christian interpretation of the Grail. He argued that Chrétien de Troyes was perhaps a converted Jew and intended his *Conte del Graal* as an allegory of Christian teaching, the result of a quest in late twelfth-century France among theologians and others for the conversion of the Jews. In this theory, the Grail procession must represent a procession of the Old Law (Sinagoga) that will be transformed into the procession of the New Law. Once the Grail question has been asked, the *graal* will become the chalice of the Last Supper carried by the beautiful damsel Ecclesia; the *tailleor* will be the paten used by Christ at the breaking of the bread at the Last Supper; and the Bleeding Lance will become the lance of Christ's Passion, carried by Longinus. This theory was strongly combated and largely discredited, most notably by Jean Frappier and Roger Sherman Loomis. (*See also* SCHOLARSHIP, MODERN ARTHURIAN.) [WWK]

Holmes, Urban T., Jr., and M. Amelia Klenke. *Chrétien, Troyes, and the Grail*. Chapel Hill: University of North Carolina Press, 1959.

Loomis, Roger Sherman. "The Grail Story of Chrétien de Troyes as Ritual and Symbolism." *PMLA*, 71 (1956), 840–52.

Frappier, Jean. "Le Conte du Graal" est-il une allégorie judéo-chrétienne?" *Romance Philology*, 16 (1962–63), 179–213, and 20 (1966), 1–31.

HOOKER, (WILLIAM) BRIAN (1880–1946), devised the eclectic libretto for Horatio Parker's oratorio *Morven and the Grail*, first performed at the Boston Handel and Haydn Society's Centenary Festival on April 13, 1915. Morven journeys in search of the Grail, refusing to tarry in Avalon (the "heaven of pleasure"), Valhalla, or Paradise. Glimpsing the Grail, he realizes man must "live on between Hell and Heaven in wonder everlastingly." [CNS]

Hooker, Brian. *Morven and the Grail, Oratorio*. Music by Horatio Parker (Opus 79). Boston: Boston Music, 1915.

HORNE, RICHARD HENRY (1803–1884), set his poetic fairy tale "The Three Knights of Camelott" (1846), in a conventionally fanciful Arthurian world peopled with goblins, satyrs, and witches. After combating a variety of such creatures, Sir Amorel, Sir Leontine, and Sir Galohault free the noble folk of a castle from an evil enchantment. [DN]

Horne, Richard Henry. *Ballad Romances*. London: Ollier, 1846.

HOUSMAN, CLEMENCE (1861–?), author of the thoughtful, though rambling, historical romance *The Life of Sir Aglovale de Galis* (1905). Housman (sister of A.E. Housman) expands imaginatively upon Malory's account to examine the ill-starred career of Aglovale, son of King Pellinore and brother of Lamorak and Percivale. Unlike other knights, Aglovale refuses to deny his failures, even when they bring him dishonor and shame. He thus serves to comment upon the hypocrisy of a court whose concern with the appearance of justice rather than its reality ultimately proves its downfall. [RHT]

Housman, Clemence. *The Life of Sir Aglovale de Galis*. London: Methuen, 1905; rev. ed. London: Cape, 1954.

HOVEY, RICHARD (1864–1900), professor of English literature at Barnard College, introduced Arthurian drama to America in a series of verse-plays intended to retell the whole story under the title *Launcelot and Guenevere: A Poem in Dramas*. Completed were two masques, *The Quest of Merlin* (1891) and *Taliesin*, and two five-act closet dramas, *The Marriage of Guenevere* and *The Birth of Galahad* (1898). The pageantic *Quest of Merlin* is exuberantly eclectic in its combination of characters from Teutonic mythology (the Norns, Valkyries, Gnomes), classical mythology (Pan, Bacchus, Aphrodite, Naiads, Satyrs), Celtic mythology via Shakespeare (Mab, Puck, Oberon, Titania, and fairies as well as the fées Nimue and Argente), and Christian mythology (angels, associated by their presence in Avalon). The scenario includes the drunkenness of Merlin, which Maynadier describes as "not only disagreeable—for Merlin does not get drunk pleasantly—but purposeless." The purpose of Merlin's quest is to ascertain from the supernatural powers the prospects for Arthur's forthcoming marriage.

In *The Marriage of Guenevere*, the marriage is effected and the plots of Morgause (whose lover is Peredur, Guenevere's brother) are thwarted by Arthur's refusal to think ill of his queen and chief knight. Hovey ameliorates criticism of the lovers' conduct by providing Arthur with several paramours—"Ay, he has been a gay dog in his day"—and sending him off to war before the marriage is consummated. Since Launcelot is her first lover, Guenevere feels justified in calling him "husband." In *The Birth of Galahad*, to avoid charging Launcelot with infidelity in the matter of Elaine of Corbenic, Hovey presents Galahad as the son of Launcelot and Guenevere, though he is passed off as the child of the recently widowed Ylen. That Hovey rejected the Victorian attitude to adultery is suggested by the angel's words to Percival in *Taliesin*: "Better the rose of love out of the dunghill of the world's adulteries/Than the maid icicle that keeps itself from stain of earth where no life is." [MAW]

Hovey, Richard. *Launcelot and Guenevere: A Poem in Dramas*. 5 vols. Boston: Small, Maynard, 1898–1907.
Maynardier, Gustavus H. *The Arthur of the English Poets*. Boston: Houghton-Mifflin, 1907.

HRAFN GUNNLAUGSSON, Icelandic director of the 1988 film *Î skugga Hrafnsins* ("In the Shadow of the Raven"), a retelling of the Tristan and Isolde story set in the year 1077, after Iceland has nominally become Christianized. This drama of "love, power and revenge" is presided over by the raven, symbol of the god Odin. [GK]

HUEMER, RICHARD, author of *A Dragon on the Hill Road* (1958), a book-length narrative poem in which Lancelot, by the magic of Merlin's horn Oliphant, is transported to twentieth-century Tennessee, where he slays a dragon (an automobile). The often-humorous poem uses the Arthurian background and Lancelot's adventures in the future to explore various types of love. [ACL]

Huemer, Richard. *A Dragon on the Hill Road*. Los Angeles: Valley Village, 1958.

HUGHES, ARTHUR (1830–1915), English painter and illustrator, began his association with the Pre-Raphaelites and Arthurian subjects in 1857, when Dante Gabriel Rossetti invited him to take part in the Oxford Union Murals project. William Holman Hunt called Hughes's own design for *The Death of Arthur* superior to the others. Hughes also contributed *The Birth of Tristram* to the Dunlop Windows (1862).

During the 1860s and 1870s, Hughes expanded his repertoire, using Tennyson as his exclusive source. Works include *The Brave Geraint* (1862, Private Collection), *Elaine with the Armour of Lancelot* (undated, Private Collection), *Sir Galahad* (1870, Walker Art Gallery, Liverpool), and *The Lady of Shalott* (1873, Private Collection). He also painted inventions upon themes from Tennyson, as in *The Rift in the Lute*

47. Arthur Hughes, *Sir Galahad*. (Courtesy Merseyside County Council, Walker Art Gallery, Liverpool.)

(1862, City Gallery, Carlisle), which was based on Vivien's song in *Merlin and Vivien*. Hughes's work is distinguished by a graceful draughtsmanship and a vivid palette. More than his contemporaries, Hughes was able to instill lyricism into his vision of Tennyson's Arthuriad. [DNM]

Gibson, Robin. "Arthur Hughes: Arthurian and Related Subjects of the Early 1860s." *Burlington Magazine*, 112 (July 1970), 451–56.

HUGHES, THOMAS, with collaborators, wrote *The Misfortunes of Arthur* for performance by members of Gray's Inn before Elizabeth I at Greenwich in 1587. Senecan in rhetoric and dramatic technique, the tragedy has dumb shows devised by Francis Bacon. Based on Geoffrey of Monmouth, it depicts Arthur's fatal revenge on Mordred, who has seduced Guenevora. [CNS]

Hughes, Thomas. *The Misfortunes of Arthur*, ed. H.G. Grumbone. Berlin: Felber, 1900.

HUME, CYRIL (1900–1966), included several Arthurian lyrics, all treating aspects of romantic love, in his collection *Myself and the Young Bowman* (1932). "To Elaine in Avalon" is a sonnet in which an "invasion" of Avalon serves as a blatantly erotic metaphor; "Dialogue" is a brief exchange of promises between Tristram and Iseult; and "Song for Camelot" is a short poetic warning about the inevitability of pain in love. In "Uther's Blood," Arthur reflects on his own failure at love while envisioning famous lovers of his court boating on the Usk at twilight. [DN]

Hume, Cyril. *Myself and the Young Bowman and Other Fantasies.* Garden City, N.Y.: Doubleday, Doran, 1932.

HUMPHRIES, ROLFE (1894–1969), American poet and translator, drew on Welsh tradition for many of his poems. "Rhonabwy's Dream" (1942) tells of Arthur's chess game with Owain ap Urien from the Red Book of Hergest; the balladlike "A Brecon Version" (1956) has Trystan and Essylt outwitting Arthur and King March; "Under Craig y Ddinas" (1958) tells of the sleeping warriors, clearly Arthur's, who are stirred when an intruder rings a bell; and "The Return of Peredwr" (1965) provides an elaborate Celtic-colored description of the hero's arrival at court. [DN]

Humphries, Rolfe. *Collected Poems.* Bloomington: Indiana University Press, 1965.

HUNBAUT, an early thirteenth-century French romance of 3,818 lines that breaks off incomplete. It tells of Gauvain's mission on Arthur's behalf to the Roi des Isles in the company of Hunbaut. The two of them demand that the king submit to Arthur and then leave in great haste. They become separated and accomplish a number of exploits, liberating various people from their oppressors.

Hunbaut is actually a Gauvain romance and is particularly interesting when compared with other Gauvain romances that contain similar episodes, such as those of the imperious host and the damsel who keeps an image of the hero so that she may recognize him when he comes her way. More particularly, the poem contains a version of the Beheading Test also found in the First Continuation of the *Perceval*, Paien de Maisières's *La Mule sans frein*, the *Perlesvaus*, and *Sir Gawain and the Green Knight*. Hunbaut functions as a kind of moralizing contrast to Gauvain, who is constantly getting into scrapes as a result of unconsidered and unreasonable behavior.

Hunbaut contains many intertextual links with the works of Chrétien de Troyes and other "epigonal romances" (in particular *L'Atre périlleux, Meraugis de Portlesguez*, and *La Vengeance Raguidel*). It is also noteworthy for a passage in which the author seems to deny plagiarizing Chrétien. We may deduce from this and allusions in other works of the period that authors of later verse romances were concerned that their poems might be unfavorably compared with those of the master. [KB]

Winters, Margaret, ed. *Hunbaut.* Leiden: Brill, 1984.
Busby, Keith. "Caractérisation par contraste dans le roman de *Hunbaut.*" *Studia Neophilologica*, 52 (1980), 415–24.
Lacy, Norris J. "The Character of Gauvain in *Hunbaut.*" *Bibliographical Bulletin of the International Arthurian Society*, 38 (1986), 298–305.

HUNTER, EVAN, prolific and versatile American author of such popular successes as *The Blackboard Jungle* (1954) and, under the pseudonym of Ed McBain, the "87th Precinct" detective series. Hunter ventured into the field of fantasy in "Dream Damsel" (1954), a humorous short story set in Arthur's court. The fair Eloise foils the plans of her champion to marry a damsel whom he conjures up in his dreams by herself dreaming up a rival for the dream-damsel's love. [RHT]

Hunter, Evan. "Dream Damsel." In *Cosmic Knights: Isaac Asimov's Magical Worlds of Fantasy # 3*, ed. Isaac Asimov, Martin H. Greenberg, and Charles G. Waugh. New York: New American Library, 1985, pp. 165–75.

HUNTER, JIM, British author of the historical novel *Percival and the Presence of God* (1978), which recounts Percival's search for Arthur and his adventures along the way, including that of the Fisher King and the Grail. The story, narrated by Percival, describes his youthful sense of divine direction, his failure either to achieve the Grail or to find Arthur, and his subsequent doubts about his heroic destiny and significance. The novel is thus the projection of an essentially twentieth-century consciousness upon the medieval character, done both skillfully and successfully. [SRR]

Hunter, Jim. *Percival and the Presence of God.* London: Faber and Faber, 1978.

HUON DE BORDEAUX, a French epic cycle elaborated from the early thirteenth century into the fifteenth in decasyllabic verse, Alexandrine verse, and prose, is set in Carolingian times but contains some important Arthurian elements. Auberon, the dwarf tutor of Huon de Bordeaux, is the son of Morgan and Julius Caesar. He was reared at Arthur's court in Faérie. Arthur and his court intervene episodically in the Continuations. The most important Arthurian insertions apart from Auberon's mother and childhood at Arthur's court are Arthur's military incursions into Faérie in attempts to seize it from Huon. These are found in *Esclarmonde* and *Clarisse et Florent.* [DK]

Schweigel, Max, ed. *Esclarmonde, Clarisse et Florent, Yde et Olive.* Marburg: Elwert, 1889.

Schäfer, Hermann. *Über die Pariser Hss. 1451 und 22555 der Huon de Bordeaux-Sage: Beziehung der Hs. 1451 zur "Chanson de Croissant"; die "Chanson de Huon et Callisse"; die "Chanson de Huon, roi de Féerie."* Marburg: Elwert, 1892, pp. 28–29.

HUPSCHES VASNACHTSPILL UND SAGT VON KÜNIG ARTUS, AIN. The full title of the anonymous fifteenth-century Shrovetide play is *Ain hupsches vasnachtspill und sagt von künig Artus, wie er siben fursten mit iren weyben zuo seinem hoff geladen het und wie si durch ain horn geschendet worden gar hupsch zuo hören* ("A Pleasing Shrovetide Play About King Arthur, How He Invited Seven Kings with Their Wives to His Court and How They Were Embarrassed by a Horn, Quite Pleasant to Hear"). The play, which derives ultimately from Robert Biket's *Lai du cor*, opens with Arthur's decision to invite seven mighty kings to a great feast where rich and poor will be wined and dined. King Arthur refuses, however, to invite his sister, the Queen of Zipper, who has offended him. To avenge the slight, she sends to Arthur's court a magic drinking horn from which all men are to drink. They learn that only a man with a faithful wife can drink from the horn without spilling a drop. The play augments the tale known from the *Lai du cor* with a scene in which a knight falsely accuses another of having committed adultery with Guenevere. Trial-by-combat clears the accused knight's name and the accuser is banished from court. [MEK]

Keller, Adelbert von, ed. *Ain hupsches vasnachtspill und sagt von künig Artus.* In *Fastnachtspiele aus dem fünfzehnten Jahrhundert: Nachlese.* Stuttgart: Literarischer Verein, 1858, Vol. 146, pp. 183–215.

Walsh, Martin W. "*Arthur Cocu:* Comic Abuse of the Round Table in Fifteenth-Century Fastnachtspiele." *Fifteenth-Century Studies,* 15 (1989), 305–21.

HYLTON, JOHN DUNBAR (1837–1893), American farmer, businessman, and vanity-press publisher, author of *Arteloise: A Romance of King Arthur and Knights of the Round Table* (1887). Although this work in rhymed tetrameters has some traditional characters, it focuses on the otherworld adventures of Beau De Main during four days and nights. The Wandering Jew guides the hero to the Towers of Arteloise, where he undergoes trials, releases maidens, and meets Griselda, Pellinore's daughter. He achieves the Holy Grail, travels to the Polar Regions to save Merlin's daughter, Ursula, and helps Arthur defeat the Romans. The poem concludes when the deathless Jew, a rabbi, marries the hero and Griselda. [MAW]

Hylton, John Dunbar. *Arteloise: A Romance of King Arthur and the Knights of the Round Table.* Palmyra, N.J.: Hylton, 1887.

IGERNE (Yguerne, Igrayne), the virtuous wife of the Duke of Tintagel, who was much desired by King Uther Pendragon but would not consent to lie with him. In the most common medieval version of the legend, reflected in Geoffrey of Monmouth, Wace, the *Estoire de Merlin*, the *Suite du Merlin* (and its imitators), and Malory, Merlin arranges for Uther to come to her in the guise of the duke, her husband, and he begets upon her the future King Arthur. That very night, the duke is killed in battle, and Uther arranges soon afterward to wed Igerne. For his services, Merlin demands and receives a boon: to be entrusted the child of the union to raise. In most medieval versions, Igerne is portrayed as a faithful and virtuous wife. [WWK]

ILAS ET SOLVAS, a French romance dating from the early fourteenth century but extant only in a 120-line fragment. The remaining lines recount the arrival of two knights who renounce their allegiance to Arthur and prepare to do battle with him. [NJL]

Langlois, Ernest. "Fragments d'un roman de la Table Ronde." *Mélanges offerts à M. Emile Picot*. Paris: Rahir, 1913, Vol. 1, pp. 383–89.

IMMERMANN, KARL LEBERECHT (1796–1840), wrote dramatic works and novels containing stylistic features of classicism, romanticism, and the new realism. Twice, he used Arthurian subject matter, first in his ambitious play *Merlin* (1832), and again in the posthumously published fragment *Tristan und Isolde: Ein Gedicht in Romanzen* (1841). The latter is the most comprehensive Tristan poem of the nineteenth century. For Immermann, Merlin is the son of Satan, who paradoxically wants to save the world. The play, which was intended to vie with Goethe's *Faust*, concludes, however, with failure and ruin, not salvation. Tankred Dorst's play *Merlin* (1981) takes inspiration from Immermann. [UM/WCM]

Immermann, Karl. *Merlin*. Leipzig: Klemm, 1832.

———. *Tristan und Isolde: Ein Gedicht in Romanzen*. Leipzig: Reclam, [1841].

Moenkemeyer, Heinz. "Immermanns 'Merlin': Die Tragödie des selbsternannten Erlösers." In *Schiller-Jahrbuch*. Stuttgart: Kröner, 1961, Vol. 5.

INTELLIGENZA, L', Italian allegorical poem (ca. 1300), dubiously attributed to Dino Compagni, that includes Erec and Enid among the portraits of lovers adorning Madonna Intelligenza's palace (stanzas 72–76), a sequence that also celebrates Lancelot and Guenevere, Rosenna and Amore (Chrétien's Soredamors), Tristan and Isolde, Fiore and Blanzifiore, Isaota Blanzemano, the Lady of the Lake, the Lady of Malehaut, Palamedes, Allessandro, Ivano, Analida (Laudine), and Merlin trapped in a cave in the Forest of Arnante. In addition, stanza 287 refers to the knights of the Round Table, including Arthur, Lancelot, and Tristan, along with their ladies, Guenevere and Isolde, and in stanza 294 a sorrowing lady sings a lay recalling Tristan. [DLH]

Mistruzzi, Vitorio, ed. *L'Intelligenza*. Bologna: Commissione per i testi di lingua, 1928.

INTERNATIONAL ARTHURIAN SOCIETY (founded 1949) comprises some 1,000 individual members and 300 institutional subscribers over the globe, but mainly concentrated in western Europe and North America. Its goal is to further Arthurian studies by enabling scholars and enthusiasts to meet and learn of each others' activities. It is organized into national branches, some of which meet annually, and a triennial international congress, which is the ultimate governing body. To facilitate contact and to provide information, it publishes an annual *Bibliographical Bulletin*, which contains a critical bibliography of all printed studies of the preceding year, an up-to-date checklist of reviews of works previously noted in the *Bulletin*, reports of scholarly activities, short research articles, a list of publications received at the Centre de Documentation Arthurienne (Paris), summaries of papers read at the triennial international congresses, and a list of members, with addresses.

The founding of the society is generally attributed to Eugène Vinaver, though credit must also be given to Jean

Frappier and Roger Sherman Loomis for its growth after the Second World War. Vinaver himself attributed the conception to a physician, Dr. Hambly Rowe, who suggested in the late 1920s that Arthurian scholars should meet in Cornwall. The First International Congress was in fact held in Truro, Cornwall, in 1930, and at that time was sponsored by the embryonic Arthurian Society of Oxford, which Vinaver had initiated in 1928. The latter was rechristened the Society for the Study of Medieval Languages and Literature, and its publication, *Arthuriana* (1929–30), was renamed *Medium Aevum*. The Second International Congress, planned for 1932, was not realized until 1948, at Quimper, where the members launched the *Bulletin Bibliographique de la Société Internationale Arthurienne*. [JLG]

Thorpe, Lewis, et al. "The First Arthurian Congress, Truro, 23–30 August 1930." *Bibliographical Bulletin of the International Arthurian Society*, 25 (1973), 179–96.

IRELAND, (SAMUEL) WILLIAM HENRY (1775 or 1777–1835), English manuscript forger. Having attracted widespread attention with a series of faked Shakespearean documents, he concocted in 1795 a "rediscovered" play, *Vortigern*. In substance, this dramatizes the British king's career as narrated by Holinshed, who derives mainly from Geoffrey of Monmouth. Vortigern is portrayed as a sort of sub-Macbeth. Quasi-Shakespearean additions include scenes in which his daughter masquerades as a man. The play shows a certain weak imitative talent but is far below Shakespeare's level and has tell-tale anachronisms. In April 1796, Sheridan staged it at Drury Lane, with deep misgivings. The audience's derisive reaction killed it on the first night. Ireland confessed his fabrications. [GA]

Mair, John. *The Fourth Forger*. London: Cobden-Sanderson, 1938.

IRISH ARTHURIAN LITERATURE. Arthurian themes acquired only modest popularity in medieval Ireland, and it moreover appears that, in many cases, Irish narratives that can now be identified as explicitly Arthurian were not originally so, the Arthurian element or sequence having been grafted onto an independent story at a later date.

Irish tradition has transmitted to us only a single work that is a direct translation of a known Arthurian story; the *Lorgaireacht an tSoidhigh Naomtha* (the "Quest of the Holy Grail") is a rendering of the French Vulgate *Queste* or, more likely, of a lost fourteenth-century English translation of it. The Irish work, dating doubtless from the mid-fifteenth century, includes some details that, as they are not found in any of the extant French manuscripts, may well reflect the original version of the French *Queste*. The Irish text is preserved in three fragmentary manuscripts, which together represent about two-thirds of the *Queste*.

In addition to this translation, several Irish compositions from the fifteenth century on make prominent use of Arthurian motifs, characters, or settings. In the *Eachtra an Mhadra Mhaoil* ("Adventures of the Crop-eared Dog"), the son of the King of India, having been transformed into a dog, regains his human form with the help of Sir Bhalbhuaidh (Gwalchmai or Gawain). A woman transformed into a deer provides the subject of the fifteenth-century *Céilidhe Iosgaide Léithe* ("The Visit of the Grey-hammed Lady"), which takes place at Arthur's court. Irish literature also preserves, in a poem in *Duanaire Finn*, a version of the chastity test involving a mantle. An obscure but fascinating Irish tale, postmedieval but of uncertain date, is *Eachtra an Amadain Mhoir* ("The Adventures of the Great Fool"), which is distantly associated both with the Perceval story and with the tempting theme found in *Sir Gawain and the Green Knight*.

A tale entitled *Eachtra Mhacaoimh an Iolair* ("The Adventures of the Youth Carried off by an Eagle," probably sixteenth century), composed by Brian O Corcráin, contains an Arthurian section, and the *Eachtra Mhelora agus Orlando* ("The Adventures of Mhelora and Orlando," seventeenth century) is cast in an Arthurian framework, although the subject is likely inspired by Ariosto's *Orlando Furioso*.

Irish Arthurian texts are not numerous, but some scholars have emphasized the possible role of Irish lore in the formation of Arthurian legends, basing their conclusions on similarities between non-Arthurian Irish tales and Arthurian texts in various languages. Accordingly, it has been suggested, for example, that the traditional Fionn stories from Ireland may provide analogues, if not actual models, for the characters of Mark, Arthur, and Perceval, and the adventures of the young Fionn bear a narrative resemblance to events in the Middle English *Sir Perceval of Galles*. In addition, the Irish tales of Diarmaid and Gráinne appear to be related, whether as source or as analogue, to those of Tristan and Isolde. [NJL]

Murphy, Gerard. *The Ossianic Lore and Romantic Tales of Medieval Ireland*. Dublin: Three Candles, 1961.
Rees, Alwyn, and Brinley Rees. *Celtic Heritage*. London: Thames and Hudson, 1961, pp. 70–72.

ISOLDE: *see* TRISTAN AND ISOLDE.

ISOLDE OF THE WHITE HANDS (Iseut [Yseut] aux Blanches Mains), sometimes known as Isolde of the Fair Hands or Isolde of Brittany. Tristan, separated from the woman he loves, marries Isolde of the White Hands because she shares his beloved's name. Their marriage remains unconsummated, and he confesses that it is because he loves another woman. Eventually, as Tristan is waiting for Isolde to arrive and heal him, his wife causes his death by informing him, untruthfully, that Isolde is not aboard the approaching ship. (*See also* TRISTAN AND ISOLDE.)

[NJL]

ITALIAN ARTHURIAN LITERATURE. Although rarely serving as the locale for the adventures of Arthur and the knights of the Round Table, Italy certainly bears literary and artistic witness to their passage. Perhaps the only indication we possess of Arthur's "physical" presence in Italy is the legend of his residence in Mount Etna (Mongibello), and it is this fabulous tale that the anonymous poet of the "Detto del gatto lupesco" evokes in a playful and comic manner. In this poem, the jongleur, who identifies himself as a "wolflike cat," meets two knights in an inn and learns of their quest for Arthur:

> Cavalieri siamo di Bretagna,
> ke vegnamo de la montagna
> ke•ll'omo apella Mongibello.
> Assai vi semo stati ad ostello
> per apparare ed invenire
> la veritade di nostro sire
> lo re Artù, k'avemo perduto
> e non sapemo ke•ssia venuto.
> Or ne torniamo in nostra terra,
> ne lo reame d'Inghilterra [ll. 25–34].

("We are knights of Brittany who come from the mountain called Mongibello. We have stayed here in the inn a long time to learn and discover the truth about our lord, King Arthur, whom we have lost, and we don't know what's happened to him. Now we are returning to our country, to the kingdom of England.")

The fascination that the *matière de Bretagne* exerted on the Italian popular imagination may be documented in at least two ways. In the twelfth and thirteenth centuries, many names of Arthurian provenance began to appear among the populace (Arturius, Galvanus, Merlinus, Tristaynus), a fact that attests both to the diffusion and to the popularity of these legends in Italy. In this same period, there were carved above the portals of some cathedrals (Modena, Bari) and depicted in the mosaic pavement of others (Otranto) knights in combat, castles and besieged towers, and other figures and events from the Arthurian cycle.

In Italian literature, the principal players in the Arthurian drama assumed a new, double life: a "symbolic" existence as emblematic figures in superficial allusions, and a "real" literary life as principal characters in a sustained narrative or sequence of episodes. On the one hand, lyric poets used these figures as standards of comparison against which they measured elements of their own experience: beauty, prowess, wisdom, and the like. On the other hand, other authors mined the rich (mainly French) Arthurian treasure trove and composed a number of prose romances, *novelle*, and *cantari*, thus creating a large and distinct body of Italian Arthurian literature.

The story of Tristan and Isolde is the most popular of the Arthurian legends in Italy, the most widely cited, and the subject of the greatest number of versions. We may therefore determine the impact of the *matière de Bretagne* on Italian literature by examining the various manifestations of this single tale. Henricus of Settimello (late twelfth century) was the first author to mention Tristan in Italy. In his *Elegia de diversitate fortunae et philosophiae consolatione* ("Elegy on the Contradiction of Fortune and the Consolation of Philosophy"), he stressed the grief associated with this famous lover in the following paronomastic verse: "Quis ille/Tristanus qui me tristia plura tulit?" ("Who is that Tristan who bore more sorrows than I?")

The Italian lyric tradition began at the court of the emperor Frederick II of Hohenstaufen in Sicily, and these vernacular poets followed the example of their Provençal forebears in their use of the Tristan legend as a source of comparisons. There, they found standards against which to measure elements of their own experience: the unsurpassed strength and courage of Tristan, the supreme beauty of Isolde, and the powerful nature and indestructible force of their love. In the following verses from his *discordo*, Giacomo da Lentini declares his own love to be much stronger than Tristan's: "Tristano a Isolda/non amau sì forte." ("Tristan did not love Isolde so strongly"; "Dal core mi vene," l. 35.) Re Giovanni alludes to Isolde's beauty in "Donna, audite como" (ll. 58–60): "E Tristan se ne godia/de lo bel viso rosato/ch'Isaotta blond'avia." ("And Tristan took great pleasure in the lovely rosy face that blond-haired Isolde had.")

In the thirteenth and early fourteenth centuries, the Italian lyric evolved both linguistically and thematically at the hands of innovative poets, such as Guittone d'Arezzo, Guido Guinizelli, Guido Cavalcanti, and Dante Alighieri. In this period of gradual transformation, the allusions to the legend of Tristan and Isolde, although less frequent, remained essentially the same. Bonagiunta da Lucca, in the *ballata* "Donna vostra belleza" (ll. 31–33), refers to the intensity of Tristan and Isolde's passion: "Ed eo . . . /'nnamorato son di vue/assai più che non fue—Tristan d'Isolda." ("And I love you, even more than Tristan loved Isolde.")

In the sonnet "Lo disioso core e la speranza" (ll. 5–8), the Florentine poet Chiaro Davanzati refers to the beauty of his lady as being greater than that of Isolde: "di voi non veggio simiglianza/né pari di bieltà sì graziosa:/ch'Isotta né Tisbïa per sembianza,/nesuna in gioia fue sì poderosa." ("I do not know anyone similar or equal to you in pleasing beauty: for neither Isolde nor Thisbe in appearance was so great in bestowing happiness.")

In a ballad on Fortune ("Se la Fortuna o 'l mondo," ll. 53–56), written in the first quarter of the Trecento, Frate Stoppa de' Bostichi first alludes to the prowess of Tristan and the other knights of the Round Table: "Tristano e Lancialotto/sono iti, benchè ancor lor fama vale./Gli altri di Camelotto/per la Fortuna feciono altrettale." ("Tristan and Lancelot have gone away, but their fame still endures. The other knights of Camelot fared the same because of Fortune.") In a subsequent strophe (ll. 79–80), he incorporates the *ubi sunt* motif in reference to the beauty of Isolde and others: "Dov'è la gran bellezza/di Ginevra, d'Isotta, e d'Ansalone?" ("Where is the great beauty of Guinevere, Isolde, and Absalom?")

There are fewer and fewer of these superficial allusions to Arthurian figures in the lyric poetry of the fourteenth century: the reason for this perhaps lies in the compilation and diffusion of numerous major and well-developed prose romances during this period. The increased familiarity with the legend and its resulting "commonness" may have vitiated the exotic quality that these allusions once possessed. Or else the disfavor into which these allusions fell may simply reflect changing attitudes toward the nature and aesthetics of poetry and indicate, in particular, the desire to avoid empty phrases and artificial conventions.

Only infrequently in the thirteenth century do we come across an allusion that seems to indicate a more specific knowledge of the Tristan legend. For example, in the *canzone* "Madonna mia, a voi mando" (ll. 41–48) Giacomo da Lentini speaks of having made a wax image of his lady, whom he compares to Isolde: "In gran dilettanza era,/madonna, in quello giorno/quando vi formai in cera/le belleze d'intorno./Più bella mi parete/ca Isolda la bronda;/amorosa, gioconda,/flor de le donne sete." ("In great delight I was that day, my lady, when I formed your beautiful image in wax. You seem to me more beautiful than Isolde; loving, joyful, you are the flower of women.") The inspiration of this allusion probably comes from the well-known "Salle aux Images" episode (Bédier's term) in Thomas's *Tristan*.

Despite this and a few other examples that suggest a knowledge of the early metrical romances, the prose version of the Tristan legend was the most widely known in Italy and furnished the basis for virtually all of the Italian redactions of the story. The several extant late thirteenth- and early fourteenth-century prose romances range from essentially literal translations of the Old French *Roman de Tristan* to liberal adaptations and compilations of diverse source materials. The earliest of the Italian Tristan romances is the *Tristano Riccardiano*, which presents freely selected portions from its Old French source, as well as numerous "new" elements and episodes. The most original of the prose romances, the *Tavola Ritonda*, combines in a harmonious whole episodes from various sources (the Prose *Tristan*, *Palamedes*, *Tristano Riccardiano*, *Mort Artu*) and a wealth of new elements and adventures, all of which give it a certain artistic autonomy and individuality. An episode in the Tristan legend, drawn primarily from Béroul—the lovers' moonlight meeting at the fountain in the garden, where Mark is hiding in a pine-tree—provides the subject for one (No. 65) of the short stories in *Il Novellino*.

Originally part of the oral tradition, the *cantari* paraphrase specific episodes from the prose romances, both Old French and Italian, and are noteworthy as examples of the art of the jongleur. Three *cantari* treat the Tristan legend: *La morte di Tristano*, *Quando Tristano e Lancielotto combattettero al petrone di Merlino*, and *La vendetta che fe messer Lanzelloto de la morte di miser Tristano*.

Other Arthurian figures were generally incorporated in Italian literature in the same manner as Tristan and Isolde: either as superficial references and allusions in lyric poetry or as the subject of major prose romances, *novelle*, and *cantari*. In the sonnet "Ben aggia ormai la fede e l'amor meo" (ll. 10–12), Guittone d'Arezzo refers to the well-known prowess of Lancelot: "Siccome a Lanzelotto omo simiglia/un prode cavaler, simil se face/a lei di fera donna a maraviglia." ("Just as one compares a valiant knight to Lancelot, so does one liken a wonderfully proud lady to her.")

In a sonnet addressed to the Compiuta Donzella di Firenza, Maestro Torrigiano compares her favorably to Guenevere (ll. 1–4): "Esser donzella di trovare dotta/sì grande meraviglia par a 'ntendre,/ca, se Ginevra fosse od Isaotta,/ver' lor di lei se ne poria contendre." ("The existence of a young woman so gifted in writing poetry seems such a marvelous thing to hear that, if Guenevere or Isolde were still alive, one could argue for her superiority over them.")

In the following verses (ll. 1–4), Chiaro Davanzati praises the outstanding beauty of his lady, who surpasses even Morgan le Fay: "Ringrazzo amore de l'aventurosa/gioia e de l'allegrezza che m'à data,/che mi donò a servir la più amorosa/che non fue Tisbia o Morgana la fata." ("I thank Love for the wondrous joy and happiness that he has given me, for he gave me to serve the most lovely one, even more so than Thisbe or Morgan le Fay.")

Allusions of this sort are common in lyric poetry, and the list could be extended to include, among others, Arthur, Merlin, Yvain, and Erec.

Dependent in large part on their Old French forerunners, the Italian prose romances treat the entire range of Arthurian material and the different generations of characters in that corpus. Basing his account on the Prose *Tristan* and the *Palamedes*, Rusticiano (or Rustichello) da Pisa (late thirteenth century) compiled the earliest Arthurian romance in Italy, the *Meliadus*, which, written in French, is extant only in fragmentary form. Its two major portions were translated early on into Italian as *Girone il Cortese* and *Il gran re Meliadus*. Merlin is the subject of two fourteenth-century romances, both of which derive from Old French sources: the *Storia di Merlino*, by the Florentine chronicler Paolino Pieri, and the later *Vita di Merlino con le sue profezie*. These numerous *volgarizzamenti* and redactions hold an important place in the history of early Italian literature, for they contributed in a major way to the establishment and expansion of Italy's heretofore relatively small literary patrimony in the vernacular.

Arthurian material is also present in the *novella* (short story) tradition. Several stories in *Il Novellino*, for example, have as their principal characters Meliadus, Lancelot, the Maid of Scalot, and Merlin. A story concerning Merlin is also included in the collection of tales called *Libro dei Sette Savi di Roma*, and another about Galehaut is found in the *Conti dei antichi cavalieri*.

The *cantari* display a much broader range in Arthurian subject matter, for they draw upon both the prose romances and the Breton lais. In addition to Tristan and Lancelot, the *cantari* feature a host of protagonists, and a survey of a few titles will give an idea of their diversity: *Pulzella Gaia*, *Bel Gherardino*, *Liombruno*, *Carduino*, *Febusso e Breusso*—all anonymous—and Antonio Pucci's *Gismirante* and *Brito di Brettagna*. The *Cantare dei cantari* allows the reader to look at the repertoire of the jongleur and to observe the literary tastes of the society he serves. In this anonymous *cantare*, the poet lists all the subjects he is able to sing about, and nine full stanzas (of fifty-nine) are devoted to Arthurian material.

Dante Alighieri was familiar with the *matière de Bretagne* and mentions the "Arturi regis ambages pulcerrimae" in *De Vulgari Eloquentia* (I,x,2) as evidence of the preeminence of the French language in vernacular prose. While not using Arthurian figures in stock allusions as preceding generations of poets had done, Dante does incorporate certain episodes from the prose romances into the literary and moral structure of the *Divina Commedia*. Most famous in this regard is his presentation of the sinful passion of Paolo and Francesca, which is played out against and defined by the episode in the Old French Prose *Lancelot*, in which Lancelot and Guenevere kiss for the first time under the guidance of the Lady of Malehaut.

In the early fourteenth-century allegorical poem *L'Intelligenza*, the poet (possibly Dino Compagni) celebrates his lady ("Intelligenza") and describes her palace. Included as integral parts of the decoration of this palace are several Arthurian figures and their stories—Tristan and Isolde, Guenevere, Merlin, and others. In his mid-fourteenth-century encyclopedic poem in *terza rima Il Dittamondo*, Fazio degli Uberti imagines himself traveling through the known world guided by the classical geographer Solinus. In his journey, he sees and comments in some detail on several places of Arthurian interest in Brittany and Great Britain.

Giovanni Boccaccio includes a chapter on Arthur in *De Casibus Virorum Illustrium* and uses Arthurian motives and allusions in the *Decameron* (the subtitle of which is "Prencipe Galeotto"), *Amorosa Visione*, *Corbaccio*, and *Elegia di Madonna Fiammetta*.

In the *Trionfo d'Amore* (Book III, ll. 79–82), Francesco Petrarca speaks in a disdainful and disparaging manner of Arthurian knights and ladies, who appear in the procession of those subjugated by Love: "Ecco quei che le carte empion di sogni,/Lancilotto, Tristano e gli altri erranti,/ove conven che 'l vulgo errante agogni./Vedi Ginevra, Isolda e l'altre amanti." ("Here are those who fill the pages of books with dreams—Lancelot, Tristan, and the other knights-errant—dreams that lead the common folk astray through desire. See Guenevere, Isolde, and other lovers.")

The final chapter in this survey of the presence of the *matière de Bretagne* in Italy concerns the conflation of the Arthurian and the Carolingian cycles. As early as the fourteenth century, the poet of the Franco-Italian epic *L'Entrée d'Espagne* endows Roland with the amorous and chivalric sensibility of a knight of the Round Table. Similarly, in the *cantare* cycles concerned with the exploits of Roland—*La Spagna* and *Li fatti di Spagna*—we find many of the marvelous trappings and adventures common to the Arthurian tradition. Andrea da Barberino imbues his late fourteenth-century narratives concerning the Matter of France—*Aspramonte*, *Storie Nerbonesi*, *Reali di Francia*—with a distinctly Arthurian spirit. Such will be the case as well with Matteo Maria Boiardo, whose *Orlando Innamorato* captures (even in its title) much of the spirit of Arthurian romance and sets the stage for Ludovico Ariosto's *Orlando Furioso*, which is replete with courtly knights and ladies and wondrous adventures. [CK]

Arese, Felice, ed. *Prose di romanzi: Il romanzo cortese in Italia nei secoli XIII e XIV.* Turin: UTET, 1950.

Branca, Daniela. *I romanzi italiani di Tristano e la Tavola Ritonda.* Florence: Olschki, 1968.

———. "Tavola rotonda: La materia arturiana e tristaniana: Tradizione e fortuna." In *Dizionario critico della letteratura italiana.* Turin: UTET, 1973, Vol. 3, pp. 471–76.

Ferrante, Joan M. *The Conflict of Love and Honor: The Medieval Tristan Legend in France, Germany and Italy.* The Hague: Mouton, 1973.

Gardner, Edmund G. *The Arthurian Legend in Italian Literature.* London: Dent, 1930.

Graf, Arturo. "Appunti per la storia del ciclo brettone in Italia." *Giornale storico della letteratura italiana*, 5 (1885), 80–130.

Heijkant, Marie-José. *La tradizione del "Tristan" in prosa in italia e proposte di studio sul "Tristan Riccardiano."* N.p.: Sneldruk Enschede, 1990.

Kleinhenz, Christopher. "Tristan in Italy: The Death or Rebirth of a Legend." *Studies in Medieval Culture*, 5 (1975), 145–58.

Viscardi, Antonio. "Arthurian Influences on Italian Literature from 1220 to 1500." In *Arthurian Literature in the Middle Ages*, ed. Roger Sherman Loomis. Oxford: Clarendon, 1959, pp. 419–29.

IVAN LEJONRIDDAREN (or *Herr Ivan*) is a Swedish adaptation of Chrétien de Troyes's *Yvain*. It is one of three works known collectively as *Eufemiavisor*, after Queen Eufemia, wife of King Hákon Magnússon of Norway (r. 1299–1319), who commissioned the work. *Ivan Lejonriddaren* is dated 1303 and is preserved in four fifteenth-century Swedish manuscripts and two Danish manuscripts. Unlike the Norwegian prose translation of *Yvain*—i.e., *Ívens saga*—*Ivan Lejonriddaren* is in verse, in rhymed couplets known as *Knittelvers*. Certain textual similarities between *Ivan Lejonriddaren* and *Ívens saga* suggest that the anonymous translator, who is thought to have been a Swede at the Norwegian court, made use of both the Norwegian saga and Chrétien's *Yvain*. *Ivan Lejonriddaren* is a fairly accurate, albeit somewhat reduced, rendering of Chrétien's romance. It has the distinction of being the only medieval Swedish Arthurian romance and the only verse translation of an Arthurian romance in the North. [MEK]

Noreen, Erik, ed. *Herr Ivan*. Uppsala: Svenska Fornskrift-Sällskapet, 1930–32; 2nd ed. 1956.

Hunt, Tony. "Herr Ivan Lejonriddaren." *Mediaeval Scandinavia*, 8 (1975), 168–86.

Ronge, Hans. "Ivan Lejonriddaren." In *Kulturhistorisk leksikon for nordisk middelalder*. Copenhagen: Rosenkilde og Bagger, 1962, Vol. 7, cols. 525–27.

"IVEN ERNINGSSON," a Norwegian ballad consisting of eighty-seven four-line stanzas, which recount an imperfect and fragmentary version of the matter contained in the Faroese "Ívints táttur" and "Galians táttur" I and II. The ballad relates how Iven spends a night with the widow Gjertrud but refuses to marry her and is cursed with a seemingly incurable illness. When Junkar, Gjertrud's son by Iven, is fifteen years old, he threatens his mother with death unless she provides a cure for his father. Henceforth his name is Galite, because his mother considers *galen* ("mad, insane") a son who would kill his own mother. She gives him a potion for Iven, and the son succeeds in finding his father and curing him. The remainder of the ballad transmits in fragmentary form Galite's encounter with trolls and his combat with his own father. The ballad concludes with the wedding of Iven and Gjertrud. Except for the name "Iven," this ballad, like "Kvikkjesprakk," no longer transmits the Arthurian motifs found in the related Faroese ballad cycle *Ívint Herintsson*. [MEK]

Bø, Olav, and Svale Solheim, eds. "Iven Erningsson." In *Folkeviser* 1 (*Norsk Folkediktning* 6), 3rd ed. Oslo: Det norske samlaget, 1967, pp. 99–111.

Kölbing, Eugen. "Beiträge zur Kenntniss der Færöischen Poesie." *Germania*, 20 (1875), 385–402.

Liestøl, Knut. *Norske trollvisor og norrøne sogor*. Oslo: Olaf Norli, 1915.

ÍVENS SAGA, an Old Norse prose translation of Chrétien de Troyes's *Yvain*. A statement in the text indicates that it was commissioned by the Norwegian king Hákon Hákonarson (r. 1217–63). There are three primary manuscripts, two fifteenth-century vellums (both defective) and one seventeenth-century paper. The latter is considerably shortened and modified but nevertheless preserves some readings, lacking in the vellums, which must be original on comparison with the French.

Íven, one of King Arthur's knights, slays the guardian of a magic fountain to avenge Kalebrant, his kinsman, who had earlier been disgraced by the knight. Íven falls in love with the guardian's widow and after a reconciliation marries her. He is aided in this by Luneta, the lady's confidante, whom Íven had once befriended at Arthur's court. When Arthur and his men later arrive, Íven successfully defends the spring. After the subsequent feasting, Valven (Gawain) persuades Íven to accompany them and preserve his reputation as a champion. His lady gives Íven leave but sets a term of a year. When Íven forgets to return, a maiden appears with a message from his lady that banishes him. In a fit of madness, Íven wanders off into the forest but is later cured with a magic ointment by another lady. He defeats an earl who is attacking this lady's lands; he then rescues a lion from a dragon, and the lion becomes his constant companion. Among his numerous adventures is an episode in which Íven rescues Luneta from being burned at the stake. Finally, a duel between Íven and Valven, each unrecognized by the other, ends in a draw, and Íven is joyfully reintroduced into Arthur's court. He must still be reconciled with his lady, however, a task that Luneta accomplishes with the aid of a ruse.

Although this saga is more a translation and less an adaptation than *Erex saga*, there are still a number of changes, presumably intentional, vis-à-vis its French original. Alliteration is used as an effective stylistic device, particularly in dramatic scenes. [FWB]

Blaisdell, Foster W., ed. *Ívens saga*. Copenhagen: Reitzel, 1979.

———, and Marianne E. Kalinke, trans. *Erex Saga and Ívens Saga*. Lincoln: University of Nebraska Press, 1977.

Barnes, Geraldine. "Arthurian Chivalry in Old Norse." *Arthurian Literature*, 7 (1987), 50–102.

Kalinke, Marianne E. *King Arthur, North-by-Northwest*. Copenhagen: Reitzel, 1981.

ÍVINT HERINTSSON, a cycle of Faroese ballads, entitled after the son of Herint, whose bridal quest is the subject of the first ballad. The cycle is extant in three redactions, presumably dating from the late Middle Ages but not written down until the late eighteenth and the first half of the nineteenth centuries. Like other Faroese heroic ballads, the cycle *Ívint Herintsson* consists of quatrains of the abcb type with a refrain at the end of each stanza and is divided into subballads, each usually containing the word *táttur* ("subballad") or *kvæði* ("poem" or "song") in the title. The longest redaction (A) consists of a cycle of five ballads: "Jákimann kongur" (eighty stanzas), "Kvikilsprang" (sixty stanzas), "Ívints táttur" (eighty stanzas), "Galians táttur I" (100 stanzas), and "Galians táttur II" (sixty stanzas). The two shorter redactions (B and C) conflate "Ívints táttur" and "Galians táttur" I and II into one ballad, entitled "Galians táttur" (B) and "Galians kvæði" (C) respectively.

"Jákimann kongur" ("King Jákimann") is a bridal-quest ballad named after the antagonist, a troll-like man, who woos the sister of King Hartan but is rejected by the desired bride in favor of Herint, another wooer. The two rivals meet in combat and Herint slays Jákimann. The ballad ends with the wedding of Herint and King Hartan's sister. "Kvikilsprang" opens with the birth of their three sons, Ívint, Víðferð, and Kvikilsprang, the youngest of whom, Kvikilsprang, sails to Girtland (Greece?) to woo Princess Rósinreyð. When Kvikilsprang is rejected by her father, he engages in battle with the king's men, but is overcome and thrown into a dungeon. His brother Ívint arrives to rescue him, and together they slay the king and all his men. The ballad ends with the wedding of Kvikilsprang and Rósinrayð. "Ívints táttur" relates how Víðferi, Herint's third son, is killed in a land of giants and poisonous springs. At the father's urging, Ívint sets out to avenge his brother. He slays a flying dragon, kills the giant Regin, and then the giant's mother. In "Galians táttur I," Arthurian allusions suggest that the person of King Hartan derives from or is identical with King Arthur. Like him, Hartan refuses to eat until some great news has been brought to his court. The ballad commences with Ívint setting out on a hunt for a wondrous hind. He spends the night with a widow, but upon leaving in the morning he informs her that he does not intend to return. She accuses him of having forcibly slept with her and mixes him a drink that leaves him incurably ill. When her son by Ívint is fifteen years old, he asks about the identity of his father and threatens to kill his mother if his father no longer lives. He departs for King Hartan's court with a potion that cures Ívint. In "Galians táttur II," the eponymous hero sets out in search of adventure and slays giants and dragons. When he returns, his father unwittingly engages his own son in combat. The ballad ends with a double wedding: Galian's and Ívint's, with the latter at last marrying Galian's mother.

The ballad cycle is based on both indigenous and imported matter. The narrative of "Kvikilsprang" presumably derives from one of the bridal quests in the Icelandic *Hrólfs saga Gautrekssonar*, while the disease-inducing potion may have been borrowed from *Mírmanns saga*. The person of Ívint seems to have been inspired by one of the knights of the Round Table, who was known in the North primarily through *Ívens saga*, the Norwegian translation of Chrétien de Troyes's *Yvain*, which also contains the motifs of the nubile widow and combat with a dragon. Other motifs presumably borrowed from the Arthurian matter are King Hartan's disinclination to eat before an adventure takes place, a fact repeatedly mentioned in "Galians táttur" I and II; the hunt for the hind; and the combat with a relative. [MEK]

"Ívint Herintsson." In *Føroya Kvæði: Corpus Carminum Færoensium*, ed. N. Djurhuus. Copenhagen: Akademisk Forlag, 1976, Vol. 5, pp. 199–242.

Conroy, Patricia L. "Faroese Ballads." In *Dictionary of the Middle Ages*, ed. Joseph R. Strayer. New York: Scribner, 1985, Vol. 5, pp. 15–17.

Kölbing, Eugen. "Beiträge zur Kenntniss der Færöischen Poesie." *Germania*, 20 (1875), 385–402.

Liestøl, Knut. *Norske trollvisor og norrøne sogor*. Oslo: Olaf Norli, 1915.

IVORY. Among the earliest ivories with Arthurian scenes are the small boxes, or caskets, intended to hold a lady's prized personal possessions. Products of the Cologne school in the thirteenth century, they are often decorated with scenes from the romance of Tristan. Figures of a man with a harp and woman with a goblet are identifiable as Tristan and Isolde.

The finest Arthurian ivories were the product of the Parisian workshops especially during the second quarter of the fourteenth century. A flourishing trade in luxury objects, such as ivory boxes, combs, mirror-cases, and hair-parters, required workshop methods of production, using set iconography and formulaic compositions; nevertheless, the

48. Parisian Ivory Casket. (The Metropolitan Museum of Art, Gift of J. Pierpont Morgan, 1917.)

many surviving objects of high quality attest to the skill of the Parisian craftsmen. Ivory jewel boxes were carved with scenes intended to appeal to the taste of noble ladies. Some of the subjects could be given a moralizing interpretation, but most represent the famous lovers of history, the attack on the Castle of Love, or the fountain of youth. Tristan and Isolde meeting by the well (the so-called Tryst Beneath the Tree), Sir Lancelot Crossing the Sword Bridge, and Sir Gawain on the Perilous Bed are the most popular Arthurian scenes, although Galahad receiving the keys to the Castle of Maidens also appears. Excellent examples of these ivory caskets may be seen in the Metropolitan Museum in New York, the Walters Gallery in Baltimore, the Victoria and Albert Museum and the British Museum in London, the Bargello in Florence, and Cracow Cathedral in Poland. The caskets differ only slightly. The Perceval Casket in the Louvre is unusual in its depiction of the youth of Perceval and was probably based on Chrétien's *Conte del Graal*. The figures of SS. Christopher, Martin, George, and Eustace decorate the lid of the Louvre Casket.

Ivory mirror-backs (Cluny Museum, Paris; Vatican Museum) were carved with the same repertoire of scenes as the caskets. Since the subject had to be composed within a roundel or quatrefoil (the square of the mirror-back originally was filled out by hunched monsters or foliage at the corners), symmetrical compositions with Tristan and Isolde spied on by King Mark or playing chess were popular. A hair-parter in Turin also has Tristan and Isolde and the face of King Mark, in a very compressed composition, and another in the Metropolitan Museum has the lovers with their little dog.

These Parisian ivories have usually been interpreted as a celebration of love and youth, with scenes from the romances considered appropriate as gifts for young ladies. Frederick Baekeland, in a psychological study of the iconography, however, has pointed out the underlying conflict and sexual tension expressed in the selection and juxtaposition of scenes, in the theme of youth and age, and the issues of sexual choice and surrender. [MS]

Baekeland, Frederick. "Two Kinds of Symbolism in a Gothic Ivory Casket." *Psychoanalytic Study of Society*, 6 (n.d.).

Koechlin, Raymond. *Les Ivoires gothiques français*. 2 vols. Paris: Picard, 1924, Vol. 1, pp. 43–44.

Loomis, Roger Sherman, and Laura Hibbard Loomis. *Arthurian Legends in Medieval Art*. London: Oxford University Press, 1938, pp. 55–54, 66–67, 70–71, 73–74, 76.

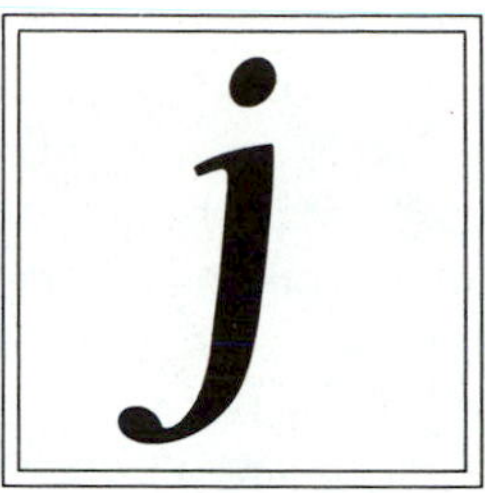

JACKSON, STEPHEN (pseudonym of John Stevenson; 1853–?), author of *The Magic Mantle* (1903), a short novel inspired by the ballad "The Boy and the Mantle." The story suggests that the tests of virtue described in the ballad, which only Sir Craydock and his wife pass, are devised by Merlin as a way of delaying the ultimate doom of Arthur's court. The second half of the story tells how the thirteenth-century descendant of Craydock and his bride prove themselves worthy of carrying on the family name, in part by undergoing the test of the magic mantle. [ACL]

Jackson, Stephen. *The Magic Mantle and Other Stories*. New York: Greene, 1903.

JACOBS, MARIA, Canadian publisher and the author of a poetic sequence based on the legend of Tristan, entitled "Iseult, We Are Barren." These twenty poems, constituting Section 3 of a larger collection with the same title (1987), are soliloquies in the voices of Iseult, Tristan, and King Mark, reflecting upon certain events and circumstances of the story. The poems are lyrical and portray well the broad range of emotions involved in the story. [SRR]

Jacobs, Maria. *Iseult, We Are Barren*. Windsor, Ont.: Netherlandic, 1987.

JAUFRÉ, the only surviving Provençal Arthurian romance. A work of some 11,000 lines, it may be the product of two authors, both of them anonymous. *Jaufré* has been variously dated from ca. 1180 to as late as 1225.

The hero is probably the same person as Chrétien de Troyes's Girflet. Most scholars who have studied *Jaufré* have noted that its author(s) had an intimate knowledge of the works of Chrétien de Troyes; their conclusions have been based on groupings of names, reflections of motifs and episodes, and some rhetorical and stylistic similarities. In a few cases (e.g., Rita Lejeune), those who propose the earliest possible dating have suggested that it might have been Chrétien who used the *Jaufré* text as inspiration, rather than the opposite.

The hero of the work sets out to avenge injuries or affronts done to Melian and Arthur by Taulat. In the process, he falls in love with Brunissen, the mistress of the castle of Monbrun. These parallel narrative lines are filled out by a number of miscellaneous episodes. The author has a taste for fantasy and comedy, and it is possible to see his work as a parody of chivalric romance.

The character attained some popularity beyond the bounds of this text, specifically in the Spanish prose *Tablante de Ricamonte y de Jofre hijo del conte Donason*. [NJL]

Brunel, Clovis, ed. *Jaufré: Roman arthurien en ancien provençal*. 2 vols. Paris: Picard, 1943.

Rémy, Paul. "Jaufré." In *Arthurian Literature in the Middle Ages*, ed. Roger Sherman Loomis. Oxford: Clarendon, 1959, pp. 400–05.

JEAN D'OUTREMEUSE, French author of *Ly Myreur des histors* ("The Mirror of Histories"), a fourteenth-century text recounting the history of the world to 1340. It offers accounts of Uther's and Arthur's reigns and includes the information that Lancelot killed Guenevere and then entombed Mordred with her body. In an effort to survive, Mordred turned to cannibalism, but the Queen's flesh did not prevent him from starving eventually. [NJL]

Borgnet, Adolphe, and Stanislas Boormans, eds. *Ly Myreur des histors*. Brussels: Hayez, 1864–80.

JEASTE OF SYR GAWAYNE, THE. Like *Golagros and Gawane*, the *Jeaste* (541 lines, but the opening is lacking) is a late fifteenth-century adaptation of events related in the First Continuation of Chrétien de Troyes's *Conte del Graal*, with a Gawain who is more humane and who magnanimously spares the lives of the father and two brothers of the girl with whom he has made love. The poem ends with the truce between the third brother, Brandles, and Gawain, who has to walk back to the court as his horse has apparently been killed. The dated manuscript (1564) contains six illustrations. [ESK]

Madden, Frederic, ed. *Syr Gawayne*. London: Bannatyne Club, 1839.

JETER, K.W., blends science fiction and fantasy in *Morlock Night* (1979), a sequel to H.G. Wells's *The Time Machine*. A reborn Arthur, initially unaware of his true identity, must restore the power of Excalibur so that he and Merlin can thwart the plans of the evil Morlocks to use the time machine to invade nineteenth-century England from the distant future. [RHT]

Jeter, K.W. *Morlock Night*. New York: DAW, 1979.

JEWETT, ELEANORE MYERS (1890–1967), American author, primarily of books for young readers. In *The Hidden Treasure of Glaston* (1946), she incorporates into the Glastonbury legend the story of Hugh, a young monk whose treacherous father slew Thomas Beckett. Hugh's lameness is cured by a vision of the Grail during the fire that destroyed much of Glastonbury Abbey in 1184. The treasure is the spiritual gift that he receives. [HT]

Jewett, Eleanore Myers. *The Hidden Treasure of Glaston*. New York: Viking; Toronto: Macmillan, 1946.

JOHN OF FORDUN, one of the most influential medieval Scottish chroniclers, wrote the Latin *Chronica Gentis Scotorum* (ca. 1385), sometimes called the *Scotichronicon*, a title more properly applied to the popular continuation of the work that Walter Bower wrote sometime between 1440 and 1447.

Apparently attempting to do for Scottish history what Geoffrey of Monmouth had done for British, Fordun drew upon earlier short chronicles and legends that gave the Scots a distinguished past and that offered evidence that Scotland was historically independent of England. Although Fordun presents Arthur as an admirable king ("beloved by almost all men"), he asserted that the British throne was not lawfully his but belonged to his legitimately conceived sister Anna or to Gawain and Mordred, the sons of Anna and her husband, the Scottish consul Lot. Arthur became king by necessity because of the threat from the Saxons and the youth of Gawain and Mordred. Mordred later rebelled because of Arthur's weak claim to the throne. Fordun's treatment of Arthur was the basis for the more hostile presentations in the later chronicles of Boece, Stewart, and Bellenden. Withrington has noted that two of the late fifteenth-century manuscripts of Fordun's chronicle, produced between 1480 and 1500, give the Latin epitaph found on Arthur's tomb at Glastonbury: *Hic jacet Arthurus rex quondam rexque futurus*. This is the same version of the epitaph found in Malory's *Morte Darthur*, the fifteenth-century metrical chronicle *Arthur*, and the manuscript of the Alliterative *Morte Arthure*, where it is added in another hand at the end of the romance. Its appearance in Fordun's Scottish chronicle offers further evidence that this version of the epitaph was fairly well known. (*See also* BOECE, HECTOR; BOWER, WALTER.) [EDK]

Johannis de Fordun. *Chronica Gentis Scotorum*, ed. W.F. Skene. Edinburgh: Edmonston and Douglas, 1871.

———. *John of Fordun's Chronicle of the Scottish Nation*, trans. F.J.H. Skene, ed. W.F. Skene. Edinburgh: Edmonston and Douglas, 1872.

Alexander, Flora. "Late Medieval Scottish Attitudes to the Figure of King Arthur: A Reassessment." *Anglia*, 93 (1975), 17–34.

Brie, Friedrich. *Die nationale Literatur Schottlands*. Halle: Niemeyer, 1937, pp. 317–53.

Fletcher, Robert Huntington. *The Arthurian Material in the Chronicles, Especially Those of Great Britain and France*. Boston: Ginn, 1906; 2nd ed. Roger Sherman Loomis. New York: Franklin, 1966, pp. 242–43.

Göller, K.H. "König Arthur in den schottischen Chroniken." *Anglia*, 80 (1962), 390–404.

Kennedy, Edward Donald. "Chronicles and Other Historical Writing." In *A Manual of the Writings in Middle English*, ed. A.E. Hartung. New Haven: Connecticut Academy of Arts and Sciences, 1981–89, Vol. 8, pp. 2679–80, 2891.

———. "John Hardyng and the Holy Grail," *Arthurian Literature*, 8 (1989), 185–206.

Withrington, John. "The Arthurian Epitaph in Malory's *Morte Darthur*." *Arthurian Literature*, 7 (1987), 103–04.

JOHN OF GLASTONBURY. In the mid-fourteenth century, John Seen, a monk of Glastonbury Abbey, composed his *Cronica sive Antiquitates Glastoniensis Ecclesie* ("Chronicle or the Antiquities of the Church of Glastonbury"), a comprehensive history of his monastery from earliest times to his own day. In his chronicle, John included a detailed account of the 1190–91 discovery of King Arthur's body in the abbey cemetery and several Arthurian genealogies. More important, he quoted fragments from the hitherto unknown prophecy of Melkin the Bard, in which the Grail of French romance tradition reappeared in a metamorphosed form as two cruets containing the blood and sweat of Jesus. [JPC]

John of Glastonbury. *The Chronicle of Glastonbury Abbey: An Edition, Translation and Study of John of Glastonbury's "Cronica sive Antiquitates Glastoniensis Ecclesie,"* ed. James P. Carley, trans. David Townsend. Woodbridge, Suffolk: Boydell and Brewer, 1984.

JOHNSON, BARBARA FERRY, American university professor and author of *Lionors* (1975), a sentimental historical romance based loosely upon Malory. It tells the story of the Earl of Sanam's daughter, who bore Arthur a child (in this instance a blind daughter). [RHT]

Johnson, Barbara Ferry. *Lionors*. New York: Avon, 1975.

JOHNSON, RICHARD (1573–1659), recounts in the euphuistical romance *Tom a Lincolne* (1599–1607) the adventures of the natural son of Arthur and Angellica, the Earl of London's daughter. He bestows the bell Great Tom on Lincoln in memory of Antonio, who fostered him after he was exposed in infancy. Marrying Prester John's daughter is the height of his brief good fortune. [CNS]

Johnson, Richard. *Tom a Lincolne*. In *A Collection of Early Prose Romances*, ed. William J. Thoms. 3 vols. London: Pickering, 1858, Vol. 2, pp. 219–361.

JONES, DAVID (1895–1974), partly construed the poet's task as the embodiment of "the mythus and deposits" constituting his or her own cultural matrix. Because no other tradition is "equally the common property of all the inhabitants of Britain," the myth of Arthur is central to Jones's writings. Most overtly Arthurian is "The Hunt" (1965) based on *Culhwch and Olwen*, while "The Sleeping Lord" (1967), *The Anathemata* (1952), and *In Parenthesis* (1937) are enriched by frequent allusion to Arthurian material. His sources are primarily Malory and the *Mabinogi*. [PD]

Jones, David. "The Myth of Arthur." In *Epoch and Artist*. London: Faber and Faber, 1959, pp. 212–59.

JONES, FRANK H., published *The Life and Death of King Arthur* in 1930. It was intended for performance by boys at Wellesley Preparatory School in Croydon, England. Three brief scenes, in prose, come from Malory; they portray Arthur drawing the sword from the stone, the institution of the quest for the Grail, and the dissolution of the Round Table. The final scene of this playlet artlessly stages lines from Tennyson's "Morte d'Arthur." [CNS]

Jones, Frank H. *The Life and Death of King Arthur*. London: Macmillan, 1930.

JONES, INIGO (1573–1652), English architect best remembered for his introduction of Renaissance architectural theory into Jacobean England. Jones devised costumes and scenery for masques presented at the Stuart court during the years 1604–40. Many of the fifty-seven masques contained chivalric allusions, but only two, *Prince Henry's Barriers* (written by Ben Jonson, presented on January 6, 1610, in honor of the prince's first bearing of arms) and *Britannia Triumphans* (written by William Lawes, presented on January 17, 1638, as the King's Twelfth Night Masque), have specific Arthurian reference, with Merlin appearing as a major character. Jones's taste for the Renaissance classical aesthetic is revealed in the few surviving drawings of these works, such as the designs for *Prince Henry's Barriers* (Collection, Duke of Devonshire), which include a costume for Merlin and the setting for Act I, "The Fallen House of Chivalry." (*See also* PAGEANT DESIGN [BRITISH].) [DNM]

Harris, John. "Jones, Inigo." In *Macmillan Encyclopedia of Architects*. New York: Free Press, 1982, Vol. 2, pp. 504–13.
Orgel, Stephen, and Roy Strong. *Inigo Jones: The Theatre of the Stuart Court*. 2 vols. London: Sotheby Parke Bernet, 1973.
Stong, Roy. *Festival Designs by Inigo Jones*. Catalogue, International Exhibitions Foundation, 1967–68.

JONES, KATHY, and LEONA AROHA, cofounders of Ariadne Productions, a community-theater association in Glastonbury concerned with myth and ritual in drama. During the 1980s, Jones wrote and directed a series of plays on mythic themes, staged in the Assembly Rooms, the former scene of Rutland Boughton's operatic activities. In 1989, she and Aroha collaborated on *Passages About Gwenhwyfar*, offering a radical reinterpretation of Arthur's queen as the Celtic grain-goddess, her true nature obscured by later legend. [GA]

JONES, THOMAS SAMUEL, JR. (1882–1932), American poet who fell under the influence of the mystical-spiritual strain of the Celtic Renaissance as exemplified by Fiona Macleod. Early Welsh Arthurian motifs and Grail imagery became prominent in his verse after his spiritual pilgrimages to Britain in the 1920s. Ten Arthurian poems, mostly sonnets, can be found in the collection *Shadow of the Perfect Rose* (1937). [DN]

Jones, Thomas Samuel. *Shadow of the Perfect Rose*. New York: Farrar and Rinehart, 1937.

JOSEP ABARAMATIA, LIVRO DE, a sixteenth-century copy of a lost Portuguese translation made in the late thirteenth or early fourteenth century of the first branch of the Post-Vulgate *Roman du Graal*. It survives also in fragmentary form in Castilian fragments (Salamanca, Biblioteca Universitaria 1877, and in Lope García de Salazar's *Libro de las bienandanzas e fortunas*). The Portuguese text (Lisbon, Torre do Tombo 643) is important for the reconstruction of the original French romance, since no French manuscript survives of the first part. However, some details, such as a reference to Wace, may indicate that the Portuguese version is not strictly a literal translation. [HLS]

Carter, Henry Hare, ed. *The Portuguese Book of Joseph of Arimathea*. Chapel Hill: University of North Carolina Press, 1967.

Castro, Ivo. "Sobre a Data da Introdução na Península Ibérica do Ciclo Arturiano da Post-Vulgata." *Boletim de Filologia*, 68 (1984), 81–98.

JOSEP ABARIMATIA, LIBRO DE, fourteenth-century fragments of a Castilian translation of the *Estoire del Saint Graal*, from the French Post-Vulgate; the narrative follows that of the Portuguese *Livro de Josep Abaramatia* but is missing the beginning and end. [NJL]

Pietsch, Karl, ed. *Spanish Grail Fragments*. Chicago: University of Chicago Press, 1924, Vol. 1, pp. 3–54.

JOSEPH OF ARIMATHEA. All four Gospels relate how Joseph, a rich man from Arimathea, obtained the body of Christ after the Crucifixion and laid it in the tomb. He is briefly sketched as a prominent Jew who had kept his discipleship a secret. In the apocryphal *Acts of Pilate* (part of a pseudo-Gospel ascribed to Nicodemus), he is said to have been imprisoned, and delivered by the risen Lord. When the Grail takes on its Christian form, and its provenance is explained in Robert de Boron's *Joseph* and the *Estoire del Saint Graal*, these hints are expanded. According to the romances, Joseph acquired the Grail and hid it in his house. When he was imprisoned, Christ appeared to him, gave him the Grail, and taught him its mysteries. It miraculously sustained him for more than forty years, till he was released by the emperor Vespasian, and set off with many companions on the adventures that brought the Grail to Britain. Its subsequent keepers were collaterally descended from him, and so was Galahad.

Joseph is also named as the founder of Christian Glastonbury. The precise relation between his two legendary roles is open to debate. No major author explicitly combines them before Tennyson. In the formative medieval phase, they are not wholly separate, but the links remain conjectural. While the romances show awareness of Glastonbury, none incontestably brings Joseph there, as monastic legend asserted. The earliest known text that does is an edition of the *De Antiquitate Glastoniensis Ecclesiae* of William of Malmesbury. Produced at Glastonbury Abbey ca. 1247, this edition declares that in A.D. 63, when the apostle Philip was in Gaul, he sent twelve missionaries to Britain under Joseph's leadership. A "barbarian king" granted them land at Glastonbury as a place to live. In honor of the Virgin Mary, they built the celebrated Old Church.

However, William's original treatise, written toward 1130, says virtually nothing of this. He notes a belief that the Old Church was built by disciples of Christ but does not commit himself to the story or give any names. The account of Joseph in the thirteenth-century recension is interpolated. It is commonly supposed that the interpolator annexed him from Grail romance, probably from the *Estoire del Saint Graal*, thus providing the community with a bogus founder who was both biblical and Arthurian and safeguarding its claim to an early beginning.

This view may be correct, but the issue is by no means as simple as it is often made out to be. As between the Grail cycle and the corpus of Glastonbury legend, the flow is not all in one direction. Robert de Boron, writing before the close of the twelfth century, knows a story of early Christians making their way to Somerset. One or two romance passages seem to show awareness of conditions at Glastonbury long before the authors' time. If these carry any weight, they must reflect abbey tradition. The abbey's date for Joseph's arrival, A.D. 63, is incompatible with the Grail version and argues another source, rather than a borrowing. John of Glastonbury's fourteenth-century *Cronica* does adapt incidents from romances, but it also includes a strange oracular text, the "Prophecy of Melkin," which mentions Joseph in terms implying—again—some other source than Grail matter.

The fundamental problem is "Why Joseph?" He is a most unlikely choice either as Grail-bearer or as missionary to Britain. Christian legend credited the island with much more impressive visitors, among them St. Paul and even St. Peter. Yet the cautious, little-traveled, and (one would think) elderly Joseph was preferred to them as hero. The usual opinion is that his role as possessor of the Grail was prior. He came to be associated with Britain because the Grail was; as its possessor, he had to be the person responsible for getting it there. The question is why he should have had the Grail, since he was certainly not present at the Last Supper. One theory is that the connection arose from ecclesiastical symbolism. At Mass, the priest laying the paten on the chalice was said by some commentators to represent Joseph closing the tomb with a stone. This would give him a link with the chalice, and hence with the Grail as prototype of all chalices. But the symbolism was not very familiar, and it may be questioned whether there is any proved instance of a motif like this creating a literal legend. Loomis's suggestion that the Grail-Joseph linkage was due to a kind of wordplay (*cors* in Old French meaning both "horn" and "body"—in this case a pagan horn of plenty and the body of Christ) failed to carry conviction.

In the absence of a clear reason for the Grail's evoking the figure of Joseph, it is reasonable to try the alternative: that he was connected with Britain first, as an early Christian who went there or as an associate of Christians who did. On this showing, he became the Grail-bearer when the Grail was given its Christian meaning and an apostolic figure had to be found who could account for its journey westward. A hagiographic tradition, strong enough to give Joseph a preferred status over St. Paul and the rest, might underlie both romance and the Glastonbury story. The simplest hypothesis, of course, is the naive one: that the legend is (in substance) true and he did come. It cannot be disproved! But a notion about his British presence could have begun with some such thing as a misunderstood inscription. The French legend of Lazarus coming to Marseilles, with his sisters Mary and Martha, was inspired by the memorial of a bishop of the same name who died there in the fifth century. An antiquarian fancy along these lines might have taken shape in Wales, as other legends of early missions did, and drifted into England and thence to France, in common with the rest of the Celtic lore that the Arthurian literary growth drew in. It may be noteworthy that Joseph is linked with Philip in an eighth-century Georgian manuscript telling how they built a church at Lydda dedicated to Mary. If this is relevant at all, its relevance is not to the romances but to the Glastonbury story, as possibly a transplanted version.

That story underwent developments. In John's *Cronica*, Joseph was made out to have been an ancestor of Arthur and to have brought to Britain not the Grail but two "cruets" containing drops of the blood and sweat of Christ. Later, he became involved in the Marseilles legend, having supposedly come to Gaul with Lazarus and his companions and then journeyed on to Britain. Also, by a misreading of the dates in the abbey's account of him, his British advent was pushed back to A.D. 31. The shift was prompted by a wish to establish seniority for the Church in England, on the ground that Joseph arrived before any Christians reached France or Spain.

Other legends are almost certainly post-Reformation. At Glastonbury, Joseph is said to have driven his staff into the ground; it became the original Holy Thorn tree, blossoming at Christmas, as its descendants still do, approximately. He is also said to have been Mary's uncle and to have brought Jesus on a visit to Britain as a boy. Defenders of the literal truth of this tale, and of others about his British career, urge the possibility that he was engaged in the tin trade. [GA]

Ashe, Geoffrey. *Avalonian Quest*. London: Methuen, 1982; rev. ed. Fontana, 1984, pp. 54–58, 76–97.

Lagorio, Valerie M. "The Evolving Legend of St. Joseph of Glastonbury." *Speculum*, 46 (1971), 209–31.

Loomis, Roger Sherman. *The Grail: From Celtic Myth to Christian Symbol*. Cardiff: University of Wales Press, 1963, pp. 224–27, 251–70.

Scott, John. *The Early History of Glastonbury*. Woodbridge, Suffolk: Boydell and Brewer, 1981, pp. 43–47.

Treharne, R.F. *The Glastonbury Legends*. London: Cresset, 1967, pp. 26–31, 39–40, 114–29.

JOSEPH OF ARIMATHIE (ca. 1375), a semialliterative Middle English fragment of 709 lines (extant only in MS Vernon), is drawn from the Vulgate *Estoire del Saint Graal*. An encomium to Joseph as an apostolic evangelist, the poem accords well with the devotional works, hagiographic writings, and other homiletic romances that comprise the manuscript. The *Joseph* is a greatly abridged adaptation of its Old French source. The author concentrates on Joseph's post-Crucifixion adventures, as he, carrying the sacred container of Christ's Precious Blood, leads his family and followers westward, and en route converts the rulers and people of the city of Sarras. The English adaptation differs from its source in two major ways. First, it treats the Holy Grail not as a wonder-working talisman linked with Arthur's reign but rather as a reliquary of the Precious Blood, with which the legendary Joseph of Arimathea was associated. Second, it consistently deemphasizes the part played by Josephe, Joseph's fictional son. Although there is no reference to England or Glastonbury, apart from one fleeting reference to the "Auenturus of Bruytayne" (ll. 231–32), the portrait of Joseph agrees with Glastonbury's spurious claim to him as founder of its abbey and protoevangelist of Britain. [VML]

Skeat, Walter W., ed. *Joseph of Arimathie*. London: Trübner, 1871.

Lawton, David A., ed. *Joseph of Arimathea: A Critical Edition*. New York: Garland, 1983.

Lagorio, Valerie M. "The *Joseph of Arimathie*: English Hagiography in Transition." *Medievalia et Humanistica*, n.s., 6 (1975), 91–101.

JOSEPHES (Josephe, Josephus), in the Vulgate Cycle, Joseph of Arimathea's son and guardian of the Grail. The *Estoire del Saint Graal* and the *Queste del Saint Graal* tell us that Josephes is the First Bishop, who was chosen by Christ, which possibly reflects a certain degree of dissent from the Church on the part of the author. In the *Queste*, Josephes uses the Grail to celebrate Mass with Perceval, Galahad, and Bors. Josephes is not to be confused with Flavius Josephus, the Jewish historian whose Latin book the *Perlesvaus* claims as its source. [SW]

JOYCE, JAMES (1882–1941), Irish writer. His *Ulysses*, though it contains elements of encyclopedic cataloguing, a technique that would achieve major emphasis in *Finnegans Wake*, makes no use of Arthurian characters. The *Wake*, however, incorporates Arthurian elements within its densely embroidered patterns, primarily because the background is Celtic, and the Arthur-Guenevere-Lancelot and Mark-Isolde-Tristan triangles parallel the Irish legend of Finn-Gráinne-Diarmaid that has its analogue in Joyce's work. *Finnegans Wake* is ostensibly set in the Dublin suburb of Chapelizod (the chapel of Isolde), and the daughter of the house is variously named Issy, Iseult, Isolde, Isabelle. Joyce relied heavily on Bédier and Wagner for the borrowings, and on Dante for the pandering Galliotto ("dantellising peaches in the lingerous longerous book of the dark. Look at this passage about Galilleotto!"). Yet Malory's *Morte Darthur* plays its part, for both author and title are cited: "melodi of malodi, she, lalage of lyonesses, and him, her knave errant"; "The merthe dirther!"

Generally, the Arthurian lore provides only a thin thread woven through the elaborate fabric, the names of the personae doubled and trebled with those of others: "lends a lot . . . erdor . . . mierlin roundtableturning" leads to "*Arthurgink's hussies and Everguin's men.*" The death of King Arthur has a particular importance in relation to the death-and-resurrection pattern of the *Wake* in association with Finn—"Arthur-honoured (some Finn, some Finn avant!)"—especially when the "Old Man" can be viewed as upended by a son-figure: "The author, in fact, was mardred." Resurrection, however, is always implied: "till Arthur comes againus." Joyce's cavalier erudition informs the text ("the matter of Brittas more than anarthur"), but the manner is often enigmatic and perhaps haphazard, as in the conflation of "Camelot, prince of dinmurk." [BBens]

Joyce, James. *Finnegans Wake*. London: Faber; New York: Viking, 1939.

JOYOUS GARD (Joyeuse Garde), Lancelot's castle, formerly called Dolorous Gard because of a sinister enchantment. Lancelot captures it and breaks the spell. Inside, he finds a tomb with his own name on it and knows this to be his destined home and eventual resting place. Arthur and Guenevere visit the castle as his guests, and "Joyous Gard" becomes its new name. When Guenevere is brought to Carlisle for execution, Lancelot rescues her and takes her to Joyous Gard; but the tragic strife that results causes it to revert to its "dolorous" name. After Lancelot's death, his body is taken there for burial.

Joyous Gard is supposedly in northern England. The Vulgate Cycle places it near the Humber, but the English preference is to put it on the site of a known castle in Northumberland. Malory offers a choice: "Some men say it was Alnwick and some men say it was Bamburgh." The Bamburgh identification may not be wholly fanciful. The present castle beside the North Sea occupies the site of a much earlier fort. Toward the middle of the sixth century, the chieftain of the Angles who had settled here, Ida, asserted his independence by taking possession and raising a stockade. Furthermore, the place was a fort of the Britons even before Ida. Its original name, preserved with various spellings in copies of Nennius, was *Din Guayrdi*. In other words, it had a name sounding rather like "Gard." Apparently, this item of topography passed through Wales to the romancers, and was reinterpreted to give Lancelot a plausible home.

If this is so, it shows that information concerning pre-Anglo-Saxon places, effaced in England by the Conquest, could survive among the Britons' descendants and be rediscovered, even repatriated. That process may explain the medieval emergence of Amesbury as an "Arthurian" town (*see* AMBROSIUS AURELIANUS) and underlie some of the associations of Glastonbury. [GA]

Morris, John. *The Age of Arthur*. New York: Scribner, 1973, pp. 231–32.

JUNG, EMMA, scientist and wife of the Swiss C.G. Jung, founder of psychoanalytic depth psychology, began in the 1930s a work on the Grail legend that was published after her death by M.-L. von Franz in 1960 under joint authorship: *Die Graalslegende in psychologischer Sicht* (published in English as *The Grail Legend*). Using alchemical writings, they explain the "Graal," using the categories of depth psychology, as a mystical symbol for the human self that bears strong traits of the female, the so-called *anima*. The book has had as great an influence in the German-speaking world as the works of Jessie L. Weston have had among English-speakers; almost all later recreations of the Grail story name it or are influenced by it. A similar effect in the nonscientific world is otherwise found only in the Grail interpretations of the anthroposophy of Rudolf Steiner, and later, in the works of French Celticist Jean Markale, the Indologist Heinrich Zimmer, and especially the feminist-oriented literary scientist Heide Göttner-Abendroth. [UM/WLS]

Jung, Emma, and M.-L. von Franz. *Die Graalslegende in psychologischer Sicht*. Zurich and Stuttgart: Rascher, 1960.

JUVENILE FICTION IN ENGLISH. Arthurian fiction and illustration specifically intended for young readers originated in the Victorian age, when the knight regained his medieval significance as an ideal figure. The chief source was Malory's *Morte Darthur*, presented in abridgments and adaptations that modernized the language (in varying degrees) but obscured the adultery of the courtly lovers and the Catholic significance of the Grail quest. As in Caxton's preface, a didactic motivation was claimed, with emphasis on the "gentlemanly" qualities of Arthur and his knights. Sidney Lanier, whose *The Boy's King Arthur* (1880) was frequently reprinted, asserted of Launcelot's "majestic manhood" that "larger behavior is not shown us anywhere in English literature." In his adaptations, *The Story of King Arthur and His Knights* (1903), *The Story of the Champions of the Round Table* (1905), *The Story of Sir Launcelot and His Companions* (1907), and *The Story of the Grail and the Passing of Arthur* (1910), Howard Pyle also emphasized moral values. Not only did the knights afford perfect examples of courage and humility, but Arthur himself was "the most honorable, gentle knight who ever lived in all the world."

While Malory is the chief source, adapters have also used Geoffrey of Monmouth's *Historia*, the Welsh *Mabinogion* (translated by Charlotte Guest in 1838–49), and Middle English romances, such as *Sir Gawain and the Green Knight*; for the Tristan story, the Old French metrical version of Thomas is sometimes preferred. Development is straightforward, with emphasis on story rather than on setting or character. Minor characters are omitted and major characters, such as the two Elaines and the various fées, may be fused. Retellings that remain reasonably faithful to Malory while accommodating their sources include Roger Lancelyn Green's *King Arthur and His Knights of the Round Table* (1953) and Rosemary Sutcliff's fine series.

Aside from recounting traditional material, modern Arthurian fiction for juveniles has taken two directions—the historical novel and the fantasy. Historical novelists like Henry Treece in *The Eagles Have Flown* (1970) or Rosemary Sutcliff in *The Lantern Bearers* (1959) generally localize the action in that period of the Dark Ages when a historical Arthur would have lived. Relying on Gildas, Bede, Nennius, and Geoffrey of Monmouth to provide characters and events, and on such historians and archaeologists as R.G. Collingwood, John Morris, and Leslie Alcock for social history, they depict the chaotic time between the withdrawal of the Roman legions from Britain in the fifth century and the establishment of Saxon kingdoms in the sixth. Artos the Bear is essentially a battle-leader, "a ruthless and possibly half-barbaric Celt" in Treece's conception, "the shining point of the arrowhead" and "one whom men would feel that they were following into the light," in Sutcliff's.

Writers of Arthurian fantasy have two paramount preoccupations—Celtic mythology and time shift. The former provides supernatural characters (e.g., Merlin, Morgan le Fay-Morrigan, the Lady of the Lake, the "Old Ones"), magical artifacts (e.g., Excalibur, the Treasures of the Tuatha De Danaan), and, most important, an otherworld consisting of a *locus amoenus* (Avalon) or a hollow hill. The hollow-hill motif associated with the legend of Arthur's sleep until the time of his return (*see* CAVE LEGEND) appears in William Mayne's *Earthfasts* (1969) and Alan Garner's *The Weirdstone of Brisingamen* (1960). Andre Norton creates an eclectic Avalon that contains Excalibur, Merlin's ring, and Huon's silver horn in *Steel Magic* (1967) and unicorns and flying saucers in *Here Abide Monsters* (1974).

Time shift may involve transition between this world and the otherworld or between the present and the past. In *Earthfasts*, the removal of the otherworld's time mechanism—a candle in Arthur's cavern beneath Garebridge Castle, Yorkshire—brings into present time a drummer boy who had disappeared in 1742, a boggart, giants, and King Arthur with his knights. Peter Dickinson's *The Weathermonger* (1968) describes the return of the Dark Ages to England because Merlin, discovered in his cavern and kept high on morphine, "was muddled and wanted everything to be just as he was used to it." Penelope Lively uses memory, both individual and collective, to bridge present and past in *The Whispering Knights* (1971), where three modern children meet Morgan le Fay. Susan Cooper's The Dark Is Rising series presents movement in both directions, with Merriman (Merlin) as the transitional agent. The hero, Will Stanton, moves into the past to observe the building of a Roman fortress, the battle of Badon, and a Victorian Christmas party, while the Grail resurfaces in modern Cornwall and Guenevere brings Arthur's son Bran to grow up in contemporary Wales.

Common elements in Arthurian fantasy are a young protagonist assisted by siblings or friends, a quest to acquire magical artifacts, a supernatural guide, a confrontation between good and evil in which the child plays a crucial role, and a good deal of folklore associated with the "Old Ones." The supreme example of the genre, T.H. White's *The Sword in the Stone*, successfully combines comic fantasy, medieval social history, and moral purpose, as the young Arthur is taught the proper use of power by means of formal lessons, forest adventures, and transformations that illustrate Merlin's precept, "Education is experience and the essence of experience is self-reliance." The continuing use of the Arthurian legends in children's literature suggests that Arthur's cry "Resurgam" is as relevant now as it ever was in the past. (*See also* BOOK ILLUSTRATION; ENGLISH, ARTHURIAN LITERATURE IN [MODERN]; GERMAN ARTHURIAN LITERATURE [MODERN].)

[MAW]

Curry, Jane L. "Children's Reading and the Arthurian Tales." In *King Arthur Through the Ages*, ed. Valerie M. Lagorio and Mildred Leake Day. 2 vols. New York: Garland, 1990, Vol. 2, pp. 149–64.

Montgomery, Catherine J. "The Dialectical Approach of Writers of Children's Arthurian Retellings." *Arthurian Interpretations*, 3 (1988), 79–88.

Thompson, Raymond H. *The Return from Avalon: A Study of the Arthurian Legend in Modern Fiction*. Westport, Conn.: Greenwood, 1985.

k

KAISER, GEORG (1878–1945), the most significant dramatist of the German Expressionist movement. However, his transitional drama *König Hahnrei* ("King Cuckold," 1910, first staged 1913)—influenced by Gottfried von Strassburg and Wagner but based primarily on Joseph Bédier—is an unsuccessful mixture of Neoromantic psychologizing and expressionistic language and setting. Mark obtains vicarious pleasure from his voyeuristic and yet repressed awareness of Tristan and Isolde's affair, whereas the lovers' attraction for each other derives from its illicit nature. Mark eliminates anyone who threatens the stability of this perverse romantic triangle. [RWK]

Kaiser, Georg. *Werke*, ed. Walther Huder. Frankfurt: Propyläen, 1971, Vol. 1.

Batts, Michael. "Tristan and Isolde in Modern Literature." *Seminar*, 5 (1969), 79–91.

Schüler, Ernst. *Georg Kaiser*. New York: Twayne, 1971.

KANE, GIL, and JOHN JAKES, authors of *Excalibur!* (1980), a fast-moving adventure story in which Guinevere and Lancelot are lovers before her marriage to Arthur but not after, Nimue is Morgan disguised, Galahad discovers that England is the Grail, and Modred poisons Arthur and fights him with Saxon troops. [MAG]

Kane, Gil, and John Jakes. *Excalibur!* New York: Dell, 1960.

KARR, PHYLLIS ANN, American author of an Arthurian murder mystery, *The Idylls of the Queen* (1982), based upon a short episode in Malory (Caxton's Book XVIII, Chapters 1–8). Narrated by Sir Kay, the novel tells of the death of Sir Patrise by poisoned apple and of Kay's attempts to discover the truth of the matter in order to clear Guinevere of suspicion. A later story, "Two Bits of Embroidery" (1988), tells the story of the Fair Maid of Astolat and her death for love of Sir Lancelot, using as counterpoint a story of a scullery maid whose love for Sir Kay leads to a better life for herself. Karr is also the author of *The King Arthur Companion*, a reference book written to support an Arthurian role-playing game, *King Arthur Pendragon* (*see* GAMES). [SRR]

Karr, Phyllis Ann. *The Idylls of the Queen*. New York: Ace, 1982.

———. *The King Arthur Companion*. Albany, Calif.: Chaosium, 1983.

———. "Two Bits of Embroidery." In *Invitation to Camelot: An Arthurian Anthology of Short Stories*, ed. Parke Godwin. New York: Ace, 1988, pp. 31–45.

KATZ, WELWYN WILTON, Canadian author of novels for younger readers, including *The Third Magic* (1988). This innovative fantasy places the opposition between Morgan le Fay and Merlin within a broader conflict between the First Magic of the Circle, wielded by women, and the Second Magic of the Line, wielded by men, originating on the world of Nwm. The Sword in the Stone, Grail, and Bleeding Head (Bran) are symbols of the Third Magic that seeks to transcend the conflict. [RHT]

Katz, Welwyn Wilton. *The Third Magic*. Vancouver and Toronto: Groundwood/Douglas and McIntyre, 1988.

KAY (Cei, Keu, Kei, Cayous), Arthur's seneschal, a ubiquitous, but never a major, character in Arthurian romance. Authors from Malory to T.H. White and beyond present him as the son of Ector or Hector, who also reared Arthur until the future king drew the sword from the stone. Kay is neither clown, coward, nor traitor, but a scoffer, scapegoat, troublemaker, and foil who contrasts with the protagonist, such as Gawain, Lancelot, or Yvain. Chrétien de Troyes invented situations that were to become typical in later narrative. In the *Chevalier au lion*, Keu unfairly insults Calogrenant for rising at Queen Guenièvre's unexpected arrival, and in the *Chevalier de la charrete* he beguiles Arthur into granting him the honor of pursuing the Queen's kidnaper, at which task he meets immediate and humiliating defeat. Such events are mimicked by imitators, like Paien de Maisières's *La Mule sans frein* and the anonymous *L'Atre* *périlleux*. Because of his behavior, he is often linked with the *gab*, an Old French word whose primary meaning was "mockery." Keu himself is a *gabeor* in the Didot-*Perceval*, and in the First Continuation of the *Perceval* he is mocked by Arthur's knights.

Chrétien's characterization depicts Keu as strangely favored by Arthur, an attitude that is very likely traceable to Celtic sources. In *Culhwch and Olwen*, Cei is an exceptional hero of mythological origins. He rides the salmon and can breathe under water for nine days and nights. He is capable of transforming himself into a giant. He is shrewd but cruel, a victorious warrior and an advocate of courtly etiquette. In *The Dream of Rhonabwy*, Cei is considered the most handsome rider in Arthur's army. Elsewhere, he appears as a hardy drinker and an angry warrior. Such traits, admirable in an epic hero like Roland, were inappropriate in the polite courtly society of twelfth-century France. Thus, scholars have assumed that Chrétien was reflecting a new social attitude while at the same time representing through Arthur the old respect for Cei, which Welsh poets maintained throughout the Middle Ages.

The German adapters follow Chrétien's lead, though Hartmann von Aue underscores Keu's maliciousness and Wolfram makes him an exemplary expression of conventional courtly order. Later French imitators, especially those who merely adopted the Arthurian framework, turned Keu into a likable character (*Durmart le Gallois*) or even a bashful lover (Girart d'Amiens's *Escanor*), but in the English romances Sir Kay retains his mocking spirit (Malory's "Tale of Gareth"; *The Avowing of King Arthur, Sir Gawain, Sir Kay, and Baldwin of Britain*). In the short Dutch *Walewein ende Keye*, he slanders Gawain and is proved a scornful liar. In sum, he underwent a blending of traditions: the revered hero, the epic warrior, the wicked seneschal, and even kitchen humorist, by a fusion of his name with Old French *keu* 'cook.' [JLG]

Dean, Christopher. "Sir Kay in Medieval English Romances: An Alternative Tradition." *English Studies in Canada*, 9 (1983), 125–35.

Gallais, Pierre. "Le Sénéchal Keu et les romanciers français du XIIe et du XIIIe siècles." Diss., Poitiers, 1967.

Gowans, Linda M. *Cei and the Arthurian Legend*. Cambridge: Brewer, 1988.

Haupt, Jürgen. *Der Truchsess Keie im Artusroman*. Berlin: Schmidt, 1971.

Herman, H.J. "Sir Kay: A Study of the Character of the Seneschal of King Arthur's Court." Diss., Pennsylvania, 1960.

KAY, GUY GAVRIEL, Canadian author of the Fionavar Tapestry (1984–86), sets this involving fantasy trilogy in the alternate world of Fionavar. Among the many champions and supernatural powers who gather to fight for the Light in a cataclysmic struggle against the Dark is Arthur the Warrior, doomed to fight whenever summoned to expiate his sin of slaying the children in his attempt to kill Mordred. In Fionavar, he finds his devoted hound Cavall, the bard Taliesin, and a reborn Guinevere; he himself revives a sleeping Lancelot on a raid to Caer Sedat (Caer Sidi). For their heroic self-sacrifice and devotion, all five are finally freed from the pattern of continuous struggle, and they sail off to their final rest. [RHT]

Kay, Guy Gavriel. *The Summer Tree: The Fionavar Tapestry Book One*. New York: Arbor House, 1984.

———. *The Wandering Fire: The Fionavar Tapestry Book Two*. New York: Arbor House, 1986.

———. *The Darkest Road: The Fionavar Tapestry Book Three*. New York: Arbor House, 1986.

KEITH, CHESTER, described his *Queen's Knight* (1920) as "neither a mere romance of adventure nor a historical novel" but a prose epic. Keith's treatment of the familiar Lancelot-Guenevere material reflects his belief that "there is only one gift a man may not give to his dearest friend—and that is the woman he loves for if he does that he breaks the thread of fate." [MAW]

Keith, Chester. *Queen's Knight*. London: Allen and Unwin, 1920.

KELLIWIC (Celliwig). A Welsh Triad lists the "Three Tribal Thrones of the Island of Britain," at places where Arthur used to hold court. The northern one, it says, was at Pen Rhionydd, possibly near Stranraer in Galloway. The Welsh one was at St. David's. The Cornish one was at Kelliwic or Celliwig. This last name preserves a tradition reaching back beyond medieval fancy. Kelliwic in Cornwall is mentioned as an Arthurian residence before any recorded ideas about Caerleon or Camelot. It figures not only in the Triads but in the Welsh tale *Culhwch and Olwen*. Patriotism would surely have located Arthur in Wales if it could. Kelliwic attests a belief that he had a home—perhaps even his principal home—outside; a belief too firmly rooted to challenge.

Kelliwic means "woodland." The best candidate is probably Castle Killibury or Kelly Rounds, a pre-Roman Iron Age hill fort near Wadebridge. Post-Roman reoccupation, as at Castle Dore, might have led to its acquiring a certain importance through proximity to the trade route from sea to sea. There are other claimants, notably Callington. In no case is there any known evidence for Arthur's literal presence. Kelliwic, however identified, is simply an attempt to give local exactitude to his deep-rooted association with the West Country. At least, it has not been proved to be more.

The Triads summarize a story making it the scene of aggression by Mordred. He and his men raided it and "consumed all," and he dragged Guenevere from her chair and struck her (or worse). A reprisal by Arthur was a major step toward the catastrophe of Camlann. Here, Arthur and Mordred sound like feuding equals. The conception of Mordred as deputy ruler and traitor seems to have originated with Geoffrey of Monmouth, who combined Welsh tradition with a separate "treachery" theme. Though he still put the catastrophe in Cornwall, he dropped Kelliwic. [GA]

Ashe, Geoffrey. *A Guidebook to Arthurian Britain*. Wellingborough: Aquarian, 1983, pp. 129–31.

Bromwich, Rachel. *Trioedd Ynys Prydein*. Cardiff: University of Wales Press, 1961; 2nd ed. 1978, pp. 3–4.

Loomis, Roger Sherman, ed. *Arthurian Literature in the Middle Ages*. Oxford: Clarendon, 1959, pp. 47, 53.

KENDON, FRANK, composed *Tristram* (1934), a narrative poem in nine sections, connected by songs sung by Tristram. Opening with the journey of the lovers from Ireland, it concludes with their death in Brittany. [RHT]

Kendon, Frank. *Tristram*. London: Dent, 1934.

KENNEALY, PATRICIA, American author of The Keltiad (1984–), a series that blends science fiction and fantasy as it transposes the ancient Celtic world and its customs into a space-faring future. Of the nine projected novels, three, known as the Aeron trilogy, have been published to date. In order to repel alien invaders, Aeron, queen of the Kelts, must recover the Thirteen Treasures that disappeared with King Arthur after the space battle of Camlann. Her guide is Taliesin's obscure poem *The Spoils of Annwn*. The author is currently engaged in writing about these earlier events in the next part of the series, the Arthurian trilogy; the first novel, *The Hawk's Gray Feather*, will follow Arthur's career up to the outer-space equivalent of Badon. [RHT]

Kennealy, Patricia. *The Copper Crown: A Novel of The Keltiad*. New York: Bluejay, 1984.

———. *The Throne of Scone: A Book of the Keltiad*. New York: Bluejay, 1986.

———. *The Silver Branch: A Novel of the Keltiad*. New York: New American Library, 1988.

KENT, WILLIAM (1685–1748), English architect and designer, began his career as a painter but soon, under the patronage of Lord Burlington, turned to architecture and landscape design. As a member of the intellectual circle around Queen Caroline, wife of George II, Kent was called on to design gardens and buildings on the grounds of Richmond Palace, where in 1735 he created one of his most popular, or notorious, works—Merlin's Cave. This "cave above ground" (as it was satirized in Bolingbroke's journal *The Craftsman*) was a decorative garden pavilion, Palladian in overall design with central block and lower flanking wings, but having a Gothic entrance and thatched roofs. Inside, in Gothic niches, wax figures represented Merlin and his secretary, Queen Elizabeth and her nurse, Elizabeth of York (queen of Henry VII), and Minerva. Edmund Curll published a description of the cave in 1736, and Swift made it the subject of satirical epigrams. Nevertheless, Merlin's Cave caught the public fancy; taverns were named after it, and the owners of a coffeehouse set up a model for the entertainment of the customers. Dryden's opera *King Arthur* was revived as *Merlin or the British Enchanter*, and Covent Garden used Kent's interior design as a set for *The Royal Chace*. Capability Brown destroyed Merlin's Cave when he redesigned the gardens later in the century.

Kent's work as an illustrator is less well known, but included illustrations for Spenser's *Faerie Queene*, done in 1751. [MS]

Allen, B. Sprague. *Tides in English Taste (1619–1800)*. Cambridge: Harvard University Press, 1937, Vol. 2, pp. 135–38.

Jourdain, Margaret. *The Work of William Kent*. London: Country Life, 1948, pp. 24, 48, 73 (ill. for *The Faerie Queene*, figs. 12 and 13).

KESTEN, HERMANN, German-born author of the story "Tristan und Isalde" (1957), an adaptation of Gottfried von Strassburg's *Tristan*. Kesten departs from his model most significantly in his accounts of the hero's parents and of the deaths of the lovers. [SSch/PWM]

Kesten, Hermann. "Tristan und Isalde." In *Ders.: Die schönsten Liebesgeschichten der Welt*. Vienna, Munich, and Basel: Desch Verlag, 1957.

KIESERITZSKY, INGO VON, along with Karin Bellingkrodt, composed a dialogue for radio entitled "Tristan und Isolde im Wald von Morois oder der zerstreute Diskurs" ("Tristan and Isolde in the Forest of Morois, or the Diffuse Discourse"), which subsequently appeared in book

49. William Kent, "Arthur Slays the Giant Orgoglio and Releases the Redcross Knight" (illustration for Spenser, *The Faerie Queene*). (Courtesy of The Newberry Library, Chicago.)

form (1987). Tristan and Isolde live in the Cave of Lovers (following Gottfried von Strassburg) but are constantly irritated with each other. Using the example of the medieval couple, the authors show, with irony, wit, and continual contemporary allusion, that love in Edenic isolation is impossible. [UM/WCM]

Kieseritzky, Ingomar, and Karin Bellingkrodt. *Tristan und Isolde im Wald von Morois oder der zerstreute Diskurs*. Graz: Droschl, 1987.

KING, BARAGWANATH, composed "The Coming of Arthur" (1925), a dramatic poem based on Geoffrey of Monmouth that describes the events surrounding the conception of Arthur by Uther and Igerna. [RHT]

King, Baragwanath. "The Coming of Arthur." In *Arthur and Others in Cornwall*. London: Macdonald, 1925, pp. 7–19.

"KING ARTHUR AND KING CORNWALL," a fragmentary ballad preserved in the Percy Folio. It bears comparison with the Old French *Pèlerinage de Charlemagne*. While engaged in a search for a Round Table that, according to the shrewish Guinevere, is infinitely superior to that which he already possesses, Arthur happens upon the castle of King Cornwall. Cornwall is a magician who exercises mastery over Arthur and his knights until they are successful in conjuring a seven-headed fiend and in procuring a magical wand, steed, horn, and sword—the instruments of Cornwall's power. [JN]

Child, Francis James, ed. *The English and Scottish Popular Ballads*. Boston: Houghton-Mifflin, 1884, Vol. 1, pp. 274–88.

"KING ARTHUR'S DEATH." Although its sources are the Stanzaic *Le Morte Arthur* and Malory, this sixteenth-century continuation of the ballad known as "The Legend of

King Arthur" affords us an interesting variation on the familiar theme of Arthur's passing. After the battle against Mordred, Lukin (as opposed to Bedivere) disposes of Excalibur and returns to the spot where he had left the dying Arthur, only to discover that the King has vanished. Notwithstanding Lukin's speculation at the conclusion of the ballad, that Arthur may be on the barge seen leaving the shore, the actual whereabouts and fate of the King remain shrouded in mystery. [JN]

Hales, John W., and Frederick J. Furnivall, eds. *Bishop Percy's Folio Manuscript*. London: Trübner, 1867-68, Vol. 1, pp. 501-07.

KINROSS, MARTHA, author of *Tristram and Isoult* (1913). This three-act play in blank verse opens at a tournament in Camelot, continues in Tintagel (where a treacherous Mark tries to kill both lovers), and concludes with the lovers' death in Brittany. Although melodramatic, it gives greater emphasis to the woman's point of view than usual. [RHT]

Kinross, Martha. *Tristram and Isoult*. London: Macmillan, 1913.

KONRAD VON STOFFELN, author of *Gauriel von Muntabel*, a verse romance (4,100 lines) written in southwestern Germany probably in the later thirteenth century. The poem is preserved in two fifteenth-century manuscripts and an earlier fragment. The texts of the full manuscripts differ substantially in length. In the longer, the work is attributed to Konrad von Stoffeln, who has not been identified but may have belonged to the noble Hohenstoffeln family.

Gauriel is rejected by his wife because he vaunts her beauty. (Apparently she is a supernatural being whose marriage to him was not to be revealed.) Before leaving him, she makes him hideously ugly so that other women will not be interested in him. After six months of suffering, he sets out to find her, accompanied by a ram he has trained to fight, and soon receives a letter from her in which she promises forgiveness and restoration of his beauty if he will bring three great heroes of Arthur's court captive to her kingdom, Fluratrone. Gauriel pitches his tent at the edge of a forest within Arthur's sight. When a damsel is sent to inquire his business, he detains her and vows to hold her prisoner until a knight defeats him. This sets in motion a long series of single combats in which Gauriel defeats many knights of the Round Table and kills some, finally triumphing over Walban, Gawan, and Iwein. With these heroes, and joined by Erec (who had been away from court on an adventure), Gauriel proceeds to Fluratrone, overcomes monstrous interdictors, and is reconciled with his wife.

Two weeks later, he decides that he must spend a year at the Round Table to make up for his detention of the damsel. Arthur gives a great feast of welcome for the five worthies. One day, Gauriel, Erec, and Pliamin hear that a daughter of the Count of Asterian has been kidnaped. They track her down, Gauriel defeats the kidnaper, and all return to Arthur's court, where Gauriel's wife joins him for the final festivities.

The narrative seems remarkably weak in proportion, motivation, and integration of episodes. Borrowings from the romances of Hartmann von Aue abound (e.g., the animal companion and the year's absence, from *Iwein*); Hartmann's literary language and style are evidently the author's model. Critics have not found a theme or central idea in the romance, and some have judged it harshly. One might suspect parody or persiflage in the figure of Arthur's knight Pontifier, so grim that he never laughs except at burning churches or fatal head-wounds, and in the four-way fight between Iwein, Gauriel, the former's lion, and the latter's ram, but the tedious bulk of the narrative does not support such suspicions. [SLW]

Konrad von Stoffeln. *Gauriel von Muntabel*, ed. Ferdinand Khull. Graz: Leuschner und Lubensky, 1885; repr. Osnabrück, 1969.

Schmitz, Wolfgang, and Hans-Jochen Schiewer, eds. "Ein bisher unbekanntes 'Gauriel-Fragmen' in München." *Zeitschrift für deutsches Altertum und deutsche Literatur*, 100 (1989), 57-76.

Schultz, James A. *The Shape of the Round Table: Structures of Middle High German Arthurian Romance*. Toronto: University of Toronto Press, 1983.

Thomas, Neil. "Konrad von Stoffeln's *Gauriel von Muntabel*: A Comment on Hartmann's *Iwein*?" *Oxford German Studies*, 17 (1988), 1-9.

KRALIK, RICHARD VON (1852-1934), a minor Catholic Neoromantic writer and editor of the Viennese religious-philosophical journal *Der Gral* (1905-37). Author of idealistic religious ballads, epics, and dramas, he reacted against the extreme aestheticism of some of his German literary contemporaries. Apart from his drama *Merlin* (1913), dealing primarily with the Niniane (here Viviane) episode, his Arthurian works are typical of the wave of *Parzival* adaptations brought on by Wagner's opera. His three-act musical drama *Der heilige Gral* ("The Holy Grail," 1912) makes use of a choir of angels as a superficial imitation of the chorus in Wagner's *Parsifal*. His poetic chronicle *Die*

Gralsage ("The Legend of the Grail," 1907), on the other hand, is an attempt to compress all of the German and some French Grail traditions into one verse epic. [RWK]

Kralik, Richard von. *Die Gralsage*. Ravensburg: Alber, 1907.
———. *Der heilige Gral*. Trier: Petrus, 1912.
———. *Gral und Romantik*, ed. Moriz Enzinger. Graz and Vienna: Stiasny, 1963.
Hermand, Jost. "Gralsmotive um die Jahrhundertwende." *Deutsche Vierteljahresschrift*, 36 (1962), 521-43.

KUBIE, WILHELM (pseudonym of Willy Ortmann; 1890–1948), Austrian writer who based several novels on historical and literary themes. In *Mummenschanz auf Tintagel* (1937, 1946), he relates Arthurian subject matter from the standpoint of the knight Bedivir, whose soul dwells in various beings and objects over the millennia. Bedivir tells the story of Tristan and Isolde from his point of view as a friend of Mark. The poetic material is treated here in a farcical manner (*Mummenschanz* = "masquerade"). The ideals of the Round Table do not coincide with reality, and the majority of the "Arthurian" knights take the part of Modred. The Arthurian realm goes to ruin in a kind of fraternal war. [SSch/WCM]

Kubie, Wilhelm. *Mummenschanz auf Tintagel*. Cologne and Leipzig: Schaffrath, 1937; rev. ed. Linz and Vienna: Österreichischer Verlag für Belletristik und Wissenschaft, 1946.

KÜHN, DIETER, respected West German author of *Der Parzival des Wolfram von Eschenbach* (1986), a "biography" that combines the subjective and the scientific to create a new genre. In its opening section, the book describes the author's own intensely personal quest for the medieval poet; as in Kühn's other medieval books, fiction is inextricably entwined with literary criticism. The second section offers an almost complete translation in unrhymed verse of *Parzival*. With the rendition by Wolfgang Mohr (1977), this version is one of the best contemporary translations of Wolfram's romance into modern German. [UM/PWM]

Kühn, Dieter. *Der Parzival des Wolfram von Eschenbach*. Frankfurt: Insel, 1986.
Kühnel, Jürgen. "Wolfram von Eschenbach als literarische Figur in der Literatur des 19. und 20. Jahrhunderts." In *Mittelalter-Rezeption I*, ed. Jürgen Kühnel, Hans-Dieter Mück, and Ulrich Müller. Göppingen: Kümmerle, 1979.

KÜNKEL, INCAPE (PETRA), feminist author in the Federal Republic of Germany, whose *auf der reise nach avalun* ("On the Way to Avalon," 1982) describes the attempt of a group of women to find themselves. "The island of apples, Avalon, a land of eternal spring" functions as the primary metaphor in the work. The Celtic Arthurian world is imagined as a better, matriarchal world, a view that may derive from the works of Jean Markale. [UM/PWM]

Künkel, incape. *auf der reise nach avalun*. Ahrensbök: Schwarze Mond, 1982.

KUNCEWICZOWA, MARIA, Polish author of a 1967 novel *Tristan 1946*, an intricate and often self-conscious transposition of the Tristan story into the period following World War II, in Cornwall and later on Long Island. The author (who, as Maria Kuncewicz, published the novel in English in 1974 as *Tristan*) exploits many of the specific events of the medieval legend: the potion, Mark's overhearing the lovers' conversation, betrayal by bloodstains on the bed, marriage to a woman resembling the object of one's love, and so on. The parallels are not pure coincidence, however, for events of the modern story are shaped to a large extent by the characters' fascination with the legend of Tristan and Isolde. [NJL]

Kuncewiczowa, Maria. *Tristan 1946*. Warsaw: Czytelnik, 1967. (English translation published in the U.S. as *Tristan* [by Maria Kuncewicz]. New York: Braziller, 1974.)

KUZUU, CHINATSU, composed, arranged, and sang *The Lady of Shalott* (Sarusuberi Records, Tokyo, 1985), which comprises ll. 1-18, 73-86, 100-17, and 154-71 from Tennyson's poem (1842), and *Elaine the Fair* (Sarusuberi, 1986), which comprises ll. 1-12 of Tennyson's "Lancelot and Elaine" (1859). Composed with a computer and reproduced on synthesizer, her unique vocal compositions defy easy classification. [TT]

"KVIKKJESPRAKK," a Norwegian ballad consisting of sixty-eight four-line stanzas and named after the protagonist, who sets out with his page to woo the fair Rosamund of Girklond (Greece?). His suit is rejected by her father; subsequently, Kvikkjesprakk is attacked by a lion, then by the kings' men, and is finally set in a dungeon. His page rides home and relates what has happened; whereupon Kvikkjesprakk's brother Iven Erningsson, himself the subject of a ballad, rescues his brother and avenges him by slaying everyone but the fair Rosamund.

This ballad together with "Iven Erningsson" belongs to a ballad cycle presumably dating from the late Middle Ages. As they have been transmitted to us, "Kvikkjesprakk" and "Iven Erningsson" do not contain Arthurian matter, but the ballads' obvious relationship to the better-preserved Faroese cycle *Ívint Herintsson*, which incorporates Arthurian material, justifies their being considered part of the Arthurian tradition. [MEK]

Bø, Olav, and Svale Solheim, eds. "Kvikkjesprakk." In *Folkeviser*, I (Norsk Folkediktning, VI), 3rd ed. Oslo: Det norske samlaget, 1967, pp. 69–78.

Kölbing, Eugen. "Beiträge zur Kenntniss der Færöischen Poesie." *Germania*, 20 (1875), 385–402.

Liestøl, Knut. *Norske trollvisor og norrøne sogor*. Oslo: Olaf Norli, 1915.

KYBER, MANFRED (1880–1933), German pacifist fiction writer, lyric poet, and dramatist, was influenced by Rudolf Steiner's anthroposophy and subscribed to the idea of the "Christianity of the Grail." The mystery play *Der Kelch von Avalon* ("The Chalice of Avalon," 1913) depicts the brotherhood of the knights of the Chalice of Avalon: Iwein, Gawein, Parzival, and Lancelot. In the temple of the holy isle of Avalon, a new king is to be crowned who will represent the Chalice of the Blood of Christ. Arthur is ushered into the brotherhood in a ritual accented by the magic numbers three, seven, and thirteen. He shows compassion toward a half-man/half-beast (in reality, Merlin), whom he recognizes as a creature of God, and allows him to drink from the Holy Grail despite the opposition of his fellow knights. This act leads to his enthronement, and henceforth he alone is permitted to distribute food at the dinner table. [EGF/PM]

Kyber, Manfred. *Drei Mysterien—Der Stern von Juda; Die neunte Stunde; Der Kelch von Avalon*, 2nd ed. Stuttgart and Heilbronn: Walter Seifert, 1921, pp. 73–96.

L

LACINA, LAWRENCE, American-born writer, composed the prose *Tristan und Isolde* to complement Salvador Dali's drypoint etchings of the Tristan legend. The plot—greatly abridged—is a compilation of Eilhart, Thomas, and Gottfried. [SSch/PWM]

Lacina, Lawrence. *Tristan und Isolde: 21 Kaltnadel-Radierungen von Salvador Dali*. Cologne: Orangerie, 1969.

LADY OF THE LAKE, a name designating several different women, although the distinction among them is frequently blurred. In addition to being known as the Lady of the Lake, or the Dame du Lac, she most often bears such names as Viviane, Éviène, or Niviene; elsewhere, she is Nimuë or (in Wordsworth) Nina. Readers of Malory will recognize her as the being who gives Excalibur to Arthur and later receives it back from him, and some works also identify her as the lady responsible for Lancelot's upbringing. In Malory, the Vulgate Cycle, and various other settings of the legend (e.g., Apollinaire), she enchants Merlin with spells he had taught her. Some texts in fact tell us that she not only enchants him but also kills him. In the *Vita di Merlino*, for example, the Lady of the Lake serves as a scribe for Merlin, recording his prophecies, after which she tricks him into lying in a tomb; then, by a charm she had learned from him, she closes the lid and seals the wizard's doom (although the author assures us that Merlin's spirit will not die). [NJL]

LAFORGUE, JULES (1860–1887), a French writer born in Uruguay, lived and traveled extensively in Germany during the period that saw the presentation of *Parsifal* (1882) and the deaths of Wagner (1883), of Wagner's patron Louis II of Bavaria, and of his father-in-law Liszt (1886). Laforgue was directly exposed to Wagnerian mythology, by meeting the Master at Bayreuth and by seeing his operas performed at Munich and Dresden in 1883. Not surprisingly, given these and other contacts, he was among the first writers to use Wagnerian themes in French letters.

In 1886, in *La Vogue*, he published *Lohengrin, fils de Parsifal* ("Lohengrin, Son of Parsifal"), using the Wagnerian form of Perceval's name. The text was later included in his *Moralités légendaires* ("Legendary Moralities," 1887). In this curious scenario, the lunar vestal Elsa is to be sacrificed in a ceremony before the "white council" of priests at the cathedral of Notre-Dame (the "temple of silence"). Eventually, the hero Lohengrin arrives from Saint-Graal (apparently considered a place) to save and marry the sacred heroine. On their wedding night, during which their love remains unconsummated, Lohengrin embraces his pillow, which is then transformed into a swan. The white bird transports him through the air, over the seas and stars, toward Saint-Graal and to his father, Parsifal.

These curious variations on the story illustrate the fantasy characteristic of the pseudo-symbolist adaptations of the legend at the time. It is first and foremost a matter of personal lyricism cultivating formal effects (exclamations, neologisms, and archaisms) and attaching itself loosely to medieval legends. But it is difficult to trace a consistent Arthurian theme through these fantasies. (*See also* FRENCH SYMBOLISM.) [RB]

Laforgue, Jules. *Moralités légendaires*. Paris, 1887; re-ed. Pascal Pia. Paris: Gallimard, 1977.

[Collective authorship.] *Laforgue aujourd'hui*. Paris: Corti, 1988.

LAGRANGE, YVAN, French director, whose film *Tristan et Yseut* (1972) reduces the well-known story to archetypal constellations and elemental forms. Experimental in the extreme, this film has no plot in the conventional sense but relies instead on symbols and imagery to convey its meaning. [UM/WCM]

Paquette, Jean-Marcel. *La Dernière Métamorphose de Tristan: Yvan Lagrange (1972)*. In *Tristan et Iseut, mythe européen et mondial*, ed. Danielle Buschinger. Göppingen: Kümmerle, 1987.

LAIS DE BRETANHA, a set of five anonymous Galician-Portuguese troubadour lyrics with prose headings that link the compositions to the Prose *Tristan* and the Prose *Lancelot* of the Vulgate Cycle. The texts probably date from the late thirteenth or early fourteenth century, the period when the French cyclical romances were translated into Galician-Portuguese. However, the poems, while recalling the use of lais in some French prose-romance manuscripts, show greater affinity with the themes and structure of medieval French and Galician-Portuguese lyric traditions than with Arthurian narrative as such. The lais are preserved in independent manuscript copies, at the beginning of the *Cancioneiro da Biblioteca Nacional* of Lisbon and in Vatican Lat. 7182. [HLS]

Pellegrini, Silvio, ed. "I lais portoghesi del codice vaticano lat. 7182." *Archivum Romanicum*, 12 (1928), 303–17.

D'Heur, Jean-Marie. "Les Lais arthuriens anonymes français et leur tradition galaïco-portugais." *Bibliographical Bulletin of the International Arthurian Society*, 24 (1972), 210.

Sh[arrer], H[arvey]. "BRETÃO, Ciclo." In *Grande Dicionário da Literatura Portuguesa e de Teoria Literária*. Lisbon: Iniciativas Editoriais, n.d., Vol. 2, p. 148.

LAMENTO DI TRISTANO ("Tristan's Lament"), fourteenth-century Italian instrumental dance, found in a unique manuscript (London, B.L. Add. 29987). The dance is in the form of an estampie, with an "afterdance," "La Rotta." [NJL]

McGee, Timothy L. *Medieval Instrumental Dances*. Bloomington: Indiana University Press, 1989, pp. 115–16, 166–69.

LAMORAK DE GALIS (Lamorat), in the Vulgate Cycle, Pellinore's son, Perceval's brother, and Morgause's lover. When Gaheris, the son of Lot (whom Pellinore killed), finds Lamorak with his mother, he kills her but spares him because he is unarmed. Lamorak, however, is eventually slain by Gaheris and his brothers. [SW]

LAMPO, HUBERT, one of the most popular and best-selling authors in the Netherlands and one of the main representatives of magic-realism. He was strongly influenced by Jung's theory of archetypes, and his essays and novels frequently interpret Arthurian elements from an archetypal point of view.

Lampo's first Arthurian novel, *De heks en de archeoloog* ("The Witch and the Archaeologist," 1967), has the Grail and its mysteries manifest themselves, apparently accidentally, in the life of a twentieth-century archaeologist. In *Wijlen Sarah Silbermann* ("The Late Sarah Silbermann," 1980), the Grail motif occurs again, this time in the context of a fictitious Brabantine town. The mysteries of Glastonbury are treated in *Zeg maar Judith* ("Judith," 1983). In 1989, Lampo published *De Elfenkoning* ("The Queen of the Elves"), another novel with Grail references.

Lampo has also published a number of essays treating Arthurian and Grail material either directly or in passing. Among them are essays included in *De zwanen van Stonehenge* ("The Swans of Stonehenge," 1970–71), *De ring van Möbius 2* ("The Ring of Möbius 2," a 1972 volume containing an essay on Glastonbury), and *Arthur* (a 1985 essay that has been translated into French, German, and English, the last as "Arthur and the Grail," 1988), *Het Graalboek* ("The Grail Book," 1985), and *Terugkeer naar Stonehenge: Een magisch-realistisch Droomboek* ("Return to Stonehenge: A Magic-Realistic Dreambook," 1988).

On commission from the BRT (Belgian Radio and Television), he wrote the script of the documentary *In de voetsporen van Koning Arthur* ("In the Footsteps of King Arthur," 1981). [VU]

Lampo, Hubert. *De heks en de archeoloog*. Amsterdam: Meulenhoff, 1967.

———. *Wijlen Sarah Silbermann*. Amsterdam: Meulenhoff, 1980.

———. *Zeg maar Judith*. Amsterdam: Meulenhoff, 1983.

———. *De Elfenkoning*. Amsterdam: Meulenhoff, 1989.

LANÇAROTE DE LAGO, a largely unedited Spanish translation of the *Lancelot* branch of the Vulgate Cycle, surviving in a sixteenth-century manuscript (Madrid, Biblioteca Nacional 9611). From linguistic evidence, the text would seem to have been rendered first into a northwestern Hispanic language, possibly Galician-Portuguese, in the late thirteenth or early fourteenth century. The surviving sections, which correspond in part to an unedited long version of the French romance, narrate Lancelot's adventures following his departure from Arthur's court after having taken a seat at the Round Table and end with a search for Tristan, the latter involving a short series of adventures extraneous to the Prose *Lancelot* but linking the Spanish version to a lost Tristan romance. Two traditional Spanish ballads are thought to have derived from the Prose *Lancelot* but not the Spanish text as it survives: "Nunca fuera caballero de damas tan bien servido" and "Tres hijuelos había el rey." The first, quoted by Cervantes in *Don Quixote*, tells of how Lancelot served Guenevere by decapitating a haughty gallant. The second reveals much affinity with the story of the "Cerf au pied blanc" as preserved in the *Lai de Tyolet* and the Dutch *Roman van Lancelot*. [HLS]

Bohigas Balaguer, Pedro. "El *Lanzarote* español del manuscrito 9611 de la Biblioteca Nacional." *Revista de Filología Española*, 10 (1924), 282–97.

Sharrer, Harvey L. *A Critical Bibliography of Hispanic Arthurian Material, I: Texts: The Prose Romance Cycles*. London: Grant and Cutler, 1977, item Aa3.

LANCELOET EN HET HERT MET DE WITTE VOET ("Lancelot and the Deer with the White Foot"), a Middle Dutch verse romance (ca. 850 lines) that has been transmitted exclusively in the *Lancelot-Compilatie*. Central to the story is the task set by a damsel to bring her the "white foot" of a deer that is guarded by lions. Lanceloet succeeds in his attempt but is cheated by a knight who leaves him severely wounded and who claims the damsel with the aid of the white foot. Walewein saves Lanceloet and defeats the impostor. The Middle Dutch text is related to the French *Lai de Tyolet* but is not based on it. The version transmitted in the *Lancelot-Compilatie* is greatly abridged. The original Middle Dutch text may date from the first half of the thirteenth century. [BB]

Draak, Maartje, ed. *Lanceloet en het hert met de witte voet*. Culemborg: Tjeenk Willink, 1979.

LANCELOT (Lancelot du Lac, Launcelot, Lanzelet, Lancilotto, Laneloet), the favored lover of Queen Guenevere. Lancelot is the central hero of three medieval romances—Chrétien de Troyes's *Le Chevalier de la charrete* (third quarter of the twelfth century), Ulrich von Zatzikhoven's *Lanzelet* (ca. 1194–1204), and the Prose *Lancelot* (ca. 1225)—and plays a prominent role in several others, most notably in Malory's *Morte Darthur*. Adaptations of the Prose *Lancelot* spread his fame into Italy, Portugal, Scotland, and the Netherlands.

In Chrétien's *Chevalier de la charrete*, Guenevere has been carried off to the land of Gorre by Meleagant, the wicked son of the good king Bademagu. After Sir Kay competes unsuccessfully for her and is captured and led away into Gorre with the Queen, both Gawain and Lancelot set off to rescue her. On his way, Lancelot encounters a dwarf driving a cart who agrees to aid him in his search if he will climb into the cart. Lancelot hesitates momentarily, for to mount into a cart was considered a sign of shame, but after two steps his love for the Queen overcomes his pride as a knight. Gawain soon happens upon them but refuses to join Lancelot in the cart. After overcoming several temptations designed to delay him in his quest or divert him altogether, Lancelot crosses over the treacherous Sword Bridge into Gorre, while Gawain chooses the easier, yet still dangerous Underwater Bridge. When he finally encounters the Queen, Lancelot is rebuffed without explanation; only much later does he learn that she is angry because of the two steps in which he let his knightly pride dominate his love for her. Guenevere eventually relents, and Lancelot spends a night of pleasure with her. He frees the captives but is himself captured by Meleagant's men. Finally released from his tower prison, Lancelot returns to Arthur's court to slay Meleagant.

Chrétien gives no background information about his hero, other than that his name is Lancelot del Lac and that he had once been given a magic ring by a fairy who had raised him as a child (ll. 2,335–50). Lancelot's cognomen may have led to his association with Niniane, the Dame du Lac, in the thirteenth-century Prose *Lancelot*, and Ulrich shows some familiarity with this motif when he has the young Lancelot carried off by a mermaid and raised in a kingdom of women until the age of fifteen. In Ulrich's *Lanzelet*, the young hero, ignorant of his name and royal birth, sets out to win a place at Arthur's court. Three times he approaches castles and slays the lord in combat, and three times he inspires the lord's daughter or niece with burning passion. The first two, after a brief dalliance, economically disappear from the story; but the third, Yblis, the daughter of Iweret of Dodone, remains his wife. By defeating Iweret in an adventure reminiscent of Yvain's at the fountain, Lanzelet avenges his foster mother for an unspecified wrong and is rewarded by being told his name and his royal kinship. He next hears that Valerin of the Tangled Wood has claimed Guenevere (much like Meleagant in Chrétien's *Charrete*) and rides rapidly to Arthur's court to defend the Queen in combat. He defeats Valerin but does not kill him, and soon Valerin proves false to his word and abducts the Queen. Lanzelet participates with the other knights of the Round Table in her rescue, which is effected with the aid of a magician. Ulrich's poem is a hodgepodge of marvelous adventures; it shares with Chrétien's the abduction theme and Lancelot's championing of the Queen, but it has no cart, no Sword Bridge, and no hint of an adulterous affair between Lancelot and Guenevere. Furthermore, there are countless adventures that have no parallels in the French poem.

Chrétien tells us at the beginning of his romance that his patroness, Marie de Champagne, had given him the material for this story, and there is no reason to doubt him on this point. Neither the character of Lancelot nor his affair with Guenevere predates *Le Chevalier de la charrete*. Where Marie got the theme, however, is much more problematic. The story of the abduction of the Queen may well be related to a Celtic abduction motif, the *aithed*, a version of which is depicted on the tympanum at Modena. Similarities between the *Charrete*, the *Lanzelet*, and the Prose *Lancelot* suggest a common source that, like the abduction motif, might ultimately have been Celtic. Ulrich's immediate source, however, was a poem written in the Anglo-Norman dialect of Old French. Ulrich clearly did not know the central theme of Chrétien's romance, the passion of Lancelot and Guenevere, so he could not have meant Chrétien's poem in his repeated references to his source. It seems likely that Marie heard a narrative much like the one later imitated by Ulrich and suggested to Chrétien that it be modified to celebrate the newly popular concept of courtly love by making Lancelot the Queen's lover.

In the thirteenth-century Prose *Lancelot*, the hero continues as the champion and lover of the Queen. As in Ulrich's poem, he is carried off after the death of his father, King Ban of Benoyc, to be raised by the Lady of the Lake, who is here identified as the fairy Niniane. He is soon joined by his orphaned cousins, Lionel and Bohort, and at the age of eighteen is taken by the fairy to be knighted at Arthur's court. There she tells him that he is of royal parentage and bestows upon him the magic ring first mentioned by Chrétien; but she does not tell him his name. At court, he meets and is enraptured by Guenevere, who bestows upon him his sword of knighthood. This bestowal symbolically divides his loyalty between Arthur and the Queen, and much of the action of the romance, as well as the eventual destruction of Arthur's kingdom in the *Mort Artu*, can be traced back to this double allegiance.

After a series of adventures, the young knight, still ignorant of his name, reaches the castle of Dolorous Gard, which he captures with help from the Lady of the Lake. There in a magic cemetery, he finds his name inscribed inside the lid of the tomb in which he will one day lie. Hundreds of pages of adventures ensue, during which Lancelot is continually referred to as "the best knight in the world." But after his adultery with the Queen, his perfection begins to tarnish, and he is shocked to learn that because of his sins he will not himself be able to fulfill the quest of the Holy Grail. This adventure will be achieved by Lancelot's son, Galahad, whom he begets on the daughter of the Grail King Pelles, with the connivance of Pelles himself, who provides a potion that makes him believe he is lying with Guenevere.

In the *Queste del Saint Graal*, a sequel to the Prose *Lancelot*, Lancelot comes to recognize his guilt and does penance for it. He is rewarded by being able to reach the Grail castle and participate in its mysteries but is denied the supreme vision, which is reserved for his son Galahad and for his companions Perceval and Bohort.

In the *Mort Artu*, the last of the Old French Vulgate romances, Lancelot relapses and recommences his affair with Guenevere. This ultimately leads to a break with Arthur and to the war that destroys his kingdom.

Much of the material from the Vulgate Cycle was reworked by Malory in the fifteenth century for his *Le Morte Darthur*, and again Lancelot is constantly at the center of the action. Thus, from its first appearance in Chrétien's *Charrete* until Malory's day, Lancelot's affair with Guenevere remained at the center of the Arthurian legend, with the curious exception of Ulrich's *Lanzelet*. In terms of secular chivalry, Lancelot was without peer, but when knighthood became impregnated with Christian ideals in the thirteenth century his adulterous relationship led not only to his own downfall, but also to the destruction of Arthur's kingdom.

In postmedieval literature, Lancelot is often presented as a somber and intense figure, plagued by guilt at the betrayal of the man who is both his king and his friend, yet unable to escape his passion for Guenevere. At the beginning of Tennyson's *Idylls of the King*, Lancelot is already recognized as Arthur's greatest knight and close adviser, and it is he who is sent along to observe and protect the youthful Gareth in the first Idyll. In one of the greatest Idylls, "Lancelot and Elaine," his face is symbolically marred by "The great and guilty love he bore the Queen," yet "Marr'd as he was, he seem'd the goodliest man/That ever among ladies ate in hall,/And noblest." But for Tennyson his tragic figure embodies the moral corruption that gnaws at the heart of Arthur's realm: haunted by the Queen, he cannot understand or accept the pure love of the honest Elaine, for "His honour rooted in dishonour stood,/And faith unfaithful kept him falsely true."

Edwin Arlington Robinson's *Lancelot* (1920) centers on the episodes of Guenevere's condemnation to the stake and Lancelot's bloody rescue of her, the apocalyptic battle on Salisbury Plain, and the last encounter of the lovers at Amesbury. It is a story of friendships betrayed—of Arthur's for Lancelot, of Lancelot's for Gawain—and of a love that betrayed the dream of Camelot.

A unique portrayal of Lancelot is that in T.H. White's tetralogy, *The Once and Future King* (1958). Not only do we witness him aging from a young man to a wise elderly statesman, but he is depicted as a sullen and physically ugly young man: "Lancelot never believed he was good or nice. Under the grotesque, magnificent shell with a face like Quasimodo's, there was shame and self-loathing." He is obsessed by virtue and virginity, which he loses to the Grail Princess Elaine, by whom he conceives Sir Galahad. He loves the Queen reluctantly and sets off voluntarily on quests to avoid her. Only when Arthur departs for the foreign wars and leaves his trusted "Lance" to look after "Gwen" does he succumb. Primary blame for the fall of Arthur's kingdom is not placed, as so often earlier, on the adulterous affair with the Queen but on the fact that the kingdom was built on Might rather than on moral Right. But ironically, it is the Right that Gawain evokes to oblige Arthur to pursue Lancelot once their adultery has been revealed.

Walker Percy's 1978 *Lancelot* is set in the world of contemporary filmmaking. In this symbolic novel, Lancelot Lamar is an alcoholic, morally corrupt filmmaker whose life reflects the wasteland that is modern America. The most successful cinematic rendering of Lancelot's legend is arguably that provided by the French filmmaker Robert Bresson's brooding *Lancelot du Lac* (1974). (For other cinematic representations, see FILMS.) [WWK]

Chrétien de Troyes. *Lancelot, or The Knight of the Cart (Le Chevalier de la charrete)*, ed. and trans. William W. Kibler. New York: Garland, 1981.

Micha, Alexandre, ed. *Lancelot: roman en prose du XIIIe siècle*. 9 vols. Geneva: Droz, 1978–83.

Malory, Sir Thomas. *The Works*, ed. Eugène Vinaver; rev. P. J. C. Field. 3 vols. Oxford: Clarendon, 1990.

Kennedy, Elspeth, ed. *Lancelot do Lac: The Non-Cyclic Old French Prose Romance*. 2 vols. Oxford: Clarendon, 1980.

Ulrich von Zatzikhoven. *Lanzelet: A Romance of Lancelot*, trans. Kenneth G.T. Webster, rev. Roger Sherman Loomis. New York: Columbia University Press, 1951.

Weston, Jessie L. *The Legend of Sir Lancelot du Lac*. London: Nutt, 1901.

LANCELOT, ROMAN VAN. The Vulgate *Lancelot* was not only adapted into Middle Dutch (*Lantsloot vander Haghedochte*) but also translated at least twice. In fragments from ca. 1350 preserved in Rotterdam (Gemeentebibliotheek, Hs. 96 A 7), a faithful prose translation has been transmitted. A verse translation has also been preserved, extant in the *Lancelot-Compilatie* and in fragments found in Brussels (Royal Library II, 115-3) and also in The Hague (Royal Library 75 H 58). The Brussels fragment contains a text that belonged to the lost first part of the *Lancelot-Compilatie*. A third Middle Dutch translation may have existed. This conjecture is based on a Ripuarian copy of before 1476, which according to the colophon is based on a Middle Dutch model. This codex is preserved in Cologne (Bibliothek des historischen Archiv, Codex W. f.° 46 Blankenheim). [BB]

Draak, Maartje. *De Middelnederlandse vertalingen van de Proza-Lancelot*. Amsterdam: Koninklijke Akademie der Wetenschappen, 1954.

Lie, Orlanda S.H., ed. *The Middle Dutch Prose Lancelot: A Study of the Rotterdam Fragments and Their Place in the French, German, and Dutch "Lancelot en Prose" Tradition*. Amsterdam: Noord-Hollandsche Uitgevers Maatschappij, 1987.

LANCELOT DO LAC, the earliest Old French prose version of the Lancelot story, probably composed between 1215 and 1220. This version, known variously as Sommer III (for its first editor), the *Marche de Gaule* (for its opening words), or the "Galehaut section," was soon incorporated into the vast Vulgate Cycle. Thirteen manuscripts conclude this section, after Lancelot and Galehaut's journey to Sorelois and the False Guenevere episode, with the death of Galehaut. In most of the manuscripts, however, the Sorelois and False Guenevere episodes contain allusions and scenes that prepare the way for Galahad's quest for the Grail, and the death of Galehaut is surrounded by episodes leading up to the prose reworking of Chrétien de Troyes's *Le Chevalier de la charrete*. The *Lancelot do Lac* presents the text of the best of the noncyclic manuscripts (Paris, B.N. fr. 768). In this version, there is no preparation for the Vulgate *Queste* or for the condemnation of illicit love in the *Mort Artu* section; everything culminates in the death of Galehaut. It is likely that the shorter noncyclic version was composed first, then incorporated into the Vulgate Cycle, rather than the longer version having been shortened and disentangled from its links to the rest of the cycle. [WWK]

Kennedy, Elspeth, ed. *Lancelot do Lac: The Non-Cyclic Old French Prose Romance*. 2 vols. Oxford: Clarendon, 1980.

Kennedy, Elspeth. *Lancelot and the Grail: A Study of the Prose Lancelot*. Oxford: Clarendon, 1986.

Micha, Alexandre. *Essais sur le Cycle du Lancelot-Graal*. Geneva: Droz, 1987.

LANCELOT OF THE LAIK, a late fifteenth-century Middle Scots adaptation of the story of Galehaut's war against Arthur in the first major division of the French Vulgate *Lancelot*. It is a fragment of 3,484 lines, written in Chaucerian five-stress couplets by an unknown author and surviving in a single manuscript (Cambridge University Library Kk. 1.5). Although the author generally follows his French source, making only minor alterations in details and sequence of events, he makes two major changes. First, he adds an introduction (ll. 1–333), indebted to the conventions of courtly literature, in which a lovesick narrator explains that he will omit Lancelot's early adventures and tell instead of the wars between Arthur and "Galiot," of Lancelot's defense of Arthur and role in establishing peace, and of Venus's rewarding Lancelot by enabling him to win his lady's love. Although the announced subject is "love ore armys," the text ends before the end of the war between Arthur and Galiot and before love becomes important to the story. The introduction, however, enables one to see the author's original plan for the romance. Second, the author expands considerably the section of the Vulgate *Lancelot* in which a wise man rebukes Arthur for his weakness and ineptness and tells him how to be a good and just ruler (ll. 1,307–2,128). Although scholars have not found much literary merit in *Lancelot of the Laik*, they have been interested in this political section of the romance because its negative portrait of Arthur has affinities with portraits of Arthur in some other Scottish works (*see* CHRONICLES, SCOTTISH) and because changes from the source suggest that the political advice was intended as an admonition to James III of Scotland. Because much of the advice is general and similar to what can be found in other works of *speculum regis* literature, there is some doubt about its applicability to James; but many scholars have felt that this work, like Blind Harry's *Wallace*, was intended for him and that the political passage was the *raison d'être* for the romance. [EDK]

Skeat, Walter W., ed. *Lancelot of the Laik*. London: Trübner, 1865.

Gray, Margaret M., ed. *Lancelot of the Laik*. Edinburgh: Blackwood, 1912.

Alexander, Flora. "Late Medieval Scottish Attitudes to the Figure of King Arthur: A Reassessment." *Anglia*, 93 (1975), 17–34.

Göller, K.H. *König Arthur in der englischen Literatur des späten Mittelalters*. Göttingen: Vandenhoeck and Ruprecht, 1963, pp. 137–42.

Lyall, R.J. "Politics and Poetry in Fifteenth and Sixteenth Century Scotland." *Scottish Literary Journal*, 3 (1976), 5–29.

Vogel, Bertram. "Secular Politics and the Date of *Lancelot of the Laik*." *Studies in Philology*, 40 (1943), 1–13.

LANCELOT-COMPILATIE. In the Royal Library at The Hague, under the signature Hs. 129 A 10, a codex is preserved from the beginning of the fourteenth century that is unique in two respects. First, the manuscript contains no fewer than ten Middle Dutch Arthurian romances (and for that reason has been called the "flagship of the Middle Dutch Arthurian fleet"). Second, the manuscript derives its unique status from the traces of use it contains. Decades after the codex was produced, someone, usually referred to as the corrector, furnished the text with comments. He corrected copyists' mistakes and tried to purge the text of Flemish dialectal peculiarities. Apart from this, he introduced changes to make the story more comprehensible to a listening audience and provided the lines of verse with directions for reading (signs in the margin) to aid recitation.

The nucleus of the *Lancelot-Compilatie*, as the collection of texts is called, is a verse translation of the Old French Prose *Lancelot*, the *Queste del Saint Graal*, and the *Mort Artu*. The translation of this trilogy is so large that it was too cumbersome for a single codex, and the text has been divided into two bindings. However, the first part of the *Lancelot-Compilatie* has been lost. The part that has been preserved (Hs. 129 A 10) begins two-thirds of the way into the translation of the Prose *Lancelot*.

In between the translations of the parts of the French cycle, seven Arthurian romances have been interpolated. Two romances were inserted before the translation of the *Queste del Saint Graal*: *Perchevael* and *Moriaen*. Another five romances were inserted between the second and third parts of the trilogy: *De Wrake von Ragisel*, *Van den Riddere metter mouwen*, *Walewein ende Keye*, *Lanceloet en het hert met de witte voet*, and *Torec*.

In the translation of the *Mort Artu*, one section has been replaced by a fragment of Jacob van Maerlant's *Spiegel Historiael*. The latter is an adaptation of the *Speculum Historiale* of Vincent of Beauvais, on which Maerlant was working in the years 1283–88.

On the final page of the codex, there is a notice that records Lodewijk van Velthem as the owner. In later times, the manuscript may have been part of the library of John IV, Count of Nassau (1410–1475). It certainly belonged to Frederik Hendrik (1584–1647) and to William IV (1711–1751). [BB]

Jonckbloet, W.J.A., ed. *Roman van Lancelot (XIIIe eeuw)*. 2 vols. The Hague, 1846–49.

Draak, Maartje. "The Workshop Behind the Middle Dutch Lancelot Manuscript The Hague K.B. 129 A 10." In *Neerlandica Manuscripta: Essays Presented to G.I. Lieftinck 3*. Amsterdam: Litterae Textualis, 1976, pp. 18–37.

Gerritsen, Willem P. "Corrections and Indications for Oral Delivery in the Middle Dutch Lancelot Manuscript The Hague K.B. 129 A 10." In *Neerlandica Manuscripta: Essays Presented to G.I. Lieftinck 3*. Amsterdam: Litterae Textualis, 1976, pp. 38–59.

———, and Frits P. van Oostrom. "Les Adaptateurs néerlandais du 'Lancelot (-Graal)' aux prises avec le procédé narratif des romans arthuriens en prose." In *Mélanges de langue et littérature françaises du Moyen Âge et de la Renaissance offerts à Charles Foulon*. Rennes: Université de Haute Bretagne, 1980, Vol. 2, pp. 105–14.

LANCILLOTTO DEL LAGO, an Italian translation (published in 1558–59) of the French *Lancelot du Lac* printed in 1533. It presents versions of the *Lancelot* proper, the *Queste*, and the *Mort Artu*. [NJL]

Gardner, Edmund G. *The Arthurian Legend in Italian Literature*. London: Dent, 1930, p. 307.

"LANETHEN MANTEL" ("Laneth's Mantle"), a fifteenth-century German *Meisterlied* ultimately deriving from *Le Mantel mautaillié*, presumably via the thirteenth-century Middle High German metrical version *Der Mantel*. In the ballad, the impetus for the mantle chastity test is vengeance: Laneth, the bearer of the garment and Arthur's niece, has been falsely accused of illicit intimacies by Guinevere. A dwarf counsels her as to how she can avenge the insult and gives her the mantle for that purpose. All the ladies but one—a young woman married to an old man—fail the mantle test. Guinevere curses the Devil for her failure, and King Arthur becomes furious with his niece for thus embarrassing Guinevere. Laneth admits that the deed was motivated by hurt and anger and that she was determined to clear her good name. [MEK]

Bruns, Paul Jakob. "Zwei Erzählungen im Meistergesang." In *Beiträge zur kritischen Bearbeitung unbenutzter alter Handschriften, Drucke und Urkunden*. Braunschweig: Reichard, 1802, pp. 143–47.

LANGE, M.R., reveals a fondness for developing obscure images in *Yseult* (1905), a dramatic poem in blank verse. Its eleven short scenes offer a romantic account of the love between Yseult and Tristan, concluding with the black-and-white sails version of their death. [RHT]

Lange, M.R. *Yseult: A Dramatic Poem*. London: Digby, Long, 1905.

LANGLAIS, XAVIER DE (1906–1975), author of *Le Roman du Roi Arthur* ("The Romance of King Arthur"), a modern retelling of the Arthurian story in five volumes (the last one completed in 1971). The work is *renouvelé* ("renewed" or "updated") largely from medieval French texts, especially the Vulgate Cycle, but with the addition of material from the *Mabinogi*, Wolfram's *Parzival*, various Tristan texts, and other sources. In addition, Langlais eliminated a number of events and invented certain details and episodes, in an attempt, he said, to restore the Arthurian story to its presumed original unity.

Langlais completed a Breton version of the same work, entitled *Romant ar roue Arzhur*, and also composed a Breton *Tristan hag Izold* (1958), an updated retelling of the story from Béroul, Thomas, and Gottfried. [NJL]

Langlais, Xavier de. *Le Roman du Roi Arthur*. 5 vols. Paris: H. Piazza, 1956–75.

——. *Tristan hag Izold*. Brest: Éditions "Al Liamm," 1958.

LANIER, STERLING E., wrote a series of tall tales for the *Magazine of Fantasy and Science Fiction* that involved his hero, Brigadier Ffellowes, in adventures with otherworldly creatures. In "Ghost of a Crown" (1976), Ffellowes aids Arthur, who in the form of one of his descendants battles Mordred and his supernatural allies beneath a castle on the Cornish coast. [DN]

Lanier, Sterling E. "Ghost of a Crown." *Magazine of Fantasy and Science Fiction*, December, 1976, 5–45; repr. in *The Curious Quests of Brigadier Ffellowes*. West Kingston, R.I.: Grant, 1986.

LANTSLOOT VANDER HAGHEDOCHTE ("Lancelot of the Cave"), a Middle Dutch verse adaptation of the Prose *Lancelot* that originally must have comprised over 100,000 lines. However, the text, dating from the second half of the thirteenth century, has been transmitted incomplete. Thirty-six fragments from one codex of ca. 1350 have been preserved. The fragments together comprise some 6,070 lines.

Lantsloot vander Haghedochte occupies a unique place among the medieval translations and adaptations of the Prose *Lancelot*, because of its freedom: the poet closely follows the main outline of the story, but within this he often goes his own way. The adaptation is characterized by three tendencies. The poet continually tries to motivate the story and to make it imaginable. Apart from this, he deviates from the "realism" of the Prose *Lancelot* by using vague spatial indications, by blurring time, and by getting rid of "historical" elements. Moreover, he tries to stylize the portraits of his main characters as much as possible according to the courtly ideal (removing familiar forms of address, idealizing the knightly combat, and so on).

It appears from these tendencies that the Middle Dutch adapter was somebody with conservative ideas. He partially reversed the modernism of the Prose *Lancelot* and tried to find links again with Arthurian romance in the style of Chrétien de Troyes. [BB]

Gerritsen, Willem P., et al., eds. *Lantsloot vander Haghedochte: Fragmenten van een Middelnederlandse bewerking van de "Lancelot en prose."* Amsterdam: Noord-Hollandsche Uitgevers Maatschappij, 1987.

Van Oostrom, Frits P. *Lantsloot vander Haghedochte: Onderzoekingen over een Middelnederlandse bewerking van de "Lancelot en prose."* Amsterdam and New York: Koninklijke Nederlandse Akademie der Wetenschappen, 1981.

LAUBENTHAL, SANDERS ANNE, author of *Excalibur*, a skillful and dramatic blending of the modern and the old. Modern characters fulfill Arthurian quests (most specifically for the Grail) as they search for Excalibur, brought to the New World by Prince Medoc and now hidden in Mobile, Alabama. They are opposed by Morgan le Fay and Morgause. [RCS]

Laubenthal, Sanders Anne. *Excalibur*. New York: Ballantine, 1973.

LAWHEAD, STEPHEN R., American author of fantasy and science fiction. The founding of Arthur's golden age on a base of Christian concepts is the theme of the Pendragon Cycle, a trilogy of fantasy novels set in post-

Roman Britain. *Taliesin* (1987) tells of the bard's strange origin, his religious conversion, and his union with the daughter of Avallach, a king of lost Atlantis who has settled with other survivors on Glastonbury Tor. It is Taliesin's mission to prepare for the coming of his son, Merlin, who in turn will prepare Britain for Arthur. *Merlin* (1988) is the enchanter's autobiography and deftly incorporates the earliest Welsh and Latin references to him. The King's story is told in *Arthur* (1989). The series displays a thorough knowledge of and appreciation for the early Welsh literature it draws on, and the religious message is for the most part subordinate to a solid narrative. [DN]

Lawhead, Stephen R. *Taliesin*. Westchester, Ill.: Crossway, 1987.
———. *Merlin*. Westchester, Ill.: Crossway, 1988.
———. *Arthur*. Westchester, Ill.: Crossway, 1989.

LAWRENCE, C(HARLES) E(DWARD) (1870–1940), releases Merlin from his confinement on the estate of a modern nobleman in the comic short story "Merlin's Oak" (1932). The contrast between ancient and modern ideals proves too much for the old wizard, who voluntarily returns to his prison, but not before instilling a sense of higher values in the nobleman's daughter. [DN]

Lawrence, C.E. "Merlin's Oak." *Cornhill Magazine*, n.s., 72 (January 1931), 56–68.

LAYAMON, author of the *Brut*, an adaptation of Wace's French *Roman de Brut* into English alliterative verse (32,241 half-lines). One of the major works of the early Middle English period, it marks the first occurrence of the Arthurian story in English. The author, a priest at Arley Regis in Worcestershire, wrote this chronicle covering the period from Brutus to Cadwalader (A.D. 689) sometime between 1189 and the mid-thirteenth century. The chronicle is dated on the basis of a reference in the prologue to Eleanor, "who was Henry [II]'s queen"; it is thus assumed that it was written after the death of Henry II in 1189 and possibly after the death of Queen Eleanor in 1204. Although Layamon mentions in his prologue two sources in addition to Wace (Bede and a book he associates with "St. Albin" and Augustine of Canterbury), his chronicle is based primarily upon Wace. He used Bede's *Historia Ecclesiastica Gentis Anglorum* (731) for at least one episode. The third source remains a mystery. Some assume that it was Alfred's translation of Bede; others, a book Layamon had seen that had contained selections by Augustine and Albin of Canterbury (or even Alcuin of York); others, that the book never existed, that Layamon, displaying what Stanley has called "doubtful erudition," thought Albin, Abbot of St. Augustine's, Canterbury (708–32), or Alcuin of York (731–804), and Augustine of Canterbury (597) were contemporaries and like many other medieval writers created what he thought sounded like a plausible source.

The chronicle survives in two manuscripts, London, B.L. Cotton Caligula A. ix and B.L. Cotton Otho C. xiii, both written between 1250 and 1325. The Caligula manuscript appears to be closer to Layamon's text, with language more archaic than that of other West Midland texts of the second half of the thirteenth century. Although some of the apparent archaisms may represent dialectal peculiarities of Worcestershire in the later thirteenth century, this manuscript indicates that Layamon, while adapting a French source, generally avoided French words, preferring English words and poetic compounds, some of which go back to the Old English period, some of which appear to be coinages designed to give his diction what Stanley calls "antique colouring." The scribe of the Otho text apparently attempted to modernize Layamon by eliminating many of the archaisms and replacing many of Layamon's English words with ones derived from French. Writing in an alliterative style and using epic formulas and a predominantly English vocabulary, Layamon was imitating native meters for an English audience at a time when most nonreligious writing was being done in Anglo-Norman or Latin. But although he was writing alliterative verse and at times manages to reproduce the Anglo-Saxon type of half-line, he also uses some rhyme and assonance, his alliteration is irregularly placed and sometimes absent, and he appears to have made little effort to produce consistently the formulas, vocabulary, and rhythm of the alliterative verse of the Old English period. In fact, the later alliterative poetry of the fourteenth century, found in works like *Sir Gawain and the Green Knight* and the Alliterative *Morte Arthure*, seems in some ways closer to classical Anglo-Saxon verse (in, for example, the absence of rhyme and assonance in the alliterative line). Layamon's lines are sometimes said to be derived from Anglo-Saxon popular poetry that is represented by some of the poems in the *Anglo-Saxon Chronicle* and that may have developed from oral poetry; they are sometimes said to have affinities with the prose of Aelfric. In any event, he was trying to write in what was primarily a pre-Conquest style.

Layamon follows the main events of Wace's account of Arthur's rise to power and conquest of Europe, but his chronicle is more than a translation. While one thinks of Wace's adaptation of Geoffrey of Monmouth as a move toward courtly romance, one thinks of Layamon's adaptation of Wace as a move back to a more heroic age. He cuts out much in Wace that was typical of courtly literature (interest in love and chivalry, for example) and adds details that depict a much rougher, more brutal society. In Wace, for example, Arthur and his men besiege Winchester; in Layamon, they burn the town and slay both old and young.

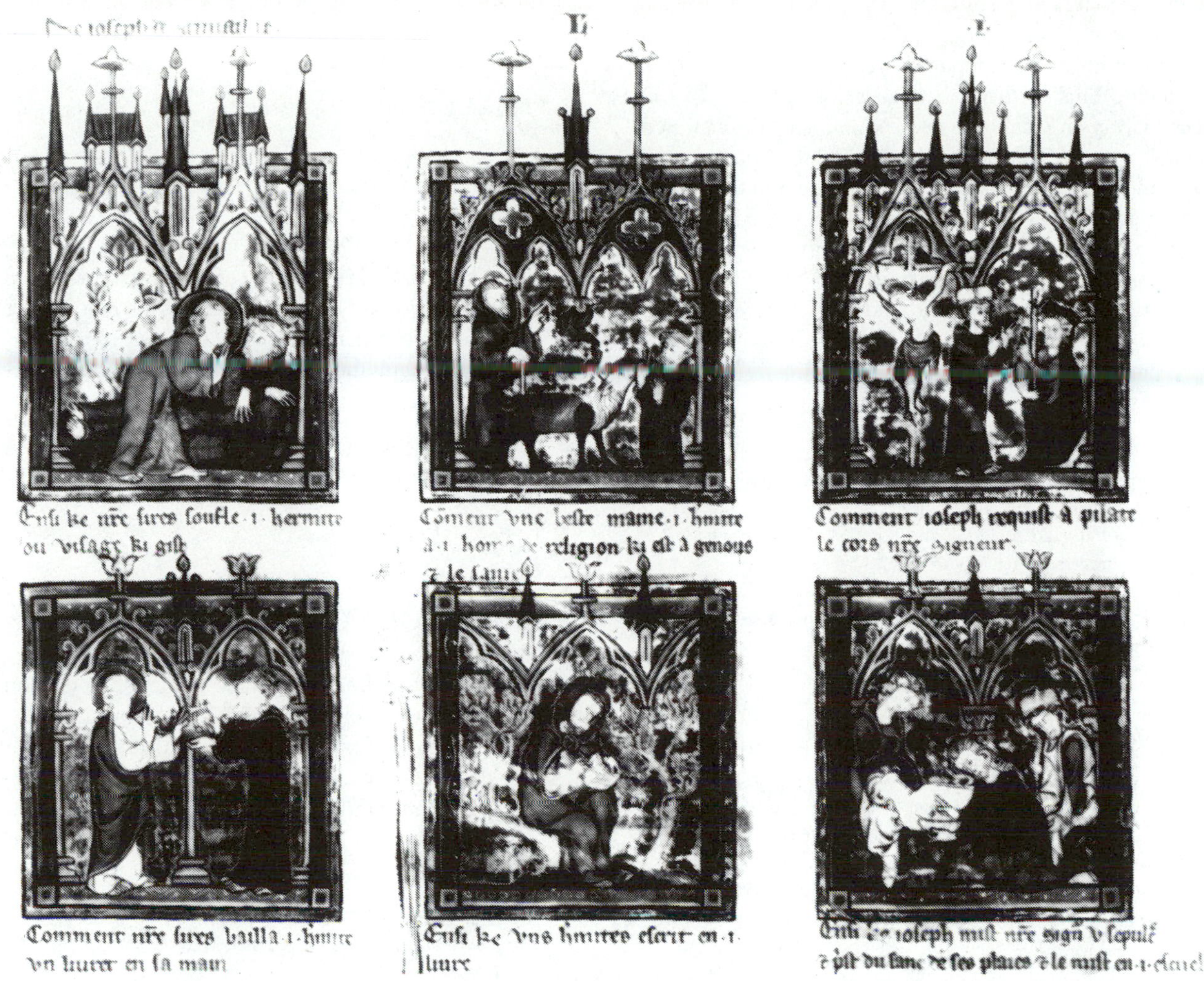

50. MS Bonn, Universitätsbibliothek, 526, fol. 1. A group of six images from *L'Estoire del Saint Graal*: Our Lord breathes breath into a hermit; An animal leads a hermit to a kneeling holy man; Joseph asks Pilate for Our Lord's body; Our Lord gives a book to a hermit; A hermit writes in a book; Joseph puts Our Lord into the sepulcher and collects the blood from his wounds in a vessel. (Universitätsbibliothek, Bonn.)

Details—such as Arthur's order, after a knight started a brawl at court, to cut off the noses of the women related to him; Arthur's dream of cutting Guenevere to pieces; and Gawain's threat, after hearing that Guenevere had sided with Modred, to have her torn apart by horses—suggest that ideals of chivalry had not had much effect upon Layamon. He expands Wace by adding concrete details that make the narrative more vivid (Arthur turns red and white when he learns that he has become king; Arthur receives fifteen wounds at his last battle, into the smallest of which one could thrust two gloves), by adding many similes that allude to nature, particularly animals, by developing descriptions of battle more fully, and by giving the characters more direct speech and thus making his episodes more dramatic (the compassion Uther Pendragon shows to the poor men asking for alms outside his castle; Arthur's nightmare that foreshadows the destruction of his kingdom just before he receives the news of Modred's rebellion). Some details that Layamon adds to his account, such as the name of Modred's son and the accounts of the elves blessing Arthur at his birth or of Arthur's being taken to Argente (Morgan) in Avalon, may come from oral Celtic traditions about Arthur.

In his attempt to write English alliterative verse and his preference for words of English rather than French origin, Layamon was undoubtedly writing for an English audience that had some nostalgia for pre-Conquest England; but his apparent sympathy for the British and his lack of sympathy for the invading Saxons, the ancestors of the English, have puzzled some modern readers. Like later English chroniclers, he may simply have felt enthusiasm for Arthur as a great hero who lived in what was to become England. He would also have seen a parallel between the Norman conquest of the English and the English conquest of the British and may have been presenting a sympathetic portrait of a people forced to defend their homeland against invaders, a situation that twelfth-century Englishmen could be expected to understand. Another possibility, which Stanley has pointed out, is that by accepting the anti-English attitude of his Anglo-Norman source Layamon was presenting to the English the moral cause for the Norman Conquest. Layamon would have known, at least through Bede, Gildas's warning that God had punished the British for their sins; and late in the Anglo-Saxon period Wulfstan, in his *Sermo Lupi ad Anglos*, had warned the English that God would similarly punish them. Layamon, in incorporating the anti-English attitude from his source, may have been thinking of the warning that God would punish the English just as he had punished the British, and the priest of Arley Regis may thus have been trying to present in his chronicle a moral explanation for the Norman Conquest. [EDK]

Layamon. *Brut*, ed. and trans. Frederic Madden. 3 vols. London: Society of Antiquaries, 1847.

———. *Brut*, ed. G.L. Brook and R.F. Leslie. London: Oxford University Press, 1963, 1978.

———. *Layamon's Brut: A History of the Britons*, trans. Donald G. Bzdyl. Binghamton, N.Y.: Medieval and Renaissance Texts and Studies, 1989.

Everett, Dorothy. "Layamon and the Earliest Middle English Alliterative Verse." In *Essays on Middle English Literature*, ed. Patricia Kean. Oxford: Clarendon, 1955, pp. 23–45.

Kennedy, Edward Donald. "Chronicles and Other Historical Writing." In *A Manual of the Writings in Middle English*, ed. A.E. Hartung. New Haven: Connecticut Academy of Arts and Sciences, 1981–89, Vol. 8, pp. 2611–17, 2781, 2798.

Le Saux, Françoise. *Layamon's "Brut": The Poem and Its Sources*. Woodbridge, Suffolk: Boydell and Brewer, 1989.

Stanley, E.G. "Layamon's Antiquarian Sentiments." *Medium Ævum*, 38 (1969), 23–37.

LEADER, MARY, American actress, journalist, and author of *Triad* (1973), a first novel of supernatural possession. Although set in the contemporary American Midwest, it incorporates not only figures from early Welsh tradition, such as Rhiannon and Branwen, but also Merlin, who is deceived yet again by Niniane. [RHT]

Leader, Mary. *Triad*. New York: Coward, McCann and Geoghegan, 1973.

LE CAIN, ERROL, wrote and illustrated *King Arthur's Magic Sword* (1968), a short children's book that makes imaginative use of illustrations to enhance the element of the marvelous. A gift from the Lady of the Lake, Excalibur is a magical sword that can change into many different things, from a boat to a toothpick, but it is eventually stolen from Arthur by Morgana le Fay. [RHT]

Le Cain, Errol. *King Arthur's Magic Sword*. London: Faber and Faber, 1968.

LEE, THOMAS HERBERT, in *The Marriage of Iseult: A Tragedy in Two Scenes* (1909), compresses the plot of the love story in order to intensify the tragedy, but the attempt is frustrated by inept and melodramatic writing. [RHT]

Lee, Thomas Herbert. *The Marriage of Iseult and Other Plays*. London: Mathews, 1909.

"LEGEND OF KING ARTHUR, THE." Although it has come to be recognized as a ballad in its own right, this poem of ninety-six lines constitutes the first part of a longer ballad in the Percy Folio entitled "King Arthur's Death." The "Legend" takes the form of a first-person narrative in which Arthur reviews the major events of his life, recalls his many military triumphs, and laments the unhappy consequences of his last great battle against Mordred. [JN]

Hales, John W., and Frederick J. Furnivall, eds. *Bishop Percy's Folio Manuscript*. London: Trübner, 1867–68, Vol. 1, pp. 497–501.

LELAND, JOHN (ca. 1503–1552), English antiquary. During the third and fourth decades of the sixteenth century, Leland traveled throughout England and Wales, examining library collections and also making detailed notes concerning architecture and landscape. A strong patriot, he was a firm upholder of Geoffrey of Monmouth's vision of the English past and defended in particular the historicity of King Arthur, whose name, he observed, was linked with many sites. Leland was the first known modern commentator to identify the legendary Camelot with South Cadbury, and he saw (and noted the inscription on) the famous leaden cross commemorating King Arthur at Glastonbury Abbey. From his notes, he composed, in 1544, his encyclopedic *Assertio Inclytissimi Arturii Regis Britanniae* (translated by Richard Robinson in 1582 as *A Learned and True Assertion of . . . Prince Arthure, King of Great Brittaine*). This text is a compilation of almost all the literary and archaeological evidence available in Tudor England on what would now be called the historical Arthur. [JPC]

Mead, W.E., ed. *The Famous Historie of Chinon of England by Christopher Middleton*. London, 1925.

Carley, James P. "Polydore Vergil and John Leland on King Arthur: The Battle of the Books." *Interpretations*, 15 (1984), 86-100.

LENAU, NIKOLAUS (1802–1850), author of a nine-part lyric poem cycle, *Waldlieder* (1843–44). Merlin the Magician is the focal point of Part V, the pivotal and longest (64-line) segment. An initiate, in harmony with the "eternal laws" of existence, Merlin is for Lenau the ultimate poet-priest-magician. In nature and the inner realm, Merlin attains the spiritual power, unity, insight, solace, and release that the despairing Lenau so ardently seeks. [RGD]

Lenau, Nikolaus. *Sämtliche Werke und Briefe*, ed. Walter Dietze. 2 vols. Frankfurt: Insel, 1971.

LEO I, Roman emperor in the East, reigning at Constantinople from 457 to 474. He supplies the only chronological fix for Arthur—that is, the only clear synchronization with known history outside Britain—that is given by any of the sources up to the time of Geoffrey of Monmouth.

Describing Arthur's expeditions to Gaul, Geoffrey portrays that country as still belonging to the empire, or at least claimed by it. However, the nature of the imperial power is ill defined. In the first expedition, Gaul is ruled by the tribune Frollo "in the name of Emperor Leo." In the second, there is an equivocal western emperor, Lucius. But Lucius has a colleague whose imperial status is definite, who is not in Rome but somewhere beyond, and whom Arthur never confronts; and this "real" emperor is still named as Leo, twice. In all three places, he can only be Leo I. Leo II was a child who succeeded him and died almost at once, and there was not another Leo for centuries. Even the allegiance of Frollo could have a factual basis. During the 460s, an interregnum occurred when Leo had no western colleague and was sole emperor.

The naming of Leo, three times, is wholly gratuitous, since he plays no part in the story. Geoffrey's general methods would suggest that when he wrote of Arthur's Gallic warfare his imagination was working (however wildly) on records putting British activities in Gaul in Leo's reign. He has a comparable chronological fix for Vortigern, making his major Saxon dealings coincide with the British mission of Germanus and Lupus, two Gallic bishops whose careers—including their visit to Britain in 429—are attested by continental records. In that instance, Geoffrey is undoubtedly drawing on older writings, and he is likely to be doing the same when he mentions Leo. (*See also* ARTHUR, ORIGINS OF LEGEND.) [GA]

Geoffrey of Monmouth. *Historia Regum Britanniae*, Book IX, Chapter 11; Book X, Chapter 6; Book XI, Chapter 1.

LEODEGRANCE (Leodegan), a character who first appears in the Vulgate *Merlin*. He is the father of Guenevere and the False Guenevere. In most accounts, it is from Leodegan that Arthur receives the Round Table, as part of Guenevere's dowry or as a gift on the occasion of her marriage to Arthur. [NJL]

LEOPARDI, GIACOMO (1798–1837), Italy's greatest modern poet, included a dialogue featuring Tristan in his *Operette Morali* (1832) and based his verse-drama *Telesilla* (1821) on Alamanni's *Gyrone*. [DLH]

Leopardi, Giacomo. "Dialogo di Tristano e di un amico." In *Operette morali. Opere*, Vol. 2: *Prose*, ed. Giovanni Feretti. Turin, 1965, pp. 272–82.

———. *Telesilla*. In *Opere*, Vol. 1: *Poesie*, pp. 255–83.

LERNER, ALAN JAY (1918–1986), wrote the libretto for *Camelot*, basing it freely on T.H. White's *The Once and Future King*. The music was by Frederick Loewe. First produced on Broadway in 1960, it was quite successful, though overshadowed by *My Fair Lady*. After a cheery opening depicting a dim-witted Arthur's marriage to Guenevere, the tone becomes more somber: Lancelot's principles and passions conflict, though the knight remains a glittering figure. Mordred is the villain of the piece but reaps no benefit. The musical is a curious mixture of comedy and chivalric sentiment, though the glorification of "one brief shining moment" of splendor struck a chord immediately after the death of John F. Kennedy. A film version of *Camelot*, directed by Joshua Logan, appeared in 1967. [CNS]

Lerner, Alan Jay. *Camelot: Book and Lyrics*. London: Chappell, 1960.

Laufe, Abe. *Broadway's Greatest Musicals*. New York: Funk and Wagnalls, 1969.

LESLIE, JOHN published his *De Origine, Moribus, et Rebus Gentis Scotorum* at Rome in 1578; it was translated into Scottish in 1596 by Father James Dalrymple. Like Boece, Bellenden, and Stewart, he limits Arthur's conquests to Britain, but he praises Arthur as noble, courageous, and honorable. He mentions Arthur's Round Table, which Leslie himself had seen, and notes that Arthur had twenty-four knights. (*See also* Boece, Hector.) [EDK]

Leslie, John. *Historie of Scotland*, trans. James Dalrymple, ed. E.G. Cody and William Murison. 2 vols. Edinburgh: Blackwood, 1888, 1895.

LEVEY, SIVORI, based two plays on Tennyson's *Idylls of the King*. *Guinevere and Arthur* (1919) and *Sir Gareth's Quest* (1920) consist of extracts from their source, adapted freely for dramatic presentation. [EB]

Levey, Sivori. *Guinevere and Arthur*. Roehampton: Fountain, 1919.
——. *Sir Gareth's Quest*. Roehampton: Fountain, 1920.

LEWIS, CHARLTON MINER (1866–1923), retells *Gawayne and the Green Knight* (1903) as an amusing fairy tale in four cantos of heroic couplets. Lewis introduces the maiden Elfinhart, whose foster mother in Fairyland devises the testing of Gawayne to prove him worthy of Elfinhart's love. [DN]

Lewis, Charlton Miner. *Gawayne and the Green Knight: A Fairy Tale*. Boston: Houghton-Mifflin, 1903.

LEWIS, C(LIVE) S(TAPLES) (1898–1963), British author of both popular and scholarly works, became a lifelong advocate of "romantic" literature after encountering the Scandinavian and Germanic myths as a child in Northern Ireland. He was drawn to the Arthurian legends later in his school years at about the time he was attempting his first serious creative work. He began *The Quest of Bleheris*, a prose romance, and apparently abandoned it before going up to Oxford in 1917, but a long narrative poem on Merlin and Nimue occupied him intermittently from 1919 to 1922. Both works have been lost.

In "Launcelot," which exists as a fragment of almost 300 lines of Alexandrine couplets, a subdued Launcelot tells Guinever of his failed Grail quest and of encounters with two maidens, each of whom displayed tombs reserved for the "three best knights." After learning that he is to be excluded from the resting place prepared for the virtuous Bors, Percivale, and Galahad, Launcelot makes his way to a palace of pleasure, where it is revealed that he is destined to there join Lamorake and Tristram in death, and at this point the poem breaks off. Probably written in the 1930s, "Launcelot" was published posthumously in 1969.

A slighter and only tangentially Arthurian work is *Mark vs. Tristram*, a series of letters initiated by Lewis's friend Owen Barfield, a solicitor as well as a writer, who claimed to represent King Mark in a lawsuit against Sir Tristram. Lewis responded with a letter from the firm of Blaise and Merlin. Two more letters from Barfield and one by Lewis completed the playful correspondence, which was exchanged in 1947 but not published until 1967.

The most notable and substantial of Lewis's Arthurian works is the novel *That Hideous Strength* (1945). In this conclusion to his Space Trilogy, Lewis uses traditional Grail characters and the idealistic essence of the legend to make his apocalyptic point. Edgestow, seat of Bracton College and a typical English country village, is being taken over by NICE (National Institute of Coordinated Experiments), an amalgam of sadistic, fascist technocrats dedicated to the principle of dehumanization and the establishment of an elite corps that would effect and then dominate a new world order. NICE plans to enlist the diabolic services of Merlin, who lies slumbering in nearby Bracton Wood. Opposing NICE is a small band of people headed by Elwin Ransom, who is called both the Pendragon and Mr. Fisher-King, and who has a painful, unhealable foot wound, the objective correlative of the NICE wasteland. Ransom and his group are the first to make contact with Merlin, who then spearheads the plan that turns NICE headquarters into a self-destructing Tower of Babel. Edgestow perishes in an apocalyptic holocaust, leaving Ransom's faithful remnant to restore civilization to their world. Ransom explains that England is two countries—Arthur's Logres and self-serving Britain, with a succession of Pendragons to uphold Logres throughout the ages. Thus, Lewis combines the belief in *Artus redivivus* with the Arthurian tradition of the Fisher King line of Grail guardians. Further, every nation is similarly dichotomized and haunted by its evil element, which must be constantly fought and overcome.

Although Lewis's *That Hideous Strength* is unabashedly reactionary with regard to scientific progress, empiricism, and atheism, his investing of human worth and hope in the Pendragon and Logres is in the mainstream of Arthurian moral realism. Moreover, his work, written in troubled modern times, strikes the dual apocalyptic theme of warning the world against encroaching disaster while affirming faith in a beneficent, providential Christian God.

In 1948, Lewis published *Arthurian Torso*, a volume for which he edited a fragmentary manuscript left by Charles Williams entited "The Figure of Arthur." It had been Williams's intention to reinterpret the legends of Arthur and the Grail in terms that supported the idiosyncratic spiritual symbolism of his own cycle of poems. Lewis elucidates Williams's plan in a lengthy commentary that proposes a sequence for reading the poems as a single work and clarifies the metaphorical geography and characterizations that inform the poetry. While conceding the obscurity that many readers of Williams's verse have encountered, Lewis's sympathy with his friend's Christian vision, so close to his own, finally ends with praise for the wisdom embodied in the poet's Arthuriad. [VML/DN]

Lewis, C.S. *That Hideous Strength: A Modern Fairy Tale for Grown-ups*. London: Lane, 1945.
———. "Williams and the Arthuriad." In *Arthurian Torso*, by Charles Williams and C.S. Lewis. London: Oxford University Press, 1948.
———. *Mark vs. Tristram: Correspondence Between C.S. Lewis and Owen Barfield*, ed. Walter Hooper. Cambridge, Mass.: Lowell House Printers, 1967.
———. "Launcelot." In *Narrative Poems*, ed. Walter Hooper. London: Bles, 1969.
Blechner, Michael Harry. "*Tristan* in Letters: Malory, C.S. Lewis, Updike." *Tristania*, 6 (Autumn 1980), 30–37.
Holmer, Paul. *C.S. Lewis: The Shape of His Faith and Thought*. New York: Harper and Row, 1976.
Moorman, Charles. *The Precincts of Felicity: The Augustinian City of the Oxford Christians*. Gainesville: University of Florida Press, 1966.
Wilson, A.N. *C.S. Lewis: A Biography*. London: Norton, 1990.

LEYDEN, JOHN (1775–1811), Scottish physician and poet whose *Scenes of Infancy* (1803) recalls, with Ossianic overtones, a Border childhood. Arthurian allusions include the Caledonian Merlin prophesying Camlann, Arthur's battles in the Cheviot Hills, and the legend of Arthur and his knights sleeping in the Eildon Hills until the horn's blast signals "proud Arthur's march from Fairyland." [MAW]

Leyden, John. *Scenes of Infancy Descriptive of Teviotdale*. Edinburgh: Ballantyne, 1803.

LIBER DE COMPOSITIONE CASTRI AMBAZIAE, Latin prose, ca. 1140. The founding legend of the House of Anjou contains a section on King Arthur, focusing on his war with Rome as an ally of Clodius. Lucius, the Roman general, is consul under the emperor Honorius. Sir Kay becomes the lord of Ambaziae. [MLD]

Marchegay, Paul Alexandre, and André Salmon, eds. *Chroniques des comtes d'Anjou*. Paris: Société de l'Histoire de France, 1856–71.

LIENHARD, FRIEDRICH (1865–1929), a versatile and prolific German journalist and writer who often employed medieval themes. In his "Parsifal und der Büsser" (1912), a poem of twelve stanzas, Lienhard depicts the protagonist as a heroic victor who changes the world. The author interprets the Grail as a symbol of German "inwardness." This orientation represents a misunderstanding of Richard Wagner. Lienhard is also the author of the play *König Arthur* (1900) and the novella *Merlin der Königsbarde* (1900). [UM/WCM]

Lienhard, Friedrich. "Parsifal und der Büsser." In *Lichtland: Neue Gedichte*. Stuttgart: Greiner und Pfeiffer, 1912.

LINDSAY, PHILIP (1906–1958), tells of Lancelot's tragic passion for Guinevere in *The Little Wench* (1935). With a wealth of medieval detail and references to many Arthurian tales, the long novel shows that love was "the poison that ate into the very heart of chivalry." Arthur remains a shadowy but charismatic figure in the background. [CNS]

Lindsay, Philip. *The Little Wench*. London: Nicholson and Watson, 1935.

LINWOOD, MARY, author of *The House of Camelot* (1858), a novel about descendants of Arthur who live in Armorica in the time of Charlemagne. After struggling against Saxon thanes who threaten his domain and seek the hand of his daughter Albinia, Avalloc, the ill-tempered Prince of Camelot, learns the superiority of Christian humility over pagan revenge. Supernatural elements, like a prophecy by Merlin, Taliessin's magic harp, and the drinking horn that protects the house of Camelot, are given rational, if implausible, explanations. [ACL]

Linwood, Mary. *The House of Camelot: A Tale of the Olden Times*. 2 vols. London: Hope, 1858.

LIOMBRUNO, an Italian *cantare* of the last third of the fourteenth century. It contains Arthurian allusions and is more permeated with fantasy—fairies, magic rings, enchanted cloaks—than other extant *cantari*. The protagonist, the son of a fisherman, is kidnaped by pirates. The fairy who saves him becomes his bride. The two are separated, but Liombruno is at last able to return to her, after many adventures. [SJN]

Levi, Ezio, ed. *Fiore di leggende: cantari antichi*. Bari: Laterza, 1914.

LIONEL, in the Third Continuation, the Vulgate Cycle, Malory's *Morte Darthur*, and modern versions, such as T.H. White's *Once and Future King*, King Bors's first son, Bors de Ganis's older brother, and Lancelot's cousin. Lionel was given his name because of a birthmark shaped like a lion. When Claudas killed Bors, he raised Bors's sons, Lionel and Bors the younger, at his own court. Bors's sons accidentally kill Claudas's son, and Seraide, one of Viviane's maidens, protects them by temporarily turning them into greyhounds. As an adult, Lionel goes with Bors, Gawain, and Bedivere on an embassy to Lucius, Emperor of Rome. He later embarks on a lengthy search for Lancelot, who had left Arthur's court in a fit of insanity that was caused by Guenevere. When Lancelot finally abandons Arthur's court, Lionel accompanies him in exile. He is slain during the battle between Mordred and Arthur, when Mordred is searching for Lancelot. [SW]

LIVELY, PENELOPE, combines details of modern life with Arthurian mystery in *The Whispering Knights* (1971), a children's tale. Three youngsters learn a lesson about responsibility when they reenact the witches' spell from *Macbeth* and conjure up Morgan le Fay. She threatens to despoil their Cotswold valley with a motor road, but her malevolence is defeated by the Whispering Knights, twenty-nine ancient standing stones outside the village. [CNS]

Lively, Penelope. *The Whispering Knights*. London: Heinemann, 1971.

LIVRE D'ARTUS, LE ("The Book of Arthur"), an independent prose continuation of Robert de Boron's *Merlin* contained only in Paris, B.N. f. fr. 337. Like the authors of the Vulgate *Merlin* and the *Suite du Merlin*, the anonymous composer of the *Livre d'Artus* felt the need to provide a transition from the material relating Merlin's conception and early marvels to the action of the Prose *Lancelot*. In a complex tapestry woven of threads from many sources (the Vulgate *Merlin* itself, Chrétien de Troyes's *Yvain* and *Erec et Enide*, and several lesser romances), the author seeks to tie up ends left dangling in texts earlier in the cycle and furnish links to episodes in subsequent books. It is indeed more closely linked to the following *Lancelot* than to the preceding *Merlin*. Following the traditional material from Robert's *Merlin*, the *Livre d'Artus* (whose real hero is actually Gawain) branches off into a long series of captures and rescues, battles and single combats, enchantments, love affairs, and the like. It continues the theme of Arthur's wars with the Saxons and presents Merlin in his usual roles of enchanter, sage, peacemaker, and prophet. [WWK]

Sommer, H. Oskar, ed. *The Vulgate Version of the Arthurian Romances*. 8 vols. Washington, D.C.: Carnegie Institution, 1908–16, Vol. 7.

Freymond, E. "Beiträge zur Kenntnis der altfranzösischen Artusromane in Prosa." *Zeitschrift für französische Sprache und Literatur*, 17 (1895), 1–128.

LLYWELYN, MORGAN, includes, among her fiction on the Celts, "Their Son" (1988), a short story about the son of Vivien and Merlin. Though he struggles against it, the young man learns to accept his destiny, which is to slay Modred at Camlann as partial recompense for his mother's depriving Arthur of his chief counselor. [RHT]

Llywelyn, Morgan. "Their Son." In *Invitation to Camelot: An Arthurian Anthology of Short Stories*, ed. Parke Godwin. New York: Ace, 1988, pp. 2–17.

LOATHLY LADY, sometimes named Ragnell; she is a character in Chaucer's *Wife of Bath's Tale* and in two English works, the romance *The Wedding of Sir Gawain and Dame Ragnell* (ca. 1450) and the ballad "The Marriage of Gawain." A knight (unnamed in Chaucer, Gawain in the others) is led to marry the hag, after which she reveals that she can be ugly by day and beautiful by night or vice versa; he is to choose. When he leaves the choice to her, she either swears eternal fidelity and constancy to him (in Chaucer) or is transformed into a perpetually beautiful lady.

The Loathly Lady theme has held limited appeal for Arthurian authors, owing perhaps to the difficulty of reconciling the idea of Gawain's marrying with his reputation, especially on the Continent, as a frivolous womanizer. Modern writers who do treat the theme often seek a rationalization of Gawain's act; Rosemary Sutcliff, for example, suggests that it is his defiant reaction to a taunt concerning his capacity for loyalty and devotion.

The Loathly Lady provided the inspiration for a 1984 children's opera, *Gawain and Ragnell*, by Richard Blackford, and the Gawain-Ragnell love story served, though awkwardly, as counterpoint to that of Lancelot and Guenevere in the 1985 CBS television film *Arthur the King*. [NJL]

LOCCUM FRAGMENTS, dated ca. 1300, contain 140 verses, many incomplete or illegible, the only remnants of Middle Low German Arthurian romance. The fragments were cut down from their original size to be used in binding a Latin prayer book from ca. 1500. Their mutilated state makes it difficult to deduce anything about the character of the narrative, but the names that occur suggest that the romance combined the Arthurian and oriental worlds. The fragments, which contain an unusually high concentration of French quotations, appear to be related to the Gahmuret-section of Wolfram von Eschenbach's *Parzival*. [MEK]

Beckers, Hartmut. "Ein vergessenes mittelniederdeutsches Artuseposfragment (Loccum, Klosterbibliothek, Ms. 20)." *Niederdeutsches Wort*, 14 (1974), 23–52.

———. "Mittelniederdeutsche Literatur—Versuch einer Bestandsaufnahme." *Niederdeutsches Wort*, 17 (1977), 25–26.

LODGE, DAVID, British author of *Small World* (1984), a comic novel that sets Grail motifs in the world of academic conferences. The plot centers on the international quest of the innocent Persse McGarrigle (= Percival) for the elusive Angelica Pabst (identical twin of Lily: cf. Spenser's *Faerie Queene* 2.66.6), which ends in his bedding the wrong twin during a Modern Language Association convention. But just before this, Persse has asked the crucial Question in a criticism section, thus miraculously (and quite inadvertently) restoring the intellectual and sexual powers of the eminent critic Arthur Kingfisher, whose release from impotence is accompanied by a sudden burst of summer weather, lifting the spirits of everyone in the midwinter wasteland of New York City. *Small World* was dramatized by Howard Schuman for Granada TV in Britain, where it was aired in six episodes during January and February 1987. [CBH/RHT]

Lodge, David. *Small World: An Academic Romance*. London: Secker and Warburg, 1984.

LOGAN, JOSHUA, American stage and film director, who in 1967 brought Lerner and Loewe's Broadway play *Camelot* to the screen as a three-hour movie. The film received mixed reviews. Logan himself had been dissatisfied with the Broadway play, whose casting and set "underwhelmed" him. Armed with a new scenario written especially for the film by Alan Jay Lerner, Logan cast Richard Harris as Arthur, Vanessa Redgrave as Guenevere, and Franco Nero as Lancelot and persuaded the producer, Jack Warner, to allow him to shoot on location in Spain.

The film is visually spectacular, and music and lyrics survive intact, despite the fact that none of the three principals is noted for his or her singing abilities. *Camelot* is limited in its approach to the story of Arthur by its genre. Both the play and the film are forced to tell a fairly one-dimensional musical version of a complex story, but both succeed admirably in doing so. [KJH]

Combs, Carl. *Camelot, The Movie Souvenir Booklet*. New York: National Publishers, 1968.

Logan, Joshua. *Movie Stars, Real People, and Me*. New York: Delacorte, 1978.

LOGRES, Celtic England, usually referring in a vague way to Arthur's kingdom. Logres is often the setting for adventure and romance, such as in Chrétien de Troyes's *Lancelot* and *Perceval* as well as in the Vulgate Cycle. Welsh texts refer to England as "Lloegyr." This is Latinized as "Loegria" and is later transformed into "Logres." ("England," which is a variant of "Angle-land," is a historical as well as a geographical designation and is technically incorrect when used to refer to Arthur's kingdom; the Anglo-Saxon conquest was still in its early stages when Arthur supposedly lived and was not completed until the ninth century, when "England" began to be used as a geographical term.) [SW]

LOHENGRIN (Loherangrin), in Wolfram von Eschenbach's *Parzival*, makes his appearance (very briefly) as the son of Parzival and Condwiramurs. His background and identity are cloaked in mystery, and his wife, the Princess of Brabant, is forbidden to ask of such matters; when she does, his fate is sealed, and he is borne away by a swan. The character and theme are treated further in the thirteenth-century German romance *Lohengrin*. In Wagner's opera *Lohengrin*, the hero explains, before his disappearance, that the Grail gives its guardians magical powers that can be maintained only so long as their identity is unknown. [NJL]

LOHENGRIN, a German Arthurian romance of 768 strophes of ten lines each, written between 1283 and 1289.

The work belongs to the Swan Knight tradition but is remarkable in that it combines the legend of the Swan Knight with the Grail legend and, furthermore, with the history of the Holy Roman Empire, the last deriving from the Saxon World Chronicle. Although the author appears to reveal his identity as "Nouhuwius" (or Nouhusius) in an achrosticon in stanzas 763–65, nothing is known about him. The hero of the romance, Lohengrin, already appears in Wolfram von Eschenbach's *Parzival* as the son of the eponymous protagonist. In *Lohengrin*, the writing on the Grail appoints the hero to champion Elsam of Brabant, who has been unjustly accused of breaking a promise of marriage. Lohengrin arrives in a ship drawn by a swan and gains victory over Elsam's accuser in judicial combat. Subsequently, he marries Elsam, but she is asked to make a promise, the nature of which the author does not reveal until the tragic conclusion: Elsam must not ask who her husband is or from where he comes. When she breaks her promise, egged on by the Countess of Kleve's suspicions that he is not of noble descent, Lohengrin reveals his identity but must now leave Elsam. The swan that brought him to Brabant takes him back to the Grail kingdom. Although there is a rich Swan Knight tradition in both French and German literature, *Lohengrin* does not derive from any of the known versions of the legend. A variant of *Lohengrin* is the fifteenth-century verse romance *Lorengel*. [MEK]

Cramer, Thomas. *Lohengrin: Edition und Untersuchungen*. Munich: Wilhelm Fink, 1971.

Lecouteux, Claude. "Zur Entstehung der Schwanenrittersage." *Zeitschrift für deutsches Altertum*, 107 (1978), 18–33.

LOHOLT (Loheant, Llacheu), in the Vulgate Cycle and various Welsh texts, such as the "Dialogue with Glewlwyd," the "Stanzas of the Graves," *The Spoils of Annwfn*, and *The Dream of Rhonabwy*, Arthur's illegitimate son. He is Arthur's legitimate son in the *Perlesvaus*. In both the *Perlesvaus* and the Vulgate, Loholt slays the giant Logrin and is in turn slain by Kay, who wants to take the credit for Logrin's death. [SW]

LOOMIS, ROGER SHERMAN (1887–1966), one of the most prolific and important scholars ever to be attracted to the Arthurian legend. Born in Japan and educated at Williams College, Harvard, and Oxford, he taught briefly at the University of Illinois and spent the remainder of his academic career at Columbia, with the exception of a year at Oxford.

Author or editor of more than twenty books and 100 articles, he is known principally as the foremost proponent of theories concerning the influence of Celtic legend and literature on Arthurian romance. From his 1927 book *Celtic Myth and Arthurian Romance* until his death, he refined his positions, adding or discarding facts and modifying interpretations, but remaining an ardent—he said "pugnacious"—champion of Celtic theories. His books and ideas provoked controversy (often heated), both because a good many scholars thought the ideas themselves radical or even fanciful and because Loomis sometimes pushed them to limits that even he eventually considered "rash." Among the formulations of his theories might be noted in particular *Arthurian Tradition and Chrétien de Troyes* (1949) and *The Grail: From Celtic Myth to Christian Symbol* (1963).

Whatever their views of Celtic theories, all Arthurian scholars are indebted to Loomis for his editing the monumental, and still standard, *Arthurian Literature in the Middle Ages: A Collaborative History* (1959). In addition, he authored, with Laura Hibbard Loomis, *Arthurian Legends in Medieval Art* (1938), the classic work on its subject. He moreover published on Chaucer (*A Mirror of Chaucer's World*, 1965), on medieval and Tudor drama, on folklore, and on other subjects. Along with Eugène Vinaver and Jean Frappier, Loomis was instrumental in the founding of the International Arthurian Society. [NJL]

Loomis, Roger Sherman. *Studies in Medieval Literature: A Memorial Collection of Essays*. With a Foreword by Albert C. Baugh and a Bibliography of Loomis by Ruth Roberts. New York: Franklin, 1970.

LORENGEL, an anonymous German stanzaic romance of the fifteenth century, which has been transmitted in two manuscripts. The romance is a variant of *Lohengrin*. Else (or Isilie) of Brabant is entrusted by her father prior to his death to a guardian, Friedrich von Dundramunt. When the latter tries to force her to marry him, she turns for assistance to the Emperor, who decrees that the matter is to be solved by judicial combat. When word reaches King Arthur's Grail kingdom that no one can be found to fight on behalf of Else, Lorengel, the son of Partzefal, is dispatched by a swan to come to the rescue. As in *Lohengrin*, the hero is victorious and marries the heiress. *Lorengel* deviates, however, in that the couple live happily ever after. Lorengel's mysterious identity does not become problematic, since the taboo concerning his background does not exist. The original contribution of the author of *Lorengel* is the incorporation of the Cologne legend of St. Ursula and the 11,000 virgins into the Swan Knight tradition. [MEK]

Buschinger, Danielle, ed. *Lorengel: édité avec introduction et index*. Göppingen: Kümmerle, 1979.

Steinmeyer, Elias. "Lorengel." *Zeitschrift für deutsches Alterthum*, 15 (1872), 181–244.

Thomas, Heinz. "Maximilian als Schwanritter: Zur Deutung und zur Datierung des 'Lorengel.'" *Zeitschrift für deutsches Altertum*, 116 (1987), 303–16.

LORGAIREACHT AN tSOIDHIGH NAOMHTHA ("Quest of the Holy Grail"), the only extant translation of a complete Grail romance into early Irish. It is the story given in the French Vulgate *Queste del Saint Graal*, although English titles and English forms of some names suggest that the immediate source of the Irish was not the French romance but an English translation of it, now lost. The Irish translation could conceivably date from the fourteenth century, although the second half of the fifteenth century is a more plausible possibility. The text is preserved in three manuscripts, all probably from the fifteenth century. All three are fragmentary; two are extensive fragments, while the third consists of two folios only. In all, about seventy percent of the narrative offered by the French *Queste* is preserved in the fragments.

In their narrative progression, the Irish and French texts consistently agree. They differ, however, on a good many details. Typical of the divergences are two examples cited by the editor of the Irish text (p. xvii). At one point, Bors notes that he has an urgent mission; in the French romance, he was to rescue Lionel, while the Irish indicates that his mission is the Grail quest. A ship containing Lancelot and the body of Perceval's sister in the French also holds the Grail table in the Irish version. Such alterations, whether due to the translator's innovations or included in his source, contribute, as Falconer notes (p. xvi), to "the heightened spiritual atmosphere of the Quest in Irish." [NJL]

Falconer, Sheila, ed. *Lorgaireacht an tSoidhigh Naomhtha*. Dublin: Dublin Institute for Advanced Studies, 1953.

LOT, King of Orkney and Lothian, husband of Morgause (or Anna)—Arthur's sister (or half-sister), and father of Gawain, Gaheris, Gareth, and Agravain. He is a rebellious vassal in Arthur's early reign but later becomes a staunch ally. He appears in all major versions of the Arthurian story from Geoffrey of Monmouth through the French prose romances and their derivations, including Malory. [KB]

LOUVRE TRAY. Arthurian heroes are among the devotees of Venus decorating a presentation tray once in the Arconati-Visconti Collection and now in the Louvre. The tray is one of the popular type known as *desco da parto*, on which gifts were brought to women after the birth of a child, a custom in fourteenth- and fifteenth-century northern Italy and Tuscany.

Six heroes—from left to right Achilles, Tristan, Lancelot, Samson, Paris, and Troilus, identified by the French form of their names—kneel in a lush meadow. All wear fashionable dress of ca. 1400. Lancelot and Tristan are represented as young lovers, while Achilles and Samson are older bearded knights. All turn and gesture toward Venus, who appears in a mandorla, flanked by winged bird-footed erotes, one of whom carries the bow and arrow of Cupid. Venus is represented as a nude, winged female wearing a crown on her long, flowing blonde hair. Beams of golden light stream from her to the heads of the knights. Such frankly sensual depiction of the theme of Venus's power, in a parody of Pentecostal iconography, heralds the Renaissance. [MS]

Whitaker, Muriel. *The Legends of King Arthur in Art*. Cambridge: Brewer, 1990, pp. 115–16.

LOVELICH, HENRY, author of *The History of the Holy Grail* (ca. 1450). This octosyllabic-couplet poem, a slavish translation of the Vulgate *Estoire del Saint Graal*, is the most complete English account of the early history of Joseph of Arimathea and the Holy Grail. Lacking the first eleven chapters, the extant work continues for forty chapters, recounting Joseph's service to the crucified Christ, his conversion, his apostolic mission as a latter-day Moses traveling westward with the ark of the Holy Grail, leading the Chosen People to the Promised Land of Britain, the conversion of Sarras, the evangelization of Britain, and the establishment of the line of Grail guardians that will extend to King Arthur's reign. Like the author of the *Joseph of Arimathie*, Lovelich consistently emphasizes the importance of Joseph over that of his fictional son, Josephe, and in Chapter 54, his most important departure from his source, he reports the burial of Joseph, Apostle of Britain, at Glastonbury Abbey.

Lovelich has also given us *Merlin* (ca. 1450), a verse translation of the Vulgate *Estoire de Merlin*. Unlike *Arthour and Merlin*, this work and the anonymous English Prose *Merlin* (ca. 1450–60) stress Merlin's role as the prophet of the Holy Grail, thereby allying him and Arthur with the vessel and its redemptive purpose. This alliance rests on four important links: 1) the Grail book, dictated by Merlin to the hermit Blaise; 2) the trinity of tables (the table of the Last Supper, the Grail table, and the Round Table; 3) the Arimathean lineage, whereby Percival, Galahad, and others are identified as "kin of Joseph of Arimathea," an honored

51. Louvre Tray, ca. 1400. (Cliché des Musées Nationaux, Paris.)

epithet; and 4) the Grail quest. Although a comparison of the English metrical and prose versions reveals a close agreement, Henry Wheatley feels that their differences indicate that the two translators worked independently from different French manuscripts. Lovelich's account ends at line 27,582 with Arthur's victory over Claudas, while the Prose *Merlin* continues until the births of Lancelot, Lionel, and Bors, and tells of the forthcoming quest of the Grail, which will test—and mark the dissolution of—Arthur's Round Table. [VML]

Lovelich, Henry. *The History of the Holy Grail* (Parts 1–4), ed. Frederick J. Furnivall. 4 vols. London: Trübner, 1874, 1875, 1877, 1878.

———. *Merlin* (Parts 1–3), ed. Ernst A. Kock. 3 vols. London: Oxford University Press, 1904, 1913, 1930.

Wheatley, Henry B., ed. *Merlin, or The Early History of King Arthur* (Parts 1–4). 4 vols. London: Kegan Paul, Trench, Trübner, 1865, 1866, 1869, 1899.

Ackerman, Robert W. "English Rimed and Prose Romances." In *Arthurian Literature in the Middle Ages*, ed. Roger Sherman Loomis. Oxford: Clarendon, 1959, pp. 485–89.

Eckhardt, Caroline D., ed. *The Prophetia Merlini of Geoffrey of Monmouth: A Fifteenth-Century English Commentary*. Cambridge: Medieval Academy of America, 1982, pp. 3–10.

Lagorio, Valerie M. "The Glastonbury Legends and the English Arthurian Grail Romances." *Neuphilologische Mitteilungen*, 4/79 (1978), 359–66.

LOVELL, GERALD, author of *Arthurian Epitaphs and Other Verse* (1976), which contains, besides the title poem, four Arthurian poems. "Arthurian Epitaphs" is a collection of eight verse epitaphs, for Arthur, Balin and Balan, Dagonet, Gareth, Gawaine, Merlin, Palamides, and Tristram. In "Mordred," Mordred is killed by the dream of Arthur even as he manages to kill it. Tristram, in "The Two Isouds," yearns toward Isoud of Brittany even as he rides toward Isoud of Cornwall and death. In "Palamides' Song" and "The Saracen and the Round Table," Palamides is shown to be alienated from love and from the faith of his father. These verses aim, through succinct language, to capture the irony or reversal in the knight's career. [PCB]

Lovell, Gerald. *Arthurian Epitaphs and Other Verse*. London: Mitre, 1976.

LOWE, SAMUEL E(DWARD), whose children's book *In the Court of King Arthur* (1918) tells the story of the page-boy Allan, who adventures with the great knights, becomes Sir Galahad and finds the Grail, and then retires with his lady fair. The story casts traditional characters into original, if uninspired, episodes. [DN]

Lowe, Samuel E. *In the Court of King Arthur*. Racine, Wis.: Whitman, 1918; repr. as *The Boy Knight*, 1922.

LOWELL, JAMES RUSSELL (1819–1891), American poet and essayist, whose poem *The Vision of Sir Launfal* (1848) tells of Launfal's quest for the Grail. The knight learns, through a dream vision, that the Grail is to be achieved not by searching throughout the world but by possessing a true spirit of charity. Lowell derived the name of his hero, though not his story, from *Sir Launfal*, by Thomas Chestre, and *Lanval*, by Marie de France, whom he considered one of the finest medieval writers.

Though not specifically Arthurian, Lowell's "A Legend of Brittany" has a knight named Mordred for its villain and a heroine who thinks of "Tristrem and of Lancilot" when she falls in love. [ACL]

Lowell, James Russell. *The Vision of Sir Launfal*. Cambridge: George Nichols, 1848.

LUCAN, Arthur's butler (or wine-steward) and a knight in the King's entourage; he is one of the last surviving knights. In the Vulgate *Mort Artu*, Arthur, grieved by the losses of his knights, embraces Lucan so strongly that he crushes him. In Malory, Lucan helps Bedivere to carry the wounded Arthur away, but he then dies of his own wounds. [NJL]

LUCIE-SMITH, (JOHN) EDWARD (McKENZIE), British writer, offers, in the laconic verses of the sequence "Fragments of a *Tristan*" that forms part of *Adam and Tristan*, a powerful version of the traditional tale. After "Tristan's Voyage" comes the chill horror of "Mariodoc's Dream." "In the Forest" portrays the fleeing lovers, and "Tristan's Madness" shows love unquenchable. *Adam and Tristan* concludes with "Adam and Tristan," which stresses the universality of the theme. [CNS]

Lucie-Smith, Edward. *Adam and Tristan*. In *Toward Silence*. London: Oxford University Press, 1968.

LUCIUS. In Geoffrey of Monmouth's *Historia*, Arthur's second and greater Gallic war is provoked by a demand for tribute from the Roman ruler Lucius Hiberius. Geoffrey hesitates over his status. He introduces him as Procurator of the Republic. "Procurator" was a title given to deputies of the emperor in minor provinces. It suggests something less than supreme authority, and that impression is reinforced by the fact that the Senate has power to give Lucius orders. Later, Geoffrey calls him an emperor; but he associates him with another, who is not in Rome, who is inactive throughout, yet whose imperial dignity is unquestioned.

In Wace and subsequent romance, Lucius becomes, simply, an emperor. However, his original ambiguity points to an awareness on Geoffrey's part of the realities of the period 455–76. During that time, the empire was breaking up in the West, and the western emperors were evanescent figures with little real power. Their eastern colleagues were still dominant, securely enthroned. Geoffrey confirms this reading of his ideas by calling Lucius's coemperor Leo. He is clearly thinking of Leo I, who reigned at Constantinople throughout most of this period,

Where he found Lucius is not so clear. No such emperor ever existed. A sustainable conjecture is that he took him from the *Chronicle* of Sigebert of Gembloux (d. 1112). Noting the late western emperor Glycerius, Sigebert gives this unfamiliar name as *Lucerius* and allots the reign, inaccurately, to the years 469–70. Thus, he gives Leo I a western colleague with a name that Geoffrey could have garbled, quite characteristically, into *Lucius*. (*See also* ARTHUR, ORIGINS OF LEGEND.) [GA]

Geoffrey of Monmouth. *Historia Regum Britanniae*, Book IX, Chapter 15, through Book X, Chapter 13.

LUCKA, EMIL (1877–1941), German writer of novels, dramas, and essays. In 1908 or 1909 appeared a "story of olden times," *Isolde Weisshand*. The tale begins after the discovery of the lovers' adultery, when Tristan is forced to leave Mark's court. He marries Isolde of the White Hands after she cures him of a wound with skills she learned from Merlin. He leaves her, however, after the wedding night and goes off in search of Isolde the Fair ("Isolde Blondhaar"). While at sea, he happens upon a ship meant to bring Isolde the Fair to her final resting place. Together they disappear into the ocean fog. [SSch/WCM]

Lucka, Emil. *Isolde Weisshand*. Berlin: Fischer, [1909?].

Schwarz, Alexander. *Sprechaktgeschichte: Studien zu den Liebeserklärungen in mittelalterlichen und modernen Tristandichtungen*. Göppingen: Kümmerle, 1984.

LUNETEN MANTEL, DER ("Lunet's Mantle"), an anonymous fifteenth-century Shrovetide play that derives ultimately from *Le Mantel mautaillié*, presumably via the thirteenth-century Middle High German version *Der Mantel*. A lady named Lunet sends a magic mantle to Arthur's court; it will be given to the woman whom it best fits—that is, a faithful woman. By shrinking and tearing as one woman after another tries on the magic garment, the mantle reveals the rampant infidelity of Arthur's court. The tone of the play is coarse, and the exposed women glibly rationalize their infidelity by pointing out the sexual inadequacies of their husbands. Not only Guenevere and the wives of mighty kings, but even the wife of the court jester, fail the test. The day is finally saved by the youngest queen present, wife of the King of Spain, the oldest monarch among those assembled. The play concludes with praise for pure wives. [MEK]

Keller, Adelbert von, ed. *Der Luneten Mantel*. In *Fastnachtspiele aus dem fünfzehnten Jahrhundert*. Zweiter Theil. Stuttgart: Litterarischer Verein, 1853, pp. 664–78.

Walsh, Martin W. "*Arthur Cocu*: Comic Abuse of the Round Table in Fifteenth-Century *Fastnachtspiele*." *Fifteenth-Century Studies*, 15 (1989), 305–21.

LUPACK, ALAN, American author of *The Dream of Camelot* (1990), a cycle of twenty-seven poems treating the Arthurian legend from the time Arthur draws the sword from the stone. Lupack deals with the affair of Lancelot and Guinevere (and that of Tristan and Isolt), and with the treachery of Morgan and later of Mordred, before turning to the Grail quest and finally to Arthur's departure for Avalon. In the last of the poems, "The Passing of Arthur," the King laments the ruin of Camelot but affirms its dream; and before boarding the boat that will bear him to Avalon, he orders Bedivere to throw his sword into the lake and "let the gentle waters/wash the blood from Excalibur." [NJL]

Lupack, Alan. *The Dream of Camelot*. Vista, Calif.: Green Chapel, 1990.

LYDGATE, JOHN (1370–1451), English poet. Drawing upon Laurent de Premierfait's French translation of Boccaccio's *De Casibus Virorum Illustrium*, Lydgate presents in *Fall of Princes* an account of Arthur's war against the Roman consul Lucius that Boccaccio had adapted from some Arthurian chronicle. Lydgate, however, eliminates most of Arthur's flaws that appear in his source and adds details that make Arthur into a greater king. Although many of Lydgate's other monarchs in *Fall of Princes* fall because of "vicious living," Arthur's tragedy is due to envious Fortune and to Mordred, who treacherously rebelled against him. [EDK]

Lydgate, John. *Lydgate's Fall of Princes* (Part 3), ed. Henry Bergen. London: Oxford University Press, 1924, pp. 898–914. (The pages on Arthur in Boccaccio and Laurent de Premierfait appear in Part 4, 1927, pp. 327–36.)

Dwyer, Richard A. "Arthur's Stellification in the *Fall of Princes*." *Philological Quarterly*, 57 (1978), 155–71.

Göller, Karl Heinz. *König Arthur in der englischen Literatur des späten Mittelalters*. Göttingen: Vandenhoeck and Ruprecht, 1963, pp. 131–36.

Withrington, John. "The Arthurian Epitaph in Malory's *Morte Darthur*." *Arthurian Literature*, 7 (1987), 103–44.

LYFE OF JOSEPH OF ARMATHY, THE, a prose translation printed by Wynkyn de Worde of Joseph's *vita* in Capgrave's *Nova Legenda Angliae*, the third in a series of legendaries of exclusively English saints, which were indicative of the rising nationalism of the English people. The *Lyfe* relies heavily on the apocryphal *Gospel of Nicodemus* and *Transitus Mariae* accounts of Joseph's post-Crucifixion activities and subsequent conversion by St. Philip. It then turns to the *Estoire* version of his apostolic journey to the Promised Land of Britain, his evangelization of Britain with his son Josephes, his imprisonment by the evil king of North Wales, and his subsequent rescue by King Mordrains. There is no mention of Joseph's Glastonbury connection.

A *Verse Lyfe of Joseph of Armathia*, printed by Richard Pynson in 1520, is a compendium of the apocryphal gospels concerning Joseph, the *Estoire* account of his journey westward and subsequent conversion of Britain, and John of Glastonbury's *Cronica* account of Joseph being sent to Britain by St. Philip and his dwelling with twelve hermits at Glastonbury, where he built Our Lady's Chapel, died, and was buried (ll. 1–232). There follows an extensive list of his posthumous miracles and an earnest entreaty for pilgrims to come to Glastonbury and pray to St. Joseph, who lies near the grave of King Arthur. Symbolizing this fusion of traditions, the Glastonbury arms appear on the title page: a white shield with drops of blood scattered over the white field, and a green, knotted cross, on either side of which is a golden ampule, representing the two cruets in which Joseph, according to Melkin's prophecy, carried the Precious Blood of Christ to Glastonbury.

"A Praysing of Joseph" follows, filled with hyperbolic epithets characteristic of a saint's litany, designed to appeal to the reader's nationalistic pride in England's own apostolic saint. The poem ends with an *Officium* consisting of liturgical prayers and responses lauding the saint. [VML]

Skeat, W.W., ed. *Joseph of Arimathie*. London: Trübner, 1871, pp. 27–32, 37–52.

Horstmann, Carl, ed. *Nova Legenda Angliae*. Oxford: Clarendon, 1901, Vol. 2, pp. 78–82.

Lagorio, Valerie M. "The Evolving Legend of St. Joseph of Glastonbury." *Speculum*, 46 (1971), 209–31.

———. "The Vita of a Grail Saint." *Zeitschrift für germanische Philologie*, 91 (1975), 54–68.

LYLE, WALTER, called *Badon Mountain* (1969), his book-length narrative in well-crafted Spenserian stanzas, a "synthetic mythology." In the poem, Britain's ancient gods arise to assist Aurelian, the Arthur figure, against the invading Saxons of Odin, and the war culminates with the taking of Hengist's stronghold on Badon. [DN]

Lyle, Walter. *Badon Mountain*. London: Mitre, 1969.

LYNETTE (Lynet, Lyonet), character who first appears in Malory's "Tale of Sir Gareth of Orkney," where she comes to Arthur's court in search of a champion to rescue her sister, Lyones. When the quest is claimed by Gareth, she is outraged and taunts him unmercifully, for she believes him no more than a kitchen knave. Gradually, however, she is won over by his patience and valor and eventually marries his brother, Gaheris.

Doubtless impressed by this pattern of female repentance for criticizing male judgment, Tennyson rewards her at the end of "Gareth and Lynette" by suggesting that the hero may have married her rather than her sister. Modern accounts of Lynette include Vera Chapman's *The King's Damosel*, where she achieves the Grail quest, and Thomas Berger's ironic novel *Arthur Rex*, where she declares, "It is far more shameful to be saved by a scullion than to be ravished by a person of one's own class." [RHT]

LYONESSE, a country of romance. In the best-known versions of the story of Tristan, he is the son of its king. It may originally have been Leonais in Brittany, or Lothian (Old French *Loenois*) in Scotland. However, it eventually becomes part of Cornwall. As such, it is more or less equated with a region known to Cornish folklore as Lethowstow. According to legend, this is now under the sea. It formerly filled the present Mount's Bay and stretched far west around Land's End and beyond, joining the Isles of Scilly to the mainland and to each other. Mostly low-lying, it contained a number of towns and 140 churches. At some indefinite date, the ocean swept in, and it has been submerged ever since.

This extension of Cornwall resembles other minor "Atlantises." Wales has its Lost Cantref (district) under Cardigan Bay, and Brittany its drowned city of Ker-Is. Lyonesse is not completely devoid of factual foundation. Part of Mount's Bay was above water and inhabited as late as the second millennium B.C. In the Scillies, remains of huts and walls below the high-water mark suggest that there was land linking some of the islands in the early Christian era. The fourth-century emperor Maximus banished a heretic to the *Sylina Insula*—the isle of Scilly. At that time, enough of the islands may have been connected to give the impression of a single main piece of land, rather than an archipelago.

In the realm of Arthur, Lyonesse is somewhat marginal. It includes a district, Surluse, that is ruled by Galahalt, and he is described as lord of the Loingtaines, or Faraway, Isles, suggesting a confused notion of the Scillies. Today, one of them is called Great Arthur, and an islet is Little Arthur. Tennyson makes Lyonesse the scene of the King's last battle; Excalibur is cast away from a "strait of barren land" suggested by Loe Bar, a ridge dividing Loe Pool from open water, where the coast east of Mount's Bay runs down to the promontory of the Lizard. In recent years, Lyonesse has become the setting for a series of "pre-Arthurian" fantasies by the American novelist Jack Vance. [GA]

Ashe, Geoffrey. *A Guidebook to Arthurian Britain*. Wellingborough: Aquarian, 1983, pp. 149–51.

Thomas, Charles. *Exploration of a Drowned Landscape*. London: Batsford, 1985, pp. 276–94.

LYSER, JOHANN PETER (pseudonym of Ludwig Peter August Burmeister; 1804–1870), German poet, folklorist, translator, graphic artist, and musician. Burmeister is responsible for one of the most curious transmutations of the Arthurian mantle tale, the oldest literary attestation of which is *Le Mantel mautaillié*. In Lyser's collection of folk and fairy tales *Abendländische Tausend und eine Nacht* (1838), there appears as the story of the 600th through 605th nights a tale entitled "Lenora" after its eponymous heroine.

In Lyser's version of the mantle tale, the heroine is falsely accused of a liaison with a black knight. The charge is brought by Guinevere and her ladies out of spite that Adolar, one of the most eligible young knights at Arthur's court, should spurn them for Lenora. The heroine's name is cleared when the chastity-testing mantle is brought to Arthur's court and she alone succeeds in the trial by mantle.

Lyser himself informs us in a note to the tale that he knew both Benedikte Naubert's *Der kurze Mantel* and Werthes's *Das Pfauenfest*. In addition, Lyser also drew on an oral version, which he does not, however, identify. [MEK]

Lyser, Johann Peter. *Abendländische Tausend und eine Nacht, oder die schönsten Mährchen und Sagen aller europäischen Völker*. Meissen: Goedsche, 1838, Vol. 8, pp. 249–54; Vol. 9, pp. 3–16.

LYTTON, EDWARD ROBERT BULWER (1831–1891), First Earl of Lytton and the son of writer Edward Bulwer-Lytton. Like his father, who wrote the Arthurian epic *King Arthur* (1848), Lytton was interested in the Arthurian stories and wrote three Arthurian poems, published under his pen-name Owen Meredith. "Queen Guenevere" (1855) paints a vivid portrait of Arthur's queen. "Elayne le Blanc" (1855) nicely captures the isolation and yearning of the young Elayne in her tower above the road, reading romances and singing songs, until she sees Launcelot through her window. All the frustration, bitterness, guilt, and longing felt by the Queen and her lover find a voice in "The Parting of Launcelot and Guenevere: A Fragment" (1855), as they argue, are reconciled, and then part. [PCB]

Meredith, Owen. *Poems*. Boston: Houghton-Mifflin, 1882.

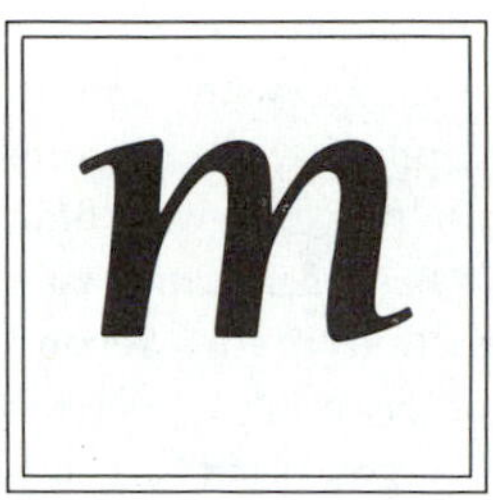

MABINOGI (MABINOGION). The four "branches" of the *Mabinogi* represent the finest flowering of the Welsh genius in the Middle Ages. Although the branches—the tales of *Pwyll*, *Branwen*, *Manawydan*, and *Math*—are only loosely connected, they are, as the metaphor suggests, sprung from the common root of inherited Celtic tradition. Sometime around the middle of the eleventh century, a single writer of considerable ability gave shape to this material in approximately the form we have it now, although the two surviving complete versions are found in manuscripts of a later period, the White Book of Rhydderch (ca. 1325) and the Red Book of Hergest (ca. 1400).

The term *mabinogi* has been subjected to close scrutiny a number of times, and for years it was understood to be built on the word *mab* 'son' and to be roughly equivalent in meaning to French *enfance*, and therefore to be a story of boyhood deeds or of youth in general. In fact, the word is used to translate Latin *infantia* in a fourteenth-century gospel of the boyhood of Jesus. (The term *mabinogion* occurs by scribal error once in the manuscripts; it was used by Lady Charlotte Guest, who thought it was a plural of *mabinogi*, as the title of her translations, which appeared 1838–49. It is still used for the sake of convenience by some scholars.) The most recent explanation of *mabinogi* is that it is a word that originally meant a collection of material relating to the British-Celtic god Maponos, or "divine youth."

This last explanation fits in well with the fact that the *Mabinogi* is heavily informed by inherited Celtic mythological traditions, and it is these traditions that scholars have long sought to unravel in their discussions of the four branches. In the first branch, for example, we find reflections of the horse-goddess Epona, a Celtic divinity worshiped virtually throughout Gaul and, adopted by Roman cavalry units, in Rome. In the many surviving depictions of Epona, we find her seated on a horse or between horses, surrounded by birds, holding a bag or cornucopia, symbols of bounteous sustenance. Her Latin nickname was *Regina*, and in the *Mabinogi* she appears as Rhiannon ("great queen, queen goddess"), riding slowly past the magical mound on which Pwyll and his retainers sit. Yet, however slowly she rides, the fastest horse in the realm cannot catch her. Later in the story, after she has been accused of destroying her son, she is driven from the court and compelled to act like a horse, carrying visitors to the court on her back. Besides her abundant equine associations, Rhiannon, like Epona, possesses a bag into which endless quantities of food can be put, and there is reference to the birds of Rhiannon in the second branch. Scholars are in agreement that her antecedents lie in Celtic traditions about the great mother goddess Epona. The fourth branch introduces us to another well-known Celtic goddess, Dôn. In Irish, she is known as Danu, mother of the mythological tribe the Túatha Dé Danann. She is tutelary goddess of the River Donau and a host of other rivers on the Continent.

And yet the stories themselves are not, superficially, concerned with myth. While we have no information about the author/redactor, the circumstances responsible for his undertaking the work, the conditions under which the stories were told or read, or the audience, it seems clear from the way in which the stories develop that the primary interest lay in their entertainment value. Whether or not she is Epona and whether or not the audience was aware of that, Rhiannon is depicted as a strong-willed woman capable of taking charge of her own destiny. She leaves her own kingdom because her people are trying to marry her to a suitor she does not want. She tells Pwyll that she wants him for a husband—and the sooner the better. Later, when he has botched the wedding feast and is in danger of losing her, she berates him for his foolishness and then patiently explains to him how he can rectify the situation. Even her punishment is undertaken with her own complicity and by her leave. Her character is strongly contrasted with that of Pwyll, who is indecisive and passive. In the third branch, her husband is Manawydan, and here too there is stark contrast between the assertive Rhiannon and her passive mate. Branwen, in the second branch, presents a different type of woman, one whose family makes decisions for her and who accepts her fate unquestioningly.

While myth may not function in an explicit way in the tales, magic and enchantment certainly do. The mound at Arberth is explicitly a place to which one goes to behold wonders. Bendigeidfran (Bran the Blessed) is so big that he can cross the Irish sea by wading and, lying across a river, be a bridge over which his army can pass. In the third branch, the kingdom of Dyfed becomes a wasteland—buildings, animals, people, all save the four principals of the story disappear. In the fourth branch, a virgin gives birth to twins while stepping across a magic wand, the brothers Gwydion and Gilfaethwy are turned into animals who mate with each other and bear offspring, a wife for Lleu is made from flowers, and so on. Although these acts of magic are integral to the stories, they are presented in a completely unselfconscious way in the narratives. Pwyll does not seem surprised when he unexpectedly encounters Arawn, king of Annwfn (the otherworld), even though Pwyll is hunting in his own kingdom. Gwydion and Gilfaethwy clearly object to being turned into animals and try to escape Math's punishment, but they get through the three years in animal form without much more apparent discomfort than if they had been away at boarding school—and without raising the eyebrows of any of the other characters. In the four branches, then, wonder, magic, and marvels are taken for granted. The storyteller's principal concern is with the characters and their relationships to one another as they move through the story. Indeed, some of the most memorable scenes in the *Mabinogi* are those involving human relationships: the pillow talk between Arawn and his wife when he returns to her after being away for a year; the scene in which Manawydan reassures the bereft Cigfa; Gwydion's grief and search for his nephew; and the scene in which Gronw and Blodeuedd fall in love at first sight, then plot their adulterous affair.

The geographical detail in the tales is for the most part authentic. The first and third branches are set in Dyfed in southwest Wales; the second is set at Harlech in mid-north Wales and in Ireland; the fourth branch is set mainly in north Wales. In the third branch, Manawydan and Pryderi travel into England to practice their crafts. It is not so easy, however, to determine the temporal setting of the tales. The characters swear by God, and there is a bishop and a priest in the third branch, but the tales are clearly pre- or at least non-Christian. The one possibly historical character named in the four branches is Caswallawn, the Welsh form of the name Cassivellaunos, who led his people in battle against Caesar in Britain in 54 B.C.; otherwise, the time frame is almost entirely obscure.

For students of Arthurian literature, the second branch holds perhaps the greatest interest. The name Bendigeidfran is a Welsh compound that means "Blessed Bran," and this figure has generally been taken to be the prototype of Bron, the Fisher King of the Grail romances. To be sure, the epithet "blessed" conjures up notions of Christian sanctity, and that is probably why this Bran was credited with introducing Christianity into Britain. (In a Welsh Triad of the "Three Saintly Lineages of the Isle of Britain," one of its early editors substituted the name of Bran the Blessed for Joseph of Arimathea.) *Bendigeid* is a clear borrowing from Latin *benedictus* and was no doubt substituted for an earlier native word that meant "blessed" in non-Christian contexts. Welsh *gwen* (masculine *gwyn*; in compounds, without initial g-) is just such a word, and it has special otherworldly and mythological connotations. In particular, it is found in many of the words for things associated with Arthur in Welsh tradition: Ehang*wen*, his dwelling; Pryd*wen*, his ship (or shield); *Gwen*hwyfar, his wife; Carn*wennan* (with diminutive suffix), his knight; *Gwenn*, the mantle that renders him invisible. Interestingly enough, the resulting form with Bran would be Branwen, the name given to Bendigeidfran's sister in the second branch. Bran's depiction in the second branch establishes him clearly as an otherworldly type. He is said to be the son of Llŷr (Lear), the sea-god (Irish *Ler*), and his ability to cross water without the aid of a ship reinforces that connection. The word *bran* in Welsh means "crow, raven" and is often used as an epithet for a warrior. Indeed, in Irish mythological tradition the scald-crow is the preeminent form assumed by the warrior-goddess.

The four branches of the *Mabinogi* constitute important reflexes of inherited Celtic tradition in the Middle Ages. Although Arthur does not appear in these tales, some of the *Mabinogi* characters—e.g., Pryderi, Pwyll, Gwydion, and Math—appear with Arthur in other branches of the tradition, and the tales depict a world in which the native Welsh Arthur would be very much at home. (*See also* WELSH ARTHURIAN LITERATURE.) [PKF]

Evans, J. Gwenogvryn, ed. *The White Book Mabinogion*. Pwllheli, 1907.

Williams, Ifor, ed. *Pedeir Keinc y Mabinogi*. Cardiff: University of Wales Press, 1930.

Ford, Patrick K., trans. *The Mabinogi and Other Medieval Welsh Tales*. Berkeley: University of California Press, 1977.

Bollard, J. K. "The Role of Myth and Tradition in *The Four Branches of the Mabinogi*." *Cambridge Medieval Celtic Studies*, 6 (1983), 67–86.

Bromwich, Rachel. *Trioedd Ynys Prydein*. Cardiff: University of Wales Press, 1961; 2nd ed. 1978.

Ford, Patrick K. "On the Significance of Some Arthurian Names in Welsh." *Bulletin of the Board of Celtic Studies*, 30 (1983), 268–73.

———. "Prolegomena to a Reading of the *Mabinogi*: 'Pwyll' and 'Manawydan.'" *Studia Celtica*, 16/17 (1981–82), 110–25.

———. "Branwen: A Study of the Celtic Affinities." *Studia Celtica*, 22/23 (1987–88), 29–41.

Hamp, Eric P. "Mabinogi." *Transactions of the Honourable Society of Cymmrodorion*, 1974–75, 243–49.

Jarman, A.O.H., and Gwilym Rees Hughes. *A Guide to Welsh Literature I*. Swansea: Davies, 1976.

MacCana, Proinsias. *The Mabinogi*. Cardiff: University of Wales Press, 1977.

McCLOSKEY, GEORGE V.A. (1883–1933), author of "The Flight of Guinevere" (1921), a collection of undistinguished dramatic monologues, in which Arthur, Guinevere, and Lancelot reflect on the sorrows of their lives. A later monologue, "Nimue to Merlin" (1927), is a poetic treatment of the imprisonment of love. [DN]

McCloskey, George V.A. *The Flight of Guinevere and Other Poems.* New York: Authors and Publishers, 1921; rev. ed. 1928.

MacCORMAC, JOHN, produced an early Arthurian foray into pulp fiction with his long story "The Enchanted Weekend" (1939), which appeared in one of the first issues of *Unknown*, a magazine of popular fantasy. The story's hero, a young American scholar in Cornwall to research the Arthurian legend, releases Merlin from his tomb and is rewarded with magical powers, which, after a series of comic adventures, enable him to win a young Lady Niniane. [DN]

MacCormac, John. "The Enchanted Weekend." In *From Unknown Worlds*, ed. John W. Campbell, Jr. New York: Street and Smith, 1948.

McDOWELL, IAN, wrote "Son of the Morning" (1983), a short fantasy in which Arthur comes to Orkney to battle a troublesome giant and discovers his paternity of Mordred. The story unevenly blends comic and religious elements with the fantastic. [DN]

McDowell, Ian. "Son of the Morning." In *Isaac Asimov's Science Fiction Magazine*, December 1983, 112–33; repr. in *Isaac Asimov's Fantasy!*, ed. Shawna McCarthy. New York: Dial, 1985.

McGOWEN, TOM (THOMAS), editor and author of *Sir MacHinery* (1971), a fantasy for juveniles. In Scotland, the demons are preparing to attack humankind but are foiled by the brownies, who enlist the aid of Merlin, a hippie scientist called Arthur, and a robot whom they mistake for a knight. [RHT]

McGowen, Tom. *Sir MacHinery*. Chicago: Follett, 1971.

MACHEN, ARTHUR (LLEWELLYN JONES) (1863–1947), Welsh novelist, journalist, translator, essayist, actor, and mystic, regarded the Grail legends as "the glorified version of early Celtic Sacramental Legends." The Arthurian knights represented Welsh saints; the "desolate enchantment of Britain," the Celtic church's defeat by the Roman; and the Grail, a persistent source of glory and power, knowledge of which was transmitted by the "Secret School." These ideas were expressed in critical articles (e.g., *Academy*, [1907]), in *The Glorious Mystery* (1924), and in two novels, *The Great Return* (1915) and *The Secret Glory* (1922). Machen uses the theory of perichoresis (cyclical return) to explain the reappearance of the Grail in modern times, an idea adopted by Charles Williams and C.S. Lewis. In *The Great Return*, a reporter investigates strange occurrences in the Welsh village of Llantrisant—an unnaturally bright light and the smell of incense in the church, the ringing of the wonderful bell of Teilo Sant, and miraculous cures. (One reviewer complained that even if there were a Grail that could return, Machen lacked good taste in making it appear to common farmers and village grocers.)

The Secret Glory combines savage criticism of the English public school with an allegorical representation of the Grail quest. The hero, Ambrose Meyrick, is so persecuted by masters and fellow students that, having established his supremacy in studies and sports, he runs away to London with a housemaid. There, he leads a free but increasingly renunciatory life. An epilogue describes his journey to Asia with the Grail, which he had seen as a boy in the possession of a Welsh farmer, Cradock, and of which he has now become the Keeper. Having completed "the most glorious Quest and Adventure of the Sangraal" by withdrawing the vessel from the materialistic world, he is crucified by Turks.

Machen also wrote a short story, "Guinevere and Lancelot" (1909), which follows Malory's account of their love affair, except that the Queen uses a sorcerer's magic spell to entrap the knight. [MAW]

Machen, Arthur. *The Great Return*. Westminster: Faith, 1915.
———. *The Secret Glory*. London: Secker, 1922.
———. *The Glorious Mystery*. Chicago: Covici-McGee, 1924.
———. *The Autobiography of Arthur Machen*, intro. Marchard Bishop. London: Richards, 1951.
———. "Guinevere and Lancelot." In *Guinevere and Lancelot and Others*, ed. Michael T. Shoemaker and Cuyler W. Brooks, Jr. Newport News, Va.: Purple Mouth, 1986, pp. 7–15.

MACHOLIN, PETER (1877–?), German writer, treated a variety of historical themes and legends lyrically and dramatically in his *Parsifal* (1928). Macholin divides his drama into a prologue (Parsifal's youth) and three acts. The author shows Parsifal torn between Klingsor and the Grail. Klingsor makes use of a vacillating Cundrie to mislead the hero and keep him from unlocking the secret of the Grail. An angel watches over Parsifal, however, and leads him to

Trevrizent. The latter tells him everything and sends him to find the Grail. Upon finding the Grail, Parsifal becomes king. Cundrie begs forgiveness and dies as a penitent. [SSch/PM]

Macholin, Peter. *Parsifal: Ein romantisches Spiel.* Nehn: Höfling, 1949.

McINTOSH, J.F. (pseudonym of James Murdoch MacGregor), Scottish author who creates a feudal culture on a planet named Avalon in his science-fiction short story "Merlin" (1960). The characters are given Arthurian names, but their behavior is only loosely modeled on that of their namesakes. [RHT]

McIntosh, J.F. "Merlin." *Fantastic*, 9 (March 1960), 6–49.

MacLEISH, ARCHIBALD (1892–1982), American poet, dramatist, essayist, teacher, and public servant. In 1927, MacLeish published "Bleheris," an Arthurian poem of nearly 200 lines. Drawing mainly on Jessie L. Weston's *From Ritual to Romance*, MacLeish recounts in a powerful Anglo-Saxon rhythm and manner the sea and land journeys of a Gawain-type Grail knight to a deserted, mysterious chapel and a Grail "castle," the ruined palace of a deserted city in an Eliotic wasteland. The next year, MacLeish included the poem as Part 3 of *The Hamlet of A. MacLeish*; Bleheris's Grail quest here contrasts with the uncertainties of MacLeish's Hamlet. When he reprinted the complete *Hamlet of A. MacLeish* in his first collected edition, *Poems 1924–1933*, MacLeish intensified this contrast by cutting out the visit to a deserted city and making even more vivid Bleheris's quest to a Grail chapel. [LL]

MacLeish, Archibald. *Collected Poems 1917–1982.* Boston: Houghton Mifflin, 1985.

Lane, Lauriat, Jr. "MacLeish at Work: Versions of 'Bleheris.'" *English Studies in Canada*, 13 (1987), 79–90.

MacLEISH, RODERICK, portrays a modern episode in the cyclical battle between the powers of light and dark in his novel *Prince Ombra* (1982). In repeated encounters, such as the Arthur-Mordred struggle, the Prince confronts the hero in the form most dreaded by him. His dark power increases or diminishes as each victory or defeat is remembered in myth. In the 1,001st battle, crippled eight-year-old Bentley Ellicott vanquishes an incarnation of himself as an unsuccessful, cynical adult. [RWK]

MacLeish, Roderick. *Prince Ombra.* New York: Congdon and Weed, 1982.

MacLEOD, FIONA (pseudonym of William Sharp; 1855–1905), adopted the persona of a reclusive Scotswoman to write numerous works colored with Celtic mysticism, including poetry with Arthurian elements and an unpublished verse play, *Drostan and Yseul*. In one unique tale, "Beyond the Blue Septentrions" (1906), young Arthur's destiny is revealed in the stars through a visionary initiation experience. [DN]

MacLeod, Fiona. "Beyond the Blue Septentrions." In *Where the Forest Murmurs.* London: George Newnes, 1906.

MacLIESH, ARCHIBALD FLEMING, American author who published, as Arthur Fleming, Fleming MacLiesh, or A. Fleming MacLiesh, over half a dozen volumes of prose and poetry. *The Destroyers* (1942) is a deterministic poetic drama about the rebellion in Roman Britain, with Arthur as the principal protagonist, aided by his Armorican kinsman Howell, and Medrawt as the main antagonist as well as Ginevra's lover. The play is concerned with treason but even more with the futility and mindless carnage of war, emphasized in the closing speeches of Ginevra and Merlin—a concern all the more pressing in 1942. [VML/LL]

MacLiesh, A. Fleming. *The Destroyers.* New York: Day, 1942.

MacVEAN, JEAN, based *The Intermediaries* (1965) on Gottfried's *Tristan*, recreating the story in Europe during the 1960s. The author closely follows Gottfried's narrative, while enhancing and updating the psychological realism. [EB]

MacVean, Jean. *The Intermediaries.* London: Gollancz, 1965.

MADAMS, H(ARVEY) H., made Dark Age Cornwall the setting of his poetic tale *Dark Encounter* (1980). On a solitary journey to rejoin his army against the Saxons, Arthur overcomes the Witch of Kenrick, who seeks an alliance with him that will restore her ancient powers. The appeal of this gothic story is diminished by the plodding blank verse, which unnecessarily extends the narrative to book length. [DN]

Madams, H.H. *Dark Encounter*. Bodmin, Cornwall: Fairhaven, 1980.

MAERLANT, JACOB VAN, a Middle Dutch poet about whom we know little. He came from Flanders and was born before 1235; he probably died shortly after 1288. Of the many works he has to his name, the best known are *Alexanders Geesten* (ca. 1260), an adaptation of the Latin *Alexandreis* of Gautier de Châtillon; the *History van Troyen* (ca. 1263), an adaptation of the *Roman de Troie* of Benoît de Sainte-Maure; *Der Naturen Bloeme* (ca. 1270), an adaptation of Thomas of Cantimpré's *De Naturis Rerum*; and the *Spiegel Historiael* (1283–88), an adaptation of Vincent of Beauvais's *Speculum Historiale*.

Jacob van Maerlant's first Arthurian romance was probably the *Torec*. This romance, of about 3,850 lines, has been transmitted exclusively in the *Lancelot-Compilatie*. The story, which contains numerous fairy-tale elements, deals with Torec's quest for a precious diadem stolen from his grandmother. He succeeds in securing the object and marries Miraude after fulfilling her condition: defeating all the knights of the Round Table in a tournament.

In his *History van Troyen*, Maerlant mentions the romance *Toerecke* as his work. This makes it probable that the text in the *Lancelot-Compilatie* is an adaptation of a Middle Dutch romance written by Maerlant sometime before 1263. He translated or adapted an Old French romance that has not survived (*Torrez chevalier au cercle d'or*).

About 1261, Maerlant was engaged in two more Arthurian romances. Commissioned by Count Adelbrecht van Voorne, he adapted the Old French prose versions of Robert de Boron's *Joseph d'Arimathie* and *Merlin*, under the titles *Historie van den Grale* and the *Boec van Merline*. In the former, he took great liberties in his adaptation; time and again, he made a stand against the way the Old French poet treated his material. He often permitted himself to make radical changes in order to reconcile the story with the Bible. Maerlant's romance has been preserved exclusively in a Middle Low German *Umschreibung* (rendering) from the Middle Dutch, in a codex dating from ca. 1425. That codex (Burgsteinfurt, Fürst zu Bentheimsche Schlossbibliothek, B 37) also contains his *Boec van Merline* and Lodewijk van Velthem's *Merlijn-Continuatie*. The *Historie van den Grale* is preserved incomplete, two pages having been torn from the manuscript during the nineteenth century; the text now comprises 1,600 lines.

In adapting the *Merlin*, Maerlant remained quite faithful to the original but allowed himself one important variation. This concerns an interpolation of about 900 lines, the so-called *Processus Satanae* ("Satan's Lawsuit"). Of the *Boec van Merline*, only 336 Middle Dutch lines have been preserved (Münster, Hauptstaatsarchiv, Dep. Landsberg-Velen), in addition to which a complete Middle Low German *Umschreibung* from the Middle Dutch is extant in the codex noted above; it comprises about 8,470 lines.

In the years 1283–88, Maerlant worked on his *Spiegel Historiael*; commissioned by the Count of Holland, Floris V. It is an adaptation of Vincent of Beauvais's *Speculum Historiale*. In 1288, Maerlant had to stop working for reasons of health. (The work was continued by Lodewijk van Velthem.) In Vincent, the history of Britain, from the arrival of Brutus up to the disappearance of Arthur, is described only briefly. Maerlant extended the description to some 1,500 lines (spread over Books 1, 5, and 6 of Part III), basing the material on Geoffrey of Monmouth's *Historia Regum Britanniae*. He explicitly distanced himself from the "fiction" of Arthurian romances in Old French (and transposed into Middle Dutch). Maerlant refused to include in his description fictional characters, such as Lancelot and Perchevael, whom, after all, he did not find in Geoffrey. [BB]

Maerlant, Jacob van. *Historie van den Grale und Boek van Merline*, ed. Timothy Sodman. Cologne: Bhohlau, 1980.

———. *Torec*, ed. M. Hogenhout and J. Hogenhout. Abcoude (Netherlands), 1978.

———. *Spiegel Historiael*, ed. M. de Vries and E. Verwijs. 3 vols. Leiden: Brill, 1863; repr. Utrecht: Hes, 1982.

Gerritsen, W.P. "Jacob van Maerlant and Geoffrey of Monmouth." In *An Arthurian Tapestry: Essays in Memory of Lewis Thorpe*, ed. Kenneth Varty. Glasgow: French Department of the University, 1981, pp. 368–88.

Knuvelder, G.P.M. *Handboek tot de geschiedenis der Nederlandse letterkunde*, 5th ed. 's-Hertogenbosch: Malmberg, 1970, Vol. 1, pp. 207–18.

MAJOR, JOHN (b. 1469/70), a Scottish historian, influenced by French humanism, who wrote the *Historia Majoris Britanniae* (1521). He bases his Arthurian account upon Geoffrey of Monmouth and John of Fordun. Major presents John's story that Arthur was illegitimate and that the true heirs to the throne were Gawain and Mordred, the sons of Loth and Anna, who here is the sister of Aurelius (not Arthur). But they were too young and Arthur was chosen king. Major expresses genuine admiration for Arthur, noting that he was noble, handsome, and chivalrous; that he conquered many foreign lands; and that he was one of the Nine Worthies. He is skeptical about magic elements in the Arthurian story and doubts that Arthur will return, although he mentions that, when Arthur was buried at

Glastonbury, people sang, "Hic jacet Arthurus rex magnus rexque futurus." [EDK]

Major, John. *Historia Majoris Britanniae tam Angliae quam Scotiae.* Paris: Ascensius, 1521.

———. *A History of Greater Britain as Well as England and Scotland*, trans. A. Constable. Edinburgh: University of Edinburgh Press, 1892.

Göller, K.H. "König Arthur in den schottischen Chroniken." *Anglia*, 80 (1962), 390–404.

Withrington, John. "The Arthurian Epitaph in Malory's *Morte Darthur.*" *Arthurian Literature*, 7 (1987), 103–44.

MALAMUD, BERNARD (1914–1986), American author of *The Natural* (1952), which concerns a talented baseball player, Roy Hobbs. The novel offers subtle but unmistakable parallels to the Perceval story. Hobbs is a naive rural man whose innate skill and wondrous bat eventually revitalize the New York Knights (managed by Pop Fisher), saving them from an impotence reminiscent of the Fisher King's wound or of the resultant wasteland. The novel was made into a film starring Robert Redford in 1984. [NJL]

Malamud, Bernard. *The Natural*. New York: Farrar, Straus, 1952.

MALORY, SIR THOMAS. Everything that we know with certainty about the author of *Le Morte Darthur* is found in his book. He was called Thomas Malory, he was a knight and a prisoner, and he finished his work during the ninth year of King Edward IV's reign (March 4, 1469, to March 3, 1470). He loved hunting, tournaments, and chivalry, had read widely in Arthurian romance, and had access to a splendid collection of such romances while he was writing. He shows few signs of having read anything non-Arthurian. His English was that of the Midlands, with some more northerly elements perhaps deliberately adopted from Arthurian poems because he felt them suitable to the stories he was telling. He could read and write French and was proud of it, but his French was far from perfect. He once describes with particular sympathy how a prison illness made one of his characters suicidally depressed, which suggests that he himself may have suffered something similar. A passage near the end of the book reproaching the English for their ingratitude to good kings suggests, since it was presumably written under the Yorkist Edward IV, that he sympathized with the ousted Lancastrian king Henry VI.

The most important of these factors for identifying the author are his name and rank. Of the six Thomas Malorys known to have been alive at about the right time, four are so obscure that they could hardly have become knights. One of them, Thomas Malory of Hutton Conyers in Yorkshire, has been suggested as the author; but as late as 1471 he was certainly not a knight. Of the two men of higher rank, Thomas Malory of Papworth St. Agnes in Huntingdonshire was not a knight at all; he is called esquire in official and personal documents throughout his life and after his death.

That leaves Sir Thomas Malory of Newbold Revel in Warwickshire, who was certainly a knight and a prisoner, although his recorded imprisonments are at the wrong time. He was born ca. 1416, succeeded his father in the family estates, and at first lived as a respectable country landowner, representing his county in Parliament in 1445. In 1450, however, he was said to have begun a spectacular career of crime, starting with the attempted murder of a local magnate and proceeding to rape, theft, extortion, cattle-rustling, sacrilegious robbery, deer-stealing, and miscellaneous vandalism. The accusations were probably politically motivated, but that does not mean they were groundless. By 1452, he was in prison in London, where he spent eight years waiting for a trial that never took place. The Yorkist leaders began to take an interest in him, and the Lancastrian authorities, presumably in consequence, showed themselves unusually determined to keep him locked up. When the Yorkists seized power in 1460, they apparently freed him; and in 1462 he followed them on a winter campaign in the north. In the mid-1460s, he again looks briefly like a respectable country landowner, but in 1468 and again in 1470 he was excluded by name from general pardons offered by King Edward. It has been suggested that he was implicated in a Lancastrian plot discovered in June 1468. Some of those involved were certainly imprisoned, and we may imagine the *Morte Darthur* being written then. The prisoners were freed by a Lancastrian invasion in October 1470, a revolution that must have brought Sir Thomas prosperity. When he died on March 14, 1471, he was expensively buried in the fashionable church of Greyfriars, Newgate.

Besides *Le Morte Darthur*, Malory may have written another English Arthurian romance, *The Wedding of Sir Gawain and Dame Ragnell*, a reworking of the traditional folktale of What Women Most Desire. There are some notable similarities between the two works in language and handling of material. The similarities are particularly striking at the end of *The Wedding*, where its author, in terms much like those that Malory uses at the end of various sections of the *Morte Darthur*, reveals that he is in prison and prays for his release. Even if *The Wedding* is by Malory, it cannot be seen as an achievement of the same order as the *Morte Darthur*—its near-doggerel versification alone would prevent that. It is easy, however, to see it as an early effort from the same author, valuable not only for itself but for the light it can throw on his development.

The *Morte Darthur* was more ambitious than *The Wedding of Sir Gawain* in almost every respect, as well as much more successful. There are two versions, one printed and one in manuscript. The former, produced by William Caxton at Westminster in 1485, survives in a perfect copy in the Pierpont Morgan Library in New York, a copy lacking eleven leaves in the John Rylands Library in Manchester, and perhaps a single leaf in Lincoln Cathedral (which has been missing for some years). Until the mid-twentieth century, this was the only known version. Editions derived directly or indirectly from it established the *Morte Darthur* as an English literary classic in the sixteenth century and reestablished it as one in the nineteenth.

The manuscript, discovered at Winchester College in 1934, is now in the British Library in London. It has lost its first and last quires and suffered minor damage elsewhere, but that did not prevent it being used as the basis for an outstanding edition by Eugène Vinaver, published in 1947, which immediately became the standard modern *Morte Darthur*. Vinaver established that neither of the surviving versions of the *Morte* derives from the other: rather, each is at least two copying stages removed from a common original. Caxton must therefore have printed from another manuscript, now lost. Nevertheless, the surviving manuscript has "offsets" of printer's ink from one type font that Caxton had begun using in 1480 and another that he had stopped using in 1483, and a parchment strip used to repair the manuscript is waste from his printing shop datable to 1489. It must therefore have been in his hands from at least 1483 until at least 1489. There has been much speculation about how Caxton obtained his manuscripts, and how the surviving one got to Winchester.

Many of the differences between the two versions of *Le Morte Darthur* are scribal errors in which one is (often obviously) wrong and the other right; but others are the result of deliberate change. One change was advertised—Caxton said in his preface that he had divided his edition into twenty-one books containing 507 chapters—but there were others, notably a drastic rewriting of the Roman-war section that was cut to half its length and restyled to match the other sections. Small changes elsewhere tended to make the Caxton version a little clearer and more modern in idiom than the manuscript version, and slightly less vivid. Vinaver assumed that Caxton had made all these changes, to make the *Morte* more attractive to potential customers. It was therefore an editor's duty to recover the unrevised *Morte* as far as possible from the manuscript version, as representing Malory's work uncontaminated by Caxton. Recently, however, it has been suggested that only Malory had the time, temperament, knowledge, and resources to revise the Roman-war story as it had been revised in Caxton's text. This raised the question of who was responsible for the other changes. It was plainly possible that both Malory and Caxton made changes and that scholarly scrutiny, however close, might often not be able to decide who had changed what. At present, these issues have not been resolved. There is therefore no scholarly consensus about the principles on which editions of the *Morte Darthur* should be produced, or (of course) on how well the available editions match up against those principles.

The discovery of the Malory manuscript focused critics' attention on the unity of *Le Morte Darthur*. The manuscript showed that Malory had organized his work into sections called either books or tales. It is now usual to call them tales, so avoiding confusion with Caxton's books, and to recognize eight of them, although Malory actually divides the fifth into two. The tales are much longer than Caxton's books, and can be seen as more self-sufficient. Each is based on a single major source and ends with an *explicit*, a short statement by the author as narrator closing the tale, and sometimes adding more information about it or the next one or himself. Some critics felt that Malory had written eight independent stories, whose *explicits* emphasized their separateness. These critics pointed to discrepancies between tales to strengthen their argument: Sir Carados, for instance, is killed in the third tale but appears in a tournament in the fourth; and Sir Tristram is mentioned as adult in all the first four tales, yet the fifth begins with the story of his birth.

Malory called his work *The Whole Book of King Arthur and of His Noble Knights of the Round Table*. (The title *Le Morte Darthur*, although now established too firmly to be challenged, came into being when Caxton mistook the title of the last tale for the title of the whole.) The phrase "whole book" shows that Malory thought of what he had written as a comprehensive and authoritative collection of Arthurian stories. The comprehensiveness lay in including everything important, not literally everything. As narrator, Malory often speaks of stories that he has not included, a feature of the *Morte Darthur* that helps to give it a kind of solidity, as part of a greater quasi-historical whole. As author, he did in fact select material from a mass of stories in different books for his tales and arranged those tales in a sequence that made a coherent account of the rise, flourishing, and fall of King Arthur and his knights.

The first tale, taken from the French Prose *Merlin*, tells how Arthur became undisputed king of Britain. Malory turned a long book about Merlin into a short book about Arthur by beginning his story at the point at which Arthur's parents meet. From then on, the tale follows its source closely, telling of Arthur's mysterious conception and secret upbringing, of his proving himself king by drawing the sword from the stone and defeating his rebellious barons in war, begetting Mordred in unknowing incest, marrying Guenivere, and obtaining Excalibur and the Round Table, and of the early adventures of the first knights of the Round Table. It ends with Lancelot and Tristram coming to court.

The second tale, taken from the English Alliterative *Morte Arthure*, tells of foreign conquest. Malory, among other things, cut his source's tragic ending, saved from death several characters needed for later tales, and increased Lancelot's part to that of Arthur's most promising young knight. The Roman emperor Lucius demands tribute from

Arthur, who, enthusiastically supported by his barons, defies him, invades France, defeats and kills Lucius, and is crowned emperor in Rome. He establishes good government there, and he and his knights return triumphantly to Britain.

The third tale consists of several episodes, mostly taken from the French Prose *Lancelot* of the Vulgate Cycle, set in a frame of Malory's making, which places the story at the end of the Roman war. However, where the main theme of the *Lancelot* was Lancelot's adulterous affair with Guenivere, the theme of this tale is his chivalry. He is said to be in love with Guenivere and undertakes his quests for her, but we never see them together, and what we hear suggests a strong, chaste, and still-distant passion. What we see is Lancelot's supreme knightly ability in one testing situation after another, bringing about justice, gaining friends and followers, and coming to be accepted as the best knight in the world—a phrase that is to echo throughout the *Morte Darthur*.

The fourth tale is taken from a lost English poem, based on a Younger Brother folktale. Its hero, Gareth, is Gawain's brother, and much of Gawain's part in the source has plainly been transferred to Lancelot, to suit their characters and the parts they are to play later. The tale is set at a time when the Round Table is at its most flourishing, and Lancelot is Arthur's friend and the greatest man in his kingdom. It tells how Gareth, by asking the King for the traditional three boons, acquires knighthood, a quest, a bride, lands, vassals, reputation, and Lancelot's friendship. That friendship displays the chivalrous natures of both men and does so all the more strikingly because it cuts across the clan loyalties of rival great families, which are emerging as an important feature of Arthur's world.

The fifth tale, which is based on the French Prose *Tristan*, is the only one not placed in time in relation to its predecessor. However, since it opens with the birth and upbringing of Tristram, who has been spoken of as adult in all the previous tales, it is natural to take the opening episode as a kind of flashback. The tale takes up almost a third of the whole *Morte Darthur*. At the beginning, Tristram, Isolde, and Mark quickly settle into the relationships that tradition had established for them. The body of the tale shows a world filled with interlaced adventures, quests, tournaments, and strange encounters. The major and minor characters of Arthurian society appear from time to time, their individual and group relationships to each other hardly changing throughout. Nor is there much, in plot development or any other way, to create an awareness of time passing. The result is to create quintessentially here what we find less perfectly in the other tales, the timeless world of romance. The absence of a real conclusion increases the effect. Malory's source had had one, a Grail story that would have been incompatible with his next tale. He did not reproduce it; but at the end a Grail episode interpolated into the *Tristan* from the Prose *Lancelot* provides a lead-in to the next tale. That episode shows that Lancelot and Guenivere's affair has almost certainly been consummated.

The world that is at its zenith in the fifth tale begins its decline in the sixth, a Grail story closely following the action of the French *Queste del Saint Graal*. The Grail appears at Arthur's court, and his knights swear to pursue it. The three best find it, but only one of them returns. The others fail and are disgraced, and some of them do not return either. Lancelot, drawn by his love for God, but unable to root out his love for Guenivere, stumbles on on the heels of the three successful knights, constantly warned that he is no longer the best knight in the world, and is granted a partial vision of the Grail.

The seventh tale consists of five episodes, two mainly from the French *Mort Artu* with some help from the English Stanzaic *Le Morte Arthur*, two from hints from other French romances, and one apparently of Malory's own invention. It opens at the end of the Grail quest, and shows Arthur's court in a kind of Indian summer before its destruction. Superficially, all is well, but Lancelot and Guenivere have begun their affair again, and each of the five episodes shows them narrowly escaping discovery.

The last tale, drawn again from the *Mort Artu* and Stanzaic *Le Morte Arthur*, shows Lancelot and Guenivere at last discovered. Their enemies trap them in compromising circumstances, and she is condemned to death. He rescues her but in doing so accidentally kills Gareth, thus earning Gawain's bitter enmity. Gawain drives Arthur to pursue Lancelot even to his own lands in France; Mordred, left as regent, attempts to seize the crown and Guenivere. Arthur returns and fights Mordred in a battle in which nearly everyone on both sides is killed. Arthur himself kills his son, who "mortally" wounds him, and he is taken away to the Vale of Avalon to be healed of his wounds. (The mortal/healing paradox goes back to Geoffrey of Monmouth.) Lancelot and Guenivere enter the religious life and undertake such penances that each dies a good death, and Lancelot's kinsmen go to the Holy Land and die fighting on Crusade.

Malory clearly had reason for believing that he had created a "whole book" on the level of plot. An exemplary study by R.H. Wilson showed that he had done the same with characterization, reconciling disparate sources and adding touches of his own. Much the same could be said of the story's ideas and ideals, of the imaginary world in which the action takes place, and of the style. In these matters, too, there are anomalies like that involving Sir Carados: Sir Bors's character in the Grail quest, for instance, is not compatible with his actions in the two final tales, and the style of parts of the Roman-war story, at least in the manuscript version, is distractingly different from that elsewhere. Such things, however, do not matter, because they are dwarfed by the massive coherence, immediacy, and symbolic power of the *Morte Darthur* as a whole, and because

Malory as narrator does not claim the authorial omniscience and omnipotence of a nineteenth-century novelist—at times even telling us that he does not know this or that. Malory as author may not have known it, but his occasional small faults as narrator act as a final grace-note in presentation: by diminishing him, they make the story greater. Evidence of the power of his storytelling lies in the many modern recreations of the Arthurian world, directly or indirectly based on his work. Knowingly or unknowingly, his whole mode of presentation makes his story stand free of him as the greatest creation in English of a romance world, a world that was not but might have been, parallel to ours and inviting comparison with it. [PJCF]

Malory, Sir Thomas. *The Works*, ed. Eugène Vinaver; rev. P.J.C. Field. 3 vols. Oxford: Clarendon, 1990.

Bennett, J.A.W., ed. *Essays on Malory*. Oxford: Clarendon, 1963.

Field, P.J.C. *The Last Years of Sir Thomas Malory*. Manchester: John Rylands University Library, 1983.

Gaines, Barry. *Sir Thomas Malory: An Anecdotal Bibliography of Editions 1485–1985*. New York: AMS, 1990.

Kennedy, Beverly. *Knighthood in the "Morte Darthur."* Cambridge: Brewer, 1985.

Life, Page West. *Sir Thomas Malory and the "Morte Darthur": A Survey of Scholarship and Annotated Bibliography*. Charlottesville: University Press of Virginia, 1980.

Lumiansky, R.M., ed. *Malory's Originality*. Baltimore: Johns Hopkins University Press, 1964.

McCarthy, Terence. *Reading the "Morte Darthur."* Cambridge: Brewer, 1988.

Parins, Marylyn J. *Malory: The Critical Heritage*. London: Routledge and Kegan Paul, 1988.

Takamiya, Toshiyuki, and Derek Brewer, eds. *Aspects of Malory*. Cambridge: Brewer, 1981.

Whitaker, Muriel. *Arthur's Kingdom of Adventure: The World of Malory's "Morte Darthur."* Cambridge: Brewer, 1984.

MANN, FRIDO, a grandson of Thomas Mann, published his first work in 1985, *Professor Parsifal: Autobiographischer Roman*. Using Wagner's *Parsifal* and Parsifal's quest for the Grail as leitmotifs, the book describes the search, by a young man of the 1968 generation, to find himself. [UM/WLS]

Mann, Frido. *Professor Parsifal: Autobiographischer Roman*. Munich: Ellermann, 1985.

MANN, THOMAS (1875–1955), perhaps the greatest twentieth-century German writer, is known primarily for such sociopolitical masterpieces as *Der Zauberberg* ("The Magic Mountain," 1924) and *Dr. Faustus* (1947). Research for *Dr. Faustus* led him to write his somewhat lighter novel *Der Erwählte* ("The Holy Sinner," 1951), which is an adaptation of Hartmann von Aue's version of the Gregorius legend. Although this work is basically not Arthurian in substance, Mann indulges his penchant for irony by enriching the medieval world of his hero with nomenclature from Wolfram von Eschenbach's *Parzival* and, to a lesser extent, from Gottfried von Strassburg's *Tristan*. Some two dozen proper names and other allusions provide the knowledgeable reader with instant, generally humorous, characterizations and the potential for multilevel interpretation.

A screen adaptation of Gottfried's *Tristan*, planned by Mann in 1923, was never realized, and plot similarities between the medieval work and Mann's novella *Tristan* (1903) are superficial. Mann's title may be merely a reference to the symbolic function of Wagner's music in the novella and in the romance of the characters it depicts, or the work may in fact be an ironic comment on Wagner's own infatuations. (*See also* TRISTAN IN MODERN GERMAN VERSIONS.) [RWK]

Mann, Thomas. *Der Erwählte*. Frankfurt: Fischer, 1951.

Weigand, Hermann. "Thomas Mann's *Gregorius*." *Germanic Review*, 27 (1952), 10–30, 83–95.

MANNING, ROSEMARY, English author who incorporates Arthurian tradition into two books of her children's fantasy trilogy about a Cornish dragon. In *Green Smoke* (1957), the 1,500-year-old dragon tells the story of Uther and Merlin; *The Dragon's Quest* (1961) describes his adventures at Camelot, where he works in the kitchens until he proves his worth on a quest, much as does his friend Gareth. Humor is generated by the contrast between appearance and reality, for despite his fearsome size and power, the dragon is civilized and kindly. [RHT]

Manning, Rosemary. *Green Smoke*. London: Constable, 1957.

———. *The Dragon's Quest*. London: Constable, 1961.

MANNYNG, ROBERT, OF BRUNNE, Lincolnshire author of *Handlyng Synne* (1303) and *The Story of England* (1338). The latter is an English verse chronicle based primarily upon the French chronicles of Wace and Pierre de Langtoft. Although Mannyng professes admiration for the French prose works about Arthur and mentions a few characters from romance, such as Blaise and Yvain, his account of Arthur generally follows Wace's *Roman de Brut*. Mannyng feels that Arthur was the greatest Christian king and regrets that little has been written about him in English. [EDK]

Mannyng, Robert. *Peter Langtoft's Chronicle (as Illustrated and Improv'd by Robert of Brunne)*, ed. T. Hearne. 2 vols. Oxford, 1725.

———. *The Story of England of Robert Mannyng of Brunne*, ed. F.J. Furnivall. 2 vols. London: Eyre and Spottiswoode, 1887.

Fletcher, Robert Huntington. *The Arthurian Material in the Chronicles, Especially Those of Great Britain and France*. Boston: Ginn, 1906; 2nd ed. Roger Sherman Loomis. New York: Franklin, 1966, pp. 204–08.

Göller, Karl Heinz. *König Arthur in der englischen Literatur des späten Mittelalters*. Göttingen: Vandenhoeck and Ruprecht, 1963, pp. 28–31.

Kennedy, Edward Donald. "Chronicles and Other Historical Writing." In *The Manual of the Writings in Middle English*, ed. A.E. Hartung. New Haven: Connecticut Academy of Arts and Sciences, 1981–89, Vol. 8, pp. 2625–28, 2811–18.

MANTEL, DER, the Middle High German metrical version of *Le Mantel mautaillié*. A fragment of nearly 1,000 lines, the text breaks off approximately halfway through the tale, after Enite has tried on the mantle. The introduction of Erec and Enite into the mantle tale is an innovation vis-à-vis the French source. The work has been ascribed to Heinrich von dem Türlin, primarily because of the advocacy of Otto Warnatsch, who argued that *Der Mantel* was written by Heinrich as the introductory episode to a larger composition that was to be devoted to the exploits of Lancelot. Bernd Kratz has argued convincingly, however, that Heinrich's authorship is dubious at best. Unlike *Le Mantel mautaillié*, *Der Mantel* has a long prologue (ll. 1–109) devoted to praising King Arthur. The German version enlarges upon the French source; there is an abundance of rhetorical ornamentation, dialogue, descriptive detail, and authorial commentary. [MEK]

Warnatsch, Otto. *Der Mantel, Bruchstück eines Lanzeletromans des Heinrich von dem Türlin, nebst einer Abhandlung über die Sage vom Trinkhorn und Mantel und die Quelle der Krone*, ed. Karl Weinhold. Breslau: Koebner, 1883.

Kratz, Bernd. "Die Ambraser *Mantel*-Erzählung und ihr Autor." *Euphorion*, 71 (1977), 1–17.

MANTEL MAUTAILLIÉ, LE ("The Ill-Fitting Cloak"), or *Lai du cort mantel*, an anonymous twelfth-century Old French version of the same chastity-test story that forms the basis of Robert Biket's *Lai du cor*, an episode from the First Continuation of Chrétien's *Percevel*, and other tales. The hero, as in Biket's version, is also called Caradoc, and the setting is likewise Arthurian. The main difference is that instead of a drinking horn the supernatural object is a cloak that shrinks or stretches so as to reveal the chastity or otherwise of those ladies of the court who try it on.

The poem is clearly a parody, and an early one at that, of certain aspects of Arthurian romance. Chronologically, it belongs to a period between Chrétien's death and the appearance of the first full-length "epigonal romances." Its *esprit gaulois* pushes it in the direction of fabliau, and it has frequently been considered by scholars something of a hybrid between comic tale and romance. The tale was adapted into Middle High German and Norwegian in the thirteenth century (*Der Mantel* and *Möttuls saga*, respectively); the Norwegian text was in turn adapted into Icelandic in the fourteenth century as the *Skikkju rimur*. [KB]

Bennett, Philip E., ed. *Mantel et Cor: deux lais du 12e siècle*. Exeter: University of Exeter, 1975.

MANUEL UND AMANDE, a late thirteenth-century anonymous German Arthurian romance of which we possess only fragments totaling 312 verses. Whether the author's reference to "daz buch" ("the book") in l. 113, which suggests that the romance may have a foreign source, is to be taken at face value is debatable. The extant verses transmit portions of a dialogue involving a figure named Jonas; a scene in which a lady accepts a knight into her service who announces that he will avenge an injustice; the conclusion of the romance in which Manuel of Greece and Amande, daughter of the Spanish king, celebrate their wedding at King Arthur's court in Karidol; and an epilogue celebrating Arthur and his queen as paragons of steadfast love. Despite the Arthurian conclusion, the names of the figures suggest that we are dealing here with a new type of "historical" romance. Noteworthy is the motif of King Arthur's battle with a monstrous cat (ll. 151–58), which occurs in Welsh, French, Dutch, and English narratives but is otherwise unattested in German literature. [MEK]

Meyer-Benfey, Heinrich, ed. "Manuel und Amande." In *Mittelhochdeutsche Übungsstücke*. Halle: Niemeyer, 1909, pp. 160–63.

Schröder, Edward. "Manuel und Amande." *Nachrichten von der Gesellschaft der Wissenschaften zu Göttingen. 1925*, Phil.-hist. Kl. (1926), 166–68.

Steinhoff, Hans-Hugo. "Ein neues Fragment von 'Manuel und Amande.'" *Zeitschrift für deutsches Altertum*, 113 (1984), 242–45.

Zingerle, Oswald. "*Manuel und Amande*: Bruchstücke eines Artusromans." *Zeitschrift für deutsches Alterthum*, 26 (1882), 297–307.

52. MS Rennes 1, fol. 1, from *L'Estoire del Saint Graal*: Christ Gives Book to Author. (Bibliothèque Municipale, Rennes.)

MANUSCRIPTS, ILLUMINATED. 1) INTRODUCTION. Illuminated manuscripts of Arthurian legends were among the most popular and the most profusely illustrated vernacular texts of the Middle Ages. They survive today in enormous numbers, particularly the lengthy Vulgate Cycle in prose, of which over 180 manuscripts survive, rivaled only by the *Roman de la rose*. Many other Arthurian manuscripts have not survived but are known from inventories, like those of the dukes of Berry and Burgundy, the counts of Flanders and Hainaut, and even lesser nobles or ecclesiastics. The exploits of the knights of the Round Table were commemorated also in stone, tiles, and textiles, or on painted walls, some of these showing scenes now lost to the illuminated-manuscript tradition.

The beginnings of Arthurian illumination are difficult to chart. Many of the earliest surviving manuscripts are unillustrated, and the earliest illustrations date from long after the beginnings of the literary traditions they depict. Hardly any Arthurian illumination survives from the twelfth century, the period of the *Mabinogi*, Geoffrey of Monmouth, Wace, Chrétien de Troyes, Marie de France, and Layamon. A small historiated initial showing King Arthur in combat with the giant of Mont St.-Michel in the Douai Manuscript of Geoffrey of Monmouth's *Historia Regum Britanniae* is all that survives (Loomis, fig. 340), while the Modena archivolt and the Otranto mosaic (dated 1165) show that, in other media, artistic interest in the Matter of Britain had already spread to the Mediterranean.

The traditional explanation for the lack of early illustrated manuscripts is that Arthurian subject matter had to await the emergence of the lay craftsman in the thirteenth century. The Loomises, in their otherwise superb and unsurpassed survey of Arthurian art, write that "monks alone in that century [twelfth] were masters of beautiful bookmaking" (p. 89). It is now acknowledged that much, even most, of the fine book illumination of the twelfth century was the work of lay craftsmen, such as Master Hugo, painter of the Bury Bible and creator of other works of art for the abbey of Bury St. Edmunds. But the major *patrons* of fine books were mainly wealthy ecclesiastics and their communities. Clearly, in such a context, books in the vernacular—history, law, medicine, epic, and poetry—took second place to the splendid Psalters and Bibles commissioned by wealthy abbots and bishops. Certain nonliturgical texts that were often illustrated, like the twelfth-century bestiaries, could no doubt be justified on the grounds that their text had a spiritual interpretation. What seems to change in the thirteenth century is that many more laypeople commissioned, purchased, and owned books, which they had read to them or, increasingly, read themselves. The fashion among noble patrons for splendidly illustrated books extended from devotional works to those read for instruction or entertainment. From the early thirteenth century, the wealthy, especially women, owned beautiful Psalters for use in private prayer, a preference that shifted at the end of the century to the illustrated Book of Hours, which remained in vogue until the end of the Middle Ages. Vernacular illustrations were produced in the same ateliers.

Against this background, it is not surprising that the earliest surviving Arthurian romance with illustrations (Rennes 255) was made in the early 1220s at a French court workshop that specialized in Psalters and also made moralized Bibles; it may have belonged to a member of the royal family. What is curious is that it contains parts of the Vulgate Cycle—the *Estoire del Saint Graal*, the *Merlin*, and the beginning of the *Lancelot*—prose versions of the Grail and Lancelot stories rather than their earlier versions in verse, by distinguished literary figures like Chrétien de Troyes. Relatively little Chrétien illustration survives; it all dates from the second third of the thirteenth century and later, and it is not of the highest quality. The Rennes manuscript contains a sequence of illuminations in the form of historiated initials interspersed at intervals in the text, a format that continued into the late Middle Ages alongside the more elaborate decorative schemes worked out later in the thirteenth and fourteenth centuries.

Paris did not maintain its reputation as the most

important center for the production of Arthurian illumination. Most of the Parisian manuscripts of the Vulgate have a single miniature at the beginning of each branch, and in general the quality of these books ranks far below the best products of Parisian ateliers in the time of St. Louis (r. 1234–70), when illuminators seem mainly to have been called upon for high-class liturgical or devotional books, or university texts. A notable exception is the *Roman de la poire* (Paris, B.N. fr. 2186), which includes a splendid sequence of full-page miniatures, unmatched elsewhere, of famous lovers, including the Arthurian heroes and heroines Tristan and Isolde and Cligés and Fénice alongside Paris and Helen and Pyramus and Thisbe.

In Germany, the full-page format is favored in the two earliest surviving Arthurian illuminated manuscripts, Wolfram von Eschenbach's *Parzival* and Gottfried von Strassburg's *Tristan*, both now in the Bayerische Staatsbibliothek in Munich (cgm 19 and cgm 51, respectively). One of the scribes in the *Parzival* also wrote the *Tristan*, but the illuminations in each are by different artists and probably of different dates; both are sets of subdivided miniatures (two registers in *Tristan*, three in *Parzival*) that were inserted into their respective manuscripts after the texts were completed. The lack of comparative material makes it difficult to date or localize these manuscripts with any certainty. They have been variously dated between the second quarter and the end of the thirteenth century, and Strassburg has been suggested as their provenance.

In France, the center of vernacular book production in general and Arthurian illumination in particular shifted by the last quarter of the thirteenth century to the northeast, to Picardie, Artois, and Flanders, as well as Hainaut, which, although in the empire, was part of the ecclesiastical province of Reims and artistically closer to France and Flanders than to Germany. These regions were especially prolific in book production during the last quarter of the thirteenth and the first quarter of the fourteenth century. Workshops produced multiple copies of Arthurian manuscripts; the surviving examples are copiously illustrated, usually with small miniatures in one text column but sometimes with historiated initials instead or as well. Complete copies of the Vulgate are Bonn 526, written in Amiens in 1286, and Paris, B.N. fr. 110, products of the same illuminator's shop, located probably in Cambrai; and London, B.L. Add. 10292–94, made after 1316 in the same shop as Oxford, Bodl. Douce 215/Manchester, John Rylands University Library fr. 1/New York, H.P. Kraus, Catalogue 165, no. 3, and London, B.L. Royal 14 E III, probably in St. Omer or Thérouanne, or possibly in Ghent. Other important Arthurian manuscripts of the fourteenth century are in New York (Pierpont Morgan Library 805–07) and Paris (Bibliothèque de l'Arsenal 5218), the latter written, illuminated, and bound by Pierart dou Tielt in Tournai. Both of these manuscripts include long miniatures that spread across the entire text, as well as historiated initials. Pierart dou Tielt is the only illuminator

53. MS Rennes 1, fol. 101, from Vulgate *Merlin*: Souls Delivered from Hell. (Bibliothèque Municipale, Rennes.)

among the group whose work is signed. In the rest of these manuscripts, there is evidence that the task of illuminating these long romances was one that depended on intermediaries of various kinds, usually in the form of written marginal notes or symbols to guide the illuminators, and suggesting—as do the division of hands within the illumination, or the slight variations within a single style—that the artistic atelier was a complex organization in which a great deal of collaboration took place on different levels: among artists, scribes, rubricators, minor decorators, and note writers. What is lacking so far is the documentary evidence to follow each stage of the process in detail.

From the fourteenth century, too, many more vernacular manuscripts survive. The French Arthurian texts were copied and illustrated in Italy, alongside Italian versions of the stories, and German versions with illustrations survive in considerable numbers. It is surprising to note the general absence of fine Arthurian manuscripts in England, although there is evidence of French or Flemish-made Arthurian books in English fourteenth-century libraries. On the Continent in the late Middle Ages, Arthurian manuscripts were owned by some of the best-known book-collectors of the period, like Gian Galeazzo Visconti or Jean, duc de Berry, and his great-grandson Jacques d'Armagnac, owners of the complete Vulgate Cycle (Paris, B.N. fr. 117–20), and Engelbert II, Count of Nassau and Vianden, owner of the *Guiron le Courtois* (Oxford, Bodl. Douce 383). These manuscripts are characterized by the general interest in realistic representation that is one of the hallmarks of the period, with spatial depth and scenic landscapes, although the selection of subjects and their position in the text changes little from the cycles worked out in the thirteenth century. The importance of the change in stylistic fashions is well exemplified by the overpainting of many of the scenes in Jean de Berry's Vulgate to suit the taste of Jacques d'Armagnac. Fortunately for the history of medieval painting, such adaptations are rare: the up-to-date patron simply preferred to commission a new copy, and the treasured images of the past remain intact. [MAS]

2) BRITISH MANUSCRIPTS. Although Arthurian romances purport to tell the history of Britain, the number of illuminated Arthurian manuscripts made by English artists is small. Of course, the English nobility imported manuscripts from France, and then in the fifteenth century from Flanders; however, some native artists also illustrated their history. Among the finest are the thirteenth-century *Prophetiae Merlini*, 1250–70, with illustrations of Merlin and Vortigern (London, B.L. Cotton, Claudius B VII), and Pierre de Langtoft's *Chronicle* ending in the year 1307 (B.L. Royal 20 A II), illustrating the early kings of Britain. In the *Chronicle*, in tinted drawings, the artist depicted Vortigern burning in his tower and Arthur as an imposing king. Arthur carries a shield on which are represented the Virgin and Child, as described by Geoffrey of Monmouth, rather than the later device of three gold crowns. The crowns of thirty kingdoms won by Arthur are ranged below his feet.

Many English manuscripts are notable for their historical interest rather than for intrinsic aesthetic value. Wace's *Brut* (B.L. Edgerton 3028) depicts Merlin transporting Stonehenge from Ireland to Salisbury Plain, the first illustration of that famous site. Of poor aesthetic quality but of great iconographical and literary interest are the illustrations to *Sir Gawain and the Green Knight* (B.L. Cotton Nero A X), ca. 1390–1400. Depicted in crude drawings and smudgy colors are four scenes: 1) Gawain holds an axe, Arthur and Guenevere sit at the table, and the Green Knight on horseback holds up his severed head; 2) Gawain in bed is tempted by his host's wife; 3) Gawain fulfills his vow by meeting the Green Knight at the Green Chapel; and 4) Gawain back in Camelot kneels before Arthur and the Queen.

King Arthur may also appear in incidental fashion, for example, in the Wheel of Fortune, a popular medieval moralizing device. Although Arthur sits at the top of the wheel, crowned as king, the turn of the wheel topples even the most powerful ruler to the ground again. Arthur and the Wheel of Fortune appear in the *Annales Cambriae* of ca. 1316 (B.L. Add. 10294). In the same manuscript are to be found the beautiful paintings of Sir Bedivere by the lake as the hand reaches up to grasp Excalibur, and the dramatic end of the fellowship of the Round Table at the battle of Camlann. [MS]

3) DUTCH MANUSCRIPTS. The history of Dutch manuscript illumination is inextricably bound to that of its more powerful neighbors, Germany and Flanders. By the fourteenth century, however, it is possible to speak of a Dutch, as opposed to Franco-Flemish or German, school of painting. Only two of the many Arthurian manuscripts made in Holland were illustrated: *Ferguut* (Leiden, Rijks-Universiteit 191) and *Walewein* (Leiden, Rijks-Universiteit Letterkr. 195). The *Ferguut*, a manuscript of ca. 1300, has only one illumination, an initial "D" enclosing a picture of the hero. The romance of *Walewein*, dated 1350 by the scribe, has a full-page, brilliantly colored illustration of Walewein and the magic chessboard, inserted in a parchment different from the rest of the manuscript. The scarcity of Arthurian illuminated manuscripts in Holland may be accounted for by the lack of wealthy nobles dedicated to a courtly ethic and the patronage of the arts and to the early emergence of towns, where practical men of affairs preferred history to romances. However, since King Arthur was considered a historical figure, his life as told by Geoffrey of Monmouth was included in histories, such as the early fourteenth-century copy of Jacob van Maerlant's *Spiegel Historiael* (The Hague, Royal Library XX). In this manuscript, Arthurian scenes occupy four of the sixty-eight illuminations. In the finest (f. 163v)—a composite scene of Mordred's death and the mortally wounded Arthur carried from the field in a cart—is a vigorous and moving depiction of the tragic end of the fellowship of the Round Table.

Many Dutch artists found employment in the court of Burgundy. The famous painter Guillaume (Willem) Vrelant, who was active in Bruges from 1454 until his death in 1481/82, was Dutch. A member of the guild of St. John and a friend of the transplanted German painter Hans Memling, he headed a large workshop that produced both religious and secular works, including illuminations for the *Chroniques de Hainaut* (1468). [MS]

4) FLEMISH MANUSCRIPTS. Flanders, the southern Netherlands, played a role in Arthurian manuscript production well before the glorious days of Burgundian ducal patronage in the fifteenth century. Chrétien de Troyes dedicated his *Conte del Graal* to Philip d'Alsace, Count of Flanders, and the *Historia Regum Britanniae* (ca. 1180) and *Prophetiae Merlini* were copied and illuminated there. A twelfth-century copy of the *Historia* contains a handsome illumination of Arthur fighting the Giant of Mont St.-Michel (Paris, Douai 880 f. 66). The adventures of the knights of the Round Table were so well known in Flanders that by the end of the thirteenth century the poet Jacob van Maerlant reported that more people read the romances than the Bible. Accounts and inventories also indicate that the Arthurian romances were as popular with the Flemish aristocracy as they were with their French relations.

Maastricht, in eastern Belgium, was the early center of manuscript production, but its style is closely associated with French work. In the thirteenth and early fourteenth centuries, the Île de France remained the center of manuscript illumination, and the books mentioned in the inventories were in all likelihood imported from Paris.

By the middle of the fourteenth century, a distinctly Flemish school appears. The *Queste del Saint Graal* (Paris, Bibliothèque de l'Arsenal 5218) was signed and dated August 15, 1351, and was illuminated by the scribe Pierart dou Tielt, who worked in Tournai. Although most of the paintings are conventional scenes of jousts and feasts, one represents the mystery of the Grail as it was revealed to Arthur's knights by angels and Bishop Josephe (f. 88). The Bleeding Lance and the Grail with the Christ child rest on a long table lit by candles. Pierart enriches the page with foliage and grotesques, including, at the bottom of the Grail page, monkey, pig, and goat musicians, and a dancing bear.

A copy of Robert de Boron's *Roman du Graal* and *Merlin*, by Johan de Loles of Hainaut (dated July 1357), includes still-visible instructions for the painter (New Haven, Yale University Library). Vivid narratives and splendid borders become important characteristics of later Flemish manuscript illumination.

In 1384, Margaret, wife of Philip the Bold, inherited Flanders from her father, and thus Flanders and Burgundy were united to form a single political unit. The power and prosperity of the later Burgundian dukes Philip the Good and Charles the Bold ensured a continuous patronage of the arts. Bruges, Ghent, and Brussels, as well as Dijon, became art centers, and the Flemish cities had thriving manuscript workshops. Philip the Good built up the greatest personal library in Europe, reputed to contain nearly 900 books. The duke ordered copies, translations, and new prose editions of Arthurian romances, including the Vulgate Cycle, *Tristan*, *Guiron le Courtois*, *Erec et Enide*, *Cligés*, and *Perceforest*. Taste was changing, however, and in the fifteenth century history, in the form of epics and chronicles, replaced romance as the most popular form of secular literature. Chronicles, such as the *Chroniques de Hainaut*, were produced in luxurious editions (Brussels, Bibliothèque Royale 9243); Volume II of the *Chroniques* contained Geoffrey's *Historia*, for Arthur was believed to have ruled Hainaut. The scribe Jacotin de Bos completed the history on December 8, 1449, and Guillaume Vrelant illuminated it in 1468. Seven of the sixty illustrations were dedicated to King Arthur. Of special interest is the wedding of Arthur and Guenevere, in which figures are depicted in contemporary costumes and are set in a meticulously rendered church interior. In other illuminations, cities and castles, extensive landscapes, and genre details (an old woman warming her feet at a fire, armorers at work before a battle) suggest the interest in realism and close observation that characterize Flemish art through the ages.

The marriage of Margaret of York, sister of Edward IV, and Charles the Bold in 1468 sealed a new Burgundian-English alliance, an alliance that enhanced trade and cultural relations between the two powers. Bruges and Ghent, already centers of manuscript production, now provided books for the English market. The *St. Albans Chronicle* (Lambeth Palace Library 6), written in English and illuminated ca. 1470, includes nine Arthurian miniatures. The lively narratives characteristic of Flemish painting are placed in a deep landscape; and the realism of the spatial setting, denied in turn by the microscopic realism of the floral borders, is a prime contribution of Flemish fifteenth-century painters to the history of art.

Among the luxury manuscripts produced by Flemish painters for the Burgundian court, of interest to Arthurian scholars is the *Guiron le Courtois* (Oxford, Bodl. Douce 383) originally made for a knight of the Golden Fleece and later vandalized; seventeen folios survive. The arms are those of Engelbert of Nassau, a lieutenant of Charles the Bold and a patron of two other important manuscripts—the *Roman de la rose* and a Book of Hours. Stylistically, *Guiron* is related to the Vienna Statutes of the Golden Fleece (Vienna, Österreichische Nationalbibliothek 2606) as well as the *Roman de la rose* (London, B.L. Harley 4425). The *Guiron* was translated by Vasque de Lucene, who came from Portugal after the marriage of Philip the Good and Isabel of Portugal. The manuscript is dated 1480–1500. The painter is a master of spacious landscape and architectural setting; and his figures act in a real space. Observable details, such as the serving hatch in the palace, contrast with elegant figures. In the borders, fanciful acanthus scrolls and centaurs balance realistic strawberries and butterflies. The subtle color scheme is enhanced with discreet use of gold highlights. [MS]

5) FRENCH MANUSCRIPTS. Despite the rich twelfth-century production of French Arthurian romances and lais by such writers as Béroul, Thomas d'Angleterre, Chrétien de Troyes, and Marie de France, that period apparently saw few manuscript copies of Arthurian (or other) works. It was only during the following century that the establishment of courtly culture in France encouraged the production of vernacular texts for a romance-loving upper-class audience. It is likely that half the Arthurian prose romances were decorated with historiated initials, rectangular miniatures, and marginalia. Initially, the prose Vulgate Cycle, consisting of *Estoire del Saint Graal*, *Merlin*, *Lancelot*, *Queste del Saint Graal*, and *Mort Artu*, provided the most popular subjects for secular workshops in northern France, the source of much notable Arthurian illumination. Many early manuscripts are folios with texts clearly written on vellum, rubrics indicating pictorial subjects, and miniatures occupying the width of a column. The bright colors range from gold, pink, and vermilion to blue, mauve, and light green. Since the workshops also produced Bibles and Psalters, the influence of pattern books is evident in repetitive battle scenes (based on illustrations for the biblical book of Kings), feasts (Marriage of Cana and Last Supper types), and the iconography of the Grail quest, which includes Adam and Eve, the Crucifixion, and the Harrowing of Hell. Subjects are often suggested by genre rather than by specific textual description.

The high point of Arthurian illumination is represented by a group of northern French manuscripts (ca. 1300–20): New Haven, Yale University Library 229; Paris,

54. MS Rennes 1, fol. 137, from Vulgate *Lancelot* Proper: Aramont Becomes Uther's Vassal; They Leave for Battle with Claudas. (Bibliothèque Municipale, Rennes.)

B.N. fr. 95; Manchester, John Rylands University Library fr. 1, 2; London, B. L. Royal 14 E III and Add. 10292–94; New York, Pierpont Morgan Library 805–07. The elegant ease of courtly society is conveyed by pictures of ladies holding lapdogs, knights playing chess or hunting, lovers naked in bed, and nobles picnicking by a fountain. Knight-errantry is visualized through jousts, tournaments, and forest encounters with damsels, evil knights, and monsters. A courtly ambience is also evoked by gold-leaf backgrounds, golden crosses, crowns, swords, goblets, and architecturally elaborate Gothic castles and monasteries with pink or blue walls and lapis-lazuli roofs. Pink, blue, mauve, and orange horses, castle-destroying flames from heaven, and demons from hell convey the wonders of Celtic magic and Christian mystery; a life remote from the real world is also suggested by the characters' unaging faces, marked, in Loomis's words, by "an incredible youthfulness, a bland sweetness, a slightly astonished expression." Despite the frequent use of conventional scenes, the superiority of these manuscripts depends partly on careful matching of image and text in climactic scenes, e.g., the sword tests, Lancelot's crossing of the Sword Bridge, the Grail questers' approach to the Ship of Solomon, the arrival of Elaine's corpse, and Bedivere's restoration of Excalibur. The symbol-studded miniatures contain no images irrelevant to the action.

After the Hundred Years' War, which inhibited book production, workshops responded to the demand of wealthy collectors for luxury editions reflecting the flamboyant, materialistic late-medieval world. Under the influence of Italian painting, composed landscapes and interiors revealing a new-found knowledge of perspective replaced architectural frames, patterned backgrounds, and frontal images. Heraldic splendors emphasized the pageantic aspect of life.

Throughout this period and well into the fifteenth century, illuminators and miniaturists continued to perfect their art, often romanticizing their subjects but also introducing greater realism into their depictions of places, people, and objects. In certain manuscripts of this period, the artists carefully reproduce contemporary dress—the men's plumed acorn hats, long velvet gowns slashed to reveal shirts, and ridiculously abbreviated doublets; the women's low-cut dresses, golden chains, and steeple headdresses. Physiognomy is equally realistic—a grey-haired, scraggy-bearded Arthur, bored and cynical courtiers, ladies exchanging sly looks as Tristan arrives at court.

The period following the Hundred Years' War saw the formation of great libraries, such as the royal library of Charles V and Charles VI. A number of illuminators from the late Middle Ages were well known and highly respected artists; among the best were Jean Fouquet (d. ca. 1481) and Michel Colombe, one of the last of the great French illuminators. But before the century ended, the painter was displaced by the woodblock cutter as the scribe was by the typesetter. Technological change made the illuminator superfluous, and although the art of illumination continued to be cultivated well into the sixteenth century, the quality of that art was declining dramatically. The great masterpieces of the genre had already been created. [MAW]

6) GERMAN MANUSCRIPTS. German nobility in the Middle Ages adopted Arthurian romances with an enthusiasm that would be repeated in the Romantic revival of the nineteenth century. Unfortunately, however, only two illuminated manuscripts have survived from the period before 1300, a *Tristan* and a *Parzival*, both mid-thirteenth century and both now in Munich. In both, the paintings are on separate leaves inserted into the manuscripts. In *Tristan* (Munich, cgm 51), fifteen leaves painted on both sides and containing eighty-four miniatures illustrate the story of Tristan's parents and the hero's exploits at the court of King Mark. The last leaves lack the finesse of the first, and the painting is clearly the work of several hands.

Even in the fourteenth and fifteenth centuries, no truly great artist worked on an Arthurian manuscript in Germany. German artists tended to use stock scenes based on religious iconography; for example, most feasting scenes resemble the Last Supper, and even the Round Table may be represented as a long rectangle. Nevertheless, German artists tend to be energetic storytellers, even when their figures are crude and their settings minimal. The drawing is often hard and angular, with bold outlines; brilliant color, abundant ornament, and twisting banners bearing texts all add to the decorative, folk-art-like quality.

In the later years of the fourteenth century, a German romance, the *Wigalois* of Wirnt von Grafenberg, was produced for Duke Albrecht von Braunschweig-Genburhagan (r. 1361–84) (Leiden, Rijks-Universiteit 537). It is signed, dated 1372, and illuminated by the scribe Jan von Brunswik, a Cistercian monk from Amelungsborn (he includes a self-portrait on the last page). In forty-seven miniatures, Jan illustrates the text of *Wigalois* with such specificity and brilliant color that Loomis related the miniatures to the Wienhausen and Brunswick embroideries. The very characteristics he notes—decorative architecture, stars and dots, four-petaled flowers of the ground and borders—also resemble fourteenth-century German and Austrian enamels.

By the fifteenth century, a truly national character emerges in German manuscript painting, a style related, in its angularity and emphasis on linear effects, to woodcuts. At this time, printers began to challenge the scribes for the attention of patrons. Just as Flanders now dominated the luxury-manuscript trade, southern German workshops turned out popular editions in large numbers. Such manuscripts as those found in the University of Heidelberg library (the earliest a *Lanzelet*, dated by the scribe to 1420, Bibliothek Palzgerm. 371) are close to folk art. Simply colored drawings suffice as illustrations for books that give the impression of being produced hastily for the trade. Surviving records of the workshop of Diebolt Lauber in the Alsatian city of Hagenau confirm this impression. Lauber was both scribe and painter, but he also had at least sixteen workers under him. It is not surprising that painters sought easy effects; the fancy dress, including plumed hats, can only strike today's viewer as amusing.

Switzerland had its manuscript shops, too. A fifteenth-century *Parzival* in Bern (Bergerbibliothek AA91), inscribed 1467 by Johann Steinhein de Constanica, was first owned by Jorg Friburger of Bern. Even the paper has a Bern watermark. Twenty-eight drawings done in an archaic style are colored with washes to give the effect of hand-colored woodcuts. Gawain on the Perilous Bed and Gawain picking the forbidden fruit are especially fine. Nevertheless, an overview of the period suggests that the most creative artists were being attracted to the new medium of printing.

[MS]

7) ITALIAN MANUSCRIPTS. Elaborately illustrated Italian manuscripts attest the popularity of Arthurian material in many centers in fourteenth-century Italy. By the late thirteenth century, cycles of Arthurian images appear in three distinct formats. Historiated initials containing one or two characters and occasional horses, bits of architecture, or a ship are the principal decorative features of several manuscripts from Bologna (Chantilly, Musée Condé 1111, *Mort Artu*, 1288; Oxford, Bodl. Douce 178, *Estoire del Saint Graal*, *Merlin*). Despite their modest format, the great number of episodes represented and the handsome color schemes (dominated by oranges, blues, and browns) make these sequences quite impressive.

Framed miniatures set into a column of text occasionally appear in Bolognese and in late thirteenth-century Venetian manuscripts (Venice, Marciana fr. App. XXIX [243], *Merlin*), but this type of scene is never as important in Italy as in France.

More distinctly Italian is the unframed miniature that fills the entire lower margin of a given folio and spreads upward into the side margins and between the columns of text. This arrangement is found throughout the group of sixteen Arthurian manuscripts recently attributed to artists working at the Angevin court in Naples between 1290 and 1320. Throughout these French texts, innovative Italian artists have executed rough but lively drawings in pen-and-ink with some touches of color. The tournament, battle, and banquet scenes follow repetitious formulas apparently developed to enhance speed of production. Representative examples with dozens of drawings are a *Tristan* and a *Lancelot*, both now in Paris (B.N. fr. 760; fr. 16998).

Most luxurious of all the Italian Arthurian manuscripts are those decorated for the Visconti courts at Pavia and Milan. The earliest of these is a *Tristan* dating to 1320–40 (B.N. fr. 755). In the lower margins of most of its 161 folios are painted complex scenes with elegantly attired figures set in exquisitely detailed palace interiors or outside of crenelated castles. The compositions borrow from French models, such as the illustrated Vulgate Cycle known to have been in the Pavia library (B.N. fr. 130), but the figure types and rendering of space reflect the innovations of Giotto. The colors are predominantly pale greens, blues, pinks, and white punctuated with deep reds or solid black. Gold crowns, utensils, and areas of background enhance the sumptuous effect.

The Lombard love of naturalistic detail and of fully developed settings reaches a peak in two Visconti manuscripts executed ca. 1380, a *Guiron le Courtois* and a volume containing the *Queste del Saint Graal* and the *Mort Artu*, also both in Paris (B.N. nouv. acq. fr. 5243; fr. 343). In the wide lower margins, knights conversing or playing chess sit in porticoes of buildings whose upper stories are glimpsed in the side and center margins. Castle towers are set obliquely to the picture plane, and their projecting balconies are filled with gossiping ladies. Tents in broad landscapes frame battle and jousting scenes. And a truly circular Round Table is depicted for the Pentecost feast, modeled on Pietro Lorenzetti's innovative Last Supper fresco of the 1320s in Assisi. Delicate tans and greys are used for the architecture, horses, and armor; contrasted with these subdued colors are the bright reds, greens, and blues of the patterned fabrics worn by knights and ladies alike. Life in the courts of Trecento Italy is here given its most vividly realistic rendering.

A coda to the story of Italian Arthurian manuscripts is found in the 289 wonderfully charming drawings of *La Tavola Ritonda* of 1446 by the Lombard artist Bonifazio Bembo (Florence, Bibliotèca Nazionale Pal. 556). Vivaciously curving pen lines delineate scenes in which ladies wear flowing robes and elaborately high coiffures, while Lancelot and Tristan don the fabulous hats and feathery cloaks of the late International Gothic style. This famous cycle reveals the persistence of the Arthurian romances in an artistic culture otherwise already far down the path of Renaissance classicism. [LA]

8) SPANISH MANUSCRIPTS. Arthurian romances were popular in Spain. King Pedro IV of Aragon, for example, acquired several Arthurian books between 1339 and 1356. Spanish authors, such as Joanot Martorell (*Tirant le Blanc*) and Guillem Torroella (*La Faula*), contributed to Arthurian literature and describe painted chambers and palace halls decorated with Arthurian subjects. However, little visual evidence of this rich art survives. A thirteenth-century French Prose *Tristan* (Paris, B.N. fr. 750) signed and dated 1278 by the scribe Petrus de Tiergevilla, was illustrated in Spain or Italy, by a Spaniard, who painted a golden three-towered castle (the arms of Castile) on Sir Kay's shield. The composition of the historiated initials is distinctive, for each letter encloses a series of events, represented in two or three registers, rather than the usual single scene. A typical illuminated manuscript of the second half of the fourteenth century, a Castilian *Guiron* (*Tristan*), contains a miniature showing the knight Branor le Brun and the women whom he assisted.

55. MS Paris, Bibliothèque Nationale, f.fr. 2186 (*Roman de la poire*), fol. 8v.: Arming of a Knight. (Paris, Bibliothèque Nationale.)

These fourteenth-century painters worked in the style of the great northern French illuminators; by the beginning of the fifteenth century, however, they fall first under the influence of the Italian Renaissance miniaturists and then under the domination of Flemish shops. The *Chronicle of the Knight Cifar* (B.N. Esp. 36), a fifteenth-century Castilian manuscript, is richly illuminated with borders of fantastic spiky foliage filled with birds and putti. Some 250 paintings, including many scenes of civic and military life, provide a rich source of information about costume, armor, architecture, and customs. Though the interior scenes are rendered with an adequate knowledge of linear perspective, the landscapes lack the sophisticated understanding of spatial relationships found in the great Flemish models. On the first folio are the arms of Castile and Leon supported by angels, a reminder that the Spanish monarchy patronized scribes and illuminators. Queen Isabel herself built up a great library in Toledo, and her accounts record many payments to scribes and painters. [MS]

9) SOME OUTSTANDING MANUSCRIPTS. *Bonn, Universitätsbibliothek, HS 526: Cycle de Lancelot* (northern France, 1286). Parchment, 477 ff. 465 × 320 mm. Text in 3 columns, 56–60 lines. 340 illustrations, mainly miniatures in one text column, and a few historiated initials. Rubrics in red above miniatures. Some marginal guides to the illuminator. The writing of this manuscript was completed in Amiens by Arnulfus de Kayo on August 28, 1286, according to a colophon at the end of the volume. The wording "qui est ambianis" suggests that Arnulfus did not usually work in Amiens, and the stylistic associations of the illumination are with manuscripts whose calendars suggest associations with other important centers, like Arras, Thérouanne, St. Omer, and particularly Cambrai. Especially close stylistically to the illustrations in this manuscript are those in the *Bestiary* formerly in the library of Sion College, now in the J. Paul Getty Museum (Malibu, Ludwig XV, 5), written in 1277; those in St. Omer 5, the second volume of a two-volume Bible; and those in Cambrai 99, a Breviary of Marquette. Less closely related stylistically, but probably also products of the same workshop are another complete Vulgate Cycle (Paris, B.N. fr. 110); a Prose *Tristan* and a fragmentary *Lancelot* (London, B.L. Add. 5474); and a *Cycle de Guillaume* (Boulogne-sur-Mer 192), written in 1295 and perhaps the same manuscript as the "livre de gestes" mentioned by Guillaume de Hainaut, Bishop of Cambrai, in his will in 1296: he says that one of the monks of St. Sépulchre, Cambrai, had had it made for him.

London, British Library, MS Additional 10292–94: Cycle de Lancelot (Flanders, after 1316). Three volumes: Add. 10292, 216 ff. 405 × 300 mm, 238 miniatures; Add. 10293, 383 ff. 405 × 300 mm, 346 miniatures; Add. 10294, 96 ff. 405 × 300 mm, 73 miniatures. Text in 3 columns, 50 lines. Miniatures in one text column, borders for the opening pages of the branches, except for *Mort Artu*, which lacks the beginning. Rubrics in red above miniatures; many marginal notes (rarely legible) in leadpoint for the rubricator and possibly also for the illuminator. Two contemporary illuminators divided the work, although they never worked in the same quire. The date 1316 is written into the miniature in Add. 10292, f. 55v, on the tombs of Nabor and le sire de Karabel, which are being sculpted. The activity of this workshop seems to have spanned the period ca. 1300–50 or later. Two other Prose *Lancelots* were produced: London, B.L. Royal 14 E III (incomplete: *Estoire, Queste, Mort Artu*), and Manchester, John Rylands University Library fr. 1, other parts of which are Oxford, Bodl. Douce 215, and New York, H.P. Kraus, Catalogue 165, no. 3. The cycles of all three manuscripts are closely related, and the first illuminator of Add. 10292–94 either worked himself on all three sets or had assistants whose style was almost identical. He also worked on the frontispiece in the Psalter of Tournai (St. Omer 270), added in 1323 when Gilbert de Sainte-Aldegonde gave the manuscript to the Charterhouse at Longuenesse near St. Omer. Also closely related, but probably earlier, are a Psalter (B.L. Stowe 17) and a fragmentary Book of Hours (B.L. Add. 28784). The second illuminator did not collaborate on the other *Lancelots*, but his work appears again in the Hours of Thérouanne or St. Omer (New York, Pierpont Morgan Library M 754, and London, B.L. Add. 36684), dated after 1318 because of the inclusion of an indulgence of that year, and in part of the Vincent of Beauvais *Speculum Historiale* (Boulogne-sur-Mer 130), a direct copy of an earlier manuscript with the same text and picture cycle (Boulogne-sur-Mer 131), made in 1297 for Eustache Gomer de Lille, abbot of the Benedictine monastery of St. Bertin at St. Omer. The associations of the workshop with St. Omer are striking, but the workshop also has close stylistic links with Ghent, and perhaps Cambrai.

Munich, Bayerische Staatsbibliothek, cgm 19: Wolfram von Eschenbach, Parzival, Titurel, Tagelieder; and Three Exemplars (Germany, ?Strassburg, second quarter or second third of the thirteenth century). Parchment, 75 ff. 295 × 210 mm. Text in 3 columns, 70–72 lines. Illustrations on both sides of two single inserted leaves, each divided into three registers, illustrating scenes from Books XII–XV of *Parzival*. The illustrations are probably fragments of a more extensive narrative sequence, of which the rest is now lost. The texts are written by seven anonymous scribes, to the first of whom has also been attributed the script of the Munich manuscript of Gottfried von Strassburg's *Tristan* (cgm 51). Though neither manuscript contains direct evidence of date or localization, both are assumed to have been written in Strassburg and have been associated with the writing-shop of the notary Meister Hesse, whose activity in Strassburg is documented between 1228 and 1236 and who is praised in the text of Rudolf von Ems's *Wilhelm von Orlens*. The Munich manuscript of *Wilhelm von Orlens* (cgm 63) has also been attributed to Strassburg, although the script is different and probably later than that of the *Parzival* or the *Tristan*. In the absence of any signed work by Meister Hesse, most scholars are now reluctant to accept him as the scribe of the *Parzival* or the *Tristan*; there is also some hesitation about the dates of all three manuscripts, owing to the lack of comparative dated material. The same problems apply to the illuminations in the books, which in the case of the *Parzival* and the *Tristan* are on separate leaves and need not have been planned with the writing of the texts. They are certainly by quite different artists and are somewhat mediocre in quality and condition, which makes the question of attribution still more vexed.

New York, H.P. Kraus, Catalogue 165, No. 3; Oxford, Bodleian Library, MS Douce 215; Manchester, John Rylands University Library, MS French 1: Vulgate Cycle (Flanders, ca. 1315–25). Parchment, Kraus i, 118 ff.; ii, 233 ff.; iii, 104 ff.; each 405 × 290 mm. Oxford 45 ff. 411 × 292 mm. Manchester i, 129 ff.; ii, 128 ff.; each 411 × 292 mm. Text in 2 columns, 44 lines. 109 miniatures in the Kraus volumes, 6 in the Oxford volume, 74 miniatures and a historiated initial in the Manchester volumes. Rubrics. Many marginal notes (particularly legible in the Kraus volumes) for the rubricator and the illuminator. Illuminations by two contemporary artists, with marginal miniatures added by a fourteenth-century artist. The first artist is the same as, or is very closely related to, the first painter in two other Prose *Lancelot* manuscripts (London, B.L. Add. 10292–94, and London, B.L. Royal 14 E III). This painter worked on all of the volumes. The second painter appears only in a few miniatures in the Oxford and Manchester volumes, but his work is important as it can also be traced in a number of other manuscripts, particularly a group of Psalters and Books of Hours associated with Ghent and Cambrai, including Oxford, Bodl. Douce 5–6, a Psalter made for the abbey of St. Peter, Blandin, Ghent; Cambridge, Trinity College B.11.22, a Franciscan Book of Hours; a Franciscan Psalter, Copenhagen, Royal Library GKS 3384 8°; and a Psalter Hours with a calendar and litany of Cambrai, Baltimore, Walters Art Gallery 82. Since the stylistic associations of the first artists are primarily with books made for St. Omer or Thérouanne, this manuscript is important in extending the parameters of the group, perhaps suggesting close collaboration between two ateliers, or perhaps the existence of several styles within a single large atelier. In either case, the location of the atelier or ateliers cannot yet be resolved with certainty.

New York, Pierpont Morgan Library, MS 805: Lancelot Proper (northern France, ca. 1315). Parchment, 266 ff. 346 × 254 mm. Text in 3 columns, 48 lines, now bound in two volumes, ff. 1–142v, ff. 143–266. 39 miniatures in 3 text columns, 136 historiated initials. 6 notes for the illuminator in the margins. The illuminations are by two main artists, with perhaps a third collaborator for f. 1. On the whole, one of the main artists painted the large miniatures and the other the historiated initials, but where there is a historiated initial on the same leaf as a miniature, it is painted by the same hand as the miniature. Both artists are anonymous, and nothing is known about the patron of the manuscript, but the artists both reappear in other manuscripts. The artist of the miniatures also painted a detached leaf in the Österreichisches Museum für angewandte Kunst (Vienna), a medical treatise by Roger of Salerno (London, B.L. Sloane 1977), and a *Vie de Sainte Benoîte* (Berlin, Dahlem Museum, Kupferstichkabinett Hs. 78.B.16), all of which contain full-page miniatures. Some idea of the date and provenance of the group is provided by the colophon of the Berlin manuscript, which was made in 1312 for Helouis d'Escoufflans, a nun at the abbey of Ste. Benoîte d'Origny (diocese of Laon). The artist of the historiated initials reappears in Paris, B.N. fr. 789, which contains three versions of the Alexander legend and the *Istoire de Judas Machabee*, and other manuscripts associated with Amiens.

Oxford, Bodleian Library, MS Douce 383 (21958): Guiron le Courtois (Flanders, ca. 1500). Parchment, 18 ff. 450 × 325 mm. Text in 2 columns, 38 lines. Rubrics. 5 large miniatures with borders. This fragmentary manuscript contains the arms of Engelbert II of Nassau and of the Order of the Golden Fleece. Its impressive miniatures have been variously attributed to painters associated with the patronage of Engelbert, particularly the *Roman de la rose*, London, B.L. Harley 4425. Other products of the same workshop include the Statutes of the Order of the Golden Fleece (Vienna, Österreichische Nationalbibliothek 2606), a number of prayer books, and another *Guiron* manuscript (Paris, B.N. fr. 358–63).

Paris, Bibliothèque de l'Arsenal, MS 5218: La Queste del Saint Graal (Tournai, 1351). Parchment, 106 ff. 285 × 196 mm. Ff. 1–91v contain the *Queste del Saint Graal* with three illuminations, one of which, painted in two columns, illustrates the mysteries of the Grail. Written, illuminated, and

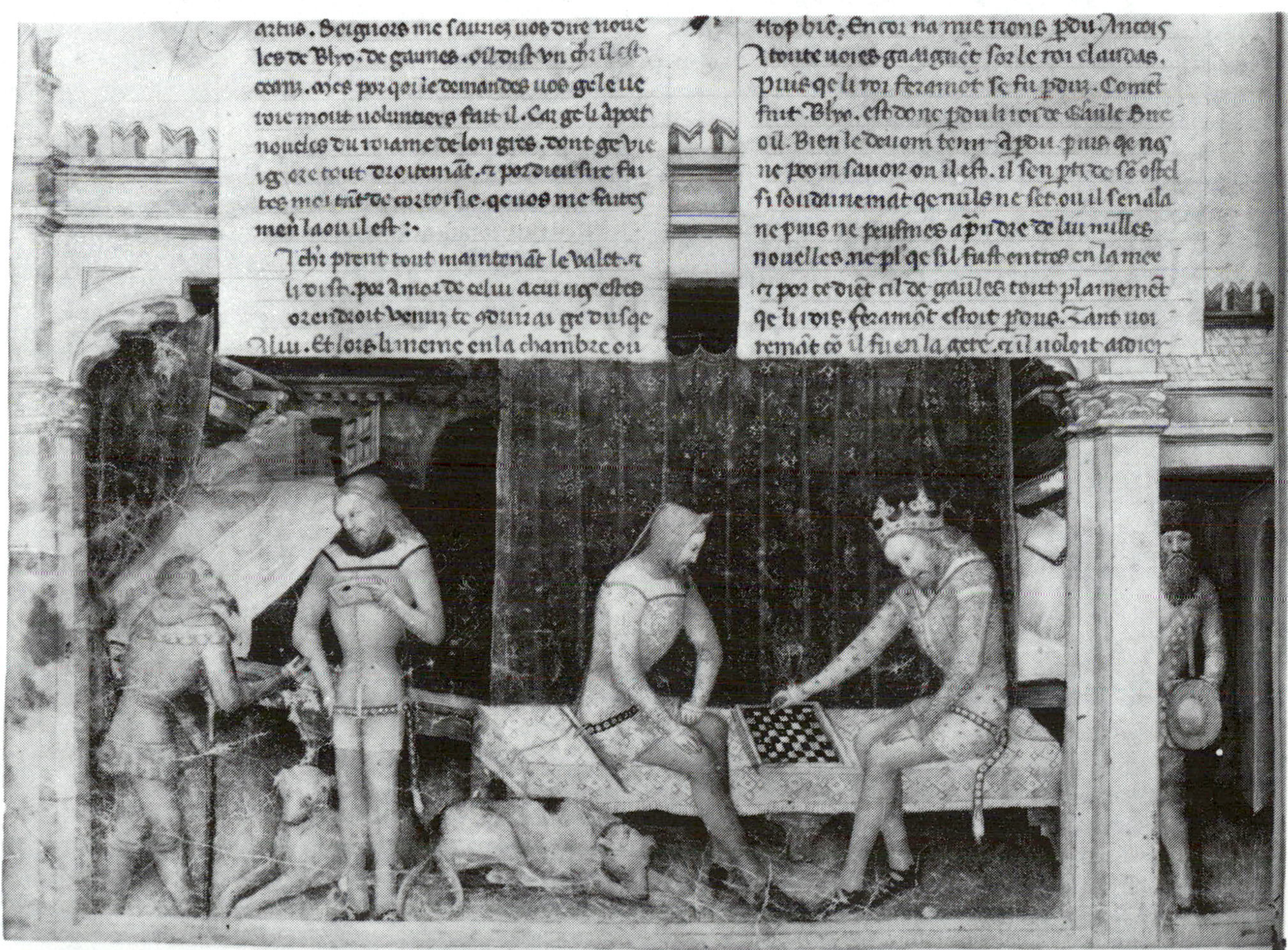

56. MS Paris, Bibliothèque Nationale, nlles. acq. 5243, fol. 3v: King Arthur Playing Chess. (Paris, Bibliothèque Nationale.)

bound by Pierart dou Tielt, in 1351, as indicated in a colophon. Pierart is documented as being responsible for the upkeep of the library at the Benedictine abbey of St. Martin at Tournai during the abbacy of Gilles le Muisit; and this manuscript includes a chronicle of the abbey. Also attributed to Pierart dou Tielt are an added miniature in a twelfth-century Gospel Book of the use of St. Martin's, Tournai (Washington, D.C., Library of Congress, De Ricci 127); *Pamphile et Galathee* (Brussels, Bibliothèque Royale 4783); a Book of Hours (Brussels, Bibliothèque Royale IV 453); and parts of the *Roman d'Alexandre* (Oxford, Bodl. 264).

Paris, Bibliothèque Nationale, MS Fr. 117–20: Cycle de Lancelot (Paris, ca. 1400). Parchment, 602 ff. in all, numbered continuously: Vol. 1, 154 ff. 494 × 341 mm, 3 miniatures; Vol. 2, 155–308 ff., 526 × 344 mm, 50 miniatures; Vol. 3, 526 × 344 mm, 50 miniatures; Vol. 4, 526 × 344 mm, 17 miniatures. Rubrics. Text in 2 columns, 65 lines, miniatures generally in one text column, a few in 2 columns, opening miniatures in four parts. These volumes comprise one of ten extant sets of manuscripts that contain the entire Vulgate Cycle. This set was purchased in 1405 by Jean, duc de Berry, for 300 *escus d'or* from the book-dealer Regnault du Montet (about whom it is also known that he sold a *Tristan* in England, and was tried for treason). This set of *Lancelot* volumes contains the arms and signature of Jean, duc de Berry, and appears in his inventories. Subsequently, it passed to Jean's great-grandson Jacques d'Armagnac, at which time substantial alterations were made to many of the miniatures. The illuminator of ca. 1400, named by Millard Meiss the Master of Berry's Cleres Femmes, also worked on a number of other manuscripts owned by Jean de Berry: Boccaccio's *Cleres et nobles femmes* (Paris, B.N. fr. 598), from which the illuminator takes his name, a manuscript given to Jean de Berry in 1404 by Jean de la Barre: a Livy (Geneva, Bibliothèque Publique fr. 77); and a *Bible Historiale* (Paris, Bibliothèque de l'Arsenal 5057–58). The anonymous illuminator who repainted parts of B.N. fr. 120 reappears in the *Lancelot* (Paris, B.N. fr. 112), where he collaborated with the illuminator Evrard d'Espingues, who also illustrated the *Tristan* (Chantilly, Musée Condé 404). B.N. fr. 112 was written in 1470 in Tournai by Micheau Gantelet, and also belonged to Jacques d'Armagnac.

Paris, Bibliothèque Nationale, MS Fr. 2186: Roman de la poire (Paris, ca. 1250). Parchment, 83 ff. 205 × 135 mm. Text in one column, 20 lines. 9 full-page miniatures, many containing two scenes in roundels or quatrefoils, 18 historiated initials. Among the prefatory full-page miniatures in this manuscript are representations of famous lovers from literature, including some of the earliest French representations of Tristan and Isolde, as well as Cligés and Fénice, Pyramus and Thisbe, Paris and Helen. Other couples in the full-page sequence are less certainly identified, but they also include the hero and heroine of the *Roman de la poire*, who appear again in the historiated initials illustrating the text. They are shown as a noble couple, both wearing heraldic garments emblazoned with the arms of France charged with *a cross or lozengy gules*. These arms are probably fictitious, as they cannot be traced in the contemporary heraldic sources, but the use of France differenced may indicate that the manuscript was made for a royal patron. The painting is of extremely high quality and the anonymous artist has been associated with a large Parisian workshop named the "Bari atelier" after a gradual now at San Nicola, Bari, which is a copy of a book made for use at the French royal *capella*.

Rennes, Bibliothèque Municipale, MS 255(148): Estoire, Merlin, Lancelot (ending incomplete) (Paris, ca. 1220–30). Parchment, 276 ff. 440 × 310 mm. Text in 3 columns, 45 lines. 57 historiated initials. This is the earliest illustrated surviving Vulgate Cycle manuscript. It can be approximately dated and localized on the basis of its codicological and stylistic affinities with a group of Psalters made in Paris for ladies of the French royal household early in the 1220s: Manchester, John Rylands University Library lat. 22; Leningrad, Saltykov-Schtschedrin State Public Library lat. Q.v.I, 67; Paris, B.N. n.a. lat. 1392, and other manuscripts, including the moralized Bibles in Vienna (Österreichische Nationalbibliothek 1179) and Toledo Cathedral Library. The decade of the 1220s is very close to the likely date of composition of the first parts of the Vulgate Cycle, and although the manuscript contains no firm evidence of patronage it is likely that this manuscript, and possibly even its texts, were also royal commissions. [MAS]

Branner, Robert. *Manuscript Painting in Paris During the Reign of Saint Louis: A Study of Styles*. Berkeley: University of California Press, 1977.

Gengaro, M.L., and L. Cogliato Arano. *Miniature lombarde*. Milan, 1970.

Loomis, Roger Sherman, and Laura Hibbard Loomis. *Arthurian Legends in Medieval Art*. London: Oxford University Press, 1938.

Meiss, Millard. *French Painting in the Time of Jean de Berry*. 2 vols. London: Phaidon, 1967.

Perriccioli Saggesse, Alessandra. *I romanze cavallereschi miniati a Napoli*. Naples: Società Editrice Napoletana, 1979.

Rasmo, N. "Il codice palatino 556 e le sue illustrazioni." *Rivista d'arte*, 23 (1939), 245–81.

Senior, Michael, ed. *Sir Thomas Malory's Tales of King Arthur*. London: Collins, 1980.

Stones, M.A. "The Earliest Illustrated Prose *Lancelot* Manuscript?" *Reading Medieval Studies*, 3 (1977), 3–44.

Whitaker, Muriel. *The Legends of King Arthur in Art*. Cambridge: Brewer, 1990, pp. 25–85.

MAP, WALTER (ca. 1140–ca. 1210), compiled *De Nugis Curialium* ("Courtiers' Trifles") in the last quarter of the twelfth century at the urging of a friend, who requested that Walter "put down in writing sayings and doings hitherto unrecorded or anything conspicuously remarkable." Born in

Hereford, Walter had a childlike fascination with the superstitious, the incredible, and the marvelous. He relates with particular relish tales of his neighbors, the Welsh. His work is a series of anecdotes taken from his own observations and experiences, from stories he has read or heard, and from contemporary and ancient history. Although none is specifically Arthurian, certain of his tales contain motifs and themes that have analogues in contemporary Arthurian literature. The fragments, gathered after Walter's death and arranged in a loosely thematic format, are preserved in a single manuscript (Oxford, Bodl. 851) of the late fourteenth century. The Vulgate Cycle of Arthurian romance is attributed, in the text itself, to Walter, but the attribution has long been recognized as false. [WWK]

Map, Walter. *De Nugis Curialium (Courtiers' Trifles)*, ed. and trans. M.R. James, rev. C.N.L. Brooke and R.A.B. Mynors. Oxford: Clarendon, 1983.

MARE AMOROSO ("Sea of Love"), a thirteenth-century Italian anthology of similes, alludes on several occasions to the Matter of Britain, referring to Morgan's Valley of False Lovers and Lancelot's adventures there, the Loathly Damsel, the Lady of Avalon, Merlin, Tristan's love potion, and the death of Iseult's brother, Chedino. [DLH]

Contini, Gianfranco, ed. "Il Mare Amoroso." In *Poeti del Duecento: Poesia Cortese Toscana e Settentrionale*. Milan, 1960, Vol. 2, pp. 301–14.

MAREK, JIŘI, Czech author and literary historian. In 1985, he published the novel *Tristan aneb O làsce* ("Tristan, or About Love"), which, using explicit and ironic references to the medieval Tristan legend, relates a love story in present-day Czechoslovakia. [UM/WCM]

Marek, Jiři. *Tristan aneb O làsce*. Prague: Československý spisovatel, 1985. (German translation published in East Berlin, 1987.)

MARIE DE FRANCE, a French poet who may have lived in England and who dedicated her *Lais* to a king presumed to be Henry II of England. She wrote during the second half, and before the last decade, of the twelfth century, but it has not been possible to date her production more accurately than that. Marie composed a version of the St. Patrick legend (*L'Espurgatoire Saint Patrice*), a collection of fables (*Ysopet*), and the lais for which she is now best known. The twelve lais and their prologue are preserved in London, B.L. Harley 978, and one or more of them are also contained in four other manuscripts; in addition, all but one were translated into Old Norse during the thirteenth century.

Although Marie is a major writer, her contribution to Arthurian literature is limited to two lais: *Chevrefueil* and *Lanval*. The former is a 118-line poem recounting a brief and passionate tryst between Isolde and the exiled Tristan. The encounter takes place in a forest, where the evocation of honeysuckle attached to a hazel branch provides a striking symbol of the lovers' entwined destinies: "Ne vus sanz mei, ne mei sanz vus" ("Neither you without me, nor I without you"). *Lanval* is longer (646 lines) and deals with an "otherworld" adventure of the hero, who leaves Arthur's court after being treated unjustly; he finds love with a fairy being who swears him to secrecy. Later, Guenevere makes advances to him, and in his own defense he is forced to reveal his love. Despite this violation of his oath, his lady arrives at the last moment to save him from punishment. A third lai, *Bisclavret*, concerning a man who periodically becomes a werewolf, is not Arthurian, but the elements of the story are taken over by the anonymous author of *Melion*, who recasts them in an Arthurian context.

Marie's accomplishment in her Arthurian lais, as in her others, resides in a combination of economical narration with effective analysis of emotion, and in her treatment of the conflicts between amorous ideals and worldly realities. [NJL]

Marie de France. *Lais*, ed. Alfred Ewert. Oxford: Blackwell, 1960.
———. *The Lais of Marie de France*, trans. Glyn S. Burgess and Keith Busby. Harmondsworth: Penguin, 1986.
Burgess, Glyn S. *The Lais of Marie de France: Text and Context*. Athens: University of Georgia Press, 1987.
Mickel, Emanuel J., Jr. *Marie de France*. New York: Twayne, 1974.

MARK (Marc, Marco), King of Cornwall, the deceived husband in the triangle with Isolde of Ireland and his sister's son, Tristan. Early versions of the legend treat Mark with sympathy: he is an essentially noble figure placed in an impossible position by the two people whom he loves best. However, his role as the deceived husband and tales like the one that he had horse's ears made him an object of ridicule, and as sympathy for the lovers grew, so Mark's character deteriorated. It reached a nadir in the French Prose *Tristan* (early thirteenth century), where he emerges as a despicable and cowardly villain, who finally murders his nephew. It is a reputation he has retained in most modern literature. (*See also* CASTLE DORE; TRISTAN AND ISOLDE.) [RHT]

Weismann-Wiedemann, Friederike. "From Victim to Villain: King Mark." In *The Expansion and Transformation of Courtly Literature*, ed. Nathaniel B. Smith and Joseph T. Snow. Athens: University of Georgia Press, 1980, pp. 49–68.

MARQUIS, DON(ALD ROBERT PERRY) (1878–1937), American humorist and satirist, and the creator of *Archy and Mehitabel*, wrote three Arthurian burlesque pieces. The first two are short poems: "Tristram and Isolt" tells how Mark traps the lovers; "Lancelot and Guinevere" comments irreverently upon how their affair brought the lovers not happiness but guilt. This idea is expanded in the stage-Irish short story "King O'Meara and Queen Guinevere," which pokes fun at people who take life too seriously.

Marquis also wrote *Out of the Sea* (1927), a melodramatic tragedy set in contemporary Cornwall with echoes of the Mark-Isolde-Tristan love triangle in the plot. [RHT]

Marquis, Don. *Sonnets to a Red-Haired Lady (By a Gentleman with a Blue Beard) and Famous Love Affairs*. Garden City, N.Y.: Doubleday, Page, 1922.

———. *Out of the Sea: A Play in Four Acts*. Garden City, N.Y.: Doubleday, Page, 1927.

———. "King O'Meara and Queen Guinevere." *Saturday Evening Post*, 202, 37 (March 15, 1930), 6–7ff.; 38 (March 22), 22–23ff.

"MARRIAGE OF SIR GAWAIN, THE," a ballad version of the Loathly Lady story, of uncertain relation to *The Wedding of Sir Gawain* and extant (with lacunae) only in the Percy Folio of 1660, though possibly of the fifteenth century. Arthur and "gentle" Gawain share the functions of answering the challenger and marrying the Lady (his sister). Family and feasting are particular concerns here. [JP]

Hales, John W., and Frederick J. Furnivall, eds. *Bishop Percy's Folio Manuscript: Ballads and Romances*. London: Trübner, 1867–69, Vol. 1, p. 103.

MARSHALL, EDISON (1894–1967), American explorer, novelist, and short-story writer, wrote *The Pagan King* (1959), a lively, if at times contrived, historical novel in which Arthur learns about illusion and reality: Vivain's friendship masks bitter enmity; the hostile Vortigern is his father; his half-brother and rival, Modred, proves a generous foe. Arthur finally resigns his kingship to wander as a bard, transforming historical fact into glorious legend. [RHT]

Marshall, Edison. *The Pagan King*. Garden City, N.Y.: Doubleday, 1959.

MARTIN, FRANK (1890–1974), Swiss composer of *Le Vin herbé* ("The Potion"), an oratorio relating the love of Tristan and Isolde as presented in Joseph Bédier's version of the story. The oratorio, completed in 1940, uses a choir of twelve and a small string orchestra, plus piano; the music is reminiscent of early polyphony. [NJL]

Martin, Frank. *Le Vin herbé, d'après 3 chapitres du Roman de Tristan et Iseut de Joseph Bédier*. Vienna: Universal Edition, 1943. (Score)

Müller, Ulrich. "Mittelalterliche Dichtungen in der Musik des 20. Jahrhunderts III: Das Tristan-und-Isolde-Oratorium von Frank Martin (nach Joseph Bédier). Mit einem Ausblick auf die Tristan-Komposition von Hans Werner Henze." In *Tradition und Entwicklung: Festschrift Eugen Thurnher*, ed. Werne Bauer, Achim Masser, and Guntram A. Plangge. Innsbruck: Innsbruck University, 1982.

MARTINE-BARNES, ADRIENNE, author of *The Dragon Rises* (1983). King Arthur turns out to have been an incarnation of The Dragon, an eternal spirit fated to be continually reborn as a successful war-leader, and in this science-fiction novel he leads his space fleet to victory in a distant future. He avoids the fatal love triangle and subsequent betrayal on this occasion by showing greater consideration for the feelings of his consort. [RHT]

Martine-Barnes, Adrienne. *The Dragon Rises*. New York: Ace, 1983.

MARTORELL, JOANOT (d. 1468) **and MARTÍ JOAN DE GALBA** (d. 1490), authors of *Tirant le Blanc*, a long and complex Catalan romance begun ca. 1460 and completed by Galba after the death of its first author. *Tirant* deals initially with the story of Guy de Warwick, who gives up chivalry and wealth to become a beggar, then with the adventures of the young Breton knight Tirant le Blanc and with his love for the Princess of Constantinople. Only one section of the work is specifically Arthurian in theme: King Arthur is at the Greek court and is sought there by

Morgan, his sister. Throughout the romance, however, the authors refer frequently to Arthurian subjects, such as the Grail quest, and characters.

The romance was translated into Castilian (*Tirante el Blanco*) and Italian (*Tirante il Bianco*) during the sixteenth century. Le Comte de Caylus translated it into French, as *Histoire du vaillant chevalier Tiran le Blanc* ("The Story of the Valiant Knight Tiran le Blanc"), ca. 1737. [NJL]

Martorell, Joanot, and Martí Joan de Galba. *Tirant le Blanc*, ed. Martí de Riquer. Barcelona: Selecta, 1947.

———. *Tirant lo Blanc*, trans. David H. Rosenthal. London: Macmillan, 1984.

McNerney, Kathleen. *"Tirant lo Blanc" Revisited: A Critical Study*. Detroit, 1983.

Vaeth, J.A. *Tirant lo Blanch: A Study of Its Authorship, Principal Sources and Historical Setting*. New York: Columbia University Press, 1918.

MARVELS AND THE MARVELOUS. The "marvelous" (French *merveilleux*) is a traditional misnomer for a body of materials and techniques that defined the characteristic "register" of the Arthurian romances and lays written throughout Europe, in various languages, from the second half of the twelfth century to the end of the Middle Ages. These materials and techniques, which one finds reused in romance after romance and lay after lay, are what made the Arthurian world extraordinary. They included, for example, stock characters like Arthur, Guenevere, Kay, Gawain, Morgan le Fay, dwarfs, and giants; props like magic salves and rings; materials like samite, squirrel fur, ermine, gold, silver, ebony, ivory, chrysolites, and carbuncles; character traits like stunning beauty, extreme forwardness, and amazing generosity; exotic places of origin like Spain, Constantinople, India, and Faërie; the conventional, unrealistic representations of time and space that scholars have come to call "romance time" and "romance space"; rhetorical devices like hyperbole and the panegyrical topics that Ernst Robert Curtius labeled "inexpressibility" and "outdoing"; "skeletal" or "archetypal" episodic structures; larger narrative paradigms including those taken over from pagan and Christian myth (like the visit to the under-, after-, or otherworld), as well as conscious, abstract, mathematical, or logical principles of organization learned in the schools (like bi- or tripartite composition) and subconscious principles and structures like those commonly associated with dreams (symbolism, displacement, repetition, and a belief in the "omnipotence of thoughts" or "infantile complexes" like the Oedipal complex); and such devices as truth claims, humorous exaggerations, and the sudden disappointment of audience expectations, which are intended to produce an ironic effect and remind the audience of the literary, artificial nature of the narrative. In the hands of a skilled author like Chrétien de Troyes, Wolfram von Eschenbach, or the author of *Sir Gawain and the Green Knight*, these elements could be woven together in such a way as to endow a narrative with an enigmatic, quasi-allegorical aura. It is this common and enduring body of materials and techniques, and not any obscure allegorical intention or mythical strata, that makes many medieval Arthurian narratives so hermeneutically provocative.

Marvels properly so-called were only one element, albeit an important one, in this larger collection of literary materials and techniques. The experience of the "marvelous" (Latin *admiratio*) was a psychological effect that was clearly defined in twelfth- and thirteenth-century scholastic circles. According to Hugh of St. Victor, for example, the human mind "marvels" when it apprehends God's power, wisdom, and goodness in and through the created universe, when it apprehends the existence of something it cannot comprehend (*De tribus diebus*). Thomas Aquinas wrote similarly that the mind "marvels" when it "sees an effect without knowing the cause" (*Summa contra gentiles*). The "marvels" one encounters in romance, of course, are fictional marvels or pseudo-marvels rather than true marvels. One knows their cause—the author. What one really wishes to know is why the author created them. It would be ridiculous to inquire after the physical cause of the lance's bleeding in the Grail episode at the Fisher King's castle in Chrétien de Troyes's *Perceval*; what one wants to know is why Chrétien introduced it into this scene. Such "marvels" are rhetorical devices that, in Clayton Koelb's words, "use the reader's disbelief to force the reader to look for the hidden kernel of truth promised by [our interpretive] tradition." Used well, pseudo-marvels contribute significantly to a narrative's enigmatic aura; used poorly, they seem nothing more than annoying flourishes or transparent *dei ex machina*.

The appearance of the Grail at the Fisher King's castle in *Perceval* is probably the episode of the medieval Arthurian romances that best exemplifies the use of the extraordinary and the marvelous to create an enigmatic aura. The episode has a strong effect on modern readers, most of whom come away from it with the impression that it is an obscure riddle with a hidden solution. Much of what has been written about *Perceval* during the last century consists of attempts to solve this riddle, to explain the central enigma of Chrétien's poem. There is, moreover, a great deal of evidence to suggest that medieval readers and listeners reacted to this episode the same way modern readers do. The numerous continuations and spin-offs, the entire Vulgate Cycle, witness to an enduring fascination with the Grail and are in their own way efforts to solve its riddles.

Chrétien does introduce two pseudo-marvels into his description of Perceval's evening at the Fisher King's castle—the drop of blood that drips from the lance tip and the brilliant radiance that accompanies the Grail—and these pseudo-marvels do play an important part in the creation of the impression that the scene is a riddle with some hidden solution. This impression is produced through the cumulative effect, rather, of the pseudo-marvels and other important elements. There is the high ceremony of the procession, its repetition, and its association with an elaborate meal, which mark it as a quasi-religious ritual. There is the play of light, colors, and rich materials: firelight, candlelight, white, red, gold, silver, precious gems. There is the hyperbole, which is concentrated in the description of the Grail itself. There is, finally, Perceval's reaction to the Grail's appearance and Chrétien's repeated allusions to it. The young knight's desire to know why this procession occurs, what the Grail is, and who is served with it is a model for the readers' or listeners' own reactions and suggests that there are things here that need to be explained. The cumulative effect of Chrétien's skillful arrangement of these elements is very strong and creates an aura of meaningfulness that provokes the curiosity of listeners or readers and makes them feel that the Grail's appearance is profoundly significant.

The Arthurian authors' recourse to this body of "extraordinary" materials and techniques, including the rhetorical use of pseudo-marvels, was a response to the situation of the aristocracy at the end of the twelfth century. It was a way of engaging a cultural and epistemological reality that was overwhelmingly ecclesiastical and a material reality that was increasingly difficult and alien. It made romance, in Glending Olson's words, "a form of discourse that is relevant to the ongoing concerns of life yet valued and enjoyed in great part as a withdrawal from them."

The extraordinary made romance into a form of social dream, an artistically produced simulacrum of dream, which imitated and explored not the world but the human heart and mind. It enabled the romance authors to portray invisible qualities in visible, narratively tractable ways. It permitted them to make their narratives immediate, dreamlike responses to their audience's (admissible and inadmissible) wishes. It allowed them to model their narratives directly on psychic, as opposed to physical, structures and processes. And, finally, it responded to the spiritual aspirations of the aristocracy and suggested that the aristocratic life had a dense and profound mystical dimension.

This last function is particularly evident, again, in the emphasis that Chrétien places on colored light in his description of the events at the Fisher King's castle. This emphasis on light is strongest in Chrétien's description of the appearance of the golden, gem-studded Grail itself, which in fact bears an uncanny likeness to the main altar of Abbot Suger's cathedral of St. Denis (described in Suger's *De administratione*, 33). Behind both Suger's description of the altar—behind, indeed, his entire rehabilitation of his cathedral—and Chrétien's description of the Grail lies a broadly influential aesthetic philosophy founded on the Neoplatonic mysticism of Pseudo-Dionysius the Areopagite (identified, in the twelfth century, with Suger's patron St. Denis), which found brillaint light to be the best symbol or material representation of spiritual and divine realities. The Fisher King's castle, as Chrétien describes it, is thus a sort of chivalric cathedral, and the Grail procession belongs to some obscure, unformulated secular liturgy. The episode was intended to suggest that aristocratic life possessed a transcendent dimension that paralleled and rivaled the transcendent dimension of ecclesiastical devotion and to endow chivalric culture with a profundity and gravity that it had not previously possessed.

The literary elaboration of an extraordinary, enigmatic world also enabled the authors of Arthurian romances and lays to define a new kind of writing within an existing, closed, homogeneous textual field dominated by ecclesiastical culture and to give written representation to the subconscious margins of that culture—the secular, the popular, the vernacular, the alien, the feminine, the immoral. This literary elaboration of an extraordinary world enabled these authors to sift reality, to transform it, to perfect it, and to imbue it with the strange imperatives of forbidden desire. It made their works into an extraordinary collective dream, one that appealed to every level of society, to all the groups one might have found at the courts of Champagne, England, or Thuringia: men and women, parents and children, older and younger siblings, great lords and simple knights, warriors and merchants, laypeople and clerks—a dream so seductive that it made the dreamers forget the material and political interests that separated them from one another. Precisely because their recourse to a body of "extraordinary" materials and techniques set romance off and apart from the material world, these authors were able to imagine an aristocratic world that redirected and resolved social, political, and economic tensions. The extraordinary was the ground and foundation of romance's participation in the unification of the aristocracy and the transformation of its dwindling material mastery into a cultural and psychological tyranny.

This common and increasingly traditional body of "extraordinary" materials and techniques remained a viable literary system well into the fifteenth century. By 1375, however, three broad developments had occurred that affected profoundly the nature of the Arthurian extraordinary. First, the Church's cultural monopolies, its grip on both spiritual and secular affairs, had been broken by 1375. It could no longer comprehensively enforce its claim to exclusive competence in the representation of all being and the determination of all meaning. As a result, secular literature was no longer limited to the vain and pleasing. The extraordinary was no longer its only and necessary ground.

The second development that changed the role of the extraordinary in romance was the evolution of a jurisprudence concerning the nobility that served as an increasingly effective regulator of the tensions and passages among social strata. As law became an ever more effective gatekeeper of the noble fortress, the cultural, ideological forms like romance, which had been entrusted with this duty, lost some of their immediate usefulness and urgency. As its importance as an instrument of social mediation diminished, the extraordinary world of romance became a more fanciful expression of aristocratic wishes.

The third broad development was the changing relation between aristocratic life in romance and in reality. In the late twelfth century, the image of aristocratic life that was created by the romance authors bore little relation to the everyday lives of aristocrats. It was, however, a desirable image that sought to justify the aristocracy's position and privileges, and the real aristocracy began to model its life on the life of their romance counterparts. This tendency grew to the point that, by 1375, romances were providing many of the models for an aristocratic life that was frequently as incredible and extraordinary as the life of an Arthurian hero.

This use of romance as a model for life created a demand for more *imitable* romances. This meant that romance had to be purged of much of its more purely psychic material and techniques or had to present this material in more imitable ways, for example, through personification allegory. In addition, romance's extraordinary elements had to be such as could be imitated or constructed in reality. The romance audience, in sum, wanted a theatrical extraordinary, one which was liable to public, dramatic representation.

This more imitable romance and theatrical extraordinary were more referential, insofar as the nobility attempted to make its own life romantic and extraordinary, but they were not therefore more "realistic." The "real" world of the fourteenth century was a grim place of warfare, floods, famine, plague, bankruptcies, and peasant revolts. The members of the nobility responded to this world, and to the numerous political, military, and economic checks with which they had met in it, by inventing an artificial, theatrical life of ritual and pageantry based in large part on romance. The extraordinary romance world, that is, became a means of escape from an unpleasant and disappointing reality, rather than being, as it had been in the late twelfth century, a way of addressing reality.

On the one hand, then, the reasons for the romance authors' recourse to the extraordinary—the Church's claim to exclusive competence in the representation and interpretation of reality, the need for cultural forms to mediate tensions among the strata of the aristocracy and among the aristocracy and other social groups—were not as pressing in 1375 as they had been in 1150. On the other hand, a strong desire existed among the nobility of 1375 for an imitable, escapist literature that could help them retire magnificently, and with as many of their winnings as possible, from the casino of public life. Extraordinary romances continued to be written after 1375, but the extraordinary underwent what Jacques Le Goff terms an "aestheticization" and became increasingly an "ornament, [a] literary and artistic technique, [a] stylistic game." It was no longer the means by which secular literature addressed its circumstances, but the means by which it composed a fanciful and pleasant alternative to them. [JR]

Guiette, Robert. *Forme et senefiance*. Geneva: Droz, 1978, pp. 29–56, 73–83.

Hanning, Robert. "The Audience as Co-Creator of the First Chivalric Romances." *Yearbook of English Studies*, 11 (1981), 1–28.

Le Goff, Jacques. *L'Imaginaire médiéval*. Paris: Gallimard, 1985, pp. 17–39.

Poirion, Daniel. *Le Merveilleux dans la littérature française du moyen âge*. Paris: PUF, 1982.

MASEFIELD, JOHN (1878–1967), Poet Laureate of England from 1930 until his death. Known especially for his poems about sailing and the sea, he published several works of poetry, one novel, and a play based on Arthurian legend. The influence of Yeats and the Celtic Revival is evident in his use of material from the Welsh Triads (Tristan as one of the Noble Swineherds of Britain, for example, and the character Gwenivach, Gwenivere's sister and rival) and in his recasting of *The Spoils of Annwfn* as "The Sailing of Hell Race."

The largest body of Masefield's Arthurian poetry (including the preceding examples) will be found in the collection *Midsummer Night and Other Tales in Verse* (1928), which includes such poems as "The Begetting of Arthur," a highly romantic account of Uther's elopement with Ygern and his murder by henchmen of her father, Merchyon of Cornwall, and "The Taking of Morgause," the story of her abduction by the pirate King Lot of Orkney. Most of the poetry is encumbered with too-pat rhyme schemes and balladlike rhythms that undercut the seriousness of its content. There are, however, poems of some power, such as "Midsummer Night," in which the narrator enters a "hollow hill" to hear Arthur and others describe their roles in the downfall of the Round Table. "The Breaking of the Links" succeeds because of the drama of the subject matter, the trial of Gwenivere; in this poem, the rhyming is more free and less obtrusive. Masefield's Arthurian poetry deals largely with conventional episodes that he recasts with situations or characters of his own invention, e.g., Arthur's divine helpers, who resemble both the *sidhe* and the classical deities.

One distinctive element in Masefield's Arthuriana is his fascination with the story of Tristan and Isolt. Evident both in the poem "The Love-Gift" and in his play *Tristan and Isolt* (1927) is his sympathy for King Mark. This play was Masefield's last, not particularly impressive, venture in the genre. To such conventional elements as the young Tristan's freeing Cornwall from tyranny, the love potion, the substitution of Brangwen for Isolt on the wedding night, and the banishment of the lovers, Masefield adds new elements that include the lovers' public avowal of their love, explicit emphasis on Tristan's political irresponsibility, and Isolt's revulsion against their love affair. This leads to her brutal repudiation of the half-mad Tristan and thus to his death, although unknown to her Mark has been killed in battle. Isolt then stabs herself over Tristan's corpse.

The strength of the drama lies in Mark's torment and in the pathos of Brangwen's unvoiced and unrequited love for him. Its structure is weakened by an overlong comic episode involving Tristan's substituting for Mark's swineherd. In contrast, the poem "Tristan's Singing," in the 1931 collection *Minnie Maylow's Story and Other Tales and Scenes*, is, with its focused lyricism, a better example of Masefield's skill.

Badon Parchments (1947) is a short, slow-paced epistolary novel of the events leading up to Arthur's defeat of the Saxon forces at Badon Hill. Arthur appears only at the beginning and at the end of the novel, which is primarily a report by John of Cos, emissary of the Byzantine emperor, on the feuding and pusillanimous behavior of British nobles. The story of Arthur was one of especial significance to an England torn and permanently changed by two wars—the vacillating and deceitful ministers of *Badon Parchments* are evidence of Masefield's concern.

Masefield also included a brief Arthurian episode in his children's novel *The Midnight Folk* (1927). The boy Kay Harker meets members of Arthur's court in one of the many dream-journeys included in the novel. He receives a promise from Arthur of help in his quest, and Lancelot, in a brief, lyrical speech, tells him that he and Guinevere are "remaking what we undid."

The Arthurian works by Masefield are not a major element of his canon, although they are of some interest in their use of Celtic elements. They exemplify convention leavened wtih moderate invention. [AAR]

Masefield, John. *The Midnight Folk*. London: Heinemann, 1927.

———. *Tristan and Isolt: A Play in Verse*. London: Heinemann; New York: Macmillan, 1927.

———. *Midsummer Night and Other Tales in Verse*. London: Heinemann, 1928.

———. *Badon Parchments*. London: Heinemann, 1947.

Sternlicht, Sanford. *John Masefield*. Boston: Twayne, 1977.

MASQUES. The masque was an elaborate form of dramatic performance that achieved its highest development in England during the first half of the seventeenth century. It combined the talents of artist, poet, musician, choreographer, and aristocratic amateur performer in a private entertainment that personified the idealized secular values of the court, expressing, in Welsford's words, "an emotional attitude towards life" (p. 360).

The masque developed from such popular entertainments as masquerades, morris dancing, carnival processions and revels, chivalric tournaments, and civic pageants, augmented by theatrical influences like morality plays and interludes (*intermedii*) between courses at banquets or acts of dramas. The performances employed sophisticated costumes, painted scenery, and stage mechanics as a setting for nobles who customarily played allegorical roles. The earliest English masques were composed for the Tudor court to celebrate aristocratic marriages and important state occasions, such as visits between royalty. Later, masque performances spread from the court to the regional seats of lesser nobility and merged with pantomime, opera, and the popular stage. Typically composed for specific patrons, they frequently expressed those patrons' personal fantasies and contained allusions recognizable chiefly to court "insiders."

Given the strong neoclassical influences of the Renaissance, masques that employed medieval Arthurian material were scarce. However, the continuing appeal of Arthur's court as a political and social precedent for an ascendant Britain, and especially of his wizard Merlin's mastery at prophecies and illusions, surfaced occasionally by means ranging from the central use of Merlin and Arthur in *The Speeches at Prince Henry's Barriers* (1610) to a single reference to "Arthur's Chair" in *The Masque of Oberon* (1611). Both were written by Ben Jonson and staged by Inigo Jones, respectively the greatest poet and designer of masque performances.

Prince Henry's Barriers celebrated the investiture of King James's fifteen-year-old elder son (who also took the part of Oberon the following year) as Prince of Wales; it cost £2,466—not an unusual sum for these sumptuous productions. The masque's allegory employs Arthur as the analogue to James, and Meliadus—in *Les Prophécies de Merlin*, a lover of the Lady of the Lake but here her son—as Prince Henry. The staging, which combined medieval and neoclassical architectural styles, was spectacular: the Lady of the Lake is discovered at floor or stage level before a landscape of ruins and water, King Arthur appears aloft as the star Arcturus, and Merlin rises from his tomb. Meliadus enters from a painted portico behind the first set, and Chivalry is revived from her sleep in a cave to the side. During the masque, the Lady of the Lake and Merlin, who speaks for Jonson as court poet and historian, present Meliadus to the king and enunciate the chivalric values of "arms and arts" that he must uphold. Arthur awards Meliadus his shield, Merlin describes the heroic achievements of the prince's ancestors, and with Chivalry's approval a mock combat (the barriers) ensues to display the prince's martial skill. The action concludes with a speech from Merlin. No other masque so successfully draws upon Arthurian traditions in its scenic and poetic style.

Other masques that incorporated Arthurian material were a lost production called *A Mask of King Arthur's Knights*

(1539); King James's composition for the marriage of the Earl of Huntly and Henrietta Stewart; Thomas Campion's *The Lord Hay's Masque* (1607); and William D'Avenant's *Britannia Triumphans* (1637). Of the first, only a record of payment "for the stuff of a mask of King Arthur's Knights" survives. James I's masque established a fashion by comparing his court with Arthur's, and Campion's prologue on the occasion of Lord Hay's marriage to Henrietta Stuart typifies this symbolic connection. D'Avenant's masque, one of the last written for Charles I before the Puritan Revolution expunged both the court and dramatic shows, was designed by Jones and illustrates how far Arthurian characterizations had drifted from their originals. His use of Merlin observes medieval tradition only in the association with prophecy; in other respects, he is a magnificently but foppishly arrayed Renaissance necromancer who serves Imposture by his command of demons. Merlin's function in this masque is to personify the stage illusion. He introduces the two antimasques—mock or rustic dances, songs, and dialogues that usually precede and counterpoise the serious message of the masque proper. The first of these is a musical dumb show of commoners in hell; the second is a brief burlesque romance in mock heroic couplets, wherein a knight attempts to rescue a damsel from a giant. The verdict of Bellerophon, the masque's hero: "How trivial and how lost thy visions are!" (*Works*, p. 282). Yet at the masque's end, Merlin returns to raise a chorus of poets who compliment the queen. Spectacle has nevertheless triumphed over poetry in the use of Arthurian legend.

The masque influenced other forms of theater both during and after its brief reign as a favorite variety of court entertainment. Thomas Hughes's tragedy *The Misfortunes of Arthur* (1588, with elaborate "devises and shows" staged by Francis Bacon and colleagues of Gray's Inn for Queen Elizabeth's court in Greenwich) combined masquelike entertainment with a Senecan treatment of King Arthur's demise. The antimasque affinity for satire was absorbed by Henry Fielding's Arthurian burlesque of classical tragedies, *The Life and Death of Tom Thumb the Great* (1730). One of the authors satirized, John Dryden, had previously written *King Arthur: or, The British Worthy* (1691), accompanied by Purcell's music, Priest's choreography, and spectacular masquelike stage effects. Fielding's satire did not lessen the appeal of Dryden's work; it was revived frequently, and other Arthurian operas appeared throughout the nineteenth and into the twentieth century. The multimedia masque influence was also combined with references to contemporary amusements in Edward Phillips's *The Royal Chase, or Merlin's Hermitage and Cave* (1735–36) and *commedia dell'arte* characters in Aaron Hill's *Merlin in Love* (1760) and Lewis Theobald's *Merlin: or The Devil of Stonehenge* (performed in 1767), *Merlin's Cave* (1750; subsequent revivals were called *A Cure for a Scold* [1788] and *Harlequin's Masquerade* [1814]), and T.J. Dibden's *Merlin's Mount* (or *Harlequin Cymraeg and the Living Leek*, 1825). John Thelwall's *The Fairy of the Lake* (1801) is a closet drama with elaborate songs, dances, and scenic embellishments. Reginald Heber's unfinished dramatic poem "The Masque of Gwendolen" (1816) employs the term more for artistic effect than technical accuracy, but *Kenilworth* (1821), by Sir Walter Scott, describes a masque for Queen Elizabeth of British, Romans, Saxons, and Normans reconciled by Merlin. Louisa May Alcott's novel *A Modern Mephistopheles* (1877) suggests the largely undocumented continuity of the form in impromptu amateur theatricals by describing the seduction of Merlin as portrayed by two characters in a privately staged performance. While most of these works are minor, they undoubtedly served—as did the masque itself—to sustain the Arthurian legend through its neoclassical period of dormancy and to signal its Romantic revival. [PHG]

D'Avenant, William. *The Dramatic Works of William D'Avenant*. New York: Russell and Russell, 1964, Vol. 2.

Jonson, Ben. *Ben Jonson: The Complete Masques*, ed Stephen Orgel. New Haven: Yale University Press, 1969.

Merriman, James Douglas. *The Flower of Kings: A Study of the Arthurian Legend in England Between 1485 and 1835*. Lawrence: University Press of Kansas, 1973.

Welsford, Enid. *The Court Masque*. Cambridge: Cambridge University Press, 1927.

MASTERS, EDGAR LEE (1869–1950), American poet best known as the author of *Spoon River Anthology*. His collection *Songs and Satires* (1916) includes two Arthurian poems, "Ballad of Launcelot and Elaine" and "The Death of Sir Launcelot," which retell in ballad stanzas the stories of the begetting of Galahad and of Launcelot's final days and holy death, respectively. [ACL]

Masters, Edgar Lee. *Songs and Satires*. New York: Macmillan, 1916.

MATIÈRE DE BRETAGNE (Matter of Britain), the traditional designation of literary material deriving from Britain (in the broadest sense, including Brittany) and of presumed Celtic ancestry. The term, which is a convenient and accepted label if something of a misleading oversimplification, comes from lines written by the French poet Jean Bodel in *Les Saisnes* (late twelfth century). Bodel divides acceptable literary material into the Matter of France (the epics or *chansons de geste*), of Rome (the romances of antiquity), and of Britain (the Breton lais and romances). The usual, but not exclusive, subject of much of the Matter of Britain is Arthur. [NJL]

MATTHEWS, JOHN, and BOB STEWART, British writers who have individually produced works approaching the Arthurian legend from literary, social, spiritual, and more esoteric perspectives. Their *Warriors of Arthur* (1987) argues for the flourishing of a Celtic revival in Arthur's time through a conglomeration of historical facts and speculation, numerous illustrations, and short stories—three by each author. Such legends as "The Beheading Game" and "Owein of the Ravens" are presented as though told to an audience in Celtic Britain.

In Matthews's poem *Merlin in Calydon*, Merlin, trapped in Brocéliande, broods on his and the world's problems but hopes that love will lead to freedom. "The Story of Grisandole" uses an adventure of Merlin before he becomes Arthur's adviser to comment on the role of women in society. Matthews's novel-in-progress, *Broceliande*, like much of his critical writing, focuses on the Grail legend. [ACL/DN]

Matthews, John. *The Grail: Quest for the Eternal*. London: Thames and Hudson, 1981.
———. *Merlin in Calydon*. Somerset: Hunting Raven, 1981.
———. "The Perilous Bed," from *Broceliande: A Novel of the Forest*. *The Round Table*, 4 (1987), 32–34.
———. "The Story of Grisandole." *The Round Table*, 4 (1987), 6–9.
———, and Bob Stewart. *Warriors of Arthur*. London: Blandford, 1987.

MAUGIN, JEAN, French author of *Le Premier Livre du nouveau Tristan Prince de Leonnois, chevalier de la Table Ronde et d'Yseulte Princesse d'Yrlande, Royne de Cornouaille* ("The First Book of the New Tristan, Prince of Leonnois, Knight of the Round Table, and of Yseulte, Princess of Ireland, Queen of Cornwall"). Updated to accommodate sixteenth-century tastes, the work, published in 1554, tended to rationalize events and to place increased emphasis on the characters' psychology; it also presented the love potion as a simple aphrodisiac. The *Nouveau Tristan* was republished in 1567, 1577, and 1586; a second book was planned but never published, and only in the 1586 edition was the announcement of a continuation dropped. [NJL]

Maugin, Jean. *Le Premier Livre du nouveau Tristan Prince de Leonnois, chevalier de la Table Ronde et d'Yseulte Princesse d'Yrlande, Royne de Cornouaille*. Paris, 1554.
Lods, Jeanne. "Le *Nouveau Tristan* de Jean Maugin." *Bibliographical Bulletin of the International Arthurian Society*, 12 (1960), 107–16.

MAYNE, WILLIAM (JAMES CARTER), English author of *Earthfasts* (1966), a serious fantasy for younger readers in which an eighteenth-century drummer-boy intrudes into the cave where Arthur rests. This causes an irruption into twentieth-century England of legendary phenomena whose impact demonstrates the value of an open mind. The schoolboy Keith returns a surprisingly menacing Arthur to his rest, but the drummer-boy must remain in the modern world.

The Hamish Hamilton Book of Heroes (1967) includes a retelling of the Welsh tale of Peredur; and *Max's Dream* (1977), a novel for younger readers set in the north of England at the close of the nineteenth century, is based upon *The Dream of Macsen Wledig*, another tale from the *Mabinogi*. [CBH/RHT]

Mayne, William. *Earthfasts*. London: Hamish Hamilton, 1966.
———. *Max's Dream*. London: Hamish Hamilton; New York: Greenwillow, 1977.

MEANEY, DEE MORRISON, sympathetically narrates the love story of Tristan and Iseult, from the latter's point of view, in *Iseult* (1985). Most of the traditional elements are retained, including the fight with the dragon and the magical love potion that binds them, though the lovers are never trapped by their enemies. Instead, since both love the noble-minded Mark, they eventually agree that Tristan should leave Mark's court. He later dies of a wound just before Iseult can arrive in response to his message; she expires on his breast. [RHT]

Meaney, Dee Morrison. *Iseult: Dreams That Are Done*. New York: Ace, 1985.

MEDIEVALISM. John Ruskin apparently coined the word *medievalism* in 1853 to distinguish one of three periods of architecture: classicism, medievalism, modernism. The term rapidly came to be employed not only for the study of the Middle Ages, which had been going on since the sixteenth century, but in particular for the use of medieval inspiration or models for almost every aspect of modern life.

The Matter of Britain has always been at the heart of medievalism in the English-speaking countries and often elsewhere, even though the two have not always advanced in step. There were always reasons for studying the Middle Ages. In the sixteenth and seventeenth centuries, the pamphlet wars of the Reformation involved elaborate study of medieval religious history and institutions. In France and the Netherlands, this was to lead to the vast series of medieval texts and documents edited by the Maurist and

Bollandist Fathers (the latter continuing today) and hence to the development of the ancillary sciences of history, in particular diplomatic, paleography, and chronology; in sixteenth-century England, the assertion of the historic independence of the English church from Rome led to the recovery and study of Anglo-Saxon. At the same time, the Matter of Britain enjoyed unprecedented influence as an important element of Tudor and Stuart policy, both foreign and domestic. This, however, was the pseudo-historical Arthur of Geoffrey of Monmouth, not the Arthur of the romantic cycle.

Already assailed by the critical historical temper (one of the more fortunate products of Renaissance humanism), this Arthur was involved in the downfall of the Stuart monarchy, and the romantic Arthur was involved in turn. In the seventeenth century, English legal medievalism was the main basis of parliamentary opposition to the Stuarts. "Magna Carta," in Coke's memorable reminder to the 1628 Parliament, "is such a fellow he will have no sovereign." Thus, medievalism and Arthurianism were for a time apparently opposed. In these centuries, only Spenser managed to handle Arthurian material effectively, in *The Faerie Queene*, and this work already had an air of antiquarianism, of revival: Malory and the Middle Ages were beginning to be something in the past. Spenser's epic, in C.S. Lewis's words, typifies in some ways "the great literature of the fifteen eighties and nineties . . . which humanism . . . would have prevented if it could."

While medievalism grew, however, the great legend—rejected by Milton as an epic subject, rendered absurd by Blackmore, redeemed from neglect only by Dryden and Purcell's *King Arthur, the British Worthy* (1691)—survived into the eighteenth century in little more than local antiquities and country ballads. The Medieval Revival of that century involved a study of the romance, but this was antiquarian rather than popular. It might be thought that the society that produced Ossian and Rowley could have handled Arthur, but, except satirically, the Romantics found the Matter unmanageable, even when they cared to attempt it. "As to Arthur, you could not by any means make a poem on him national to Englishmen. What have we to do with him?" asked Coleridge.

By the end of the eighteenth century, everything was ready for the great outburst of historical study that was to characterize the nineteenth century. Vast collections of documents had been asssembled and edited, principally in France; Voltaire, Vico, and Herder had devised philosophies of approach to the past; Scott would show how history might be told ("Scott taught Europe to write history," said Thierry); the Middle Ages, if not respectable, were at least fashionable. The greater part of nineteenth-century historical writing was to be medieval, increasingly as it became recognized what society owed to medieval institutions, to parliament rather than senate, jury rather than tribune, and to medieval "representation" rather than Greek "democracy."

Scholarship apart, there were powerful social impulses to medievalism. In *Le Génie du Christianisme* (1802), Chateaubriand undertook to show that medieval literature and art were superior to pagan by reason of their Christianity. The argument was useful to Protestant and Catholic alike, and as employed by A.W. Pugin and John Ruskin it was to have a wide-ranging effect in England and America. Political motives to medievalism were even stronger than religious. In eighteenth-century France, it had been necessary to invent "feudalism" in order that the Revolution might overthrow it, but the loss of political direction following the downfall of Napoleon could only be reconciled with national pride by recalling what Michelet called "the epic of the people" in its largely medieval entirety. In Germany, the demand for political and economic unity was to be supported by recalling the cultural heritage of the medieval German empire, while the English preferred to attribute their power and prosperity to the slow maturing of their medieval institutions rather than to industrialization.

The Arthurian recovery was signaled by the republication of Malory after almost 200 years: the two editions of 1816 and Southey's of 1817 were the first since 1634. Meanwhile, medievalism had become not only respectable but necessary. The Oxford Movement in religion, the Arthurian Revival in art, the Gothic Revival in architecture, and the Young England movement in politics illustrate a dominance that was to last through the 1860s and yield ground only slowly until 1914. The first of Tennyson's Arthurian poems, "The Lady of Shalott," came in 1832; myth was restored and the pseudo-historical Arthur now troubled only historians. Tennyson spoke for his age: his high moral treatment of the legend inspired not only the Pre-Raphaelite poets and artists and their successors on the one hand but on the other the new, or reformed, public schools of England, which were satisfying the demand for an enlarged middle class of professional men, administrators, and soldiers. This public-school ethos proved equally assimilable in the United States, as shown by the popularity of a native work, Sidney Lanier's *The Boy's King Arthur* (1880).

Around the turn of the century, the fortunes of both medievalism and Arthurianism changed significantly: both were enlarged by new studies, such as anthropology, and new social interests, such as occultism. J. Comyns Carr's *King Arthur* (1895), with designs by Burne-Jones and music by Sir Arthur Sullivan, both summed up Victorian Arthurianism and heralded a wave of drama and poetry that, expanding to include prose fiction in the thirties, continues unabated: the poetry reached a peak with large-scale treatments by Edwin Arlington Robinson, T.S. Eliot, Charles Williams, and David Jones.

The First World War dealt a serious blow to the public ethos of chivalry and the dominance of medievalism as a social force: after 1914, Europe no longer looked to the past for models. Medievalism remained strong in particular contexts, such as Thomist philosophy in Roman Catholic circles, Gothic Revival architecture in the Bauhaus, and economic medievalism (which had powerfully influenced Karl Marx and William Morris earlier) in the English Labour movement. Meanwhile, medieval, including Arthurian, scholarship was being steadily consolidated and institutionalized: the Medieval Academy of America was founded in 1925, the International Arthurian Society, in 1949.

Even greater changes occurred after the Second World War. By about 1960, it became apparent that the great age of collection (in all the arts), textual establishment, and editing was virtually over, and that medieval art and literature were now available for critical appreciation and popular enjoyment, as shown by the current popularity of medieval music, dance, and drama ensembles. In Arthurian studies, the most dramatic change has been the emergence of a third Arthur, the Arthur of history. Finally, medievalism in general, and certainly Arthurian subcreation, have benefited immeasurably from the readmission of fantasy to the canons of literary acceptance in the last thirty years. (*See also* ARTHURIAN REVIVAL.) [LJW]

Chandler, Alice. *A Dream of Order: The Medieval Ideal in Nineteenth-Century English Literature*. Lincoln: University of Nebraska Press, 1970.

Clark, Kenneth. *The Gothic Revival*. London: Constable, 1928; rev. ed. 1962.

Ferguson, Wallace K. *The Renaissance in Historical Thought*. Boston: Houghton Mifflin, 1948.

Fraser, John. *America and the Patterns of Chivalry*. Cambridge: Cambridge University Press, 1982.

Girouard, Mark. *The Return to Camelot: Chivalry and the English Gentleman*. New Haven: Yale University Press, 1981.

Kenney, Alice P., and Leslie J. Workman. "Ruins, Romance, and Reality: Medievalism in Anglo-American Imagination and Taste 1750–1840." *Winterthur Portfolio*, 10 (1975), 131–62.

Merriman, James D. *The Flower of Kings: A Study of the Arthurian Legend in England Between 1485 and 1835*. Lawrence: University Press of Kansas, 1973.

Simpson, Roger. *Camelot Regained: The Arthurian Revival and Tennyson, 1800–1849*. Woodbridge, Suffolk: Boydell and Brewer, 1990.

MELEAGANT (Meliagrant, Melwas), in Caradoc's *Vita Gildae*, King of Somerset, who abducts Guenevere from Arthur's court and holds her prisoner at Glastonbury Abbey until Gildas intervenes. (A reconciliation is reached and Guenevere is returned.) This is the first account of Guenevere's abduction as well as the first reference to Glastonbury Abbey in connection with Arthur. In Chrétien de Troyes's *Lancelot*, the Vulgate Cycle, and Malory's *Morte Darthur*, Meleagant is portrayed as a jealous and evil man. In Chrétien, Lancelot fights him several times and eventually kills him. Malory tells us that, while Guenevere is at Meleagant's castle, Lancelot breaks into her room and spends the night with her. The following morning, Meleagant notices blood stains on Guenevere's bed, which are the result of Lancelot's injuring his hands while tearing out the window bars of Guenevere's room, and openly accuses her of adultery. During Meleagant's and Lancelot's combat, the former refuses to rise after being struck, thereby forcing Lancelot to agree to fight partially armed and bound. Nevertheless, Meleagant is slain. [SW]

MELEKH ARTUS ("King Artus"), a Hebrew prose translation of sections from two romances found in the Vulgate Cycle, the *Estoire de Merlin* and the *Mort Artu*. The immediate source of the work was almost certainly a lost north Italian (Tuscan) version; its single transmitting manuscript, dated 1279 and preserved in the Vatican Library, consists of five closely written folios. The anonymous translator was well read in both religious (biblical and Talmudic) and secular literature—in addition to the two works translated, he shows familiarity with at least the Prose *Lancelot* and the *Queste del Saint Graal*. The *Merlin* passage recounts the infatuation of Uther for the wife of the Duke of Tintagel, Uther's war with the Duke, Merlin's assistance in the deception of Igerne, and the birth of Arthur. The selection from the *Mort Artu* begins with Bohort's ("Borz") return to Camelot from the Grail quest. It then narrates the passion of Lancelot and the Queen ("Zinevra"), his visit with the Lord of Escalot and the amorous daughter, and Lancelot's disguised participation in the tournament at Winchester. The transmission breaks off in mid-sentence, at the point where Lancelot fells Bohort and joins in the mass battle. The *Merlin* episode represents a strongly abbreviated, "digest version" (Leviant) of the Vulgate story; the *Mort Artu* is a close translation. The translator eliminates all specifically Christian elements except Lancelot's visit to confession and introduces Jewish associations through his use of biblical and rabbinical terminology (compare the redactional technique in the Old Yiddish *Widwilt*). A brief preface to the stories bears some significance for an assessment of medieval Jewish interest in Arthurian literature. Seeking Talmudic justification for his preoccupation with such secular material, the translator cites the example of a rabbi who was reported to have read fox-fables and parables in addition to Torah. His conclusion: "The stories that I have translated are no less worthy than the . . . parables; on the contrary, they are far more excellent and distinguished." [RGW]

Leviant, Curt, ed. and trans. *King Artus: A Hebrew Arthurian Romance of 1279*. Assen: Van Gorcum; New York: KTAV, 1969.

MELIADUS, father of Tristan and one of the heroes of the romance *Palamedes*. His adventures, including his abduction of the Queen of Scotland and the consequent war with the Scottish king, are sufficiently prominent that the first half of the romance was often known as *Meliadus*. [NJL]

Foerster, Wendelin, ed. *Li Chevaliers as deux espees*. Halle: Niemeyer, 1877.

Busby, Keith. "Diverging Traditions of Gauvain in Some of the Later Old French Verse Romances." In *The Legacy of Chrétien de Troyes*, ed. Norris J. Lacy, Douglas Kelly, and Keith Busby. 2 vols. Amsterdam: Rodopi, 1988, Vol. 2, pp. 93–109.

Thompson, Raymond H. "Le Serviteur de la société: la composition structurale dans *Li Chevaliers as deus espees*." *Studia Neophilologica*, 49 (1977), 95–100.

MELION, an anonymous French lai (600 lines), dating from ca. 1200, that tells essentially the same story as Marie de France's *Bisclavret* but places it in an Arthurian setting. The narrative concerns a knight whose magic ring enables him to become a werewolf and then regain his human form. His wife steals the ring, requiring him to remain a werewolf until her treachery is discovered. The knight, Melion, is apparently the same character as the Meliant de Lis who appears in a number of Arthurian texts, and the story also includes Arthur, Gauvain, Yvain, and Ydel (or Yder). [NJL]

Tobin, Prudence Mary O'Hara, ed. *Les Lais anonymes des douzième et treizième siècles*. Geneva: Droz, 1976.

MERINGTON, MARGUERITE, author of *The Testing of Sir Gawayne* (1913). Of the many adaptations of Arthurian material for children's theater, Merington's is notable for its craftsmanship, though it strives to do no more than elicit "innocent merriment" from its young audience. Arthur's court on the Eve of All-Hallowmas is the setting for this completely sanitized version of Gawayne and the Loathly Lady. [DN]

Merington, Marguerite. *Festival Plays*. New York: Duffield, 1913.

MÉRIADEUC (or *Le Chevalier aux deux épées*), a French romance of 12,352 lines probably composed in the second quarter of the thirteenth century. The Knight of the Two Swords is so called because he won a second weapon at Arthur's court after unfastening a sheath about the waist of Lore of Caradigan. Lore wishes to marry the anonymous knight, who has since disappeared. The sword had in fact come from the corpse of the hero's father, Bleheri, killed in his war against Brien de la Gastine. After the hero comes by chance to his mother's castle, and discovers his identity and the nature of his father's death (Brien had tricked Gauvain into helping him and Gauvain had unwittingly slain Bleheri), he avenges him, is reconciled with Gauvain, and marries Lore. A subplot tells how Gauvain searches for Mériadeuc and eventually fights incognito with him, defeats the traitor Brien des Illes, and consummates his relationship with a girl he had championed earlier.

This poem is a quintessential Gauvain romance, containing motifs and episodes found elsewhere, all woven into a well-structured and well-written whole. Despite its conventional nature, however, the direct intertextual links with other romances are less evident than in other romances of the same period. The basis of the poem's structural composition is, as in *Hunbaut*, a comparison between the career of the hero and that of Gauvain. Mériadeuc must first equal and then surpass the great Gauvain, whose reputation as knight and lover informs much of the work. [KB]

MERLIN (Myrddin). 1) ORIGINS. As a literary figure, the great prophet and magician Merlin is a creation of Geoffrey of Monmouth. In Geoffrey's work, he is a composite of two persons. One of them is more likely to be historical than the other. This "original Merlin" is said to have been a Briton who was crazed by a battle at Arfderydd in Cumbria, ca. 575. He wandered through the Caledonian Forest in southern Scotland, an inspired madman, gifted or cursed with second sight.

While similar characters are found in the folklore of other countries, this one has a shadowy historical role in the life of St. Kentigern, the patron of Glasgow. According to the hagiographers, his name was Lailoken. The Welsh, however, had their own legends and poems about him, notably the *Afallennau* ("Apple-Trees"). (*See* MYRDDIN POEMS.) They gave him the alternative name Myrddin. This related him somehow to the Welsh town of Carmarthen, though the notion that the town was named after him is certainly false. In his Myrddin guise, he was portrayed with more dignity, suffering deeply in his exile, afraid of powerful enemies, lamenting a happier past, yet also uttering great public prophecies that foreshadowed a Celtic revival. In Welsh poetry, "Myrddin" occasionally seems to refer to inspiration—even to a god or spirit of inspiration—rather than to a human individual; Lailoken may have acquired the sobriquet as being inspired, a Myrddin-man, so to speak. A statement in the White Book of Rhydderch that the first name of the island of Britain was "Myrddin's Precinct" closely implies that the word had a different and more mysterious meaning.

Geoffrey of Monmouth took up Myrddin before he took up Arthur. He Latinized the name as *Merlinus*, changing a letter because his prospective Norman-French readers would dislike *Merdinus* as suggesting the offensive *merde*. In a short work entitled *Prophetiae Merlini* ("The Prophecies of Merlin"), Geoffrey paraphrased some of the existing Myrddin material, and added more of his own, most of it in a highly cryptic style. Then he incorporated these "Prophecies" in his major book, the *Historia Regum Britanniae*, completed toward 1138. He puts them in the mouth of Merlin as a character in the story, identifying him with a young prophet in an episode taken from Nennius—who, however, calls the lad Ambrosius. Merlin is presented as born in Carmarthen (or, to be precise, the town subsequently so named), the offspring of a daughter of the king of Dyfed. She took up residence in a convent and was visited there by an incubus who begot the marvelous child. As a boy, Geoffrey relates, Merlin was in danger of death at the hands of Vortigern, but he saved himself by his paranormal powers.

On the face of it at least, this was all a blunder. Not knowing when Myrddin lived, Geoffrey identified him with someone more than a century earlier and pulled him back into a totally erroneous context. But there was more to it than that. By going on to invent more exploits for him, such as transferring Stonehenge from Ireland and contriving the conception of Arthur, he created a character of irresistible fascination. The later romancers kept Merlin in the fifth century, and expanded him further into the superhuman sponsor of Arthur's regime.

Geoffrey himself found out more about the original northerner and tried to reconcile the discrepancies in a long poem, the *Vita Merlini* ("Life of Merlin"), written ca. 1150. The romancers did not quite ignore his attempted fusion—it has left a slight imprint on the Prose *Merlin*, for instance—but in general they took little interest in it and simply enlarged the Merlin of the *Historia*. Giraldus Cambrensis accepted his existence, a tribute to Geoffrey's persuasiveness, but went no further. He would not admit the equation with the northerner, and accordingly recognized two separate Merlins. So do medieval Welsh poems and triadic matter. (A sixteenth-century Welshman, Elis Gruffudd, tries to identify the two by reincarnation.) [GA]

2) MERLIN IN MEDIEVAL LITERATURE. Merlin first appears in the vernacular around the year 1200 in the Old French verse *Merlin*, by Robert de Boron, a continuation of his *Joseph d'Arimathie*. Only a fragment of Robert's poem remains, but there are two prose redactions, in the Vulgate Cycle and in the so-called *Suite du Merlin*, or *Huth Merlin*. Robert's *Merlin* is heavily indebted to Geoffrey, but Robert's religious conception of his material causes Merlin to take on an important redemptive and prophetic role. *Merlin* opens with an assembly of devils plotting to bring about the ruin of humankind by creating a prophet to rival Christ who would be half-human, half-devil. One of their number drives a wealthy man to despair and cohabits with one of his daughters in her sleep. However, she tells her confessor Blaise and is signed with the cross so that, when her son is born, he has a hairy body and preternatural knowledge but not his father's will to evil. Because of his father, he knows the past; and God, because of his mother's goodness, allows him to foretell the future. At baptism, the infant is named Merlin. He soon shows his special powers by saving his mother from a sentence of death; and before he is three years old he dictates to his mother's confessor the story of Joseph of Arimathea and the transferral of the Holy Grail to Britain and tells of his own supernatural conception.

57. Aubrey Beardsley, "Merlin" from the Dent *Morte D'Arthur*.

The setting is now fifth-century Britain, where King Constant has just died, leaving three sons, Moine, Pendragon, and Uter. The first is murdered and his place usurped by his seneschal, Vertigier, who eventually allies himself with the Saxons. Pendragon and Uter flee abroad. Vertigier attempts to build an impregnable tower, but three times it collapses. On the advice of his astronomers, he sends for a "fatherless child," whose blood is to be mixed with the mortar. Merlin is produced and explains that the tower is unstable because it is set on the back of two dragons, who move around under its weight. He explains that the two dragons symbolize King Constant's sons and Vertigier, and that Vertigier will be killed in a great struggle between them. And indeed, three months later Pendragon and Uter land at Winchester, and Vertigier perishes in the flames of his own tower. Pendragon now reigns and with the help of Merlin persuades the Saxons to leave Britain. But they soon return and Pendragon is slain, as Merlin has predicted, in a great battle at Salisbury. His brother defeats the enemy and assumes the throne, taking the name Uterpendragon. On Merlin's advice, he has the Round Table constructed, an exact replica of the Grail table fashioned by Joseph of Arimathea, which in turn was a replica of the table of the Last Supper. During a great Christmas celebration at Carduel, Uter falls in love with the virtuous Ygerne, wife of his vassal the Duke of Tintagel. Merlin casts a spell that causes her to believe that Uter is her husband, and through this deception Arthur is conceived in the castle of Tintagel. The duke is killed that same night, and Uter soon weds Ygerne, who confides to him how she had been victimized. On Merlin's advice, Uter does not reveal to her that he is the father and instead has Merlin give the child to foster parents unaware of his royal descent. After Uter's death, the young Arthur proves himself the rightful heir by pulling the sword from the stone.

In the prose Didot-*Perceval*, which is likewise thought to have been based on a poem by Robert, Merlin assists Perceval in his adventures at the Grail castle. After Perceval assumes his place as the Grail King and fills the Siege Perilous at Arthur's Round Table, Merlin retires to the woods near the Grail castle in company with his mother's confessor, Blaise, who will write down for posterity the adventures of the Round Table and the Grail.

In Robert's conception, Merlin, rescued from the devils by the holiness of his mother, plays a redemptive role as mediator between earthly chivalry and the heavenly plan of salvation: he oversees the conception and early education of Arthur, creates the symbolism of the Round Table, and prepares Perceval for the Grail quest.

Robert's *Merlin* was given two continuations, designed to link Arthur's early years to the *Lancelot-Graal* story: the "historical" one of the Vulgate and the "romantic" one of the *Huth Merlin*. Both tell of the early years of Arthur's reign and his wars against rebellious vassals, but the *Huth* continuation emphasizes such familiar episodes as the birth of Mordred, the revelation of Arthur's parentage by Merlin, his combat with Pellinor, the obtaining of Excalibur from the lake, the tragic tale of Balain, the installation of the Round Table at Arthur's court, the enchantment of Merlin by Viviane, Morgain's plots to destroy Arthur, as well as many other adventures. Merlin's role as prophet is still important, but there is increased exploitation of his skills as a necromancer. In the French *Lancelot-Graal*, where Perceval's quest is superseded by that of Galahad, Merlin's role is reduced to a minimum: he does not appear in person but is remembered as the prophet of the Grail.

In England, the legend of Merlin was well known through Geoffrey of Monmouth, his French translator Wace, the French prose romances, and English adaptations of the French material. Robert Mannyng included a translation of Wace's *Roman de Brut* as the first part of his *Story of England* (1338), where the legends of Merlin occupy some 7,000 lines. Besides Malory's well-known adaptations, there are three other English tales involving Merlin: *Arthour and Merlin* (about 10,000 lines; composed in Kent in the second half of the thirteenth century); Lovelich's nearly 30,000-line translation of only half of the Vulgate *Merlin*; and the English Prose *Merlin* of ca. 1450, which is a fairly literal translation of the Vulgate *Merlin*.

In all these romances, both English and French, Merlin is constantly at the center of the action, predicting events and using his magical powers to control history. He is puckish and benevolent and constantly makes use of his shape-shifting powers to aid and befuddle. He is the creator of the Round Table, and its prophet. Robert and his continuators judiciously mingle Merlin's prophetic and magical powers to create what is certainly the most colorful and one of the most ubiquitous characters in Arthurian romance. [WWK]

3) MERLIN IN MODERN LITERATURE. In the modern world, Merlin has exerted a particular fascination on writers and readers. During the seventeenth and eighteenth centuries, when the vogue of Arthurian subjects declined significantly, Merlin was the most popular of the familiar characters, though even he suffered at the hands of writers. He became primarily a figure in nursery rhymes and children's songs, and he is sometimes shown (e.g., by Aaron Hill) as a lascivious and somewhat ridiculous old man. In France, he figured in a number of light plays and ballets, often influenced by Cervantes, and most of them contributed further to the decline of the sorcerer's reputation.

From the early nineteenth century to the present, Merlin has continued to be an extremely popular subject for Arthurian writers. Owing to his nature, he was an unusually versatile character: he was sometimes of interest for his symbolic or metaphoric value, often for his status as magician (more often than prophet). Some writers exploited his demonic origin and character; others explored his relationship with Viviane and his basic humanity. And in a good many cases, it was his death and entombment that fascinated authors.

Owing to his immortality and to his subjugation by Viviane/Nimue, Merlin could be a symbol of freedom or of enslavement. In Edgar Quinet's *Merlin l'enchanteur* ("Merlin the Magician," 1860), he was both, representing the French spirit in temporary decline but destined for eventual liberation and triumph. Most often, writers exploited the theme of his enslavement; he represented the lover symbolically imprisoned by the lady in an 1835 poem by Heinrich Heine, and he was emblematic of Jean Cocteau's opium addiction in Cocteau's play *Les Chevaliers de la Table Ronde* ("The Knights of the Round Table," 1937).

Particularly in Germany, a number of poets, such as Christoph Martin Wieland, Ludwig Tieck, and Karl Immerman, have been drawn to the theme of Merlin's entombment rather than his general role in the Arthurian story. This situation offered an opportunity for Merlin to make prophetic announcements or, more often, to lament the state of the world.

In 1889, Mark Twain popularized a new vision of a diminished Merlin, who is only a magician, and a poor one at that. Twain's novel *A Connecticut Yankee in King Arthur's Court* contrasts the protagonist's superior knowledge and technology with Merlin's fraudulent magic. The notion of a Merlin deficient even in magic recurs in Nicholas Seare's 1983 *Rude Tales and Glorious*, where he is further diminished and is a mere trickster, rather than a magician: the Sword in the Stone is a simple deception involving a hollow rock with Merlin inside.

Both Merlin's magic and his traditional longevity or immortality make his return a tempting theme. He may return to combat forces intent on dominating the world, as in C.S. Lewis's *That Hideous Strength* (1945), or, incarnated as a professor, he may offer protection and aid to children, as in Susan Cooper's The Dark Is Rising series. A darker dimension is added to Merlin's character in Roger Zelazny's 1979 story "The Last Defender of Camelot," where, having survived, he is a well-intentioned but wrong-headed man who plans to use force and magic to impose good on the modern world.

To Merlin the Magician are ascribed some curious traits, beyond his traditional immortality and his mixture of demonic and saintly characteristics. In T.H. White, he lives backward, so that he knows the future but cannot remember the past. In Peter David's 1987 novel *Knight Life*, he is an eight-year-old boy who serves as adviser and defender of an Arthur returned to the modern world. And, as noted, he has sometimes been either a lascivious old man or an enchanter whose powers are seriously limited.

White's Merlin is doubtless the one most familiar to modern readers. He is Arthur's tutor, transforming the young man into various animals in order that the future king might learn lessons about war, work, and freedom. In later volumes, the magician-prophet becomes the vehicle for White's misanthropic vision, hinting at catastrophes in store for Arthur and (in the person of a certain Austrian tyrant and his stormtroopers) for us.

Some modern works restore Merlin to his traditional dignity, as prophet and enchanter but also, in many cases, a complex and fallible being. In English, one thinks of the series by Mary Stewart, who tells Merlin's history and makes him a surprisingly human character, appealing and plausible. In French, René Barjavel's *L'Enchanteur* ("The Magician," 1984) offers a Merlin in love with Viviane, painfully denying his desires and appetites in order to pursue his high moral purpose: directing the Grail quest.

Few generalizations can be made about the modern figure of Merlin. His very unreality and his immortality lead authors to cast him in fantasy or science-fiction stories, to use him to comment on modern society, or to express a personal and often idiosyncratic vision. Elsewhere, his magic powers (and his love for Viviane/Nimue) simply offer the opportunity for fun and comedy. In a small number of modern texts, he is, as often was the case in medieval literature, a prominent secondary character providing advice, direction, and support for King Arthur. He himself tends more often to assume center stage, with Arthur receding to a secondary position or entirely absent. In such cases, whether the appeal is myth, mysticism, mystery, or magic, he is an Arthurian character only by tradition. (*See also* MERLIN AND THE PROPHETIC TRADITION.) [NJL]

Bromwich, Rachel. *Trioedd Ynys Prydein*. Cardiff: University of Wales Press, 1961; 2nd ed. 1978, pp. 469–74.

Gollnick, James, ed. *Comparative Studies in Merlin from the Vedas to C.G. Jung*. Lewiston, N.Y.: Mellen, 1990.

Goodrich, Peter, ed. *The Romance of Merlin: An Anthology*. New York: Garland, 1991.

Harding, Carol E. *Merlin and Legendary Romance*. New York: Garland, 1989.

Loomis, Roger Sherman, ed. *Arthurian Literature in the Middle Ages*. Oxford: Clarendon, 1959.

Markale, Jean. *Merlin l'enchanteur, ou l'éternelle quête magique*. Paris: Retz, 1981.

Stewart, R.J., ed. *The Book of Merlin: Insights from the First Merlin Conference, London, June 1986*. Poole, Dorset: Blandford, 1987, pp. 17–46.

Tolstoy, Nikolai. *The Quest for Merlin*. London: Hamish Hamilton, 1985.

Zumthor, Paul. *Merlin le prophète: un thème de la littérature polémique, de l'historiographie et des romans*. Lausanne: Payot, 1943.

MERLIN AND THE PROPHETIC TRADITION. The Celtic tradition of Merlin as a prophet culminates in Geoffrey of Monmouth's *Prophetiae Merlini*, written in the 1130s and later included, as Book VII, in the *Historia Regum Britanniae*. Geoffrey's prophecies begin with a prediction of the victories of Arthur and the ultimate triumph of the Saxons and proceed through a series of cryptic utterances to a final apocalyptic vision. The *Prophetiae* was translated into several languages, and its popularity led to the writing of other works based on the prophetic tradition, such as the thirteenth-century French *Prophécies de Merlin*, ascribed to Maistre Richart d'Irlande. In the Middle Ages and the Renaissance, prophecies of Merlin were used to support various political and religious claims, including Welsh nationalism and the Reformation.

In 1641, Thomas Heywood's (1573–1641) *Life of Merlin* used purported prophecies of Merlin as the basis for a history of England up to the beginning of the reign of Charles I. Merlin's name was also frequently used by astrologers and writers of almanacs in the seventeenth century. From 1644 onward, William Lilly (1602–1681) published almanacs under the names of Merlinus Junior and Merlinus Anglicus, and in the late seventeenth and early eighteenth centuries John Partridge produced an almanac under the name of Merlinus Liberatus. Jonathan Swift (1667–1745) parodied these prophecies by predicting, in the Bickerstaff papers, that Partridge would die on March 29, 1708, and then after that date writing that the prediction had in fact proved true (though Partridge did not actually die until 1715). Swift also mocked the abuse of prophecies attributed to Merlin in "A Famous Prediction of Merlin, the British Wizard, Written Above a Thousand Years Ago and Relating to the Present Year 1709."

The notion of Merlin as a prophet has also influenced modern Arthurian works as diverse as Richard Hovey's play *The Quest for Merlin*, Mary Stewart's novels, and John Boorman's film *Excalibur*. [ACL]

Heywood, Thomas. *The Life of Merlin, Surnamed Ambrosius; His Prophecies and Predictions Interpreted, and Their Truth Made Good by Our English Annals: Being a Chronographical History of All the Kings and Memorable Passages of This Kingdom, from Brute to the Reign of King Charles*. London: J. Okes, 1641; repr. Carmarthen: J. Evans, 1812.

Paton, Lucy Allen, ed. *Les Prophécies de Merlin*. 2 vols. New York: Heath, 1926.

Thomas, Keith. *Religion and the Decline of Magic: Studies in Popular Beliefs in Sixteenth and Seventeenth Century England*. London: Weidenfeld and Nicolson, 1971.

MERVEILLES DE RIGOMER, LES ("The Marvels of Rigomer"), an incomplete French verse romance of 17,271 lines written in the second half of the thirteenth century by an author who calls himself Jehan. At the request of Dionise, mistress of the Castle of Rigomer, Lancelot sets out to free it from enchantment but is rendered powerless, by a magic lance and ring, and becomes a servant. Gauvain sets out to free Lancelot, is himself imprisoned but freed by his mistress Lorie, before freeing Lancelot and the Castle of Rigomer. He refuses to marry Dionise and returns to court. A second plot involves Arthur's restoring to the heiress of Quintefuele her heritage. The poem breaks off without a conclusion.

Les Merveilles de Rigomer is one of the last Old French Arthurian romances to have been written in verse, and its author shows a detailed knowledge of both the verse and prose traditions, in particular of the works of Chrétien and the Prose *Lancelot*. While its length may create the impression that the narrative wanders somewhat aimlessly, it is structured around the same principle of multiple quests used in, say, *Claris et Laris*. There is much uproarious comedy in the romance, such as an episode in which Gauvain, while defending himself against another knight, retreats onto the rung of a revolving mill-wheel, which promptly catapults him into the air; he lands next to a beautiful damsel on a bed, situated on the deck of a barge that happens to be passing by. The author also excels at inventing supernatural creatures, such as talking birds, flame-breathing panthers, other savage cats, and a man-eating falcon. It would be wrong to talk of the degeneration of romance in cases such as this, and more accurate to conclude that its function has shifted in the direction of pure entertainment. [KB]

Foerster, Wendelin, and H. Breuer, eds. *Les Merveilles de Rigomer*. 2 vols. Dresden: Gesellshaft für romanische Literatur, 1908–15.

Vesce, Thomas E., trans. *The Marvels of Rigomer (Les Mervelles de Rigomer)*. New York: Garland, 1988.

Busby, Keith. "Diverging Traditions of Gauvain in Some of the Later Old French Verse Romances." In *The Legacy of Chrétien de Troyes*, ed. Norris J. Lacy, Douglas Kelly, and Keith Busby. 2 vols. Amsterdam: Rodopi, 1988, pp. 93–109.

MICHAELS, PHILIP (pseudonym of Philippe van Rjndt), Canadian author of *Grail* (1982), a horror novel in which a cup made by Lucifer as a "life force" for a race of demons was lost by them and refashioned into the cup used by Christ. When the Grail is removed from the sacred ground of the Vatican where it has been kept for centuries, modern Fisher Kings try to prevent the race of demons from obtaining it and using its power to multiply and ultimately to take over the world. [ACL]

Michaels, Philip. *Grail*. New York: Avon, 1982.

MILÁN, VICTOR, in the story "Soldatenmangel" (1981), brings Merlin forward to Germany during the Thirty Years' War, where he duels unsuccessfully with another wizard. [RHT]

Milán, Victor. "Soldatenmangel." In *Dragons of Darkness*, ed. Orson Scott Card. New York: Ace, 1981, pp. 165–80.

MILLAY, EDNA ST. VINCENT (1892–1950), American poet and author of two Arthurian works. In "Elaine" (1921), the abandoned Elaine meditates wistfully on her love for Lancelot. The succinct, intense four-part poem *Tristan* (1954) is told from the lover's viewpoint: he describes his rejection of the love potion for the immediacy of their passion, the preparation of Isolde's gown for her first encounter with King Mark, and Tristan's morning-memories after the avowal of their love. The poem ends with his meditations as he awaits his death. [AAR]

Millay, Edna St. Vincent. *Collected Poems*, ed. Norma Millay. New York: Harper, 1956, pp. 477–81.

MILMAN, H(ENRY) H(ART) (1791–1868), poet, historian, and Dean of St. Paul's, London, began *Samor, Lord of the Bright City* (i.e., Gloucester) as an Eton schoolboy and published it in 1818 on graduating from Oxford. In the twelve-book "heroic poem," a fictional Samor raises Uther Pendragon to unite the British against Vortigern, the confederate of the Saxon invaders under Hengist and Horsa. A youthful Arthur appears in one episode, and Merlin prophesies that he will be the foundation of Britain's glory. [CNS]

Milman, Rev. H.H. *Samor, Lord of the Bright City*. London: Murray, 1818.
Anonymous. Review. *The Quarterly Review*, 1818, 328–47.
Milman, Arthur. *Henry Hart Milman*. London: Murray, 1900.

MISERICORDS, hinged seats in the choir stalls of medieval churches that when tipped up offer shelflike support for the person who must stand during a lengthy service (their name implies "indulgence"). The brackets under these hidden seats are often carved, displaying figures and scenes inspired by fables, romances, or incidents of daily life. Popular Arthurian subjects include Tristan and Isolde under the spreading branches of the tree in which King Mark is concealed (Chester and Lincoln Cathedrals, fourteenth century) and Yvain plunging through the turreted castle gate as the portcullis bisects his horse (Chester, Lincoln, Boston, Entville, late fourteenth century; New College, Oxford, late fifteenth century). [MS]

Anderson, M.D. *Misericords*. Harmondsworth: Penguin, 1954.
———. *The Choir Stalls of Lincoln Minster*. Lincoln, 1951.
Bond, Francis. *Woodcarvings in English Churches, Misericords*. London: Clarendon, 1910, Part 2, Sec. 7.
Loomis, Roger Sherman, and Laura Hibbard Loomis. *Arthurian Legends in Medieval Art*. London: Oxford University Press, 1938, pp. 68, 79; figs. 131–32, 168–70.

MITCHELL, DAVID M., English poet, dramatist, and author of *Sir Tristram: A Tragedy in Four Acts* (1927). Mitchell's play, written in competent blank verse interspersed with graceful short lyrics, relies heavily on the versions of the Tristan legend by Thomas and Béroul. The lovers, although passionate, are quickly repentant, and Mark is depicted as alternately benevolent and brutal. The dramatic tension of this retelling is slight; Mitchell uses the motif of fate to exonerate the lovers. [AAR]

Mitchell, David M. *Sir Tristram: A Tragedy in Four Acts*. London: Wright, 1927.

MITCHELL, MARY, in *Birth of Legend* (1956), tells the story of Lohengrin, the son of Perceval. The mysterious arrival of the Swan Knight to defend a maiden in trial-by-combat arouses suspicions in minds unprepared to accept a miracle with simple faith when their own interests are affected. [RHT]

Mitchell, Mary. *Birth of a Legend*. London: Methuen, 1956.

MITCHISON, NAOMI (MARGARET HALDANE), Scottish playwright and novelist, wrote the thoughtful ironic fantasy *To the Chapel Perilous* (1955), which creates humor by introducing the press into the Arthurian world, then sending reporters with modern professional standards to investigate conflicting claims that the Holy Grail has been found: is it cauldron of plenty, stone, spear, dish, or cup? Truth turns out to be more complex than we expect. [RHT]

Mitchison, Naomi. *To the Chapel Perilous*. London: Allen and Unwin, 1955.
Nellis, Marilyn K. "Anachronistic Humor in Two Arthurian Romances of Education: *To the Chapel Perilous* and *The Sword in the Stone*." *Studies in Medievalism*, 2 (1985), 57–77.

MODENA ARCHIVOLT. Possibly the earliest representation of an Arthurian theme in monumental sculpture appears on the Cathedral of Modena in northern Italy. On the north portal, known as the Porta della Pescheria, the archivolt and lintel are carved in high relief with secular scenes: archivolt figures are identifiable as Arthurian from the inscriptions; the lintel has decorative sculpture including birds, animals, and a man riding a sea-horse.

The action depicted on the archivolt centers on a moated, stone castle having a shield hung on the wall and

58. Cathedral of Modena, Archivolt of Porta della Pescheria. (Photograph by Norris J. Lacy.)

timber towers as outworks. A woman (Winlogee) is held prisoner by a man (Mardoc). On the left, three mounted knights (Artus de Bretania, Isdernus, and an unnamed knight) charge with lances set; the tower is defended by a thug with a pick-axe. On the right, two knights (Carrado and Galvagin) attack each other with lances, while two more knights (Galvariun and Che) gallop along with their lances at rest over their shoulders. The sculptor, known as the Arthur Master, works with more energy than finesse, but he faithfully records the details of military architecture and knightly equipment. His artistic source and the date of his work have been the subject of long and often heated debate.

Scholars of Arthurian literature and the history of Italian Romanesque art have argued over the sculpture of Modena Cathedral. The cathedral, begun in 1099, is universally considered to be one of the masterpieces of Romanesque art, and its sculpture—especially the work of Wiligelmo on the west façade—is some of the earliest and finest work in Italy. If an early date is also accepted for the sculpture of the north portal, then the sculpture would antedate the earliest written Arthurian romance. Arthurian legends could have come to Italy even before they were brought by Crusaders and the Norman conquerors of southern Italy. Archaeological and art-historical evidence and analysis, however, suggest a date in the second quarter of the twelfth century, no earlier than 1120. Loomis never ceased arguing for a date at the beginning of the century; however, in recent work Stiennon dated the sculpture between 1120 and 1140.

With few exceptions, scholars have agreed on the Arthurian interpretation of the sculpture. The story is that of Carrado of the Dolorous Tower. Winlogee (Guenevere), while riding with the knight Isdernus in the forest, is abducted by a giant, Carrado, who takes her to the Dolorous Tower and turns her over to Mardoc. Artus de Bretania, Galvagin (Gawain), Galvariun, and Che (Kay), joined by Isdernus, set out to rescue her. They approach the castle by the two wooden gates, but Burmalt holds off one party with his club, while Carrado and Galvagin fight at the other gate. According to one story, Galvagin was given Carrado's magical sword in order to kill him and enter the castle. Once in the castle, he found the shields of vanquished knights hanging on the walls; finally, he was able to restore the Queen to Arthur. Loomis has made a convincing case for the Breton origin of the names engraved on the arch and identified Winlogee as Guenevere, Mardoc as Mordred, and Carrado as Curoi. He argued that the story comes from the Vulgate *Lancelot*, although the names Winlogee and Mardoc do not appear in the French romance, and Galvagin (Gawain) replaces Lancelot as the hero. He argued further that in an early version of the story of Guenevere's abduction Gawain rather than Lancelot was the rescuer. Other scholars have suggested that the sculpture illustrates the romance of Yder rather than Gawain or Lancelot, and also suggest that Arthur himself rescued Guenevere, with the help of his knights. Lejeune also regards the sculpture on the tower at Modena as Arthurian in inspiration. [MS]

Hutchings, Gweneth. "Isdernus of the Modena Archivolt." *Medium Ævum*, 1 (1932), 204–05.

———. "Gawain and the Abduction of Guinevere." *Medium Ævum*, 4 (1935), 61–66.

Loomis, Roger Sherman. "Modena, Bari, and Hades." *Art Bulletin*, 2 (1923–24), 71–74.

———. "The Date, Source, and Subject of the Arthurian Sculpture at Modena." In *Medieval Studies in Memory of Gertrude Schoepperle Loomis*. Paris: Champion, 1927, pp. 209–28.

Stiennon, Jacques, and Rita Lejeune. "La Légende arthurienne dans la sculpture de la cathédrale de Modène." *Cahiers de civilisation médiévale*, 6 (1963), 281–96.

Whitaker, Muriel. *The Legends of King Arthur in Art*. Cambridge: Brewer, 1990, pp. 86–88.

MONACO, RICHARD, American writer of fiction, poetry, and screenplays. His series on the Grail, loosely based on Wolfram von Eschenbach's *Parzival*, is unequaled in Arthurian literature for its depiction of violence both graphic and senseless. *Parsival* (1977) interlaces the story of the naive prince's awakening from innocence to bitter experience, and his (much-altered) Grail-castle adventures, with the search for him by a new character, the faithful servant Broaditch. *The Grail War* (1979) rationalizes and despiritualizes the Grail quest. Broaditch's last quest and that of Parsival for his son, Lohengrin, are interwoven in *The Final Quest* (1980). The series continues with the anticlimactic *Blood and Dreams* (1985), in which Parsival, pursued by many enemies, discovers only emptiness at the heart of the Grail mystery.

The novels are all antiromances of the most extreme sort, with many scenes of murder and mayhem, rape and cannibalism, among other atrocities. As in the originals by Chrétien de Troyes and Wolfram, Gawain's adventures are counterpointed with Parsival's, but neither emerges as admirable; the contrast between the best worldly and best spiritual knight disappears, as Parsival continually rejects his mission as Grail savior, first in extreme knightly brutality, and then in his turning to family life for comfort from the horror of a harsh, feudal, plaguey, hungry, and war-torn world—a true wasteland. Gawain, even more than his medieval counterpart, is a womanizer and an unchivalrous warrior. Opposed to both Gawain and Parsival is Clinschor, his role greatly expanded from Wolfram into that of a frightening representative of the powers of darkness seeking to gain the Grail. Another new character, John of Bligh, emblemizes the forces behind medieval peasant revolts and crazed cults. Throughout, the Grail appears as a nebulous, perhaps nonexistent, source of wealth and power, of which Parsival is (wrongly) thought to have the secret. In the bittersweet ending of the third book, the hero seems to discover the light of the Grail within himself, although his problems—including a mistress as well as a disillusioned wife and family—seem insoluble. Morgan le Fay and Mordred join the cast of the fourth book, in which Parsival is again besieged by a host of foes greedy for the Grail power. He again returns to his family, this time to rescue them.

Monaco has begun another fantasy series that again treats Arthurian legend in a highly unorthodox way. Events are set anachronistically in the strife-torn years before Augustus established imperial rule in Rome. *Runes* (1984) deals with the adventures of Arthur's parents, here the son of Spartacus the Gladiator and a British slave. *Broken Stone* (1985) continues their story and introduces the young Arturus (Arthur) to his half-sister Morga (Morgan le Fay). The forces of good (Avalon) are engaged in a supernatural struggle against those of evil, and the latter seem to have all the advantages as they scheme to reunite the three stones of the Black Grail. They are, however, frustrated finally by their own ambition and treachery. [MF/RHT]

Monaco, Richard. *Parsival or a Knight's Tale*. New York: Macmillan, 1977.

———. *The Grail War*. New York: Pocket Books, 1979.

———. *The Final Quest*. New York: Putnam, 1980.

———. *Runes*. New York: Ace, 1984.

———. *Broken Stone*. New York: Ace, 1985.

———. *Blood and Dreams*. New York: Berkley, 1985.

MONTALVO, GARCI RODRÍGUEZ DE, author of *Amadís de Gaula* (1508), a chivalric romance in prose, the major contribution in Spanish to Arthurian literature. Montalvo, a Castilian nobleman of whom little is known, restyled and shortened the primitive anonymous fourteenth-century version (also in Castilian) consisting of three books, adding a fourth. His non-Arthurian *Sergas de Esplandián* (1510) is the fifth book or sequel. Books I and II of the primitive *Amadís* were composed ca. 1340, probably in Castile, by a single author who adapted Arthurian motifs and characters from French sources (principally the Vulgate Cycle and the Prose *Tristan*) to create a new, unified story. The pseudohistorical narrative takes place not long after Christ and before the time of Arthur, whose reign is foretold. The central plot coincides with the legends of Lancelot and

Tristan, in that the love between the hero and the daughter (not the wife) of his king compels them to conceal their secret passion. They must undergo separation, tests of fidelity and jealousy, penitential exile, and love-madness. The originality of the primitive *Amadís* stems from its transposition of adulterous and "courtly" love into the "true" fidelity of Amadís to Oriana. He is himself son of an illicit marriage between royal parents, separated from them at birth and destined to gain fame and kingdoms through his skill and bravery. His career, aided by Urganda the enchantress (based on Morgan le Fay), follows a schema traditional in myth and folklore. Oriana is daughter of Lisuarte, King of Britain. They become lovers from childhood; but separated by his enigmatic ancestry, career-in-arms, and, in Montalvo's redaction, her father's political aims, they are obliged to conceal their "secret" marriage and the birth of their son from her father for almost the entire length of the story. Book III of the primitive version introduced materials from Hispanic versions of the *matière de Rome*, telling of Amadís's death at the hands of his young son and Oriana's suicide. Montalvo suppressed this outcome and in Book IV depicts Amadís as a moral and military leader and father figure. Recent study has moved from debate on sources and authorship to analysis of style, structure, and theme and evaluation of Montalvo's originality. He preserved the archaic charm of the Arthurian materials in Books I and II, including magical and supernatural forces, while interpolating his views on love and morality. The fame of *Amadís de Gaula*—as a model of chivalric conduct and courtly speech, as a portrait of medieval pageantry and ritual, or as an inventive and stately interlacing on a grand scale, the first in modern prose fiction—is owed to his craft.

One or more books of the *Amadís* were soon translated into a number of languages. The French version, by Nicolas de Herberay, ca. 1540, proved to be the most productive, being itself rendered into Dutch (last quarter of the sixteenth century), English (by Anthony Munday and Lazarus Pyott, 1590–1618), and German (ca. 1670). Direct translations from the Spanish original were made into Hebrew by Jakob Ben Moses Algaba (ca. 1535) and into Italian by Mambrino da Fabriano (ca. 1545). [LAM]

59. From *Monty Python and the Holy Grail* (1975).

Montalvo, Garci Rodríguez de. *Amadís de Gaula*, ed. E.B. Place. 4 vols. Madrid: CSIC, 1959–69.

———. *Amadís of Gaula*, trans. E.B. Place and H.C. Behn. 2 vols. Lexington: University of Kentucky Press, 1974, 1975.

Pierce, Frank. *Amadís de Gaula*. New York: Twayne, 1976.

MONTY PYTHON AND THE HOLY GRAIL (1975), a film by the comedians known collectively as Monty Python: John Cleese, Graham Chapman, Terry Gilliam, Eric Idle, Terry Jones, and Michael Palin. Gilliam and Jones directed it. The Arthurian element—the Grail quest—serves as a skeletal pretext for extended humorous sketches, such as the Black Knight who continues to fight after Arthur hacks him to bits and the attack by a killer rabbit. Characters include Arthur, Launcelot, Galahad, Bedivere, Gawain, and others, and the filmmakers show an acquaintance with many Arthurian conventions, even though there are few reflections of actual traditional motifs or narrative sequences. The film makes extensive use of slapstick physical comedy, exaggerations, anachronisms, verbal humor, and parody of film conventions, such as voice-overs and sound effects; it is a masterpiece of comic absurdity, if not a lasting contribution to Arthuriana. [NJL]

Monty Python and the Holy Grail (Book), designed by Derek Birdsall, photographs by Drew Mara. London: Methuen, 1977 (includes first draft and last version of screenplay).

MOORE, GEORGE (1852–1933), contrasts decadence with naiveté in *Peronnik the Fool* (1924), a story closely analogous to Perceval's Grail quest. An illiterate cowherd attuned to nature, Peronnik journeys with the crippled Sir Gilles de Lacenaire to Grey Castle and, overcoming temptation, wrests the fateful Bowl and Spear from the sorceress Redemonde. The drought breaks in Peronnik's home village, St.-Jean-de-Braie, but he is not allowed to remain; as a knight, he must go forth to seek further adventure. Arthur also appears briefly in *Héloïse and Abélard* (1921). [CNS]

Moore, George. *Peronnik the Fool*. New York: Boni and Liveright, 1924.

———. *Héloïse and Abélard*. London: Cumann Sean-Eolais na h-Éireann, 1921.

MORDRED (Modred, Medraut), Arthur's nephew. Early Welsh tradition is generally favorable to Mordred, whose name (as *Medraut*) appears almost as early as does that of Arthur. The *Annales Cambriae* record that in 539 both fell in the battle of Camlann but do not make clear whether they were friends or foes. Though opponents in *The Dream of Rhonabwy*, both seek to avoid a conflict caused by others. This tale may have been influenced by Geoffrey of Monmouth, who first identifies Mordred as the son of Arthur's sister Anna, and thus brother of Gawain. Camlann becomes the climax of his attempt to seize both his uncle's kingdom and his wife. Since most medieval writers condemn this revolt, they portray Mordred as a villain and traitor.

The Vulgate *Mort Artu* takes the treachery a step further by making Mordred the issue of Arthur's incest with his half-sister Morgause, though the couple are unaware of their relationship at the time. Guenevere, who is in love with Lancelot, is still the object of Mordred's passion, but she rejects him with horror. At Camlann, Arthur kills Mordred, but he receives his mortal wound in the process. In the *Suite du Merlin*, Arthur unsuccessfully arranges for his infant son to be exposed in a boat.

The incest motif is preserved in romances based upon the *Mort Artu*, including Malory's, but Mordred remains no more than Arthur's nephew elsewhere. The Alliterative *Morte Arthure* offers a sympathetic portrait of Mordred as a figure who suffers genuine remorse for his deeds. Some Scottish chronicles even support Mordred as the true heir to the throne usurped by the illegitimate Arthur.

Since the Middle Ages, the incest motif has been retained (Rosemary Sutcliff) or rejected (Tennyson), depending upon the vision of the author. Mordred's mother is usually Morgause, occasionally Morgan le Fay. Mordred is regularly evil, but a few authors do portray him as a human being trapped by a fate he seeks to avoid (Edward Frankland, Henry Treece, Phyllis Karr, Mary Stewart). [RHT]

Bruce, J.D. "Mordred's Incestuous Birth." In *Medieval Studies in Memory of Gertrude Schoepperle Loomis*, ed. Roger Sherman Loomis. Paris: Champion, 1927, pp. 197–208.

Varin, Amy. "Mordred, King Arthur's Son." *Folklore*, 90 (1979), 167–77.

MORGAN, CHARLES (1894–1958), sets *Sparkenbroke* (1936) in contemporary Cornwall. In creating a new version of "Tristan and Isolde," the hero, an author, writes of his own life. Arthurian allusions are minimal. [EB]

Morgan, Charles. *Sparkenbroke*. London: Macmillan, 1936.

MORGAN, RICHARD WILLIAMS, published his "classic tragedy" *The Duke's Daughter* in 1867 with his authorship designated only by initials at the end of the introduction. Antiquarianism and a sense that true nobility is in the spirit, not the blood, appear to be the inspiration of this dramatization of the story of Lady Ida's alleged infidelities, Lady Claudia's bold acceptance of guilt, and her death in shame and sorrow at the hands of her father, the "Haut Duke" Claudius, who himself expires in grief as Arthur looks on. [CNS]

Morgan, R.W. *The Duke's Daughter*. London: Trübner, 1867.

MORGAN LE FAY (Morgaine). Although their theories are not universally accepted, many scholars trace the origins of the figure of Morgan le Fay to the Celtic deities Morrigan, Macha, and Modron (a divine mother). Morgan first appears in Geoffrey of Monmouth's *Vita Merlini* as the eldest and most beautiful among nine sisters living on the Isle of Avalon. Not only can she change her shape and fly through the air, but she is also kindly and greatly skilled in the art of medicine. Thus it is that Arthur journeys there to be healed of his mortal wound after the battle of Camlann. Chrétien de Troyes notes not only her healing powers, but also her relationship as Arthur's sister. In the French verse romances, Morgan remains a powerful and generally benevolent fay, but in the prose romances her reputation declines progressively.

In the Vulgate Cycle, Morgan is still on good terms with her brother, whom she carries off in a boat after the battle of Camlann. However, after her affair with Guiomar is broken up by his cousin, Guenevere, she grows to hate the Queen and constantly seeks either to seduce Lancelot from her side or to expose their affair. In the Prose *Tristan*, she tries to send to Arthur's court a magic drinking horn from which no unfaithful lady can drink without spilling, but it finds its way instead to the court of King Mark of Cornwall. In the Post-Vulgate Cycle, Morgan, here the wife of King Urien and mother of Yvain, becomes Arthur's enemy as well after he executes one of her lovers, and she incites another lover, Accolon, to try to kill the King with his own sword.

From a fay untouched by time, Morgan degenerates into a mortal who must conceal her age through magic arts; her once-prized favors are condemned as promiscuity in romances that favor the devotion of courtly lovers; the famed healer now schemes to destroy others, almost invariably with humiliating results. This is how Morgan is pictured by Malory, but she was paid little attention in English literature (a notable exception being *Sir Gawain and the Green Knight*) until rediscovered by modern fantasy writers.

Authors like Jane Curry and Penelope Lively offer a conventional portrayal of an evil enchantress from the past who threatens a new generation of heroes. More recently, however, her character has been undergoing a reappraisal. She is the protagonist of an ongoing series of novels by Fay Sampson, and in novels by Parke Godwin, Marion Zimmer Bradley, and Joan Wolf she has even become Arthur's first and only true love, replacing Morgause as the mother of Mordred. This sympathetic approach marks a new and welcome phase in the development of this fascinatingly ambiguous figure. [RHT]

Bogdanow, Fanni. "Morgain's Role in the Thirteenth-Century French Prose Romances of the Arthurian Cycle." *Medium Ævum*, 38 (1969), 123–33.

Paton, Lucy Allen. *Studies in the Fairy Mythology of Arthurian Romance*. 1903; 2nd ed. Roger Sherman Loomis. New York: Franklin, 1960.

MORGAUSE (Morgawse, Margawse), one of three daughters of Gorlois and Igraine and thus Arthur's half-sister. The Vulgate *Merlin* mentions Igraine's three daughters but names only the third, Morgan, while noting that her oldest sister was married to King Lot and became the mother of Gawain, Agravain, Gerehes (Gareth), Gaheries (Gaheris), and Mordred. Malory names all three: Margawse, Elayne, and Morgan le Fay.

In a good many other accounts, Morgause is renamed, eliminated, or conflated with Morgan. Tennyson called the mother of Gawaine and Mordred Bellicent, not Morgause; Mary Stewart makes her an illegitimate daughter of Uther; and in John Boorman's *Excalibur*, it is Morgan with whom Arthur lies to engender Mordred. [NJL]

MORHOLT (Morold), beginning with Béroul's and Eilhart's Tristan romances, a giant-sized warrior, brother of the Queen of Ireland and uncle of Isolde. Morholt travels to Cornwall and demands a tribute on behalf of his country. He is slain by Tristan in single combat, and his body is returned to Ireland as the "tribute." This episode marks the beginning of Tristan's affair with the Irish court, specifically Isolde, who learns that it was by Tristan's sword that Morholt met his death when she discovers a fragment of Tristan's sword embedded in her uncle's skull. [SW]

MORIAEN, a Middle Dutch work from the second half of the thirteenth century. The main character is a Moorish knight in search of his father. Walewein and Lancelot also play important parts; at the request of Arthur, they go in search of Perchevael. Both quests are brought to a successful conclusion, and the romance ends with the marriage of Acglovael, Moriaen's father, to the Moorish queen.

The text has been transmitted in two ways. A version included in the *Lancelot-Compilatie* numbers 4,720 lines. A fragment in the Royal Library at Brussels (MS IV 1059), dating from the first half of the fourteenth century, contains 176 lines, which agree almost word for word with the corresponding lines in the *Lancelot-Compilatie*. [BB]

Paardekooper-van Buuren, Haaneke, and Maurits Gysseling, eds. *Moriaen*. Zutphen: Thieme, 1971.

Weston, Jessie L., trans. *Morien: A Metrical Romance Rendered into English from the Middle Dutch*. London: Nutt, 1901.

Wells, D.A. "Source and Tradition in the *Moriaen*." In *European Context: Studies in the History and Literature of the Netherlands Presented to Theodoor Weevers*, ed. P.F. King and P.F. Vincent. Cambridge: Modern Humanities Research Association, 1971, pp. 36–51.

———. "The Middle Dutch *Moriaen*, Wolfram von Eschenbach's *Parzival*, and Medieval Tradition." *Studia Neerlandica*, 2 (1971), 243–81.

MORLAND, HAROLD, author of *The Matter of Britain* (1984), a sequence of eleven poems, surprisingly readable for narratives written in haiku verse. Morland discusses the problem of finding meaning in a world of change while loosely following the outline of the Arthurian legend through the stories of characters like Merlin and Perceval. [ACL]

Morland, Harold. *The Matter of Britain*. London: Graal, 1984.

MORRIS, WILLIAM (1834–1896), English poet, novelist, designer, and socialist. Morris recreates episodes from Malory's *Morte Darthur* in the four Arthurian poems that open his first and most highly praised book of verse, *The Defence of Guenevere, and Other Poems* (1858). This group contains two pairs of poems: "The Defence of Guenevere" and "King Arthur's Tomb" treat the adulterous love of Launcelot and Guenevere; the much shorter "Sir Galahad, A Christmas Mystery" and "The Chapel in Lyoness" treat the quest for the Holy Grail.

"The Defence of Guenevere" begins abruptly as Arthur's queen, threatened with burning at the stake for her adultery, attempts to counter the accusations of infidelity brought against her by Gauwaine. In her monologue, Guenevere defends her difficult choice of Launcelot's passionate attentiveness over "Arthur's great name and his little love." She recalls the first arrival of Launcelot at Arthur's court, her subsequent joyful sexual encounters with him, and the "bitter day in *la Fausse Garde*" when the stealthy Mellyagraunce discovered the wounded Launcelot's blood on her bed. Despite the self-incriminating nature of her recollections, which tend more toward her condemnation than toward her exoneration, Guenevere appears to evoke pity in Gauwaine by the passion of her defense. Nevertheless, Gauwaine ultimately turns away from Guenevere, leaving her to her execution, which is forestalled only by the sudden arrival, at the very end of the poem, of her rescuer, Launcelot. In "King Arthur's Tomb," set after the death of Arthur, Guenevere's stance toward Launcelot and Arthur has markedly changed. At the beginning of the poem, a weary, confused, and morally uncertain Launcelot rides to meet Guenevere at Glastonbury, and there they reminisce about their unlawful yet exhilarating love. Upon his arrival, he falls asleep, exhausted and unsuspecting, on Arthur's tomb. Guenevere, preparing herself privately to receive her former lover, offers an impassioned prayer, in which her attention wavers between love of Christ and love of Launcelot. The last meeting of Launcelot and Guenevere (whose setting derives partly from Dante Gabriel Rossetti's 1855 watercolor of *Arthur's Tomb*) reveals frustrated passion, remorse, and misunderstanding. While Guenevere cannot conceal her abiding love for the still-attentive Launcelot, she rebukes him for being untrue to Arthur, whom she now acknowledges as her rightful lord and as "the greatest king/that ever lived." The third poem of Morris's Arthurian group begins with Galahad's monologue, in which he recounts his arrival at a chapel, his dejection at the prospect of the solitary and endless search for the Grail, his awesome vision of Christ, who has assured him that he will receive, for his purity, a heavenly love surpassing earthly love, and his visitation by two angels and four saints, who promise to bring the Grail to him while he sleeps. The poem continues with dramatic dialogue, in which an angel directs Galahad, now awake, to seek his father, Launcelot, and informs him of the imminent arrival of Bors, Percival, and Percival's sister, the only three persons other than Galahad himself who are sufficiently pure to see the Grail. The poem ends as Bors tells Galahad of the destruction and disarray of the other knights who have sought the Grail in vain. In the final poem of the group, Galahad renders spiritual aid to the dying and tormented knight Ozana.

The poems of Morris's Arthurian group succeed, through retrospection and allusion, in suggesting within a restricted compass the larger patterns of the Arthurian legend. They manage to combine their modern poetic concerns (the minutely accurate yet symbolic presentation of physical phenomena sought by Morris and his Pre-Raphaelite friends, and the tracing of mental processes and psychic states developed by Robert Browning in the dramatic monologue) with profound respect for their traditional source. Morris shares with his friend Rossetti, to whom the 1858 volume is dedicated, and with his more famous contemporary Tennyson, a deep affection for Malory's narrative. Far more than Tennyson, Morris restrains himself in his Arthurian poems from tracing a moral or parabolic significance for the Victorian era in the grand Arthurian themes of earthly love and spiritual aspiration.

For Morris's other poems on Arthurian themes, see "Near Avalon" and "A Good Knight in Prison" from the *Defence* volume, as well as the fragments "The Maying of Queen Guenevere," "St. Agnes' Convent," and "Palomydes' Quest." [MDC]

Morris introduced Edward Burne-Jones to the Arthurian poetry of Tennyson while they were classmates at Exeter College, Oxford, in 1853. Together, they read Malory's *Morte Darthur* in 1855, and in 1857 Morris read the saga aloud to Burne-Jones and Dante Gabriel Rossetti as they painted in the latter's studio.

Morris's renditions of the legend in painting and drawing include only studies for unfinished works, such as *Iseult on the Ship* (1858) and the finished watercolor *Queen Guenevere* (1858, Tate Gallery, London). He painted one mural and the ceiling in the Oxford Union Murals project (1857), and he directed the Dunlop Windows project (1862), for which he designed five of the panels. His firms Morris and Company and Merton Abbey Tapestry Works sponsored many Arthurian projects, and he planned an edition of *Le Morte Darthur*, to be illustrated by Burne-Jones and published by the Kelmscott Press, but the project was abandoned at his death.

Morris's major contribution to the history of Arthurian art was his influence upon other artists. His poetry suggested an alternative source, his decorative-art projects joined Pre-Raphaelite designs with Arthurian themes, and his continual choice of Malory over Tennyson was crucial for the Pre-Raphaelite interpretation of the Arthurian legend. [DNM]

Morris, William. *The Defence of Guenevere, and Other Poems*. London: Bell and Daldy, 1858.

Aho, Gary L. *William Morris: A Reference Guide*. Boston: G.K. Hall, 1985.

Henderson, Philip. *William Morris: His Life, Work and Friends*. London: Thames and Hudson, 1967.

Raymond, Meredith B. "The Arthurian Group in *The Defence of Guenevere and Other Poems*." *Victorian Poetry*, 4 (1966), 213–18.

Silver, Carole. *The Romance of William Morris*. Athens: Ohio University Press, 1982.

William Morris and the Middle Ages. Manchester: University Press, 1984.

MORTIMER, JOHN (ca. 1741–1779), British history painter, was the only artist to paint the subject *The Discovery of Prince Arthur's Tomb by the Inscription on the Leaden Cross* (ca. 1767); his source was John Speed's *The History of Great Britaine* . . . (1611). The painting is lost and known only through drawings (National Gallery of Scotland, Edinburgh, and Victoria and Albert Museum, London) and an engraving by J. Ogborne (1797). Mortimer also designed illustrations for John Bell's *The Faerie Queene* (1778) and painted subjects from Spenser, *Sir Arthegal the Knight of Justice* (1778) and *A Head of Despaire* (1779). [DNM]

Sunderland, John. "Mortimer, Pine and Some Political Aspects of English History Painting." *Burlington Magazine*, 116 (June 1974), 317–26.

60. John Hamilton Mortimer, *The Discovery of Prince Arthur's Tomb by the Inscription on the Leaden Cross*. (Courtesy National Galleries of Scotland.)

MOSCHINO, ETTORE (1872–1941), Italian author of *Tristano e Isolde* (1910), a verse drama in the style of Gabriele d'Annunzio. [DLH]

Moschino, Ettore. *Tristano e Isolde*. Milan, 1910.

MÖTTULS SAGA, an Old Norse prose translation of the French fabliau *Le Mantel mautaillié*. A statement in the text indicates that the work was undertaken at the behest of the Norwegian king Hákon Hákonarson (r. 1217–63). A single vellum leaf from ca. 1300 contains the beginning of the text. A vellum from ca. 1400 preserves the text in fragmentary form: one leaf from approximately the middle and a leaf and a half from the end. Two copies of the latter manuscript, both seventeenth-century paper, have the full text.

King Arthur is preparing for a feast at Pentecost at which knights and ladies from all over will be his guests. He refuses to begin, however, until some great event has been related or taken place (a trait also mentioned in *Parcevals saga*). A young man comes rushing in; he is in possession of a lovely mantle. Each of the ladies present, starting with the Queen, must try on this mantle, which will fit only a lady who has been faithful to her husband or beloved. All of the ladies, including the Queen, fail the test, much to the surprise and chagrin of the men. Finally, a maiden is discovered who had remained in an upper room because she was slightly indisposed. She comes down, the mantle fits perfectly, and the feasting begins. Afterward, she and her knight take leave of Arthur. The tale ends on the note that good women should always be welcomed and praised.

Comparison of the vellums (and the seventeenth-century copies) with the French demonstrates that the original translation must have been fuller and closer to the French than any of the individual preserved texts; that is, all show condensation. However, the tale as it now stands evinces a skillful use of amplification and various stylistic features, such as alliteration. Notable is an explicit authorial presence, unlike anything in the other Old Norse Arthurian works. An extended opening encomium of Arthur coupled with the tale's content produces a clever parody of the Arthurian scene. [FWB]

Kalinke, Marianne E., ed. *Mǫttuls saga*, with an edition of *Le Lai du cort mantel* by Philip E. Bennett. Copenhagen: Reitzel, 1987.

———, trans. "The Saga of the Mantle." In *The Romance of Arthur III*, ed. James J. Wilhelm. New York: Garland, 1988, pp. 55–68.

———. *King Arthur, North-by-Northwest*. Copenhagen: Reitzel, 1981.

Mancoff, Debra N. *The Arthurian Revival in Victorian Art*. New York: Garland, 1990, pp. 149–50, 254–57.

61. D.G. Rossetti, from *The Palace of Art*:

Or mythic Uther's deeply-wounded son
In some fair space of sloping greens
Lay, dozing in the vale of Avalon,
And watch'd by weeping queens.

(Courtesy of the Kenneth Spencer Research Library, University of Kansas.)

MOXON TENNYSON, a collection of Alfred Tennyson's early writings published as *Poems* (London: Moxon, 1857), illustrated by artists chosen by the poet, with the assistance of publisher Edward Moxon. The artists, both traditional Academic figures and Pre-Raphaelite painters, were given specific subjects, and their finished drawings were translated to wood blocks by the Dalziel Brothers. In this volume, Tennyson's Arthurian poetry was first published with illustrations.

Of the fifty-five subjects, only six were Arthurian. Academician Daniel Maclise designed "Arthur Obtains Excalibur" and "Arthur in the Death Barge" for "Morte d'Arthur." William Holman Hunt and Dante Gabriel Rossetti each submitted a design for "The Lady of Shalott," and Rossetti also interpreted "Sir Galahad" and "The Palace of Art." Rossetti unjustifiably complained that he had been given the unwanted subjects and that the Dalziel Brothers

62. Daniel Maclise, *Arthur Obtains the Sword Excalibur*. (Courtesy of the Kenneth Spencer Research Library, University of Kansas.)

butchered his designs, but the Moxon Tennyson established his public image as an Arthurian artist. Although not a financial success, the Moxon Tennyson influenced book illustration into the early twentieth century. [DNM]

Layard, George Somes. *Tennyson and His Pre-Raphaelite Illustrators: A Book About a Book*. London: Paternoster Row, 1894.

MUIR, EDWIN (1887–1959), poet, journalist, and teacher, was born and educated in the Orkney Islands. He composed two Arthurian poems, "Merlin" (1937) and "Tristram's Journey" (1937, originally entitled "Tristram Crazed" when it first appeared in 1932). The former, famous for its first line, "O Merlin in your crystal cave," is a nostalgic evocation of a lost age of magic. The latter, based on the story of Tristram's madness as found in the Prose *Tristan* and Malory, presents Tristram's disordered perceptions of his world as he wanders insane. [AAR]

Muir, Edwin. *Collected Poems*, 2nd ed. Oxford: Oxford University Press, 1965, pp. 64–66, 73–75.

MUMFORD, ETHEL WATTS, author of "Merlin and Vivian" (1907), verse lyrics for a short music drama by Henry Hadley that tells how Vivian learned Merlin's spells and imprisoned him forever. [AEG]

Hadley, Henry. *Merlin and Vivian*. Opus 52. New York: Schirmer, 1907.

MUNN, H(AROLD) WARNER (1903–1982), author of the fantasy trilogy *King of the World's Edge* (1939), *The Ship from Atlantis* (1967) (published together in 1976 as *Merlin's Godson*), and *Merlin's Ring* (1974). The books trace the journey of Ventidius Varro, a centurion in Arthur's army, and Myrdhinn (Merlin) in Arthur's ship Prydwen after the battle of Camlann; their struggle to establish a kingdom in the New World; and the return and subsequent adventures of Varro's son Gwalchmai over the centuries and across continents. [MAG]

Munn, H. Warner. *Merlin's Ring*. New York: Ballantine, 1974.
———. *Merlin's Godson*. New York: Ballantine, 1976.

MURALS (MEDIEVAL). Literary references to mural paintings with Arthurian subjects abound; however, few secular paintings remain from the Middle Ages. Secular painting is especially vulnerable: domestic architecture is remodeled regularly in accord with changes in fashion; castles or royal residences are damaged or destroyed in times of war or civil unrest. Thus, those few surviving secular murals are often in isolated provincial centers and do not represent the work of the leading artists of the day or (with a few exceptions, such as Runkelstein) the taste of major patrons. Furthermore, many paintings have suffered from ill-advised restoration or repainting. Arthurian murals must often be studied second hand, in early photos or watercolor reproductions.

The most famous Arthurian murals in literature are surely those painted by Sir Lancelot himself on the walls of the chamber in which he was imprisoned by Morgan le Fay. Here, he recalled his love for Queen Guenevere, and later, when Morgan entertained King Arthur in the room, the murals revealed the deception practiced on the King. Again, in the romance of *Perlesvaus*, Sir Gawain learned of his illegitimacy from the paintings on chapel walls. Throughout medieval literature, descriptions of palaces include lists of the subjects of wall paintings: the castle hall in Boccaccio's *Amorosa Visione*, Martorell's description of the decoration of the palace at Constantinople in *Tirant le Blanc*, or Guillem Torroella's description, in *La Faula*, of mural paintings in Morgan le Fay's palace. Chaucer, too, included Tristan and Isolde in his mural of ill-fated lovers, and the Alsatian poet Altswert described the Palace of Venus as decorated with paintings of Arthur and his knights. These simple lists of subjects lack any reference to composition or style. They do suggest, however, the popularity of Arthurian material, especially of the great lovers, Tristan and Isolde and Lancelot and Guenevere.

Typical of the surviving Arthurian mural complexes are the great tower of the chateau of St.-Floret near Issoire in the Auvergne in France, mid-fourteenth century; the ceiling of the Palazzo Chiaramonte in Palermo, Sicily, from the 1370s; the Summer House of Schloss Runkelstein (Castel-Roncolo), two kilometers north of Bolzano in the Tyrol, ca. 1400; and the great hall of the castle of La Manta near Turin, ca. 1430.

The St.-Floret paintings have been dated to the fourteenth century on the basis of the will drawn up for Athon de St.-Floret in 1364, as well as on the type of armor represented in the painting. Today, the paintings can be studied best in watercolor copies made at the beginning of the twentieth century, for they are not well preserved and are located high on the walls. Best preserved are the stories of the knights Branor le Brun and Tristan, on the north and south walls, respectively. Texts accompanying the paintings indicate that the painters' sources were the Prose *Tristan* and the *Meliadus*. In one of the best-preserved scenes, Isolde pretends to see a strange fish in the fountain in order to call Tristan's attention to the reflection of King Mark.

Tristan and Isolde also appear on the ceiling of the Palazzo Chiaramonte in Palermo; however, the figures on the beams are at such a great distance that they are barely visible. The owners of the Palazzo were a Norman family who established themselves in Sicily in the twelfth century. The palace built by Manfredi I between 1307 and 1321 was refurbished by Manfredi III, the powerful ruler of Palermo. The painted ceiling was part of his commission, and an inscription records the names of three Sicilian painters who executed the ceiling between 1377 and 1380.

King Arthur appears in his role as one of the Nine Worthies in the great hall of the fourteenth-century castle of La Manta in the Piedmont south of Turin. The owners, Valerano and Clemensia Provana, commissioned the paintings ca. 1430. Valerano's father, Tommaso, had composed a poem, *Le Chevalier errant*, in which he described the Palace of Fortuna as having a hall with the seats of the Nine Worthies. The poem may have suggested the theme for the decoration of the actual castle hall. At La Manta, the painters represented the Worthies as life-sized armed figures standing amid flowers and trees. King Arthur, on his blue shield and surcoat, bears the three gold crowns identified in the inscription as Britain, Scotland, and England.

Other examples of mural painting may be studied conveniently in reproductions published by Loomis, for many of them are recorded in watercolors and drawings. They include the story of Yvain, in a thirteenth-century house in Schmalkalden in Thuringia; Perceval, in a house in Lübeck (ca. 1330, recorded in watercolor before its destruction) and a house in Constance (drawing preserved); and the three Christian Worthies, in the castle in Sion, Switzerland. (*See also* Boston Public Library Murals; Dyce, William; Oxford Union Murals; Pisanello; Runkelstein Murals.)

[MS]

Loomis, Roger Sherman, and Laura Hibbard Loomis. *Arthurian Legends in Medieval Art*. London: Oxford University Press, 1938, figs. 92–105 (St.-Floret), 106–16 (Palermo), 60–75, 171–201 (Schloss Runkelstein), 14 (La Manta), 159–66 (Schmalkalden), 150–54 (Lübeck), 149 (Constance), 17 (Sion).

Nickel, Heinrich L. *Mittelalterliche Wandmalerei*. Leipzig, 1979, pp. 280–83 (Schmalkalden).

Whitaker, Muriel. *Legends of King Arthur in Art*. Cambridge: Brewer, 1990, pp. 121–136.

MUS, DAVID. A tree on a hillside, which was used by Tristram to convey a message to Isolde, serves as the focal image for four poems drawn from a twelfth-century lai. "Before the Hill" (1988), as the sequence is called, examines a contemporary relationship through its parallels in "The *Chevrefoil* of Marie de France," which is retold in polished free verse. The incident and Tristram's motivation are explored in the other poems: "Hillside," "Terrain," and "Tree."

[DN]

Mus, David. "Before the Hill." In *Wall to Wall Speaks*. Princeton: Princeton University Press, 1988.

MUSCHG, ADOLF, professor of German literature and one of the most important modern Swiss-German writers. Muschg is the author of the trilogy *Der rote Ritter* ("The Red Knight"), a retelling of Wolfram's *Parzival*. In Muschg's version, the rape of Jeschute and the unknightly killing of Ither, followed by the theft of his red armor, are sins sufficient to make Parzival fail as a member of the Arthurian court and as a model of courtly ideals. The Grail quest reconciles the hero with himself, and at the end he becomes the Grail King.

[WW]

Muschg, Adolf. *Der rote Ritter*. 3 vols. Frankfurt am Main: Suhrkamp, 1991.

MUSIC. Music inspired by Arthurian characters and themes has been a vital element of the Arthurian tradition from the Middle Ages to the present. Centuries of development, a variety of languages, and wide geographical distribution have led to complex interrelationships of romance, music, and folklore.

1) THE MIDDLE AGES, RENAISSANCE, RESTORATION. Surviving Medieval music in the Arthurian tradition is often lyrical and makes only passing reference to Arthur and the principals of his court (*see* Troubadours). Alfonso IX in thirteenth-century Spain was responsible for four Arthurian works in the *Cantiga de Santa Maria*. For example, in the cantiga "Dereit e dess'end 'achar mal quen fillar' perfia" ("It Is Fitting That Whoever Works Evil Against the Virgin Mary Should Come to a Bad End") Merlin debates a Jewish theologian over Christ's divinity. Merlin also takes a central role in Thibaut de Navarre's (1201–1253) "Dex es ausi li pellicans" ("God Is Like the Pelican"), in which Merlin's prophecies as found in Geoffrey's *Historia* are used to support Christian charity and sacrifice. A number of fifteenth-century Spanish ballads make reference to Ginebra (Guenevere) and Gálvan (Gawain), but only three extant ballads can be termed Arthurian: "Herido está don Tristán" ("Sir Tristan Is Wounded"; apparently derived from the Prose *Tristan*), "Nunca fuera caballero" ("Never Was a Gallant Knight"), and "Tres hijuelos había el rey" ("Three Tender Striplings Had the King").

In medieval Italy, Arthurian music found its audience in the popular *cantari*, the narrative ballads built on traditional motifs and often utilizing several major Arthurian characters. Antonio Pucci (ca. 1310–1388) is thought to be the author of *Gismirante*, a story of bride-winning by a knight in Arthur's court, and *Brito di Brettagna*, which recounts a hero's efforts to earn a lady's love. Another song sometimes attributed to Pucci is *I Cantari di Carduino*, which contains an *enfances* of Perceval. Other songs in this popular urban tradition include *I Cantari di Tristano*, *Li Chantari di Lancellotto*, *Quando Tristano e Lancielotto combattettero al petrone di Merlino* ("When Tristan and Lancelot Fought at Merlin's Tomb"), and *La vendetta che fe messer Lanzelloto* ("The Vengeance Taken by Sir Lancelot"). An instrumental piece also survives from fourteenth-century Italy: the *Lamento di Tristano*.

Arthurian songs from Scandinavia center exclusively on the story of Tristan. "Tristram's kvæði," a fifteenth-century Icelandic ballad, derives from a thirteenth-century Norwegian translation of Thomas's *Tristan*. Recounting events from Tristan's wounding to his death, it contains the intertwining rose and briar motif, though here it is tree branches that bring the lovers together in death. Also from the fifteenth century is the Danish ballad "Tistram og Jomfru Isolt"; all three extant versions focus on Tristan's wooing of Isolde over her mother's objections. A sixteenth-century Danish Tristan ballad, "Tistrum og Isalt," recounts the arrangements for a tryst between the lovers and the deception of King Magnus, Isalt's husband, by her trusted handmaiden. A final Tristan ballad, this from the Faroe Islands, does not appear to be related to the other Scandinavian ballads except that Tristan is its central figure. "Tístrams táttur" is a unique account of Tristan's death by hanging at the hands of the King of France.

In Great Britain, the earliest examples of Arthurian music are known only by report and in entries in the *Stationers' Register*. In 1565–66, the broadside ballad "a pleasaunte history of an adventurus knyghte of knygges Arthurs Couurte" was licensed by a Richard Jones. In 1603, Edward Alde licensed "The noble Actes nowe newly found of Arthure of the round table," and in 1624 the ballad "When Arthur first in Court" was entered. The latter ballad was apparently appropriated by Thomas Deloney, who published it in 1631 as "Noble Acts of *Arthur* of the Round Table to the tune of, Flying Fame." It was this version that Falstaff was trying to sing in Shakespeare's *Henry IV, Part 2* and that appeared in plays by Marston, and Beaumont and Fletcher.

The history of Arthurian music in Britain is linked to the appearance of the great ballad collections in the eighteenth century. From the first general collection, published in 1723, there began an intense interest in this form of literature. In 1765 appeared the first edition of Bishop Percy's *Reliques of Ancient English Poetry*. Six ballads on Arthurian themes are found in the *Reliques*. "The Legend of King Arthur" is an account by Arthur of his life history; its source has been variously identified as the fifteenth-century chronicle of Gerard de Leew, Malory, and a fifteenth-century play. "King Arthur's Death" is a sixteenth-century continuation of "The Legend of King Arthur" recounting Arthur's story to his last battle with Mordred. Its source is Malory, though it has been compared with the Stanzaic *Le Morte Arthur*. The fragmentary "Sir Lancelot du Lake" is a version of "When Arthur first in court." "King Ryence's Challenge," a fourth ballad in Percy's *Reliques*, follows Malory, with the arrogant king demanding Arthur's beard to trim his cloak. Also derived from Malory is "The Boy and the Mantle" (Child No. 29), in which husbands and wives are put to a series of chastity tests. "The Marriage of Sir Gawain" (Child No. 31), the sixth Arthurian ballad in Percy, is built on the ancient motif of a woman's transformation from loathsome hag to lovely damsel and tells the same story as the fifteenth-century romance *The Wedding of Sir Gawain and Dame Ragnell*. A seventh ballad, not in the *Reliques* but appearing in the Percy Folio, is "King Arthur and King Cornwall." The ballad, featuring supernatural transformations, fiends, and fiery steeds, has no known antecedents in courtly literature.

Restoration music, still under the influence of Renaissance art, which sought to recreate the spirit of the ancient world, turned on occasion to the Arthurian idea for inspiration. *King Arthur, the British Worthy* (1691) is John Dryden's "Dramatik Opera," produced in collaboration with the composer Henry Purcell (1659–1695). Extremely popular, the opera was frequently performed throughout the eighteenth and nineteenth centuries. The action of *King Arthur* is, as one critic notes, "enveloped in an aura of myth and fantasy," the plot centering on contemporary political allegory rather than the well-known stories of Arthur's knights. Dryden had written "this trifle," as he called it, in 1684 for performance in honor of Charles II. Charles died before it could be staged, however, and the work was put aside. Dryden reworked the text extensively to make it acceptable to the new king, William, and it was further modified by Purcell as he composed the music. Purcell is usually credited with creating an exceptionally fine score, though the music has not survived in complete form. It was not printed during Purcell's lifetime, and surviving manuscripts contain omissions.

The preference for dramatic spectacles in which music played a major part, as seen in Dryden and Purcell's *King Arthur*, also found expression in a number of musical pieces on Merlin. The contemporary assessment of Merlin as diabolical and antirational is reflected in such titles as *Merlin: or the Devil of Stone-Henge*, by Lewis Theobald (1688–1744); *Merlin: or the British Inchanter* (1760), by William Giffard; and *Merlin in Love, or Youth Against Magic* (1760), by Aaron Hill (1685–1750).

Eighteenth-century satire and burlesque ventured into music on Arthurian ideals in Thomas Arne's (1710–1778) *The Opera of Operas, or Tom Thumb the Great* (1733), after Henry Fielding, with libretto by Eliza Heywood (1693?–1756), with music first by Thomas Arne (1710–

1778) and in the next year with new music by John Frederick Lampe (1703–1751).

2) OPERA. Composers throughout the nineteenth and twentieth centuries continued to recognize the dramatic possibilities of Arthurian subjects and produced a diverse body of operas and entertainments. Over thirty have found their sources in traditional ballads, Malory and Wolfram von Eschenbach, such modern authors as Sir Walter Scott, Thomas Hardy, and Joseph Bédier, and the Arthurian operas of Richard Wagner. Although many of these works hold little interest today, the efforts of a few opera composers are significant in the history of the Arthurian legend.

The verse tale *The Bridal of Triermain*, by Sir Walter Scott (1771–1832), inspired two early operatic adaptations of Arthurian materials. In "Lyulph's Tale," his original Arthurian contribution in *The Bridal of Triermain*, Scott combined familiar characters, traditional magic, and the core motif of Sleeping Beauty in a fanciful romantic story. The story provided the basis for J.L. Ellerton's operetta *The Bridal of Triermain* (1831) and Isaac Pocock's musical entertainment *King Arthur and the Knights of the Round Table* (1834), as well as an orchestral and choral composition, *The Bridal of Triermain* (1886), by Frederick Corder.

Isaac Albéniz (1860–1909), a major figure in the history of Spanish piano music, also produced theater music of quality. Following the libretto of Francis Coutts after Malory, Albéniz composed the vocal score of *Merlin* (written 1901), the first of a projected opera trilogy to be entitled *King Arthur. Lancelot*, the second work, was never completed, and *Guinevere* was not begun. This promising trilogy remained incomplete and unperformed due to Albéniz's preoccupation with his masterpiece, the *Suite Iberia*, which he was composing at the same time, and to the onset of the illness that would silence him seven years later.

The fate of Albéniz's trilogy is typical of many Arthurian music projects, which often begin with a grand design but never come to be realized. Henry Irving, for example, eager to dramatize Arthurian legends, commissioned J. Comyns Carr (1849–1916) to write a *King Arthur*, with Arthur Sullivan to compose the incidental music and Edward Burne-Jones to produce the scenery, costumes, and armor. Sullivan himself conducted the opening-night performance at the Lyceum in January 1895. Reviews of the performance were generally highly favorable ("the best specimen of the stage art of our time"), and Sullivan was moved to begin a full Arthurian opera with Comyns Carr again writing the libretto. Nothing further was composed, however, or at least nothing survives of this new project. After Sullivan's death, the original incidental music to *King Arthur* was published with concert arrangements by Wilfred Bendall (1904).

Claude Debussy (1862–1918), the French Impressionist composer, began but never completed five operas, one of which was to be based on Bédier's *Roman de Tristan et Iseut*, with a libretto by Gabriel Mourey (1865–1943). The work would be composed with an Impressionist emphasis on tone and delicate voluptuousness that suggested meaning rather than stated it. Debussy reportedly worked enthusiastically on the libretto of Mourey's newly renamed *L'Histoire de Tristan*. In August 1907, the collaboration was announced in the press, and in July of the next year he sold first-performance rights to the Metropolitan Opera House in New York. Problems over an exclusive license for theater adaptations granted by Bédier to his cousin Louis Artus brought the enterprise to a halt, though Artus did manage to have his own adaptation, *Tristan et Iseut*, performed with incidental music by Paul Ladmirault in Nice in 1929.

Not all Arthurian music projects were abandoned or resulted in mediocre work, of course, and without question some of the greatest music ever composed has its beginnings in the story of Arthur. Richard Wagner (1813–1883) set about to reform the lyric drama, both its themes and its music. For his subject matter, he looked to myth as the ideal source, while his music became a blend of sound and poetry. In three of his operas, for which he wrote both the music and librettos, Wagner used the Arthurian legend as the vehicle for his beliefs about society, art, religion, love, and passion.

Lohengrin (1845) had its beginnings in the last 100 lines of Wolfram's *Parzival*; *Der jungere Titurel*, by Albrecht, which tells of the Holy Grail and Lohengrin's life; the thirteenth-century poems *Der Schwanen-Ritter* and *Lohengrin*; and international folklore motifs. Wagner transforms these sources into a masterly musical work of power and beauty. Lohengrin enters society from above, the Grail realm of Monsalvat, to transform and reform the world. Monsalvat is a realm of moral absolutes and purity, and the hero, revealed as the son of Parzival the Grail King, is its finest representative.

Tristan und Isolde, completed in 1859, was immediately acknowledged as a musical "revolution." It has been said that the opera "questioned and eroded" the musical tradition of centuries and is the beginning of modern music. After six years of struggling to find a company willing and able to perform the opera, the composer finally saw it produced in Munich in 1865. Wagner's source is Gottfried von Strassburg's *Tristan*. The Tristan story questions the adequacy of passion and transcendental love and, particularly, erotic love. Wagner holds up the dream of lovers, that their love is everlasting and of supreme value, as a destructive belief, an illusion. The emphasis on the wish for death in *Tristan und Isolde* is not central in Gottfried and is here a reflection of Wagner's interest in Schopenhauer's philosophy.

Six months before his death in 1882, Wagner directed the first performance of *Parsifal*. He had first read Wolfram von Eschenbach's *Parzifal* in 1845 and had long intended to compose an opera based on the story. By 1865, he had finished the outline, and in 1877 he completed the libretto. The theme of this profound drama of Christianity is redemption.

63. MS Paris, Bibliothèque de l'Arsenal 5218, fol. 88: Grail Liturgy, from *La Queste del Saint Graal*. (Paris, Bibliothèque de l'Arsenal.)

Two composers, one French, the other British, were motivated by Wagner's achievements to write their own operas. In 1886, Ernest Chausson (1855–1899) revealed that he was working on the libretto for a projected opera, *Le Roi Arthus*. Inspired initially by Wagner's *Tristan und Isolde*, Chausson found himself in an eight-year struggle to break free of Wagner's influence. Chausson wrote his own libretto, choosing as his subject the Lancelot story and the death of King Arthur. However, concern that his opera would seem too derivative kept Chausson from completing *Le Roi Arthus* for nearly a decade, and even then it was not performed until 1903, four years after his death.

Rutland Boughton (1878–1960) combined in his life and art a commitment to socialist goals and the music drama of Wagner. With the poet Reginald Buckley, he wrote *The Music Drama of the Future* (1911), setting forth their beliefs on the decline of Christianity and the rise of the socialist state. Music drama was at the heart of this future world, and Boughton, Buckley, and artist Christina Walshe determined to be part of it by creating a commune of artists in Glastonbury, where they would compose music drama along Wagnerian lines. From 1914 to 1927, they mounted 350 performances at the Glastonbury Festival, with a cycle of Arthurian operas at their center. Boughton and Buckley collaborated on the first two operas, *The Birth of Arthur* and *The Round Table*. In 1926, Boughton's *The Lily Maid* (the Elaine and Lancelot story) was performed at Stroud. The last two works of the cycle, *Galahad* (1943–44) and *Avalon* (1944–45), have not been performed.

Both Chausson and Boughton were for a time dominated by the power of Wagner's style and achievements, but each was able finally to produce exceptionally fine compositions—Chausson, because he explored the lyrical qualities of the French language, Boughton, because he employed the simple melodic line of English folksong.

In Germany, Johann Gottfried von Herder (1744–1803) provided an Arthurian theme for early musical compositions. His German translation of the English ballad "The Boy and the Mantle" was apparently the inspiration for Benedikte Naubert's novel *Der kurze Mantel* (1819), which was the immediate source of Carl Franz van der Velde's opera libretto *Der Zaubermantel* (1827) and a *Singspiel* by F.A.C. Werthes. The magic mantle that tests its wearer's chastity is also the subject of "Die Ausgleichung," a folksong from the collection of Clemens Brentano and Achim von Arnim, *Des Knaben Wunderhorn* (1806–08). All the compositions on the magic-mantle motif appear to derive ultimately from *Le Mantel mautaillié*, an anonymous twelfth-century French poem.

Later German-language operas returned to the character of Merlin, basing their librettos on Karl Immermann's play *Merlin*, which appeared in 1832. Hungarian composer Karl Goldmark (1830–1915) used Immermann's play for his own *Merlin*, performed first in Vienna in 1886 and revised in 1904. Goldmark's music was heavily influenced by Hungarian folk culture, Impressionism, and Wagnerian opera style. Felix August Bernhard Draeseke (1835–1913) was highly successful in employing Immermann's play to develop his own *Merlin* (written 1900–05), performed in 1913 shortly after his death. Poet Richard von Kralik (1852–1934), who was to write his own Merlin play in 1913, composed the music drama "Der heilige Gral" ("The Holy Grail") the year before.

Merlin, Gawain, Lancelot, and Tristan have continued as the central figures in twentieth-century opera. French composer Victorin de Joncières completed his "lyric drama" *Lancelot* in 1900. Willem Pijper (1894–1947), a Dutch composer and teacher, began his *Merlijn* during the Second World War. The symphonic element of the production predominates over an episodic structure related to the twelve astrological signs of the Zodiac. Richard Blackford is responsible for two Gawain operas, *Gawain and the Green Knight* (1978–79) and *Gawain and Ragnell* (1984). Ian Hamilton's *Lancelot* appeared in 1985. Two Tristan operas continue the long tradition of works on the hero, Gillian Whitehead's *Tristan and Isolt* (first performed in 1978) and Timothy Porter's *Trystan and Essylt* (1980). A "music drama" by Gordon Crosse, to a libretto by Alan Gardner, *Potter Thompson* was first performed in 1975 (published by Oxford University Press in 1985). The opera is a retelling of the Arthurian cave legend.

3) CHORAL AND INSTRUMENTAL MUSIC. Since the late nineteenth century, composers of choral and instrumental music have produced many compositions of enduring quality. Most of the music appears to fall into two categories: those compositions meant for concert performance and usually named for a familiar Arthurian character, and those written as incidental or accompanying music for plays, radio broadcasts, and movies. Some representative pieces: Ernest Chausson's symphonic poem *Viviane* (1882); English organist Reginald Steggale's scena *Elaine* (1896); Henry Hadley's music drama *Merlin and Vivian*, with lyrics by Ethel Watts Mumford (written 1903, published 1907 by Schirmer); G.A. MacFarren's choral piece *The Lady of the Lake*, published by Novello; Wilfred Bendall's *The Lady of Shalott* for female voices, also published by Novello; Rutland Boughton's *Chapel in Lyonesse* (1905) and *King Arthur Had Three Sons*; English composer Arnold Bax's *Tintagel: A Symphonic Poem*, first performed in 1917 (it uses the "sick Tristan" motif and is strongly influenced by Celtic folklore); Brian Hooker's oratorio *Morven and the Grail* (1915); Ludomir Michel Rogowsky's (1881–1954) three symphonic poems influenced by Slavic folksong; Swiss composer Frank Martin's (1890–1974) *Le Vin herbé* ("The Potion"), a secular oratorio for twelve solo voices with string and piano accompaniment, based on three chapters of Bédier's *Roman de Tristan et Iseut*; Elinor Remick Warren's oratorio *The Passing of Arthur* (1939), based on Tennyson's *Idylls of the King;* and Dan Welcher's 1980 *The Visions of Merlin*, an instrumental suite in six sections.

4) INCIDENTAL, THEATRICAL, POPULAR MUSIC. A number of orchestral pieces were composed as incidental music for dramatic productions. Arthur Sullivan's music for J. Comyns Carr's *King Arthur* and Paul Ladmirault's music for the *Tristan et Iseut* of Bédier and Artus, mentioned above, are two such works. Also of interest is Vincent Thomas's music to Ernest Rhys's three Arthurian plays, *Gwenevere: A Lyric Play* (written 1895, performed 1905), *Enid: A Lyric Play* (1908), and *The Masque of the Grail* (1908). Sir Edward Elgar's Arthurian compositions are some of the finest examples of incidental orchestral music. For many years, Elgar was invited to collaborate by playwright Laurence Binyon. Finally, when in 1923 Binyon's play *Arthur* was to be performed at the Old Vic, Elgar accepted the commission to write the incidental music. His task was to provide introductions and entr'actes for the play's nine scenes. The score was completed in February 1923, and the play received exceptional reviews when it opened a month later. Elgar's music, unpublished during his lifetime, survives as an orchestral suite.

A 1938 radio play based on T.H. White's *The Sword in the Stone* provided the occasion for incidental music written by Benjamin Britten; Cocteau's movie *L'Éternel Retour*, for music by Georges Auric. Popular musical treatments of the Arthurian legend have been very successful. Frederick Loewe and Alan Jay Lerner's Broadway play *Camelot* (1960), later made into a film, is based on White's *The Once and Future King*. Richard Rodgers and Lorenz Hart's *A Connecticut Yankee* and a 1949 musical movie starring Bing Crosby are based on Twain's *A Connecticut Yankee in King Arthur's Court*. *Monty Python and the Holy Grail* (1975) contains rollicking songs spoofing Arthurian ideals. Rick Wakeman's 1975 album *The Myths and Legends of King Arthur and the Knights of the Round Table*, and popular songs by such performers as Al Stewart, represent recent musical versions.

5) CELTIC MUSIC. Some critics have used Gaelic traditional songs with Arthurian themes to shed light on the origins of Arthurian romance. "Am Bròn Binn" ("The Sweet Sorrow"), a Scottish Gaelic song still sung in oral tradition, tells the story of Arthur or Sir Bhalbha, who rescues a maiden from a castle on an island in the sea. "Bas Artuir" ("The Death of Arthur") is an abbreviated version of "Am Bròn Binn" with its own oral tradition. "Laoidh an Bhruit" ("The Lay of the Mantle") employs the familiar chastity test; it first appears in the sixteenth-century Book of the Dean of Lismore. "Laoidh an Amádain Mhóir" ("The Lay of the Great Fool") is a work with an uncertain date of composition, probably sixteenth or seventeenth century. Although Arthur is not specifically named in the text, its subject matter and hero, the Great Fool, find parallels elsewhere in Arthurian prose texts recounting the testing of the Fair Unknown.

Two modern songs with political implications are part of Cornish Arthurian musical history. Ralph Dunstan's "Merlin the Diviner," a soprano solo, was first sung at a meeting of the Royal Institution of Cornwall in Truro in 1927. "Arta Ef A Dhe" ("He Shall Come Again") is sung each year at the *Gorsedd*, the meeting of Cornish bards. Each has played a role in efforts to maintain and revive Cornish culture and language.

Welsh compositions also have political implications, either because they stress the importance of perpetuating the Welsh language or because they emphasize the return motif of the Arthurian legend. An opera composed in the 1960s by William Mathias, *Culhwch ac Olwen*, has a dual-language libretto written by Gwyn Thomas. It is scored for narrator, choral speech group, chorus, percussion, and piano duet. *Arthur* is a musical drama for male voices by Hugh Davies with words by W.G. Williams. Among modern Welsh songs are "Marchogion Arthur" ("Arthur's Knights"), with music by John Henry, Welsh lyrics by Bryfdir, and English lyrics by T. Gwynn Jones; "Arthur yn Cyfodi" ("Arthur Is Arising"), by Silyn Roberts with English translation and music by W.S. Gwynn Williams (1924); "Ymadawiad Arthur" ("The Passing of Arthur"), also by W.S. Gwynn Williams (1935); "Caledfwlch" ("Excalibur"), a musical setting from the ode *The Passing of Arthur*, by T. Gwynn Jones (1931); and "Ďraw Dros y Don," on the passing of Arthur from *Tri Darlun*, by Arwel Hughes (1975). [BJW]

Child, Francis James, ed. *The English and Scottish Popular Ballads*. Boston: Houghton-Mifflin, 1884.

Hales, John W., and Frederick J. Furnivall, eds. *Bishop Percy's Folio Manuscript*. London: Trübner, 1867–68.

Hunt, Tony. "Ernest Chausson's 'Le Roi Arthus.'" *Arthurian Literature*, 4 (1985), 127–54.

Nitze, William A. *Arthurian Romance and Modern Poetry and Music*. Chicago: University of Chicago Press, 1940.

Percy, Thomas. *Reliques of Ancient English Poetry Consisting of Old Heroic Ballads, Songs and Other Pieces of Our Earlier Poets*. 3 vols. London: Dodsley, 1765.

Tower, John. *Dictionary-Catalogue of Operas and Operettas*. 2 vols. Morgantown, W.Va., 1910. (Cites twenty-nine operas based on Arthurian themes.)

Ward, Barry J. "King Arthur and Traditional Music." *Keystone Folklore*, 2 (1984), 23–33.

MYERS, JOHN MYERS (1906–1988), American writer, sends the protagonist of his exuberant fantasy classic *Silverlock* (1949) on a picaresque journey through a land filled with memorable characters from literature, including Arthurian. Encounters with figures like Nimue and Gawain (on his way to meet the Green Knight) teach him a fuller appreciation of life. In a sequel, *The Moon's Fire-Eating Daughter* (1981), a university science professor develops his literary talents on a similar journey, during which he encounters famous authors and poets, like Taliesin and Walter Map. He is guided by supernatural beings, among whose manifestations are Merlin and Morgan le Fay. [RHT]

Myers, John Myers. *Silverlock*. New York: Dutton, 1949.

———. *The Moon's Fire-Eating Daughter*. Virginia Beach, Va.: Donning, 1981.

MYRDDIN POEMS, a group of brief (18–225 lines) Welsh texts preserved in manuscripts from the twelfth into the fifteenth centuries (e.g., the Black Book of Carmarthen and the Red Book of Hergest), but surely predating those manuscripts by several centuries. Although unconnected, they mostly concern Myrddin's prophecies about early Welsh history. Two of the poems also present Myrddin's sister: *Cyfoesi Myrddin a Gwenddydd ei Chwaer* ("The Conversation of Myrddin with His Sister Gwenddydd") and *Peirian Faban* ("Commanding Youth"). *Hoianau* ("Greetings") records Myrddin's greetings to his only companion, a piglet; this text, along with *Afallennau* ("Apple-Trees"), deals with the prophet's years of madness in the Caledonian Wood. *Ymddiddan Myrddin a Thaliesin* ("The Dialogue of Myrddin and Taliesin") presents predictions by both bards, and an entombed Myrddin issues prophecies in *Gwasgargerdd Fyrddin yn y Bedd* ("The Song Sung by Merlin in His Grave"). [NJL]

Bollard, John K., trans. "The Myrddin Poems." In *The Romance of Merlin: An Anthology*, ed. Peter Goodrich. New York: Garland, 1991.

Jarman, A.O.H. "The Welsh Myrddin Poems." In *Arthurian Literature in the Middle Ages*, ed. Roger Sherman Loomis. Oxford: Clarendon, 1959, pp. 20–30.

MYSTERY AND SUSPENSE FICTION. The narrow conventions of the modern mystery story, in which a protagonist typically solves a crime involving murders, missing objects, and hidden motives, seem remote from the world of Arthurian romance. Indeed, in the few instances where authors have set such stories in Camelot, the results have been notable primarily for the novelty of the approach, as in Maxey Brooke's short story "Morte d'Alain" (1969) and Phyllis Ann Karr's novel *Idylls of the Queen* (1982), where the murder-solving detectives are Merlin and Sir Kay respectively. Yet the Arthurian legend, following the appealing premise that it is based in historical fact, has successfully provided material for mystery and suspense fiction set in modern times, often in the form of such legendary artifacts as the Holy Grail.

As the vessel used by Christ at the Last Supper, the Grail has not been entirely dependent on its role in Arthurian romance for its literary perpetuation. In Vincent Starrett's short story "The Case of the Two Flutes" (1944), his Sherlock Holmes–like detective solves a Grail-related murder that owes nothing at all to Arthurian story, and in other mysteries involving thefts of the Grail, the borrowings from medieval literature are oblique at best, as when protagonists rise to untypically chivalric stature as they pursue their quests. Such is the case of the heroes in Jonathan Gash's *The Grail Tree* (1979) and Richard Ben Sapir's *Quest* (1987).

Some stories involving the Grail, however, have explicitly drawn on its Arthurian background. In Nelson DeMille's *The Quest* (1975), the four characters who seek the relic's hiding place in a hidden Ethiopian monastery have obvious counterparts in the medieval stories. In other novels, the settings include places with strong Arthurian associations, notably Glastonbury in Alice Campbell's *The Murder of Caroline Bundy* (1932) and Cadbury Hill, a key archaeological site in James Goldman's *The Man from Greek and Roman* (1974).

The spiritual implications of possessing the Grail have provided the focus for stories of secret societies and international conspiracies. An ancient knightly order of prominent Britons, for example, guards the Grail in Francis Gerard's *Secret Sceptre* (1937), though in Michael Delving's *Die Like a Man* (1970), the Grail is protected by common folk who practice medieval rituals in an isolated Welsh village. Geoffrey Household, in *Summon the Bright Water* (1981), portrays a neopagan cult in the Forest of Dean that treasures a golden cauldron believed to be the Grail. The novel also features a character who anticipates Arthur's return to combat the corruption of the modern world.

The theme of the return has appealed to other authors as well. In *Shadows on the Sceptered Isle* (1980), Jo Anne Stang presents a conspiracy devised by a wealthy industrialist to restore Britain's national purity in Arthur's name, the plan having been fueled by the discovery of the leaden cross from Arthur's grave. The plot of Elizabeth Peters's *The Camelot Caper* (1969) involves a less ambitious plan to create an Arthurian archaeological site in Cornwall by salting it with fifth-century artifacts, including a golden crown that may have been Arthur's. Cornwall is also the setting of a romantic mystery involving the kidnaping of a foreign prince in Gavin Holt's *Dark Lady* (1933), in which a group known as the Order of the Round Table appears. And a suspense novel that incorporates considerable speculation about the historical Arthur is Anthony Price's *Our Man in Camelot* (1975), in which American, British, and Russian spies become involved in a scheme to discredit the United States for destroying the site of Badon Hill during the construction of an airfield.

Even the best of these novels can scarcely be considered genuine developments of the Arthurian tradition; they represent, rather, adjuncts to it. But they also serve as illustrations of the extent to which the tradition has become part of our common literary currency. [DN]

NABOKOV, VLADIMIR (1899–1977), author of the 1952 story "Lance." Set sometime in the future, the story presents Lancelot Boke's experiences as a member of "the first interplanetary expedition" and reflects Nabokov's preoccupation with time. Evoking Lanceloz del Lac, the *Chevalier de la charrete*, and the Sword Bridge leading to the otherworld, the story implicitly relates space exploration to chivalric adventure, and the author notes that "the future is but the obsolete in reverse." [NJL]

Nabokov, Vladimir. "Lance." In *Nabokov's Dozen*. New York: Doubleday, 1958.

NATHAN, ROBERT (1894–1985), prolific American author who drew on Arthurian legend for three of his novels, all gently ironic fantasies though quite different in content and treatment. *Sir Henry* (1955) recounts the comic adventures of an aging knight and is set in the nominally Arthurian Middle Ages. *The Fair* (1964) is set in the historical period following the defeat of Arthur by the Saxons and concerns the journey of a young Celtic girl and an angel. *The Elixir* (1971) takes place in modern Britain, where an American professor becomes involved with Nimue and Merlin. Entertaining and sometimes sentimental, Nathan's stories are well-crafted light reading. [DN]

Nathan, Robert. *Sir Henry*. New York: Knopf, 1955.
———. *The Fair*. New York: Knopf, 1964.
———. *The Elixir*. New York: Knopf, 1971.

NAUBERT, BENEDIKTE (1756–1819). Not until two years before her death, with the publication of her novel *Rosalba*, did Benedikte Naubert divulge her name. More than eighty original works and translations were published anonymously by her. In the years 1789–93, she published a volume of tales entitled *Neue Volksmährchen der Deutschen*. In this collection is a novel entitled *Der kurze Mantel*, a recreation of the tale about the chastity-testing mantle, the oldest literary version of which is the late twelfth- or early thirteenth-century *Le Mantel mautaillié*. The primary sources for Naubert's novel, however, were presumably a sixteenth-century prose version of the fabliau, *Le Manteau mal taillié*, and the English ballad "The Boy and the Mantle." Naubert also drew on the folktale of Frau Hulda, or Frau Holle, a good fay who punishes the lazy but rewards the diligent, especially those who occupy themselves with spinning. In general, the novel contains all the essential elements of the mantle story. There is one significant change, however: the magic mantle is not woven by supernatural creatures but unwittingly by the heroine herself, although this is not divulged until the very end of the novel, when the mantle has attested the heroine's chaste way of life.

Naubert's work is characterized by pronounced criticism of the Arthurian world, which she depicts as being controlled by lascivious and cunning women. The novel expresses disdain for court society and glorifies proletarian virtues.

Der kurze Mantel was not only translated into English (by George Soane in *Specimens of German Romance*, London, 1826) but also inspired a *Singspiel* by Friedrich August Clemens Werthes, an opera libretto by Karl Franz van der Velde, and a short prose version by Johann Peter Lyser. [MEK]

Naubert, Benedikte. *Der kurze Mantel. Und: Ottilie. Zwei Volksmährchen*. Vienna: Armbruster, 1819.
Soane, G. *Specimens of German Romance: Selected and Translated from Various Authors*. London, 1826.

NELSON, MICHAEL L. (1953–1988), poet and writer who published three works on the Grail legends. The short story "Perceval and the Holy Grail" (1979) and the poem "Sir Bors and the Holy Grail" (1979) use first-person narrative to expose the Christian mystery of the triumph of the confused and unlikely. *The Way to Carbonek: The Quest for the Grail* (1981), a long narrative poem in a variety of verse forms, treats the entire Grail quest, with an emphasis on Lancelot's failure. The poem includes embedded narratives of Percival and of Bors (a revised version of "Sir Bors"), and it closes with a complete Christmas Mass of the Holy Grail. [PCB]

Nelson, Michael L. "Perceval and the Holy Grail." *Brushfire*, 28 (1979), 2–3.

———. "Sir Bors and the Holy Grail." *Brushfire*, 29 (1979), 12–14.

———. *The Way to Carbonek: The Quest for the Grail*. Fallon, Nev.: Sand Mountain, 1981.

NENNIUS, a monk of Bangor in north Wales, commonly named as compiler of a *Historia Brittonum* ("History of the Britons"), which was used by Geoffrey of Monmouth and has figured largely in attempts to reconstruct a historical Arthur. The principal version is a copy in an early twelfth-century hand, one of a medley of items in the British Library manuscript Harley 3859. Copied with it in that context are the *Annales Cambriae* and a collection of Welsh genealogies. There are other manuscripts of the *Historia* alone. Formerly, it was sometimes ascribed to Gildas, but its Latin is cruder than his, and the apparent date of composition is much later—near the beginning of the ninth century. While the ascription to Nennius is itself uncertain, his name may be used for convenience.

In his preface—which, even if spurious, is apt and well invented—he says that he has "made one heap of all he has found" rummaging among old documents. This gives him a kind of credibility. At least, he has genuinely "found," not invented; he hardly seems capable of invention. However, while most of his materials are prior to the ninth century, they are so full of legends, errors, inconsistencies, and matter that was probably oral rather than written that they seldom inspire much trust.

Early sections offer various notions about the first peopling of the British Isles. These include a fantasy elaborated by Geoffrey, tracing the origin of the Britons to a party of migrating Trojans. Britain's Roman phase is covered by a confused narrative of the few emperors who were specially concerned with the island. One is Maximus, proclaimed in Britain in 383. The *Historia* mentions the tradition that British soldiers whom he led overseas remained on the Continent and founded Brittany.

Nennius portrays the Britons as becoming independent by killing the Roman *duces* ("commanders"). In the fifth century, he gives an account of Vortigern, his hiring of Saxon auxiliaries, and their mutinous attack on their British employers, which forms the basis of Geoffrey's account of the same disaster. After a digression about St. Patrick, Nennius prefaces his chapter on Arthur with the words: "In that time the Saxons strengthened in multitude and grew in Britain." It is not clear when "that time" is meant to be, except that it is still in the fifth century; a reference to the death of the Saxon chief Hengist is a parenthesis and useless for dating. Nennius goes on to enumerate twelve victories won by Arthur over the Saxons and perhaps allies of theirs. "Arthur fought against them in those days with the kings of the Britons, but he himself was leader of battles [*dux bellorum*]." The first battle is said to have been fought at the mouth of the River Glein; the next four by another river, Dubglas, in the district Linnuis; the sixth by another river, Bassas; the seventh in the Caledonian Wood; the eighth in Fort Guinnion; the ninth in the City of the Legion; the tenth by the River Tribruit; the eleventh on the "hill that is called Agned"; and the twelfth on Mount Badon, where Arthur personally slew 960 of the enemy in a single charge.

This list is thought to be based on a lost Welsh poem in Arthur's praise. There is no literary reason why such a poem should have been contemporary or anything like it. In fact, a poem in Welsh could not have been contemporary with an Arthur much before the middle of the sixth century, because the language had not then taken shape. The implications for history are thus uncertain. Most of the place-names are obscure, a fact that makes deliberate fabrication less likely. The Glein could be the Glen in the south of Lincolnshire. Linnuis is probably Lindsey, the northern portion of the same county. Most nearly certain are the Caledonian Wood, which was in southern Scotland, and the City of the Legion, which, to judge from the *Annales Cambriae*, means Chester. Badon is the major success mentioned by Gildas, at which the Britons' leader is here said to have been Arthur.

Nennius gives him a military paramountcy among the Britons. Nothing shows whether this is political as well. Clues to the dating of his battles are hard to reconcile. The Caledonian Wood seems to imply that he fought Picts, and Bede names them as allies of the auxiliaries in their revolt, but not later. Chester seems to imply enemy raiding right across the country, and Gildas mentions this as occurring in the revolt, but not later. Hence, both the identifiable battle sites point to that phase. The revolt may have been a long-drawn and sporadic ordeal rather than a brief cataclysm, but it cannot be stretched far outside the period 440–60. Badon, however, was fought round about 500. Arguably, Arthur's singlehanded exploit proves his association with Badon to be a product of legend. Nennius's "kings of the Britons" are no help: the plural does not imply Britain's political breakup toward the close of the fifth century, because he speaks of regional rulers under a high king at an earlier stage. Nor can the list be simplified by rejecting some of the battles on the ground that a single leader could not have ranged so widely. Well-attested campaigns in later times show that he could. This does not prove that the battles are all authentic or indeed that any of them are, only that picking and choosing is unsafe.

After the Arthur section come chapters of mainly northern history and genealogy, some of it fairly acceptable. Notes that follow give a date, 425, for Vortigern's rise to power, and another, 428, for the first authorized Saxon settlement. These are expressed in Roman style, with the names of the consuls for the year, and supply Nennius's best chronological fixes.

An appendix of *Mirabilia* ("Marvels") may be a little later than the rest of the book, but not much. Among the marvels are two local legends showing that such tales were already attaching themselves to Arthur in the ninth century. One concerns a stone marked with a paw-print of his dog Cabal. It lies on a heap, and if anybody takes it away, it returns to the heap. This is in the "region of Buelt" in south-central Wales. The other marvel is a tomb near Licat Amr—Gamber Head, a spring in Herefordshire—said to contain the body of Arthur's son Amr, whom he killed himself in some unrecorded tragedy. The "marvelous" feature is that it changes in size. [GA]

Nennius. *Historia Brittonium*, ed. and trans. John Morris under the title *British History and the Welsh Annals*. In *History from the Sources*. Chichester: Phillimore, 1980, Vol. 8.

———. *The Historia Brittonum: The "Vatican" Recension*, ed. David Dumville. Cambridge: Brewer, 1985.

Alcock, Leslie. *Arthur's Britain*. London: Penguin, 1971, pp. 29–41, 55–71.

Jackson, Kenneth Hurlstone. "The Arthur of History." In *Arthurian Literature in the Middle Ages*, ed. Roger Sherman Loomis. Oxford: Clarendon, 1959, pp. 1–11.

NEWBOLT, SIR HENRY (1862–1938), whose poetic drama *Mordred: A Tragedy* (1895) modifies Malory's account of the fall of the Round Table. It is distinguished by its sympathetic portrayal of the main characters, including Mordred, all of whom struggle to maintain right conduct as they see it. Though never staged, the play develops both plot and character relationships effectively. Newbolt was also the author of *Aladore* (1914), a mock-medieval prose romance in the manner of William Morris; the hero is named Sir Ywain. [RHT]

Newbolt, Sir Henry. *Mordred: A Tragedy*. London: Unwin, 1895.

———. *Aladore*. Edinburgh and London: Blackwood, 1914.

NEWELL, WILLIAM WELLS, American folklore scholar and author of the poem *Isolt's Return* (1907), a defense of Béroul's nonromanticized version of the tale. Wells appends an essay about the origins of the Tristan legend to his poem, which is narrated by a minstrel entertaining his young mistress with a poem about her namesake, Isolt. To the young girl's distress, Isolt returns to Mark after the forest episode. [AAR]

Newell, William Wells. *Isolt's Return*. Wayland, Mass.: Published by the author, 1907.

NEWMAN, ROBERT, author of *Merlin's Mistake* (1970), in which Brian, a sixteen-year-old squire; Tertius, a boy whom Merlin has mistakenly gifted with future knowledge; and young Lianor, disguised as a crone, join forces as their separate quests lead them to Nimue's castle and Merlin. This fantasy for adolescents makes humorous use of Arthurian conventions to teach lessons about appearance and reality. However, in the sequel, *The Testing of Tertius* (1973), the tone becomes more complex and serious, as the young people face Nimue and the evil wizard Urlik to rescue Merlin and Blaise and to keep Arthur and Britain safe. [JW]

Newman, Robert. *Merlin's Mistake*. New York: Atheneum, 1970.

———. *The Testing of Tertius*. New York: Atheneum, 1973.

NEWMAN, SHARAN, author of an Arthurian trilogy: *Guinevere* (1981), *The Chessboard Queen* (1984), and *Guinevere Evermore* (1985). Newman emphasizes Guinevere's upbringing in one of the last fully Roman households and the difficulty with which she adjusts to the sweeping and radical social changes inherent in Arthur's reign. Newman intermingles traditional Arthurian episodes with new material, most of which deals with the interweaving of a fantastic otherworld and its creatures, especially a unicorn, with Guinevere's own world. In the story "The Palace by Moonlight" (1988), Newman writes a brief sequel to her "Guinevere" trilogy: the bard Miniffer confronts the reality of the end of the Arthurian era and resolves, after meeting the widowed Guinevere, to preserve the story in the vernacular. [AAR]

Newman, Sharan. *Guinevere*. New York: St. Martin, 1981.

———. *The Chessboard Queen*. New York: St. Martin, 1984.

———. *Guinevere Evermore*. New York: St. Martin, 1985.

———. "The Palace by Moonlight." In *Invitation to Camelot: An Arthurian Anthology of Short Stories*, ed. Parke Godwin. New York: Ace, 1988, pp. 201–21.

NICOLÒ DEGLI AGOSTINI retold the love of Tristan and Isolde in his *Innamoramento di messer Tristano e di madonna Isotta* ("Sir Tristan and Lady Isolt Fall in Love," 1520) and the love of Lancelot and Guenevere in the *Innamoramento di Lancilotto e di Ginevra* (1521–26), which was completed by Marco Guazzo. Both romances are based on traditional Italian *cantari*. [DLH]

Gardner, Edmund G. *The Arthurian Legend in Italian Literature*. London: Dent, 1930, pp. 308–09.

NÍELS JÓNSSON (1782–1857), an Icelandic writer whose *œuvre* is extant mostly in manuscript. Like his better-known countryman Sigurður Breiðfjörð, Niels Jónsson was inspired by the Danish chapbook *En tragoedisk Historie om den aedle og tappre Tistrand* ("A Tragic Tale of the Noble and Courageous Tistrand") to compose *rímur*, or cantos, about Tistrand and Indiana, entitled *Rijmur af þeim Tistrani Hrobjartar Hertogasyni af Borgund og Indíaunu Drottníngu Mógols Dóttur af Indíalandi* ("Verses About Tistran Hrobjart, Son of the Duke of Burgundy, and Queen Indiana, Daughter of the Ruler of India"). The work, which consists of seventeen *rímur*, has been published only in part. The author's revised version (ca. 1850) of the *rímur* written in 1844 is preserved in his own manuscript (Lbs 982 8vo) in the National Library, Reykjavik. [MEK]

Níels Jónsson. *Tistrans rímur og Indíönu*. In *Sýnisbók íslenzkra rímna: Specimens of Icelandic Rímur*, selected by William A. Craigie. Reykjavik: Leiftur, 1952, Vol. 3, pp. 195–98.

NINE WORTHIES (*les neuf preux*), a group of historical personages considered to be particularly worthy of admiration or veneration. First formulated during the early fourteenth century, in Jacques de Longuyon's *Les Voeux du paon*, the list comprises three pagans (Hector, Caesar, Alexander), three Christians (Arthur, Charlemagne, Godefroy de Bouillon), and three Jews (Joshua, David, Judas Maccabeus). The notion of the Nine Worthies quickly gained popularity and provided material for numerous poets, such as Guillaume de Machaut, Eustache Deschamps, and the anonymous author of the Alliterative *Morte Arthure*, in which this motif is joined with that of the Wheel of Fortune: in a dream, Arthur sees the wheel to which the other eight are attached, and it is revealed that he will be the ninth, distinguished but doomed. Perhaps predictably, the Worthies were soon joined, as the result of Deschamps's inventiveness, by Nine Female Worthies but then also, less predictably, by a tenth male: Bertrand du Guesclin, the great Breton warrior. Once integrated into the Nine Worthies group, Arthur served (e.g., in vernacular history writing) along with the others as an example of glory, valor, and splendor, although it was most often his image as warrior that engaged the interest of authors and artists. The entire group, or the trio of Christian Worthies alone, frequently appeared in the visual arts. The best-known example is the Nine Worthies tapestry now in the Metropolitan Museum (Cloisters), New York. Other examples are a series of mural paintings in the castle of La Manta, Piedmont (early fifteenth century); a series of three windows in the Lüneburg Rathaus; frescoes in Dronninglund, Denmark (shortly after 1500), and at Sion, Switzerland; woodcuts in the Hôtel de Ville of Metz (mid-fifteenth century); tapestries in the château of Langeais (Loire Valley, sixteenth century); and a number of manuscript miniatures. [NJL]

64. Cloisters Tapestry: Arthur as one of the Nine Worthies. (The Metropolitan Museum of Art, The Cloisters Collection; Munsey Fund, 1932.)

Tyson, Diana B. "King Arthur as a Literary Device in the Fourteenth Century." *Bibliographical Bulletin of the International Arthurian Society*, 33 (1981), 237–57.

NORMAN, DIANA, English novelist who wrote *King of the Last Days* (1981), a historical novel that revolves around the attempt of a prioress, a knight, and a monk to deliver

Excalibur, discovered when Arthur's grave is unearthed at Glastonbury, to the ailing and beleaguered King Henry II of England. [ACL]

Norman, Diana. *King of the Last Days*. London: Hodder and Stoughton, 1981.

NORMAN, ELIZABETH, tells the story of the young Igraine in a slight and fanciful romance novel, *Silver, Jewels and Jade* (1980). More fairy tale than fantasy, the story's major Arthurian element is found in Merlin, whose magic supports the heroine against the plotting of a sorceress-stepmother. [DN]

Norman, Elizabeth. *Silver, Jewels and Jade*. New York: Ballantine, 1980.

NORTON, ANDRE (or André; legal name change from Alice Mary Norton), author of *Merlin's Mirror* (1975), which retells the story of Merlin and Arthur as science fiction. Merlin is the product of cross-breeding with alien beings, and his powers are attributed to extrasensory perception. Here, as elsewhere in her extensive canon, Norton focuses on the alienated and powerful outcast (often as the shaman), human ambivalence, and emotional dilemmas. In her juvenile fantasy *Steel Magic* (1965), three children enter Avalon and recover the talismans of power stolen from Merlin, Arthur, and Huon of the Horn. In "Pendragon: Artos, Son of Marius," a tale from a companion volume, *Dragon Magic* (1972), four boys of different nationalities assemble appropriately matched dragon puzzles, one of which takes Artie Jones into historical Britain to participate in the rise, fall, and secret burial of Artos, the Pendragon and *dux bellorum*. *Witch World* (1963), the first volume of Norton's most extensive and most emulated series, uses the Siege Perilous to transport Simon Tregarth from a deadly, post-World War II world to another realm, the magical and matriarchal Witch World, to find his true home and destiny. *Huon of the Horn* (1951) is Norton's adaptation of Sir John Bourchier's *Boke of Duke Huon of Burdeux* (1534), a portion of the Charlemagne cycle. In it, Huon and Arthur amicably resolve the rule of the Land of Faery in anticipation of King Oberon's passing. [RCS]

Norton, Andre. *Huon of the Horn, Being a Tale of that Duke of Bordeaux Who Came to Sorrow at the Hand of Charlemagne and Yet Won the Favor of Oberon, the Elf King, to His Lasting Fame and Great Glory*. New York: Harcourt, Brace, 1951.

———. *Witch World*. New York: Ace, 1963.

———. *Steel Magic*. Cleveland: World, 1965 (later title: *Grey Magic*, 1967).

———. "Pendragon: Artos, Son of Marius." In *Dragon Magic*. New York: Crowell, 1972.

———. *Merlin's Mirror*. New York: DAW, 1975.

Schlobin, Roger C. *Andre Norton: A Primary and Secondary Bibliography*. Boston: G.K. Hall, 1980.

———. "The Witch World Series by Andre Norton." In *Survey of Modern Fantasy Literature*, ed. Frank N. Magill and Keith Neilson. La Canada, Calif.: Salem, 1983, Vol. 5, pp. 2139–49.

NOSSACK, HANS ERICH (1901–1977), transposes the familiar motifs of Gottfried's *Tristan* to postwar Germany in his deceptively simple novel *Spätestens im November* (1955). When the predestined love between a writer and a rich industrialist's wife, both outsiders, remains unopposed and therefore mundane in our tolerant society, the lovers seek to transcend their unfulfilling life and love through death. [RWK]

Nossack, Hans Erich. *Spätestens im November*. Berlin: Suhrkamp, 1955. (Published in the U.S. as *Wait for November*. New York: Fromm, 1982.)

Batts, Michael S. "Tristan and Isolde in Modern German Literature: L'Éternel Retour." *Seminar*, 5 (1969), 79–91.

NOVELLINO, IL (or *Cento Novelle Antiche*), a collection of short tales written by an anonymous Florentine ca. 1300. Materials are drawn from classical mythology, the Bible, medieval legends, miracle stories and saints' lives, and historical anecdotes both ancient and medieval. Five tales focus on Arthurian matters. In No. 26, Merlin, appearing as an isolated seer, rebukes a woman for encouraging her husband's sinful usury in order to buy herself a dress. In No. 45, Lancelot fights with the Saxon knight Alibano, who, on discovering the identity of his foe, laments, "Your name undoes me more than your prowess." In No. 63, King Meliadus frees his own enemy, who, without recognizing Meliadus, has defended the king's superiority over himself. In No. 65, Tristan and Isotta, perceiving that King Mark is watching their tryst from a pine-tree, deceitfully convince him of their innocence. No. 82 ("Damigella di Scalot") describes the death of the Lady of Scalot. There is also a reference in No. 28 to the story of Lancelot's riding on the cart of shame. [JLS]

Segre, Cesare, ed. "Il *Novellino*." In *La prosa del Duecento*, ed. Cesare Segre and Mario Marti. Milan: Riccardo Ricciardi, 1959, pp. 793–881.

D'Ancona, Alessandro. "Del Novellino e delle sue fonti." *Studi di critica e storia letteraria*, 2 (1912), 2–163.

Gardner, Edmund G. *The Arthurian Legend in Italian Literature*. London: Dent, 1930, pp. 88–94.

Viscardi, Antonio. "Arthurian Influences on Italian Literature from 1200 to 1500." In *Arthurian Literature in the Middle Ages*, ed. Roger Sherman Loomis. Oxford: Clarendon, 1959, pp. 419–29.

NYE, ROBERT, author of *Merlin* (1978), a bawdy, farcical *tour de force* in four books (Black, White, Red, and Gold). Narrated by Merlin from the crystal cave, the book recounts his own and Arthur's conception, birth, and Grail quest in surrealistic, phantasmagoric vignettes, transformed by the alchemy of language into a psychology of sexual fantasy. Earlier, Nye had published the juvenile novel *Taliesin* (1966), an accomplished account of the rebirth of Gwion as Taliesin and of his career as a court poet, drawn from the *Mabinogi* and the Welsh poems of Taliesin. Nye also published an Arthurian poem, "To Hell with the Graal!" (1961), a complicated dialogue between Parsifal and "Merrymaid" about the meaning of the Graal and what kind of quest will achieve it, if it exists outside of choice itself. [MAG/PCB]

Nye, Robert. *Juvenilia I*. Northwood, Middlesex: Scorpion, 1961.

———. *Taliesin*. London: Faber and Faber, 1966.

———. *Merlin*. London: Hamish Hamilton, 1978.

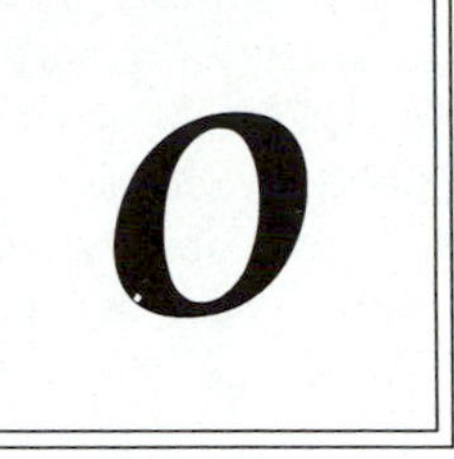

OGIER LE DANOIS, ROMAN D', a long fourteenth-century French verse composition that tells the traditional story of Ogier, known through epic poems, and then appends the account of his shipwreck and subsequent adventures on an island inhabited by Arthur and his knights, as well as by Morgan, who offers him perpetual youth and her love. The text was prosified during the fifteenth century, but both verse and prose remain unedited. [NJL]

Togeby, Knud. *Ogier le Danois dans les littératures européennes.* Munksgaard: Danske Sprog- og Litteraturselskab, 1969, pp. 140–54.

OLD SWEDISH LEGENDARY contains legends about Christ, the Virgin Mary, and the saints and was presumably composed by a Dominican friar at the end of the thirteenth or the beginning of the fourteenth century. The *Legendary* is arranged in chronological order, and a curious anecdote about King Arthur is injected between the legends of St. Ursula (ca. 452) and St. Remigius (ca. 500). After an introductory section that relates how Arthur died, an exemplum is told about a knight named Walwanius (Gawain), who appears one Midsummer's Eve to a priest in his sleep and invites him to attend an Arthurian feast. The feasting ends, however, with a battle in which all are slain. The priest is told that this is a daily ritual to which King Arthur must submit until the Day of Judgment because in life his deeds had been performed for worldly gain. The priest is instructed to have chalices made from King Arthur's golden goblets. When he awakes, he finds the vessels and does as Walwanius has bidden him. The tale of warriors who are slain each day, rise up to feast, and then battle once more is presumably modeled after the Norse myth of the slain warriors who are taken to Valhalla, where they engage in battle each day but feast at night. [MEK]

Stephens, George, ed. *Ett forn-svenskt Legendarium.* Stockholm: Norstedt, 1858, Vol. 2, pp. 685–86.
Cross, J.E. "King Arthur in the Old Swedish Legendary." *Medium Ævum*, 30 (1961), 80–88.

O'MEARA, WALTER (ANDREW) (1897–?), advertising copywriter, journalist, and author of the historical novel *The Duke of War* (1966), in which events surrounding Arthur's victory at Badon are chronicled by a young Romano-British girl. Since her villa is used as Arthur's campaign headquarters, she is well placed to observe his domestic, as well as his military and political, problems. [RHT]

O'Meara, Walter. *The Duke of War.* New York: Harcourt, Brace and World, 1966.

ORMEROD, JAMES (1883–1947), author of three Arthurian poems. "Tristram's Tomb," a ballad, describes how "Iseult of Ireland now hath wed/Sir Tristram in Death's orat'ry," their union symbolized by the embracing briar rose. "Meliagrance and Guenevere," a blank-verse drama in two scenes, relates the consequences of Guenevere's maying. "St. Joseph of Arimathea," a closet drama in blank verse, gives Joseph's account of the Crucifixion, Easter morning, Pentecost, and the eventual transference of the Grail to Glastonbury. [MAW]

Ormerod, James. *Tristram's Tomb and Other Poems.* London: Mathews and Marrot, 1928.

OSTROGA, YVONNE, author of *Quand les fées vivaient en France* ("When Fairies Lived in France," 1923), a collection of children's tales about the magical fairies of France, particularly Brittany. Most of the stories are Arthurian. Some focus on Viviane's adventures in Brocéliande, including her caring for the baby Lancelot and her marriage to Merlin; others treat Morgane, who learns her magic from Merlin. Allusions are made to Arthur, Gauvin, Lanval, and Genièvre. [BTL]

Ostroga, Yvonne. *Quand les fées vivaient en France.* Paris: Hachette, 1923.

OTRANTO MOSAIC. King Arthur, identified by the inscription *Rex Arturus*, is represented as wearing a crown, holding a scepter or club, riding on a goatlike animal, and confronting a giant cat (possibly the Capalus, or giant cat of Lausanne) among the Old Testament figures on the floor mosaic in the nave of the Norman cathedral of Otranto, Italy. The mosaic was made in 1165 by the priest Pantaleone, at the request of Archbishop Jonathan. In a section of the mosaic depicting the history of humanity beginning with Adam and Eve, King Arthur appears with Cain and Abel and has been interpreted as an allegory on the fall and subsequent impurity of humankind. The goat-riding figure may also represent Arthur as a supernatural or fairy king, part of the legend of the immortal Arthur who dwelt in a magical subterranean kingdom entered through a cave (or Mount Etna) in Sicily. [MS]

Gianfreda, G. *Il mosaico pavimentale della Basilica Cattedrale di Otranto*, 2nd ed. Casamari, 1965.

Haug, Walter. *Das Mosaik von Otranto: Darstellung, Deutung und Bilddokumentation*. Weisbaden: Reichert, 1977.

Loomis, Roger Sherman, and Laura Hibbard Loomis. *Arthurian Legends in Medieval Art*. London: Oxford University Press, 1938, p. 36; figs. 9, 9a.

Petrucci, Alfredo. *Cattedrali di Puglia*. Rome: Bestetti, 1960, pp. 97–98.

OWAIN (or *The Lady of the Fountain*), probably dating to the thirteenth century, is one of three Middle Welsh prose tales commonly referred to as "the three romances," the others being *Geraint and Enid* and *Peredur*. All three have some as-yet-undefined relationshp with romances by Chrétien de Troyes—*Yvain*, *Erec et Enide*, and *Perceval*. It has been claimed that the Welsh tales derive directly (either by formal translation or by retelling from memory) from the French; another view is that both Welsh and French texts stem from a common Old French source that was itself based on Welsh or Breton materials. Other critics see the three Welsh tales as having a single author who used dynastic themes reflecting sovereignty myths for patriotic purposes and whose work underlies Chrétien's poems, though the Welsh stories in their extant forms reveal French influence. In fact, the three Welsh stories differ in the extent of their resemblance to the French, and they are best examined separately. It should be emphasized that none can be shown to be a word-for-word translation and that stylistically all are excellent examples of traditional Middle Welsh prose writing. *Owain* is the story of the defeat by one of Arthur's knights of the Knight of the Fountain and his subsequent marriage to the widow, the Lady of the Fountain. His return to Arthur's court leads to his forgetting his wife, but the realization of his neglect causes him to lose his reason. He is restored to health, overcomes adversaries with the help of a lion, and regains his position as knight and husband. The theme of the "romance" appears to be Owain's path to critical self-awareness and maturity. Such a theme, together with the courtly setting, places this story in a different category from most other Middle Welsh tales and suggests strongly that it is an attempt to adapt chivalric romance to the conventions of the native Welsh narrative tradition. [BFR]

Thomson, R.L., ed. *Owain*. Dublin: Dublin Institute for Advanced Studies, 1970.

Jones, Gwyn, and Thomas Jones, trans. *The Mabinogion*, 2nd ed. London: Dent, 1974.

Jarman, A.O.H., and Gwilym Rees Hughes. *A Guide to Welsh Literature I*. Swansea: Davies, 1976.

OWEN, FRANCIS, in *Tristan and Isolde* (1964), adapts the traditional tale for younger readers by providing a happy ending: the lovers are rescued by Palomides and Dinadan, and they live out their lives at Joyeuse Garde, where they are joined by Lancelot and Guenevere after Arthur's death. [RHT]

Owen, Francis. *Tristan and Isolde: A Romance*. Ilfracombe, Devon: Stockwell, 1964.

OXFORD UNION MURALS. In 1857, Dante Gabriel Rossetti was asked by the Oxford Union Committee to design a program of ten murals in the Debating Hall of the new Union Building. Rossetti saw the project as an opportunity to provide an alternative to the frescoes in the Queen's Robing Room. In accordance with John Ruskin's teachings, Rossetti and his staff—Edward Burne-Jones, Arthur Hughes, John Hungerford Pollen, William Morris, Valentine Prinsep, and Rodham Spencer Stanhope—all in sympathy with Pre-Raphaelite ideas, took only materials and lodging for payment.

The design of the building was inappropriate for murals; the second floor walkway, the designated area, was punctuated with large windows, and the excessive illumination forced the artists to whitewash them to see to paint.

Rossetti chose the following subjects from Malory: *King Arthur Obtains the Sword Excalibur from the Lady of the Lake* (Pollen), *The Jealousy of Sir Palomedes* (Morris), *Sir Pelleas Leaving Lady Ettarde* (Prinsep), *Sir Gawain Meets Three Ladies at the Well* (Stanhope), *The Death of Merlin* (Burne-Jones), *The Death of Arthur* (Hughes), *Lancelot's Vision of the Sangrael*, *Lancelot in the Queen's Chamber*, and *How Sir Galahad, Sir Bors and Sir Percival Saw the Sangrael* (all Rossetti). The work began in August 1857, but by November Rossetti left, and the others, excepting Burne-Jones, followed. Only Morris had finished his mural, and painted the ceiling, and Burne-Jones completed his by the following spring. In June 1859, the Union Society hired William and Breton Riviere to finish the work.

Technically, the murals were a disaster. The excessive illumination made viewing impossible, and by 1870 they had deteriorated on the damp, absorbent walls, which had not been treated. The Society asked Morris and Rossetti to advise about restoration; Morris suggested wallpaper, Rossetti, whitewash. Despite a restoration supervised by E.W. Tristram in 1936, the present state of the murals is lamentable. They can be seen only poorly from the infrared photographs taken by John Renton in 1975. The murals are significant for linking the Pre-Raphaelites with Arthurian subject matter and attest their preference for Malory over Tennyson, and for romantic over heroic subjects. [DNM]

Christian, John. *Oxford Union Murals*. Chicago: University of Chicago Press, 1981.

Mander, Rosalie. "Rossetti and the Oxford Murals." In *Pre-Raphaelite Papers*, ed. Leslie Parris. London: Tate Gallery, 1984, pp. 170–83.

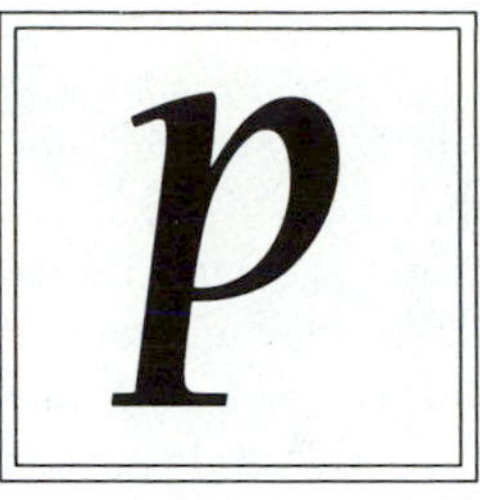

PADMORE, E.S., author of *The Death of Arthur, The Story of the Holy Grail* (1936), a play that covers events from Arthur's marriage to his death. Mordred, a cynical malcontent, seeks to destroy the spiritually minded Arthur by revealing the sin that surrounds him. Though disillusioned, the King retains something of his mystical vision. [RHT]

Padmore, E.S. *The Death of Arthur, The Story of the Holy Grail.* London: Jenkins, 1936.

PAGEANT DESIGN (BRITISH). During the Elizabethan and Jacobean periods (sixteenth and early seventeenth centuries), the cult of chivalry surrounding the monarchs led to renewed interest in the etiquette and mythology of King Arthur and his knights of the Round Table. When Queen Elizabeth visited Leicester at Kenilworth, for example, she was received with a pageant in which Morgan le Fay welcomed her as Arthur's heir. Spectacles produced for the entertainment of the court—tilts, tournaments, barriers, pageants of every kind—adopted the imagery of Arthurian romances. Sir Henry Lee (1533–1611), the Master of the Armory and Queen Elizabeth's personal champion, began a great series of pageants by challenging all comers on the Queen's Accession Day, November 17, 1558. He created a drama at the entry of each contestant to enhance the spectacle in the tiltyard. In the pageant held at Woodstock in 1575, the Faerie Queene made her first appearance. When George Clifford, third Earl of Cumberland, succeeded as champion in 1580, he appeared in the Accession Day pageant as the Knight of Pendragon Castle, and arrived for the tilt on a sham-castle surrounded by Arthurian figures (see Nicholas Hilliard's portrait of the earl in costume for the event). The Accession Day tilts (changed to March 24, after James I's accession in 1603) continued to be held until 1621.

Arthurian imagery inspired the pageants known as the barriers, that is, mock tournaments held in settings made up of mock fortifications. In 1610, for his first public appearance in arms, Prince Henry chose an Arthurian theme. He took the name of Meliadus, Lord of the Isles, and with six companions challenged all comers. As surveyor to the prince, Inigo Jones designed and staged the event, and Prince Henry's barrier was performed in the Banqueting House at Whitehall on Twelfth Night. As the pageant began, the Lady of the Lake was "discovered" in mourning near Merlin's Tomb, bewailing the fall of the House of Chivalry. The scene shifted to a neo-Gothic setting, St. George's portico, where King Arthur appeared and presented the prince with a shield. The prince and his six companions set out to revive knighthood in England, and the tourney began.

The Arthurian imagery chosen by Prince Henry was appropriate, for he was a descendant of King Arthur, or so his father, James I, claimed. For James's triumphal entry into London in 1604, triumphal arches and two seventy-foot pyramids illustrating this claim were erected at the entrance of the Strand. In effect, James was claiming "Arthur's seat," and thus fulfilled Merlin's prophecy of the union of the two kingdoms England and Scotland. Anne of Denmark, queen of James I and a patron of the arts, also commissioned works with Arthurian themes. She introduced the court masque and commissioned Ben Jonson and Inigo Jones to create spectacular entertainments for the court. In the Christmas masque in 1610/11, Prince Henry took the role of Oberon, son of King Arthur and the ruler of the fairy kingdom. The untimely death of the prince in 1612 and his mother in 1619 ended the attempt to combine a neomedieval ideal of chivalry with the new art of the continental Baroque. (*See also* MASQUES.) [MS]

Orgel, Stephen, and Roy Strong. *Inigo Jones: The Theatre of the Stuart Court.* 2 vols. London: Sotheby Parke Bernet, 1973.

Strong, Roy. *Festival Designs by Inigo Jones.* Catalogue, International Exhibitions Foundation, 1967–68.

———. *Artists of the Tudor Court.* Catalogue, Victoria and Albert Museum, London, 1983.

PAIEN DE MAISIÈRES (perhaps a pseudonym parodying the name Chrétien de Troyes), the author of *La Mule sans frein* ("The Mule Without a Bridle"), a brief French romance of 1,136 lines, dating from the time of Chrétien's works or shortly after. The "hero," Gauvain, is more precisely an antihero, as he undertakes (with uncharacteristically single-minded devotion) a quest to recover a bridle. In the process, he undergoes a number of comical trials and remains unaware of far more momentous events unfolding around him. The work is preserved in the same manuscript as *Le Chevalier à l'épée*, which may be by the same author. [NJL]

Johnston, R.C., and D.D.R. Owen, eds. *Two Old French Gauvain Romances*. New York: Barnes and Noble, 1973.

PALAMEDES, a French prose romance of the thirteenth century, predating the cyclic version of the Prose *Tristan*. The work, which is anonymous (although attributed in the prologue to Elie, or Hélie, de Borron), is preserved as part of the *Compilation* of Rusticiano da Pisa and, in fragmentary form, in several manuscripts. The full title of the work (according to some manuscripts) identifies its heroes as Palamedes, Meliadus (the father of Tristan), and Guiron le Courtois. The last two of them play prominent roles, respectively, in the two halves of the romance; in fact, the two parts of the work could be—and often were—considered to be independent texts, and the titles *Meliadus* and *Guiron* (or *Gyron*) *le Courtois* were attached to them.

Palamedes offers stories of an older Arthurian generation, involving the fathers of such figures as Palamedes, Arthur, Tristan, and Erec. The convoluted narrative recounts, among other adventures, the abduction of the Queen of Scotland by Meliadus, who is then attacked by the King of Scotland but aided by Guiron. The latter's lady is abducted but then rescued, and they both are then captured; although he is later freed, she dies in childbirth. The second book continues these series of abductions, battles, and seemingly random adventures. In spite of the apparent formlessness of the work, it achieved remarkable popularity. [NJL]

Gyron le Courtoys. Paris: Antoine Vérard, 1501; repr. with intro. by Cedric E. Pickford. London: Scolar, 1980.
Meliadus de Leonnoys. Paris: Galliot du Pré, 1528.

PALLEN, CONDÉ BENOIST (1858–1929), tells of Launcelot's last years as a penitent monk in over 600 lines of blank verse in "The Death of Sir Launcelot" (1902). Acknowledging the ruin of Arthur's kingdom caused by his sin with Guinevere, Launcelot endures a painful spiritual struggle and is transfigured into a holy man. [DN]

Pallen, Condé Benoist. *The Death of Sir Launcelot and Other Poems*. Boston: Small, Maynard, 1902.

PARCEVALS SAGA, an Old Norse prose translation of Chrétien de Troyes's unfinished *Perceval* (or of roughly the first 6,500 lines; the remainder is preserved separately as *Valvens þáttr*). There is no internal indication of circumstance of origin, but it is assumed that the translation was connected with the court of the Norwegian king Hákon Hákonarson (r. 1217–63), responsible for the translation of *Tristrams saga* and (probably) *Ívens saga*. The primary manuscripts are a vellum from ca. 1400 (one leaf) and a vellum fragment from ca. 1350. Some ten lines of the latter correspond to lines now lost in the former.

Parceval, son of a champion (now deceased) and a captured princess, has been raised in the wilderness. When he is twelve, he meets five knights in the forest, asks one if he is God, learns that King Arthur dispenses the splendid arms, and determines to find this king. His mother gives him a quantity of good advice and sorrowfully parts with him. After meeting a woman alone in a tent and taking from her a kiss and a ring, Parceval proceeds to Arthur's court, where the Red Knight has taken the King's gold goblet, insulted the Queen, and challenged Arthur for his kingdom. Parceval asks Arthur to make him a knight, but Kæi (Kay) tells him to take the arms from the Red Knight. He does so. He then meets Gormanz, who teaches him the use of arms and gives him more good advice. Parceval next rescues Blankiflúr and her castle from a besieging army but must move on to find his mother (he later learns she died). There follows the episode at the Grail castle, with suffering king and Bleeding Lance. Following Gormanz's advice, Parceval does not ask about any of this. After several more encounters, Parceval is brought back to Arthur's court by Valven (Gawain). The story then follows Valven on a series of adventures but returns to Parceval for the Good Friday encounter. Parceval confesses to a hermit, his mother's brother, who tells him about the Grail and admonishes him to go to church. In an abrupt conclusion, Parceval returns to Blankiflúr, marries her, and is always victorious in combat.

The overlapping lines in the two vellums suggest that the original translation was much closer to the French source than either preserved text now is; both show condensation. The saga contains some interesting stylistic effects for emphasis, such as alliteration, assonance, and rhyme, especially at the end of some chapters. [FWB]

Kölbing, Eugen, ed. *Riddarasögur*. Strassburg: Trübner, 1872.
Barnes, Geraldine. "Arthurian Chivalry in Old Norse." *Arthurian Literature*, 7 (1987), 50–102.
Kalinke, Marianne E. *King Arthur, North-by-Northwest*. Copenhagen: Reitzel, 1981.

PARLEMENT OF THE THRE AGES, THE, a fourteenth-century alliterative dream-vision debate (665 lines) written in the North Midlands of England ca. 1350–

90. A young hunter dreams that he overhears a debate among three men: thirty-year-old Youth, sixty-year-old Middle Age, and one-hundred-year-old Old Age. The latter, lecturing the others on the transience of earthly things, describes Arthur among the Nine Worthies, giving a brief summary of his career and death (ll. 462–512) that draws upon both chronicles and the French Vulgate Cycle and includes some details that appear to be original with the author. Gawain, for example, throws Arthur's sword into the lake, and not Girflet (Vulgate *Mort Artu*) or Bedivere (Stanzaic *Le Morte Arthur*). [EDK]

Offord, M.Y., ed. *The Parlement of the Thre Ages*. London: Oxford University Press, 1959.

Gardner, John, trans. *The Alliterative Morte Arthure, The Owl and the Nightingale, and Five Other Middle English Poems*. Carbondale: Southern Illinois University Press, 1971.

PARSAFORESTO, an Italian translation (printed in 1556–58) of the French *Perceforest*. Like its French original, *Parsaforesto* links up Arthurian history with that of Alexander the Great, who installs Arthur's ancestor Parsaforesto as King of Britain. [NJL]

La dilettevole historia del valorosissimo Parsaforesto re della Gran Brettagna, con i gran fatti del valente Gadiffero re di Scotia, vero essempio di Cavalleria. 6 vols. Venice: Tramezzino, 1556–58.

PATERSON, KATHERINE, American author of *Park's Quest* (1988), a children's novel about Park, a young boy whose father has died in Vietnam. His quest is to find information about his father. The action is interspersed with Park's reveries about the Arthurian legend, and his story parallels that of Chretien's Perceval. [ACL]

Paterson, Katherine. *Park's Quest*. New York: Lodestar/Dutton, 1988.

PAUL, EVELYN, translator and illuminator of *The Romance of Tristram of Lyones and La Beale Isoude . . .* (1920). This mostly prose version of the story is taken from the Prose *Tristan* with some episodes derived from the Old French *Queste del Saint Graal*; the author simply gives Lancelot's adventures to Tristan. Paul provides original verse-interludes and pious introductory and concluding passages. The book is most notable for the elaborate embellishment of color plates and illuminated initials. [AAR]

Paul, Evelyn. *The Romance of Tristan of Lyones and La Beale Isoude, Drawn Out of the Celtic French and Illuminated by Evelyn Paul*. London: Harrap, 1920.

PAYNE, JOHN (1842–1916), English poet and translator whose "The Romaunt of Sir Floris" (1870) is based on a Provençal legend found in *Le Violier des histoires Provenciaux*. The Grail poem, in octosyllabic couplets, describes an allegorical dream-journey to a brilliant otherworld garden, ruled by a lord (Christ) whose face can be seen only when the quest is completed. Floris defeats a sequence of monsters; in each case, a beautiful flower (a virtue) blossoms from the monster's blood. Galahad directs Floris to Sarras, where he joins other Grail knights in experiencing the mystic vision. Inspired by the dream, Floris leads a saintly life and achieves salvation. [MAW]

Payne, John. *The Poetical Works of John Payne*. 2 vols. London: Villon Society, 1902.

PEACOCK, THOMAS LOVE (1785–1866), an employee of the East India Company for thirty-seven years, devoted his leisure to writing poetry and novels and cultivating literary friendships. Arthurian interest was first revealed in "Calidore" (ca. 1816), a poetic fragment in which Arthur and Merlin send the protagonist from a classical otherworld to Wales in search of a wife and a disputatious philosopher. "The Round Table; or, King Arthur's Feast" (verse, 1817) describes Merlin's attempt to entertain his bored monarch by summoning to their otherworld castle all subsequent British rulers.

Peacock's major contribution was a satirical-historical romance, *The Misfortunes of Elphin* (1829), set in sixth-century Wales. Peacock's interest in history and legend increased after his marriage to Jane Gryffydh, who made accessible to him materials then unavailable in English translations, such as *The Myvyrian Archaiology of Wales*, the *Mabinogion*, and the *Hanes Taliesin*. The flooding of Gwaelod through Prince Seithenyn's neglect, the mysterious birth and heroic life of the bard Taliesin, and Gwenhyvar's kidnapping by Melvas as told in Caradoc's *Vita Gildae* are combined through the device of an Arthurian court in Caerleon. Bardic songs and Triad materials are also used. Taliesin, the protagonist who links the main characters, effects the rescue of his future father-in-law, Elphin, and of Gwenhyvar. Opportunities for satire arise from ironic comparisons between nineteenth-century England and sixth-century Wales (when people, lacking polluted water and air, paper money, steam engines, and poorhouses, were "lost in the grossness of beef and ale") and from allegorical identifications of Seithenyn's rotten dam with the English constitution, and the "plump, succulent" monastery at Avallon with the Established Church, for example. Comic invention reaches a peak in the characterization of Seithenyn, a gargantuan drunkard who proclaims, "Wine is my medicine; and my quantity is a little more." Peacock was reportedly proud of the fact that Welsh archaeologists treated *The Misfortunes* as a valuable addition to Welsh history. [MAW]

Peacock, Thomas Love. *Calidore and Miscellanea*, ed. Richard Garnett. London: Dent, 1891.

——. *The Misfortunes of Elphin*. London: Hookham, 1829.

——. *Nightmare Abbey, The Misfortunes of Elphin, Crotchet Castle*, ed. Charles B. Dodson. New York: Holt, Rinehart, and Winston, 1971.

Felton, Felix. *Thomas Love Peacock*. London: Allen and Unwin, 1973.

PEARE, CATHERINE OWENS, American author of *Melor, King Arthur's Page* (1963), a work for younger readers. Melor learns from the thoughtless mistakes he keeps making, and he eventually redeems himself by saving Arthur's life from a huge boar named Troynt (Twrch Trwyth). [RHT]

Peare, Catherine Owens. *Melor, King Arthur's Page*. New York: Putnam, 1963.

PÉLADAN, JOSÉPHIN (1858–1918), a French writer who in 1888 was profoundly influenced by Wagner at Bayreuth. From that time on, he considered himself a "priest of the Grail." In 1890, he founded the Order of "la Rose+Croix du Temple et du Graal" ("The Rosy Cross of the Temple and Grail"), of which he was the Grand Master. The purpose of the order was to reinstate the Christian esoteric tradition.

Péladan also instituted "Salons de la Rose+Croix" in an effort to establish a "new chivalry" that would create in France an aesthetic climate analogous to that of Bayreuth. His desire was to foster all idealistic tendencies congenial to legend, myth, and dream. The composer Erik Satie opened the first of these Salons in 1892 by performing the prelude to *Parsifal* on the trumpet.

In 1893, Péladan published *Le Mystère du Graal* ("The Mystery of the Grail") and *De Parsifal à don Quichotte* ("From Parsifal to Don Quixote"), which unfortunately have not had modern editions. These are aesthetic and critical essays, in which the author joins the Grail legend, Wagnerian myth, and eastern traditions in a highly debatable esoteric syncretism. [RB]

Péladan, Joséphin. *Théâtre complet de Wagner*. Geneva: Slatkine, 1981.

David-Neel, Alexandra. *Le Sortilège du mystère*. Paris: Plon, 1983.

Doyon, René-Louis. *La Douleureuse Aventure de Péladan*. Paris: La Connaissance, 1946.

PELLAM, one of the Grail-keepers, appearing first in the *Suite du Merlin*. He is the father of Pelles and Pellinore, great-grandfather of Galahad. Wounded by Balin with the Dolorous Stroke, he is henceforth known as the Maimed King until eventually healed by Galahad. [NJL]

PELLES (of Listeneise), a descendant of Joseph of Arimathea, Pellam's son, Pellinore's brother, Elaine of Corbenic's father, and Galahad's grandfather. In some texts, Pelles is one of the Fisher Kings. In Chrétien's *Perceval*, the name of the Fisher King is never given. The *Perlesvaus* states that Pelles is Joseus's father and Perlesvaus's uncle but does not indicate that he is the Fisher King. In the Didot-*Perceval*, the Fisher King is not Pelles but Bron, Perceval's grandfather. In the Vulgate Cycle and Malory's *Morte Darthur*, Pelles is the Fisher King once again and receives visits from Galahad, Perceval, and Bors during their quests for the Grail. The *Queste del Saint Graal*, however, is inconsistent; we are led to believe that Pelles is the Fisher King but are told at least once that he and the Fisher King are two distinct characters. [SW]

PELLINORE, King of the Isles, brother of Pelles, and father of Lamorak. In some texts, Pellinore is also Perceval's father. While in pursuit of the Questing Beast, Pellinore meets Arthur, who challenges him to a joust. During their joust, Arthur breaks the sword that he had drawn from the stone and is given a replacement, Excalibur, by Merlin and the Lady of the Lake. In the rift that causes the eventual dissolution of the Round Table, Pellinore slays Lot and is later slain by Lot's sons, Gawain and Gaheris. [SW]

PENDRAGON, a title Geoffrey of Monmouth applies to Uther, the father of King Arthur. When there appears a star with a single ray ending in a fireball shaped like a dragon, Merlin associates the star and the dragon with Uther. Having later become king, Uther has two gold dragons made, one for the cathedral of Winchester, the other to take into battle. Geoffrey tells us that thenceforth he is called Uther Pendragon, which in the British tongue means "dragon's head" and which recognizes both his symbol and his sovereignty as chieftain or king. (In fact, the word apparently means "head dragon"—"foremost leader.") In *Arthour and Merlin*, Pendragon is the name of Arthur's brother.

There is a Pendragon Castle in Cumbria, Westmorland, which dates from the twelfth century and is now in ruins; it is sometimes contended, on the basis of the name, that this is the site of an earlier fortification belonging to Uther. [NJL]

Ashe, Geoffrey. *A Guidebook to Arthurian Britain.* Wellingborough: Aquarian, 1980, pp. 166–67.

PENNINC and PIETER VOSTAERT, Middle Dutch authors of the *Roman van Walewein*; they are known exclusively for this work. They are assumed to have been Flemings who wrote their poem in the second half of the thirteenth century. Penninc, the more important of the two, began the romance but stopped after some 7,800 lines. Pieter Vostaert completed the work, which numbers about 11,200 lines and is one of the undisputed high points among Middle Dutch Arthurian romances.

The story deals with Walewein's quest for the Floating Chessboard, which Arthur is determined to acquire. Walewein must fulfill a number of tasks that arise one from the other (King Wonder, for instance, agrees to part with the Floating Chessboard only if Walewein captures the miraculous Sword with the Two Rings for him). This main action is regularly interrupted by sudden challenges to adventure. Walewein always accepts the challenge, completes the adventure, and then resumes the quest for the chessboard. He is assisted on his journey by a speaking fox, Roges, who regains his human shape once Walewein has accomplished his tasks. Eventually, Walewein returns to Arthur with the chessboard and with Roges, as well as his beloved Ysabele.

The *Roman van Walewein* is a fairy tale rewritten into an Arthurian romance, a variant of Aarne-Thompson 550, to which belong Grimm's *Der goldene Vogel* and the story known in Russia as *Of Iwan Tsarewitsj, the Firebird, and the Grey Wolf.*

The *Roman van Walewein* has been transmitted to us complete in a codex dating from 1350 (Leiden, University Library, ltk. 195). The inserted leaf before the beginning of the text contains the well-known miniature depicting Walewein on horseback pursuing the Floating Chessboard. In addition, fragments are preserved at Ghent (University Library, 1629) from the second half of the fourteenth century, containing 388 lines from the *Roman van Walewein*. [BB]

Van Es, G.A., ed. *De jeeste van Walewein en het schaakbord van Penninc en Pieter Vostaert.* 2 vols. Zwolle: Tjeenk Willink, 1957.

Draak, A. Maartje E. *Onderzoekingen over de "Roman van Walewein."* Haarlem, 1936; 2nd ed. Groningen: Bouma, 1975.

PERCEFOREST is a romance of heroic proportions; early editions publish it in six parts, and when it is edited in its entirety, it will occupy some twelve thick octavo volumes (perhaps about 7,000 pages of text), thus being more considerable than either the Vulgate Cycle or the Prose *Tristan*. Its popularity is nevertheless attested by the fact that it survives in French in four manuscripts (only one is complete) and two printed editions of 1528 and 1532, and that it was translated into Italian and Spanish toward the end of the sixteenth century. It was completed in the first half of the fourteenth century, and certainly before 1344, probably by a cleric and clearly at the court of Hainaut. The author's knowledge of the Low Countries is obvious, and the Count of Hainaut himself is credited in an elaborate and misleading prologue with having procured the original, Greek, manuscript from which the romance derives.

"Greek" because the romance's premise brings together two of the great chivalric heroes of the Middle Ages, Alexander the Great and King Arthur. The story, which the writer presents carefully not as fiction but as a chronicle perfectly consistent with Geoffrey of Monmouth, the Alexander legends, the history of Rome, and the Arthurian cycle, is predicated on the contention that Alexander is swept by a storm at sea to the remote island of Britain, where he finds a kingdom riven by dissension, to which he appoints rulers. The dynasties that he founds and the son whom he fathers while in Britain are to be the direct ancestors of King Arthur. This grandiose historical sweep has been lost to view, the author contends, because of successive invasions of the country; it has been his good fortune to rediscover the facts, and his only role has been to embellish the stark historical record.

The audacity of the original conception is matched by the execution. One of the most remarkable features of the romance is the sense of discipline that the writer achieves in controlling his vast canvas. Two distinct matrices are developed. The first is sociopolitical: the history of this pre-Arthurian Britain is presented as a search for political stability and religious purity. Under Perceforest and his heirs, the country undergoes a series of cyclical vicissitudes: ideal chivalric kingdom, invasion and devastation by the Romans under Julius Caesar, regrowth and pacification, new devastation by the Danes. Always in the background, the unscrupulous forces of evil, often using sorcery, threaten the peace and stability that the writer posits as the ultimate political good and preach a dangerous polytheism. Against these forces stand chivalry, courtliness, and an ideal, austere religion preaching a single God. The romance culminates with the coming of the Grail to Britain and the propagation of the new Christian faith. The second matrix is structural. Not only does the romance explain the Arthurian kingdom, it also prefigures it. Thus, for instance, Perceforest introduces the Order of the Franc Palais, which mirrors the Round Table; Perceforest's son Betides, who betrays Britain to the Romans, is a reflection and prefiguration of Mordred; and Gallafur, the perfect knight, prefigures Galahad.

Within the broad sweep of these two guiding threads, the work is a tissue of romance themes and motifs. Quests and tournaments, adventures chivalric and supernatural, proliferate and interlace across some 200 years of supposed history. But these too the writer is able to vary and animate: he has an endlessly inventive fantasy and a lively sense of the ridiculous, and his huge cast of characters includes a number who are vividly imagined and original, from the accident-prone Estonné to the delicate and subtle young girl Lyriope, from the Rabelaisian child Passelion to the Puck-like Zéphir. It is a measure of the writer's remarkable success that the reader's sympathies engage with the heroes and heroines, and that we arrive at the end of the sixth book breathless perhaps, but neither lost nor bored. [JHMT]

Taylor, Jane H.M., ed. *Le Roman de Perceforest, première partie*. Geneva: Droz, 1979.

Roussineau, Gilles, ed. *Perceforest, quatrième partie*. 2 vols. Paris and Geneva: Droz, 1987.

———, ed. *Perceforest, troisième partie*. Paris and Geneva: Droz, 1988.

Lods, Jeanne. *Le Roman de Perceforest: origines, composition, caractères, valeur et influence*. Geneva: Droz, 1951.

PERCEVAL (Parsifal, Parzival, Perchevael, Pressivalle), introduced in the *Conte del Graal*, by Chrétien de Troyes, but obviously related to the hero of the Welsh *Peredur*. In Chrétien's text, he makes a rapid, if painful, transition from bumpkin to Grail hero. His mother has kept him ignorant of chivalry, which she blamed for his father's death; once he learns of the existence of knights, however, he disregards his mother's grief and leaves for Arthur's court. He receives some basic chivalric instruction from Gornemanz and soon embarks on his first adventures. As a guest in a strange castle, he is witness to the Grail procession, but having been advised to talk little he does not inquire about what he sees. Later, he learns that his question would have cured the infirm Fisher King. He sets out to expiate his sin, but the unfinished state of Chrétien's romance prevents him from completing his quest. Throughout the work, Perceval shows himself to be precocious in the acquisition of chivalric skills but deficient in responsibility and understanding.

In the Continuations of Chrétien's *Conte del Graal*, Perceval meets first with partial success (in the Second Continuation) and is then crowned Grail King (in the Third). In the Didot-*Perceval*, the young man has the same brashness he had demonstrated in Chrétien, but the charm and naiveté that had characterized him earlier are lacking. Despite the modification of his character, this romance and others (e.g., the Prose *Joseph* and *Merlin*) trace his success in bringing the quest to a conclusion and curing the Fisher King.

Perceval was initially a popular figure, giving rise to a number of other works, for example, the *Parzival* of Wolfram von Eschenbach and the Middle Dutch *Perchevael*, a literal translation of Chrétien's work. With the Vulgate, however, authors began to focus on other heroes, and perhaps because Perceval was tainted by sin (with Blanchefleur, as well as in the Grail castle), Galahad replaced him as the perfect Grail knight.

In Wagner's opera, Parsifal is the Pure Fool, whose role as the Grail knight is long unrecognized either by the young man himself or by those around him. His destiny in Wagner requires absolute purity, including sexual abstinence, a condition not imposed on him in most earlier traditions.

Various modern treatments of Perceval have shown him either rejecting his messianic role (e.g., Richard Monaco) or failing to achieve his goal and expressing serious doubts about himself (e.g., Jim Hunter.) In a number of instances, writers (notably T.S. Eliot) have been drawn less to Perceval himself than to the theme of the Wasteland. (*See also* PEREDUR.) [NJL]

Owen, D.D.R. "The Development of the Perceval Story." *Romania*, 80 (1959), 473–92.

Weston, Jessie L. *The Legend of Sir Perceval: Studies upon Its Origin, Development and Position in the Arthurian Cycle*. 2 vols. London: Nutt, 1906, 1909.

PERCHEVAEL, a Middle Dutch translation of Chrétien de Troyes's *Perceval* (*Le Conte del Graal*) originating in the first half of the thirteenth century. Of this translation, some 1,150 lines have been preserved, the majority in fragments dating from the last quarter of the thirteenth century (Liège, University Library 1333). The other fragments are kept in Brussels (Royal Library II 115–2), Prague (Museum of National Literature 392/zl), and Düsseldorf (Landesund Stadtbibliothek F. 23).

A much-abridged version of this translation (relating only the adventures of Walewein) is included in the *Lancelot-Compilatie*, followed by an adaptation of the first part of the anonymous Old French First Continuation of Chrétien's romance. Moreover, new episodes are inserted to adjust the *Perchevael*-translation to the compositional properties of the *Lancelot-Compilatie*. The *Perchevael* in the *Lancelot-Compilatie* comprises almost 6,000 lines. [BB]

Gysseling, Maurits, ed. *Corpus van Middelnederlandse teksten (tot en met het jaar 1300)*, II, 1. The Hague: Nijhoff, 1980, pp. 501–19.

Jonckbloet, W.J.A., ed. *Roman van Lancelot*. 2 vols. The Hague: van Stockum, 1846–49, pp. 247–84.

Fuehrer, M.R. *A Study of the Relation of the Dutch Lancelot and the Flemish Perchevael Fragments to the Manuscripts of Chrétien's "Conte del Graal."* Diss., University of Washington, 1939.

PERCY, THOMAS (1729–1811), an antiquarian bishop whose historically significant *Reliques of Ancient English Poetry* (1765) included six Arthurian ballads. "Sir Lancelot du Lake" (124 lines) recounts Lancelot's battle with Tarquin (Malory, Book VI, Chapters 7-9). "The Boy and the Mantle" (196 lines) describes chastity tests at Arthur's court. "The Marriage of Sir Gawain" (160 lines) retells the Middle English romance *The Wedding of Sir Gawain and Dame Ragnell*. In "King Ryence's Challenge" (42 lines), sung before Queen Elizabeth at Kenilworth in 1575, the Welsh king demands Arthur's beard to decorate his mantle. "King Arthur's Death" (184 lines) closely follows Malory's account from Gawain's dream to the King's departure. "The Legend of King Arthur" (96 lines) reproduces Geoffrey of Monmouth's account of Arthur's genealogy and wars. [MAW]

Percy, Thomas. *Reliques of Ancient English Poetry Consisting of Old Heroic Ballads, Songs and Other Pieces of Our Earlier Poets*. 3 vols. London: Dodsley, 1765.

Davis, Bertram H. *Thomas Percy: A Scholar-Cleric in the Age of Johnson*. Philadelphia: University of Pennsylvania Press, 1989.

PERCY, WALKER (1916–1990), American physician and author of *Lancelot* (1978), which transposes the Grail quest into the contemporary world of filmmaking. The predicament of the narrator-hero, Lancelot Lamar, who has watched his early promise and idealism fade after an unhappy marriage, reflects the spiritual wasteland that is modern America. He seeks escape in alcohol, just as others do in the illusion provided by Hollywood. Viewing himself as the "Knight of the Unholy Grail," Lancelot sets out to expose the corruption that lies behind the glittering façade. This he achieves by recording on videotape the sexual promiscuity of both his wife and daughter. Since he is so deeply corrupted by the very sins that he condemns, however, he too is destroyed in the final cataclysm. This is a symbolic novel, and the Arthurian borrowings, which include the figures of Merlin and Percival, deepen the significance of the symbols. The powerful vision of spiritual desolation in the modern world gives fresh meaning to the myth of the Grail quest. [RHT]

Percy, Walker. *Lancelot*. New York: Farrar, Straus and Giroux, 1978.

Bugge, John. "Arthurian Myth Devalued in Walker Percy's *Lancelot*." In *The Arthurian Tradition: Essays in Convergence*, ed. Mary Flowers Braswell and John Bugge. Tuscaloosa: University of Alabama Press, 1988, pp. 175–87.

PERCY, WILLIAM ALEXANDER (1885–1942), puts Arthurian material to fanciful use in several poems in *Enzio's Kingdom* (1924). "In the Cold Bright Wind" is a brief lyrical account of Merlin's passing to Fairyland, and "The Green Bird Seeth Iseult" is a colorful impression of the drinking of the love potion. The romance of Tristan and Iseult also provides a counterpoint to a modern love story in "A Brittany Idyll." [DN]

Percy, William Alexander. *Enzio's Kingdom and Other Poems*. New Haven: Yale University Press, 1924.

PEREDUR, one of "the three Welsh romances" probably dating from the thirteenth century. (The others are *Geraint and Enid* and *Owain*). Peredur is brought up by his mother, in the company of females and far from chivalric society, in an attempt to protect him from the dangers of knightly pursuits and tournaments, which have killed his father and brothers. The appearance of three knights kindles the boy's imagination, and he makes his way to Arthur's court to be dubbed. His rustic appearance and naiveté create welcome relief at court. Setting out to avenge Cei's insult to a dwarf, Peredur undergoes a series of adventures that bring out his innate chivalry; but his education is continued at the courts of two of his uncles. The first uncle, who is lame, advises him never to enquire about the significance of what he sees. At the court of the other, he sees being carried in procession a bleeding lance and a head upon a salver. More adventures follow, including a period spent at the court of the witches of Caerloyw, who instruct him in arms, before he returns at last to Arthur's court. Peredur embarks upon another round of adventures culminating in a period of fourteen years when he rules with "the empress of great Constantinople," an episode that contains many clear remnants of a sovereignty myth. The story returns abuptly to Arthur's court, where Peredur is berated by a loathly damsel for failing to ask the meaning of the marvels he saw at his uncle's castle, for that question would have restored the king to health and the land to prosperity. After many adventures, it is revealed that the witches of Caerloyw had beheaded Peredur's cousin and lamed his uncle and that Peredur has been fated to avenge them. In spite of the story's obvious resemblances to Chrétien de Troyes's *Perceval*, the differences are nevertheless striking. The order of events is changed, the head upon the salver replaces the Grail, and the episodes culminating in the fourteen years' sojourn with the empress are not found in the French version. Independent references show that Peredur was a figure well established in Welsh tradition, and it is possible that *Peredur* is a retelling in Welsh of material found in, or used by, Chrétien, combined with independent folklore and dynastic traditions about the hero. The Grail and its attendant mysteries are represented in Welsh by the head, and the tale becomes one of vengeance for the slaying of a kinsman. [BFR]

Goetnick, Glenys, ed. *Historia Peredur vab Efrawc*. Cardiff: University of Wales Press, 1976.

Jones, Gwyn, and Thomas Jones, trans. *The Mabinogion*, 2nd ed. London: Dent, 1974.

Bollard, John K. trans. "The Story of Peredur Son of Efrog." In *The Romance of Arthur II*, ed. James J. Wilhelm. New York: Garland, 1986.

Jarman, A.O.H., and Gwilym Rees Hughes. *A Guide to Welsh Literature I*. Swansea: Davies, 1976.

PERILOUS CHAPEL, in Malory's *Morte Darthur* (Caxton, Book IX), a chapel that has been taken over by the sorceress Hellawes, in order to entrap Lancelot. While riding in the forest, Lancelot encounters the knight Sir Meliot de Logres, who has been mortally wounded and whose bleeding can be staunched only with a piece of the shroud of the dead knight who lies in the Perilous Chapel. Despite many harrowing adventures, Lancelot bravely rides to the chapel, obtains a small piece of the shroud, and heals the wounded knight. [SW]

PERILOUS SEAT (Siege Perilous, Siège Périlleux), a vacant seat at the Round Table, to be occupied eventually by the knight destined to accomplish the Grail quest. In the Didot-*Perceval*, Perceval sits there, causing darkness and the splitting of a stone, whereupon a voice rebukes Arthur for permitting this act. As the *Queste del Saint Graal* informs us, Galahad is the knight for whom the seat is reserved. (*See also* ROUND TABLE.) [NJL]

***PERLESVAUS*,** an early Old French Grail romance in prose, dating from the beginning of the thirteenth century. It is extant in three manuscripts, two fragments, and an early printing. The name of the hero, Perlesvaus, is a variant of Perceval, explained as *perd-les-vaux* ("to lose the vales") of Kamaalot, his heritage.

The plot is too lengthy and complex to summarize, but it involves a pilgrimage by Arthur to Cornwall to repent of his inactivity and the lengthy adventures of Gauvain (who sees the Grail and Lance but fails to ask the question), of Lancelot (including one of the Beheading Test analogues of *Sir Gawain and the Green Knight*), and of Perceval (who avenges his mother and frees the Grail castle from the King of Castle Mortal). The end of the romance concerns a political intrigue, in which Brien des Illes is the central villain, and the story of Perceval's retirement from the world.

The *Perlesvaus* follows Robert de Boron's *Joseph* in that the Arthurian story, and in particular the quest for the Grail, is interpreted in a religious spirit. Here, the spirit is militant

65. Edward Burne-Jones, The Grail (frontispiece for The High History of the Holy Grail [*Perlesvaus*]; trans. Sebastian Evans). (Courtesy of The Newberry Library, Chicago.)

and is dominated by the opposition of the New Law and the Old Law, of Christians and heathens. The religious spirit is mixed with a large dose of the supernatural and savage bloodshed, which gives the whole romance a wild and anarchic feeling. Symbolism and allegory are also prevalent. In some ways, the *Perlesvaus* is unconventional: it contains, for example, the only full-length account of Arthur and Guenevere's legitimate son, Loholt, whose death causes the Queen to die of grief, thereby modifying Lancelot's subsequent behavior considerably.

The author seems to have known Chrétien de Troyes's *Perceval*, its early Continuations, and the work of Robert de Boron, but the romance certainly predates the Vulgate *Queste del Saint Graal*. In its turn, it seems to have influenced the *Mériadeuc* (in the prominent role given to Brien des Illes) and *Fouke Fitz Warin* (in which a whole episode from the *Perlesvaus* was rewritten in verse). There are grounds for associating the romance with Glastonbury Abbey and the British Isles in general. A Middle Welsh adaptation exists under the title *Y Seint Greal*. [KB]

Nitze, William A., and T.A. Jenkins, eds. *Le Haut Livre du Graal: Perlesvaus*. 2 vols. Chicago: Chicago University Press, 1932–37.

Bryant, Nigel, trans. *The High Book of the Grail*. Ipswich: Brewer, 1978.

Kelly, Thomas E. *Le Haut Livre du Graal, Perlesvaus: A Structural Study*. Geneva: Droz, 1974.

PERROS RELIEF, an early-medieval granite relief on a pier in the Romanesque church of St. Efflam in Perros-Guirec on the north coast of Brittany. It illustrates two male figures, one holding a crozier and one nude, spraddled, and displaying large sexual organs. The scene is traditionally considered to represent Arthur and the Irish saint Efflam of Brittany. The saint vanquished a dragon through prayer after Arthur failed to kill the monster in a day-long battle. [MS]

Renouard, Michel. *Art roman en Bretagne*. Rennes: Ouest-France, 1978.

PERSEFORES, HISTORIA DEL NOBLE REY ("Story of the Noble King Persefores"), a late sixteenth-century Spanish translation by Fernando de Mena of the first two parts of the fourteenth-century French Alexander and Arthurian romance *Perceforest*, surviving in an unedited manuscript (Madrid, Biblioteca de Palacio 266–67) bearing the title *La antigua y moral historia del noble rey Persefores y del esforçado Gadifer su hermano, reyes de Inglaterra y Escoçia*. The Mena translation, based perhaps on a manuscript copy and a 1531 imprint of the French in the library of Philip II, tends to abbreviate the French text but at the same time reveals the translator's interest in presenting an accurate and smooth rendering of the original. Although never printed, the *Persefores* forms part of the great vogue of sub-Arthurian chivalric romances in sixteenth-century Spain and Portugal and may have been intended as a mirror of princes and chivalry. [HLS]

Michael, Ian. "The Spanish *Perceforest*: A Recent Discovery." In *Studies in Medieval Literature and Languages in Memory of Frederick Whitehead*, ed. W. Rothwell, W.R.J. Barron, David Blamires, and Lewis Thorpe. Manchester: Manchester University Press, 1973, pp. 209–18.

PHILATELY. On September 3, 1985, to celebrate the fifth centenary of the publication of Malory's *Le Morte Darthur*, the British Post Office issued a set of four stamps on the subject of the Arthurian legend. Designed by illustrator Yvonne Gilbert, they portray Merlin advising King Arthur (17 pence), the Lady of the Lake holding Excalibur (22 pence), Lancelot riding with Guenevere mounted behind him (31 pence), and Galahad experiencing the Grail vision (34 pence).

The legend of the Glastonbury Thorn, said to have taken root on the spot where Joseph of Arimathea thrust his staff into the earth, and to blossom every Christmas Eve, is commemorated in the 13-pence stamp, designed by Lynda Gray and issued as the first of a set of five Christmas stamps on November 18, 1986. The design was used also in the 12-pence stamp, issued on December 2, 1986, as part of the Christmas-mail discount offer.

66. Arthurian stamp, Arthur and Merlin. Yvonne Gilbert, designer (1985).

Of related interest is a set of four stamps designed by Richard Gay and issued on September 29, 1976, to commemorate the 500th anniversary of the establishment of the printing press in Britain by William Caxton. [RHT]

Barden, Mike. "Arthurian Legend." In *Royal Mail Special Stamps, 1985*. London: The Post Office, 1985, pp. 20–22.

———. "Christmas." In *Royal Mail Special Stamps, 1986*. London: The Post Office, 1986, pp. 28–29.

PHILIBIN, AN (pseudonym of John Hackett Pollock), Irish author of *Tristran and Iseult* (1924). Philibin's "Dramatic Poem" centers on the beginning of the love affair, with all of the action taking place on the ship and ending with Brangwaine's prophecy of their fated, immortal love. The poem's blank verse is competently handled, with good use of a storm as a device of pacing and mood. [AAR]

Philibin, An. *Tristran and Iseult: A Dramatic Poem*. Dublin: Talbot, 1924.

PHILIP, NEIL, gathered both familiar and obscure medieval Arthurian stories into his collection for young readers, *The Tale of Sir Gawain* (1987). The Green Knight adventure and Gawain's marriage to the loathly lady are among the stories that a dying Gawain tells his squire at the siege of Lancelot's castle, but there is little attempt to present his reflections on his life. The emphasis is instead on the telling of the stories. [DN]

Philip, Neil. *The Tale of Sir Gawain*. Cambridge: Lutterworth; New York: Philomel, 1987.

PHILLIPS, STEPHEN (1868–1915), best known for romantic dramas like *Paolo and Francesca* (1900), included his blank-verse "Parting of Launcelot and Guinevere" in his *New Poems* of 1908. He paints a Pre-Raphaelite scene in Tennysonian language to evoke the suppressed sexuality of the knight's last meeting with the Queen in the nunnery to which she had retired. [CNS]

Phillips, Stephen. *New Poems*. London: Bodley Head, 1908.

PIERI, PAOLINO (fl. 1300–05). A Florentine writer best known for the *Cronica delle cose d'Italia*, Paolino is also author of *La Storia di Merlino*, a prose text recounting Merlin's youth and recording his prophecies. The prologue explains that the Emperor Frederick had a translator prepare a French text of the Merlin story and that Paolino Pieri is putting that text into Italian. [NJL]

Pieri, Paolino. *Storia di Merlino*, ed. Ireneo Sanesi. Bergamo: Istituto Italiano d'Arti Grafiche, 1898.

PIERRE DE LANGTOFT (d. ca. 1307), author of a *Chronicle* written in Anglo-Norman alexandrines, probably in England. Condensing material from Geoffrey of Monmouth in order to treat the history of England up to the death of Edward I, Pierre condemns Guenevere and praises Arthur as the greatest of kings. [NJL]

Pierre de Langtoft. *The Chronicle of Pierre de Langtoft*, ed. Thomas Wright. 2 vols. London: Longmans, Green, 1866–68.

PINGET, ROBERT, French author of *Graal Flibuste* (1955; definitive edition, 1966). The novel is a curious piece of Arthuriana, if indeed it is Arthuriana at all. The narrator makes a voyage, or undertakes a quest, to a strange land inhabited by fantastic creatures, including a cross between butterflies and monkeys. The country is a wasteland, a land of "desolation and stench," in the middle of which is a castle inhabited by its monarch, Graal Flibuste (an untranslatable name that juxtaposes the Grail with the word for "piracy" or "buccaneering"). The narrator is told that nothing can be done to remedy the aridity of the land (the adjective *impuissant*, reminiscent of the medieval Fisher King, suggesting both "powerless" and "impotent"). If the book narrates a quest, however, it is indeed an odd, even absurd one: it is not clear why the narrator has come there or what, if anything, he is seeking; the journey seems to have no beginning or end; it does not seem to progress, and the character does not see, much less achieve, a Grail. Pinget's novel, a parody of travel narrative, is only a distant, though very imaginative, reflection of the Grail legend, and the overwhelming presence and profusion of "unreal" elements in the strange kingdom serve to cast into doubt the presumed reality of the universe the reader inhabits. [NJL]

Pinget, Robert. *Graal Flibuste*. Paris: Minuit, 1966.

Henkels, Robert M., Jr. *Robert Pinget: The Novel as Quest*. University: University of Alabama Press, 1979.

67. Pisanello, Tournament Scene, mural from the Ducal Palace, Mantua. (Courtesy of Joanna Woods-Marsden.)

PISANELLO (Antonio Pisano, known as; ca. 1395–1455). Only a single series of large-scale paintings depicting an Arthurian romance has survived from early Renaissance Italy: the recently discovered mural cycle in the Sala del Pisanello of the Ducal Palace in Mantua. Commissioned in the late 1440s by the ruler of Mantua, Marchese Lodovico Gonzaga, the frescoes were begun—but left unfinished—by Pisanello, one of the most famous artists of his day. *Sinopie* (drawings on the first layer of plaster) were discovered on three walls of the Sala (or hall), which measures approximately 57 by 31.5 feet, but only one wall reached the point of being partially painted. On the basis of French inscriptions in the *sinopie*, the iconography can be identified as an episode taken from the Prose *Lancelot*. The story chosen by the Gonzaga tells of the hero Bohort's visit to King Brangoire's castle, his participation in a tournament and a banquet, and his love intrigue with King Brangoire's daughter, which results in the conception of Helain Le Blanc.

Inventories of the princely libraries of the Courts of Milan, Ferrara, and Mantua reveal that north Italian princes were avid readers of Arthurian romance during the fourteenth and fifteenth centuries, often preferring the texts in the original language. In the 1407 inventory of the Gonzaga library, for instance, sixty-seven volumes out of a total of 392 codices were in French, of which seventeen were Arthurian prose romances.

Although only the scenes showing the tournament and some of the knights' vows at the banquet have survived in the Sala del Pisanello, suggestive parallels can be drawn between Pisanello's pictorial design for the mural cycle and the narrative techniques, especially that of *entrelacement* or interlacing, of the Vulgate *Lancelot*. Whether deliberately or fortuitously, the thirteenth-century French romance and the fifteenth-century Italian frescoes convey related aesthetic values. [JW-M]

Woods-Marsden, Joanna. *The Gonzaga of Mantua and Pisanello's Arthurian Frescoes*. Princeton, N.J.: Princeton University Press, 1988.

PLATIN, CLAUDE, sixteenth-century French author of *Giglain et Geoffroy*, a prose retelling of the story of Guinglain, taken largely from Renaut de Beaujeu's *Le Bel Inconnu*, but also incorporating narrative elements of *Jaufré*. [NJL]

Platin, Claude. *L'Hystoire de Giglan, filz a messire Gauvain . . . et de Geoffroy de Maience son compaignon, tous deux chevaliers de la Table Ronde*. Lyon: Claude Nourry, [1530?].

PLEIER, DER, author of three lengthy Arthurian romances: *Garel von dem blühenden Tal* ("Garel of the Flowering Valley"), 21,310 short lines in rhymed couplets (the beginning, ca. 100 lines, is missing); *Tandareis und Flordibel* (18,339 short lines mostly in rhymed couplets); and *Meleranz* (12,834 short lines in rhymed couplets). Little is known about the author. He wrote between 1240 and 1270; his rhymes point to Austria, perhaps to the Salzburg area. His pen name probably means "(glass) blower" and perhaps refers metaphorically to his writing technique of using old materials, melting them up, and fusing them into "new" works.

In *Garel*, Ekunaver of Kanadic provokes Arthur and his court by sending his messenger, the giant Karabin, who announces, after a year's term, a campaign of revenge. Arthur accepts this declaration of war. Garel, one of his young knights, follows Karabin in order to explore Ekunaver's lands. On his journey, he becomes involved in several adventures; defeats many knights and princes and helps others, obliging all of them to provide him with troops; and finally frees Queen Laudamie of Anferre from her oppressor, the monstrous Vulganus, and marries her. With his old and new troops, he is able to conquer Ekunaver before Arthur arrives at the battlefield. The hostile parties arrange a reconciliation, there follows a splendid celebration at Arthur's court, several marriages are concluded, and on the battlefield Ekunaver and Garel have a monastery built.

The *Garel* story was meant as a reaction to *Daniel von dem blühenden Tal*, by Der Stricker (ca. 1230). Daniel is an overly cunning and ruthless hero, an antihero in the view of Der Pleier, who raises his own protagonist again to the level of high knightly and courtly ideals.

Tandareis und Flordibel tells how the youthful prince Tandareis of Tandernas and Flordibel, an oriental princess, fall in love at Arthur's court. They cannot admit this publicly, however, because Arthur had assured her that he would kill anybody who wanted to come into the possession of her love. The couple flee to Tandernas. Arthur besieges the castle, and several fights take place. But Gawan is able to bring about a reconciliation between Arthur and the couple under the condition that Flordibel entrust herself to Arthur's wife, Queen Jenover; Tandareis must journey to foreign countries in order to establish himself as a real knight.

In two series of adventures, Tandareis defeats robbers and giants and frees imprisoned knights and ladies, among them the oppressed queen Albiun. Arthur keeps hearing about the young knight's victories and tries to get him back to court, but his attempts fail. He then decides to organize a tournament once a month for a whole year. Tandareis appears three times incognito and wins, every time in a different guise. He is recognized but refuses to return to court. Arthur tries other ways to get him back and finally succeeds. The King and Tandareis come to a lasting reconciliation, the couple is reunited, and after some more complications (other ladies claim Tandareis!) the wedding takes place at Arthur's court, where at a splendid celebration several other couples are also married. Tandareis and Flordibel return to his kingdom, where the coronation feast is celebrated at Pentecost.

Meleranz relates how a prince of France decides to go to Arthur's court at the age of twelve. On his way there, Meleranz encounters the young queen Tydomie of Kameric under a lime-tree. They fall in love, but Meleranz rides on to court. Two years later, he is dubbed a knight; on this occasion, he receives from Tydomie belt, wreath, and clasp, clear signs of her lasting love, and he resolves to return to the place under the lime-tree. On the way back, he gets involved in three interconnected adventures. He is victorious in all three but learns that Tydomie is in danger of being married to King Libers by her uncle Malloas. Meleranz defeats both of them. During a splendid celebration, attended by King Arthur as well as the King of France, the wedding takes place; the narrator predicts that the marriage will be happy and blessed with two sons and one daughter.

Although Der Pleier claims French narratives as sources for his works, none has been found. His achievement appears to consist in recombining narrative plots and motifs found in "classical" Arthurian works by Hartmann von Aue, Wolfram von Eschenbach, Wirnt von Grafenberg, Gottfried von Strassburg, and Der Stricker into new stories that are well constructed and pleasantly narrated. The author also takes most characters from earlier German romances; in doing so, he draws heavily upon the genealogies of Arthur's family and other dynasties that are to be found in Wolfram's *Parzival* and *Titurel*, developing the characters and filling in narrative lacunae. There are strong restorative trends in these works, and a decidedly nostalgic flavor. Der Pleier must have appealed to a reading public well versed in Arthurian fiction. (The popularity of *Garel*, at least, is attested by the murals, ca. 1400, from Schloss Runkelstein that depict scenes from the romance.) He consciously and adroitly establishes a comprehensive but specific narrative world, and the reading or listening pleasure of his public probably consisted mainly in recognizing and enjoying the old in the new as well as the new in the old. Although Der Pleier is not an original writer, he is a fascinating figure particularly because of his revival of Arthurian literature in German lands after several generations of neglect. [PWT]

Pleier, Der. *Garel von dem blüenden Tal*, ed. Wolfgang Herles. Vienna: Halosar, 1981.

———. *Tandareis und Flordibel: Ein höfischer Roman*, ed. Ferdinand Khull. Graz: Styria, 1885.

———. *Meleranz*, ed. Karl Bartsch. Hildesheim: Olms, 1974.

Gottzmann, Carola L. *Artusdichtung*. Stuttgart: Metzler, 1989.

Kern, Peter. *Die Artusromane des Pleier: Untersuchungen über den Zusammenhang von Dichtung und literarischer Situation*. Berlin: Schmidt, 1981.

Riordan, John Lancaster. "A Vindication of the Pleier." *Journal of English and Germanic Philology*, 47 (1948), 29–43.

Schultz, James A. *The Shape of the Round Table: Structures of Middle High German Arthurian Romance*. Toronto: University of Toronto Press, 1983.

POMEROY, FLORENCE M., English poet, brought out her *Tristan and Iseult: An Epic Poem in Twelve Books* in 1958. This blank-verse narrative follows the details of the "complete" story of the two lovers as it is found in Bédier, and it is presented in a deliberately archaic diction composed of extended quasi-Homeric simile and recondite vocabulary. [AAR]

Pomeroy, Florence M. *Tristan and Iseult: An Epic Poem in Twelve Books*. Oxford: Lane, 1958.

POPULAR CULTURE. If the Arthurian legend has attracted many hundreds of important writers, artists, composers, and scholars, it has also permeated popular culture to an extraordinary degree: film and television, comics and cartoons, festivals, objects and memorabilia, the pervasive use of Arthurian names, especially in commercial ventures—these are only a few of the categories under which the subject can be studied. In many cases, it is not possible to draw a definite line between artistic and popular treatments of the legend. A series of Arthurian stamps, for example, were designed as serious art (by Yvonne Gilbert) but were disseminated to the general public.

Literary retellings of Arthur's story, especially for juveniles, and most often illustrated, have traditionally been not only the vehicle by which the King is introduced to successive generations but also objects of popular culture. The same is true of certain films. The Disney version of *The Sword in the Stone* is both art and popular artifact. Most often, films made for television, at least in the United States, are by intent geared more to popular than to high culture; an example is NBC's unfortunate 1990 retelling of *A Connecticut Yankee in King Arthur's Court*, which features a small girl whose "magic" resides in a Polaroid camera.

The frequency with which Arthurian stories find their way into film and especially onto television is evidence of the intimate link that exists between Arthur and popular culture. Animated films and cartoons have often depicted Arthur, his knights, or Merlin. The nature and quality of these offerings vary widely, from the wonderful animation of *The Sword in the Stone* to the series, drawn but barely animated, *King Arthur and the Knights of the Round Table* (early 1980s, from Ziv International, Inc.) to a great many cartoons of a type illustrated by the titles *Bugs Bunny in King Arthur's Court*, *Square Knights of the Round Table*, and *Superboy Meets Merlin*. Although Arthurian themes in these pieces are merely convenient vehicles and not serious subjects, that very fact confirms their currency and their popular acceptance.

Arthuriana have often been celebrated or disseminated by festivals, which in some cases include the performance of serious texts or music, while others, without historical or cultural intent, simply capitalize on those themes or exploit Arthurian names. In the former category are the Glastonbury Festival (inaugurated in 1914 and long since defunct, though revived in 1963 and 1964) and several annual festivals in Normandy or Brittany, such as the "Lancelot du Lac" festival held in July and August at Elven, near Vannes. The less substantial category is represented by the annual Arthurians' Ball in New Orleans, held at "Arthur's Winter Palace": after "Arthur" arrives, Merlin taps ladies with his magic wand to select them as the annual Guenevere and her court. Arthur has turned up in Trinidad. For the 1988 Trinidad Carnival, a band of celebrants wore elaborate costumes with tall gold headdresses, two to three feet in height, depicting King Arthur's sword, embedded in a stone and flanked by two lions rampant. Although such costumes are intended to be disposable, these, fortunately, were saved and included in a traveling Caribbean exhibit.

Many people believe, or simply assume, that the story of Arthur is historically based, and some presumed Arthurian artifacts survive to support those assumptions. During the 1950s, a cup located in a Welsh castle and thought by many to be the Grail came into the possession of an Englishwoman. The vessel, called the Holy Cup of Nanteos, is the object of multiple legends: it may, depending on the particular account, be the Holy Grail or a cup made later from the Cross. Other objects have been promoted as the Grail as well: Genoa, Valencia, and Montserrat all claim it, with Genoa adding that the vessel preserved in a museum there was once owned by King Solomon. A number of objects that commemorate Arthurian scenes or motifs are commercial enterprises, although some of them may have value as decorative art as well. Arthurian jewelry and figurines fall into this group, and two other widely promoted examples are the successful "King Arthur Plates" designed by James Marsh and the Franklin Mint's 1989 promotion of a historically inaccurate Excalibur.

American comics and cartoons constitute one of the fertile sources of popular Arthuriana. In addition to comics of the *Prince Valiant* and *Camelot 3000* variety, Arthurian subjects often appear in humorous strips or cartoons, with the Sword in the Stone being the most popular motif by far.

Such subjects have surfaced often in *The Wizard of Id*, drawn by Brant Parker and Johnny Hart, and Gary Larson's *The Far Side*. Parker and Hart have referred to the necessity to replace the sword in the stone frequently (because young people continue to steal it) or to the marketing of trusses to those who try to remove it. One strip has a carving knife stuck in a meatloaf: the man who can pull it out is destined to be the next cook. Larson, too, uses the sword motif. For example, as a portly, middle-aged, bespectacled woman withdraws the sword to the accompaniment of trumpets played by angels, a character calls, "Stop the music! There's something wrong here!" In another drawing, Arthur rebukes Lancelot and Galahad for sticking gum under the Round Table. Elsewhere, we encounter Camelot—similar to a car lot, but with camels as the commodity. If the humor suffers in narration, these examples nonetheless give an idea not only of the extent to which the creators of such strips are drawn to Arthurian themes, but also of the fact that their readers can be expected to recognize the reference and respond to it. These and other examples also suggest what would be in any event a reasonable assumption: that those readers are most familiar with the Sword in the Stone, but beyond that they are aware of a limited number of Arthurian names (Arthur, Lancelot), places (Camelot), artifacts (the Round Table), and other motifs (Excalibur rising from the lake).

The association of Arthurian names and stories with hundreds of geographical areas and topographical features is treated elsewhere in this volume, but these surely fall also into the category of popular culture as much as folklore or history, particularly because such associations continue to be created. The alignments of menhirs at Carnac, in Brittany, are traditionally explained as the work of St. Cornély; yet residents of the region have occasionally transferred the legend to Merlin instead.

Arthurian names are regularly attached to objects, buildings, and places. One of the most striking instances is the "King Arthur" class of locomotives used on England's Southern Railway from 1925 until the 1960s; in all, seventy-four locomotives carried the names of Arthurian characters and locations (information courtesy of C.N. Smith).

Arthurian nomenclature, however, is most prevalent in the United States. Peter David, in an afterword to his 1987 novel *Knight Life*, points out that "Arthurian" places mentioned in the book—a men's store named Arthur's Court, and the Camelot Building, housing the Lady Guinevere Theatre—correspond to real New York establishments. Examples could be multiplied many times over in New York or in almost any city. St. Louis, for example, boasted in 1990 the Camelot Apartments, Camelot Day Care Center, Camelot Music (a chain), Camelot Pools, and Camelot Residence for Senior Adults. Near the city are the Camelot Coin Laundry and the Camelot Carwash. There is also a Camelot subdivision, and there are streets named Sir Bors Court, Sir Lancelot, Galahad Drive, Guenevere Drive, Isolda, and King Arthur Drive, Court, Lane, and Spur. While Camelot is clearly the most popular of Arthurian names, Merlin, Arthur, Excalibur, Avalon, Pendragon, and others are far from rare; and they may be attached to virtually anything: buildings, jewelry stores, pubs, automobiles (the Excalibur), streets—and, of course, locomotives. Round Table Pizza is a nationwide chain. In 1990 the world's largest hotel opened in Las Vegas; it is named The Excalibur.

Thus, from films and television to stage plays (including a *Merlin* show by magician Doug Henning); from comics, cartoons, and jokes to all sorts of games; from items that properly belong to the decorative arts to others unabashedly created for profit; from local legends and festivals to names of commercial establishments—the legends surrounding King Arthur flourish in the popular culture of Britain and often reach the level of a virtual cult in the United States. The examples offered here are miscellaneous but entirely representative. The King who attracted Geoffrey of Monmouth, Chrétien de Troyes, Malory, and Tennyson also has the power to appeal to the masses. The popular notion of Arthur appears to be limited, not surprisingly, to a few motifs and names, but there can be no doubt of the extent to which a legend born many centuries ago is profoundly embedded in modern culture at every level. (*See also* COMICS; FILMS; FOLKLORE; GAMES; PHILATELY; TELEVISION SERIES; TOPOGRAPHY AND LOCAL LEGENDS.) [NJL]

PORTER, TIM, has written and composed the music for numerous dramatic works based on Celtic myth and legend that have been staged in regional productions throughout Britain. His Arthurian plays include the musical *Sir Gawain and the Green Knight* (1970) and *The Entertaining of the Noble Head* (1973), which joins the myth of Bran to that of Arthur. A darker work than most of Porter's lighter-hearted entertainments, *Trystan and Essylt* (1980) is an operatic treatment of the story with Trystan as a Pictish warrior and his lover one of the Tuatha De Danaan. *The Marvels of Merlin* (1981) incorporates the winning of Olwen into a comic framework of traditional Merlin episodes, and *Lancelot: The Tale of the Grail* (1984) is a verse play enlivened by original plot twists and comic dialogue. [DN]

POST-VULGATE CYCLE (or the *Post-Vulgate Romance of the Grail* or *Roman du Graal*), a rehandling of the Vulgate Cycle of Arthurian prose romances composed between 1230 and 1240 by an anonymous writer but attributed to "Robert de Boron." (Hence, this work was once known as the "pseudo-Robert de Boron" cycle.) The author's aim was to create out of the several branches of the Vulgate a more homogeneous unity, one that would center on Arthur and the Grail rather than on the love of Lancelot and Guenevere.

The Post-Vulgate has not been preserved in its complete form; it has had to be reconstructed from the scattered French fragments that have only gradually come to light and from certain Portuguese and Spanish translations. Like the Vulgate, the Post-Vulgate probably began with a history of the Grail in pre-Arthurian times (the *Estoire del Saint Graal*). To judge from the Galician-Portuguese *Livro de Josep Abarimatia* and the fragmentary Castilian *Josep*, the Post-Vulgate *Estoire del Saint Graal* did not differ substantially from the Vulgate version. This was followed, as in the Vulgate, by the prose rendering of Robert de Boron's *Merlin*. The Vulgate *Merlin* continuation, however, is replaced by a brief account of Arthur's early wars against the rebel kings and the Saxons (adapted from the Vulgate) together with a new series of adventures, including such episodes as Arthur's begetting of Mordred, the revelation of Arthur's parentage, his combat with Pellinor, the obtaining of Escalibor from a hand in the lake, the wars against Rion and Lot, the tragic tale of Balain, the story of Merlin and Niviene, and the adventures of Gauvain, Yvain, and Le Morholt. The Post-Vulgate *Suite du Merlin* was rendered into Galician-Portuguese, Castilian (*El Baladro del Sabio Merlin*, Burgos, 1498; Seville, 1535), and English (Malory's "Tale of King Arthur"); it is known in French in the main from two fourteenth-century manuscripts: the so-called Huth Manuscript (London, B.L. Add. 38117), which like the *Baladro* lacks the account of Arthur's wars against the rebel kings, and the manuscript Add. 7071 of Cambridge University Library, identified by Eugène Vinaver in 1945. Both the Huth and Cambridge manuscripts are incomplete at the end. The conclusion of the adventures of Gauvain, Yvain, and Le Morholt—missing in both but appearing in Malory—was discovered in 1895 by Eduard Wechssler in a fifteenth-century compilation of Arthurian prose romances (B.N. f. fr. 112); a small section of it has also been preserved in a manuscript first identified in 1989 by Monica Longobardi (Imola, Biblioteca Comunale 135, *A.A.*2. 5 n.°9[7]).

No branch corresponding to the Vulgate *Lancelot* formed part of the Post-Vulgate. Referring to the contents of his *livre*, the Post-Vulgate author admits having excluded *la grant hystore de Lanscelot*, as it would have made "the middle portion three times as big as the other two." To supply a transition to the last part of his "book" (versions of the *Queste del Saint Graal* and the *Mort Artu*), he adapted a few relevant incidents from the Agravain section of the Vulgate *Lancelot* and from the first version of the Prose *Tristan* and combined them with his own inventions. This section of the *Suite* (*La Folie Lancelot*), which was discovered in 1957 by F. Bogdanow and which largely bridges the gap between the adventures of Gauvain, Yvain, and Le Morholt and the final section of the romance, is found in B.N. f. fr. 112 and in a late thirteenth-century codex, B.N. f. fr. 12599; a small portion of it has also been preserved in another late thirteenth-century manuscript (Cracow, Biblioteca Jagiellońska, Berol. Gall. F. 188).

The redactions of the *Queste del Saint Graal* and *Mort Artu* that complete the *Roman du Graal* (based on the Vulgate but completely remodeled so as to link up with the earlier portions of the narrative) have been preserved in almost-complete form in Galician-Portuguese (*Demanda do Santo Graal*) and partially in Castilian (*Demanda del Sancto Grial*). Of the French original, the only fragments known for a long time were those incorporated into certain manuscripts of the second version of the Prose *Tristan* and other later compilations, notably B.N. f. fr. 112, 116, 340, and 343. But recently, Monica Longobardi discovered in the State Archives of Bologna a fragment of the Post-Vulgate *Queste* previously known only from the Iberian versions, while F. Bogdanow found in a manuscript in Geneva (Bodmer 105) a considerable section of the Post-Vulgate *Mort Artu* and in another one in Oxford (Bodleian Library, Rawlinson D 874) an extensive section of the Post-Vulgate *Queste*, both including sections similarly hitherto unknown in French.

In the Vulgate Cycle, the combination of such incompatible themes as that of the Grail and Lancelot's love for Guenevere produced an inevitable clash of ideologies. This *double esprit* and the *joie de vivre* so characteristic of the early parts of the *Lancelot* proper are absent from the Post-Vulgate. *Fin'amors* is condemned unequivocally throughout the narrative. The author treats it from a severely ascetic and tragic angle. Influenced no doubt by the mystical theology of St. Bernard of Clairvaux—for whom all faults, even those perpetrated unknowingly, are imputable sins—the Post-Vulgate conceives of Arthur's kingdom as the *roiaume aventureux*, the land in which the monarch and many of his knights are doomed to commit, unwittingly, outrages that the whole country will have to expiate. The two main tragedies to befall the Arthurian world—the adventures of the Grail inaugurated by Balain's Dolorous Stroke and the destruction of the realm brought about by Arthur's incestuous son Mordred—are both interpreted as divine punishment for sins committed inadvertently, through pure mischance.

Structurally, too, the Post-Vulgate is more closely knit than the Vulgate. The author, who conceived his Arthuriad as a whole, was anxious not only to reinterpret Arthurian history but to motivate the various peripeties better than his predecessors had done. He achieved this, like most thirteenth-century prose writers, not psychologically but structurally, supplying the material antecedents of the events to be elucidated. Long narrative sequences begun in the early portions of the *Romance*, notably the *Suite du Merlin*, foreshadow themes in the *Queste* and *Mort Artu*. The sections dovetail to form an indestructible whole.

All this enables us to comprehend the significance of the tripartite division of the *Romance* both on the purely narrative plane and on the symbolic level. The sections cut across those of the Vulgate Cycle: the first part, for example, ends not with the *Estoire del Saint Graal* but in the midst of Balain's adventures. But if we regard the Post-Vulgate as a single "book," the story of Arthur's kingdom—which is also *La Haute Escriture del Saint Graal*, the title significantly given by the author to the *whole* romance—it falls logically into three parts, corresponding to the three phases in the history of the kingdom. First comes the story of Logres before the beginning of the Grail adventures; this ends at the point where Balain sets out on the quest during which he will strike the Dolorous Stroke. The second part shows us Logres suffering for Balain's action. The last part, beginning with the news of the coming of the Good Knight who will achieve the adventures of the Grail, includes not only the *Queste* but also an account of Arthur's death. On the allegorical level, the second part broadly represents the history of the world subsequent to the Fall (Balain's Dolorous Stroke being likened by the author to the sin that renews that of Eve), while the third part symbolizes the world since the coming of Christ to whom Galaad is likened and concludes with a dire warning that if man fails to repent and to abstain from sinning the fate of the world will be similar to that of the Arthurian kingdom. [FB]

Bogdanow, Fanni, ed. *La Folie Lancelot: A Hitherto Unknown Portion of the Suite du Merlin Contained in MSS. B.N. fr. 112 and 12599*. Tübingen: Niemeyer, 1965.

———, ed. *La Queste del Saint Graal et la Mort Artu Post-Vulgate, Troisième Partie du Roman du Graal*. Paris: SATF, 1991.

Bogdanow, Fanni. "The *Suite du Merlin* and the Post-Vulgate *Roman du Graal*." In *Arthurian Literature in the Middle Ages*, ed. Roger Sherman Loomis. Oxford: Clarendon, 1959, pp. 325–35.

———. *The Romance of the Grail: A Study of the Structure and Genesis of a Thirteenth Century Arthurian Prose Romance*. Manchester: University of Manchester Press, 1966.

———. "A Hitherto Unknown Manuscript of the Post-Vulgate." *French Studies Bulletin*, 16 (1985), 4–6.

POVEST' O TRYSHCHANE ("The Romance of Tristan"), known as the *Byelorussian Tristan*, is found in a single manuscript (MS 94) located in the Raczynski Public Library in Poznan, Poland. Written by an anonymous author-translator ca. 1580, this is the only extant Slavic version of the Prose *Tristan*. Despite the statement at the outset that "Here begins the tale of the knights from Serbian books, in particular the famous knight Tristan," no Serbian version is known.

The *Povest' o Tryshchane* can be divided into two parts: the longer first part is faithful to French and Italian texts, especially to the fifteenth-century Italian *Tristano Veneto*, which is considered a direct prototype. In the second part, roughly the last third of the manuscript, the story drastically changes. Interesting new episodes appear; new characters are introduced, and old characters, especially Tristan, undergo transformation. In contrast to other versions, *Povest' o Tryshchane*, particularly in its second part, is characterized not by the love story but by knightly adventures and battle scenes that are at times quite violent. This is an adventure story, and folkloric usages and devices produce the feeling of a Byelorussian story rather than a French romance. [ZK]

Sgambati, Emanuela, ed. *Il Tristano biancorusso*. Florence: Casa Editrice le lettere, 1983.

Veselovskii, A., ed. "*Belorusie povesti o Tristane*. . . ." In *Iz istorii romana i povesti*. Sanktpeterburg, 1888.

Kipel, Zora, trans. *The Byelorussian Tristan*. New York: Garland, 1988.

POWELL, ANTHONY, novelist noted for penetrating depictions of the comedies and tragedies of upper-class life in Britain. In *The Fisher King* (1986), a crippled photographer on a cruise ship is identified as an incarnation of the title character, complete with virginal attendant. The analogy is expanded with the appearance of a Perceval and a Loathly Lady, and ultimately the legend seems to dictate the fate of the major figures. [DN]

Powell, Anthony. *The Fisher King*. London and New York: Norton, 1986.

POWER, NORMAN, Anglican clergyman in Birmingham who wrote *The Forgotten Kingdom* (1970) for young readers. The novel is set in Firland, an imaginary, vaguely medieval land, and includes many Arthurian allusions. It involves Michael, the sixteen-year-old squire to Sir Roland in Arthur's court, who defends the Firlanders alongside the youthful Sir Galahad. The characters swear by the Grail, and the wizard of Firland is a cousin to Merlin.[EB]

Power, Norman. *The Forgotten Kingdom*. London and Glasgow: Blackie, 1973.

POWERS, J(AMES) F(ARL), American writer who won the National Book Award for fiction in 1963 for his novel *Morte D'Urban*, the story of a worldly priest transferred from Chicago to a struggling Minnesota retreat house. In a career that parallels Arthur's, Father Urban has his victories and establishes a new order, but he also experiences betrayal by his champion, and his story ends with an ironic "death." [DN]

Powers, J.F. *Morte D'Urban*. Garden City, N.Y.: Doubleday, 1962.

POWERS, TIM, author of *The Drawing of the Dark* (1979), a fantasy that transforms the Turkish siege of Vienna in the sixteenth century into part of the struggle between good and evil. The former is led by the Fisher King and Merlin, who brings back from Avalon the spirit of King Arthur, temporarily resurrected as an Irish soldier of fortune. The process of his self-discovery is marked by both thoughtfulness and humor. [RHT]

Powers, Tim. *The Drawing of the Dark*. New York: Ballantine, 1979.

POWYS, JOHN COWPER (1872–1963), English-born author of three Arthurian novels, *A Glastonbury Romance* (1932), *Morwyn* (1937), and *Porius* (1951), as well as the marginally Arthurian *Maiden Castle* (1936). Powys's books are concerned as much with metaphysical issues as with event and character; this is quickly established in *A Glastonbury Romance*, Powys's best-known work, which deals with the lives of a family in and around Glastonbury. In the midst of their mundane concerns with business, with inheritances, and especially with love in all of its varieties, they find that they must deal with the powerful ambience of the legendary ruins and with those who seek to exploit the human desire to partake in or perform the miracles associated with the Holy Well of Glastonbury.

A Glastonbury Romance is Arthurian not simply in its Glastonbury setting and its invocation of the magic associated with the Grail but also in the constant permutations of the Arthurian roles among its characters, from the betrayed "ruler" and women who resemble Celtic fays to the eventually mad scholar seeking the truth behind the mysterious "esplumoir Merlin." Powys interweaves the events of this novel with tortuous passages exploring love and, more frequently, sexual freedom. In this, the book, as does *Morwyn*, bears some resemblance to the work of D.H. Lawrence. One of the strengths of the novel is the author's clear-sighted depiction of human frailties even in the midst of his various advocacies. This immense, flawed novel is nevertheless influential in modern Arthurian fiction, most notably in its references to the Great Goddess and the remnants of her influence and religion.

There are similarities between *A Glastonbury Romance* and Powys's novel *Maiden Castle*, although the Arthurian connections are more tenuous in the latter. Powys again superimposes Celtic/Arthurian patterns on daily life in a small town, this time Dorchester, and the title refers to a neolithic earthwork outside the town. Enoch Quirm, the long-lost father of the protagonist, takes the name of Uryen, seeing himself as the present-day channel of the erotic forces he believes were worshiped by the ancient Celts; the tension between his beliefs and the entanglements, mostly erotic, of the other characters forces him into madness and death. In this, he is the counterpart to the mad scholar of *A Glastonbury Romance*.

Morwyn, the least successful of Powys's Arthurian novels, impinges on the Arthurian legend only in that Taliesin and Merlin put in appearances. A fantastic journey through hell experienced by the middle-aged narrator, his dog, and the object of his passion, the young female Morwyn, the novel is a thinly disguised diatribe against the dual oppressors science and religion, both of which, in the narrator's view, torture for the sake of truth.

The action of *Porius* takes place during one week of A.D. 499. Porius, the son of a Romano-Celtic family, decides to join Arthur's cause. His rites of passage are extended: he must free himself from the domination of his parents and of the remnants of the old religion represented by his three aunts, while accepting the burdens laid on him by the mad sorcerer Myrddin Wyllt. His personal struggle is complicated by the conflicts of his village, as an increasingly intolerant Christian community attempts to suppress participation in the rites of the Goddess or of Mithras. Arthur makes one brief appearance (although not to Porius). Taliesin appears as an inspired bard and cook, and Medraut is depicted as already forming treacherous alliances with the Saxons and Arthur's Celtic enemies. *Porius* contains more humor than Powys's other Arthurian fiction: Porius, a young giant of a man, resembles the classic fairy-tale hero, and his dilemmas are viewed with a certain amusement.

The difficulties and infelicities of Powys's prose style will keep his works from the status of great fiction, but they must be reckoned with in any study of twentieth-century Arthurian literature. [AAR]

Powys, John Cowper. *A Glastonbury Romance*. New York: Simon and Schuster, 1932.

———. *Maiden Castle*. New York: Simon and Schuster, 1936.

———. *Morwyn: or, The Vengeance of God*. London: Cassell, 1937.

———. *Porius: A Romance of the Dark Ages*. London: Macdonald, 1951.

PRATT, FLETCHER (1897–1956), among the first American authors in the field of popular literature now known as "adult fantasy." In the opening sequence of his long story "The Spiral of the Ages" (1954), Pratt's protagonist travels in time to Arthur's Britain, where he foils Mordred's conspiracy, thereby altering subsequent history and the world to which he returns. [DN]

Pratt, Fletcher. "The Spiral of the Ages." *Startling Stories*, 32 (Summer 1954), 10–66.

PRE-RAPHAELITES. One of the stated aims of the original Pre-Raphaelite Brotherhood, founded in 1848, was "to have genuine ideas to express." As early as 1849, they turned to the Arthurian poetry of Tennyson for these ideas, as seen in the unfinished *Mort d'Arthur* (Tate Gallery, London) by F.G. Stephens (1828–1907). In 1850, William Holman Hunt (1827–1910) drew a subject from *The Lady of Shalott* (National Gallery of Victoria, Melbourne), and at the same time Hunt and Stephens became acquainted with the fresco project in the Queen's Robing Room, through a renewed association with Hunt's former drawing instructor William Dyce. Among the other Pre-Raphaelites, Elizabeth Siddal (?1831–1862) painted Arthurian themes.

After the Brotherhood was dissolved in 1853, Dante Gabriel Rossetti undertook responsibility to perpetuate the Pre-Raphaelite ideals of reform in painting, and he turned to Arthurian themes of his own invention in 1854, painting *King Arthur's Tomb* (Private Collection), a subject with no discernible source in the literature. Arthurian subjects were linked to the Pre-Raphaelite movement, first through the Moxon Tennyson (1857) and then through an exclusively Pre-Raphaelite endeavor, the Oxford Union Murals (1857), Rossetti's response to the Queen's Robing Room. The latter project solidified the connection between Pre-Raphaelitism and Arthurian subjects, drew Edward Burne-Jones and William Morris among others into the movement, and broke the Pre-Raphaelite link with Tennyson, forging one instead with Malory, a bond that endured to the end of the Arthurian Revival.

Arthurian subjects remained a standard of Pre-Raphaelite painting. Group projects continued, as in the Dunlop Windows (1862). The preferred narrative, in contrast to the Academic tradition, was of forbidden love. Artists associated with the movement, Arthur Hughes, Frederick Sandys (1832–1904), and Frederic Shields (1833–1911), explored and invented themes outside the literature while maintaining the Pre-Raphaelite aesthetic of slender figures, jewel-toned palette, and meticulous detail. Former associates continued to interpret Arthurian subjects: Hunt painted *The Lady of Shalott* (1886–1905, Wadsworth Athenaeum, Hartford), and Thomas Woolner (1826–1892) sculpted marbles of *Guinevere* and *Elaine* (1870s, both unlocated). The Pre-Raphaelite love of evocative subject matter and highly naturalistic detail became a ubiquitous feature of the late Arthurian Revival, influencing the styles of Academic painters James Archer, John Lyston Byam Shaw, Joseph Noël Paton, George Frederick Watts, and John William Waterhouse. The Pre-Raphaelites left an indelible mark on the course of the Arthurian Revival, expanding both the corpus and the iconography and offering an alternative interpretation to the heroic and moral subjects preferred by the government and the Royal Academicians. [DNM]

Fredeman, William E. *Pre-Raphaelitism: A Bibliocritical Study*. Cambridge: Harvard University Press, 1965.

Mancoff, Debra N. *The Arthurian Revival in Victorian Art*. New York: Garland, 1990.

Parris, Leslie, ed. *Pre-Raphaelite Papers*. London: Tate Gallery, 1984.

Tate Gallery. *The Pre-Raphaelites*. London: Tate Gallery, 1984.

PRESBYS HIPPOTES, HO ("The Old Knight"), a brief Greek verse text, dating from ca. 1300 and perhaps taken from the *Compilation* of Rusticiano da Pisa. The title refers to an old man whom Palamedes, Gawain, Lancelot, and Tristan are unable to defeat. [NJL]

Breillat, Pierre. "La Table Ronde en orient: le poème grec du *Vieux Chevalier*." *Mélanges d'Archéologie et d'Histoire Publiés par l'École Française de Rome*, 55 (1938), 308–40.

PRIESTLEY, J(OHN) B(OYNTON) (1894–1985), lightheartedly interweaves Arthurian magic with satire of modern advertising techniques and reflections on the nature of time in *The Thirty-first of June* (1961). Melicent, princess of Peradore, a kingdom owing allegiance to Arthur, gazes into an enchanted mirror and falls for Sam, a painter who works for an advertising agency in London. [CNS]

Priestley, J.B. *The Thirty-first of June*. London: Heinemann, 1961.

PRINCE, AELIAN (pseudonym of Frank Carr; also known as Launcelot Cross), English poet whose *Of Palomide, Famous Knight of King Arthur's Round Table* (1890), written in blank verse, is based on Malory's "Book of Sir Tristram." Palomide, descended from Norse gods, is supernaturally inspired to court King Mark's wife, Isonde, who in turn loves Tristram. When the marriage is dissolved because of Mark's adultery, Isonde and Tristram retire to Lancelot's Joyous Gard. Love-sick and weary of his quest, Palomide is welcomed to the castle, "a miraculous realm of joy." Tristram promises a boon as a gesture of hospitality. When the two

68. William Holman Hunt, *The Lady of Shalott*. (Courtesy Wadsworth Atheneum, Hartford, Ella Gallup Sumner and Mary Catlin Sumner Collection.)

knights subsequently confront one another at the Tournament of Lonazep, the boon demanded is Tristram's spear. Tristram keeps his promise by lodging the weapon in his opponent's body. The poem ends with prophecies of future trouble. [MAW]

Prince, Aelian. *Of Palomide, Famous Knight of King Arthur's Round Table*. London: Allen, 1890.

PRINCETON UNIVERSITY CHAPEL WINDOWS. The Milbank Choir of the Chapel (Cram and Ferguson, architects, 1925–28) includes windows depicting the four Christian epics of Bunyan, Milton, Dante, and Malory executed by the Boston stained-glass artist Charles J. Connick (1875–1945). *Le Mort d'Arthur* is found in the central bay of the north wall, where scenes organized thematically rather than narratively are grouped into three tiers (bottom to top): *Life and Death of Arthur*, *Aspirations of Chivalry*, and *The Quest of the Holy Grail*, with *The Mystical Vision of Christ* surmounting all. Thirty-six individual panels contain "portraits" (e.g., Malory, Modred, Percival) as well as key events (*Modred Kills Arthur*, *Galahad Achieves the Grail*). [JFO'G]

Stillwell, Richard. *The Chapel of Princeton University*. Princeton, N.J.: Princeton University Press, 1971.

69–72. Princeton University Chapel Windows: the Malory window, Charles J. Connick, artist. (Courtesy of Charles J. Connick Foundation. Reproduced by permission of Princeton University Press from Richard Stillwell, *The Chapel of Princeton University* (Princeton University Press, 1971).)

69. *As May Moneth Floreth and Floryssheth*

70. *Lete Every Man of Worship Florysshe his Herte in this World.*

PROPHÉCIES DE MERLIN, LES, attributed to Maistre Richart d'Irlande and composed in the 1270s. Ostensibly translated from Latin, the work is unrelated to Geoffrey of Monmouth's *Prophetiae Merlini.* Although various Arthurian characters are introduced, the text consists essentially of conversations between Merlin and several scribes. In the course of these conversations, Merlin makes prophecies that are in fact references to political events of the twelfth and thirteenth centuries. The author criticizes religious abuses and exhorts readers to be properly obedient to the Church. [NJL]

Berthelot, Anne, ed. *Les Prophesies de Merlin.* Cologne: Bodmer, 1990.

Paton, Lucy Allen, ed. *Les Prophécies de Merlin.* 2 vols. New York: Heath, 1926.

PROSA-LANCELOT. a German prose version (ca. 1250) of the Vulgate *Lancelot* that exists in one complete manuscript (Heidelberg, Pal. germ. 147 [*P*], ca. 1460–80) and in three important fragments. The narrative may have been by more than one translator. The *Prosa-Lancelot* is divided into three parts that deal with Lancelot's life and death: Galahad, the Grail quest, and the death of Arthur. It offers a compendium of characters and locales found in traditional Arthurian literature up to the time of its composition, as well as new personalities, such as Lancelot's cousins Lionel and Bohort; his half-brother, Hestor/Hector; King Claudas, a renegade Arthurian knight who is the mortal enemy of Lancelot's father, Ban, and the rival of King Arthur; Lancelot's friend Galahot; and his son, Galaad, destined to replace Perceval in the Arthurian tradition as the Grail hero.

71. *Fyrst Vnto God and Next Vnto the Joye*

72. *Of Them That He Promysed his Feythe Vnto*

Also of interest in the *Prosa-Lancelot* is the conception of chivalry, which is viewed within the framework of the history of salvation. The chivalric way of life is legitimized by the Lady of the Lake as a *militia christiana*, a prefiguration of the new type of fulfilled spiritual knighthood that finds its culmination in the figure of Galaad. Thus, the Arthurian chivalric order is viewed as a necessary and valuable, if less perfect, prerequisite for the new order of knighthood. [FGG]

Kluge, Reinhold, ed. *Lancelot*. 3 vols. Berlin: Akademie, 1948, 1963, 1972.

———, ed. *Der Karrenritter: Episode des mhd. Prosa-Lancelot*. Munich: Fink, 1972.

Gottzmann, Carola L. *Artusdichtung*. Stuttgart: Metzler, 1989.

Schröder, Werner, ed. *Wolfram-Studien IX: Schweinfurter "Lancelot"-Kolloquium 1984*. Berlin: Erich Schmidt, 1986.

PROSE *BRUT*, the title scholars give to a group of Anglo-Norman, English, and Latin prose chronicles written in the late thirteenth, fourteenth, and fifteenth centuries that cover, in their early chapters, the history of Britain. They include the familiar story of Arthur's rise to power, his conquest of the Romans, and his fall through the treachery of Mordred.

The earliest of these chronicles is the Anglo-Norman *Brut*, of which at least two redactions were written; it survives in at least forty-seven manuscripts. It appears to have been originally compiled from several sources shortly after 1272, but most manuscripts include continuations to 1333. It has never been edited.

The English *Brut* was translated from the Anglo-Norman *Brut* a little before 1400, but continuations carry events in some manuscripts past the mid-fifteenth century. The survival of over 170 manuscripts indicates that it was one of the most popular works written in English in the Middle Ages. It also has the distinction of being the first English chronicle to appear in print: Caxton published an edition in 1480 entitled *The Chronicles of England*. Eleven more editions followed in the fifteenth and sixteenth centuries, and it was an important source for other English chroniclers of the sixteenth century. Although Brie's edition of 1906 and 1908 made a version of the *Brut* accessible to modern readers, several English versions of this chronicle have never been published, and it is not yet clear how they are all related.

The amount of Arthurian material in the different versions ranges from a short paragraph in some to the long account found in many manuscripts and edited by Brie. Here, Arthur appears as the ideal king who attracts knights to his Round Table from many foreign lands and as a champion of Christianity fighting the pagan Romans. He is "wel bilouede of al men," "the most worthi lord of renoun that was in al the worlde," a model for future kings to follow.

Fifteen manuscripts have been described as Latin *Bruts*, but these represent at least three or four different chronicles. Brie discusses four manuscripts that he feels represent two different translations into Latin from the Anglo-Norman *Brut*. Kingsford describes as the Latin *Brut* ten other manuscripts representing two versions of a different chronicle, and he adds still another manuscript that he describes as a peculiar version of the Latin *Brut*. Kingsford believes that all these manuscripts represent a translation into Latin from the English *Brut*. Kingsford's Latin *Brut*, however, has Arthurian material not found in most versions of the English *Brut*, including information drawn from the Latin chronicle of John of Glastonbury and the Vulgate *Mort Artu*. [EDK]

Brie, Friedrich, ed. *Geschichte und Quellen de mittelenglischen Prosachronik The Brute of England oder The Chronicles of England*. Marburg: Elwert, 1905.

———, ed. *The Brut or the Chronicles of England*. London: Oxford University Press, 1906, 1908.

Fletcher, Robert Huntington. *The Arthurian Material in the Chronicles, Especially Those of Great Britain and France*. Boston: Ginn, 1906; 2nd ed. Roger Sherman Loomis. New York: Franklin, 1966, pp. 214–20.

Gransden, Antonia. *Historical Writing in England II ca. 1307 to the Early Sixteenth Century*. Ithaca, N.Y.: Cornell University Press, pp. 73–77, 222–27.

Kennedy, Edward Donald. "Chronicles and Other Historical Writing." In *A Manual of the Writings in Middle English*, ed. A.E. Hartung. New Haven: Connecticut Academy of Arts and Sciences, 1981–89, Vol. 8, pp. 2629–40, 2818–33.

Kingsford, C.L. *English Historical Literature in the Fifteenth Century*. Oxford: Clarendon, 1913, pp. 113–39.

Meyer, Paul. "De Quelques Chroniques anglo-normandes qui ont porté le nom de *Brut*." *Bulletin de la Société des Anciens Textes Français*, 1878, 104–45.

PROSE *EREC*, an anonymous French text dating from the thirteenth century. Although its editor considered it to be a vestigial Erec romance, it is less an autonomous work than a narrative sequence interlaced with other prose episodes in *La Folie Lancelot*. Despite its title, the Prose *Erec* is only distantly related to Chrétien de Troyes's romance about Erec (Enide is absent, and there are only a few narrative echoes of the earlier poem); nor is it to be confused with the fifteenth-century *L'Histoire du noble et vaillant chevalier Erec*, a prose adaptation of Chrétien's romance (*see* CHRÉTIEN DE TROYES, BURGUNDIAN ADAPTATIONS OF).

The text recounts the quest conducted by a number of knights who are seeking Lancelot; Erec is among them, and it is in this quest that he first demonstrates his abilities and establishes his reputation as a knight. Eventually, the quest is abandoned, and the second half of the work recounts miscellaneous episodes (e.g., a series of battles with Gauvain) that are not part of a linear or logical sequence of events but are elaborations of a specific motif, character, or scene. [NJL]

Pickford, Cedric E., ed. *Erec: roman arthurien en prose*. Geneva: Droz, 1968.

PROSE *MERLIN* (1), the early thirteenth-century prosification of a verse *Merlin* of which only 504 lines are extant. The important prose text is attributed to Robert de Boron, who twice names himself in his work. At a time when verse was considered to be incompatible with truth, the prose form, of which the *Merlin* is one of the earliest examples in romance, appeared better able to present the historical role of Arthurian chivalry in the divine project: prose is the vehicle of truth.

The Prose *Merlin* is not an autonomous work. A sequel to the *Joseph d'Arimathie* (the prosification of the *Estoire dou Graal*, which is also by Robert de Boron), it is followed by the Didot-*Perceval*, a romance of uncertain attribution. These three texts constitute the earliest Arthurian cycle in prose. The *Merlin* provides the link between the origins of the Grail and its transfer to the West, on the one hand, and the Arthurian period and the quest for the Holy Vessel undertaken by the knights of the Round Table, on the other. Soon after, the *Merlin* was detached from this shorter cycle and integrated into the *Lancelot-Graal* (or Vulgate) cycle, where it stands between the *Estoire del Saint Graal* and the *Suite-Vulgate*, and also into the Post-Vulgate, where it is followed by a *Suite-Huth*. The manuscript tradition clearly reflects the work's fate: the manuscripts divide into two families, α and β, the latter group having revised key passages in order to respond to the demands of a larger cycle.

The story, strongly influenced by Wace's *Roman de Brut*, describes the conception and birth of Merlin, the son of an incubus who seduced a virgin. His diabolical origin gives him knowledge of the past, while God endows him with prescience. These abilities enable Merlin to contribute to the fall of the usurper Vertigier and to restore the legitimate reign of King Constant's sons. He advises King Pandragon on ways to defeat the Saxon enemy. But above all, it was during the reign of Uterpandragon that Merlin played a major role in inaugurating Arthurian grandeur by creating the Round Table, the *tierce table* ("third table") that recalls the Table of the Last Supper and the Grail Table and establishes symbolic correspondences between them. After bringing together the king and Igerne, Merlin has the newborn Arthur delivered to him and has him reared by a wise man named Antor. Arthur will eventually be revealed as king only after a test (withdrawing the sword from the stone), which will identify his reign with an exceptional destiny. Finally, the *Merlin* introduces a motif that Arthurian prose was to treat frequently: references, within the fictional context of the work, to a fictitious book that synthesizes the history of the Grail and its guardians and that is also the source from which the romance is derived. [C-AVC]

Micha, Alexandre, ed. *Merlin: roman du XIIIe siècle*. Geneva: Droz, 1979.

Loomis, Roger Sherman, ed. *Arthurian Literature in the Middle Ages*. Oxford: Clarendon, 1959, pp. 251–62, 295–335.

Micha, Alexandre. *Etude sur le "Merlin" de Robert de Boron, roman du XIIIe siècle*. Paris and Geneva: Droz, 1980.

Zumthor, Paul. *Merlin le prophète: un thème de la littérature polémique, de l'historiographie et des romans*. Lausanne: Payot. 1943.

PROSE *MERLIN* (2), a mid-fifteenth-century English translation of the Vulgate *Estoire de Merlin*, extant only in Cambridge University Library MS Ff 3 11 (a fragment of a related manuscript survives in Bodleian MS Rawlinson Misc. olim 1262, later 1370). The French source-manuscript of the Prose *Merlin* was like, but not identical to, that used by Lovelich in his contemporary verse translation of *Merlin*. The Cambridge manuscript breaks off shortly after Gawain receives the imprisoned Merlin's last message, but it lacks only a little of the Vulgate *Merlin*'s ending. There is no particular reason to think the translator intended a whole cycle in the manner of Malory's *Morte Darthur*. The *Estoire de Merlin*, also reworked in the romance *Arthour and Merlin*, seems itself to have been of interest in England.

The Prose *Merlin* covers Merlin's history from his demonic conception to his final imprisonment by Nimiane. His activities as strategist, counselor, and politico-military tactician for the Arthurian regime are paramount. Several apparently digressive anecdotes, such as his appearances in Rome as a white hart and laughing wild-man, reinforce this role: in non-Arthurian contexts, he remains "Merlin of Nothumbirlande, the maister counseller of kynge Arthur of Breteyne," whose powers are harnessed to the quasi-eschatological task of establishing the Arthurian reign, not used for personal dominance.

Merlin's foresight is crucial in Arthur's complex series of wars against rebel British kings, invading Saxons, and the Romans. In the numerous accounts of melées, battles, and single combats (e.g., Bohors and Amaunt's moving combat "body for body"), the translator often draws on native alliterative and doublet traditions without abandoning the practice of anglicizing French words into English lexis (cf. Malory's "play" for "wound"). Though he follows the structure and theme of his French original closely, he permits himself more radical assimilations and innovations stylistically: the *matière* is fully "translated." His profound respect for this legendary British history ensures that the translator keeps carefully all his source's authenticating references to textual transmission but does not obtrude his own role at all. [JP]

Wheatley, Henry B., ed. *Merlin, or The Early History of King Arthur: A Prose Romance.* 2 vols. London: Kegan Paul, Trench, Trübner, 1865, 1899.

PROSE *TRISTAN*, a lengthy French romance that has been transmitted in two basic versions, dating from the second and third quarters of the thirteenth century. Many manuscripts are extant as well as printed editions based on the latest manuscript version. Both attributions, of the first version to Luces de Gat (Gaut, Galt) and of the second to Hélie de Borron, are almost certainly false.

The Prose *Tristan* is the first great Arthurian prose romance written after the Vulgate Cycle and is profoundly influenced in almost all aspects by it. The authors of this romance were the first to "Arthurianize" properly the story of Tristan and Iseut, a process barely begun in Béroul and Thomas. Tristan is an Arthurian knight and member of the Round Table, King Mark becomes a villain, and the moral issues of the adulterous love affair are greatly simplified insofar as they survive at all. The chivalric values and problems presented in the Prose *Tristan* are simple, much more so than in Chrétien's romances or in the Vulgate Cycle.

The romance begins with the story of Tristan's ancestors and birth, a common tendency of literature of the period being to elaborate on the prehistory of a popular hero. After the murder of Tristan's father, Meliadus, the young knight is taken to the court of King Pharamont of Gaul by his tutor, Governal, and then on to the court of Mark. Here, the narrative more or less rejoins the story told in the poems, and the author seems to have known both the Béroul-Eilhart and Thomas-Gottfried versions. After his marriage to Iseut of the White Hands, Tristan returns to Cornwall and his first love before Mark banishes him from Cornwall for good. After proving himself as a knight, he is made a member of the Round Table and occupies the seat left vacant by Le Morholt, whom he had killed. Some versions of the Prose *Tristan* include a traditional version of the hero's death, while others have Mark kill him treacherously with a poisoned lance as he is singing a lay for Iseut.

Into this basic framework are woven innumerable adventures of Tristan, Palamedes, and many Arthurian heroes; and frequently whole episodes from other romances, in particular the Vulgate *Queste* and *Mort Artu*, are interpolated. The whole shows a tendency toward creating a *summa arthuriana*.

It is the life of the knight-errant and his quest for adventure that dominate the Prose *Tristan*, resulting in long descriptions of tournaments and jousts. Any other departure from the norm of Arthurian romance and from the Tristan story can also generally be explained in the same way. This is not to say that the characters do not express noble and idealistic sentiments but rather that they do not enter into the typically courtly form of analysis. Palamedes, for example, an invention of the Prose *Tristan*, is desperately in love with Iseut but unfailingly loyal to Tristan. Despite his unrequited love, Palamedes never conducts inner dialogues with himself about the hopelessness of his position. Paradoxically, perhaps, Dinadan, another invention of the Prose *Tristan*, constantly calls into question the most fundamental concepts of the Arthurian world: he enters into a discussion about the point of jousting with a knight who has just challenged him; he condemns love as folly, since it tortures its servants and even causes their death. Yet Dinadan is a valiant knight and a passionate friend of Tristan, whose death leaves him dazed and wondering about the purpose of life.

Perhaps because of the way in which the various versions of the Prose *Tristan* came into being (often by accretion and interpolation), the narrative structure has been seen as wanting in some respects. Although partly based on the idea of *entrelacement* so successfully employed in the Vulgate Cycle, the narrative does not appear to use the device as consistently as do the earlier texts. Episodes seem to have little relationship with what precedes or follows, and conclusions are difficult to draw about the placement of a particular episode and its consequences for the interpretation of the whole. This may be related to the expectations of the audience of the prose romances of the time, who probably read them episode by episode, keeping only a general overview of the lengthy whole. Such reading habits may have partly determined the manner of composition. The digressive and rambling shape of the narrative is therefore more apparent rather than real.

The popularity of the Prose *Tristan* was enormous: more than fifty manuscripts survive in Old French, as well as innumerable fragments; a printed version is among the earliest French printed books. It was imitated in the Italian *Tavola Ritonda* and in Spanish, Danish, Russian, and Polish, not to mention the adaptation by Malory. In France, later romances, such as the *Palamedes* (otherwise known as *Meliadus* and *Guiron le Courtois*), the Compilations of Rusticiano da Pisa, Jean Vaillant, and Michot Gonnot, and the *Prophécies de Merlin*, derive from the Prose *Tristan*. As yet, there is no complete edition of this important text, whose complex manuscript tradition has long deterred editors. Some progress, however, is being made. [KB]

Curtis, Renée L., ed. *Le Roman de Tristan en prose.* 3 vols. Vol. 1, Munich: Hueber, 1963; Vol. 2, Leiden: Brill, 1976; Vol. 3, Cambridge: Brewer, 1985.

Ménard, Philippe, ed. *Le Roman de Tristan en prose*. Geneva: Droz, 1987, Vol. 1.

Baumgartner, Emmanuèle. *Le Tristan en prose: essai d'interprétation*. Geneva: Droz, 1975.

Löseth, Eilhert. *Le Roman en prose de Tristan*. Paris: Champion, 1891.

Van Coolput, Colette-Anne. *Aventures querant et le sens du monde: aspects de la réception productive des premiers romans du Graal cycliques dans le "Tristan en prose."* Leuven: Leuven University Press, 1986.

PROSE *YVAIN*, an episodic French romance preserved in a single manuscript from the fourteenth century. The work consists of seven separate episodes, only the first of which concerns Yvain directly (although he is mentioned in others). The first part recounts the rescuing of the lion, and the details of the adventure do not differ substantially from those given by Chrétien de Troyes. The other sections relate a series of adventures of various knights, including Gawain, Tristan, and Lancelot. The fifth episode contains an interesting debate concerning the relative merits of various knights of Uther's and Arthur's courts. Although the work as a whole is historically interesting, the talent of the author is decidedly deficient. [NJL]

Muir, Lynette R. "A Reappraisal of the Prose *Yvain* (National Library of Wales MS. 444-D)." *Romania*, 85 (1964), 335–65.

PUCCI, ANTONIO (ca. 1310–1388), a popular poet whose lyrics are interesting for their glimpses of everyday life in fourteenth-century Florence. He wrote two *cantari* based on Arthurian themes: *Gismirante* and *Brito di Brettagna*. The first *cantare*, in two parts, recounts the adventures of Gismirante, the son of a former knight of the Round Table who, on his deathbed in Rome, sends him to Arthur's court to become a knight. Once there, Gismirante wins the admiration and affection of the entire court. After seven years, the opportunity comes for Gismirante to prove his mettle: the absence of tales of new adventure has caused the court to abstain from eating. Gismirante saves the court from starvation with the help of a fairy, who tells him about the most beautiful woman in the world and gives him a single strand of her golden hair. Enamored of this princess and undaunted by the attendant difficulties in courting her, he sets out to win her as his bride. The remainder of the *cantare* recounts his numerous adventures before and after winning the princess and includes a number of marvelous and folkloristic elements. He saves three beasts—a griffin, an eagle, and a hawk—all of which return to assist him at crucial junctures; he receives a magic horse from another fairy; the princess possesses a magic wand that can alter a river's flow. One long episode concerns a giant ("un uomo selvaggio") who abducts the princess and holds her and forty-three other ladies captive in an enchanted castle. To defeat the giant, Gismirante must discover the secret place where his heart is hidden. The giant's heart is guarded by a "Chinese box" arrangement of animals, consisting successively of a wild boar, a hare, and a swallow. The *cantare* concludes with the marriage of Gismirante and the princess at Arthur's court.

In *Brito di Brettagna*, Pucci bases his story on that found in the *De Amore* of Andreas Capellanus (Book II, Chapter 8) and employs a similarly striking array of motifs (a vaunt, single combats, the quest) and marvelous elements (a magic horse, a sumptuous banquet in the field), all of which derive from Arthurian literature. Brito's lady promises to grant him her love if he will bring her three items from King Arthur's castle: a sparrowhawk, two hunting dogs, and the scroll containing the rules of love. He learns from a fairy that to obtain these things he must declare that his lady is more beautiful than that of any other king and demonstrate the validity of this "vaunt" by winning in single combat. Further, to gain access to Arthur's court, he must first win the hawk's glove, which is guarded at the bridge of gold by two giants. After the successful conclusion of his quest, Brito returns to his lady. [CK]

Sapegno, Natalino, ed. *Poeti minori del Trecento*. Milan and Naples: Ricciardi, 1952, pp. 869–81.

Gardner, Edmund G. *The Arthurian Legend in Italian Literature*. London: Dent, 1930, pp. 247–52.

Levi, Ezio. "I cantari leggendari del popolo italiano nei secoli XIV e XV." *Giornale storico della letteratura italiana*, Supp. 16 (1914), 92–113.

PULZELLA GAIA, LA ("The Merry Maiden"), an Italian *cantare* of the third quarter of the fourteenth century, concerns the tribulations of Morgana's daughter. It presents Morgana, however, only in passing; at the end of the first *cantare*, she speaks in the accents of a woman of the people. Probable sources include Marie de France's *Lanval*, the anonymous lai *Graelent*, and the *Tavola Ritonda*. It is also known as *La ponzela gaia*. [SJN]

Levi, Ezio, ed. *Fiore de leggende: cantari antichi*. Bari: Laterza, 1914.

Varanini, G., ed. *Ponzela gaia, cantare dialettale inedito del secolo XV*. Bologna: Commissione per i testi di lingua, 1957.

PURCELL, HENRY (1658–1695), composed the music for John Dryden's *King Arthur*, first performed in

1691. The collaboration resulted in an outstanding example of so-called Restoration semiopera. Dryden provided, together with a heroic theme, a text offering many opportunities for instrumental and choral ensembles, solo singing, dance, and spectacular effects to musical acccompaniment. Purcell rose to the challenge of creating music for situations as diverse as Druidical rites, rural jollification, and a scene celebrating the Order of the Garter, during which the soprano sings the air "Fairest Isle." Owing much to the traditional masque and to familiar English music forms, Purcell also looks to the Continent for inspiration. Though the music is very highly rated, complete performances of *King Arthur* are now rare. [CNS]

Purcell, Henry. *The British Worthy*. London: W. Strahan, 1770.
Moore, R.E. *Henry Purcell and the Restoration Theatre*. London: Heinemann, 1961.

PURCELL, SALLY, British poet who, in "Lancelot Speaks" and "Loquitur Arthurus" (1968), suggests that the great sins committed in ignorance, the fathering of Galahad and Mordred, were necessary elements in a greater pattern of events. The poems were subsequently incorporated with three others—"Sarras," "The Holly Queen," and "Magician Meditating" (1971)—in a sequence of lyrics. This portrays the sad fate of the Arthurian world in images that evoke a sense of ancient, mysterious forces at work. [DN]

Purcell, Sally. *The Holly Queen*. London: Anvil Press Poetry, 1971.

PURNELL, CHARLES WILLIAM, New Zealand poet, in "The Modern Arthur" (1912) tells how the spirit of Arthur, sickened by the modern world's preoccupation with commerce and gain, voyages to New Zealand, only to discover that here too the human soul "Is but a mirror of the age." [RHT]

Purnell, Charles William. "The Modern Arthur." In *The Modern Arthur and Other Poems*. London and Christchurch: Whitcombe and Tombs, 1912, pp. 3–21.

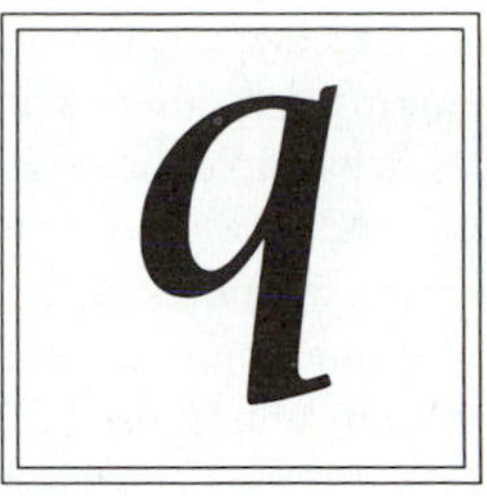

QUANDO TRISTANO E LANCIELOTTO COMBATTETTERO AL PETRONE DI MERLINO ("When Tristan and Lancelot Fought at the Tomb of Merlin"), an Italian *cantare* believed to represent a fairly late (fifteenth-century) stage in the development of the tradition. In the story, Merlin's tomb has been chosen as the site of a duel between Tristan and Palamedes. Lancelot arrives there accidentally and reads on the tombstone an inscription predicting that the two best knights in the world are to do battle there. Thinking the knights indicated must be Tristan and his own son Galasso (also spelled, in Italian tradition, Galeatto or Galeazzo), Lancelot lingers at the tomb, hoping to separate the two. Tristan arrives and engages Lancelot in combat, believing him to be Palamedes. The misunderstanding is finally resolved. [SJN]

Branca, Daniela Delcorno. "I cantari di Tristano." *Lettere italiane*, 23 (1971), 289–305.

QUESTING BEAST (French, *beste glatissant*), a strange beast or monster that reappears frequently, beginning with the *Suite du Merlin* and *Perlesvaus*, in French, Spanish, and Italian romance and in Malory. Malory describes it as "the strongeste beste that ever he [Arthur] saw or herde of." From the beast's belly, there came a noise like the barking, or questing, or "thirty coupyl houndes." The beast is pursued in Malory's Book I by Pellinore, in French romance and the rest of Malory by Palamede, and in Spanish and Italian texts by Perceval. [NJL]

Muir, Lynette R. "The Questing Beast: Its Origin and Development." *Orpheus*, 4 (1957), 24–32.

QUILLER-COUCH, SIR ARTHUR (1863–1944), British educator, scholar, journalist, and author who wrote frequently under the pseudonym "Q," was associated all his life with Cornwall, and he uses the region as the setting for his novel *Castle Dor* (1961), which was completed from his notes by English novelist Daphne du Maurier (1907–1989). The story of Tristan and Isolde is transposed into the nineteenth century, to the vicinity of Castle Dore, Mark's reputed fortress. Most of the traditional motifs and characters, including the love potion and the spying dwarf, are woven into a fascinating plot involving a Breton fisherman, an elderly innkeeper, and his headstrong young wife. The connection between past and present is made explicit through the researches of a local physician, yet despite his knowledge he fails "to stay a senseless repetition of one of the saddest love stories in the world." The triumph of fate over human will powerfully evokes the spirit of the original legend.

Quiller-Couch earlier had written "The Legend of Sir Dinar" (1895), which recounts the fate of Dinar, knight of the Round Table and son of Geraint. As a punishment for shooting her hawk, Morgan le Fay lays a spell upon him that compels him to dance forever. He is relieved from his anguish by Galahad, who transforms him into a withered leaf, dancing in the wind. [RHT]

Quiller-Couch, Arthur. "The Legend of Sir Dinar." In *Wandering Heath: Stories, Studies, and Sketches*. London: Cassell, 1895, pp. 215–24.

———, and Daphne du Maurier. *Castle Dor*. Garden City, N.Y.: Doubleday, 1961.

QUINET, EDGAR (1803–1875), French author of *Merlin l'enchanteur* ("Merlin the Magician," 1860), in which he exploited Arthurian themes to provide a vehicle for his attacks on Louis-Napoleon, whom he introduces into the novel in the guise of the infidel Hengist. In this bizarre and enormous epic (in twenty-four books and nearly 900 pages), Quinet chose Merlin as a symbol of the French nation and spirit, whose glorious accomplishments of an earlier time were succeeded by a period of torpor and pathetic disarray. The enchanter also represents Quinet himself, the victim of a lengthy exile from France during the period he saw as its decadence.

In its barest outlines, the work generally follows tradition in the presentation of Merlin. The son of Satan and a mortal mother, he grew up to achieve power and fame, brought about Arthur's coronation, established a vast Round

Table (which served as a sort of cornucopia, providing food and drink for all), and fell hopelessly in love with Viviane. Such details, however, simply provide a pretext or frame for Quinet's often jarring innovations: during a long exile, the enchanter traveled throughout the world, performing various exploits (just as, in Quinet's view, France had formerly distinguished itself among nations) and meeting numerous personages of note, including Robespierre, Mirabeau, Robin Hood, Faust, Don Juan, and Hamlet's father. Returning to France, he found that Arthur had fallen into a deathlike sleep, while France itself was languishing in darkness and decadence. Viviane, using a spell he revealed to her, imprisoned him in an enormous tomb, where she remained with him, sharing his love and bearing his child, also named Merlin. Eventually, Arthur awakened, and France began to emerge from its darkness, plague, and strife; Merlin thereupon undertook his greatest task, the conversion of Satan.

Quinet's work includes most of the major Arthurian characters, including Tristan, Yseut, Genièvre, Lancelot, Gauvain, Parceval and his son Lohengrin, and others, but sometimes doubles them. There are, for example, both an Yvain and an Owein, as well as an Yvan and an Yvanet. The Arthurian figures are, moreover, intermingled on occasion with characters from other traditions: at one point, we find Brunhild seated with Yseut aux Blanches Mains, and Chriemhild with Genièvre. (*See also* SECOND EMPIRE.) [NJL]

Quinet, Edgar. *Merlin l'enchanteur*. 2 vols. Paris: Michel Lévy, 1860.

Crossley, Ceri. *Edgar Quinet (1803–1875): A Study in Romantic Thought*. Lexington, Ky.: French Forum, 1983.

Dakyns, Janine R. *The Middle Ages in French Literature, 1851–1900*. London: Oxford University Press, 1973.

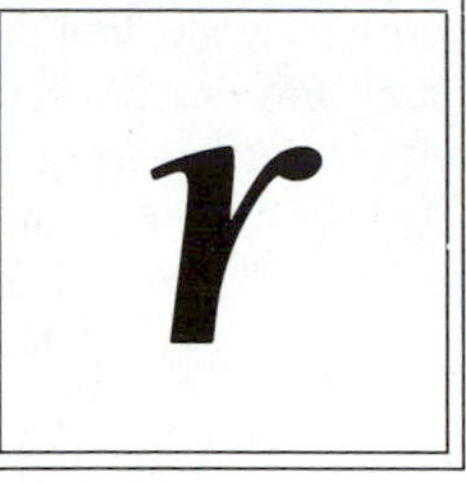

RAO, RAJA, one of the "Great Three" Indian novelists writing in English. Rao's second novel, the strongly autobiographical *The Serpent and the Rope* (1960), has a protagonist who lives sometimes in India and sometimes in Europe; his attempt to embrace the cultures of the two worlds finally founders on the synthesis of both. His relationship to a young married Indian woman is depicted with specific reference to the *Tristan* of Thomas d'Angleterre. The story of Parsifal and his search for the Grail, as interpreted by Richard Wagner, also plays an important role in the structure of the novel. [UM/WLS]

Rao, Raja. *The Serpent and the Rope*. London: Murray, 1960.

Müller, Ulrich, and William C. McDonald. "Tristan in Deep-Structure: Raja Rao's 'The Serpent and the Rope' (1960), a Paradigmatic Case of Inter-Cultural Relations." *Tristania*, 12 (1986–87), 44–47.

RAOUL DE HOUDENC, author of *Meraugis de Portlesguez*, possibly of *La Vengeance Raguidel*, and a number of shorter allegorical and didactic pieces. Active in the first quarter of the thirteenth century, Raoul de Houdenc is probably to be identified with Radulfus de Hosdenc, a knight, of Hodenc-en-Bray in the Beauvaisis.

Meraugis de Portlesguez, a verse romance of 5,938 lines, is concerned with the rivalry of two friends, Meraugis de Portlesguez and Gorvain Cadrut, for the love of the beautiful Lidoine. One of the main issues is whether Meraugis (who loves Lidoine for her *courtoisie*) or Gorvain (who loves her for her beauty) has the better claim to her love. When Guenièvre and her damsels find in favor of Meraugis, Lidoine sends him off to prove himself worthy of her, while Gorvain leaves in high dudgeon, complaining of the lack of justice to be found at Arthur's court. Gauvain in the meantime sets out to seek the *Espee as Estranges Renges* ("Sword of the Strange Hangings") and becomes involved in many adventures, some of them burlesque and comic. In one such, he defeats the guardian of an island and becomes the new guardian until such time as he is himself defeated; he then fights with Meraugis before recognizing him and devising a plan by means of which they can escape from the island (it involves Meraugis dressing up in women's clothes).

Raoul is one of Chrétien's most successful epigones, and his achievement lies in a clearly thought-out treatment of some complex emotional problems arising from the initial situation, a carefully structured plot, and a deft touch of comedy. He also has a penchant for dialogue and inner dialogue and was clearly influenced by dialectic and logic. *Meraugis* differs from the work of Chrétien in a number of respects: there is a clear shift away from concerns of chivalry in the direction of amorous debate; the comedy is sometimes broader; and the roles played by Arthurian characters are less notable (in this respect, *Meraugis* might be compared with *Cligés*). Raoul de Houdenc nevertheless makes good use of Chrétien, rewriting for his own ends the sparrowhawk episode from *Erec et Enide*, the role of Laudine from *Yvain* (which he uses in his portrayal of Lidoine), and linking his romance intertextually to *Perceval* and the Continuations.

Raoul's shorter didactic poems, in particular *Le Roman des Eles*, are concerned with issues similar to those at the heart of the romance and may assist in interpreting it. Raoul was a gifted and productive poet who was admired in the Middle Ages, as witnessed by the praise allotted to him by Huon de Mery in his *Tournoiement de l'Antéchrist* (thirteenth century), where he is mentioned in the same breath as Chrétien as one of the masters of French poetry. [KB]

Raoul de Houdenc. *Meraugis de Portlesguez*, ed. Mathias Friedwagner. Halle: Niemeyer, 1897.

———. *"Le Roman des Eles": The Anonymous "Ordene de Chevalerie,"* ed. Keith Busby. Amsterdam: Benjamins, 1983.

Blumenfeld-Kosinski, Renate. "Arthurian Heroes and Convention: *Meraugis de Portlesguez* and *Durmart le Gallois*." In *The Legacy of Chrétien de Troyes*, ed. Norris J. Lacy, Douglas Kelly, and Keith Busby. 2 vols. Amsterdam: Rodopi, 1988, Vol. 2, pp. 79–92.

Busby, Keith. "*Le Roman des Eles* as Guide to the 'sens' of *Meraugis de Portlesguez*." In *The Spirit of the Court*, ed. G.S. Burgess and R.A. Taylor. Cambridge: Brewer, 1985, pp. 79–89.

Kundert-Forrer, Verena. *Raoul de Houdenc: Ein französischer Erzähler aus dem XIIIe Jahrhundert*. Zurich: Juris, 1960.

RAWE, DONALD R., British author of plays, in the style of the medieval *Cornish Ordinalia*, for Piran Round, a theater-in-the-round. *Geraint: Last of the Arthurians* (1972) is about the death of Geraint, King of Cornwall, the last survivor of Arthur's Round Table, and the conflict over Cornish succession in the face of Saxon incursions. Rawe struggles in the play to reconcile several conflicting traditions: one from Arthurian romance, which sees Geraint as the romantic warrior-prince who wins Enid; another from the *Life of St. Teilo of Llandaff*, which makes him a Christian saint; and a local Cornish tradition, which gives him an elaborate Celtic funeral in the pagan manner. [PCB]

Rawe, Donald R. *Geraint: Last of the Arthurians*. Padstow: Lodenek, 1972.

READE, JOHN (1837–1919), Irish-born Canadian clergyman, whose blank-verse poem "The Prophecy of Merlin" (1870) reveals the influence of Tennyson. To comfort Bedivere as he mourns the departure of Arthur for Avalon, Merlin prophesies the future greatness of Britain, culminating in the glorious reign of the "Good Queen" Victoria and the "Blameless Prince" Albert. [RHT]

Reade, John. "The Prophecy of Merlin." In *The Prophecy of Merlin and Other Poems*. Montreal: Dawson, 1870, pp. 3–28.

REED, HENRY, contemplates, in his poem "Tintagel" (1946), the sea-battered ruins of the ancient castle. Linking human emotion with the forces of nature and the march of time, he meditates on the "perpetually recurring" story of one of the world's great romances. The four sections are: "Tristram," "Iseult Blaunchesmains," "King Mark," and "Iseult la Belle." [CNS]

Reed, Henry. "Tintagel." In *A Map of Verona*. London: Jonathan Cape, 1946.

RENAUT DE BEAUJEU, author of *Le Bel Inconnu* ("The Fair Unknown"), a verse romance of 6,266 lines written ca. 1185–90; Renaut has recently been identified with Renaud de Bâgé, Lord of Saint-Trivier (ca. 1165–ca. 1230). The poem relates the story of Gauvain's son, Guinglain, who is assigned the task of liberating the daughter of the King of Wales, transformed into a serpent by two enchanters. Although young and inexperienced, Guinglain goes to Sinaudon, conquers the two enchanters, Mabon and Evrain, releases Esmeree from the spell, and marries her. As with most romances of this type, the basic plot (also present in the Italian *Carduino*, the Middle High German *Wigalois*, and the Middle English adaptation of Renaut, Chestre's

73. MS Paris, Bibliothèque Nationale, f.fr. 120, fol. 524v: Galahad and the Perilous Seat. (Paris, Bibliothèque Nationale.)

Libeaus Desconus) is enhanced by motifs to be found elsewhere: sparrowhawk contest, seduction by a fairy, prevention of the rape of a damsel. Also interesting is the theme of the *Fier Baiser* by means of which Guinglain releases Esmeree from the enchantment. This, like much else in Arthurian romance, is of Celtic origin, and is related more or less distantly to the various versions of the Loathly Lady story, as found in Chaucer's *The Wife of Bath's Tale*.

Le Bel Inconnu is one of the earliest post-Chrétien verse romances and still shows unmistakable signs of Chrétien's influence, especially of *Erec et Enide*. Specifically, Renaut adapts the sparrowhawk episode in a deftly ironic manner while at the same time retaining its narrative function at the beginning of a series of adventures. The poet has given his romance a clear and logical structure, a quest for love that is threatened by the complication of the encounter with the fairy before being brought to a happy conclusion. Renaut adds a personal touch when he says that he is writing his romance for one to whom he has given his own heart. Despite its chronological proximity to Chrétien, it is difficult to argue that Renaut is concerned with the same issues as his predecessor. There is no question of the conflict between love and chivalry, for example, so central to Chrétien's first four romances, or of religion, so central to the meaning of *Perceval*. The conflict in *Le Bel Inconnu*, however, is between love and love, one of the romance's most interesting structural principles being that of the hero's relationship with two women, La Pucelle aux Blanches Mains and Esmeree la Blonde.

The story of Gauvain's son is also related elsewhere, particularly in the First Continuation of Chrétien's *Perceval* (where he is called Lionel and not Guinglain), and there are grounds for believing that the story may originally have been associated with Gauvain himself and that Guinglain may be seen as a double of his father. In the early sixteenth century, Claude Platin wrote a prose *Giglain et Geoffroy*, in which he combined the story of Guinglain with that of Jaufré, hero of a Provençal romance. [KB]

Renaut de Beaujeu. *Le Bel Inconnu*, ed. G. Perrie Williams. Paris: Champion, 1929.

Boiron, Françoise, and Jean-Charles Payen. "Structure et sens du *Bel Inconnu* de Renaut de Beaujeu." *Le Moyen Age*, 76 (1970), 15–26.

Fierz-Monnier, Antoinette. *Initiation und Wandlung: Zur Geschichte des altfranzösischen Romans im zwölften Jahrhundert von Chrétien de Troyes zu Renaut de Beaujeu*. Bern: Francke, 1951.

RETURN, LEGENDS OF ARTHUR'S. The possibility of Arthur's return has figured significantly in his story since William of Malmesbury (1125), Henry of Huntingdon (ca. 1139), and Wace (1155) repeated the "Breton hope" apparently popular in folk tradition. Although most medieval chroniclers refuted the claim, it enjoyed such a firm hold in the popular imagination that, according to Hermann of Tournai (*De Miraculis Sanctae Mariae Laudunensis*, 1146), violence erupted at an 1113 religious gathering when a churchman declared that Arthur was actually dead. Malory cautiously recorded the legend of the *Rex quondam Rexque futurus* (using the Latin inscription he found in the mid-fourteenth-century Alliterative *Morte Arthure*), remarking that "men say that he shall come again. . . . I will not say it shall be so, but rather I will say, here in this world he changed his life." Despite popular credence in the myth of the return, medieval romances almost never recorded its fulfillment. In Étienne de Rouen's Latin poem *Draco Normannicus* (ca. 1169), Arthur writes a letter warning Henry II to leave Brittany alone, for he has returned from Avalon to marshall troops against Henry's intrusions. And the late thirteenth-century German verse *Manuel und Amande* maintains that after his apparent death Arthur returned to reign another twenty-five years. Otherwise, romances treated the return as a promise for the future. Medieval and Renaissance writers occasionally depicted Arthur awaiting his return in Avalon (or in less traditional locations, such as Sicily or the island of Brasil), surrounded by former companions or by fairy ladies, and perhaps restored annually by the Grail, but these descriptions by and large appeared in the essentially non-Arthurian accounts of such figures as Loquifer, the Bâtarde de Bouillon, and Ogier the Dane, who visited Arthur's magic isle in their travels.

In his poem "The Grave of King Arthur" (1777), Thomas Warton memorialized the traditional debate over whether Arthur would return. But depiction of that second coming awaited nineteenth- and twentieth-century British and American writers, who in most instances have described the return or survival of his associates more often than of the King himself. Walter Scott's *Bridal of Triermain* (1813) recounts the awakening of Arthur's daughter in Plantagenet England. Thomas Love Peacock, who in "The Round Table; or King Arthur's Feast" (1817) described Arthur's boredom in Avalon, in "Calidore" (ca. 1816) depicted the King, impatient to return, dispatching a young knight to nineteenth-century England to assess whether the time was right. The most significant version of the myth in the nineteenth century is that of Alfred Tennyson, who treated Arthur's promised return in two imaginative ways: "The Epic" (1842), the modern frame for his earliest tale of the death of Arthur (the "Morte d'Arthur"), depicts the King returning in the narrator's dream as "a modern gentleman/ Of stateliest port," thereby suggesting that the medieval ideals of the Round Table could be maintained in the nineteenth century, though necessarily in modern forms. The expanded version of "The Passing of Arthur" (1869) that concludes the *Idylls of the King* implies that Arthur's departure from this world is actually a return to his proper home, where he is welcomed "beyond the limit of the world" like "a king returning from his wars."

In the twentieth century, John Masefield remained closer to medieval tradition in the title poem of *Midsummer Night and Other Tales in Verse* (1928), which relates how on midsummer night the King and his knights awaken, again turning to stone at the end of the hour, and ends with the hope of Arthur's return. The mythic possibility of this return seized the popular imagination with new force during World War II, when newspaper editorials announced that England's need had never been greater and writers of the period used the material to dramatize the threat of totalitarianism. The myth furnished the collective title *The Once and Future King* (1958) for books that T.H. White had published separately, beginning in 1939. The novel concludes with Arthur imagining his return to establish a brighter world. Adapting the prophecy to a modern setting, C.S. Lewis's novel *That Hideous Strength* (1945) shows Merlin awakening to help destroy an organization that aims to recondition the human race. Arthur himself never returns; however, various Arthurian figures appear throughout the work, and finally both Merlin and Mr. Fisher King, who heads the resistance against the evil organization, like Arthur go to another sphere. Martyn Skinner used the myth similarly in two satiric epics. In *Merlin; or, The Return of Arthur* (1951), Merlin recalls Arthur from Avalon, first taking him to hell to view a documentary film about the sickening realities of the modern world; *The Return of Arthur: A Poem of the Future* (1955) brings Arthur to England about the year 2000 to overthrow a totalitarian regime.

Recent science-fiction writers have employed the mythic return to depict a cosmic conflict between good and evil. In *Merlin's Mirror* (1975), Andre Norton, while focusing on Merlin in his medieval setting, adapts the story of Arthur's survival through the device of time travel, showing the wounded King being put in a life-suspension chamber to await the arrival of space travelers with advanced medical arts. Other writers follow the more common pattern of showing Arthur's companions rather than the King himself returning to the modern world: Morgan le Fay, Lancelot, and Merlin reappear in locations ranging from Cornwall to San Francisco and Mobile, Alabama. This concentration on Arthurian characters other than the King emphasizes that the most significant "return" of Arthur has been not in particular accounts of his second coming but in the revitalization of the entire body of Arthurian material after its relative dormancy between the Middle Ages and the nineteenth century. (For the legend of Arthur's Return in folklore, *see* CAVE LEGEND; FOLKLORE; TOPOGRAPHY AND LOCAL LEGENDS.) [BT]

Loomis, Roger Sherman. "The Legend of Arthur's Survival." In *Arthurian Literature in the Middle Ages*. Oxford: Clarendon, 1959, pp. 64–71.

REYNOLDS, ERNEST RANDOLPH, English scholar and sometime actor, was awarded, in 1930, the Kirke White Prize of Nottingham University for his poem *Tristram and Iseult*. The sixty-five eight-line stanzas are divided into a prelude and three parts, each describing, in images of flowers and gems, a particular scene from the story. In his preface, Reynolds calls it "pictorial poetry" and acknowledges an indebtedness to Wagner. In his musical drama *Mephistopheles and the Golden Apples* (1943), which was the first part of a projected poetic drama called *Martinsmoon*, Mephistopheles provides such entertainments as appearances by Galahad, Lavaine, and Bedivere, an Interlude of Merlin at Tintagel, Merlin's Pantomime, an Interlude at Tintagel, and a song, "Tristram and Iseult," that celebrates their love affair. [SRR/RHT]

Reynolds, Ernest Randolph. *Tristram and Iseult*. Nottingham: Clough, 1930.

———. *Mephistopheles and the Golden Apples: A Fantastic Symphony in Seven Movements*. Cambridge: Heffer, 1943.

RHYS, ERNEST (1859–1946), English editor, poet, dramatist, Rhys was one of the most productive of the many authors from the turn of the century who were inspired by the Arthurian legend. His long poem "The Story of Balin and Balan: From the *Morte d'Arthur*" is collected in *The Garden of Romance* (1897). His next collection, *Welsh Ballads and Other Poems* (1898), contains five short Arthurian poems inspired by Welsh tradition, one of which deals with a version of the widespread cave legend. *Lays of the Round Table and Other Lyric Romances* (1905) contains twenty-four short Arthurian poems, and *The Leaf Burners and Other Poems* (1918), three: based upon Malory, they ponder the mysteries of love, the Grail, and death.

Rhys's three Arthurian plays were all written for music composed by Vincent Thomas. *Gwenevere: A Lyric Play*, which was first performed in 1905 at the Coronet Theatre, London, is based upon Malory's account of the Queen's life. It was followed in 1908 by *Enid: A Lyric Play* and *The Masque of the Grail*, both performed at the Court Theatre. The former is derived from the Welsh tale of Geraint, but it compresses the plot and combines the hero's enemies in one figure, Earl Dwrm; the latter mingles Welsh and French tradition in a short play about Galahad, confronted by the choice of seeking glory or staying home to care for the sick Pelleas. Rhys's treatment of Arthurian legend is romantic and mystical, though he demonstrates more talent than most of his contemporaries, particularly in the creation of a lyrical and pensive mood well suited to the music. [RHT]

Rhys, Ernest. *The Garden of Romance*. London: Kegan Paul, Trench, Trübner, 1897.

———. *Welsh Ballads and Other Poems*. London: Nutt, 1898.
———. *Lays of the Round Table and Other Lyric Romances*. London: Dent, 1905.
———. *The Leaf Burners and Other Poems*. London: Dent, 1918.
Starr, Nathan Comfort. *King Arthur Today: The Arthurian Legend in English and American Literature 1901–1953*. Gainesville: University of Florida Press, 1954.

RIDDERE METTER MOUWEN, DIE ("The Knight with the Sleeve"), an original Middle Dutch verse romance written probably in the second half of the thirteenth century. The main character is Miraudijs, who is called the Knight with the Sleeve after Clarette has given him a white sleeve at the beginning of the story as a token of attachment. After many tribulations, the knight gains the hand of his beloved, finds his lost father, and is witness to the marriage of his parents.

The text has been transmitted to us in two ways. A complete version of 4,020 lines has been preserved as part of the *Lancelot-Compilatie*. In addition, the Royal Library at Brussels possesses a fragment (MS IV 818) dating ca. 1360–70. It contains 320 lines of a more original and much more elaborate version. The compiler of the *Lancelot-Compilatie* abridged the text to one-third. This makes it probable that the *Riddere metter mouwen* originally numbered some 13,500 lines. [BB]

De Kruyter, C.W., ed. *Die Riddere metter mouwen*. Leiden: New Rhine, 1975.
De Haan, Max J.M., L. Longen, B.C. Damsteegt, M.J. Van der Wal, and A. Neesen, eds. *Roman van den Riddere metter mouwen*. Utrecht: HES, 1983.

RIETHMÜLLER, CHRISTOPHER JAMES, who published a number of works in the period 1843–83, intended his first play, the tragedy *Launcelot of the Lake*, for Macready at Drury Lane Theatre, London, but the great actor retired before it could be produced. In five acts of blank verse with some spectacular effects (e.g., for Morgan le Fay's chariot), Arthur's kingdom is brought low as Launcelot and Gwenever fall in love under the spell of Morgan, who is abetted by Mordred. In one striking scene, Launcelot delivers the Queen from the stake and bears her off to Joyous Gard. [CNS]

Riethmüller, C.J. *Launcelot of the Lake: A Tragedy in Five Acts*. London: Chapman and Hall, 1843.

RILEY, JAMES WHITCOMB (1849–1916), American author known as "the Hoosier poet," wrote two Arthurian poems. "An Idyl of the King," which contains virtually no traditional Arthurian material, tells the story of Raelus, who lies to Arthur to get the help of his knights in tracking down the woman he loves. In "Guinevere," the Queen describes the love that overwhelmed her. [ACL]

Riley, James Whitcomb. "Guinevere." In *The Poems and Prose Sketches of James Whitcomb Riley*. New York: Scribner, 1914, Vol. 15: *Early Poems*.
———. "An Idyl of the King." In *Armazindy*. Indianapolis: Bobbs-Merrill, 1894.

RIOTHAMUS. *Riothamus* is the style given in continental documents to a fifth-century "king of the Britons," whose career may underlie parts of the account of Arthur in Geoffrey of Monmouth. It Latinizes a title or honorific in the British language—that is, the parent tongue from which Welsh, Cornish, and Breton evolved.

The known context is the disintegrating Roman Gaul of the late 460s. The north was dominated by Syagrius, a man of imperial loyalty ruling a fragment of the empire. Within his sphere of influence were Franks who cooperated with him, and lately arrived Britons in Armorica, the pioneer Bretons. Southward were the Burgundians, with rulers of their own but friendly to Rome. Hostile Saxons, however, were settled along the lower Loire, and a serious threat came from the southwest, where the Visigothic king Euric was powerful on both sides of the Pyrenees and had ambitious designs.

In 467, the eastern emperor Leo I appointed Anthemius, a Byzantine noble, as his western colleague. A pressing need was to check Euric. Britain had been out of the empire for decades, but Anthemius, possibly encouraged by a pro-Roman trend among its rulers, negotiated a British alliance. The "king of the Britons," Riothamus, came to Gaul in 468 "by the way of Ocean" with 12,000 ship-borne troops (thus the sixth-century historian Jordanes). The Britons were temporarily stationed north of the Loire and may have assisted in a campaign against the Saxons near Angers. But Gaul's imperial prefect, Arvandus, was acting treacherously. He wrote to Euric urging him not to come to terms with the "Greek emperor," meaning Anthemius, but to crush "the Britons posted north of the Loire" and carve up Gaul with the Burgundians. Arvandus was detected and brought to justice, but the empire's hollowness in Gaul was exposed.

Meanwhile, Riothamus moved into Berry and occupied Bourges. Probably in this phase, the Gallo-Roman author Sidonius—formerly city prefect of Rome, now bishop of Clermont, or shortly to become so—wrote to him on behalf of a landowner whose slaves the Britons were enticing away, doubtless to employ them as bearers or mercenaries. Riothamus advanced to Déols near Châteauroux. There, Euric pounced on him with an overwhelming force, "before the Romans [presumably the troops of Syagrius] could join him." The Britons were defeated and Euric drove them from Bourges. Riothamus escaped with a remnant of his army into the nearby territory of the friendly Burgundians, in late 469 or early 470.

Some historians have minimized him as simply a chief of Bretons—i.e., settlers in Armorica—but at that time the Armorican settlement was too sparse. The scattered colonies could not have fielded an army with any prospect of checking Euric; and Arvandus's proposal to him would have made little sense, since he would have achieved nothing by overrunning them. Jordanes's testimony that the Britons came "by the way of Ocean" seems decisive. An army from Britain would have done so, the Armorican settlers would not, since they were on the Continent already and had been for years. A king of the Britons might have gathered recruits from them and counted them as still his subjects. In the judgment of James Campbell, Riothamus is credible as "a British ruler having authority on both sides of the Channel." Ian Wood remarks on his "extraordinary career," viewing him as a man who, beyond doubt, led an expeditionary force to the Continent and presumably did so not under any compulsion but as an act of policy, still seeing his island in the context of a greater world. That he was prepared in 468 to take soldiers out of Britain, and stay overseas for at least a year, helps in dating Ambrosius Aurelianus. Action against the Saxons in the island, under Ambrosius's leadership, had apparently convinced its rulers that they were contained and neutralized.

The Latin form *Riothamus*, used with slight variants in continental texts, corresponds to the British *Rigotamos*. *Rig*, with the added *o* in a compound, meant "king"; *tamos* was a superlative suffix. As a noun, this word would mean "kingmost" or "supreme king" (cf. the modern word *generalissimo*). As an adjective, it would mean "most kingly," "supremely royal." It appears later as a proper name, becoming *Riatham* in Breton and *Rhiadaf* in Welsh. But in the fifth-century setting—in Sidonius's letter, for instance—it looks like a designation for a ruler whose name was something else. Cognate in sense with *Vortigern* and *Vortimer*, and applied to a king of the Britons, it suggests that he was one of the high kings of the period—recasting the style, perhaps, to dissociate himself from discredited predecessors. To judge from the cross-Channel context, he probably held territory in the southwest, but at that time, when the Britons' unity under Rome was still remembered, he might have claimed paramountcy over a much wider area. At any rate, it is hard to believe that his parents happened to give him a name that turned out to be so apt for the office he held as an adult.

As a noun, "supreme king," *Riothamus* would be a title. Similarly, "Genghis Khan," meaning "very mighty ruler," is the accepted designation of a Mongol chieftain whose name was Temujin. As an adjective, "supremely royal," *Riothamus* would be an honorific. Again, the first Roman emperor, whose name was Octavian, adopted the epithet *Augustus*, meaning "majestic," with an overtone of sacredness; after which every emperor was Augustus, "His Majesty." Plutarch records a Greek word, *Basileutatos*, exactly equivalent to *Riothamus*, which was definitely not a name but a term of honor bestowed on Minos of Crete.

The fact that this king of the Britons would have had a separate name—and could have had another one even if *Riothamus* was his name—has inspired attempts to give him substance in Britain by identifying him with someone else. Fleuriot makes him out to be Ambrosius. One of several objections is that Gildas, the single real authority, describes Ambrosius as a general only. But Fleuriot acknowledges that the story of Riothamus, whoever he was, has gone into the making of the story of Arthur. Geoffrey of Monmouth portrays Arthur campaigning in Gaul and makes him contemporary with persons living in Riothamus's time, notably Leo I. Nor is he the only author who does so. (For the traces of an identification or semi-identification, *see* ARTHUR, ORIGINS OF LEGEND.)

A Riothamus appears in Breton genealogies who may be the King, correctly or incorrectly dated. But there were certainly other men so called in the sixth century. [GA]

Gregory of Tours. *History of the Franks*, Book II, Chapter 18.

Jordanes. *Gothic History*, Chapter 45.

Sidonius Apollinaris. *Letters*, Book I, 7; Book III, 9.

Ashe, Geoffrey. "A Certain Very Ancient Book." *Speculum*, 56 (1981), 301–23.

———. *The Discovery of King Arthur*. New York: Doubleday, 1985, pp. 53–56, 96–100.

Campbell, James, ed. *The Anglo-Saxons*. Ithaca, N.Y.: Cornell University Press, 1982, p. 37.

Fleuriot, Léon. *Les Origines de la Bretagne*. Paris: Payot, 1980, pp. 118, 168–73.

Jackson, Kenneth Hurlstone. *Language and History in Early Britain*. Edinburgh: Edinburgh University Press, 1953, p. 457.

Wood, Ian. "The Fall of the Western Empire and the End of Roman Britain." *Britannia*, 18 (1987), 251–62.

ROBBINS, RUTH, inspired by illuminated manuscripts and ancient carvings seen on a visit to England and Wales, illustrated her own children's story of *Taliesin and King Arthur* (1970). After relating the riddle of his birth at the Grand Esteddfod, held at Yuletide in Arthur's court at Caerleon, young Taliesin is proclaimed "the greatest bard of all." [HT]

Robbins, Ruth. *Taliesin and King Arthur*. Berkeley: Parnassus, 1970.

ROBBINS, SHIRLE DOROTHY, author of three Arthurian poems. "Elaine" is a sonnet in which Elaine confesses her deep love to the unyielding Launcelot, in an attempt to move him to pity, if not love. Another sonnet, "Song of Tristan," expresses the dying Tristan's joy to be in the embrace of Isolt one last time before they join in eternity. "Solitude" speaks of a friend seeking solitude in woods so enchanted that Vivien's footprint and Merlin's oak are there. The friend becomes himself like a wizard in that haven. [PCB]

Robbins, Shirle Dorothy. *Tender Is My Song: Poems*. N.p.: Privately printed by Lenora and Anatole Robbins, 1948.

ROBERT DE BLOIS. During the second half of the thirteenth century, Robert de Blois, who is best known for such didactic works as *Enseignements as Princes*, composed *Beaudous*, a verse romance about Gawain's son, the Fair Unknown, that is preserved in a unique manuscript (Paris, B.N. f. fr. 24301). The hero's mother conceals his name from him so that he may win renown for his own achievements, not just because of his lineage. This he accomplishes during a series of adventures that culminate when he gains a kingdom and the love of its princess. To lure him back to his court, Arthur holds a three-day tournament, but Beaudous changes his shield on successive days to hide his identity. He defeats Arthur's finest knights, including Perceval, Kay, Lancelot, Cligés, Yvain, and Erec, before an inconclusive encounter with Gawain. The poem concludes with a recognition scene, followed by the double wedding and coronation of father and son, for Gawain belatedly decides to marry Beaudous's mother when he succeeds his father as king.

The romance follows the traditional pattern of the Fair Unknown story, retold by Renaut de Beaujeu and others, and the account of the tournament owes much to the works of Chrétien de Troyes, particularly *Cligés*. Because it suffers by comparison with these romances, *Beaudous* has been too readily dismissed and ignored by critics. It possesses a charm of its own, however, and its picture of knighthood interestingly reflects the author's didactic concerns. Moreover, Robert does introduce some untraditional features, notably Gawain's marriage and his succession to his father's throne (in Ireland, not Orkney). That he should choose to marry his lady only after their son is old enough to join in a double ceremony reveals the rich ironic potential in the situation, but it is not developed. [RHT]

Robert de Blois. *Sämmtliche Werke: I. Beaudous*, ed. Jacob Ulrich. Berlin: Mayer, 1889.

Lamarque, Gisèle Andrée, ed. "*Le Roman de Biaudeaus*: A Critical Edition." Diss., North Carolina, 1968.

ROBERT DE BORON, a Burgundian poet who composed the first cycle of Grail romances. About this author we know only what he himself has revealed in his work, his name and the name of his noble patron: "Meistres Robers dist, de Bouron,/Se il voloit dire par non" (l. 3,156); "A ce tens que je la retreis/O mon seigneur Gautier en peis,/Qui de Mont Belyal estoit . . ." (l. 3,490). This Gautier has been identified as Gautier de Montbéliard, Lord of Montfaucon, who took the cross and set out on the Fourth Crusade in 1202, never to return to his homeland. He died in 1212. About eighteen kilometers from Montbéliard, there is the village of Boron, presumably Robert's place of origin. The most logical conclusion, supported by the majority of critics, is that Robert, a cleric from Boron in the Franche-Comté, was the author of the works that bear his name and that he was in the service of or somehow close to the Lord of Montbéliard, to whom he recounted (*retreis*) his romance before Gautier's departure (*en peis* 'at peace,' or 'at rest'), in any case before his involvement in the events of the Fourth Crusade.

Robert is the author of a trilogy written in French octosyllabic verse, the *Joseph d'Arimathie* (so-called by scholars, although it was edited under the title *Le Roman de l'Estoire dou Graal*), the *Merlin*, and in all probability a *Perceval*, generally known as the Didot-*Perceval*. Of the original cycle, only the *Joseph* and the initial 504 lines of the *Merlin* survive in their original verse form, but a prose adaptation of the three romances was made by an anonymous redactor shortly after their composition. It was this prose version that ultimately gave rise to the vast cycle of Arthurian prose romances known as the Vulgate. (*See* PROSE *MERLIN* [1]; DIDOT-*PERCEVAL*.)

The *Joseph* has been variously dated. We must consider that Robert had completed most or all of the romance prior to 1202, the date of Gautier's departure for the Holy Land. The early limit is somewhat more difficult to establish, though it is widely thought that the Vales of Avalon mentioned in the romance are to be identified with the area around Glastonbury in Somerset, where the bones of Arthur and his queen were supposedly discovered in 1191. The years 1191–1202 thus limit considerably the period of composition and support the conclusion that Robert's *Joseph* postdated Chrétien de Troyes's *Perceval* and that he derived certain crucial details from the work of the Champenois poet.

After a prologue relating the Fall of Man and leading up to the Passion, Robert tells how the vessel of the Last Supper was given by Pilate to the obscure disciple Joseph of Arimathea, who in turn used it to collect the blood of the crucified Christ after the Deposition. Joseph is imprisoned by the Jews, but the risen Christ visits him and delivers the twice-hallowed vessel into his possession and reveals to him the secrets bound up with it. After the passage of many years, the emperor Vespasian, cured of the foulest disease by Veronica's cloth, arrives in Judea to avenge the death of Christ. Vespasian discovers Joseph alive in prison, miraculously sustained by the precious vessel, and is converted to Christianity by his words.

Suddenly, the narrative takes an unusual turn. Joseph's sister, Enygeus, and her husband, Hebron (or its shortened form Bron), appear as if from nowhere and in the company of some followers leave Judea with Joseph and go into exile in some "distant land." After an initial success, their crops fail, owing to the sin of lechery, of which some of the company were guilty. To separate the innocent from the guilty, Joseph is directed by the Holy Spirit to set up, in memory of the table of the Last Supper, a second table where will be celebrated the service of the Grail (but not so-named until later). Bron is sent to catch a fish that will occupy a place at the table close to the vessel. When all is ready, the followers are bidden to seek a place at the table, but mysteriously only those who are untainted with the sin of lust can approach, and their hearts are filled with ineffable delight. (Here, the Grail is named and is derived in typical medieval fashion from the verb *agreer* 'to delight.') One of the banished sinners, Moysés by name, attempts to take a place at the table against the dire warning of Joseph and is swallowed up in the earth. Twelve sons are born to Enygeus and Bron, of whom eleven marry and adopt the earthly life. The twelfth is named Alain; he will take charge of his brothers and lead them toward distant lands in the West, preaching the name of Christ. A future offspring of this Alain, the "third man" (Perceval?), will be the ultimate keeper of the Grail. Another follower of Joseph, Petrus, is also to travel to the West, to the Vales of Avalon, and there await the coming of Alain's son. Finally, Bron, henceforth to be called the Rich Fisher, will take possession of the holy vessel and follow the others to the West to wait for the third man to whom the vessel will be entrusted. All of this comes to pass and the significance of the Holy Trinity is fulfilled. Joseph returns to Arimathea to end his days.

Robert is a sorry poet, often confusing in detail and on occasion even guilty of self-contradiction. But what he lacks in graceful expression and elegant poetic turn of phrase is made up for by a magnificent vision of universal history centered on the Holy Grail. He was the first to identify the vessel of the Last Supper with the mysterious *graal* of Chrétien's *Perceval* and describe how this sacred vessel was used by Joseph of Arimathea to collect the blood of Christ. It was this bold vision that bridged the gap between sacred history and the world of Arthurian Britain (the Round Table was the "third table," in keeping with Trinitarian symbolism) and gave the impulse to the thorough Christianization of the Grail myth. [RO'G]

Robert de Boron. *Le Roman de l'Estoire dou Graal*, ed. William Nitze. Paris: Champion, 1927.

———. *Merlin, roman du XIIIe siècle*, ed. Alexandre Micha. Geneva: Droz, 1980.

Roach, William, ed. *The Didot-Perceval*. Philadelphia: University of Pennsylvania Press, 1941.

Nitze, William. "Messire Robert de Boron: Enquiry and Summary." *Speculum*, 28 (1953), 279–96.

O'Gorman, Richard. "The Prose Version of Robert de Boron's *Joseph d'Arimathie*." *Romance Philology*, 23 (1970), 449–61.

———. "La Tradition manuscrite du *Joseph d'Arimathie* en prose de Robert de Boron." *Revue d'Historie des Textes*, 1 (1971), 145–81.

ROBERT OF GLOUCESTER. The two versions of the late thirteenth-century verse chronicle in English attributed to Robert of Gloucester appear to have been the work of at least three people. Both the longer version (ca. 12,000 lines, surviving in seven manuscripts) and the shorter (ca. 10,000 lines, seven manuscripts) incorporate an earlier presumably anonymous English chronicle from Brutus to the death of Henry I in 1135. Although it is possible that Robert of Gloucester wrote this early section of the chronicle, it is certain only that sometime near the beginning of the fourteenth century he wrote the continuation of this earlier chronicle to 1270 that is found in the longer version. Someone else appears to have written the shorter version, which adds to the earlier anonymous chronicle to 1135 some details from Geoffrey of Monmouth's *Historia Regum Britanniae* and Layamon's *Brut* and a continuation to the accession of Edward I in 1272.

Nothing much is known about the Robert of Gloucester to whom the whole work was once attributed. He may have been a secular clerk, since the chronicle seems in some ways to belong to the secular tradition of historiography and since none of the manuscripts appears to have originated in a monastic library. If so, he would have had some associations with Oxford and Gloucester. Most scholars, however, assume that he was a monk of St. Peter's, Gloucester.

The chronicle was widely read in the Middle Ages and later and was a source for many antiquarians of the sixteenth, seventeenth, and eighteenth centuries. The Arthurian story, which belongs to the earlier, presumably anonymous, part of the chronicle, is the second chronicle, after Layamon, to tell the story of Arthur in English. Presenting, like most chroniclers, a heroic picture of Arthur, the author follows Geoffrey of Monmouth closely, with some details added from Henry of Huntingdon and some that suggest knowledge of Arthurian romance. (Merlin is described as an enchanter; Gawain is the "flour of corteysye.") The author adds considerably to the glory of Arthur's court, noting, for example, that the final battle at Camlann was greater than any battle except that of Troy. Unlike Layamon, who confined his narrative to the period originally covered by Geoffrey of Monmouth, this author followed the lead of twelfth- and thirteenth-century Latin chroniclers and produced the first vernacular chronicle that incorporated this material into the whole history of Britain and England. In the section that Robert of Gloucester actually seems to have written, there is a reference to the discovery of Arthur's bones at Glastonbury during the reign of King Richard. [EDK]

Robert of Gloucester. *The Metrical Chronicle of Robert of Gloucester*, ed. W.A. Wright. 2 vols. London: Eyre and Spottiswoode, 1887.

Fletcher, Robert Huntington. *The Arthurian Material in the Chronicles, Especially Those of Great Britain and France*. Boston: Ginn, 1906; 2nd ed. Roger Sherman Loomis. New York: Franklin, 1966, pp. 193–98.

Gransden, Antonia. *Historical Writing in England, c. 550 to c. 1307*. London: Routledge and Kegan Paul, 1974, pp. 432–38.

Hudson, Anne. "Tradition and Innovation in Some Middle English Manuscripts." *Review of English Studies*, n.s., 17 (1966), 359–72.

Kennedy, Edward Donald. "Chronicles and Other Historical Writing." In *Manual of the Writings in Middle English*, ed. A.E. Hartung. New Haven: Connecticut Academy of Arts and Sciences, 1981–89, Vol. 8, pp. 2617–21, 2798–807.

ROBERTS, SIR CHARLES G.D. (1860–1943), Canadian Confederation poet, animal-story writer, and teacher. Roberts's "Launcelot and the Four Queens" (1880) is a narrative poem based on the account in Malory. Launcelot is imprisoned by Morgan le Fay and her royal companions in an unsuccessful attempt to force him to choose one of them as his lady. [RHT]

Roberts, Sir Charles G.D. "Launcelot and the Four Queens." In *Orion and Other Poems*. Philadelphia: Lippincott, 1880; repr. in *The Collected Poems of Sir Charles G.D. Roberts: A Critical Edition*, ed. Desmond Pacey and Graham Adams. Wolfville, Nova Scotia: Wombat, 1985, pp. 38–46.

ROBERTS, DOROTHY JAMES (1903–1990), American author of three historical novels based on Malory. *The Enchanted Cup* (1953) recreates the ill-fated love of Tristram and Isoud. *Launcelot, My Brother* (1954) is the account by Bors (here Launcelot's brother rather than cousin) of Launcelot's love for Guinevere and the destruction of the Round Table. *Kinsmen of the Grail* (1963) focuses upon the Grail quests of Perceval and Gawin, a quest for what all search for but few find: the meaning of life. All three novels are written with clarity and emotional insight, particularly the last, which brings a fresh, modern perception into both theme and the psychology of character. [MAG]

Roberts, Dorothy James. *The Enchanted Cup*. New York: Appleton-Century-Crofts, 1953.

———. *Launcelot, My Brother*. New York: Appleton-Century-Crofts, 1954.

———. *Kinsmen of the Grail*. Boston: Little, Brown, 1963.

ROBERTS, REV. PETER (1760?–1819), published in 1811 an English translation of a Welsh chronicle of the early British kings, similar in all respects to that of Geoffrey of Monmouth. The translation's principal source was a work found in a manuscript in the Welsh language, the *Brut Tysilio*, supplemented by Welsh copies that reposed in the "Archaiology of Wales" and two privately owned manuscripts. Roberts hoped to produce something even more correct than Aaron Thompson's 1718 translation of Geoffrey. [JHW]

Roberts, Rev. Peter, trans. *The Chronicle of the Kings of Britain*. London, 1811.

ROBERTS, THEODORE GOODRIDGE (1877–1953), Canadian author of three Arthurian novelettes and nine short stories in *Blue Book Magazine* (1947–52). Inspired by Malory, these romantic comedies laugh gently at the foibles of chivalry. The short stories deal with the adventures of Dinadan, an impractical romantic who hides behind the pose of cynicism. [RHT]

Thompson, Raymond H. *The Return from Avalon: A Study of the Arthurian Legend in Modern Fiction*. Westport, Conn.: Greenwood, 1985.

ROBINS, MADELEINE E., in her fantasy "Nimuë's Tale" (1988), describes how the youthful Nimuë learns the bitter realities of power and love through her relationship with Merlin, Pelles, and Viviene, the Lady of the Lake. [RHT]

Robins, Madeleine E. "Nimuë's Tale." In *Invitation to Camelot: An Arthurian Anthology of Short Stories*, ed. Parke Godwin. New York: Ace, 1988, pp. 145–64.

ROBINSON, EDWIN ARLINGTON (1869–1935), American-born poet, composed three Arthurian works: *Merlin* (1917), *Lancelot* (1920), and *Tristram* (1927). All three are lengthy blank-verse narratives set in the last days of Arthur's realm, and all are characterized by an ambience of fatality. The events described do not depart much from those given in Malory, except in *Tristram*. The style of the poems is primarily that of extended meditation and self-analysis, with some scenes of dramatic interaction. In terms of style, the dialogues can only with difficulty be considered as mimetic. They are, rather, dialectical argument recast as speech.

Merlin begins with the meditations of Dagonet, the "fool" knighted by Arthur, who muses on speculations by other knights about the fate of the realm, but Merlin is the central focus of the poem. Despite his passion for Vivian, the sage cannot submit to a life of ease and blandishment, depicted in an extended and elaborate flashback, and must return to Arthur even if he can do nothing. The poem ends with Merlin exacting an oath of fealty from the despairing Dagonet as they go to join the King.

Lancelot centers on the catastrophe set in motion by the love affair of Lancelot and Guenevere. The poem could easily be entitled "Lancelot and Gawaine," since it is the tragedy of friendship betrayed that informs the greater portion of the work. Dramatic dialogue predominates as Gawaine tries and fails to warn Lancelot; as Gawaine's brothers plot; as Lancelot and Guenevere struggle with the dissolution of their affair and of their world; and, most movingly, as Arthur is torn between love and law, in a scene that shows him skirting the edges of madness on the day of Guenevere's scheduled execution. The poem is flawed by occasional passages of overwrought pseudo-Shakespearian diction, but this is swept aside when characters speak with simple feeling, as Arthur does in the passage just mentioned, or as Gawaine does when he learns of his brothers' deaths at Lancelot's hands. Lancelot and Guenevere part at her convent, but Robinson chooses to depict Lancelot as an eternal wanderer, a departure from the symmetry of the traditional ending of their story.

Of Robinson's three Arthurian poems, *Tristram* is the most unified in lyric focus and original in its approach to the material of legend; the lovers' language in both *Lancelot* and *Merlin* becomes in *Tristram* as much philosophy as passion. The poem begins and ends in pathos as Isolt of the White Hands waits in Brittany for Tristram's arrival, watching the sea, and watching still after his death. This Isolt is preserved from mawkishness by the poet's insistence on her clear-sighted appraisal of her hopes despite her passion for Tristram.

The lyric focus of the poem is loss. For risking one last rendezvous, Tristram is banished on the night of Mark's wedding with Isolt of Ireland. Mark loses his nephew and retainer, and he never possesses the love of Isolt. Isolt, who remains in the background for much of the poem, is slowly destroyed by Tristram's absence. Like Isolt of Brittany, she sees clearly, more so than Tristram, that the affair can end only in death; in a reversal of the conventional details of the legend, it is Tristram who comes to her deathbed, with Mark's consent, there to be slain treacherously by the jealous Andred.

Robinson reduces the multiple episodes of lovers' meetings and deceptions of Mark to the wedding-night encounter and the extended idyll at Joyous Garde after Tristram is summoned from Brittany to Arthur's court. He thus emphasizes the deprivation that robs Tristram of any joy in his marriage and drains life itself from Isolt of Ireland, so that when she is abducted by Mark's men from Joyous Garde she yields slowly to death. Relief from the intensity of the characters' emotion is provided by Morgan le Fay, sometime rescuer of Tristram and an ironic observer of the affair's progress. On the other hand, Morgan is implicated in the lovers' final catastrophe by Mark, who suspects her of further inflaming Andred's insane jealousy of the lovers. These three characters, Mark, Andred, and Morgan, who establish essentially negative relationships, are thus set in opposition to the three lovers.

As one might expect in poems written in a relatively brief timespan and having common subject matters, there are specific mutual correspondences, especially among the minor characters, such as Gawaine and Bedivere. Gawaine, lighthearted and in love with life, is troubled by the events around him, but he is incapable of real engagement until personal tragedy strikes. Bedivere is a mixture of resignation and hope. He is Arthur's oldest and most clear-sighted knight, if one discounts the wise folly of Dagonet, yet he is the one who can envision a new world beyond the downfall of Arthur's kingdom.

Further correspondences among the poems can be found in the pervasive motif of the passage of time and the emblematic imagery of the colors of hair, eyes, and complexion for female characters. All three poems are characterized by vivid contrasts in the use of inner and outer spaces—rooms, castles, gardens, and forests, and, in *Tristram*, the sea; the contrasts are generally ironic, since the characters in the poems are all prisoners of their circumstances.

The structural complexity of *Merlin* is not repeated in the other two poems. *Lancelot* is structured according to the events of the legend, and Robinson does not use the additional framing furnished by the character of Dagonet in *Merlin* or of Isolt of the White Hands in *Tristram*. The dramatic action of *Lancelot* flows consistently from the weaknesses of the characters rather than from their strengths; it is only final renunciations that do not go awry. Published over a ten-year period, Robinson's three Arthurian poems show not so much a progression in poetic technique as a varied experimentation in the presentation of traditional material. [AAR]

Robinson, Edwin Arlington. *Merlin*. New York: Macmillan, 1917.

———. *Lancelot: A Poem*. New York: Seltzer, 1920.

———. *Tristram*. New York: Macmillan, 1927.

Winters, Yvor. *Edwin Arlington Robinson*. New York: New Directions, 1971.

74. Henry Peach Robinson, "The Lady of Shalott." (The Royal Photographic Society, Bath.)

ROBINSON, HENRY PEACH (1830–1901), English photographer, whose narrative photographs of literary subjects included two Arthurian images: "Elaine Watching the Shield of Lancelot" (1859–60) and "The Lady of Shalott" (1860–61). The latter, a composite of several negatives (the technique was Robinson's speciality), is derived from John Everett Millais's painting *Ophelia* (1851–52). Robinson later repudiated the theatricality of much of his early work, describing "The Lady of Shalott," in particular, as "a ghastly mistake." [JL]

Harker, Margaret. *Henry Peach Robinson: Master of Photographic Art, 1830–1901*. Oxford: Blackwell, 1988.

ROGERS, MARK E., wrote and illustrated "A Samurai Cat in King Arthur's Court" (1986), an anachronistic parody of Arthurian romance and popular films in which a cat trained to fight as a samurai warrior wins a tournament against the finest knights of the Round Table, overcomes the magic of Morgan Le Fairchilde, and returns in a bi-plane with Wisconsin Platt (Indiana Jones) in time to save Arthur from Mordred's savage hordes. [RHT]

Rogers, Mark E. "A Samurai Cat in King Arthur's Court." In *More Adventures of Samurai Cat*. New York: Doherty, 1986, pp. 9–47.

ROHMER, ERIC, French director of *Perceval le Gallois* (1978), a faithful setting of the text of Chrétien de Troyes's last work. This eccentric and beautiful film (with Fabrice Luchini as Perceval and André Dussollier as Gauvain) begins with Perceval's encounter with knights in his mother's forest and presents all the major scenes dealing with Perceval—his battle with the Red Knight, his instruction by Gornemant, scenes at Blancheflor's castle, the Grail castle and Fisher King, the drops of blood on the snow, and the Good Friday episode—but only the first two episodes of the Gauvain section of the original. Rohmer effectively depicts the naiveté of Perceval, who, as in Chrétien's text, moves through the story like a marionette, understanding little of what is happening to him until the final scene, when the holy hermit reveals to him his mother's death and the secrets of the Grail castle.

The text is a modernized rendering of Chrétien's own, but very archaic nonetheless, with the vocabulary and syntax in many cases taken directly from the Old French; the dialogue, however, can be followed without difficulty. The characters not only speak the words assigned to them, but they also provide narrative, often speaking of themselves in the third person, as when Blancheflor says of herself, "she weeps," and then does so. This kind of narration is contributed also by singers and various nameless characters, whose function is to provide transitions and announce action. Rohmer systematically shuns realism, a characteristic most evident in his use of scenery composed of heavily stylized trees and buildings. The effect is similar to that of a medieval miniature and is theatrically more like a pageant or a morality play than a drama.

Other than the omission of the later Gauvain episodes, the film departs strikingly from Chrétien's work only in the conclusion. Whereas the Old French romance noted simply that Perceval learned that "Dieu el vendredi rechut/ Mort et si fu crucefiiez" ("God was crucified and killed on [Good] Friday," ll. 6,510–11), Rohmer adds a Latin sequence, a kind of passion play that depicts the stations of the Cross and dramatizes both Christ's agony in crucifixion and Perceval's rebirth. [NJL]

Avant-Scène du Cinéma, 221 (February 1, 1979), 1–68. (Contains screenplay and related documents.)

"Dossier-Auteur: Eric Rohmer à la recherche de l'absolu." *Cinéma*, 242 (February 1979), 7–32.

Tesich-Savage, Nadja. "Rehearsing the Middle Ages." *Film Comment*, 14 (September–October 1978), 50–56.

ROMERO, GEORGE A., American director, best known for such horror films as *Night of the Living Dead* and *Dawn of the Dead*. Romero's 1981 *Knightriders* retells the story of Arthur in terms of a quest for the American dream. Set in contemporary western Pennsylvania, the film follows the adventures of Billy (Ed Harris in the role of Arthur) and his companions, a troupe of motorcycle enthusiasts who travel armor-clad from country fair to country fair to joust for groups of spectators who routinely fail to share their quest for a simpler and better America. The cast of characters includes a Lancelot, a Guenevere, a Morgan—here a man—and a Merlin, as well as a Pippin and a Friar Tuck. Together, Billy and his troupe do battle with corrupt law-enforcement officials and the encroaching threat that crass commercialism poses to their way of life.

Although overlong, *Knightriders* stands as a worthy attempt to show that Arthur is both once and future king. Released by coincidence during the same week as John Boorman's *Excalibur*, *Knightriders* initially failed to attract an audience but then went on to become a cult film on the midnight circuit of repertory film houses. [KJH]

Gagne, Paul R. *The Zombies That Ate Pittsburgh: The Films of George A. Romero*. New York: Dodd, Mead, 1987.

75. D.G. Rossetti, "Sir Tristram and La Belle Yseult Drinking the Love Potion." (Courtesy of the Trustees, The Cecil Higgins Art Gallery, Bedford, England.)

ROSEN, WINIFRED, in *Three Romances* (1981), retells the stories of three of the more perplexing Arthurian love affairs: Gawain and Ragnell, Enid and Geraint, and Merlin and Niniane. The author, with a modern romance-fiction sensibility, emphasizes the resolution of the characters' problems. [DN]

Rosen, Winifred. *Three Romances: Love Stories from Camelot Retold*. New York: Knopf, 1981.

ROSSETTI, DANTE GABRIEL (1828–1882), became interested in chivalric stories in his youth. His first Arthurian subject, *King Arthur's Tomb* (1854, Private Collection), was his own invention. After designing three subjects for the Moxon Tennyson (1857), he organized the Oxford Union Murals project, using Malory as his text. Of his own contribution, *Lancelot's Vision of the Sangrael* and *Lancelot in the Queen's Chamber* are known only through drawings, and *How Sir Galahad, Sir Bors and Sir Percival Saw the Sangrael* was not begun. He also participated in the Dunlop Windows project.

His later Arthurian subjects were refinements of earlier designs, such as *How Sir Galahad, Sir Bors and Sir Percival Were Fed with the Grael; but Sir Percival's Sister Died by the Way* (1864, Birmingham City Galleries) and *Sir Tristram and La Belle Yseult Drink the Love Potion* (1867, Cecil Higgins Art Gallery, Bedford). By the end of the 1860s, Rossetti was concerned with writing his own Arthuriad, *God's Graal*, which was never finished; by the 1870s, Arthurian subjects vanished from his work. Rossetti's influence was crucial in the Arthurian Revival. He urged other artists, notably Edward Burne-Jones, Arthur Hughes, and William Morris, to undertake Arthurian subjects; his own style was associated with the romantic facet of Arthurian painting, and he added erotic and mystic subjects to the Victorian repertoire. [DNM]

Faxon, Alicia Craig. *Dante Gabriel Rossetti*. New York: Abbeville, 1989.

Surtees, Virginia. *The Paintings and Drawings of Dante Gabriel Rossetti (1828 to 1882): A Catalogue Raisonné*. 2 vols. Oxford: Clarendon, 1971.

ROUBAUD, JACQUES, French author of *Graal Fiction* (1978) and of *Le Roi Arthur au temps des chevaliers et des enchanteurs* ("King Arthur in the Time of Knights and Enchanters," 1983). *Graal Fiction*, announced as the first of twenty-six volumes, combines retellings of the stories of Merlin, the Lady of Shalott, Joseph of Arimathea, and others with a commentary on the tales and on narrative methods.

Le Roi Arthur retells the early portions of the Arthurian story. After a brief survey of the reigns of Brutus, Constant, and Vortiger, it offers the story of Uther and Ygerne (whose husband is named Mark) and of Arthur's conception. Concentrating on Arthur's early career (the sword in the anvil, Merlin's role, Arthur's marriage to Guenièvre and his establishment of the Round Table, and Excalibur), the account breaks off after his victory over the Saxons; the conclusion hints at further adventures to come and, in the last paragraph, announces the arrival of the Green Knight at court. This uneven retelling of Arthur's story is enlivened by touches of humor and by the narrator's frequent objections that the Arthurian legend has so many variants that the truth is not easily discerned. Roubaud appends to his story a *dossier* presenting some facts concerning chivalry, courtly love, and Arthurian history and legend.

Roubaud and Florence Delay are also the authors of *Graal Théâtre* (1977–), a series of dramas expected to run to ten volumes. (*See also* DELAY, FLORENCE.) [NJL]

Roubaud, Jacques. *Graal Fiction*. Paris: Gallimard, 1978.

———. *Le Roi Arthur au temps des chevaliers et des enchanteurs*. Paris: Hachette, 1983.

ROUND TABLE. King Arthur's celebrated Round Table is first mentioned by Wace in 1155 in his *Roman de Brut*. In lines 9,747–58, he ascribes the origin of the table to Arthur's desire to prevent quarrels of precedence among his barons and to promote a sense of equality: "On account of his noble barons, each of whom thought himself the best and none of whom accounted himself the worst, Arthur made the Round Table, of which Britons tell many fabulous tales. There sat his vassals, all noble and all equal; they sat equally at table and were equally served. No one of them could boast of sitting higher than his peer."

Layamon, in his adaptation of Wace's *Brut* in the early thirteenth century, expanded his source by creating a fierce quarrel over precedence at a Yuletide feast, with many dead and wounded. A Cornish carpenter, hearing of this fight, created a great Round Table that could seat 1,600 and more men, yet was easily portable. Both Wace and Layamon refer to Breton storytellers as the source for this Round Table, and in spite of the hesitations of some scholars there is no compelling reason to doubt them on this point. An ancient Celtic custom had warriors sit in circles around their king or the bravest warrior, and certain specific details recounted in Celtic stories (the number of warriors, the quarrel of precedence) recur in Wace and Layamon.

By a later tradition, recounted in prose texts of the thirteenth century, the origin of the Round Table is ascribed to Merlin. In the prose redaction of Robert de Boron's *Merlin* (ca. 1200), Merlin recalls in a celebrated passage Christ's table of the Last Supper and Joseph of Arimathea's Grail table, each of which had twelve places and one empty seat, in memory of Judas's betrayal. At Uther Pendragon's request, Merlin has a third table constructed to seat fifty knights. He tells Uther that one seat must remain empty and will be filled only after Uther's death by the knight who will achieve the Grail quest. In the Didot-*Perceval*, a continuation of Robert's *Merlin*, the number of places is again thirteen, with one still empty "por le senefiance del liu u Judas sist." Since Merlin had left this place empty at Uther's table, Arthur does not dare fill it now. However, Perceval, after defeating the knights of the Round Table in a tournament, demands Arthur's permission to occupy the empty seat. This provokes an earthquake and occasions the "enchantments of Britain," which will not end until one of the knights then at table will surpass all others in chivalry, reach the abode of the rich Fisher King, and ask concerning the Grail.

In the opening pages of the *Queste del Saint Graal* (the principal source of Malory's "Tale of the Sankgreal"), Galahad is led forward to occupy this seat, now known as the Siege Perilous. He goes on to achieve the adventure of the Sword in the Stone and assists at the great evening meal at Camelot at which all at the Round Table are fed miraculously from the Holy Grail. (*See also* PERILOUS SEAT; ROUND TABLES; WINCHESTER.) [WWK]

Loomis, Roger Sherman. *Arthurian Tradition and Chrétien de Troyes*. New York: Columbia University Press, 1949, pp. 61–70.

Tatlock, J.S.P. *The Legendary History of Britain*. Berkeley: University of California Press, 1950, pp. 471–77.

ROUND TABLES, festive events involving jousting and dancing in imitation of Arthur and his knights. The first known Round Table took place in Cyprus in 1223, to celebrate a knighting, and such pageants remained popular throughout much of Europe during the remainder of the Middle Ages. In many cases, the participating knights assumed the names and arms of Arthur's knights, and René d'Anjou even built an "Arthurian" castle for a Round Table he held in 1446. (*See also* BALTIC REGION, ARTHURIAN CLUBS IN; PAGEANT DESIGN [BRITISH]; ROUND TABLE; TOURNAMENTS.) [NJL]

Loomis, Roger Sherman. "Arthurian Influence on Sport and Spectacle." In *Arthurian Literature in the Middle Ages*. Oxford: Clarendon, 1959, pp. 551–59.

RUNKELSTEIN MURALS. Schloss Runkelstein (properly, Castel Róncolo, for it now lies in Italy) guards the southern approaches to the Brenner Pass just north of the Italian city of Bolzano in the southern Tyrol. The thirteenth-century castle was purchased in 1385 by the bankers and patrons of the arts Nikolas and Franz Vintler. Before his death in 1413, Nikolas Vintler added a summer house and decorated the castle with paintings. In 1500, the emperor Maximilian acquired the castle and between 1503 and 1511 ordered the restoration of the paintings. In the nineteenth century, the castle was restored again and given to the town of Bolzano by the emperor Franz Joseph.

The Summer House where the Arthurian paintings are to be found was an open structure with gallery and loggia. In the gallery are paintings of the Nine Worthies including King Arthur, knights seated at the Round Table, three pairs of lovers including Tristan and Isolde, and giants and giantesses. The romance of Tristan, following the version of Gottfried von Strassburg, rendered in grisaille, is found in the so-called Ladies' Chamber. Additional grisailles (with touches of green and red) in the loggia illustrate the adventures of Wigalois as told by the Austrian poet Wirnt von Grafenberg. Although badly damaged and defaced, the latter subject can be identified by the repeated inscription "Vigelas"; furthermore, an inventory of 1493 lists a "Vigelas sal."

The thirteenth-century romance *Garel von dem blühenden Tal*, by the Austrian author Der Pleier, also found a place among the paintings in the Summer House, in the room known as the "Library." Ten of twenty-two paintings survive, from ca. 1400; although also repainted in the sixteenth century and restored in the nineteenth, they are in slightly better condition than those of Wigalois, and the artist's attention to details lends a note of human interest to the fantasy of the romance. For example, in the representation of Garel at Arthur's Round Table the table stands in a meadow under a leafy tree where musicians entertain the King and his knights. Above, a pennant bearing Arthur's emblem of three crowns flutters from a long trumpet, and one hungry knight reaches for food from the central platter. [MS]

Loomis, Roger Sherman, and Laura Hibbard Loomis. *Arthurian Legends in Medieval Art*. London: Oxford University Press, 1938, pp. 60–75, 79–84; figs. 60–75, 171–83, 184–201.

RUSTICIANO DA PISA, or Rusticien de Pise, has a double claim to the attention of posterity. As a prisoner in Genoa in 1298, he wrote an account in French of the adventures of his fellow prisoner, Marco Polo. Earlier in his career, he had composed a vast Arthurian *mélange* in prose known as the *Roman de Roi Artus* (or the *Compilation*) that, although written in French, is the first Arthurian romance by an Italian. This *Compilation*, apparently derived from a book that had been in the possession of Edward I of England when he journeyed through Italy on his way to the Crusade in the Holy Land in 1272, is a large interpolation in manuscripts that preserve *Palamedes*. In the sixteenth century, the *Compilation* was divided into two volumes and printed as the *Gyron le Courtois* (Verard, 1501?) and the *Meliadus de Leonnoys* (Janot, 1528, 1532). The rambling *Meliadus* contains the adventures of Tristan's father; the *Gyron*, less connected to the adventures of Tristan and the knights of the Round Table, celebrates the House of Bruns and its most notable representative, Gyron. The *Compilation* influenced a Greek poem of ca. 1300 (*Ho Presbys Hippotes*), the Spanish *Tristán de Leonís*, and most subsequent prose versions of *Tristan* in Italian. [DLH]

Gardner, Edmund G. *The Arthurian Legend in Italian Literature*. London: Dent, 1930, pp. 47–50.

Löseth, Eilert. *Le Roman en prose de Tristan*. Paris: Champion, 1891.

RYONS (Rience), a king, descended from Hercules (according to the Vulgate Cycle), who was killed by Arthur. In Malory, Ryons pursues a custom of trimming his cloak with the beards of his defeated enemies. Attempting to complete the project with Arthur's beard, he is instead defeated by the King, assisted by Balin and Balan. [NJL]

S

SABERHAGEN, FRED, popular American science-fiction author, wrote *Dominion* (1982), an involving horror novel set largely in modern Chicago. Merlin shakes off the enchantment that bereft him of power in time to frustrate Nimue's diabolical plan to bring from the past an evil sorcerer who seeks dominion over the world. The novel is part of Saberhagen's Dracula series (1975–). [RHT]

Saberhagen, Fred. *Dominion*. New York: TOR, 1982.

SACHS, HANS (1494–1576), the most prolific sixteenth-century German dramatist and *Meistersinger*. Sachs is known to the non-German world primarily through Richard Wagner's opera *Die Meistersinger von Nürnberg*. The celebrated shoemaker of Nürnberg composed approximately 4,400 *Meisterlieder* and close to 130 dramas in his lifetime, not to mention his Shrovetide plays. In his most productive period, Sachs produced up to 450 titles per year. In the years 1545–53, he composed one drama and seven *Meisterlieder* inspired by the *matière de Bretagne*.

Sachs's first Arthurian composition is the *Meisterlied* "Die Ehbrecherbruck" ("The Adulterers' Bridge"), dated March 17, 1545. The poem relates how a suspicious King Arthur had a magic bridge built that would not carry unfaithful persons and would announce their infidelity by the sounding of a bell. At a great feast, the King and Queen lead a procession across the bridge. The knights and ladies fall off to right and left, but Arthur's wife safely crosses the bridge. Sachs concludes by observing that many a person would not be able to cross the bridge today.

The drama *Tragedia von der strengen Lieb, Herr Tristrant mit der schönen Königin Isalden* ("Tragedy of the Severe Love of Sir Tristrant and the Beautiful Queen Isalde"), dated February 7, 1553, is based on the chapbook *Ein wunderbarliche vnd fast lustige Historij von Herr Tristrant vnd der schönen Isalden* ("A Marvelous and Quite Pleasing Tale of Sir Tristrant and the Beautiful Isalde"), first published in 1484. The drama is composed in seven acts and commences and concludes with didactic considerations (*see* TRISTAN IN MODERN GERMAN VERSIONS).

Sachs's Arthurian *Meisterlieder* that are devoted to the Tristan matter commemorate specific events in the life of the lovers: the spying episode in the orchard, the lovers' sojourn in the woods, Tristrant's battle with Morhold, the slaying of the dragon, Tristrant disguised as a fool, and Tristrant's death. The first five *Meisterlieder* were composed in December 1551, the last in March 1553, shortly after Sachs had written the drama. [MEK]

Sachs, Hans. "Tragedia mit 23 personen, von der strengen lieb herr Tristrant mit der schönen königin Isalden, unnd hat 7 actus." In *Hans Sachs*, ed. Adelbert von Keller. Tübingen: Litterarischer Verein, 1879, Vol. 12, pp. 142–86.

Könneker, Barbara. *Hans Sachs*. Stuttgart: Metzler, 1971.

Sobel, Eli. *The Tristan Romance in the Meisterlieder of Hans Sachs*. Berkeley: University of California Press, 1963.

SAGA AF TRISTRAM OK ÍSODD (or *Tristrams saga ok Ísoddar*), a shortened retelling from Iceland of the Tristan story, dated to the fourteenth century. Some episodes have been drastically changed or deleted, while others have been added. In this saga, Mark is called Mórodd. His sister's knight is killed in a joust, and she falls in love with his slayer, Kalegras. She sends for him and they remain in bed for three years. She gives birth to Tristram but dies of grief when Kalegras is killed. After being kidnaped by African warriors and sold as a slave, Tristram arrives at the court of Mórodd. The saga deviates from other versions in that a piece of sword lodges in Tristram's head. In Ireland, he is cured by Ísodd, and the queen offers Tristram her daughter as a reward for killing the dragon. He demurs and says that his uncle is a more suitable husband. During the voyage to England, Tristram and Ísodd drink from a horn, but it is not stated that this is a love potion. Indeed, it is made clear that Ísodd is already quite fond of Tristram. The remainder of the text abounds in further deviations. From his union with the other Ísodd, here called Ísodd the Dark, Tristram has a son who becomes king of England. The author mentions that there is a great saga about his children.

Opinions about this saga are varied: it was once thought to be based on an unknown source, while others saw it as an inaccurate and clumsy retelling of Brother Robert's version. More recently, Paul Schach has suggested that it may have been a satire, because so many events in the story have been reversed, often with humorous effect. The Icelandic fairy tales and Scandinavian ballads about Tristan show greater similarity to this version than to Robert's. [MCH]

Brynjúlfsson, Gísli, ed. *Saga af Tristram ok Ísodd i Grundtexten med oversættelse*. In *Annaler for nordisk Oldkyndighed og Historie*. N.p., 1851, pp. 3–160.

Hill, Joyce, trans. "The Icelandic Saga of Tristan and Isolt (Saga af Tristram ok Ísodd)." In *The Tristan Legend: Texts from Northern and Eastern Europe in Modern English Translation*. Leeds: University of Leeds, Graduate Centre for Medieval Studies, 1977, pp. 6–28.

Schach, Paul. "The Saga af Tristram ok Ísodd: Summary or Satire?" *Modern Language Quarterly*, 21 (1960), 336–52.

———. "Tristrams saga ok Ýsoddar as Burlesque." *Scandinavian Studies*, 59 (1987), 86–100.

SAGREMOR (Sagramore, Saigremor), a knight of the Round Table whose importance varies with each text. In Chrétien de Troyes's *Perceval*, Sagremor interrupts Perceval's reverie that is induced by the three drops of blood on the snow. In the Vulgate Cycle, he is slain by Mordred in the battle between Mordred and Arthur. In the Prose *Tristan*, Sagremor is Tristan's messenger, who brings his shield and sword when he (Tristan) is dying. In Froissart's *Meliador*, he has an affair with Sébille. The only other romantic intrigue associated with the knight occurs in Tennyson's *Idylls of the King*, where a weary Sagremor stumbles into a maiden's bedroom in Arthur's castle and falls asleep. (Public opinion forces the couple to marry, but they are content.) Finally, the Vulgate says that Sagremor is the nephew of the Emperor of Constantinople and that he has an illness that attacks him without warning, which is a source of derision for Kay, who calls Sagremor "le mort jeune" ("the young corpse"). [SW]

ST. JOHN, NICOLE (pseudonym of Norma Johnston), American editor and author of *Guinever's Gift* (1977), a gothic romance that transposes the Arthur-Guenevere-Lancelot triangle to a contemporary setting. [RHT]

St. John, Nicole. *Guinever's Gift*. New York: Random House, .

SAINTS' LIVES. Like other Celtic lands, Wales in the so-called Dark Ages has innumerable saints, not all of them generally recognized. Their written "Lives" are seldom early or factual enough to carry much documentary weight. Traditions were handed down and embroidered for centuries, often in a community founded by the saint, before an official Life was compiled. The resulting texts usually contain a small amount of authentic matter embedded in a mass of fiction, miracles, and would-be edification. The monastery of Llancarfan in Glamorgan was a major hagiographic center, and five of the Llancarfan Lives, all in Latin, introduce Arthur. That of St. Cadoc, the monastery's own founder, is ascribed to Lifris, who taught there in the late eleventh century. That of Gildas is the work of Caradoc in the twelfth. Arthur also appears in Lives of SS. Illtud, Carannog, and Padarn, written during the same period.

Llancarfan's account of Cadoc begins by telling how he was born. His mother eloped with a local ruler in southern Wales, and Arthur, together with his knights Cai and Bedwyr (Kay and Bedivere), prevented her father from reclaiming her. She married her lover, and Cadoc was their firstborn. Long after, when Cadoc was abbot of Llancarfan, he gave sanctuary for seven years to a man who had killed three of Arthur's soldiers. Arthur at last found out where he was and came to complain. Supported by David and other saints, Cadoc confronted the angry leader across the River Usk and defended his right to grant long-term sanctuary. Arthur demanded 100 cows as compensation, making awkward conditions. When Cadoc supplied them, they became bundles of fern. Arthur, nonplussed, withdrew his objections.

The Life of Illtud says briefly that he was Arthur's cousin and served him as a soldier before turning to the religious life. That of Carannog tells of the saint going to Somerset, where Arthur ruled at Dunster as co-prince with Cato (who figures in Geoffrey of Monmouth's *Historia* as Cador). Arthur had stolen Carannog's portable altar. The saint banished a giant serpent that Arthur had been pursuing without success, and the altar was restored to him. In the Life of Padarn, the saint is in his monastery near Aberystwyth when "a certain tyrant named Arthur," from foreign parts, tries to rob him of a fine tunic. Padarn says, "Let the earth swallow him up," and it does. Arthur has to beg forgiveness before he can extricate himself. (For the more important *Vita Gildae*, or Life of Gildas, *see* GILDAS.)

These stories disclose a discrepancy in Welsh clerical views of Arthur. Whereas Nennius and the *Annales Cambriae* make him a Christian champion, winning battles by celestial aid, most of the Llancarfan matter presents him unfavorably. He is not an outright heathen; much less is he (as some have imagined) a demon in disguise, since a demon would not have repented as he does in the stories; but he is a most unsatisfactory son of the Church and a troubler of the saints. This portrayal is more likely to reflect convention than fact. Arthur is cast in the role of the Recalcitrant King, a stock character in this class of literature, who is brought in so that the saint can teach him a lesson through supernatural powers or superior virtue. His rapacity may be an echo of clashes between abbots and warrior chiefs, requisitioning monastic goods to supply their forces, but nothing can safely be inferred about a real Arthur's real behavior.

Arthur's status in the saints' lives has the same ambiguity as in Welsh tradition generally. Sometimes he is the leader of a war-band, sometimes he is a regional despot, twice he is called King of Britain. His kingship has an air of limitation and uncertain legitimacy. Doubt also overhangs the indications of place and time. While he is spoken of as having a residence at Dunster, and as being a foreigner at Aberystwyth, the stories spread so widely that they fail to define any convincing home territory. As for the chronology, it stretches him out too far. St. Carannog supposedly is a grandson of the Welsh patriarchal hero Cunedda, who belongs early in the fifth century, so that Carannog belongs in that century, too, and so, by implication, does Arthur. A young St. Illtud in Arthur's service likewise implies the fifth century. Gildas, however, was not even born till ca. 500, and Cadoc's abbacy cannot have begun much before the middle of the sixth century, while David's presence beside him could point to an even later date.

Clearly, some of the hagiographers have shifted Arthur in time so as to work him in. But is he a fifth-century figure wrongly associated with saints who lived long afterward, or is he a sixth-century figure, contemporary with Cadoc and wrongly made to flourish much earlier by writers on other saints? While the saints' lives give no certain answer, those of Gildas and Cadoc, in putting him very late, also betray what looks like a fundamental unsoundness by making him an anachronism. Both credit him, at some stage of his career, with a national kingship however questionable. He could have had this after a fashion in the fifth century but not in the time of the two saints, after Britain's breakup into small kingdoms. The passages where the title occurs allow him to be a fifth-century high king ignorantly or irresponsibly transplanted. They rule him out as an authentic contemporary of Gildas or Cadoc. Of course, his sovereignty may be a purely legendary accretion; the value of this clue can be assessed only in the context of other evidence.

Brittany has a Life of St. Efflam with an episode like the Carannog tale, in which the saint overcomes a monster that has proved too much for Arthur. The Arthurian passage in the Life of Goeznovius, also of Breton provenance, is a text of a different type and not part of the hagiographic legend itself. [GA]

Chambers, E.K. *Arthur of Britain*. London: Sidgwick and Jackson, 1927, pp. 80–85, 243–49, 262–64.

Loomis, Roger Sherman, ed. *Arthurian Literature in the Middle Ages*. Oxford: Clarendon, 1959, pp. 1–2, 54.

Morris, John. *The Age of Arthur*. New York: Scribner, 1973, pp. 120–23.

SALA, PIERRE, author of nine French works from the late fifteenth and early sixteenth centuries. Three of his compositions are Arthurian. The first is a modernized verse redaction of *Le Chevalier au lion*; Sala omitted certain of the episodes from Chrétien de Troyes's original and condensed others. His *Hardiesses de plusieurs roys et empereurs* includes several Arthurian episodes from the Vulgate *Merlin* and the *Prophécies de Merlin*. Finally, between 1525 and 1529, Sala wrote a prose *Tristan*, depicting the adventures and the illicit loves of Tristan and Lancelot. This lively and well-constructed narrative, which appears to constitute an implicit critique of Arthurian chivalry, is considered to be Sala's masterpiece. [NJL]

Sala, Pierre. *Tristan en prose*, ed. Lynette R. Muir. Geneva: Droz, 1958.

Lacy, Norris J. "The Arthurian Ideal in Pierre Sala's *Tristan*." *Arthurian Interpretations*, 1 (1987), 1–9.

SALAZAR, LOPE GARCÍA DE, author of *Libro de las bienandanzas e fortunas* ("The Book of Prosperity and Fortune"), a late fifteenth-century Spanish universal history containing a largely legendary summary of the history of England, from its founding by Brutus of Troy to the reign of Edward III. The principal sources for the legendary material are a variant version of the fourteenth-century Spanish pseudo-historical romance *Sumas de historia troyana*, by Leomarte, and the three branches of the Post-Vulgate *Roman du Graal*. Salazar makes free use of his sources, most notably the substitution of seamen's accounts of the mythical North Atlantic island of Brasil for the story of Arthur's passing to the Isle of Avalon. Salazar also interpolates material from the *Roman du Graal* and the Prose *Tristan* in his narration of French and Flemish history. Within his history of the reign of the Spanish king Pedro the Cruel, taken from the fourteenth-century chronicle of the king's rule by Pedro López de Ayala, Salazar includes verbatim the text of a prophecy attributed to Merlin. [HLS]

Salazar, Lope García de. *The Legendary History of Britain in Lope García de Salazar's "Libro de las bienandanzas e fortunas,"* ed. Harvey L. Sharrer. Philadelphia: University of Pennsylvania Press, 1979.

SAMIVEL (pseudonym of Paul Gayet-Tancrède), author and illustrator of *La Grande Nuit de Merlin* ("The Great Night of Merlin," 1943), a charming play in seven brief acts about magical happenings in the forest of Brocéliande during a full moon. Merlin l'Enchanteur and Viviane, Prince and

Princess of the Fairies and the Elves, work various miracles not traditionally associated with the Arthurian legend. The play includes a poem called "The Song of Merlin" as well as a ballad about Gauvain and alludes to the adventures of Galaad and Lancelot. [BTL]

Samivel. *La Grande Nuit de Merlin*. Paris: IAC, 1943.

SAMMES, AYLETT (1636?–1679?), author of *Britannia Antiqua Illustrata* (1676). Sammes tried to present a comprehensive argument that ancient British culture resulted from Phoenician exploration and settlement. He sweeps aside all claims that British roots went back to Troy through Brutus, a theory that underpinned Geoffrey of Monmouth's history of British kings. He depicts Arthur as a pathetic, beleaguered young monarch, pressured constantly by threats from Picts and Scots within Britain as well as Saxons from without. But Sammes does accept the historicity of Arthur as son of Uther and the Duchess of Cornwall, elevated to the throne at not more than fifteen years of age. Nennius's claims for Arthur's twelve great victories are challenged as lacking credibility. Sammes cites Mount Badon as the only clear military success. Sammes feels the greatest proof of Arthur's existence was the celebrated grave at Glastonbury. [JHW]

Sammes, Aylett. *Britannia Antiqua Illustrata, or the Antiquities of Ancient Britain*. London, 1676.

SAMPSON, FAY, British author of *Wise Woman's Telling* and *White Nun's Telling* (both 1989), the first two books of a sequence of novels dealing with Morgan le Fay. *Wise Woman's Telling* describes Morgan's strong attachment to her father and her hatred of Uther and Arthur after her father is killed. *White Nun's Telling* is a masterly presentation of the power of Morgan's personality even as a child, as she manipulates a nun at the convent of Tintagel who has been charged with controlling her but who cannot keep her from participating in the rites of the old religion. [ACL]

Sampson, Fay. *White Nun's Telling*. London: Headline, 1989.
———. *Wise Woman's Telling*. London: Headline, 1989.

SAMSONS SAGA FAGRA ("Saga of Samson the Fair"), a fourteenth-century Icelandic work that has been repeatedly linked to the *matière de Bretagne* because the hero is the son of one King Arthur of England. This is not the famous ruler of legend, however. The saga relates the adventures encountered by Samson in his search for his beloved Valentina, daughter of King Garlant of Ireland and a maid-in-waiting at Arthur's court. The saga's sole link to the Arthurian matter is the appearance of the chastity-testing mantle—this is actually a blind motif—which has been borrowed from *Möttuls saga*. The author of *Samsons saga* supplements the information provided by *Möttuls saga* with matter concerning the origin of the mantle, its magic properties, and its subsequent appearance at the legendary Arthur's court. The author adds that there is a tale about the last, called *Skickiu saga*, and this is an alternative title for *Möttuls saga*. [MEK]

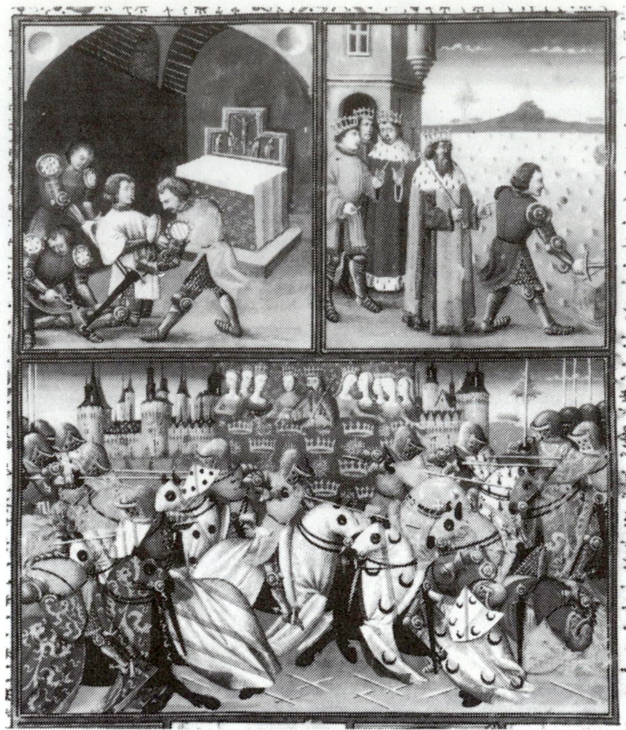

76. MS Paris, Bibliothèque Nationale, f.fr. 99, fol. 56r: Tristan scenes. (Paris, Bibliothèque Nationale.)

Wilson, John, ed. *Samsons saga fagra*. Copenhagen: Samfund til Udgivelse af gammel nordisk Litteratur, 1953.
Simek, Rudolf, trans. *Die Saga vom Mantel und die Saga vom schönen Samson. Möttuls saga und Samsons saga fagra*. Vienna: Braumüller, 1982.

SARMATIAN CONNECTION, term coined by C. Scott Littleton in 1978 for a complex of material about the "historical Arthur," and of motifs in the Arthurian legends, that cannot be readily explained as Celtic.

The Sarmatians and their cousins, the Alani, were Iranian horse-nomads from the Eastern European steppes. In A.D. 175, Emperor Marcus Aurelius hired 8,000 Sarmatian cavalrymen from Pannonia (today's Hungary) as auxiliaries for the Roman army; 5,500 of them were sent to Britain to fight the Picts. After their twenty-year term of service expired, they were not repatriated but were settled in a kibbutz-like military settlement—the only one of its kind in the western Roman Empire—at *Bremetennacum* (now Ribchester in Lancashire). There, a *cuneus veteranorum Sarmatorum* ("troop of Sarmatian veterans") was still documented in 428. The Sarmatians imported in 175 were attached to the Legio VI Victrix; the praefectus of this legion was a certain Lucius Artorius Castus, who had served in Pannonia and led a punitive expedition from Britain to Gaul. Later, during the Migration Period, Sarmatians and Alani came to western Europe as the cavalry arm of the better-known Germanic tribes, such as Goths, Vandals, and Burgundians, and settled in Gaul, Spain, and even North Africa, after the fall of the Roman Empire.

Sarmatian warriors were heavy-armored cavalry. They fought under dragon standards as their battle ensigns, worshiped as their tribal war-god a naked sword set upright in the ground or on a platform, had shamans as their tribal spiritual leaders, and used sacred cauldrons for burning hemp leaves to induce religious visions by inhaling the fumes. Their princes were buried in river banks; the next flooding would obliterate all traces of the grave as a precaution against grave-robbing. The parallels to Arthur's "knights," the Pendragon standard, the Sword in the Stone, the magician Merlin, the Grail vessel, and Arthur's unknown grave are obvious, though of course the Sarmatian hashish cauldron would be only one of several sources for the Grail.

The sole surviving speakers of a Sarmatian tongue today are the Ossetians of the Caucasus. Though now severely curtailed as free-roaming nomads, they still have a rich and colorful heritage of epics about a legendary tribe of heroes, the Narts. The main hero of the Narts is Batradz, who among other features has his life bound up with his magic sword, which has to be thrown into the sea by his last companion, after he is mortally wounded. The warrior trusted with the disposal of the sword tries to deceive Batradz twice, as Bedivere does, in order to save the wonderful sword, but he has to throw it into the water at the third attempt and wait for the "sign" to be reported back to Batradz as proof. Other heroes of the Narts, Soslan and Sosryko, collect the flayed beards of their defeated enemies for a fur-trimmed cloak, a clear parallel to King Ryons's mantle. There is even the corresponding detail of the one empty spot still to be filled on Soslan's cloak.

Further eastern connections may be present in some Arthurian names, such as Ban (Hungarian *ban*, Slavic *pan* 'lord'), Bors (Alanic *boz* 'king,' Turkic *bos/bas* 'leader,' *böri* 'hero,' cf. Russian *Boris*), Bedwyr (Hungarian *bator*, Turkic *batir* 'brave'; Polish *bohater*, Russian *bogatyr*, Turkish *bahadur* 'hero'), Kay (Iranian *kai* 'hero, warrior'), Pendragon (*pan* 'lord,' Central Asian *tarkhan* 'leader'), Avalonia (Slavic *iablonia* 'apple-tree'). Also, the name of the praefectus Artorius might have been remembered among the Sarmatian troopers in Britain and their descendants as a synonym for "the General," as the name Caesar became a title for the Romans, and lived on as Kaiser and Tsar among further generations. (*See also* CAVALRY, ARTHURIAN.) [HN]

Bachrach, Bernard S. "The Origin of Armorican Chivalry." *Technology and Culture*, 10 (1969), 166–71.

Dumézil, Georges. *Le Livre des Héros: légendes sur les Nartes*. Paris: Gallimard, 1959.

Littleton, C. Scott, and Ann C. Thomas. "The Sarmatian Connection: New Light on the Origin of the Arthurian and Holy Grail Legends." *Journal of American Folklore*, 91 (1978), 513–27.

Nickel, Helmut. "The Dawn of Chivalry." In *From the Lands of the Scythians*. New York: Metropolitan Museum of Art/Los Angeles County Museum of Art, 1975, pp. 150–52. (Exhibition catalogue.)

———. "The Fight About King Arthur's Beard and for the Cloak of Kings' Beards." *Interpretations*, 16 (Fall 1985), 1–7.

———. "Wer waren König Artus' Ritter?: Über die geschichtliche Grundlage der Artussagen." *Waffen- und Kostümkunde*, 1 (1975), 1–28.

Peterson, Linda A. "The Alan of Lot: A New Interpretation of the Legends of Lancelot." *Folklore and Mythology Studies*, 9 (Fall 1985), 31–49.

Phillips, E.D. *The Royal Hordes: Nomad Peoples of the Steppes*. New York: McGraw-Hill, 1965, pp. 92–93.

Richmond, I.A. "The Sarmatae, Bremetennacum Veteranorum and the Regio Bremetennacensis." *Journal of Roman Studies*, 35 (1945), 15–29.

Sulimirski, T. "The Forgotten Sarmatians." In *Vanished Civilizations*, ed. Edward Bacon. New York: McGraw-Hill, 1963, pp. 279–98.

SARRAS, in the Vulgate Cycle, the mystical city to which Perceval, Galahad, and Bors sail on Solomon's ship. Galahad's quest for the Grail ends in Sarras; he has a vision of the Grail and dies in ecstasy. [SW]

SAUL, GEORGE BRANDON (1901–1986), American scholar and poet, wrote a dramatic poem in 700 blank-verse lines, "The Fair Eselt." Divided into a large number of short scenes held together through the narration of a "Master of Revels," it recounts the story of Tristan and Eselt, replacing the magical elements of the traditional tale with psychological explanations and ending with a moral about passion in the modern world. [SRR]

Saul, George Brandon. "The Fair Eselt." In *Hound and Unicorn: Collected Verse—Lyrical, Narrative, and Dramatic.* Philadelphia: Walton, 1969, pp. 217–53.

SCANDINAVIAN ARTHURIAN LITERATURE. In the introduction to *Tristrams saga ok Ísöndar*, the Norwegian translation of Thomas's *Tristan*, we hear that 1,226 years after the birth of Christ the story of Tristram was written down in Norwegian by a certain Brother Robert at the request of King Hákon Hákonarson, or Hákon IV, king of Norway from 1217 to 1263. To judge by authorial commentary in other *riddarasögur*, or chivalric sagas, the name given to Old Norse-Icelandic translations of continental literature, Hákon also commissioned the translation of twenty-one Breton lais, known in Norwegian as *Strengleikar*, among them the Arthurian *Januals ljóð* (= *Lanval*) and *Geitarlauf* (= *Chevrefueil*), as well as *Ívens saga*, which derives from Chrétien de Troyes's *Yvain*, and *Möttuls saga*, a translation of the anonymous *Lai du cort mantel* or *Le Mantel mautaillié*. Two other works of Chrétien de Troyes are presumed to have been translated during Hákon's reign, although the works themselves are silent regarding royal patronage: *Erex saga* (= *Erec et Enide*) and *Parcevals saga* with *Valvens þáttr* (= *Perceval*). The earliest Arthurian fiction in Scandinavia thus consists of four romances and three lais.

Two reasons have been adduced for Hákon's program of translation, which also included non-Arthurian works, such as *Elis saga*, a translation of *Elie de St. Gille*, a *chanson de geste*: edification and entertainment. Earlier scholarship interpreted the Norwegian translations as didactic documents intended to instruct the Norwegian nobility in the ideals and duties of chivalry. This interpretation of the function of the Norwegian translations, however, ignores the fact that *Tristrams saga* glorifies adultery, that the portrayal of King Arthur is not entirely positive in the sagas, and that Arthur's court is depicted in a negative light both in *Januals ljóð* and especially in *Möttuls saga*. Internal testimony suggests that the primary function of the translations was entertainment. In the prologue to *Möttuls saga*, we are told that this tale about a curious and amusing incident at Arthur's court was translated at Hákon's request to provide entertainment and amusement. A similar statement is found in *Elis saga*. The prologue of the *Strengleikar* reiterates that the lais are meant as entertainment. If one considers the fact that Arthurian literature has continued to be a source of amusement and pleasure in our own day, then it is unlikely that Hákon's Norwegian court was not more entertained than edified by the latest fiction from France.

Although the four romances and three lais named above became known in Scandinavia in Norwegian translation, only *Geiterlauf* and *Januals ljóð* are extant in a Norwegian manuscript (from ca. 1270). The other works are known to us only in Icelandic manuscripts, the oldest of which is a single leaf of *Möttuls saga* from ca. 1300, the youngest—but the oldest complete redaction of *Erex saga*—a manuscript from the middle of the seventeenth century.

In addition to the romances and lais, Geoffrey of Monmouth's *Historia Regum Britanniae*, a major portion of which is devoted to King Arthur, also became known in the North through *Breta sögur* and *Merlínusspá*. The *Breta sögur*, extant only in Icelandic manuscripts, are an early thirteenth-century translation of the *Historia*. Both Norway and Iceland have been proposed as transmitters of the *Historia*, but proof for either thesis is wanting. *Merlínusspá* ("The Prophecy of Merlin"), however, is the work of an Icelander: it is a metrical version of Merlin's prophecies in Book VII of the *Historia*, composed ca. 1200 by Gunnlaugr Leifsson (d. 1218 or 1219), a monk at the Benedictine monastery of Þingeyrar.

The one Arthurian work that is associated with neither Norway nor Iceland in the Middle Ages is *Ivan Lejonriddaren*, or *Herr Ivan*, a Swedish translation of Chrétien de Troyes's *Yvain*. *Ivan Lejonriddaren*, which dates to 1303, is one of three works (the other two being *Hertig Fredrik av Normandie* and *Flores och Blanzeflor*) that are collectively known as *Eufemiavisor*, after Queen Eufemia, the German wife of King Hákon Magnússon of Norway (r. 1299–1319), who instigated the translation of these works on the occasion of her daughter's engagement and marriage to Duke Erik of Sweden.

Ivan Lejonriddaren is unique not only because it is the sole translation of an Arthurian work into Swedish but also because it is written in rhymed couplets. All the other works belonging to the *matière de Bretagne* are translations into prose. Although there are stylistic differences from work to work, the prose of the Old Norse-Icelandic *riddarasögur* is on the whole highly rhythmical and rhetorical, characterized by synonymous and antithetical collocations as well as alliteration. Occasionally, one finds rhyming couplets in passages where the author wishes to emphasize the content. The prose of *Parcevals saga* in particular is interspersed with short rhyming verses that are usually at the end of a chapter. The couplets may be the work of the translator but may also be by a later redactor. The prose of the translated sagas is thus quite unlike the laconic and elliptic prose known from the indigenous Sagas of Icelanders.

Although the Old Norse-Icelandic Arthurian literature was presumably written during a relatively short period—during the reign of Hákon IV—the Arthurian sagas display considerable diversity in the extent to which they reproduce their sources. The three lais are relatively faithful translations, but the longer romances are considerably shorter than their French counterparts. Passages devoted to psychological analysis and interior monologue are, if not completely missing, greatly reduced. Earlier scholarship had ascribed the reduction of text in the *riddarasögur* to a lack of understanding and a distaste for extensive reflections and sentimental discourses on the nature of love. Recent manuscript evidence, however, enables us to postulate relatively faithful Norwegian translations that were condensed and modified by Icelandic redactors during centuries of manuscript transmission.

Erex saga is the most extreme example of the modification of the content and style of a thirteenth-century Norwegian translation that presumably reproduced Chrétien's *Erec et Enide* in most of its details. The seventeenth-century versions in which the saga is extant reflect a work that is the result of a systematic and intentional revision of the structure of the tale. By interpolating two new adventures encounters with a flying dragon and with seven armed men—an anonymous Icelandic redactor produced a work that is structurally distinct from the French romance, a work that must be considered a recreation of the tale.

Although the Arthurian *riddarasögur* may be said to transmit the substance of the French romances and lais from which they derive, certain additions and modifications in the sagas vis-à-vis their sources suggest a process of acculturation. Most of the discrepancies between the *riddarasögur* and the French originals are the work of one or more Icelandic redactors rather than the Norwegian translator. In *Ívens saga* and *Erex saga*, for example, the position of women is somewhat different from that in the French romance. After Íven has rescued 300 enslaved maidens, the lord of the castle offers the hero his daughter as reward, but Íven replies sanctimoniously that he would never bargain for a woman in such a manner, that the daughter is a free agent. In *Erex saga*, the hero falls in love with Evida (Enide) at first sight and immediately proposes. The father is pleased but informs Erex that Evida must make the decision herself. A similar deference to woman occurs in the Earl Placidus (Count of Limors) episode. Unlike the French count, who marries Enide over her objections, the Scandinavian earl heeds his courtiers' admonitions—that it is contrary to God's law to marry Evida unless she herself assents—and so does not marry her. *Ívens saga* is extant in two redactions, and in the younger version one observes a systematic revision of the saga. The mistress of the spring is portrayed as a decisive and aggressive individual who reserves the right to make independent decisions and is not subject to the desires of her courtiers.

In a work like *Möttuls saga*, which is extant in manuscripts dating from ca. 1300 through the middle of the nineteenth century, we can observe the process of modification and interpolation that the sparse manuscript evidence from *Erex saga* only allows us to postulate. Like its French source, *Möttuls saga* is a hilarious account of a chastity test conducted at King Arthur's court by means of a magic mantle. One by one, beginning with Guenevere, the ladies of the illustrious knights must submit to the trial. The peculiar manner in which the mantle does not fit permits Kay to interpret the exact nature of the sexual transgression. The serial nature of the plot encouraged interpolation and thus, at the same time that relatively accurate copies of a medieval manuscript of the saga were produced in the seventeenth and eighteenth centuries, there are also deviating redactions in which new female characters and further mantle tests are introduced. In the French lai and in the Norwegian translation, the chastity test is entirely unmotivated, but two early nineteenth-century manuscripts of the saga provide fuller information about the origin of the mantle and the motivation of the woman who sent it to King Arthur's court.

Most scholars consider *Tristrams saga ok Ísöndar* the first work translated at Hákon's court, but it is also possible that the *matière de Bretagne* was introduced into Norway by way of *Möttuls saga*. The evidence for such a hypothesis is the saga's prologue, which is independent of the French lai; it is an encomium of Arthur and the most extended portrait of the monarch in Scandinavian literature. Had the Norwegian court been ignorant of the Arthurian tradition when *Möttuls saga* was translated, a portrayal of Arthur and his court would have been necessary if Hákon's retainers were to appreciate fully the farcical nature of the plot.

Icelanders not only transcribed the thirteenth-century Norwegian translations through some six centuries but were also inspired to produce original Arthurian literature. Of the works belonging to the *matière de Bretagne*, the Norwegian *Tristrams saga* had the greatest influence on Icelandic literature. In Icelandic romances as well as Sagas of Icelanders, the several motifs from the saga recur, such as the embedded sword-fragment, the voyage for healing, and the ambiguous oath. Analogues to the Hall of Statues episode proliferate. The impact of *Tristrams saga* can be seen in an important episode of *Grettis saga*, the *Spesar þáttr*, in which the married Spes must undergo an ordeal to prove her fidelity; the episode seems to have been inspired by and modeled after the analogous episode in *Tristrams saga*. Similarly, an abduction episode in *Kormáks saga*, which is devoted to the life of the famous skald, appears to derive from the episode relating Ísönd's abduction by an Irish harper.

The Norwegian *Tristrams saga* also inspired one of the most curious of Icelandic romances, the fourteenth-century *Saga af Tristram ok Ísodd*, which Henry Goddard Leach dismissed as a "boorish account of Tristram's noble passion" but which in recent times has been interpreted as a parody of the Norwegian *Tristrams saga*. The Icelandic *Tristram* appears to be a parody not only of the Tristram romance but also of Arthurian romance in general through the exaggeration and humorous use of such motifs as Erec's *recreantise* and Perceval's drops-of-blood episode.

The contribution of other Arthurian romances to Icelandic literature is more modest. The Grateful Lion motif from *Ívens saga* recurs in six late-medieval Icelandic romances and in a post-Reformation folktale. In the indigenous romances, the serpent of *Ívens saga* metamorphoses into a flying dragon, which in turn has an effect on the nature of the episode as we know it from the Arthurian romance. In the Icelandic romances, the episodes depict the dragon in flight with its claws dug into the helpless lion. The rescued lion takes on anthropomorphic features, for example, in *Sigurðar saga þǫgla* ("Saga of Sigurðr the Silent"), which is set in the days of King Arthur; in this saga, the beast shows its gratitude by weeping. The author of the folktale *Vígkæns saga kúahirðis* ("Saga of Vígkænn the Cowherd") appears to have been influenced by Arthurian romance in the composition of his charming narrative. The tale contains a grateful-lion episode, indebted to both *Ívens saga* and the *Physiologus*, in which the animal that accompanies Vígkænn is a weak lioness who has just given birth to a stillborn cub. Once the protagonist and the beast become partners, the lioness assumes the functions of a dog by guarding Vígkæn's horses and protecting his father's property.

The character of Vígkænn seems patterned after that of Parceval. Like the famous Arthurian hero, Vígkænn sets out for a career at court totally ignorant of the ways of knighthood. In the late-medieval *Vilmundar saga viðutan* ("Saga of Vilmundr the Absentminded"), there are similar reminiscences of *Parcevals saga*, especially in Vilmund's innocence when he spends a night in a princess's chambers and his ignorance of chivalric ways when he appears before the king and his courtiers.

Like *Sigurðar saga þögla*, *Samsons saga fagra* ("Saga of Samson the Fair") is set in the days of a King Arthur, who is identified as being married to a Queen Filippia. The author of *Samsons saga* was familiar with the Arthurian *Möttuls saga* and its chastity-testing mantle and embellished the early history of the famous garment. It was woven by four elf-women who had been in the habit of stealing wool from a certain King Skrymir. As punishment for their theft, they were forced to weave for the king a wondrous garment that could expose not only unfaithful women but also thieves. The saga contains one mantle test, which is, however, not motivated, since the woman in question has been faithful. The saga concludes by informing us that the mantle eventually came into the possession of a viking who took it to Africa, and from there it was sent by a lady named Elida to King Arthur of England. As a result of this concluding intelligence, *Samsons saga* has repeatedly been linked to the Arthurian matter, both in the disposition of manuscripts, where the saga regularly appears between *Erex saga* and *Möttuls saga*, and by literary historians.

The French metrical romances and lais were turned into prose in Norway. Subsequently, the prose sagas generated not only prose imitations but also metrical narratives, known as *rímur*, a popular genre in Iceland in the late Middle Ages and even as late as the nineteenth century. Of the medieval Arthurian *riddarasögur*, only *Möttuls saga* generated a *rímur*-version, entitled *Skikkju rímur* ("Mantle Verses"). The *Skikkju rímur* contain three *rímur*, or cantos. The individual stanzas of each *ríma* are bound by end-rhyme and alliteration. Although *Möttuls saga* is the primary source of the *Skikkju rímur*, the author was also familiar with other romances, such as *Erex saga*, from which he borrowed not only Erex and his beloved but also the wedding guests. The *Skikkju rímur* alone explain how the Round Table came into being and contain additional mantle tests. The interpolated material in the *rímur* was in turn the source of the interpolations in two of the eighteenth-century manuscripts of *Möttuls saga*.

At the end of the Middle Ages, the Tristan matter found its way into Icelandic, Danish, and Faroese ballads. The Icelandic "Tristrams kvæði," dating probably from the fifteenth century, relates the tale from the wounding of Tristan to his death. In Denmark, several versions of the ballad of "Tistram og Jomfru Isolt" are known, the oldest believed to date from the fifteenth century. Unlike the Icelandic ballad, the Danish versions depart drastically from the classical Tristan tale, and only one version, in which Tistram and Isolt are brother and sister, has a tragic conclusion. One ballad, entitled "Tistram og Isold," and known through manuscripts of the sixteenth and seventeenth centuries, celebrates a nocturnal lovers' tryst under a linden-tree. The most unusual of the Scandinavian Tristan ballads is the Faroese "Tístrams táttur," in which Tístram refuses to marry the daughter of the French king, is hanged, and is then avenged by his beloved Ísin, who subsequently dies of a broken heart.

Imperfect reminiscences of the Arthurian matter in *Ívens saga* are found in a cycle of Faroese ballads entitled *Ívint Herintsson*, which contains, depending upon the redaction, three or five ballads. Like King Arthur, King Hartan refuses to eat until news of an adventure has reached him. Like his Arthurian namesake, Ívint gets involved with a widow and suffers from an illness that can be cured only by magic. Related to the Faroese cycle are two Norwegian ballads, "Iven Erningsson" and "Kvikkjesprakk." The ballads have evolved so drastically, however, that their affinity to the Arthurian matter is attested solely by virtue of their relationship to the Faroese cycle.

During the Middle Ages, the *matière de Bretagne* was imported into Norway from France. The Norwegian translations were transmitted in Icelandic manuscripts and inspired original compositions. In the seventeenth century and later, there occurred a second wave of foreign importations into Scandinavia. This time, the literature came from Germany, was translated in Denmark, and was subsequently translated from Danish into Icelandic.

In 1656, the Danish chapbook *Her Viegoleis med Guld Hiulet* was published. The Danish prose romance derives from an anonymous fifteenth-century German prose redaction of the medieval romance *Wigalois*, by Wirnt von Grafenberg. In the same century that the German chapbook was translated into Danish, the Danish chapbook was translated into Icelandic and entitled *Gabons saga ok Vigoles*.

As already mentioned, the thirteenth-century Norwegian *Tristrams saga ok Ísöndar* had considerable impact on indigenous Icelandic literature, more so than the other translated Arthurian romances. The same phenomenon occurs in modern times with the eighteenth-century Danish chapbook *En tragoedisk Historie om den ædle og tappre Tistrand*, which inspired the composition of two Icelandic *rímur* cycles in the nineteenth century. Unlike the Norwegian *Tristrams saga*, which may be considered a fairly accurate rendering of Thomas's *Tristan*, the Danish chapbook is a drastic revision of its source, the fifteenth-century German chapbook *Ein wunderbarliche vnd fast lustige Historij von Herr Tristrant vnd der schönen Isalden* . Although most of the characteristic motifs and situations of the Tristan matter are found in the Danish chapbook, the romance has been rewritten in such a manner as to remove what might be offensive to eighteenth-century sensibilities. Instead of an adulterous relationship, we are told about a case of platonic love. Tistrand and Indiana—as Isolt is called in the chapbook—have children by Innanda and King Alfonsus, respectively. The strongest expression of love that Tistrand is permitted is a chaste kiss on Indiana's hand.

Not only was the Danish chapbook translated into Icelandic in the eighteenth century (*Tistrans saga ok Indiönu*) but it also inspired the composition of two *rímur* cycles, those by Sigurður Breiðfjörð (1831) and Níels Jónsson (1844–50). (*See also* TRISTAN IN SCANDINAVIA.) [MEK]

Barnes, Geraldine. "Arthurian Chivalry in Old Norse." *Arthurian Literature*, 7 (1987), 50–102.

Kalinke, Marianne E. *King Arthur, North-by-Northwest*. Copenhagen: Reitzel, 1981.

Leach, Henry Goddard. *Angevin Britain and Scandinavia*. Cambridge: Harvard University Press, 1921.

Mitchell, P.M. "Scandinavian Literature." In *Arthurian Literature in the Middle Ages*, ed. Roger Sherman Loomis. Oxford: Clarendon, 1959, pp. 462–71.

Schlauch, Margaret. *Romance in Iceland*. Princeton, N.J.: Princeton University Press, 1934.

SCARBOROUGH, ELIZABETH ANN, American author who combines science fiction and fantasy in her short story "The Camelot Connection" (1988). The application of modern psychiatric techniques at Arthur's court comically backfires when a romantic young woman and a pop psychiatrist travel back in time to occupy jointly the body of a revived Merlin in an Arthurian world based on T.H. White's *The Once and Future King*. [RHT]

Scarborough, Elizabeth Ann. "The Camelot Connection." In *Invitation to Camelot: An Arthurian Anthology of Short Stories*, ed. Parke Godwin. New York: Ace, 1988, pp. 47–82.

SCHAEFFER, ALBRECHT (1885–1950), prolific German author from the circle of Stefan George. He lived in exile in the United States from 1939 to 1950 but returned home shortly before his death. Using Wolfram von Eschenbach, Robert de Boron, and Richard Wagner as sources, he composed *Parzival* (1922), a popular epic poem of over 20,000 lines. This "story of the spirit" (*Seelengeschichte*) is characterized by polished and picturesque language and a plethora of images, motifs, and allusions. Schaeffer only briefly considers the Arthurian court and the death of Arthur. [UM/WCM]

Schaeffer, Albrecht. *Parzival*. Leipzig: Insel, 1922.

Schulze, Ursula. "Ideologisierung durch Strukturverlust." In *Akten des DFG-Symposions zur Mittelalter-Rezeption*, ed. Peter Wapnewski. Stuttgart: Metzler, 1985.

SCHALLER, ROBERT CLARK. Wistful sonnets and ballades, many on fairy and romance themes, predominate in Schaller's verse collection *The Throne of Merlin* (1937). In the title poem, Arthur's disillusioned wizard magically crafts a throne, the Siege Perilous, that will transport one to Avilion, but he destroys it at the command of the Lady of the Lake. The "Ballade of Avilion" provides an ecstatic picture of the land of desire, and Arthurian allusions abound in other poems as well. [DN]

Schaller, Robert Clark. *The Throne of Merlin*. Chicago: Argus, 1937.

SCHIBLER, ARNIM (1920–1986), a leading Swiss composer, whose *La Folie de Tristan: mystère musicale pour chanteurs et récitants, orchestre, choeur mixte, groupe Jazz-rock et bande électronique d'après Marie de France, "Le Roman de Tristan et Iseut," renouvelé par Joseph Bédier et "Das Unverlierbare" d'Arnim Schibler (adaptation française: Daniel Reichel)* ("Tristan's Madness: Musical Mystery Play for Singers, Orchestra, Mixed Choir, Jazz-Rock Group, and Electronic Band . . .") was written in 1976–79. As the title makes clear, the lengthy and demanding composition makes use of texts by Marie de France, Bédier, and the composer himself. In 1982, these texts were printed in Schibler's calligraphy. The premiere performance of the work at the 1981 Festival de Musique in Montreux met with great success, and a recording appeared two years later (Zurich, PAN, 1983, No. 130085). [UM/PWM]

Schibler, Arnim. *Antoine und die Trompete: Texte 75–82*. Adliswil and Lottstetten: Kunzelmann, 1982.

Müller, Ulrich. "Mittelalter-Musicals. Eine kommentierte Übersicht: Mit einem Anhang über mittelalterliche Themen in der U- und E-Musik 1977–1984." In *Forum: Materialien und Beiträge zur Mittelalter-Rezeption I*, ed. Rüdiger Krohn. Göppingen: Kümmerle, 1986.

SCHIRMER-IMHOFF, RUTH, German author among whose works are a Tristan novel (1969) and a "romance of love at the Arthurian court," *Lancelot und Ginevra* (1961). She treats Arthurian subject matter from the parentage of Merlin to the fall of Arthur's realm, using as source (according to her own testimony) the Old French Vulgate Cycle. Both novels are successful poetic adaptations of traditional material. [SSch/WCM]

Schirmer-Imhoff, Ruth. *Lancelot und Ginevra, ein Liebesroman am Artushof.* Zurich: Manesse, 1961.

———. *Der Roman von Tristan und Isolde.* Zurich: Manesse, 1969.

SCHLEGEL, FRIEDRICH (1772–1829), **and AUGUST WILHELM SCHLEGEL** (1767–1845), through their literary journal *Athenäum*, were the fathers and leading theoreticians of German Romanticism. The enthusiasm of these two brothers for medieval culture led ultimately to the promotion of the German tradition of medieval literature throughout the nineteenth century. Unfortunately, their creative contributions to Arthurian literature are more limited. The *Geschichte des Zauberers Merlin* ("Story of Merlin the Magician"), published by Friedrich in 1804, is merely a translation by his future wife, Dorothea, of the medieval French *Roman de Merlin*. August Wilhelm Schlegel promoted German Arthurian works in his many popular lectures and even began a verse translation of Gottfried's *Tristan*, which he planned to complete from French sources. He abandoned this undertaking after the first canto of ninety-one stanzas (published in 1811), which takes Tristan up to his kidnaping by Norwegian merchants. [RWK]

Schlegel, August Wilhelm. *Sämtliche Werke*, ed. E. Böcking. Leipzig, 1846, Vol. 1.

Schlegel, Friedrich. *Sammlung von Memoiren und romantischen Dichtungen des Mittelalters aus altfranzösischen und deutschen Quellen*, ed. L. Dieckmann. Paderborn, Munich, and Vienna: Schöningh, 1980.

Eichner, Hans. *Friedrich Schlegel.* New York: Twayne, 1970.

Golther, Wolfgang. *Tristan und Isolde in den Dichtungen des Mittelalters und der neuen Zeit.* Leipzig: Hirzel, 1907, pp. 261–68.

SCHOLARSHIP, MODERN ARTHURIAN. 1) INTRODUCTION. Many of the major issues that have occupied twentieth-century scholars were studied no less attentively in the nineteenth century. We have more information now; and new approaches, techniques, and interpretations are characteristic of modern scholarship. But, as this survey will show, in producing texts, in studying the Grail's origins, in searching for the historic Arthur, and in many other areas of Arthurian studies, the nineteenth century provided the background against which the work of the twentieth century should be viewed.

One measure of the flourishing of Arthurian scholarship in this century can be seen in attempts to cover the field. James Douglas Bruce's impressive two-volume study *The Evolution of Arthurian Romance* (1922, 2nd ed. 1928) addressed virtually every aspect of Arthurian literature before 1300, provided résumés of many works, and surveyed much of previous scholarship. By the 1950s, a new "survey of the field" was needed, but it was impossible that the work could be undertaken by one person. Thus, *Arthurian Literature in the Middle Ages* (1959), edited by Roger Sherman Loomis, was a collaborative effort by a number of scholars prominent in specialized areas. In more recent years, scholars have generally concentrated on single authors, single works, or even limited aspects of a particular author or work; but we also have essays that survey scholarship and outline problems yet to be solved. Recent broadly titled collections reflect a wide range of individual essays—for example, *The Passing of Arthur: New Essays in Arthurian Tradition* (1988) and *The Arthurian Tradition: Essays in Convergence* (1988).

Bibliography has become an increasingly complex but necessary adjunct to Arthurian studies. Bruce compiled an extensive and authoritative bibliography of Arthurian studies and editions, and it was supplemented by A. Hilka in 1928. Eugène Vinaver, with H.J.B. Gray and then with F.M. Williams, produced one-year bibliographies in *Arthuriana* in 1929 and 1930. John J. Parry, later with Margaret Schlauch, produced cumulative bibliographies for 1922–29, 1930–35, and 1936–39; beginning with Volume 1 of *Modern Language Quarterly* (1940), Parry issued yearly bibliographies until 1955, when Paul A. Brown continued the work up to 1962. Meanwhile, the International Arthurian Society began in 1949 to publish a yearly bibliography in its *Bulletin bibliographique*. A measure of the proliferation of twentieth-century Arthurian studies can be seen in the *Bulletin*'s increased length over the years. Until the late 1980s, it listed editions, books, and articles dealing only with Arthurian material produced before 1500. Therefore, none of the growing body of work on, for example, the Arthurian creations of Victorian poets is included. Nevertheless, the 226 entries in the 1949 bibliography had more than tripled by 1987 to an even 700 for the one year (including reviews). Reflecting the international scope of modern Arthurian studies, entries typically come from the United States, Great

Britain, France, Germany, Belgium, the Netherlands, Scandinavia, Spain, Italy, and, since 1975, from Japan.

The need to collate this bibliographic material was long recognized. *The Arthurian Bibliography* (Vol. 1, Pickford and Last, 1981; Vol. 2, Pickford, Last, and Barker, 1983; Vol. 3, Last, 1985) is a list of nearly 10,000 entries compiled from these previous bibliographies. Volume 1 of another large bibliographic project was published in 1984; it is the first of two volumes of more than 400 pages each, edited by Edmund Reiss, Louise Horner Reiss, and Beverly Taylor. This first volume of *Arthurian Legend and Literature: An Annotated Bibliography* includes Arthurian material of the Middle Ages and selected studies of that material; Volume 2, which will cover Arthurian poetry and fiction from the Renaissance to the present and the growing body of commentary on this latter field, has not yet appeared.

But so large is the amount of material to be listed or described that bibliographies of individual works and authors have also been found necessary or helpful. Malory studies provide a good example. Vinaver's first edition of the Winchester manuscript (1947) listed only ninety-one books and articles on Malory, whereas his 1967 list of critical works, with some omissions, numbered 177. Within fewer than twenty years, Toshiyuki Takamiya brought this 1967 bibliography up to date (1985) by the addition of 235 new books and articles on Malory's work (*Aspects of Malory*, updated issue, 1986). Much of this bibliographic material, as well as a number of nineteenth-century periodical and review articles and brief commentary on Malory from earlier centuries, has been collected in a book-length work by Page West Life, *Sir Thomas Malory and the "Morte Darthur": A Survey of Scholarship and Annotated Bibliography* (1980); another Malory bibliography, by Barry Gaines, was published in 1990. Other bibliographies issued recently include those on the *Morte Arthure* (Michael Foley, *Chaucer Review*, Vol. 14), the *Gawain*-poet (Malcolm Andrew, 1980), Wolfram (Joachim Bumke, reissued 1970), and Chrétien (Douglas Kelly, 1976). And still, these modern bibliographical listings seldom include literary histories and other general studies, such as Bernhard Ten Brink's *History of English Literature* (in German 1877–93; in English 1883–96) or Albert Baugh's *Literary History of England* (2nd ed. 1967), which address many Arthurian works and problems.

Another area of Arthurian scholarship that has received increased attention of late is the study of the Arthurian legend itself—not in its historic development but in the ways Arthurian romance, in various forms, has been perceived and drawn upon in particular periods and societies since its birth. Early studies in this area include Mungo MacCallum's *Tennyson's Idylls of the King and Arthurian Story* (1894) and Howard Maynardier's *The Arthur of the English Poets* (1907). Contributions by Ronald Crane (1919), William Edward Mead (1925), Roberta F. Brinkley (1932), Charles Bowie Millican (1932), and Nathan Edelman (1946) all deal with the reception and treatment of Arthurian romance in the sixteenth and seventeenth centuries. There are also studies on the treatment of Arthurian characters in later literature; Maurice Halperin's study (1931) of Tristan and Isolde in the nineteenth and twentieth centuries is an example, as is Nathan Comfort Starr's survey of twentieth-century Arthurian works, *King Arthur Today* (1954). More general studies include Alice Chandler's *A Dream of Order* (1970), Geoffrey Ashe's *Camelot and the Vision of Albion* (1971) and other works, and Richard Barber's *King Arthur: Hero and Legend* (1986). James Douglas Merriman's *The Flower of Kings* (1973) studies the Arthurian legend in England from 1485 to 1835, and *The Return of Arthur* (1983), by Beverly Taylor and Elisabeth Brewer, considers nineteenth- and twentieth-century Arthurian literature. Raymond H. Thompson's *The Return from Avalon: A Study of the Arthurian Legend in Modern Fiction* was published in 1985. These books, while concerned mainly with literary treatments of the Arthurian legend, also provide some discussion of the scholarly treatment as well. Cedric Pickford discussed *Changing Attitudes Towards Medieval French Literature*, much of it Arthurian romance, in a 1966 publication and examined "the way in which critics and readers . . . after the Middle Ages reacted to and enjoyed (or otherwise)" the French prose romances (*Bulletin bibliographique*, 1982). Stephen Knight's *Arthurian Literature and Society* (1983) addresses the ways in which individual romances, such as *Culhwch and Olwen*, Chrétien's *Chevalier au lion*, Malory's *Morte Darthur*, and Tennyson's *Idylls of the King*, represented and commented upon dominant elements of the societies from which they arose. A recent collection of essays, *The Changing Face of Arthurian Romance* (1986), reflects the "reshaping" of Arthurian prose romances, "in response to changing taste and fashion" from ca. 1200 to 1500, and Christopher Dean's *Arthur of England* (1987) examines the (in his view limited) "popular" awareness of the Arthurian legend in medieval and Renaissance England. As this brief survey of bibliographies and general works has suggested, the field of Arthurian studies is vast indeed. To take another example, Boydell and Brewer's "Arthurian Studies Series," begun in 1981 with *Aspects of Malory*, now includes twenty titles. No single essay can attempt to give more than general outlines even in particular areas; therefore, the remainder of this entry deals briefly with some major points in three areas of Arthurian scholarship; publication of texts, Grail studies, and the historical Arthur.

2) TEXTS. The development of Arthurian scholarship has been in large part determined by the accessibility of appropriate texts. An essential contribution of the nineteenth century was the publication, from manuscript or from early printed editions, of most of the poems and prose romances associated with Arthur and his knights.

Reflecting the growth of various antiquarian interests in late eighteenth-century England, for example, Bishop Percy's *Reliques of Ancient English Poetry* (1765), including six Arthurian ballads, was enormously popular; before the end

77. W. Russell Flint, illustration for Malory's *Le Morte d'Arthur* (1910–11). (Courtesy of The Newberry Library, Chicago.)

of the eighteenth century, similar collections by Pinkerton and Ritson appeared containing Gawain and Lancelot poems, and two translations into English of Le Grand d'Aussy's modern *French Fabliaux, or contes du XIIe et du XIIIe siècles* (1779–81), which included Arthurian lais of Marie de France. The growing influence of Romanticism, with its interest in the medieval past and its rejection of many Neoclassical standards for literature, no doubt contributed to an enhanced market for the longer Arthurian works that were published after the turn of the century. In addition, Thomas Warton's ambitious *History of English Poetry* (1774–81) had featured some discussion of the origins of Arthurian romance as well as consideration, with some summary, of individual French romances. More scholarly was Joseph Ritson's "Dissertation on Romance and Chivalry," the preface to his *Ancient Engleish Metrical Romanceës* (1802), a carefully edited collection that included *Ywaine and Gawin* and *Lybeaus Disconnus*. George Ellis's *Specimens of Early English Metrical Romances* (1805) also had a "Historical Introduction on the Rise and Progress of Romantic Composition in France and England"; Ellis furnished brief extracts pieced together by his own prose paraphrases of such Arthurian poems as *Arthour and Merlin* and the Stanzaic *Le Morte Arthur*.

French Arthurian material, too, became more accessible in England in the early nineteenth century. John Colin Dunlop's *History of Fiction* (1814) provided English prose summaries of several long French romances, mainly from the Vulgate Cycle but including also romances of Perceval and Tristan. Robert Southey's introduction to an 1817 edition of Malory's *Morte Darthur* also summarized or commented upon the French romances "from which the Morte Arthur has been compiled." Drawn mainly from French printed editions of the fifteenth and sixteenth centuries, which Southey was able to borrow from the libraries of friends and collectors like Richard Heber and David Laing, his summaries and descriptions included the Vulgate *Merlin*, *Lancelot*, the Prose *Tristan*, and a Prose *Perceval*.

Besides these collections and summaries, longer romances, both French and English, were published in increasing volume through the century. Sir Walter Scott's *Sir Tristrem* (1804), from the Auchinleck Manuscript, also included an "elegant precis" by George Ellis of what are now known as the Douce fragments of Thomas's twelfth-century *Tristan*. Two inexpensive (and poorly edited) editions of Malory, the first since 1634, appeared in 1816, followed by a more elaborate edition with Southey's introduction in 1817. By 1900, there would be seven more complete editions of Malory and numerous abridgments and adaptations.

Beginning in 1812 with the Roxburghe Club, the founding of book clubs and literary and publishing societies both reflected and encouraged an interest in the publication of older literature. These groups sponsored variously the publication of several Arthurian editions, including the Stanzaic *Morte* (1819), *Arthour and Merlin* (1838), and Sir Frederic Madden's Gawayne collection in which *Sir Gawain and the Green Knight* was first printed (1839). The Society of Antiquaries made possible Madden's edition of Layamon's *Brut* (1847), which remained the standard edition until 1963. In addition, Lady Charlotte Guest's translations from the *Mabinogion* began appearing in 1838, and in 1847 the first edition of the Alliterative *Morte Arthure* was published. The introductions to many of these editions, especially those of Madden, reflect the progress and the problems of Arthurian scholarship at about mid-century. Madden drew upon the work of French scholars like Gervais de la Rue, Francisque Michel, and Paulin Paris.

Publication of romances continued with Frederick J. Furnivall's edition of Lovelich's *History of the Holy Grail* (1861–63), the French Vulgate *Queste* (1864), and another Stanzaic *Morte* (1864). Furnivall founded the Early English Text Society in 1864, and among its early publications were a fragmentary English poem, *Arthur* (1864), and the text of the English Prose *Merlin* (1865–69). The introduction planned for the Prose *Merlin* was delayed for a number of years, initially because of the discovery in 1869 of the *Huth Merlin*, or *Suite du Merlin*, which would be edited and published by Jacob Ulrich and Gaston Paris in 1886.

Other EETS publications in the Arthurian field were Skeat's edition of four short Joseph of Arimathea romances (1871) and Leon Kellner's *Caxton's Blanchardyn and Eglantine*

(1890). Skeat's introductory material drew on the work of Paulin Paris, Henry Morley (*English Writers*), F.G. Bergmann (*The San Greäl*, in French 1842; in English 1870), and the Flemish scholar W.J.A. Jonckbloet. Meanwhile, H. Oskar Sommer had been publishing a three-volume scholarly edition of Malory (1889–91) that included copious source comparisons. Sommer also produced the first complete edition of the French Vulgate romances (1908–16).

The developing pattern of publication was somewhat similar, if less extensive, in France. In the late eighteenth century, summaries of the romances began to be published out of the great collections. The Comte de Tressan wrote modernized summaries of old romances, including a *Tristan de Leonis* praised by Sir Walter Scott as "an elegant and beautiful abridgement" (*Sir Tristrem*). Dunlop's English summaries, mentioned above, were also translated into French and German and reprinted. Paulin Paris had described several medieval Arthurian texts in *Les Manuscrits françois de la Bibliothèque du Roi* (1836–48) and had himself produced a modernized version of the Vulgate Cycle under the title *Les Romans de la Table Ronde mis en nouveau langage* (1868–77). Among early editors, Francisque Michel published an incomplete version of the Thomas *Tristan* fragments along with Béroul (1835–39; Bédier's edition of Thomas would not appear until 1903); Michel also edited *Le Roman du Saint Graal* (1841), which contained Robert's *Joseph d'Arimathie* and *Merlin*. Hersart de la Villemarqué had published a popular collection of old Breton ballads, *Barzaz Breiz*, some of them containing Merlin material, in 1839; not until 1868 was it revealed that la Villemarqué had treated his materials with the same freedom that Bishop Percy had used, altering and adding passages to his originals.

In 1849, Jonckbloet edited the Dutch *Roman van Lancelot* with an appendix consisting of his edition of Chrétien's *Lancelot*. Potvin, whose edition of Chrétien's *Perceval* (1866–71) included an edition of the *Perlesvaus*, and Foerster brought out editions of all Chrétien's romances by the century's end. In 1875, Gaston Paris and Paul Meyer founded the Société des Anciens Textes Français, under whose auspices Paris and Ulrich published the *Huth Merlin*. In his introduction to this edition and in the pages of the periodical *Romania*, founded in 1872, Paris made important contributions to Arthurian scholarship. The Prose *Tristan* was not substantially edited until the twentieth century (R.L. Curtis, 1963, 1976, 1985), but Eilert Löseth provided a useful summary in 1891.

In Germany, too, the nineteenth century saw the publication of editions of Arthurian romances of Eilhart, Gottfried, Hartmann, and Wolfram. An edition of Gottfried's *Tristan* had appeared as early as 1785 and was followed by several editions in the 1800s. The German *Lanzelet* appeared in 1845, and Albert Schulz published in German selections from the Red Book of Hergest (1842), several Merlin romances and fragments (*Die Sagen von Merlin*, 1853), and Geoffrey of Monmouth (1854). Notable also were Bartsch's edition of Wolfram (1875–77) and Kolbing's edition of the Scandinavian *Tristrams Saga ok Ísöndar* (1878). The persistence and thoroughness of nineteenth-century German editors are suggested if perhaps exaggerated by Furnivall in a statement of the aims of the newly formed EETS in 1864. He is quoted by H.B. Wheatley as saying that none of the Society's early participants should rest "till Englishmen shall be able to say of their early literature what the Germans can now say with pride of theirs—'every word of it is printed, and every word of it is glossed.'"

Most of the texts here mentioned were published out of manuscript or early printed editions for the first time in the nineteenth century, and scholarship owes a debt to the energetic and dedicated editors of the period. However, some of the work was undertaken in haste, with more enthusiasm than care, in a time when linguistic studies were not far advanced. In addition, many early nineteenth-century editions were out of print and again difficult of access by the mid-twentieth century. Consequently, almost every major Arthurian work here mentioned has been edited anew, as a number of fine scholarly editions have appeared during the last thirty or so years. Even at the end of the 1980s, a team of scholars was reediting the romances of Chrétien de Troyes. These new editions have in turn stimulated fresh examinations and assessments of the works themselves. And the discovery of new material, though rare now, does occur. Obvious examples are Malory's Winchester manuscript, discovered in 1934, and a second manuscript of the *Suite du Merlin* found in 1945. Fragments of romances have been found quite recently, as separate leaves or as incorporations into other works; findings of this sort have been reported, for example, by Fanni Bogdanow (*Bulletin bibliographique*, 1976) and Ceridwen Lloyd Morgan (*Bulletin bibliographique*, 1979).

A recent development in this area is the publication of a quite large number of English translations of Arthurian romances. Some translations, of course, had been done in the nineteenth century. Sebastian Evans's translation of the *Perlesvaus* (1898), for example, was long the only available English version of that work, but it has lately been translated by Nigel Bryant (*The High Book of the Grail*, 1978). Jessie Weston translated Wolfram's *Parzival* (1894), *Sir Gawain and the Green Knight* (1894), Gottfried's *Tristan* (1899), the English *Sir Cleges* and *Sir Libeaus Desconus* (1902), and *Four Lays of Marie de France* (1904). Through the first half of the twentieth century, however, not much more was done; *Medieval Romances*, by Loomis and Loomis (1957), filled a clear need with its prose translations of several romances including Chrétien's *Perceval*, *Sir Gawain and the Green Knight*, and Gottfried's *Tristan*, although the latter was, in fact, Weston's 1899 version.

From the 1960s and increasingly after 1975, this picture changed completely, and numerous translations of Arthurian romances in Middle English, French, German, Scandinavian languages, Italian, Latin, and Russian are now available, many appearing in Garland Publishing's Library of Medieval Literature. A team of translators is preparing, for example, an English version of the French Vulgate and Post-Vulgate for Garland.

3) GRAIL STUDIES. The Holy Grail has fascinated generations of scholars. However, considerations of the origins of this vessel are enmeshed in a complex of related problems. The study of Celtic origins has brought to light Irish and Welsh analogues but also numerous theories about the transmission of Celtic material to French romance. Attempts to trace the origin of Grail stories have led to necessary study of the chronology and relationships of the works of Robert de Boron, Chrétien and his continuators, and Wolfram, as well as the Vulgate Cycle, the Welsh *Peredur*, the *Perlesvaus*, and the Post-Vulgate *Roman du Graal*. The study of these relationships has in turn produced conflicting opinions on the nature and process of romance composition, opinions that affect dating and that are used to support or attack various theories about whether the Grail's entry into Arthurian romance better represented a Celtic survival or a Christian impulse.

In the nineteenth century, the debate over the origin of the Grail in Christian or Celtic sources was complicated by two factors: the chronology of existing romances was faulty, and the authenticity of Celtic material, especially the Welsh, was held in question.

Sir Frederic Madden's contribution to Arthurian studies was considerable, but his remarks about chronology, like those of his distinguished French colleague Paulin Paris, contained inaccuracies that would be uncritically repeated for decades. Chief among these was the notion that French prose romances preceded metrical ones, that Chrétien's works, for example, appeared to have been drawn from the prose romances. Madden dated Chrétien's works closely enough (1170–95), but because he and other scholars believed the Vulgate Cycle to have been composed mainly by Robert de Boron and Walter Map—because of numerous manuscript attributions to these authors—they necessarily dated these romances too early, to the reign of Henry II (d. 1189), at whose court Map was known to have served. These problems along with the question of a Latin original, sometimes also attributed to Map, for the *Estoire del Saint Graal* made it difficult for such early researchers as Madden, Paris, de la Rue, Michel, and Bergmann to come to a clear understanding of the Grail's first entry into Arthurian romance (now generally accepted as having occurred in Chrétien's *Perceval*) and its subsequent development therein. By 1883, however, with the publication of Gaston Paris's "Le Conte de la Charrette" (*Romania*, Vol. 12), the notion that prose romances had provided Chrétien's sources was put to rest, as Paris showed that Chrétien's poem was undoubtedly the direct source of the corresponding episodes in the Prose *Lancelot*.

The authenticity of early Welsh material, especially that pertaining to Arthur, had been defended by Sharon Turner as early as 1803, and much early material was made available in the *Myvyrian Archaiology of Wales* (1801–07), edited by Owen Jones, Edward Williams, and William Owen Pughe. Pughe's *Cambrian Biography* (1805) made additional Welsh material readily available, as did the later publication of the *Mabinogion*. But beginning with Pughe, there developed a tendency to see the Celtic material as the repository (in somewhat altered form) of esoteric ancient doctrines and rituals and to view it as useful primarily for elucidating these doctrines and religious practices. The work of Edward Davies (1804 and 1809) on Druidical lore in the Welsh material extended this attitude with unsubstantiated claims and was exceeded by the bizarre theories about pagan Druidism of the Arthurian period put forth by Algernon Herbert (*Britannia After the Romans*, 1836, 1841); Herbert also declared that the "Alcoran of Arthurian Romance" was the "Book of the Saint Greal," which he said was later translated into Latin perhaps by Map and then into French, but had been composed in Welsh in the year 717. These excesses in England led to an opposite extreme in the debunking work of D.W. Nash. In *Taliesin* (1858), and in related essays published or cited by Furnivall in the intro-

78. Florence Harrison, "Lancelot and Guenevere Kissing"; illustration for Tennyson's *Guinevere and Other Poems* (London: Blackie, 1912). (Courtesy of The Newberry Library, Chicago.)

ductory matter of his Arthurian editions of the 1860s, Nash insisted that surviving Welsh materials could not be dated before the twelfth and thirteenth centuries and implied that therefore the material in them could be no older. He found much influence from Geoffrey and from later romances and said that there was nothing in the "genuine remains of Irish or Welsh 'story' which can be taken as the germ of the [Grail] legend." Matthew Arnold's lectures "On the Study of Celtic Literature" (1865–66, published 1867) restored some balance and no doubt some respectability to the study of Celtic literature partly through his suggestions that Nash's work of demolishment, though useful, had gone too far, that the nature of the Celtic genius as expressed in its literature lay in the evocation of "an older, pagan, mythological world." This older world and its survival in folktale and romance would be most fruitfully explored by Alfred Nutt in his *Studies on the Legend of the Holy Grail* (1888), a landmark in Grail studies.

While finding it neither "necessary, or even advisable" to incorporate what the *Encyclopædia Britannica* (1878) and "some other English 'authorities' say about the Grail legends," Nutt included a "Sketch of the Literature Connected with the Grail Cycle" that surveyed the contributions, theories, and Grail-romance editions of a number of continental scholars and a few English ones. The reader is directed to this chapter for an admirable summary of the views of such scholars as la Villemarqué (who early argued for the Celtic origin of the Grail legend), Albert Schulz (Christian), Simrock, Rochat, Paulin Paris, Potvin, Hucher, Zarncke, Birch-Hirschfeld (at length), E. Martin, and W. Hertz. Nutt disagreed with Birch-Hirschfeld's conclusion (*Die Sage vom Gral*, 1877) that the Grail was Christian in origin but considered his work "at present the only basis for sound criticism." In other related areas, Birch-Hirschfeld had been among the first to question Walter Map's supposed authorship of the *Queste*, thus helping to clear the way for more accurate chronology, and also expressed the then-unpopular view that Wolfram's only major source for *Parzival* was Chrétien and that the Provençal "Kyot" was an invention of Wolfram's to justify his departures from Chrétien's version of the Grail story.

Nutt's hypothesis was that the story surrounding the Grail had its origin in Celtic myth and in stories of the Great Fool type. The Grail itself, he believed, was in its earliest form the Celtic cauldron of knowledge and regeneration, and the visit to the Grail castle was originally a visit to the Celtic otherworld. However, Nutt agreed that once the vessel became connected to Joseph and thus to Christ, it became in subsequent romances a Christian symbol, although he noted that these later romances retained many of the archaic features that mark them as Celtic in ultimate origin.

Besides this hypothesis, Nutt's most important specific contributions were three: he emphasized the importance of little-utilized Irish analogues; he identified much of the confused material of the various romances as originating in two formulas, a feud quest and an unspelling quest; and he insisted that the incidents found in the Grail romances were "not variants of one, and that an orderly and logical original."

This single-source theory, which Nutt wished to dispel, had grown out of nineteenth-century theories about the process by which the romances had been composed, theories that lasted into the twentieth century and accounted in part for the postulation of so many "lost sources." The idea was that many shorter works, such as Chrétien's poems, as well as longer works, such as the *Suite du Merlin*, that seemed to consist of fragments of narrative clumsily stitched together, represented in degenerated form pieces of earlier, more complete, and more coherent romances. Ferdinand Lot had introduced the term *entrelacement* in his study of the Vulgate *Lancelot* (1918) to explain the process by which later romances were composed of intertwining segments, and Eugène Vinaver's work developed this theory to undermine the long-held notion that behind virtually every romance was a more perfect version (see *The Rise of Romance*, 1970, as well as Fanni Bogdanow's summary of work in this area, her introduction to the *Romance of the Grail*, 1966). But Nutt's assertion that there never existed "a Grail legend, a definite fixed sequence of incidents," of which Chrétien and others had produced more or less corrupt versions, did much to clear the way for the work of later proponents of the Celtic origin of the Grail. No longer looking for whole originals, John Rhys, A.C.L. Brown, Lucy Paton, Helaine Newstead, and R.S. Loomis found numerous analogues from Celtic myth to explain incidents and objects of the Grail legend and other Arthurian romances.

Meanwhile, the theory of Christian origin had found many champions in the nineteenth century. Some nineteenth-century editors and authors (Furnivall, Henry Morley, and Ernest Rhys are examples) made much of the way in which the quest of the Holy Grail added a high spiritual quality to the stories of Arthur and his knights, perhaps to provide an antidote to their uneasiness about the immoralities that occurred elsewhere in, for instance, Malory's *Morte Darthur*. This concept of the elevating spiritual role of the Grail accounted in part for a reluctance to see in its origins barbaric crudities, such as witches' cauldrons and bleeding heads on platters. Robert's *Joseph d'Arimathie* and the Vulgate *Estoire del Saint Graal* were more acceptable as providing the original background for later developments. But more serious scholars continued to support the Christian-origin theory on the grounds of problems with the transmission (and transformation) of the Celtic elements and the absence of a coherent Celtic original. These latter were among the objections raised by J.D. Bruce in his summary of three theories of origin (*Evolution of Arthurian Romance*, 1928). Bruce, then, favored a Christian origin over Celtic. Other notable scholars who minimized the Celtic content of Grail and other Arthurian romances include Wendelin Foerster, Joseph Bédier, Edmond Faral, and Albert Pauphilet. Pauphilet, for example, recognized the ultimately Celtic *origin* of the material but was more concerned with the spirit of Cistercian piety that pervaded the Vulgate *Queste* (*Études sur la Queste del Saint Graal*, 1921).

Bruce also discussed a third theory, which, although it had been suggested by Simrock as early as 1842, had been fully launched, perhaps with the influence of Frazer's *Golden Bough*, in the decades following Nutt's work. This was the ritual theory—that the concept of the Grail, the elements in the Grail procession, and the Maimed King sprang from the (consciously or unconsciously preserved) rituals of vegetation cults like those dedicated to the worship of Osiris or Adonis. Two major proponents of this theory were W. A. Nitze and Jessie L. Weston, and although the intelligence and lucidity of Weston's presentations have been regarded with respect, the ritual theory has failed to find favor except insofar as vegetation myth is seen to form some of the background of the Celtic material.

Bruce's work is invaluable as a survey of earlier scholarship, but to assess what aspects of his own work and the work he discusses have held up and what have been superseded by later findings, one must turn to *Arthurian Literature in the Middle Ages*. Here, essays by Roger Sherman Loomis support the Celtic origins of the Grail stories, and essays by other scholars—Kenneth Hurlstone Jackson, I.L. Foster, Rachel Bromwich, Helaine Newstead, and Jean Frappier, for example—establish and show the use of Celtic sources by later romancers. (Frappier, while he acknowledged Celtic sources for Chrétien's Grail romance, emphasized that Chrétien's handling of his sources was individual and deliberate.) In several other books and articles, Loomis developed and supported his view of the Celtic origins of the Grail and other Arthurian stories. Loomis's work has seemed to establish beyond question that Chrétien's *Perceval*, and much of the Grail material of later romances, grew out of Irish saga, passed on to the Welsh, and combined with other narratives that were transmitted orally to the French and Anglo-Normans, at which time the platter or cauldron acquired Christian attributes that were rapidly extended to other elements of the story.

These findings have not been challenged in the main in more recent years, although questions of the precise form and manner in which the Celtic "Grail" material reached Chrétien and others have been raised. The theory of oral transmission from Wales through the Bretons and thus to the French had been suggested by Sharon Turner in 1799 and supported by George Ellis in 1805, although it is more often associated today with Heinrich Zimmer's studies of the 1890s. D.D.R. Owen's *The Evolution of the Grail Legend* (1968) explores five possible avenues of transmission, favoring the route "from the Welsh to the Bretons and thence to the Anglo-Normans." Owen has also postulated, as background to Chrétien's *Perceval* and some later romances, the development of a story of the Fair Unknown type with elements drawn from other Celtic sources, a story necessarily altered in particular thematic aspects for an Anglo-Norman audience and thus passed to Chrétien.

Not all scholars have accepted without question the comparative literary methods used to establish sources for Chrétien's works. One recent attack has come from Claude Luttrell in *The Creation of the First Arthurian Romance* (1974). Luttrell challenges Celtic analogues to *Perceval* suggested by Loomis and criticizes Owen's hypothetical source story for that romance, contending that "originals have been assumed which are in fact ghosts conjured up from Chrétien's works." Tony Hunt, pointing out some strengths and weaknesses of this book's argument (*Bulletin bibliographique*, 1978), notes that Luttrell "has compelled Chrétien scholars to re-examine their assumptions." But perhaps more typical of post-Loomis work is a report of research in progress by Jean-Claude Lozachmeur and Shigemi Sasaki (*Bulletin bibliographique*, 1982), which draws on Loomis's views of the origin and development of the Grail story—with a few modifications—to develop a theory of the two archetypes (Vengeance and Magic; cf. Nutt above), adding the probable derivation of the latter from the former to explain some of the obscurities of Chrétien's Grail story and other Grail romances. See also Lozachmeur's article "Recherches sur les origines indo-européenne et ésoteriques de la légende du Graal" (*Cahiers de civilisation médiévale*, 30 [1987]) and Sasaki's "Etat présent relatif à la chronologie de la légende du Graal" (*Kenkyu-Kiyo*, 21 [1985]).

This is not to say that other theories of the Grail's origin have not been proposed, nor that its meaning in Chrétien or Wolfram has not been explored. Noting the problems that have arisen from confusion of *Perceval*'s sources with its actual twelfth-century meaning, Urban T. Holmes and M. Amelia Klenke argued in *Chrétien, Troyes, and the Grail* (1959) that Chrétien, perhaps a converted Jew, intended his *Perceval* to represent the possible great good that would come from the conversion of the Jews to Christianity. In this Judeo-Christian interpretation, the Grail castle symbolizes the Temple of Solomon in Jerusalem, and the objects of the Grail procession are drawn from medieval iconography of the Church Triumphant as presented in the Synagoga (old-law)/Ecclesia (new-law) motif in medieval art.

Henry and Renee Kahane in collaboration with Angelina Pietrangeli proposed another origin of the Grail material in *The Krater and the Grail: Hermetic Sources of the Parzival* (1965). According to this theory, the word *grail* derives from the Greco-Latin *crater* and is related to the Krater of Hermetism, a sort of gnostic, non-Christian philosophy that arose probably in the second or third century A.D. Several Hermetic treatises were preserved in the *corpus hermeticum*, and from them, in this view, "Kyot," Wolfram, and possibly Chrétien culled various myths and motifs to make a kind of *Urparzival*. Another fascinating theory of the origin of the Grail has been presented in articles by C. Scott Littleton and Ann C. Thomas (*Journal of American Folklore*, 1978, 1979).

"The Sarmatian Connection" notes the existence of a magical cup, the Amonga, with qualities like those of the Grail, in the epic traditions of the Sarmatians, warrior tribes of the Caucasus. The cup never runs dry and can be possessed only by those free of fault or demonstrating great courage. According to these reports, some 5,500 Sarmatian auxiliaries, posted to Britain in the second century to serve under Lucius Artorius Castus, established there a colony whose traditions featured mounted warriors, a dragon banner, and the stories of the cup and also of a mortally wounded king brought to the shore of a sea into which he bids his companions throw his sword; they hide the sword and lie, he tells them to go again, and when the sword is thrown in, the sea turns blood-colored and turbulent.

4) THE HISTORICAL ARTHUR. In his introduction to an edition of Malory's *Morte Darthur* (1868), Edward Strachey said that "most recent critics are disposed to prefer Gibbon's belief to Milton's skepticism as to the actual existence of Arthur." In his *History of Britain*, Milton had said Arthur's existence has been doubted heretofore, "and may again with good reason." Gibbon based his "belief" on Nennius's account of Arthur's twelve battles, although he added, without naming a source, that "the declining age of the hero was imbittered by popular ingratitude and domestic misfortunes." He traced additions to the legend made by Geoffrey and others through the long prose romances and said that, through an unjust reversal of public opinion toward these obvious exercises in imagination, his own age questioned the very existence of Arthur.

Writing some twenty years after Gibbon's first edition, Sharon Turner took a similar approach, saying that to deny Arthur's actual existence simply because of later embellishments is an objectionable extreme. Unlike Gibbon, Turner was familiar with much early Welsh material and used it in his account: ". . . this victory [Badon] only checked the progress of Cerdic and does not appear to have produced any further success. . . . Arthur was, therefore, not the warrior of irresistible strength. . . . This state of moderate greatness suits the character, in which the Welsh bards exhibit Arthur. They commemorate him; but it is not with that excelling glory, with which he has been surrounded by subsequent tradition" (*History of the Anglo-Saxons*).

Although he had apparently read the Welsh materials about Arthur that Turner had used, Joseph Ritson distrusted their authenticity and believed Geoffrey of Monmouth's work to have influenced some of the Welsh accounts of Arthur. As displayed in *The Life of King Arthur* (1825), published twenty-two years after Ritson's death, his knowledge of the early Arthurian material is impressive, as is his rigorous skepticism about much of it. He called Gildas "querulous," recognized the ambiguities in Gildas's "forty-four years" passage (which could provide either of two dates for the battle of Badon Hill), derided Geoffrey's "miraculous history," and claimed that the monks of Glastonbury "filled their monastery with forgery and falsehood." But he acknowledged that the Britons had popular stories about Arthur before Geoffrey, such as the tradition that Arthur did not die. Exactly what Ritson believed to be true and authentic about Arthur is harder to determine from this book, but in the preface to *Ancient Romanceës* (1803) he had declared it "manifest from authentick history" that Arthur was a brave warrior and probably a petty king.

British historians of the following decades offered even more cautious views about Arthur's existence, and the distrust of Celtic material posed problems here as in Grail studies. Sir Francis Palgrave found British history before the introduction of Christianity to the Anglo-Saxons to be derived from "the most obscure and unsatisfactory evidence." Noting the tradition that Gildas is supposed to have thrown the real history of Arthur into the sea, Palgrave adds that "the same misfortune appears to have fallen on all the British annals of the next three centuries" (*Rise and Progress of the English Commonwealth*, 1832). In *History of the Anglo-Saxons* (1831), although he mentions such figures as Ambrosius Aurelianus and Vortigern, Hengist and Horsa, with some skepticism, Palgrave moves through an account of the English conquest without mentioning the name Arthur.

A popular *History of the Anglo-Saxons* by the poet and novelist Thomas Miller (1848) went through five editions; Miller, acknowledging Sharon Turner as his guide, found no record of Arthur's deeds besides the "slight mention" in Gildas and Nennius and what tradition has preserved in the "lays of Welsh bards." His account of Arthur's battles does not lend an air of clear authenticity: "His twelve battles have a glorious indistinctness,—they sink behind the other in the sunset. . . ."

Some eighty years later, in a work first published in 1926, G.M. Trevelyan was still cautious. He mentions a "half mythical King Arthur" leading Celts against the heathen, but notes the lack of "authentic chronicles of the Saxon Conquest. . . . The most important page in our national annals is a blank. The chief names of this missing period of history—Hengist, Vortigern, Cerdic, Arthur—may be those of real or of imaginary men" (*History of England*). However, R.G. Collingwood, in *Roman Britain* (1924, rev. ed. 1932) and in *Roman Britain and the English Settlements* (1936), was more positive in postulating the existence of a Romanized Celt named Artorius, whose "mobile field army" harried the Saxons in various parts of Britain, or that at the very least the "legend" stood for a "fact"—that "isolated and crippled as she was, Britain preserved for a time her Roman character and went down fighting."

In the meantime, the nature of the written record was being examined anew. R.H. Fletcher's *Arthurian Material in the Chronicles* (1906) provided a detailed chronological discussion of Arthurian material from Gildas through fifteenth- and sixteenth-century chronicles. Fletcher allowed that Nennius's account suggested the existence of a "bold warrior and an energetic general" who "sustained the falling fortunes of his country" but advised caution, given the possibility that even Nennius's "modest eulogy" was based not on fact but on "the persistent stories of ancient Celtic myth or the patriotic figments of the ardent Celtic imagination." E.K. Chambers's *Arthur of Britain* first appeared in 1927 and is still useful as the source of early Latin texts concerning Arthur. Newer editions of Geoffrey and the Welsh Triads and poems especially have made some of Chambers's comments outdated, but his presentation of the evidence is careful, and the 1964 reissue contains a valuable supplementary bibliography by Brynley F. Roberts.

This added material points out later studies in several areas covered by both Fletcher and Chambers. J.S.P. Tatlock's *Legendary History of Britain* (1950), for example, was openly skeptical about the historic value of most Welsh material and saints' lives. Tatlock, sounding at times like a latter-day Ritson, believed *Culhwch and Olwen*'s presentation of Arthur to have been influenced by Geoffrey of Monmouth's work, and he stated that the "earliest indication that Arthur was known to either tradition or history" is in the composite work attributed to Nennius. However, more recent publications have taken a different view. Particular attention should be called to essays by Jackson, A.O.H. Jarman, Foster, and Bromwich in *Arthurian Literature in the Middle Ages*. These essays and other more recent works have argued for the authenticity of early Arthurian Welsh material and made more probable the existence of a person named Arthur. Jackson answered the question "Did Arthur exist?" by saying, "The only honest answer is, 'We do not know, but he may well have existed.' The nature of the evidence is such that proof is impossible." Jackson found no evidence of historic value in Nennius's *Mirabilia*, in Welsh saints' lives, or in Geoffrey, but he did give an ingenious explanation of Gildas's failure to mention Arthur by name. He cited lines about Arthur from the early Welsh *Gododdin* but noted the possibility of interpolation. Jackson cited as evidence for a real Arthur the fact that several persons in Celtic Britain were named Arthur in the late sixth and early seventh centuries. In addition, he discussed possible sites for some of the battles named by Nennius; he concurred in the suggestion first made by H.M. Chadwick and Nora K. Chadwick (*The Growth of Literature*, 1932) that Nennius's list of twelve Arthurian battles had its origin in an early Welsh battle-listing poem. Rachel Bromwich, among others, has further suggested that Nennius's list contained battles not originally Arthur's at all.

Discussion of these battle sites is often linked with questions of Arthur's original sphere of activity, northern or southern Britain. J.S. Stuart Glennie, in an essay attached to the EETS Prose *Merlin* (1869), had argued at length that Arthur was originally a hero of the north—that is, of southern Scotland and the Border Country. W.F. Skene and D.W. Nash also leaned toward northern claims over southern ones. More recently, Bromwich (*Studia Celtica*, 1975–76, and elsewhere) has put forth cogent arguments supporting the view that "the earliest traditions of Arthur belonged to the *corpus* of north British material which was preserved and developed in Strathclyde and from there transmitted to North Wales" during the ninth century or earlier. Nora Chadwick, too, calling the evidence for a historical Arthur "highly unsatisfactory," referred to a "growing body of opinion" that views early traditions about Arthur as the model of a hero-warrior as originating in north Britain (*Celtic Britain*, 1963).

However, Jackson, in the essay in *Arthurian Literature in the Middle Ages*, and probably a majority of nineteenth- and twentieth-century explorers of this topic, have supported a southern locale—Somerset, Cornwall, or Wales—as Arthur's probable center of activity. When *ALMA* appeared in 1959, efforts that would lead to the excavation of South Cadbury hill were just getting underway. As Edward Strachey, among others, had pointed out in the nineteenth century, the hill had been identified as Camelot by John Leland, the Tudor antiquary, in 1542, and the nearby River Cam provides one of the conjectural sites for the battle of Camlann. Archaeological work at Cadbury in the 1960s revealed, among several layers showing some 4,000 years of periodic occupation of the site, evidence of British refortification on a large scale between ca. 460 and 500. Details of the excavation and similar work from such sites as Glastonbury and Castle Dore are attractively illustrated in *The Quest for Arthur's Britain* (1968). In this book, Geoffrey Ashe and Leslie Alcock conclude that the British rampart of the late fifth century was built "to defend the home or headquarters of a great British chieftain." His name cannot be established, but the evidence points to the real existence of a military leader, in a place traditionally associated with Arthur, in the right period, "a person big enough for the legends to have gathered round him." *Arthur's Britain* (1971), by Alcock, is a detailed historical and archaeological study of the period 367–634. Alcock reviews and evaluates many of the problems of dating associated with Nennius, the Easter annals, Gildas, and the *Anglo-Saxon Chronicle*, provides a historical background to the period, and discusses archaeological findings to conclude that there is "acceptable historical evidence that Arthur was a genuine historical figure," who led Celts against the English during the late fifth and early sixth centuries, achieving a major victory at Mount Badon ca. 490; Alcock points out, though, that this victory did not materially affect the character of the English settlement of Britain. If this sounds as though nothing much has changed since Sharon Turner made similar statements, the difference lies in the fact that the Latin and Welsh Arthurian material has been studied and tested in ways not available to early historians, and archaeology has provided evidence unknown to them.

In the nearly twenty years since, however, there has been considerable challenge to belief in the existence of a "real" Arthur. In the volume of the Oxford History of England (1936) where Collingwood had been eloquently supportive of the strong likelihood of an historical figure like Arthur, M.L. Myres had discussed possible dates of Mount Badon without finding it necessary to mention Arthur. In his recent revision of *The English Settlements* (his subject in the 1936 volume), Myres breaks that silence: "The fact is that there is no contemporary or near-contemporary evidence for Arthur playing any decisive part in these events at all. No figure on the borderline of history and mythology has wasted more of the historian's time" (*Oxford History of England*, Volume IB, 1986).

Recent work by David Dumville, Kathleen Hughes, and M. Miller has seriously undermined attempts to use the *Annales Cambriae*, the *Gododdin*, or Nennius's *Historia Brittonum* to make a case for the existence of a historical Arthur. Myres does allow that the "siege of Mons Badonicus . . . seems to have marked a temporarily decisive check to the progress of Saxon settlement" but attributes this check tentatively to Ambrosius "and his unrecorded successors." Dumville regards Arthur as "a man without position or ancestry in pre-Geoffrey Welsh sources" (*History*, 62 [1977]). Alcock has continued and expanded his cogent interpretations of the findings at Cadbury, but as to the Arthur of history, has declared his position to be "one of agnosticism" (*Proceedings, British Academy* [1982]). Similarly, Peter Salway in the new Oxford History volume *Roman Britain* (Volume IA, 1981) is "not prepared to say whether Arthur was a real figure or not—least of all that he was a national British leader . . . —till a new and convincing case has been made one way or the other."

But pendulums do swing to both sides of center, and no doubt the search for and the desire to have a "real" Arthur will continue. It is interesting to note in this connection that even Geoffrey of Monmouth's "spurious" historicity is being, in part, rehabilitated. Recent studies by Geoffrey Ashe and others suggest that there may have been a germ of historical truth in Geoffrey's account of Arthur's continental victories. Chambers had published an extract from the Latin "Life" of the Breton St. Goueznou (Goeznovius), possibly written in 1019, which speaks of Arthur as having won many victories in Gaul as well as Britain. Ashe (*Speculum*, 56 [1981]) has recalled attention to this passage and proposed a link and a source for Geoffrey's account of Arthur on the Continent in the fifth-century Riothamus, who took a British army to Gaul. (Dumville, however, has suggested accounts of Maximus as the "literary source of inspiration" for Arthur's continental exploits in Geoffrey.) In addition, the ruins of what was long thought to be an early Celtic monastery at Tintagel—thus showing how nonhistorical Geoffrey had been to choose it as the locale of Gorlois's (or anyone's) stronghold—have been recently reinterpreted "as a secular site with impressive natural defences" (Alcock, *Proceedings, British Academy*, 1982, citing articles by I.C.G. Burrow, 1973, and C. Thomas, 1982). [MJP]

SCHWEMER, HERMANN, German writer who, according to Rudolf Mirbt's epilogue, wrote his drama *Parzival* in an English prison camp. The play recounts Parzival's second arrival at the Grail castle, his conversation with Trevrizent, the encounter with Feirefiz, and eventual coronation as Grail King. The play concludes with a conversation between two World War II German prisoners of war, who highlight such contemporary themes as Parzival's search for meaning and discovery of salvation, Herzeloyde's love and faithfulness, Klingsor's malice and thirst for power, and reconciliation after the acknowledgment of guilt.

[SSch/PM]

Schwemer, Hermann. *Parzival: Ein geistliches Spiel zur Vergegenwärtigung der mittelalterlichen Dichtung des Wolfram von Eschenbach*. Kassel: Barenreiter, 1948.

SCOTT, SIR WALTER (1771–1832), wrote only one work of Arthurian inspiration, the verse tale *The Bridal of Triermain*. This is surprising, for his edition of *Sir Tristrem*, first published in 1804, was well received, and he revealed an interest in Malory in the introduction and notes to *Marmion* (1808). Composed during the period of his major successes in verse narrative, just after *Rokeby* and immediately before *The Lord of the Isles*, *The Bridal of Triermain* is a curious work, one that Scott himself did not take with complete seriousness. He was secretive about writing it and had it published anonymously, taking an unholy delight when the critics were uncertain how to judge it.

"Lyulph's Tale," the Arthurian episode of *The Bridal of Triermain*, is one of two romances that Arthur, a nineteenth-century young gentleman, relates to his beloved, Lucy; the other is an account of the twelfth-century Roland de Vaux's search for a Sleeping Beauty. For "Lyulph's Tale," Scott invents a traditional Arthurian story, adding some irreverence and a spice of satire. Arthur comes to a magic castle where he falls in love with Guendolen. After tarrying for three months, he feels obliged to return to Camelot, but he promises that, should a daughter be born and later come to court, she should marry the knight who proves most valiant in a tourney. A decade and a half later, Gyneth presents herself, and Arthur must fulfil his vow. Her charms are so great that the knights are enthralled, and the tourney becomes a bloodbath. The fighting is stopped only when Merlin imposes peace after a young man is slain, and the magician sentences Gyneth to a centuries-long slumber. She is not awakened until Sir Roland de Vaux discovers her. This amalgam of Arthurian romance and a Sleeping Beauty tale formed the basis of two stage works, J.L. Ellerton's operetta *The Bridal of Triermain* (1831) and Isaac Pocock's "chivalric entertainment" *King Arthur and the Knights of the Round Table*

(1834), as well as Frederick Corder's orchestral and choral composition *The Bridal of Triermain* (1886). [CNS]

Scott, Sir Walter. "The Bridal of Triermain." In *Poetical Works*. London: Longman, 1813.

Johnson, Edgar. *Sir Walter Scott*. 2 vols. London: Hamish Hamilton, 1973.

SEARE, NICHOLAS (pseudonym of Rod Whitaker), American professor of drama, wrote *Rude Tales and Glorious* (1983). The novel is a cross between Malory and Rabelais, in which a hag and a beggarman, claiming to be Elaine and Sir Lancelot, win bread and shelter from a hard-hearted Baron by telling indecent stories about Arthur and his companions. [SRR]

Seare, Nicholas. *Rude Tales and Glorious, Being: The Only True Account of Diverse Feats of Brawn and Bawd Performed by King Arthur and His Knights of the Table Round*. New York: Potter, 1983.

SECOND EMPIRE. During the French Second Empire in the nineteenth century, the Middle Ages were the subject of perpetual controversy. Critical and creative writers saw in them the image of an idealized or sinister past, a detested present, or a longed-for future. For Ultramontane Catholics, the Middle Ages represented a lost paradise. Republicans, scornful of attempts on the part of Louis-Napoleon's regime to present itself as an age of chivalry revived, loathed them as a malignant presence in the land. Liberal Catholics, and some republicans, strove to dissociate certain favored enclaves in medieval literature and society from imperial contamination and set them up as an antidote to it, a source of refreshment and consolation. One such enclave was Arthurian legend and romance, popularized by T.H. de la Villemarqué (*Les Romans de la Table Ronde et les contes des anciens Bretons*, 1842; 3rd ed. 1860; *La Légende celtique en Irlande, en Cambrie, et en Bretagne*, 1859; and *Myrdhinn ou l'enchanteur Merlin*, 1862) and Paulin Paris (*Romans de la Table Ronde mis en nouveau langage*, 1868–77). Some critics denounced the Arthurian matter as immoral and expressed distaste for its un-Christian dwarfs and fairies, its cult of Woman, and its glorification of adulterous love, but republicans, such as the Celtophile Henri Martin (*Histoire de France*, 4th ed. 1858), extolled its Gallic, dissident, and "prerevolutionary" character and the "democratic" nature of the Round Table.

The essay *La Poésie des races celtiques* (1854), by the Breton intellectual historian Ernest Renan (1823–1892), had an important influence on other writers, including Matthew Arnold. Renan (a covert opponent of the empire in his writings on the Middle Ages) praises the originality and refinement of the Celtic genius, as well as its thirst for the infinite, attachment to lost causes, and unorthodox, non-Roman spirit. When Arthurian legend spread to the Continent, these qualities brought about a profound modification in European sensibility. The mood of the essay is elegiac, a lament for the passing of a doomed world, which is set against the immorality and vulgar materialism of modern bourgeois society. The Round Table was nobly egalitarian; the central role accorded to women was a civilizing factor. Unaware that Lady Charlotte Guest's version of the *Mabinogion* was expurgated, Renan denies that the Arthurian legend in its primitive Welsh or Breton form was immoral and accuses later French imitators of it, such as Chrétien de Troyes, of coarsening and sensualizing its refined ideal of love. Renan also frowned on the reuse of this material by modern creative writers of his own day: the poetry of past ages, in his opinion, could be evoked only by critics and historians. However, Edgar Quinet (1803–1875), who was best known for his earlier poetic drama *Ahasvérus* (1833), exploited Arthurian legend in *Merlin l'enchanteur* (1860).

This prolix utopian fantasy in two volumes, sensational in its own day as an attack, launched from exile, on the empire, is now read mainly by Quinet specialists, who detect in it some "extraordinary moments." Influenced by Henri Martin, who had glorified Merlin as a "political prophet," Quinet identifies with his hero throughout and uses him as a mouthpiece to denounce Louis-Napoleon (who features as the pagan villain Hengist). Viviane, Quinet's second wife, furnished the second edition with explanatory notes. Merlin reconciles the nations of the world at the Round Table, the ideal federation of future republics. His servant Jacques Bonhomme, who joins a traveling circus, enticed by the bright clothes offered to him, represents the common people of France seduced by the tawdry glitter of the empire. Political and social life under the empire are censured through the vehicle of King Arthur's sleep (the eclipse of the Republic) and Merlin's entombment (Quinet's exile and France under imperial rule). In the end, Arthur awakens (each time he has turned over in his sleep, an enslaved nation has thrown off the shackles of oppression); Merlin emerges from his tomb; Jacques sees the error of his ways; and the nations of Europe are roused from their slumber one after the other. Tyrannical governments are overthrown everywhere, while Merlin converses with his brother Jonathan the Yankee across the ocean (by electric cable, according to Viviane Quinet's gloss). Quinet was obliged, his wife says, to "follow the guiding thread of legend," but the reader receives little inkling of this, despite the occasional surface archaism and echo of Béroul's *Tristran*.

Another, much shorter, Arthurian fantasy, *La Tour d'ivoire* (1865), was produced by Quinet's friend and fellow opponent of the empire, the poet Victor de Laprade (1812–1883). This insipid verse narrative tells of a knight in quest of the Grail who braves a series of temptations to find ideal Love in the shape of a noble and ethereal lady in an ivory tower awaiting him at the end of his quest. His adventures along the way in the perilous forest form a sequence of oblique allusions to the immorality and materialism of the empire. Both *Merlin l'enchanteur* and *La Tour d'ivoire* were praised by critics as modern Arthurian ventures immeasurably superior to their medieval predecessors. [JRD]

Crossley, Ceri. *Edgar Quinet (1803–1875): A Study of Romantic Thought*. Lexington, Ky.: French Forum, 1983.

Dakyns, Janine R. *The Middle Ages in French Literature, 1851–1900*. London: Oxford University Press, 1973.

Wardman, H.W. *Ernest Renan: A Critical Biography*. London: Athlone, 1964.

SEEGER, ALAN (1888–1916), Harvard-educated American poet who enlisted in the French Foreign Legion in 1914 and died in battle in 1916. Remembered chiefly as a war-poet, he wrote three poems with vaguely Arthurian references, all appearing in the posthumous *Poems* (1916). "Vivien," "Broceliande," and "Lyonesse" all use rich language to call up enchanted landscapes. Vivien is shown in Broceliande, like a Siren, causing knights to forget their quests. [PCB]

Seeger, Alan. *Poems*. New York: Scribner, 1916.

SEGREMORS, a German romance the protagonist of which is one of the knights of the Table Round who also appears in Wolfram von Eschenbach's *Parzival*. The romance is transmitted in only three fourteenth-century fragments that depict Segremors's search for Gawain; his leave-taking from his beloved; a magic isle ruled by a fay for whose love knights must engage in combat with her champion; a combat between the friends Segremors and Gawain. The romance is composed in rhymed couplets conjoined into sections that conclude on a rhyming triplet. [MEK]

Meyer-Benfey, Heinrich, ed. "Segremors." In *Mittelhochdeutsche Übungsstücke*. Halle: Niemeyer, 1909, pp. 175–87.

Hoffmann von Fallersleben, Heinrich. "Gawain: Drei Bruchstücke." *Altdeutsche Blätter*, 2 (1840), 152–55.

Köhler, Reinhold. "Bruchstücke eines Gedichts aus dem Artuskreise." *Germania: Vierteljahrsschrift für deutsche Alterthumskunde*, 5 (1860), 461–63.

79. John Rylands University Library, MS 1, fol. 109v: Fire Consumes an Occupant of the Perilous Seat. (Courtesy John Rylands University Library.)

SENIOR, DOROTHY, author of *The Clutch of Circumstance* (1908), a sentimental historical romance inspired by Malory. Set in Arthur's day, it includes nontraditional figures like Cormac, King of Leinster. [RHT]

Senior, Dorothy. *The Clutch of Circumstance: or The Gates of Dawn*. London: Black, 1908.

***SEPT SAGES DE ROME, LES,* CONTINUATIONS OF.** The *Roman des Sept Sages de Rome*, one of the Old French prose versions of the Seven Sages cycle, gave rise to a continuation, the *Roman de Marques de Rome*, in which a short version of the second part of the *Cligés* story of Chrétien de Troyes is incorporated as an exemplum. The influence of the works of Chrétien de Troyes and the Matter of Britain becomes particularly marked in its sequel, the *Roman de Laurin*, which unlike its two predecessors in the cycle is not a *roman à tiroir*, or a frame-story that interpolated tales, but a *roman d'aventures* into which Chrétien's

Matter of Britain is introduced, transforming it into a predominantly Arthurian romance. The Matter of Britain was apparently introduced into the cycle of the Seven Sages of Rome by the author of *Laurin* after he had exhausted the themes, chiefly misogynous, that he had inherited from the Seven Sages legend and from the *Marques de Rome*. That he turned to the tales of King Arthur and his knights to pad his story attests to their popularity and freshness in France a century after Chrétien de Troyes, especially in the new prose form in which we find them in the Vulgate Cycle. It points up, too, not only the change in narrative structure but also a change in spirit in the cycle, substituting an interest in chivalric action for the earlier attraction of folk wisdom, encompassed in the interpolated tales and exempla, that characterized the Seven Sages material.

The Arthurian element in the *Roman de Laurin* is explicit. The hero, Laurin, Emperor of Constantinople and son of Marques, the seneschal of Rome, decides to seek adventure at the court of Arthur. Arriving in Great Britain and traveling under the name of Alyenor, he rescues Baudemagus and later liberates four more members of the Round Table: Gyglain, Orenyaus, Pinel le Roux, and Mordred. The knights go on to Winchester, where they are welcomed by King Arthur, Perceval, and others, and Baudemagus relates his adventures to Lancelot, Kay, and their companions. Laurin arrives in Winchester, meets such celebrities as Yvain, Erec, Perceval, and Lancelot, and wins the day in the Winchester tourney. The White Knight appears at court with a girl on a white palfrey. Laurin, as Arthur's champion, meets the mysterious White Knight in single combat and forces him to reveal himself to the assembled court as Gawain. After a celebration, the entire court moves on to Camelot to meet Queen Guinevere. She welcomes Gawain warmly but is annoyed with Lancelot for not winning the tourney at Winchester. Later, the knights of the Round Table, to whose numbers have been added Laurin and his companions, are sent by Arthur to help Marques in Aragon, where they gain a notable victory.

The *Roman de Cassidorus*, which follows the *Laurin* in the cycle of the Seven Sages, is, like the later works in the cycle, less obviously Arthurian, although much of its narrative depends heavily on the Matter of Britain. Differing totally in this respect from *Laurin*, it represents a reversion within the cycle to the frame-story type of narrative, and therefore contains not only a running narrative constituting essentially a complicated romance of chivalry but also two series of interpolated tales or exempla in which allusions to Arthurian names and places are often found: one recounts the story of a sodomite king of Logres; in another, a version of the tale of the Loathly Damsel, the maltreated maiden makes her appearance at the court of Uther at Windsor Castle. The principal Arthurian feature of *Cassidorus*, however, occurs not incidentally in the interpolated stories but as a major episode of the frame-story itself, namely in an adaptation of the Knight of the Lion story from Chrétien's *Yvain*, in which Helcana, the wife of Cassidorus, has the role of Yvain.

The Knight of the Lion motif reappears in the *Roman de Pelyarmenus*, sequel to the *Cassidorus* and the *Roman de Helcanus*, but in this romance the role of Yvain falls to the emperor Cassidorus himself. In the immediately preceding romance, Helcanus, the son of Cassidorus, repairs to Britain to seek his father and like Laurin before him meets the Arthurian heroes of that legendary place. In the final romance of the cycle, the *Roman de Kanor*, sequel to *Pelyarmenus*, the motif of Chrétien's *Chevalier de la charrete* provides the dominant Arthurian theme. (*See also* SEVEN SAGES OF ROME, THE.) [JPal]

Keller, Heinrich Adelbert von, ed. *Li Romans des Sept Sages*. Tübingen, 1836.

Alton, Johann, ed. *Le Roman de Marques de Rome*. Tübingen, 1889.

Thorpe, Lewis, ed. *Le Roman de Laurin*. Cambridge: Bowes and Bowes, 1950.

Palermo, Joseph, ed. *Le Roman de Cassidorus*. 2 vols. Paris: Picard, 1963, 1964.

Niedzielski, Henri, ed. *Le Roman de Helcanus*. Geneva: Droz, 1966.

Brodtkorb, Lorna Bullwinkle, ed. *Le Roman de Pelyarmenus*. Ann Arbor, Mich.: University Microfilms, 1965.

McMunn, Meradith Tilbury, ed. *Le Roman de Kanor*. 2 vols. Ann Arbor, Mich.: University Microfilms, 1978.

Runte, Hans R., J. Keith Wikeley, and Anthony J. Farrell. *The* Seven Sages of Rome *and the* Book of Sindbād: *An Analytical Bibliography*. New York: Garland, 1984.

SERVICE, PAMELA F., American author of an ongoing fantasy adventure series for young readers. After 500 years of nuclear winter, Britain is still in a new Dark Age that is, once again, the setting for a conflict between Arthur and Merlin and their old enemy Morgan La Fay. In *Winter of Magic's Return* (1985), Merlin revives in the body of a teenager and, with the help of two friends, brings Arthur out of Avalon. In *Tomorrow's Magic* (1987), the trio help Arthur in his struggle to reunite the feuding kingdoms of Britain against Morgan and her horde of mutant invaders. The external struggle is mirrored by an internal one, as the protagonists learn to come to terms with their growing magical powers. [RHT]

Service, Pamela F. *Winter of Magic's Return*. New York: Atheneum, 1985.

———. *Tomorrow's Magic*. New York: Atheneum, 1987.

***SETTE SAVI DI ROMA*,** the Italian version of the Seven Sages cycle. There are nine extant redactions of this *roman à tiroir* (frame-story with interpolated tales). In the frame-story, a Potiphar's Wife analogue, a wicked stepmother attempts by means of exempla to persuade her imperial husband to execute his son for allegedly attempting to rape her; seven wise men alternate with her in telling exempla to sway their master the other way. The penalty for false accusation being capital, this is also a *Halsgeschichte*, like the frame of the *Thousand and One Nights*. Each of the Italian versions includes the story known as *Sapientes*, in which Merlin plays a major role. *Sapientes*, which is one of the tales told by the emperor's wife, is in fact strikingly similar to the Vortigern's Tower episode of the Merlin narrative cycle: a king—of England in the most popular version, the 1542 *Erasto* (in two earlier redactions he is named Herod)—who is overreliant on the counsel of seven sages, is powerless to leave the city without losing the faculty of sight, just as Vortigern is powerless to erect a fortress. Eventually, the king learns that a certain Merlin may be able to solve his predicament. In the *Libro dei sette savj di Roma*, as in the *Vita di Merlino*, the messengers sent out to find Merlin come across him playing with other children, one of whom taunts him with his lack of a father. Merlin accepts the royal summons and on his arrival instructs the monarch to uncover the source of his infirmity by digging—which reveals not two dragons, as in the Merlin legend, but seven cauldrons, which can be extinguished (thereby restoring the king's strength) only when each of the seven sages has been decapitated. Though Geoffrey of Monmouth's *Historia Regum Britanniae* is the most probable ultimate source of *Sapientes*, the latter in its turn influenced later versions of the story of Merlin, such as Paolino Pieri's *Storia di Merlino*.

[JKW]

D'Ancona, Alessandro, ed. *Il libro dei sette savj di Roma*. Pisa: Nistri, 1864.

Erasto et i suoi compassionevoli avvenimenti, che gli successe. Venice: Francesco di Leno, 1542. (At least thirty other editions by 1599.)

Gardner, Edmund G. *The Arthurian Legend in Italian Literature*. London: Dent, 1930.

Krappe, A.H. "Studies on the *Seven Sages of Rome: Sapientes*." *Archivum Romanicum*, 8 (1924), 398–407.

Runte, Hans R., J. Keith Wikeley, and Anthony J. Farrell. *The* Seven Sages of Rome *and the* Book of Sindbād: *An Analytical Biography*. New York: Garland, 1984.

Wikeley, J.K. "Italian Versions of the *Seven Sages of Rome*." Thesis, Alberta, 1983.

SEVEN SAGES OF ROME, THE, a cycle of stories, has been summarized by Campbell: a young prince is tempted by his stepmother, the empress. Rebuffed, she accuses him of attempting to violate her, and he is condemned to death. Seven wise men, however, secure a stay of execution by entertaining the emperor for seven days with tales showing the wickedness of woman; the empress meanwhile recounts stories to offset those of the sages. On the eighth day, the prince, who has remained silent up to that time, speaks in his own defense, and the empress is put to death.

The story has its ultimate roots in the oriental *Book of Sindbād the Philosopher* (fifth century B.C.), the oldest extant version of which is the Syriac *Sindban* (tenth century). From the *Sindbād* are derived two western narrative traditions, the *Dolopathos* (in Latin, French, and German) and *The Seven Sages* proper. The latter was disseminated throughout Europe in eight distinct versions: K (French), C (French), D (French), A (French, English, Italian, Swedish, Welsh), H (Latin, with translations into virtually all languages), I (Italian), L (French), and M (French). With the exception of K, the oldest western text, variously dated between the middle and the last third of the twelfth century, and of parts of C, all versions are in prose.

By origin, genre, and theme, *The Seven Sages* is firmly grounded in medieval didacticism. Grown out of the wisdom literature of the east, cast in the form of the frame-narrative reminiscent of the *Thousand and One Nights*, and based on the folklore motif of Potiphar's Wife, *The Seven Sages* shares more characteristics with medieval collections of exempla or fabliaux than with romance. Yet, as the starting point for a full-fledged Seven Sages cycle, it may be compared with the thirteenth-century phenomenon of the Vulgate Cycle of Arthurian romances. *The Seven Sages* not only offers an example of derhyming (from K to D and, less directly, to A), but through the French continuations ultimately based on A it also partakes in the literary trend toward cyclical adaptation and amplification.

Although the influence of the Matter of Britain is greatest in the French continuations of the Seven Sages cycle, *The Seven Sages* proper, originating as it does in the time of Wace, Marie de France, and Chrétien de Troyes, is not devoid of Arthurian echoes. From the last third of the twelfth century on, references to Arthur's return (cf. Wace, *Roman de Brut*, ll. 4,709–16) may be proverbial expressions of a senseless faith in unlikely eventualities, as in the early example from the tale *Gaza* in French Version K, where a prodigal sage refuses to save for the future since he "ne creoit pas en Artur" (l. 2,875). Furthermore, much of the frame-story of *The Seven Sages* is devoted to detailed accounts of the education of the prince, recalling the pervasive educational theme in Arthurian (Perceval, Lancelot, Tristan) and other romances. Given the work's didactic orientation, the prince's education is less chivalric than clerical. *The Seven Sages* is not only an antifeminist diatribe but a *miroir du prince*, in which the empress teaches by example about political power and the perfidy of counselors.

Beyond the frame-story, various analogues have been proposed for the embedded tales. The "Faithful Dog" (*Canis*) constitutes one episode in the Latin *Arthur and Gorlagon* (fourteenth century), an Arthurian version in dialogue form of the werewolf legend (cf. *Bisclavret*, by Marie de France); *Vidua*, the easily consoled widow of the "Matron of Ephesus" story, has been likened to Laudine in Chrétien's *Chevalier au lion*; elements of *Inclusa*, a tale about an immured wife and her paramour, also appear in Marie de France's *Guigemar* and *Yonec*, as well as in the *Roman de Flamenca*; some of the exploits of the fabled Vergil (*Virgilius*), including the *Salvatio Romae*, which one Middle English version attributes to the same Merlin who is featured in *Sapientes* of French Version A, are also told in the *Cléomadès*, by Adenet le Roi. None of these parallels demonstrates the link between the Matter of Britain and that of the Seven Sages as convincingly as do the French continuations; yet even the faintest echoes attest not only the ubiquity of the Arthurian myth but also the unlimited receptiveness of the frame-genre, in which the legends of the Celts, of antiquity, and of the orient may coexist. (*See also* SEPT SAGES DE ROME, LES, CONTINUATIONS OF; SETTI SAVI DI ROMA.) [HRR]

Kittredge, George L., ed. "Arthur and Gorlagon." *Harvard Studies and Notes in Philology and Literature*, 8 (1903), 149–275.

Speer, Mary B., ed. *"Le Roman des Sept Sages de Rome": A Critical Edition of the Two Verse Redactions of a Twelfth-Century Romance*. Lexington, Ky.: French Forum, 1989.

Campbell, Killis. *The Seven Sages of Rome*. Boston: Ginn, 1907.

Cosman, Madeleine P. *The Education of the Hero in Arthurian Romance*. Chapel Hill: University of North Carolina Press, 1965–66.

Gier, Albert. "'Il ne creoit pas en Artur': *Roman des sept sages*, V. 2875." *Romanische Forschungen*, 93 (1981), 367–71.

Kelly, Douglas. *Medieval Imagination: Rhetoric and the Poetry of Courtly Love*. Madison: University of Wisconsin Press, 1978.

Niedzielski, Henri, Hans R. Runte, and William L. Hendrickson, eds. *Studies on the* Seven Sages of Rome . . . *Dedicated to the Memory of Jean Misrahi*. Honolulu: Educational Research Associates, 1978.

Runte, Hans R., J. Keith Wikeley, and Anthony J. Farrell. *The* Seven Sages of Rome *and the* Book of Sindbād: *An Analytical Bibliography*. New York: Garland, 1984.

SHAKESPEARE, WILLIAM (1564–1616). In *The Fairy Mythology of Shakespeare*, Alfred Nutt points out that Shakespeare derived the idea of a fairy realm from the medieval romance, particularly that of the Arthurian legend. In his fairy realm, Shakespeare reproduced the external trappings of a medieval court, and Shakespeare's ladies are similar to those of the faroff island of Avalon. Shakespeare also inherited certain philosophical concepts that emphasized a hierarchical structure in society, particularly as it relates to nobility. For instance, in Malory's *Morte Darthur* this idea is illustrated in Book I (young Arthur and the sword), Book III (the account of Torre, supposedly a son of a cowherd but actually son of King Pellinor), and Book VII (the account of Sir Gareth). In *Cymbeline*, the king's sons Guiderius and Arviragus, brought up in the mountains of Wales, show the strengths of nobility despite their ignorance of their lineage.

In more specific ways, the Arthurian influence on Shakespeare is seen in two references to the Merlin legend. In *I Henry IV*, Act III, scene i, Hotspur says: "He angers me with telling me of the moldwarp and the ant, of the dreamer Merlin and his prophecies. . . ." In *King Lear*, Act III, scene ii, the fool declares: "This prophecy Merlin shall make." These references to Merlin as a prophet probably came from Geoffrey of Monmouth, Layamon, or Caxton. Shakespeare's knowledge of Arthur and Merlin was commonly accepted in the seventeenth and eighteenth centuries: the title page of the play *The Birth of Merlin* indicates William Shakespeare and William Rowley as the authors. The scholar C.F. Tucker Brooke lists the play as one of the apocryphal works attributed to Shakespeare, but recent criticism has attempted to show Shakespeare's presence in the play. *Merlin* was first published in 1662 by Thomas Johnson for Francis Kirkman and Henry Marsh. The play was obviously written much earlier, though the date is uncertain.

Roland Smith has argued that Shakespeare was influenced by Arthurian material for some of the events and characters in *King Lear*. By paying particular attention to the madness scenes, Smith points out more than a dozen parallels between Lear and Merlin and suggests that other characters in Shakespeare's subplot may have come from Arthurian material. Smith believes that lost sources—*Uter Pendragon*, *Arthur King of England*, *Hengist and Vortigern*, and three plays registered under the title of *Valentine and Orson*—were used by Shakespeare. In addition, the Arthurian prose romance by Richard Johnson known as *Tom a Lincolne* (entered in the Stationers' Register in 1607) and a twelfth-century Latin text, *Vita Merlini*, may have been source material for characters such as Lear, the fool, Gloucester, Edmund, and Edgar.

Taking a somewhat different tack in her discussion of *Lear*, Guilfoyle shows Arthurian imagery throughout many passages. She argues that Shakespeare deliberately clouded the localization of his play so that his characters could move in a mysterious country where history and legend intermingle. The journey to Dover with its emphasis upon spiritual failure borrows heavily from the Arthurian legend. The magic forest in Arthurian legends was a place of testing, and those who were able to survive its deadly perils were reborn. Dover is the place where Lear and Arthur have much in common. In Malory's *Morte Darthur*, Arthur leads an army from France and lands at Dover to confront a would-be usurper of his throne. In some ways, both Cordelia and Arthur play somewhat the same role—"two scions of the rightful houses of Britain." By detailing structural parallels, plot, and similar imagery, Guilfoyle makes a convincing case for the Arthurian presence in *King Lear*. (*See also* BIRTH OF MERLIN, THE; IRELAND, [SAMUEL] WILLIAM HENRY.) [JPM]

Berkeley, David, and Donald Edison. "The Theme of *Henry IV, Part 1*." *Shakespeare Quarterly*, 19 (1969), 25–31.
Dominik, Mark. *William Shakespeare and The Birth of Merlin*. New York: Philosophical Library, 1985.
Guilfoyle, Cherrell. "The Way to Dover: Arthurian Imagery in *King Lear*." *Comparative Drama*, 21 (1987), 214–28.
Hawkes, Terence. "The Fool's Prophecy in *King Lear*." *Notes and Queries*, 205 (1960), 330–32.
McRoberts, J. Paul. *Shakespeare and the Medieval Tradition: An Annotated Bibliography*. New York: Garland, 1985.
Nutt, Alfred. *The Fairy Mythology of Shakespeare*. London: Nutt, 1900.
Smith, Roland M. "*King Lear* and the Merlin Tradition." *Modern Language Quarterly*, 7 (1946), 153–74.
Tucker, Brooke C.F. *The Shakespeare Apocrypha*. Oxford: Oxford University Press, 1908.

SHALOTT, LADY OF, the form given by Tennyson and other modern writers to the French name "Escalot," although many of them create a parallel character called the Lady of Astolat (often named Elaine). The theme of the lady who falls in love with Lancelot and dies when her love remains unrequited became a favorite of writers and artists alike; the dozens of visual representations include paintings by William Holman Hunt and John W. Waterhouse, an engraving by Gustave Doré, and the first known photograph of an Arthurian subject (1861), by Henry Peach Robinson. (*See also* ELAINE OF ASTOLAT.) [NJL]

SHARPE, RUTH COLLIER, author of *Tristram of Lyonesse* (1949), one of the very few complete treatments of the Tristan legend in modern fantasy. The story, placed in a disconcertingly anachronistic setting that recalls the eighteenth century, is transformed into a tediously long and sentimental gothic melodrama with a convoluted plot and a happy ending. [RHT]

Sharpe, Ruth Collier. *Tristram of Lyonesse: The Story of an Immortal Love*. New York: Greenberg, 1949.

SHERRELL, CARL, author of the sword-and-sorcery novel *Raum* (1977). The title character is a creature from hell who visits a Britain in which Arthur's armored knights combat Viking raiders. Seeking the aid of Merlin to help discover his destiny, the demonic hero battles several of Arthur's knights and ultimately falls in love with the Lady Viviene. [DN]

Sherrell, Carl. *Raum*. New York: Avon, 1977.

SHERRIFF, ROBERT CEDRIC, British screenwriter in the 1930s and later an amateur archaeologist, composed a play, entitled *The Long Sunset* (1955), about a Roman family in Britain in A.D. 410, when the legions were withdrawing to the Continent. Arthur is called upon to help establish a new system of defense for this family and their neighbors. [SRR]

Sherriff, Robert Cedric. *The Long Sunset*. London: Elek, 1955.

SHORT METRICAL CHRONICLE, written ca. 1307 in English four-stress couplets, was probably intended to teach history through recitation or memorization. Although it was originally only 900 lines long, later redactors added to it, with one of the five known recensions consisting of about 2,400 lines. While one manuscript (London, B.L. Add. 19677) devotes only a few lines to Arthur, others (Auchinleck, Royal) draw upon the chronicle account of Arthur's war against Lucius and add Yvain (Royal) and Lancelot (Auchinleck) from romance. Auchinleck develops with some originality the story of Lancelot and Guenevere, having Lancelot build Guenevere a castle at Nottingham and offer to defend her honor at Glastonbury. [EDK]

Zettl, Ewald, ed. *An Anonymous Short Metrical Chronicle*. London: Oxford University Press, 1935.
Fletcher, Robert Huntington. *The Arthurian Material in the Chronicles, Especially Those of Great Britain and France*. Boston: Ginn, 1906; 2nd ed. Roger Sherman Loomis. New York: Franklin, 1966, pp. 198–99.
Kennedy, Edward Donald. "Chronicles and Other Historical Writing." In *A Manual of the Writings in Middle English*, ed. A.E. Hartung. New Haven: Connecticut Academy of Arts and Sciences, 1981–89, Vol. 8, pp. 2622–24, 2807–09.

SHORTHOUSE, J.H. (1834–1903), in *Sir Percival* (1886), transposes the Grail quest to a contemporary Victorian setting in order to launch a sanctimonious attack upon women committed to socialism. [RHT]

Shorthouse, J.H. *Sir Percival: A Story of the Past and of the Present*. London and New York: Macmillan, 1886.

SHWARTZ, SUSAN, American journalist, editor, and author of fantasy fiction, including "Seven from Caer Sidi" (1988), a short story based upon the early Welsh poem *The Spoils of Annwfn*. To save the lives of his loyal followers, Arthur voyages to the otherworld in search of the magic cauldron that revives the slain. In Heirs to Byzantium, a trilogy set in a world with an alternate history, stories are told of "Arktos the Bear," and both Gereint and Olwen play major roles in *The Woman of Flowers* (1987) and *Queensblade* (1988). In the story "The Count of the Saxon Shore," Artos survives Camlann, is reconciled with Gwenhwyfar, and passes on to the son whom she bears a rebuilt kingdom in which Briton and Saxon live together peacefully. [RHT]

Shwartz, Susan. *The Woman of Flowers*. New York: Warner/Popular Library, 1987.

———. *Queensblade*. New York: Warner/Popular Library, 1988.

———. "Seven from Caer Sidi." In *Invitation to Camelot: An Arthurian Anthology of Short Stories*, ed. Parke Godwin. New York: Ace, 1988, pp. 109–30.

———. "The Count of the Saxon Shore." In *Alternatives*, ed. Robert Adams and Pamela Crippen Adams. New York: Baen Books, 1989, pp. 121–63.

SIGURÐUR BREIÐFJÖRÐ (1798–1846), an Icelandic poet who gained fame as the author of over twenty-five cycles of *rímur* (narrative poems, of medieval origin, divided into groups of stanzas, each division called a *ríma*). Among Sigurður Breiðfjörð's *rímur* are the "Rímur af Tistrani og Indiönu," published in 1831, which derive from the eighteenth-century Danish chapbook *En tragoedisk Historie om den ædle og tappre Tistrand*. The Tistran-*rímur* consist of fourteen *rímur* with a variable number of stanzas ranging from forty-nine to eighty. The stanzas of one *ríma* follow the same metrical pattern, but the patterns vary from *ríma* to *ríma*. The stanzas are bound by end-rhyme and alliteration. [MEK]

Sigurður Breiðfjörð. *Rímur of Tistrani og Indiönu*. Copenhagen, 1831.

SILVA, ANTÓNIO DA, MESTRE DE GRAMÁTICA, an obscure eighteenth-century Portuguese author of popular chapbooks who borrowed heavily from Arthurian and other romances, ostensibly Spanish prose versions, to create new short chivalric tales for the contemporary Lisbon public. In four of his chapbooks—*Lançarote do Lago* (1746), *Grinalda de Flores* (1747), *Labyrntho Affectuoso* (1750), and *Dário Lobondo Alexandrino* (1750), to use shortened titles—we find situations, adventures, stock characters, and even whole passages taken from the Prose *Tristan*, the *Tablante de Ricamonte*, possibly the Post-Vulgate *Roman du Graal*, and, in the case of *Lançarote do Lago*, from Cervantes's novel *Don Quixote*. These Silva texts, like other chapbook romances of medieval origin that continued to be printed into the twentieth century in Spain, in Portugal, among the Portuguese in New England, and in Brazil, where chapbook literature continues to flourish, exemplify the perennial attraction of the medieval chivalric myth, despite Cervantes's death knell to the romance of chivalry in his satiric treatment of the genre in *Don Quixote*. [HLS]

Sharrer, Harvey L. "Two Eighteenth-Century Chapbook Romances of Chivalry by António da Silva, Mestre de Gramática: *Lançarote do Lago* and *Dário Lobondo Alexandrino*." *Hispanic Review*, 46 (1978), 137–46.

———. "Eighteenth-Century Chapbook Adaptations of the *Historia de Flores y Blancaflor* by António da Silva, Mestre de Gramática." *Hispanic Review*, 52 (1984), 59–74.

SIR CLEGES, a late fourteenth-century verse romance in twelve-line stanzas, preserved in two fifteenth-century manuscripts. It is a folktale or secular saint's legend. The hero's virtue is rewarded when a cherry-tree bears fruit at Christmas, whereby he gains the royal favor with which to punish those who mocked him. The work's only Arthurian element is the king's name, Uther Pendragon; the hero bears no relation to the protagonist of Chrétien de Troyes's *Cligés*. [SNI]

McKnight, George H., ed. *Middle English Humorous Tales in Verse*. Boston: Heath, 1913, pp. 38–59, 71–80.

SIR CORNEUS, ROMANCE OF, a brief fifteenth-century English verse account of the traditional chastity test involving a drinking horn that spills its contents on drinkers whose wives are unfaithful. Arthur and others are shown to be cuckolds, but, apparently undisturbed by the revelation, they join in a happy dance. The work, also known as *The Cukwold's Daunce*, shares its theme with Robert Biket's *Lai du cor*, among other works. [NJL]

Hartshorne, Charles Henry, ed. *Ancient Metrical Tales*. London: Pickering, 1829, pp. 206–29.

SIR DEGREVANT, a romance of 1,920 lines, written about the turn of the fifteenth century in sixteen-line tail-rhyme stanzas. The work survives in two manuscripts of the mid-century, one of which is the famous Thornton Manuscript (Lincoln Cathedral A.5.2.), which also includes the romance of *Sir Perceval of Galles*. The romance relates how

Sir Degrevant regains his lands from a neighboring earl and wins the earl's daughter's love. It is Arthurian only in its assertion that the hero is a knight of the Round Table and knows Arthur and Guenevere. [SNI]

Casson, L.F., ed. *The Romance of Sir Degrevant: A Parallel-Text Edition*. London: Oxford University Press, 1949.

SIR GAWAIN AND THE GREEN KNIGHT, the finest Middle English Arthurian romance, is preserved in a single manuscript, London, B.L. Cotton Nero A x Art. 3, which dates from ca. 1400. Written in alliterative stanzas of irregular length, each followed by a rhymed "bob-and-wheel," the poem itself is usually dated from the last quarter of the fourteenth century, but there is no precise evidence for this except the language, which may be (but probably is not) removed considerably from the author's original. The dialect of the sole extant copy, which may also be the author's dialect, is generally Northwest Midland; it has been localized more precisely as that of a small area in southeastern Cheshire or northeastern Staffordshire. About the author nothing is known except what may be deduced from the poem. It is widely assumed—based on the evidence of similarity of dialect, moral concerns, and literary techniques, as well as some verbal similarities—that the other three poems in the manuscript, *Pearl*, *Cleanness*, and *Patience*, are by the author of this romance, but the case is far from proved. Specific identifications of the author, usually based on the supposed anagrams and numerological codes, with members of Northwest Midland families, are even less securely based, though both John de Massey and Hugh de Massey have been seriously proposed. Above the beginning of the poem on fol. 91r of the manuscript appears "Hugo de" in a fifteenth-century hand, but whom it refers to is not clear.

The poet promises his audience "an outtrage awenture of Arthurez wonderez" (l. 29), and the poem lives up to this description. Fitt I tells how, at the splendid New Year's Day feast at Camelot, Arthur, in accordance with his custom, refuses to eat until he has heard or seen a marvel or until some incident has enlivened the proceedings. Scarcely has the first course been served than "Þer hales in at þe halle dor an aghlich mayster" (l. 136), handsome and elegantly dressed but bigger than an earthly man, colored green and wearing green garments, and riding on a big green horse. In one hand, he bears a holly branch and in the other a green axe, "hoge and vnmete" (l. 208). Though he explains that the holly branch is a symbol of peace and that he has come to Camelot only for "a Crystemas gomen" (l. 283), his behavior is provocatively aggressive and contemptuous and the contest he proposes is dangerous: he will allow one of Arthur's knights to strike him a single blow with the axe, if in a year's time, should he survive, he is permitted to return the blow. Though Arthur, offended at the Green Knight's disparagement of his court, is angered into undertaking the contest himself, his council persuades him to give it to Gawain, who duly beheads the man. But the Green Knight recovers his head, remounts his horse, and reminds Gawain of his promise to receive a return blow at the Green Chapel a year hence. He leaves the axe as a memento.

In Fitt II, Gawain prepares to meet his commitment. On November 2, after Arthur's feast of All Saints, Gawain sets out on his quest, dressed in the finest armor available and bearing on his shield the device of the pentangle to symbolize his human perfection. He journeys through Wales and the northwest of England "in peryl and payne and plytes ful harde" (l. 733), seeking but failing to find the Green Chapel. He spends Christmas at a splendid castle he chances upon; he is entertained lavishly by the lord, his beautiful wife, and a mysterious old lady dressed in black. His host tells him that the place he seeks "is not two myle henne" (l. 1,078) and invites Gawain to spend the last three days of the year at the castle. He further proposes an exchange-of-winnings game whereby whatever he gains while hunting is to be Gawain's and whatever Gawain gains while taking his ease in the castle is to become his host's.

Fitt III is taken up with this game. His host presents Gawain on three successive days with venison, a boar, and a fox skin; in return, Gawain gives him the kisses (though he refuses to reveal where he got them) that he had received from the host's wife, who on each of three mornings had attempted to seduce him in his bedroom. He does not give up, however, a green girdle that she gives him as a talisman to protect his life.

At the beginning of Fitt IV, on New Year's Day, Gawain sets out for the Green Chapel accompanied by a guide his host has provided. Before he leaves Gawain, the guide seeks to dissuade him from keeping his appointment by describing his adversary's terrifying deeds. But Gawain persists, and though the Green Chapel turns out to be "nobot an olde caue/Or a creuisse of an olde cragge" (ll. 2,182–83) the Green Knight appears dressed as before, with another axe. His first two blows are feints, to unnerve Gawain, but the third cuts his neck slightly. Gawain, having survived the blow, rejoices, but his spirits are dashed when the Green Knight explains to him that the three blows were related to his performance in the exchange-of-winnings game; by keeping the green girdle when he should have given it up, Gawain "lakked a lyttel" (l. 2,366), and the blow is a fittingly slight punishment for that moral lapse. For the Green Knight reveals himself as none other than Gawain's host at the castle, Sir Bertilak de Hautdesert, who had himself set his wife to tempt Gawain. He also reveals that the old lady in black was Morgan le Fay, the enchantress, who had set up the whole adventure to test "þe grete renoun of þe Rounde Table" (l. 2,458) and to frighten Guenevere. Gawain returns to Camelot wearing the green girdle as a sign of his blameworthiness, but the rest of Arthur's court adopt similar garments in his honor.

On one occasion, the author says that he had "herde" the story he tells (l. 31), but most scholars have assumed that he used written sources like the "boke of romaunce" (l. 2,521) he refers to elsewhere. The "beheading game" first appears in the Middle Irish *Fled Bricrend* (ca. 1100), where Cuchulainn one day beheads a giant challenger and then next day makes himself ready to receive the return blow: but the axe is merely drawn down thrice with its edge reversed on Cuchulainn's neck. In another variant of the story from the same source, three heroes in turn behead the challenger before Cuchulainn, but only Cuchulainn is brave enough to reappear for the return blow. Similar tests of courage and honor appear in Arthurian literature, but none is exactly as in *Sir Gawain and the Green Knight*. In *Le Livre de Caradoc*, part of the anonymous First Continuation of Chrétien's *Perceval*, the challenger interrupts Arthur's feast on horseback, and the period between blows is a year. But the feast is at Pentecost; the hero is Caradoc; the weapon is a sword; there is no journey and there are no feinted blows; and the adversary turns out to be Caradoc's father. In the *Perlesvaus*, Lancelot beheads a knight and in a year's time is faced by his brother, who appears sharpening an axe (cf. ll. 2,199-207). After a feinted blow, from which he flinches, Lancelot is spared when a lady appeals for his life. The incident causes the enchantment on a waste city to be lifted. In Paien de Maisières's *Mule sans frein*, Gawain is the hero involved: but the incident takes place one day in a strange castle and involves as adversary a *vilain*, who on the following day lifts his axe but does not strike the return blow. In the Middle High German *Diu Crône*, by Heinrich von dem Türlin, appears a similar version of the story: but here the adversary is the enchanter Gansgouter, who lifts his axe twice but does not strike Gawain. In *Hunbaut*, there is no return blow, for Gawain prevents the *vilain* challenger from recovering his head after the first contest.

Parallels to the Lady's temptation of Gawain are plentiful in romance, though they are not very exact. In *Yder*, a queen, at her husband's instigation, makes explicit advances to the hero, but he rebuffs her in a grotesquely comic and physical way. In the Prose *Lancelot*, Morgan le Fay incites her maid to seduce the hero while he is in bed, but he resists. In *Hunbaut*, his host makes Gawain kiss his daughter but is offended when he does so more than once. In *Le Chevalier à l'épée*, an imperious host causes Gawain to sleep with his daughter, but a magic sword wounds him every time he makes advances to her. No extant romance, however, makes the outcome of the beheading game depend upon the hero's moral behavior in relation to temptations, and it may well be that the author of *Sir Gawain and the Green Knight* put together for himself the elements he had encountered in several romances. He certainly appears to have been widely read in this genre: he almost certainly derived the character of Bertilak, for example, from the enemy of the Round Table who appears in the continuation of the French *Estoire de Merlin*, from which he probably took also the general concept of the youthfulness of Arthur and his court (ll. 85-89).

The materials of the poem are therefore disparate. And the poet frequently turns aside from his story to dwell upon details in long, formal, technical descriptions of a sort characteristic both of romance and of Alliterative Revival poetry: there are accounts of a banquet (ll. 107-29), the Green Knight and his horse (ll. 136-220), the turning of the seasons (ll. 500-35), the arming of the hero (ll. 567-668), a provincial castle (ll. 763-802), and an old lady and a young lady (ll. 943-69), and three highly specialized and exact descriptions of a deer hunt (ll. 1,133-77, 1,319-71), a boar hunt (ll. 1,414-67, 1,561-1,618), and a fox hunt (ll. 1,690-1,730, 1,894-1,921). But the narrative impetus, despite these pauses, is maintained.

Certain narrative procedures emphasize the symmetry and shapeliness of the work. Significance is pointed up by means of parallels and contrasts. The most obvious is the highly wrought parallel between the three hunts that enclose the Lady's three temptations of Gawain, and the three blows of the Green Knight's axe (ll. 2,345-57). But parallels are implied also between Arthur's court and Bertilak's, between Gawain's journey from Camelot and his journey back, and between the two memorials of the encounter with the Green Knight—the axe left at Camelot (ll. 476-80) and the green girdle (ll. 2,513-21)—symbols respectively of success and partial failure. Among the most striking contrasts that the poet makes are those between the privations of the harsh winter landscapes through which the hero travels and the welcoming warmth and opulence of the courts at which he is entertained, between the noisy movement and dangerous physicality of the hunting field and the quiet, static moral drama played out in Gawain's bedroom at Hautdesert, and preeminently between the pentangle symbolizing Gawain's moral excellence and the compromising green girdle, what he calls the "syngne of my surfet" (l. 2,433). But a circular movement encloses the poem, emphasized by the fact that the opening line, "Siþen þe sege and þe assaut watz sesed at Troye," is virtually repeated in line 2,525, the last line of the poem apart from the final five-line "bob-and-wheel." Critics have seen significance in this arrangement of fives and have linked it with the five sets of five virtues associated with the pentangle (ll. 619-65). Significance has also been seen in the fact that the poem (like *Pearl*) has 101 stanzas—a number interpreted as indicating a flawed perfection.

The poet, therefore, has a sure grasp of form but also a gift for the dramatic incident or image, an instinct for suspense, and a finely judged sense of high comedy, seen at its best in those sections in which the Lady attempts to seduce the embarrassed Gawain, whose reluctance is somewhat disabled because she plays on his reputation as a seducer of women (ll. 1,290-1,301). Above and beyond this, however, the poet is a moralist: that is perhaps why somebody attached "Hony soyt qui mal pence"—the motto of the Order of the Garter—to the poem at an early stage on fol. 124v. But the poem is not only celebratory: the author wishes to test his embodiment of human perfection to his limits.

It is difficult to describe and assess the nature and extent of Gawain's moral faultiness, and there has been much scholarly debate on the matter. Some, pointing to the statement that Morgan le Fay organized the Green Knight's challenge to test the renown of the Round Table, argue that the poem centrally concerns itself with fame and reputation and that the humbling of Gawain's pride is the main issue: "Þe loke of þis luf lace schal leþe my hert" (l. 2,438). Some give emphasis to Bertilak's explanation of Gawain's action in terms of his love for his life (l. 2,368) and link that with Gawain's own strictures on his "cowarddyse" (ll. 2,374, 2,508). Some point to Gawain's admitted "couetyse," in its various broad and narrow senses, as his most important fault (ll. 2,374, 2,508). Occasionally, the part that the "wyles of wymmen" (l. 2,415) had in his downfall has been stressed. Alternatively, his undoing is caused by what he calls "Þe faut and þe fayntyse of þe flesche crabbed" (l. 2,435), particularly the sin of sloth. Most scholars, however, prefer to see the hero's fault in more general terms as a failing in courtesy, or as an example of "vnleute" (l. 2,499), or "vntrawþe" (l. 2,509).

That there is a problem over the seriousness of Gawain's fault is clear, for the poem suggests various ways of looking at it. On the one hand, there is the relieved, perhaps approving, but certainly accommodating laughter of the Arthurian court (ll. 2,513–21), and on the other the shamefaced, obsessive self-condemnation of Gawain (ll. 2,374–88, 2,505–12). Bertilak's criticism, which is perhaps meant to be taken as authoritative, is relatively mild: the hero may have shortcomings, but "As perle be þe quite pese is of prys more/So is Gawayn, in god fayth, bi oþer gay knyȝtez" (ll. 2,364–65). The poet's assessment of chivalric behavior may not be tolerant, but it is understanding and compassionate. [VJS]

Tolkien, J.R.R., and E.V. Gordon, eds. *Sir Gawain and the Green Knight*; 2nd ed. Norman Davis. Oxford: Clarendon, 1967.

Borroff, Marie, trans. *Sir Gawain and the Green Knight*. New York: Norton, 1967.

Andrew, Malcolm. *The Gawain-Poet: An Annotated Bibliography*. New York: Garland, 1979.

Benson, Larry D. *Art and Tradition in Sir Gawain and the Green Knight*. New Brunswick, N.J.: Rutgers University Press, 1965.

Brewer, Elisabeth, trans. *From Cuchulainn to Gawain: Sources and Analogues of Sir Gawain and the Green Knight*. Cambridge: Brewer, 1973.

Burrow, J.A. *A Reading of Sir Gawain and the Green Knight*. London: Routledge and Kegan Paul, 1965.

Howard, Donald R., and C.K. Zacher, eds. *Critical Studies of Sir Gawain and the Green Knight*. Notre Dame, Ind.: University of Notre Dame Press, 1968.

SIR GAWAN AND SIR GALERON OF GALLOWAY, a Middle Scots poem of 715 lines divided into fifty-five stanzas, composed ca. 1440. Part I narrates how, while hunting, Arthur, Gaynour (Guenevere), and Gawan encounter the ghost of Gaynour's mother. The ghost describes its misery and advises them to display humility and charity and to eschew pride. In Part II, a knight, Sir Galeron, appears before Arthur at supper and claims his lands, which had been conquered by Arthur. Gawan offers to fight him and does defeat him. Galeron's lady intercedes with Gaynour, and Gaynour with Arthur, who returns Galeron's lands, gives him lands in Wales, and makes him a knight of the Round Table. Gaynour orders Masses for her mother. [SNI]

SIR LAMBEWELL, a sixteenth-century lay of 316 rhyming couplets that, like *Sir Landeval* and *Sir Lamwell*, is thought to be derived from a Middle English translation (now lost) of Marie de France's *Lanval*. Although close in subject to *Sir Landeval*, *Sir Lambewell* contains a number of original passages in which its author seeks to lend added emphasis to two motifs that are of central importance in both works—the sanctity of Lambewell's oath to his mistress and her status among women as the fairest of the fair. *Sir Lambewell* survives in the Percy Folio. [JN]

Hales, John W., and Frederick J. Furnivall, eds. *Bishop Percy's Folio Manuscript*. London: Trübner, 1867–68.

SIR LAMWELL, a sixteenth-century lay that survives in three fragments. The first, ninety lines in length, is preserved in Cambridge University Library Kk V.30; it betrays a strong Scottish influence in its diction and spellings. In subject, the Cambridge text corresponds closely to the opening ninety lines of the second *Lamwell* fragment, a sixteenth-century (?) printed text of eight damaged leaves and 420 lines (Oxford, Bodl. Malone 941). Except for a passage of about fifty lines, which correspond more closely in style and content to the third fragment (Bodl. Douce fragments e. 40), the Malone *Lamwell* affords a relatively faithful rendition of the Launfal story as recorded in lines 1–420 of *Sir Lambewell*. [JN]

Furnivall, Frederick J., ed. *Captain Cox, His Ballads and Books; or Robert Laneham's Letter*. London: Taylor, 1871.

Hales, John W., and Frederick J. Furnivall, eds. *Bishop Percy's Folio Manuscript*. London: Trübner, 1867–68.

"SIR LANCELOT DU LAKE," a fragmentary ballad preserved in the Percy Folio that has its origins in the Tarquin episode of Malory's *Morte Darthur.* Lancelot sets out from Arthur's court to prove his valor, encounters a maiden, and engages Tarquin in fierce single combat. The conclusion and missing central portion of this late Elizabethan ballad survive in a seventeenth-century printed version. [JN]

Hales, John W., and Frederick J. Furnivall, eds. *Bishop Percy's Folio Manuscript.* London: Trübner, 1867–68.

SIR LANDEVAL, a lay of 535 lines in short couplets dating from the first half of the fourteenth century. It is thought to have its origins in the same Middle English translation (now lost) of Marie de France's *Lanval* as do *Sir Lambewell* and *Sir Lamwell.* Preserved in Oxford, Bodl. Rawlinson C 86, *Sir Landeval* is close in subject to the French *Lanval* and to Thomas Chestre's *Sir Launfal*; indeed, Chestre's immediate and primary source would appear to have been a version of *Sir Landeval* not very different from that which survives in the Rawlinson Manuscript. [JN]

Bliss, A.J., ed. *Sir Launfal.* London and Edinburgh: Nelson, 1960.

SIR PERCEVAL OF GALLES, an anonymous short English romance of 2,288 lines, composed ca. 1300–40 and extant only in the Thornton Manuscript (Lincoln Cathedral A.5.2, fol. 161r–76r). It has many striking resemblances to Chrétien de Troyes's *Perceval* but omits the central Grail theme altogether. The poem opens with a history of Perceval's parents, including an account of the father's murder by the Red Knight. Young Perceval is raised by his mother in the forest of Wales, and after he meets the three knights (identified as Gawain, Ewain, and Kay) he sets out for Arthur's court. He encounters the sleeping Maiden of the Hall, with whom he exchanges rings. At King Arthur's court, he comes into contact with the Red Knight and kills him with his dart. He then kills the Red Knight's mother, meets his own uncle, and learns of the plight of the damsel Lufamour (who replaces Blancheflor in this poem). He goes to Lufamour's castle in Maidenhead (where he is joined by Arthur, Gawain, Ewain, and Kay), defeats the besieging Sultan in combat, beheads him, and then marries Lufamour. Next, he remembers his mother and vows to return to the forest. When he encounters the Wretched Maiden for a second time, he discovers that it was the exchange of rings that rendered him invulnerable. He also learns of his mother's sorrow over his supposed death. He is then reunited with his mother (at the same well where the poem began), takes her home to Lufamour, and finally ends his days in the Holy Land.

Early scholars interpreted *Sir Perceval of Galles* as a debased rendition of a now-lost primitive source for Chrétien's poem and suggested that the author did not himself know the French *Perceval.* More recently, however, it has been argued that *Sir Perceval of Galles* is a deliberate adaptation of Chrétien; the author has consciously tightened the plot, defined family relationships, increased the *enfances* aspect of the story, and clarified the revenge motif. Sir Perceval's final reconciliation with his mother, moreover, thematically replaces the Grail episodes. The poem is organized around one individual and has a principle of almost circular coordination, with key episodes and even phrases balancing one another. It is in many ways typical of English tail-rhyme romances but is more sophisticated than most. As a comic parody, too, it anticipates Chaucer's *Sir Thopas*, for which it may indeed have been a model. [JPC]

Campion, J., and F. Holthausen, eds. *Sir Perceval of Galles.* Heidelberg: Winter, 1913.

Rodriguez, Marcia. "*Sir Perceval of Gales*: A Critical Edition." Diss., Toronto, 1976.

Fowler, David C. "*Le Conte du Graal* and *Sir Perceval of Galles.*" *Comparative Literature Studies*, 12 (1975), 5–20.

SIR TRISTREM, a Middle English romance of 3,344 lines, dating probably from the end of the thirteenth century, and found only in the Auchinleck Manuscript, 1330–40. The dialect was originally identified as northern, showing modifications by a southern scribe, and subsequently as essentially Southeast Midland. The early attribution of the poem to Thomas of Erceldoune or Thomas of Kendale is now considered unreliable. The poem follows closely, though in a condensed form, the fragmentary Old French *Tristan* by the Angevin poet Thomas.

Tristrem, son of Duke Roland of Ermonie and Blanchefleur, sister of King Mark of England, is brought up in ignorance of his parentage. At fifteen, he comes by chance to Mark's court, where he charms all by his courtly accomplishments and knowledge of hunting. Discovering that Mark is his uncle, he serves him by defeating Moraunt, brother of the Queen of Ireland, and later by bringing back her daughter, Ysonde, as bride for Mark. On the voyage, however, Tristrem and Ysonde drink the potion intended for the royal couple and fall irrevocably in love. At court, they continue their affair by a series of stratagems designed to lull Mark's mounting suspicions. Finally, Tristrem flees to Brittany, where he marries Ysonde of the White Hands but does not consummate the marriage. With her brother Ganhardin, he returns to England to see Queen Ysonde and there is wounded. The folio containing the poem's conclusion is missing.

The poem uses a distinctive eleven-line stanza form, of eight three-stress lines followed by a one-stress "bob" and two more three-stress lines, rhyming ababababcbc. Alliteration also enhances the meter and frequently links the bob to the preceding line. This complex form poses difficulties that the poet cannot always overcome. His tags and metrical fillers, along with the ballad techniques of telescoped action, unattributed dialogue, and anticipation of events, result in a narrative that despite moments of genuine vigor is often obscure and hard to follow. [DBM]

The Auchinleck Manuscript: National Library of Scotland, Advocates MS. 19.2.1. Introduction by Derek Pearsall and I.C. Cunningham. London: Scolar, 1977.

Kölbing, Eugen, ed. *Sir Tristrem*. In *Die nordische und die englische Version der Tristan-Sage*. Heilbronn: Henninger, 1882, Vol. 2.

McNeill, George P., ed. *Sir Tristrem*. Edinburgh: Blackwood, 1886.

Pickford, Cedric E. "*Sir Tristrem*, Sir Walter Scott and Thomas." In *Studies in Medieval Literature and Languages in Memory of Frederick Whitehead*, ed. W. Rothwell, W.R.J. Barron, David Blamires, and Lewis Thorpe. Manchester: Manchester University Press, 1973.

Rumble, T.C. "The Middle English *Sir Tristrem*: Towards a Reappraisal." *Comparative Literature*, 11 (1959), 221–28.

SKIKKJU RÍMUR ("Mantle Verses"), a fourteenth-century Icelandic metrical version of *Möttuls saga*, the thirteenth-century Norwegian translation of *Le Mantel mautaillié*. The *Skikkju rímur* consist of three *rímur*, or cantos, with a variable number of stanzas, each stanza consisting of four lines connected to each other both by alliteration and end-rhyme. The *rímur* relate how a chastity-testing mantle is sent to Arthur's court. The magic garment exposes all women but one as unfaithful wives or lovers. The anonymous author of the *Skikkju rímur* augments and modifies the narrative as told in *Möttuls saga* by having the wives of visiting monarchs also submit to the mantle test. The interpolated guests are borrowed from the wedding scene in *Erex saga*. The author of the *Skikkju rímur* also provides more detailed information concerning the origin of the magic mantle; his source presumably was *Samsons saga*. [MEK]

Jónsson, Finnur, ed. *Skikkju rímur*. In *Rimnasafn: Samling af de ældste islandske rimer*. Copenhagen: Samfund til Udgivelse af gammel nordisk Litteratur, 1913–22, pp. 327–56.

Driscoll, Matthew James. "Skikkja skírlífisins." *Ný saga*, 3 (1989), 65–74.

SKINNER, MARTYN, English poet and farmer, prided himself on having won prizes in both professions. Between 1950 and 1966, he wrote, and published in several parts, a comic epic of 14,000 lines in rhyme-royal stanzas and in the manner of Byron's *Don Juan*. Consisting of *Merlin; or, The Return of Arthur* (1951) and *The Return of Arthur* (1955, 1959; these parts collected and concluded in 1966), the epic recounts Arthur's return to England in the 1990s to save Europe from a Marxist technocracy. [SRR]

Skinner, Martyn. *The Return of Arthur: A Poem of the Future*. London: Chapman and Hall, 1966.

SLAUGHTER, FRANK G., American bestselling author, whose *The Thorn of Arimathea* (1959) is a romantic fictionalization of the founding of the first Christian church in Britain. Though not specifically Arthurian, the novel identifies Gastonbury with Avalon and follows Joseph of Arimathea and Veronica (of the Veil) as they travel there from the Near East to spread the new faith. [GK]

Slaughter, Frank G. *The Thorn of Arimathea*. Garden City, N.Y.: Doubleday, 1959.

SMITH, GEORGE HENRY, American science-fiction author, wrote *Druids' World* (1967), a novel of fast-paced adventure. When mind-controlling aliens invade Annwn, a world ruled by descendants of Arthur, the hero recovers Excalibur from the Dark Lake, where it is guarded by the spirit of Morgan le Fay, and uses it to destroy the revolving castle that forms the gateway between their different worlds (and through which Arthur first gained access to Annwn). [RHT]

Smith, George Henry. *Druids' World*. New York: Avalon, 1967.

SMITH, JOHN MOYR (fl. 1872–89), a designer of transfer-printed ceramic tiles for English firms, notably Mintons China Works, for which he provided twelve illustrations of scenes from Tennyson's *Idylls of the King* for a set of six-inch-square tiles, ca. 1875. [TLS]

Austwick, Jill, and Brian Austwick. *The Decorated Tile: An Illustrated History of English Tile-making and Design*. New York: Scribner, 1981.

SMITH, KEN, British poet who wrote *Tristan Crazy* (1978), a sequence of ten poems based on the Tristan legend. The poems allude to traditional events and motifs, such as Mark's turning Isolde over to the lepers, Tristan as harper, and the black and white sails, but are more lyric than narrative and nicely convey both the maddening sorrow and the beauty of love. [ACL]

Smith, Ken. *Tristan Crazy*. Newcastle upon Tyne: Bloodaxe, 1978.

SOBOL, DONALD J., author of *Greta the Strong* (1970), a slight juvenile novel set in the lawless years following Arthur's reign. The last Round Table knight, Sir Porthal, sends the strong but sensitive young heroine on a quest to recover the lost Excalibur. In the end, she rejects the sword as the method of achieving peace and justice. [DN]

Sobol, Donald. *Greta the Strong*. Chicago: Follett, 1970.

SONE DE NAUSAY, a late thirteenth-century adventure romance of 21,321 octosyllabic lines in rhymed couplets. A prose prologue claims as the author a certain Branque, who is said to have written the work when he was 105 years old and a cleric for Fane de Baruch, allegedly a descendant of Sone. The romance focuses on adventures in foreign lands, tournaments, and a Holy War against the Saracens in Italy and Palestine.

Although *Sone* is not an Arthurian romance strictly speaking, several episodes include Grail material drawn from some version of the Joseph of Arimathea legend. The Grail, as well as the Holy Cross and Lance, are found at Galoches Abbey; they contribute to the plot principally because of their suggestive marvelous features. Joseph of Arimathea is buried there as well, and serves as patron saint of Norway. The theme of the poem, however, is hardly virginity or chastity, as in the prose-romance tradition. Sone receives Joseph's sword, which makes him invincible in combat with a giant. Later, in a nearby cemetery, Sone frees the region from a pestilential corpse, that of the heathen wife of Joseph. Despite the Crusading motifs at the end, the romance focuses on love and chivalry, particularly Sone's youthful but hopeless love for Yde in the first half, followed by his turning to the faithful Odee of Norway, whom he finally marries. [DK]

Goldschmidt, Moritz, ed. *Sone de Nausay*. Tübingen: Laupp, 1899.

SŌSEKI, NATSUME (1867–1916), author of *The Phantom Shield* (1905), dealing with a story of courtly love remotely set in the Arthurian background, and *Kairo-kō: A Dirge* (1905), the only major prose resetting of Arthurian themes in Japanese.

Inspired by both Malory and Tennyson (and probably by *The Faerie Queene* as well for the description of Merlin's mirror), *Kairo-kō* consists of a brief introduction and five sections. "The Dream" relates a meeting between Lancelot and Guenevere, her recounting a dream in which the two are bound together by a coiled snake, and Lancelot's departure for a tourney. In "The Mirror," the Lady of Shalott, to continue living, may look at the world only through a mirror. When Lancelot passes, she turns and gazes directly at him; before dying, she puts a curse of death on him. In "The Sleeve," Elaine of Astolat prevails on Lancelot to wear her sleeve on his shield at the tourney. In "The Transgression," Guenevere learns of Lancelot's apparent love for, or dalliance with, Elaine, and Mordred and others denounce the Queen for her sin with Lancelot. "The Boat" tells how Elaine, grieving for the wounded and absent Lancelot, dies; her body is placed in a boat and borne to Camelot, along with a letter proclaiming her love.

Though spiced with images of violence and pain, with which love is associated, this elegant and lyrical work is a striking blend of western material (both medieval and Victorian) with Japanese and Chinese textures. The author's intention has long been a matter of controversy, since Jun Eto produced a radical theory that *Kairo-kō* carried Sōseki's secret message suggesting his own supposed adulterous relationship with his sister-in-law, a theme that was to develop in later novels. Sōseki's choice of antiquated, and sometimes enigmatic, Japanese prose style may have resulted from this situation as well as from Pre-Raphaelite and fin-de-siècle paintings and art design, often entwined and interlaced, which he must have encountered during his traumatic stay in London in 1900–02. [TT]

Sōseki, Natsume. *Kairo-kō: A Dirge*, trans. Toshiyuki Takamiya and Andrew Armour. *Arthurian Literature*, 2 (1983), 92–126.

SOUTHWORTH, MARY E., prolific compiler of American cookbooks, also wrote a novel, *Galahad, Knight Errant* (1907). Dismissing the analysis of symbolism, which "destroys the exquisite beauty," she identifies the Grail as a golden cup set with a stone from Lucifer's crown. In forty-two pages, she combines Malory's version with the *Parzival* of Wolfram von Eschenbach (Amfortas, the questions, Loathly Maiden, Castle of Maidens, and Blanchfleur). Galahad shows that "it is possible to have the strength to overcome the bad and the grace to remain unsullied." [MAW]

Southworth, Mary E. *Galahad, Knight Errant.* Boston: Gorham, 1907.

SPAGNA, LA, a late fourteenth-century Italian text of the Carolingian expedition to Spain familiar from the *Chanson de Roland.* There are two principal versions: the "maggiore," consisting of forty *canti,* and the "minore," in thirty-four *canti.* Termed a *summa* of this material, the poem begins with preparations for departure; recounts the reconquest of numerous cities, Ganelon's treason, and the tragedy at Roncevaux; and closes with the execution of Ganelon. Like other Franco-Italian and Italian narratives based on French epic, *La Spagna* emphasizes the theme of the Maganzi traitor family and diminishes Charles's mythic stature and unquestioned authority. Innovations suggest the influence of romance: Paris is the royal capital, to which Charles returns to recover both his throne and his queen on the wings of a friendly devil, and where *cortesia* reigns in an ambience of luxury and refinement. The poet also stresses *cortesia* in the Charles-Roland relationship, at least until Roland's departure for the orient, where the amorous princess Dionés contributes to Arthurian tonality. Additional Arthurian associations include a number of traditional motifs, including quests, giants, and enchantments. *La Spagna* enjoyed wide diffusion in Italy and exercised direct influence on Pucci, Boiardo, and Ariosto. [NB-C]

Catalano, Michele, ed. *La Spagna: poema cavalleresco del secolo XIV.* 3 vols. Bologna, 1939.

SPANISH AND PORTUGUESE ARTHURIAN LITERATURE. The Arthurian legend reached medieval Spain and Portugal mainly by way of France. Although remote in time and space, it had a larger impact upon the culture and society of the Iberian peninsula than is generally recognized. Allusions to the Matter of Britain are found in the early literatures of the various linguistic and political divisions of the peninsula and date as far back as 1170. Arthurian material in Wace's *Roman de Brut* was translated in the thirteenth century as part of a now-lost Navarrese version of the *Liber Regum,* and a well-known episode concerning Merlin and Uther Pendragon from Geoffrey of Monmouth's *Historia Regum Britanniae* was used to illustrate the doctrine of transubstantiation in a fifteenth-century Spanish vernacular sermon, but there is no evidence that the verse romances of Thomas, Béroul, or Chrétien de Troyes were rendered into any of the Ibero-Romance languages. Rather, it was translations of the widely popular thirteenth-century French prose romances—the Vulgate Cycle, the Prose *Tristan,* and the Post-Vulgate *Roman du Graal*—that became, with their emphasis on heroic adventure, the primary vehicle for the transmission of the legend in the peninsula. From the early fourteenth century to the mid-sixteenth, these translations and their later reworkings—extant in twenty-six manuscript and printed texts, some merely fragments—lexically enriched the Ibero-Romance languages, provided inspiration to poets and prose writers, and played an important role in influencing social customs and individual attitudes and morals, especially among the aristocracy.

Catalonia was particularly receptive to the Arthurian legend and showed considerable originality in its literary treatment of the subject. Of apparent Catalan authorship are *Jaufré,* a verse romance much influenced by works of Chrétien, and *Blandín de Cornualha,* a verse narrative that reveals the impact of the prose-romance cycles in its Cornish setting and emphasis on action over the love theme. A Spanish prose adaptation of the *Jaufré,* the *Tablante de Ricamonte* (first printed in 1513), was known to Cervantes; it continued to be printed down to the late nineteenth century and has even survived in Tagalog translation. *La Faula,* a verse narrative by the Mallorcan poet Guillem de Torroella, makes use of a variety of Arthurian sources in recounting the poet's imaginary voyage on a whale to a distant island and his encounter there with Morgan le Fay and King Arthur. Allusions and references to Arthurian names and places abound in Catalan and Valencian poetry, historiography, and romance from the late twelfth century to the end of the Middle Ages—for example, in troubadour lyrics of Guerau de Cabrera, Guillem de Berguedà, Ramon Vidal de Besalú, and Guillem de Cervera; the chronicles of Bernat Desclot and Ramon Muntaner; the lyric poetry of Jaume March, Andreu Febrer, Arnau March, Ausiàs March, Joan Rocafort, and Bernat Hug de Rocabertí; such miscellaneous works as Bernat Serradell's *Testament,* Ramon Perellos's *Viatge al Purgatori de Sant Patrici,* and Jaume Roig's *Spill*; and the romances *Curial e Güelfa* and *Tirant lo Blanc.* And, in addition to the surviving Vulgate and Prose *Tristan* texts, the translation and circulation of the cyclical romances, as well as the importation of *Meliadus, Palamedes, Guiron le Courtois,* and the *Prophécies de Merlin,* are attested to in numerous Catalan and Aragonese documents and letters. From such sources, we also learn of tapestries of the Nine Worthies (one presumably being Arthur) and the knights of the Round Table, and the depiction of the story of *Jaufré* in wall paintings at Saragossa. The neo-Arthurian prose romance *Perceforest* may have been known to the anonymous Catalan author of the poem *Frayre de joy e sor de plaser*; the first two parts of the *Perceforest* were eventually translated into Spanish in the mid-sixteenth century by Fernando de Mena. The prose romances came under attack, however, from the Dominican friar Antoni Canals (ca. 1352–1415), who condemned the reading of the *Lancelot* and the *Tristan* in his epistle *De Modo Bene Vivendi* (wrongly attributed to St. Bernard).

r dist li contes que lende
main de la pentecouste fist
li rois artus venir devant
li tous les cōpaignons q
furent de la queste · ⁊ qnt
il furent tout asis · si apr
la li rois artus devant li ses rois ⁊ ses contes

80. John Rylands University Library, MS 1, fol. 114v: Arthur Convokes the Grail Questers. (Courtesy John Rylands University Library.)

In the western part of the peninsula, the Matter of Britain also took early root. Arturus was a name used in Salamanca in 1200, and in Portugal we find the name Merlinus in 1190 and Galvam in 1208. On the model of Provençal troubadours, poets writing in Galician-Portuguese in the thirteenth and fourteenth centuries often allude to Arthurian subjects, taking their material primarily from the cyclical prose romances; e.g., Martin Soares, Alfonso X, Gonçal' Eannes do Vinhal, Estevão da Guarda, Fernand' Esguio, and the anonymous poet of the five *Lais de Bretanha*. The Post-Vulgate *Roman du Graal*, which must be reconstructed to some extent from the surviving Hispanic texts, was translated into a western Ibero-Romance language by Brother Juan Vives (or João Bivas) ca. 1313–14. Versions of all three branches of the cycle survive in Galician-Portuguese and Portuguese—the *Livro de Josep Abaramatia*, copied ca. 1543–44, early fourteenth-century fragments of the *Merlin* discovered in bindings at the Biblioteca de Catalunya, and the *Demanda do Santo Graal*, copied in the fifteenth century—as well as in Spanish, but the evidence points to a Leonese or Galician-Portuguese origin. The fourteenth-century *Livro de Linhagens*, or *Nobiliário*, of Dom Pedro, Count of Barcelos, contains a reworking of the Wace material in the Navarrese *Liber Regum*, incorporating details from a version of the *Roman du Graal*. Similar material is also found in the Spanish *Crónica de 1404* and Martín de Larraya's fifteenth-century copy of the *Libro de las generaciones*. The Prose *Tristan* and the Vulgate *Lancelot* were apparently translated in the northwest at about the same time as the *Roman du Graal*, but only a short Galician-Portuguese manuscript fragment of the *Tristan* survives. Elements of Arthurian romances linked to Cistercian authorship, such as the Vulgate *Queste*, have been traced in a tale in the fifteenth-century Portuguese exempla collection *Horto do Esposo*. References to Arthurian characters in Fernão Lopes's chronicles of the reign of João I (1385–1433) make it clear that the prose romances were widely read at the Portuguese court. We know that the library of Dom Duarte, João's son by Philippa of Lancaster, contained a *Livro de Tristam*, a *Merlim*, and a *Livro de Galaaz* (probably the *Demanda*). The *Perceforest* may also have been known to the fifteenth-century Portuguese chronicler Gomes Eanes de Zurara. And late-medieval and early sixteenth-century courtly lyrics gathered by Garcia de Resende in his *Cancioneiro geral* (1516) include a number of allusions to Arthurian characters.

In northern and central Spain, we find early references to Arthur's fatal battle with Mordred in annals attached to a manuscript of the Navarro-Aragonese *Fuero general de Navarra* (ca. 1196–1212) and in the Castilian *Anales toledanos primeros* (1217). The earliest surviving Spanish romance of chivalry, the *Libro del caballero Zifar* (ca. 1300), contains several Arthurian references, to the story of Yván (probably Yvain) and to Arthur's fight with the Cath Palug (an apparent borrowing from the Vulgate *Merlin*). The library of Carlos III of Navarre (1361–1425) included a now-lost Navarrese translation of the Vulgate *Lancelot* as well as a copy in French. A long version of the *Lancelot* was translated from a northwestern dialect into Castilian by 1414 but is extant only in a partial mid-sixteenth-century copy, with an appended set of chapters linking the Lancelot story to that of Tristan. Two medieval Spanish ballads concerning Lancelot survive: "Nunca fuera caballero de damas tan bien servido" (cited by Cervantes in *Don Quixote*) and "Tres hijuelos había el rey" (still surviving in modern oral tradition). The widely influential neo-Arthurian romance *Amadís de Gaula*, probably composed in the first half of the fourteenth century, was modeled in large part on the plot and style of the Prose *Lancelot* and also the Prose *Tristan*. The language of the original text is much disputed, some claiming Galician or Portuguese priority, others Spanish or even Catalan, but French now seems unlikely. The three branches of the *Roman du Graal* are preserved in two manuscript versions from the late fifteenth century (one shows marked Leonese features and the other, by the Vizcayan chronicler Lope García de Salazar, is heavily condensed and reworked, especially in the account of King Arthur's passing to the island of Brasil) and the last two branches in several printed versions, titled the *Baladro del Sabio Merlín* (Burgos, 1498; Seville, 1535) and the *Demanda del Sancto Grial* (Toledo, 1515; Seville, 1535). The 1535 imprint of the *Baladro* interpolates a set of cryptic prophecies attributed to Merlin concerning late-medieval Spanish history, derived from an earlier text preserved in Catalan and Spanish manuscripts. Merlin texts are known to have formed part of the libraries of the Count of Benavente and Queen Isabella, the latter also possessing a Spanish version of the *Demanda*. Elements from the early Grail history as found in the Vulgate or Post-Vulgate *Estoire del Saint Graal* are included in Spanish and Portuguese incunabula adaptations of the French prose romance *Destruction de Jerusalem*, titled *La estoria del noble Vespasiano* (Toledo, ca. 1490; Seville, 1499) and *Estória do mui nobre Vespasiano, emperador de Roma* (Lisbon, 1496). The fourteenth-century Catalan *Storia del Sant Grasal* translates a portion of the French *Queste*.

The Prose *Tristan* may have been translated into Aragonese and Spanish through a Catalan intermediary, although the theory of an Italian origin has not been totally disproven. A mixed Castilian/Aragonese version, the *Cuento de Tristán de Leonís*, seems generally closer to the surviving Catalan fragments than the other extant Spanish Tristan texts. The Prose *Tristan* would seem to have inspired the medieval Spanish ballad "Herido está don Tristán," which comes down to us in several fragmentary versions; and elements from the romance were interpolated by García de Salazar in his *Libro de las bienandanzas e fortunas*. Arthurian allusions are common in Spanish texts of the late Middle Ages and early sixteenth century and constitute another reflection of the continuing vogue of the prose romances, especially among the aristocracy; examples are Juan Ruiz's *Libro de buen amor*, Rodrigo Yáñez's *Poema de Alfonso XI*, Pero López de Ayala's *Crónica de don Pedro I* (in his *Rimado de Palacio*, Ayala also disparages the *Amadís* and the *Lancelot* as time-wasting works read when he was young), Fernán Pérez de Guzmán's *Mar de historias*, the *Libro del conocimiento de todos los reinos*, Alfonso Martinez de Toledo's *Corbacho* (or *Arcipreste de Talavera*), Gutierre Díez de Games's *Victorial* (or *Crónica de don Pero Niño*), Juan de Flores's *Triunfo de amor*, and numerous poems by court and church poets from the late fourteenth and fifteenth centuries, such as Pero Ferrús, Alfonso Álvarez de Villasandino, Fray Migir, Juan Alfonso de Baena, Juan de Dueñas, Fray Gauberte del Monge, Francisco Imperial, the Marquis of Santillana, Diego Martínez, Ruy Paes de Ribera, Alfonso de Córdoba, and Juan del Encina. Authors of several sentimental romances of the fifteenth century were influenced by Arthurian material: Juan Rodríguez del Padrón reworked elements from the Prose *Tristan* and the tale of King Arthur's passing in his *Siervo libre de amor*; and Diego de San Pedro, in his *Cárcel de amor*, made use of the episode of Lancelot's rescue of Guenevere from the stake in the *Mort Artu*. In turn, excerpts from Juan de Flores's sentimental romance *Grimalte y Gradissa* are found in the *Libro del esforçado cavallero don Tristán de Leonís*, a Spanish version of the Prose *Tristan* printed in 1501 and also surviving in editions dated 1520 and 1528 as well as a 1534 reworking with sequel, the *Corónica del buen cavallero don Tristán de Leonís y del rey don Tristán de Leonís, el joven su hijo*, later translated into Italian. A sixteenth-century manuscript copy of an epistolary exchange between Isolde and Tristan contains additional material from *Grimalte y Gradissa*; and the extant incunabulum fragment of Mossèn Gras's *Tragèdia de Lançalot*, a Catalan reworking of the Vulgate *Mort Artu*, also reveals rhetoric associated with sentimental romances.

Throughout Christian Spain and Portugal, Arthurian literature served as an exemplar for aristocratic society, prompting the mimicry of Arthurian tourneys and jousts, even molding the behavior of individuals. In Muntaner's *Crónica*, we learn of "round tables" (i.e., jousting, feasting, and dancing) held at Barcelona, Saragossa, Calatayud, and Gascony in the thirteenth century. The nature of such activities is described at length and contrasted with Arthur's Round Table in *La gran conquista de Ultramar*. Alfonso the Magnanimous of Aragon is said to have used the arms of Tristan on his shield in a tourney held at Barcelona. In the *Libro de la montería*, attributed to Alfonso XI of Castile and León, a Galician noble is chided for hunting a giant called the "Dragón Negro de la Lana Encantada" instead of proper beasts of venery. In the *Crónica do Condestabre de Portugal Nun' Alvares Pereira* and in the first part of Fernão Lopes's *Crónica del Rei Dom João I*, we read that Dom Nuno Alvares Pereira, Constable of Portugal, was an avid reader of the Galahad story and that he emulated the model of celibacy exemplified by Galahad. In the second part of Lopes's *Crónica*, historical personages are mocked through comparisons of their deeds with those of Tristan, Lancelot, Kay, Galahad, and Arthur. In 1434, an extraordinary imitation of chivalric adventure took place in the province of León, described for us by a witness, Pero Rodríguez de Lena, in the *Libro del passo honroso*: with the permission of Juan II of Castile, a young knight named Suero de Quiñones held control of a bridge over the River Órbigo as a tribute to his lady-love. In a series of tourneys, Suero and nine companions faced sixty-eight Spanish and foreign knights; Suero and all but one of his friends were wounded; among the challengers one was killed and many others injured.

In the late Middle Ages, the practice of giving Arthurian names to children and even to animals also reflects the popularity of the romances. Alfonso X's brother Enrique had two falcons named Lanzarote and Galván. Lanzarote was also given as a Spanish baptismal name in 1344. Juan I of Aragon read contemporary Merlin prophecies as a youth and called one of his hounds Merlin. In García de Salazar's *Bienandanzas e fortunas*, we find various individuals in Spain's northern provinces bearing the names Tristán, Galaz, Persival, and Florestán (Amadís's half-brother); and in Fernando de Rojas's *Tragicomedia de Calisto y Melibea*, there is a fictional servant by the name of Tristán. Zurara's *Crónica da tomada de Ceuta* and *Crónica da Guiné* and Resende's *Cancioneiro geral* also reveal the use of the names Tristão, Lançarote, and Lionel in fifteenth-century Portugal.

Although the Arthurian legend appealed primarily to the nobility and clergy, by the end of the Middle Ages, particularly as a result of the advent of printing, the legend also had an impact upon the middle class. Though some medieval and Renaissance writers condemned the chivalric romances as frivolous, the Arthurian texts were widely read for more than 300 years, either in the original or in translation. The vogue for Arthurian romance also gave rise to Spain's most influential romance of chivalry, the *Amadís de Gaula*, reworked by Garci Rodríguez de Montalvo and printed in 1508. This and other Hispanic romances, such as *Tirant le Blanc* and *Palmerín de Inglaterra*, caused an important rebirth of the romance of chivalry throughout Europe in the sixteenth century. (*See also* TRISTAN IN SPAIN AND PORTUGAL.) [HLS]

Entwistle, William J. *The Arthurian Legend in the Literatures of the Spanish Peninsula*. London: Dent, 1925.

Malkiel, María Rosa Lida de. "Arthurian Literature in Spain and Portugal." In *Arthurian Literature in the Middle Ages*, ed. Roger Sherman Loomis. Oxford: Clarendon, 1959, pp. 406-18.

Sharrer, Harvey L. *A Critical Bibliography of Hispanic Arthurian Material*. London: Grant and Cutler, 1977, Vol. 1: *Texts: The Prose Romance Cycles*.

———. "Notas sobre la materia artúrica hispánica, 1979-1986." *La Corónica*, 15 (1986-87), 328-40.

SPENSER, EDMUND (1552-1599), began work sometime during the 1570s on his romantic epic *The Faerie Queene*, of which he completed slightly more than half before his death in 1599. Arthur is the hero of this allegorical poem; he is intended to be at once a model of the ideal nobleman and a representation of the Aristotelian virtue of magnanimity, or "magnificence," as Spenser terms it, the virtue that is the sum of all the rest. The epic is set in motion when Uther Pendragon is attacked by Octa, son of Hengist, and his kinsman Eosa. Arthur is still a prince. Having seen Gloriana, the Faerie Queene, in a dream vision, Arthur has fallen in love with her. As he searches for her, he encounters trials through which he demonstrates his virtue and prowess. Had Spenser lived to complete his poem, presumably Arthur would have been united with Gloriana—that is, magnanimity would have been joined with glory—in a climactic embodiment of Spenser's theme that the return of the house of Arthur (the Tudors) restores the glory of England. In developing this theme, however, Spenser makes scant use of the traditional Arthurian story. Arthur and Merlin are the only characters who figure importantly, and Arthur himself has none of his usual adventures; indeed, his very quest for Gloriana is based on Chaucer's anti-Arthurian *Tale of Sir Thopas*. Only one of Arthur's knights, Tristram, even has a role, and that an insignificant one. To compliment both Elizabeth I and the Order of the Garter, Spenser substitutes the Order of Maidenhead, who are Gloriana's knights, for the Round Table. By the very nature of his role in *The Faerie Queene*, Spenser's Arthur has to be essentially invincible; in part because of his infallibility, he is neither the most important nor the most memorable of Spenser's knights. *The Faerie Queene* is a great poem, but not a great Arthurian poem. [LRG]

Spenser, Edmund. *The Faerie Queene*. In *Poetical Works*, ed. J.C. Smith and E. de Selincourt. London: Oxford University Press, 1912.

Hieatt, A. Kent. "The Passing of Arthur in Malory, Spenser, and Shakespeare: The Avoidance of Closure." In *The Passing of Arthur: New Essays in Arthurian Tradition*, ed. Christopher Baswell and William Sharpe. New York: Garland, 1988.

Millican, Charles Bowie. *Spenser and the Table Round: A Study in the Contemporaneous Background for Spenser's Use of the Arthurian Legend*. Cambridge: Harvard University Press, 1932.

SPICER, JACK (1925-1965), American poet who published among his last works a series of forty-nine free-verse lyrics under the title of *The Holy Grail* (1964). The work is divided into seven books, each of which recounts the response of one of the principal Arthurian characters to the Grail; under this guise, through a reinterpretation of the Grail's significance and through an almost "metaphysical" and often humorous juxtaposition of medieval and modern images, Spicer raises questions about poetry in the modern world. [SRR]

Spicer, Jack. *The Holy Grail*. San Francisco: White Rabbit, 1964.

SPOILS OF ANNWFN, THE (PREIDDEU ANNWFN), a short Welsh poem (dating ca. 900) in the Book of Taliesin. An enigmatic text, it describes an expedition by Arthur and his followers to a city (which doubtless represents the Celtic otherworld) where he obtains a magic cauldron. (*See also* WELSH ARTHURIAN LITERATURE.) [NJL]

Evans, J. Gwenogvryn, ed. *Poems from the Book of Taliesin*. Llanbedrog: Tramvan, 1915, pp. 26-41.

STAINED GLASS. Representations of King Arthur in stained glass are unknown before the fifteenth century. In spite of the popularity of sculptured "galleries of kings" on church façades of the twelfth and thirteenth centuries, there appear to be few counterparts in stained glass of that period. Apart from the glazed series of imperial figures at Strasbourg Cathedral (ca. 1200) and representations of the first thirty-six kings of France at Reims Cathedral (thirteenth century), the subject of kingship in stained glass was limited to the ancestors of Christ in biblical genealogies (Matthew 1:1-17; Luke 3:23-38).

In England, by the fifteenth century, there was a conscious attempt to link King Arthur with the English royal line; the Tudor king Henry VII claimed descent from Arthur and named his eldest son Arthur in 1486. Several stained-glass programs are known to include depictions of King Arthur alongside other secular kings and ecclesiastics (e.g., east window of York Minster, 1405-08; north window in antechapel originally in library of All Souls College, Oxford, 1441-47; St. Mary's Hall, Coventry, 1450-1500). Another factor that may have contributed to the growth in popularity of King Arthur in the fifteenth century, particularly by the last quarter of the century, was Caxton's publication of Malory's *Morte Darthur*. [NK]

The revival of Arthurian subjects in modern stained glass corresponded to the renewed interest in secular medieval themes by the Pre-Raphaelites. In 1861, William Morris, in partnership with Edward Burne-Jones, Dante Gabriel Rossetti, Ford Madox Brown, and others, founded the London decorating firm of Morris, Marshall, Faulkner & Co. In the same year, the firm produced a *King and Queen*, most probably Arthur and Guenevere, now in the Victoria and Albert Museum, London. A series of designs for the story of Tristan and Isolde followed in 1862. The Bradford City Art Gallery possesses two panels in this series, the *Fight with Sir Marhaus* and *Tristram Leaving the King of Ireland*. Cartoons for the *Birth of Tristram* and *Tristram's Madness* are in the possession of the Birmingham City Art Gallery. In Kirkby Lonsdale are panels of Lancelot and Elaine dating ca. 1870-82. In 1886, Burne-Jones designed four panels for the firm, showing episodes of Lancelot, Gawain, Galahad, and the Holy Grail (now in the Victoria and Albert Museum). Burne-Jones also designed tapestries on this theme at about this time.

Louis Comfort Tiffany's windows also include Arthurian themes, often based on well-known paintings. *Sir Galahad*, in the 1902 Ogden Cryder Memorial window in St. Andrew's Dune Church, Southampton, N.Y., was copied from Frederick Watts's painting *Sir Galahad* (1862), now in the Fogg Art Museum, Cambridge, Mass. A drawing of Sir Galahad sustained by the Holy Grail while in prison was illustrated in the Tiffany studio's promotional booklet *Tributes to Honor*. One of Tiffany's better-known windows is the 1917 three-panel composition of the *Red Cross Knight* (after Spenser's *Faerie Queene*) in the National Headquarters of the American Red Cross, Washington, D.C.

In England, a number of Arts and Crafts designers continued Arthurian themes, for example Veronica Whall, with her series in "King Arthur's Hall" at Tintagel, Cornwall, in 1933. Another set was made by Arnold Robinson, a pupil of Christopher Whall, Veronica's father, ca. 1914. The windows are now in the possession of Robinson's son, Geoffrey, director of Joseph Bell & Son, Bristol. A cartoon for one of these windows was illustrated in the catalogue *The Pre-Raphaelite Era* (Delaware Art Museum, 1976, No. 6-7), wrongly attributed to Louis Davis. In 1901, Dorothy C. Smyth designed a panel showing Isolde holding the love potion, set near the main entrance of Mackintosh's Glasgow School of Art. In this same tradition, the Boston stained-glass artist Charles J. Connick produced a large series of panels on the Grail legend in 1922 for an alcove in Princeton University's Proctor Hall, and the *Morte Darthur* window in the Epic Series for the university's chapel. Other American firms produced Arthurian windows; notably J. Gordon Guthrie (a Galahad window) and Willet Stained Glass Studios (a Quest for the Grail, in the Fort Lincoln Cemetery, Washington, D.C., and a Parsifal, after Wagner's opera, in the Allegheny Cemetery, Pittsburgh). [VCR]

Caviness, Madeline Harrison. *Stained Glass Before 1540: An Annotated Bibliography*. Boston: G.K. Hall, 1983.

Cormack, Peter (William Morris Gallery, London), and Helene Weis (Willet Studios, Philadelphia). Unpublished research.

Duncan, Alastair. *Tiffany Windows*. New York: Simon and Schuster, 1980.

Loomis, Roger Sherman, and Laura Hibbard Loomis. *Arthurian Legends in Medieval Art*. London: Oxford University Press, 1938.

Nelson, Philip. *Ancient Painted Glass in England 1170-1500*. London: Methuen, 1913.

Sewter, A. Charles. *The Stained Glass of William Morris and His Circle*. 2 vols. New Haven: Yale University Press, 1974.

STANMORE HALL TAPESTRIES. In 1891, Australian mining millionaire W.K. D'Arcy commissioned a six-panel tapestry ensemble for the dining room of his Uxbridge estate, Stanmore Hall, from Morris and Company. Burne-Jones designed the cartoon, illustrating the quest for the Holy Grail, and the panels were made by another of Morris's firms, the Merton Abbey Tapestry Works. The ensemble, completed in 1894, included *The Knights of the Table Summoned to the Quest by a Strange Damsel*, *The Arming and Departure of the Knights*, *The Failure of Sir Lancelot*, *The Failure of Sir Gawain*, *The Achievement of Sir Galahad Accompanied by Sir Percival and Sir Bors*, and *The Slip*. A verdure panel of a thick forest, festooned with shields, was designed to cover the dado. The tapestries, now in the collection of the Duke of Westminster, were copied twice: for Laurence Hodson

(1895–96, Birmingham City Galleries) and for D'Arcy's partner George McCulloch (1898–99, Private Collection). [DNM]

Marillier, H.C. *History of the Merton Abbey Tapestry Works*. London: Constable, 1927.

Parry, Linda. "The Tapestries of Edward Burne-Jones." *Apollo*, 102 (November 1975), 324–28.

STANZAIC *LE MORTE ARTHUR*, an English verse romance of 3,969 lines, generally believed to have been written in the fourteenth century. The poem survives in only one manuscript, London, B.L. Harley 2252, a miscellany compiled by the London mercer and bookseller John Colyns in the early sixteenth century. The poem occupies fols. 86–133, forming an originally independent booklet, which can be dated between 1460 and 1480. The dialect of the poem has been identified as belonging to the northern border of the West Midlands; however, the two scribes who copied the poem were probably from the East Midlands and the southern border of the East Midlands, respectively. A leaf has been lost from the manuscript between fols. 102 and 103, which probably contained an account of the funeral of the Maid of Ascolat.

The romance is written throughout in eight-line stanzas of four-stress lines. There are ten short stanzas; the irregularity may be attributed to scribal error, since nine of them are in the hand of the second scribe. The rhyme-scheme is abababab, and the prevailing rhythm iambic, though variations on both rhyme-scheme and rhythm occur. The poet also makes considerable use of alliteration; it appears in forty-two percent of the lines. Some lines have as many as four alliterated syllables, though two or three are more common. The alliteration is not merely decorative: it frequently coincides with the stress register, indicating the rhythm, and, although some alliterative phrases function merely as metrical fillers, many others carry the emphasis or meaning of the lines. The blend of initial alliteration, stress, internal alliteration, assonance, and end-rhyme creates a distinctive sound texture. Detractors of the poem have termed it "minstrel-like" because of the limited rhymes and frequent use of stock phrases and metrical fillers; supporters of the poem point to its balladlike simplicity, economy, and power. Economical changes of scene or speaker at stanza-breaks, an emphasis on dialogue, and an absence of motivational explanation help to move the narrative swiftly, giving it an objective quality in which character and action speak for themselves.

The action of the poem falls into two unequal parts. Four years after the quest of the Grail, Arthur calls a tournament at Winchester. Lancelot attends in disguise, is wounded by his brother Ector, and inspires the love of the Maid of Ascolat; he refuses her courteously but agrees to wear her sleeve at the tournament, and he leaves his armor with her at Ascolat afterward. This action causes Gawayn to believe that Lancelot is the Maid's lover, and Gaynor (Guenevere), the Queen, to rebuke him for his infidelity to her and drive him away. Thus, when she is unjustly accused by Sir Mador of murdering his brother with a poisoned apple, she has no champion to defend her. By law, she must be burned, but Lancelot arrives in time to defeat Mador and restore harmony at court.

The second part of the poem puts Gaynor in deadlier peril, as the result of an ambush of the two lovers in the Queen's chamber by Aggrawayne and his fellows. Lancelot survives the ambush and rescues Gaynor from burning, but in the fighting at the fire Gawayn's brothers Gaheries and Gaheriet are killed. Gawayn swears revenge on Lancelot and pursues it implacably, even after the pope has persuaded Arthur to be reconciled with the Queen. Gawayn and Arthur besiege Lancelot and his kinsmen in his own country, Benwicke, till they are forced by the news from England to return. Mordred, Arthur's nephew and son, who had been left as regent in England, has usurped the crown and attempted to marry the Queen, who escaped to the Tower of London.

In the ensuing battles between Arthur's army and Mordred's, Gawayn is killed. An attempt at a truce is made as the two suspicious hosts face each other on Salisbury Plain, but an adder appears from a bush, a sword is drawn to kill it, and the battle is joined. Mordred is killed and Arthur fatally wounded. Though a ship full of weeping ladies carries him away to the vale of Avalon, his tomb is found the next day by the faithful Bedwere at the hermitage founded by the former Archbishop of Canterbury. Later, Lancelot, searching for Gaynor, finds that she has taken the veil; after a poignant farewell, he becomes a hermit, living out his last seven years with his kinsmen at the archbishop's hermitage, which subsequently becomes the Abbey of Glastonbury.

The stanzaic poem is based on the French *Mort Artu*. The poet has considerably condensed his source, omitting such episodes as Arthur's visit to Morgan's castle (where he sees Lancelot's paintings), his defeat of the Roman emperor in Burgundy, and the seizure of power after Arthur's death by Mordred's sons, who are subsequently defeated by Lancelot. He has also provided many original touches, such as the adder in the bush and the farewell scene between the lovers. (Only one late French manuscript contains a brief account of such a meeting, and it is probably an interpolation.) The greater emphasis on dialogue and action and the omission of the explicit philosophizing on Fortune that characterizes the French romance produce a narrative in which tragedy results from a complex interweaving of character and accident rather than from the power of Fate. Gaynor's imperiousness, Lancelot's chivalry, and Gawayn's intransigence affect the plot as powerfully as chance details, such as Gaheriet's failure to wear armor at Gaynor's execution and the adder on Salisbury Plain.

The Stanzaic *Le Morte Arthur* is one of the primary sources of the final two tales of Sir Thomas Malory's *Le Morte Darthur*, "The Tale of Lancelot and Guinevere" and "The Morte Arthur Saunz Guerdon" (Caxton's Books XVIII–XXI). Malory rearranges the episodes of the first part of the poem and adds original episodes in his seventh tale, but his eighth tale is directly dependent on the stanzaic poem, with frequent verbal reminiscences. [DBM]

Bruce, J.D., ed. *Le Morte Arthur: A Romance in Stanzas of Eight Lines*. London: Oxford University Press, 1903.

Hissiger, P.F., ed. *Le Morte Arthur: A Critical Edition*. The Hague: Mouton, 1975.

Schmidt, A.V.C., and Nicolas Jacobs, eds. *Medieval English Romances, Part Two*. London: Hodder and Stoughton, 1980.

Stone, Brian, trans. *King Arthur's Death*. Harmondsworth: Penguin, 1988.

Jansen Jaech, Sharon L. "The Parting of Lancelot and Gaynor: The Effect of Repetition in the Stanzaic *Morte Arthur*." *Interpretations*, 15 (1984), 59–69.

Knopp, Sherron E. "Artistic Design in the *Stanzaic Morte Arthur*." *Journal of English Literary History*, 45 (1978), 563–82.

Wertime, Richard A. "The Theme and Structure of the Stanzaic *Morte Arthur*." *PMLA*, 87 (1972), 1075–82.

STEEDMAN, MARGUERITE COUTURIER, American journalist and author who based *Refuge in Avalon* (1962) on the legend that Joseph of Arimathea brought Jesus to Britain as a young boy. Here, Jesus meets Taliesin and Bran the Pendragon. The rest of this long novel is concerned mainly with Jesus's life in Palestine, but it ends with Joseph's return to Britain after the Crucifixion. [EB]

Steedman, Marguerite. *Refuge in Avalon*. Garden City, N.Y.: Doubleday, 1962.

STEINBECK, JOHN (1902–1968), American Nobel Laureate, evinced a career-long interest in matters Arthurian, and especially in Malory. His first novel, *Cup of Gold* (1929), a historical fiction about the Welsh pirate Sir Henry Morgan, presents Merlin (or his descendant—it is unclear which) as an incidental character who prophesies his career to the boy Morgan. More fully in *Tortilla Flat* (1935), he attempted to impose a Malorian pattern upon the story of his twentieth-century *paisano* losers; but its author's preface and his chapter titles *à la* Caxton do nothing to make Danny's Monterey house like the Round Table or his friends like its knights. Critics, sometimes with hints from Steinbeck, have also seen Arthurian motifs in other works, such as *Of Mice and Men* (1937) and *Cannery Row* (1945). Yet none of these emerges as an appropriate modern analogue for the *Morte Darthur*: their antiheroes and antiheroic plots prove a recalcitrant fit. A much more ambitious attempt at modernizing Malory is the posthumously published "translation" *The Acts of King Arthur and His Noble Knights* (1977). Moving with increasing freedom of invention through the Winchester version, Steinbeck retells its Tales I and III (Vinaver ed.). Reduced to about one-fifth of its original, this is truly "more Acts than Morte," as Steinbeck said. Only minor changes, mostly to suit its author's conception of modern taste, appear in the early parts. Rather more originality emerges in the triple quest of "Gawain, Ewain and Marhalt," with lively dialogue and the kind of incidental humor at which Steinbeck excelled. Most expanded of the Malorian stories is the "Lancelot," where the tutelage of Lionel becomes more explicit than in the original, and Lancelot and Guinevere discover their love more explicitly than in Malory. Thematic differences between the more literal and the more imaginative parts of the work make a jarring contrast, and the latter, more original tales are occasionally marred by Steinbeck's recurrent tendency toward sentimentality. [MF]

Steinbeck, John. *The Acts of King Arthur and His Noble Knights, from the Winchester MSS of Thomas Malory and Other Sources*, ed. Chase Horton. New York: Farrar, Straus and Giroux, 1976.

Hayashi, Tetsumaro, ed. *Steinbeck and the Arthurian Theme*. Muncie, Ind.: Ball State University Press, 1975.

STEPHENS, G. ARBOUR, in "Christmas Interlude at the Court of King Arthur" (1939), presents the traditional story of Sir Cleges in the form of a one-act play for children. Generosity is rewarded and greed punished when Cleges presents Arthur with his gift of cherries that miraculously ripened on the tree at Christmas. [RHT]

Stephens, G. Arbour. "Christmas Interlude at the Court of King Arthur." In *Cameo Plays, Book 2*, ed. George H. Holroyd. Glasgow, Leeds, and Belfast: Arnold, 1939, pp. 86–96.

STERLING, SARA, author of *A Lady of King Arthur's Court* (1909). Subtitled "A Romance of the Holy Grail," this insubstantial novel chronicles the happy outcome of the love of Dieudonnée and Anguish, Prince of Ireland, who after much suffering achieves a vision of the Grail. [AEG]

Sterling, Sara. *A Lady of King Arthur's Court*. London: Chatto and Windus, 1909.

STETTNER, LEO, German teacher and writer. In Stettner's play *Tristan und Isôt* (1964), the legendary characters step out of a tapestry and perform their story, from Isôt's healing of the hero to their time together in the forest. The work deviates from tradition in that Tristan does not kill Morold, nor Brangäne administer the love potion. [SSch/PWM]

Stettner, Leo. *Tristan und Isôt: Ein Spiel nach einem alten Wandteppich*. Munich: Buchner, 1964.

STEWART, MARY, British novelist and sometime lecturer in English literature, has written four Arthurian novels, three focusing on Merlin and one on Mordred. In *The Crystal Cave* (1970), she depicts Merlin as bastard son of Ambrosius Aurelianus (in Nennius, his cognate character) by a Welsh princess. Tutored by the sage Galapas in the cave that he eventually himself inhabits, Merlin seeks and discovers his father, whom he serves as seer until the former's death. Performing a like function for his uncle, Uther Pendragon, he moves the monoliths of Stonehenge from Ireland and presides at the conception of Arthur, as in traditional story.

The Hollow Hills (1973) is largely an untraditional account of Merlin's mostly long-distance supervision of Arthur's *enfances*, his search for the sword of Macsen Wledig (whose Celtic legend Stewart conflates with the conventional motif of the Sword in the Stone), and his abetment of Arthur's winning the throne. The climax of the book, Morgause's (here deliberate) seduction of the young monarch and her conception of Mordred, is an important foreshadowing of Stewart's later novels.

In *The Last Enchantment* (1979), Stewart continues to recount Merlin's supervision of Arthur's reign. In an interesting conjunction, she lays the blame for Merlin's traditional madness, as in the Welsh Myrddin poems, upon his poisoning by Morgause. The latter continues as chief villain, while Merlin's love for Nimue, who succeeds him as physician and seer to Arthur, is presented as idyllic and nondestructive; his disappearance is self-willed and not permanent. Guinevere's lover—a flexible role usually filled since Chrétien by Lancelot—is played by Bedivere.

In *The Wicked Day* (1984), Stewart turns her attention to Mordred, here a sympathetic character who is the unwilling instrument in the debacle of his battle with Arthur. His mother, Morgause, is the decisive agent of revenge in what has always been a family feud. But no one can forestall the wicked day, which, as traditionally, is precipitated by an Edenic snake.

Stewart uses various sources—Geoffrey of Monmouth, Celtic myth, Chrétien, and Malory among others—plus her own imagination to recreate the Arthurian story. Her plots are absorbing examples of their kind, the popular romance, and her characters' psychology is mostly convincing. In her use of Merlin's and Mordred's *enfances*, she restores to twentieth-century readers one of the most popular medieval Arthurian modes of explaining subsequent plot and character. While self-conscious narrators, especially in the Merlin trilogy, and occasional self-pity in the Mordred novel, somewhat vitiate her literary achievement, Stewart's use of early British history and her rationalization of the marvelous in Arthurian legend remain artful. [MF]

Stewart, Mary. *The Crystal Cave*. London: Hodder and Stoughton, 1970.

———. *The Hollow Hills*. London: Hodder and Stoughton, 1973.

———. *The Last Enchantment*. London: Hodder and Stoughton, 1979.

———. *The Wicked Day*. London: Hodder and Stoughton, 1984.

STEYNOR, MORLEY, used sober blank verse and some spectacular effects to dramatize the traditional tragic tale in *Lancelot and Guenevere*, which was first performed at the Bijou Theatre, London, on April 8, 1904. On the same day and in the same theater, his *Lancelot and Elaine* also had its premiere. Mingling prose and verse, it tells of Elaine's unrequited love for the knight and of Guenevere's unwarranted suspicions. The character of Arthur is not fully developed in either tragedy. [CNS]

Steynor, Morley. *Lancelot and Guenevere: A Play in a Prologue and Four Acts*. London: Bell, 1909.

———. *Lancelot and Elaine: A Play in Five Acts*. London: Bell, 1909.

STONE, EUGENIA (1879–1971), American author of two delightful Arthurian juvenile novels. In *Page Boy for King Arthur* (1949), Tor, a peasant boy, rescues Sir Lancelot and is rewarded by being made a page to Sir Galahad. In *Squire for King Arthur* (1955), Tor rescues the son of Pellinore from the Saxons, warns Arthur of a Saxon invasion, and is rewarded by being made Pellinore's squire. [ACL]

Stone, Eugenia. *Page Boy for King Arthur*. Chicago: Wilcox and Follett, 1949.

———. *Squire for King Arthur*. Chicago: Follett, 1955.

STONEHENGE. Geoffrey of Monmouth calls this monument on Salisbury Plain the Giants' Ring—*Chorea Gigantum*, suggesting a circular dance. He says that the stones composing it were brought from Africa to Ireland by giants and arranged in a circle on "Mount Killaraus." Rituals were performed there, and the stones had healing properties. When Aurelius Ambrosius wanted to create a worthy memorial for 460 nobles massacred by Hengist's Saxons, Merlin proposed transplanting the Giants' Ring to Britain. An expedition headed by Uther, with Merlin as adviser, crossed to Ireland. The Britons failed to shift the stones, so Merlin employed his arts to dismantle them. They were shipped to Britain, and he arranged them in the same formation around the nobles' mass grave. Aurelius, Uther, and Arthur's successor, Constantine, were also buried there.

In a folkloric version of this tale recorded by John Wood (*Choir Gaure*, Oxford, 1747), Merlin enlists the help of the Devil, who steals the stones from an old Irishwoman, ties them into a bundle, and flies over to Salisbury Plain.

So far as Geoffrey's giants have any reality, they are the pre-Celtic megalith-builders, imagined as huge because of the size of the stones. In the case of Stonehenge, the architectural design and implied skill could readily have suggested that ordinary mortals would have needed magical aid. Actually, the monument was built on its present site, in stages, long before Merlin. But a smaller circle inside the larger one has provoked speculation relating to him. Archaeologists have maintained that the stones composing it could not have been quarried anywhere nearer than the Prescelly Mountains in southwest Wales. If they were quarried there, they would doubtless have been floated up the Bristol Channel on rafts, and Geoffrey's account of seaborne stones from the west could preserve a factual tradition. Some geologists dispute the necessity of such a faraway origin, but the weight of evidence is now generally acknowledged to be in its favor. [GA]

Geoffrey of Monmouth. *Historia Regum Britanniae*, Book VIII, Chapters 10–12.

Chippindale, Christopher. *Stonehenge Complete*. London: Thames and Hudson, 1983.

Grinsell, L.V. *Legendary History and Folklore of Stonehenge*. St. Peterport: Toucan, 1975.

STORIA DEL SANT GRASAL, a Catalan work, surviving in a manuscript dated 1380, offering a faithful translation of the Vulgate *Queste del Saint Graal*, from Galahad's arrival at court to the completion of the Grail quest. [NJL]

Crescini, Vincenzo, and Venanzio Todesco, eds. *La versione catalana della Inchiesta del San Gral*. Barcelona: Institut d'Estudis Catalans, 1917.

STRAUSS, VICTORIA, American author of the parallel-world fantasy *Worldstone* (1985). In the mythology underlying this novel, Arthur was the last to reign over united realms of magic and technology. After Arthur died and the worlds of Mindpower and Handpower separated, Percival stole the worldstone (the Grail) from Bron and harbored it in the world of Mindpower. The novel is about a quest to return the stone to the world of Mindpower after it has been taken to our world, the modern world of Handpower, by a descendant of Bron. [PCB]

Strauss, Victoria. *Worldstone*. New York: Macmillan, 1985.

STRENGLEIKAR ("Stringed Instruments") is the name given to a collection of twenty-one lais and a prologue translated into Norwegian from French sources during Hákon Hákonarson's reign (1217–63). Preserved in codex De la Gardie 4–7 (Uppsala University Library) and in one other fragment, this compilation contains eleven lais attributed to Marie de France, six anonymous lais found in other collections, and four lais not attested in other sources. These translations represent the third major collection of lais in existence and belong to the literary activity associated with the Norwegian court during the first half of the thirteenth century. The *Strengleikar* collection is possibly the work of a cleric connected with Hákon's court. Some scholars have suggested that Brother Robert, the translator of *Tristrams saga*, may have participated in the translation of the lais.

The fidelity of the translation varies considerably. Some tales have extensive omissions and abridgment, while others display a complete and careful rendering of the French. In each case, the translator has transformed the verse lais into Norwegian prose often characterized by an ornate style that encourages rhetorical embellishments, rhythmic prose, and artistic elaboration.

81. John Rylands University Library, MS 1, fol. 223v: A Knight Who Wants to Kill Gauvain Gives Poisoned Fruit to Guenevere, But she Offers It to Another Knight. (Courtesy John Rylands University Library.)

Of the lais collected in *Strengleikar*, only *Geitarlauf* and *Januals ljóð* have Arthurian subjects. The first, a translation of Marie de France's *Chevrefueil*, recounts the meeting of Tristram and Ísönd in the forest. The tale centers on a message inscribed by Tristram on a piece of hazelwood. In a striking deviation from the French, the Norwegian version clarifies the exact content of Tristram's communication. Otherwise the translation follows closely the original with few omissions. Like other translations written at Hákon's behest, *Geitarlauf* displays stylistic embellishments, especially alliteration, as well as textual amplification. Because of a missing leaf in the manuscript, *Januals ljóð*, which translates Marie de France's *Lanval*, begins with line 157 of the French. Approximately three-quarters of the remaining 490 lines are translated. This abridgment does not alter the overall plot. The Norse version still recounts quite faithfully the adventures of Janual (Lanval), a knight from Arthur's court who is befriended by a fairy mistress and who finally escapes with her to Avalon. Like *Geitarlauf*, *Januals ljóð* exhibits stylistic embellishments (alliteration, repetition) as well as marked amplification (and at times reduction) of the text.

The compositions in the *Strengleikar* preserve a tradition that even outside of Scandinavia was limited. That they reached Norway attests the interest in French and especially Arthurian literature favored by Hákon's court. [IJR]

Cook, Robert, and Mattias Tveitane, eds. *Strengleikar: An Old Norse Translation of Twenty-one Old French Lais*. Oslo: Kjeldeskriftfondet, 1979.

Leach, Henry G. *Angevin Britain and Scandinavia*. Cambridge: Harvard University Press, 1921.

Meissner, Rudolf. *Die Strengleikar: Ein Beitrag zur Geschichte der altnordischen Prosalitteratur*. Halle: Niemeyer, 1902.

STRICKER, DER, flourished in the first half of the thirteenth century. He was a commoner, as his name indicates, probably from Franconia, who later lived and worked in Austria. He had a solid knowledge of practical theology and German literature. Rudolf von Ems mentions him in his *Alexander* and *Willehalm von Orlens* and appreciates his talents as narrator.

Der Stricker is among the early representatives of the genres of didactic poetry and exempla; he deals with religious themes and practical morality but also with courtly love and praise of women (*Frauenehre*). He excels in his popular stories and anecdotes on everyday situations, where comical and burlesque elements prevail, his best-known story being the *Pfaffe Amîs* ("Priest Amîs").

Among his epic works are *Karl*, an adaptation of Konrad's *Song of Roland* to the literary taste and style of his time, and the Arthurian romance *Daniel von dem blühenden Tal* (8,482 lines), for which no direct source is known. The romance relates the adventures of the young knight Daniel, who, attracted by the fame of Arthur's court, offers his services to Arthur. He sets out on a series of combats against the forces of evil, which he successfully overcomes not only by his intrepidity but also by cunning. The setting is the world of fairy tale and legend, inhabited by supernatural creatures and outfitted with magic objects. Correspondences can be established with ancient Greek myths (the myths of Polyphemus and of the Gorgon), with Christian legends (the legend of Silvester), with Arthurian romances (*Jaufré*, the Prose *Lancelot*, and especially Hartmann's Arthurian romances), and with the *Song of Roland* and the *Song of Alexander*. Unlike other courtly Arthurian romances, *Daniel* is characterized by the spirit of heroic epic. King Arthur actively engages in hostilities, the precourtly ideal of vassalage plays an important role, and specifically courtly values are not developed. Later in the thirteenth century, *Daniel* inspired another Arthurian verse romance, *Garel von dem blühenden Tal*, by Der Pleier. [KRG]

Stricker, Der. *Daniel von dem blühenden Tal*, ed. Michael Resler. Tübingen: Niemeyer, 1983.

———. *Der Stricker: Daniel of the Blossoming Valley*, trans. Michael Resler. New York: Garland, 1990.

De Boor, Helmut. "Der Daniel des Stricker und der Garel des Pleier." *Beiträge zur Geschichte der deutschen Sprache und Literatur*, 79 (1957), 67–84.

Gottzmann, Carola L. *Artusdichtung*. Stuttgart: Metzler, 1989.

Hart, Thomas Elwood. "'Werkstruktur' in Stricker's *Daniel*? A Critique by Counterexample." *Colloquia Germanica*, 13 (1980), 106–41.

Henderson, Ingeborg. "Stricker's *Daniel* in the Recently Found *Ms. germ. 1340*." *Journal of English and Germanic Philology*, 86 (1987), 348–57.

Schultz, James A. *The Shape of the Round Table: Structures of Middle High German Arthurian Romance*. Toronto: University of Toronto Press, 1983.

STUCKEN, EDUARD (1865–1936), a widely traveled and versatile German author. Between 1901 and 1924, he wrote eight plays, which he arranged according to the story of Arthur and collected under the title *Der Gral: Ein dramatisches Epos*: *Gawan* (1901), *Lanval* (1903), *Lanzelot* (1909), *Merlins Geburt* (1913; later title: *Lucifer*), *Tristram und Ysolt* (1916), *Das verlorene Ich* (1922; later title: *Uter Pendragon*), *Vortigern* (1924), and *Zauberer Merlin* (1924). These dramatic works, which combine religious mysticism and *Jugendstil* (or fin-de-siècle aesthetic), were for the most part performed and enjoyed success on important stages of Europe. Most famous were *Gawan*, *Lanval*, and *Lanzelot*. They were highly praised for their hypnotic effect but are now largely forgotten. [UM/WCM]

Stucken, Eduard. *Der Gral: Ein dramatisches Epos.* Berlin: Reiss, 1924.

Carlson, Ingeborg L. *Eduard Stucken: Ein Dichter und seine Zeit.* Berlin: Haude and Spener, 1978.

STURGEON, THEODORE (pseudonym of Edward Hamilton Waldo; 1918–1985), American author of science fiction and fantasy, wrote one Arthurian piece, "Excalibur and the Atom" (1951). A Sam Spade-like private eye, named Guinn after his mother, is hired by a lady, Morgan, to find a cup that was last known to be in the possession of a shepherd named Percival and that has the power to render H-bombs useless. Guinn ultimately "remembers" that he was formerly Galahad; reincarnations of Merlin, Gareth, Lynnette, and Mordred also play significant roles in the story. [SRR]

Sturgeon, Theodore. "Excalibur and the Atom." *Fantastic Adventures*, 13 (August 1951), 8–51.

STURM, FRANK PEARCE (1879–1942), English physician who was a friend of Yeats, a student of the occult, and an admirer of French symbolism. Sturm's writings include five Arthurian poems published in the Aberdeen literary magazine *Bon-Accord*. "The Questing Host" (1902) and "Palomide Remembers the Quest" (1903) use Palomide of the Hopeless Quest as the emblem the poet's search for peace and wisdom. In "Launcelot Praises Guenevere with Rhymes," "Launcelot Tells of the Enchanted Islands," and "The Monk Launcelot Remembers Guenevere" (all 1905), the love of Launcelot and the Queen is shown as passionate and pure, edged with mortality and guilt, yet defiant and proud. [PCB]

Sturm, Frank Pearce. *Frank Pearce Sturm: His Life, Letters, and Collected Work*, ed. Richard Taylor. Urbana: University of Illinois Press, 1969.

SUITE DU MERLIN. A mid-thirteenth-century French amplification of the prose reworking of Robert de Boron's *Merlin*, the *Suite du Merlin* ("Continuation of *Merlin*") has been preserved in two fourteenth-century manuscripts, both incomplete: London, B.L. Add. 38117 (often referred to as the *Huth Merlin*) and Cambridge University Library Add. 7071. The publication of the former in 1886 was an important step toward the rehabilitation of the Arthurian prose romances. The Cambridge manuscript, discovered in 1945 by Eugène Vinaver, is far more complete, but it remains unpublished. This *Suite du Merlin* forms a part of the so-called *Roman du Graal* or Post-Vulgate Cycle of Arthurian romances; indeed, it is about all that remains of the cycle in French.

Both the Vulgate and Post-Vulgate accounts of Merlin begin with common material drawn from Robert de Boron's *Merlin*. They recount the birth of Merlin (begat by an incubus on a virtuous girl in a moment of anger) and his powers to know the past (given him by the Devil) and the future (a gift from God, because his mother had sincerely repented). In an episode well known from Malory, Merlin allows Vertiger (Vortigern) to complete his tower by having the two dragons undermining it meet and destroy one another. This first part continues with the destruction of Vortigern's tower, the reigns of Aurelius Ambrosius and his brother Uther Pendragon, including their victory over the Saxons with Merlin's aid, the building of Stonehenge, the establishment of the Round Table with its *Siège périlleux*, the conception of Arthur at Tintagel, and Arthur's recognition as legitimate heir through the Sword in the Stone. Throughout this first part, Merlin is a shape-changer, prophet, and magician figure. But at this point, the stories diverge and the *Suite du Merlin* largely replaces the historiographically oriented account of Arthur's wars with the rebel lords and Saxons found in the *Estoire de Merlin* section of Vulgate Cycle with a more fantastic account of the origins of the Arthurian world. In this second part, the *Suite* proper, which is no longer dependent on Robert de Boron's account, Merlin becomes the sad victim of Viviane's magic and is entombed forever by her womanly wiles. Here, we have the incestuous conception of Mordred, the revelation of Arthur's parentage, the obtaining of Excalibor, Arthur's marriage to Guenevere, and Balain's Dolorous Stroke, which at one and the same time begins the downfall of Arthur's kingdom and sets off the momentous quest for the Grail. The conclusion of the *Merlin* is missing in the Huth and Cambridge manuscripts but has been identified in B.N. f. fr. 112.

The *Suite du Merlin* was the source of the Merlin sections of the Castilian *Demanda del Sancto Grial* and Galician-Portuguese *Demanda do Santo Graal* but is best known as the primary source of the first four books of Sir Thomas Malory's *Morte Darthur*. [WWK]

Paris, Gaston, and J. Ulrich, eds. *Merlin*. 2 vols. Paris: Didot, 1886.

Baumgartner, Emmanuèle, trans. *Merlin le prophète ou le Livre du Graal*. Paris: Stock + Plus, 1980. (Modern French translation of much of the preceding edition.)

Rosenberg, Samuel N., trans. "Episodes from the Prose *Merlin* and the *Suite du Merlin*." In *The Romance of Arthur II*, ed. James J. Wilhelm. New York: Garland, 1986.

SULPICIUS. According to Geoffrey of Monmouth, Gawain's father sent him to Rome as a boy to serve in the household of Pope Sulpicius, who dubbed him a knight. Sulpicius is also mentioned in the Latin romance *De Ortu Waluuanii*, but the allusion derives from Geoffrey and does not imply any separate account.

No such pope ever existed. Tatlock and others have explained Sulpicius as a product of Geoffrey's waywardness or imperfect memory. He picked up the name of a real pope, Simplicius, and modified it. Simplicius succeeded to the papacy in 468 and held office till 483. Geoffrey's apparent reference to him is unhistorical, but it hints that background reading may have led him to passages in chronicles where Simplicius figured. This is in keeping with his evident awareness of the reign of the eastern emperor Leo I, six years of which (468–74) overlapped Simplicius's pontificate. Use by Geoffrey of known sources relating to the period could have supplied him with the pope's name as well as the emperor's. (*See also* ARTHUR, ORIGINS OF LEGEND.)

[GA]

SUMARIO DE HISTORIA DE LOS REYES DE BRETAÑA ("Summary of the History of the Kings of Britain"), a lost thirteenth-century Navarrese work derived from Wace's *Roman de Brut*. It survives with modifications in a Portuguese genealogical register and in two Hispanic universal chronicles: the *Livro Velho* or "Old Book" section of the Portuguese *Livro de Linhagens* (also called *Nobiliário*), compiled in the fourteenth century by Dom Pedro, Count of Barcelos; the Spanish *Crónica de 1404*, or *Crónica general de 1404*, originally written in Portuguese; and Martín de Larraya's late fifteenth- or early sixteenth-century copy of the Navarrese *Libro de las generaciones*. Some details in the *Livro de Linhagens* account were probably based upon the *Mort Artu* of the Vulgate Cycle; additions in the *Crónica general de 1404* were in all likelihood taken from the Post-Vulgate *Roman du Graal*. [HLS]

Catalán, Diego, and María Soledad de Andrés, eds. *Edición crítica del texto español de la Crónica de 1344 que ordenó el Conde de Barcelos don Pedro Alfonso*. Madrid: Gredos & Universidad de Madrid, Seminario Menéndez Pidal, 1971, Vol. 1, pp. lvii, lix–lx, 239, 274–90.

Catalán Menéndez Pidal, Diego. *De Alfonso X al Conde de Barcelos: cuatro estudios sobre el nacimiento de la historiograffa romance en Castilla y Portugal*. Madrid: Gredos & Universidad de Madrid, Seminario Menéndez Pidal, 1962, pp. 360–401.

SUTCLIFF, ROSEMARY, English novelist, has written six books based on Arthurian themes, four of them for younger readers. All of them are evocative, insightful, and readable. *Sword at Sunset* (1963) is the longest and most sophisticated. It retells Arthur's story in the first person—a daring conception, since he must die at the end. His remembrance begins with Ambrosius giving the young Artos the sword of Maximus; continues with his seduction by Ygerna, his half-sister, whose issue, Medraut, will destroy him; moves on to the buying of horses on the Continent, where he meets and takes into service Bedwyr, the Harper, who becomes his friend and his wife's lover. Guenhumara, a chieftain's daughter who nurses his wounds after a battle, is given to him in marriage with a dowry of 100 men. The novel captures the loneliness and hardship of her life as the wife of Arthur, delivering her child among the Ancient People of the Hills, blaming her husband when the child later dies, turning to Bedwyr in her loneliness, being betrayed by Medraut. Though the story departs significantly from that of Malory, Sutcliff retains the twin themes of incest, with its consequent retribution, and the breaking of the brotherhood, through the illicit love between the Queen and the King's best friend.

The Lantern Bearers (1959), set in the pre-Arthurian period, describes the struggle of Vortigern and Ambrosius, as seen through the eyes of Aquila, a young Romano-British Decurion who defects when the troops are recalled to Rome. Captured by Saxons, he spends three years as a thrall in Juteland, but when his master emigrates to his homeland Aquila escapes and joins Ambrosius in the struggle against the invaders. He finds personal peace, however, only after he learns to forgive his enemies.

The other four books are retellings of the legend. *Tristan and Iseult* (1971) tries to return to the Celtic original as far as possible. It omits the love potion and the role of Brangain and ends with the stories of the black and white sails and the hazel and honeysuckle growing over the lovers' single grave. A condensation of this book is included in *The Sword and the Circle* (1981), which follows Malory "in the main" for its account of the early years of Arthur's kingdom but also draws upon other sources. Sutcliff here succeeds admirably in the difficult task of combining a well-known collection of legends in a unified and absorbing tale. Two other of Sutcliff's books follow Malory more closely. *The Light Beyond the Forest* (1979) is a simplified but never condescending account of the Grail quest. Though Sutcliff pays equal attention to chivalric adventure and Christian allegory, she preserves a sense of Celtic mystery and unexplained happenings. *The Road to Camlann* (1981) concludes with the tragic story of the fall of Arthur and the Round Table. [MAG]

Sutcliff, Rosemary. *The Lantern Bearers*. London: Oxford University Press, 1959.

———. *Sword at Sunset*. London: Hodder and Stoughton, 1963.

———. *Tristan and Iseult*. London: Bodley Head, 1971.

———. *The Light Beyond the Forest: Quest for the Holy Grail*. London: Bodley Head, 1979.

———. *The Road to Camlann*. London: Bodley Head, 1981.

———. *The Sword and the Circle: King Arthur and the Knights of the Round Table*. London: Bodley Head, 1981.

Thompson, Raymond H. *The Return from Avalon: A Study of Modern Arthurian Fiction*. Westport, Conn.: Greenwood, 1985.

ŠVARC, EVGENIJ L. (1896–1958), Russian writer, actor, and journalist, wrote several fairy-tale plays for youth theater. In *Drakon* ("Dragon," 1943), the dragon-slaying knight Lanzelot, clearly patterned after the Arthurian knight, reveals that people who are used to dictatorship and oppression are reluctant to be helped. The play was aimed at German fascism, but since it criticized dictatorships of all kinds it was forbidden by Stalinist censorship. In 1961, three years after the author's death, it was performed for the first time, in Nova Huta; since then, it has appeared on many stages of the world. A German operatic version with the title *Lanzelot*, by dramatist Heiner Müller and the well-known composer Paul Dessau, had a successful premiere at the State Opera of Berlin on December 19, 1969. [UM/WLS]

Švarc, Evgenji [sic] L. *Drakon*. Moscow, 1943.

SWANWICK, MICHAEL, author of "The Dragon Line" (1989), in which Mordred and Merlin survive into modern times and Mordred enlists the magician's aid in a futile effort to save the world from pollution. The principal innovation of the story is to make Merlin Mordred's grandfather; the magician, we learn, had killed the infant Arthur and instead delivered his own son, Mordred's father, to be reared by Ector. At the end of the story, Merlin's powers are destroyed by a genital wound reminiscent of the Fisher King's. [NJL]

Swanwick, Michael. "The Dragon Line." *Isaac Asimov's Science Fiction*, June 1989, 109–23.

SWINBURNE, ALGERNON CHARLES (1837–1909), English poet, turned to the Arthurian legends early in his career, not because of any special interest in the material but because of the Pre-Raphaelite fascination with the Arthurian stories and in particular the Arthurian verse of William Morris. Swinburne's Arthurian work falls naturally into three divisions: the early poetry of the late 1850s, written under the direct influence of Morris; *Tristram of Lyonesse* (1882); and *The Tale of Balen* (1896).

There are four early Arthurian poems: *Queen Yseult*, a long unfinished work in six cantos, based on the romance of *Sir Tristrem* and following the career of Tristram from his birth until his marriage to Yseult in Brittany; "Joyeuse Garde" (78 lines), a possible continuation of *Queen Yseult*, which depicts the love of Tristram and Yseult; "The Day Before the Trial" (44 lines), a soliloquy by King Arthur on the day before his wife's trial, suggested by Morris's "The Defence of Guenevere"; and "Lancelot" (327 lines), a version of Lancelot's quest for the Grail, similar to Morris's portrait of Galahad in "Sir Galahad: A Christmas Mystery" and taking the form of a dialogue between Lancelot and an angel.

Swinburne's major Arthurian creation is *Tristram of Lyonesse*. Divided into a prelude and nine sections, it focuses on Tristram's love, his subsequent sufferings, his marriage, and his tragic death. Angered by Tennyson's recreation of the Arthurian world and in particular his treatment of the Tristram story, Swinburne makes the fatal passion the poem's center. Selecting the lyrical moments of the medieval romance, he fashions his own account of the fatal grandeur of human love. Arguably the finest and most famous treatment of the Tristram legend in the English language, the poem is a celebration of sexual love realized in all its beauty and tragedy.

Late in his career, Swinburne returned to the Arthurian world to write *The Tale of Balen*, which closely follows Malory's version of the Balin story. Divided into seven sections, the poem is a further exploration of fate's power in human affairs, but it lacks the lyrical intensity of his more original recreation of the Tristram story.

Swinburne's Arthurian work, initially a consequence of his interest in Pre-Raphaelite poetry, reflects his permanent fascination with the implications of the Tristram story. *Tristram of Lyonesse* is that exceptional vehicle that allows a writer to depict the medieval world in a poetic celebration of his own understanding of the human condition. [DS]

Swinburne, Algernon Charles. *Tristram of Lyonesse*. London: Chatto and Windus, 1882.

———. *The Tale of Balen*. London: Chatto and Windus, 1896.

———. *The Complete Works of Algernon Charles Swinburne*, ed. Edmund Gosse and T.J. Wise. 20 vols. London: Heinemann, 1925–27.

Cochran, Rebecca. "An Assessment of Swinburne's Arthuriana." In *King Arthur Through the Ages*, ed. Valerie M. Lagorio and Mildred Leake Day. 2 vols. New York: Garland, 1990, Vol. 2, pp. 62–82.

McSweeney, Kerry. "The Structure of Swinburne's 'Tristram of Lyonesse.'" *Queen's Quarterly*, 75 (1968), 690–702.

Staines, David. "Swinburne's Arthurian World." *Studia Neophilologica*, 50 (1978), 53–70.

SWORD IN THE STONE. According to traditional accounts, Arthur's royalty is revealed when, as a young man, he is able to withdraw a sword from a stone or from an anvil placed on a block of stone. This motif, absent from Geoffrey of Monmouth, apparently originated with Robert de Boron, in his *Merlin* romance. That work exists only in a fragment, but scholars are agreed that it survives in two prose redactions (the *Suite du Merlin* and the Merlin portion of the Vulgate Cycle). In Robert's work, and also in Malory, the sword is embedded in an anvil, but some later writers omitted the anvil, and the sword and stone have become standard elements of Arthur's early history. Robert had partially explained the significance of the objects—the sword represents justice; the stone doubtless symbolizes Christ—thereby establishing Arthur as defender of the faith and as king by divine right. This special relationship of Arthur to God is not so strongly emphasized by later writers, and the symbolism of sword and stone is similarly deemphasized; the withdrawal of the sword, a test often arranged by Merlin, becomes a means not of divine selection of a king but of his revelation. In most accounts, the sword is first given to Kay, whose possible claim to the kingship is disproved when he is unable to repeat the sword's removal.

In the Vulgate and thereafter, the test of the Sword in the Stone also serves to reveal Galahad as the preordained Grail knight. Malory, for example, tells us how Merlin inserted Balin's sword into a marble stone, where it remained until Galahad was able to remove it. [NJL]

Micha, Alexandre. "L'Épreuve de l'épée." *Romania*, 70 (1948–49), 37–50.

Morris, Rosemary. *The Character of King Arthur in Medieval Literature*. Cambridge: Brewer, 1982, pp. 36–49.

SWORD OF THE STRANGE HANGINGS, in the Vulgate *Queste del Saint Graal*, a wonderful sword that can be gripped only by the chosen knight, who will be Galahad. Much earlier, Varlan had used this sword to strike Lambar (the father of the king who would be known as the Maimed King), and the blow had led to the devastation known as the Wasteland. The sword received its "strange hangings" when Perceval's sister replaced its belt by one woven from her own hair. [NJL]

SYBERBERG, HANS JÜRGEN, film director, member of the "New German Cinema." Syberberg's controversial filming of Richard Wagner's *Parsifal* (1981–82) is no mere record of a stage performance but is rather an attempt to accord the plot and music a fresh dimension through cinematic imagery. The opera is overlaid with an ornate web of visual symbols and evocative allusions that simultaneously "explain" Wagner's work and make it more hermetic; the central staging device, for example, is a towering death mask of the composer. Syberberg exploits episodes from medieval sources that Wagner either omits or merely points to, such as the incident of the three drops of blood in the snow and the tale of Parsifal's ancestors, conveyed here with the aid of doll actors. The film is impressive not only for its technical refinement but for the acting of the cast, especially Edith Clever as Kundry. [UM/WCM]

Syberberg, Hans Jürgen. *Parsifal: Ein Filmessay*. Munich: Heyne, 1982.

SYMONS, ARTHUR (1865–1945), British poet, critic, editor, and a leading member of the Decadent Movement, was inspired by Wagner's opera to write *Tristan and Iseult* (1917). In this poetic drama in the Symbolist tradition, Tristan and Iseult, who are not lovers, drink the love potion by mistake. Surprised by Mark, Tristan is repentant, Iseult defiant. Tristan marries Iseult of Brittany, is stabbed, and, after the episode of the black and white sails, dies. Arriving too late, Iseult of Ireland dies at his side. Mark laments that, had he known all, he would have surrendered Iseult to his nephew.

Symons also composed several short lyric Arthurian poems. Apart from "Parsifal," which was written at Bayreuth in 1897 in response to Wagner's opera, they give voice to the passion that Tristan feels for Iseult. [AEG/RHT]

Symons, Arthur. *Tristan and Iseult*. London: Heinemann, 1917.

———. *The Collected Works of Arthur Symons*. 9 vols. London: Secker, 1924.

SYRE GAWENE AND THE CARLE OF CARLYLE, a short English romance (ca. 1400) that exists in two versions; both of them are incomplete, but since the texts overlap and complement one another the entire poem can be reconstructed. The longer and certainly less inferior poem is the one discussed here (the other being *The Carle off Carlile*). It lacks the beheading scene, which reshapes the Carl both physically and spiritually into a normal human being and is therefore crucial to our understanding of the plot. Yet there is no gap in the manuscript, which points to an incomplete exemplar. The poem itself is a test of courtesy and its related virtues of valor and obedience. During a hunt, Bishop Baldwin, Kay, and Gawain get lost and have to ask for shelter from the ill-famed Carl of Carlyle. Kay boasts that he will teach him a lesson but soon changes his mind when he sees the four pets (a bull, a boar, a lion, and a bear) and giantlike stature of his host. The Carl says that he can offer them only a carl's courtesy, which is supposedly a rough variant of the sophisticated courtesy of Arthur's court. In the same way, the poem is a crude imitation of the courtly romance, and yet neither the Carl nor the poem is entirely without merit. There is a humorous sneer at the clergy when the Bishop, threatened by the Carl, exclaims: "Don't, I'm a man of holy orders!"—he will not fight but did not hesitate to go hunting. Kay shows himself similarly ill-bred. Only Gawain passes the tests of courtesy and obedience toward his host and is rewarded with his daughter. Remarkable features are the obedience shown the Carl first by his pet animals and later by his wife, whom he presses to go to bed with Gawain but stops at the last moment, and his daughter, who is summoned to sleep with Gawain instead. Although the names of the main characters are identical, the poem bears no relationship to *The Avowing of King Arthur*. [ESK]

Madden, Frederic, ed. *Syr Gawayne*. London: Bannatyne Club, 1839.

Kurvinen, Auvo, ed. *Sir Gawain and the Carl of Carlisle in Two Versions*. Helsinki, 1951.

TABLANTE DE RICAMONTE, the short title of a Spanish prose romance adapted probably from a lost late-medieval French prosification of the thirteenth-century Provençal poem *Jaufré*. The earliest known Spanish version was printed at Toledo in 1513: *La coronica de los nobles caualleros Tablante de Ricamonte y de Jofre hijo del conde Donason*. Notably absent is the *Jaufré* poet's use of irony and humor. In the Spanish version, the hero Jofre's adventures as a newly armed knight from Arthur's court are given serious treatment, reflecting it would seem the late-medieval interest in resurrecting chivalric ideals of the past. The text underwent numerous reprintings across the years, surviving as a popular chapbook down to the late nineteenth century. The chapbook version was translated into Tagalog verse, and episodes from it were also adapted by an eighteenth-century Portuguese chapbook author, António da Silva. [HLS]

Bonilla y San Martín, Adolfo, ed. *Cronica de los muy notables caualleros Tablante de Ricamonte y de Jofre hijo del Conde Don Ason* [Estella, 1564]. In *Libros de caballerías, primera parte*. Madrid: Bailly-Baillière, 1907, pp. 457–99.

TABLANTE DE RICAMONTE SAMPO NANG MAGASAUANG SI JOFRE AT NI BRUNIESEN ("Tablante de Ricamonte Together with the Couple Jofre and Bruniesen"), a nineteenth-century Tagalog translation and condensation of the Spanish *Tablante de Ricamonte*, itself an adaptation of the Jaufré story. The Tagalog text depicts the conflict of Taulot and Jofre and the latter's love for Bruniesen, with the events taking place in the Kingdom of "Camalor." (*See also* SPANISH AND PORTUGUESE ARTHURIAN LITERATURE.) [NJL]

Dinaanang Buhay ni Tablante de Ricamonte sampo nang magasauang si Jofre at ni Bruniesen sa Caharian nang Camalor na nasasacupan nang Haring Si Artos at Reina Ginebra. Manila, 1902. (Text.)

Fansler, Dean S. "Metrical Romances in the Philippines." *Journal of American Folklore*, 29 (1916), 217–22. (Translation.)

TAFT, LINWOOD (1877–1935), composed *Galahad: A Pageant of the Holy Grail* (1924) for schools. Each of ten episodes is introduced by a chronicler and accompanied by music as the action unfolds. Based largely upon Malory, the work depicts important events in Galahad's career, some of them traditionally attached to Perceval. [RHT]

Taft, Linwood. *Galahad: A Pageant of the Holy Grail*. New York: Barnes, 1924.

TALBOT, NORMAN, British-born Australian poet, demonstrated the potential of the story of Tristan and Isolde for diverse treatments in half a dozen poems in each of two collections, *Poems for a Female Universe* (1968) and *Son of a Female Universe* (1971). The lovers are cast in modern roles in "He Drinks to Isolde on the Liner" and as figures of the Celtic past in "2 Poems for Isolde's Mother." The poems range in mood and imagery from the light romance of "A Poem About 3 True Lovers," to the ominously grim "Isolde Jealous II," to the graphically violent "Tristan Mad." [DN]

Talbot, Norman. *Poems for a Female Universe*. Sydney: South Head, 1968.

———. *Son of a Female Universe*. Sydney: South Head, 1971.

TALIESIN. Although there is doubt about his historicity, Taliesin is believed to be a sixth-century poet, and he is listed in the Triads as one of the three chief Christian bards of the Isle of Britain. Twelve of his poems survive, including three panegyrics to Urien's son Owein.

Taliesin also figures as a character in early Welsh poetry, and he is sometimes identified with Merlin as a manifestation of the archetypal poet reincarnated in various eras. The prose tales in *Hanes Taliesin*, written down from the late sixteenth to eighteenth centuries, tell how Gwion Bach learns wisdom from the cauldron of Ceridwen. He tries to elude the goddess by changing shape but is swal-

82. Galehaut Tapestry, Northern French or Flemish. (The St. Louis Art Museum.)

lowed as a grain of wheat and reborn as Taliesin. Exposed on the sea in a leather bag, he is caught in the weir of King Gwyddno and raised by his son Elphin, whom he later saves from the wrath of King Maelgwn. For his many exploits, he earns the title Chief of the Bards and goes to Arthur's court. There, he engages in such adventures as the raid on the otherworld described in *The Spoils of Annwfn* (though dating from ca. 900, the poem is collected in the Book of Taliesin, a fourteenth-century manuscript containing the poet's supposed works). Taliesin's development, from historical poet to poet-prophet-magician, follows a traditional pattern in folklore and literature.

Taliesin was largely ignored outside of Welsh tradition until rediscovered by modern writers, most notably Charles Williams. He uses the bard to represent the poetic imagination, and it is through his eyes that the world is most often viewed in *Taliessin Through Logres* (1938) and *The Region of the Summer Stars* (1944). [RHT]

Taliesin. *The Poems of Taliesin*, ed. J.E. Caerwyn Williams and Ifor Williams. Dublin: Dublin Institute for Advanced Study, 1968.

Guest, Charlotte, trans. "Taliesin." In *The Mabinogion*. 1849; London: Dent, 1906, pp. 263–85.

Wood, Juliette. "Virgil and Taliesin: The Concept of the Magician in Medieval Folklore." *Folklore*, 94 (1983), 91–104.

TAPESTRY. Prized for their intrinsic value, workmanship, and unique ability to turn cold, barren halls into sumptuous, warm chambers, suites of tapestries were sought by the nobility to enhance their owners' comfort and prestige. These splendid hangings—like paintings made of colored wool and linen with silk, gold, and silver threads—were given and received as diplomatic gifts, taken as booty and spoils of war, and considered excellent investments. In Spain, in 1356 and 1368, Queen Leonor, wife of Pedro IV of Aragon, acquired tapestries with the stories of King Arthur and the knights of the Round Table. In England, "cloth of arras," that is, tapestry, is often listed in inventories. The English apparently preferred the stories of Lancelot and Perceval, although King Arthur was included as a figure in tapestries of the Nine Worthies. The fifteenth-century inventories of King Charles VI of France list 150 tapestries, several with Arthurian subjects: a quest for the Grail, the Nine Worthies, and the story of Yvain. Charles's wife, Queen Isabelle of Bavaria, owned a Perceval and a large Holy Grail tapestry, and his uncles, the royal dukes, also collected tapestries. Louis of Anjou owned seventy-six tapestries, including the Nine Worthies, the Three Christian Worthies, two with stories of Lancelot, and several with Tristan. The bibliophile Jean de Berry had a Nine Worthies tapestry worked with gold and silver thread. Philip the Bold, Duke of Burgundy, who had a taste for sumptuous materials and magnificent scale, owned a King Arthur tapestry so large that he had it divided into four pieces for storage. His inventory also lists tapestries illustrating the jousts of Lancelot and the story of Perceval. He sent his largest Perceval tapestry (sixty-four feet wide) as a diplomatic gift to the Duke of York, uncle of the King of England.

The finest surviving tapestry of King Arthur is from a suite of the Nine Worthies, now in the Metropolitan Museum, The Cloisters Collections, New York. King Arthur is seated in an elaborate Gothic niche surrounded by tracery and figures of bishops and cardinals. Arthur wears over his armor a tabardlike garment and he carries a banner; both tabard and banner are decorated with the three golden crowns symbolizing the kingdoms of North Wales, South Wales, Logres. The style and technique of weaving resemble that of the well-known Angers Apocalypse; thus, this tapestry may be the work of Nicolas Bataille, and a date of ca. 1385 has been suggested. The tapestry may have been made for Jean de Berry (1340–1416), although it is not listed in the inventory made at the time of the duke's death. The entire set must have been very impressive; even this fragment measures fourteen feet by nearly ten feet.

By the end of the fifteenth century, wealthy burghers also could afford the luxury of tapestry; Mathias Eberle of Basel, for example, owned a tapestry of the Three Christian Worthies (now in the Historical Museum at Basel). In it, Arthur is represented as an elegant, fashionably dressed youth holding a banner displaying the three crowns. A number of other museums possess tapestries with Arthurian scenes. For example, a large wool tapestry (French, dating from ca. 1500) in the St. Louis (Missouri) Art Museum presents a scene involving Galehaut but depicting events not yet identified in literary sources.

Arthurian tapestries were again produced during the nineteenth-century Arthurian Revival. In 1879, Herbert Bone designed tapestries on Arthurian subjects, such as the departure of Arthur on the death barge; the set was executed by the Royal Windsor Tapestry Manufactory. The best-known modern example of Arthurian tapestry is a series of six, on the theme of the Grail quest, designed by Edward Burne-Jones for Stanmore Hall and woven in 1894 at the Merton Abbey Tapestry Works, a company organized by William Morris. The set was later copied twice. [MS]

Goebel, Heinrich. *Wandteppiche*. 2 vols. Leipzig, 1923, 1928.

Loomis, Roger Sherman, and Laura Hibbard Loomis. *Arthurian Legends in Medieval Art*. London: Oxford University Press, 1938, pp. 27–30, 38–40; figs. 12, 15.

Salet, Francis, and Geneviève Souchal. *Masterpieces of Tapestry*. Paris: Éditions des Musées Nationaux, 1973, pp. 34–38.

TAROT, MERLIN. This Tarot deck, designed by R.J. Stewart and illustrated by Miranda Gray, is discussed by

Stewart in *The Merlin Tarot* (1988). The author, who has written a number of books offering mystical interpretations of the Grail legend and the life of Merlin, uses as a basis the adventures of Merlin as found in Geoffrey of Monmouth's twelfth-century texts. He offers a detailed examination of the twenty-two Trumps and a system of relating them to mystical cosmology and psychology, sections on the Court and Elements cards, and methods for laying out and working with the cards. Although modern in conception, the work seeks to recover a Western, Celtic tradition that predates the earliest known set of Tarot cards. [RHT]

Stewart, R.J. *The Merlin Tarot: Images, Insight and Wisdom from the Age of Merlin*. Wellingborough: Aquarian, 1988.

TATUM, EDITH, American novelist and poet, author of "The Awakening of Iseult" (1913), a verse narrative of the lovers' first meeting. Tatum is writing a romance for adolescents, and so the poem, although faithful to its sources, ends with Tristan's departure from Ireland after his true identity is discovered. Tatum's verse is reasonably graceful, making much of the youthful beauty of her protagonists, and her language is only mildly archaic. [AAR]

Tatum, Edith. *The Awakening of Iseult*. Oglethorpe, Ga.: Oglethorpe University Press, 1933.

TAVOLA RITONDA, LA ("The Round Table"), a text in the Tuscan dialect dating from the second quarter of the fourteenth century, bears witness to the popularity of Tristan in Italy. While echoes of Dante, especially *Inferno* V, certify a fourteenth-century date for the text in its present form, there are references to a (possibly spurious) history of the book deriving from a volume that Piero, Count of Savoy (d. 1268), took to England as a gift for King Edward I, a book "now" in the possession of the Pisan Gaddo de' Lanfranchi. The volume may have been the same one known to Italy's earliest Arthurian, Gaddo's fellow Pisan Rusticiano. If this ancient book is not a fiction, it has undergone considerable revision before achieving its current form preserved in ten manuscripts of the fourteenth and fifteenth centuries, three of which—Mediceo-Laurenziana, Pluteo XLIV 27; Florence, Magliabecchiana Biblioteca Nazionale Centrale; and one in the Biblioteca Comunale in Siena—provided the base texts for Polidori's modern edition.

While clearly derived from the Prose *Tristan*, the *Tavola* is an eclectic text indebted to such additional direct and indirect sources as Robert de Boron's *Merlin*, the *Tristan* of Thomas d'Angleterre, the *Palamedes*, the Vulgate *Queste* and *Mort Artu*, and an as yet unidentified source that the *Tavola* shares with the *Tristano Riccardiano*. Inventions of the *Tavola* include a number of original lyrics, the tale of Ferragunze and his four boasts, the attempted seduction of Dinadano, the adventures of Burletta della Diserta and Sir Lasancis, and additional combats serving to inflate the reputation and prowess of Tristano: combats against Sigurans lo Bruno, a 170-year old knight of the Old Table, against the giant who had captured Sir Gabrionello, against Sir Fellone, and three times (instead of only once) against Lancilotto at Merlin's *perron* ("stone"), a sequence clearly designed to show Tristano's parity with the epitome of Arthurian chivalry, Messer Lancilotto. The most original invention, however, is the tale of the entrapment of the two pairs of lovers, Tristano and Isotta, and Lancilotto and Ginevra (Guenevere), in the magic castle of the Dama del Lago (Lady of the Lake), an episode that creates a unique celebration of secular love in the moments before Galasso (Galahad) and the Grail quest intervene to question the value of earthly love, or at least to provide an alternative.

The *Tavola*, like Malory's *Morte Darthur*, attempts to provide a *summa* of the Arthurian cycle but chooses Tristano rather than Lancilotto as the exemplar of its ethic. While preserving the Italian textual tradition of distinguishing between the Tavola Vecchia ("Old Table") presided over by Uther Pendragon and Arthur's Tavola Nuova ("New Table"), the *Tavola* quickly dispenses with this formality to concentrate on the contrasting careers of Tristano and Lancilotto. Both Malory and the *Tavola* are concerned with Lancilotto's "instability," his wavering from fidelity to Guenevere when called to the Grail quest. Malory, however, finds this wavering the essence of his strength and profundity; the *Tavola* condemns it and finds Tristano's refusal to join the quest proof of his fidelity to Isotta and the love that defines him. For this fidelity until death (even, it would seem, at the risk of his soul), Tristano achieves deification of a kind at the end of the *Tavola* when the vines issuing from his grave are allegorized and symbolically associated with both the wine of Dionysos and the wine of the communion. The *Tavola* reinvests the Tristan legend with the passion of the verse redactions, a passion considerably reduced in the French prose versions. [DLH]

Polidori, Filippo-Luigi, ed. *La Tavola Ritonda o l'istoria di Tristano*. Bologna: Romagnoli, 1864–65.

Shaver, Ann, trans. *Tristan and the Round Table: A Translation of "La Tavola Ritonda."* Binghamton, N.Y.: Medieval and Renaissance Texts and Studies, 1983.

Branca, Daniela Delcorno. *I Romanzi Italiani di Tristano e la Tavola Ritonda*. Florence, 1968.

Gardner, Edmund G. *The Arthurian Legend in Italian Literature*. London: Dent, 1930.

Kleinhenz, Christopher. "Tristan in Italy: The Death or Rebirth of a Legend." *Studies in Medieval Culture*, 5 (1975), 145–58.

Shaver, Ann. "The Italian Round Table and the Arthurian Tradition." In *Courtly Romances*, ed. Guy Mermier. Detroit, 1984.

TAX, E(RVIN) H., produced one of the more unusual battlefield compositions of World War II in *The Wraith of Gawain* (1948), which relates the knight's story from a youthful quest to his death and beyond in almost 9,000 lines of Miltonic blank verse. The enchanted adventures of the earlier episodes, in spite of diction rather too poetic, form a bright prelude to the grim worldview of the conclusion. [DN]

Tax, E.H. *The Wraith of Gawain*. Prairie City, Ill.: Decker, 1948.

TAYLOR, ANNA, British author of the historical novel *Drustan the Wanderer* (1971). Drustan (Tristan) tells the story of his love for Essylt (Isolde). This tale of blind passion and ill fate in a world itself torn asunder by political and religious strife draws upon earlier romances rather than Malory, and it uses the findings of recent historical and archaeological research to recreate the historical setting. [SRR]

Taylor, Anna. *Drustan the Wanderer: A Novel Based on the Legend of Tristan and Isolde*. London: Longmans, 1971.

TAYLOR, KEITH, author of a sword-and-sorcery series about an Irish bard wandering through Europe after the battle at Badon, where he fought for Artorius, Count of Britain. In *Bard* (1981), *Bard III: The Wild Sea* (1986), and *Bard IV: Ravens' Gathering* (1987), his adventures lead to encounters with Vivayn, here the British daughter-in-law of Cerdic of the West Saxons, as well as with many of Artorius's followers and barbarian foes. [RHT]

Taylor, Keith. *Bard*. New York: Ace, 1981.
———. *Bard III: The Wild Sea*. New York: Ace, 1986.
———. *Bard IV: Ravens' Gathering*. New York: Ace, 1987.

TAYLOR, T(HOMAS) HILHOUSE (1861–?), Australian clergyman and author of *Parsifal* (1906), a four-act play in blank verse based on Wagner's opera. Left vulnerable by his pride and his love for Kundry, Amfortas loses the Sacred Spear to the evil Klingsor, who wounds him in the side. Parsifal, the "Simple One and Pure," redeems Kundry, recovers the Spear, destroys Klingsor, and heals Amfortas, whom he succeeds as King and Guardian of the Holy Grail. [RHT]

Taylor, T. Hilhouse. *Parsifal: A Romantic Mystery-Drama*. Sydney: Angus and Robertson, 1906; 2nd ed. Melbourne: Lothian, 1907.

TAYLOR, U. ASHWORTH, begins his romantic novel *The City of Sarras* (1887) with a reading of Malory's account of the death of Galahad, who is seen as representing an ideal for the mystical union of the soul with the divine. Similarly, Sarras is a spiritual place to be found "wherever man's spirit lives in its purity," but it constitutes an ideal too high for most human beings, and the characters in the novel, to attain. [EB]

Taylor, U. Ashworth. *The City of Sarras*. Edinburgh and London: Blackwood, 1887.

TEASDALE, SARA (1884–1933), American poet, wrote several short Arthurian works. In "Guenevere" (1911), a dramatic monologue in blank verse, the Queen laments the consequences of discovery, complaining that she is "branded for a single fault" and that the sweetness of love between her and Lancelot is turned to bitterness; "Galahad in The Castle of Maidens" (1911) describes the reaction of the maidens to their rescue; and in "At Tintagil" (1926), Iseult, though lonely for Tristan, refuses to regret their love. [EB/RHT]

Teasdale, Sara. *Helen of Troy and Other Poems*. New York: Putnam, 1911.
———. *Collected Poems*. New York: Collier, 1967.

TELEVISION SERIES on the Arthurian legend have usually been prepared for younger viewers. An early example is *The Adventures of Sir Lancelot*, produced in the mid-1950s by Sapphire Film Productions for the Incorporated Television Programme Company in Britain. Lancelot, played by William Russell, performs a number of untraditional deeds of knight-errantry, such as leading a band of shepherds against some robber knights who have been preying upon them. Greater realism was achieved in another British series, *Arthur of the Britons*. The twenty-four episodes, which were shown on HTV in the early 1970s, reveal the harshness of life in the Dark Ages.

The Legend of King Arthur, a coproduction of the BBC, Time-Life Television, and the Australian Broadcasting Commission that was first shown on BBC-TV in the late 1970s, follows the traditional story more closely, from the conception of Arthur to the last meeting of Lancelot and Guinevere after the battle of Camlann. The series stars Andrew Burt as Arthur, Felicity Dean as Guinevere, and David Robb as Lancelot, but it is Morgan le Fay, played by Maureen O'Brien, who provides the main link between the twelve episodes with her thirst for revenge against Arthur. Shortened to eight episodes to focus more strongly upon the role of Lancelot, the series was shown on PBS and the Arts and Entertainment cable network in North America.

Some Arthurian tales, such as "The Marriage of Sir Gawain," were among the fables and traditional tales dramatized in *Story Theatre*, an American syndicated series from the early 1970s produced by Winters-Rosen. Using the cast and director (Paul Sills) of the Broadway hit upon which it was based, it employed the techniques of improvised theater, with the performers speaking their lines in narrative as if reading from a book.

The Arthurian legend also figures in stories placed in a modern setting. In *Raven*, a series that appeared in the mid-1970s on ATV in Britain, with screenplay by Jeremy Burnham and Trevor Ray, a conservationist movement saves an ancient network of caves that is linked with Arthur's cave legend. It is strongly implied, moreover, that their leader is none other than Arthur reborn, and that the cranky archaeologist who helps him is Merlin. Merlin appears again briefly in a TV Ontario series from the late 1970s, *Read All About It!*, this time so that he can use his magic to transport some children to another world. Merlin's power also lies behind the upheavals that take place in *The Changes*, a popular series in the 1970s that was developed for BBC-TV from Peter Dickinson's trilogy.

The 1980s have continued the trend of placing Arthurian characters in a modern setting. Early in the decade viewers in North America saw a short-lived situation comedy called *Mr. Merlin*. Merlin, now a garage-owner, raises a few laughs in his efforts to teach his apprentice, a typical California teenager, the responsibilities involved in using magic. David Lodge's novel *Small World* (1984) was dramatized by Howard Schuman for Granada TV in Britain, airing in six episodes during January and February 1987. The series was directed by Robert Chetwin, produced by Steve Hawes, and starring Barry Lynch as Persse McGarrigle. A 1989 episode of the long-lived British science-fiction/fantasy series *Dr. Who* pitted the Doctor against Morgan le Fay and Mordred in a struggle for Excalibur. Although this encounter took place in a contemporary setting, it was suggested that the three had met before and that the Doctor was none other than Merlin! [RHT]

Davies, Andrew. *The Legend of King Arthur*. London: Fontana/Armada, 1979.

Endersby, Clive. *Read All About It!* Toronto: Methuen, 1981.

Groom, Arthur. *The Adventures of Sir Lancelot, Book 2*. London: Adprint, 1958.

Paton, John. *The Adventures of Sir Lancelot*. London: Adprint, 1957.

TENNYSON, ALFRED LORD (1809–1892), father of the Arthurian renaissance in Victorian England, who spent much of his life recreating the legends in his poetry.

By the early nineteenth century, the Arthurian legends had become a literary anachronism. Tennyson's poetry brought about a rebirth of interest in the material and eventually placed it on a new plateau of respect and significance for writers and artists of the later nineteenth century.

The past always exerted a powerful attraction for Tennyson, functioning as a mirror that might indicate the moral condition of the present. By nature nostalgic, Tennyson sought in the past not a retreat from the plight of his time but a barometer of the moral temper of Victorian England. And throughout his life, the Arthurian legends were his most powerful inspiration.

"The vision of Arthur as I have drawn him," he wrote, "had come upon me when, little more than a boy, I first lighted upon Malory." In the figure of Arthur, Tennyson found a character whose life would stand as an example for Victorian readers of the need for an idealistic spiritual vision. Although Malory always remained Tennyson's major source of knowledge of the legends, the poet also studied all available histories and commentaries that might clarify his understanding of the medieval world. In his twenties, he was already searching for a proper avenue into a poetic recreation of the legends. His early Arthurian efforts reveal a thorough knowledge of medieval texts, a commitment to a recreation of the story of Camelot, and a constant experimentation with varying degrees of source fidelity, from faithful adaptation to almost complete originality. His early attempts to depict the King and his realm are an important preparation for his final commitment to an Arthurian epic, *Idylls of the King*, which would occupy much of his attention from the 1850s until his death.

Outlines and sketches of possible Arthurian works show the variety of Tennyson's early plans. A prose sketch from ca. 1833 emphasizes the splendor and beauty of Camelot, qualities that would appeal to the young disciple of John Keats; another sketch concerns itself with an allegorical interpretation of the legends; there is also a draft of a five-act play.

Tennyson's first published Arthurian poem, "The Lady of Shalott," written by May 1832, is based on a medieval Italian novelette, *Donna di Scalotta*. This version of a maiden's helpless love for Lancelot provides the Arthurian setting for a study of the artist and the dangers of personal isolation from the world. At this time, Tennyson seemed ignorant of Malory's story of Elaine: "I doubt whether I should ever have put it in that shape if I had been then aware of the Maid of Astolat in Mort Arthur."

Tennyson had already employed an Arthurian setting in "Sir Launcelot and Queen Guinevere: A Fragment," which was "partly if not wholly written in 1830." The five extant stanzas, the opening of a projected poem, focus on the beauty of nature and the beauty of Guinevere: the blossoming springtime becomes a backdrop for the youthful and innocent Guinevere and Lancelot. The poem is an attempt to create a highly visualized story involving central figures from the Arthurian world.

"Sir Galahad," written by September 1834, employs an Arthurian figure as a vehicle for exploring the virtue of chastity. In this reflective lyric, Galahad is a pure knight, the paragon of virtue, whose love of the divine motivates all his actions. The essential character of Galahad, derived from Malory, Tennyson presents in terms of the virtue—chastity—that makes him the outstanding knight. Yet Galahad's introspection, his exuberant joy bordering on arrogance, his ceaseless desire for activity and movement, are all qualities that make him a distinctly Victorian figure, a precursor of the Galahad of the Pre-Raphaelites.

The last of Tennyson's early Arthurian poems, "Morte d'Arthur," completed by October 1834, is the poet's most faithful recreation of Malory's structure and language. The poem is a careful expansion of Malory's account of the final moments in King Arthur's life. Taking an essentially dramatic moment, Tennyson retells the episode with a degree of embellishment that does not violate, but rather enriches, the source. Written shortly after the death of Tennyson's best friend and mentor, Arthur Henry Hallam, the poem chronicles the death of another Arthur, the mythic King who here is presented with the same idealization as is Hallam himself in *In Memoriam* (1850).

In the four early poems, Tennyson focuses on the three major concerns of the Arthurian world that will dominate his ultimate achievement in the *Idylls of the King*. In "Sir Launcelot and Queen Guinevere," he studies the nascent love of the knight and his queen. In "Sir Galahad," the chastity of the knight is a prelude to a brief description of the Holy Grail, which will vex the poet's imagination and retard his Arthurian epic for many years. In the "Morte d'Arthur," Tennyson turns to Arthur as ideal ruler, the symbolic embodiment of the perfection of the old order. Out of these three themes will come a focal point that will provide the poet with a coherent structure for his final treatment of Camelot.

With the publication of the widely acclaimed *In Memoriam* in 1850, and with the poet's acceptance that same year of the Laureateship, the Arthurian world beckoned Tennyson even more strongly than before. In 1852, he published two socially hortatory poems, "The Third of February, 1852" and "Hands All Round," under the pseudonym "Merlin."

Tennyson's first new Arthurian poem takes as its plot the seduction by Nimuë (Vivien) of Merlin, drawn from Southey's translation of the *Estoire de Merlin*, which had appeared in the introduction to his 1817 edition of Malory. "Vivien" is a detailed narrative account of the corrosive power of lust and the destructive nature of wanton sensuality. An antidote to the negative horror of Vivien, "Enid," Tennyson's next Arthurian poem, is a similar portrait of a female character, but one who is the embodiment of truth. The story of Enid's patient submission to her jealous husband Geraint, drawn from Lady Charlotte Guest's *Mabinogion*, forms a much longer narrative than the more focused "Vivien."

Printed together in a trial edition in 1857, *Enid and Nimuë: The True and the False*, the two poems constitute a separate work in their own right, but they also exist, more powerfully, as part of an incomplete context suggested by the framework that Tennyson adds to the story of Enid. The plot from the *Mabinogion* offered an excellent contrast to the completed study of Vivien, yet it also gave Tennyson an opportunity to expand his brief study of an ideal order that Arthur was intent on establishing. In "Enid," this order is not fully organized, yet the sin of adultery already exists at its center; in "Vivien," the destruction of Merlin is only part of a wider decay operating throughout Camelot.

Even before the publication of the trial edition, Tennyson was contemplating a successor to the two Arthurian poems. The successor was "Guinevere," the portrait of a complex woman at war with her own being, one who partakes of both Enid's ennobling goodness and Vivien's destructive sensuality. In "Guinevere," a dramatic rendition of the final meeting of Arthur and his queen (a scene the poet himself invented), Arthur is an almost divine force trying to lead humanity to the highest realization of its capability; Guinevere is a passionate and intelligent woman, conscious of human complexity and ultimately aware of the necessity for a proper response to the demands of an ideal vision.

"Elaine," Tennyson's next Arthurian poem, allowed a return to the story of the Lady of Shalott, seen now through the light of Malory's version. Vividly depicting Elaine as the victim of her unreciprocated love, the poem shows the destructive power of Guinevere's sin as it begins to influence innocent human beings. Tennyson retells Elaine's story in the light of the particular world already presented in "Vivien," "Enid," and "Guinevere." This quartet of poems about women became the foundation of Tennyson's long-anticipated Arthurian epic. The original title of the quartet, *The True and the False*, was changed to *Idylls of the King*; the phrase on the title page, "Flos Regum Arthurus" ("Arthur, Flower of Kings"), taken from Joseph of Exeter, emphasizes the importance of King Arthur to the world of these four idylls, which were published together in a single volume in 1859.

To complete his developing Arthurian epic, Tennyson knew that he had to compose a version of the Grail quest, yet he feared the task: "I doubt whether such a subject could be handled in these days, without incurring a charge of irreverence. It would be too much like playing with sacred things. The old writers *believed* in the Sangreal." He shied away from the topic until 1867, when he found a suitable approach: he would use one of the questers, specifically a failed quester, to narrate the story. "The Holy Grail" follows the *Queste del Saint Graal* by making Percivale a soiled contrast to the perfect Galahad. Inspired by Malory, Tenny-

83. William Waterhouse, *The Lady of Shalott*. (Tate Gallery, London/Art Resource.)

son goes on to create his own portrayals of six questers: the perfect Sir Galahad and Percivale's faultless sister, the slightly deficient Percivale, the sinful Lancelot, the selfless Bors, and the despicable Gawain. In Tennyson, the quest accelerates the decay of the Round Table, functioning as an external force that harms a world already wounded by the Queen's adultery. By implying that the absence of the Grail is dependent upon Guinevere's sin, Tennyson subtly links the external force of destruction with the sin at the center of the realm.

After completing "The Holy Grail," Tennyson created a frame for his Arthurian work. In the early "Morte d'Arthur," he found his natural conclusion. His next new poem was to comprise the beginning. "The Coming of Arthur" is an account of Arthur's birth that employs Malory's version but sets it within a context of conflicting stories and rumors that undercut its credibility. The resulting confusion emphasizes the poem's focus—not Arthur's origin, but how others come to accept him. A new order automatically raises suspicions about its origin and validity.

The next idyll, "Pelleas and Ettarre," is the direct continuation of "The Holy Grail," and it depicts the younger generation of knights who have come to fill the void created by the Grail quest. Drawn from a brief incident in Malory, Tennyson's poem makes Pelleas the embodiment of the confusion and despair that confront the idealistic man looking upon the decay of Camelot.

With a few lines added to the beginning and end, the "Morte d'Arthur" became "The Passing of Arthur" and allowed another quartet of Arthurian poems to be made ready for publication. Titled *The Holy Grail and Other Poems*, the volume appeared in December 1869; the following month, the collected edition of the eight *Idylls of the King* was published.

Two more idylls were added to the series in the 1870s: "The Last Tournament" and "Gareth and Lynette," both natural outgrowths of "Pelleas and Ettarre." "The Last Tournament," a somber study of the autumn of the Round Table, continues the tragic movement of the Pelleas idyll by focusing on Camelot's disintegration; the society that drove

Pelleas to madness must now endure the consequence of that madness—the transformation of Pelleas into the evil Red Knight of the North. The idyll also includes Tennyson's version of the Tristram story, ending with Tristram's brutal murder by Mark. Malory's Tristram, second only to Lancelot as an ideal knight, here becomes a cynical realist dedicated to the practice of free love, an example of the beast to which man has returned.

"Gareth and Lynette," the happiest idyll, is a direct contrast to "Pelleas and Ettarre." Its springtime setting and the growth of its young characters into noble adulthood are taken directly from Malory; they display the perfection that once belonged to Arthur's realm. The poem offers the only fully developed study of Camelot as Arthur envisioned it, and it dramatizes the power of such an ennobling world on a young knight who is similar to Pelleas. At this time, however, Camelot allows the youthful Gareth to realize his ideal vision.

The two new idylls were published together in 1872 and incorporated into an edition of the *Idylls* in January 1873. Tennyson also made small additions to strengthen the humanity of the King and to maintain narrative clarity and consistency with the new idylls. This edition also divided the original "Enid" into two parts, marking a definite step toward the final creation of an epic poem in twelve books. Also added was the epilogue, "To the Queen."

Believing that some introduction to his account of Merlin and Vivien was necessary, Tennyson turned to Malory's story of "Balin, or the Knight of the Two Swords" for the twelfth member of the sequence. "Balin and Balan," published in 1885 and incorporated into the whole series in an 1886 edition, is a study of the destructive power of self-denial. Balin chooses self-denial as the seemingly proper road to self-improvement; Malory's Pellam becomes a heathen king whose conversion to Christianity is a flight into self-denying asceticism. Malory's presentation of an unestablished realm and the natural chaos of a disordered world has become the barometer of the early decay of the established realm.

Idylls of the King reshapes the medieval accounts of Arthur's career into a vehicle for the poet's own vision of an idealistic philosophy significant to his generation. "The general decay of faith/Right through the world" finds a remedy and a hope in Arthur; the decaying Camelot serves as an indictment of Victorian England. Tennyson's recreation of the Arthurian world is an attempt to reform his generation by showing the effects of sensuality, materialism, and spiritual blindness.

Tennyson's interest in the Arthurian world and his own epic did not abate with the completion of the *Idylls*. In "Merlin and the Gleam," written in 1889, Tennyson composed his "literary history," choosing Merlin to represent the poet in pursuit of his vocation. At the same time, he was also contemplating a great stage drama on the legend of Tristram of Lyonesse, since he had been obliged to cut down the story for its inclusion in the *Idylls*. The project, however, remained unrealized.

The second half of the nineteenth century saw an unprecedented interest in the world of Camelot, and the Arthurian painting and literature of the period reveal Tennyson's pervasive influence. The Pre-Raphaelite Brotherhood took Tennyson's Sir Galahad as their standard-bearer. For the 1857 Moxon edition of Tennyson's *Poems*, Dante Gabriel Rossetti contributed five illustrations, three of them Arthurian, representing his first extended treatment of this material. Rossetti's associates, Edward Burne-Jones, Holman Hunt, Daniel Maclise, and John Everett Millais, also entered the Arthurian world under Tennyson's guidance; their Arthurian paintings are either illustrations of Tennyson's poems or depictions of incidents originating in Tennyson's Arthurian world.

Poets were also conscious of Tennyson's influence. Matthew Arnold, disapproving of Tennyson's medieval characters, created his own version of the Tristram story in his only foray into the Arthurian world. William Morris, who shared Arnold's dislike of Tennyson's Arthurian poetry, composed a series of Arthurian poems. However, his plan to create an Arthurian cycle may have been dimmed by the popularity of the *Idylls*, for it never materialized. So too, Swinburne, whose method of handling the legends is both a direct criticism of Tennyson's method and an acknowledgment of his influence.

A final testimony to Tennyson's importance is the sudden emergence in the later nineteenth century of scholarly commitment to medieval Arthurian texts, including Malory. Moreover, in 1862, James Knowles compiled *The Story of King Arthur and His Knights of the Round Table*, the first modernization of Malory and a volume destined to pass through seven editions before 1900. The book is dedicated to Tennyson: "This attempt at a popular version of the Arthur legends is by his permission dedicated, as a tribute of the sincerest and warmest respect." Five more modernizations appeared before the end of the century, and each noted Tennyson's role in the steadily growing interest in King Arthur. [DS]

Tennyson, Alfred Lord. *Idylls of the King*, ed. J.M. Gray. New Haven: Yale University Press, 1983.

———. *The Poems of Tennyson*, ed. Christopher Ricks. London: Longmans, 1969.

Buckley, Jerome H. *Tennyson: The Growth of a Poet*. Cambridge: Harvard University Press, 1960.

Rosenberg, John D. *The Fall of Camelot: A Study of Tennyson's Idylls of the King*. Cambridge: Belknap, 1973.

Simpson, Roger. *Camelot Regained: The Arthurian Revival and Tennyson, 1800–1849*. Woodbridge, Suffolk: Boydell and Brewer, 1990.

Staines, David. *Tennyson's Camelot: The Idylls of the King and Its Medieval Sources*. Waterloo, Ont.: Wilfrid Laurier University Press, 1983.

Tennyson, Hallam Lord. *Alfred Lord Tennyson: A Memoir*. 2 vols. New York: Macmillan, 1897.

THEATER DER FIGUREN, West German puppet-theater ensemble in Braunschweig. In 1988, the group successfully produced *König Artus: Ein Schauspiel für Figurentheater* ("King Arthur: A Play for Theater of Images"), with script by Michael Schmidt and direction by Carsten Busch. The play, which draws from Malory, focuses on the archetypal patterns in the material. Accordingly, the fall of the Round Table, the result of existential tragedy and human failure, augurs a new epoch. [UM/WCM]

THELWALL, JOHN (1764–1834), English lecturer and pamphleteer, contributed a closet drama, *The Fairy of the Lake* (1801), to the Gothic Revival. Drydenesque in its combination of mythology, legendary history (Hengist, Rowenna, Vortigern), magic spells, stagey songs, and spectacles, the work reveals the Lady of the Lake as the *dea ex machina* who rescues Guenevere from Vortigern's incestuous designs and Rowenna's necromancy to unite her with an ineffectual Arthur. [MAW]

Merriman, James Douglas. *The Flower of Kings: A Study of the Arthurian Legend in England Between 1485 and 1835*. Lawrence: University Press of Kansas, 1973.

THOMAS, EDWARD (1878–1917), English novelist, poet, and essayist, who wrote two Arthurian sketches, "Bronwen: A Welsh Idyll" (1903) and "Isoud." As is characteristic of Thomas's writings, both are strongly imbued with his love of the English countryside. "Bronwen" is the story of the love that awakens between a Welsh princess and Sir Agravaine. "Isoud" is a fantasy on Malory's brief episode of Sir Kehydius, one of Tristram's rivals, who dies for love of Isoud; Thomas alters Malory's ambiguous denouement to suggest that he dies at the hands of Tristram. [AAR]

Thomas, Edward. *Cloud Castle and Other Papers*. London: Duckworth, 1922, pp. 81–89, 157–66.

THOMAS, JOHN, wrote *The Story of Sir Launcelot* (1958) for children. The story, illustrated by Treyer Evans, is carefully bowdlerized to give no hint of the love between Guinevere and Launcelot, who ends his days as a hermit, wandering the countryside and succouring the sick and distressed. [EB]

Thomas, John. *The Story of Sir Launcelot*. London: Muller, 1958.

THOMAS, R(ONALD) S(TUART), Welsh poet whose work includes three Arthurian poems. In "Taliesin 1952" (1955), Taliesin is reborn in each age to point to a new world, one incarnation being Merlin. In the clever "A Welshman to Any Tourist" (1955), Thomas indicts the Welsh by suggesting that Arthur and his sleeping knights are hiding in shame. "Remembering David Jones" (1983) links the soldiers of Jones's poems with the quest for the Grail. [PCB]

Thomas, R.S. *Song at the Year's Turning: Poems 1942–1954*. London: Hart-Davis, 1955.

———. *Later Poems: 1972–1982*. London: Macmillan, 1983.

THOMAS D'ANGLETERRE. The legend of Tristan was recorded twice in Old French verse of the twelfth century: once by Béroul and once by a certain Thomas. Both drew on traditional Celtic materials that have now been lost. Thomas's retelling has been variously dated from ca. 1150 to 1200, but most critics today place it ca. 1170–75. Thomas composed his work in England, possibly for the court circle of Henry II Plantagenet and his queen, Eleanor of Aquitaine. We know little of the poet's life, other than his name.

Thomas's *Tristan* is extant in only eight fragments from five different manuscripts. It is written in the octosyllabic rhyming couplets traditional for romance. There is some overlapping, but all the fragments come to about one-sixth of what the whole is estimated to have been. The beginning of the tale, which recounts Tristan's early years, his skills in hunting and music, and the fight with the giant Morholt that led to his first encounter with Iseut the Blond, has been entirely lost, as has the episode in which the lovers consume the fatal love potion on the sea as Tristan is escorting Iseut from Ireland to Cornwall to become King Mark's queen. This material is known only through comparisons with other tellings of the legend, particularly that by Gottfried von Strassburg.

The Cambridge fragment (52 lines) recounts the discovery of the lovers in the orchard by Mark, who has been brought there by a dwarf, and Tristan's tearful farewell to Iseut. The Sneyd fragment (888 lines) tells of Tristan's marriage to Iseut of the White Hands in an attempt to forget his love for the queen. It is characterized by two lengthy interior monologues: one as Tristan determines to marry her; a second when he regrets his action and determines to do penance by never consummating the marriage. The fragment ends with Iseut the Blond's grief when Cariados tells her of Tristan's marriage.

The two Turin fragments (now lost; 256 lines and 3 lines) begin with Tristan in the Chamber of Images, where he laments his sad fate and uncertainties before statues of Iseut and Brangain, her serving girl and confidante. They tell also of Iseut's unwilling submission to Mark and of Iseut of the White Hands's admission to her brother Kaherdin that her marriage has not been consummated. The first Strasbourg fragment (68 lines; destroyed by fire in 1870) tells of Kaherdin's wonder as he first beholds Iseut the Blond.

The final three fragments (Douce, 1,815 lines; Sneyd, 839 lines; Strasbourg, 151 lines—destroyed) narrate the end of the poem, including Brangain and Iseut's quarrels, Tristan's return disguised as a leper, Tristan le Nain, Tristan wounded, the ship with the white sail, and the death and interment of the lovers.

There remains considerable controversy over which French version came first, Thomas's or Béroul's, but there is no question that the two texts are fundamentally different in inspiration. Whereas Béroul's text is marked by an underlying and occasionally even overt violence, by fantastic elements and supernatural intervention, and by a sometimes illogical or frankly self-contradictory plot, Thomas's *Tristan* is more rational in its development and action, and the behavior and motivation of the characters show more logic. Thomas eliminated or reworked certain overly "realistic" episodes (including the harp and lyre, Iseut and the lepers, life in the forest of Morois, hermit scenes) and gave the poem a more elevated and introspective tone. The material becomes thus less a series of seemingly random external happenings and more a sequence of love-motivated inner adventures.

But Thomas did not simply rework certain episodes of the inherited materials, he imposed a new courtly tone and manner on the legendary materials he inherited. His version is characterized throughout by a courtly concern for the depiction of the birth, growth, and sufferings of love. In lengthy monologues and lyric laments, the characters reveal their psychological states: their hopes, fears, hesitations, and passions. In substantial interventions, the narrator in turn comments on the progress of their love. The very different views of the nature of love that distinguish the two French versions can best be seen in the treatment of the love potion. For Béroul, the potion is a tangible intervention of destiny with a specified duration of three years; although the lovers are aware of their sin, they are essentially guiltless because they are powerless against the supernatural nature of the potion. For Thomas, on the other hand, the potion is an eternal symbol of the value and intensity of Tristan and Iseut's love. This love is predicated on the individual merits of the lovers and is a product of their own free will. They take full responsibility for their love, and it becomes their only morality, their only law, alienating them from society and elevating them in their struggle to avoid detection. They loved before the potion, will continue to love afterward, and therefore the potion has no fixed duration.

Thomas's and Béroul's poems were both eclipsed in French in the thirteenth century by the Prose *Tristan*, but not before Thomas's conception of the legend was integrated into the great Middle High German *Tristan* of Gottfried von Strassburg. [WWK]

Thomas. *Les Fragments du Roman de Tristan, poème du XIIe siècle*, ed. Bartina H. Wind. Geneva: Droz, 1960.

———. *Le Roman de Tristan par Thomas*, ed. Joseph Bédier. 2 vols. Paris: SATF, 1902–05.

Gottfried von Strassburg. *Tristan, with the "Tristan" of Thomas*, trans. A.T. Hatto. Harmondsworth: Penguin, 1960.

Baumgartner, Emmanuèle. *Tristan et Iseut: de la légende aux récits en vers*. Paris: Presses Universitaires de France, 1987.

Bromiley, Geoffrey N. *Thomas's* Tristan *and the* Folie Tristan d'Oxford. London: Grant and Cutler, 1986.

THOMPSON, AARON (1681 or 1682–?), in 1718 became the first translator into English of Geoffrey of Monmouth's epic history of early British kings almost 600 years after Geoffrey had written his history. Thompson's translation includes a 111-page introduction in which he makes an impassioned and well-reasoned case that Geoffrey's work was in truth based on an actual manuscript acquired in Armorica (Brittany) and written in the "British tongue." This lengthy statement also repudiates the allegations of Polydore Vergil, William of Newburgh, Gerald of Wales, William Camden, and other notable chroniclers who had at the least cast doubt on Geoffrey's claim that Brutus was discoverer of Albion and founder of the British race. [JHW]

Thompson, Aaron. *The British History, translated in English from the Latin of Jeffrey of Monmouth*. London, 1718.

THÜRING VON RINGOLTINGEN (ca. 1415–1483) published in 1474 a German prose translation of Couldrette's metrical romance *Mellusigne*, written ca. 1401. The German version, entitled *Von einer Frawen genandt Melusina die ein Merfaye was* ("Concerning a Woman Named Melusina Who Was a Mermaid"), is not an Arthurian romance, yet it contains a noteworthy episode that shows the reception of Arthurian narrative in the early stages of the prose novel in German literature. The episode tells the tragic tale of an anonymous knight of the Arthurian Round Table, a relative of Tristan, who had the arrogance to attempt to win a great treasure not destined for him, which was guarded in a mountain by ferocious monsters. After killing a dragon, a bear, and other beasts, he at last confronts a Cyclopean monster that guards the iron door leading into the mountain and to the treasure. The monster bites the knight's sword in two and thereupon swallows him. The episode anticipates the arrival of the knight destined to gain entry into the mountain. In the prologue to *Melusina*, Thüring boasts of his having read many books about Arthur's court and the Round Table, notably the romances of Iwein, Lanzelot, Tristan, and Parzival. In addition to the Arthurian episode, others, such as one involving a sparrowhawk, show the general influence of Arthurian romance on *Melusina*. [MEK]

Thüring von Ringoltingen. *Melusine*, ed. Karin Schneider. Berlin: Schmidt, 1958.

Roloff, Hans-Gert. *Stilstudien zur Prosa des 15. Jahrhunderts: Die Melusine des Thüring von Ringoltingen*. Cologne and Vienna: Böhlau, 1970.

THURBER, JAMES (1894–1961), American humorist, sets his fairy tale *The White Deer* (1945) in a nonsense world quite different from that of Arthurian romance, but the malevolent power whose jealousy has caused all the trouble turns out to be Nagrom Yaf: Morgan (le) Fay spelled backward. [CBH]

Thurber, James. *The White Deer*. New York: Harcourt, Brace and World, 1945.

TIECK, LUDWIG (1773–1853), is generally classed as an early German Romantic because of his close association with the founders of the movement. He was, however, a prolific writer in all genres and active during all stages of the Romantic period. He was particularly interested in the Middle Ages and also in English literature. In his *Leben und Thaten des kleinen Thomas, genannt Däumchen* ("Life and Times of Little Tom Thumb," 1811), the dwarf Thomas, whose birth was prophesied by Merlin from his grave, uses Merlin's seven-league boots to aid Arthur in his war against the Saxons. Tieck's excellent translation of the Elizabethan drama *The Birth of Merlin, or The Childe Hath Found His Father (Die Geburt des Merlin oder Das Kind hat seinen Vater gefunden*, 1829) had an influence on later German works, such as Immermann's *Merlin: Eine Mythe* (1832). [RWK]

Tieck, Ludwig. *Schriften*. Berlin: Reimer, 1828, Vol. 5.

Weiss, Adelaide Marie. "Ludwig Tieck." In *Merlin in German Literature*. Washington, D.C.: Catholic University of America Press, 1933, pp. 81–94.

TINTAGEL, a place on the north Cornish coast, the scene of the begetting of Arthur according to Geoffrey of Monmouth and subsequent romancers. The conventional reading of the story makes it his birthplace, too, though Geoffrey gives no actual warrant for this. King Uther, he says, had an ungovernable desire for Ygerna, the wife of Duke Gorlois of Cornwall. The consequent quarrel between the king and the duke led to a local war. Gorlois put his wife in Tintagel Castle, supposedly out of Uther's reach. But the king made his way to her, magically disguised as her husband. Thus Arthur was conceived. Since Gorlois had just been killed, Uther was able to revert to his true shape and make Ygerna his queen.

Tintagel village is at the head of a ravine that runs downhill to a cove. The locale that Geoffrey has in mind is a huge rocky promontory above the cove, with ruins of a castle. It is almost an island, being connected with the mainland only by a ridge. The ridge has crumbled, so that today a visitor to the ruins and the rest of the promontory has to cross by a footbridge and climb a long flight of steps. In past times, when the ridge was much higher, the crossing from the adjacent hill on the mainland was correspondingly easier, but the path would have been so narrow that a small force could have kept Uther out if he had approached in a normal manner.

Geoffrey's most obvious motive in his choice of this place was therefore topographical. However, a further question arises. The castle was started not earlier than 1141 by Reginald, Earl of Cornwall. But Geoffrey had completed his *Historia* before 1138. When he wrote, the headland was bare, without visible traces of any relevant buildings. To invent an important stronghold on an empty spot, with no previous associations, would have been out of keeping with his habitual practice. The *Historia* as we have it may be a second edition, and he could have added Tintagel after the castle was begun—perhaps to please a half-brother of Reginald's, Earl Robert of Gloucester, from whom he hoped for favor. But this is guesswork, and archaeology offers another explanation.

Dotted about the promontory are the remains of a number of stone buildings quite different from the castle, which were excavated during the 1930s by C.A. Ralegh Radford. In and around these structures, Radford discovered what has sometimes been called Tintagel pottery. He identified fragments of high-quality vessels, some of them of a type used for expensive goods, such as wine and oil. They were not of British make; they had been imported from the Mediterranean region, probably the eastern part, and could be dated to the later fifth century or the sixth. Thus, they provided, for the first time in Britain, an archaeological means of proving occupation in a broadly "Arthurian" span of time. Foreign ware of this kind, classifiable into types, has since come to light in many other places. Where it occurs, it suggests the presence of a wealthy household, importing costly commodities from remote lands.

At Tintagel, Radford interpreted the scattered complex of buildings as a monastery. More recent study, in the light of work on other sites, makes it likelier that the pottery came from a fifth-century ruler's fortress. There is now in

84. Tintagel, aerial view. (Britain on View Photographic Library, BTA/ETB.)

fact good reason to think that Tintagel was an important center, perhaps a regional seat of government. The inference is that Geoffrey knew an authentic tradition, probably not of actual persons but of the place's occupation in the right period and suitability for his story. Something of the sort may be implied also by his putting Arthur's origin in Cornwall at all, when we might expect him to prefer Wales. For whatever reason, he sensed that Cornwall was correct.

Rock formations around the headland have been given fanciful names, such as Arthur's Chair, and Arthur's Cups and Saucers. A Cornish folk-belief that he turned into a bird has a local version: usually, he is said to have become a raven (a tale known to Cervantes), but a variant makes him a red-legged chough, such as may occasionally be seen perching on Tintagel's cliffs. Further legends aver that the castle was built by giants, that it was painted in a checker pattern of green and blue, and that it vanished on two days of the year. In the neighborhood, folklorists have reported a megalith called Arthur's Quoit and a pond from which the Round Table rises if watched for on the right night.

Other characters are involved with Tintagel besides Arthur. In the Tristan romances, Tintagel Castle belongs to King Mark. Starting from the cove at the foot of the headland, a natural tunnel runs right through its base, and this is Merlin's Cave. The enchanter's ghost reputedly haunts it. When the tide is rising, the sea works its way slowly through the cave, making impressive and eerie sounds.

Tennyson, wishing to get rid of Uther's misconduct but keep Tintagel, invented a legend of his own in which Arthur, as an infant, is mysteriously washed ashore in the cove and taken up from the water by Merlin. In another story (reported by Snell, who cites folklorist Miss M.A. Courtney), perhaps as recent as Tennyson's, Arthur's life not only begins but ends here. Mortally wounded at Slaughter Bridge on the River Camel, he is said to have been brought to Tintagel and to have died in the castle. His body was conveyed to Glastonbury for burial. The sea moaned and the wind sighed around the promontory till he was laid in his grave. [GA]

Cornish Studies, 16 (1989). (Special Tintagel issue.)

Padel, O.J. "Tintagel: An Alternative View." In *A Provisional List of Imported Pottery in Post-Roman Western Britain and Ireland*, ed. Charles Thomas. Redruth: Institute of Cornish Studies, 1981.

Radford, C.A. Ralegh. "Tintagel." In *The Quest for Arthur's Britain*, ed. Geoffrey Ashe. London: Pall Mall, 1968, pp. 75-94.
Snell, F.J. *King Arthur's Country*. London: Dent, 1926, pp. 13-21.
Thomas, Charles. "Tintagel Castle." *Antiquity*, 62 (September 1988), 421-36.

"TISTRAM OG ISOLD," a Danish ballad preserved in nine manuscripts that date from the sixteenth and seventeenth centuries. The ballad tells of a tryst between Sir Tistram (in the manuscripts: Thisterum, Tristum, Thristrum, Thistronn) and Lady Isold (in the manuscripts: Isoldt, Isolt, Isalt, Isaldt). Tistram sends a page to arrange for a secret nocturnal meeting. A handmaiden accompanies Isold to the meeting place, and Tistram and Isold spend the night under a linden-tree. At daybreak, the handmaiden admonishes the lovers that they must part. Isold's angry husband, King Magnus, awaits the women, but the handmaiden succeeds in having him believe that they had aided a woman in childbirth. [MEK]

Olrik, Axel, ed. "Tistram og Isold." In *Danmarks gamle Folkeviser*. Copenhagen: Gyldendal, 1905-19, Vol. 8, pp. 29-36.
Bradley, S.A.J. "The Danish Ballads of Tristan and Isolt." In *The Tristan Legend: Texts from Northern and Eastern Europe in Modern English Translation*, ed. Joyce Hill. Leeds: University of Leeds, Graduate Centre for Medieval Studies, 1977, pp. 144-55.
Schach, Paul. "Tristan and Isolde in Scandinavian Ballad and Folktale." *Scandinavian Studies*, 36 (1964), 281-97.

"TISTRAM OG JOMFRU ISOLT," a Danish ballad extant in three redactions. The oldest of these probably dates from the fifteenth century. In the oldest version, Tistram decides to woo the emperor's daughter, Isolt. The latter falls in love with him despite her mother's opposition, and during the emperor's absence from the country the two elope, return to Tistram's country, and presumably live happily ever after. The second version is similar to the first except that the mother attempts to poison the lovers, only to be forced to drink the poison herself. Only the third version of the ballad is tragic: Tistram and Isolt are brother and sister, children of the King of Denmark. The mother does not love Isolt and sends her out of the country to be fostered by the Empress of Rome. Without knowing that she is his sister, Tistram woos Isolt as in the other versions. When the empress tells them that they are siblings, Isolt refuses to believe her. The lovers attempt to elope but Isolt is imprisoned in a tower. When Tistram manages to join her there, the empress poisons them. [MEK]

Olrik, Axel, ed. "Tistram og Jomfru Isolt." In *Danmarks gamle Folkeviser*. Copenhagen: Gyldendal, 1905-19, Vol. 8, pp. 37-46.
Bradley, S.A.J. "The Danish Ballads of Tristan and Isolt." In *The Tristan Legend: Texts from Northern and Eastern Europe in Modern English Translation*, ed. Joyce Hill. Leeds: University of Leeds, Graduate Centre for Medieval Studies, 1977, pp. 144-55.
Schach, Paul. "Tristan and Isolde in Scandinavian Ballad and Folktale." *Scandinavian Studies*, 36 (1964), 281-97.

"TÍSTRAMS TÁTTUR," a Faroese ballad belonging to the Tristan matter but showing no affinity to any of the other Scandinavian versions. The ballad is extant only in a version recorded by V.U. Hammershaimb in 1848 from a seventy-seven-year-old Faroese woman. The ballad, thirty-seven stanzas of four lines each, relates how Tístram's parents separated him from his beloved Ísin by sending him to France, where he was to marry the daughter of the French king. He refuses and is hanged. Upon hearing the news, Ísin herself sails to France and sets the countryside ablaze. To the French king, who asks why she is burning him to death, she replies that she is avenging the fact that Tístram has been taken from her. She removes Tístram from the gallows and then dies of a broken heart. [MEK]

Djurhuus, N., ed. "Tistrams táttur." In *Føroya kvæði: Corpus Færoensium*. Copenhagen: Akademisk Forlag, 1968, Vol. 5, pp. 283-85.
Lockwood, W.B. "The Faroese Ballad of Tristan." In *The Tristan Legend: Texts from Northern and Eastern Europe in Modern English Translation*, ed. Joyce Hill. Leeds: University of Leeds, Graduate Centre for Medieval Studies, 1977, pp. 156-58.
Schach, Paul. "Tristan and Isolde in Scandinavian Ballad and Folktale." *Scandinavian Studies*, 36 (1964), 281-97.

TISTRANS SAGA OK INDIÖNU (or *Sagan of Tistran ok Indiönu*), an Icelandic translation of the eighteenth-century Danish chapbook *En tragoedisk Historie om den ædle og tappre Tistrand*. The saga is extant in three manuscripts from the eighteenth and nineteenth centuries that are preserved in the National Library, Reykjavik. [MEK]

TODHUNTER, JOHN, author of *Isolt of Ireland: A Legend in a Prologue and Three Acts* (1927), a play that shows much influence of Wagner's *Tristan und Isolde*, although there are also elements of Thomas d'Angleterre's version, such as the presence of the second Isolt. Isolt is the most strongly depicted character, her self-awareness contrasts with Tristan's blind passion, and Mark is a noble and idealistic lover; Brangwaine, consenting to Isolt's trickery, comes to love him. The play avoids being purely derivative by the skillful use of contrasts among all the characters. [AAR]

Todhunter, John. *Isolt of Ireland: A Legend in a Prologue and Three Acts*. London and Toronto: Dent, 1927.

TOLSTOY, NIKOLAI, British historical writer, turned to the Celtic Dark Ages in his speculative study of the origins of Merlin, *The Quest for Merlin* (1985), and his historical fantasy *The Coming of the King* (1988), the first in a projected Merlin trilogy. The novel is set in a completely un-Romanized northern Britain two generations after Arthur. Myrddin, called from his grave by a British king, recounts his life story and in the process details a vast historical and mythological background to his time. The richly digressive narrative, which proceeds from Myrddin's birth and initiatory adventures to a great battle against the Saxons, draws on the legends of Wales predominantly, but also those of other northern European cultures. Myrddin himself, as a character who moves among Celtic deities as well as such figures of history and legend as Belisarius and Beowulf, remains appropriately enigmatic. [DN]

Tolstoy, Nikolai. *The Quest for Merlin*. Boston: Little, Brown, 1985.
———. *The Coming of the King: The First Book of Merlin*. London and New York: Bantam, 1988.

TOM THUMB, King Arthur's dwarf, a popular literary character in England during the seventeenth and eighteenth centuries. Several popular ballads and literary compositions feature Tom, but he owes his greatest fame to Henry Fielding (1707–1754), whose satiric drama *Tom Thumb, A Tragedy* (1730; reworked the following year as *The Tragedy of Tragedies; or the Life and Death of Tom Thumb the Great*) depicts Tom loved by the Queen of the Giants but in love with Arthur's daughter Huncamunca. The popularity of Fielding's drama led to the composition of operas and other musical treatments of Tom's story (*see* Fielding, Henry). [NJL]

TOMASZEWSKI, HENRYK, Polish director of a mime troupe whose play *Rycerze Krola Artura* ("The Knights of King Arthur") premiered in Wroclaw in 1981. The play depicts the founding of the Round Table, when in a moment of chaotic disorder Arthur's knights literally tear apart the table in his court and he, inspired by a vision of the history of the Grail, directs them in the reconstruction of a symbolically round one. Mordred, cruel and bitter, destroys Arthur's order; but, in the final scene, Galahad finds the Grail within himself and the ideal is kept alive. [ACL]

TOPOGRAPHY AND LOCAL LEGENDS. Places associated with Arthur fall into two groups. Only a few, though probably a significant few, belong to both. The first group comprises those where attempts have been made to establish his historical presence. The second comprises those where his name appears, or where local folklore or legend has something to say about him. Other Arthurian characters occasionally appear in the same way. In the first group, the number of places counted depends on the number of speculations judged worth considering; but within the bounds of serious scholarship, this group is not large. The second can be defined more objectively. It embraces about 160 locations in Britain, plus a few more in Brittany.

Several places in the first group correspond, conjecturally, to battle sites listed in Nennius's *Historia Brittonum*. This text supplies "the mouth of the River Glein," "the River Dubglas in the district Linnuis," "the River Bassas," the "Forest of Celidon" or "Caledonian Wood," "Fort Guinnion," "The City of the Legion," "the River Tribruit," "the hill that is called Agned," and "Mount Badon"—a total of ten names, plus an eleventh, "Breguoin," which appears instead of "Agned" in some manuscripts. The problem in finding locations that these names may be thought to represent is that several seem to have been effaced when Anglo-Saxon settlement imposed a different language, while even the rest are, in varying degrees, questionable.

Philological scrutiny has yielded some credible equations. *Glein* means "clear" or "pure," and there are rivers still called Glen in southern Lincolnshire and Northumberland. Both flow into larger rivers and have no "mouth" on the sea, but the word could be used for a confluence. *Dubglas*, meaning "blue-black" or "the black stream," has a cluster of variants—such as Douglas, Dulas, Dawlish, Divelish—and is not helpful. But *Linnuis* probably derives from *Lindenses*, the dwellers in or around *Lindum*, and points to what is now Lindsey, the northern portion of Lincolnshire. In conjunction with *Glein*, it could suggest that Arthur came to this part of the country to oppose Anglo-Saxon encroachments via the Wash and Humber.

Bassas and *Guinnion* are baffling, but the Caledonian Wood and the City of the Legion are the nearest to being sure. The former spread over the southern uplands of Scotland, and the latter, in this context, is almost certainly Chester. *Agned*, according to Geoffrey of Monmouth, is Edinburgh, but he is no longer taken seriously. One guess is that the name may come from a record of British activities in Gaul after the first migration to Armorica, and that *Agned* is a scribally contracted and garbled version of *Andegavum*, Angers. There, Saxon settlers in the Loire valley were defeated ca. 469 by an imperial force that may have included Britons. The alternative *Breguoin* is believed to denote *Bremenium*, the Roman fort of High Rochester in Northumberland, but a poetic allusion to a battle there in the late sixth century hints that its connection with Arthur is anachronistic and therefore spurious (which may also be the case with any of the others, though nothing comparable suggests it).

As for *Badon*, the major victory, it has been detected in several areas. The surviving place-name Badbury is often invoked. On this basis, two former Iron Age hill forts, Badbury Rings in Dorset and Liddington Castle in Wiltshire, which has a village called Badbury close by, have both been favored; the latter perhaps more plausibly. However, Geoffrey's identification of Badon with Bath is approved by some historians, who have stressed the potentialities of hill forts neighboring it, such as Little Solsbury.

Two further Arthurian places have been looked for with an eye to historical fact. These are Camlann (or Camlan) and Camelot. *Camlann* probably means "crooked bank" and refers to a winding river, beside which Arthur could have fought against Mordred in his last battle. A present-day Camlan in Merioneth has attracted little attention. Geoffrey chooses the River Camel in Cornwall, not an absurd idea but usually dismissed as a mistake. The Somerset Cam has some support. Much has been made of the Roman fort *Camboglanna* on Hadrian's Wall, because this name would have evolved into *Camlann* in Welsh, but the early legend of Arthur and Mordred implies a Cornish tradition and has no trace of a northern origin. Camlann remains elusive. As for Camelot, fanciful identifications with Winchester, Caerwent, and Camelford rest on the misconception that the Camelot of romance was a real city. The only original reality here would have been some sort of Arthurian headquarters, from which the notion of the King's having a personal capital might have been derived. In that sense, the claim of the Somerset hill fort Cadbury Castle carries unrivaled weight.

Places proposed as Kelliwic, Arthur's Cornish home, may be allotted to this group, though even the likeliest of them cannot be given much credence as the residence of a real Arthur. The most favored site is Castle Killibury or Kelly Rounds, a hill fort near Wadebridge. Five other candidates include Callington, across Bodmin Moor, and Callywith, nearer to Bodmin.

Finally, one major Arthurian place raises no problem as to what or where it was, because it still exists under its old name. This is Glastonbury. The question is whether the connection with Arthur has anything in it, allowing Glastonbury's inclusion among places where he may literally have been. Important here is the claim of the monks at Glastonbury Abbey to have found his grave. While many scholars assume that this was fraudulent, some have argued for a prior tradition and even for a bare chance of genuineness.

If we turn to what may loosely be called Arthur's folklore map, this had demonstrably begun to take shape by the ninth century. An appendix to Nennius listing various *Mirabilia*, or Marvels of Britain, mentions two that involve him. The first is in Buelt in central Wales, where Builth Wells preserves the name. This is a stone marked with a dog's paw-print, made by Arthur's dog Cabal during the hunting of the boar Twrch Trwyth, an adventure told at length in *Culhwch and Olwen*. It lies on top of a heap and cannot be removed, because, after a day and a night, it always reappears on the heap. Not far from Rhayader is a hill called Corngafallt, Cabal's Cairn, but it is uncertain whether this is the place intended. The second "marvel" is in Ercing, a district that stretched across Herefordshire. Near the spring Licat Amr, the writer says, is the burial mound of Arthur's son Amr. Arthur killed him there and buried him. The mound changes in size, being anything from six feet long to fifteen at different times. *Licat* means "eye" and also the source of a river, the place from which water flows. The spring is Gamber Head, the source of the Gamber; the mound may have been Wormelow Tump, which no longer exists and therefore cannot be measured.

Two other scraps of local lore are on record before Geoffrey of Monmouth. Hermann of Tournai describes a journey through Devon and Cornwall in 1113, during which the travelers were informed that they were in Arthur's country and were shown Arthur's Chair and Arthur's Oven, probably rock formations or prehistoric stone structures. Arthur's Chair cannot now be identified; Arthur's Oven may have become King's Oven on Dartmoor.

Numerous features of the landscape have acquired names like these. As a rule, it is quite impossible to tell when. Some are natural objects. Some are megaliths, dating from long before any imaginable Arthur. Largest of all is a mountain, Ben Arthur in Argyllshire. Britain has at least six stones known as Arthur's Stone and eleven more known as Arthur's Quoit, most of them in Wales. Four hills show a vaguely saddlelike configuration—a double top with a dip between—that has inspired the name Arthur's Seat, the one beside Edinburgh being the most famous. Cornwall has Arthur's Bed, a large stone lying flat with a hollow in its upper surface; Arthur's Hall, perhaps a misunderstood medieval reservoir; and Arthur's Hunting Lodge, the hill fort Castle-an-Dinas. Earthworks and other formations are "Round Tables," to the number of five at least, a curious instance being at the center of King's Knot below Stirling Castle, once a formal garden of the Royal Stuarts.

The legend of Arthur and his knights lying asleep in a cave has at least fifteen locations. Cadbury Castle is one of them. Others are in Wales, Cheshire, Yorkshire, Northumberland, and Scotland. (*See* CAVE LEGEND.) Normally, the cave is an enchanted underground chamber that is entered only under peculiar circumstances and can never be found otherwise. In addition, two real caves bear Arthur's name, one near Monmouth, one in Anglesey.

At Tintagel, the scene of Arthur's conception and presumably birth, and at Glastonbury, linked with him in several ways, local legends have been created by known literature, such as Geoffrey's *Historia* and the Grail romances. A literary theme that has given other places an Arthurian aspect is the casting-away of Excalibur. This is said to have happened at Pomparles Bridge just outside Glastonbury, where there would then have been an expanse of water; but it is also said to have happened at Llyn Llydaw in Snowdonia, at Bosherston in Dyfed, and at Dozmary Pool on Bodmin Moor and Loe Pool near Helston, both in Cornwall.

Guenevere, Lancelot, Kay, Mark, and Tristan are also encountered here and there, but, next to Arthur himself, Merlin is the character who figures most frequently and widely. Besides various spots around Carmarthen, his reputed birthplace, he is mentioned at Drumelzier in Peebles and Marlborough in Wiltshire, having been buried in both; at Tintagel, where his ghost haunts Merlin's Cave under the castle headland; and at other Cornish locations. Also, he is in a magic retreat on the Welsh island of Bardsey, keeping the Thirteen Treasures of Britain and a seat on which he will enthrone Arthur when the King returns.

Since only four sites of this type can be proved before Geoffrey—Nennius's pair and Hermann's pair—it is plausible to conclude that literature rather than genuine folklore accounts for most of them, as it does at Tintagel. Of those that clearly reflect romance, some may be surprisingly recent in their Arthurian guise. Dozmary Pool, for instance, has real folkloric associations, but they are not with Arthur. They are with Jan Tregeagle, a figure of popular legend whose ghost roams the moor. The Excalibur story may have been imposed on this atmospheric tarn in the course of the Arthurian vogue started by Tennyson. Even when a place's Arthurian character is spelled out in a medieval text, the lack of any tradition older than that may be fairly obvious. Thus, Guildford is alleged to be Astolat, the home of the lily maid Elaine, and Malory says so. But his only apparent reason is that his plot requires Astolat to be a halting place on the road from London to Camelot. Since he locates Camelot at Winchester, a glance at the map shows Guildford to be a natural choice. There is no need to postulate any prior folk-belief.

Yet explanations of this kind actually have only a limited scope. Considering how long the romance-image of "King Arthur and the Knights of the Round Table" has been the familiar one, it is remarkable how little it has stamped itself on the landscape. Most of the Arthurian sites are in places that the romances never mention, often obscure and out of the way. The assorted Stones, Quoits, and so forth are things of immemorial age having nothing to link them with an idealized medieval court. Legends attached to them are apt to portray an Arthur who sounds like some timeless titan or demigod in a barbaric fairyland.

Whereas in his literary guise he fights giants, his topographic lore sometimes makes him a giant himself. Seated on King's Crags in Northumberland, he tossed a huge boulder at Guenevere on Queen's Crags—which are half a mile away. It bounced off her comb and now lies on the ground between, showing the toothmarks. On another occasion, walking through Carmarthenshire, he felt a pebble in his shoe and threw it aside, and it flew seven miles, landing on top of a heap of stones in the Gower peninsula. That pebble is still there, the capstone of what is actually a megalithic burial chamber, and it weighs twenty-five tons. Tales like this, whatever their true age, owe nothing to medieval romance. They are rooted in the soil of Celtic imagination, *Culhwch and Olwen* country, with its superhuman denizens who can run along treetops, drink whole seas dry, and hear the stirring of an ant at a fifty-mile range.

The central contrast appears in the two main versions of Arthur's survival. Romance puts him in the isle of Avalon. Geoffrey introduces this literary motif in his *Vita Merlini*. Describing the western "island of apples," he shows acquaintance with Celtic myth, and probably with popular Breton ideas. Even so, the island retreat never commended itself to the folklore of Wales. There and elsewhere in Britain, Arthur lives on as the sleeper in the secret cavern, with attendant knights around him. In this case, we have two expressions of the same theme, and it is not the one known to romance that inspires local legends.

There is a further consideration. Taken together, the two versions, island and cave, amount to evidence for a common source long before Geoffrey—indeed, before Arthur himself, whose legend here seems to have annexed a senior one. In A.D. 82, an official named Demetrius, on a visit to Roman Britain, noted one of the few myths of the British Celts ever to be recorded in plain terms. His report, or some of it, is transmitted by Plutarch in two dialogues, *Concerning the Face That Appears in the Orb of the Moon* and *The Obsolescence of Oracles*. The Britons told of a god lying asleep in a cave on an island, a warm and pleasant place "in the general direction of sunset," with attendant spirits around him. Unfortunately, Plutarch follows the practice of his time by giving not the god's Celtic name but the name of a classical deity with whom he can supposedly be equated. Plutarch's chosen equivalent is Cronus, Zeus's father and predecessor in sovereignty, who presided over a golden age but went into exile on his son's rise to power. It is likely that both versions of Arthur's immortality derive ultimately from this British Cronus, the departed ruler who slept in a cave on a paradisal western isle. Certainly, it emerges that Arthur's cave legend has a remote Celtic antecedent, which supplied the mold, at whatever stage this particular hero was fitted into it.

To appraise the list of sites as a whole, in relation to the map, is to bring out a further point. For eight centuries, romance has depicted Arthur as king of all Britain, yet very little indeed of the topographic lore has developed in those areas where Anglo-Saxon dominance has been fullest. Arthur, it has been remarked, is more widespread than anybody except the Devil; so perhaps he is, but he is not everywhere. Preponderantly, the place-names and local legends belong to the West Country, Wales, Cumbria, southern Scotland—to the Celtic fringe, where Celtic people, descendants of Arthur's people, maintained a measure of identity longest, and in some cases still do. They occur in Brittany also, the overseas extension of the same fringe. In most of England, on the other hand, they are scanty. Arthur's folkloric presence belongs almost wholly to regions where he might have been active and where descendants of the Britons did create a saga of him before medieval romance began. The inference is that the saga, not the romance, was the main foundation for local lore and that, however late some of this may be, it has generally depended on deep and authentic popular roots. Nothing necessarily follows, of course, about folk-memory of historical fact, though in a few instances (as at Cadbury) archaeology supplies grounds for suspecting it. (*See also* CAVE LEGEND; FOLKLORE; RETURN, LEGENDS OF ARTHUR'S.) [GA]

Alcock, Leslie. *Arthur's Britain*. London: Penguin, 1971, pp. 160–65.

Ashe, Geoffrey. *A Guidebook to Arthurian Britain*. Wellingborough: Aquarian, 1983.

Chambers, E.K. *Arthur of Britain*. London: Sidgwick and Jackson, 1927, pp. 183–97.

Rhys, John. *Celtic Folklore*. 2 vols. Oxford: Clarendon, 1901, Vol. 1, pp. 20–23; Vol. 2, pp. 457–61, 538–39.

Snell, F.J. *King Arthur's Country*. London: Dent, 1926.

Westwood, Jennifer. *Albion: A Guide to Legendary Britain*. London: Granada, 1985, pp. 5–8, 18–21, 27–29, 292–93, 305–08, 313–15.

TORROELLA, GUILLEM, the fourteenth-century Mallorcan author of *La Faula* ("The Tale"), one of the most original Hispanic adaptations of a French Arthurian text. Composed in verse (1,269 lines) and written in Catalan with some dialogue in French, *La Faula* narrates the purportedly autobiographic vision of the poet involving his fantastic voyage on a whale to the Enchanted Island—identified by modern critics with Sicily—where King Arthur and his sister Morgana wait for Arthur's messianic return to Britain. The poet describes in detail Arthur's palace, where he sees paintings depicting deeds of leading knights of the Round Table and then observes an infirm but young-looking Arthur lamenting the decline of chivalry. Arthur informs the poet of how Morgana brought him to the island after the battle of Salisbury Plain, how every year the Holy Grail provides him with youth-giving nourishment, and how figures depicted on his sword Excalibur provide a moral lesson for kings. Arthur charges the poet with recounting this lesson to the world together with all else he has seen. Torroella skillfully combines material from the Vulgate *Mort Artu* with topics and narrative devices found in other French courtly romances. His style is noteworthy for its use of *amplificatio* in the description of objects, animals, and places. [HLS]

Torroella, Guillem. *La Faula*, ed. Pere Bohigas and Jaume Vidal Alcover. Tarragona: Tarraco, 1984.

Ors, Joan. "De l'encalç del cérvol blanc al creuer de la balena sollerica: la funció narrativa del motiu de l'animal guia." In *Studia in honorem prof. M. de Riquer*. Barcelona: Quaderns Crema, 1986, Vol. 1, pp. 565–77.

TOURNAMENTS. Tournaments originated as training exercises for deadly warfare; the early tournaments, known as Round Tables, were immensely popular exercises of both military and carousing skills. By the time tournaments became fashionable court entertainments, however, the mounted knights had lost their effectiveness on the battlefield. Henry V of England's victory over the French at Agincourt in 1415 completed the rout. Tournaments continued, and in fact reached new popularity, in the nostalgic revival of a romantic chivalry in the fifteenth century under such enthusiasts as King René I of Naples and Anjou and the Tudor monarchs in England (who came to power in 1485). King René wrote the finest book of tournament ceremonial (Paris, B.N. fr. 2692; 1460–65), in which he described and illustrated every detail of the pageant.

Heralds, whose function of announcing and identifying the participants had expanded into that of judges, scorekeepers, and ultimately genealogists who recorded and authenticated coats-of-arms, also had their tournament rolls. The military roll of arms, known as *Sir Thomas Holmes' Book* (1448), illustrated with pairs of jousting knights, recorded arms of knights of the shires. The ceremonial extended into literature; King Arthur and his knights also had their personal coats-of-arms, recorded in such manuscripts as the *Names and Blazons of the Knights of the Round Table* (New York, Pierpont Morgan Library 16). Specific events might also be recorded; *The Great Tournament Role of Westminster* depicts a tournament, held in honor of the birth of a son to Henry VIII and Catherine of Aragon, on February 12–13, 1510/11. The procession at the entrance, the king tilting, and the exit of the participants are depicted in a continuous narrative.

Tournaments continued to be popular under Elizabeth and James I. The Queen's Champions organized spectacular Accession Day Tilts, which were pageants designed around allegorical themes often based on the stories of the knights of the Round Table. (*See also* Arms and Armor; Heraldry; Round Tables.) [MS]

Anglo, S. *The Great Tournament Role of Westminster*. Oxford, 1968.

Brault, Gerard J. *Early Blazon: Heraldic Terminology in the Twelfth and Thirteenth Centuries with Special Reference to Arthurian Literature*. London: Oxford University Press, 1972.

Marks, Richard, and Ann Payne. *British Heraldry from Its Origins to ca. 1800*. London: British Museum, 1978.

Sandoz, Edouard. "Tourneys in the Arthurian Tradition." *Speculum*, 19 (1944), 389–420. (Edition of *La Forme des tournois*.)

TOURNIER, MICHEL, French author of *Tristan et Iseut* (1979), a retelling of the Prose *Tristan*. Tournier also wrote "Tristan Vox," a story in *Coq de bruyère*, which acquires Arthurian overtones when the main character, a radio announcer who calls himself "Tristan," begins receiving love letters from a woman signing herself "Isolde." [NJL]

Tournier, Michel. *Coq de bruyère*. Paris: Gallimard, 1978.

TOYNBEE, THEODORE PHILIP (1916–1981), based *Tea with Mrs. Goodman* (1947), a surrealistic novel set in the modern world, on the theme of quest. The Graal is presented as an enduring personal symbol of spiritual reality. [EB]

Toynbee, Theodore Philip. *Tea with Mrs. Goodman*. London: Horizon, 1947. (Published in the U.S. as *Prothalamium*. Garden City, N.Y.: Doubleday, 1947.)

TRAGOEDISK HISTORIE OM DEN ÆDLE OG TAPPRE TISTRAND, EN. The full title of this eighteenth-century Danish chapbook about Tristan and Isolt is *En tragoedisk Historie om den ædle og tappre Tistrand, Hertugens Søn af Burgundien, og den skiønne Indiana, den store Mogul Kejserens Daatter af Indien* ("A Tragic Story of the Noble and Courageous Tistrand, Son of the Duke of Burgundy, and Indiana, Daughter of the Great Ruler, the Emperor of India"). According to the title page, the anonymous novel had been translated from German into Danish, but the Danish version is unlike any extant German text. The oldest dated imprint of the Danish chapbook was published in 1775 in Christiania, now Oslo. Three subsequent imprints were issued in Copenhagen, in 1785, 1792, and 1800. The chapbook was popular: there exist six additional undated imprints from Copenhagen, presumably from the eighteenth century, and at least six Norwegian imprints from the nineteenth century. The *Tragoedisk Historie* was not only translated into Icelandic under the title *Tistrans saga ok Indiönu* but also inspired two nineteenth-century authors, Sigurður Breiðfjörð and Niels Jónsson, to write *rímur*, that is, metrical narratives, about Tistran and Indiana.

Although the Danish *Tistrand* retains most of the significant motifs and episodes of the medieval Tristan legend, such as the fight with the dragon, the love potion, the sword between the lovers, and the marriage to the second Isolt, the author of the chapbook has rewritten the romance as an exemplum. Isolt is depicted as an individual governed by reason, and her comportment as wife and queen is above reproach.

The source for the unusual names in the Danish *Tistrand* is not known. The protagonists are Tistrand of Burgundy and Indiana of India. Tistrand marries Innanda, whose appearance and name remind him of his beloved Indiana. Tistrand's uncle and Indiana's husband is King Alfonsus of Spain, and Indiana's handmaiden is called Galmeye. A relatively minor figure in the German chapbook, the protagonist's cousin Auctrat, is named Røderich in the Danish novel and plays a major role throughout. At the beginning of the novel, the as-yet-unmarried King Alfonsus declares that one of his two nephews is to succeed him as king: thus, the author introduces into the Tristan matter an otherwise unknown narrative strand dealing with Røderich's machinations to become king of Spain. He envies Tistrand's favored position and plots at one time or another to kill Tistrand, Alfonsus, and even Indiana.

Compared with the classical medieval Tristan legend, the Danish *Tistrand* may seem a blunder. Tistrand and Indiana do not commit adultery—their signs of affection do not go beyond a kiss on Indiana's hand and a pat on Tistrand's cheek—and both Indiana and the narrator are given to moralizing about behavior appropriate to a wife and queen. Not until the lovers have died is the existence of the magic potion revealed and their heroic virtue recognized. Tistrand's and Indiana's bodies do not decompose, thus attesting their blameless lives, and Pope Cleo canonizes them. Because of the changed and singular character of the Tristan matter in the chapbook, Golther concluded in his survey of the Tristan legend that the Danish novel must have been written by an enlightened and semilearned, but prudish, author.

The deviation of the chapbook from the classical Tristan legend is so striking and the didactic elements concerning royal behavior are so pervasive that one can justifiably interpret the novel as a "king's mirror," or handbook of royal ethics. Despite the intelligence on the title page of the oldest dated imprint that the work is a translation from the German, a case can be made for composition in the Danish realm. In 1775, the former queen of Denmark, Caroline Mathilde, sister of King George III of England, died in exile at the age of twenty-four. Three years earlier, her marriage to Christian VII of Denmark (1749–1808) had been dissolved because of her flagrant adultery with Johann Friedrich Struensee (1737–1772), the king's German physician in ordinary, who had acquired such power that over a period of sixteen months he was sovereign of Denmark in fact, if not in name. In 1772, Struensee was publicly executed, and Caroline Mathilde was deported to Celle in Germany. So striking are the similarities between the fictional Tristan-Isolde-Mark and the historical Struensee-Caroline Mathilde-Christian VII triangles that the traditional Tristan romance would have been read as a *roman à clef* in late eighteenth-century Denmark. Instead, the presumably Danish or Norwegian author modified and subverted the classical legend. The political rise and subsequent downfall of the fictional antagonist Røderich mirrors the fate of the historical Struensee, who was executed in the same manner as his fictional counterpart. By means of the exemplary behavior of Tistrand and Indiana, the anonymous author illustrates how the Struensee-Caroline Mathilde tragedy could have been averted. [MEK]

En tragoedisk Historie om den ædle og tappre Tistrand, Hertugens Søn af Burgundien, og den skiønne Indiana, den store Mogul Kejserens Daatter af Indien, Nu nyligen af Tydsk paa Dansk oversat. Christiania, 1775.

Golther, Wolfgang. *Tristan und Isolde in den Dichtungen des Mittelalters und der neuen Zeit.* Leipzig: Hirzel, 1907, pp. 248–53.

TRASK, KATRINA (1853–1922), American author of *Under King Constantine* (first published anonymously). The book contains three long poems set in the time immediately following Arthur's death, when, according to Malory, Constantine, son of Cador of Cornwall, ruled England. Trask's newly invented knights and ladies learn moral lessons in a setting that suggests none of the devastation of a land torn by civil strife. The traditional Arthurian material in the poems consists of allusions to Arthurian characters and a quest for the Grail by a knight named Kathanal. [ACL]

Trask, Katrina. *Under King Constantine*, 2nd ed. New York: Randolph, 1893.

TRAVERS, P(AMELA) L., known as an authority on traditional storytelling themes and techniques as well as for her Mary Poppins books, retold part of the Grail quest in the short tale "Le Chevalier Perdu" (1987). The young Perceval unknowingly receives a lesson from the very counselor he is seeking, a hermit who was once the greatest knight in the world. [DN]

Travers, P.L. "Le Chevalier Perdu." *Parabola*, 12 (February 1987), 14–17.

TREECE, HENRY (1912–1966), British poet, historian, and novelist, wrote three historical novels using Arthurian material. Believing that the Age of Migration provided one of the "crossroads of history," when "individuals of opposing sides meet and learn from one another, merge and come to terms," Treece brings his protagonists in contact with an unromantic, fifth-century Arthur, "a ruthless and possibly half-barbaric Celt, who had adopted Roman manners and military methods." The Bear's missing eye, teeth, and fingers and his tattooed cheeks and lame leg indicate a violent life. In the juvenile novel *The Eagles Have Flown* (1954), two boys, Festus, a Romanized Celt, and Wulf, a Jute, provide the narrative view of Arthur's battles, a theme expanded in the adult novel *The Great Captains* (1956). Camlann and Camelot are identified with Colchester. In *The Green Man* (1966), Amleth (Hamlet), a berserk type motivated by visions and lust for vengeance, travels from Jutland to Geatland, Arthur's Britain, and Pictish Caledonia, where he encounters three aggressive societies. The large cast of characters includes Gwenhwyvar, Ygerne, Kei, Bedwyr, Gavin, Medreut, a Pictish queen descended from Clytemnestra, and Beowulf, the hero's nemesis. Treece rationalizes some mythic elements—the Sword in the Stone is Caliburn deliberately buried in an oak bole; the Round Table is Arthur's shield around which the Welsh kings unhierarchically sit—but retains Merlin's prophetic powers and the green man's fertility rites. He demonstrates his view that an author should "tell his real readers about real life" by emphasizing the terror and violence of battle, murder, rape, mutilation, cannibalism, and unbridled cruelty. His Arthurian world is derived from the chronicles of Gildas and Nennius, the architecture and artifacts of Roman Britain, modern archaeological research, and his own observation of British landscape and seascape.

Treece also deals with Arthurian legend in other literary forms. "Princes of the Twilight" (1947) combines poetry and prose to create a series of symbolic scenes and images in which death and loss dominate. This brief, impressionistic outline of Arthur's career is thus haunted by a sense of doom. "The Tragedy of Tristram," produced by Dafydd Gruffydd, was broadcast from Cardiff by BBC radio in 1950. A dramatic reverie in free verse, it brings together on a Breton heath the ghosts of Tristram, Mark, and Yseult Blanchemain. Their final tragedy is that they must continually retell their story throughout eternity. "Gorlois and Tintagel—Fifth Century" (1959) dramatically recreates for younger readers the story of Arthur's conception, as part of a collection of short stories describing memorable events associated with thirteen British castles. [MAW/RHT]

Treece, Henry. "Princes of the Twilight." In *The Haunted Garden*. London: Faber and Faber, 1947, pp. 23-31.
——. "The Tragedy of Tristram." In *The Exiles*. London: Faber and Faber, 1952, pp.13-39.
——. *The Eagles Have Flown*. London: Allen and Unwin, 1954.
——. *The Great Captains*. London: Bodley Head, 1956.
——. "Gorlois and Tintagel—Fifth Century." In *Castles and Kings*. London: Batsford, 1959, pp. 11-31.
Anonymous. "Henry Treece: Lament for a Maker." In *Only Connect*, ed. Sheila Egoff, G.T. Stubbs, and L.F. Ashley. Toronto: Oxford University Press, 1969.
Fisher, Margery. *Henry Treece*. London: Bodley Head, 1969.

TREVELYAN, R(OBERT) C(ALVERLY) (1872-1951), relates in the blank verse of *The Birth of Parsival* (1905) how Frimutel, son of Titurel, the keeper of the Grail, loved the heathen princess Herzeloida. In a rage, he smashed the magic sword and cursed anyone who should weld it anew, unwittingly dooming his son. For Herzeloida bears Parsival, and when she is ordered by her father to expose the baby, Kundry finds and cherishes him.

The tone is quite different when Trevelyan makes intellectual mockery of Wagnerian pretension in his verse "operatic fable" *The New Parsifal* (1914). After an introduction poking fun at the self-importance of both Wagner and the Lord Chamberlain (the British dramatic censor), we see Klingsor transported to Circe's Isle. The potency of the Grail is questioned, British professors appear, and the unlikely new Parsifal arrives in an airplane. [CNS]

Trevelyan, R.C. *The Birth of Parsival*. London: Longmans, Green, 1905.
——. *The New Parsifal*. London: Chiswick, 1914.

TREVISA, JOHN (ca. 1342-1402), during the 1360s and 1370s lived at Oxford, where he may have helped translate the Lollard Bible. After becoming Vicar of Berkeley (ca. 1380), he translated into English Higden's *Polychronicon* (1387), Aegidius Romanus's *De Regimine Principum*, and Bartholomaeus Anglicus's *De Proprietatibus Rerum* (1398). His translation of the Arthurian section of the *Polychronicon* includes a lively protest against Higden's doubts about the truth of the Arthurian stories, doubts based largely on the silence about Arthur in foreign chronicles. The gospel of John contains much, Trevisa reminds us, omitted by Mark, Luke, and Matthew; similarly, Geoffrey of Monmouth's account contains much about which others were ignorant. (*See also* HIGDEN, RANULF.) [EDK]

Trevisa, John. *Polychronicon Ranulphi Higden*, ed. C. Babington and J.R. Lumby. 9 vols. London: Longman, 1865-86, Vol. 5, pp. 328-38.
Taylor, John, ed. *The Universal Chronicle of Ranulf Higden*. Oxford: Clarendon, 1966, pp. 134-42.
Fowler, D.C. "John Trevisa: Scholar and Translator." *Transactions of the Bristol and Gloucestershire Archaeological Society*, 89 (1970), 99-108.
——. "New Light on John Trevisa." *Traditio*, 18 (1962), 289-317.
Kennedy, Edward Donald. "Chronicles and Other Historical Writing." In *A Manual of the Writings in Middle English*, ed. A.E. Hartung. New Haven: Connecticut Academy of Arts and Sciences, 1981-89, Vol. 8, pp. 2656-61, 2866-77.

TREVOR, (LUCY) MERIOL, English author of three novels that make use of Arthurian tradition. *Merlin's Ring* (1957) is a didactic juvenile fantasy about a boy transported briefly, through the power of Merlin's ring, back to the months preceding Arthur's victory at Badon. After witnessing the political scheming among the Britons, he learns the dangers of ambition, spite, and greed.

That the Britons themselves failed to grasp this lesson is demonstrated in *The Last of Britain* (1956), a historical novel for adults that records events just prior to the British defeat at Dyrham in 577. Neither the memory of Arthur nor the chastisement of Gildas can restrain the ambition and treachery that undermine the heroic resistance against the Saxons.

The Sparrow Child (1958) is another didactic juvenile novel, this time about a quest for the Holy Grail in modern-day Cornwall. Elements of the traditional Grail story are reflected in both the setting and the characters, who find the lost "Glastonbury Chalice" only after they recognize and atone for their sins, the "dolorous strokes" to their own spirit. [RHT]

Trevor, Meriol. *The Last of Britain*. London: Macmillan, 1956.
——. *Merlin's Ring*. London: Collins, 1957.
——. *The Sparrow Child*. London: Collins, 1958.

TRIADS, summaries of Welsh bardic lore, grouped in sets of three. The series known as the "Triads of the Island of Britain" relates to a semilegendary heroic age when the Britons were still predominant—or, at least, had not entirely succumbed to the Saxons—and records the names and exploits of the principal heroes, together with several villains. More than a dozen of these Triads introduce Arthur, and most of the characters who are mentioned belong, like him, to a period stretching from the Roman twilight into the seventh century. However, the heroic age is vague and blends with the pre-Roman, so that Julius Caesar's opponent Cassivellanus also appears, as does the euhemerized god Beli, supposedly his father. Among the post-Roman characters, some are historical or have real originals. Others are doubtful or fictitious.

The triadic form in general may reflect Celtic ideas about the mystique of the number three. But in the "Island of Britain" series, the Triad is a mnemonic device. Bards arranged their topics in threes under headings that applied in common, so that any member of the Triad would bring the others to mind. By way of illustration, a modern storyteller who told stories from Shakespeare might link *Othello*, *Cymbeline*, and *The Winter's Tale* by means of a Triad like this:

> Three Jealous Islanders:
> Othello in Cyprus,
> and Posthumus in Britain,
> and Leontes in Sicily.

The tale of Othello would be a reminder of the plays with Posthumus and Leontes in them, supplying encores. Some of the Welsh Triads are brief like this example, others amplify. Many are late, influenced by Geoffrey of Monmouth or Arthurian romance, and quite a number are outright forgeries. The most valuable are in manuscripts of the thirteenth, fourteenth, and fifteenth centuries, which despite their date contain matter far older than Geoffrey. In a few instances, Nennius or the *Mabinogion* may preserve a story complete. Usually, however, the story is lost and only the triadic summary survives.

Arthur's elevation above other characters is shown not only by the frequency of his appearances but by the fact that several Triads have been enlarged into tetrads to bring him in. Thus, the Triad of the "Three Exalted Prisoners" lists them as Llyr, Mabon, and Gwair. It then adds that there was a prisoner still more exalted, namely Arthur, and notes three places of confinement from which his cousin Goreu released him.

Such traditions suggest guerrilla warfare or solitary adventuring rather than kingship. Most of the Triads that say anything of consequence about Arthur, and are free from Geoffrey's influence, do tend to have a primitive air. He is seldom portrayed as a mighty war-leader against the Saxons. In fact, the battle of Badon is never mentioned. The battle of Camlann is: it is one of the "Three Futile Battles," the outcome of a conflict between Arthur and Mordred, which sounds more like a feud of barbaric equals than a case of treason. According to another Triad, the "Three Unrestrained Ravagings," Mordred came to Arthur's court at Kelliwic in Cornwall, where his men consumed all the food and drink, and their leader struck Guenevere. Arthur retaliated with a similar raid on Mordred's court.

The triadic Arthur is apt to be unexpected. For instance:

> Three Frivolous Bards of the Island of Britain:
> Arthur,
> and Cadwallawn son of Cadfan,
> and Rahawd son of Morgant.

In *Culhwch and Olwen*, Arthur justifies the description in some degree by making up a short verse, at which Cai takes offense. Another Triad makes Arthur guilty of one of the "Three Wicked Uncoverings" or "Unfortunate Disclosures"—the digging up of the head of Bran, buried on Tower Hill in London as a talisman against foreign dangers. Arthur removed it, on the ground that the Britons should rely on the military effort under his leadership. The magic was gone and in due course the Saxons conquered. In another Triad, he is one of the "Red Ravagers." Wherever he walked, neither grass nor plants would spring up for seven years.

Tristan, as "Drystan," also appears in several Triads. The most remarkable makes him one of the "Three Powerful Swineherds." Strictly speaking, he was a deputy swineherd. He looked after Mark's pigs while their usual guardian took a message to Iseult for him. Arthur tried to raid the herd but failed to get a single pig, whether by force, deception, or stealth.

Guenevere, as "Gwenhwyfar," occurs a few times apart from her husband. She is added to the Triad of the "Three Faithless Wives" as "one more faithless than those three." A puzzling Triad lists Arthur's "Three Great Queens" and says they were all called Gwenhwyfar. This may be a case of multiple personality such as is found here and there in Celtic legend, being derived, it seems, from ancient representations of deities (notably the Great Mother) in triple form. There may be a connection with the True and False Gueneveres in the Vulgate Cycle. [GA]

Bromwich, Rachel. *Trioedd Ynys Prydein*. Cardiff: University of Wales Press, 1961; 2nd ed. 1978.

———. "The Welsh Triads." In *Arthurian Literature in the Middle Ages*, ed. Roger Sherman Loomis. Oxford: Clarendon, 1959, pp. 44–51.

TRISTAN. Only one fragment has been preserved of the Middle Dutch adaptation of the *Tristan* of Thomas d'Angleterre (Vienna, Österreichische Nationalbibliothek, Series Nova 3968). The fragment numbers 158 lines and dates from the middle of the thirteenth century. The text has been transmitted in a Low Frankish dialect. The adaptation originated at the end of the twelfth century or the beginning of the thirteenth. [BB]

Smet, G., and Maurits Gysseling, eds. "Die niederfrankischen Tristan-Bruchstüke, Cod. Vind. ser. Nova 3968." *Studia Germanica Gandensia*, 9 (1967), 197–234.

TRISTAN ALS MÖNCH ("Tristan as Monk"), a brief German romance (2,705 lines) from the first half of the thirteenth century and originating in the South Franconian/Alemannic dialect area. It has been transmitted in two manuscripts: *R*, Hs. Nr. 14697 in the Bibliothèque Royale de Belgique (Brussels); and *S*, Cod. ms. germ. 12 in the Staats- und Universitätsbibliothek Hamburg (missing since World War II). *S* is a copy of a lost manuscript from Strassburg, *S**. *R* contains, in addition to *Tristan als Mönch*, the *Tristan* of Gottfried von Strassburg and the conclusion of the *Tristan* continuation of Ulrich von Türheim. Both manuscripts date from the fifteenth century.

The source is uncertain, although it is probably to be found in French. The work belongs to the "disguise" category of *Tristan* narratives and is quite similar to *Tristan Ménestrel*, by Gerbert de Montreuil, in which Tristan disguises himself as a minstrel in order to meet again with Isolde. Nowhere else, however, does Tristan take on the disguise of a monk.

The connection with the Arthurian matter is tangential. Arthur has invited Tristan and Isolde of the White Hands to a festival at Caridol. Tristan dreams of Isolde and desires to see her once again. He changes identity with a dead knight and enters a monastery and assumes the name of "Brother Wit." The dead knight, whom everyone assumes to be Tristan, ostensibly wished to be buried in Cornwall and the funeral procession, accompanied by Brother Wit in his capacity as chaplain, journeys to Cornwall, and all connection with Arthur ceases. In Cornwall, Tristan reveals himself to Isolde, who, in order to bring Tristan to her in privacy, feigns sickness. Tristan disguises himself as a physician, and he and Isolde enjoy the intimacy of one another's company. Isolde is "cured," and Tristan takes his leave with the profuse thanks of King Mark. [FGG]

Bushey, Betty C., ed. *Tristan als Mönch*. Göppingen: Kümmerle, 1974.

Jungreithmayr, Anna. "*Tristan als Mönch*: Ansätze zu einem Textverständnis." *Sprach-Text-Geschichte*. Göppingen: Kümmerle, 1980, pp. 409–40.

TRISTAN (Tristran, Tristram, Tristrem) **AND ISOLDE** (Isolt, Iseut, Yseut). The legend of Tristan and Isolde was one of the most popular love stories of the Middle Ages and was widespread throughout Europe. With the coming of the Renaissance, it shared the obscurity into which Arthurian legend lapsed until its revival in the nineteenth century. This interest culminated in the early decades of the twentieth century, but it has since declined again.

As the story spread, details were altered and added, but its basics may be summarized as follows. The love between Tristan and Isolde is anticipated by that between the hero's parents, Rivalin, King of Lyonesse, and Blancheflor, sister to Mark, King of Cornwall (or Meliadus and Elizabeth, as they are named in the prose romances). They marry, but she dies in childbirth, and her son's name commemorates this loss. The boy is raised by a tutor, Governal, who becomes his faithful companion. Together, they travel to Cornwall to seek adventure, though in some versions Tristan is kidnaped and put ashore there.

Concealing his identity, he distinguishes himself for his skill in both harping and hunting before he undertakes his first major feat, the combat with Morholt. Morholt is the brother-in-law and champion of Anguish, King of Ireland,

85. Woodcut, "Tristano e Isotta per mare," from Daria Banfi Malaguzzi, *Storia di Messer Tristano* (Milan, 1927). (Courtesy of The Newberry Library, Chicago.)

who demands tribute from Cornwall; he is slain by his youthful opponent after a long struggle. Tristan's wounds refuse to heal, however, because Morholt's weapons were poisoned. In despair, he has himself set in an open boat, which drifts to Ireland, though in later accounts he goes there deliberately in search of Isolde, Anguish's only daughter, who has special healing skills. Concealing his identity under the name of Tantris, he makes a slow recovery. In some accounts, Isolde's love for Tristan begins to develop while she learns harping from him during his convalescence. Later, Anguish offers his daughter's hand in marriage to the knight who can slay a dragon that is ravaging the land. Tristan, who has returned seeking her as a bride for his uncle, King Mark, slays the dragon and cuts out its tongue but is overcome by its poisonous fumes. When the king's steward produces the dragon's head and claims the reward, Isolde finds Tristan and nurses him back to health again. Though angry when she discovers that he slew her uncle, Morholt, she spares his life so that he can refute the claim of the steward, whom she detests. In prose versions, Tristan wins her for Mark by defending her father in trial-by-combat.

On the voyage back to Cornwall, Tristan and Isolde accidentally drink the love potion intended for the bridal couple, and thereafter cannot escape their love. To disguise her loss of virginity, Isolde persuades her faithful maid, Brangwain, to take her place in Mark's bed on the wedding night, but fearing betrayal she arranges her murder, though she later repents and spares her. This is the first of many deceptions that the lovers practice, including the Tryst Beneath the Tree; but the plotting of courtiers who envy Tristan finally traps the lovers, usually by marks of blood in flour scattered around Isolde's bed.

In some versions, the lovers are condemned to death, but Tristan escapes and rescues Isolde from a group of lepers to whom she was given as punishment; in others, she tricks Mark by swearing a false oath in an ordeal by hot iron, but is later banished with Tristan. They seek refuge in the forest, but Isolde eventually returns to Mark, while Tristan goes into exile.

In the course of his wanderings, he meets and marries Isolde of Brittany, also known as Isolde of the White Hands. Since Tristan cannot forget his love for Isolde of Ireland, however, the marriage remains unconsummated. In the prose romances, Tristan is murdered by the treacherous Mark, but in the verse romances he receives a poisoned wound while aiding his brother-in-law and friend, Kaherdin. He summons Isolde of Ireland to heal him, but when his jealous wife reports that the ship has black sails, not the white that were the signal that her rival is coming, he dies in despair. Isolde of Ireland dies from grief, and the lovers are buried side by side. From his grave there grows a vine, from hers a rose; they meet and intertwine.

The traditions out of which this story developed have prompted much conjecture. While some have sought its historical roots near Castle Dore in Cornwall, others have argued for north Britain, since the hero's name in Welsh tradition, Drystan son of Tallwch, can be traced to the Pictish Drust son of Tallorc. He is mentioned in several of the Triads, most notably as one of the Three Powerful Swineherds of the Isle of Britain. Despite all their efforts, Arthur and three of his best warriors were unable to obtain as much as one pig from him. The Celtic basis of the legend has long been recognized: the hero's rescue of a princess from her fate as forced tribute and her recognition of him in his bath in time to refute false claimants appear in the tenth-century Irish saga *The Wooing of Emer*; the love story is found in *The Pursuit After Diarmaid and Gráinne*, which dates from the ninth century. Source studies have further revealed that various features of the legend survive in these and other Irish tales, as well as in classical, Germanic, and oriental sources, such as the Persian *Wîs and Râmîn*.

Some scholars believe that the legend passed through Brittany to France, where an archetypal *Ur-Tristan* was composed ca. 1150. This was closely followed by verse romances of the so-called common version, most notably the German *Tristrant* of Eilhart von Oberge (ca. 1170) and the Anglo-Norman *Roman de Tristran* by Béroul (late twelfth century). This version of the legend emphasizes dramatic action and elemental passion.

The archetype was refined and rationalized by the Anglo-Norman Thomas d'Angleterre (ca. 1170). His poem was the source for Gottfried von Strassburg's *Tristan* (ca. 1210), and thus the many German versions based upon it (*see* TRISTAN IN MODERN GERMAN VERSIONS); for Brother Robert's Norse *Tristrams saga ok Ísöndar* (1226), the only complete treatment of this version of the legend, and thus for various Icelandic sagas and romances derived from it, including the parody in the fourteenth-century *Saga af Tristram ok Ísodd* (*see* SCANDINAVIAN ARTHURIAN LITERATURE); and for the English verse *Sir Tristrem* (late thirteenth century). Works in this group comprise the "courtly version."

There also developed a prose tradition, in which Tristan becomes a knight of the Round Table, second in valor only to Lancelot, and encounters many chivalric adventures typical of the prose romances. This starts in the second quarter of the thirteenth century with the French Prose *Tristan*, which exists in first and second (or enlarged) versions. The romance proved so popular that it largely superseded the poetical versions. In France, it was added to in successive redactions, and it formed the basis of later romances, such as the *Palamedes* (*see* PROSE *TRISTAN*); though widely popular in the Iberian peninsula, it has survived mostly in fragmentary translations (*see* TRISTAN IN SPAIN AND PORTUGAL); but in Italy, where it was equally popular, it inspired such works as the fourteenth-century *La Tavola Ritonda*, which combines elements from other sources as well (*see* ITALIAN ARTHURIAN LITERATURE); Danish, and Russian adaptations also survive, while in England Sir Thomas Malory condensed it into "The Book of Sir Tristram de Lyones" as part of *Le Morte Darthur* (1485).

Gottfried's poem remained influential in postmedieval treatments of the Tristan legend in German, culminating in Wagner's opera *Tristan und Isolde* (1865). In other languages, the prose version dominated. Prose Tristan romances were popular in the sixteenth century, though they had little impact on literature. Once they passed out of fashion, the love story attracted little attention until the nineteenth-century revival of interest in Arthurian legend. Alfred Lord Tennyson uses Tristan to illustrate the moral decline of Arthur's followers in "The Last Tournament" (1871), but both Matthew Arnold's *Tristram and Iseult* (1852) and Algernon Swinburne's *Tristram of Lyonesse* (1882) are more sympathetic to the lovers. The legend reached the height of its postmedieval popularity in the largely romantic poems and plays composed in the opening decades of the twentieth century by writers like Arthur Symons and Edwin Arlington Robinson. Since then, interest has waned.

The lovers may be presented as heroic figures caught in the grip of an implacable fate or as unscrupulous and self-centered adulterers. Tristan may be an artist-figure whose heightened sensitivity causes him acute anguish or a valiant knight serving his lady with splendid deeds; Isolde may be a lonely Irish exile seeking tenderness in a hostile court or a proud queen, graciously rewarding her devoted lover. Yet, whether victims or villains, true-hearted or tricksters, they remain for most people the symbol of a tragic love. (*See also* GOTTFRIED VON STRASSBURG.) [RHT]

Buschinger, Danielle, ed. *La Légende de Tristan au Moyen Âge: Actes du Colloque des 16 et 17 Janvier 1982*. Göppingen: Kümmerle, 1982.

de Rougement, Denis. *Love in the Western World*, trans. Montgomery Belgion, rev. ed. Princeton, N.J.: Princeton University Press, 1983.

Eisner, Sigmund. *The Tristan Legend: A Study in Sources*. Evanston, Ill.: Northwestern University Press, 1969.

Ferrante, Joan M. *The Conflict of Love and Honor: The Medieval Tristan Legend in France, Germany and Italy*. The Hague: Mouton, 1973.

Golther, Wolfgang. *Tristan und Isolde in den Dichtungen des Mittelalters und der neuen Zeit*. Leipzig: Hirzel, 1907.

Newstead, Helaine. "The Origin and Growth of the Tristan Legend." In *Arthurian Literature in the Middle Ages*, ed. Roger Sherman Loomis. Oxford: Clarendon, 1959, pp. 122–33.

Schoepperle, Gertrude. *Tristan and Isolt: A Study of the Sources of the Romance*. Frankfurt and London, 1913; 2nd ed. Roger Sherman Loomis. New York: Franklin, 1959.

TRISTAN IN MODERN GERMAN VERSIONS.

The relationship of the Tristan story to the Arthurian corpus is a tenuous one, and in Germany at least the development proceeded largely unaffected by the *matière de Bretagne*. Perhaps because the story became the basis for one of the most brilliant literary achievements of German medieval literature, or perhaps because the story in its German form appealed so strongly to something in the German character, it has remained a constant source of material for German writers. The number of literary recreations, excluding editions and translations, is consequently so large that no attempt can be made here to survey or even list them. Emphasis will therefore be placed on a few periods at which interest seems to be peculiarly intense.

Gottfried von Strassburg makes it clear at the beginning of his *Tristan* that he has been careful to seek out the "genuine" source; Eilhart von Oberge's version is not acceptable to him. Gottfried's source is Thomas d'Angleterre, whose work he seems to use freely, although comparison is not easy, given the fragmentary nature of the Thomas manuscripts and the lack of an ending to Gottfried's work. The essential feature of the story as related by Gottfried is the positive attitude toward the love relationship. The effect of the love potion is absolute, permanent, and fully accepted by the lovers. The poem depicts the emotional relationship as a supreme experience but one that conflicts with contemporary social and religious norms. The story is not placed in relation to the Arthurian world.

When Gottfried's work was completed by later writers—Ulrich von Türheim in 1235 and Heinrich von Freiberg in 1290—these poets turned to Eilhart as a source and to a tradition in which the love relationship was brought about by a force, the potion, that was not permanent (it was usually limited to four years) and was seen rather as an unfortunate aberration than as a positive experience. This became the dominant tradition through the following centuries, as the story was told and retold in prose, sometimes with the inclusion of figures from the Arthurian world; already in Heinrich von Freiberg's version, Tristan spends some time at Arthur's court. In the chapbooks that appear every ten to twenty years from 1484 to 1664, the basic elements of the story remain much the same: parentage, battle with Morold, cure, wooing mission, love potion, intrigues, banishment, marriage to Isolde Weisshand, visits to Isolde, second poisoned wound, black and white sails, death. Only once, approximately in the middle of this period, is the story taken up by a major poet, and his attitude toward the material may be taken as representative of the prose works in general.

Hans Sachs (1494–1576) treated the story in two ways. In 1553, he completed a seven-act tragedy on the topic (*Tragedia von der strengen Lieb, Herr Tristrant mit der schönen Königin Isalden*, "Tragedy of the Severe Love of Sir Tristrant and the Beautiful Queen Isalde") and wrote also the last of a series of seven fairly short *Meisterlieder*. His source is the chapbook published in Worms in 1550. He adheres closely to the substance of it. Each poem treats only one aspect of the story, but the drama takes the lovers through the usual sequence of events. The seven "acts" are little more than scenes in which 1) Tristan kills Morold; 2) Tristan obtains a cure for his wound, returns to Ireland, and kills the dragon; 3) Tristan wins Isolde for Marke and shares the love potion with her; 4) the lovers engage in intrigues but successfully deceive the king; 5) they are caught, condemned to death, escape to the forest, and are finally separated; 6) Tristan visits Isolde in fool's clothing; 7) Tristan is wounded and dies, Isolde arrives too late and dies also. The work closes with a speech by the "Herold" in which the audience is encouraged to take heed of the fate of the lovers and to resist love's blandishments in favor of honorable marriage. The chapbook of 1484 had ended with a similar warning against worldly love.

The development of an interest in Germany's literary past and the Romantic revival of the Middle Ages in particular are the prime factors in the rediscovery and further development of the Tristan story at the end of the eighteenth and beginning of the nineteenth century. There were editions and translations both of Gottfried's work and of the chapbooks. Academic reaction was for the most part hostile to the content of the story while grudgingly admitting the poetic qualities of Gottfried's version. One might have expected the Romantic poets to take up the story with enthusiasm; that they did not is symptomatic of their essentially conservative stance in moral matters (the most scathing condemnation of Gottfried ever written is from Eichendorff's pen). Typical of the Romantics, too, is the existence of many fragmentary attempts to treat the material. A.W. Schlegel, Friedrich Rückert, and many others left fragments of translations and poetic or dramatic versions, of which only that by Immermann is at all extensive.

August von Platen (1796-1835) planned the earliest Tristan drama in the 1820s; a complete but brief plan seems to have been drawn up in June of 1827 (*Sämtliche Werke*, ed. Max Koch and Erich Petzet. Leipzig: Hesse, 1910, Vol. 10, pp. 373-82). However, nothing further came of this plan, which envisaged five acts, beginning with the situation after Isolde's arrival in Cornwall. The meeting between Tristan and Isolde is betrayed to Marke by Auctrat, who wounds Tristan with a poisoned arrow, since banishment is in his view not a sufficient punishment. It is also Auctrat who tells Tristan of the black sail; there is no second Isolde.

The first part of a dramatic version by Friedrich Roeber (1819-1901) was published in 1840, but it is not clear from the subsequent edition of this version together with a revised version in 1898, whether or not the whole had been completed at the earlier date (*Tristan und Isolde. Eine Tragödie. In zwei nach Inhalt und Form verschiedenen Bearbeitungen,* "Tristan and Isolde. A Tragedy. In Two Versions, Differing in Content and Form." Leipzig: Baedeker, 1898). The dates are given here as 1838 and 1898. Roeber's concern is with the morality of the action, and he therefore has Brangane as a regular substitute for Isolde in the first version, while in the second the marriage, and the moral dilemma, are continually postponed. Brangane is in any case in love with Marke, and her feeling is reciprocated in the later version. It is Roeber's view that tragedy can be convincing only if the tragic characters are morally sound.

Karl Immermann (1796-1840), too, was perplexed by the problem of morality, but he takes a different approach in his dramatic poem *Tristan und Isolde*, which remained unfinished at his death in 1840 and which has been both fulsomely praised and condemned as extraordinarily bad (Düsseldorf: Schaub, 1841). It is certainly of very uneven quality, lacking in concentration, and would, if completed, have been inordinately long. The most interesting aspect is Immermann's attempt to change the function of the ordeal. Isolde demands the ordeal without any plan for falsifying the oath, and she even rejects Tristan's offer of rescue by force. She survives the ordeal, because she knows in her heart that she wishes to be pure and is acting only under the influence of the potion. The passing of the test she sees as a sign of grace, and this enables her to regain the moral strength to refrain from sin, even though her love for Tristan does not die; she insists on the separation.

A number of plays on the Tristan material appeared in the latter half of the nineteenth century, most of them in blank verse and all of them designated either as tragedies or as *Trauerspiele*. Josef Weilen's (1828-1889) play *Tristan* appeared in 1860 (Breslau: Max), presumably too early to be influenced by Wagner, whose opera had been published in 1859 but was not performed until 1865; there are, however, clear signs of the influence of Immermann—for example, in the figure of Ritter John and in the lovers' intention to commit suicide by throwing themselves from the ship. Tristan is betrayed by Marke before the lovers have any assignation, but after his departure Isolde refuses to marry Marke and falls into a decline. When Tristan returns in the guise of a pilgrim, he claims to be able to cure Isolde, but when she is brought before him, the true story of their innocent and compulsive love is told, at which point Tristan gives Isolde to Marke and kills himself. Isolde dies of grief. The tenor of the work as a whole is pessimistic rather than genuinely tragic. "Das höchste Recht auf Erden ist die Liebe" ("the highest right on earth is love," p. 122), but love cannot thrive in society as it is.

A better work is Ludwig Schneegans's (1842-1922) *Tristan* (Leipzig: Wigand, 1865), for here the plot has been purged of medievalisms and subplots. Tristan and Isolde fall in love on the voyage (without a love potion), and their attempt to suppress their feelings and renounce their love on the day that Isolde marries Marke is thwarted only because their parting is betrayed to the king. He banishes them on the spot but later, when he finds them in a cave, literally drags Isolde from Tristan, who flees and attempts to find solace with the second Isolde. The main issue in this work is the right to love. Marke is guilty of marrying Isolde without love, and Tristan and Isolde are "guilty" of attempting renunciation.

Albert Gehrkes's (1840-1896) *Isolde* (Berlin: Heimann, 1869) avoids many of the problems posed by the medieval plot, for Tristan and Isolde are openly in love before Tristan is revealed as the killer of Morhold (in this work Isolde's father). There is nevertheless a potion, but Isolde is told by its guardian, the Marshall, that it is a "hate potion," for it is his hope that she will drink it with him in order to be freed from his importunate love. In Cornwall, prior to the marriage ceremony, the Marshall assassinates Tristan but is then deceived by Isolde, who puts poison rather than the love/hate potion into the wine, thus avenging the death of both her father and Tristan.

Adolf Bessel's (1856–1936) short work *Tristan und Isolde* (Kiel: Lipsius und Tischer, 1895) also simplifies the plot considerably. Here, Tristan and Isolde are in love before Marke sends Tristan to woo for him, and the love potion is deliberately administered and the lovers told of this by Brangane, who wants them to declare themselves. Immediately after the marriage, however, the lovers are caught with the usual ruse. Tristan is condemned to death and Isolde is forced to swear loyalty to Marke in order to save Tristan (which naturally causes doubts in his mind about her loyalty). In the final scene, she forgets to hoist the white flag and Tristan stabs himself; they exchange last words before Tristan dies and Isolde stabs herself. The emphasis in this work is firmly on the innocence of the lovers, caught in an impossible situation. When Marke learns the truth, he sets out to save them but comes too late.

The first decades of the twentieth century produced a large number of editions, translations, and reworkings of the Tristan story, many of them based on Gottfried, and most of them again in dramatic form. Of the prose versions, the best known is probably the novella by Thomas Mann (1903), but this work, set in the modern context of a sanatorium, is better seen as a satire on Wagner and his relationship with the Wesendonks. In 1923, Mann also drafted the plot for a film version, based primarily on Gottfried, a project that was never carried out. The only major change that he makes in his plot summary is to substitute for the earlier episodes a situation in which Tristan and Isolde know of each other by repute and are attracted to each other prior to their meeting. Their love develops during the wooing mission, and the potion only has the effect of releasing them from the restrictive bonds of duty. Mann planned, rather surprisingly, to retain most of the subsequent episodes of intrigue.

Other prose works, such as Emil Lucka's (1877–1941) *Isolde Weisshand* (Berlin: Fischer, 1909) and Will Vesper's (1882–1962) *Tristan und Isolde* (Munich: Langewiesche-Brandt, 1911), are much inferior to the dramatic works. There is a stronger tendency to embroider on the original in the prose, but neither here nor in the stage works is there more than the occasional attempt to modernize the medieval situation entirely. One such exception is *Tristans Ehe* ("Tristan's Marriage"), by Karl Albrecht Bernouilli (1868–1937) (Leipzig: Reclam, 1926; an earlier version perhaps in 1916). In this work, Marke is an American millionaire, and there are modern equivalents of traditional episodes, including a dwarf, a miniature dog, and "Tristan" as a clown. The action revolves around Isolde's unbalanced state of mind after "Tristan's" disappearance and the efforts made by the psychiatrist to cure her. In the final scenes, he seems to have succeeded, for, despite a near-riot in the mental asylum, the two couples—"Marke" and "Isolde," and "Tristan" and the second "Isolde"—are reunited!

Returning to more traditional paths, Albert Geiger's (1866–1915) play is entitled *Tristan* (Karlsruhe: Bielefeld, 1906) but consists of two parts, "Blanscheflur" and "Isolde." The first part follows the Gottfried plot fairly closely, except that Riwalin dies immediately after taking Blanscheflur to his bed and she is then rejected by her brother Marke (as much, it would seem, on Riwalin's account as on hers). Tristan's mother lives to bring him up, and it is an altercation over an apparent love affair and her fear that Tristan is displaying inherited tendencies that bring about her death. The Tantris–Tristan plot and the garden scene are distinctly Wagnerian. In the strange final scene, Tristan is dying of a wound received while saving his beleaguered and plague-stricken country from the enemy; he is found in an inn by Isolde, who has been wandering the world in search of him. She, too, is dying—in her case from the plague.

In contrast with Geiger's work, Emil Ludwig's (1881–1948) play *Tristan und Isolde* (Berlin: Oesterfeld, 1909) begins, like Wagner's opera, with the shipboard scene, although with a genuine love potion. Thereafter, though, the plot is much more in line with Eilhart: the lovers are caught and condemned to death; Tristan escapes from the chapel and frees Isolde from the lepers. Marke finds them in the forest and exchanges swords. At this point, there is a voluntary separation, during which Tristan meets and marries the second Isolde. In the guise of a fool, he receives the death wound on a visit to Isolde. The ending is the traditional one.

Ernst Hardt's (1876–1946) *Tantris der Narr* ("Tantris the Fool"; Leipzig: Insel, 1907) explores in detail the love-hate relationship in which the main characters are enmeshed. This drama is restricted to a single episode, based on Tristan's visit to Isolde in the guise of a fool. The crisis is precipitated by a report that Tristan has been seen but has fled on being challenged in the name of Isolde. This angers Isolde, who feels doubly betrayed, because Tristan has denied her and yet rendered her life forfeit, under the terms of the ambiguous oath, by his presence. Marke condemns her but has his doubts; Denovalin, in love with Isolde, wavers between the desire to protect or destroy her. Finally, Isolde herself is unable to recognize Tristan in the fool, even when he shows detailed knowledge of her past. Only Tristan's dog, Husdent, recognizes him, and with the dog Tristan leaves the palace as Isolde realizes her error too late. In part because Hardt concentrates on a single episode, this is one of the most successful of modern recreations.

In Georg Kaiser's (1878–1945) play *König Hahnrei* ("King Cuckold"; Berlin: Fischer, 1913), the medieval situation is retained, but it has no real significance. The central figure here is the king, and the entire plot revolves around his sexual problems. He is almost senile and experiences vicarious pleasure through his knowledge of the relationship between the lovers. He therefore does his best to conceal, not to discover, their secret and is disturbed only by feelings of jealousy with regard to Isolde's fondness for her much younger brother. The king's overt encouragement of their passion has the effect eventually of destroying it. Urged to embrace, they feel only revulsion and are united in death when the king's spear transfixes them both as they stand passively before him.

Like many plays, Eduard Stucken's (1865–1936) *Tristram und Yseult* (Berlin: Reiss, 1916) begins with the Tantris-Tristan plot and the shipboard scene. In this case, Tristan and Isolde think they are taking poison and declare their love as the ship arrives in Cornwall. The marriage is put off for a while and Tristan and Isolde are able to escape to the forest. Here, the lovers are found by Marke's men, and Isolde is forced to return to Marke in order to save Tristan's life. She is again forced to deny Tristan when he comes in the guise of a pilgrim, since his presence is known to the king. In the conclusion, Isolde comes to Tristan and the misunderstanding is clarified, but Isolde does not die of grief; she is strangled by the dying Tristan!

Maja Loehr's *Tristans Tod* ("Tristan's Death"; Vienna: Heller, 1919) has little to recommend it beyond the economy of action. The emphasis is on the two Isoldes, the first of whom believes herself betrayed by Tristan's subsequent marriage and therefore is more generous to Marke, while the second Isolde feels herself equally betrayed by the discovery of the real reason for Tristan's coldness after the marriage ceremony. In the final scene, after the usual betrayal and remorse, Tristan stabs himself and Isolde takes poison.

The dramatic *Trilogie der Leidenschaft: Ysot, Marke, Tristan* ("Trilogy of Passion"; Munich: Musarion, 1922), by Robert Prechtl (pseudonym of Robert Friedländer; 1874–1950), has little action despite its length, for most of the plot is narrated in the course of the dialogue. Thus, the first part begins with the report of the death of Morolt, Ysot's brother, and the arrival almost simultaneously of Tristan to woo on behalf of Marke. Ysot's hatred gradually turns to love, which is openly expressed when Tristan is willing to accept poison from her hands, as he in turn loves her and prefers death to dishonor. The second part revolves entirely around the false oath. Tristan and Ysot genuinely desire to renounce their relationship at the moment of taking the ordeal. After successfully undergoing the ordeal, they separate voluntarily, but Ysot subsequently makes it plain to Marke that love between them is impossible. The third and last part is restricted to the death of Tristan, who is waiting for both Ysots. Here, there is a strange variation, as it is the lover of Kaedin, maddened by his death, who tells Tristan of the black sail and then kills herself. The two Ysots are reconciled at Tristan's deathbed, not knowing at the end whether it is one or both of them or love itself that is the object of Tristan's desire. Throughout the work, there is an emphasis on the demonic, destructive nature of love, underlined by a brief love scene between two of Tristan's youthful followers in his sickroom.

86. John Rylands University Library, MS 1, fol. 240v: After Entrusting Guenevere to Mordred, Arthur Assaults Lancelot. (Courtesy John Rylands University Library.)

Another lengthy work is Joseph Hurter-Ammann's *Tristan und Isolde* (Zurich: Amaltha, 1928). The first part ends with the love potion, while the second begins with Tristan's arrival in Karke to aid Kaherdin, thereby avoiding all difficulties with regard to the episodes of deception. The work is marred by many extraneous and at times tedious passages of "medievalizing" detail, such as the scenes with the doctors who disagree about the possible cure for Tristan.

Recreators of the story of Tristan and Isolde face two basic problems, the one technical and the other intellectual. On the one hand, they must modify the medieval aspects of the story sufficiently to make the material palatable to a modern public, and on the other hand they must find a critical point around which to build the plot. The first problem clearly can impinge on the second. In the works that have been cited here, the major elements that have been redefined by the authors are the love potion, the ordeal, and the death of the lovers. The potion is generally no longer the source of their love, which develops by itself. The death of the lovers seems at times unnecessarily complicated, as authors strive to avoid what is apparently the unacceptable idea of Tristan's death by mischance and Isolde's death from a broken heart. Yet the idea of suicide—the death of the lovers at their own hand—may flow from the authors' desire to strengthen the tragic quality of their end.

The ordeal is the element that most closely relates to the general line of modern dramatic interpretations, which can be summed up largely in one word: renunciation. By this is not meant the "if only I had known" type of renunciation indulged in by Marke, who is willing to renounce his claim to Isolde (too late). It is rather the lovers' own attitude toward their love that is the specifically modern feature. As morally sound individuals (to use Roeber's term), they recognize the impossibility of their situation and the need to renounce any thought of union. They part or plan to part voluntarily, and they can survive the ordeal because they are willing to renounce. Only rarely is there any suggestion that their love is a positive force, something that might take precedence over worldly considerations, something that should be rejoiced in rather than suppressed.

The exploration of this theme produces little genuine tension, as the plot movement is based essentially on misunderstandings, accidents, and so forth. The only element that appears to be successful in generating the kind of dramatic tension that holds the public's interest is the relationship between Tristan and Isolde after separation. In a sense, the medieval situation of Marke, wavering between belief and disbelief, is transferred to the lovers, who are led by circumstances to waver between trust and mistrust, to doubt the steadfastness of each other's love. This aspect plays a role in many of the works and it is the sole topic in Hardt's work, probably the most successful of the modern dramatic versions.

In the last few decades, literary versions in German have been few and far between. The cause may lie in the radically changed attitude to myth and legend. These stories are no longer retold in modified form but completely recreated in a modern idiom and frequently in an "alien" form. Thus, there have been versions of the Tristan story in music, ballet, or film where only the essence is preserved; characters, situations, and medium are all transposed to our era. It is difficult to consider such transpositions as modern versions of a given medieval text, and, while novels like Hans-Erich Nossack's (1901–1977) *Spätestens im November* ("At the Latest in November"; Berlin: Suhrkamp, 1955), may be based on the Tristan story and may take that concept to its (for our age) ultimate conclusion, consideration of this and similar works belongs rather in the realm of motif research and not in the pages of an Arthurian encyclopedia. This and other works suggest, however, that the story of Tristan and Isolde is still very much alive. (*See also* WAGNER, RICHARD.)

[MSB]

TRISTAN IN SCANDINAVIA. Names, episodes, and motifs from the love tragedy of Tristan and Isolde abound in medieval Icelandic sagas and in Scandinavian ballads. The story, modified and reinterpreted over the centuries, embodies elements of fate and tragedy seen also in such tales of the North as those of Hagbard and Signe and of the Nibelungs. (Jan de Vries in fact characterized Tristan as an anti-Sigurd.) The works that lay behind these numerous versions are a matter of disagreement among scholars, who are strangely reluctant to acknowledge *Tristrams saga ok Īsöndar*, the oldest known Scandinavian example of the Tristan story, as their direct or ultimate source. An exception is the Dane Paul V. Rubow, who in 1928 declared that *Tristrams saga* had provided the Icelanders with both the model and the impetus for the literary recreation in the sagas of the lives of their illustrious forebears.

Tristrams saga, a Norwegian prose adaptation of the *Tristan* of Thomas d'Angleterre, was composed in 1226 at the command of King Hákon Hákonarson (r. 1217–63) by a certain Brother Robert. (The work is preserved in Icelandic manuscripts: two vellums from ca. 1450, three complete or almost complete paper transcripts from the seventeenth and eighteenth centuries, and two résumés from the same period.) Robert made a faithful rendering of the narrative but expunged most of Thomas's psychological analysis. Since several sagas about native heroes, or *Īslendingasögur*, antedate *Tristrams saga*, this translation could not have marked the inception of the genre; but it did serve as a model for individual sagas.

If a borrowed episode or theme in a Scandinavian work is unique to the Thomas, or "courtly," branch of the romance, it is plausible to regard *Tristrams saga* as the source. One such borrowing is the Hall of Statues episode, which is perhaps the invention of Thomas. In the saga, after subduing the giant Moldagog, Tristram has artisans fashion statues of Īsönd, her companion Bringvet, the scheming dwarf, the giant Moldagog, the king's evil counselor, a huge lion, and Īsönd's dog. Tristram and Moldagog arrange the lifelike figures in a subterranean hall. Tristram frequently visits the hall to kiss and embrace the likeness of Īsönd and, when angry or depressed, to vent his wrath on the image of the evil dwarf. (Here, Robert improved on the French text, according to which Tristan berated the statue of Isolde rather than that of the dwarf.)

Þidreks saga, which was compiled at the Norwegian court two or three decades after *Tristrams saga*, contains three variants of this episode. In the first, Velent the Smith creates a likeness of the man who stole his money and tools and sets it at a place where the king will be certain to see it; when the king catches sight of the statue, he addresses it by name. In *Herburts þáttr*, another episode in the saga, Herburt is sent to sue for the hand of Hildr Artúsdóttir for his uncle, King Þidrekr. When she asks him to trace a picture of his uncle on the wall, Herburt draws such a dreadful face that Hildr is horrified. She suggests that Herburt woo her for himself, and they elope. The third variant in *Þidreks saga* occurs in *Īrons þáttr jarls*. Īron's wife is irked because the earl spends all his time hunting and pays little attention to her. She goes into the garden, takes off her clothing, and falls into the snow. Showing the earl the impression of her body, she suggests that he do his hunting closer to home. The compiler of *Þidreks saga* made certain that his readers would associate this passage with its source: the name Īron occurs in *Tristrams saga* immediately preceding the Hall of Statues episode, and both the wife and daughter of Jarl Īron bear the name Ísodd (also spelled Ísolld), as do two of Þidrek's wives. One of their sons is named Tristram.

In the fourteenth-century *Rémundar saga keisarasonar*, the Hall of Statues episode is skillfully integrated into the narrative. Rémundr falls in love with a maiden who appears to him in a dream. He secretly has a likeness of her set up. His father, the Emperor of Saxland, is offended when the statue does not reply to his greeting. One day, when Rémundr is kissing and caressing the statue, he is attacked by Eskupart, who claims to be the lover of the maiden. Rémundr kills him but receives a blow to the head that leaves a sword fragment embedded in it. Before Eskupart dies, he declares that the wound can be cured only by the most beautiful woman in the world. Rémundr sets out in a carriage in quest of healing. After many adventures, he is healed in India by Elína, his dream girl. Thus, the Hall of Statues episode precipitates a duel, which necessitates the quest for healing, which is telescoped with the bridal quest. *Tristrams saga* was presumably the major source of this story, and *Rémundar saga* in turn became the immediate source of numerous borrowings in later sagas.

Schlauch interpreted *Haralds saga Hringsbana* as a deliberate reply to the Tristan story. Haraldr is sent by his father, King Hringr of Denmark, to woo Signý of Constantinople for him. Signý, however, prefers Haraldr, who refuses to become a betrayer of his lord. When Signý begs Haraldr never to let her see King Hringr, he is so moved by pity and love that he finds a substitute bride, also named Signý, for his father. The old king is happy with his young bride, but when he learns of the deception, he attempts to kill his son, who is forced to commit patricide in self-defense. When Haraldr is attacked by a man who wishes to punish the crime, he kills his assailant but is wounded in such a way that he must undertake a quest for healing. In the older version of the saga, preserved only in *rímur*, Haraldr becomes king of Denmark and marries Signý. Hertryggr, Harald's friend, marries the young widow, and they become king and queen of Constantinople.

The fourteenth-century *Saga af Tristram ok Ísodd* (also known as *Tristrams saga ok Ísoddar*), on the other hand, is a deliberate travesty, a burlesque treatment of the story. Kalinke has characterized it as a humorous commentary on Arthurian romance in general. The author achieves his purpose by grotesquely distorting and exaggerating basic themes and motifs of *Tristrams saga*. When Blenziblý sees Kalegras kill her sweetheart in a joust, she has him summoned to her bower, where they remain for three years. The abduction episode, found only in the Thomas branch, contains a blind motif: before releasing Tristram on the shore of Cornwall, his abductors shave his head and rub tar into it. As in *Rémundar saga*, the hero must seek healing with a sword fragment embedded in his head. After drinking the love potion, Ísodd and Tristram tarry at sea for three months before proceeding to Cornwall. The behavior of characters is at times contradictory or incredible. Although Tristram is repeatedly urged to marry Ísodd, by the girl herself, by her mother, and by his uncle, who even offers him the kingdom to do so, he steadfastly refuses. (We have here a mingling of echoes from *Rémundar saga* and *Haralds saga*.) The vacillation of the king is also exaggerated. Immediately after declaring that Tristram visits Ísodd's bed merely to keep her innocently amused during his own absence, the king has the adulterous lovers banished to a cave, where he can closely monitor their words and deeds. The author directly reveals his parodic intent through the names of the two royal counselors: Kæi the Courteous and Dunce the Clever. He furthermore interjects comments about the ignorance and stupidity of the king and the inappropriateness of Kæi's epithet, since Kæi was, of course, the very embodiment of incivility in Arthurian romance.

The most obvious Tristan reminiscence in the *Íslendingasögur* is found in the *Spesar þáttr* in *Grettis saga* (first half of the fourteenth century). Grettir's slaying is avenged by his brother Þorsteinn in Constantinople. Here, Þorsteinn becomes involved with a prominent woman named Spes. Accused by her husband of infidelity, Spes agrees to a trial. On the way there, she is carried over a pool of water by Þorsteinn disguised as a beggar. He falls down with her on dry land, and his hand brushes her bare thigh. During the trial, she swears that she has never suffered defilement by any other man than her husband and the beggar who touched her thigh with his filthy hand. Through the support and gifts of her friends and kinsmen, she is awarded a divorce. The scene is clearly an adaptation of the ambiguous-oath episode in *Tristrams saga*. There are, in addition, significant verbal and phrasal similarities between the two sagas. In this case, the donor text is less coherent than the receiving one.

The work of this genre most frequently associated with *Tristrams saga* is *Kormáks saga*, the tragic biography of a lovelorn poet. The donor text here casts light on the garbled imitation. Einarsson relates Kormák's rescue of his beloved Steingerðr from her viking abductors to the harp-and-rote episode of the Tristan story, and in fact the severely abridged passage in *Kormáks saga* can be understood only by comparison with its source, which relates events unique to the Thomas branch of the story.

Influence of a less specific nature is more difficult to demonstrate. It is generally assumed that love triangles, such as the one in *Kormáks saga*, were inspired by the Tristan legend. Heroines who die of a broken heart, like Hrefna in *Laxdœla saga*, are often compared with Ísönd. The rhythmic style and the "statuesque" characters of *Laxdœla saga* are also reminiscent of the translated romances.

The most beautiful treatment of a Tristan theme in Old Norse literature is the Icelandic ballad "Tristrams kvæði" ("The Poem of Tristram"), composed ca. 1400. The mortally wounded hero longs for the arrival of Ísodd bjarta ("the fair"), who alone can save his life. The ship bearing his sweetheart is flying blue sails to indicate that she is on board. Three times, however, Tristram's wife, Ísodd svarta ("the dark"), declares: "Black are the sails on the ships." The poem ends with the entwining branches of trees that spring up from the lovers' graves. In one of the two recensions of the ballad, each stanza is followed by the melancholy refrain "For them, it was fated only to part." In the second version of the poem, this refrain has been replaced by "He is blissful who is lucky enough to fall asleep beside her." As Kalinke notes, this refrain mitigates the poem's somber tone and makes the image of the branching trees a stronger symbol of hope.

The intertwining of two plants as a symbol of the union of the two lovers is also the subject of the Norwegian prose lai of the honeysuckle known as *Geitarlauf* ("Goatleaf"). This translation of Marie de France's *Chevrefueil* is believed to have been made at the behest of King Hákon Hákonarson, perhaps by the translator of *Tristrams saga*. Just as the entwined hazel-tree and woodbine die when severed, so Tistram and the queen must perish when parted. This lai is characterized by an unusual subtlety of style, in which the careful choice of words and intertwining alliteration reflect the union of the plants and the lovers.

The Faroese "Tístrams táttur" is a poem of savage heroism. To prevent Sir Tístram from marrying Lady Ísin, his parents send him to the King of France with a letter instructing that he be put to death if he does not marry the king's daughter. Tístram refuses to be unfaithful to his beloved. When Ísin hears of his death, she devastates France and burns the king to death in his castle. She removes Tístram from the gallows and lays him on a green meadow. Then, like Ísönd in *Tristrams saga*, Ísodd fagra in the *Saga af Tristram*, and Ísodd bjarta in "Tristrams kvæði," Ísin dies of a broken heart. The only motivation for the killing of Tístram is the statement that his mother was "evil in counsel," which suggests the motif of the evil stepmother.

One of the two Danish Tristan ballads, "Tistram og Jomfru Isolt" (fifteenth century) shows points of similarity with "Tístrams táttur." The love triangle has been replaced by the incest motif. To avert the prophesied tragedy, the queen sends Isolt to the Emperor of Rome, who rears her as his own child. When the inevitable comes to pass, the empress poisons them, and Isolt dies in Tístram's arms. In a later version of this ballad, the incest motif is replaced by the evil stepmother, Grimoldt, who is forced to drink the poison by the two lovers. This version of the poem ends with Isolt sleeping in the hero's arms.

The other Danish ballad, "Tistram og Isold" (sixteenth–seventeenth century), is even more flippant. Lady Isold and Sir Tistram meet at night in a wood—in chastity and honor, the poet assures us. Upon her return to the castle, Isold is confronted by an angry husband. Her pert maid-in-waiting, however, who is a counterfeit of Bringvet, assuages his wrath and suspicion by assuring him that she and Isold spent the evening helping a woman in childbirth (an echo of the leechcraft theme). Golther was probably correct in interpreting this ballad as a composite reflection of the many clandestine meetings between the two lovers. The form of the heroine's name—Isall/Issalt in the manuscripts—suggests influence from the prose version of the *Tristrant* of Eilhart von Oberge, where the name is spelled Isalde.

The connections between the many versions of the Icelandic folktale about Tristram and Ísól (also spelled Ísódda) and the Norwegian and Icelandic sagas is even more tenuous. (*See* "Tristram og Ísól bjarta.") None of the five versions published in Árnason's *Íslenzkar þjóðsögur og æevintýri* is a self-contained story. Each contains motifs from the two sagas, but, like the ballads, they can be fully appreciated only by those who are well acquainted with the entire legend. Furthermore, some of their motifs are drawn from other legends and traditions.

Eilhart's *Tristrant* is the ultimate source of a later, independent version of the story. A Danish translation of the German prose version of this poem was published in 1857 but was probably known much earlier. The second Danish account, the eighteenth-century *En tragoedisk Historie om den ædle og tappre Tistrand* ("A Tragic Story of the Noble and Courageous Tistrand"), which also derives from Eilhart, retains the plot but changes almost all personal names and place-names. This Danish novel inspired the Icelandic *Rímur af Tistrani og Indiönu* (1831) by Sigurður Breiðfjörð. [PS]

Einarsson, Bjarni. *Skáldasögur. Um uppruna og eðli ástaskáldasagnanna fornu*. Reykjavík: Bókaútgáfa Menningarsjøðs, 1961.

Golther, Wolfgang. *Tristan und Isolde in den Dichtungen des Mittelalters und der neuen Zeit*. Leipzig: Hirzel, 1907.

Hill, Joyce, ed. *The Tristan Legend: Texts from Northern and Eastern Europe in Modern English Translation*. Leeds: University of Leeds, Graduate Centre for Medieval Studies, 1977.

Kalinke, Marianne E. *King Arthur, North-by-Northwest*. Copenhagen: Reitzel, 1981.

Leach, Henry Goddard. *Angevin Britain and Scandinavia*. Cambridge: Harvard University Press, 1921.

Schach, Paul. "Some Observations on the Influence of *Tristrams saga ok Ísöndar* on Old Icelandic Literature." In *Old Norse Literature and Mythology*, ed. Edgar C. Polomé. Austin: University of Texas Press, 1969, pp. 81–129.

———. "Tristan and Isolde in Scandinavian Ballad and Folktale." *Scandinavian Studies*, 36 (1964), 281–97.

Schlauch, Margaret. *Romance in Iceland*. Princeton, N.J.: Princeton University Press, 1934.

TRISTAN IN SPAIN AND PORTUGAL. The story of Tristan reached Spain from France, together with other Arthurian material, in the second half of the twelfth century. The Catalan troubadour Guiraut de Cabrera first mentioned tales of Arthur, Erec, Gawain, and Tristan and

Isolde ca. 1170. Scattered allusions persist in the works of other Catalan writers of the late twelfth century and throughout the thirteenth and probably reflect a continuing but limited interest in the Tristan legend. This interest increased markedly in the fourteenth and fifteenth centuries, as the French Prose *Tristan* was more widely circulated. Two manuscript fragments of Catalan translations of the Prose *Tristan* have survived. One from Arxiu d'Andorra (second half of the fourteenth century) describes Tristan's marriage to Isolde of the White Hands, his receipt of a letter from Isolde the Fair asking him to return to Cornwall, and his arrival there with Kaherdin. The second fragment (late fourteenth century) recounts the story of Tristan's birth.

In Castile, references to Tristan as well as to other Arthurian heroes appear predictably later than in Catalonia. Alfonso X the Wise, Castilian monarch from 1252 to 1284, mentioned Tristan, Arthur, and Merlin in his poetry written in Galician-Portuguese; there is also a late fourteenth-century Tristan fragment in Galician-Portuguese. As in Catalonia, however, interest was probably restricted to courtly and aristocratic circles until the fourteenth century, when Juan Ruiz, Archpriest of Hita, noted the currency of the popular Tristan legend (*Libro de buen amor*, "The Book of Good Love," 1703). Allusions to Tristan and Isolde in particular and Arthurian characters in general proliferate in Castilian texts of the late Middle Ages, especially in the works of court and church poets represented in the *Cancionero de Baena* (1445). A *romance*, or ballad, "Herido está don Tristán," based on the account of Tristan's death in the Prose *Tristan*, circulated at the court of Ferdinand and Isabella and survives in some ten or more texts in addition to fragments preserved in other sources.

Several medieval Spanish texts ultimately descend from the Prose *Tristan*: a late fourteenth-century Castilian fragment (one folio); a late fourteenth or early fifteenth-century Castilian and Aragonese manuscript, the *Cuento de Tristán de Leonís* ("The Story of Tristan of Leonis," 131 folios); a printed edition, the *Libro del esforçado cauallero don Tristán de Leonís y de sus grandes fechos an armas* ("The Story of the Valiant Knight Sir Tristan of Leonis and of His Great Feats of Arms"; Valladolid: Juan de Burgos, 1501); several subsequent imprints (1511, 1525, 1528) of the 1501 edition; and a 1534 imprint, the *Corónica nuevamente emendada y añadida del buen cavallero don Tristán de Leonís y del rey don Tristán de Leonís el joven su hijo* ("Newly Revised and Expanded Chronicle of the Great Knight Sir Tristan of Leonis and of His Son, King Tristan of Leonis, the Younger"), which reworks the earlier romance and appends a sequel, Book 2, that relates the adventures of Tristan and Yseo, offspring of the original lovers, after their parents' death. (The 1534 text was translated into Italian as *I due Tristani*, published in Venice in 1555.) Finally, there is the *Carta enviada por Hiseo la Brunda a Tristán; respuesta de Tristán* ("Isolde's Letter to Tristan; Tristan's Reply"), a sixteenth-century manuscript copy of a letter of complaint from Isolde the Fair after Tristan's marriage to Isolde of the White Hands and a response from Tristan defending his actions.

A disproportionate amount of Hispanic Tristan scholarship has focused on textual tradition. The marked verbal similarity of the single folio fragment and the 1501 and subsequent imprints clearly indicates that these texts represent the same manuscript tradition. The structural correspondence between these versions and the Castilian-Aragonese *Cuento*—despite an almost absolute lack of verbal coincidence—suggests that these texts represent two independent translations of a common archetype not written in Spanish and not based on any known version of the Prose *Tristan*. Since the Hispanic romances and the Italian *Tristano Riccardiano* and *Tavola Ritonda* share certain important features not found in extant Old French versions of the Prose *Tristan*, an Italian source for the Spanish translations has been proposed; more recent research has suggested a lost French or Catalan intermediary.

The question of source is important in establishing historical connections between the peninsular derivations and the Old French archetypes, in editing the Tristan texts, and in interpreting historical, cultural, artistic, or ideological differences between the translations and the French originals. It has, however, unnecessarily sidetracked attention away from critical readings of the peninsular versions, which span a period of more than 150 years. Preliminary research suggests that the Hispanic Tristan romance was remarkably susceptible to reworking and reinterpretation in accordance with prevailing political values or literary tastes. For example, while the *Cuento de Tristán* retains the ambiguous realistic depiction of knighthood of the Prose *Tristan*, the 1501 *Libro* presents a serious and expurgated view of the courtly-chivalric way of life reflecting and propagating the prochivalric ethos of Isabelline Castile. The 1534 edition and sequel introduce a new chivalric ideal, the *miles christianus* (somewhat akin to the Esplandián figure in the *Amadís* cycle) and purports to influence or correct the political program of Charles V. Authors of sentimental romances of the fifteenth century both influenced and were influenced by the story of Tristan and Isolde. The capacity of the Tristan romance for reinterpretation in the Spanish texts and the ongoing renewal of its significance illustrates, and explains, the pervasiveness and continuity of the Tristan myth on the Iberian peninsula. (*See also* SPANISH AND PORTUGUESE ARTHURIAN LITERATURE.) [DS-N]

Corónica nueuamente emendada y añadida del buen cauallero don Tristán de Leonís y del rey don Tristán de Leonís, el jouen su hijo. Seville: Domenico de Robertis, 1534.

Bonilla y San Martín, Adolfo, ed. *Libro del esforçado cauallero don Tristán de Leonís y de sus grandes fechos an armas (Valladolid, 1501)*. Madrid: Sociedad de Bibliófilos Madrileños, 1912.

Northrup, George Tyler, ed. *Cuento de Tristán de Leonís*. Chicago: University of Chicago Press, 1928.

Eisele, Gillian. "A Comparison of Early Printed Tristan Texts in Sixteenth-Century Spain." *Zeitschrift für romanische Philologie*, 97 (1981), 370–82.

Hall, J.B. "A Process of Adaptation: The Spanish Versions of the Romance of Tristan." In *The Legend of Arthur in the Middle Ages: Studies Presented to A.H. Diverres by Colleagues, Pupils, and Friends*, ed. P.B. Grout et al. Cambridge: Brewer, 1983, pp. 76–85, 235–37.

Seidenspinner-Núñez, Dayle. "The Sense of an Ending: The Tristan Romance in Spain." *Tristania*, 7 (1981–82), 27–46.

Sharrer, Harvey L. "Malory and the Spanish and Italian Tristan Texts: The Search for the Missing Link." *Tristania*, 4 (1978–79), 37–43.

TRISTAN STONE, a monolith, some seven feet tall, located near Fowey in Cornwall. A Latin inscription on the stone (which probably dates from the sixth century) indicates that this is the grave-marker of one Drustanus, son of Cunomorus. The name *Drustanus* is the equivalent of Tristan, and the stone is taken in popular lore as the gravestone for Isolde's lover. If Cunomorus (or Cynvawr) is Mark—as he is reputed to be in Wrmonoc's Life of Paul Aurelian—the poets made a significant change in identifying him as Tristan's uncle, rather than his father. In any event, we have no proof that the Tristan named on the stone corresponds to the Tristan of romance. (*See also* CASTLE DORE.) [NJL]

Ashe, Geoffrey. *A Guidebook to Arthurian Britain*. Wellingborough: Aquarian, 1983, pp. 105–07.

***TRISTANO PANCIATICCHIANO*,** named for the manuscript that preserves it (the Codice Panciatichiano 33, Florence) and described by Gardner as an "Arthurian medley," is an eclectic romance of the early fourteenth century based on the same "unorthodox" French redaction as the *Tristano Riccardiano* until Tristano departs for Little Britain; thereupon, it turns to a source much like the one Malory used for his version of the Tristan story, except that, owing either to an authorial decision or to a lacuna in the original, all of the adventures in the Forest Perilous are eliminated; when Tristano leaves Little Britain, he arrives in Cornwall without delay. The five sections of the "medley" recount with relative brevity the Grail quest, the birth of Tristano and his life until Isotta receives the false report of his death, a portion of *Mort Artu*, the adventures of Tristano leading up to the Tournament at Lonezep (Verzeppe) and the adventures of Palamides in the Red City, and the death of Tristano and Isotta (which Parodi has edited to provide a conclusion to the incomplete *Tristano Riccardiano*). The *Panciaticchiano* account of the death of Tristano is remarkable for the detail and sentiment of its treatment of the dual demise of the lovers and the spectacular tomb, richer than that of Galeotto (Galehaut), prepared for them by Marco. The lovers are interred richly but, apparently, permanently, since the text provides no hint of the symbolic vines rooted in the hearts of the lovers. [DLH]

Parodi, E.G., ed. *Il Tristano Riccardiano*. Bologna: Romagnoli, 1896.

Gardner, Edmund G. *The Arthurian Legend in Italian Literature*. London: Dent, 1930, pp. 114–20.

***TRISTANO RICCARDIANO*,** composed after Rusticiano's *Compilation* (later than 1272) but before 1300, is the earliest Arthurian romance in Italian. Preserved in the Codice Riccardiano 2543 and considered a "magnificent fragment" by Gardner, it is a derivative of the French archetype of the Hispanic Tristans. The narrative begins with an account of the three sons of Filicie (Meliadus, the brother rather than the brother-in-law of Marco, the second son of Filicie, and the third son, Pernam). Marco treacherously murders Pernam and is condemned by Meliadus, who in his own kingdom marries Eliabel, who gives birth to Tristano in a forest, where she has gone to seek her husband, who has been led away by an enchantress. She dies in childbirth, and the life of Tristano follows its usual course, with a few variations in the order of incidents and the names of characters. Although the prose tradition is generally held to develop an interest in Tristan's chivalry at the expense of his love, the *Tristano Riccardiano* seems to exaggerate this tendency. Nearly half of the romance as it is preserved concerns Tristano's marriage and his adventures in Little Britain. While the desire to see Isotta once again motivates his decision to return to Cornwall, it is his adventures in the desert of Nerlantes and his rescue of Arthur from enchantment that claim the author's attention. It is a bibliographical accident that the concluding pages of the *Tristano Riccardiano* have been lost, but it is true to the spirit of this redaction that the hero is last seen in an (original) encounter with Pressivalle lo Gallese at the Fountain of Adventure and never actually completes his journey to the perpetually anticipating Isotta. [DLH]

Parodi, E.G., ed. *Il Tristano Riccardiano*. Bologna: Romagnoli, 1896.

Gardner, Edmund G. *The Arthurian Legend in Italian Literature*. London: Dent, 1930, pp. 68–84.

***TRISTANO VENETO*.** Preserved in a late fifteenth-century manuscript in Vienna (Palatine 3325), the *Tristano Veneto* is a faithful fourteenth-century translation in Venetian dialect of the Old French Prose *Tristan*, which also follows the versions of certain episodes found in the *Tristano Riccardiano* and in the *Compilation* of Rusticiano da Pisa. Although interesting for its combination of various redactions, the *Tristano Veneto* has been studied primarily for its importance to research in Italian dialectology and linguistics. [CK]

Arese, Felice, ed. *Prose di romanzi: Il romanzo cortese in Italia nei secoli XIII e XIV.* Turin: UTET, 1950, pp. 261–75.

Parodi, E.G., ed. "Dal *Tristano Veneto*." In *Nozze Cian—Sappa-Flandinet*. Bergamo, 1894, pp. 105–29.

Gardner, Edmund G. *The Arthurian Legend in Italian Literature.* London: Dent, 1930, p. 265.

"TRISTRAM OG ÍSÓL BJARTA." The Tristan matter was known in Iceland primarily through the Norwegian translation of Thomas d'Angleterre's *Tristan* (*Tristrams saga ok Ísöndar*) and a parodistic Icelandic version of the Tristan legend (*Saga af Tristram ok Ísodd*). There exist also several versions of a folktale about the lovers that has only a tenuous affinity to the classic medieval romance. Five versions of the folktale—each with a different title—have been published: "Sagan af Fertram og Ísól bjarta," "Sagan af Tístram og Ísól björtu," "Tristram og Ísól bjarta," "Sagan af Tristram og Ísoddu," and "Sagan af Helgu kóngsdóttur." The folktales have a number of distinguishing motifs that place them in the category of the Wicked Stepmother tale. The infant Tristram (or Ísól) floats in a chest onto the shores of a foreign kingdom; the royal couple already have a child (Tristram or Ísól) and adopt the foundling; Tristram and Ísól are reared together; the queen dies and the king marries again; the wicked stepmother throws Ísól into a ditch in the woods intending for her to die; the stepmother's own daughter impersonates Ísól and is to marry Tristram; she is pregnant by a thrall and to avoid detection on the nuptial night she exchanges roles with a peasant girl who is the real Ísól; Tristram learns of the impersonation and the true identity of the peasant girl. The folktales end on a happy note with the wedding of Tristram and Ísól. [MEK]

Árnason, Jón. *Íslenzkar þjóðsögur og ævintýri*, 2nd ed. Árni Böðvarsson and Bjarni Vilhjálmsson. Reykjavik: Bókaútgáfan þjóðsaga, 1954, 1956, Vol. 2, pp. 308–17; Vol. 4, pp. 486–95.

Schach, Paul. "Tristan and Isolde in Scandinavian Ballad and Folktale." *Scandinavian Studies*, 36 (1964), 281–97.

Sveinsson, Einar Ól. *Verzeichnis isländischer Märchenvarianten mit einer einleitenden Untersuchung.* Helsinki: Suomalainen Tiedeakatemia, Academia Scientiarum Fennica, 1929, pp. 126–30.

"TRISTRAMS KVÆÐI" ("The Poem of Tristram"), an Icelandic ballad of uncertain date, but most probably from the beginning of the fifteenth century. The ballad is extant in four redactions of unequal length, the longest of which contains thirty-two stanzas. The stanzas are a variant of the quatrain with only two stresses in the second and fourth lines. "Tristrams kvæði" derives ultimately from *Tristrams saga ok Ísöndar*, the early thirteenth-century Norwegian translation of Thomas d'Angleterre's *Tristan*. Certain correspondences between "Tristrams kvæði" and the later Icelandic *Saga af Tristram ok Ísodd*, which presumably derives from the Norwegian translation but possibly also from oral tradition and is dated ca. 1400, suggest that the ballad either postdates the Icelandic saga and borrowed from it or that the ballad antedates the saga, in which case the saga author was influenced by the ballad, which would then be older than any other extant Icelandic ballad.

"Tristrams kvæði" focuses on the events from the wounding of Tristram to his death. The female antagonists are contrasted through the use of the epithets "fair" and "dark" (Ísodd bjarta, Ísodd svarta). Three of the four redactions are punctuated by the ominous refrain "þeim var ekki skapað nema að skilja" ("For them, it was fated only to part"), whereas one redaction contains the more optimistic refrain "Og er sá sæll, sem sofna náir henni" ("He is blissful who is lucky enough to fall asleep beside her"), which presumably alludes to the eventual union of Tristram and Ísodd in death. Despite their being buried on either side of the church, their union is represented symbolically by the intertwining branches of the two trees that grow from their graves. [MEK]

Helgason, Jón, ed. *Íslenzk fornkvæði. Islandske folkeviser.* Copenhagen: Munksgaard, 1962, 1963, 1965, Vol. 1, pp. 137–43; Vol. 3, pp. 198–201; Vol. 4, pp. 221–26; Vol. 5, pp. 22–25.

Hill, Joyce. "The Icelandic Ballad of Tristan." In *The Tristan Legend: Texts from Northern and Eastern Europe in Modern English Translation.* Leeds: University of Leeds, Graduate Centre for Medieval Studies, 1977, pp. 29–38.

Ólason, Vésteinn. *The Traditional Ballads of Iceland: Historical Studies.* Reykjavik: Stofnun Árna Magnússonar, 1982, pp. 213–20.

Schach, Paul. "Tristan and Isolde in Scandinavian Ballad and Folktale." *Scandinavian Studies*, 36 (1964), 281–97.

TRISTRAMS SAGA OK ÍSÖNDAR is of great importance not only for students of Icelandic and Norwegian literature but also for those who want to understand the history of the Tristan material in Europe, because the saga is the sole complete representative of the Thomas d'Angleterre branch of the romance. The preface of the saga states that Brother Robert translated it in 1226 at the instigation of

King Hákon Hákonarson (r. 1217–63). On the basis of this date, many scholars assume that it was the first French romance to be translated into a Scandinavian language. Because there was no tradition of longer verse narrative in Norwegian vernacular literature, the translation of Thomas's romance into Norwegian required the development of a suitable prose style. The result is the so-called "court style," which takes many features from earlier religious literature. Its characteristics are shared by many of the translated romances, and include frequent use of the present participle, alliteration, and amplification.

Comparison of Thomas's and Gottfried's incomplete versions shows that Robert neither leaves out episodes nor changes their order. However, the intense psychological interest and introspective passages in Thomas are shortened dramatically; the scene in which Tristan contemplates marriage covers 368 lines of verse in Thomas's version, but only eight lines of prose in *Tristrams saga*. It is assumed that Robert consciously deleted material that would have been unpalatable to an audience unfamiliar with romantic literature. Certain changes in Robert's text tend to make the characters more sympathetic. For example, the unseemly accusations that Isolt and Brengvein fling at each other (ll. 1–344 in the Douce fragment of Thomas) are greatly reduced in the saga. There are several brief additions in the saga, including a short prayer that Ísönd piously utters before her death.

Although *Tristrams saga ok Ísöndar* was translated for a Norwegian king, all existing manuscripts are from Iceland, which attests the popularity of the saga in that country. There are numerous borrowings from the Tristan material, including the *Saga af Tristram ok Ísodd*, several ballads, and episodes in native romances and family sagas. [MCH]

Kölbing, Eugen, ed. *Tristrams saga ok Ísöndar. Mit einer literaturhistorischen Einleitung*. Heilbronn: Gebrüder Henninger, 1878; repr. Hildesheim: Olms, 1978.

Schach, Paul, trans. *The Saga of Tristram and Ísönd*. Lincoln: University of Nebraska Press, 1973.

———. "The Style and Structure of Tristrams saga." In *Scandinavian Studies: Essays Presented to Dr. Henry Goddard Leach on the Occasion of His Eighty-fifth Birthday*, ed. Carl F. Bayerschmidt and Erik J. Friis. Seattle: University of Washington Press for the American-Scandinavian Foundation, 1965, pp. 63–86.

TRISTRANT UND ISALDE, a German prose version of Eilhart von Oberge's *Tristrant*. The oldest extant incunabulum of this chapbook, the full title of which is *Ein wunderbarliche vnd fast lustige Historij von Herrn Tristrant vnd der schönen Isalden* ("A Marvelous and Quite Pleasing Tale of Sir Tristrant and Beautiful Isalde"), was printed in Augsburg in 1484. The text was reprinted fifteen times between 1484 and 1664, and there exist seven modern printings or editions, the most recent dating from 1966. In general, the anonymous author of the chapbook is faithful to his medieval source, but there are explanatory or didactic intercalations, and occasionally Eilhart's vivid vocabulary and imagery are toned down. The author of the chapbook also tended to substitute indigenous German vocabulary for French loan words and modern equivalents for words perceived to be outdated. [MEK]

Brandstetter, Alois, ed. *Tristrant und Isalde: Prosaroman*. Tübingen: Niemeyer, 1966.

———. *Prosa Auflösung: Studien zur Rezeption der höfischen Epik im frühneuhochdeutschen Prosaroman*. Frankfurt: Athenäum, 1971.

Melzer, Helmut. *Trivialisierungstendenzen im Volksbuch: Ein Vergleich der Volksbücher "Tristrant und Isalde," "Wigoleis" und "Wilhelm von Österreich" mit den mittelhochdeutschen Epen*. Hildesheim: Olms, 1972.

TROUBADOURS. The troubadours, who in the twelfth and thirteenth centuries used the Occitan, or Provençal, language to write lyric poetry in what is now southern France and adjoining territories, prove the early and broad dissemination of Arthurian themes. The troubadours referred to the stories surrounding Arthur and Tristan even before the known French references and works began shortly after 1150. By the time of Chrétien de Troyes, a generation of troubadours had been familiar with oral and possibly written versions of the Matter of Britain; it even seems likely that the "Bréri" cited by Thomas d'Angleterre as a source told tales of Tristan at the court of Poitiers. Such southern precociousness should not surprise us, given that by the early twelfth century Arthurian stories penetrated as far as northern Italy, as shown in personal names as well as on the archivolt of Modena.

In what is probably the first known Occitan reference to Tristan and Isolde, Cercamon (fl. 1137–48) refers to *lo cor tristan* ("the heart of Tristan") in "Ab lo pascor," line 38, apparently meaning "a heart like Tristan's" or "Tristan's feelings." Although this reading has been much debated, and some critics take *tristan* as the only known occurrence of an adjective meaning "sad," the fact that the passage concerns a lady "who sleeps with two or three" makes it hard not to see a reference, even if only by pun, to Isolde.

Somewhat later, Bernart de Ventadorn (fl. 1147–80) writes, "I endure greater suffering from love than Tristan the amorous, who suffered many pains for Iseut the Blonde" ("Tant ai mo cor," ll. 45–48). In addition, four of Bernart's poems use Tristan as a *senhal* (secret name for a lady, a friend, or a patron). Some scholars believe that this *senhal* designates Raimbaut d'Aurenga, who himself, ca. 1169, refers to the love potion, an unworn shirt given Tristan by Isolde, and Isolde's making her husband believe "that no man born of a woman had ever touched her" ("Non chant," ll. 27–47).

In all, the troubadours name Tristan twenty-seven times and use the name six times as a *senhal*; they name Isolde twelve times, some in the same passages as Tristan, plus, once each, Brangien and Lamorat, a hero of the Prose *Tristan*. (These data follow Chambers.) In addition, we find other echoes, as in the medieval biography of Guilhem de Cabestanh, where the unfortunate lovers are, like Tristan and Isolde, united in the tomb.

Arthur, not being associated with the troubadours' prime subject, love, receives less attention, with sixteen references. In the first known of these, Marcabru says, "I shall henceforth be lost like Arthur" ("Al prim comens," version of MS *A*, l. 60); since this reference probably dates from 1137, it is tempting to connect it to the success of Geoffrey of Monmouth's *Historia*, completed ca. 1136. Typically, the troubadours use Arthur as a measure of nobility ("Neither Charlemagne nor Arthur was worth more," in Gaucelm Faidit's "Fortz chausa es," l. 16) or of antiquity ("Never in the time of Arthur or now," beginning a *tenso*, or debate, between Aimeric de Peguilhan and Sordel). In general, they depict Arthur as both more courageous and more courtly than does French literature. They also frequently evoke, often as a comparison to the lover's unfulfilled hope, "the hope of the Bretons" that Arthur would eventually return to his people.

Other Arthurian references comprise twelve to Gawain, four to Gawain and to Erec and/or Enide, three to Merlin, two to Lancelot and Yvain, and one to Kay and to Estout de Vertfolh, a character in *Jaufré*. Usually, like Arthur himself, they exemplify a given quality, though not always those qualities brought out by other sources, like Chrétien: bravery, amorousness, sorcery. Thus, "Gawain was not more valiant in arms, nor did Yvain know more of courtliness, nor did Tristan undergo so many trials of love" (Aimeric de Peguilhan, fl. 1195–1230, "Era par ben," ll. 14–16). Other times, we find more developed descriptions: "Just as Perceval, in the time when he was alive, become so enraptured gazing that he never was able to ask what was the use of the Lance and the Grail . . ." (Rigaut de Berbezilh, fl. 1140–63 or 1170–1210, "Atressi com Persavaus," ll. 1–6). There are also references to places of Arthurian resonance, such as the forest of Brocéliande and Arthur's castle of Cardolh (Carlisle); these come in the context of frequent evocations of the Breton language, customs, music, geography, and historical figures.

87. John Rylands University Library, MS 1, fol. 255v: Arthur Tarries at the Castle of Dover After Sending the Body of Gauvain to Camelot and Before Going to Fight Mordred. (Courtesy John Rylands University Library.)

There are Arthurian references in several *ensenhamens*, or didactic poems, which list literary, legendary, and historical characters, works, and authors that good jongleurs were said to be expected to have in their repertory. Guiraut de Cabreira's "Cabra joglar" testifies that the names of Arthur, Cardolh, Erec, Gawain, Tristan, Isolde, and (probably) Mark were familiar in Catalonia already ca. 1160. Shortly after 1200, Guiraut de Calanso's "Fadet joglar" mentions Lancelot and Marescot, a knight in *Les Merveilles de Rigomer*. And ca. 1240, the "Gordo" of Bertran de Paris de Roergue names Arthur, Tristan, Mark, Yvain, and Merlin.

Arthurian characters are mentioned in some ten other nonlyric works, such as Peire de Corbian's *Thezaur* (ca. 1250) and Arnaut Guilhem de Marsan's *ensenhamen* (ca. 1170), which refers to the French *Lai d'Ignaure*, the name of whose hero, under the form Linhaura, Gaucelm Faidit and Guiraut de Bornelh use, also ca. 1170, to designate Raimbaut d'Aurenga. Even more notably, the works recited at the heroine's wedding in the non-Arthurian thirteenth-century romance *Flamenca* include the *Lai de Cabrefoil* ("Lay of the Honeysuckle," a possible reference to Marie de France), a *Lai de Tristan*, and "the one that Yvain made" (ll. 600–03); and other jongleurs go on to tell a whole series of Arthurian tales evidently derived from Chrétien and related sources (ll. 662–92).

Lejeune points out that the troubadours make many more references to Arthurian characters than do the trouvères. She and some others believe that a number of Occitan Arthurian romances were lost, alongside the surviving texts, which are *Jaufré*, the marginally Arthurian *Blandín de Cornualla*, and two fragments of a Provençal translation of the Vulgate *Merlin*. Evidence for this belief includes Torquato Tasso's unsupported statement that the troubadour Arnaut Daniel (fl. 1180–1210) wrote of Lancelot, details and episodes mentioned by the troubadours that do not seem to correspond to any other known source, and tantalizing references to lost romances and unknown characters.

In the first half of the twelfth century, then, Arthurian motifs, spreading probably from the courts of Poitiers and Barcelona, gained vernacular expression in the South before reaching the North. Then, as if in return for the concept of courtly love, which did not appear in French literature until Chrétien's two troubadour-inspired lyric poems, the South took back a plenitude of references to the characters universalized by Chrétien's romances. It is likely that Eleanor of Aquitaine (1122–1204) and her two royal families (particularly her daughter Marie de Champagne, Chrétien's patroness) did much for this literary exchange. In the thirteenth century, the chief purveyor of Arthurian themes to the South became the French prose romances, along with any lost Occitan Arthurian romances at whose existence we can only guess. Even poets of the fourteenth-century "decadence," such as Raimon de Cornet and Peire de Ladils, helped keep Arthurian traditions alive; and, as if to usher in the Renaissance, a play was put on in Avignon in 1481 concerning *The Triumph of King Arthur.*

In sum, though the troubadours did not elaborate on the Arthurian material that they inherited, they were perhaps unequaled in exploiting its poetic value. A familiar Arthurian name, with or without a line or two of development, served to evoke, often by comparison, a whole courtly world and ethos, in which the troubadours liked to imagine themselves—and in the love lyric their ladies—as participants. [NS]

Anglade, Joseph. *Les Troubadours et les Bretons.* Montpellier: Société des Langues Romanes, 1929.

Chambers, Frank M. *Proper Names in the Lyrics of the Troubadours.* Chapel Hill: University of North Carolina Press, 1971.

Lejeune, Rita. "The Troubadours." In *Arthurian Literature in the Middle Ages*, ed. Roger Sherman Loomis. Oxford: Clarendon, 1959, pp. 393–99.

Pirot, François. *Recherches sur les connaissances littéraires des troubadours occitans et catalans des XIIe et XIIIe siècles: les "sirventes-ensenhamens" de Guerau de Cabrera, Guiraut de Calanson et Bertrand de Paris.* Barcelona: Real Academia de Buenas Letras, 1972, pp. 435–525.

TRYST BENEATH THE TREE (or beneath the pine), a motif first presented in Béroul's *Tristran* and destined to be depicted innumerable times in various artistic media. The tryst, which opens Béroul's fragmentary text, is between Tristran and Iseut, who have a rendezvous under a tree in which her husband, King Mark, is hiding to entrap them. Seeing his reflection in a fountain, the lovers dramatically proclaim their innocence and thus convince Mark that his suspicions are baseless.

Both because the scene was vivid and dramatic and because visually it was adaptable to many surfaces and shapes, the tryst motif was popular with medieval artists, who repeatedly painted, embroidered, or carved it. It was depicted in several manuscript miniatures and in the murals of the château of St. Floret, on English misericords, on corbels (one from the palace of Jacques Coeur in Bourges, one formerly on the façade of the town hall in Bruges), on ivory caskets, on mirror-backs, on cups, and on other objects. In at least one instance, a manuscript presents a miniature of the scene and then moralizes it, with Mark representing the Father who sees all (*see* CY NOUS DIT). [NJL]

TUCKER, IRWIN ST. JOHN (1886–?), American author of such works as *Poems of a Socialist Priest* and *The Sangreal* (1919), a four-act play in blank verse. The play reshapes the traditional accounts of the Grail quest and death of Arthur to condemn hypocrisy and divisions between class and nation. Galahad succeeds Arthur, who falls in battle against the rebellious Lancelot, and, with the blessing of the Holy Grail, he promises a new age in which "all the hosts of men shall dwell in peace." [RHT]

Tucker, Irwin St. John. *The Sangreal.* Chicago: Published by the author, 1919.

TUMIATI, DOMENICO (1874–1943), composed two dramas on Arthurian subjects, *La Regina Ginevra* and *Merlino e Viviana*, that revive the legends with a passion and style derived from Gabriele d'Annunzio. [DLH]

Tumiati, Domenico. *La Regina Ginevra.* Milan: Società Editrice Unitas, 1925.

———. *Merlino e Viviana.* Milan: Fratelli Treves, 1927.

TURKE AND GOWIN, THE (ca. 1500), has been preserved, together with three other Gawain stories (*The Carle off Carlile*, *The Grene Knight*, and *The Marriage of Sir Gawain*), in the Percy Folio (ca. 1660), a collection of (near) contemporary verse and late and much-debased versions of medieval romances. The poem as we have it numbers 335 lines, but about half of it is lost because halves of pages were torn out and used to light the fire by the maids of a one-time owner. Some guesswork is necessary for the interpretation of the text. It combines the challenge and beheading plot of *Sir Gawain and the Green Knight* with that of a series of three tests in the land of giants. The character of the Turk is as dualistic as the plot, for at Arthur's court he behaves like the traditional fierce challenger, whereas he metamorphoses into the helpful fairy once Gawain has to face the contests with the giants of the King of Man. In the end, the two plots come together when Gawain by decapitating the Turk lifts the spell on the enchanted Sir Gromer, who is subsequently made King of Man (this ending is similar to that of *The Carle off Carlile*). The only parallel to the testing episode is in the Old French *Pèlerinage de Charlemagne* (twelfth century), which agrees in the presence of a spherical object (a brass tennis ball and a *pelotte*), in the cauldron of molten lead, in the vanishing garment, and in the assisting figure. As it is unlikely that the *Pèlerinage* served as a direct source for *The Turke*, both the Charlemagne and the Arthurian romances may go back to a story, now lost, about a king who pays a visit to the court of a rival, situated in the otherworld. [ESK]

Madden, Frederic, ed. *Syr Gawayne*. London: Bannatyne Club, 1839.

TURNBULL, E(LEANOR) LUCIA, and H(AROLD GEORGE) DALWAY TURNBULL, authors of English textbooks, supplement prosaic dialogue with song and historical costume in *Through the Gates of Remembrance* (1933), three playlets for the schoolroom on the theme of Glastonbury. The first shows the founding of the Abbey; the second, *The Return of Arthur*, depicts the desecration of Arthur's grave, for though King Henry II protests that he acts for England's unity, the Abbot predicts doom; the prophecy is fulfilled with the spoliation of Glastonbury in the final episode. [CNS]

Turnbull, E. Lucia, and H. Dalway Turnbull. *Through the Gates of Remembrance*. London: Nelson, 1933.

TURNER, ROY, author of *King of the Lordless Country* (1971). This historical romance is an involving, if improbable, account of Arthur's rise to power, culminating in his victory at Badon. Bedwyr relates how he and Arthur are recruited into the Circle, a band of warriors led by Gwenhwyfar and dedicated to noble ideals. [RHT]

Turner, Roy. *King of the Lordless Country*. London: Dobson, 1971.

TURTON, GODFREY E., contemporary English lexicographer and author of *The Emperor Arthur* (1967), a historical novel narrated by Pelleas as a nostalgic retrospective. The characters are Romanized Celts, and the story employs a pronounced pagan-Christian opposition: even the Grail quest is depicted as a Church-fomented plot. The traditional story of Pelleas and Ettard is woven in among the series of conspiracies that form most of the action. [AAR]

Turton, Godfrey E. *The Emperor Arthur*. New York: Doubleday, 1967.

TWAIN, MARK (pseudonym of Samuel Langhorne Clemens; 1835–1910), apparently first encountered Arthurian legend when some member of his household purchased Sidney Lanier's *The Boy's King Arthur* in 1880, and he at least dipped into Malory in 1884 during a reading tour with George C. Cable. He started work in earnest on what was to become *A Connecticut Yankee in King Arthur's Court* in the winter of 1884/5, but he put it aside before finishing it in a creative burst in time for publication on December 10, 1889. The attractive illustrations were the work of Daniel Beard, who collaborated closely with the author. Initial sales were disappointing, but the novel soon established itself and has retained its popularity. It has been made into a film several times and turned into a musical comedy by Richard Rodgers and Lorenz Hart.

The novel is a characteristic Twainian amalgam of fantasy and fun, observation and satire, that both amuses and provokes reflection as it confronts the customs of olden times with the brash values of the New World. Hank Morgan travels back in time to the days of King Arthur, and he uses his technological expertise to gain power. He humorously exposes the follies and ignorance of medieval society and the exaggerations of the world of romance. However, we gradually discover that his own values are no better. Despite his professed concern for the rights of the individual, Hank is prepared to further his own interests with a callous disregard for human life and dignity. When he uses electric wire and gatling machine guns to slaughter his enemies in their thousands, he reveals that technological progress has not changed humanity's destructive nature.

Yet despite the satire against the ignorance and cruelty of both medieval and modern society, and the comedy aimed at the exaggerations of the world of romance, there remain in the novel an underlying admiration and an affection for Arthurian legend itself, witnessed in the generosity and heroism of Lancelot and Arthur. [CNS/RHT]

Twain, Mark. *A Connecticut Yankee in King Arthur's Court*. New York: Webster, 1889.
Gerber, John. *Mark Twain*. Boston: Twayne, 1988.
Knight, Stephen. *Arthurian Literature and Society*. New York: St. Martins, 1983.

TYOLET, an anonymous Old French lai from the end of the twelfth century that imitates, in the first part, the story of Perceval's childhood from Chrétien's romance, with supernatural additions characteristic of the lai. In the second part, probably the original lai, Tyolet succeeds in cutting off the white foot of a stag for the daughter of the King of Logres—this where others had failed. He is, however, attacked by lions and left for dead. Gauvain finds Tyolet and foils a false knight who claimed that he had achieved that white-foot quest. Tyolet marries the princess.

The white-foot episode occurs elsewhere, notably in the Second Continuation of the *Perceval*, the Didot-*Perceval*, the Welsh *Peredur*, and the Middle Dutch *Lanseloet en het hert met de witte voet*. The author of *Tyolet* seems to have known Marie de France's *Lanval*. [KB]

Tobin, Prudence Mary O'Hara, ed. *Les Lais anonymes bretons*. Geneva: Droz, 1976.

UHLAND, LUDWIG (1787–1862), a popular German poet of the so-called "Swabian" school of later Romanticism. He is known for his interest in folk literature and for the lyricism of his own folk ballads, many of which were set to music by such composers as Schubert, Schumann, Liszt, and Brahms. The important role of nature in his poetry is reflected in *Merlin der Wilde* ("Merlin the Wild Man," 1829; published 1831), which relates the essentially non-Arthurian tradition of Merlin from Geoffrey's *Vita Merlini*. A depressed Merlin, King of Demetia, wishes to return to his forest retreat but is detained by King Roderick, his twin sister's husband. Merlin exchanges a prophecy about the infidelity of his sister for permission to leave. She discredits the prophecy, but Merlin is still allowed to return to his beloved forest, the source of his strength and insight. [RWK]

Uhland, Ludwig. *Werke*, ed. Hans-Rüdiger Schwab. Frankfurt: Insel, 1983, Vol. 1.

Weiss, Adelaide Marie. "Ludwig Uhland." In *Merlin in German Literature*. Washington, D.C.: Catholic University of America Press, 1933, pp. 94–104.

ULRICH VON TÜRHEIM. In line 26 of his *Tristan*, written ca. 1235, Ulrich von Türheim informs us that a certain "Kuonrât der schenke von Wintersteten" asked him to write a conclusion to Gottfried von Strassburg's unfinished *Tristan*. In the prologue to his continuation, Ulrich praises Gottfried's literary art and laments the fact that the great master had been snatched from life so prematurely. Ulrich's *Tristan*, a work of some 3,700 lines, picks up the tale with Tristan's decision to marry the other Ŷsôt. Ulrich's continuation is greatly indebted to Eilhart von Oberge's *Tristrant*, from which he borrows, for example, the magic-pillow episode and Tristan's sojourn as fool at Mark's court. Compared with the work of the more gifted Heinrich von Freiberg, who also wrote a continuation of Gottfried's *Tristan*, Ulrich's effort is pedestrian and uninspired. [MEK]

Ulrich von Türheim. *Tristan*, ed. Thomas Kerth. Tübingen: Niemeyer, 1979.

Kerth, Thomas. "The Denouement of the Tristan-*Minne*: Türheim's Dilemma." *Neophilologus*, 65 (1981), 79–93.

ULRICH VON ZATZIKHOVEN, identified by many scholars with the "capellanus Uolricus de Cecinchoven plebanus Loumeissae," a cleric named as a witness on a document of 1214 from Lommis near Zezikon (= Zatzikhoven) in Switzerland. He is known to have composed only one work, the Middle High German *Lanzelet*. Ulrich claims that his source was "ein welschez buoch" that had been brought to Germany by Huc (Hugo) von Morville, one of the nobles who remained as hostage at the court of the emperor Henry VI after Richard the Lionhearted returned to England in 1194. One assumes therefore that *Lanzelet* was composed sometime after 1194, but not later than 1205, and that it is based on a lost French or, more likely, Anglo-Norman source.

Like most Arthurian romances, *Lanzelet* (some 9,400 lines of verse) is composed of a series of more or less independent episodes, which in this case fall into three occasionally overlapping categories. The work begins when Lanzelet's father is overthrown by his vassals and the infant hero is abducted by a water-fay queen. He grows up in her magical kingdom, ignorant of his name and ancestry; he will learn these, he is told, only when he defeats Iweret, the best knight alive. After a series of unrelated adventures, Lanzelet does kill Iweret, thereby winning the hand of his daughter, Iblis, and the kingdom of Dodone; soon after, a messenger appears and reveals Lanzelet's name. Falling at the center of the work, these episodes are by far its most elaborate. In the last two episodes, after a second series of unrelated adventures, Lanzelet finally claims his father's throne and then returns with Iblis to take possession of Dodone. Thus, the beginning, middle, and end of the work constitute a single group of episodes distinguished by a single constellation of interwoven themes: exile and return; loss and recovery of identity; winning Iblis and her kingdom.

The second category of episodes comprises those in which Lanzelet defeats a knight, each time winning a kingdom and a bride. In his first adult adventure, Lanzelet kills Galagandreiz and wins his nameless daughter; in the next episode, he defeats Linier and wins his niece, Ade; after a few intervening adventures comes the central episode, in which Lanzelet wins Iblis by killing Iweret. One observes in this series an increase in courtliness both of the combats (Galagandreiz: knife-throwing; Linier: fighting giants, a lion, and Linier; Iweret: single combat) and of the women won (Galagandreiz's daughter offered her love to two other guests before coming to Lanzelet; Ade helps Lanzelet out of charity; the love of Iblis is elaborated with all the familiar topoi of romance love). Surprisingly, however, Lanzelet's conquests do not end with Iblis. A few episodes after winning her, Lanzelet sets out and "wins" the Lady of Pluris, who keeps him for a year as her captive lover.

The third category of episodes traces Lanzelet's increasing integration into the world of Arthur's court. After Lanzelet's first adventure, word of his prowess reaches Arthur; after the second, Walwein (Gawain) is dispatched to locate the new hero. In the third episode, Lanzelet fights Walwein until they are interrupted, and then he distinguishes himself at a tournament before Arthur's court. In these episodes, Arthur seeks Lanzelet; in the second half of the romance, however, after Lanzelet has overcome Iweret and learned, along with his name, that he is Arthur's nephew, the relation is reversed: now Lanzelet seeks Arthur, in whose behalf he performs a series of adventures. On arriving at court, Lanzelet discovers that Valerin has claimed the Queen, but Lanzelet defends her successfully in judicial combat. On returning from his captivity at Pluris, Lanzelet discovers that Valerin has abducted the Queen, and he is active in her rescue. This pattern of increasing involvement with the world of Arthur culminates in the last two episodes of the work, where it finally unites with the other two episode series (regaining identity; winning wife): Arthur accompanies Lanzelet and Iblis as they celebrate their coronation first in his father's kingdom, then in hers.

Ulrich's *Lanzelet* is the first German representative of the European Lancelot tradition, with which it shares a number of features: infant abduction by a water fay; childhood in a magical kingdom; suppression of identity; championship of Guenevere. Yet it differs from this tradition in ways that are even more striking. Most remarkably, there is not even a hint of what the tradition is best known for, the adulterous love of Lancelot and Guenevere. Further, even though Lanzelet defends the Queen, he never actually rescues her. Finally, questions of kingship and succession play an uncharacteristically large role (revolt against Lanzelet's tyrannical father; defeat of the violent Galagandreiz; the lengthy portrayal of Lanzelet's accession and kingly virtues).

Lanzelet is the second of the German Arthurian romances, falling chronologically after Hartmann von Aue's *Erec* but before his *Iwein* and Wolfram von Eschenbach's *Parzival*; like them, it is composed in the four-stress rhymed couplets characteristic of Middle High German courtly narrative. Ulrich's work has often been taken to task for the ways in which it differs from those of Hartmann and Wolfram: its hero is regarded as flawless throughout; its narrator lacks the literary self-consciousness of his more celebrated contemporaries; as a consequence the work does not seem to question the commonplaces of romance ideology and literary convention, as do those of Hartmann and Wolfram. Yet in all these ways, *Lanzelet* agrees with the rest of the lesser-known Middle High German Arthurian romances—among which, because of its balanced proportions, the variety of its episodes, and its easy, slightly ironic tone, it has always been a favorite.

Although Ulrich was not as well known as Hartmann or Wolfram, he was not forgotten by later authors: Heinrich von dem Türlin incorporated elements from *Lanzelet* into *Diu Crône*, and Ulrich was twice praised by Rudolf von Ems (*Alexander*, l. 3,199; *Willehalm*, l. 2,197). Two complete manuscripts of *Lanzelet* survive (W, thirteenth century; P, 1420) as well as fragments of three others (B, early thirteenth century; G and S, fourteenth century). [JAS]

Ulrich von Zatzikhoven. *Lanzelet: Eine Erzählung*, ed. K.A. Hahn. Frankfurt: Brönner, 1845.

———. *Lanzelet: A Romance of Lancelot*, trans. Kenneth G.T. Webster, rev. Roger Sherman Loomis. New York: Columbia University Press, 1951.

Gottzmann, Carola L. *Artusdichtung*. Stuttgart: Metzler, 1989.

Pérennec, René. "Artusroman und Familie: *das welsche buoch von Lanzelete*." *Acta Germanica*, 11 (1979), 1–51.

Schultz, James A. "'Lanzelet': A Flawless Hero in a Symmetrical World." *Beiträge zur Geschichte der deutschen Sprache und Literatur* (Tübingen), 102 (1980), 160–88.

———. *The Shape of the Round Table: Structures of Middle High German Arthurian Romance*. Toronto: University of Toronto Press, 1983.

Thoran, Barbara. "Zur Struktur des 'Lanzelet' Ulrichs von Zatzikhoven." *Zeitschrift für deutsche Philologie*, 103 (1984), 52–77.

ULTIME IMPRESE E MORTE DI TRISTANO, LE ("The Last Deeds and Death of Tristan"), an Italian *cantare* that condenses many episodes from Arthurian romance. (*See also* CANTARI DI TRISTANO.) [SJN]

Branca, Daniela Delcorno. "I cantari di Tristano." *Lettere italiane*, 23 (1971), 289–305.

UNDERHILL, EVELYN (1875–1941), English author of numerous influential writings on mysticism. The novel *The Column of Dust* (1909), dedicated to her friend Arthur Machen, is set in contemporary England. In the course of a journey of spiritual discovery, the heroine encounters, and later reluctantly accepts guardianship of, the Holy Grail. From it, she learns that spiritual glory lies behind unassuming physical appearance, not only of the relic, but of the whole world and the people within it—even the least promising. [RHT]

Underhill, Evelyn. *The Column of Dust*. London: Methuen, 1909.

UNERMAN, SANDRA, tells of the tests undergone by Cei, Bedwyr, and Gawain in *Trial of Three* (1979). This juvenile novel of rebellion early in Arthur's reign is set in a well-conceived Celtic court and borrows incidents and characters from early Welsh literature. [DN]

Unerman, Sandra. *Trial of Three*. London: Dodson, 1979.

UPDIKE, JOHN, American novelist who wrote "Four Sides of One Story" (1965), an epistolary short story in which the Tristan and Iseult legend is retold through letters by Tristan, the two Iseults, and King Mark. Updike cleverly works the medieval characters and incidents, such as the drinking of the love potion, into a modern setting. [ACL]

Updike, John. "Four Sides of One Story." *The New Yorker*, October 9, 1965, 48–52; repr. in *The Music School: Short Stories*. New York: Knopf, 1966, pp. 87–100.

URIEN (Urbgen [of Gore]), King of Rheged, Owain's father. Urien is mentioned in Nennius's *Historia Brittonum* as having waged battles with military prowess against the Angles in the sixth century. Urien's battle at Brewyn is often listed as one of Arthur's victories and replaces the traditional battle of Agned. Urien appears, with his son Owain, in Geoffrey of Monmouth's *Historia Regum Britanniae* and in the Welsh Triads. He is mentioned as Yvain's father in Chrétien's *Yvain*. In *Claris et Laris*, Urien is the father of Yvain and Marine. In the Vulgate Cycle and Malory's *Morte Darthur*, he is one of the kings who initially rebels against Arthur but is later reconciled with him. Malory tells how Urien remains loyal to Arthur when Morgan, his wife, tries to kill him and subsequently leaves Arthur's court. Urien eventually dies while fighting Mordred with Arthur. [SW]

UTHER PENDRAGON, Arthur's father in Geoffrey of Monmouth. After a youth spent in Breton exile with his elder brother, Aurelius Ambrosius, he returns to Britain with him to dethrone Vortigern. Aurelius, as king, sends Uther and Merlin to Ireland to bring back the Giants' Ring, otherwise Stonehenge. When Aurelius is poisoned, a celestial portent appears. Merlin interprets this as forecasting the glories of Uther and his unborn offspring. Its main feature is a luminous dragon, whence Uther's sobriquet "Pendragon." Geoffrey explains it as meaning "a dragon's head"; more probably, it means "head dragon," which may be interpreted as "foremost leader" or "chief of warriors."

Uther becomes king. He holds court in London and is smitten with desire for Ygerna, the wife of Gorlois, Duke of Cornwall. Observing his advances, Gorlois leaves without permission and immures his wife in Tintagel Castle, approachable only by a narrow isthmus, easily guarded. Taking his conduct as an insult, Uther leads an army to ravage the ducal lands. Merlin magically turns him into a replica of Gorlois, enabling him to enter Tintagel and reach Ygerna, who supposes him to be her husband. Thus, Arthur is begotten. Since the real Gorlois has fallen in battle, Uther can resume his true shape and marry the lady. The remainder of his life is troubled by ill health and aggressive Saxons. After about sixteen years, he dies—like Aurelius, by Saxon poison—and is buried beside him at Stonehenge.

An early Welsh poem mentions "Uthr Pendragon." However, there is no proof that he was a real person. Pendragon Castle in Cumbria allegedly stands on the site of an older fort that Uther built, but the story cannot be traced back far. *Uthr* in Welsh means "terrible, awe-inspiring." The connection with Arthur could perhaps be a mere mistake, since the poetic phrase "Arthur the terrible" might have been misconstrued as "Arthur son of Uthr." [GA]

Geoffrey of Monmouth. *Historia Regum Britanniae*, Book VI, Chapters 5, 8; Book VIII, Chapters 1, 11, 14–24.

Bromwich, Rachel. *Trioedd Ynys Prydein*. Cardiff: University of Wales Press, 1961; 2nd ed. 1978, pp. 520–23.

VAILLANT DE POITIERS, JEAN, assembled for Louis II de Bourbon (1337–1410) a vast prose compilation of Arthurian adventures, drawn principally from *Guiron le Courtois*. To that material, he added a translation of Geoffrey of Monmouth's story of the giants, an abridgment of Wace's *Roman de Brut*, a prosified episode of Chrétien's *Erec et Enide*, and interpolations taken from prose Arthurian romances, such as the Vulgate *Lancelot*, Prose *Tristan*, and *Alixandre l'Orphelin*. The work is preserved in its most complete form in manuscripts Paris, B.N. fr. 358–63. In another manuscript (Geneva, Bodmer 96 1–2), which only partly parallels the Paris manuscripts, Jean Vaillant claims to have completed his work in 1391. The seventeen miniatures of manuscript Oxford, Bodl. Douce 383, correspond exactly to passages in manuscripts 358 and 363 and constitute a third, but very fragmentary, witness. [C-AVC]

Bogdanow, Fanni. "The Fragments of *Guiron de Courtois* Preserved in Ms. Douce 383, Oxford." *Medium Ævum*, 33 (1964), 89–101.

Lathuillère, Roger. *Guiron le Courtois: étude de la tradition manuscrite et analyse critique*. Geneva: Droz, 1966.

———. "Le Manuscrit de *Guiron le Courtois* de la Bibliothèque de Martin Bodmer à Genève." *Mélanges de langue et de littérature du Moyen Âge et de la Renaissance offerts à Jean Frappier*. Geneva: Droz, 1970; Vol. 2, pp. 567–74.

Pickford, Cedric E. *L'Évolution du roman arthurien en prose vers la fin du moyen âge d'après le manuscrit 112 du fonds français de la Bibliothèque Nationale*. Paris: Nizet, 1960.

VAL SANS RETOUR (or Valley of No Return), a lush valley that, according to the Vulgate Cycle, Morgan sealed off by an enchantment, establishing invisible prison walls within which she traditionally imprisoned her lovers. Legendary associations place the Val Sans Retour in Brittany's Forest of Paimpont, the Brocéliande of romance, and a valley in the forest still bears that name. [NJL]

VALLET À LA COTE MAL TAILLIÉE, LE, a brief French fragment (from the thirteenth century) concerning a young man whose desire to serve at Arthur's court is championed by Gawain. [NJL]

Meyer, Paul, and Gaston Paris. "Fragment du *Vallet a la Cote Mal Tailliee*." *Romania*, 26 (1897), 276–80.

VALVENS ÞÁTTR, a continuation of *Parcevals saga*, the Old Norse prose translation of Chrétien de Troyes's unfinished *Perceval* (from line 6,514 to the end). Because this part deals exclusively with Valven (Gawain), it was—at some now indeterminable point—separated from *Parcevals saga* and treated as an individual work. The primary manuscripts are a vellum from ca. 1400 (the same one for *Parcevals saga*) and a single vellum leaf from perhaps fifty years earlier, which contains the beginning, corresponding roughly to the first page of the former.

Valven leaves the castle where he had been staying and comes upon a seriously wounded knight and a sorrowing girl under a large oak. He rouses the knight, who tells him that another knight is stationed on the road ahead and kills all who come past. Valven promises to return. He helps a lovely but arrogant girl, who says she will follow him—but to his disgrace. Valven returns to the injured knight and heals him through his knowledge of herbs, whereupon the ingrate steals Valven's horse. They meet again later, fight, and Valven recovers his steed. In an enchanted castle, he survives a shower of crossbow bolts and the attack of a giant lion, thereby freeing the castle from its spell. In a series of adventures, Valven defeats another knight, meets his own sister (of whose existence he has been unaware), and returns to his arrogant female companion. Her nature has now changed completely—for the better. Valven sends a man to King Arthur to announce that he may be present at an impending duel, and the tale comes to an abrupt end.

The fragmentary nature of the work is clear, but of course the French original was itself incomplete. Notable is the absence of the stylistic features that characterize *Parcevals saga*. [FWB]

Kölbing, Eugen, ed. *Riddarasögur*. Strassburg: Trübner, 1872.

Kalinke, Marianne E. *King Arthur, North-by-Northwest*. Copenhagen: Reitzel, 1981.

VAN ASTEN, GAIL, sets her involving fantasy *The Blind Knight* (1988) in England during the reigns of Stephen and Henry II. A long-lived Uther Pendragon, here a prince of Fairie as well as the brother of Merlin, trains a blind albino youth to become his spiritual heir and husband of his daughter (through her mother she is also the granddaughter of Launcelot and Guenivere). The new Lord Pendragon claims his inheritance after many trials, and he uses Excalibur to locate the tomb of Arthur in Glastonbury for King Henry, before returning the sword to the Lady of the Lake. [RHT]

Van Asten, Gail. *The Blind Knight*. New York: Ace, 1988.

VANCE, JACK (John Holbrook Vance), American author of science fiction and fantasy. Vance's Lyonesse series is set on the mythical Elder Isles (south of Ireland, west of France) two generations before Arthur. *Lyonesse: Suldrun's Garden* (1983) and *Lyonesse: The Green Pearl* (1985) are sprinkled with Arthurian allusions. *Lyonesse: Madouc* (1989) has as two of its many plot elements an irreverent search for the Holy Grail and the struggle for possession of the great table Cairbra an Meadhan, the "model for the 'Round Table' which graced King Arthur's court at Camelot." Like all Vance's work, these fantasies are marked by sly wit, extravagant invention, and loose plotting, although they are noteworthy for their unusual blending of tragedy and humor. For Arthurians, the series offers a rare glimpse of a purely invented "background world" lying behind the better-known legends of Camelot. [GK]

Vance, Jack. *Lyonesse: Suldrun's Garden*. New York: Berkley, 1983.
———. *Lyonesse: The Green Pearl*. San Francisco and Columbia, Pa.: Underwood-Miller, 1985.
———. *Lyonesse: Madouc*. Novato, Calif., and Lancaster, Pa.: Underwood-Miller, 1989.

VAN DER VELDE, CARL FRANZ (1749–1824), who has been called the German Walter Scott because of his many historical novels, was inspired by Benedikte Naubert's *Der kurze Mantel* to produce in the years 1816–17 an opera libretto entitled *Der Zaubermantel*. Like Naubert's modern adaptation of *Le Mantel mautaillié*, van der Velde's libretto expresses a disdain for the aristocracy and glorifies the virtues of the working man. The weaknesses of Arthur and his knights are made manifest in the libretto. King Arthur worries about his gout and cannot get along without a midday siesta. Impotent in the face of Guenevere's wiles and machinations, Arthur is cast in the role of the long-suffering husband.

Although van der Velde hoped that Carl Maria von Weber might be interested in his libretto, *Der Zaubermantel* failed to find a composer. [MEK]

van der Velde, C.F. *Der Zaubermantel. Oper in drei Akten. Die böhmischen Amazonen. Romantisches Gemälde in zwei Akten*. Dresden: Arnoldische Buchhandlung, 1827.

VANSITTART, PETER, British author whose novel *Lancelot* (1978) offers an antiromantic picture of the decline of Roman Britain and the ensuing material and moral chaos. In laconic prose, Lancelot, sensitive, solitary, and aging, recalls first his youth in a villa, then his period of service under Ambrosius Aurelianus, during which he met the whore Gwenhever. Artorius emerges toward the end as an engimatic, half-barbaric figure.

Vansittart returns to the Arthurian legend in *Parsifal* (1988), a reflective novel that follows the adventures of the long-lived hero at different places and times in history: from primitive pre-Roman Britain; through the courts, first of the Duke of Burgundy, then of the Holy Roman Emperor, at the end of the Middle Ages; finally to the collapsing Third Reich. Throughout, Parsifal remains a naive innocent, both puzzled and puzzling. His simplicity inspires a range of responses, from affection and devotion, to mistrust and hostility, but wherever he goes he is a disturbing presence. [CNS/RHT]

Vansittart, Peter. *Lancelot*. London: Owen, 1978.
———. *Parsifal*. London: Owen, 1988.

VASNACHTSPIL MIT DER KRON, DAS ("The Shrovetide Play with the Crown"), an anonymous fifteenth-century Shrovetide play, contains a variant version of the Arthurian chastity test transmitted in the *Lai du cor* and *Le Mantel mautaillié*. A wondrous crown, sent to King Arthur by the King of Abian, is to be tried on by all men present. It will be given to the king or lord whom it best fits. One king after another tries on the crown only to have horns grow out of his head to indicate that he has enjoyed illicit love. In each case, the wronged wife berates her husband and receives feeble excuses. The game is short-lived, and the play ends with a decision to return the crown to its sender. [MEK]

Keller, Adelbert von, ed. *Das vasnachtspil mit der kron*. In *Fastnachtspiele aus dem fünfzehnten Jahrhundert. Zweiter Theil*. Stuttgart: Litterarischer Verein, 1853, pp. 654–63.

Walsh, Martin W. "*Arthur Cocu*: Comic Abuse of the Round Table in Fifteenth-Century *Fastnachtspiele*." *Fifteenth-Century Studies*, 15 (1989), 305–21.

VEITCH, JOHN (1829–1894), Scottish professor, published *Merlin and Other Poems* in 1889. The 450-line title poem, a source for Tennyson's "Merlin and the Gleam" (1889), features Merlin Caledonius and loosely follows the legend of Merlin in the Welsh poem *Afallennau*, from the Black Book of Carmarthen. However, Veitch's is distinctly a nineteenth-century version in its themes of Faustian aspiration and doubts about immortality. (LH]

Veitch, John. *Merlin and Other Poems*. Edinburgh and London: Blackwood, 1889.

Hughes, Linda K. "Text and Subtext in 'Merlin and the Gleam.'" *Victorian Poetry*, 23 (1985), 161–68.

VELTHEM, LODEWIJK VAN, a Middle Dutch poet about whom little is known. He came from Brabant, and he lived and worked in the second half of the thirteenth century and the first half of the fourteenth. Velthem became known mainly as the executor of Jacob van Maerlant's literary testament. His continuation of Maerlant's *Spiegel Historiael* (1283–88), which treats the period 1248–1316, was intended for the Lord of Voorne, Gerard, son of Albrecht of Voorne. One of the many events that he describes concerns a Round Table organized by King Edward I of England, a festive performance in which the participants appeared as Arthurian knights (*Spiegel Historiael* V, Book 2, Chapters 15–20).

Velthem continued two other works by Jacob van Maerlant, the *Historie van den Grale* and the *Boec van Merline*: in 1326, he completed his *Merlijn-Continuatie*, an adaptation of the *Suite du Merlin*. His verse romance was intended as a sequel to the work by Maerlant, who had transposed Old French prose versions of Robert de Boron's *Joseph d'Arimathie* and *Merlin* into Middle Dutch verse ca. 1261.

In Middle Dutch, Velthem's adaptation has been transmitted in fragmentary form. Some 1,650 lines have been preserved, in fragments from the second half of the fourteenth century (Leiden, University Library ltk. 1107; Maastricht, Public Record Office 167 III 10; and Münster Hauptstaatsarchiv, Dep. Landsberg-Velen). In addition, a complete version of Velthem's work is preserved in a Middle Low German *Umschreibung* (rendering) from the Middle Dutch, in a codex from ca. 1425 (Burgersteinfurt, Fürst zu Bentheimsche Schlossbibliothek B 37). This manuscript, which has always been in the possession of the counts of Bentheim, also contains Middle Low German *Umschreibungen* of Maerlant's *Historie van den Grale* and *Boec van Merline*. Velthem's work comprises almost 26,000 lines.

Even this does not exhaust Velthem's concerns with Arthurian romance. A notice on the last leaf of the *Lancelot-Compilatie* indicates that he was the owner of this codex. The questions of whether he was also responsible for the composition of the compilation, and of whether he perhaps even transposed the Old French *Lancelot–Queste–Mort* into Middle Dutch, have not yet been answered. [BB]

Stallaert, K.F., ed. "De Merlijn van Jacob van Maerlant." *Nederlandsch Museum*, 1 (1880), 51–63.

De Pauw, Napoleon, ed. *Middelnederlandsche gedichten en fragmenten*. Ghent, 1903, Vol. 2, pp. 66–72.

Sodmann, Timothy, ed. "Die münsterschen Fragmente von Lodewijks van Velthem *Boec van coninc Arthur*." *Niederdeutsches Wort*, 23 (1983), 39–81.

Te Winkel, Jan. *De Ontwikkelingsgang der Nederlandsche Letterkunde*. Haarlem, 1922–27; repr. Utrecht: Hes, 1973, Vol. 1, pp. 490–500.

VENDETTA CHE FE MESSER LANZELLOTO DE LA MORTE DI MISER TRISTANO, LA ("Lancelot's Revenge for the Death of Sir Tristan"), an Italian *cantare*, the plot of which departs somewhat from the main body of Tristan literature in recounting Lancelot's revenge. Variants of this *cantare* appear in several codices that contain *Le ultime imprese e morte di Tristano*. [SJN]

Branca, Daniela Delcorno. "I cantari di Tristano." *Lettere italiane*, 23 (1971), 289–305.

VENGEANCE RAGUIDEL, LA ("The Avenging of Raguidel"), a French verse romance of 6,182 lines, dating from the first quarter of the thirteenth century, written by a certain Raoul, possibly to be identified with Raoul de Houdenc. The story centers on Gauvain's quest to avenge the death of Raguidel, whose body arrives at Arthur's court on a boat. With the aid of Yder, the quest is eventually achieved and the murderer, Guengasoain, brought to justice. Within the framework of this quest, many other adventures are related, often in a humorous and burlesque style: the Pucele du Gaut Destroit, infatuated with Gauvain, who plans to guillotine him when he scorns her love, or the faithless Ydain, who deserts Gauvain for another knight, and is then given to the hunchback Druidain.

La Vengeance Raguidel may be seen as an anti-Gauvain parody, the parody being centered largely on Gauvain's reputation with women. The guillotine episode is an example, and in the episode where Ydain deserts Gauvain (a version of which is found in *Le Chevalier à l'épée*), it is suggested that she does so because the other knight is better endowed sexually. The broader conventions of courtly romance are also objects of humor; for example, Gauvain departs to avenge Raguidel but forgets the lance-point he needs for the vengeance and has to return shamefacedly to court. On occasion, specific episodes from Chrétien are parodied, most notably the crisis between hero and heroine from *Erec et Enide*, which underlies the salubrious and unsuccessful affair between Gauvain and Ydain. There are other intertextual links to *Yvain* and *Perceval*. *La Vengeance Raguidel* was adapted into Middle Dutch as *Die Wrake van Raguisel* in the thirteenth century. [KB]

Friedwagner, Mathias, ed. *La Vengeance Raguidel*. Halle: Niemeyer, 1909.

Busby, Keith. *Gauvain in Old French Literature*. Amsterdam: Rodopi, 1980, pp. 272–94.

Schmolke-Hasselmann, Beate. *Der arthurische Versroman von Chrestien bis Froissart*. Tübingen: Niemeyer, 1980, pp. 106–15.

VERA HISTORIA DE MORTE ARTHURI ("True History of the Death of Arthur"), a Latin prose text dating perhaps from the late twelfth century and extant in three manuscripts (London, Gray's Inn 7; London, B.L. Cotton Cleopatra D.III; London, B.N. Cotton Titus A.XIX). This version of Arthur's final battle and death describes his wound from a poisoned spear, his funeral rites, and the mysterious disappearance of the King's body from the bier during a thick mist. [MLD]

Lapidge, Michael, ed. "An Edition of the *Vera Historia de Morte Arthuri*." *Arthurian Literature*, 1 (1981), 19–93.

———. "Additional Manuscript Evidence for the *Vera Historia de Morte Arthuri*." *Arthurian Literature*, 2 (1982), 163–68.

VERE, B.D., wrote *King Arthur: His Symbolic Story in Verse* (1930), a five-act play in blank verse for an enormous cast. A prologue, with Jesus at Tintagel, is followed by the episode of the Sword in the Stone. The final scene in the Grail Chapel, after the death of Arthur, represents the achievement of the Grail and the death of Galahad. The style is declamatory, with a chorus explaining what is happening before the beginning of each act. [EB]

Vere, B.D. *King Arthur: His Symbolic Story in Verse*. King Arthur's Hall, Tintagel, 1930.

VERGIL, POLYDORE. Trained in the new humanist tradition, the Italian Polydore Vergil came to England in 1502 and remained there until 1553. During this time, he wrote his *Anglica Historia*, of which the earliest manuscript copy can be dated to 1512–13. In the early parts of this work, Vergil set about to debunk Geoffrey of Monmouth; in particular, he attacked Geoffrey's accounts of Brutus and Arthur. Brutus is dismissed altogether and Arthur emerges with considerably diminished stature. What Vergil is willing to grant as factual concerning Arthur, after discrediting the "anilibus fabellis" ("silly little tales" of medieval writers), is even less than the earlier skeptic William of Malmesbury had accepted: Arthur ruled after Uther and would have perhaps reunited Britain for a time if he had lived longer. Contemporary patriotic reaction against Vergil was often vitriolic, and ultimately he was pilloried by the Arthurians as "that most rascall dogge knave in the worlde" (Hay, p. 159). [JPC]

Carley, James P. "Polydore Vergil and John Leland on King Arthur: The Battle of the Books." *Interpretations*, 15 (1984), 86–100.

Hay, Denys. *Polydore Vergil*. Oxford: Clarendon, 1952.

VESPER, WILL (1882–1962), German author with strong nationalistic (later Nazi) tendencies. He adapted traditional material in *Parzival* and *Tristan und Isolde*, both published in 1911 as part of the popular series Bücher der Rose. Vesper trivializes his medieval antecedents. Parzival appears, for example, as a prefascist conqueror and savior-figure. [UM/WCM]

Vesper, Will. *Parzival*. Ebenhausen bei München: Langewiesche-Brandt, [ca. 1911].

———. *Tristan und Isolde*. Ebenhausen bei München: Langewiesche-Brandt, 1911.

Schulze, Ursula. "Ideologisierung durch Strukturverlust." In *Akten des DFG-Symposions zur Mittelalter-Rezeption*, ed. Peter Wapnewski. Stuttgart: Metzler, 1985.

VIAN, BORIS (1920–1959), French author of *Le Chevalier de Neige* ("The Snow Knight"), which was a drama and later an opera about Lancelot, both with music by Georges Delerue. The drama, which had the subtitle *Les Aventures de Lancelot*, was presented in the château of Caen during the Normandy drama festival of 1953. Running nearly four hours and using three dozen speaking roles, plus songs, dances, and mimes, the play concentrates on the story of Lancelot and Guénièvre (taken largely from Jacques Boulenger's modernization of the Vulgate Cycle), to the exclusion of the Grail quest and other traditional themes. The drama received enthusiastic critical acclaim, and its seven performances were seen by almost 70,000 people.

The title refers to Lancelot, brought to Arthur's court by the Lady of the Lake and identified only by his white armor. Subsequent events follow the Vulgate selectively but accurately: the birth of the adulterous love, the Lady of Escalot (Shalott) story, the condemnation of the Queen and her rescue by Lancelot, the war between Lancelot and Arthur, Mordret's treason, and Arthur's departure for Avalon.

Vian and Delerue turned the drama into a three-act opera that was presented at Nancy in January 1957; unfortunately, it was not recorded, nor has it been presented or recorded since. The opera was scheduled for presentation in Paris, but owing to financial and personnel problems at the Opéra-Comique it was withdrawn from the program after five rehearsals. Additional songs written for the projected revival have been preserved. [NJL]

Vian, Boris. *Le Chevalier de Neige*. Paris: Union Générale d'Éditions, 1974.

VILAIN QUI DEVINT RICHE ET PUIS PAUVRE, LE ("The Man Who Became Rich and Then Poor Again"), also known as *Merlin Merlot*, is an anonymous French text included in the thirteenth-century compilation of edifying tales entitled *La Vie des anciens peres* ("The Lives of the Fathers"). It recounts the story of a poor man whose wish to be wealthy and powerful is granted by Merlin. The man's initial gratitude and respect for Merlin are gradually replaced by casual indifference and then scorn, at which point the magician threatens to restore his original poverty. He ignores the threat only to have his children die and his money stolen by his neighbor. [NJL]

VINAVER, EUGÈNE (1899–1979), eminent Arthurian scholar and one of the founding members of the International Arthurian Society. Among his invaluable contributions to Arthurian scholarship is his work on the Prose *Tristan* and its relation to Malory, as well as his definitive edition of Malory's *Morte Darthur, The Works of Sir Thomas Malory*. This edition grew out of his identification of the Malory manuscript discovered at Winchester by W.F. Oakeshott in 1934. In his later years, Vinaver enhanced understanding of and appreciation for Arthurian romance in books and articles that identify and describe medieval aesthetic principles. In these works, especially *À la recherche d'une poétique médiévale* (1970) and *The Rise of Romance* (1971), he illuminates formal principles, such as interlace, analogy, and repetition, underlying much medieval romance. [SNI]

VINES, SHERARD (1890–?), satirizes religious cults of the 1920s in *Return, Belphegor!* (1932), a modern Grail story that blends realism with fantasy. The unexpectedly sadistic last chapters contrast jarringly with the humor of the earlier parts of the novel. [EB]

Vines, Sherard. *Return, Belphegor!* London: Wishart, 1932.

VINEY, JAYNE, author of a historical novel, *The Bright-Helmed One* (1975), which follows Arthur's career by focusing, successively, upon the fortunes of one of his warriors, of his half-Jutish wife Winifrith (Guenevere), and of Cai. The result is a disjointed exploration of the theme of loyalty and betrayal. [RHT]

Viney, Jayne. *The Bright-Helmed One*. London: Hale, 1975.

VIRUNNIUS, PONTICUS, a fifteenth-century humanist, native to Treviso, who, under a commission, abbreviated Geoffrey of Monmouth's history of British kings for the family of the Badaer, prominent Venetians who were originally from Britain. The first edition was probably printed at Augsburg sometime prior to Ponticus's death in 1490. [JHW]

Virunnius, Ponticus. *Viri Doctissimi Britannicae, Historiae Libri Sex, Magna et Fidi, Pontici Virunni*, ed. David Powel. London, 1585.

VISUAL ARTS. Any attempt to construct a comprehensive history of the Arthurian legend in the visual arts will prove to be an elusive endeavor. Surveying the known examples of Arthurian imagery, diverse in age, geographic origin, and medium, we can discern only a single thread of continuity: Arthurian art was dependent upon Arthurian literature; each surge of development in the written tradition was followed by a manifestation in the arts. This symbiotic relationship has characterized Arthurian imagery from its emergence in the twelfth century to its zenith during the late Middle Ages, from its decline during the Renaissance to its revival in Victorian England. There exists even today a vestigial interest in the arts.

Just as its narrative subjects have been drawn from literature, the aesthetic conventions of Arthurian art have reflected contemporary taste. No single stylistic mode can be labeled exclusively Arthurian. As the legend was recast for each succeeding audience, the visual vocabulary was translated to satisfy the current canon. In its dependency upon literary tradition, and in its chameleonlike adaptability, Arthurian imagery defies broad generalizations. Although comprehensive surveys exist, such as Scherer's, the survey approach may simply address an assemblage of images with little insight into the art-historical problems of style and iconography. The sheer diversity of this corpus is best understood as a series of separate phases, each with an individual aesthetic, iconography, and iconology.

The true breadth and variety of Arthurian iconography in the medieval era are cloaked in uncertainty. Sacred themes supplanted the profane during the Middle Ages, and, as Roger Sherman Loomis and Laura Hibbard Loomis have pointedly observed (*Arthurian Legends in Medieval Art*, pp. 3–4), the inferiority of secular objects, as well as their rarity, has diminished the attention given to them. It is true that no lay patron rivaled the munificence of the Church in its commission of luxurious objects, embellished with sacred themes. It was not until the fourteenth century that the laity emerged as a substantial force in art patronage, but at no time did the splendor and extravagance of secular works vie with the finest of the sacred.

The perishability of some of the media—textiles, delicate wood and ivory carvings, single-leaf woodcuts—presents another obstacle and constitutes a major loss. Metal objects were often melted for reuse; fresco disappeared beneath coats of whitewash. Private collections suffered the ravages of time to a far greater extent than ecclesiastical collections; the riches of the laity often vanished during civil unrest and social reversal, while the treasures of the Church enjoyed the security of the vaults of the cathedrals and monasteries. What has survived has been selected on the basis of coincidence and circumstance.

Arthurian objects have often survived only in a state of partial preservation. A late Flemish luxury manuscript of *Guiron le Courtois* (ca. 1480; Oxford, Bodl. Douce 383) retains only seventeen folios of what was believed to have been a lavishly illustrated work (Loomis, pp. 128–30). The "Frauenlob" murals in Constance and the Parzival murals in Lübeck are known only from postmedieval copies, the former through black-and-white copies made in 1860, shortly after their discovery, the latter (destroyed in 1929) through watercolor drawings by Wilhelm Boht, now in the St. Annen Museum, Lübeck (Loomis, pp. 37, 75–76). The depiction of Arthur in the stained-glass ensemble in St. Mary's Hall in Coventry was heavily restored twice, in 1783 and in 1893, and its original appearance is obliterated (see *Walpole Society Annual*, 19 [1931], 103ff.). The modification of objects, combined with questions of identification, impedes the compilation of a comprehensive catalogue. Loomis has rightly observed (pp. 6–7): "Omniscience alone can determine how many illustrations of the Round Table legend remain to be discovered under a coat of whitewash or in some provincial museum or in an art dealer's shop, and only Fortunatus' purse and at least a lifetime of patience would serve to discover and reproduce every miniature from an Arthurian MS, every woodcut from incunabula, and every illustration of Arthur among the Nine Worthies."

Written records do suggest that the surviving objects represent only a small fraction of the whole tradition. For large-scale interior decorative programs that have vanished, such as "Arthur's Hall" and "Guenevere's Chamber" at Dover Castle (ca. 1250), a manuscript's tinted drawing is often the sole evidence (for the example of Dover Castle, see Loomis, p. 138). Inventories of vast private collections, now dispersed, suggest the popularity of Arthurian iconography. The collection of Louis, Duke of Anjou, documented during the years 1364–65, contained tapestries depicting the Nine Worthies and scenes from the romances of Lancelot as well as gilt-and-enameled cups decorated with subjects from the legend of Tristan. Commission orders—such as a request for roof tiles sent by Pedro IV of Aragon to his counselor Johan Ximenez of Huesca, discussing a chamber in Aljaferia painted with the history of Jaufré—allude to vanished programs.

Literary descriptions, although unreliable as documentation of lost works, were likely based on actual types and bear witness to the demand for elegant secular objects. Vivid descriptions of complex painted and sculpted programs suggest the compositional ideas and the techniques that were employed. In Thomas d'Angleterre's *Tristan*, the grieving lover builds a "Hall of Images" populated with lifelike statues of Queen Ysolt and her entourage. The Vulgate *Lancelot* describes an intricate painting, complete with incriminating inscriptions, executed by Lancelot when he was held captive by Morgan le Fay. Arthur's discovery of the telltale picture is illustrated in a manuscript of the *Lancelot* (ca. 1470; Paris, B.N. fr. 112, Vol. II, fol. 193), an illumination that indicates the size and disposition of figures in such an ensemble. Another popular type, a procession in which Arthur, his champions, and their ladies ride in a cavalcade, is described in detail by Boccaccio in *Amorosa Visione*, Cantos XI and XXIX.

On the basis of surviving monuments, it appears that the history of Arthurian art begins in the twelfth century. Arthurian iconography seems to have appeared almost at random, and the literary inspiration for the early subjects remains a topic for speculation. The crude Perros relief, carved on a nave pier in the church of St. Efflam in Brittany (ca. 1100), was more likely based on a local saint's legend than a strictly Arthurian source. Arthurian iconography emerges as an independent motif in an archivolt sculpture on the Porta della Pescheria, the north portal of Modena cathedral (1100–40). Loomis (p. 75) has hypothesized that the source was oral tradition, for Arthur's adventures were probably disseminated by Breton troubadours passing through Italy en route to the Holy Land. The remaining history of Arthurian art in the twelfth century is fragmentary, and few other monuments have been identified.

The impetus for a continuous development came with the burgeoning of the romance tradition at the end of the twelfth century. The visual arts responded, but in an evolution subsequent, not parallel, to the literature. From the thirteenth through the fifteenth centuries, Arthurian imagery enjoyed generous patronage and pan-European popularity. The influence of courtly society was clearly manifest in the arts. Subjects became focused and distinct, and the execution and visual conventions attained an unprecedented refinement, typical of the arts commissioned by courtly patrons.

Both the material remains and the documentation reveal that Arthurian subjects appeared in all forms of the visual arts, and the prevailing demand was for objects for

88. Sicilian wall hanging, fourteenth century, Tristan scenes. (By courtesy of the Board of Trustees of the Victoria and Albert Museum.)

private rather than public appreciation. Manuscripts, wall paintings, carved and enameled works, and tapestries and other textiles were adorned with Arthurian motifs. Yet the appearance of such objects in public art, particularly in the sacred realm, was not unknown and accounts for most of the sculpture and stained glass in the tradition.

The repertoire of subjects grew in direct response to the growth of the literature. Furthermore, this repertoire was shared by all the visual arts; subjects were used freely in all media. For example, in the fourteenth and fifteenth centuries, the iconography of the Nine Worthies appeared in manuscript illumination, sculpture, stained glass, and tapestry with equal regularity. A romance subject, such as the Tryst Beneath the Tree from the Tristan legend, was favored for toilette articles—jewel caskets, mirror-backs, combs—but also appeared on architectural elements, such as corbels, and in furniture carving, such as misericords. It is through the study of the development of the media, rather than that of a single motif, that we can demonstrate the intricate breadth of the whole.

The proliferation of Arthurian subject matter in manuscript illumination was a natural consequence of the development of the romance. Loomis and Loomis do note, however, that patronage for such manuscripts arose nearly a century later, suggesting (pp. 37–39) that in the twelfth century Arthurian romances were read aloud and the texts were unadorned. They credit the growth of an illuminated tradition to the expansion of courtly culture in the thirteenth century, as well as the simultaneous establishment of lay scriptoria (there were, for example, seventeen lay illuminators working in Paris by 1292).

Illuminated manuscripts combined text with various forms of decoration, from modest borders and tinted drawings to lavish historical initials and, in the finest luxury manuscripts, full-page miniatures. The manuscript tradition flourished in France, Flanders, and Italy and to a lesser extent in England, Germany, Holland, and Spain. In each case, the style reflected national taste. France was the uncontested leader in the production of both sacred and secular illuminated manuscripts in the Gothic era. During the thirteenth and fourteenth centuries, the Vulgate *Lancelot* and *Queste del Saint Graal* provided the most popular subjects. The fifteenth century was graced by luxury manuscripts, enriched with full-page, narrative illustrations, such as two manuscripts in the Bibliothèque Nationale, a *Lancelot* (ca. 1405; fr. 117–20), once owned by Jean, duc de Berry, and the *Estoire-Merlin-Lancelot* (ca. 1466; fr. 96). At the same time, the tournament book was introduced as a heraldic guide to the arms of Arthur's champions. By the end of the century, named artists, such as Evarard d'Espingues and Jean Colombe, appear, suggesting an association of illuminators with specialized subject matter.

The early Flemish illuminators turned to historical works, like Geoffrey of Monmouth's *Historia Regum Britanniae* (ca. 1180; Douai 880), practicing a plain, blunt aesthetic, but by the fourteenth century they emulated the French models; such works as the *Queste del Saint Graal* (ca. 1350; Paris, Bibliothèque de l'Arsenal 5218) attained a refinement that was maintained through subsequent decades. Guilame Vrelant was an important figure in the mid-fifteenth century, as Flanders shed the cloak of medieval anonymity. Illuminators from Italy displayed a distinctive style, incorporating the classicizing, natural concept of the figure. Lombard manuscripts (ca. 1295–1325), the earliest pictorial transcriptions of the Arthurian story, were crude, but by the mid-fourteenth century such works as the Prose *Tristan* in the Bibliothèque Nationale (ca. 1320–40; fr. 755) and the *Meliadus* (fourteenth century; London, B.L. Add. 12228), featuring French texts, equaled Flemish achievements. The Italian tradition waned earlier than others, fading out of fashion by the mid-fifteenth century.

In England, the clear preference was for historical works that associated Arthur with other monarchs, such as the *Flores Historium*, illustrated by Matthew Paris (ca. 1230–50; Manchester, Chetham's Library 6712), and Pierre de Langtoft's *Chronicle* in the British Library (ca. 1207; Royal 20 A II). The indigenous romance tradition, which did not emerge until the late-medieval era, did not attain French or Flemish standards. In Germany, subjects reveal a national bias, with manuscripts of *Parzival* and *Tristan* reigning supreme from the mid-thirteenth through the fifteenth centuries. In Holland, the tradition was weaker, and such manuscripts as the *Spiegel Historiael* (ca. 1325; The Hague, MS XX) were often concerned only in part with Arthurian iconography. Spain developed a hybrid tradition, wherein Norman scribes worked with Spanish illuminators, as in the Prose *Tristan* (ca. 1278; Paris, B.N. fr. 750).

Courtly taste had a strong influence upon decorative arts. Delicate ivory jewel caskets, combs, and mirror-backs were carved with Arthurian motifs for female patrons. In the thirteenth century, the Cologne School was prominent, only to be surpassed by the Parisian School in the fourteenth century. Romance subjects were preferred: the ill-starred love of Tristan and Isolde, the lives of Perceval and Galahad, the adventures of Lancelot. Scenes from Arthurian romance were often combined or contrasted with other vignettes to present a commentary on love.

Arthurian motifs were widely used in interior decoration. Pavements, such as those in Otranto Cathedral (ca. 1165) and Chertsey Abbey (ca. 1270), depicted single subjects and full narratives. Fresco and mural painting was practiced throughout Europe, as evidenced in the Great Tower of the St.-Floret Chateau in the Auvergne (ca. 1350), the Summer House in the Castle Runkelstein in the Tyrol (ca. 1400), the Great Hall of the Castle of La Manta of Saluzzo (ca. 1430), and the Hall of the Round Table in the Palazzo Ducale in Mantua, painted by Pisanello (before 1455). Ensembles often combined sources, illustrating romance subjects and the Nine Worthies in a single program. Arthur figured prominently in the art of tapestry as well; the

Nine Worthies was a favored motif, as in the Parisian King Arthur Tapestry (fourteenth century, Metropolitan Museum of Art, New York). Other textiles of less monumental scale, such as embroidered hangings and bed quilts, were enhanced with romance subjects.

Sculpture is rare among surviving objects and its tradition is obscure. Appearances seem random and oddly located, as the capital carved with Lancelot crossing the Sword Bridge at St. Pierre in Caen (ca. 1350) or the fourteenth-century misericord carvings in the cathedrals at Lincoln and Chester. A life-sized painted stone sculpture of King Arthur as one of the Nine Worthies has been identified in the Hall of the Hanseatic League in the Rathaus in Cologne (ca. 1325).

The diversity of subject matter, the persistent use of contemporary detail, and the variety of media prevented the amalgamation of a single, distinctive style. Artists did not formulate individual physical types: Arthur appeared sometimes bearded, sometimes clean-shaven, with or without a crown, and the absence of heraldry or previous knowledge of the subject impeded comprehension. It was the literature and the courtly taste of the patron that provided the tenuous continuity of the development of medieval Arthurian imagery.

The association of Arthurian imagery with an elite audience ended with the advent of printing in the mid-fifteenth century. The combination of printed text with woodcut illustrations in an inexpensive and easily reproduced format popularized the legend. Single-leaf woodcuts could grace the wall of a modest home, and the rising merchant, who would find the price of an illuminated manuscript prohibitive, could afford a printed volume, illustrated with woodcuts. We see this development throughout Europe: in the shops of Jean Dupré in Paris and of Anton Sorg in Augsburg and in the Spanish broadside tradition. Outstanding among the illustrated editions was the *Morte Darthur* printed in 1498 by Wynkyn de Worde, heir to William Caxton's London enterprise.

The succeeding century, with its shift in cultural ideals, saw the first decline in Arthurian interest. During the Renaissance, Arthurian subjects waned in the popular realm but were occasionally employed by monarchs, particularly in England, as political propaganda. The Winchester Round Table, likely crafted for a tournament in the fourteenth century, was given a fresh coat of paint by Henry VII in 1485 and changed to Tudor colors and devices. Henry VIII (who repainted the table again in 1522) carried banners lauding Arthur as a world conqueror when he met Francis I at the Field of Cloth of Gold in 1520. In Germany, Emperor Maximilian turned to Arthurian monarchical iconography in his commission of the bronze statue of the King at Innsbruck from the workshop of Peter Vischer the Elder in 1513.

The passing of the sixteenth century marked the full decline of Arthurian imagery. Aside from a rare Arthurian costume in Queen Elizabeth's Accession Day Tilts and Prince Henry's revival of the monarchical symbol in his commission of *Prince Henry's Barriers* (1610), by Ben Jonson with designs by Inigo Jones, the subjects vanished from the artist's repertoire. Throughout the remainder of the seventeenth century and the first half of the eighteenth, interest in Arthur languished. The literature declined, but the art disappeared.

In the eighteenth century, particularly in England, a new interest in medieval heritage arose. As early as the 1720s, garden follies, such as Merlin's Cave in Richmond, by William Kent, were built to evoke a romanticized vision of the past. The Gothic Revival pursued "ancient" literature with unprecedented zeal, but it was *The Faerie Queene* of Edmund Spenser that inspired the artists. Illustrated editions of *The Fairie Queene* served to increase public interest. In the last quarter of the eighteenth century, paintings based on Spenser's poem, especially those of Henry Fuseli and John Hamilton Mortimer, were featured at Thomas Macklin's Poets Gallery in London (1788–1800). In every case, only the subjects were Elizabethan, for in style these paintings reflected the classicizing standards espoused by the Royal Academy of Art.

The Gothic Revival in literature brought Malory's *Le Morte Darthur* out of almost 200 years of obscurity, with three new editions in the early nineteenth century. A similar interest among artists did not arise until the Victorian era, and no Arthurian work of art based on a source other than *The Faerie Queene* predates the year 1849. The legend came to be regarded as a paradigm of modern behavior, the result of popular medievalism, which redefined chivalry as a modern behavioral code, and the reinterpretation of the legend by contemporary poets for their own audience, so that Arthurian iconography was introduced into Victorian painting as a new national allegory. In 1848, the government commissioned William Dyce to paint an ensemble of frescoes for the Queen's Robing Room in the new palace at Westminster, illustrating the virtues of national character as exemplified in the Arthurian legend. Dyce edited all incidents of sin and pessimism out of the legend. This expurgated version, the first Victorian Arthuriad in the visual arts, foreshadowed the interpretive mode of Tennyson's *Idylls of the King*, and it began a revival that would endure until the end of the century.

During the 1850s and the 1860s, every sector of the Victorian art world embraced Arthurian subject matter. Three sources provided the inspiration: Tennyson's poetry, Malory's *Morte Darthur*, and Dyce's frescoes. The Pre-Raphaelite artists, most prominently Edward Burne-Jones, William Morris, and Dante Gabriel Rossetti, explored the potential of the new subject, in painting, as in the Oxford Union Murals (1857), and in decorative arts, such as the Dunlop Windows (1862) and the Stanmore Hall Tapestries (1891–94). Academic artists, such as James Archer, Joseph Noël Paton, Thomas Woolner, and John William Waterhouse, addressed similar themes, but with greater moral content. The most popular subjects were Sir Galahad, Elaine, Tristan and Isolde, Lancelot and Guenevere, the Lady of Shalott, and the Death of King Arthur, but subjects were limited only by the artist's familiarity with the literature. Book illustrations also flourished; notable among the many illustrated editions were the Moxon Tennyson (1857) and the *Idylls of the King* illustrated by Gustave Doré (1868) and by Julia Margaret Cameron (1874). Parodies appeared as well, as in the work of George du Maurier.

The Arthurian Revival waned with the century, as a new generation rejected chivalric idealism and the canon of aestheticism drained the heroic figures of their power. Aubrey Beardsley's drawings for the Dent *Morte D'arthur* (1893–94) typify the late decadent phase. The Arthurian Revival differed from the medieval manifestation of the legend in several ways. Primarily, it was brought into being as a royal, sanctioned allegory with a clear, moral iconology. Also, the visual arts in the Victorian era developed in parallel rather than subsequent to the literature. Further, artists developed definite prototypes, assigned physical characteristics to characters, and formulated a clear iconography. The Victorian era borrowed only the superficial trappings from the medieval achievements; in interpretation, form, and influence, the revival marked a distinct new phase of development.

A minor interest in Arthurian imagery was manifest outside of England in the nineteenth century. In France, the subject matter was restricted to the decorative arts, as in the work of Victor Adam. In Germany, interest was revived through the works of Wagner, which inspired stage design by Heinrich Döll and the elaborate palace decorations at Neuschwanstein and Schlossberg commissioned by Ludwig II of Bavaria (1860–80). It was also through Wagnerian influence that the Belgian Symbolists, such as Paul Delville, turned to Arthurian themes. In America, the model was English, as evidenced by Edwin Austen Abbey's murals for the Boston Public Library (1895). Only England, however, enjoyed a full-scale revival of the legend in the arts.

Vestiges of the revival continued into the twentieth century in England and America. It remained a minor theme in British painting until World War I. In both countries, book illustration, particularly for the juvenile audience, became the dominant expression. British illustrators included Walter Crane, Edmund Dulac, and Arthur Rackham, while Howard Pyle and N.C. Wyeth developed an independent American tradition. Arthur and his champions also appeared in British public-school decoration and, in rare instances, in American institutions, such as the Princeton Chapel Windows design by Charles Connick (1931).

By the 1940s, Arthurian subjects had fallen into neglect. The self-expressive trend in European and American painting disdained literary subjects, and the nonrepresentational vocabulary of the modern painter expressed formal rather than narrative ideas. From the 1960s to the present, cinema has been the major medium for exploration of Arthurian subjects. The films of John Boorman, Robert Bresson, and Eric Rohmer provide personal visions of the legendary world. It is too early in the development to assess cinema's position in the history of Arthurian art; it may be a response to the current wealth of new fiction, a new force in the arts, or a brand of escapist entertainment.

The history of Arthurian art is riddled with discontinuity. Its origins have yet to be discovered, while its current manifestations await evaluation. Two major phases can be recognized, but these phases were distinct in their style, their interpretation, and their motivation. They shared only the legendary subject matter, and ultimately it is the literature that lends structure to the study of the Arthurian art. (*See also* Decorative Arts [Medieval].) [DNM]

Loomis, Roger Sherman, and Laura Hibbard Loomis. *Arthurian Legends in Medieval Art*. London: Oxford University Press, 1938.

Mancoff, Debra N. *The Arthurian Revival in Victorian Art*. New York: Garland, 1990.

Scherer, Margaret R. *About the Round Table*. New York: Metropolitan Museum of Art, 1945.

Whitaker, Muriel. *The Legends of King Arthur in Art*. Cambridge: Brewer, 1990.

VITA DI MERLINO CON LE SUE PROFETIE

("The Life of Merlin, with His Prophecies"), also known as *Historia di Merlino*; a free Italian translation of the prose version of Robert de Boron's *Merlin*. The work offers a number of departures from the French text and includes some "prophecies" that appear to refer to recent Italian events. [NJL]

La Historia di Merlino. Venice: Tramezzino, 1480.

VIVES, BROTHER JUAN (or João Bivas), the early fourteenth-century Spanish translator of the French Post-Vulgate Cycle. His translation is known through Spanish and Portuguese redactions and fragments, such as *Estoria de Merlín*, *Livro de Josep Abaramatia*, *Libro de Josep Abarimatia*, *Baladro del sabio Merlín*, *Lançarote*, and *Demanda del Sancto Grial*. [NJL]

Entwistle, William J. *The Arthurian Legend in the Literatures of the Spanish Peninsula*. London: Dent, 1925, pp. 172ff.

VOLLMÖLLER, KARL GUSTAV (1878–1948), film pioneer, engineer, businessman, and Neoromantic poet from the circle of Stefan George who worked on Hollywood films until his death. Vollmöller's early creation, the poem cycle *Parcival* (1897–1900; published 1902), is considered to be the most "modern" treatment of the subject, one reason being its imagistic language. The poem by Wolfram von Eschenbach, here framed in the diction of the *Jugendstil*, is made to mirror the modern period. [UM/WCM]

Vollmöller, Karl Gustav. *Parcival*. Milan: Treves, 1902.

Schulze, Ursula. "Ideologisierung durch Strukturverlust." In *Akten des DFG Symposions zur Mittelalter-Rezeption*, ed. Peter Wapnewski. Stuttgart: Metzler, 1985.

VON FÜRSTENBERG, VEITH, film director and member of the "New German Cinema," shot the first German fantasy film, *Feuer und Schwert—Die Legende von Tristan und Isolde*, in Ireland ("Fire and Sword . . . ," 1981); it was not a commercial success. In part, von Fürstenberg gives the medieval subject matter a new interpretation. Isolde, for example, offers the love potion to Tristan with premeditation. The film is distinguished by its poetic images, but it inclines to an apathy that does not do justice to the material. It neither attains the forceful imagery of Boorman's *Excalibur* (which was filmed at exactly the same time, also in Ireland), nor does it exhibit the extreme, but convincing, stylization of Rohmer's *Perceval le Gallois*. [UM/WCM]

VORTIGERN, a fifth-century British ruler, blamed by the Welsh for the Saxons' settlement in Britain, and thus for their eventual takeover of what is now England. Vortigern's friendship with them is the cause of the troubles that Arthur temporarily ends.

"Vortigern" in Welsh is *Gwrtheyrn*, and the king figures in the Triads as Gwrtheyrn the Thin. Despite his bad reputation, one or two places in Wales are named after him, such as Nant Gwrtheyrn by Caernarvon Bay. Nennius's *Historia Brittonum* makes him reign during a vague forty-year period after the end of Roman rule. When the Saxon brothers Hengist and Horsa land with three ships, Vortigern allows them to live in the isle of Thanet and to bring more of their heathen compatriots from the Continent. He promises to maintain them if they will fight the Picts and Scots who are harassing Britain. They do so but also exploit Vortigern's failings to seize more territory. Hengist gives him his daughter as a wife, in exchange for Kent. Later, he tricks Vortigern into arranging a conference at which the British nobles are massacred; Hengist then imprisons him and extorts further lands.

Nennius names Ambrosius as Vortigern's chief British rival. This is Ambrosius Aurelianus. However, the narrative adds little to what is known of him. He appears in a legendary tale: Vortigern tries to build a fortress among the Welsh mountains, but supernatural happenings halt the work. The king's magicians say that he must find a boy with no father, kill him, and sprinkle his blood on the building site. A boy whose mother claims to have conceived without intercourse is brought to the spot. He challenges the magicians to tell what is under the foundations. When they cannot, he reveals a pool with two serpents—one red, one white—that fight each other. The boy interprets them as representing the Britons and Saxons. His name turns out to be Ambrosius (in Welsh, *Emrys*—the place is still called Dinas Emrys). Vortigern, shaken, gives him authority over western Britain.

With all this, Nennius interweaves legends of St. Germanus, who visited Britain twice to oppose the Pelagian heresy, a doctrine of British origin. The first visit was in 429 with another bishop, Lupus; the second was possibly six years later. However, Nennius's Germanus episodes, like his tale of Ambrosius, are too fanciful to be much use in linking Vortigern with history. The saint and the king clash, but with no reason given, apart from scandal about Vortigern living in incest with his daughter. Nennius offers several versions of his end. The most credible is that he wandered from place to place amid general hate, "until his heart broke and he died without honor."

Geoffrey of Monmouth adopts and expands most of this, prefacing it with a story making Vortigern an unscrupulous usurper and closing with his death when the rightful princes return. (*See* AURELIUS AMBROSIUS; CONSTANTINE [1].) In Geoffrey's version, the prophetic youth becomes Merlin. Vortigern's Saxon settlers remain in Britain, and the glories of Arthur are founded on a campaign that subdues them for many years.

Despite the fantasy, Vortigern did exist. He appears in sources unaffected by Welsh legend. Gildas speaks of a *superbus tyrannus*, or "preeminent ruler," who, in concert with a council, brought in the Saxons, and while he leaves this man anonymous, the English historian Bede in 731 calls him Vortigern. Also, the *Anglo-Saxon Chronicle* refers to Vortigern as the Britons' king at the time of a battle in Kent.

Nennius gives a genealogy suggesting a Gloucestershire background for him and makes him an ancestor of a Welsh royal house. He is mentioned on a ninth-century monument near Llangollen in north Wales, the Pillar of Eliseg. According to this, St. Germanus gave a blessing to one of his sons (an incident known to Nennius), and Vortigern's wife, who bore this son, was a daughter of Maximus, an emperor proclaimed in Britain. After Maximus's downfall in 388, his young daughters became imperial wards. An eventual marriage of one of them to a British noble could have been part of a treaty transferring authority to him, which he might then have exploited to achieve sovereign power. A title that Geoffrey alleges Vortigern held seems to give an oblique hint at the Maximus connection.

Appended to the *Historia Brittonum* is a note dating Vortigern's supremacy from 425. Geoffrey says his surrender of Kent occurred at the time of Germanus's first visit, in 429, and this is at least compatible. As to his status when he reigned, the meaning of "Vortigern" itself is a clue. Though found later as a name, it is probably a title here, or, at any rate, a designation. In the British language, it would have meant "over-chief" or "over-king." Taken in conjunction with other royal designations, such as "Vortimer," it indicates that the Britons, like their Celtic kinsfolk in Ireland, had high kings—kings with paramountcy at least in theory over a number of regional rulers—and the man called Vortigern was one, his personal name being unrecorded. It is noteworthy that Nennius names a ruler of Kent whom Vortigern sets aside by superior authority in his deal with Hengist. Gildas's phrase *superbus tyrannus* would be a Latin rendering of the "high king" dignity, the word *tyrannus* in the Latin of the time implying not so much tyranny as doubtful legitimacy. The high kingship seemingly remained unstable and ill-defined, never evolving a standard form of the title, and faded out as Britain disintegrated.

Historians have suggested that Vortigern was a nationalist, sponsoring the Pelagian heresy as a British version of Christianity, this being the truth behind Germanus's conflict with him. The idea is speculative. But the advent of the Saxons (a term comprising the Saxons proper and their associates the Angles and Jutes, all destined to blend as "English") is a fact of history. A few were already in Britain early in the fifth century, possibly as squatters. Larger groups came later, apparently as "federates"—barbarians allotted land and maintenance in return for military service. This was Late Roman practice; in Britain, the federates got out of hand, and many more of their kinsfolk arrived in their wake, without permission. Bede puts the first authorized settlement around the middle of the fifth century. This dating reflects a confusion in Gildas, and archaeology proves it to be too late. The notes appended to Nennius make the process begin in 428, Vortigern's fourth year. The real extent of his personal responsibility is uncertain. [GA]

Nennius. *Historia Brittonum*, Chapters 31, 36–49, 66.

Geoffrey of Monmouth. *Historia Regum Britanniae*, Book VI, Chapter 6, through Book VIII, Chapter 2.

Alcock, Leslie. *Arthur's Britain*. London: Penguin, 1971, pp. 33–34, 102–09, 359.

Bromwich, Rachel. *Trioedd Ynys Prydein*. Cardiff: University of Wales Press, 1961; 2nd ed. 1978, pp. 392–96.

Chadwick, N.K., ed. *Studies in Early British History*. Cambridge: Cambridge University Press, 1954, pp. 18–19, 26–33, 254–61.

Dumville, David. "Sub-Roman Britain: History and Legend." *History*, 62 (1977), 173–91.

VORTIMER, in Nennius's *Historia Brittonum*, Vortigern's eldest son, who breaks with him and makes war on the Saxons he has settled in Kent. Vortimer fights them four times and drives them out but dies soon after. They return with Vortigern's acquiescence and resume their depredations. Geoffrey of Monmouth expands the story, saying that the Britons, angry at Vortigern's pro-Saxon stance, deposed him and made Vortimer king instead. When he won the Kentish victory, his Saxon stepmother poisoned him, and Vortigern was back in power.

As a figure of history, Vortimer eludes definition. If he existed at all, he probably did die before Vortigern, because there is no hint of a succession. Morris, one of the few modern historians to take him seriously, equates three of his battles with three recorded in the *Anglo-Saxon Chronicle* and dated 455, 457, and 465. Since Vortigern is unlikely to have lived beyond the mid-450s, this attempt to pin Vortimer down involves pulling back the *Chronicle* dates ten years or more. Geoffrey puts his campaign earlier still—contemporary with the mission of Germanus and Lupus in 429. This, however, is a product of his dynastic fictions. In 429, any Saxons settled in Britain as auxiliary troops would still have been few and controllable.

When he writes of Vortimer, Nennius employs the Welsh spelling *Guorthemir*. This has variants of its own, but the fifth-century original from which it derives is a British form *Vortamorix*, which, like *Vortigern*, would probably have been a title or designation. The syllable *vor* meant "over"; *tamo-* was a superlative suffix; *rix* meant "king." As *Vortigern* is the "over-king," so *Vortimer* is the "over-most" or "highest" king. Whether or not he was actually Vortigern's son, he may have put up a rival claim to authority, adopting a distinctive and grander form of the royal style. [GA]

Nennius. *Historia Brittonum*, Chapters 43–44.

Geoffrey of Monmouth. *Historia Regum Britanniae*, Book VI, Chapters 13–14.

Bromwich, Rachel. *Trioedd Ynys Prydein*. Cardiff: University of Wales Press, 1961; 2nd ed. 1978, pp. 386–88.

Morris, John. *The Age of Arthur*. New York: Scribner, 1973, pp. 80–83.

VULGATE CYCLE (also called the Lancelot-Grail Cycle or the Pseudo-Map Cycle), one of the major literary monuments that mark the shift from verse to prose in the writing of Arthurian romance. In the twelfth century, when Chrétien de Troyes was composing his chivalric tales in verse, prose was reserved largely for translations of Latin works, commentaries or paraphrases of sacred texts and sermons in particular. In the thirteenth century, prose became the medium of vernacular chronicles, such as those by Robert de Clari and Villehardouin, followed by Joinville's *Histoire de Saint Louis*. When authors begin to cast the Arthurian material into prose ca. 1210, the scope of these tales becomes simultaneously more historical and more religious: the focus shifts from the courtly knight to the Grail quester, and the material is organized into cycles of tales that attempt to recount the entire history of the Grail from its origin in the Passion of Christ to the successful accomplishment of the quest by the chosen hero. The earliest example of this tendency is found in the *Roman du Graal*, a prose trilogy that is attributed to Robert de Boron and that recounts the biblical history of the Grail vessel (*Joseph d'Arimathie*), its arrival in Great Britain along with the discovery of the future King Arthur (*Merlin*), the quest for the Holy Grail, and the subsequent demise of Arthur's world (*Perceval*).

The Vulgate Cycle (ca. 1215–35) offers a more elaborate version of this literary scenario, expanding the Prose *Perceval* into two separate tales: the *Queste del Saint Graal* and the *Mort (le roi) Artu*, and adding a lengthy rendition of the *Lancelot* story to make a total of five roughly sequential narratives. The *Lancelot propre* (or Prose *Lancelot*), the *Queste*, and the *Mort Artu* were written first, and supplemented by the *Estoire del Saint Graal* and the *Estoire de Merlin* (or Vulgate *Merlin*), although the latter two are designed to head the sequence in terms of narrative chronology.

Though the cycle is anonymous, it contains elaborate scenarios of fictive authorship. The *Queste* and *Mort Artu* are attributed to Walter Map, a scribe at the court of Henry II who died before the composition of the texts he is supposed to have written. The *Estoire* and the *Merlin* bear the name of Robert de Boron, purported author of the *Roman du Graal* and its predecessor in verse. Emphasis is placed particularly in the *Queste* on genealogies of narrative transmission. The tale is said to have passed from the oral deposition of knights who recount their adventures at King Arthur's court, to a scribal copy of this narrative, to a Latin version later translated into French. The *Merlin* results ostensibly from Merlin's dictation to his scribe Blaise, who combines accounts of the Arthurian past with those of Christ's miracles. The *Estoire* claims to issue directly from the mouth of God and from a book that Christ, the divine author, gave the vernacular "author" to copy.

Appeal is thus made to two distinct traditions of authority: the Divine Book has its secular counterpart in King Henry's written records, and the all-powerful voice of God has its vernacular rival—the oral tales of King Arthur's knights. This conflation of written and oral modes is played out in the very pages we read, since the tales committed to writing are recounted to us by the textualized and highly ambiguous voice of *li contes*. This fictive voice usurps the traditional role of author and narrator by speaking, becoming silent, ending one narrative segment to begin another. Scholars have argued for both single and multiple authorship of the cycle—the most convincing theory postulates an original "architect" whose plan for the *Lancelot*, *Queste*, and *Mort Artu* was carried out by a series of authors—but the historical authors of the Vulgate Cycle remain well concealed behind the voice of *li contes* and the fabricated attributions of authorship accompanying it.

An elaborate matrix of cross-references involving prophecy and family lineage serves to thematize the conjunction of sacred and secular modes that is cultivated throughout the cycle. The *Lancelot* announces at its beginning that Lancelot was given the baptismal name of Galahad, thus forging a crucial link between the archetypal knight-lover and the chosen hero of the *Queste del Saint Graal*. At the end of the *Lancelot*, we learn that Lancelot is in fact Galahad's father, having engendered the Grail hero during a visit with King Pelles's daughter at Corbenic, although the son far surpasses the more courtly Lancelot in spiritual achievement. Galahad represents the ideal conjunction of religious and chivalric modes, and of past and future epochs. Descending from David and Joseph of Arimathea on his father's side, and from the Grail kings on his mother's, he is the embodiment of biblical history destined to cure the ills of the troubled Arthurian world.

The belated prologue to the Vulgate Cycle supplied by the *Estoire* recasts this father/son scenario in yet a more religious vein. A highly Christianized version of Robert de Boron's *Joseph*, this tale adds to the story of the Grail-keeper, Joseph of Arimathea, the narrative of his son, Josephe, whose purity and chastity qualify him to become the first Christian bishop. Joseph catches Christ's blood in the Holy Vessel after the Crucifixion, miraculously survives forty-three years in prison, and, when liberated, transports the sacred object to Sarras (the imaginary land of the Saracens). It is, however, Josephe who has a privileged vision of Christ while contemplating the Grail and becomes the spiritual leader of the Christians. The evangelization of the East and West ensues in highly stylized accounts of conversion: Mordred, Nascien, and Celidoine are instructed in succession to journey to a desert isle where each falls prey to a bewitching temptress until a *prudhomme* (holy man) offers spiritual guidance and release. A final voyage leads the faithful to Great Britain, where the Grail, sign of the covenant between God and his chosen people, performs a series of miracles. When Josephe dies, he confers the Grail on Alain, the first Fisher King, who places it in Corbenic Castle, where its guardians await the arrival of the *Bon Chevalier*. Without drawing directly on biblical apocrypha, this romance invents episodes that imitate the apocryphal tradition, mixing them with incidents modeled after Breton saints' lives, Tristan stories, and other Old French romances to provide an elaborate "preview" of the tales to come.

In the *Estoire de Merlin*, the most chronicle-like of the

Vulgate stories, Merlin as prophet and enchanter becomes the nexus where chivalric and sacred threads of the narrative cross. With a knowledge of the past, inherited from his incubus father, and a divine gift of foresight, Merlin confounds onlookers with his ability to explain mysterious events and predict the future. After using his magic to disguise King Uther as the Duke of Tintagel so that the king can lie with Igerne, the duke's wife, and engender Arthur, Merlin establishes the future king's authority—by having him pull the sword from the stone—and assures his military supremacy—by inventing ingenious combat strategies. Chivalry here dons a supernatural dimension, however, as the Round Table, originally characterized as a meeting place of Arthur's most valiant knights, becomes an exact replica of the Grail table—itself fashioned after the table of the Last Supper. The principal heroes of this tale are Arthur and Gawain, who with Merlin's help score repeated victories against Arthur's rebellious barons. Their military successes are developed in detail in a narrative *suite* (the *Suite du Merlin* or historical *suite*) that links the *Merlin* proper to the *Lancelot*. It is also in this portion of the tale that we learn of Arthur's marriage to Guenevere, Merlin's love of Viviane, and the birth of Lancelot.

The *Lancelot*, which alone accounts for half of the Vulgate Cycle, details the adventures of its most popular if flawed chivalric hero. Drawing on the scenario recounted in Chrétien de Troyes's *Chevalier de la charrete*, and on the *enfances* provided by a lost Anglo-Norman tale (predecessor of the German *Lanzelet* by Ulrich von Zatzikhoven, ca. 1200), the Vulgate *Lancelot* enlarges the legendary biography of its hero by adding a long series of highly stylized adventures. Lancelot's role as outlined by the Lady of the Lake, a fairy mentor who holds her power from Merlin and the Devil, is essentially secular: to combine earthly chivalry with charitable acts, defending the Church and protecting the weak. Lacking specific instruction in chastity or spirituality, Lancelot falls in love with Guenevere and, to prove his worth, undertakes a series of exploits that form the bulk of the tale. Although these episodes are highly repetitive, they fall into three major patterns—imprisonment and release, deception and perception, wounding and healing—patterns that characterize both the captive state of Logres awaiting the chosen hero, and the captive nature of the romance text, which, while claiming to possess the authority of Scripture, indulges wholeheartedly in the verbal trap of secular narrative. In addition to being arranged in patterns, the disparate adventures of the many knights are carefully knit together in the *Lancelot* through a technique of *entrelacement*, the interweaving of narrative segments within a remarkably consistent chronology.

A lengthy segment of the tale is devoted to Galehaut, who is the go-between for Lancelot and Guenevere during a period when their love is threatened by the False Guenevere and Morgain, and when Arthur himself is seduced by the enchantress Camille. Gauvain and Hector become principal chivalric heroes in this segment, only to be eclipsed by Lancelot in the "Conte de la charrete" portion of this tale. Lancelot's activities deviate significantly from those recounted in the cemetery scene of Chrétien's *Charrete*: the tombstone that previously named Lancelot as the future liberator of Gorre is here replaced by two tombstones. The hero's failure at the second one, attributed to his lust for Guenevere, predicts his subsequent exclusion from the Grail quest. As Lancelot's behavior becomes demonstrably more flawed, his cousin Bohort emerges as one of the elect who will join Perceval and Galahad on the final quest of the Grail.

The *Queste* begins with a description of Galahad's uncanny powers as chosen hero and ends with his privileged viewing of the mysterious Grail vessel. The bulk of the tale is concerned, however, with attempts of less-successful knights: Lionel, Hector, and Gauvain, who form the elite of earthly questers, and Perceval and Bohort, who are chosen but less accomplished than Galahad. Drawing on Chrétien's *Conte del Graal* and its First and Second Continuations, this text combines mythic elements from the Matter of Britain—the Perilous Seat, the Sword in the Stone, the abolition of evil customs—with more Christianized motifs. The Bleeding Lance and Broken Sword, found in Robert de Boron's unfinished Grail trilogy and in the Didot-*Perceval*, become the lance of Longinus and King David's sword. The Grail itself is the vessel from which Christ ate the paschal lamb with his disciples.

To substantiate the text's authority and give the illusion that it advances didactic truth, the exploits, visions, and dreams recounted in the course of this tale are routinely interpreted by resident hermits who offer to tell the *senefiance* and *vérité* of what we read. This unusual method of composition has led scholars to read the *Queste* allegorically: as a spiritual treatise promulgated by the Cistercian order of monks, who used the romance mode for purely didactic purpose. Such an undertaking, however, raises the complex problem of transcribing the ineffable into language. If the ethereal Grail exists, as we are told, beyond the realm of mortal speech, how can one possibly represent it in a romance text? The problematic rapport between Lancelot and Galahad as representatives of the secular and sacred worlds is here reproduced in another form, as the secular strives to achieve what lies clearly beyond its grasp.

The *Mort Artu* provides a *suite* for the *Queste* and a conclusion to the entire cycle. The holocaust on Salisbury Plain, in which Arthur and his bastard son Mordred kill each other, is preceded by an inexorable succession of narrative events set in motion by the renewed love affair between Lancelot and Guenevere and complicated by incidents of misunderstanding and misinterpretation. These two narrative strains are established early in the tale when Lancelot, who comes to the Winchester tournament in disguise, is accused of adultery with the Queen and suspected of loving the Dame d'Escalot. When the Queen is charged subsequently with poisoning a knight at Arthur's court, Lancelot comes to her defense and accidentally kills Gauvain's brother, Gaheriet, inciting Arthur and his nephew to declare war against Lancelot and his family. When departing for battle, Arthur entrusts his kingdom to Mordred, who usurps the royal power, prompting the King's return and the mortal combat between father and son. Before dying, Arthur orders his squire Girflet to throw the famed sword Excalibur into the lake, where a disembodied hand catches it. A boat bearing Morgain and her enchanted attendants then carries Arthur out to sea. Continuing some narrative incidents established in the Prose *Lancelot*, this tale also builds on the adultery scenario of the Tristan legends and develops the military schema laid out in Geoffrey of Monmouth's *Historia Regum Britanniae* and *Vita Merlini* and the end of the Didot-*Perceval*. But the *Mort Artu* is distinguished from these predecessors and all other volumes of the Vulgate Cycle by the dramatic alignment of events in an inexorable chain of cause and effect proceeding relentlessly from a harmless chivalric tournament to a bloody cataclysmic battle.

Despite its emphasis on chronological sequence, however, this chronicle of Arthur's last days does not come to a definitive close. The text's apparent grounding in linear time and secular history is undermined in the final pages by a timeless openendedness reminiscent of scriptural narrative. Arthur, though dead and buried, is expected to return miraculously at a later date, effecting a human resurrection in line with the Second Coming. And the Arthurian narrative, having come to an apocalyptic end, will similarly be continued in subsequent romance texts. [EJB]

Frappier, Jean, ed. *La Mort le roi Artu: roman du XIIIe siècle*. Geneva: Droz, 1954; 3rd ed. 1959.

Hucher, Eugène, ed. *Le Saint-Graal*. 3 vols. Le Mans: Monnoyer, 1875–78.

Micha, Alexandre, ed. *Lancelot: roman en prose du XIIIe siècle*. 9 vols. Geneva: Droz, 1978–83.

———, ed. *Merlin: roman du XIIIe siècle*. Geneva: Droz, 1979.

Pauphilet, Albert, ed. *La Queste del Saint Graal*. Paris: Champion, 1923.

Sommer, H. Oskar, ed. *The Vulgate Version of the Arthurian Romances*. 8 vols. Washington, D.C.: Carnegie Institution, 1908–16.

Cable, James. trans. *The Death of King Arthur*. Harmondsworth: Penguin, 1971.

Corley, Corin, trans. *Lancelot of the Lake*. Oxford: Oxford University Press, 1989. (Abridged translation of the short version of *Lancelot*.)

Lacy, Norris J., et al., trans. *The Lancelot-Grail Cycle*. 5 vols. New York: Garland, forthcoming.

Matarasso, P.M., trans. *The Quest of the Holy Grail*. Harmondsworth: Penguin, 1969.

Burns, E. Jane. *Arthurian Fictions: Re-reading the Vulgate Cycle*. Columbus: Ohio State University Press, 1985.

Kennedy, Elspeth. *Lancelot and the Grail: A Study of the Prose Lancelot*. Oxford: Clarendon, 1986.

Leupin, Alexandre. *Le Graal et la littérature*. Lausanne: L'Âge d'Homme, 1982.

Micha, Alexandre. *Essais sur le cycle du Lancelot-Graal*. Geneva: Droz, 1987.

WACE. What little we know about the life of Wace, we owe to the autobiographical asides in his *Roman de Rou*. He tells us that he was born on the Norman isle of Jersey early in the twelfth century (ca. 1110?). As a child, he was taken to be educated at Caen in Normandy and later in the Île de France, possibly at Paris or Chartres. He returned after many years to Caen and took up a literary career. His earlier works, like those of Chrétien de Troyes, were translations from the Latin to *romanz* (the Old French vernacular). Of the many occasional pieces he must have composed in this period, only three can be identified with certainty: *La Vie de Ste. Marguerite* ("The Life of St. Margaret," a fragment of 420 lines), *La Vie de St. Nicholas* ("The Life of St. Nicholas," about 1,500 lines), and *La Conception Nostre Dame* ("The Conception of Our Lady"), all of which are signed "G[u]ace" or "Maistre G[u]ace." Wace's first long poem was his *Roman de Brut* ("Romance of Brutus"), which, he informs us at the end, he completed in 1155. This work, which his English translator Layamon tells us was presented by Wace to Eleanor of Aquitaine, probably attracted the attention of her husband, the English king Henry II, for whom he began in 1160 the *Roman de Rou*, a verse history of the dukes of Normandy. It was at about this time, too, that he was given the canonry of Bayeux, perhaps as a sort of retainer. Around 1175, however, after having composed over 16,000 lines covering Norman history down to the battle of Tinchebray in 1106, Wace was supplanted in his task as court historian, at Henry's insistence, by Benoît de Ste.-Maure, author of the successful *Roman de Troie*. We have no reliable information regarding the date of Wace's death.

Wace's *Brut* is a key text in Arthurian studies, for it is among the earliest works to introduce Celtic matter into French. His principal source, since he could not immediately locate a copy of Geoffrey of Monmouth's *Historia Regum Britanniae*, may have been the *Britannici sermonis liber vetustissimus* (possibly by the archdeacon Walter of Oxford), composed in the early 1130s to ingratiate the Celtic part of the population with the new Norman overlords by stressing the Britons' claim to Britain, tracing its history back to the Trojans, in particular to Aeneas, with the help of early Welsh chronicles and Nennius. According to these sources, Aeneas's great-grandson Brutus led the Trojans out of Greek captivity to Britain (< Brytt < Brutus, by popular etymology). It was this text that Geoffrey of Monmouth subsequently reworked into his prose *Historia* (ca. 1138) and that was then expanded by Wace into some 15,000 Old French octosyllabic lines. Wace's text is extant in eighteen complete manuscript copies and several fragments.

Wace omits the names of some minor characters, abbreviates purely religious history, and deletes some brutal passages, such as Arthur's torturing of the Picts and Scots. His work contains several episodes that presage the spirit of courtly love (King Aganippus's love "from afar" for Cordeïlle, King Leïr's youngest daughter, and Uther Pendragon's love at first sight for Ygerne); but he also stresses the catastrophic consequences of love-passion (in, for example, Locrin's and Mordred's adulterous relationships). While he eliminates the most fantastic elements in his source, such as Merlin's prophecies, his additions are of particular interest for the study of Arthurian romance. He is the first to mention the Round Table; he alludes to Breton storytellers and the existence around 1150 of an oral tradition concerning Arthur; he adds topical details based most likely on personal travels in southwestern Britain; he comments on the "Breton Hope" of Arthur's messianic return from the Isle of Avalon. Also important in this regard is a passage in the *Roman de Rou* concerning the forest of Brocéliande.

Wace is noted for his skill in description, his honesty in treating his material, and his lively style. He had enormous influence on subsequent French authors of Arthurian materials: on Chrétien de Troyes and Marie de France, as well as on the anonymous authors of the Vulgate *Merlin*, the *Mort Artu*, the Didot-*Perceval*, the *Suite du Merlin*, and the *Livre d'Artus*. Around 1200 Layamon, a priest of Arley Regis in Worcestershire, adapted the *Brut* into Middle English, swelling it to over 32,000 lines. It is Layamon who reports that Wace had dedicated his work to Eleanor of Aquitaine. (*See also* GEOFFREY OF MONMOUTH; LAYAMON.) [WWK]

Wace. *Le Roman de Brut*, ed. I. Arnold. 2 vols. Paris: SATF, 1938–40.

———. *Le Roman de Rou de Wace*, ed. A.J. Holden. 3 vols. Paris: SATF, 1970–73.

——— and Layamon. *Arthurian Chronicles*, trans. Eugene Mason. Dent: London, 1912.

Foulon, Charles. "Wace." In *Arthurian Literature in the Middle Ages*, ed. Roger Sherman Loomis. Oxford: Clarendon, 1959, pp. 94–103.

Pelan, Margaret. *L'Influence du "Brut" de Wace sur les romanciers français de son temps*. Paris: Droz, 1931.

WAGNER, RICHARD (1813–1883). The mention of Wagner in an Arthurian context immediately calls to mind two of his greatest operas, *Tristan und Isolde* and *Parsifal.* Yet his fascination with such subjects is suggested as early as 1850, in his marginally Arthurian *Lohengrin,* which presents the story of King Parsifal's son. The Holy Grail theme occurs at various points through the opera, but its significance is explained only in the final act, when the hero's "narrative" offers details of Monsalvat, the castle where the Grail is guarded by a group of holy knights. Those knights have magical powers, so long as their identity is not known. Lohengrin reveals his ancestry and the fact that he has been sent by the Grail.

Wagner's first contact with Arthurian legend had probably been in Dresden, where he studied medieval literature. He no doubt studied Gottfried von Strassburg's *Tristan* and may have been familiar with the earlier works of Thomas d'Angleterre, Béroul, and Eilhart von Oberge. Wagner mentions Wolfram von Eschenbach's *Parzifal* in his correspondence, and it is likely that he also knew Chrétien de Troyes's *Perceval.* The Tristan and Parzifal stories must have impressed the composer deeply, for he returned to the medieval texts and used them as the basis for two of his greatest operas (presented in 1865 and 1882). However, he uses his music-drama as a showcase for philosophical ideas that had for some time been taking form in his mind. His philosophy necessitated several important changes in the legends, as did the demands of a musical presentation. Wagner's dramas, although based on the medieval texts, are new and personal creations.

In the interest of dramatic simplicity, Wagner had to condense the plot of Gottfried's *Tristan.* The action of the opera is very simple, being reduced to three main dramatic situations corresponding to the three acts of the opera. The battles and adventures that occupy the first part of Gottfried's romance and establish Tristan's chivalric reputation are reduced to a few lines in the first act. Gottfried's vivid hunting scenes are practically eliminated, merely alluded to musically with hunting-horn sounds in the second act. Wagner reduces the group of conspirators against Tristan to one person, Melot, and completely does away with Isolde of the White Hands. By limiting the number of characters, Wagner is able to rivet the spectator's attention on the tragic couple and thus intensify the drama.

Both Gottfried and Wagner emphasize the change in the two main characters after the drinking of the love potion. In Gottfried's version, the gentle Isolde is willing to sacrifice Brangaene's virginity to hide her own guilt. Later on, she actually commands two of her squires to kill the innocent Brangaene, a task they are unable to perform. After the potion, Isolde's reason and her sense of justice are overshadowed by her all-consuming passion. Wagner underlines this change by emphasizing the music in the last two acts. In the first act, the music had served to highlight the text. This is consistent with Wagner's essay on the synthesis of the arts published in 1851, *Oper und Drama,* where he preaches a complete union of word and tone. The music and text would be fused to form an indivisible unit he called "die Versmelodie" ("melodic verse"). The melodic line is dependent on the words to which it is united; the music then helps to extend the emotional content of the words into the more expressive sphere of music. This is the central exposition of Wagner's "Gesamtkunstwerk." The text is enhanced by the music, but the words of the drama are still prominent. We are still in a rational, conceptual world. With the drinking of the love potion, we enter a new world, a world dominated by music. The voice is often lost under the weight of the orchestra. Wagner sometimes extends vowel sounds to such an extent that the meaning of the word is lost. The emotion is all-important. The wonderful second-act love duet contains many passages of free canonic imitation. The lovers sing at the same time, but the one sings words the other has already finished. Naturally, the words are difficult to understand; the conceptual gives way to the passion of the moment.

This shift of emphasis from the textual to the musical, so appropriate in the Tristan drama, is probably due in part to Wagner's reading of the German philosopher Arthur Schopenhauer. Schopenhauer held music to be a superior art, being independent of the world as representation in that it does not derive its material from phenomena and is thus closer to the metaphysical will itself. Music after *Tristan und Isolde* plays a more important and a more independent role than in the earlier operas. The leitmotifs are less strictly associated with a particular text or with a particular object.

Wagner's interest in Schopenhauer may also have influenced some of the changes he made in the text. In Gottfried's version, the lovers drink the potion by mistake, thinking it to be wine. Isolde truly hates Tristan, and there is no love until after the potion has been mistakenly drunk. In Wagner, Isolde reveals that her supposed hatred is in fact love. Knowing that she can never find happiness in this world, she decides to drink the death potion and to avenge herself of Tristan's rejection by having him drink of it also. Tristan also expresses a death wish and gladly downs the potion. Having drunk what they believe to be poison, they are free to confess their love: Isolde free of her shame and Tristan free of his duty to King Mark. Rather than cause their love, the potion in Wagner's opera simply permits them to voice their love.

The pair engage in a Schopenhauerian dialogue in the love duet of the second act. The idea of love is inexorably tied to the idea of death. They embrace and cry out, "löse von/der Welt mich los!" ("separate me from the world!"), and later, "So stürben wir,/um ungetrennt,/ewig einig" ("so we would die, to be united, forever one"). They express a desire to lose themselves in the infinite (Schopenhauer's universal will): ". . . in ungemess'nen Räumen/übersel'ges Träumen./Du Isolde,/Tristan ich,/nicht mehr Tristan,/nicht Isolde" (". . . in boundless spaces, blissful dreams; you Isolde, I Tristan; no longer Tristan, nor Isolde").

The "night and day," "dark and light," symbolism is important throughout the opera. The day seems to represent the world and worldly reality; the night, death or an escape from that reality. The light of day is the lover's enemy. In the opera, Tristan and Isolde can meet only at night. The lovers must remain separated until the light of Brangaene's torch is extinguished. When the lovers are discovered in the garden, Tristan turns to Isolde and asks: "Wohin nun Tristan scheidet,/willst du, Isold', ihm folgen?/Dem Land, das Tristan meint,/der Sonne Licht nicht scheint" ("Will you, Isolde, follow Tristan where he is going? To the land, Tristan means, where the sun's light does not shine"; Act II, scene iii). With Isolde's promise to follow, Tristan drops his guard and, inviting death, is mortally wounded. The symbolism continues in the third act. Tristan regains consciousness and tells Kurvenal that he has been in the endless realm of "earthly night." But he cannot find peace because "accursed day" still shines on Isolde. The lovers will never find rest until they both find the peace of eternal night and are united in death. Gottfried's ending, where Tristan, betrayed by his wife, dies of despair before Isolde arrives, was rejected by Wagner. The lovers must die in each other's arms. Isolde must keep her promise and follow Tristan to the land where "sunlight has no gleams." When Isolde arrives, Tristan rips off his bandages, once again attempting suicide, this time successfully. Isolde follows him after assuring the audience that Tristan lives again "calmly happy," having at last found release.

In Gottfried's version, Tristan and Isolde consummate their love immediately after drinking the potion. In a later episode, they do so eight times in as many days, and Gottfried insists that this pair of lovers "did not play the prude." Wagner allows the lovers very little time together and never permits total union until the final union in death; nevertheless, the music of the opera is intensely sensual. There are three moments of highest passion depicted in the orchestra, but each time the lovers are foiled. They have only a few minutes together to confess their love after drinking the potion before they land in Cornwall. The sailors interrupt their bliss by announcing the world of reality and ending their dream: "Heil dem König!/Kornwall Heil!" The music of the love duet in the second act modulates to an ever-higher key as the passion of the lovers rises. But Brangaene interrupts them twice with her eerie and significant warning, "Habet Acht!/Habet Acht!/Schon weicht dem Tag die Nacht" ("Be careful! Be careful! Already the night is yielding to the day"). The lovers continue their song but are finally interrupted by the sudden entrance of Kurvenal, King Mark, and the traitor Melot, announced in the orchestra by a tremendous dissonance. The music is exquisitely sensual in the final scene, when Isolde sings the famous "Liebestod." Isolde ends the opera alone, for Tristan has already died in the previous scene, but the union of their spirits is imminent.

Both Gottfried and Wagner depict society and the official marriage of Isolde and King Mark as an obstacle to

89. Woodcut, King Arthur and His Knights, from *Tristan de Leonnoys* (Paris: Antoine Vérard, 1506).

Tristan's and Isolde's true love. In the opera, as in many medieval romances and in most troubadour poetry, the lovers find love outside of marriage. Yet Wagner seems to suggest not only that love and marriage are incompatible but that love and any sort of tangible or temporal satisfaction are incompatible. The lovers believe that the only true fulfillment is in death.

The two lovers' yearning for death and their dissatisfaction and uneasiness in this world are expressed eloquently in the music, which modulates unceasingly from bar to bar, all but abolishing any sense of tonal center. Wagner increases the tension over long periods of time, denying the resolution to the listener, who finds release only when the lovers die. The B-major chord at the end of the "Liebestod," awaited since the love duet of the second act, floats upward into infinity, and the listener can exhale at last after forty-five minutes.

Wagner's music reveals the intent of the spoken word, and the listener is immediately aware if the speaker is sincere, sarcastic, or lying. The orchestra is constantly commenting upon the action, and the music adds its power to the dialogue. Although Wagner's libretto is not great poetry, the combination of music and drama produces a powerful effect.

The music plays perhaps a greater role in Wagner's last opera, *Parsifal*, than in any of the preceding. Whereas in *Tristan* the words are sometimes unintelligible owing to prolonged separation of syllables or simultaneous singing of different vocal lines, *Parsifal* goes a step farther and quite often has no spoken dialogue at all. It is interesting to note that although *Parsifal* is one of Wagner's longest operas in presentation time, the libretto is the shortest. Gestures and music are accorded great importance. This can be explained partially by the fact that *Parsifal* is an opera of Christian ritual. In the scenes that portray, for instance, the partaking of communion by the knights, Kundry's baptism, or the anointing of Parsifal, the gesture is all-important. Music intensifies the action and translates the character's reaction to the event.

The music also reveals truths that may or may not be evident to the characters on stage. Parsifal's role as the Pure Fool who will redeem the Grail Brotherhood is revealed to the audience before any of the characters, including Parsifal, is aware of the fact. This is accomplished by means of the famous Wagnerian leitmotif. The distinctive Pure Fool motive, characterized by a descending diminished fifth, rising major sixth, and descending perfect fifth, is prepared by Gurnemanz ("ihm hilft nur eines, nur der Eine") and is finally introduced by Amfortas, who explains that only "der reine Thor" can heal him. The complete motive ("Durch Mitleid wissend, der reine Thor, harre sein', den ich erkor") is sung by Gurnemanz, who explains to four squires the promise issued from the Grail. The squires immediately repeat the motive in four-part harmony. This rendition of the motive directly precedes news of Parsifal's shooting of the swan and his entrance on stage. Parsifal is thus associated with the Pure Fool theme by juxtaposition. He is present at the Hall of the Grail when young boys, invisible above the stage, again sing the complete motive in four-part harmony. But no one recognizes Parsifal as the promised one, and Gurnemanz chases Parsifal from the hall, proclaiming him "nothing but a fool." The orchestra, however, insists on the true identity of Parsifal by quietly playing the Pure Fool motive, which is now clearly associated in the listener's mind with the Grail's promise. To insist further upon the fact, a solo voice sings the words "Durch Mitleid wissend, der reine Thor" ("Knowing through pity, the purest fool") just after Parsifal's departure.

The opera as a whole is highly chromatic. The harmony is forever changing and, as in *Tristan*, provides few satisfying cadences. Half and deceptive cadences predominate, lending the work a sense of restlessness. The few passages of extended diatonicism offer a welcome contrast; they are most often related to the Grail, to the Grail Brotherhood, or to Parsifal. "The Good," then, is represented by the relative stability of the diatonic passages, which in turn suggests the peace offered to the servants of the Holy Grail. The Grail theme itself has not a single accidental, staying completely within one key. This theme, besides being reassuringly diatonic and familiar in a sea of chromaticism, would no doubt have been recognized by Wagner's contemporaries as the Dresden Amen. Mendelssohn had already capitalized on the theme's religious connotations in his Reformation Symphony, and Wagner most probably also counted on its associations to add to the solemn atmosphere of his opera.

Amfortas's first-act speech to the Grail Brotherhood effectively translates his suffering; its chromaticism is all the more effective owing to the diatonic harmony established as the Grail Knights proceed to the communion tables immediately before Amfortas speaks. The purity and peace of the diatonic and relatively stable harmonic structure of the music associated with the knights is supported by a regular and stately rhythm. Amfortas's music, on the other hand, is characterized by an irregular rhythm whose frequent rests and off-beat accents betray his agitation. Amfortas's physical and mental sufferings are recounted in the text, as is his feeling of isolation. But it is the music that renders the passage so moving.

One of the most distinctive and poignant musical motives of Amfortas's monologue is the triplet figure in the orchestra, the last note of which is suspended into the following chord and then resolved upward, the dissonance of the suspension emphasizing Amfortas's yearning. This figure helps link Amfortas musically to Kundry and Parsifal, whose destinies are so closely intertwined with his own. The figure recurs as Kundry bemoans her servitude to Klingsor, and as Parsifal, after Kundry's kiss, realizes the cause of Amfortas's suffering.

As he had in *Tristan*, Wagner condenses the medieval legend to fit his dramatic ends. He once again organizes the story around three main dramatic situations that correspond to the three acts of the opera. Wagner's immediate source was Wolfram von Eschenbach, whom he had already incorporated as a character in his *Tannhäuser*. He greatly reduces the number of characters, completely eliminating Gawain, who rivals Parzival himself in importance in Wolfram's romance and who plays an important role in Chrétien's account as well. Wagner concentrates the action on only four main characters: Kundry, Klingsor, Amfortas, and Parsifal (Wagner changed the spelling in the belief that two Arabic words, *Fal parsi*, meant "pure fool"). A fifth major character, Gurnemanz, serves as a kind of narrator, filling in information as necessary.

Wagner's characters are sometimes more complex than their counterparts in Wolfram's romance. The opera's Kundry is much more developed than Wolfram's Cundrie, a sorceress. Kundry, who in some respects resembles the Loathly Damsel of other Arthurian tales, is a woman of strong contradictions. She desires to do good and makes great sacrifices to help the Brotherhood of the Grail. But at the same time, owing to Klingsor's magic powers, she is an agent of evil and has even occasioned the downfall of the leader of the Grail Brotherhood. Klingsor refers to Kundry as Gundryggia, a wandering spirit of Nordic mythology, and as Ahasuerus, the man who laughed in the face of Christ and who became the Wandering Jew. The link between the two is, of course, their restlessness and search for peace.

Amfortas is also characterized by his restlessness and yearning. Wagner's Amfortas, like Wolfram's Anfortas, is plagued by a wound that will not heal. But Wagner changes more than the spelling of the name. Whereas Anfortas was wounded in the genitals (as was the *Roi Pêcheur* in Chrétien's tale), Amfortas of the opera is wounded in the side. The medieval rendition of the legend is consistent with fertility myths of earlier cultures in which the king's fertility is intimately linked with the land's productivity. Wagner aligns his Amfortas with Christian tradition, having him wounded by the same spear that pierced Christ's side. Amfortas, unlike his counterpart in the medieval romance, suffers mentally as well as physically. The keeper of the Holy Grail has betrayed the Brotherhood through his weakness and now must continue to serve, his wound an all-too-obvious mark of his sin. His guilt is compounded in the third act, when the Grail Brotherhood degenerates and his father, Titurel, dies because of Amfortas's reluctance to reveal the Grail. Amfortas's wound and its consequences seem designed to accentuate his failure by the suggested comparison with Christ. The sinful Amfortas is wounded in the same place and by the same spear as the blameless Christ. And whereas Christ, the Son of God, is sacrificed to save humankind, Amfortas sacrifices his father and the Brotherhood rather than endure the pain of revealing the Grail.

Parsifal puts an end to Kundry's and Amfortas's restlessness and yearning, just as the diatonicism associated with the young hero finally gains dominance over the chromaticism of the opera. In the third act, Parsifal returns to transform discord into harmony, giving Kundry a kiss of pure love in return for her lecherous one of the second act, and returning the holy spear to the Grail Brotherhood, making Amfortas whole.

The act that enables Parsifal to "redeem" the others is his renunciation of Kundry's advances. Total sexual abstinence is certainly not required in Wolfram's rendition, nor is it necessarily part of Christian tradition. This aspect of Wagner's opera may be due to Schopenhauer's idea of total renunciation.

In the years between *Tristan* and *Parsifal*, Wagner's focus shifts from the individual couple to universal compassion. In *Parsifal*, the disdain for the material world extends to the body itself as an objectification of the will. Individual or sexual love is replaced by the broader and nobler love of humankind. He turns from eros to agape, or, in the context of *Parsifal*, to *Mitleid*.

Wagner is best known as a composer, and it is certainly the music, more than anything else, that infuses his operas with their magic. He has, however, made an important contribution to opera history by the care he takes with all elements of his music-drama. In both *Tristan und Isolde* and *Parsifal*, Wagner combines a powerful medieval legend and a talent for music and drama to create a new work of art that is at the same time personal in its uniqueness and universal in its application. [FLT]

Beckett, Lucy. *Richard Wagner: Parsifal*. Cambridge: Cambridge University Press, 1981.

Ingenhoff, Anette. *Drama oder Epos? Richard Wagners Gattungstheorie des Musikalischen Dramas*. Tübingen: Niemeyer, 1987.

Newman, Ernest. *The Wagner Operas*. New York: Knopf, 1949.

Stein, Jack M. *Richard Wagner and the Synthesis of the Arts*. Westport, Conn.: Greenwood, 1973.

WAITE, A(RTHUR) E(DWARD) (1857–1942), British poet and mystic, argues in *The Hidden Church of the Holy Graal* (1909) and in *The Holy Grail: Its Legends and Symbolism* (1924), that the Grail legend's religious elements were derived from practices of the Celtic Church that the Latin rite had displaced after the Council of Whitby (663/4). In *The Book of the Holy Graal* (1921), blank-verse poems alternate with short lyrics, presenting subjective religious experiences in Grail imagery. Like Dante, Waite sees a beautiful woman, Beata Mea or Eva, as the bridge between physical and spiritual love. [MAW]

Waite, A.E. *The Book of the Holy Graal*. London: Watkins, 1921.

———. *The Hidden Church of the Holy Grail*. London: Rebman, 1909.

———. *The Holy Grail: Its Legends and Symbolism*. London: Rider, 1924; reissued as *The Holy Grail: The Galahad Quest in the Arthurian Literature*. New Hyde Park, N.Y.: University Books, 1961.

WALEWEIN ENDE KEYE, a Middle Dutch verse romance, written probably during the second half of the thirteenth century, that comprises some 3,660 lines. It has been transmitted exclusively in the *Lancelot-Compilatie*. Keye accuses Walewein of bragging, after which Walewein angrily leaves the court and performs so many heroic deeds that he disproves Keye's accusation. The humiliated Keye is eventually removed from the court. [BB]

Jonckbloet, W.J.A., ed. *Roman van Lancelot*. 2 vols. The Hague: van Stockum, 1846–49, Vol. 2, pp. 126–51.

WARD, CHRISTOPHER (1868–1943), gently burlesqued the stories of Arthur, Lancelot, Gareth, Tristram, and Galahad in comic verse narratives. The Arthurian poems are collected with similar treatments of other literary characters in *Sir Galahad and Other Rimes* (1936). [DN]

Ward, Christopher. *Sir Galahad and Other Rimes: Pass-Keys to the Classics*. New York: Simon and Schuster, 1936.

WARREN, ELINOR REMICK, American composer, produced *The Passing of Arthur* (1939), an hour-long oratorio based on Tennyson's "Morte d'Arthur." An episodic presentation of the narrative is dramatically enhanced by Warren's late-romantic, highly descriptive style. There are moments of sublime choral writing, and sensitively orchestrated passages support the unfolding drama throughout. This setting is regarded as one of the composer's major works. The oratorio was first performed in Los Angeles in 1940 by the Los Angeles Philharmonic with the Los Angeles Oratorio Society, Albert Coates conducting. [TJD]

Warren, Elinor Remick. *The Passing of Arthur*. New York: H.W. Gray, 1939.

WARTBURGKRIEG ("Wartburg War"), a thirteenth-century compilation of poems that belong to the learned-dialogue tradition, the German *Spruchdichtung*. Two figures associated with the Arthurian matter appear, the poet Wolfram von Eschenbach and one of his fictional characters, Klingsor the magician, known from *Parzival*. The setting is a poets' competition, a learned battle of "mastersingers," at the Wartburg before the Landgrave Hermann of Thuringia to see who can compose the best praise poem in honor of an illustrious prince. The competition assumes the character of a judicial combat with the vanquished poet liable to loss of life. Of interest from an Arthurian perspective is the subsequent competition of solving riddles that is fought out between Klingsor and Wolfram. Klingsor poses the riddles that the famous poet must solve, and one of these elicits from Wolfram the story of Lohengrin. [MEK]

Rompelmann, Tom Albert, ed. *Der Wartburgkrieg*. Amsterdam, 1939.

Krogmann, Willy. "Studien zum Wartburgkrieg." *Zeitschrift für deutsche Philologie*, 80 (1961), 62–83.

Ragotzky, Hedda. *Studien zur Wolfram-Rezeption: Die Entstehung und Verwandlung der Wolfram-Rolle in der deutschen Literatur des 13. Jahrhunderts*. Stuttgart: Kohlhammer, 1971, pp. 45–91.

WARTON, THOMAS (1728–1790), Oxford professor and critic, encouraged the Gothic Revival with *Observations on the Faerie Queene of Spenser* (1754), which defended chivalry as a civilizer of "savage and ignorant people" and discussed Spenser's use of Malory. His *History of English Poetry* (1774–81) included Arthurian romance. "The Grave of King Arthur" (1777), an ode in octosyllabic couplets, countered the tradition of *Rex Quondam, Rexque Futurus* with the claim of a Glastonbury burial. [MAW]

Warton, Thomas. *History of English Poetry*. London: Dodsley, 1774–81.

Johnston, Arthur. *Enchanted Ground: The Study of Medieval Romance in the Eighteenth Century*. London: Athlone, 1964.

WASTELAND, a motif, of probable Celtic origin, that relates the fertility of the land to the condition of its king or leader. In Chrétien de Troyes's *Perceval*, the land lies barren so long as the Fisher King's wound (in the genitals) remains uncured; had Perceval asked about the Grail, he would have cured the king. Texts gradually place more emphasis on the king's wound than on the restoration of the wasteland, and in some works, such as the *Queste del Saint Graal*, there is no mention of a wasteland related to the infirmity of the king. Other romances, such as *Perlesvaus*, suggest that the king's condition and the troubles of the land (whether barrenness or, more often, a perpetual state of war and crime) are the *result* of the hero's failure, rather than a condition that preceded it.

Modern literature has seen some strikingly original settings of the wasteland motif. One of the more curious is that of Julien Gracq, who in *Le Roi Pêcheur* inverts it to show the manor being strangled by a lush vegetation wildly out of control. The best-known modern treatment is of course T.S. Eliot's *The Waste Land*, in which the poet, inspired by Jessie L. Weston's book *From Ritual to Romance*, appropriates the wasteland as a metaphor applicable to the city, the modern world, and the human condition. [NJL]

WEDDING OF SIR GAWAIN AND DAME RAGNELL, THE, a tail-rhyme version in 855 lines of the Loathly Lady story, extant in the early sixteenth-century Rawlinson Manuscript, though probably written in the fifteenth century. Dame Ragnell and Arthur's challenger, Sir Gromer Somer Joure, are siblings, but the emphasis is less on family relations than on courtly shame and honor, here treated via a comedy of manners.

The court is horrified when Gawain, according to his promise, marries Dame Ragnell, who had saved Arthur's life. Guinevere begs for a quiet wedding; the court anxiously investigates the nuptial chamber the next morning to see if Gawain has survived. Dame Ragnell's ugliness is twice elaborately described and her monstrous appetite dwelt on. Her insistence on a public wedding, as well as her inversion of the beauty topos, answers the court's inversion of *curtesye*, whereby gratitude for her rescue of Arthur is given only after she becomes beautiful.

The author is versed in romance convention: Arthur finds adventure initially by pursuing a deer, Gawain has an attack of postnuptial *recreantise*, and so forth. Gawain is a pleasantly youthful romance figure; he loyally and optimistically helps Arthur by collecting a whole book of answers to the question of what women most desire, and he readily assents to the wedding. But his experience deepens, for his openness and courtesy permit Dame Ragnell's transformation and his own recognition that the question of whether she shall be beautiful publicly by day or privately by night is too hard for him. He gives her sovereignty, she publicly gives him obedience. A son, Gyngalyn, is conceived, and after five years Dame Ragnell dies, much mourned by Gawain.

Similarly, the romance itself deepens and extends its initial ethical vocabulary. A narratorial explicit invokes God as "veray kynge ryalle," yielding body and soul to him in hope of redemption from prison. The anonymous author, though no Chaucer, develops interesting problems and implications from the source matter. This is a better late-medieval romance than is usually allowed. [JP]

Sumner, L., ed. *The Weddynge of Sir Gawen and Dame Ragnell.* Northampton, Mass.: Smith College, 1924.

Wilhelm, James J., ed. "The Wedding of Sir Gawain and Dame Ragnell." In *The Romance of Arthur III*. New York: Garland, 1988.

WEINBERGER, MILDRED, wrote "Elaine: A Poetic Drama" (1923), in which two people witness the unfolding of their lives in an earlier incarnation as Elaine of Corbenic and Lancelot. In this account, Vivienne places a spell on Lancelot, who is saved when Elaine invokes the power of the Grail. The knight, whose dedication to Guinevere is innocent, truly loves Elaine but recognizes that the story will be told differently in later ages. [RHT]

Weinberger, Mildred. "Elaine: A Poetic Drama." *Poet-Lore*, 34 (1923), 72–110.

WEINGARTEN, ROMAIN, French author of *Le Roman de la Table Ronde, ou le livre de Blaise* ("The Romance of the Round Table, or the Book of Blaise," 1983). Through Blaise, who in traditional accounts had been Merlin's master and eventually the scribe to whom Merlin dictated his prophecies, Weingarten presents the Arthurian story from the birth of Merlin and Arthur to the death of the King. Included are most of the familiar events of the legend—the sword in the anvil, the establishment of the Round Table, and the Grail quest, but not the story of Tristan and Isolde. Weingarten uses a method of interlace reminiscent of medieval texts to narrate the adventures of Perceval (including his naive introduction to knighthood), Lancelot, Galahad, and Gawain. Curiously understated in the novel is the Lancelot-Guenevere-Arthur triangle, and the account of Arthur's death is presented briefly and factually almost to the point of flatness. [NJL]

Weingarten, Romain. *Le Roman de la Table Ronde, ou le livre de Blaise*. Paris: Albin Michel, 1983.

WELSH ARTHURIAN LITERATURE. To a degree, all of the countries that produced Arthurian literatures in the Middle Ages were once occupied by the Celts. Celtic tribes and their kingdoms were dominant from the Iberian peninsula to the Balkans, from Cisalpine Gaul to the British Isles. The Romans changed much of that, however, and by the beginning of the Christian era Celtic strengths lay chiefly in the British Isles. By the end of the Dark Ages, the Celtic regions had further shrunk to western and northern Britain, Ireland, and northwestern France (Brittany). To scholars, the term "Celtic" is essentially a linguistic one, though that implies a cultural unity as well. The two main branches of Celtic (a sister language group to Germanic, Italic, Indo-Iranian, etc., in the Indo-European family) are Goidelic and Brythonic. The former includes in its modern descendants Irish Gaelic, Scottish Gaelic, and Manx Gaelic; the latter, Welsh, Cornish, and Breton. The traditions about King Arthur arose among the Brythonic Celts. Where then do we find Arthur in the early Celtic sources, and what is his nature?

The problem that faces the scholar here is that of dating. The earliest manuscripts written in the vernacular and mentioning Arthur are not much earlier than the middle of the thirteenth century, although in some instances (e.g., the tale of *Culhwch and Olwen*) it can be demonstrated on linguistic grounds that the material belongs to a considerably earlier period. Some of the material, such as the "Dialogue of Arthur and Gwenhwyfar," is found only in late manuscripts. Perhaps the oldest reference to Arthur in our Celtic sources is a line in the *Gododdin* to the effect that a particular hero fought bravely, "though he was no Arthur." Tradition ascribes this poem to the late sixth century, though it exists in a manuscript of the late thirteenth century, in a language that cannot be older than the ninth to tenth century. But if it is authentic and tradition is true, then this would surely be the earliest reference to Arthur, portrayed here as a paragon of heroic virtues.

The Welsh Triads contribute an important source of early information about the native Arthur. Their editor has demonstrated that the manuscript transmission of the Triads goes back to the early twelfth century, but it is clear that this body of traditional lore in triadic form has its roots in much earlier oral tradition. It is also clear that some of the Triads are late and owe their existence to such literary texts as Geoffrey's *Historia Regum Britanniae*. In all, there are some two dozen mentions of Arthur and his court in the Triads, plus another eight Triads that form a text known as the "Twenty-four Knights of Arthur's Court." Taken together, they constitute an important body of tantalizing references to the Arthur of native Celtic tradition.

Arthur figures prominently in one poem and is mentioned in several others in the mid-thirteenth-century manuscript known as the Black Book of Carmarthen. In "The Stanzas of the Graves," a poem about the burial places of a number of heroes, it is said that the grave of Arthur is an eternal wonder—that is, no one knows where it is. Another series of stanzas speak of the hero Geraint, and one of the stanzas claims that Arthur was present with Geraint at a battle in a place called *Llongborth* (site unknown). The most important poem in the Black Book of Carmarthen is in the form of a dialogue between Arthur and Glewlwyd Gafaelfawr ("Glewlwyd of the mighty grasp"). In *Culhwch and Olwen*, Glewlwyd is Arthur's own porter; here, he is porter of a fortress to which Arthur and his men seek admission. In the ninety surviving lines of this poem, Arthur identifies his retinue for the porter, naming Cei and Bedwyr (Kay and Bedivere), Mabon son of Modron, Manawydan son of Llŷr (Lear), and other characters known from various texts that reflect Celtic mythological tradition. The poem also celebrates adventures with witches, lions, a fierce cat, dog-headed warriors, and the like.

The Book of Taliesin, a manuscript of ca. 1275, contains several arcane poems that mention Arthur, treating him as an eminent figure, the object of the adulation of certain sages. For example, Arthur is named toward the end of the poem known as *Cad Goddeu* ("The Battle of the Trees"), a poem in which Gwydion and Math from the fourth branch of the *Mabinogi* are named as prominent magicians. Much of this poetry is obscure, though it is clear at times that the setting is the Celtic otherworld and that some of the characters named in them belong to inherited myth. One of these poems, clearer than the others, has attracted considerable attention and has been edited and translated several times; it is known as *The Spoils of Annwfn* (Annwfn being the name for the otherworld in Welsh). This remarkable poem tells of a raid by Arthur and his men on Annwfn to acquire its spoils or treasures. Several things deserve notice here: Annwfn is depicted as a place located at sea or across water, for Arthur and his men travel there in his ship Prydwen (the name given to Arthur's shield in Geoffrey's *Historia*!). Annwfn is variously called in this poem "the fairy fort," "the fort of intoxication," and "the glassy fort." In it is the well-outfitted prison of a certain Gweir. Among its treasures is a beautifully decorated cauldron from which emanates poetic inspiration and which contains a special sword; the cauldron, it is stated, will not boil the food of a coward. Three boatloads of men went with Arthur. The fort was guarded by 600 men, and from the expedition only seven returned.

The Spoils of Annwfn is set squarely in the mainstream of Celtic tradition in Wales, and it has clear analogues in Welsh literature. It makes reference to the tale of Pwyll, the central figure of the first branch of the *Mabinogi*, and his son, Pryderi, who is also mentioned in the second, third, and fourth branches. In the second branch, *Branwen*, we hear of a raid by Bendigeidfran ("Bran the Blessed") on Ireland, nominally to avenge his sister's churlish treatment at the hands of her husband, Matholwch the Irishman. Branwen's son, Gwern, is there, too, and a pivotal role is played by a cauldron, one into which dead warriors are cast and from which they are taken revivified. When the treacherous Efnisien is thrown into it, he breaks it. The forces of Bendigeidfran defeat the Irish in a dire battle, and from it only seven escape. In the tale of *Culhwch and Olwen*, one of the tasks set by the giant is to acquire the cauldron of Diwrnach the Irishman and the sword of Wrnach, names that would appear to be doubtlets. Arthur and his men set out for Ireland and finish by taking the cauldron—full of Irish treasures—by force, thanks to the magical use of another sword. The parallels among the three texts are obvious, and it has been suggested that in *Branwen* and *Culhwch and Olwen* we have a euhemerized version of the raid on the otherworld—that is, that Ireland has been substituted in those tales for the Annwfn of the Book of Taliesin poem.

The reference to the otherworld as "the glassy fortress" is significant. Giraldus Cambrensis, in his *De Principis Instructione* (1195), states that Glastonbury was the site of the legendary Avalon. In the British tongue, he wrote, it was called the glassy isle, and that is why the Saxons called it afterward *Glæstingabyrig* ("the fort of glass"). According to Welsh tradition, Merlin was imprisoned by his lover in a glass house, where he was also custodian of the thirteen treasures of the Isle of Britain—treasures, perhaps, like those that Arthur sought from "the glassy fort."

Surely, the most important text that belongs to Celtic Arthuriana is the tale of *Culhwch and Olwen*. Though it is found in manuscripts of the fourteenth century, scholars generally agree on linguistic grounds that it belongs at least to the early eleventh century in its present form. The tale is remarkable in several ways. At one level, it has been recognized as a tale type of the Giant's Daughter. A destiny is sworn upon the hero that he will wed the giant's daughter; her father imposes a series of "impossible" tasks, hoping thereby to destroy the unwanted suitor; but with supernatural assistance the hero accomplishes the tasks, the giant is slain, and the bride is won. In this instance, the supernatural aid comes from Arthur and his men, and Culhwch and his bride-to-be are forgotten for much of the story. In fact, the largest single episode in the tale is the pursuit of the giant boar Twrch Trwyth. Traditions of this boar, which date back to Nennius's *Historia Brittonum* (ca. 800), are evocative of other supernatural pigs in Celtic tradition, including some from Gaul and Ireland. The boar's human characteristics are "explained" in the story by the statement that the beast had been a king, but God turned him into a boar because of his sins. In other exploits on Culhwch's behalf, Arthur frees Mabon son of Modron (who had been imprisoned in a stronghold located in a body of water), destroys a powerful witch, and in general participates in a world very much like that of the dialogue poem with the porter and the otherworldly Annwfn. His companions include Cei and Bedwyr and a catalogue of other heroes capable of supernatural feats. His court is located at Celliwig (site unknown) in Cornwall, and though it is well provisioned it is much more primitive than the resplendent courts of later English and continental romance.

The Dream of Rhonabwy is a literary composition that belongs to the early thirteenth century. It is unique in that its geographical and historical background is indicated clearly. Also, it employs a dream-vision form not at all common in traditional Welsh literature. The story within the story, Rhonabwy's dream, is a surrealistic presentation of Arthur and his field court just before the battle of Mount Badon; the battle of Camlann has already taken place, and in that respect the story indulges in an anachronism. The strange events that transpire invite an allegorical interpretation, and a colophon confirms the fact that the story is the creation of an individual author whose penchant was for richly descriptive detail.

The poem known as the "Dialogue of Arthur and Gwenhwyfar" is probably in reality a dialogue between Gwenhwyfar and her abductor Melwas, reflecting an episode known from Caradoc's *Vita Gildae* and Chrétien de Troyes's *Lancelot*. The "Dialogue of Arthur and the Eagle," in which the Eagle identifies himself as a grandson of Uther Pendragon, is essentially a religious poem. These two poems exist in manuscripts only from the sixteenth century, though both are surely older.

Celtic traditions concerning Merlin existed independent of Arthurian connections, though that character was eventually drawn into the Arthurian orbit. The earlier Merlin is a prophet and madman, mad in the sense of frenzied or possessed. This is a state associated with the practice of divinely inspired poetry and supernatural wisdom and is one well documented in Celtic tradition. Most of the poetry attributed to this Merlin is vaticinatory and supports political themes for the most part. In Welsh tradition, Taliesin and Merlin were presumed to be the same person (archetypal poet) alive or living among men at different periods. Both are said to have lived at the time of Arthur, and to both are ascribed political prophecies.

It can be seen from this brief summary that Arthur's appearances in early Welsh literature place him firmly in the mythological traditions of the Celts. He operates largely in the supernatural community, abetted by a retinue of supernaturally gifted heroes. His opponents are giants, witches, princes of the otherworld, and men-turned-beasts. Like the Arthur of romance, his origins were obscure and his end a mystery. By the twelfth century, the Bretons were eagerly awaiting Arthur's return, and among the Welsh poets of the twelfth to fourteenth century Arthur was held up as a paragon of heroic and courtly virtues.

Finally, it should be pointed out that, while Arthur's origins are to be found among the British Celts, his name itself may not be Celtic. It is assumed that the name is one of several in the post-Roman period (after, say, A.D. 410) that derive from Latin—in this case, from Artorius; Patricius is another noteworthy example. Still, it must be remembered that the Welsh form of the name, "Arthur," is evocative of the Welsh word for "bear," *arth*, and that in Celtic tradition gods were often assimilated to certain animals—that is, they had a zoomorphic aspect. The bear was one of these, and in Gaul there were divinities with such names as *Dea Artio* 'bear goddess,' *Andarta* 'powerful bear,' *Artgenos* 'bear's son,' and *Artaios* 'bearlike.' In this connection, it is perhaps significant that our Arthur has no patronymic prior to Geoffrey of Monmouth's work and that there is no mention of Arthur at all in the early Welsh genealogies. (*See also* ARTHUR, ORIGINS OF LEGEND; IRISH ARTHURIAN LITERATURE; *MABINOGI*; MUSIC; MYRDDIN POEMS; TRIADS.) [PKF]

Bollard, John K., trans. "Arthur in the Early Welsh Tradition." In *The Romance of Arthur*, ed. James J. Wilhelm. New York: Garland, 1984. (Translations and commentary.)

Bromwich, Rachel. *Trioedd Ynys Prydein*. Cardiff: University of Wales Press, 1961; 2nd ed. 1978.

———, and D. Simon Evans, eds. *Culhwch ac Olwen*. Cardiff: University of Wales Press, 1988.

Ford, Patrick K., trans. *The Mabinogi and Other Medieval Welsh Tales*. Berkeley: University of California Press, 1977.

———. "The Death of Merlin in the Chronicle of Elis Gruffydd." *Viator*, 7 (1976), 379–90.

Jackson, Kenneth Hurlstone. "Arthur in Early Welsh Verse." In *Arthurian Literature in the Middle Ages*, ed. Roger Sherman Loomis. Oxford: Clarendon, 1959, pp. 12–19.

———. *The Gododdin: The Oldest Scottish Poem*. Edinburgh: Edinburgh University Press, 1969.

Jarman, A.O.H. "The Arthurian Allusions in the Black Book of Carmarthen." In *The Legend of Arthur in the Middle Ages: Studies Presented to A.H. Diverres*, ed. P.B. Grout, R.A. Lodge, C.E. Pickford, and E.K.C. Varty. London: Brewer, 1983, pp. 99–112.

Jones, Thomas. "The Black Book of Carmarthen 'Stanzas of the Graves.'" *Proceedings of the British Academy*, 53 (1967), 97–137.

Loomis, Roger Sherman. *Wales and the Arthurian Legend*. Cardiff: University of Wales Press, 1956.

WERTHES, FRIEDRICH AUGUST CLEMENS

(1748–1817), was well known for his many dramas that were performed at the Vienna Hofburgtheater. He collaborated with the celebrated composer Johann Rudolf Zumsteeg to produce a *Singspiel* entitled *Das Pfauenfest* ("The Peacock Feast"), which was premiered at the Stuttgart Hoftheater on February 24, 1801.

Das Pfauenfest is a dramatization, with musical interludes, of the Arthurian mantle tale that derives ultimately from the medieval French fabliau *Le Mantel mautaillié*. Werthes's source, however, was Benedikte Naubert's *Der kurze Mantel*. Although the *Singspiel* was well received at the court of Duke Friedrich I of Württemberg, it has fallen into oblivion. [MEK]

Werthes, F.A.C. *Das Pfauenfest: Ein Singspiel in zwey Akten*, with music by J.R. Zumsteeg. Leipzig: Breitkopf und Härtel, n.d.

WESTON, JESSIE LAIDLAY (1850–1928), indefatigable translator of Arthurian romances from Old French, Middle English, Middle High German, and Dutch. Weston also published monographs on Gawain (1897), Lancelot (1901), and Perceval (1906–09). She is known especially for her study of the origins and development of the Grail legend, *From Ritual to Romance* (1920), which was a major influence on T.S. Eliot's *The Waste Land*. Although largely discredited, her "Ritualist theory" is still often featured in nonscholarly studies of the Grail. Weston traces the Grail legend back to the classical cult of Adonis, whom she identifies with the maimed Fisher King. The Wasteland was brought about, she claims, by the death of the Vegetation Spirit. Perceval's quest will restore life, and the Grail and Lance are, respectively, symbols of the female and male sexual organs. [WWK]

Reid, Margaret J.C. *The Arthurian Legend: Comparison of Treatment in Modern and Mediaeval Literature*. Edinburgh and London: Oliver and Boyd, 1938.

WESTWOOD, THOMAS (1814?–1888), one of Tennyson's first imitators, published privately *The Sword of Kingship: A Legend of the Mort D'Arthur* (1866), a rendering in blank verse of Malory's opening chapters (Book I, Chapters 3–7), with emendations to avoid offending Victorian sensibilities and additions to present Arthur as a Christ-type. *The Quest of the Sancgreall* (1868) mingles vague quests, magic artifacts, and sexual temptations, but, true to the medieval source, identifies the Grail as the Catholic eucharistic vessel. [MAW]

Westwood, Thomas. *The Sword of Kingship: A Legend of the Mort D'Arthur*. London: Whittingham and Wilkins, 1866.

———. *The Quest of the Sancgreall, The Sword of Kingship, and Other Poems*. London: Smith, 1868.

WHEATCROFT, JOHN, American poet, in "Gawain" (1971), has the dying hero recall the dawning of his youthful powers and awareness of his destiny. "Lancelot, Tonsured, Walks the Field at Dover" (1977) presents the knight's less than penitent remembrance of Guenever, even as he surveys the horror of the battlefield. [DN]

Wheatcroft, John. "Gawain." *Literary Review*, 14 (Spring 1971), 320–21.

———. "Lancelot, Tonsured, Walks the Field at Dover." *Four Quarters*, 27 (Autumn 1977), 13.

WHEATLEY, JEFFERY, British author of *Prince Arthur* (1981), a chapbook collection of fourteen short poems that are episodes in Arthur's various returns to Britain in time of need. The poems use satire and humor to comment on modern disarray and corruption. The longest, "The Tintagel Manifesto," a parody of the Credo, catalogs important things until they become trivial and absurd. [PCB]

Wheatley, Jeffery. *Prince Arthur*. Kingston-upon-Thames: Court Poetry, 1981.

WHEELER, THOMAS GERALD, author of the light fantasy novel *Loose Chippings* (1969). An American professor visits an unknown British village built in the Vale of Avalon, where, among other wonders, the tomb of Arthur is found under the ruins of an ancient abbey. [DN]

Wheeler, Thomas Gerald. *Loose Chippings*. New York: Phillips, 1969.

WHITE, T(ERENCE) H(ANBURY) (1905–1964), sometime public schoolteacher and freelance writer of short stories, poems, journalism—and five novels based on the Arthurian legend. First published separately, *The Sword in the Stone* (1938), *The Witch in the Wood*—later retitled *The Queen of Air and Darkness* (1939), and *The Ill-Made Knight* (1940) eventually appeared with *The Candle in the Wind* as a tetralogy: *The Once and Future King* (1958). A later work, *The*

Book of Merlyn, intended originally by White to be part of his *magnum opus* and duplicating some of its incidents, was published in 1977. White's main medieval source is Malory's *Morte Darthur*, and his novels contain some of the best modern commentary on their original.

The Sword in the Stone, eventually made into a Walt Disney film, treats Arthur's *enfances*, always vague in medieval versions of his story. Here, Merlin trains the future monarch (in counterpoint to his conventional knightly grooming), leading him through shape-shifting transformations that mimic Darwinian evolution. As fish, ant, wild goose, and badger, Arthur learns that Might should work for Right and that the best rule is the freest. Essentially a comedy, the book ends with a delightful version of the Sword in the Stone episode and a coronation. In the latter, all those who have participated in his education, both men and beasts, either attend or send gifts.

Comedy mixed with tragedy appears in the second novel, *The Queen of Air and Darkness*. Interwoven narrations include Arthur's early wars against the rebel kings; the comic adventures of Pellinore, Grummore, and Palomides; and the tragic education (or neglect of education) of Gawain and his brethren by their mother, Morgause of Orkney. Tragic, too, is the book's climax, Morgause's deliberate seduction of her half-brother, Arthur, which will lead to Mordred's birth.

This movement from the comedy of the first book to the mixed genre of the second yields to more serious concerns in *The Ill-Made Knight*, which features a physically ugly Lancelot. His perception of himself as monkeylike colors both his complementary feeling of sinfulness and the ever-growing and mutual attraction he feels to the beautiful Guenevere. A notable addition to Malory's account is Lancelot's prizing of his virginity, which he loses to the Grail Princess Elaine before his adultery with Guenevere, whom he had previously loved unwillingly and virtuously. Such familiar episodes as the Roman War, Lancelot's madness, and his initial rescue of the Queen from the stake are also reworked. In White, the Grail quest is unimportant—Lancelot's relation to God is direct. It is told in retrospect as its participants return to Arthur's court (thus from a *Mort Artu*/Stanzaic *Morte Arthur* viewpoint). White further alters conventional Arthurian characterization: Gawain is almost parodically braid Scots in his speech; Elaine of Astolat gets fat; and Lancelot, Guenevere, and Arthur demonstrably age.

The final book is *The Candle in the Wind*. It treats the clan feuds of the house of Pellinore and Lot, the discovery of Lancelot and Guenevere's adulterous relationship, Arthur's revelation of Mordred's parentage (here rather like that in the *Mort Artu*), and Guenevere's further rescues by her lover. New is Arthur's unsuccessful replacement of knight-errantry with common law as a novel attempt to harness Right to Might. After a moving account of the Lancelot-Gawain feud, the tetralogy ends *in medias res* before the battle of Salisbury, as Arthur commands his young page—no less than Thomas Malory—to withdraw to safety in order to tell his king's story. (This latter episode, along with much in the last two novels, inspired the Broadway musical *Camelot*, which, however, is an oversimplification and—in spite of its lovely songs—lessening of White's work.)

In the posthumous *Book of Merlyn*, some material White included in his tetralogy is repeated. The enchanter appears one last time before Arthur in his tent at Salisbury. His invocation of their former teacher-student relationship leads to his taking Arthur, once again, back to the animals of the first book, this time to learn about the abolition of war. Didactically and unconvincingly presented, the book's theme is humanity's patent inferiority to the animals. So incongruent is this idea with White's earlier books that his publisher's refusal to issue it with them is understandable.

T.H. White's achievement in *The Once and Future King*, if not in his *Merlyn*, is undoubtedly the finest in twentieth-century Arthurian prose. Setting aside the rampant misanthropy of the *Merlyn*, one may say of his work that it is inventive, perceptive, and above all newly creative of its medieval materials. Its narrator is detached, omniscient, and implicative of an authorial presence much like that of the historical White (as is true of Malory's narrator, and this is perhaps one of their meeting points). The story moves, with relative ease, from an anachronistic, quasi-children's book through stages of comedy and tragedy, to the final catastrophe. Like the Brontës, White has "domesticated" romance, especially in the wonderful Lancelot-Guenevere-Arthur scenes of *The Candle in the Wind*. He draws upon a wide and scholarly range of knowledge in medieval history, beast lore (he also translated a twelfth-century bestiary), practical naturalism, and all periods of literature to make a new and often enchanting Arthuriad.

Much in his books is both political and autobiographical. White's concern with communism, fascism, and pacifism (he refused to fight in World War II) emerges everywhere, as does his concomitant guilt. Additionally, his own miserable childhood, lifelong loneliness, and sexual ambiguity, together with his love of animals, are transmuted into this compellingly readable narrative. If White's personal quest to "find an antidote to war" results, in his work, only in the failure of Arthur's belated discovery of law, that is as much the burden of the Arthurian matter he chose as of his own valiant effort to reorder it as a parable for his time. [MF]

White, T.H. *The Once and Future King*. London: Collins, 1958.

———. *The Book of Merlyn*, ed. Sylvia Townsend Warner. Austin: University of Texas Press, 1977.

Gallix, François. *T.H. White: An Annotated Bibliography*. New York: Garland, 1987.

Thompson, Raymond H. *The Return from Avalon: A Study of the Arthurian Legend in Modern Fiction*. Westport, Conn.: Greenwood, 1985, pp. 126–28, 135–38, 144–45.

Warner, Sylvia Townsend. *T.H. White: A Biography*. London: Chatto and Windus, 1967.

WHITTEMORE, REED, included Arthurian characters among his witty verse portraits in *Heroes and Heroines* (1946). In "Merlin," the mean-spirited wizard muses about his role in Camelot's fall, while in "Guinevere" the Queen reconsiders her acts of treason. "Sir Bedivere" provides an ironic commentary on commitment in the dying Arthur's surprisingly breezy farewell to his knight. Whittemore also took a pointed look at the values of Arthurian heroes in a later sonnet, "The Bad Knight" (1963). [DN]

Whittemore, Reed. *Heroes and Heroines*. New York: Reynal and Hitchcock, 1946.

———. "The Bad Knight." In *Poems: New and Selected*. Minneapolis: University of Minnesota Press, 1967.

WIBBERLEY, LEONARD (1915–1983), Irish-born novelist who wrote *The Quest of Excalibur* (1959), a mildly satiric account of Arthur's return to a bureaucratic England. With the help of an English princess and a California graduate student (a modern Guenevere and Lancelot who ultimately put duty before their love), Arthur helps to ease the government restrictions that control individual lives.

Under his Christopher Webb pseudonym, which he used for juvenile historical fiction, Wibberley wrote one of the more inventive Grail stories, *Eusebius the Phoenician* (1969). Brought to Britain on his search for the Cup of Life, the merchant Eusebius encounters an aging Arthur, here a tribal king appointed Count of the Saxon Shore by the departing Romans. Eusebius's quest is finally achieved in Glastonbury. [ACL/DN]

Wibberley, Leonard. *The Quest of Excalibur*. New York: Putnam, 1959.

Webb, Christopher. *Eusebius the Phoenician*. New York: Funk and Wagnalls, 1969.

WIDWILT, an Old Yiddish Arthurian verse romance of some 4,200 lines, composed probably in the fifteenth century and transmitted in three sixteenth-century Hebrew-letter manuscripts, found today in the Trinity College Library, Cambridge, and the State-University Library in Hamburg. All manuscripts point to northern Italy, then a center for Yiddish literary production, as their place of origin.

The work is a revision of the much longer Middle High German *Wigalois*, by Wirnt von Grafenberg. The Jewish redactor was probably a professional entertainer with at least some knowledge of German courtly literature. Though by no means a noteworthy poet, he is an accomplished storyteller with a good imagination and sense for the organization of his adopted narrative material. He retains the rhymed-couplet form and, except for a transformation of the ending and the conversion of Wigalois's main opponent into a giant and his enchantress mother, follows the main outlines of his model. He consolidates several scenes, or recasts them into other narrative situations, and deletes Wirnt's moralizing sections on courtly and Christian ethics. There is a marked tendency to reduce the hero to human proportions; twice, Widwilt is effortlessly defeated by the giant's mother and slinks away from her castle like an Arthurian *shlemiel*.

The clear redactional goal of the Old Yiddish revision is the long, tongue-in-cheek wedding finale. Widwilt, though promised to Lorel, daughter of a king whom he had rescued from his metamorphosis as a stag, is claimed by another king as husband for *his* daughter. The wedding is announced and guests arrive from afar—Lorel and her family, Widwilt's parents, and his friends from King Arthur's court, all hoping to hear word of the lost knight. Widwilt coyly refuses to reveal his identity until recognized by one of Lorel's retinue. The dilemma of the bridegroom claimed by two brides is resolved by King Arthur, who grants Lorel priority as the first-betrothed.

During the seventeenth and eighteenth centuries, *Widwilt* was itself the basis for three major revisions in Hebrew letters. The first was published in 1671 by the Amsterdam printer Josel von Witzenhausen under the title *Ain shen mayse fun Kinig Artis hof . . . un fun dem barimten Riter Widwilt* ("A Fine Story of King Arthur's Court . . . and of the Famous Knight Widwilt"; only extant copy in the University Library, Erlangen). Josel's changes are primarily linguistic: the Old Yiddish is modernized, and Hebrew components not found in the medieval text are added. A vulgarization of the language causes the hero to appear as somewhat of a braggart. An addition to the wedding scene reflects actual historical circumstance. As compensation to the disappointed bride, King Arthur arranges her marriage to his nephew, the Grand Duke of Tuscany. At the end of the sixteenth century, the Tuscan Grand Duke had protected Jewish refugees, primarily expellees from the Papal States, a memory still fresh in the minds of coreligionists north of the Alps.

The most interesting reworking of *Widwilt* is *Kinig Artis hof*, published between 1671 and 1679 in the printing office of Israel ben Jehuda Katz in Prague (single known copy in the Bodleian Library). On the basis of Josel's revision, the romance is completely recast in around 580 ottava-rima stanzas, a form known in Yiddish literature since the early sixteenth century (a century before its introduction into German literature). A curious technique of the unknown redactor is the double narration of numerous scenes, usually by having one of the characers involved in a previously described action repeat the incident as personal experience. Although the plot of the stanzaic version is close to that of its model, its social character has been transformed to the bourgeois world of merchant-class values. The motifs of money and education are prominent, and there is a notable interest in travel and the ways of the road: Ritter Gawein orders five carriages and a lackey for the journey to his son's wedding; and the hero's mother, also on her way to the wedding, is advised to ask traveling beggars, the people "who know the world best," for information about her missing son. Not a major literary achievement, *Kinig Artis hof* is nevertheless an important document of Jewish attaction to, and probably participation in, the life of the upper middle class of the sixteenth and seventeenth centuries.

The last Hebrew-letter adaptation of *Widwilt, Riter Gavein*, was published in 1789 in Frankfurt an der Oder. Its language is no longer Yiddish and scarcely standard German. Both the form, a truncated (nine-folio) prose retelling, and the story are vastly changed. Gawein's abductor in the prologue is Kaduk, Emperor of China, and the main story leads Widwilt through Greenland, Russia, Albania, and England before the final reunion and reconciliation in Sardinia. The work is of value only as an example of the literary taste and interest in the exotic, particularly the orient, of the Yiddish-reading public in the eighteenth century.

One final curiosity in the three-century history of the Old Yiddish material is a 1786 German version, *Vom Könige Artus und von dem bildschönen Ritter Wieduwilt: Ein Ammenmährchen* ("Of King Arthur and the Fair Knight Wieduwilt: A Nursery Tale"; copies in the Library of Congress and University Library, Marburg). The work is essentially a prose translation of Johann Christoph Wagenseil's transcription edition, written by the Nuremberg pastor and prolific popular author Johann Ferdinand Roth. Two elements raise the rendition to a level of genuine interest. Roth recasts the story as a nursery tale, divided into three weeks, each with seven evening readings ("Abendstündchen"). In an unusually personal and candid three-part preface—directed to "my dear maid Gertraud" (the nurse to whom the book is also dedicated), to "the gentlemen reviewers," and to "the readership"—and in occasional remarks interspersed through the evening readings, the author airs his views on the ills of eighteenth-century German society, from the profligacy of upper-class mothers (including his own) to social injustice and the financial plight of young authors. [RGW]

Landau, Leo, ed. *Arthurian Legends, or the Hebrew-German Rhymed Version of the Legend of King Arthur*. Leipzig: Avenarius, 1912.

Dreessen, Wulf-Otto. "Zur Rezeption deutscher epischer Literatur im Altjiddischen: Das Beispiel 'Wigalois'—'Artushof.'" In *Deutsche Literatur des späten Mittelalters*, ed. W. Harms and L.P. Johnson. Berlin, 1975.

Warnock, Robert G. "Wirkungsabsicht und Bearbeitungstechnik im altjiddischen 'Artushof.'" *Zeitschrift für deutsche Philologie*, 100 (1981), 98–109.

———. "Frühneuzeitliche Fassungen des altjiddischen 'Artushofs.'" In *Akten des VII. Internationalen Germanisten-Kongresses Göttingen 1985*. Tübingen: Niemeyer, 1986, Vol. 5, pp. 13–19.

WIELAND, CHRISTOPH MARTIN (1733–1813), one of the principal writers of the eighteenth-century German Rococo and Enlightenment. Wieland was familiar with the available Arthurian stories from foreign sources, particularly the summaries in Count Tressan's Bibliothèque universelle des romans (1775–89). His brief prose summary of Merlin's life, *Merlin der Zauberer* ("Merlin the Magician," 1777), is probably taken from Tressan, as is his *Geron der Adelige* ("The Noble Geron," 1777), which is essentially a translation, in blank verse, of the medieval French *Guiron le Courtois*. His first acquaintance with the prophet and magician Merlin, to whom he merely alludes in his *Don Quixote* imitation *Don Sylvio von Rosalva* (1764) and his verse tale *Oberon* (1780), came from Ariosto's *Orlando Furioso*, on which *Oberon* is based. In Wieland's long elegiac poem *Merlins weissagende Stimme aus seiner Gruft* ("Merlin's Prophetic Voice from His Grave," 1810), Merlin, after 1,000 years in his grave, laments the loss of the golden age of Arthurian chivalry. This reflects the older Wieland's despair at the passing of the German Classical age of Weimar. Still, the mood of despair is broken at the end of the poem when Merlin prophesies great things for the yet-unborn son of the fairy Viviane, and, by implication, for Germany. [RWK]

Wieland, Christoph Martin. *Werke*, ed. Fritz Martini and Hans Werner Seiffert. Munich: Hanser, 1966.

McCarthy, John A. *Christoph Martin Wieland*. Boston: Twayne, 1979.

Weiss, Adelaide Marie. "Wieland." In *Merlin in German Literature*. Washington, D.C.: Catholic University of America Press, 1933, pp. 55–69.

WIGAMUR, a German romance of somewhat over 6,000 lines, is poorly preserved. One fifteenth-century manuscript (W) transmits the whole tale but with many lacunae; two fragmentary manuscripts from ca. 1300–50 (M, S) supply some material missing from W but cover only a third of the story. The text in W is replete with flaws suggesting scribal indifference. The romance is generally dated to the mid-thirteenth century, but without firm evidence.

Wigamur, son of King Paldriot of Lendrie, is abducted by a "wild-woman" named Lesbia, who raises him in a cave.

A semihuman sea monster then carries him off to an underwater realm, training him in certain manly skills and later sending him ashore. Wigamur finds a warhorse in the ruins of a sacked castle. On it, he defeats the knight Glakotelesfloyer, then returns to the castle and discovers the maiden Pioles. She is affianced to the King of Nordein, who is away at a tournament. Wigamur passes two chaste nights with her, then gives her over, apparently for protection, to a dwarf at a nearby castle. Received by Arthur's uncle, Yttra, Wigamur completes his chivalric education. He intervenes in a fight between an eagle and a vulture; the grateful eagle accompanies him thereafter, so he is known as the Knight with the Eagle. He champions a damsel in a property dispute before Arthur but declines her hand and lands because he holds himself unworthy and is ignorant of his parentage.

Wigamur accompanies Arthur to aid Queen Ysope, besieged by the heathen king Marroch. He then discovers his identity by nearly championing King Atroclas against Paldriot, his father, and marries Atroclas's daughter, Dulceflur. After defeating Lypondrigan at a tournament held by Queen Dinifogar, the hero reunites Pioles with her fiancé; he again defeats Lypondrigan, who had abducted Dulceflur, and presumably retires with his wife to Lendrie.

This story has many parallels in German Arthurian romances (e.g., the animal companion in Hartmann von Aue's *Iwein* and Konrad von Stoffeln's *Gauriel von Muntabel*; exotic names in Wolfram von Eschenbach's *Parzival*). Wigamur is a naive but modest and chaste hero, perhaps a deliberate counterpart to the protagonist of *Lanzelet*, by Ulrich von Zatzikhoven. Though no philosophical or aesthetic subtlety has been discovered in the romance, it has a number of vivid and engaging sequences beside many commonplace descriptions and enumerations. Its poor transmission and the lack of a critical edition are obstacles to evaluation and appreciation. [SLW]

Kraus, Carl von, ed. *Mittelhochdeutsches Übungsbuch*, 2nd ed. Heidelberg: Winter, 1926, pp. 108–67. (Fragments M, S, and parallels in W.)

von der Hagen, F.H., and J.G. Büsching, eds. *Wigamur*. In *Deutsche Gedichte des Mittelalters*. Berlin, 1808, Vol. 1, Part 4. (Manuscript W.)

Blamires, David. "The Sources and Literary Structure of *Wigamur*." In *Studies in Medieval Literature and Languages in Memory of Frederick Whitehead*, ed. W. Rothwell, W.R.J. Barron, David Blamires, and Lewis Thorpe. Manchester: Manchester University Press, 1973, pp. 27–46.

Ebenbauer, Alfred. "Wigamur und die Familie." In *Artusrittertum im späten Mittelalter: Ethos und Ideologie*, ed. Friedrich Wolfzettel. Giessen: Schmitz, 1984, pp. 28–46.

Gottzman, Carola L. *Artusdichtung*. Stuttgart: Metzler, 1989.

Martin, Ann G. "The Concept of *reht* in *Wigamur*." *Colloquia Germanica*, 20 (1987), 1–14.

Schultz, James A. *The Shape of the Round Table: Structures of Middle High German Arthurian Romance*. Toronto: University of Toronto Press, 1983.

WIGOLEIS VOM RADE ("Wigoleis of the Wheel"), a condensed German prose version of Wirnt von Grafenberg's Arthurian romance *Wigalois*, composed ca. 1200–15. The oldest incunabulum of the chapbook was printed by Johann Schönsperger in 1493 in Augsburg. This text is based upon a prose redaction in manuscript—now lost—from the years 1472–83. The chapbook was translated into Danish (*see* HER VIEGOLEIS MED GULD HIULET) and from Danish into Icelandic (*see* GABONS SAGA OK VIGOLES). [MEK]

Brandstetter, Alois. *Prosa Auflösung: Studien zur Rezeption der höfischen Epik im frühneuhochdeutschen Prosaroman*. Frankfurt: Athenäum, 1971.

WILLIAM OF MALMESBURY (ca. 1095–1143). In 1125, William, a monk in the abbey of Malmesbury, wrote two of his most important works, one of which was the *Gesta Regum Anglorum*. William mentions Arthur twice in it. First, Arthur aided Ambrosius Aurelianus in holding back the barbarians—that is, the Saxons, whom William wrongly calls Angles. At the siege of Mount Badon, Arthur, with the image of the Virgin Mary on his armor, singlehandedly defeated 900 of the enemy. Second, while the tomb of Walwen, Arthur's nephew, had been found during the reign of William I, Arthur's tomb still remained undiscovered in 1125. Noting that the British had created fables about Arthur, William was of the opinion that because of his achievements he deserved to be commemorated not in fiction but in authentic history. [KGM]

William of Malmesbury. *Gesta Regum Anglorum*. In *Willelmi Malmesbiriensis Monachi de Gestis Regum Anglorum Libri Quinque*, ed. William Stubbs. 2 vols. London: Eyre and Spottiswoode, 1887–89.

Gransden, Antonia. *Historical Writing in England, c. 550 to c. 1307*. London: Routledge and Kegan Paul, 1974.

WILLIAM OF NEWBURGH (1135/6–ca. 1198). Between 1196 and 1198, William wrote his *Historia Rerum Anglicarum* at the request of Ernald, abbot of Rievaulx. Although the *Historia* begins with William of Normandy's conquest of England, its preface is devoted to the place of Arthur and Merlin in history. Using the historical works of Gildas and especially Bede, William subjected Geoffrey of Monmouth's history of Arthur and Merlin to harsh but careful criticism. He pointed out that Bede had never mentioned Arthur and that Geoffrey told of activities that should have made Arthur famous and known to other writers—who in fact know nothing of him. For these and other reasons,

William concluded that Geoffrey's Arthur and Merlin were fictional creations of the British. [KGM]

William of Newburgh. *Historia Rerum Anglicarum*. In *Chronicles of the Reigns of Stephen, Henry II, and Richard I*, ed. Richard Howlett. London: Longman, Trübner, 1885, Vol. 1.

———. *William of Newburgh: The History of English Affairs, Book 1*, ed. and trans. P.G. Walsh and M.J. Kennedy. Warminster: Aris and Phillips, 1988.

Gransden, Antonia. *Historical Writing in England, c. 550 to c. 1307*. London: Routledge and Kegan Paul, 1974.

Partner, Nancy C. *Serious Entertainments: The Writing of History in Twelfth-Century England*. Chicago: University of Chicago Press, 1977.

WILLIAMS, ANTONIA R., English poet and author of *Isolt: A New Telling* (1900). This dramatic poem is both derivative of Wagner, with much musical imagery and actual song, and cast in a symbolic mold, carefully detailed in the *dramatis personae* of the piece. Williams evades the consummation of the affair, insisting on the lovers' innocence, and Marc ends the play by giving Isolt to Trystan. [AAR]

Williams, Antonia. *Isolt: A New Telling*. London: Published by the author, [1915].

WILLIAMS, CHARLES (1886–1945), among modern English poets, the foremost reshaper and recreator of Arthurian mythology. Williams's Arthuriad is composed of two cycles of poems, *Taliessin Through Logres* (1938) and *The Region of the Summer Stars* (1944). At his death, he left an unfinished prose work on "The Figure of Arthur," which was edited by his friend C.S. Lewis and published with Lewis's own commentary on the poems in *Arthurian Torso* (1948). Williams's first published novel, *War in Heaven* (1930), depicts a modern reappearance of the Holy Grail.

The poems in the Arthurian cycle are complex both in structure and interrelationships, but the overall structure is clear. *Taliessin Through Logres* portrays the establishment, growth, and fall of the realm of Arthur. In a sense, it shows the progress through the earthly kingdom. The poems of *The Region of the Summer Stars* (the "third heaven" of poets and lovers) take up the same themes, but from a perspective *sub specie aeternitatis*.

Williams's original contribution to Arthurian legend lies in his development of the myths of King Arthur and the Grail, their gradual coalescence, and the further history of the Grail. Other elements, such as the story of Lancelot and Guinevere, are represented only in passing. From the outset, the empire of King Arthur is concerned with the Grail quest, which Williams treats as being mystic, unchivalric, and ascetic. The union of the legendary kingdom and the Grail is a highly complex symbol of the fusion of Empire and Christendom, and thus of Christ's Second Coming.

The cycle begins with the coronation of the King. Even at this early point, the reader is haunted by premonitions of disaster. Merlin does not take part in the coronation ceremonies. Instead, he sits in the steeple of St. Stephen's and meditates on the inevitable downfall of the realm. He foresees the Dolorous Blow, the wounding of the Grail-keeper with the Sacred Lance. Man wounds himself, and this is an image of Original Sin, of the Fall. The result is the destruction of order and the spread of anarchy. Balin kills his brother, Balan, without recognizing him. The Fall and the first murder destroy the innocence of the kingdom; the disease of disorder spreads throughout the land.

Even Arthur is affected. In the early versions of the Matter of Britain, Mordred was nephew to the King, but in later versions he became the son conceived in incest. This crime was usually recounted by medieval authors without explicit comment, even though they recognized that the result was the traitor Mordred, the destroyer of the Arthurian world. In Williams's Taliessin cycle, however, incest has become a symbol of egotistic self-love, which Williams calls "Gomorrha," and Arthur has thus become an antagonist of the Grail, which he betrays through his egotism, as well as his lack of *caritas* and *largesse*.

Arthur is an unmoved mover, the passive center of his kingdom. Another must act in his stead, and as in Malory this is Lancelot, beloved by both King and Queen. He serves as the poet's example for the Way of Affirmation, just as the nun Dindrane, who sacrifices her blood for a leper, is an example of the Negative Way of the soul's quest for the Eternal. ("This also is thou; neither is this thou," *The Region of the Summer Stars*.) Guinevere is marginal for Williams: he feels no sympathy for her. And so she can only sit, wait, and love. Galahad, the purest of knights, cannot be born from her. His mother must stem from the family of the Grail kings; his father must belong to the leaders of secular knighthood. Originally, Williams considered making Arthur the father of Galahad but gave up the plan because the fate of the Round Table had to be determined through the King. With Galahad's conception, Merlin's task is fulfilled; he disappears into the mystic darkness whence he came. In the person of Galahad, the symbols of stone and shell are united: the geometric and the vital, Byzantium and Brocéliande. Williams calls this process the finding of identity. Galahad is an image of the New Man, exemplary incarnation of the union of Arthur's world and the Grail.

The poem on Galahad closes with Taliessin's vision of the ascent of the soul to the inner heaven. Like Dante, Williams regards the planetary spheres as levels of holiness and as grades of spiritual development. The first planet is Mercury, the god of opposition and of change, an image of competition among the planetary houses. Venus is the sphere of orientation and decision, that is, "of preference." Jupiter, with its two moons, refers to irony and defeated irony, which does not take umbrage at the unavoidable vicissitudes of this world but smiles at the apparent absurdity of things. Saturn is the planet of loneliness and meditation, promise and symbol of a future Golden Age. Logres, Arthur's kingdom, has so far reached only the sphere of Jupiter. There, Galahad and Lancelot live side by side, the unrest of the human heart and the misery of existence. But the path of the future is already clearly recognizable. The enormous forces of Brocéliande have created Galahad but have exhausted themselves in the effort. Logres becomes Britain. Carbonek and Camelot are farther apart than ever before.

Like Galahad, who has already seen the Holy Grail in Camelot, Perceval and Bors are the Elect of the Grail. They are living flesh and blood but at the same time incarnations of typical attitudes toward life. Perceval is the pure lover, full of spiritual questions and problems; Bors is the ordinary mortal, married and the father of children, a person striving toward perfection but entangled in the needs and problems of everyday life. Galahad, however, is of a different make. He is not a "Christlike figure" but a symbol of the divine spark in human beings, that is, the human "capacity for Christ." In Carbonek, after Galahad has healed the wounded king, he sees a vision of Christ in the Holy Grail. As instructed, he travels to Sarras, where he disappears from sight. This marks the final separation of the Arthurian world and the Grail. Arthur's thoughts center more and more on his own power, which results in his loss of *caritas* and *largesse*. He begins war with Lancelot; Mordred betrays the King; father and son kill one another.

The poem "The Prayers of the Pope" both ends and summarizes the cycle. The young pope remembers in his prayers the sufferings that result from the spread throughout the Empire of the betrayals and divisions that destroyed the Round Table and Logres. As each province asserts its independence, it shatters the harmony (or coinherence, as Williams calls it) that gives protection against external forces, and so falls victim to invasion by savage hordes. Even the pope feels within himself the schism that is destroying the Empire, that allows the return of chaos and leads to spiritual death. The vision of the development of humanity toward the Epiphany has dissolved. A magnificent opportunity has remained unused. Each of the pope's prayers repeats the anguished refrain, "Send not, send not the rich empty away."

But Williams does not dismiss us without hope. Although formally dissolved, Taliessin's household will remain, each member serving the higher vision. Above all, there is the hope of Brocéliande, which Williams describes in "The Figure of Arthur" as "a place of making." The roots of the forest grip and neutralize the tentacles of the octopods of P'o-l'u (hell): the inherent goodness of creation thus holds in check the unnatural growths of evil.

The constellation of characters, symbols, and images in Williams's Arthuriad is mapped out in a universe of the poet's own creation. Logres stands for both the genuine realm of Britain and the mythic world of Arthur. The visionary city of Byzantium, like London, is the navel of the Empire, the legendary New Jerusalem, and the emperor who reigns there is a symbol of God-in-action, the Divine Mover, or even Fate. The vision recedes; Logres is, on the surface of things, lost. But Brocéliande, the realm of forest and sea, points the way to hope. It stands for the untapped resources of the subconscious, the future path of the soul on its quest. In apperant defeat, humiliation, and even death rests the seed of salvation. The poems leave us with the certainty of the ultimate good The rites of passage lead on.

Williams has widened the dimensions of the Arthurian story, reminding us of Milton and his representation of the Fall. Heaven and earth are united in a new mythic empire, which is not the less real because it never existed. Indeed, the poet has always in mind the spiritual reality behind the façade of material appearances. His Arthuriad is not a stylized portrait of a utopian *phantastikon* but a universally valid representation of the modern human situation.

The same tenor of thought underlies the plays and novels of the author, as well as his essays on literature and on Christianity. In many aspects, it is related to views shared by his Oxford companions C.S. Lewis and J.R.R. Tolkien, particularly in a tendency toward elements of fantasy and the supernatural. Certain themes echo throughout Williams's work: the primacy of the transcendental, the nature of love as a mirror of the Divine and as a mystical perception of the whole human relationship, the painful way of the soul in quest of perfection, and the image of the City as an image of the Church.

Williams returns the Holy Grail to a modern setting in his novel *War in Heaven* (1930), in which the struggle between good and evil for possession of the Grail takes place on both the physical and spiritual levels. The inadequacy of human reason to comprehend the reality of the mystical world again leaves humankind spiritually impoverished.

"The Figure of Arthur" starts as a survey of the historical and literary origins of the legends of both Arthur and the Holy Grail. Before it breaks off incomplete, however, it begins to discern patterns that are developed in Williams's poetry, revealing, as C.S. Lewis observes in "Williams and the Arthuriad," "an insight into the process whereby his own Arthuriad came into existence."

Early in his career, Williams also wrote a sequence of poems, "The Advent of Galahad." The preoccupation with the Grail anticipates his later work, but the lack of control over the material marks his youthful inexperience. Williams never tried to publish them as a group, but forty-five survive in typescript and several appear in *Heroes and Kings* (1930), *Three Plays* (1931), and *New English Poems*, ed. Lascelles Abercrombie (1931).

It can only be regretted that the work of Charles Williams, and in particular his poetry, has not yet found the appreciation it deserves. Williams recognized the potential of the Arthurian myth better than his predecessors, and he expressed what others have only vaguely anticipated. [KHG/RHT]

Williams, Charles. *War in Heaven*. London: Gollancz, 1920.

———. *Heroes and Kings*. London: Sylvan Press, 1930.

———. *Three Plays*. London: Oxford University Press, 1931.

———. *Taliessin Through Logres*. London: Oxford University Press, 1938.

———. *The Region of the Summer Stars*. London: Editions Poetry London, 1944.

———. "The Figure of Arthur." In *Arthurian Torso*, by Charles Williams and C.S. Lewis. London: Oxford University Press, 1948.

———. "On the Arthurian Myth." In *The Image of the City and Other Essays*, by Charles Williams, ed. Anne Ridler. London: Oxford University Press, 1958.

Abercrombie, Lascelles, ed. *New English Poems*. London: Gollancz, 1931.

Cavaliero, Glen. *Charles Williams: Poet of Theology*. London: Macmillan, 1983.

Göller, Karl Heinz. "From Logres to Carbonek: The Arthuriad of Charles Williams." *Arthurian Literature*, 1 (1981), 121–73.

Hadfield, Alice Mary. *Charles Williams: An Exploration of His LIfe and Work*. New York: Oxford University Press, 1983.

Kollman, Judith. "Charles Williams' *Taliessin Through Logres* and *The Region of the Summer Stars*." In *King Arthur Through the Ages*, ed. Valerie M. Lagorio and Mildred Leake Day. 2 vols. New York: Garland, 1990, Vol. 2, pp. 180–206.

Lewis, C.S. "Williams and the Arthuriad." In *Arthurian Torso*, by Charles Williams and C.S. Lewis. London: Oxford University Press, 1948.

WILLIAMSON, JOANNE S., American author of *The Iron Charm* (1964), a juvenile novel that cleverly incorporates traditional Arthurian elements in the story of Marco, a young Roman patrician sold into slavery. In Dark Age Britain, Marco witnesses the ritual wedding of Ambrosius (Arthur) and the Gwenifer or White Lady, then joins the fight at Badon Hill. [DN]

Williamson, Joanne S. *The Iron Charm*. New York: Knopf, 1964.

WILMER, LAMBERT A. (1805–1863), wrote his poetic drama *Merlin*, which was first published in three installments of one act each in the Baltimore *North American* (Autumn 1827), in an attempt to counter the suicidal despair that overcame Edgar Allan Poe when his marriage to Sarah Elmira Royster was forbidden by her parents. Merlin conjures up spirits to conquer evil and unite Alphonso and Elmira. [CNS]

Wilmer, Lambert A. *Merlin, Together with Recollections of Edgar A. Poe*, ed. Thomas Ollive Mabbot. New York: Scholars' Facsimiles and Reprints, 1941.

WILSON, ALAN, and A.T. BLACKETT, researchers who identified the legendary Arthur with a sixth-century king of south Wales in such works as *Artorius Rex Discovered* (1986). They fictionalized their theories in *Arthur the War King* (1982), in which Arthur is credited with everything from defeating the Saxons to initiating the Christmas holiday and founding Cambridge University. [DN]

Blackett, Baram, and Alan Wilson. *Artorius Rex Discovered*. Cardiff: Byrd, 1986.

Wilson, Alan, and A.T. Blackett. *Arthur the War King*. Cardiff: Byrd, 1982.

WILSON, PETER LAMBORN, American author, translator, and editor, infuses Sufi and Ismaili mysticism into his short story "Glatisant and Grail: An Arthurian Fragment" (1984). Reconstructed from fragments in romance tradition, the work offers an impressionistic account of Palamydes's life, culminating in his discovery of the harmony at the heart of the "seeming paradoxes" in the Grail mythos and Glatisant, the Questing Beast. [RHT]

Wilson, Peter Lamborn. "Glatisant and Grail: An Arthurian Fragment." In *At the Table of the Grail: Magic and the Use of the Imagination*, ed. John Matthews. London: Routledge and Kegan Paul, 1984, pp. 219–42.

WILSON, T(HADDEUS) HOWARD, reveals the influence of Tennyson and a fondness for extended dialogue in *The Quest Everlasting: Launcelot and Guinevere Cycle* (1950), a long poem in blank verse. Modred and Vivian conspire to destroy the Round Table by revealing the love between Launcelot and Guinevere, a love that has endured from their previous incarnations as Adam and Eve, Anthony and Cleopatra. [RHT]

Wilson, T. Howard. *The Quest Everlasting: Launcelot and Guinevere Cycle*. Los Angeles: House-Warven, 1950.

WINCHESTER, cathedral city in Hampshire, formerly the Roman *Venta Belgarum*. Its chief Arthurian significance lies in its identification with Camelot, which is asserted by Malory.

In the post-Roman decline of urban Britain, *Venta Belgarum* probably survived better than most towns. It may have passed with no complete break into the small domain initiated by Cerdic, the putative founder of the West Saxon dynasty, from which English royalty is descended. With its new name, Winchester was the capital of Wessex under Alfred the Great. For many years afterward, it rivaled London as a place for coronations and royal entombments.

Vague recollections of Winchester's age and dignity explain its importance in the imagined Britain of Arthur. Geoffrey of Monmouth introduces it several times. In his *Historia*, Constans, the eldest son of Arthur's grandfather Constantine, is educated here for the monastic life. Hengist captures the city; Merlin mentions it in the *Prophetiae*; Aurelius Ambrosius restores it after the Saxon devastation, and dies here. Arthur himself fights Mordred at Winchester, and after his passing one of Mordred's sons seizes the place and holds it till he, too, is defeated and slain.

Malory's Winchester = Camelot equation became known to many readers through Caxton's edition, published in 1485 (though the preface shows, curiously enough, that Caxton rejected it himself). One result was that Henry VII, who tried to exploit the Arthurian mystique, had his heir-apparent baptized in the cathedral and named Arthur. The intention was that he should reign as Arthur II and, in the eyes of his subjects, fulfill the prophecy of the King's return. Unfortunately for the plan, he died young. Royal interest in Winchester may have had something to do with its college's possession of a Malory manuscript antedating the Caxton edition. This was discovered in 1934.

At some point during the Middle Ages, the city's association with Arthur led to its acquiring the most famous relic of him. Caxton, in his preface, says the Round Table is at Winchester. It is not; but a Round Table imitative of it is still on view in the great hall of the castle. This is what Caxton supposed to be the original, as did Hardyng thirty-five years earlier.

Strictly speaking, it is a table-top only, since the legs—twelve of them, to judge from the mortise holes—are gone. It is made of oak, and is eighteen feet across and two

90. Winchester Round Table. (Britain on View Photographic Library, BTA/ETB.)

and three-quarter inches thick. The weight is about a ton and a quarter. Today, it is fixed to the wall high above the floor and is painted in twenty-four segments, green and white, allotted to knights whose names appear around the rim. They would have been rather crowded, shoulder to shoulder, and all the more so because there is also a place for Arthur himself with a picture of a king. At the center is a rose.

The paintwork is easier to date than the table. Henry VIII had it done in 1522 for a state visit by the emperor Charles V. The pictured king is Henry himself, with the beard that he had recently grown, and the rose is a Tudor rose. The whole design was repainted in the eighteenth century without change. As for the table itself, one conjecture is that it was made for Edward III in 1344, when he formed a project for reviving the Arthurian knighthood (he gave up the notion and founded the Order of the Garter instead). In 1976–77, the table was moved out from the wall and subjected to a series of tests. Indications in the method of carpentry, and tree-ring patterns in the wood, appeared to support the Edward III theory, but carbon-dating suggested a slightly earlier time.

It now seems likely that this massive piece of furniture was made for a type of aristocratic festival known as a Round Table. Quite a number were held during the Middle Ages, in England and overseas. Nobles played Arthurian roles, danced, banqueted, and competed in jousts. The apparent age of the Winchester table would fit it into the reign of Henry III or that of Edward I. Henry was born at Winchester and might have presented the table to his birthplace, if he had it made for himself. During at least part of his reign, he disapproved of Round Tables and tried to ban them, but he may not have been entirely consistent, and several were held while he was king if not under his auspices. Edward I, however, is more promising. An Arthurian enthusiast, he favored such functions and attended at least five, organizing a lavish one himself in 1299 to celebrate his second marriage. The Winchester table could have been made for that occasion. [GA]

Geoffrey of Monmouth. *Historia Regum Britanniae*, Book VI, Chapters 5, 16; Book VII, Chapter 4; Book VIII, Chapters 9, 14; Book XI, Chapters 2–3.

Malory, Sir Thomas. *Le Morte Darthur*, Book XVIII, Chapter 10.

Ashe, Geoffrey. *A Guidebook to Arthurian Britain*. Wellingborough: Aquarian, 1983, pp. 209–11.

Loomis, Roger Sherman. "Arthurian Influence on Sport and Spectacle." In *Arthurian Literature in the Middle Ages*. Oxford: Clarendon, 1959, pp. 553–59.

WIPPERSBERG, W.J.M., Austrian director who also writes children's books and screen and radio plays. King Arthur, Queen Guinevere, and many Arthurian knights play a significant if untraditional role in the plot of *Erik und Roderik* (1977). The heroes of the book are two young neighbors who quarrel continually about a small plot of land in a farcical petty war. But when the aging and impoverished King Arthur wants Eric and Roderik to house him and his knights, they join forces to trick the King and prevent him from pillaging France in a "holy war." [SSch/PM]

Wippersberg, W.J.M. *Erik und Roderik: Eine Rittergeschichte*. Innsbruck and Vienna: Obelisk, 1977.

WIRNT VON GRAFENBERG, author of *Wigalois*, a romance of about 11,700 lines written ca. 1200–15. Wirnt, who names himself twice (ll. 141, 10,576), is the central figure of a didactic poem by Konrad von Würzburg written ca. 1250, *Der Welt Lohn* ("World's Reward"), but little is known of his life. *Wigalois* reveals his familiarity with great romances of Hohenstaufen culture, such as *Erec* and *Iwein*, by Hartmann von Aue, and *Parzival* (at least the first six books), by Wolfram von Eschenbach. Many scholars believe that Wirnt belonged to an influential family seated near Grafenberg, Bavaria. Thus, he appears integral to the florescence of Arthurian literature in German between 1180 and 1220. It is likely that Wirnt's story derives from French sources, written or oral, though no direct relationships have been found. The early part of *Wigalois* is much like Renaut de Beaujeu's romance *Le Bel Inconnu* (ca. 1200). Allusions to *Wigalois* are found in German literature from ca. 1220 on; nearly forty complete or fragmentary manuscripts preserve it; a large series of fourteenth-century murals in a Tyrolian castle, Schloss Runkelstein, depicts episodes from it; and a prose redaction was published in 1493 (*Wigoleis vom Rade*, "Wigalois of the Wheel") and often thereafter. *Wigalois* belongs among the more popular German castings of Arthurian lore.

In the story, an unknown knight comes to Arthur's court and offers the Queen a beautiful girdle, vowing to challenge Arthur's knights the next day should she choose not to keep it. The girdle has marvelous powers, but the Queen returns it, and with its help the stranger defeats all opponents, Gawein being the last. With Gawein as prisoner, he returns to his fabulous country: there, Gawein marries his niece, Florie, but after some blissful months leaves her to visit Arthur. Lacking the girdle, Gawein cannot find his way back to Florie; she bears a son, Wigalois, who excels in manly virtue and, at the age of twenty, goes in search of his father.

He comes to Arthur's court, seats himself on a stone that rejects all but the most excellent, and is accordingly welcomed. Gawein becomes his mentor, although neither perceives their relationship. When a damsel comes to Arthur seeking a champion for a dread adventure, Wigalois gains the commission—much to her distress, for she doubts the prowess of this young and unknown knight. Traveling with her, Wigalois defeats four separate knights and a pair of giants and thus wins her confidence. At her mistress's castle, Roimunt, he learns that, ten years before, the heathen Roaz had assassinated King Lar and usurped his country, Korntin. The legitimate heiress, Larie, dwells at Roimunt and is to marry the hero who liberates her land. Wigalois and Larie fall in love. He finds his way into Korntin by following a strange beast; this is transformed into the spirit of King Lar, who tells Wigalois that Gawein is his father and equips him to fight a dragon. Though he kills the dragon, he is gravely injured and robbed of his armor. Restored to strength by the widow of one of the dragon's victims, he is nearly killed by a monstrous forest-woman, slays a powerful dwarf, and so reaches Glois, the fortress of Roaz. The bridge into Glois is blocked by a turning water-wheel studded with swords and axes. God answers the hero's prayer and brings the wheel to a stop. Entering the city, Wigalois kills a centaur and two guards, then fights all night with Roaz, finally killing him. The wife of Roaz, Japhite, dies of grief.

In Korntin, the hero marries Larie in the presence of several Arthurian knights, including Gawein, whose relationship to him is joyfully acknowledged. A messenger reports that King Amire of Libia has been slain by Lion of Namur—this for love of Queen Liamere, second cousin to Larie. Wigalois and Gawein mount a punitive expedition; after much fighting, Gawein kills Lion. Father and son travel to Arthur's court, Gawein learning on the way that Florie has died; then Wigalois and Larie return to Korntin, where she bears a son of whom amazing adventures are told.

Stylistically facile, though not distinguished, *Wigalois* is carefully constructed. The hero's adventures are framed by stories of his father; his great mission, the liberation of Korntin, proceeds through stages of escalating peril; the final conflict at Namur confirms his manhood and cements the bond with his father. An atmosphere of the sinister and supernatural grows ever stronger as he approaches the devilish Roaz at Glois; his success depends not only on his courage and hardihood but also on God's direct intervention. The victory of Christian over heathen (e.g., Gawein over Lion) is an important motif. Numerous details associate Wigalois's adventures with Christian tradition, notably with elements in the Revelation of John (discussed by Wirnt, ll. 10,272–305), suggesting that the author's many pious excurses express an important part of his character. Unlike the heroes of Hartmann and Wolfram, Wigalois is not a gravely flawed knight achieving reconciliation with God and man through selfless adventure. He seems instead to embody the knight in full harmony with Fortune (hence his emblem, the wheel). Wirnt wants his audience to reflect on the excellence and final happiness of one whose behavior so reflects God's will that life withholds nothing from him. The relative disfavor of *Wigalois* among modern readers may arise in this unproblematic essence, for the poem is very interesting in story, composition, atmosphere, and authorial presence. [SLW]

Wirnt von Grafenberg. *Wigalois, der Ritter mit dem Rade*, ed. J.M.N. Kapteyn. Bonn: Klopp, 1926.

———. *Wigalois, the Knight of Fortune's Wheel*, trans. J.W. Thomas. Lincoln: University of Nebraska Press, 1977.

Cormeau, Christoph. *"Wigalois" und "Diu Crône": Zwei Kapitel zur Gattungsgeschichte des nachklassischen Aventiureromans*. Zurich and Munich: Artemis, 1977.

Gottzmann, Carola L. *Artusdichtung*. Stuttgart: Metzler, 1989.

Grubmüller, Klaus. "Artusroman und Heilsbringerethos: Zum 'Wigalois' des Wirnt von Gravenberg." *Beiträge zur Geschichte der deutschen Sprache und Literatur*, 107 (1985), 218–39.

Schröder, Werner. "Der syncretistische Roman des Wirnt von Gravenberg: Unerledigte Fragen an den *Wigalois*." *Euphorion*, 80 (1986), 235–77.

Schultz, James A. *The Shape of the Round Table: Structures of Middle High German Arthurian Romance*. Toronto: University of Toronto Press, 1983.

Thomas, Neil. *A German View of Camelot: Wirnt von Gravenberg's Wigalois and Arthurian Tradition*. New York: Peter Lang, 1987.

WODEHOUSE, P.G. (1881–1975), wrote an Arthurian story, "Sir Agravaine" (1912), in which a knight, who has suffered much because he has neither strength nor handsome appearance, is at long last given a quest and, at its end, finds his heart's desire. The story is told with typical Wodehousian wit, and its many anachronistic references help to establish Sir Agravaine as something of a modern man lost in the medieval world. [SRR]

Wodehouse, P.G. "Sir Agravaine." *Collier's National Weekly*, 49 (June 29, 1912), 18–19; repr. in *The Man Upstairs*. London: Methuen, 1914; reissued in book form as *Sir Agravaine*. Poole, Dorset: Blandford, 1984.

WOLF, JOAN, author of *The Road to Avalon* (1988), a historical-romance version of Arthur's story. Morgan is here Arthur's aunt, his lifelong lover, and the mother of Mordred. The unusual relationships and some inventive treatments of traditional episodes are the most interesting aspects of an otherwise unremarkable novel. [DN]

Wolf, Joan. *The Road to Avalon*. New York: New American Library, 1988.

WOLFE, GENE, American author of *Castleview* (1990), a novel about the interfacing of the fairy world and the normal world in a small Illinois town called Castleview. The Arthurian content in this hodgepodge of folklore and mythology in a modern setting revolves around a character named Viviane Morgan (a blend of Morgan le Fay and the Lady of the Lake), who succeeds in bringing about the death of a contemporary Arthur figure but who loses Excalibur in the process. [ACL]

Wolfe, Gene. *Castleview*. New York: Tor, 1990.

WOLF-FEUER, KÄTHE, follows primarily Chrétien de Troyes and Wolfram von Eschenbach in her two-part dramatic presentation, "Parcival-Spiel" (1970). Although Wolf-Feuer greatly condenses her models, she does add a scene in which the smith Trebucet repairs the broken Grail sword and then dies. [SSch/PWM]

Wolf-Feuer, Käthe. "Parcival-Spiel." In *Reimen und mit Noten*. Stuttgart: Mellinger, 1974.

WOLFRAM VON ESCHENBACH, the greatest German epic poet of the high Middle Ages, that period of extraordinary literary and artistic achievement around the year 1200. He was recognized as such by some of his contemporaries, and his reputation has remained alive throughout the centuries. To be sure, he was no innovator like Hartmann von Aue, who with his classical style introduced Arthurian literature to Germany, nor was he a consummate master of language and love like Gottfried von Strassburg. On the contrary, Wolfram's style is anything but polished. It is obscure and complex, frequently with the immediacy of conversation, but his works show an intense grappling with the problems of human existence that sets him apart from his contemporaries. In recent years, appreciation of Wolfram's genius has spread beyond German-speaking areas, so that he is now recognized as one of the great poets of world literature.

Wolfram's works include his monumental *Parzival*, which is a reworking, expansion, and completion of Chrétien de Troyes's *Conte del Graal*; his unfinished *Willehalm*, a tragic romance based on *Aliscans*, an Old French *chanson de geste*; two fragments commonly known by the title *Titurel*, but actually dealing with the love of young Schionatulander and Sigune, two of the characters in *Parzival*; and nine lyric poems, mostly dawn songs (possibly the first in German), attributed to Wolfram in the various collections of *Minnesang*. The chronology of Wolfram's works is not completely clear. One thing is certain: his *Parzival* preceded his *Willehalm*, because Wolfram mentions the former in the prologue to the latter. Most scholars believe that his lyric poems came before *Parzival* and that the *Titurel* fragments, written in strophic form, were composed either immediately before or during the work on *Willehalm*. One historical event, the destruction of vineyards during the siege of Erfurt in 1203–04, is mentioned in Book VII of *Parzival*, so that the beginning of work on *Parzival* is believed to lie between 1200 and 1210. In *Willehalm*, there is a mocking reference to the coronation of Otto IV in October 1209, and in the same year a new siege weapon, the tribocco mentioned in *Willehalm*, was supposedly introduced into Germany. Wolfram names Landgrave Hermann of Thuringia as the provider of the Old French source for his *Willehalm* and appears to refer to him as deceased in the last book. Hermann died on April 25, 1217, so that *Willehalm* was probably begun after ca. 1212 and left unfinished sometime after 1217, maybe as late as the 1220s.

Despite the fact that Wolfram, or at least the first-person narrator of his works, makes numerous references to himself and his circumstances, very little concrete biographical knowledge is actually available. Eschenbach is probably the old Middle Franconian city of Ober-Eschenbach southeast of Ansbach, today Wolframs-Eschenbach in Bavaria. Mention is made of Wolfram's grave there in the Frauenkirche as late as the middle of the fifteenth century and the early seventeenth century, and a von Eschenbach family is known there from 1268 to the second half of the fourteenth century. Wolfram was probably not of the nobility, but rather a poor man, dependent on patronage from the powerful and wealthy for his livelihood. He does call himself a soldier on one occasion, but that is no reason to assume that he was even a *ministerialis*. He spent at least some time at the court of Hermann of Thuringia, who undoubtedly commissioned *Willehalm*, and the Count of Wertheim may have been an early patron. Geographical references in his works indicate that he traveled about, even as far as Styria.

Wolfram claims to be illiterate (*Parzival*, Chapter 115, ll. 27–30), yet he also is proud of his wealth of knowledge and is eager to display it. He is acquainted, for example, with lists of precious stones and the Arabic names of planets that are both probably derived from written sources. Nevertheless, he surely did not enjoy a traditional clerical education, for he shows no knowledge of the Latin school authors. He did know some French, but certainly not very well, because he probably misunderstood his French sources on occasion. Scholars have continued to speculate on Wolfram's literacy and how he actually composed, but perhaps it is significant that Wolfram always says: "as I heard tell" or "the story says"; he never says, "as I read" or "as it is written." He is well acquainted with the German literature of his day: Heinrich von Veldeke, Hartmann von Aue,

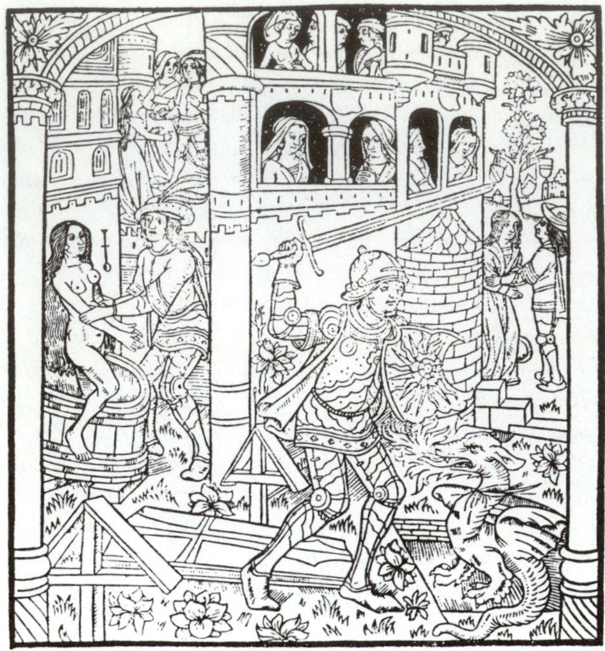

91. Woodcut from first known printed *Lancelot* (1488). (Courtesy of The Newberry Library, Chicago.)

Walter von der Vogelweide, and Neidhart von Reuental are all mentioned. He knew the German *Alexander*, *Rolandslied*, *Kaiserchronik*, Eilhart von Oberge's *Tristrant*, the *Nibelungenlied*, and other heroic sagas, and apparently engaged in a literary feud with Gottfried von Strassburg. His professed analphabetism could well be part of his reaction to the obviously learned Hartmann and Gottfried, for Wolfram does not hesitate to heap scorn on those who keep referring to their literary sources. He relies instead on his own divinely inspired creative sense (*Willehalm*, Chapter 2, ll. 16–22) for his artistic achievements. Nevertheless, Wolfram is acutely aware of the importance of sources and repeatedly refers to his *aventiure* or to the *maere* that he is retelling.

Wolfram's best-known work is his *Parzival*, an Arthurian epic of some 25,000 lines, written in rhymed couplets. It may also have been the most popular German courtly epic, if one may judge by the unusually large number of extant manuscripts. His chief source is undeniably Chrétien de Troyes's *Perceval*, or *Le Conte del Graal*, but Wolfram's version differs from Chrétien's in many respects. Two differences are immediately apparent. First, Chrétien's *Perceval* remains fragmentary, having been left unfinished after 9,234 lines (there are, of course, numerous Continuations, which Wolfram probably did not know, with the possible exception of the First Continuation and the so-called *Bliocadran Prologue*), whereas Wolfram has brought his story to a satisfactory conclusion. Second, Wolfram has expanded his *Parzival* by the addition of two books that describe the adventures of Parzival's father, Gahmuret, in the East and his ultimate marriage to Herzeloyde, who later gives birth to Parzival after Gahmuret's death. Also, Wolfram's concept of the Grail and the Grail society is quite different from Chrétien's. Wolfram's Grail family goes beyond the courtly family of King Arthur to function as a divinely ordained instrument in the affairs of the world. Parzival is related to the Arthurian family through his father and to the Grail family through his mother. Wolfram is keenly aware of family relationships and has almost all characters of any importance related to one another in some way. Furthermore, Wolfram gives names to characters nameless in Chrétien and changes some others. Nevertheless, the general sequence of events is preserved by Wolfram in the parts that correspond to Chrétien's work, although some episodes are shortened or expanded.

In an epilogue to *Parzival*, Wolfram finds fault with Chrétien for not having done justice to the story, indicating clearly that he must have been acquainted with Chrétien's version. Earlier, however, he had mentioned a certain "Kyot" as his source. According to Wolfram, Kyot was a Provençal who had provided the true story of the Grail, a story written in Arabic that he had found discarded in Toledo. That manuscript contained a report about the Grail and the Grail family by an astronomer named Flegetanis, who was part Jewish and who had read about the Grail in the stars. Kyot, the Christian, had to learn Arabic in order to read what Flegetanis had written. Thereupon, he searched through Latin chronicles to find the story of the Grail family, which he finally located in Anjou. This is patently a fantastic fabrication to impress the gullible and to delight the cognoscenti in Wolfram's audience.

Along with his invention of Kyot, Wolfram exhibits a very different concept of the Grail from the one found in Chrétien. What was there a dish or bowl has become a stone, named enigmatically *lapsit exillis*, quite possibly an intentionally distorted "Latin" term, although there have been many attempts at explanation, none of which has been completely convincing. It was to this stone that God had banished the angels who had remained neutral in the struggle between God and Lucifer. Later, a human family was entrusted with the protection of the Grail and lived from the food and drink that it miraculously provided. The Grail could be carried only by a virgin and had the power to keep anyone who came into its presence from dying for the next week. Wolfram's Grail is practically inaccessible, being guarded by an order of knights in a castle that cannot be found by those who seek it. Children are named to the Grail by means of an inscription that appears on the stone. They grow up there as knights and ladies to be sent out later to occupy thrones that lack rulers. The ladies are sent out openly—such was the case with Herzeloyde, Parzival's mother—but the men are sent out secretly.

The "templars," as Wolfram calls the Grail knights, are not allowed to marry or have a love relationship with women while guarding the Grail. Only the Grail King may be married, but Anfortas, the current king, had defied that stipulation and, performing chivalric deeds in the service of a lady, had been wounded in the groin by a poisoned spear. The wound cannot be healed, and his sufferings are intense, yet he cannot die because of the presence of the Grail. At length, a message appears on the Grail, stating that a stranger will come to the Grail castle who is to ask the question that will release Anfortas. No one must inform him of the situation, and he must ask the question on the first night, otherwise he will lose the opportunity to become king, and Anfortas will not be healed.

Parzival, of course, is the one chosen by the Grail to free Anfortas. He had been raised far from courtly life: after the tragic death of his father, Gahmuret, his mother had purposely kept him away from court, but the genetic inheritance from his adventure-loving father is not to be denied, and Parzival goes out into the world, dressed as a fool, seeking King Arthur in order to become a knight. He eventually does become one, but only after killing a relative unwittingly in the process. He rescues and marries the beautiful Condwiramurs, whom he then leaves to visit his mother, only to arrive at the Grail castle. Mindful of all he had been taught about knightly behavior, Parzival sees the Grail procession and the bloody spear and hears the lamenting of the people. He receives a sword from Anfortas, who is obviously suffering. He remains silent, however, and on the next morning the Grail company has mysteriously disappeared. Two days later, Parzival arrives at Arthur's court and is accepted as a knight of the Round Table. At this crowning moment of his knightly career, Parzival suffers the bitter humiliation of being cursed publicly by the ugly Grail messenger, Cundrie, for having failed to ask the question.

The narrative then divides, with Gawan occupying the foreground in his quest for four queens and 400 maidens held captive in Schastel Merveile; yet Parzival hovers in the background, angry with God and determined to find the Grail again. Gawan's adventures are interrupted in the middle when the narrative returns to Parzival on Good Friday, to his meeting with his hermit uncle, Trevrizent, who tells him about his family, his relationship to Anfortas and the Grail, about his mother's death and the murder of his relative. He hears Parzival's confession and gives him insight into God and His ways with man, so that Parzival loses his anger toward God, yet he still hopes to find the Grail.

Gawan eventually succeeds in freeing the queens. He gains the hand of the proud Orgeluse and arranges for Arthur to come to see his culminating duel with Gramoflanz. Parzival, however, intervenes, fights first with Gawan (unaware of his identity), then in Gawan's stead with Gramoflanz. King Arthur is left with the problem of reconciling Gramoflanz with Gawan, and Parzival leaves the ensuing joyous celebration, only to encounter his heathen half-brother, Feirefiz, in combat that almost costs Parzival his life before his brother magnanimously reveals his identity first. Parzival, having learned to know God and having proven himself, is now ready to be called to the Grail by Cundrie. Accompanied by Feirefiz, he is conducted to the Grail; asks what ails his uncle, Anfortas, who is then miraculously cured; and assumes the kingship of the Grail, his wife and twin sons joining him shortly thereafter.

Wolfram's story clearly deals with two realms, the Arthurian world of preeminent chivalry, with Gawan, the perfect knight, as its leading figure, and the Grail-world, a transcendent realm with a definite relationship to God, one that demands a suitable electus as its savior and new leader. Both Parzival and Gawan are exemplary knights in the eyes of the world, and both succeed in their quests, but it is Parzival who must undergo the purification process that will enable him to assume his rightful heritage. The courtly world of Arthur, implicit in the first two books in the life of Parzival's father, is sought at first by Parzival in his ignorance. It is a world of the highest courtly virtues, but Parzival must learn that for him it is not sufficient. He has a higher calling.

King Arthur does not appear in Wolfram's *Willehalm*, an unfinished tragic romance of some 13,000 lines, yet the spirit of courtly love and chivalry is very much present. It is remarkable that here Wolfram portrays not only the Christians but also the heathens as noble knights in the service of ladies, and he lavishes praise on the heroes of both sides, quite in contrast to his Old French source, *Aliscans*.

The *Titurel* fragments, also placed in a courtly setting, are likewise without the presence of King Arthur. They are composed in strophes of four long lines each, similar to those of the *Nibelungenlied*. The two groups of fragments, comprising approximately 170 strophes (there are questions about the authenticity of some strophes), present the love story of two young people, Schionatulander and Sigune. The first group describes the development of their love; the second tells of a hunting dog with a magnificent long leash that has an artistically worked story on it. The hound tears itself loose from Sigune's hands, but she wishes to learn the whole story and asks Schionatulander to retrieve it, saying that she will not grant him her love until he does. Here, the fragment breaks off, but we know from Wolfram's *Parzival* that Schionatulander meets his death in the attempt and that Sigune spends the rest of her life doing penance and grieving over the body of her lover.

Titurel was continued and brought to a conclusion in an enormous work, known as *Der jüngere Titurel*, by a certain Albrecht, who actually passes himself off initially as Wolfram. Thus, Wolfram was generally considered to be the author throughout the fourteenth and fifteenth centuries. If one adds *Der jüngere Titurel* to his *Parzival* and *Willehalm*, one should not be surprised that Wolfram was highly regarded by his successors. He is even credited with participation in the famous singing contest at the Wartburg (*see* WARTBURGKRIEG), and his style was consciously imitated by other poets. Today, he is viewed as a highly individualistic artist who transformed his sources with masterly skill into new creations and imbued them with an ethical and spiritual dimension that was unique in his time. [SMJ]

Wolfram von Eschenbach. *Wolfram von Eschenbach*, ed. Karl Lachmann. Berlin, 1833; 6th ed. Berlin; de Gruyter, 1926; repr. 1965.

———. *Wolfram von Eschenbach* (edition of *Parzival*), ed. Albert Leitzmann. 5 vols. Halle, 1905–06; 6th ed. Wilhelm Deinert. Tübingen: Niemeyer, 1965.

———. *Willehalm*, ed. Werner Schröder. Berlin and New York: de Gruyter, 1978.

———. *Parzival*, trans. A.T. Hatto. Harmondsworth: Penguin, 1980.

———. *Willehalm*, trans. Marion E. Gibbs and Sidney M. Johnson. Harmondsworth: Penguin, 1984.

———. *Wolfram von Eschenbach:* Titurel *and the Songs*, ed. and trans. Marion E. Gibbs and Sidney M. Johnson. New York: Garland, 1988.

Bumke, Joachim. *Wolfram von Eschenbach*. Stuttgart: Metzler, 1964; 5th ed. 1981.

Gärtner, Kurt, and Joachim Heinzele, eds. *Studien zu Wolfram von Eschenbach*. Tübingen: Niemeyer, 1989.

Gottzmann, Carola L. *Artusdichtung*. Stuttgart: Metzler, 1989.

Poag, James F. *Wolfram von Eschenbach*. New York: Twayne, 1972.

Sacker, Hugh D. *An Introduction to Wolfram's "Parzival."* Cambridge: Cambridge University Press, 1963.

Weigand, Hermann J. *Wolfram's "Parzival,"* ed. Ursula Hoffmann. Ithaca, N.Y.: Cornell University Press, 1969.

Wynn, Marianne. *Wolfram's "Parzival": On the Genesis of Its Poetry*. Frankfurt am Main: Peter Lang, 1984.

WOMEN, ARTHURIAN. From the first Arthurian fictions to the most recent transformations of the legend, the role of women at Arthur's court and in the lands beyond has been both centrally important and highly problematic. Although it is difficult to generalize about the vast corpus of Arthurian materials, it is clear that the early legend established a pattern that subsequent reworkings have modified but never completely undone. Arthur's knights are the active subjects who embark upon quests and fight in tournaments; the women play more restricted, although by no means passive, roles as the objects of the knights' protection, love, or fear. We first witness this dynamic of male-female relations when Geoffrey of Monmouth recounts the insistence of the ladies at Arthur's court on marrying only men who have proved themselves skillful warriors. The effect of what has become known as the "chivalry topos," according to which a knight performs more valorously because he is in love, is to relegate the beloved lady literally to the sidelines.

In the eleventh and twelfth centuries, the representation of woman as inspiration may have reflected the social aspirations of landless youths striving to better themselves through marriage. In later periods, female figures reflect fears and fantasies rather than political goals. The enduring legacy of the Arthurian lady is the mirror she holds up to the psyche of creator and reader: the idealized women of Arthurian literature reflect the social mentalities and sexual preoccupations of their eras.

The literary theme of women as spectators of and inspirations for chivalric exploits found its historic counterpart in the medieval audience, where women played a vital part as early patrons, readers, and listeners. Eleanor of Aquitaine has been credited by some scholars as being the patron of Wace's *Roman de Brut*, Thomas's *Tristan*, and numerous non-Arthurian works, although some of these attributions are speculative. More certain proof of female patronage occurs when an author inscribed the name of a female dedicatee in the text, as did Chrétien de Troyes for Marie de Champagne in the *Chevalier de la charrete*, Manessier for Jeanne de Flandre in the third Continuation of the *Perceval*, and Gerbert de Montreuil for Marie de Ponthieu in the fourth Continuation; Girart d'Amiens's *Escanor* may have been dedicated to Eleanor of Castille. Dedications to an anonymous or imaginary lady beloved of the poet occur in *Le Bel Inconnu* and *L'Atre périlleux*. Such inscriptions are evidence of medieval women's participation in the court culture that fostered Arthurian literature, of the class privileges afforded a few highly placed ladies, and of the apparent appeal of Arthurian fiction to noblewomen. Within the romances' narratives, however, the lady's idealization and cultural privilege are often attenuated by dependent status or marginalization, just as it was for historical noblewomen from the twelfth through the fifteenth centuries.

Both the early Tristan poems and the romances of Chrétien de Troyes present rich female figures whose ambiguities later romancers will develop. In Béroul and Thomas, Iseut is both a hapless victim of her fate to love Tristan, rather than her husband King Mark, and a clever schemer who is able to defend herself and fulfill her passionate desire, at least occasionally. Although the poets praise her resourcefulness, the narrator's admiration in some versions, such as Thomas's and Gottfried von Strassburg's, is qualified by outbursts of antifeminism.

In Chrétien's romances, Enide, Fenice, Laudine, and Lunete provide complex characterizations of women whose powers as observer, manipulator, or autonomous ruler in chivalric society are ultimately circumscribed within a male order that legitimates feudal marriage. In *Le Chevalier de la charrete*, Guenevere functions doubly as a helpless victim of male machinations and as an imperious lady whose motivations are elusive. In *Le Conte del Graal*, Perceval's neglect of his mother and Gauvain's flirtations could be construed to point subtly to an underlying fear of women and of female sexuality.

These ambiguous female characters are the precursors of a rich gallery of female figures in Arthurian literature, ranging from benevolent and malevolent fairies to besieged ladies, from scheming temptresses to chaste, well-born maidens ripe for a feudal alliance. The world beyond the court is populated not only by damsels in distress, but also by wives, mothers, nuns, orphans, sisters. In some romances, such as *Durmart le Gallois* and *Le Bel Inconnu*, the heroine is an idealized love object, a fantasy woman who might well have appealed to landless bachelor knights seeking a successful marriage. The heroine's youth, wealth, and beauty promise fecundity and prosperity. Other portrayals of Arthurian women in verse romance reflect clerical antifeminism rather than chivalric idealization. In *La Vengeance Raguidel*, Gauvain encounters women who threaten his masculinity, and he ultimately launches into a diatribe wherein he compares the fidelity of women unfavorably with the companionship of dogs. In the Vulgate Cycle, the focus shifts more sharply to the spiritual progress of the knights, and the view of women becomes even more dichotomized between the poles of Eve's sin and Mary's redemption. Within the religious framework of the Grail quest, woman represents the carnal pleasures that tempt man to sin, but she can also be the vehicle for revelation and salvation. Thus, Guenevere, the most fully individualized woman in the Arthurian world, is both the sole inspiration for Lancelot's worldly honor and the supreme obstacle to his spiritual ascent. The fairy Morgan, jealous of Guenevere, schemes to seduce Lancelot and to destroy the couple by revealing their affair. But at the other end of the spiritual scale from these are women who function as helpful messengers and spiritual guides; an example is Perceval's sister, who dubs Galahad as God's knight and leads him to the marvelous ship. Throughout the Prose *Lancelot* numerous anonymous damsels seem to know the way even as they lead the knight to stray from the direct route, thereby conspiring with the wandering voice of the tale itself in its digressions and amplifications. The association of a mysterious, elusive female voice with an otherworld of fable and fiction-making opposed to the straight and narrow of the conventional chivalric order may have appealed as much to clerks and knights seeking to transcend social boundaries as it did to women.

Female characters retain their ambiguity and their importance in the German reworkings of Chrétien, and their treatment often reflects an author's moral preoccupation. Hartmann von Aue's *Erec* seems to present an even more restricted sense of woman's proper station; Ulrich von Zatzikhoven's *Lanzelet* makes no mention of Guenevere's adulterous affair with Lancelot. Gottfried's *Tristan* fully develops Isolde's early hatred of Tristan as her uncle's assassin, as well as the animosity between Isolde and Brangien and the jealousy between the two Isoldes. Although, as in the French romances, women are never the principal protagonists of these stories, they nonetheless function as the principal obsession of the hero and consequently engender the romances' moral complexity and psychological intensity.

In Middle English Arthurian literature, women continue to be both marginal and central, a source of poetic preoccupation and consternation. In *Sir Gawain and the Green Knight*, the contrast between the male "public" world of the hunt and the female "private" world of the bedchamber structures the dichotomy between the feminine order of pleasure and sensuality and the "masculine" order of male-to-male feudal obligations. Although the dispute between Morgan and Guenevere is the ultimate source of the poem's erotic tensions, female power is displaced to the margins of the story. If we believe the fictional example of Chaucer's feistiest heroine, Arthurian romance widened its appeal for women in the English audience, extending beyond the aristocracy. It is significant that when the Wife of Bath chooses to tell her story, she deploys the Arthurian genre to express her fantasy of youth and beauty.

Nonetheless, male authorship of pre-twentieth century Arthurian fictions is the rule, and the representation of women reflects the mentalities of male authors. Although knights continue to dominate the Arthurian landscape, the troublesome presence of ladies becomes increasingly the focus of narrators' attention. By telescoping the Vulgate's structure to emphasize sentimental dramas more sharply, Malory highlights the characters of Guenevere, Morgause, Morgan, and Nimue in a way that will capture the fancy of nineteenth-century readers. Less doctrinaire than the Vulgate author(s), Malory is both moralistic and sympathetic toward Guenevere: an adulteress, she nonetheless exemplifies "trewe love," constant as she is in her affection for Lancelot, and, in her reclusion, she comes to a "goode ende."

As Arthurian conventions are reworked more self-consciously in the Renaissance, women's function not as "real" entities but as projections of male fear and desires is more acutely dramatized. In the psychological epics of Spenser and Ariosto, the chaste woman and the lascivious temptress adopt a multiplicity of roles and disguises representing the warring forces within the hero's psyche. An arresting example is that of the transvestite Britomart, the maiden warrior of *The Faerie Queene*.

The dichotomized image of women as either pure or lascivious persists in nineteenth- and twentieth-century Arthurian fictions. Even more sharply than Malory's version, Tennyson's *Idylls of the King* is structured around problematic male-female relationships, on pairings of Arthur's men and their women. He portrays virtuous love in the character of Enid, manipulative and destructive female lust in Vivien, self-destructive female desire in Elaine, and a complex web of guilt and faith in Guinevere. For the Victorian and Pre-Raphaelite poets, the sexual enchantresses and extramarital lovers of Arthurian fiction exerted a strong attraction. Guenevere, Isolde, and Nimue are celebrated as beautiful spellbinders who may have allowed their creators to fantasize relationships free of the strictures of Victorian society, and whose unconventional morality may have appealed to both men and women in the reading public. Whatever the underlying social causes, by the late nineteenth century and well into our own, in the high art of Wagner as well as in more popular fiction, films, and the musical comedy *Camelot*, the adulteresses Isolde and Guenevere emerge as the preeminent medieval heroines.

Arthurian female characters thus mirror fantasies about and fears of women within the ages that produced them. In keeping with women's emergence in the twentieth century, many contemporary Arthurian fictions are more female-centered than ever before. Written by women authors, they are directed primarily at female audiences, and they depict the lives of their otherworld heroines in the intimate detail of realistic fiction. But increased attention to the Arthurian ladies has not, for the most part, liberated fictional women from their traditional feminine roles. In Sharan Newman's Guinevere trilogy, where Guinevere's emotional development is analyzed in depth, the heroine is fully absorbed in a private, sentimental dilemma shared with numerous heroines in popular contemporary romance. A more radical revision of the legend, written from a more overtly feminist perspective, is Marion Zimmer Bradley's *The Mists of Avalon*, which retells the story from Morgaine's view and offers an imaginative reconstruction of a region largely unexplored in previous renditions: the female world of magic, pagan ritual, and sisterly friendship. [RK]

Burns, E. Jane. "La Voie de la voix: The Aesthetics of Indirection in the Vulgate Cycle." In *The Legacy of Chrétien de Troyes*, ed. Norris J. Lacy, Douglas Kelly, and Keith Busby. 2 vols. Amsterdam: Rodopi, 1988, Vol. 2, pp. 151–67.

Cavanagh, Sheila. "'Beauties Chace': Arthur and Women in *The Faerie Queene*." In *The Passing of Arthur: New Essays in Arthurian Tradition*, ed. Christopher Baswell and William Sharpe. New York: Garland, 1988, pp. 207–20.

Chênerie, Marie-Luce. "Le Chevalier, la Femme, et l'Amour." In *Le Chevalier Errant dans les romans arthuriens en vers des XIIe et XIIIe siècles*. Geneva: Droz, 1986, pp. 410–501.

Fisher, Sheila. "Leaving Morgan Aside: Women, History, and Revisionism in *Sir Gawain and the Green Knight*." In *The Passing of Arthur: New Essays in Arthurian Tradition*, ed. Christopher Baswell and William Sharpe. New York: Garland, 1988, pp. 129–51.

Krueger, Roberta. "Love, Honor and the Exchange of Women in *Yvain*: Some Remarks on the Female Reader." *Romance Notes*, 25 (1985), 302–17.

Lefay-Toury, Marie-Noëlle. "Roman breton et mythe courtois: l'évolution du personnage féminin dans les romans de Chrétien de Troyes." *Cahiers de civilisation médiévale*, 15 (1972), 193–204, 283–93.

Lejeune, Rita. "La Femme dans les littératures française et occitane du XIe au XIIIe siècle." *Cahiers de civilisation médiévale*, 20 (1977), 201–18.

Payen, Jean-Charles. "La Destruction des mythes courtois dans le roman arthurien: la femme dans le roman en vers après Chrétien de Troyes." *Revue des langues romanes*, 78 (1969), 213–28.

Silver, Carole. "Victorian Spellbinders: Arthurian Women and the Pre-Raphaelite Circle." In *The Passing of Arthur: New Essays in Arthurian Tradition*, ed. Christopher Baswell and William Sharpe. New York: Garland, 1988, pp. 249–63.

WOOLLEY, PERSIA, American author of *Child of the Northern Spring* (1987), in which Guinevere describes her youth as princess and heir of the kingdom of Rheged and her marriage to Arthur, the young High King. Events largely follow those in Malory, with special attention paid to psychological motivation of the characters. This novel, the first part of a Guinevere trilogy, is continued by *Queen of the Summer Stars* (1990). This is closer to medieval romance in plot and incident, but the story is revalued by an imaginative use of new motivations and relationships, making it more realistic in terms of present-day conceptions of human nature. [RHT/GA]

Woolley, Persia. *Child of the Northern Spring*. New York: Poseidon, 1987.

———. *Queen of the Summer Stars*. New York: Poseidon, 1990.

WORDSWORTH, WILLIAM (1770–1850). In "The Egyptian Maid" (begun in 1828 and published in 1835), Merlin, "provoked to envious spleen" by a lovely ship that seems to float in the air, destroys the ship; an Egyptian princess is cast ashore. At the instruction of Nina, Lady of the Lake, Merlin takes the innocent and unconscious princess to Arthur's court. The maid's father, earlier freed by Arthur, had promised to become a Christian and betroth his daughter to one of Arthur's knights. One by one, the knights touch her hand; at Galahad's touch, she returns from death and the two are married. Wordsworth changes the traditional characters Merlin and Galahad to create a symbolic account of his own turning from youthful freedom toward moral responsibility. As such, the poem is much less successful than the "Immortality" ode. [JW]

Wordsworth, William. *The Poetical Works of William Wordsworth*, ed. E. de Selincourt and Helen Darbishire. 2nd ed. Oxford: Clarendon, 1954, Vol. 3, pp. 232–43.

Merriman, James D. *The Flower of Kings: A Study of the Arthurian Legend in England Between 1485 and 1835*. Lawrence: University Press of Kansas, 1973.

WORKSHOP MOOSACH, German experimental and alternative theatrical group founded in 1977 in Moosach near Munich, best known for the dramatic piece *Flechtungen: Der Fall Partzifall* ("Weavings: The Partzifall Case"). The "case" of Parzival (in the Wolfram version) is here joined to a modern story of a schizophrenic. Common to both, the authors and players (Ulrike Doepfer, Rudi Roth, Axel Tangerding) believe, is the abnormality of the protagonists. The play was produced with great success between

1978 and 1981 in Germany, Austria, Yugoslavia, Canada, and the United States (at the La Mama Theater in New York). [UM/WCM]

Müller, Ulrich. "Parzival 1980." In *Mittelalter-Rezeption II*, ed. Jürgen Kühnel, Hans-Dieter Mück, Ursula Müller, and Ulrich Müller. Göppingen: Kümmerle, 1982.

WRAKE VAN RAGISEL, DE ("The Avenging of Ragisel"), a Middle Dutch adaptation of the Old French *La Vengeance Raguidel*, dating from the first half of the thirteenth century. The Middle Dutch poet increases the tension of certain situations in a courtly fashion (Walewein is depicted as a courtly lover, more so than Gauvain in the *Vengeance*). About 900 lines have survived; the fragments, from two manuscripts, are preserved in Düsseldorf, Landes- und Stadtsbibliothek F. 26a and F.26b, and Cologne, Historisches Archiv W. f°. 317. One of the two manuscripts dates from 1260–80.

The *Lancelot-Compilatie* includes a greatly abridged version of the Middle Dutch adaptation that numbers 3,414 lines. The compiler of the *Lancelot-Compilatie* inserted two chapters in his abbreviation and, moreover, followed it with two more chapters. One of the two inserted chapters completes two fabliaulike stories with an antifeminist moral. The other three chapters are intended to adjust the *Wrake* adaptation on the one hand to the compositional properties of the *Lancelot-Compilatie* (such as putting the figure of Lancelot back into prominence) and on the other hand to the narrative technique of the historical Arthurian romances (narrative threads have to be brought to a logical and compositionally justified end). [BB]

Gerritsen, W.P., ed. *Die Wrake van Ragisel*. 2 vols. Assen: van Gorcum, 1963.

92. 1498 woodcut, Wynkyn de Worde, scenes from Malory's *Morte Darthur*: "How Syr Tristram jousted and smote downe Kynge Arthur and Syr Uwayne and woldne not telle theym his name." (Courtesy of The Newberry Library, Chicago.)

WRIGHT, S(IDNEY) FOWLER (1874–1967), composed three poems based on Malory. *The Ballad of Elaine* (1926), in six-line stanzas, presents a whitewashed Lancelot whose refusal to marry Elaine of Astolat depends not on his love for Guenevere but on his vow of chastity. *The Riding of Lancelot* (1929) is a blank-verse narrative in twenty-four parts from Malory's *Morte Darthur*, Book VI. *Scenes from the Morte d'Arthur* (1920), published under the pseudonym Alan Seymour, shows Tennysonian influence in its form, treatment of nature, and comprehensiveness. Of nineteen parts, the most extensive are "Uther and Igraine" and "Gareth and Lionore." [MAW]

Seymour, Alan. *Scenes from the Morte d'Arthur*. London: Macdonald, 1920.

Wright, S. Fowler. *The Ballad of Elaine*. London: Merton, 1926.

———. *The Riding of Lancelot*. London: Merton, 1929.

WYNKYN DE WORDE. The first illustrated edition of Malory's *Morte Darthur* was published in London in 1498 by Wynkyn de Worde. Jan van Wynkyn, from Worth in Alsace, had been William Caxton's foreman in Bruges. He moved to England with Caxton in 1476 and took over the press when Caxton died in 1491. Wynkyn moved the press from Westminster to Fleet Street and finally to St. Paul's churchyard, the center of London's new printing trade. There, he worked until his death in 1534–35.

In spite of the intention of the printers to produce books in relatively large numbers for profitable commercial distribution, only one copy of Wynkyn de Worde's illustrated Malory survives (Manchester, John Rylands University Library). Caxton had published the original edition of the *Morte* in 1485. Wynkyn now added illustrations at the heading of each chapter for his 1498 edition. Woodblocks, about four by five inches, are crudely cut, with heavy angular lines and shading created by blocks of parallel strokes. Elongated figures move like puppets, but in the best illustrations, such as Lancelot's madness, the birth of Tristram, and the enchantment of Merlin, a childlike directness carries considerable power. In early woodblocks, the drawing and the cutting of the block were not necessarily done by the same person, and here the inventiveness is not matched by skill in cutting. Deep spatial settings suggest the artist's debt to Flemish painting; landscapes with distant towns, castles, and even windmills spread out under skies filled with flying birds. Wynkyn reissued the Malory in 1529 and also reused some of the blocks in later books, such as the *Recuyles of ye Hystories of Troye* (1502). [MS]

Hind, Arthur M. *An Introduction to a History of Woodcut*. London: Constable, 1935, Vol. 2, pp. 728–29; fig. 463.

Loomis, Roger Sherman, and Laura Hibbard Loomis. *Arthurian Legends in Medieval Art*. London: Oxford University Press, 1938, pp. 143–44; figs. 415–20.

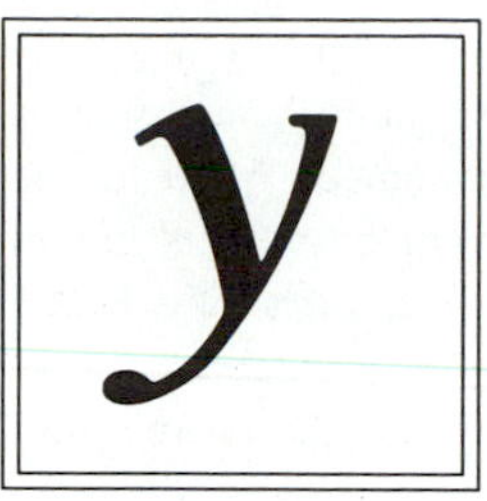

YARBRO, CHELSEA QUINN, American author who applies her talent for supernatural horror fiction to Arthurian legend in "Night Mare" (1988), an ironic tale about the childhood of Mordred. Resentful at the slights he receives because of his illegitimacy, he asks the magical wish-horse for three wishes that will feed his pride: "to be Artus' son, to be his heir and to be remembered as long as he is remembered." [RHT]

Yarbro, Chelsea Quinn. "Night Mare." In *Invitation to Camelot: An Arthurian Anthology of Short Stories*, ed. Parke Godwin. New York: Ace, 1988, pp. 166–99.

YDER, a French romance of 6,769 lines, extant in one manuscript; it was composed probably in the second quarter of the thirteenth century. The illegitimate Yder attempts to win the love of Queen Guenloie by deeds of arms. He rescues an ungrateful Arthur, then joins Arthur's enemy, Talac de Rougemont, and is treacherously wounded by Kay. Cured by Guenloie and reconciled to Arthur, he joins the Round Table and rescues Guenièvre from a bear. When Guenièvre claims that she would have preferred Yder to Arthur if she had had the choice, Arthur tries in vain to kill the hero. Yder fulfills all of Guenloie's conditions, marries her, and then legitimizes his own birth with the wedding of his mother and his father, Nuc. The romance is noteworthy for its portrayal of an odious Arthur and Kay and for its links with an old tradition according to which Yder was the lover of Guenièvre, for whose sake he kills a bear.

Yder can be viewed as an anti-Arthur romance, in which good and evil have been polarized, everything that has to do with Arthur and the court being evil, and everything non-Arthurian (especially the hero), good. There is potential for criticism of Arthur and Kay in earlier romance, but it is rarely as severe or explicit as in *Yder.* [KB]

Adams, Alison, ed. *Yder.* Cambridge: Brewer, 1983.

Adams, Alison. "The *Roman d'Yder*: Individual and Society." In *The Legacy of Chrétien de Troyes*, ed. Norris J. Lacy, Douglas Kelly, and Keith Busby. 2 vols. Amsterdam: Rodopi, 1988, Vol. 2, pp. 71–77.

Schmolke-Hasselmann, Beate. *Der arthurische Versroman von Chrestien bis Froissart*. Tübingen: Niemeyer, 1980, pp. 76–85.

YEO, MARGARET (1887–1941), dedicated *The Everlasting Quest* (1915) to Arthurian scholar and translator Sebastian Evans. In archaic prose, Yeo describes Messire Galain's yearning for "strange and far-off things," his adventures, and his eventual discovery that "the love of Our Lord is above all others, . . . and that the Quest of the Grail is the Eternal Quest." The work has a High Anglican tone. [EB]

Yeo, Margaret. *The Everlasting Quest*. London: Society of SS. Peter and Paul, 1915. (Two chapters were earlier published in *The Treasury* and *The Academy*.)

YOLEN, JANE, American writer of fantasies, has written several works using Arthurian motifs. A children's book, *The Acorn Quest* (1981), tells of an owl named Earthor, King of Woodland, who, upon the advice of his wizard Squirrelin, sends four of his knights (animals with names such as Sir Runsalot and Sir Belliful) on a quest to find the Golden Acorn, which will save the creatures of Woodland from starvation. Intended for adults, *Merlin's Booke* (1986), the first volume in a projected trilogy, is a collection of thirteen poems and stories related to Merlin (about half of them previously published). Loosely based upon the medieval legends, they describe a number of separate events from the sorcerer's birth to his entrapment and, ultimately, to the discovery of his grave in the twenty-first century. A poem in the voice of Guinevere, "Amesbury Song" (1987), reflects upon the stages of her life and the roles that she played as maiden, queen, and nun. Closely related to the material in *Merlin's Booke* is the story "Meditation in a Whitethorn Tree" (1988), in which Merlin, entrapped, reflects upon his betrayal by Igraine, Morgaine, and Guinevere; Niniane, he says, did not betray him but provided him with an opportunity to discover the truth about the other three. [SRR]

Yolen, Jane. *The Acorn Quest*. New York: Crowell, 1981.

———. *Merlin's Booke*. New York: Ace, 1986.

———. "Amesbury Song." *Mythlore*, 50 (Summer 1987), 63.

———. "Meditation in a Whitethorn Tree." In *Invitation to Camelot: An Arthurian Anthology of Short Stories*, ed. Parke Godwin. New York: Ace, 1988, pp. 223–42.

YOUNG, ROBERT F., wrote "A Knyght Ther Was" (first published in *Analog Science Fiction* in 1963), a humorous science-fiction story in which a time-thief's plot to steal the Holy Grail from the castle of Carboneck is thwarted. Marooned in the past, he eventually realizes that he is none other than the Thomas Malory destined to write *Le Morte Darthur*. [RHT]

Young, Robert F. "A Knyght Ther Was." In *Cosmic Knights*, ed. Isaac Asimov, Martin H. Greenberg, and Charles G. Waugh. New York: New American Library, 1985, pp. 201–49.

YOUNG, STARK (1881–1963), professor of English and theater critic for the *New Republic*, describes, in his blank-verse play *Guenevere* (1906), how the Queen and Launcelot are trapped by the plots of an ambitious Mordred. It concludes with her death in a convent and her burial, by Launcelot, beside her husband at Glastonbury. [HT]

Young, Stark. *Guenevere: A Play in Five Acts*. New York: Grafton, 1906.

YSAÏE LE TRISTE, a long, anonymous prose romance, surviving in two fifteenth-century manuscripts (now in Darmstadt and Gotha) and four sixteenth-century printed editions. The work dates from the late fourteenth or early fifteenth century, the very end of the medieval French Arthurian tradition. A tissue of allusions to Arthurian themes, characters, and motifs, it is conceived as a dynastic continuation of the Prose *Tristan* and a thematic continuation of the Vulgate Cycle.

The surprising starting point of the romance is the premise that Tristan and Yseut have a son, born just before their deaths and a few years prior to the destruction of the Arthurian kingdom at the battle of Salisbury. The romance relates the stories of Ysaïe and his own son, Marc, whose mission is the elimination of evil customs that have flourished in the anarchic Britain left after Arthur's death. The two life stories are interlaced, in a variety of heroic and sometimes comic episodes; the climax, in a Britain to which peace has been restored by their efforts, is the double marriage of the two heroes to their loves, Marthe and Orimonde.

Enhancing the flavor and originality of the romance is the invention of the dwarf Tronc, who is Ysaïe's and later Marc's companion and guardian angel—paradoxically, since he is demonically ugly. The son of Julius Caesar and Morgan la Fée, Tronc is destined to remain hideous until his two *protégés* fulfill their mission. At their marriages, and now rebaptized Auberon, he is transformed into a magically beautiful being and disappears into fairyland. Tronc's narrative function is to act as a focus for comedy. His extreme ugliness and the effect it produces on bystanders are in themselves a source of humor; on a more sophisticated level, Tronc fills the folklore role of the cunning rogue always getting into scrapes and using his ingenuity to escape from them.

The romance, however, is not simply a chaotic succession of seriocomic episodes orchestrated by Tronc. The author resembles many of the writers of romance in the late Middle Ages in that his prime concern is the political cycle: the rise and fall of kingdoms, the responsibility of the king and leader. Chivalric incident is subordinated to a narrative and thematic structure that reflects a horror of social and political disorder and a longing for harmony. Most single combats have as their *raison d'être* the ending of evil customs; many tournaments oppose Ysaïe and the forces of wickedness; and the heroes' endless interlaced journeys are governed by reforming zeal. Beneath the comedy, then, and beneath the derivative trappings of the romance mode, is a seriousness that makes this one of the most interesting of the late Arthurian romances. [JHMT]

Giacchetti, André, ed. *Ysaÿe le Triste: roman authurien du moyen âge tardif.* Rouen, 1989.

Taylor, Jane H.M. "The Fourteenth Century." In *The Legacy of Chrétien de Troyes*, ed. Norris J. Lacy, Douglas Kelly, and Keith Busby. 2 vols. Amsterdam: Rodopi, 1987–88, Vol. 1, pp. 267–332.

Zeidler, Julius. "Der Prosaroman *Ysaye le triste*." *Zeitschrift für romanische Philologie*, 25 (1901), 175–214, 472–89, 641–68.

YUNGE-BATEMAN, ELIZABETH, sets her juvenile novel *The Flowering Thorn* (1961) in modern-day Wales, where five young people set out to find the Grail. They achieve spiritual contentment from their charitable deeds along the way. [RHT]

Yunge-Bateman, Elizabeth. *The Flowering Thorn*. N.p.: Published by the author, 1961.

YVAIN (Ivain, Owein, Ywain), the son of Urien. He appears in the Book of Taliesin and then in *The Dream of Rhonabwy*, in which he plays a game with Arthur. The major developments of his character occur in Chrétien de Troyes's *Yvain* (*Le Chevalier au lion*) and in the Welsh *Owein*; in those works, he kills a woman's husband, marries her, loses and eventually regains her love. Yvain also appears in a number of later romances, and his prominence in the *Mort Artu* is indicated by the fact that he is one of the last knights to die (at Mordred's hand) before the death of the King himself. (*See also* OWEIN; CHRÉTIEN DE TROYES.) [NJL]

YWAIN AND GAWAIN, a clear adaptation from Chrétien de Troyes's *Yvain* (*Le Chevalier au lion*). *Ywain and Gawain* is the only one of Chrétien's romances to survive in an English version (the Middle English *Sir Perceval de Galles* does not go back to the *Perceval*). Preserved in a single manuscript of the early fifteenth century (London, B.L. Cotton Galba E. ix.), it was probably composed some hundred years earlier, in the north. The uniqueness of the text and of the manuscript appears to confirm the impression, created by the lack of references to Chrétien in Middle English poetry and the slight influence of his works, that Chrétien was far less popular with English-speaking than with French-speaking audiences. The English adapter reduced the number of lines by approximately a third (6,808 against 4,032). Most of Chrétien's long and penetrating musings on the workings of love have been clipped or completely discarded by the English poet, who instead concentrates on the more realistic elements of the story, such as Ywain's chivalric exploits and his heroic qualities. Women, the goddesses to men in truly courtly poetry, have been reduced to a position of inferiority, as if the adapter were writing for a male audience more interested in life's realities than in love's ideals. Also, high chivalric notions expressed by such words as *enor* 'honor' or *honte* 'shame' do not play a part in the English *Ywain*; the words for honor and shame do not even occur in it. However, the changes show a coherent pattern and were apparently deliberately introduced by an adapter whose aims or audience must have been different from Chrétien's. His skillful control of the story, the swift succession of events, the powerful diction, the often lively colloquial language, as well as the competent handling of the octosyllabic line, explain why the poem has been called one of the most successful romances in Middle English. [ESK]

Friedman, Albert B., and Norman T. Harrington, eds. *Ywain and Gawain*. London: Oxford University Press, 1964.

Hamilton, Gayle. "The Breaking of the Troth in *Ywain and Gawain*." *Mediaevalia*, 2 (1976), 111–35.

ZELAZNY, ROGER, American writer, makes extensive use of many legends in his science fiction and fantasy. Zelazny's Amber series generally follows the pattern of the Grail quest and wasteland themes. The parallels are strongest in *The Guns of Avalon* (1972), in which Lancelot makes a brief appearance. In "The Last Defender of Camelot" (1980), Lancelot fights against intolerance when he forms an untraditional alliance with Morgan le Fay to prevent a reawakened Merlin from imposing his will upon a new age. [RHT]

Zelazny, Roger. *The Guns of Avalon*. Garden City, N.Y.: Doubleday, 1972.

———. "The Last Defender of Camelot." In *The Last Defender of Camelot*. New York: Pocket, 1980, pp. 271–94.

Yoke, Carl. *Roger Zelazny*. West Linn, Ore.: Starmont, 1979.

***ZIFAR* (or *CIFAR*), *LIBRO DEL CABALLERO*,** the first indigenous Spanish romance of chivalry, composed ca. 1300, perhaps by Ferrán Martínez, Archdeacon of Madrid in the church of Toledo. The *Zifar*'s debt to Arthurian romance is nebulous, although there are specific allusions (e.g., Arthur's fight with the Cath Palug as found in the Vulgate *Merlin* and the figure of Yván, son of King Orián, recalling Chrétien de Troyes's hero Yvain) as well as distinct parallels (the accusation of adultery and the sentencing to the stake of Grema, the hero Zifar's wife, as happens to Guenevere in the Vulgate Cycle; and the supernatural adventures of the Caballero Atrevido, or Bold Knight, involving a Lady of the Lake and those of Zifar's son Roboan, who travels to the Islas Dotadas, recalling Geoffrey of Monmouth's Insulae Fortunatae). Critics have also pointed to the possible influence of various French lais. In general, however, the work is essentially a Byzantine romance with a strong didactic and religious (but not mystical) tone, revealing oriental and epic influences, as well as much in common with the Placidas/St. Eustace legend. [HLS]

González Muela, Joaquín, ed. *Libro del caballero Zifar*. Madrid: Castalia, 1982.

González, Cristina, ed. *Libro del caballero Zifar*. Madrid: Cátedra, 1983.

Olsen, Marilyn A., ed. *Libro del cauallero Çifar*. Madison: Hispanic Seminary of Medieval Studies, 1984.

Walker, Roger M. *Tradition and Technique in "El Libro del cavallero Zifar."* London: Tamesis, 1974.

Index

This index includes all Arthurian authors, artists, and important themes and motifs discussed in this volume; it also lists most historical figures and major literary characters. All Arthurian titles are given, with cross-references to the author, if known, but we have generally omitted non-Arthurian titles mentioned in passing. We have indexed very selectively, especially in regard to characters and places, some of which are mentioned many dozens of times in the text. For those, we have listed only a few of the most substantial discussions. In addition, for the most general essays, such as the survey of modern English literature, we index only the principal essay and related surveys (for example, "Juvenile Fiction"), but we have made no effort to list all specific entries that belong to that category. The listing of entries at the beginning of the volume will enable users to locate such related entries.

In cases where authors or subjects receive substantive treatment in several places, the page numbers printed in bold type identify the primary entry devoted to that subject.

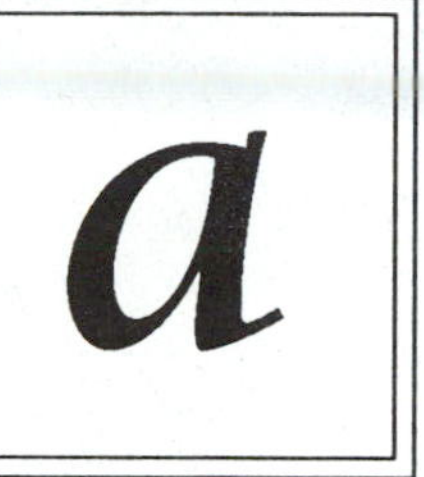

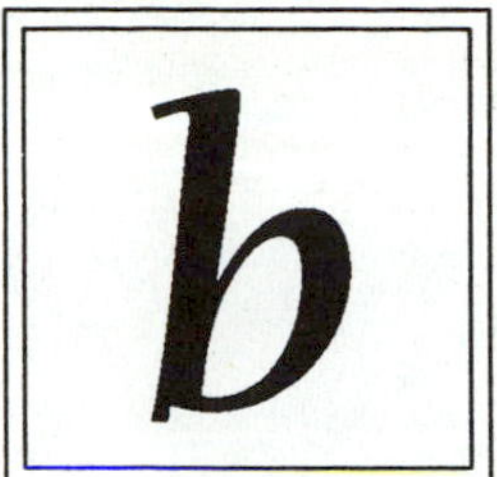
b

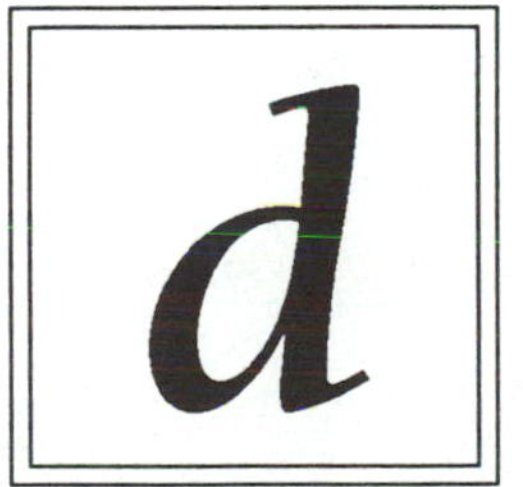

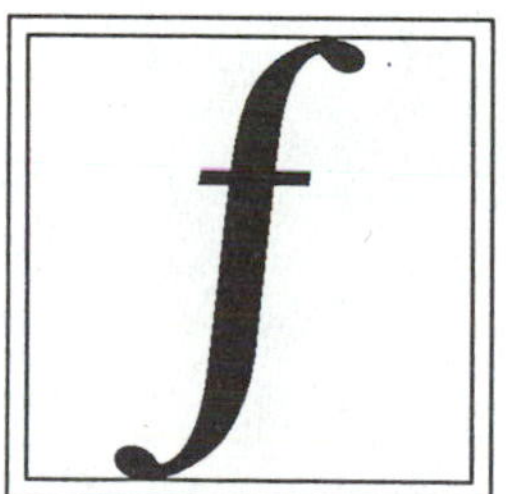

h

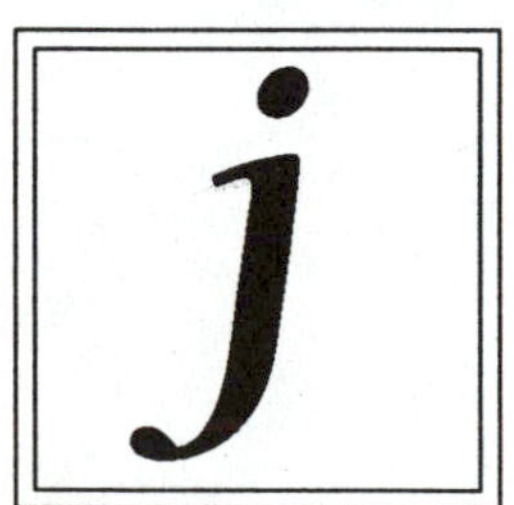

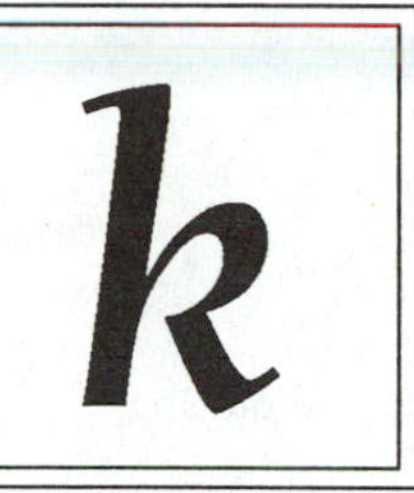

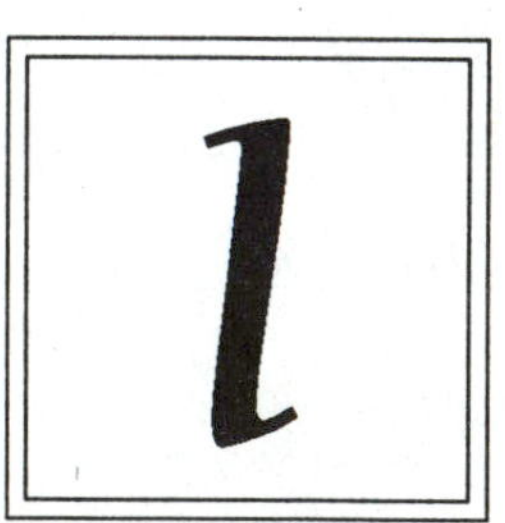

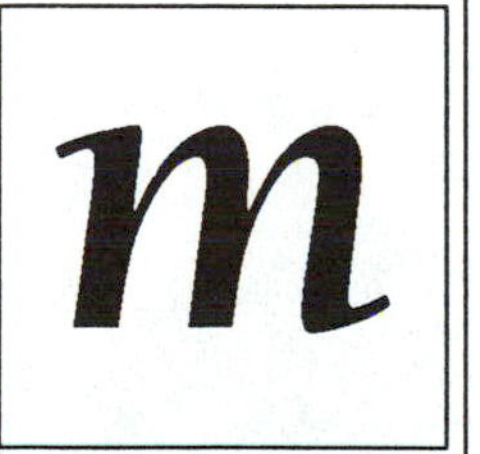

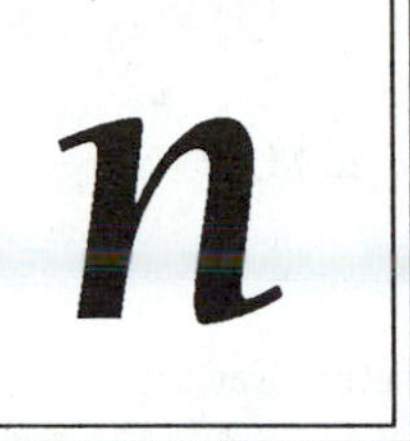

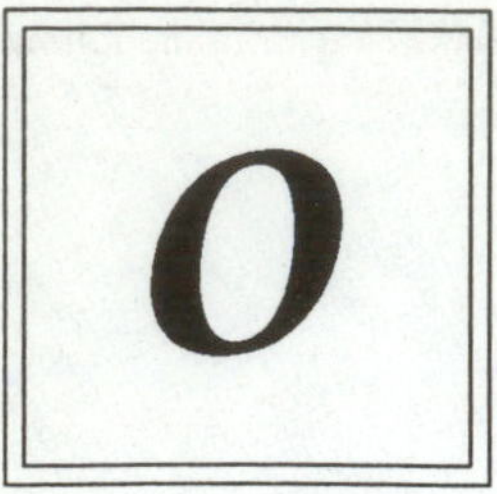

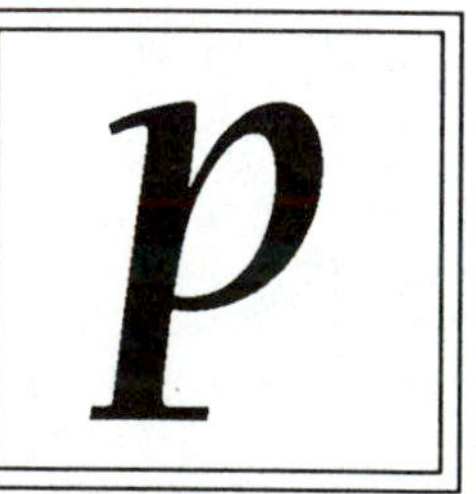

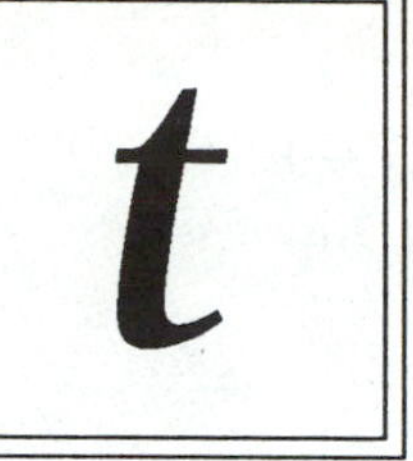

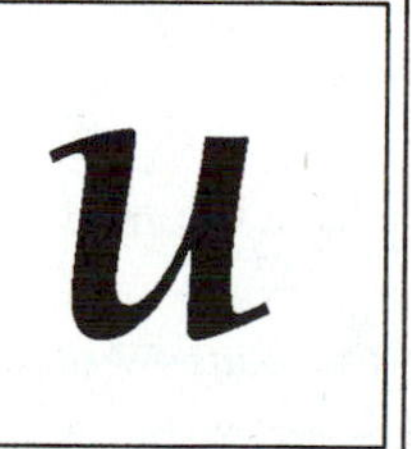

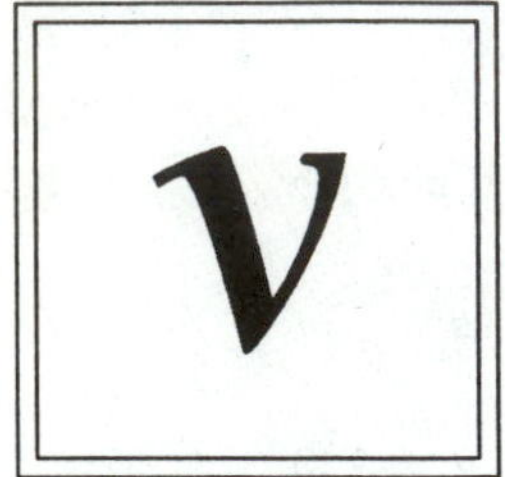

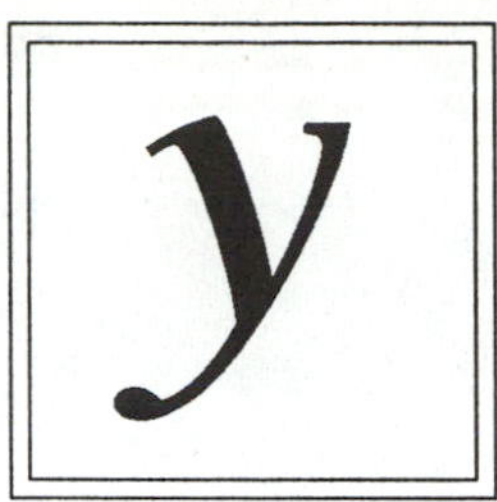

Supplement 1990-1995

Following the publication of *The New Arthurian Encyclopedia* in 1991, the editors, struck by the amount of new Arthuriana—novels, poems, films, computer games, and the like—appearing annually or even monthly, determined to prepare periodic supplements. The first of those appeared in *The Arthurian Yearbook III* (1993), pp. 229-71. The present supplement includes the roughly seventy-five entries from that first one and adds over one hundred others. Although most of the entries treat material that is newly published or created, we also include some texts that we originally omitted, in a few cases by oversight, more often because the Arthurian content was not prominent. Those texts include a medieval fragment and several works by noncontemporary authors (e.g., Galdós, Hawthorne, Fitzgerald, Claudel). This supplement also provides a longer essay on modern French versions of the Tristan legend, a subject that was treated only briefly in the *Encyclopedia*. In this supplement, we have sought to be inclusive rather than selective, in an effort to provide a full record of contributions, especially very recent ones, to the constantly expanding corpus of Arthurian literature, film, and other media.

Because most of the new material is British or American, primary editorial responsibility for the supplements is shared by the original editor, Norris J. Lacy, and the associate editor whose province was modern English-language material, Raymond H. Thompson. The other three associate editors of *The New Arthurian Encyclopedia*—Marianne E. Kalinke, Geoffrey Ashe, and Sandra Ness Ihle—have participated in the planning of these supplements, and Kalinke is also a contributor.

The entries published here follow the form of those included in the body of the *Encyclopedia*. We treat authors, filmmakers, and composers in entries given under their names, and in cases of multiple authorship we use cross-references to direct readers to the main entry. Within entries, we also provide cross-references where needed to direct users to *The New Arthurian Encyclopedia* (identified as *NAE*). For further information, readers are referred to the preface, above (p. vii).

The seventeen contributors to this supplement are identified by initials enclosed in brackets following each entry. Those contributors and their institutional affiliations are as follows:

GMA Grace Morgan Armstrong
Bryn Mawr College

FB Frank Brandsma
University of Utrecht

JTG Joan Tasker Grimbert
Catholic University of America

KJH Kevin J. Harty
La Salle University

MEK Marianne E. Kalinke
University of Illinois, Urbana

NJL Norris J. Lacy
Washington University, St. Louis

ACL Alan C. Lupack
Rossell Hope Robbins Library, University of Rochester

BTL Barbara Tepa Lupack
Rochester, New York

DOM Daniel Octavio Mosquera
Washington University, St. Louis

UM Ulrich Müller
Universität Salzburg

DN Daniel Nastali
Kansas City, Missouri

ELO Eduardo Lage Otero
Washington University, St. Louis

SSch Siegrid Schmidt
Universität Salzburg

RS Roger Simpson
University of East Anglia

HT Hilary Thompson
Acadia University

RHT Raymond H. Thompson
Acadia University

WW Werner Wunderlich
Hochschule St. Gallen

AHERN, JERRY and SHARON, together wrote the short story "Siege Perilous" (1992). Two American priests and their friends foil the attempt of neo-Nazis to seize a Grail embellished with runic inscriptions that hold the key to great power. [RHT]

Ahern, Jerry, and Sharon Ahern. "Siege Perilous." In *Grails: Quests, Visitations, and Other Occurrences*, ed. Richard Gilliam, Martin H. Greenberg, and Edward E. Kramer. Atlanta: Unnameable, 1992. Republished as *Grails: Visitations of the Night*. New York: Roc/Penguin, 1994, pp. 191–212.

ANDERSON, DENNIS LEE, author of *Arthur, King*, a 1995 novel about Arthur's return in the hour of Britain's greatest need, the London Blitz. Mordred, his mortal enemy, takes control of a Nazi officer and originates the plan to bomb London civilians and, later, Coventry. Thwarting his son's plan to assassinate Churchill and the king, Arthur, with the aid of Merlin and Excalibur, eventually defeats Mordred and then, accompanied by the woman he has come to love (Jenny), returns to his own age. [NJL]

Anderson, Dennis Lee. *Arthur, King*. New York: HarperPrism, 1995.

APSLEY, BRENDA, CHARLES PEMBERTON, and LESLEY SCOTT combined their talents to create *Dr. Who: Journey Through Time* (1985), a collection of stories and cartoon strips dealing with adventures of the characters in the British television series (*see NAE*, p. 446). In "The Creation of Camelot," the Doctor unmasks his mortal foe, The Master, who has taken on the title of the Merlin, but not before the latter has "initiated the birth of Mordred," here the son of Morgan le Fay. The Doctor does, however, advise Arthur to adopt the Round Table as a means of avoiding arguments over precedence at court. [RHT]

Apsley, Brenda, Charles Pemberton, and Lesley Scott. "The Creation of Camelot." In *Doctor Who: Journey Through Time*. New York: Crescent, 1985, pp. 124–30.

AQUINO, JOHN, author of "The Sad Wizard" (1985), a fantasy short story about a young man at the court of Queen Elizabeth I whose life is transformed by an encounter with Merlin. Whether for good or ill is uncertain. [RHT]

Aquino, John. "The Sad Wizard." *Fantasy Book* (December 1985), 34–39.

ARLANC, SYLVAIN: *see* TRISTAN AND ISOLDE IN MODERN FRENCH VERSIONS.

ARMSTRONG, ANTHONY (pseudonym of George Anthony Armstrong Willis, 1897–1976), was a prolific writer of crime and historical novels, and of humorous short stories, among which is "Sir Borloys and the Dark Knight" (1933). This recounts the rescue of a damsel in distress by a knight of the Round Table whose taste for food proves stronger than his admiration of female beauty. [RHT]

Armstrong, Anthony. "Sir Borloys and the Dark Knight." *The Strand Magazine* (December 1933), 634–43; rpt. as "Sir Borlays and the Dark Knight." In *The Camelot Chronicles*, ed. Mike Ashley. London: Robinson, 1992, pp. 273–86.

ATTANASIO, A.A., author of *Kingdom of the Grail* (1992), a historical novel set in twelfth-century Wales. A young woman arrives from the Holy Land claiming to be the aged mother of a tyrannical Norman lord miraculously rejuvenated by the Holy Grail. Grail imagery and themes pervade the story, which includes a character's retelling of a legend in which Arthur became the Fisher King. [DN]

Attanasio, A.A. *Kingdom of the Grail*. New York: HarperCollins, 1992.

BAUDINO, GAEL, author of the Dragonsword series of novels set in the alternate world of Gryylth. Created in the mind of a professor who specialized in the archaeology of fifth-century Britain, this world contains a number of Arthurian parallels, including a society fighting for survival against barbarian invaders, the sorcerer Mernyl (Merlin), Pellam the Maimed King, and the Holy Grail. Into this society, with its male-dominated warrior values, comes Suzanne, a feminist and pacifist who finds herself transformed into a skilled female warrior. The series explores the conflict between her beliefs and her role as guardian of this world. [RHT]

Baudino, Gael. *Dragonsword*. New York: Roc, 1991.
———. *Duel of Dragons*. New York: Roc, 1991.
———. *Dragon Death*. New York: Roc, 1992.

BENNETT, LAURA GILMOUR (pseudonym of Laura Bennett and Jean Gilmour Harvey), American authors who have collaborated on several works of popular fiction. Their *A Wheel of Stars* (1989) is a romantic fantasy novel that features the Holy Grail, black magic, and modern reincarnations of thirteenth-century Cathar lovers. Possession of the Grail ties the present-day story line to the historical novel neatly woven through it. [DN]

Bennett, Laura Gilmour. *A Wheel of Stars*. London: Viking, 1989;

Harmondsworth: Penguin, 1990; American edition retitled *By All That Is Sacred*. New York: Avon, 1991.

BERGH, WALTER, and WALTER COUVOISIER, in 1916, published an opera entitled *Lanzelot und Elaine*; it was first performed at the Hoftheater Munich in November 1917. The opera, with libretto by Bergh and music by Couvoisier, deals freely with the lovestory of Lanzelot and Elaine in which both die. When Lanzelot's love for Ginevra becomes public, he is exiled to Ireland. Before leaving, he assumes a fictitious name and participates in a tournament at the court of the Duke of Astolat, whose daughter falls in love with the unknown KNIGHT. He suffers severe injury even though he emerges as victor in the fight, and the daughter nurses him back to health. Lanzelot is already betrothed to Ginevra, however, and Elaine dies of a broken heart ("Liebestod"). Lanzelot collapses when he sees her body. [SSch]

Bergh, Walter, and Walter Couvoisier. *Lanzelot und Elaine: Musikdrama in vier Aufzügen*. Munich: Drei Masken-Verlag, 1916.
Schmidt, Siegrid. *Mittelhochdeutsche Epenstoffe in der deutschsprachigen Literatur nach 1945: Beobachtungen zur Aufarbeitung des Artus- und Parzival-Stoffes in erzählender Literature für Jugendliche und Erwachsene mit einer Bibliographie der Stoffkreise Artus, Parzival, Tristan, Gudrun und Nibelungen 1945–1981*. [= GAG Nr. 495 I/II] Göppingen: Kümmerle, 1989.

BETANCOURT, JOHN GREGORY, in the story "Dogs Questing" (1992), describes, in terms that recall the Quest for the Holy Grail, canine attempts to find "Man" again and restore their ancient bond. [RHT]

Betancourt, John Gregory. "Dogs Questing." In *Grails: Quests, Visitations, and Other Occurrences*, ed. Richard Gilliam, Martin H. Greenberg, and Edward E. Kramer. Atlanta: Unnameable, 1992. Republished as *Grails: Visitations of the Night*. New York: Roc/Penguin, 1994, pp. 20–22.

BIRTWISTLE, SIR HARRISON, British composer, whose operatic version of *Sir Gawain and the Green Knight* premiered at Covent Garden in May 1991 and garnered almost universally favorable reviews, if not raves. In 1963, Birtwistle had set a modernized version of a portion of *Sir Gawain* to music for chorus; the result was entitled "Narration: A Description of the Passing of a Year."

With a libretto in modern English by David Harsent, Birtwistle's Gawain reinterprets the medieval poem along Jungian lines, according to which Morgan le Fay is central throughout the retelling of the tale. In the poem, her role as instigator is unknown until nearly the end of the narrative; in the opera, she has the first and last words and everywhere haunts Arthur's court. In the three-hour opera's most spectacular scene, Gawain appears naked for a ritual bath in blood after cutting off the head of the Green Knight.

The opera casts Gawain as a knight who does not recognize himself as the hero and redeemer he is. Nor, as Wilfrid Mellers notes, does the hero "achieve self-fulfillment to become the arbiter of his destiny, though he does attain a point at which he learns that self-realization is a consummation devoutly to be wished." [KJH/NJL]

Driver, Paul. "A Knight to Remember." [London] *Sunday Times*, June 2, 1991, sec. 5.6.
Mellers, Wilfrid. "Music for Everyman," *Times Literary Supplement*, June 14, 1991, p. 18.
Porter, Andrew. "Knight's Progress." *The New Yorker*, 67 (July 1, 1991), 77–80.
Smith, Patrick J. "A Towering Masterpiece." *Opera News*, 56 (October 1991), 4.

BLACKWOOD, GARY, author of "Ethan Unbound" (1992), a short story for young adults in which Morgan le Fay's plans to turn a boy into a library book are foiled by Merlin. [RHT]

Blackwood, Gary. "Ethan Unbound." In *Short Circuits*, ed. Donald R. Gallo. New York: Delacorte, 1992; rpt. New York: Dell, 1993, pp. 60–74.

BLAYLOCK, JAMES P., author of *The Paper Grail*, a 1991 fantasy/mystery novel set in northern California. Howard Barton, a museum curator seeking to acquire a nineteenth-century Japanese sketch, eventually learns that the sketch can be folded into numerous forms and that it had apparently once been shaped into a cup in which blood was gathered. This "paper Grail" is in the possession of Michael Graham, a Fisher King figure whose age and infirmity limit his physical activity to fishing. After a series of adventures involving not only the sketch, but also a machine that produces the spirit of John Ruskin, as well as a divining rod reputedly made from the armbones of Joseph of Arimathea, Howard obtains the Grail and succeeds Graham as its keeper. [NJL]

Blaylock, James P. *The Paper Grail*. New York: Ace, 1991.

BLOCH, ROBERT (1917–1994), author of many works of science fiction and fantasy. In the humorous short story "A Good Knight's Work" (1941), Merlin sends one of King Arthur's knights forward in time to retrieve a special table on which to place the Holy Grail. [RHT]

Bloch, Robert. "A Good Knight's Work." *Unknown* (1941); rpt. in *Unknown*, ed. Stanley Schmidt. New York: Baen, 1988, pp. 187–215.

BOSSUAT, ROBERT: *see* TRISTAN AND ISOLDE IN MODERN FRENCH VERSIONS.

BRADLEY, MARION ZIMMER, the author of *The Mists of Avalon* (*see NAE*, p. 50), also wrote two short stories in which Arthurian motifs occur: "Chalice of Tears, or I Didn't Want That Damned Grail Anyway" (1992) describes the transfer of the Grail to a new Guardian and the lesson in humility that it teaches in the process; "Here There Be Dragons?" (1995) sends a magician to an otherworld where she finds a helpful sword in a stone. [RHT]

Bradley, Marion Zimmer. "Chalice of Tears, or I Didn't Want That Damned Grail Anyway." In *Grails: Quests, Visitations, and Other Occurrences*, ed. Richard Gilliam, Martin H. Greenberg, and Edward E. Kramer. Atlanta: Unnameable, 1992. Republished as *Grails: Quests of the Dawn*. New York: Roc/Penguin, 1994, pp. 27–35.

———. "Here There Be Dragons?" In *Excalibur*, ed. Richard Gilliam, Martin H. Greenberg, and Edward E. Kramer. New York: Warner, 1995, pp. 183–92.

BRAKMAN, WILLEM, a leading Dutch novelist, published a collection of short stories entitled *Een familiedrama* ("A Domestic Drama") in 1984. "Artorius," the bizarre and intriguing final story, describes Arthur's conception, which mirrors that of the eccentric Merlin: Egyrne (Ygraine), dressed as a nun, asks the man she believes to be her husband, really Uther in disguise, to play the part of the devil when he comes to her bed. The domestic drama takes place between Gorlois and his wife, a relationship often neglected in traditional accounts of the conception. [FB]

Brakman, Willem. "Artorius." In *Een familiedrama*. Amsterdam: Querido, 1984, pp. 110–47.

BROOKE, MAXEY, author of "Morte d'Alain" (*see NAE*, p. 56), set another mystery story in Arthur's court. In "Morte d'un Marcheant" (1992), Merlin deduces who is responsible for destroying financial records and assaulting his assistant. [RHT]

Brooke, Maxey. "Morte d'un Marcheant." In *The Camelot Chronicles*, ed. Mike Ashley. London: Robinson, 1992, pp. 243–52.

BROUWER, SIGMUND, author of *Winds of Light*, a series of six short historical novels for younger readers. Set in the fourteenth century, it chronicles the struggle between Merlins, an enlightened movement founded by Merlin, and evil Druids, and it involves the Holy Grail. [RHT]

Brouwer, Sigmund. *Merlin's Destiny*. Wheaton, Ill.: Victor, 1993.

BRUNNER, JOHN, author of *Father of Lies* (*see NAE*, p. 57), also introduced Arthurian tradition into his short story "An Entry That Did Not Appear in Domesday Book" (1988). Officials gathering data for William the Conqueror's Domesday Book stumble upon the Isle of Avalon, though only the sole Englishman in the party of Normans is granted a vision of Arthur sleeping in a chapel. [RHT]

Brunner, John. "An Entry That Did Not Appear in Domesday Book." *Amazing*, 62 (March 1988), 12–25.

BUECHNER, FREDERICK, Presbyterian minister and author, recounts the life of Brendan the Navigator in his novel *Brendan* (1987). During a visit to Wales, the Irish saint befriends Gildas, who is writing his diatribe against the rulers of Britain; and he comforts an aged King Artor, who is befuddled with drink and grief at his betrayal by Gwenhwyfar and Llenlleawg. [RHT]

Buechner, Frederick. *Brendan*. New York: Atheneum, 1987.

BYATT, A.S., English novelist, subtitled her award-winning *Possession* (1990) a romance. Roland, her hero, consciously lives within that form, in "a vulgar and a high Romance simultaneously" (p. 425). Postmodern as he is, he is aware that he is moving within the patterns of the Chase, the Race, and the Quest. Allusions to Arthurian romance include Nimue/Vivien and Merlin, the Fatae Morganae, and Elaine the Lily Maid of Astolat, to whom the heroine Christabel compares herself. In the nineteenth-century documents found by Roland, the tragic lovers Tristan and Iseult are embodied in the lover-poets Christabel LaMotte and Randolph Henry Ash, who love as if possessed by demons and whose star-crossed passion ends with a journey to Brittany. [HT]

Byatt, A.S. *Possession*. London: Chatto and Windus, 1990.

BYERS, RICHARD LEE, author of two Arthurian short stories: in "Castle of Maidens" (1992), a Christian knight and bishop find the Grail in, of all places, a Turkish harem; in "St. Paul's Churchyard, New Year's Day" (1995), Arthur draws the Sword from the Stone but is more interested in punishing personal slights than building a better world. [RHT]

Byers, Richard Lee. "Castle of Maidens." In *Grails: Quests, Visitations, and Other Occurrences*, ed. Richard Gilliam, Martin H. Greenberg, and Edward E. Kramer. Atlanta: Unnameable, 1992. Republished as *Grails: Visitations of the Night*. New York: Roc/Penguin, 1994, pp. 65–80.

———. "St. Paul's Churchyard, New Year's Day." In *Excalibur*, ed. Richard Gilliam, Martin H. Greenberg, and Edward E. Kramer. New York: Warner, 1995, pp. 241–47.

CACEK, P.D., in his short story "Here There Be Dragons" (1994), recounts how Merlin, with the aid of his pet dragon, abducts a reluctant American psychiatrist and takes him back to Arthur's court in sixth-century Britain to seek the Holy Grail. [RHT]

Cacek, P.D. "Here There Be Dragons." In *Grails: Visitations of the Night*, ed. Richard Gilliam, Martin H. Greenberg, and Edward E. Kramer. New York: Roc/Penguin, 1994, pp. 263–74.

CADIGAN, PAT, introduces the Grail and bleeding Lance into a modern hospital in the short story "A Deal with God" (1992). They are used by a doctor to cure the very sick, but once again the foolish "quester" fails to ask the right question. [RHT]

Cadigan, Pat. "A Deal with God." In *Grails: Quests, Visitations, and Other Occurrences*, ed. Richard Gilliam, Martin H. Greenberg, and Edward E. Kramer. Atlanta: Unnameable, 1992. Republished as *Grails: Visitations of the Night*. New York: Roc/Penguin, 1994, pp. 328–50.

CAIDIN, MARTIN, like Rob MacGregor, has been officially licensed by Lucasfilm to write a number of novels for a series based on its film character Indiana Jones (*see NAE*, p. 155). In *Indiana Jones and the White Witch* (1994), the dauntless archaeologist comes to the aid of a white witch who wields not only magical powers but also the sword Caliburn and its protective scabbard, given originally by Merlin to King Arthur. Together they pursue a merciless villain who is trying to find a treasure of gold bullion and ancient coins. (*See also* MACGREGOR, ROB.) [RHT]

Caidin, Martin. *Indiana Jones and the White Witch*. New York: Bantam, 1994.

CAINE, ERIN, pseudonym of an author who introduces Arthurian legend to the realm of the erotic novel in *Knights of Pleasure* (1992; reissued in 1994 as *Avalon Nights* under another pseudonym, Sophie Danson). A sorceress compels Arthur and his noblest knights to confess, in lurid detail, their most shameful sexual adventure. How little they deserve their reputation for chivalry to ladies is demonstrated by the revelations of what really occurred between Lancelot and Elaine, Gawain and Bercilak's wife, Erek and Enid, Galahad and Perceval's sister, Arthur and Margaise, among others. [RHT]

Caine, Erin. *Knights of Pleasure*. London: Nexus/Virgin, 1992. Reissued as *Avalon Nights*, by Sophie Danson. London: Black Lace/Virgin, 1994.

CARMICHAEL, DOUGLAS, author of *Pendragon* (*see NAE*, p. 73), returned to Arthurian legend in the short story "The Grievous Stroke" (1989). This account of Balin's maiming of Pellam is based upon Malory but transposed to a Dark Age setting. The spear and cauldron in Pellam's care are sacred to the mysteries of the Celtic deities Cernunnos and Coventina, respectively. [RHT]

Carmichael, Douglas. "The Grievous Stroke." *The Round Table*, 5 (1989), 25–34.

CARRY ON LAUGHING, popular 1970s British television series noted for its Monty Pythonesque spoofs of other television series and conventions. Two of the spoofs were sendups of the Arthurian legend. "Under the Round Table," first broadcast in October 1975, tells the tale of Sir Pureheart, tall, handsome, strong, but (alas) chaste. "Short Knight—Long Daze," also broadcast in October 1975, tells the tale of a famous doctor who surgically excises a boil from Arthur's posterior and is rewarded for his service to the King by being dubbed "Sir Lancelot." (*See also* TELEVISION.) [KJH]

CASTLE, MAGRANNE, is a member of the Pleiades, a group of poets that includes Pamela Constantine. Her Arthurian poems, such as "Galahad's Departure," "Guinevere Camellard," "Lancelot's Lament," and "Wizardcraft" (1993), reveal a fascination with the working of destiny in the legend. (*See also* CONSTANTINE, PAMELA.) [RHT]

The Pleiades. *The Celtic Collection*. Upminster, Essex: The Sharkti Laureate, 1993.

CASTRO, ADAM-TROY, placed his short story "Jesus Used a Paper Cup" (1994) in "a crass alternate universe" where Jesus is accidentally run down in a parking lot outside a shopping mall and where the "Holy Paper Cup" from which he last drank is found in a garbage dump by Arthur's knights, with unexpectedly sordid results. [RHT]

Castro, Adam-Troy. "Jesus Used a Paper Cup." In *Grails: Visitations of the Night*, ed. Richard Gilliam, Martin H. Greenberg, and Edward E. Kramer. New York: Roc/Penguin, 1994, pp. 183–90.

CAZENAVE, MICHEL: *see* TRISTAN AND ISOLDE IN MODERN FRENCH VERSIONS.

CHAMPION, PIERRE: *see* TRISTAN AND ISOLDE IN MODERN FRENCH VERSIONS.

CHAPMAN, RAYMOND, wrote five "Sonnets on the Arthurian Legend" (1947), which do not form a chronological sequence but provide reflections upon the virtues required by the Grail quester to release the stricken land from the power of death. [RS]

Chapman, Raymond. *Prince of the Clouds and Other Poems*. London: Fortune, 1947.

CHAPMAN, VERA, author of The Three Damosels trilogy (*see NAE*, pp. 80–81), also wrote "Belle Dame, Sans Merci" (1992), described as a self-contained extract of an unpublished novel. It tells of the hopeless love of a young knight for Vivian, here sister to Morgause and Morgan. [RHT]

Chapman, Vera. "Belle Dame, Sans Merci." In *The Camelot Chronicles*, ed. Mike Ashley. London: Robinson, 1992, pp. 10–26.

CHARRETTE, ROBERT N., graphic artist and author of science fiction and fantasy, has begun a trilogy about the clash between magic and high technology. In *A Prince Among Men* (1994), as the otherworld of faery moves toward convergence with the world of humanity in a future dominated by megacorporations and crime-plagued urban sprawl, Nym (Nimue) awakens the sleeping Artos. He sets out to recover Caliburn from the Lady of the Lake, but he does not find it easy to distinguish friend from foe among the factions that seek to aid or kill him for their own ends.

Factional conflict continues unabated in *A King Beneath the Mountain* (1995). Here, Artos's role is reduced to that of a weakened and disoriented figure who is rescued from the custody of the dwarfs. The conclusion, *A Knight Among Knaves*, was scheduled for publication in 1995. [RHT]

Charrette, Robert A. *A Prince Among Men*. New York: Warner, 1994.
———. *A King Beneath the Mountain*. New York: Warner, 1995.

CHEVALIERS DE LA TABLE RONDE: *see* LLORCA, DENIS.

CHIZMAR, RICHARD T., is the author of a short story entitled "The Sinner King" (1994). After stealing a cup used in emulation of the Holy Grail by a religious cult, a Philadelphia journalist flees to a remote wilderness cabin, only to find himself trapped in the role of the Fisher King. The old man living in the cabin takes on the role of the Sinner King. [RHT]

Chizmar, Richard T. "The Sinner King." In *Grails: Visitations of the Night*, ed. Richard Gilliam, Martin H. Greenberg, and Edward E. Kramer. New York: Roc/Penguin, 1994, pp. 213–28.

CHOPRA, DEEPAK, author of several books on healing, turned to fiction for the first time in *The Return of Merlin* (1995). The novel begins with a brief account of the fall of Camelot under the assault of Mordred's black magic, then moves to the modern era, when Mordred and Merlin confront one another once again. Merlin's Stone, the Grail, and Excalibur all reappear, and many of the characters involved in the action turn out to be reincarnations of their Arthurian predecessors, their recognition of which proves vital to the eventual unharnessing of their own power to resist Mordred's evil designs for humanity.

Arthurian tradition is extensively adapted and reinterpreted in order to present Chopra's message of spiritual healing: that people can awaken from the drab wasteland into which they have sunk if they can restore, through love, trust, and forgiveness, the role of Merlin and magic in their lives. [RHT]

Chopra, Deepak. *The Return of Merlin*. New York: Harmony, 1995.

CLARE, THOMAS, English archaeologist and historian, turned to fiction to present his theory that Arthur should be identified with Urien, king of Rheged (Cumbria) in the sixth century (*see NAE*, pp. 441 and 483). In *King Arthur and the Riders of Rheged* (1992), against a carefully reconstructed historical background, the author blends elements from early traditions attached to Arthur, Urien, Myrddin, and St. Kentigern (the son of Owen and grandson of Urien) into an account of this northern leader's heroic but doomed attempt to unite the Britons under his rule and to drive the Germanic invaders from the land. [RHT]

Clare, Thomas. *King Arthur and the Riders of Rheged*. Kendal, Cumbria: Rheged, 1992.

CLAUDEL, PAUL (1868–1955), French author of *Partage de midi* ("Division of Noon," 1905, definitive version 1948–49). The drama depicts the meeting of Mesa and Ysé, the wife of De Ciz, aboard a ship bound for the Orient. They have an affair, and she becomes pregnant. She has the baby and later kills it; eventually, she returns to Mesa, to die with him. Beyond the similarity of the names Ysé and Yseut, the play offers few overt resemblances to the Tristan legend. Claudel scholars, however, have long recognized the influence of Richard Wagner on Claudel, and more particularly of Wagner's *Tristan und Isolde* on *Partage de midi*. Michel Lioure has pointed out that the dramatic structures of Wagner's opera and Claudel's play (especially the second acts) are identical, that the themes of the play, concerning the conflicts inherent in an illicit love, were inherited from Wagner, and that Mesa and Ysé are the "poetic incarnations" of Tristan and Yseult/Isolde. [NJL]

Claudel, Paul. *Partage de midi*. Paris: L'Occident, 1906; definitive version, Paris: Gallimard, 1949.

Lioure, Michel. *L'Esthétique dramatique de Paul Claudel*. Paris: Colin, 1971.

COCHRAN, MOLLY, and WARREN MURPHY, authors of *The Forever King* (1992), a fantasy novel in which Arthur returns as a young Chicago boy and Galahad as a failed FBI agent. With Merlin's aid, they battle one of history's great villains, Saladin, for possession of the ancient cup that has given him immortality. The central section of the book, recounting Saladin's life in Camelot, reworks traditional versions of Arthur's career, the story of Merlin and Nimue, and the Grail quest to tie them to the modern story line. [DN]

Cochran, Molly, and Warren Murphy. *The Forever King*. New York: Tor, 1992.

COLANDER, VALERIE NIEMAN, composed *The Naming of the Lost* (1989), a narrative poem in which Merlin and Nimue meet again in the modern age and are at last reconciled: "We'll sing together a song, and arches raise/ of a new Camelot which shall not fall." [RHT]

Colander, Valerie Nieman. *The Naming of the Lost*. *The Round Table*, 5 (1989), 4–10.

CONNEMARA: *see* GROSPIERRE, LOUIS.

CONSTANTINE, PAMELA, was founder of the New Renaissance Movement, which includes strong Celtic elements. A dominant theme in many of her Arthurian poems, such as "Call to Arms," "Conjuration," "Excalibur," "Kingdom of the Grail," "Return to Camelot," "The Land Is Empty Now," "The Return," and "Say No More King Arthur Sleeps" (1988–93), is the spiritual inspiration of both the Arthurian dream and the Grail quest. [RHT]

The Pleiades. *The Celtic Collection*. Upminster, Essex: The Sharkti Laureate, 1993.

A Round Table of Contemporary Arthurian Poetry, ed. Barbara Tepa Lupack and Alan Lupack. Rochester, N.Y.: Round Table, 1993, pp. 1 and 48.

COSIER, TONY, a Canadian schoolteacher, has published widely in literary magazines. To date, six excerpts have been printed from his unpublished novel *Perceval*, a contemporary version of the Perceval-Amfortas story. Other short stories and poems, particularly "Finding the Church" (1981) and "The Plow" (1993), also include Arthurian overtones. [RHT]

Cosier, Tony. "Amfort's Final Meditation." *The Coffee House*, 3 (May 1983).

———. "Peter Amfort the Scholar Remembers His Boyhood." *Focus*, 1.3 (June 1984), 18–19.

———. "Amfort's Meditation." *The Round Table*, 1.2 (Fall 1984), 29–31.

———. "Peter Amfort the Scholar Remembers Norma." *Yellow Silk*, 14 (Spring 1985), 8.

———. "Peter Amfort the Poet and the Temptations of St. Anthony." *Sonoma Mandala* (1986).

———. "Norma." *Carousel*, 4 (1987/88), 53–55.

———. "Finding the Church." *The Antigonish Review*, 85/86 (Spring/Summer 1991), 88.

———. "The Plow." In *A Round Table of Contemporary Arthurian Poetry*, ed. Barbara Tepa Lupack and Alan Lupack. Rochester, N.Y.: Round Table, 1993, pp. 14–15.

COUPERUS, LOUIS (1863–1923), Dutch novelist and poet, published a chapter of *Het zwevende schaakbord* ("The Floating Chessboard") in the magazine *De Haagsche Post* weekly from October 1917 to June 1918. The full text was published in 1923 in a slightly revised form. Couperus based his nostalgic story on Penninc and Vostaert's *Roman van Walewein* (*see NAE*, p. 355) and medievalized his own somewhat decadent style by adapting words and phrases from his source. In *Het zwevende schaakbord*, Gawain, after ten years of adventureless idleness, is confronted once again by the threefold quest for the floating chessboard, magic sword, and beautiful princess Ysabele, described in the Middle Dutch romance. This time, however, the adventures are created by Merlin and Morgaine, who have magically mastered the technological innovations of the author's own day. As a knight of the old order, Gawain is unable to prevail over the challenges of the modern world, and his death signals a sad end to the belief in wondrous adventures. [FB]

Aardse, Karel. "Couperus te Camelot." *Literatuur*, 1 (1984), 120-28.

Couperus, Louis. *Het zwevende schaakbord*. Amsterdam: Maatschappij voor Goede en Goedkoope Lectuur, 1922 [= March 1923]; rpt. Amsterdam: Veen, 1994.

COUVOISIER, WALTER: *see* BERGH, WALTER.

CROW, DONNA FLETCHER, in *Glastonbury* (1992), centers upon Glastonbury her reverent account of the history of British Christianity from its legendary beginnings to the dissolution of the monasteries. The Arthurian story permeates this long, epochal novel, from the opening section in which Joseph of Arimathea brings the cup of the Last Supper to Celtic Britain, to the romance writers of Norman England. The third section, "The Anointing of the King: Arthurian Britain," substantially retells the central story of Arthur as a historical Christian king, with the roles of the major characters carefully sanitized and traditional medieval marvels rationalized. Merlin, for example, is identified as Merlinus Ambrosius Dubricius, archbishop of Caerleon, in this sentimentally religious work. [DN]

Crow, Donna Fletcher. *Glastonbury: The Novel of Christian Britain.* Wheaton, Ill.: Crossway, 1992.

CROWLEY, JOHN, author of *Ægypt* (1987), the first volume of a "philosophical romance" tetralogy in which a modern scholar, Pierce Moffett, is intent on exploring the secret history of the world as created by centuries of heretics and magicians. A Perceval figure—an association explicitly made at several points—Pierce finds his "Grail" in the draft of a dead author's historical novel, portions of which are incorporated in the text. A passage about John Dee tells of the Elizabethan astrologer's visit to Glastonbury, where he recounts Arthur's glory for his son and attempts his own Grail quest. The second book in the series, *Love and Sleep*, was published in 1994. [DN]

Crowley, John. *Ægypt.* New York: Bantam, 1987.

CROWLEY, SUSAN HANNIFORD, wrote "Heartleaf" (1991), a one-page story that tells how a damsel falls in love with Lancelot, only to suffer heartbreak when she learns of his affair with Guinevere. [RHT]

Crowley, Susan Hanniford. "Heartleaf." *Marion Zimmer Bradley's Fantasy Magazine*, 14 (Fall 1991), 31.

CROWTHER, PETER, in his short story "All We Know of Heaven" (1995), relates how a young boy, inspired by the tale of Arthur drawing the Sword from the Stone, disconnects his mother, who has been left in a permanent coma by a car accident, from her life-support system. [RHT]

Crowther, Peter. "All We Know of Heaven." In *Excalibur*, ed. Richard Gilliam, Martin H. Greenberg, and Edward E. Kramer. New York: Warner, 1995, pp. 131–47.

CUNQUEIRO MORA, ALVARO (1911–1981), Galician writer of both Galician and Spanish stories. In 1955, he published *Merlin e familia* ("Merlin and Family"), in which he blends the Galician magical world with the mythical tradition of Merlin and the Arthurian legend. In this novel, Felipe de Amancia, Merlin's servant, narrates the stories of his master when they were in Miranda, where people came from all over the world to ask for Merlin's advice. The action of the story often serves as a means to convey the poetic descriptions of the Galician landscape. [ELO]

Cunqueiro Mora, Alvaro. *Merlin e familia.* Vigo: Galaxia, 1955.

DANSON, SOPHIE: *see* CAINE, ERIN.

DARBY, CATHERINE, in her fantasy novel *A Dream of Fair Serpents* (1979), follows the lives of a group of people who are reincarnated in different eras but always retain a link with their initial location on the Isle of Anglesey in North Wales. They embody archetypes, several of which are drawn from Arthurian tradition (Merlin, Vivien, Morgan, Kay, Guinevere, and Gawain), and their interaction demonstrates the dangers of betraying one's gifts and true destiny for selfish reasons. [RHT]

Darby, Catherine. *A Dream of Fair Serpents.* New York: Popular, 1979.

DELAVOUËT, MAS-FELIPE: *see* TRISTAN AND ISOLDE IN MODERN FRENCH VERSIONS.

DE LINT, CHARLES, author of *Spiritwalk* (1992), a collection of related fantasy stories that serves as a sequel to the author's 1984 novel *Moonheart* (*see NAE*, pp. 113-14). De Lint again sets his characters in a world in which the borders between modern Canada and the realm of Faerie continually dissolve. *Ascian in Rose*, first published separately in 1986, is a novella in which the evil queen Glamorgana is clearly based on Morgan le Fay. More explicitly Arthurian is the short story "Merlin Dreams in the Mondream Wood" (1990), in which a young girl's love frees Merlin from his oak-tree prison in the garden of a mysterious house in Ottawa.

De Lint also wrote *The Fair in Emain Macha* (1985), a heroic fantasy set in a Dark Age "Ireland that never was." Colum, one of Artor's captains, returns from exile in search of revenge for past wrongs. This he accomplishes with help from Myrddin. De Lint's short story "Passing" (1995) deals, in a modern setting, with a sister of the Lady of the Lake who gave Excalibur to Arthur. [RHT/DN]

De Lint, Charles. *Ascian in Rose.* Seattle: Axolotl, 1986.
———. *The Fair in Emain Macha. Space & Time*, 68 (1985). Rev.

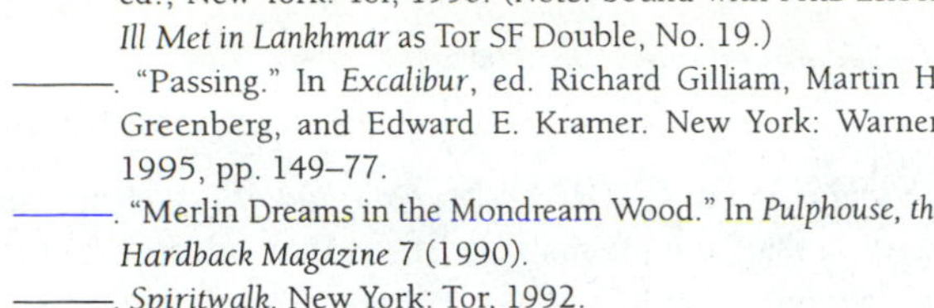
ed., New York: Tor, 1990. (Note: bound with Fritz Leiber, *Ill Met in Lankhmar* as Tor SF Double, No. 19.)

———. "Passing." In *Excalibur*, ed. Richard Gilliam, Martin H. Greenberg, and Edward E. Kramer. New York: Warner, 1995, pp. 149–77.

———. "Merlin Dreams in the Mondream Wood." In *Pulphouse, the Hardback Magazine* 7 (1990).

———. *Spiritwalk*. New York: Tor, 1992.

D'ESPEZEL, PIERRE: *see* TRISTAN AND ISOLDE IN MODERN FRENCH VERSIONS.

DEXTER, SUSAN, in her short story "Where Bestowed" (1995), tells how a survivor of Camlann searches Dozmary Pool for Excalibur in the hope that it will rally the disunited Britons. As a reward for his self-sacrifice, the Ladies of the Lake transform him into a unicorn with the sword as his horn, and in this form he rescues a woman and her two daughters from Saxon raiders. [RHT]

Dexter, Susan. "Where Bestowed." In *Excalibur*, ed. Richard Gilliam, Martin H. Greenberg, and Edward E. Kramer. New York: Warner, 1995, pp. 363–75.

DORR, JAMES S., composed "Dagda" (1992), a poem in which the Irish god muses upon the past. He reveals that the Grail that caught the blood of Christ as He hung on the cross is none other than his cauldron and that he is the Fisher King, living in the revolving glass castle he himself built. Perceval failed in his quest, not because he did not ask the right questions, but because he fled, offended by the Dagda's earthy tales. [RHT]

Dorr, James S. "Dagda." In *Grails: Quests, Visitations, and Other Occurrences*, ed. Richard Gilliam, Martin H. Greenberg, and Edward E. Kramer. Atlanta: Unnameable, 1992. Republished as *Grails: Quests of the Dawn*. New York: Roc/Penguin, 1994, pp. 90–95.

DORST, TANKRED (*see NAE*, pp. 118–20), wrote a libretto for an opera about Merlin and published his scenario for a film about Parzival (1992). A German stage presentation, *König Artus oder Aufstieg und Fall des Abendlandes* ("King Arthur or Rise and Fall of the West"), was produced by the "Ensemble 90" and performed in 1992 in the Hannover off-theater workshop; it deals with questions of war and love, magic and religion, drawing on Dorst's play *Merlin* and Marion Zimmer Bradley's novel *The Mists of Avalon*. [UM/WW]

König Artus: Aufstieg und Fall des Abendlandes. Hannover: "Theaterwerkstatt Hannover," 1992 [unpublished playbook].

Krohn, Rüdiger. "Der Wilde: Exposé für einen Film 35mm Farbe, ca. 90 Minuten, von Tankred Dorst." *Forum, III: Materialien und Beiträge zur Mittelalter-Rezeption*. (Göppingen: Kümmerle, 1992), pp. 53–79.

DU BOSE, HORACE M.: *see* YOUTH GROUPS, ARTHURIAN.

ECO, UMBERTO, Italian author of the 1988 *Il pendolo di Foucault* (published in English as *Foucault's Pendulum*), in which three editors become obsessed with a theory that, if correct, could reveal to them a source of extraordinary power. The complex and convoluted theory involves a presumed secret society of adepts who possess knowledge of the source of that power. The central element of the secret is the Templars, but scarcely less crucial are druidic and Catharist dimensions, the philosopher's stone, and the Holy Grail (which is considered sometimes a stone, sometimes the Chalice of the Last Supper). One of Eco's characters explains that the Grail "was taken to France by Joseph of Arimathea" and adds that it is "a symbol representing power, a source of immense energy. It nourishes, heals wounds, blinds, strikes down" (p. 119). Eco uses Wolfram von Eschenbach's *Parzival* (whence the Grail as a stone) as the link connecting the Templars to the Grail, presumably kept in "the mythical Monsalvat." [NJL]

Eco, Umberto. *Il pendolo di Foucault*. Milan: Bompiani, 1988. Published in English as *Foucault's Pendulum*, trans. William Weaver. New York: Ballantine, 1990.

EDGERTON, TERESA, borrows extensively from Welsh and Arthurian tradition in her fantasy series set in the land of Celydonn. Although Arthurian borrowings are largely confined to personal names in most of the novels, in *The Grail and the Ring* (1994) they include the motifs of the Grail, Maimed King, and Wasteland. [RHT]

Edgerton, Teresa. *The Grail and the Ring*. New York: Ace, 1994.

EFFINGER, GEORGE ALEC, author of numerous works of science fiction and fantasy, among them a series of parodies about Maureen Birnbaum, "a totally cool prep-school senior who became a socially aware . . . swordsperson." Most of the short stories take place in the imaginative worlds created by other authors, but in "Maureen Birnbaum and the Saint Graal" (1993) she sets out, with Joseph of Arimathea and Bohort (Bors), to seek, not the Grail, but the "berry bowl" used by Jesus at the Last Supper. Despite her prowess, it is her verbal pronouncements that have most impact upon friend and foe alike: "Holy Grail is a male-supremacist, sexist, revisionist term using religion to hide the devious conspiracy to rob women of their innate power and authority granted to them by the Goddess," she informs her stunned companions. [RHT]

Effinger, George Alec. "Maureen Birnbaum and the Saint Graal." In *Maureen Birnbaum, Barbarian Swordsperson*. N.p.: Guild America, 1993, pp. 96–117. Rpt. in *Grails: Visitations of the Night*, ed. Richard Gilliam, Martin H. Greenberg, and Edward E. Kramer. New York: Roc/Penguin, 1994, pp. 351–72.

ELLIOTT, JANICE, British author of the Sword and the Dream trilogy of juvenile fantasy novels set in a "post-Catastrophe" future. In the first of the two books published to date, *The King Awakes* (1987), Arthur, awakened from the sleep that followed his battle with Modret, helps a young man and his family escape from savage pursuers to the Isles of the Blest. In *The Empty Throne* (1988), the characters are again assisted by Arthur, who accompanies them in disguise as they search for "Jerusalem," the site of the throne of Britain. [DN]

Elliott, Janice. *The King Awakes*. London: Walker, 1987; new ed., 1989.

———. *The Empty Throne*. London: Walker, 1988; new ed., 1989.

ELLIS, PETER BERRESFORD: *see* TREMAYNE, PETER.

ENDERSBY, CLIVE, Canadian actor, novelist, and screenwriter for *Read All About It!*, a television series that includes the figure of Merlin, has also written *Young King Arthur* (1983). First performed in 1980 at Theatre Aquarius in Hamilton, Ontario, this play adapts for young audiences the story of the Sword in the Stone. Arthur is squire for a humorous bumpkin, Sir Kay, while Guinever (Gwen) is disguised as a squire chosen by Sir Mordred. His evil matches that of Morgan, who tries to prevent Arthur's accession. The play has limited but effective audience participation. [HT]

Endersby, Clive. *Young King Arthur*. In *Young King Arthur and The Adventures of Robin Hood*. Toronto: Playwrights Canada, 1983, pp. 1–44.

ENGSTROM, INGEMO, director and writer of *Ginevra*, a German film shown during the 1992 Berlin and Edinburgh film festivals. In the film, Cecilia Linné, an actress with more pretentions than skill who has adopted the stage-name Ginevra, suffers a nervous breakdown, after which she divides her affections between two boyfriends, the physician Luc and the painter Artus. Although intended as a modern version of the Camelot triangle, the film is amateurish, and the Arthurian parallel is never fully realized. [KJH]

Elley, Derek. Review. *Variety*, March 16, 1992, p. 60.

ESPINOSA, GERMÁN, Colombian novelist, essayist, diplomat, and journalist, is the author of a story entitled "El Píxide" ("The Pyx"), written in 1977 and published in 1988. In the story, a portion of the pseudo-history of the Holy Grail is reconstructed and set in the context of the siege against the Albigensians in the Castle of Montségur in 1244. The story weaves Christian history with Arthurian myth, historical with mythical characters. [DOM]

Espinosa, Germán. "El píxide." In *Noticias de un convento frente al mar*. Bogotá: Editorial La Overja Negra, 1988.

FABRE, LUCIEN: *see* TRISTAN AND ISOLDE IN MODERN FRENCH VERSIONS.

FAWCETT, BILL, in his short story "Demon Sword" (1995), adopts a revisionist approach to the enmity between Morganna and Arthur. The former is a druidess who risks her life to steal the king's sword because it exercises an evil and oppressive power over people. [RHT]

Fawcett, Bill. "Demon Sword." In *Excalibur*, ed. Richard Gilliam, Martin H. Greenberg, and Edward E. Kramer. New York: Warner, 1995, pp. 377–97.

FENN, LIONEL, in "The Awful Truth in Arthur's Barrow" (1992), a short story about the discovery of the "Holy G(r)ail," parodies the cliches in adventure films of archaeological discovery, such as the Indiana Jones series (*see NAE*, p. 155). [RHT]

Fenn, Lionel. "The Awful Truth in Arthur's Barrow." In *Grails: Quests, Visitations, and Other Occurrences*, ed. Richard Gilliam, Martin H. Greenberg, and Edward E. Kramer. Atlanta: Unnameable, 1992. Republished as *Grails: Quests of the Dawn*. New York: Roc/Penguin, 1994, pp. 309–34.

***FIRST KNIGHT*:** *see* ZUCKER, JERRY.

***FISHER KING*:** *see* GILLIAM, TERRY.

FISK, ALAN, author of *The Summer Stars* (1992), a historical novel in the form of the autobiography of Taliesin, recorded at the end of his life as a Christian monk at Glastonbury. Born the bastard son of a west-country lord, the bard encounters most of the prominent figures of sixth-cen-

tury Britain, which is still enjoying the peace established by Arthur in the years just before the story opens. Taliesin's blandly recounted adventures take him from the courts of Welsh kings to the Saxon lands in Kent, where he marries and lives among the Germanic settlers, returning to the Celtic lands only after the death of his wife. Assuming his traditional role as the bard of Urien of Rheged, Taliesin meets, among others, the battle-crazed bard Myrddin. [DN]

Fisk, Alan. *The Summer Stars*. Llandysul, Dyfed: Gomer, 1992.

FITZGERALD, F. SCOTT (1896–1940), the great chronicler of America's Jazz Age, was fascinated by the medieval throughout his lifetime, and he incorporated traditional medieval and Arthurian motifs, especially the wasteland and the Grail quest, into both his novels and his short fiction.

Amory Blaine, the romantic egotist and protagonist of Fitzgerald's first novel, *This Side of Paradise* (1922), reads works that he christens "quest books" and realizes ultimately that life can be either an amusing game or a more noble "seeking for the grail." In *The Great Gatsby* (1925), Jay Gatsby, Fitzgerald's most fully developed questing hero, pursues Daisy Fay Buchanan with the ardor and courtesy of a medieval courtly lover because, from their first meeting, "he found that he committed himself to the following of a grail." Even when Daisy's enchantment fades and she herself proves to be as false, or fey, as her maiden name suggests (a name that, not coincidentally, links her to Morgan le Fay), he remains true to his noble ideal of her. Gatsby's quest, though unsuccessful, nevertheless becomes for Fitzgerald a paradigm of contemporary man's search for honor.

The wasteland, a related and recurring image appropriated from T.S. Eliot and used by Fitzgerald to convey the deterioration of social values in the first half of the twentieth century, also appears in much of Fitzgerald's best fiction. Most notably, *The Great Gatsby*'s Valley of the Ashes, which separates the privileged but sterile world of the Long Island Eggs from the corrupt city of New York, is a dismal place where "ashes grow like wheat" and "ash-grey men move dimly . . . through the powdery air"; and the Valley's ashes become part of the foul dust that, after Gatsby's untimely death, floats in the wake of his dreams of Daisy and of the orgiastic future. Arthurian motifs figure in other works too: the main character of "O Russet Witch!," one of the fantasies in *Tales of the Jazz Age* (1922), is Merlin, a modest bookstore owner scorned by his son, Arthur, who cannot understand the magic "Old Merlin [gets] from his books."

Fitzgerald's love for medievalism and for the Arthurian legends carried over into his personal life as well. In his correspondence, he refers repeatedly to the need for a chivalric code of conduct. His daughter, Scottie, who remembered the "Histomaps" of the Middle Ages that hung on the walls of her father's workroom and the toy soldiers that he deployed on marches around the Christmas tree, recalled playing "Knights of the Round Table" with paper dolls that had been elaborately painted by Zelda Fitzgerald in a dollhouse described by Scott in his story "Outside the Cabinet-Maker's." [BTL]

Fitzgerald, F. Scott. *The Great Gatsby*. New York: Scribner, 1925.
———. "O Russet Witch!" In *Tales of the Jazz Age*. New York: Scribner, 1922, pp. 234–72.
———. *This Side of Paradise*. New York: Scribner, 1922.
———. "Outside the Cabinet-Maker's." In *Afternoon of an Author: A Selection of Uncollected Stories*, ed. Arthur Mizener. New York: Scribner, 1957, pp. 137–41.

FORBUSH, WILLIAM BYRON: *see* YOUTH GROUPS, ARTHURIAN.

FREEMAN, DAVID, Australian-born director, considered by some one of modern opera's *enfants terribles*, whose more recent work has been for the dramatic stage. In 1990, Freeman wrote and directed a seven-hour dramatic adaptation of Sir Thomas Malory's *Morte Darthur*. The production, which premiered in London on 19 July 1990, was staged in two venues on successive nights. Part One opened in the Lyric Hammersmith's proscenium stage and after the interval moved to the nearby *faux* Gothic Church of St. Paul's for Part Two. The second night opened at St. Paul's and moved after the interval back to the Lyric's stage for the concluding Part Four. Freeman discussed his vision for the play in an interview with Clare Colvin in the London *Times*: "The quest for the Holy Grail was incompatible with Camelot, which was based on compromise. . . . It is not the love affair between Lancelot and Guinevere, which Arthur had chosen not to see, that destroyed Camelot. It is the search for the Grail, which represented the moral absolute."

Set in the fifth century, Freeman's text calls for a troupe of fifteen actors, playing multiple roles. His intent, according to a program note, is "to find a theatrical form to express Malory, rather than press him into any readily available theatrical form." The result is unsuccessful, and critical response to the production was universally negative. The parts of the production that work best are those that were set in St. Paul's, which might have served as the sole venue for a streamlined, more effective attempt to dramatize Malory. [KJH]

Clovin, Caire. "Arthur Goes Walkabout in W6." [London] *Times*, July 16, 1990, 19.
Harty, Kevin J. Review. *Arthurian Interpretations*, 4 (Spring 1990), 88–90.
[Reprints of Major London Reviews.] *London Theatre Record*, 16 (July 30–August 12, 1990), 1010–16.

FRIESNER, ESTHER M., deals with Arthurian legend in three short stories. In "The Death of Nimue" (1985), an aged Nimue returns to the oak in which she imprisoned Merlin, only to learn that he actually wanted to be rid of the burden of his magic powers all along. When he refuses to take them back, her daughter takes them instead to give her mother release. "Up the Wall" (1990) offers a humorously unflattering account of the truth behind, not only the story of how Arthur came to the throne but also the early career of Beowulf. In "Goldie, Lox, and the Three Excalibearers" (1995), high-flown rhetoric and the lofty machinations of magicians prove no match for a practical teenage waitress in a Brooklyn deli. Even if she is the reincarnated Lady of the Lake and has succeeded in passing on Excalibur to an also reincarnated Arthur, she is not about to accept the great king's offer of marriage if he cannot prove that he is Jewish too! [RHT]

Friesner, Esther M. "The Death of Nimue." *Fantasy Book* (June 1985), 59–60.

———. "Up the Wall." 1990; rpt. in *Smart Dragons, Foolish Elves*, ed. Alan Dean Foster and Martin Harry Greenberg. New York: Ace, 1991, pp. 246–75.

———. "Goldie, Lox, and the Three Excalibearers." In *Excalibur*, ed. Richard Gilliam, Martin H. Greenberg, and Edward E. Kramer. New York: Warner, 1995, pp. 193–225.

GAIMAN, NEIL, in "Chivalry" (1992), tells, with gentle humor, how an old-age pensioner buys the Holy Grail in an Oxfam shop but then gives it to Galaad in exchange for the Philosopher's Stone and the Egg of the Phoenix, both of which, she decides, will "look nice on the mantelpiece." [RHT]

Gaiman, Neil. "Chivalry." In *Grails: Quests, Visitations, and Other Occurrences*, ed. Richard Gilliam, Martin H. Greenberg, and Edward E. Kramer. Atlanta: Unnameable, 1992. Republished as *Grails: Quests of the Dawn*. New York: Roc/Penguin, 1994, pp. 344–57.

GALDÓS, BENITO: *see* PÉREZ GALDÓS, BENITO.

GAMES. The California-based company Chaosium has issued a number of new publications to augment its popular Arthurian role-playing game *King Arthur Pendragon* (*see NAE*, p. 175). *Savage Mountains* (1991), *Blood and Lust* (1991), and *The Spectre King* (1992) are modules, each of which contains several adventures by different designers. Four game supplements have also been published: in *Knights Adventurous* (1990), Greg Stafford offers guidelines for creating characters from outside Arthurian tradition; in *The Boy King* (1991) Stafford provides additional information on Arthur's early years; *The Pagan Shore* (1994) by John Carnahan and *Beyond the Wall* (1995) by several authors describe respectively Ireland and Britain north of Hadrian's Wall, integrating history and legend with the information found in Malory. The most recent edition of the game itself is the fourth, *King Arthur Pendragon* (1993) by Stafford; it has been substantially expanded to include additional information. (*See also* STAFFORD, GREG.)

In 1980, Metagaming introduced *Grail Quest*, a supplementary module for use with the Fantasy Trip role-playing game system. The object of the game is to find the Holy Grail and return with it to Camelot, performing deeds of knight-errantry on the way.

Spirit of Excalibur is an interactive computer game whose premise is that King Arthur has died and the Round Table is weakened. The player assumes the identity of Arthur's successor, Lord Constantine, who must go to Camelot to assume power; along the way, he faces dangers from beasts, magic spells, and hostile knights (including the sons of Mordred). The game, based loosely on characters and events from Malory, was produced in 1990 by Virgin Mastertronic and programmed by Alan Clark, John Conley, and Michael Branhyam. For Apple or IBM.

Arthurian lore is also included in *Quest: In Search of the Dragontooth* (1994) by Michael Green, a game in which the players seek a Perilous Dragontooth with the aid of such objects as a map and a mage's notebooks. [RHT/NJL]

Stafford, Greg. *King Arthur Pendragon*. 4th ed. Oakland: Chaosium, 1993.

GARETH, DAVID, author of "Sir Mador Seeks the Grail" (*see NAE*, p. 176), completed "Prelude to the Quest" (1989), another short story in his projected collection dealing with the quest for the Grail. Lancelot here ponders the paradox of his love for both Guinevere and Arthur, and for what they represent, as he prepares to set out in search of the Grail.

Gareth also composed the poem "Arthur's Lament for Merlin" (1993), in which the King recognizes his lost mentor's influence upon "all that my kingdom will become." [RHT]

Gareth, David. "Arthur's Lament for Merlin." In *A Round Table of Contemporary Arthurian Poetry*, ed. Barbara Tepa Lupack and Alan Lupack. Rochester, N.Y.: Round Table, 1993, pp. 6–7.

———. "Prelude to the Quest." *The Round Table*, 5 (1989), 37–42.

GARNIER, PIERRE: *see* TRISTAN AND ISOLDE IN MODERN FRENCH VERSIONS.

GARTON, JAMES ARCHIBALD (1891–1969), British author, wrote *The Bowman* (1931), a four-act play in which a minstrel from King Arthur's court rescues a nun from

Sir Murdrid. Because in "service . . . lies the key / to all we hope for Eternity," the hero's self-effacing love for this nun leads to his achieving the Vision of the Holy Grail. [RS]

Garton, J.A. *The Bowman*. Eton: Spottiswoode, Ballantyne, 1931.

GASTAUD, ELYANE: *see* TRISTAN AND ISOLDE IN MODERN FRENCH VERSIONS.

GAUTIER, BLAISE: *see* TRISTAN AND ISOLDE IN MODERN FRENCH VERSIONS.

GIBSON, WILFRED WILSON (1878–1962), British author, contributed to *North Country Magazine* two Arthurian poems that were not later included among his *Collected Poems*. In "The Song of the Lough Maiden" (May 1901) Arthur still holds his court under the waters of Broomlea Lough in Northumberland. "The Rousing of the King" (August 1901) retells the story of the sleeping king under the Castle of the Seven Shields. [RS]

Gibson, Wilfred Wilson. "Song of the Lough Maiden" and "Rousing of the King," *North Country Magazine*, 2 (1901).

GILLARD, HENRI: *see* TRÉHORENTEUC.

GILLIAM, RICHARD, preserves some traditional motifs in "Storyville, Tennessee" (1992), his short story about an encounter with the Grail in America in 1917. Most notable are the purifying bowl, various associated "maidens," and the figure of the fool (Perceval) who misses a wonderful opportunity. [RHT]

Gilliam, Richard. "Storyville, Tennessee." In *Grails: Quests, Visitations, and Other Occurrences*, ed. Richard Gilliam, Martin H. Greenberg, and Edward E. Kramer. Atlanta: Unnameable, 1992. Republished as *Grails: Quests of the Dawn*. New York: Roc/Penguin, 1994, pp. 149–70.

GILLIAM, TERRY, formerly a member of the Monty Python group and co-director of *Monty Python and the Holy Grail* (*see NAE*, p. 328), directed *The Fisher King*, a 1990 Tri-Star film with screenplay by Richard LaGravenese. It concerns Lucas, a disc jockey who unintentionally inspired a mass murder and became a guilt-ridden alcoholic as a result, and Parry, a medievalist who was driven mad when his wife was among those murdered. Meeting accidentally several years after the tragedy, the two men become friends, and the film depicts their mutual redemption.

The film is in no way a retelling of the Arthurian story, but it contains a number of references to, and images of, the Fisher King, the Grail, and related motifs. Parry tells Lucas a story of the infirm Fisher King, who could be cured only by drinking from the Holy Grail. Eventually, the Grail was brought to him by a fool, who did it neither for glory nor for the challenge, but because "I only knew you were thirsty." In the film, but not in the original screenplay, the King was required to spend time alone in the wilderness to prepare himself spiritually, and he was injured when he had to reach into fire for the Grail.

The object that Parry takes to be the Grail in the film is a simple trophy, a photograph of which he saw in a magazine. Lucas eventually saves Parry by stealing the "Grail" for him; in the process, he also saves the life of the trophy's owner. [NJL]

LaGravenese, Richard. *The Fisher King: A Screenplay*. Hill/Obst Productions, 1988; revised 1989.

GINEVRA: *see* ENGSTROM, INGEMO.

GIONO, JEAN (1895–1970), French author of the 1948 novel *Un Roi sans divertissement* ("A King Without Diversions"), which is tightly woven around references to the scene of Perceval's trance over the blood drops on the snow in Chrétien de Troyes's *Le Conte del Graal* (*see NAE*, pp. 90-91). Chrétien downplays the violence responsible for this red-white contrast, which catalyzes his hero's first prolonged experience of aesthetic and emotional contemplation. In contrast, Giono emphasizes the abundance of blood, whose contrast with the snowy mountain landscape of Haute Provence mesmerizes a host of characters: the poacher Bergues, whom Giono specifically compares to Perceval; the murderer M.V., whose obsession moves him to select victims according to their red or white complexions; the wolf, hypnotized by the blood of its victim, which passively awaits its own death; and the hero Langlois, who has a goose killed in order to experience the same trancelike state. The wolf and M.V. are the initiators of the violence that entrances them. They thus catalyze ritual, sacrificial ceremonies, which distract the winter-weary villagers and so affect the observer Langlois that he, unlike Perceval, who grows out of his violence in the trance scene, internalizes it to the point of killing himself. [GMA]

Giono, Jean. *Un Roi sans divertissement*. Paris: Gallimard, 1948.

GRAY, PHOEBE: *see* YOUTH GROUPS, ARTHURIAN.

GRIFFITHS, PAUL, English author of *The Lay of Sir Tristram*, a 1991 novel that intertwines details from Richard

Wagner's life with elements of the Tristan/Tristram story, from Tristram's birth through the love potion to the lovers' death. This is less a retelling of the Tristram legend than a record of the attempt to draw a coherent story out of "the intricate multiplicity of alternative accounts" (p. 102) in which "there is so much . . . that we have to conflate or omit" (p. 89). The narrator may have second thoughts about his choices ("there may even be a brief scene inserted in the previous chapter," p. 18; or "no, no, that must be a mistake," p. 1); he may offer hypotheses ("quite possibly Tristram is somewhere in the room," p. 21); and he laments the point at which literary sources fail us (p. 102). At one point (Chapter 7), he speculates about "how to get Tristram back to Ireland," and he offers four possible solutions.

The novel, however, is the account not only of a narrator's attempt to reconstruct the story, but of Wagner's efforts to construct an opera, to transform Tristram and Yseult into *Tristan und Isolde*. The composer is thus shown writing at his desk, conducting the first rehearsals of the opera, and in other scenes. The two narratives intersect frequently; for example, Griffiths describes a musical contest (at King Mark's court) in which we hear "just three notes—a rise, a fall—and then the promised chord" (p. 64), which can only be Wagner's own famous Tristan chord. [NJL]

Griffiths, Paul. *The Lay of Sir Tristram*. London: Chatto and Windus, 1991.

GROSPIERRE, LOUIS, writer and director of *Connemara*, a film that premiered in Paris in June 1990. In the distant past, Loup is sent to bring his uncle Mark's fiancée, Sedrid of the long red tresses, back to Connemara. Of course, Loup and Sedrid fall in love with each other, and the ensuing romantic triangle has only the expected tragic consequences. Except for the change in name for two of the three characters in the love triangle, the film, set in Ireland rather than in Cornwall, is nothing more than an unremarkable retelling of the legend of Tristan and Isolde. [KJH]

Tous les films 1990. Paris: Éditions chrétiens-médias, 1991.

GUINEVERE: *see* TAYLOR, JUD.

GYGAX, GARY, recounts the story of Arthur's career from the point of view of Caliburnus/Excalibur in his short story "Duty" (1995). Given magical powers and sentience by Viviane, the sword recognizes the ambition and tyranny of Arthur and Merlin, and it works, along with its creator, to bring an end to an unjust rule marked by "degeneracy . . . savagery and death." [RHT]

Gygax, Gary. "Duty." In *Excalibur*, ed. Richard Gilliam, Martin H. Greenberg, and Edward E. Kramer. New York: Warner, 1995, pp. 429–58.

HALDEMAN, JACK C., II, added to his many works of science fiction and fantasy the short story "Ashes to Ashes" (1992). A private investigator from New York is brought to Amsterdam to locate some bones and ashes that are kept with the Holy Grail. The former are being sought by rival groups intent on wielding their supernatural power for personal gain. [RHT]

Haldeman, Jack C., II. "Ashes to Ashes." In *Grails: Quests, Visitations, and Other Occurrences*, ed. Richard Gilliam, Martin H. Greenberg, and Edward E. Kramer. Atlanta: Unnameable, 1992. Republished as *Grails: Visitations of the Night*. New York: Roc/Penguin, 1994, pp. 238–62.

HAMLETT, CHRISTINA, American actress, director, and playwright, introduces elements of fantasy into her romance novel *The Enchanter* (1990). A Washington reporter falls in love with a stage magician, only to discover that they are both reincarnations, he of Merlin and she herself of a damsel of the Lake. Together, they recover Excalibur, which had been stolen by the evil Nimue and brought forward in time for concealment in the twentieth century. They travel with it back to Dark Age Britain, where they destroy the pursuing Nimue with the help of the Lady of the Lake, here identified as the Goddess. They then return to live out their lives together. [RHT]

Hamlett, Christina. *The Enchanter*. New York: Evans, 1990.

HARSENT, DAVID, British poet whose verse drama *Gawain* was developed into an opera through collaboration with composer Harrison Birtwistle and first presented in a well-received production at Covent Garden in 1991. Based on *Sir Gawain and the Green Knight* (*see NAE*, pp. 419–20), the story of Gawain's testing is here presented as Morgan le Fay's lesson about the failings of human nature, which undermine both the placid gentility of the court and Arthur's yearning for marvels and heroism. (*See also* BIRTWISTLE, HARRISON.) [DN]

Harsent, David. *Gawain*. London: Universal Edition, 1991.

HART, JACK, American author of a narrative poem, *The Lady of the Fountain* (1986), which retells the traditional story with humorous digressions on such topics as heroic literature, literary interpretation, and the problems of writing verse. The effect is of a somewhat inept minstrel who regrets ever starting upon the tale: "You know it must be true, / because its telling hardly flatters me." [RHT]

Hart, Jack. *The Lady of the Fountain*. Independence, Mo.: International University Press, 1986.

HARVEY, JEAN GILMOUR: *see* BENNETT, LAURA GILMOUR.

HAVILL, JUANITA, author of the short story "The Cat and Uther Pendragon" (1989), in which various animals appear at a banquet held by Uther to honor the birth of Arthur. Each offers the child the gift of a particular virtue with which it is associated, but the cat's gift of listening is rejected by Uther, too drunk to appreciate its value until too late. [RHT]

Havill, Juanita. "The Cat and Uther Pendragon." *The Round Table*, 5 (1989), 46–52.

HAWKE, SIMON, has published five more fantasy novels in his humorous Wizard series (*see NAE*, p. 225), set in a future where magic provides the energy source for technology. In *The Wizard of Rue Morgue* (1990), Wyrdrune, Kira, and Modred, descendants of the three daughters of Gorlois, defeat three of the Dark Ones who are lurking in the sewers of Paris. They are aided by the spirits of both Gorlois and Merlin, who share the body of their mutual descendant, a cockney punk rocker named Billy. In *The Samurai Wizard* (1991), the same group defeats a Dark One in Tokyo. Modred is killed, but his essence moves into Wyrdrune, who changes shape between the two personalities. In *The Wizard of Santa Fe* (1991), the six characters in their three bodies destroy another Old One in the city of Santa Fe. Billy is killed but revives when Merlin and Gorlois release their life force into the body all three share. This "transmogrification" blends all three into a single personality for the first time.

The Wizard of Camelot (1993) moves back in time chronologically to describe how Merlin is released from the oak tree in which he was imprisoned, and how he saves the world, where civilization is collapsing into a new Dark Age, by introducing magic as an energy source for technology. *The Wizard of Lovecraft's Cafe* (1993) continues the story of the struggle against the evil Dark Ones, two more of whom are destroyed by the various descendants of Gorlois, this time in New York. Modred is (again) almost killed in a necromantic ambush, but his essence survives, albeit in dormant state, by transferring to the body of a policeman named John Angelo. [RHT]

Hawke, Simon. *The Wizard of Camelot*. New York: Warner, 1993.
———. *The Wizard of Lovecraft's Cafe*. New York: Warner, 1993.
———. *The Wizard of Rue Morgue*. New York: Popular Library/Warner, 1990.
———. *The Samurai Wizard*. New York: Warner, 1991.
———. *The Wizard of Santa Fe*. New York: Warner, 1991.

HAWTHORNE, NATHANIEL (1804–1864), American author of short stories and novels, wrote "The Antique Ring," in which he tells of an aspiring American author who, when asked to provide a fictional history for the engagement ring he gives his fiancée, creates a tale of its having been the ring given by Merlin to his (unnamed) lover. Merlin made a spirit to dwell in the ring who, so long as the love was true, could work only good; but if the love proved false the spirit could "work his own devilish will." [ACL]

Hawthorne, Nathaniel. "The Antique Ring." In *The Snow Image and Uncollected Tales*, ed. William Charvat, Roy Harvey Pearce, and Claude M. Simpson. The Centenary Edition of the Works of Nathaniel Hawthorne, Vol. 11. Columbus: Ohio State University Press, 1974.

HELBLING, HANNO, Swiss writer, translator, and journalist. In 1991, he published a small volume entitled *Tristans Liebe: Abendstücke* ("Tristan's Love: Evening Serenade"). This postmodern "new novel" combines the medieval Tristan legend, Wagner, and some contemporary events. Rather than tell a story, it delivers meaningful fragments about departures and returns. [UM]

Helbling, Hanno. *Tristans Liebe: Abendstücke*. Munich: Piper, 1991.

HERBERT, KATHLEEN, completed a trilogy of historical novels set in north Britain during the Dark Ages. In *Ghost in the Sunlight* (1986), which deals with the struggle between Oswy of Northumbria and Penda of Mercia in the mid-seventh century, Oswy's half-Cumbrian children can still recall the heritage of Urien and Owain from Arthurian tradition. *The Lady of the Fountain* (1982), which retells the story of Owain and Taniu, the parents of St. Kentigern, was revised and reissued as *Bride of the Spear* (1988). The first volume of the trilogy is *Queen of the Lightning* (1983). (*See NAE*, p. 234.) [RHT]

Herbert, Kathleen. *Ghost in the Sunlight*. London: Bodley Head, 1986.
———. *Bride of the Spear*. London: Bodley Head, 1988.

HESCOTT, BOB, author of a seven-part children's fantasy adventure, *Wail of the Banshee*, shown on British Independent Television in 1992. In this inventive ecological allegory about the misuse of magic (= modern technology), a group of modern children seeks Arthur's help in saving Planet Earth. [RS]

HOFBAUER, FRIEDL, Austrian author who composed a fantasy story for young readers, using historic and literary sources. *Die Insel der weissen Magier: Ein Merlin-Roman* ("The Island of the White Magician: A Merlin Romance") takes place in a generation preceding King Arthur: Merlin, who was assumed dead, helps to free Wales and the British Isles from black magic and from invading Scandinavian enemies. He assists Jorinde and Joringle (a couple known from Grimm's fairy tales) to ascend to the throne. The book ends with a vision of a dream that was inspired by Martin Luther King's address of 1967. [SSch]

Hofbauer, Friedl. *Die Insel der weissen Magier: Ein Merlin-Roman.* Vienna: Herder, 1987.

HOFFMAN, LEE, transposes the Grail legend to the American West in his short story "Water" (1992). A cowboy uses an ancient Indian lance to help recover the Grail for its three keepers (mother, crone, and maiden). He thereby breaks the drought that has gripped the land. [RHT]

Hoffman, Lee. "Water." In *Grails: Quests, Visitations, and Other Occurrences*, ed. Richard Gilliam, Martin H. Greenberg, and Edward E. Kramer. Atlanta: Unnameable, 1992. Republished as *Grails: Quests of the Dawn.* New York: Roc/Penguin, 1994, pp. 112–32.

HOLDER, NANCY, introduced Arthurian elements in two short stories. "To Leave if You Can" (1992) demonstrates how the Grail and Arthurian legends inspire one man to make the sacrifices necessary to organize immigrant Mexican farmworkers into a union. The anachronistic "Prayer of the Knight of the Sword" (1995) includes not only Excalibur but also Joseph of Arimathea, Igraine, and Arthur. "Only those who love can save England, and the world" from its suffering, she concludes. [RHT]

Holder, Nancy. "To Leave if You Can." In *Grails: Quests, Visitations, and Other Occurrences*, ed. Richard Gilliam, Martin H. Greenberg, and Edward E. Kramer. Atlanta: Unnameable, 1992. Republished as *Grails: Visitations of the Night.* New York: Roc/Penguin, 1994, pp. 416–29.

———. "Prayer of the Knight of the Sword." In *Excalibur*, ed. Richard Gilliam, Martin H. Greenberg, and Edward E. Kramer. New York: Warner, 1995, pp. 91–105.

HOLDSTOCK, ROBERT, added three fantasies to those in which he makes use of Arthurian tradition (*see NAE*, p. 238). The first is "The Shapechanger" (1989), a short story in which an abused child's daydreams of a glorious Arthurian world, so different from his own, impinge upon the real world of eighth-century England.

Holdstock's dark-fantasy novel *The Fetch* (1991) tells the story of a young boy with the psychic power to "fetch" objects across time and space and who is obsessed with a need to retrieve the Holy Grail. Fisher King and Wasteland motifs are central to the novel, though the Arthurian associations are limited to the boy's insatiable appetite for Grail-quest stories. In *The Hollowing* (1993), which continues the author's Mythago series, a father searches for his missing son in a magical wood shaped by dreams of a primitive version of the story of Gawain and the Green Knight. [DN]

Holdstock, Robert. *The Fetch.* London: Macdonald/Orbit, 1991.

———. *The Hollowing.* London: HarperCollins, 1993.

———. "The Shapechanger." *G.M.: The Independent Fantasy Roleplaying Magazine*, 1.8 (April 1989), 48–57.

HOLMES, LILLIAN: *see* YOUTH GROUPS, ARTHURIAN.

HOLT, TOM, British author of *Grailblazers* (1994), a humorous novel about a knight of Arthur's court named Sir Boamund. He wakes from an enchanted sleep to lead a group of knights (Bedevere, Turquine, Pertelope, Lamorak, and Galahaut) on three quests that must be accomplished before they undertake the quest for the Holy Grail. Holt presents the Grail as a "terracotta washing-up bowl," which is transformed into blue plastic after Christ uses it to wash the dishes dirtied at the Last Supper. Although the novel is not one of the more interesting modern treatments of the Grail legend, Holt's Pythonesque humor produces some very funny scenes. [ACL]

Holt, Tom. *Grailblazers.* London: Orbit, 1994.

HUMPHREYS, SION, director of *Outside Time*, a four-part dramatization of stories from the *Mabinogi*; made for Ffilimiau Bryngwyn, it first aired on Britain's Channel Four in 1991. The thirty-minute episodes are entitled *A Prince Goes Hunting*, which tells the story of Pwyll and his chosen wife, Rhiannon; *The Cauldron of Rebirth*, which recounts the events leading up to the marriage of Branwen to the Irish king Matholwch; *The Making of Arthur*, which introduces the character of Arthur as part of the story of Pryderi and Manawydan; and *Alternative Heroes*, which details how Arthur consults Merlin for advice. [KJH]

Capsule Reviews and Summaries. *Radio Times* [London], August 10–16, 1991, p. 47; August 17–23, 1991, p. 49; August 24–30, 1991, p. 51; and August 31–September 6, 1991, p. 59.

HUNT, PAUL, director of *Merlin*, a 1992 fantasy-adventure film from October 32nd Productions. The story is by Hunt and Nick McCarty; the screenplay is by the latter.

Exploiting fanciful, if not confused, Arthurian associations, the film centers on "Crystal," who is both the Lady of the Lake and the daughter of Merlin; the villain is Pendragon, "son of Mordred." Following an initial sequence set vaguely in the Middle Ages, the main story involves Merlin's daughter, reborn as California reporter Christy Lake, who successfully battles the reincarnated Pendragon for the possession of the sword. [NJL]

JAMMERS, EWALD: *see* WIEDENMANN, REINHOLD.

JOHNSTON, ANNIE FELLOWS (1863–1931), American author of the popular "Little Colonel" series for girls. In one of these novels, *Two Little Knights of Kentucky* (1899), two boys put on a pageant based on James Russell Lowell's *Vision of Sir Launfal* in order to raise money to help a homeless waif. Because of their good deed, the boys are called "little Sir Galahads." Johnston also wrote *Keeping Tryst: A Tale of King Arthur's Time* (1906), the story of the page Ederyn, who hopes to become a knight. A minstrel tells him of Arthur, who wants to establish "round him at his court a chosen circle whose fidelity hath stood the utmost test." After a series of trials, in all of which Ederyn keeps tryst, he is knighted by Arthur. [ACL]

Johnston, Annie Fellows. *Keeping Tryst: A Tale of King Arthur's Time*. Boston: Page, 1906.

———. *Two Little Knights of Kentucky: Who Were the "Little Colonel's" Neighbours*. Boston: Page, 1899.

JOHNSTONE, PAUL, depicts Artorius as a loyal captain in the army of Ambrosius Aurelianus in his short story "Up, Red Dragon!" (1950). His courage, steadfastness, and generosity to a proud Pictish warrior help to save post-Roman Britain from both Saxon invaders and British traitors. [RHT]

Johnstone, Paul. "Up, Red Dragon!" *Blue Book*, 90.5 (March 1950), 104–16.

JONES, COURTWAY, began his projected Dragon's Heir Trilogy with *In the Shadow of the Oak King* (1991). This historical romance recasts Malory's story in a Dark Age setting and tells it from the point of view of Pelleas, here the son of Uther and a Pictish princess. Reared with Nithe (Nineva) and Arthur by Merlin, Pelleas learns from his mentor the skills of both blacksmith and warrior before helping his half-brother claim the throne of a Britain torn by the strife among the various races and political factions. This volume concludes with the defeat of those who oppose Arthur's rule and the union of Pelleas and Nithe.

The second book of the trilogy, *Witch of the North* (1992), is narrated by Morgan and covers events from the conception of her half-brother Arthur to the death of Gawaine at Dover at the outset of Mordred's rebellion. Morgan, whose enmity to her half-brother is muted, emerges as a sympathetic character: she takes her responsibilities to those in her care very seriously and fiercely opposes those who arrogantly trample on the rights of others. The author observes, "[while] I have tried to keep events within the compass outlined in Malory's work . . . I admit I have given everything else a twist to make the story come out the way I wanted." [RHT]

Jones, Courtway. *In the Shadow of the Oak King*. New York: Pocket, 1991.

———. *Witch of the North*. New York: Pocket, 1992.

JONES, MARY J., introduced many traditional characters in her fantasy novel *Avalon* (1991), described by the publisher as a "lesbian Arthurian romance." Argante, the daughter of Gwenhyfar, becomes the Lady of the Lake, defending Avalon in the name of the Goddess against Annis, evil queen of the Wastelands. [DN]

Jones, Mary J. *Avalon*. Tallahassee: Naiad, 1991.

KARR, PHYLLIS ANN, author of a number of Arthurian works, including *The Idylls of the Queen* (*see NAE*, pp. 175 and 259), adopts unfamiliar viewpoints in two short stories. In "The Truth About the Lady of the Lake" (1990), a sorceress and warrior woman from another world (and literary series) stray into that of Arthurian legend, where they accidentally provide Arthur with Excalibur. In "The Coming of the Light" (1992), a Saxon captive denounces Arthur and his knights as brutal murderers of peaceful farmers, rather than heroic defenders of embattled Britain. [RHT]

Karr, Phyllis Ann. "The Truth About the Lady of the Lake." In *The Best of Marion Zimmer Bradley's Fantasy Magazine*, ed. Marion Zimmer Bradley. New York: Warner, 1994, pp. 188–92.

———. "The Coming of the Light." In *The Camelot Chronicles*, ed. Mike Ashley. London: Robinson, 1992, pp. 360–73.

KENNEALY, PATRICIA, in *The Hawk's Gray Feather* (1990) continues her science-fantasy series The Keltiad (*see NAE*, p. 261), which transposes the ancient Celtic world into a space-faring future. In this, the first of the Tales of Arthur trilogy, Taliesin recounts Arthur's early wars to restore to the High Kingship the royal house of which he is a member. Not only must he fight against the forces of the powerful Druid who has usurped the throne, but he must also cope with tensions within the royal camp, particularly in his dealings with his cousin Gweniver. The novel culminates with Arthur's defeat of the usurper's regent, Owein Rheged, and his warriors known as the Ravens at the Battle of Cadarachta (Catraeth). Kennealy imaginatively adapts traditional elements of the Arthurian legend to a new context, while exploring the conflict between the warlike and peaceful sides of the Kelts.

In the second of the Tales of Arthur trilogy, *The Oak Above the Kings* (1994), the author (under the name Patricia Kennealy-Morrison) continues The Keltiad. Here Taliesin recounts Arthur's defeat of the Druid who has usurped the throne and his punishment of those who supported him. He and Gweniver marry and rule as High King and High Queen, but a new foe arises: his half-sister Marguessan (Morgause). The novel incorporates, albeit radically transformed, such traditional elements as the hunting of the boar Twrch Trwyth (from *Culhwch and Olwen*); the thirteen treasures of Britain, including the Grail; the Tristan and Isolde love story; and Uther's entrance into Tintagel in the guise of Gorlois. [RHT]

Kennealy, Patricia. *The Hawk's Gray Feather*. New York: Roc, 1990.
Kennealy-Morrison, Patricia. *The Oak Above the Kings: A Book of the Keltiad*. New York: Roc, 1994.

KIDS OF THE ROUND TABLE: *see* TINNELL, ROBERT.

KING, CLIVE, author of the juvenile historical novel *Ninny's Boat* (1981), the story of a young Pictish prince who was captured at an early age by raiders and raised as a slave among the Angles. Returning to Britain with a group of settlers, he encounters a band of soldiers heading north to join Medraut at Hadrian's Wall, where he witnesses the Battle of Camboglanna and the fatal blows of Medraut and Arturius. The boy helps deliver the body of Arturius to a small island, where his own identity is established, but as the novel ends he returns to East Anglia to rejoin the sympathetically portrayed settlers among whom he was raised. [DN]

King, Clive. *Ninny's Boat*. New York: Macmillan, 1981.

KLESSMANN, ECKART, German lyric poet and writer of historical and literary nonfiction. In 1980, he published a collection of poems, *Botschaften für Viviane* ("Messages to Vivian"). This title derives from a love poem in the collection, "Botschaften Merlins an Viviane" ("Merlin's Messages to Vivian"), seven stanzas of free verse about Merlin's bewitching by Vivian. Merlin, the speaker of the poem, celebrates erotic fascination, which he experiences as a fulfillment of his need for love. [WW]

Klessmann, Eckart. *Botschaften für Viviane*. Hamburg: Hoffmann und Campe, 1980, pp. 42–44.
Wunderlich, Werner. "The Arthurian Legend in German Literature of the Nineteen-Eighties." *Studies in Medievalism*, 3 (1991), 423–42.

KONIG ARTUS ODER AUFSTIEG UND FALL DES ABENDLANDES ("King Arthur, or The Rise and Fall of the Occident"), a German stage presentation produced by the "Ensemble 90" and performed in August 1992 in the Hannover off-theater workshop. The play is built around questions of war and love, magic and religion, drawing on Tankred Dorst's drama *Merlin* (*see NAE*, pp. 118-20) and Marion Zimmer Bradley's novel *The Mists of Avalon* (*NAE*, p. 50). In the sequence of the seasons, the play shows the evolution and the eventual destruction of utopian visions of peace and fortune by ruthless ambition, and it dramatizes the greed for sex and power after Christianity displaced the old Celtic nature goddesses. [WW]

KRAMER, EDWARD E., author of "The Power in Penance" (1994), a short story in which the Holy Grail consumes in flames all the humans who try to drink from it, but not the bishop's cat named Percy (Perceval). [RHT]

Kramer, Edward E. "The Power in Penance." In *Grails: Visitations of the Night*, ed. Richard Gilliam, Martin H. Greenberg, and Edward E. Kramer. New York: Roc/Penguin, 1994, pp. 161–71.

KURTI, RICHARD, director and writer of *Seaview Knights*, a British film shown at the 1994 Cannes Film Festival. As the film opens, would-be bank robber Arthur suffers a blow to the head and thinks he is England's legendary king returned to save the realm. The garbled and confusing ploy that follows includes a taxi driver named Merlin, who organizes a group of Blackpool thieves to make up a new Round Table, and an Arab plot to blow up Parliament that Arthur manages, for reasons never explained, to foil. The film is not a high point in the long and varied history of Arthurian cinema. [KJH]

McCarthy, Todd. Review. *Variety*, June 13, 1994, p. 62.

KUTTNER, HENRY (1915-1958), wrote many pieces of science fiction and fantasy with contributions from his wife, C.L. Moore, another respected author in the field. Their science-fantasy novelette "The Dark World" (1946) includes Merlin among the characters with special powers in an alternate world. As he once did for Arthur, he again gives crucial advice to the hero in his battle against evil foes. [RHT]

Kuttner, Henry. "The Dark World." *Startling Stories*, 14 (Summer 1946), 9ff. Republished as *The Dark World*. New York: Ace, 1965.

LACKEY, MERCEDES, popular American science-fiction author, has written two short stories that incorporate Arthurian elements. In "The Cup and the Cauldron" (1992), two young women, one a follower of the Goddess, the other a Christian nun, are chosen to become Grail Maidens after they learn to overcome their religious prejudices. In "Once and Future" (1995), an Irish shipyard worker who has just lost his job finds Excalibur and learns that he is a reincarnated King Arthur. Aware of the complexities of modern life with its legal quagmires and smut-seeking tabloids, however, he chooses to sell the sword to a pawnbroker rather than try to save the world. [RHT]

Lackey, Mercedes. "The Cup and the Cauldron." In *Grails: Quests, Visitations, and Other Occurrences*, ed. Richard Gilliam, Martin H. Greenberg, and Edward E. Kramer. Atlanta: Unnameable, 1992. Republished as *Grails: Quests of the Dawn*. New York: Roc/Penguin, 1994, pp. 2–19.

———. "Once and Future." In *Excalibur*, ed. Richard Gilliam, Martin H. Greenberg, and Edward E. Kramer. New York: Warner, 1995, pp. 327–38.

LACY, NORRIS, author of *The Mordred Manuscript* (1994), a story in which Mordred offers to a scribe his own interpretation of the situation at Arthur's court, harshly criticizing Lancelot and Merlin. The latter, he insists, serves as "propaganda advisor," helping to create the popular image of the noble King Arthur. Mordred finally rebels against his father in order to save the lives of those threatened by the latter's grandiose plan of world conquest. [RHT]

Lacy, Norris. *The Mordred Manuscript*. Rochester, N.Y.: Round Table, 1994.

LAGRAVENESE, RICHARD: *see* GILLIAM, TERRY.

LANGHAM, TONY, author of *King Arthur's Mouse* (1988), a lively novel for children. Set in Camelot, it describes the fur-raising adventures of the court's mice, who are terrorized by Morgana's evil cat. One Christmas Eve, two brave mice discover and foil a plot by Morgana and Modred to kill King Arthur. In a seasonably charitable mood, Arthur imposes mere banishment on the offenders, but he remains wholly unaware of the rodents' intervention. [RS]

Langham, Tony. *King Arthur's Mouse*. Illustrated by Dandi. Leeds: Arnold, 1988.

LAWHEAD, STEPHEN R., American author residing in England, added a fourth novel to his Pendragon Cycle some five years after he had ostensibly ended the series with an account of Arthur's life in *Arthur* (1989; *see NAE*, pp. 273–74). *Pendragon* (1994) covers some of the same ground as the previous book, though here Merlin is the narrator and he adds further information about Arthur's early years, complete with portentous marvels. The greater part of the narrative deals with the war against Vandal invaders of Ireland and Britain, which enables Arthur to consolidate the support of the British kings. As in the earlier novels, the author develops his fully conceived fantasy world from early Celtic sources infused with a strong Christian message. [DN]

Lawhead, Stephen R. *Pendragon*. New York: Morrow/AvoNova; Oxford: Lion, 1994.

LECHNER, AUGUSTE, the best-known Austrian author of books for young readers. With her many re-creations of medieval themes (the Nibelungen, Dietrich von Bern, Gudrun, Parzival), she succeeded in influencing the perception of the Middle Ages for young Austrian readers during the 1950s and 1960s. The medieval world as presented by Lechner is unique in certain aspects, as in the presentation of love relationships, which are reduced to a functional minimum. Lechner's view of the world is determined by a conservative Catholic philosophy.

The source for her Parzival narrative (*Parzival*, 1977; published in the 1950s under the title *Das Licht von Montsalvat* ["The Light of Montsalvat"]) is clearly Wolfram's epic. For her later Arthurian novels (*Artus*, 1985; *Iwein*, 1988), she uses sources from Geoffrey to Malory, as she indicates in her concluding commentary. [SSch]

Lechner, Auguste. *Parzival: Für de Jugend erzählt*. Innsbruck, 1977.

———. König Artus. *Die Geschichte von König Artus, seinem geheimnisvollen Ratgeber Merlin und den Rittern der Tafelrunde*. Innsbruck, 1985.

———. *Iwein. Der Ritter mit dem Löwen*. Innsbruck, 1988.

LE DANTEC, JEAN-PIERRE, Breton author of the 1985 French novel *Graal-Romance* ("Grail Romance"). The novel takes place ten years after Arthur's death, when Lancelot and Gautier de Bath, the latter a cleric commissioned by Arthur to write the full story of his reign, come to Brocéliande to visit Merlin and Guenièvre. Viviane, Merlin, and the Queen tell Gautier numerous stories and give him access to documents, and as he tries to separate fact from fiction Gautier interjects his own recollections of a drunken and mad King Arthur, sunk into self-pity at the realization of his failure.

Among Arthur's personal tragedies (and Le Dantec's innovations) is his relationship with Mordret. When the young man, thought to be Arthur's nephew, tries to usurp power, he mortally wounds Arthur; before dying, the latter refers to Mordret as his son. Moved by this revelation, the son tries to embrace Arthur and in so doing impales himself on Excalibur.

Le Dantec offers a peculiar reinterpretation of the Grail. At the beginning of the quest, there had been only the name "Grail," and no one knew what it designated. The notions of cauldron or chalice, of Fisher King and the associations with Joseph of Arimathea, had been added after the fact. At the end, Gautier comes to understand that the Grail was a gnostic myth mixed with Christian beliefs. [NJL]

Le Dantec, Jean-Pierre. *Graal-Romance*. Paris: Michel, 1985.

LEE, TANITH, British fantasy author, turns to Grail legend in her short story "Exalted Hearts" (1992), in which a knight returns, successful after long years on his quest, only to discover that all at court have grown old and the land waste. Ironically, the cup brings no healing, only desolation. [RHT]

Lee, Tanith. "Exalted Hearts." In *Grails: Quests, Visitations, and Other Occurrences*, ed. Richard Gilliam, Martin H. Greenberg, and Edward E. Kramer. Atlanta: Unnameable, 1992. Republished as *Grails: Visitations of the Night*. New York: Roc/Penguin, 1994, pp. 1–7.

LEIGH, JOSEPH, Welsh-born American author of *Illustrations of the Fulfilment of the Prediction of Merlin: Occasioned by the Late Outrageous Attack of the British Ship of War the Leopard on the American Frigate Chesapeake, and the Measures Taken by the President, Supported by the Citizens Thereon*. This 1807 treatise takes the form of a prophecy of Merlin that is interpreted as predicting the attack of the British ship *Leopard* on the American vessel *Chesapeake*, seen by modern historians as a significant event leading to the War of 1812. The "prophecy" is constructed in such a way as to predict dire consequences for Britain unless reparations are made for the attack. [ACL]

Leigh, Joseph. *Illustrations of the Fulfilment of the Prediction of Merlin: Occasioned by the Late Outrageous Attack of the British Ship of War the Leopard on the American Frigate Chesapeake, and the Measures Taken by the President, Supported by the Citizens Thereon*. Portsmouth, N.H., 1807.

LINAWEAVER, BRAD, sets his short story "Under an Appalling Sky" (1992) in an alternate universe where Hitler was not defeated. A Nazi expedition to the Himalayas in search of the Grail finds not only the vessel but a most unwelcome judgment. In "The Other Scabbard" (1995), Merlin tricks a woman of the Little People, who are deeply hostile to humanity, into helping him create an anti-Excalibur that eventually saves England from attack in the far future. [RHT]

Linaweaver, Brad. "Under an Appalling Sky." In *Grails: Quests, Visitations, and Other Occurrences*, ed. Richard Gilliam, Martin H. Greenberg, and Edward E. Kramer. Atlanta: Unnameable, 1992. Republished as *Grails: Visitations of the Night*. New York: Roc/Penguin, 1994, pp. 91–106.

———. "The Other Scabbard." In *Excalibur*, ed. Richard Gilliam, Martin H. Greenberg, and Edward E. Kramer. New York: Warner, 1995, pp. 249–64.

LIND, HELENA, and MICHAEL TAYLOR, German musicians who released a 1991 CD with eleven ballads taken from their major project, *The Magic World of Avalon*. They play with variations of the theme of Avalon, Glastonbury, and "The Spirit of Stone." Additional CDs with script were planned for release. The producer plans to create a full-evening musical from this material. [SSch]

Lind, Helena, and Michael Taylor. "The Magic World of Avalon: The Sound of Eternity." Hamburg, 1991. [CD]

LLORCA, DENIS, contemporary French theater and film director who, at Besançon in 1986, staged an eleven-hour spectacle recounting the quest for the Holy Grail. This theatrical production subsequently served as the basis for Llorca's film *Les Chevaliers de la Table Ronde* ("Knights of the Round Table"). The film was produced in 1989 and released in Paris in November 1990, but it has not had a wide distribution. Critical reaction to the film found it overly long—it runs three hours and fifty minutes—and more theatrical than cinematic. The film recounts the quest for the Grail, the birth of Merlin, the foundation of the Round Table, the coronation of Arthur, the love of Lancelot and Guinevere, the vengeance of Morgana, and the triumphant return of Galahad to the castle of the Fisher King. [KJH]

Review. *Film français*, 2321 (October 16, 1990), 13.

Review. *Revue du cinéma / Image et son*, 465 (November 1990), 29.

Review. *Revue du cinéma / La Saison cinématographique*, 37 (1990), 27.

LOOMIS, RICHARD, author of "The Testing of Cadog" (1989), a humorous short story about St. Cadog, told in the traditional style of the Old Welsh. Arthur, Kei, and Bedwyr ride to the monastery at Llancarfan "to watch Cadog defend his sanctuary of learning and wisdom against the brutish Cynon." The saint repels the raider by placing a curse upon him. [RHT]

Loomis, Richard. "The Testing of Cadog." *The Round Table*, 5 (1989), 12–18.

LOUIS, RENÉ: *see* TRISTAN AND ISOLDE IN MODERN FRENCH VERSIONS.

LUSTBADER, ERIC, popular fantasy author, sets his short story "Lassorio" (1995) in Camelot one hundred years after Arthur's death. On a hunting trip, the local warlord meets Merlin and recovers Excalibur from the lake, but after learning to prize life more than death he rejects the former's invitation to seek the power that once was Arthur's. [RHT]

Lustbader, Eric. "Lassorio." In *Excalibur*, ed. Richard Gilliam, Martin H. Greenberg, and Edward E. Kramer. New York: Warner, 1995, pp. 29–46.

McCARTY, NICK: *see* HUNT, PAUL.

McDOWELL, IAN, in "The Storming Bone" (1991), continued the account of Mordred's life that he began in "Son of the Morning" (*see NAE*, p. 291). Mordred describes how he avenges the murder of his mother by King Lot, magically conjuring up a storm in which his stepfather is killed. [RHT]

McDowell, Ian. "The Storming Bone," *Amazing Stories* (September 1991); rpt. in *The Camelot Chronicles*, ed. Mike Ashley. London: Robinson, 1992, pp. 57–78.

MacGREGOR, ROB, like Martin Caidin, was licensed by Lucasfilm to write novels for a series based on its film character Indiana Jones. His contributions included both *Indiana Jones and the Last Crusade* (1989), a novel based upon the filmscript of Jeffrey Boam (*see NAE*, p. 155), and *Indiana Jones and the Dance of the Giants* (1991), in which the intrepid archaeologist foils the attempt of a would-be dictator to seize the power once wielded by Merlin. After excavating Merlin's dwelling and finding a "golden scroll" supposedly written by him, Indy travels to Stonehenge, where he has a vision of the ancient seer himself. (*See also* CAIDIN, MARTIN.) [RHT]

MacGreger, Rob. *Indiana Jones and the Last Crusade*. New York: Ballantine, 1989.
———. *Indiana Jones and the Dance of the Giants*. New York: Bantam, 1991.

McKENNITT, LOREENA, Canadian musician, arranger, and singer, who has found inspiration in Celtic music. Her fourth album, *The Visit* (1991), voted Best Roots/Traditional album at the Juno Awards (Canadian equivalent of the Grammy Awards), includes "The Lady of Shalott," an abbreviated version of Tennyson's poem, for which McKennitt composed a haunting musical arrangement. [JTG]

McKennitt, Loreena. *The Visit*. Stratford, Ont.: Quinlan Road, 1991. [CD]

McKENZIE, NANCY, acknowledged the influence upon her historical novels *The Child Queen* (1994) and *The High Queen* (1995) of the vision of fifth-century Britain found in Mary Stewart's Arthurian fiction (*see NAE*, p. 432), particularly for her treatment of Merlin and Niniane and of Morgause and her sons. In the first novel, Guinevere tells the story of her early life: her childhood riding across the hills of northern Wales; her marriage to King Arthur, which evokes the jealous fury of Elaine, her cousin and companion; the love that binds her, Arthur, and Lancelot; and finally her betrayal by Elaine, who helps Melwas abduct the Queen, then tricks Lancelot into marriage.

In the second novel, Guinevere brings her story to its tragic conclusion, wrought by a combination of misfortune, the selfish ambition of various rulers, and the irresponsible behavior of Arthur's own kindred. Mordred proves a worthy heir to Arthur, as well as a fervent admirer of both the King and the Queen, but his mother, Morgause, and his turbulent half-brothers (except Gareth) show an arrogant disregard for the laws of civilized conduct. The strife that they and others foment finally dooms Arthur's kingdom, despite the conciliatory efforts of his most trusted advisers, particularly Guinevere herself. Although guilt-ridden by her failure to produce an heir, the queen is deeply loved by her husband, to whom she provides comfort amid the stress of rule. [RHT]

McKenzie, Nancy. *The Child Queen: The Tale of Guinevere and King Arthur*. New York: Del Rey/Ballantine, 1994.
———. *The High Queen: The Tale of Guinevere and King Arthur Continues*. New York: Del Rey/Ballantine, 1995.

MARSHALL, LAURA: *see* SERVICE, PAMELA F.

MARY, ANDRÉ: *see* TRISTAN AND ISOLDE IN MODERN FRENCH VERSIONS.

MATTHEWS, CAITLIN, and JOHN MATTHEWS, English authors who have individually written numerous critical and creative Arthurian works, usually from an esoteric perspective. Together, they produced *The*

Arthurian Book of Days (1990), in which condensed versions of traditional Arthurian stories are supplied for each day of the year. The book is beautifully illustrated from medieval manuscripts. [RHT]

Matthews, Caitlin, and John Matthews. *The Arthurian Book of Days*. New York: Macmillan, 1990.

MAYHAR, ARDATH, in her short story "The Weapon" (1995), describes how an engineer working for a shopping-mall developer unearths Excalibur. Transported back in time, he hands over to King Arthur both the sword and the gold medallion that belongs to his employer, thereby ensuring that civilization will show more care for the environment. [RHT]

Mayhar, Ardath. "The Weapon." In *Excalibur*, ed. Richard Gilliam, Martin H. Greenberg, and Edward E. Kramer. New York: Warner, 1995, pp. 307–17.

MERLIN: *see* HUNT, PAUL.

MIDDLETON, HAYDN, an English writer, draws upon the Tarot symbol of the Tower, Charles Williams's poem "Mount Badon," and the story of Vortigern, Rowena, and Merlin, in his novel *The Collapsing Castle* (1990). This material is introduced into an account of infidelity in a modern marriage. Gradually, however, the mythic and the real worlds converge in Oxford, culminating in horrific death and destruction, as the ancient curse of the Britons against their invaders is finally fulfilled during the May Day celebration in front of Magdalen Tower. [RHT]

Middleton, Haydn. *The Collapsing Castle*. London: Hamilton, 1990.

MILLER, ARTHUR MAXIMILIAN (1901–1992), German writer of Swabian dialect stories and historical novels. In 1982, he published the play *Der Gral* ("The Grail"), a lofty blending of Wolfram's courtly epic *Parzival* and Wagner's opera *Parzifal*. Miller shows the path of Percival, chosen and enigmatic, through human guilt and sin to religious purification. The hero reaches mercy and glory through his Grail quest, triumphing over ignorance, doubt, and fear by his qualities of learning, perseverance, and humility. Miller uses the Perceval figure to show that the spiritual elevation that marks Wolfram's and Wagner's Percival is considered a timeless model for the redemption of humankind through the saving power of the Grail. [WW]

Miller, Arthur Maximilian. *Der Gral*. Kempten: Allgäuer Zeitundsverlag, 1982.

MILLER, RANDY, transposes elements of Arthurian legend to the setting of modern baseball when a scout named Oslin (Merlin) discovers a phenomenally talented player named Arturo Reyes and gives him a special bat (Excalibur) in the short story "The Scout, the Slugger and the Stripper" (1995). Arturo, however, rejects his mentor's guidance when he falls in love. [RHT]

Miller, Randy. "The Scout, the Slugger and the Stripper." In *Excalibur*, ed. Richard Gilliam, Martin H. Greenberg, and Edward E. Kramer. New York: Warner, 1995, pp. 289–305.

MNOOKIN, WENDY, author of *Guenever Speaks* (1991), a sequence of thirty-one lyric poems. Beginning with her journey to Camelot to marry Arthur and ending with her last days among the nuns at Almesbury, the poems expand upon incidents in the Queen's life as portrayed in Malory. She speaks of Arthur's insensitivity to her needs as a woman and of her passionate love for Lancelot. [RHT]

Mnookin, Wendy. *Guenever Speaks*. Illustrated by Deborah Davidson. Rochester, N.Y.: Round Table, 1991.

MOERMAN, ERNST: *see* TRISTAN AND ISOLDE IN MODERN FRENCH VERSIONS.

MOORE, C.L.: *see* KUTTNER, HENRY.

MORAES, DOM, Indian author, composed "Merlin," a sequence of ten short poems. Merlin, who has awakened in the twentieth century, narrates how he has fulfilled Arthur's prophecy that he would return at the "worst time" in human history. His ancient magic is no longer effective in a modern world that is poisoned by pollution. Publicly scorned as a crazy mendicant, he longs for his lost tomb but is condemned to endless suffering on earth. [RS]

Moraes, Dom. "Merlin." In *Collected Poems 1957–1987*. Harmondsworth: Penguin, 1987.

MUENCH, JAMES F., author of "Arthur" (1989), a short story in which Arthur prepares for and wins the Battle of Badon Hill against the Saxons. In this curious mixture of historical fiction and T.H. White–influenced comedy, the characters include such traditional medieval figures as Launcelot, Tristram, and Pellinore. [DN]

Muench, James F. "Arthur." *Arthurian Interpretations*, 4 (Fall 1989), 86–102.

MÜLLER, WALTER, Austrian author who wrote for the Salzburg Landestheater the highly successful play *Ein Parzival* (premiere September 29, 1994). Drawing on Wolfram's epic, it is centered on the topics of growing up and of violence. [WW]

Müller, Ulrich, and Michael Westreicher. "'Am Anfang war Gewalt': 'Ein Parzival' von Walther Müller" (1994). In *"bickelwort" und "wildiu maere": Festschrift für Eberhard Nellmann*, ed. Dorothe Lindemann et al. Stuttgart: Heinz, 1995, pp. 167–83.

MURDOCH, IRIS, though born in Dublin, has lived most of her life in England. She has written works of philosophy, as well as poetry, plays, and novels—most recently *The Green Knight* (1993), in which the lives of a group of people living in contemporary London are transformed by an encounter with a mysterious stranger who intrudes unexpectedly into their midst. There are echoes of Arthurian figures and motifs, including the quest for the Holy Grail and the Arthur-Guenevere-Lancelot love triangle; the strongest echoes, however, are with those found in the fourteenth-century poem *Sir Gawain and the Green Knight*. Murdoch adapts this material freely, as one of her characters recognizes: "Pieces of the story are there, but aren't they somehow jumbled up and all the wrong way round? . . . It isn't really like the poem, yet it is too." [RHT]

Murdoch, Iris. *The Green Knight*. New York: Viking Penguin, 1993.

MURPHY, WARREN: *see* COCHRAN, MOLLY.

MURRAY, DOUG, in his short story "The Unholy" (1994), describes the attempt of Morganna to wield the power of the Unholy Grail, the evil counterpart of the Holy Vessel, against Arthur through his illegitimate son Giles. The plot fails, but the chalice that "dirties whatever it touches" sparks the fatal attraction between Lancelot and Guinevere. [RHT]

Murray, Doug. "The Unholy." In *Grails: Visitations of the Night*, ed. Richard Gilliam, Martin H. Greenberg, and Edward E. Kramer. New York: Roc/Penguin, 1994, pp. 30–51.

NICHOLSON, WILLIAM: *see* ZUCKER, JERRY.

NICOLL, GREGORY, in his short story "From Camelot to Deadwood" (1992), offers an account of how bandits steal the Grail from a traveling missionary during a stagecoach robbery and how these events provide the basis for Mark Twain's *Connecticut Yankee in King Arthur's Court*. [RHT]

Nicoll, Gregory. "From Camelot to Deadwood." In *Grails: Quests, Visitations, and Other Occurrences*, ed. Richard Gilliam, Martin H. Greenberg, and Edward E. Kramer. Atlanta: Unnameable, 1992. Republished as *Grails: Visitations of the Night*. New York: Roc/Penguin, 1994, pp. 81–90.

NOGARE, PIERRE DALLE: *see* TRISTAN AND ISOLDE IN MODERN FRENCH VERSIONS.

NORTON, ANDRE, who has made use of Arthurian legend throughout her career (*see NAE*, p. 345), has written "That Which Overfloweth" (1992), a short story about the Grail brought to Glastonbury by Joseph of Arimathea. Raiders pillage the shrine, but they overlook the simple earthen cup that is the greatest treasure of all, for "It cleanses evil." [RHT]

Norton, Andre. "That Which Overfloweth." In *Grails: Quests, Visitations, and Other Occurrences*, ed. Richard Gilliam, Martin H. Greenberg, and Edward E. Kramer. Atlanta: Unnameable, 1992. Republished as *Grails: Quests of the Dawn*. New York: Roc/Penguin, 1994, pp. 20–26.

NYE, JODY LYNN, in her short story "Sword Practice" (1995), explores the difficult learning process that the newly crowned Arthur, but twelve years old, must go through as he strives to win the respect of more experienced leaders, particularly King Lot of Lothian. [RHT]

Nye, Jody Lynn. "Sword Practice." In *Excalibur*, ed. Richard Gilliam, Martin H. Greenberg, and Edward E. Kramer. New York: Warner, 1995, pp. 339–61.

OUTSIDE TIME: *see* HUMPHREYS, SION.

PARISI, OSVALDO: *see* WIEDENMANN, REINHOLD.

PAUPHILET, ALBERT, French author of *La Roue des fortunes royales, ou La Gloire d'Artus Empereur de Bretagne* ("The Wheel of Royal Fortunes, or The Glory of Arthur, Emperor of Britain"). This 1977 work by a distinguished medievalist is a retelling of the Arthurian story drawn primarily from the French *Mort Artu*. Pauphilet's purpose, however, was to provide a balanced account not only of Arthur's fall but also of his rise, conquests, and glory; to that end, he borrowed also from Wace and the Modena *Perceval*, and he included an epilogue drawn from the Welsh *Dream of Rhonabwy*. [NJL]

Pauphilet, Albert. *La Roue des fortunes royales, ou La Gloire d'Artus Empereur de Bretagne*. Alfortville: Piazza, 1977.

PAXSON, DIANA L., American author, deals with aspects of Arthurian legend in several works. *The White Raven* (1988) is a novel about the turbulent love between Drustan and Esseilte (Tristan and Isolde), narrated by Branwen, cousin of the Esseilte and daughter of the Morholt. Taking the place of Esseilte on her wedding night, Branwen enters into the "Great Marriage" with Marc'h, a mystical union between the ruler and the land. As a consequence, she falls in love with the king, who is here portrayed as noble in character, but she conceals her feelings until after her cousin's death.

"The Feast of the Fisher King" (1992) is a masque in verse, based upon the account of Perceval's visit to the Grail Castle as given by Chrétien de Troyes. It was first created for performance at the Mythopoeic Conference in 1981.

"The God-Sword" (1995) is a short story about Excalibur, a holy sword brought to Britain by Sarmatian auxiliaries of the Roman army (*see NAE*, pp. 396-97). With the aid of a druid's daughter and the god he serves, the warrior-priest charged with its custody preserves the sword from tribesmen raiding across Hadrian's Wall after the withdrawal of the legions. Dying, he is given a vision of their descendants, culminating in Arthur, who is destined to wield the weapon. [RHT]

Paxson, Diana L. *The White Raven*. New York: Morrow, 1988.

———. "The Feast of the Fisher King: A Masque in Verse (with narrative inclusions)." In *Grails: Quests, Visitations, and Other Occurrences*, ed. Richard Gilliam, Martin H. Greenberg, and Edward E. Kramer. Atlanta: Unnameable, 1992. Republished as *Grails: Quests of the Dawn*. New York: Roc/Penguin, 1994, pp. 36–59.

———. "The God-Sword." In *Excalibur*, ed. Richard Gilliam, Martin H. Greenberg, and Edward E. Kramer. New York: Warner, 1995, pp. 3–28.

PEMBERTON, CHARLES: *see* APSLEY, BRENDA.

PÉREZ GALDÓS, BENITO (1843–1920), Spanish novelist, playwright, and journalist. His last novel, *Tristana* (1892), records the eponymous heroine's struggle to transcend the boundaries that nineteenth-century society set for women. Literary allusions abound, both to high romance (Don Juan, Don Quixote, and Tristan) and to popular genres (farce, *fabliau*, *folletín*). Tristana, her lover Horacio, and her seducer/guardian Don Lope initially recall the Tristan/Isolde/Mark triangle, but the myth is cruelly subverted by the intrusion of reality: Horacio is uncomfortable with Tristana's artistic aspirations, and a temporary separation causes him to lose interest in their idyll even before Tristana contracts an illness that leads to the amputation of a leg—and of her dream of independence. Tristana eventually consents to marry Don Lope and to settle into a life of comfortable domesticity. Luis Buñuel's film *Tristana* (1970) considerably alters the novel's tone and emphasis. [JTG]

Grimbert, Joan. "Galdós's *Tristana* as a Subversion of the Tristan Legend." *Anales Galdosianos*. [Forthcoming.]

Pérez Galdós, Benito. *Tristana*. In *Obras completas*, ed. Federico C. Sainz de Robles. 6 vols. Madrid: Aguilar, 1965, Vol. 5, pp. 1541–1612.

PHELPS, ELIZABETH STUART (1844–1911), American author, was born Mary Gray Phelps but later took her mother's name. Phelps wrote three stories in which she translates Arthurian characters into a nineteenth-century setting. Her Lady of Shalott (in "The Lady of Shalott," 1879) is a sickly seventeen-year-old girl living in a slum and supported by a sister who earns a poverty wage doing piecework. When the mirror through which she views the world is broken by street urchins throwing rocks, she succumbs to her harsh environment and dies. Phelps's Galahad (in "The Christmas of Sir Galahad," 1871) is a man who, despite his love for another woman, remains faithful to his wife though she is "crazy" and "takes opium" and though she only occasionally returns to his home. Not until after her death does he marry, on Christmas Day, the woman he loves. Phelps's Arthur, Guenever, and Launcelot (in "The True Story of Guenever," 1879) are a carpenter, his wife, and a boarder they take in. In the last of these stories, the narrator says, "I rebel against the story" because she "cannot bear to leave her [Guenever] there upon the convent floor." She redeems Guenever by suggesting that her running off with Launcelot occurs in a dream induced when the Queen mistakenly takes laudanum for a toothache. Thus, she can wake, morally unblemished, to a loving Arthur.

In 1891, Phelps also published three short poems on the Arthurian characters treated in her stories: "Elaine and Elaine" presents a cryptic picture of Elaine, who keeps her "secrets sweet" even in death; "Guinevere" offers a rereading of Tennyson in which Guinevere's "one short song" is meant to alter the traditional view of the guilty Queen; and "The Terrible Test" suggests that it is "Enough, to know that once [i.e., in the person of Christ] the clay / Hath worn the features of the God," the implication being that Galahad, so pure that he had "no human pulses," is less than ideal because less than human. [ACL]

Phelps, Elizabeth Stuart. "The Christmas of Sir Galahad." *Independent*, 23 (December 7, 1871), 1.

———. "The Lady of Shalott" and "The True Story of Guenever." In *Sealed Orders*, 1879; rpt. New York: Garrett, 1969, pp. 48–64; 65–80.

———. "Elaine and Elaine," "Guinevere," and "The Terrible Test." Boston: Houghton Mifflin, 1891, pp. 77–78, 59–63, 92–93.

PHILATELY. On March 10, 1992, to mark the centenary of the death of Alfred, Lord Tennyson, the British Post Office (*see NAE*, pp. 359–60) issued a set of four stamps. Designed by Irene Von Treskow, they feature portraits of the poet at different stages of his life, superimposed upon paintings by well-known Victorian artists illustrating scenes from his poems. Two of these are Arthurian: *The Beguiling of Merlin* by Sir Edward Burne-Jones, which illustrates "Merlin and Vivien" (24 pence), and *"I am half sick of shadows," said The Lady of Shalott* by John William Waterhouse, which illustrates "The Lady of Shalott" (33 pence).

A recent set of stamps from Grenada, issued to celebrate the work of UNICEF, featured figures from children's stories. King Arthur in full plate armor, mounted on horseback, appears on the half-cent and 25-cent stamps.

Of related interest is a set of four stamps issued by the British Post Office on June 15, 1993, to commemorate the Roman invasion of Britain 1,950 years earlier. Designed by John Gibbs, they display the heads of the emperor Claudius (24 pence), the emperor Hadrian (28 pence), the goddess Roma (33 pence), and Christ (39 pence). [RHT]

Shackleton, Tim. "Roman Britain." In *Royal Mail Special Stamps, 10.* London: Royal Mail, 1993, pp. 23–25.

"Tennyson." *British Philatelic Bulletin*, 29.6 (February 1992), 123–26.

POWELL, PERRY EDWARDS: *see* YOUTH GROUPS, ARTHURIAN.

POWERS, TIM, author (*see NAE*, p. 367) of the 1992 *Last Call*, a fantasy/suspense novel in which the ancient renewal of the reign of the goddess-queen and her consort, the young king who replaces the old, is re-enacted in Las Vegas among a group of gamblers whose destinies are determined by a Tarot card game. The protagonist is explicitly identified with the Fisher King, and events, characters, and imagery echo those of Arthurian and Grail literature throughout. [DN]

Powers, Tim. *Last Call*. New York: Morrow, 1992.

RECHEIS, KÄTHE, a well-known Austrian author of books for young readers. In 1974, she published an Arthurian novel, *König Arthur und die Ritter der Tafelrunde* ("King Arthur and the Knights of the Round Table"), which is strongly in the tradition of Malory. She makes significant cuts, however, and focuses as a narrator on Arthur, Parcifal, Galahad, Gawain, Erek, and Iwein. In the latter case, she closely follows the literary tradition of Hartmann von Aue. [SSch]

Recheis, Käthe. *König Arthur und die Ritter der Tafelrunde*. Munich: dtv, 1974.

Schmidt, Siegrid, *Mittelhochdeutsche Epenstoffe in der deutschsprachigen Literatur nach 1945*. Göppingen: Kümmerle, 1989.

RESNICK, LAURA, author of "A Fleeting Wisp of Glory," a short story in an anthology of speculative fiction about the Kennedy family. In a postnuclear future, an old man passes on to a young boy the myth of the king who will return, blending traditional elements of the Arthurian legend with events and characters of President John F. Kennedy's era. (*See also* TURTLEDOVE, HARRY.) [DN]

Resnick, Laura. "A Fleeting Wisp of Glory." In *Alternate Kennedys*, ed. Mike Resnick. New York: Tor, 1992.

REZABECK, KARL: *see* TRÉHORENTEUC.

RHEINISCHE MERLIN ("The Rhenish Merlin"), the name given to a Ripuarian text of 324 lines that has been dated to 1330–1350. The fragment is a strange combination of material from the lives of the prophet Merlin and a local Rhenish saint (never canonized), Lüthild (Lüfthildis). There is no break in the text between the statements that Merlin died without flaw only a short time ago (ll. 230–32) and that much can be told about Christ, who revealed himself in the life of a young girl, St. Lüthild (ll. 233–39). Merlin is the type of the *puer senex*, characterized by wisdom and the powers of prophecy, which he has received from Christ. He is depicted as an anchorite, who can be captured only by a pure maiden and whose life is an imitation of Christ in that he submits to trials, insults, and even threats to his life. The fragment may be said to transmit a hagiographic version of Merlin's life. If *Der rheinische Merlin* is understood as sacred legend, the life of Merlin complements the *vita* of Lüthild, for in both, the workings of Christ are revealed and both are persecuted, Merlin for his prophetic gifts, Lüthild for her good deeds. [MEK]

Beckers, Hartmut, ed. *Der rheinische Merlin: Text, Übersetzung, Untersuchungen der "Merlin" und "Lüthild"-Fragmente*. Paderborn: Schöningh, 1991, pp. 23–54. [Facsimile and critical edition, modern German translation.]

Bauer, G., et al. "Der historische Hintergrund des 'Rheinischen Merlin.' Exkurs: Das Drachensymbol als englisches Herrschaftszeichen." "Eine rheinische Merlin-Legende?—

Überlegungen zur literarischen Einordnung. Exkurs: Der institutionalisierte Funktionstyp 'Legende.'" In Beckers, *Der rheinische Merlin* [see previous entry], pp. 94–146.

RICE, ROBERT, author of the historical novel *The Last Pendragon* (1991), in which Bedwyr, the last of Arthur's companions, reluctantly joins forces with the son of Medraut to retake Camelot (Cadbury hill fort) from the Saxons. [DN]

Rice, Robert. *The Last Pendragon*. New York: Walker, 1991.

RICHARDS, LAURA E. (1850–1943), a prolific children's writer, created the operetta "Good King Arthur" (1916). She uses popular airs like "The Campbells Are Coming!" to present the nursery rhyme "When Good King Arthur Ruled This Land." Arthur steals the barley, Guinever makes the bag pudding, and the court enjoys the dessert. This operetta was first performed at the summer camp that the Richards ran in Maine. [HT]

Richards, Laura E. "Good King Arthur." In *Fairy Operettas*. Boston: Little, Brown, 1916, pp. 71–79.

ROBERTS, THEODORE GOODRIDGE (1877-1953), wrote a series of humorous short stories about Sir Dinadan in the early 1950s (*see NAE*, p. 387); he also planned a novel about the knight's early life, though he completed only a draft of the opening chapter. This chapter, published as "Mountainy Madness" (1992), describes an encounter between a love-struck Dinadan, a prophetic Merlin, and some superstitious mountain men. [RHT]

Roberts, Theodore Goodridge. "Mountainy Madness." In *The Camelot Chronicles*, ed. Mike Ashley. London: Robinson, 1992, pp. 409–18.

SABERHAGEN, FRED, author of *Dominion* (*see NAE*, p. 393), returned to Arthurian legend in *Merlin's Bones* (1995). In this playful fantasy novel, Merlin's bones are the source of great power sought, for their own often obscure purposes, by the competing forces of the Fisher King, Morgan le Fay, Mordred, and Woden. Merlin's spirit, meanwhile, has plans of its own to return and rebuild Camelot in the otherworld of Logres. The search involves time travel, as characters move from the twenty-first century to the time of Vortigern, though most of the action takes place in the years soon after the fall of Camelot. In the process, some, notably Vivian and Elaine, find themselves unexpectedly taking on the traditional roles of their Arthurian predecessors. [RHT]

Saberhagen, Fred. *Merlin's Bones*. New York: Tor, 1995.

SAMPSON, FAY, in 1991 concluded her fantasy series Daughter of Tintagel (*see NAE*, p. 396). Sampson follows the career of Morgan the Fay, making use of incidents from Malory transposed to a Dark Age setting. *Black Smith's Telling* (1990) covers the period from Morgan's arrival in Rheged as Urien's bride until the birth of Modred; *Taliesin's Telling* (1991) brings the story to its conclusion at the Battle of Camlann. The conflict between Arthur and his sisters stems largely from his reluctance to share power with them. The union of the two forces in the realm, male and female, is symbolized by the sword Caliburn and its magical scabbard. Morgan's reclaiming of the scabbard reflects the divisions and rivalry that ultimately destroy the realm, despite her own spasmodic efforts to bring about a reconciliation with her brother.

Although the narrative was brought to an end in *Taliesin's Telling*, Sampson's *Herself* (1992) reconsiders the main events of the first four books, but this time from the point of view of Morgan le Fay. She admits that the contradictions in her love-hate relationship with Arthur are partly her own fault but lays most of the blame on her half-brother's unwillingness to share love and power with her. Each chapter is preceded by her ironic comments upon how she is treated by different authors throughout Arthurian tradition. [RHT]

Sampson, Faye. *Black Smith's Telling*. London: Headline, 1990.
———. *Herself*. London: Headline, 1992.
———. *Taliesin's Telling*. London: Headline, 1991.

SCARBOROUGH, ELIZABETH ANN, author of "The Camelot Connection" (1988; *see NAE*, p. 401), wrote another humorous short story, "The Queen's Cat's Tale" (1991). Guinevere's cat reveals not only that Mordred's plot to trap Lancelot in her mistress's bedchamber was orchestrated by Morgan le Fay, who had taken on the shape of a cat to work her spells at court unobserved, but that the seemingly invulnerable Lancelot had an embarrassing weakness: he was extremely allergic to cats. [RHT]

Scarborough, Elizabeth Ann. "The Queen's Cat's Tale." In *Catfantastic II*, ed. Andre Norton and Martin H. Greenberg. New York: DAW, 1991, pp. 235–52.

SCHUTTING, JULIAN, Austrian novelist of the 1994 *Gralslicht* ("Grail's Light"), "a lyrical opera for reading." In a railway car in the late nineteenth century, three persons called P(arsifal), G (Don Giovanni), and K(undry) discuss and mix medieval and modern topics, ending with modern fascism; subjects include the medieval Grail story and Wagner. [UM]

Schutting, Julian. *Gralslicht: Ein Theater-Libretto*. Salzburg: Residenz, 1994.

SCHWEITZER, DARRELL, author of both scholarly and creative works, several of which include Arthurian elements. In "Midnight, Moonlight, and the Secret of the Sea" (1981), first published as "The Faces of Midnight" (1981), both the Maimed King and the Wasteland appear (*see NAE*, pp. 354 and 506); "L'Envoi" (1981) briefly describes an encounter of a knight from a later era with three of Arthur's knights, still seeking the Holy Grail; "Told by Moonlight" (1992) recounts a meeting between the remorseful ghosts of Mordred and Lancelot; in "The Epilogue of the Sword" (1995), an aged Lancelot is summoned by the spirit of Guinevere from the monastery to which he has retired to pray for his sins, and given Excalibur by the three queens so that he may save Constantine and the Britons from defeat and death at the hands of the Saxons. [RHT]

Schweitzer, Darrell. "The Faces of Midnight." In *Distant Worlds* (1981). Revised as "Midnight, Moonlight, and the Secret of the Sea." In *We Are All Legends*. Virginia Beach, Va.: Donning/Starblaze, 1981, pp. 171–86.

———. "L'Envoi." In *Nightflights (Myrddin #5)* (1981). Revised in *We Are All Legends*. Virginia Beach, Va.: Donning/Starblaze, 1981, pp. 187–89.

———. "Told by Moonlight." In *The Camelot Chronicles*, ed. Mike Ashley. London: Robinson, 1992, pp. 374–79.

———. "The Epilogue of the Sword." In *Excalibur*, ed. Richard Gilliam, Martin H. Greenberg, and Edward E. Kramer. New York: Warner, 1995, pp. 459–70.

SCIESZKA, JON, author of *Knights of the Kitchen Table* (1991), a short illustrated book in his humorous Time Warp Trio series for younger children. Three young American boys travel back in time to the court of King Arthur. After defeating the dreaded Black Knight, they save Camelot from a giant and a dragon. [RHT]

Scieszka, Jon. *Knights of the Kitchen Table*. Illustrated by Lane Smith. New York: Viking Penguin, 1991.

SCOTT, LESLEY: *see* APSLEY, BRENDA.

SEAVIEW KNIGHTS: *see* KURTI, RICHARD.

SERVICE, PAMELA F., returned to Arthurian legend (*see NAE*, p. 414) to recount the youth of Merlin in a children's book brightly illustrated by Laura Marshall. *Wizard of Wind and Rock* (1990) begins with "Monk Geoffrey" (of Monmouth) hunched over his desk. After this acknowledgment of her sources, Service describes how Merlin comes by his name and discovers his magical powers during a lonely boyhood. These powers are tested when he faces an enraged Vortigern, thwarted by a sinking fortress. While the story is exciting and dangerous, pictures of sympathetic animals ameliorate the loneliness and fear of Merlin. Likewise, exaggerated facial features add humor when Merlin overcomes the threat of death and asserts his control over prophecy. [HT]

Service, Pamela. *Wizard of Wind and Rock*. Illustrated by Laura Marshall. New York: Atheneum, 1990.

SHECKLEY, ROBERT: *see* ZELAZNY, ROGER.

SHWARTZ, SUSAN, author of novels and short stories that include Arthurian elements (*see NAE*, pp. 417–18), returns to Arthurian legend in *The Grail of Hearts* (1992). Based upon Wagner's *Parsifal*, this account of the legend of the Holy Grail is told primarily from the point of view of Kundry, who is a variant of the Wandering Jew. Cursed to wander the earth without rest for laughing at Christ on the Cross, she falls under the power of the evil sorcerer Klingsor, at whose command she seduces and betrays Amfortas, the Fisher King. Despite bitter regret for her sins, Kundry, like Amfortas, is unable to overcome the pride and despair that bar her from true repentance. She must suffer at great length, reliving the events leading up to the Crucifixion, witnessing the anguish of Amfortas, whom she has grown to love, and being rejected by Parsifal, before she finally attains redemption and release in death.

In the short story "Troubled Waters" (1995), Niviene, the Lady of the Lake, angered at the destructive folly of men that has culminated in the ruin of Camlann, sets off for Avalon, determined to end the cycle of senseless suffering by slaying Arthur. She is dissuaded by Morgan le Fay, who argues that the hope of a better world makes the pain and sacrifice worthwhile. [RHT]

Shwartz, Susan. *The Grail of Hearts*. New York: Tor, 1992.

———. "Troubled Waters." In *Excalibur*, ed. Richard Gilliam, Martin H. Greenberg, and Edward E. Kramer. New York: Warner, 1995, pp. 399–425.

SKINNER, MARTYN, author of *Merlin* (1951) and *The Return of Arthur* (1955–1956; *see NAE*, p. 423), also wrote and published anonymously *Sir Elfadore and Mabyna* (1935), a poem written in a style that foreshadows his later Arthurian works. It is the story of the rescue of two fairies from Avalon, also called Elfland: Mabyna, who is kidnaped by a gnome, and Elfadore, her rescuer, who is said to be superior to Lancelot. Aside from the setting, the Arthurian content consists of allusions to Camelot, Arthurian knights, and the Grail quest. [ACL]

Skinner, Martyn. *Sir Elfadore and Mabyna: A Poem in Four Cantos*. Oxford: Printed for the Author, 1935.

SMITH, L(ISA) J., includes Morgana Shee as a mighty sorceress whom four California youngsters must rescue in order to save their world from invasion from the otherworld in *The Night of the Solstice* (1987). [RHT]

Smith, L.J. *The Night of the Solstice.* New York: Macmillan, 1987; Rpt. New York: HarperCollins, 1993.

SMITH, ROSAMOND (pseudonym of Joyce Carol Oates), American author of psychological suspense novels, including *You Can't Catch Me* (1995), a convoluted version of the Tristan legend. When Tristram Heade, a reclusive bibliophile, arrives in Philadelphia to visit antiquarian bookstores, his striking resemblance to one Angus T. Markham brings him into contact with a beautiful young woman, Fleur, with whom he is instantly smitten. Vowing eternal love, she persuades him to rescue her from an unhappy marriage to a prominent philanthropist, Otto Grunwald, a misogynist who collects wives and murders them once he tires of them. When Tristram's attempt to kill Otto is aborted, it is Otto's nephew Hans who succeeds—and who collects the prize (Fleur). Tristram realizes he has been set up by the young lovers when he sees a photograph of them at a benefit performance of *Tristan und Isolde*. More disturbing still is the protagonist's increasing identification with Markham, who vanished the day Tristram arrived in Philadelphia and whose past conduct with women appears to have been as perverted as Otto's. [JTG]

Smith, Rosamond. *Your Can't Catch Me.* New York: Dutton, 1995.

SNEYD, STEVE, British author of two chapbooks of Arthurian verse, *The Rex Quondam File* (1976) and *What Time Has Use For: Arthurian Poems* (1992). The poems of the former generally see the legend from an ironic perspective or use it to comment on the modern world. The 1992 poems make use of the Celtic background of the legends and links between Arthurian myth and historical fact.

In the poem "A Time of Buried Questioning" (1993), Sneyd combines popular and topographical traditions and literary allusions to present an Arthur who is both a historical and a mythic figure. In the author's own words, "the mortal Arthur" is a "human equivalent of the 'lightning flash' of Excalibur (and in a sense of poetry itself)." [ACL]

Sneyd, Steve. *The Rex Quondam File: 13 Poems on Arthurian Themes.* Norfolk: Excello and Bollard, 1976.

———. "A Time of Buried Questioning." In *A Round Table of Contemporary Arthurian Poetry*, ed. Barbara Tepa Lupack and Alan Lupack. Rochester, N.Y.: Round Table, 1993, pp. 35–42.

———. *What Time Has Use For: Arthurian Poems.* Stamford, Lincolnshire: K.T., 1992.

SOMTOW, S.P. (pseudonym of Somtow Sucharitkul), Thai writer, brings Perceval, who has "traversed the burning desert of time itself," to a remote Thai village in his short story "The Steel American" (1992). In this island of peace amid the wasteland of brutal war, the knight finds the Grail and sexual fulfillment in the arms of the beautiful village shaman. [RHT]

Somtow, S.P. "The Steel American." In *Grails: Quests, Visitations, and Other Occurrences*, ed. Richard Gilliam, Martin H. Greenberg, and Edward E. Kramer. Atlanta: Unnameable, 1992. Republished as *Grails: Visitations of the Night.* New York: Roc/Penguin, 1994, pp. 107–25.

STAFFORD, GREG, is the president of Chaosium, Inc., for which he has designed *King Arthur's Knights* (1978), a board game in which the player tries to prove himself worthy of joining the Round Table, and *King Arthur Pendragon* (1985), the popular role-playing game set in Arthur's kingdom. For the latter, he provided new editions in 1988 and 1993; he compiled five game supplements, *The Pendragon Campaign* (1985), *Noble's Book* (1986), *King Arthur Pendragon* (1990), *Knights Adventurous* (1990), and *The Boy King* (1991); and he co-authored three adventure modules, *Tournament of Dreams* (1987), *Savage Mountains* (1991), and *Blood and Lust* (1991). He also designed *Prince Valiant, the Storytelling Game* (1989), based upon the comic strip created by Hal Foster (*see NAE*, pp. 97–98), and another board game, *Merlin* (1980), for Heritage USA. (*See also* GAMES.) [RHT]

Stafford, Greg. *King Arthur's Knights.* Albany, Calif.: Chaosium, 1978.

———. *King Arthur Pendragon.* Albany, Calif.: Chaosium, 1985.

———. *Prince Valiant, the Storytelling Game.* Albany, Calif.: Chaosium, 1989.

STRICKLAND, BRAD, in his short story "The Sword in the Net" (1995), describes how a fifteen-year-old hacker named Arthur Armour seizes control of all government computers using a Merlin computer with Roundtable modem. [RHT]

Strickland, Brad. "The Sword in the Net." In *Excalibur*, ed. Richard Gilliam, Martin H. Greenberg, and Edward E. Kramer. New York: Warner, 1995, pp. 319–23.

STURDZA, GRIGORI: *see* TRISTAN AND ISOLDE IN MODERN FRENCH VERSIONS.

STUTTS, ROBERT E., author of a short story and three poems on Arthurian legend. The story, "On the Borders of the Green" (1991), describes an encounter of a daughter of

Guinevere and Arthur with her half-brother Medraut, who is wracked by guilt at his incestuous origins; in "White Moon's Daughter" (1991), Guinevere wonders whether her overly sheltered life left her unprepared for her responsibilities as queen; "Passant D'Arthur" (1993) and "Fath Mo Dhuilichinn" (1993) both describe Arthur's passing, the former from Arthur's point of view, the latter from Morgan's. [RHT]

Stutts, Robert E. "On the Borders of the Green" and "White Moon's Daughter." *Snow Island Review*, 1.1 (Spring 1991), 19–24, 4–6.

———. "Fath Mo Dhuilichinn" and "Passant D'Arthur." In *A Round Table of Contemporary Arthurian Poetry*, ed. Barbara Tepa Lupack and Alan Lupack. Rochester, N.Y.: Round Table, 1993, pp. 44 and 43.

SUTCLIFF, ROSEMARY (1920–1992), author of several books on the Arthurian legend, published *The Shining Company* (1990), a historical novel based upon *The Gododdin* (*see NAE*, pp. 203, 436). Inspired by tales of Arthur and his Companions, Mynyddog the Golden, king of the Gododdin (a British kingdom around Edinburgh) ca. A.D. 600, gathers and trains a band of warriors drawn from throughout Britain. He sends them against the Angles at Catraeth, accompanied by his bard Aneirin, but he is unable to rally the Celtic tribes in their support, for he is not Arthur. The heroic sacrifice of these warriors, who die rather than be forsworn, is movingly recounted, and it marks another lost opportunity for the Celts to fulfill Arthur's dream of unity against the invaders. [RHT]

Sutcliff, Rosemary. *The Shining Company*. London: Bodley Head, 1990.

TARR, JUDITH, American fantasy author, has Merlin speak from his imprisoning oak tree in "Silver, Stone, and Steel" (1995). His dreams of Christ's betrayal, of Joseph of Arimathea's bringing of the cup to Glastonbury, and of Arthur's rise and fall lead him to an understanding of the oneness that links "Coin, staff, cup, sword." [RHT]

Tarr, Judith. "Silver, Stone, and Steel." In *Excalibur*, ed. Richard Gilliam, Martin H. Greenberg, and Edward E. Kramer. New York: Warner, 1995, pp. 227–39.

TAYLOR, JUD, director of *Guinevere*, a made-for-television movie that first aired in the United States on the Lifetime Cable Channel in May 1994. The film, with a script by Ronni Kern, presents a conflation of the stories of the female-centered Arthurian world found in the novels of Persia Woolley (*see NAE*, p. 526). Here, the youthful Guinevere is a skilled negotiator, swordfighter, and even kickboxer intent upon marrying her schoolmate Lancelot. Fate, however, intervenes, and she is forced by circumstance to marry Arthur while still loving Lancelot. Guinevere's influence in the film is far-reaching. When a carpenter inquired how he should make a table for her, she promptly replies, "Make it round!" [KJH]

Masson, Charles. "'Camelot,' 'Guinevere': Like Knight and Day." *Times-Picayune* [New Orleans], May 1, 1994, p. T4.

TAYLOR, KEITH, Australian fantasy writer, has added to his Bard series (*see NAE*, p. 445) a novella, "The Brotherhood of Britain" (1992). This account of the abduction of the Queen by Lamorak and her recovery by Artorius, with assistance from the Irish bard Felimid, takes place on the eve of Badon. It also introduces traditional tales of an earlier Arthur who fought against the invading Romans. [RHT]

Taylor, Keith. "The Brotherhood of Britain." In *The Camelot Chronicles*, ed. Mike Ashley. London: Robinson, 1992, pp. 128–98.

TAYLOR, MICHAEL: *see* LIND, HELENA.

TELEVISION. Mary Stewart's *The Crystal Cave* (*see NAE*, p. 432) was dramatized by the BBC, in six thirty-minute episodes, as *Merlin and the Crystal Cave*. It was produced by Hilary Bevan Jones, and the role of Merlin as child, adolescent, and adult was played by three different actors. The series, which deals with Merlin's early years and which endeavors to re-create an authentic Dark Age setting, was aired on BBC1 in November and December 1991. There were plans to continue the story by dramatizing more of Stewart's books.

In North America, during the 1991–92 season, the popular adventure series *MacGyver* dealt with Arthurian legend in two dual episodes. The first borrows from Mark Twain's *Connecticut Yankee in King Arthur's Court* the device of sending the hero to Arthur's court by means of a blow to the head. There, he sides with Merlin against the evil Morgana, who has invented gunpowder. The second double episode recalls the film *Indiana Jones and the Last Crusade,* as MacGyver helps an enthusiastic young anthropologist to find the Grail, also known as the cauldron of regeneration. The screenplay is by Stephen Downing. (*See also* HESCOTT, BOB.)

In 1992, Bohbot Entertainment produced *King Arthur and the Knights of Justice*, an animated series about the exploits of an American college football team from Connecticut that is transported back in time to the days of King Arthur. Helped by the magic of Merlin, they take on the roles of the original King Arthur and his "Knights of Justice," who have been imprisoned in a Castle of Glass by the evil Morgana, and wage war against her and her stone warlords. Screenplay was by Jean Chalopin.

Another animated series that appeared in 1992 was *The Legend of Prince Valiant*. Based upon the characters in Hal Foster's comic strip (*see NAE*, pp. 97–98), it was produced in France and Korea by the Sei Young Animation Company for the Family Channel. The series was developed for television and produced by David J. Corbett, with Dianne Dixon as story editor, and episodes deal with such modern issues as the conflicting demands of conservation and commercial development. (*See also* HUMPHREYS, SION.) [RHT/RS]

THACKERY, ANNE, author of the historical fantasy novel *Ragnarok* (1989), which describes how attempts to safeguard a Romanized culture after Arthur's defeat at Camlann result in the heroic Arthurian legend being preserved among the Saxons of the fledgling kingdom of Bernicia. [RS]

Thackery, Anne. *Ragnarok*. London: Bantam, 1989.

THOMAS, FRANCES, author of three juvenile novels that tell the story of the bard Taliesin: *The Blindfold Track* (1980), *A Knot of Spells* (1983), and *The Region of the Summer Stars* (1985). Set in the post-Arthurian world of the northern Celts, this trilogy begins with a reworking of the tale of Taliesin's origin, from his discovery in a coracle by Elphin, through his acquisition of supernatural powers in an out-of-body experience, to his magical rescues of Elphin from Maelgwn's prison and Merddyn from his madness. The subsequent novels involve Taliesin in events of great moment in the borderland between legend and history—a perilous journey that results in the reunion of Urien and Owain, and the story of the fall of the house of Urien, an event foreseen by a Taliesin powerless to stop it. Although intended for young readers, the novels are more mature in incident and tone than most modern historical fantasies. [DN]

Thomas, Frances. *The Blindfold Track*. London: Macmillan, 1980; rpt. Port Talbot, West Glamorgan: Barn Owl, 1981.

———. *A Knot of Spells*. Port Talbot, West Glamorgan: Barn Owl, 1983.

———. *The Region of the Summer Stars*. Port Talbot, West Glamorgan: Barn Owl, 1985.

THOMSEN, BRIAN M., describes the death of Perceval in his short story "Reunion" (1992). Though preserved from aging after he finds the Holy Grail, he eventually dies from a wasting disease in a modern nursing home, like the Maimed King grateful for release. [RHT]

Thomsen, Brian M. "Reunion." In *Grails: Quests, Visitations, and Other Occurrences*, ed. Richard Gilliam, Martin H. Greenberg, and Edward E. Kramer. Atlanta: Unnameable, 1992. Republished as *Grails: Quests of the Dawn*. New York: Roc/Penguin, 1994, pp. 335–41.

TILTON, LOIS, in her short story "Sanctuary" (1994), identifies as the Holy Grail the cup stolen from the dragon's hoard in the Old English epic *Beowulf*. [RHT]

Tilton, Lois. "Sanctuary." In *Grails: Visitations of the Night*, ed. Richard Gilliam, Martin H. Greenberg, and Edward E. Kramer. New York: Roc/Penguin, 1994, pp. 23–29.

TINNELL, ROBERT, Canadian director of *Kids of the Round Table*, which premiered at the 1995 Cannes Film Festival. With a screenplay by David Sherman based on an original short story by Tinnell, the film begins with a familiar enough plot device, a modern-day would-be knight stumbles upon Excalibur. Here the knight is an eleven-year-old named Alex, who faces off against a neighborhood bully. Fleeing the bully, Alex stumbles upon Excalibur and Merlin, who instructs him in how to use the sword and its special powers. Alex soon turns the table on the bully and goes on to derail a bank robbery and kidnaping. The film, light and entertaining, is clearly intended for younger audiences. [KJH]

Kelly, Brendan. Review. *Variety*, May 22, 1995, p. 109.

TOLMIE, SARAH, in her poem "The Story of the Meeting of Cuculainn and Arthur" (1993), brings the Irish hero to Britain. He follows the hound Cabal to an island in a lake, where he witnesses the young Arthur's discovery of Excalibur. [RHT]

Tolmie, Sarah. "The Story of the Meeting of Cuculainn and Arthur." In *A Round Table of Contemporary Arthurian Poetry*, ed. Barbara Tepa Lupack and Alan Lupack. Rochester, N.Y.: Round Table, 1993, pp. 20–28.

TRANTER, NIGEL, author of many popular historical novels about Scotland, in *Druid Sacrifice* (1993) draws upon both medieval saints' legends and Arthurian tradition for the story of Thanea. The daughter of King Loth of Lothian, she is raped by Owen ap Urien, then condemned to death by her father, who holds her responsible for the disgrace of the resultant pregnancy. She survives exposure in an oarless coracle, however, and her son, known as Mungo or Kentigern, becomes a noted Christian missionary, the founder and patron saint of Glasgow. When her half-brother Mordred rebels against their uncle Arthur, the high king, Thanea and her son help Lancelot to rescue Guinevere, whom Mordred has imprisoned. The author displays considerable interest in Scottish topography. [RHT]

Tranter, Nigel. *Druid Sacrifice*. London: Hodder and Stoughton, 1993.

TRÉHORENTEUC, a small village at the western edge of the Forest of Paimpont (*see NAE*, p. 55), near the Val sans Retour (the Valley of No Return; *see NAE*, p. 485). During the early 1940s, Abbot Henri Gillard, rector of the small church in Tréhorenteuc, began to refurbish it with windows and decorations depicting local and regional legends. A notable example is a Grail window created in 1943. In 1945, Gillard enlisted the services of released German prisoners-of-war Karl Rezabeck, a painter, and Peter Wisdorff, a cabinetmaker. For two years, these two executed altarpieces, paintings, and other decorations illustrating the same legends. Among the Arthurian paintings is one that, in the style of medieval miniatures, depicts Arthur's knights at the Round Table. A striking series illustrates the Stations of the Cross, located at recognizable sites in the Valley of No Return; one scene includes both the fallen Christ and Morgan le Fay. [NJL]

Arz, Claude, *et al. Brocéliande, ou l'obscure des forêts*. La Gacilly: Artus, 1990, pp. 97–99.

TREMAYNE, PETER (pseudonym of Peter Berresford Ellis), author of the short story "The Oath of the Saxon" (1992). Modreuant (Mordred), resentful that his uncle rather than he has been chosen high king, has the head of Bran the Blessed dug up and the blame attached to Artios for an action that removes its protection against invasion. [RHT]

Tremayne, Peter. "The Oath of the Saxon." In *The Camelot Chronicles*, ed. Mike Ashley. London: Robinson, 1992, pp. 79–103.

TRISTAN AND ISOLDE IN MODERN FRENCH VERSIONS. Although the Tristan legend was popular throughout the Middle Ages, its incorporation into the Arthurian tradition in the early thirteenth century caused it to share that tradition's decline in popularity starting in the sixteenth century. Tristan continued to enjoy the reputation of a great knight of the Round Table in the abridged retellings of the prose romances published in popular collections like the Comte de Tressan's *L'Histoire de Tristan de Léonois* ("The Story of Tristan of Lyonesse," 1781), but his love for Isolde was hardly the stuff of tragedy. In the nineteenth century, two events occurred that would restore to the legend its peculiar force and determine its orientation in modern French literature and film: the discovery and publication by Francisque Michel (in 1835–39) of the extant fragments of the Old French Tristan poems by Béroul and Thomas and the performance of Richard Wagner's powerful "music drama" *Tristan und Isolde* (1865).

Wagner's impact on French artists and writers was both immediate and far-reaching (*see NAE*, p. 164). His retelling of Gottfried von Strassburg's version primarily as a quest for transcendence propelling the lovers toward an ardently desired death had tremendous appeal for poets like Baudelaire, Mallarmé, Verlaine, and their symbolist successors, whose devotion extended to the founding in 1885 of the *Revue Wagnérienne*. Wagner's reduction of the legend to a tale in which love's inception is inextricably intertwined with a death wish was to fascinate not only the decadent poets, for whom it had a morbid appeal, but also all those who appreciated its mythic power, including Denis de Rougemont. In *L'Amour et l'Occident* (1939, translated as *Passion and Society* and *Love in the Western World*), de Rougemont based his seductive interpretation of the medieval legend and its impact on society principally on Wagner, who he believed had grasped the essence of the legend. Wagner's and de Rougemont's combined influence can be seen in the emphasis given in many modern French interpretations to the spiritual dimension of the legend.

The discovery of the fragments of the poems by Béroul and Thomas, representing the two main Tristan traditions of the Middle Ages, was to provide the impetus for the research undertaken on the legend by a preeminent medievalist whose influence was prodigious. Joseph Bédier's credentials lent authority not only to his painstaking attempts to construct the two traditions for scholars but also to his celebrated *Roman de Tristan et Iseut* ("Romance of Tristan and Iseut," 1900; *see NAE*, p. 34), a reworking of material from the Béroul tradition designed for the general public, which was a surprise bestseller and an instant classic.

Most of the French retellings of the legend in the first half of the twentieth century were in dramatic form. Following in the wake of Armand Silvestre's *Tristan de Léonis* (1897) came Saint-Georges de Bouhélier's *Tragédie de Tristan et Iseult* (1923; *see NAE*, p. 165), Ernst Moerman's *Tristan et Yseult* (Brussels, 1936), and Lucien Fabre's *Tristan et Yseult* (1945). They naturally reflected Wagner's influence, but Bédier also had a role in shaping them; he even wrote a play of his own with Louis Artus, *Tristan et Iseut* (1929; *see NAE*, p. 34), featuring music by Paul Ladmirault. Other works that combined drama and music and drew inspiration from both Wagner and Bédier, are *Le Vin herbé* ("The Potion"), an oratorio completed in 1940 by Swiss composer Frank Martin (*see NAE*, p. 310), and *Tristan et Yseut: version nouvelle d'après la légende des trouvères* ("New Version Based on the Legend of the Trouvères," 1943), an opera by Sylvain Arlanc (and Paul Gautier?).

The only major French dramatists to treat the Tristan material were Paul Claudel and Jean Cocteau, who both offered fascinating modern versions. In *Partage de midi* ("Division of Noon," 1948), Claudel treated the conflict inherent in human love between the appeal of the flesh and that of the spirit. The structure of the play is reminiscent of Wagner, but Claudel portrays the lovers' passion—whose consummation they vainly resist—as highly destructive, a rupture with all that is good and decent. Only in death do they achieve a meaningful union, one that is wholly spiritual. (*See also* CLAUDEL, PAUL; for Cocteau, *see NAE*, pp. 96–97.)

Cocteau wrote the screenplay for Jean Delannoy's film *L'Éternel Retour* ("The Eternal Return," 1943; *see NAE*, p. 152), which features music by Georges Auric. Situating the legend in the twentieth century, Cocteau adhered remarkably well to the traditional story by employing some ingenious transpositions: the Morholt is a barroom bully from whom Patrice (Tristan) rescues Nathalie (Isolde); Patrice's main enemies are the Frossin family, including the malevolent dwarf Achille, who serves up the love potion, which he believes to be poison; when Patrice is banished, he finds work in a garage run by an old friend whose sister he considers marrying. Although it is clear that Cocteau was following Bédier's romance, Wagner's influence can still be seen in the designation of the Morholt as Nathalie's fiancé, in the connection established between potion and poison, and especially in the determination to keep the "lovers" untainted by any physical or moral misconduct. Cocteau also wrote the texts for another film, André Swoboda's *Noces de sable* ("Wedding in the Dunes," 1949), a retelling of an Islamic legend in which he saw analogies with the Tristan legend.

The versions of the legend that have appeared in the past fifty years owe a much less obvious debt to Bédier and Wagner; indeed, some reveal a concerted effort to resist those influences. This is particularly clear in the case of medievalists who endeavored to surpass Bédier as a storyteller. Bédier's authority may well have discouraged any but André Mary (*Tristan*, 1937) from presenting rival retellings during his lifetime, and although several took up the challenge after his death in 1938, they took care to pay respectful homage to their illustrious mentor. Whereas Pierre Champion (*Roman de Tristan et Yseut*, 1947) avoided the problem by adapting a fifteenth-century prose version, Robert Bossuat (*Tristan et Iseut*, 1951), Pierre d'Espezel (*Tristan et Iseut*, 1956), and René Louis (*Tristan et Iseult*, 1972) reworked the same sources as Bédier. They found ample justification for their enterprise in the interest that France had begun to take in its Celtic heritage, stimulated in part by the studies of Celticist scholars Henri Hubert, Jean Marx, and Jean Markale. Bossuat, d'Espezel, and Louis all felt that Bédier, despite his determination to present a version that adhered closely to the so-called archetype of the legend, had retained too much of the courtly and chivalric context with which they believed the twelfth-century poets had infused it. Moreover, in his desire to weave the elements of his sources into a unified whole, Bédier had glossed over many of the primitive traits that revealed the legend's pre-Christian legacy. Of Bédier's three rival storytellers, Louis is the most militant in his determination to return the story to its Celtic roots. His most daring innovation shows Brangien and Iseult reasserting in the potion scene the power that women had in the Celtic analogues of the legend to choose their own mates: the women are both aware of the real contents of the cup that Brangien gives to Iseult, who drinks of it and passes it to Tristan.

The attempt to take the legend back beyond the earliest extant sources has led naturally to ever more mythical reconstructions. A retelling by Michel Cazenave (*Tristan et Iseut*, 1985) envisions Iseut and Tristan as creatures of the sun and moon, respectively, intimately linked with all living creatures in a universe presided over by a pre-Christian god of love. Cazenave substitutes for the traditional ending a more optimistic fate, in which the lovers are laid side by side in an open boat and pushed out to sea bound for a land where they are not constrained by the laws of society.

Some retellings, especially those adorned with prints, betray a desire to appeal to popular tastes. Blaise Gautier's *Tristan et Iseult* (1958), illustrated by Jean Garcia, is a fairly streamlined version, and Michel Manoll's *Tristan et Yseult*, illustrated by Gilles Valdès (1959) and then by Michel Gourlier (1971, 1981), is a relatively chaste retelling. Much less restrained is Marcelle Vioux's *Tristan et Yseult, amants éternels* ("Tristan and Yseult, Eternel Lovers," 1946), which appeared in a collection focusing on "romantic destinies" (allusion is made to a bond the lovers shared before being reunited on earth). Vioux's novelistic treatment depicts the lovers and Marc as honorable characters making the best of their impossible fate. She explores their feelings, supplying modern psychological motivation for their decisions. She also rationalizes certain episodes: the dragon that threatens the Irish is actually a Nordic pirate ingeniously disguised.

In general, the most idiosyncratic retellings are offered by poets. Yves Viollier sets his *Un Tristan pour Iseut* ("A Tristan for Iseut," 1972) in a small village in contemporary Vendée. Tristan, wounded in a fight with another youth, Morhout (whom he kills), receives herbal treatments from Morhout's father at a local farm, where he meets Iseut. Despite the attraction felt by the two, Iseut's loyalty to her cousin Morhout precludes marriage. Their passion becomes uncontrollable after they taste an aphrodisiac mint on the night before Iseut's marriage to "Monsieur Marc." Their inevitable separation leads a languishing Tristan to Iseut aux Blanches Mains, who is none other than death.

In all the poetic renderings, the lovers share an intimate bond with nature. The sea is often the dominant element. Versions that do not claim to recount the entire legend often begin with an episode that takes place on the sea and end with the lovers reunited in death on the Breton coast; earlier episodes are then related as dreamy flashbacks. Such is the case in Pierre Dalle Nogare's contemplative prose poem *Tristan and Iseut* (1977), which begins with a somewhat delirious Tristan recalling the combat with the

Morholt as he lies languishing in the boat he hopes will take him to a mythical island where he can be cured. In this "long chant full of dreams and fatality," the lovers are curiously passive; they follow their destined path less as protagonists than as wondering spectators. Mas-Felipe Delavouët's 500-line poem in Provençal, "Ço que Tristan se disiè sus la mar" ("What Tristan said while on the sea," 1971), also begins with the ailing hero adrift at sea: like his "older brother" Ulysses, he longs to rediscover his beloved and his homeland. In Pierre Garnier's innovative "spatial poem" *Tristan et Iseult* (1981), images of the sea and other natural elements combine with key components of the legend (Tristan, Iseult, life, death) to form on the page constellations seen to be in a relationship of creative tension. The lovers, rejected by society which they in turn reject, take refuge in the unity of nature, and their love is accomplished in eternity.

Garnier's desire to detach Tristan and Isolde from their textual tradition and to inscribe them in a timeless framework actually continues the Wagnerian-Rougemontian impulse to relegate the legend to the status of myth. But the legend, when stripped of all its detail, also lends itself to demystification, an impulse that informs many recent treatments of medieval France's most celebrated works. Yvan Lagrange's stunning film *Tristan et Yseut* (1972; *see NAE*, p. 267) situates the legend at the intersection of the four elements and effectively subordinates the lovers' passion to more basic instincts, such as that of individual survival. The need to engage in constant combat leaves Tristan little time to tend to Yseut's emotional and sexual needs, and the two are eventually returned to the primordial chaos.

The demystifying impulse can be seen as well in three plays that focus on the female characters. Agnès Verlet's *Yseult et Tristan* (1978) is a feminist play that restores to the heroine the magical, mysterious power that she had in the Irish analogues of the legend, portraying an insignificant and weak Tristan as a pawn of patriarchal society, whose death is caused by his unwillingness to give up the view of women held by that society. The two other dramatic works view the legend from the vantage point of the "other" Isolde: *An Isild A-Heul* or *Yseult seconde* ("The Second Yseult," 1964; *see NAE*, p. 229) is a three-act tragedy with epilogue composed in Breton by Per-Jakez Hélias (with facing translation in modern French); and *Yseut aux Blanches Mains: tapisserie d'un long hiver* ("Yseult of the White Hands: tapestry of a long winter," 1975) is a dramatic prose poem in six "chants" by Elyane Gastaud. Both works offer a pointed contrast between the love of a wife and that of a lover, for the patience and realism that characterize Brittonic Isolde constitute a calm refuge from the furious, unrealistic passion Tristan shares with Irish Isolde.

Demystification of a different sort can be found in works that infuse the legend with a twentieth-century sensibility. Grigori Sturdza's *Tristan sans Isolde, roman d'après les cahiers de Stanislas Tugomir* ("Tristan Without Isolde, a Novel Based on the Notebooks of Stanislas Tugomir," 1972) recounts how a wealthy young man becomes infatuated with a simple village girl whom he resists the impulse to possess. Having nourished his obsession on that refusal, he then determines to cure himself by turning the experience into a novel, a project he also puts off indefinitely in order to continue savoring his impossible love. The dangerously seductive power of the Tristan myth is also clear in Michel Tournier's short story "Tristan Vox" (in *Coq de bruyère*, 1978; *see NAE*, p. 459). A radio announcer takes the name "Tristan Vox" and assumes a persona so powerful that a woman, "Isolde," begins sending him love letters, as does his own secretary. When a picture of another person is published with the name "Tristan Vox," he is confronted by that person, who then takes over the show and begins receiving letters from the first announcer's wife.

Finally, there is François Truffaut's film *La Femme d'à-côté* ("The Woman Next Door," 1981), no doubt the most depressingly successful confrontation between the legend and modern mores. It is a fairly realistic adaptation so redolent of contemporary values that the venerable old story takes on the look of a modern-day soap opera. The protagonists, Bernard and Mathilde, are former lovers whose relationship had failed. Now married to others and finding themselves neighbors in a small town near Grenoble, they are unable to resist such tempting proximity and resume their liaison. But the tensions created are unbearable. After suffering a nervous breakdown, Mathilde decides to move away. A final meeting in the empty house results in her shooting Bernard and then herself. The story is narrated by Odile, a woman who became disabled when, in love and despairing, she jumped out a window. It is she who finally makes explicit the link between the legend and this sorry *fait divers* when she remarks that these lovers will not be buried in the same tomb and proposes as their epitaph: "Ni avec toi, ni sans toi" ("Neither with you, nor without you"). This transformation of the famous verse from Marie de France's *Chevrefueil*, "Ne vuz sanz mei, ne je sanz vus" ("Neither you without me, nor I without you") offers a twist that is thoroughly modern: despite their strong mutual attraction, it is their own incapacity to commit fully to each other that constitutes the ultimate obstacle to fulfillment. [JTG]

Grimbert, Joan, ed. *Tristan and Isolde: A Casebook*. New York: Garland, 1995, esp. pp. lxv–lxxix.

TRUFFAUT, FRANÇOIS: *see* TRISTAN AND ISOLDE IN MODERN FRENCH VERSIONS.

TURTLEDOVE, HARRY, author of "A Massachusetts Yankee in King Arthur's Court" (1992), a short comic fantasy in which a modern druid sends John F. Kennedy back in time to an unromanticized Camelot. After making love to Guinevere, he is returned to the modern world by

Merlin, here presented as an Egyptian wise man. (*See also* RESNICK, LAURA.) [DN]

Turtledove, Harry. "A Massachusetts Yankee in King Arthur's Court." In *Alternate Kennedys*, ed. Mike Resnick. New York: Tor, 1992.

UHLIG, WOLFGANG, German author of the 1986 poem *Gralslicht* ("Grail's Light"). The Grail is here stylized into a supernatural object of desire and a source of secret knowledge, which only a chosen few can come to possess by virtue of self-denial. [WW]

Uhlig, Wolfgang. *Gralslicht. Fantasia*, 28/29 (1986), 166.

Wunderlich, Werner. "The Arthurian Legend in German Literature of the Nineteen-Eighties." *Studies in Medievalism*, 3 (1991), 423–42.

UPDIKE, JOHN, author of "Four Sides of One Story" (1965; *see NAE*, p. 483), returned after many years to the story of Tristan and Iseult in his novel *Brazil* (1994), for which, he acknowledged, Bédier's *Romance of Tristan and Iseult* "gave me my tone and basic situation." Set in Brazil, the novel tells the story of Tristão, a dark-skinned slum dweller, and Isabel, a light-skinned daughter of wealthy parents. *Brazil* combines elements of the realistic novel and of South American magic realism with the tone and occasional motifs from medieval romance, such as Tristão and Isabel's ill-fated love at first sight, which survives almost overwhelming trials, their sleeping with a sword between them, and occasional references to Tristão as a knight. The novel ends with Tristão's death at the hands of robbers from the slums such as he himself once was. Though Isabel remembers the story of a woman who willed herself to die beside her dead lover, when she lies next to Tristão she does not die because "the spirit is strong, but blind matter is stronger." Thus, in the end, realism is dominant over the romance and magic in the novel. [ACL]

Updike, John. *Brazil*. New York: Knopf, 1994.

VERLET, AGNÈS: *see* TRISTAN AND ISOLDE IN MODERN FRENCH VERSIONS.

VIOLLIER, YVES: *see* TRISTAN AND ISOLDE IN MODERN FRENCH VERSIONS.

VON TRESKOW, IRENE: *see* PHILATELY.

WAGNER, KARL EDWARD, in his ironic short story "One Paris Night" (1992), recounts how two nineteenth-century adventurers melt down a chalice, which turns out to be the Holy Grail, in order to make silver bullets to shoot a werewolf. [RHT]

Wagner, Karl Edward. "One Paris Night." In *Grails: Quests, Visitations, and Other Occurrences*, ed. Richard Gilliam, Martin H. Greenberg, and Edward E. Kramer. Atlanta: Unnameable, 1992. Republished as *Grails: Visitations of the Night*. New York: Roc/Penguin, 1994, pp. 8–19.

WATT-EVANS, LAWRENCE, science-fiction and fantasy author, demonstrates his fondness for irony in "Visions" (1992), a short story about an insurance adjuster who sees a vision of the Holy Grail. Rather than pursue it, he decides that he has "plenty of old quests to finish up," and he sets about putting his life in better order. [RHT]

Watt-Evans, Lawrence. "Visions." In *Grails: Quests, Visitations, and Other Occurrences*, ed. Richard Gilliam, Martin H. Greenberg, and Edward E. Kramer. Atlanta: Unnameable, 1992. Republished as *Grails: Quests of the Dawn*. New York: Roc/Penguin, 1994, pp. 301–08.

WEATHERHILL, CRAIG, Cornish author of a fantasy novel, *The Lyonesse Stone* (1991), in which a young boy and girl, descendants of the ancient rulers of Cornwall, discover a gem that opens their world to creatures both good and evil from the ancient past. Arthurian associations are abundant in, if not central to, the story, which includes a retelling of the legend of the sinking of Lyonesse in the sixth century as punishment for Medraut's crimes. An account of Arthur's passing is also given, Merlin's tomb is visited, and the sword of Tristan plays an important part in what was to be the first in a series of novels. [DN]

Weatherhill, Craig. *The Lyonesse Stone: A Novel of West Cornwall*. Padstow: Tabb House, 1991.

WEIN, ELIZABETH E., author whose first novel for young readers, *The Winter Prince* (1993), tells the story of Medraut, the bastard son of Artos the King. Having grown to manhood in self-exile from Britain after Artos has named his legitimate son, Prince Lleu, heir to the throne, Medraut returns to Britain, where he comes under the influence of his mother, Morgause, the sister of the King. Her plot to overthrow Artos by kidnaping his heir fails when Medraut finally declares his allegiance to his younger half-brother, who has overcome his own frailties through Medraut's tutelage.

The fate of the brothers is revealed in the short story "Fire," also published in 1993. Darker in mood than the novel, it tells of the captivity of Prince Lleu by the Saxons following the destruction of Artos's forces at Camlan. After several years, his freedom is purchased by Medraut, who apparently fled the country after the last battle. The story ends with Lleu's return to his father's villa at Camlan, which he finds in ruins. [DN]

Wein, Elizabeth E. *The Winter Prince*. New York: Atheneum, 1993.
———. "Fire." In *L. Ron Hubbard Presents Writers of the Future, Volume IX*, ed. Dove Wolverton. Los Angeles: Bridge, 1993, pp. 3-33.

WEIR, IAN, author of the BBC radio drama *Passings* (1984), blends elegiac poetry and skeptical humor to portray the ambivalence of myth. While Arthur is dying, his career is reviewed in a series of flashbacks contrasting his public glory with his private sins. After Arthur's death, Bedwyr restarts the mythologizing process. [RS]

WHITE, STEVE, introduces Arthurian legend into his science-fiction novel *Legacy* (1995), the sequel to his *The Disinherited*. The hero starts out in the twenty-third century, fighting aliens bent on subjugating the human race, but time travelers from the distant future not only rescue him after he has been taken prisoner but send him back to the time of King Arthur, where he plays the role of Bedwyr. Weaving together the theories of both Geoffrey Ashe, who identifies Arthur with Riothamus, and C. Scott Littleton, who proposes the "Sarmatian Connection" (*see NAE*, pp. 20–21, 383–84, 396–97), the story deals with the King's campaign in Gaul during the fifth century, culminating in his defeat by Euric, king of the Visigoths. This defeat remains ironically necessary to the eventual development of a progessively minded western civilization. [RHT]

White, Steve. *Legacy*. New York: Baen, 1995.

WHYTE, JACK, Scottish-born Canadian actor and author, is currently (1995) writing A Dream of Eagles, a four-volume cycle of historical novels set in Britain from A.D. 367 to 448. Three novels have been published to date, the first two of which are narrated by Publius Varrus, a retired Roman officer and master blacksmith. *The Skystone* (1992) deals with the foundation, in the far southwest, of "The Colony," a community of British-born Romans who seek to achieve economic and military self-sufficiency in anticipation of the collapse of the Roman Empire. The title refers to a meteorite from which Excalibur is eventually forged in *The Singing Sword* (1993).

This second novel follows events up to the withdrawal of the legions from Britain. The colonists build their headquarters on an old hill fort that they rename Camulod, and the families of their leaders intermarry with the royal house of the neighboring Celts. From these unions, Uther Pendragon and Merlyn are born. The conflict between traditional Roman virtues and latter-day decadence is mirrored in the feud between the narrator and a wealthy Roman patrician.

In the third novel, *The Eagles' Brood* (1994), Merlyn continues the story begun by his great-uncle, recounting the long and devastating war between the Colony and Lot of Cornwall. It culminates in the deaths of Uther, Lot, and Ygraine and in Merlyn's discovery of the infant Arthur. [RHT]

Whyte, Jack. *The Skystone*. Toronto: Viking, 1992.
———. *The Singing Sword*. Toronto: Viking, 1993.
———. *The Eagles' Brood*. Toronto: Viking, 1994.

WIEDENMANN, REINHOLD, German musician who, together with the Argentine-born lutenist Osvaldo Parisi, is committed to reviving the medieval tradition of epic singing. Wiedenmann is reconstructing musical performances of medieval and Arthurian epics written in stanzas: Wolfram's *Titurel* (1986), *Der Wartburgkrieg* (1988), *Der Winsbecke* (1989). Using a melody proposed by Ewald Jammers, he has even sung parts of Wolfram's *Parzival* (1991). [UM]

Müller, Ulrich. "Aufführungsversuche zur mittelhochdeutschen Sangversgeert." In *Festschrift Manfred Lemmer*. Frankfurt: Lang, 1993, pp. 87–103. [CD (Koch-Records) announced for 1995].

WILBER, RICK, in "Greggie's Cup" (1992), recounts how a young boy suffering from Down's syndrome transcends time when he meets Lancelot in the ruins of an old Roman fort. The boy's innocence and generosity inspire both the knight and the boy's father to commit themselves to a noble course of action. [RHT]

Wilber, Rick. "Greggie's Cup." In *Grails: Quests, Visitations, and Other Occurrences*, ed. Richard Gilliam, Martin H. Greenberg, and Edward E. Kramer. Atlanta: Unnameable, 1992. Republished as *Grails: Quests of the Dawn*. New York: Roc/Penguin, 1994, pp. 368–84.

WILCOX, DON, science-fiction writer and portrait painter, wrote "Blueflow" (1992), a short story about a painter who uses paints enchanted by Merlin for a portrait of Arthur and Guinevere sitting together. When moonlight falls on the figure of the King, however, it is transformed into that of Lancelot, changing back again in the daylight. [RHT]

Wilcox, Don. "Blueflow." In *The Camelot Chronicles*, ed. Mike Ashley. London: Robinson, 1992, pp. 104–27.

WILLIAMS, ANTONIA R., author of the dramatic poem *Isolt: A New Telling* (1900; *see NAE*, p. 515), also contributed "Elaine" to the *English Illustrated Magazine* in 1904. This poem, a single quatrain, celebrates the way the heroine's love transcends all the conventional joys of earthly life. The poem was accompanied by an illustration in a lush, late Pre-Raphaelite style by Charles E. Dawson. [RS]

Williams, Antonia R. "Elaine." *English Illustrated Magazine*, N.S. 32 (December 1904), 243.

WILLIS, GEORGE ANTHONY ARMSTRONG: *see* ARMSTRONG, ANTHONY.

WISDORFF, PETER: *see* TRÉHORENTEUC.

WOLF, JOAN, author of *The Road to Avalon* (1988; *see NAE*, p. 520), completed her trilogy of historical novels of Dark Age England with *Born of the Sun* (1989), which tells the story of Ceawlin, the king of Wessex who defeats the Britons at Deorham, near Bath, in 577. He marries a British princess, for whom tales of Arthur's glories contrast with her people's present decline. She realizes, however, that the best hope for preserving the vision for which Arthur fought lies in supporting a king who respects the rights of all his subjects, Saxon and Briton alike. *The Edge of Light* (1990) describes the struggle of Alfred against the Danes; in her afterword, the author comments, "Alfred holds in real history the place which romance gives to Arthur . . . . Alfred is Arthur reincarnated." [RHT]

Wolf, Joan. *Born of the Sun*. New York: NAL, 1989.
———. *The Edge of Light*. New York: NAL, 1990.

WOOLLEY, PERSIA, completed her trilogy on Guinevere (*see NAE*, p. 526) with *Guinevere: The Legend in Autumn*, which deals with the quest for the Grail and the fall of the Round Table. The story follows that of Malory, with borrowings from other romances, but it endeavors to provide motives for the behavior of the characters that would be more credible to a modern audience. Guinevere herself emerges as a lively and sympathetic figure, on the one hand struggling to help Arthur deal with his fractious followers, particularly the members of his own family, while on the other maintaining her independence in the face of patriarchal attitudes toward women. [RHT]

Woolley, Persia. *Guinevere: The Legend in Autumn*. New York: Poseidon, 1991.

WURTS, JANNY, in her short story "That Way Lies Camelot" (1992), tells how a young boy dying of leukemia in our era changes places with Perceval. Both thus fulfill their dearest dream: the former to win a place at the Round Table, the latter to "go on to God's glory, to meet His most beautiful angels." [RHT]

Wurts, Janny. "That Way Lies Camelot." In *Grails: Quests, Visitations, and Other Occurrences*, ed. Richard Gilliam, Martin H. Greenberg, and Edward E. Kramer. Atlanta: Unnameable, 1992. Republished as *Grails: Quests of the Dawn*. New York: Roc/Penguin, 1994, pp. 264–88.

YOLEN, JANE, author whose *Merlin and the Dragons* (1991) tells of a young Arthur troubled by bad dreams until his anxiety is relieved by Merlin's tale of his own youthful dream about Vortigern's tower. This children's story was written as part of a collaborative project produced in several media. An animated version, narrated by the actor Kevin Kline, with music by Michel Rubini, was produced on videotape. The story has also been released as a recording with the text in an accompanying booklet illustrated by Iain McCraig.

Yolen (*see NAE*, p. 529) also wrote "The Quiet Monk" (1988), "The Question of the Grail" (1992), and "The Question of the Sword" (1995). The first is a short story in which a long-lived Lancelot turns up at Glastonbury Abbey in 1191 and excavates the grave of Arthur and Guenevere in search of absolution (*see NAE*, p. 200). The last two are short poems: the first considers several theories concerning the origins of the Grail before favoring its identity with the female, life-giving principle; the second is similar, in that it "could argue" for the association of Excalibur with its creation by blacksmiths or its use in war, but again "would rather argue" its links with women, "bringing life" and "the ending of it." [DN/RHT]

Yolen, Jane. *Merlin and the Dragons*. New York: Lightyear Entertainment, Stories to Remember series, 1991 [video]; Lightyear Records/BMG Music S106-2-LR, 1991 [CD]; New York: Dutton Children's Books, 1991 [book].
———. "The Quiet Monk." *Isaac Asimov's Science Fiction Magazine*, (March 1988); rpt. in *The Camelot Chronicles*, ed. Mike Ashley. London: Robinson, 1992, pp. 380–92.
———. "The Question of the Grail." In *Grails: Quests, Visitations, and Other Occurrences*, ed. Richard Gilliam, Martin H. Greenberg, and Edward E. Kramer. Atlanta: Unnameable, 1992. Republished as *Grails: Quests of the Dawn*. New York: Roc/Penguin, 1994, p. 1.
———. "The Question of the Sword." In *Excalibur*, ed. Richard Gilliam, Martin H. Greenberg, and Edward E. Kramer. New York: Warner, 1995, pp. 1–2.

YORGASON, BRENTON and MARGARET, turn to Arthurian legend to provide a fictional frame for their didactic novel *Family Knights* (1986). Their anachronistic story draws little from tradition, however, focusing instead upon the importance of love and understanding in the family. [RHT]

Yorgason, Brenton and Margaret. *Family Knights*. Salt Lake City: Bookcraft, 1986.

YOUTH GROUPS, ARTHURIAN. In 1893, a minister named William Byron Forbush (1868–1927) founded the first of what was to become a network of American clubs for boys called the Knights of King Arthur. In the course of his membership, a boy progressed through the stages of Page, Esquire, and Knight. To help him focus on particular virtues, each boy took the name of a knight or of some hero, ancient or modern, and tried to emulate him. Each club, called a "castle," was guided by an adult "Merlin." The Merlin helped the boys organize "tournaments" (usually athletic), competitions, and "quests," which were cooperative good deeds. These clubs were seen as a way of channeling what was believed to be an instinctive tendency in adolescent males, that of forming gangs, into a means of doing good deeds and developing character. In 1902, a female parallel to the Knights of King Arthur, known as the Queens of Avalon (originally Queens of Avilion), was established. Whereas the boys' clubs were directed by a Merlin, the girls' were guided by a "Lady of the Lake." These clubs remained in existence until at least 1940.

Another minister, Perry Edwards Powell, founded a strikingly similar organization, which he described in a book called *Knights of the Holy Grail: A Solution to the Boy Problem* (1906). Though he claims his order was original, the borrowing from Forbush is evident. Powell's Knights went through two of the three degrees that Forbush's did, esquire and knight, and were led by a Merlin. Powell's Knights of the Holy Grail seems to have remained a relatively small group and not to have had the national membership that Forbush's Knights achieved.

Yet another organization, the Knighthood of Youth, was directed by the National Child Welfare Association and focused on school children from seven to twelve years of age. The Knighthood of Youth was designed to provide moral training in a manner analogous to the training in health habits provided in the schools, that is, through a program by which improvement could be measured; but it also was meant to appeal to the child's imagination. One of the principal ways of doing this was through stories of King Arthur and his knights.

The combined membership of these clubs was in excess of half a million. The Arthurian youth groups also inspired retellings of the Arthurian legends as well as original novels for children, such as Horace M. Du Bose's *The Gang of Six: A Story of the Boy Life of Today* (1906), which describes the efforts of a young man to transform six street urchins by founding for them a club based on the model of the Round Table, and two didactic novels, each with the same title (*Little Sir Galahad*), one by Lillian Holmes (1904), the other by Phoebe Gray (1914); both of them show how moral courage on the knightly model can overcome adversity. [ACL]

Forbush, William Byron. *The Queens of Avalon*. 4th ed. Boston: The Knights of King Arthur, 1925.

———, and Dascomb Forbush. *The Knights of King Arthur: How to Begin and What to Do*. Oberlin, Ohio: The Knights of King Arthur, 1915.

———, and Frank Lincoln Masseck. *The Boys' Round Table: A Manual of the International Order of the Knights of King Arthur*. 6th ed., rewritten. Potsdam, N.Y.: Masseck, 1908.

Powell, Perry Edwards. *The Knights of the Holy Grail: A Solution of the Boy Problem*. Cincinnati: Jennings and Graham, 1906.

ZELAZNY, ROGER (1937–1995), **and ROBERT SHECKLEY,** authors of *Bring Me the Head of Prince Charming* (1991). Parsifal and Excalibur make brief appearances in this humorous fantasy about how a demon's efforts to subvert the tale of Sleeping Beauty are frustrated by the contradictions of human nature and Hell's own obstructive bureaucracy. (For Zelazny, *see NAE*, p. 533.) [RHT]

Zelazny, Roger, and Robert Sheckley. *Bring Me the Head of Prince Charming*. New York: Bantam, 1991.

ZUCKER, JERRY, director of *First Knight*, a 1995 film for Columbia Pictures; the screenplay is by William Nicholson. En route to her marriage to the much older Arthur of Camelot, Guinevere, the Lady of Leonesse, is rescued from Prince Malagant's forces by Lancelot, an itinerant commoner with loyalties to no one, who makes a living by fighting with his sword. Safely delivered to Camelot, Guinevere is soon abducted by Malagant, only to be rescued once again by Lancelot. Guinevere and Arthur marry, and Arthur makes Lancelot a knight of the Round Table. When Malagant lays waste Leonesse, Arthur, Guinevere, and the Knights of the Round Table ride out to defeat him. They are partially successful, but Arthur soon stumbles upon Guinevere and Lancelot in a passionate embrace—the extent of their disloyalty and infidelity in the film. At a trial for treason, they escape condemnation when Malagant attacks, wounds Arthur, and dies at the hand of Lancelot. In the film's final scene, Arthur's corpse is set adrift on a burning pyre.

The time frame in *First Knight* is indefinite, though vaguely medieval. Malagant's forces, all of whom need to wash their faces, favor two weapons, serrated broad swords and hand-held crossbows. Leonesse looks genuinely medieval enough, but Camelot resembles something more Disneyesque. The dialogue is wooden and at times unintentionally humorous. [KJH]

McCarthy, Todd. Review. *Variety*, June 26, 1995, pp. 78, 85.